MW00770082

THE BUILDINGS OF ENGLAND

FOUNDING EDITOR: NIKOLAUS PEVSNER

DORSET

MICHAEL HILL
JOHN NEWMAN
AND
NIKOLAUS PEVSNER

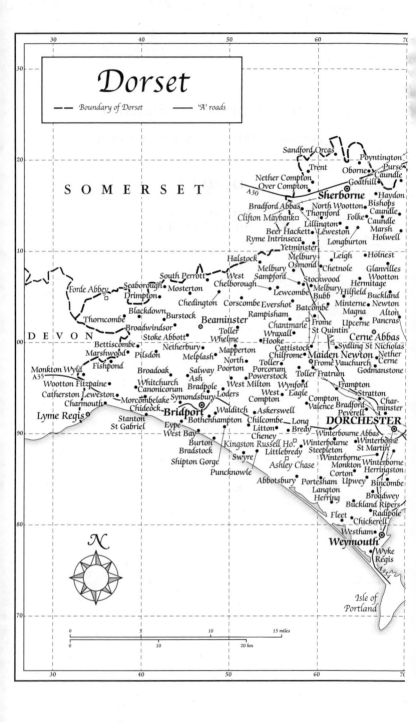

Dorset

- - - Boundary of Dorset   ——— 'A' roads

SOMERSET

Sandford Orcas
Poyntington
Trent
Oborne • Purse
Nether Compton • Caundle
Over Compton • Goathill
A30
Sherborne • Haydon
Bradford Abbas • North Wootton • Bishops
Clifton Maybank □ • Thornford • Caundle
Lillington • Folke • Caundle
Beer Hackett • Leweston • Marsh
Ryme Intrinseca • Longburton • Holwell
Yetminster
Halstock • Leigh • Holnest
Melbury • Chetnole • Glanvilles
Melbury Osmond • Wootton
South Perrott • West • Sampford • Stockwood • Hermitage
Chelborough • Lewcombe • Melbury • Hilfield • Buckland
Forde Abbey □ Seaborough • Mosterton • Bubb • Minterne • Newton
Drimpton • Corscombe • Evershot • Batcombe • Magna • Alton
Chedington • Rampisham • Frome • Pancras
Thorncombe • Blackdown • Burstock • **Beaminster** • Chantmarle • St Quintin • Upcerne
Broadwindsor • Stoke Abbott • Toller • Wraxall • **Cerne Abbas**
DEVON • Whelme • Hooke • Cattistock • Sydling St Nicholas
Bettiscombe • Netherbury • Mapperton • Chilfrome • **Maiden Newton** • Nether
Marshwood • Pilsdon • Melplash • North • Frome Vauchurch • Cerne
Monkton Wyld • Fishpond • Broadoak • Salway • Poorton • Toller • Godmanstone
A35 • Ash • Porcorum • Toller Fratrum
Wootton Fitzpaine • Whitchurch • Bradpole • West Milton • Wynford • Frampton
Catherston Leweston • Canonicorum • Loders • West • Eagle • Stratton
Charmouth • Morcombelake • Symondsbury • Compton • Bradford • Char-
Lyme Regis • Chideock • **Bridport** • Walditch • Valence • Peverell • minster
Stanton • Bothenhampton • Chilcombe • Long • **DORCHESTER**
St Gabriel • Eype • Litton • Bredy • Winterbourne Abbas • Winterborne
West Bay • Cheney • Winterbourne • St Martin
Burton • Kingston Russell Ho.□ • Steepleton • Winterborne
Bradstock • Swyre • Littlebredy • Winterborne • Monkton • Herringston
Shipton Gorge • Ashley Chase • Corton
Puncknowle • Abbotsbury • Portesham • Upwey • Bincombe
Langton • Broadwey
Herring • Buckland Ripers • Radipole
Fleet • Chickerell
Westham • **Weymouth**
Wyke
Regis

Isle of
Portland

0   5   10   15 miles
0   10   20 km

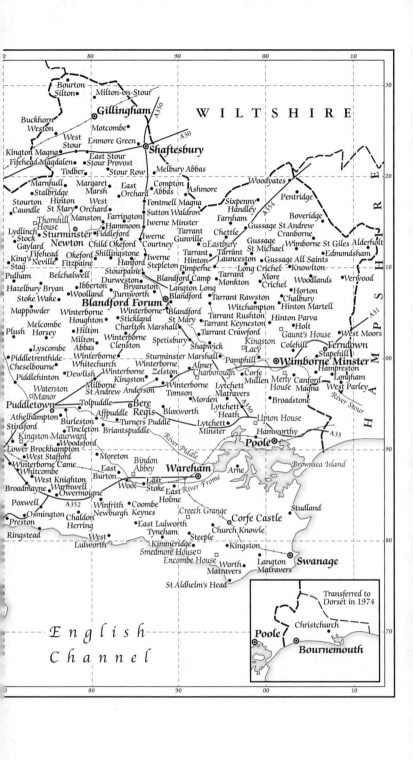

Dorset

BY

MICHAEL HILL

JOHN NEWMAN

AND

NIKOLAUS PEVSNER

THE BUILDINGS OF ENGLAND

YALE UNIVERSITY PRESS
NEW HAVEN AND LONDON

YALE UNIVERSITY PRESS
NEW HAVEN AND LONDON

302 Temple Street, New Haven CT 06511
47 Bedford Square, London WC1B 3DP
www.pevsner.co.uk
www.lookingatbuildings.org.uk
www.yalebooks.co.uk
www.yalebooks.com

Published by Yale University Press 2018
2 4 6 8 10 9 7 5 3 1

ISBN 978 0 300 22478 8

Originally published in 1972,
© John Newman and Nikolaus Pevsner
Revised in 2018, new material © Michael Hill

Printed in China
through World Print
Set in Monotype Plantin

The 1972 edition of Dorset was dedicated

AS A MEMENTO FOR CORDELIA,
PAM, HELEN AND ALLAN

AND

FOR KATRINA

2018 dedication

WITH GRATITUDE TO
D.O., D.L. AND P.H.

CONTENTS

LIST OF TEXT FIGURES AND MAPS

Every effort has been made to trace or contact all copyright holders. The publishers will be glad to make good any errors or omissions brought to our attention in future editions.

MAPS

PHOTOGRAPHIC ACKNOWLEDGEMENTS

The majority of photographs were specially taken for this book by James O. Davies. We are also grateful for permission to reproduce the remaining photographs from the sources as shown below.

Country Life Picture Library: 91
Courtesy of Jonathan Stone: 72
© Historic England Archive: 127
Michael Hill: 73, 100
robertharding / Alamy Stock Photo: 5

MAP AND ILLUSTRATION REFERENCES

The numbers printed in italic type in the margin against the place names in the gazetteer of the book indicate the position of the place in question on the INDEX MAP (pp. ii–iii), which is divided into sections by the 10-kilometre reference lines of the National Grid. The reference given here omits the two initial letters which in a full grid reference refer to the 100-kilometre squares into which the county is divided. The first two numbers indicate the *western* boundary, and the last two the *southern* boundary, of the 10-kilometre square in which the place in question is situated. For example, Abbotsbury (reference 5080) will be found in the 10-kilometre square bounded by grid lines 50 (on the *west*) and 60, and 80 (on the *south*) and 90; Yetminster (reference 5010) in the square bounded by the grid lines 50 (on the *west*) and 60, and 10 (on the *south*) and 20.

The map contains all those places, whether towns, villages or isolated buildings, which are the subject of separate entries in the text.

ILLUSTRATION REFERENCES are given as marginal numbers for photographs, and as marginal *italic* cross-references for images on other pages of the text.

FOREWORD AND ACKNOWLEDGEMENTS

My first encounter with Dorset was on family holidays at Swanage in the early 1960s. Awareness of approaching a special place started as we passed over the heathlands to the north (later understood as Hardy's 'Egdon Heath'), and further on, the shattered slabs of Corfe Castle, sitting atop its conical hill in the glittering Purbeck landscape. Colour changed too. In our part of the Cotswolds we were used to the pinkish russet of rubble stone and the rich orange of Stonehouse brick, and trains were maroon or chocolate-and-cream; but in Dorset the trains were green and, when we ventured to Bournemouth (always by the chain ferry from Studland), there were curiously smooth-shaped trolleybuses in banana yellow with a thin red stripe. And the stone around Corfe and Swanage was reflective-silver, under huge stone-slab roofs.

One day my father brought home a copy of David Verey's *The Buildings of England: Gloucestershire, The Cotswolds*. (He was chairman of the local planning committee, and I think he was hoping to see which buildings weren't mentioned so that they could be cleared for new housing.) I like to believe that reading the book changed his mind about the preservation of the past; it certainly formed my mindset when (as soon as I had a car) I toured myself around the Cotswolds. From Portsmouth, where I studied architecture, my adventures took me out to Chichester and Surrey and to houses by Lutyens and Voysey. And as my appreciation for the 'pattern of English building' took hold, so did my amazement at the great achievement that is the *Buildings of England* series. So, in the privileged position of revising Dorset, my astonishment at what Nikolaus Pevsner completed was amplified.

Revising a volume in the series now is, in theory at least, easier than writing one of the first editions. Architectural history has blossomed as a specialist subject, especially since the 1960s when the research for the original Dorset volume was carried out, and access to documents has, in general, become easier with the advent of the internet. (What we no longer have, alas, is the ability to browse thoughtfully through the ranks of red boxes at the National Monuments Record, first at Fortress House in Savile Row, later moved to Swindon, and now partially available online.)

So, despite the corrections and expansion, I remain in admiration of Pevsner and John Newman and their work for the 1972 edition. Together with the baseline of data, much of their writing has been retained, for example John Newman's introductory description of Corfe Castle: highly evocative, and, as far as I'm concerned, yet to be bettered. Much of the preliminary research was conducted by Robert Gibbs but, most importantly, the authors had access to information gathered by the Royal Commission on the Historical Monuments of England for their county inventory series. Pevsner's driver for Dorset was David McLaughlin (who was Conservation Architect at Bath City when I worked there briefly in the late 1980s), and his hosts during art of the tour were Mr and Mrs Bagg. The town entries received a read-through by David Lloyd, whose invaluable article on Dorchester (*Proceedings of the Dorset Natural History and Archaeological Society* 89, 1968) was the basis of the original entry on that place. Finally, a major slice of Poole was researched and written by Nicholas Taylor. His thorough listing of 1930s and post-war buildings has been frustrating to revisit on account of the level of demolition and replacement there.

And so to the present book. The geographical coverage remains as before, i.e. ignoring the transfer in 1974 of Bournemouth and Christchurch from Hampshire (to be covered in the forthcoming *Hampshire: South* volume). Since the first edition the scope has enlarged so that, for example, all churches are included, apart from the odd recent example where the building is off-the-peg and displays no architectural features of being a church or chapel. Descriptions of church furnishings have been greatly expanded, although most moveable items are no longer included; nor is church (or civic) plate. The most heavily revised sections are chiefly those where most change has taken place since 1972. For example, Poole has undergone major redevelopment, while immediately west of Dorchester is an entirely new settlement: Poundbury.

For the first edition, the archaeological introduction and entries were by Roger Peers, and the building materials chapter by Alec Clifton-Taylor. The last, written in Clifton-Taylor's inimitable style, has been retained for this edition, corrected by Paul Ensom where necessary. The new specialist introductions are by Paul Ensom (Geology); Peter and Ann Woodward (Archaeology); and Bob Machin (Traditional Rural Houses). Peter and Ann Woodward also provided revised archaeological entries for the gazetteer, including an extended introduction to pre-medieval Dorchester. Sadly, Peter Woodward died before the new edition went to press.

The gathering of information for this new edition was inevitably a team effort. Many have contributed on a large or small scale, resulting in a richness of detail that no individual could possibly provide alone. I am extremely grateful to those who have gone out of their way to supply information, or proffer opinions on early drafts. Of those who read through much of the text, particular thanks are due to Richard Jones (who made many comments on the church entries), Anthony Jaggard (whose knowledge of all things architectural in Dorset continues to be invaluable), Tim Connor, Peter Howell, Michael Whitaker and Roger White. Geoff Brandwood kindly provided notes from the ICBS church files, and the late Nick Antram gave copies of his reports on Roman Catholic churches. Notes by George

McHardy were particularly interesting, made available in the bundle of documents held in the Historic England archive. I have been on a sharp learning curve on Victorian (and later) stained glass, and these entries would have been much less reliable had Alan Brooks not responded so fully to my constant questions. Michael Kerney and Peter Cormack have also answered specific queries on glass, indicated in the text by (MK) or (PC). I am also in debt to Anne Andrews (gardens), Maureen Attwooll, Maureen Boddy, Pru Bollam and Colin Ellis (Weymouth), Susie Barson and John Cattell (St Giles's House), Anna Butler, Ken Mumford and Jenny Cripps (Dorset County Museum), Pat Clark (Lady Wimborne Cottages), Rosie Dilke and Anna Bright (Old Shire Hall, Dorchester), Geoffrey Fisher (C17 and C18 church monuments, indicated by (GF) in the text), Brian and Moira Gittos (medieval monuments), Michael Hall (G.F. Bodley), Rachel Hassall (Sherborne School), Richard Horden (C20 houses in Poole), Stuart Morris (Portland), Tony Nicholson (C.E. Ponting), Philip Proctor (Shaftesbury), Martin Self (Hooke Park), Richard Sims (Bridport and West Bay), Ann Smith (Sherborne Castle and all things Sherborne), the late Gavin Stamp (Sir George Gilbert Scott), Caroline Stanford (Belmont, Lyme Regis), Hilary Townsend (Stalbridge), David Watkins (Poole Museum) and Peter White (Sherborne Old Castle). The former Conservation Officer for East Dorset, Ray Bird, read through the entries for that area, as did Barbara Willis (at the Priest's House Museum), and both provided many useful observations. Benjamin Webb, Conservation Officer for Purbeck District, also kindly read through parts of the text for that area. Many other people not listed here – you will know who you are – have also helped out on various aspects, and all deserve my gratitude.

For the towns, villages and country houses, most of my research was carried out at the Dorset History Centre in Dorchester. I would like to thank Sam Johnston, Dorset County Archivist, his predecessor Hugh Jaques, and all of the staff for their help. Archives related to churches are also to be found in Dorchester, but my work mostly revolved around the Diocesan Archives held at the Wiltshire and Swindon History Centre in Chippenham. On each visit stacks of files were brought forth in a continual flow, helping me get the most from this wealth of material. I would also like to thank the many incumbents and churchwardens who happily unlocked those churches that are not normally open. I am pleased to say, however, that many remain unlocked.

Much of my research for the country houses was conducted for previous books on that subject (published by Spire Books in 2013 and 2014). I would like to repeat my thanks here to those who have been especially generous with their time: the Earl and Countess of Sandwich, the Earl of Shaftesbury, Lord Cranborne, Lord Digby, Lord Fellowes and Lady Kitchener Fellowes, Lord Rockley, Lady Susan Bradbury, Sir Mervyn Medlycott, Sir Richard Glyn, Sir William Hanham, Sir Philip Williams, the Hon. Mrs Charlotte Townshend, Jan Biggs, Anthony Boyden, Katharine Butler, Mrs Caroline Carlyle-Clarke, Dr Harold Carter, Patrick

Cooke, Mrs Jennifer Coombs, James Gibson Fleming, Richard Frampton Hobbs, James Gaggero, Mrs Patricia Jaffé, John and Betty Langham, Roby Littman, Dr Philip Mansell, Harry Ross Skinner, Mrs Julia Smith, Capt. and Mrs Nigel Thimbleby, the late Dr Christopher Upton, the late Wilfrid Weld, Raymond Williams and Edward Wingfield Digby. The late Major-General Mark Bond corresponded about the sad story of Tyneham, while the late Edward Bourke told me much about Chettle and sent copies of his extensive notes on Nathaniel Ireson (later worked up into a monograph by Peter Fitzgerald).

My gratitude is also owed to school staff at Bryanston, Clayesmore, Hanford, Leweston, Lytchett Minster, Milton Abbas and Port Regis. Frank Ahern at Canford School was especially helpful with reference to its archives, as was Martin Papworth of the National Trust (who read through and commented on my revisions for Kingston Lacy and Corfe Castle). Robin Harcourt-Williams, curator at Hatfield House, was also helpful for information on Cranborne Manor. At this point I should add that, while many country houses open either regularly or occasionally to the public, they remain private property, and mention in this book is not intended to imply that access will be allowed.

Colleagues revising other volumes in the *Buildings of England* series have been generous with their time, especially Julian Orbach, James Bettley and Alan Brooks. Research through the libraries of periodicals in London has been provided by Karen Evans and Michael Breen. Others who have helped in various ways (some quite some time ago when I was embarking on my Dorset work) include Nicholas Kingsley, Timothy Mowl and Edward Peters.

This book was commissioned by Sally Salvesen at Yale University Press and was seen through to publication by her successor Mark Eastment. Simon Bradley as editor has guided me through the process, sorting out some of my more tangled arguments and supplementing my researches with extra information, especially that gleaned from local newspapers. Elizabeth O'Rafferty gathered the illustrations, including the spectacular colour photography specially taken for this book by James O. Davies, assisted by Rebecca Lane; and the county, town and building plans drawn by Martin Brown. Linda McQueen has carefully assembled text and pictures, seeing the book through to printing. Thanks are also due to Hester Higton (copy editor), Charlotte Chapman (proofreader) and Judith Wardman (indexer). With all of this checking and cross-checking some errors may yet have crept through and for these I take full responsibility. Finally I would like to thank my artist wife, Kim Jarvis, who put up with my constant disappearances to Dorset, and on the most congenial days accompanied me, providing an informed extra pair of eyes.

Michael Hill
January 2018

INTRODUCTION

There are no cities in Dorset; nor are there any cathedrals or motorways. As in 1972, when the first edition of this book was published, the county is one of countryside and coast, towns and villages, heathland and downs. So apart from the SE corner, where Poole has developed suburbs connecting seamlessly with Bournemouth, Dorset is a rural county. Market towns, located chiefly on rivers, are widely spaced throughout the landscape. So far, modern development has done little to harm their traditional character or relationship with their surroundings. Beyond Poole, population densities are low, comparable with similar counties such as Somerset, Suffolk, Wiltshire and Devon. It is therefore the countryside that predominates. This may broadly be subdivided into three areas: the round-hilled, western clay valleys centred on Sherborne, Beaminster and Bridport; the zigzag of the sparsely populated, sheep-grazing, wide and high chalk downs running diagonally from the NE near Shaftesbury, SW to the Dorchester area, turning SE to meet the sea W of Lulworth, before returning E to Ballard Point; and the pine-wooded heathlands stretching from eastern Purbeck to the N of Poole and linking with the New Forest in Hampshire.

The 'isles' of Purbeck and Portland are curiously distinct places that require separate treatment. Purbeck is sharply separated from the heathland by the slender chalk ridge of the Purbeck Hills, which acts as a climatic barrier. So weather in Purbeck is often warm and sunny while, to the N, cloud may cover much of the county. And the light in Purbeck has a sparkling character, enhanced by the white-grey of the ubiquitous local stone and the ever-present sea. Portland, with its even whiter stone likewise highlighting the bleak scene and surrounded to a greater extent by sea, is so curious a place as to be almost beyond description. The coastline in general, the so-called Jurassic Coast, is a series of curiosities: Chesel Beach, Durdle Door, Lulworth Cove, Kimmeridge Bay and the Old Harry rocks.

After the heroic days of the prehistoric hill-forts, Maiden Castle, Hambledon Hill, Pilsdon Pen and the rest, settlement in Dorset progressed slowly until the creation of the fortified Saxon *burhs* under King Alfred: Shaftesbury, Bridport and Wareham. He also walled the old Roman town of *Durnovaria* – present-day Dorchester. Bridport and Wareham were early ports, both eventually overshadowed by the development of Poole from

9   the C14 onwards, one of the medieval new towns. Corfe, the
location of the most dramatically sited Norman castle in the
region, and Newtown Studland were towns founded by King
John and Edward I respectively, although the latter seems
never to have taken hold, perhaps too overshadowed by nearby
Wareham. Other early towns grew chiefly under the influence of
major churches or abbeys, such as Sherborne, Wimborne and
Milton Abbas.

Control of the land by country estates is a consistent theme in
Dorset. The earliest medieval lay estates were generally smaller
and in the W. To the E larger estates emerged especially after
the Dissolution. And to come at last to architecture, we find the
western estate owners erecting structures in a Perp, late medieval tradition in the C16, much influenced by the master masons
of Hamdon Hill, just over the border in Somerset, while later
houses in the classical tradition are generally found on the more
extensive chalkland estates of the centre and E. The heathland
was left largely undeveloped by the country estates, and not
much settled until the C20. Within this setting there are many
villages of thatched cottages nestling in the valley bottoms, and
few buildings of the first rank in size or importance in the history
of English architecture; but again, though scale may be lacking,
there is abundant character.

Apart from quarrying (*see* below), major industrial activity has also been slight, with the exceptions of brick and tile
manufacture in the Poole area and rope-making at Bridport.
These have sharply declined, as too has light engineering, which
flourished after 1950. Nuclear research had a major establishment
at Winfrith, opened in 1957, but a decommissioning programme
began here in the 1990s. Oil and gas extraction started at Wytch
Farm, the largest onshore oilfield in Europe, on the W side of
Poole Harbour in 1973 and production has continued to expand.
However, the associated structures are mercifully screened by
the surrounding woodland. The military had a major impact
on the county during the Second World War, and many training grounds continue in use, especially around Lulworth; also
at Tyneham, where the village remains unoccupied, its country
house reduced to a ruin.

As one might expect of a county with such a spectacular
coastline, tourism has flourished. George III's treatment for his
2   nervous condition by sea bathing at Weymouth in 1789 – an
p. 645 early date in the national context – and his annual visits between
1791 and 1802 saw the growth of that resort from a humble port.
Swanage was developed largely for sea-bathing visitors from the
1820s onwards. Lyme Regis also became popular from the early
C19, and by the early C20 was joined by the coastal suburbs of
Poole at Branksome Park and Canford Cliffs.

THE GEOLOGY OF DORSET
BY PAUL ENSOM

The sediments forming the surface geology of Dorset were deposited in a variety of environments over the last 201 Ma (million years/million years ago). Overlying much older and deeply buried rocks, they have responded to periods of compression and tension throughout their history; they have been faulted, folded and tilted, sometimes dramatically, as seen at Lulworth Cove and Stair Hole (West Lulworth). These strata provide the medium from which the Dorset landscape has been sculpted, and from which the building stones described by the late Alec Clifton-Taylor (*see* p. 7) have come. The exceptional geology and

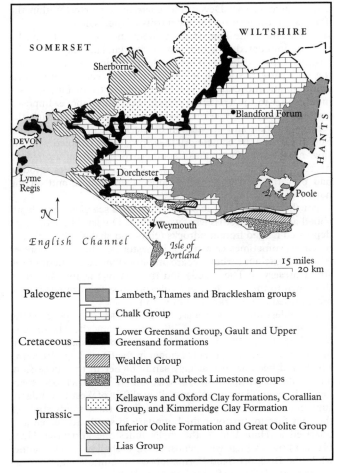

Simplified geological map of Dorset

geomorphology of much of the Dorset coast led to its inscription on the World Heritage List in 2001 as part of the Jurassic Coast.

At depth, the rocks below Dorset are an extension of those which are exposed in parts of Devon and Somerset. These Devonian and Carboniferous rocks (older than 299 Ma) form Dorset's 'basement'. They carry scars of ocean closure and continental collision, facets of the plate-tectonic processes which continue to make and break continents and shape the Earth as we know it. These strata dip down to the E beneath Dorset and have been glimpsed in the cores recovered from boreholes drilled in the search for hydrocarbons; at Wytch Farm on the shore of Poole Harbour they are present at around 9,000 ft (c. 2,750 metres), and 5,500 ft (c. 1,670 metres) at Cranborne. Overlying the eroded landscape formed by these basement rocks are PERMIAN and TRIASSIC red-beds (299–201 Ma) laid down in arid conditions and familiar in east Devon and parts of Somerset. Within the Triassic mudstones are thick deposits of rock salt.

At the end of the Triassic, after an absence of around 100 Ma, the sea inundated a featureless terrestrial landscape and the JURASSIC period began. The sea floors during this period, and the CRETACEOUS which followed, were subject to both subtle and dramatic movements. Some were related to the buried basement, some to the Triassic rock salt mentioned above. Imposed on these 'internal processes', astronomical cycles involving the relative position and orientation of the Earth in relation to our Sun influenced the climate. All these processes, coupled with the slow northward movement of southern Britain from around 30 degrees N at the start of the Jurassic to over 50 degrees N today, had powerful and interrelated impacts on climate and on the nature of the sediments deposited.

For the ensuing Jurassic period (56 Ma), a sea of varying depth ebbed and flowed across what we know as Dorset. The sediments deposited ranged from mudrocks (clays and shales), through silts to sands, sometimes calcareous. Limestones, which are more or less pure calcium carbonate, are an important constituent of the strata preserved. These beds and the rest of the Jurassic strata dip down to the E so that, as a rule, progressively younger strata are exposed as one travels from W to E.

The oldest Jurassic strata are the LIAS GROUP, exposed along the coast as far E as Burton Cliff, and flooring the Marshwood Vale. The strata consist of grey-blue clays, black shales and thin limestones, the last especially evident in the BLUE LIAS FORMA-TION, and become increasingly sandy higher in the succession. This culminates in the BRIDPORT SAND FORMATION, spectacularly exposed in the golden-yellow cliffs E of West Bay. Inland, sunken lanes are especially characteristic of these sandy strata of the Lias Group. Just over the boundary in south Somerset, and quarried at Ham Hill, is the shelly limestone known as HAM HILL STONE which was deposited in a shallow tidal channel while the Bridport Sand Formation was accumulating.

Above the Bridport Sand Formation is the INFERIOR OOLITE FORMATION. A series of fossiliferous, often iron-rich, oolitic and

sometimes rubbly limestones, they are best developed in north
Dorset. They have been quarried as building stone. The overlying FULLER'S EARTH, FROME CLAY, FOREST MARBLE and
CORNBRASH formations comprise the GREAT OOLITE GROUP.
The lower formations of this group consist predominantly of
mudrocks, though calcareous units occur such as the FULLER'S
EARTH ROCK and WATTONENSIS BEDS. Oyster banks are
preserved within the Frome Clay Formation along the Dorset
coast. The uppermost two formations, the Forest Marble and
Cornbrash, become increasingly dominated by carbonates. The
middle of the Forest Marble is characterized by impersistent,
coarse shelly limestones that originated in tidal channels. These
have been widely quarried and will take a polish, hence the name
'marble'. Below, the lower argillaceous (mudrock) sequence is
relieved by thin sandy limestones which have been used in buildings. Above the shelly limestones are more mudrocks; these are
overlain by the Cornbrash Formation, in which thin and often
rubbly beds of limestone dominate.

The progressive shallowing of the sea that may be deduced
from the sediments and their fossils within the Great Oolite
Group was reversed with the deposition of the KELLAWAYS
and OXFORD CLAY formations; fossiliferous sandy clays, clays
and shales, the last sometimes bituminous, underlie parts of the
Weymouth lowlands and Blackmore Vale. Both these 'lowland'
areas are crossed by more pronounced ridges formed by resistant strata in the overlying Corallian Group which separates the
Oxford Clay from the younger Kimmeridge Clay formations.
The CORALLIAN GROUP is a sequence of clays, sands and limestones representing shallower water conditions over a sea floor
which was influenced by underlying tectonic processes; composition and thicknesses of beds vary laterally, especially in north
Dorset. Useful building stones have been quarried from them.

The overlying marine KIMMERIDGE CLAY FORMATION,
named after the village on the Dorset coast, comprises a great
thickness of clays and shales with carbonate-rich stone bands
common at certain levels. These strata were deposited in deeper
water and often in anoxic conditions. These conditions are
responsible for a high bituminous content, which at its most
extreme forms the waxy shale known as 'Kimmeridge Coal' that
has been used in industrial processes and for the domestic hearth
alike. In addition to invertebrates, these richly fossiliferous strata
contain a remarkable fauna of fishes and reptiles. Terrestrial
dinosaurs and flying reptiles have also been found.

Shallowing seas once again brought about a significant change
in the sediments deposited. The PORTLAND SAND FORMATION
heralds a change in environment, with muddy silts and fine
sands dominating, and in turn is overlain by the most famous
of Dorset's limestones, Portland Stone. The PORTLAND STONE
FORMATION, named from the Isle of Portland where it has been
exploited extensively, is present across parts of southern Dorset.
Deposited in warm shallow seas often with strong currents, the
sediment particles were sometimes laid down as submarine dunes,

providing thick beds of clean and well-sorted sediment – a perfect stone for building. Shelly horizons are present, such as the decorative Roach, in which many of the shells of the abundant fossils have been dissolved, leaving empty moulds.

At the end of the Jurassic (145 Ma), the sea was replaced by extensive lagoons and shallow lakes across southern Dorset. This heralded another terrestrial interlude of around 20 Ma in the early Cretaceous, during which the PURBECK LIMESTONE and WEALDEN groups were laid down. The former continues to be an important source of building and decorative stones, including the celebrated PURBECK MARBLE; the latter provides clay for specialist brick and tile manufacture. During this time, earth movements to the W and N led to the erosion of varying thicknesses of previously deposited sediments.

Around 125 Ma the sea once again inundated parts of Dorset, depositing the LOWER GREENSAND GROUP. The full extent of this incursion from the E is unclear, but we know that a more extensive transgression covered more of the eroded landscape with marine clays, silts and sands, sometimes calcareous, comprising the GAULT and UPPER GREENSAND formations. Evidence for localized uplift and folding can be seen in the cliffs at Ringstead Bay, E of Weymouth, where the Gault and Upper Greensand formations rest unconformably on the inclined Kimmeridge Clay Formation and Portland and Purbeck Limestone groups. Similarly in west Dorset, the summits of the hills composed of the much older Lias Group are capped unconformably by these same sediments: e.g. at Golden Cap, Lewesdon Hill and Lambert's Castle. Beds of the siliceous rock CHERT are especially well developed in the Upper Greensand Formation of west Dorset, where they have been worked as a building stone. The Cretaceous culminated in the deposition of the great thickness of the CHALK GROUP across the whole of Dorset. Today this distinctive rock type, sometimes rich in FLINT, forms the ridgeways of Dorset, stretching up into Wiltshire, Hampshire and beyond.

The Cretaceous period ended 66 Ma. Over the ensuing millions of years, several episodes of uplift saw the Chalk Group and underlying strata eroded from parts of southern and western Dorset; PALEOGENE sediments (LAMBETH, THAMES and BRACKLESHAM groups) were deposited on an eroded Chalk surface across the W end of the Hampshire Basin and beyond. From around 37 Ma Dorset entered what might be thought of as the geological equivalent of the Dark Ages. The only sediments identified from this time interval were deposited in the last 2.5 Ma. The continuing northward movement of Africa to collide with Europe created the Alps, and reactivated faults and folds along the line of the Chalk ridgeway running from Abbotsbury to the Isle of Purbeck, and E to form the spine of the Isle of Wight. At Ballard Point (Swanage), Lulworth Cove and Stair Hole, the sea has carved through steeply inclined strata, providing spectacular evidence of the effects of these plate-tectonic processes. The rocks of central and north Dorset also responded to this episode of folding, forming a landscape which has been sculpted to create the Dorset we recognize today.

BUILDING MATERIALS
BY ALEC CLIFTON-TAYLOR*

For the possession of natural building materials of the highest aesthetic quality, Dorset ranks with Somerset and Gloucestershire as one of the three most fortunate of all the English counties. There is a good deal less to be seen, especially in the field of outstanding churches, than in either of the other two, but the debt of the rest of England for stone is greater to Dorset than to any other county whatsoever.

The STONE here is not the whole story, but it must of course come first. In the Middle Ages there was the early Cretaceous Purbeck marble, not a true marble but a gastropod-rich limestone which will take – and when protected from the weather retain – a high polish; this stone enjoyed immense popularity, mainly for church architecture, between the beginning of the C13 and the second quarter of the C14. The late Jurassic and early Cretaceous rocks were also yielding, even as early as this, other limestones much more important to the Dorset scene: limestones from nearly a dozen beds in the Isle of Purbeck, some with hardly any shells, like the splendid stone known as 'Purbeck-Portland'; and then Portland itself, with stone worked locally from Norman times, and by the C14 already finding its way in some quantity as far afield as Exeter. But the great age of Portland stone did not begin until the C17. It was the patronage of Sir Christopher Wren which turned it into the most famous stone in England, and after three hundred years this is what it still remains.

There are three great beds of Portland stone. The uppermost is the Roach, fairly coarse and shelly, and therefore rich in texture when employed for building. Then comes the Whitbed, on which the great reputation of Portland principally rests: a magnificent building stone, close-grained, even in texture because relatively free from shell fragments, and the whitest of all the Jurassic limestones. Below this is the Basebed, even more uniform in its composition. All three can be seen in a variety of Dorset buildings, mainly in the southern part of the county. Had Portland stone been less hard and therefore less expensive to work, and had it not been situated, despite the advantage of proximity to the sea, on a remote and for centuries almost uninhabited peninsula, there can be no doubt that it would have been used in its own county much more extensively than it was.

Formerly there were many other oolitic limestone quarries serving local needs, not one of which is now working, nor has been for generations. The town of Sherborne is largely constructed of the local Inferior Oolite, known locally as Sherborne Building Stone.

The Victorians, often attracted to polished surfaces, revived to some extent the fashion for Purbeck marble, which can be

---

* Slightly revised for this edition.

107 seen in particular profusion in the remarkable church which
G.E. Street built for the 3rd Earl of Eldon at the hill village of
Kingston, overlooking Corfe Castle. This stone was hewn on
Lord Eldon's estate.

The Purbeck quarries also supplied the county with many of
its beautiful stone roofing tiles. Purbeck stone tiles were already
popular before the end of the C15, and by 1700 were being used
all over Dorset by everyone who could afford them; but their
great weight meant that they were always relatively expensive, as
was the very robust wooden framework required to support them.
Though still produced, most of those that survive in present-day
Dorset were quarried some time ago.

Even among the Jurassic stones, the tally of Dorset's resources
is not yet by any means complete. From the Corallian Group in
the N of the county comes a coarse but very serviceable building stone, well seen at Sturminster Newton. The main quarries
were at Marnhull, three miles N of Sturminster. There were also
other 'marbles' – limestones, that is – which could be polished
for internal use: septarian nodules prised from the Oxford Clay
Formation at Melbury Bubb, near Evershot, and a shell-rich
limestone from the Forest Marble Formation at Longburton,
s of Sherborne. In west Dorset, limestones from the Blue Lias
Formation were at one time extensively worked; the older parts
of Lyme Regis itself are largely built of it. But the finest Liassic
limestone in Dorset, it must be admitted, is not native to the
county; this came from Ham Hill, a few miles across the border
with Somerset. The NW part of Dorset owes a great debt to this
31 glorious golden-brown stone. It is seen to specially good effect
on the ashlar-faced walls of the nave of Sherborne Abbey. In
32 Tudor times it travelled s at least as far as Charminster (for the
church tower).

Of the younger Dorset stones the most enjoyable is that from
the Upper Greensand Formation of the Shaftesbury district,
where it was used extensively both in Shaftesbury itself and for
churches as far s as Blandford and Charlton Marshall. *Vanbrugh*
76 availed himself of this stone for Eastbury; and when, after its
builder's death, all but one wing of that great house was demolished, it is said that much of the material was reused by *Wyatt*
at Bryanston (1778). The surviving outbuildings from his house
seem to bear this out. In cottage walls this stone is particularly
pleasing when chequered with flint.

At Wimborne Minster, stone from the Upper Greensand Formation, which was no doubt floated down the Stour, can be
seen in combination with a dark rust-brown conglomerate of
the Paleogene period that underlies parts of the heathlands (e.g.
Hardy's 'Egdon Heath') in the SE portion of the county. Two
kinds of stone so different not only in colour but also in tone have
produced, in combination, a 'spotted dog' effect which is not
easy to admire. The conglomerate stone is neither attractive to
look at nor a good building material, but in times when transport
was laborious and no better material was at hand locally, it was
doubtless welcome, as for the church at Wool.

Between these two, and in Dorset much more prominent than either, is another of the limestones: Chalk. This was important both for itself and also because it yielded flint. Nearly half the surface of the county consists of rolling chalk downs; from Cranborne Chase in the NE a broad belt of Chalk sweeps across the centre of the county almost as far as Beaminster, and then doubles back past Dorchester to the coast between White Nothe and Lulworth, and then to Swanage. This Chalk belt is decidedly more sparsely populated than the rest of Dorset; agriculture was less rewarding here, and village buildings were humbler. But the harder Chalk bands were good enough to be used for building. Nevertheless, Chalk masonry is rare by comparison with flint, which for centuries was used for walling throughout the Chalk areas. The best effects were obtained when the flint was employed in combination with local stone in alternating bands and chequers, a practice which can be seen to better effect in Dorset and Wiltshire than anywhere else in England. It was no doubt a convenient method of making the much more expensive limestone go further, but fortunately it is also both durable and decorative. In Dorset, bands are much the commoner of the two forms; at the E end of the county bands of flint sometimes alternate – less attractively – with brick, as commonly in Hampshire.

From the Chalk belt also came – to leave now the subject of stone – the famous Dorset COB, which is in fact mud. In many parts of England cottages and farm buildings were formerly built of mud, but not every county could provide chalky mud, which was the best, as the lime acted as a binder, and, mixed with straw, yielded a stronger wall. Some parts of Dorset have few or no cob buildings, but on the Chalk it is surprising how many survive: far more than is generally realized, because it is always rendered or at least whitewashed, which means that it is no longer visible. All the cottages at Milton Abbas, for example, a showpiece of Dorset village architecture, are of this material. The Winterbornes, among other villages, preserve a number of cob walls, still occasionally with the coping of thatch with which they were all provided originally.

THATCHED ROOFS are still plentiful in Dorset. The advent of the combine harvester has led to a shortage of long straw, and ordinary straw thatch is gradually disappearing, here as elsewhere. But the material known as Dorset reed (because it is laid like true reed, with the butt-ends of the stalks forming the exposed surface) is still obtainable; this is, in fact, specially selected wheat straw of a variety which grows to about 3 ft (90 cm.), and which escapes bruising at harvest time by being passed through a device known as a comber, attached to the threshing drum. This kind of thatch, which looks more urbane than ordinary straw thatch, is virtually confined to Dorset and Devon. In recent years, true reed (*Phragmites communis*), such as grows so profusely in the broads and marshes of Norfolk, has been cultivated at Radipole close to Weymouth, and at Abbotsbury.

TIMBER FRAMING was never a favourite building method in Dorset and is now decidedly rare (*see* p. 52). BRICK AND TILE manufacture, on the other hand, was carried on increasingly in some parts of the county from the C17, and there are even modest examples of brickwork from the time of Henry VIII (*see* p. 44). The first large houses do not, however, go back earlier than the reign of James I: the core of Bloxworth House dates from 1608 and Anderson Manor from 1622. But the county is not lacking in good brick clays, notably the Oxford Clay and Kimmeridge Clay formations and the rather narrow band of Paleogene clays which overlie the Chalk in the SE, describing an arc from the Hampshire boundary near Cranborne to Wimborne Minster and Broadmayne near Dorchester, thence back eastwards to Studland. Most of Dorset's brick architecture is in towns, the stimulus for which was sometimes provided by bad fires, as at Dorchester in 1613, 1725 and 1775, at Gillingham in 1694, and at Blandford in 1731. Excellent Georgian brick buildings can be enjoyed at Poole (despite improper demolitions), Wareham, Weymouth, Bridport, Dorchester and above all Blandford, where the fine brickwork is of several colours. Broadmayne was known for its speckled bricks, owing to the presence in the clay of small nodules of manganese oxide, which only become evident after firing. Tiles were made chiefly in SE Dorset, where was also the principal demand. The works at Chickerell (Kellaways and Oxford Clay formations) supplied Weymouth. These are no longer in operation; most of the local brick and tile works, as unhappily all over England, have had no alternative but to close.

PREHISTORIC AND ROMAN REMAINS
BY PETER WOODWARD AND ANN WOODWARD

Dorset in prehistory

Handaxe scatters and concentrations in Dorset river-gravel quarries identify hominin occupations of the PALAEOLITHIC period, beside ancient rivers in an environment very different from that of today. In the Broom gravel quarries at Thorncombe, by the confluence of the Axe and Blackwater rivers, are the bedded silts and sand deposits of an ancient meandering river. Here, a large concentration of Acheulean handaxes of chert indicates several generations of activity, hunting on a shallow ridge with heath and mainly coniferous woodland, during a warmer interglacial period between 339,000 and 245,000 B.P. (Before Present). Scatters of Acheulean handaxes in SE Dorset, from quarries along the Frome, with concentrations in Moreton and Corfe Mullen parishes, identify occupation on two ancient rivers, the Frome and Solent, flowing E and S through land now inundated by the sea.

A few flint axes identify a human presence in the UPPER PALAEOLITHIC period, between 60,000 and 13,000 B.P., but there are no known occupation sites until the following MESOLITHIC period. With the retreat of the last glaciers, the

consequent rising sea levels, coastal erosion and cutting of
the English Channel (from *c.* 11,000 B.C.) to form the British Isles,
there were dramatic changes in the environment. In the EARLY
MESOLITHIC, 10,000–7500 B.C., the rapid growth of deciduous
and coniferous woodland in a warmer climate provided rich and
diverse resources for recolonization by hunter-gatherer groups,
exploiting river valleys and surrounding uplands. In the LATER
MESOLITHIC, 7500–4000 B.C., hunter-gatherer groups managed
woodland tracts rich in game (auroch, deer and pig), maintaining
glades for seasonal camps within climax woodland of oak, elm
and ash, with some pine. Groups from Weymouth Bay westwards
exploited marine resources of shell and fish. A number of sites
have been excavated and some radiocarbon-dated (*c.* 6000–4000
B.C.): Blashenwell, Corfe Castle (5700–4600 cal B.C.); Culverwell,
Southwell, Portland (shell midden 6220–5300 cal B.C., a hearth
6210–5750 cal B.C.); Down Farm, Sixpenny Handley (4340–4040
cal B.C.); Whitcombe Hill, Winfrith Newburgh; Boyne's Lane,
Iwerne Courtney; and Ulwell (Swanage).

Evidence of the first farmers appeared in the EARLIER NEO-
LITHIC period, around 4000 B.C. Remains of domestic animals
and cereals indicate that both arable and pastoral farming were
practised, and clearance of the wooded landscape began. Technological innovations included the production of polished stone
tools, especially axes for wood-felling, and the first pottery. Large
chunks from sets of finely made bowls and jars were sometimes deposited deliberately in pits. Such deposits are common
in south Dorset, as at Rowden (Winterbourne Steepleton) and
Maiden Castle (Winterborne St Martin). However, few traces of
any buildings survive.

The earliest man-made monuments were LONG BARROWS.
Each barrow is a mound formed mostly from soil and subsoil dug
out from ditches alongside, and, as occasionally on Cranborne
Chase, around the rear end. Radiocarbon-dating has shown that
long barrows were built between 3800 and 3300 B.C., but the
active history of each was often short, and few were in use at
any one time. Most contained structures at the wider end, and
these may have been constructed from large timber posts or
megalithic stones. Such chambers often contained groups of
human remains; these were usually disarticulated, but sometimes
whole skeletons were deposited. Earthen long barrows have been
excavated at Wor Barrow (Sixpenny Handley), Hambledon Hill
(Iwerne Courtney) and Alington Avenue (Dorchester), and the
remains of stone chambers can be seen at the Grey Mare and
Her Colts (Long Bredy) and the Hell Stone (Portesham). Long
barrows of exceptional length are known as BANK BARROWS;
the largest are at each end of the South Dorset Ridgeway, at
Broadmayne and Martin's Down (Long Bredy), and at Maiden
Castle (Winterborne St Martin).

The larger communal monuments, known as CAUSEWAYED
ENCLOSURES – enclosures with single or multiple circuits of
causewayed ditches and banks – have been dated between the
late C38 and the late C36 B.C. Evidence for structures within them

is rare, but the ditch fillings often contain rich deposits of debris, including animal bones, cereals, pottery, digging tools and stone implements. Isolated human bones also occur. First interpreted as settlements or pastoral enclosures, causewayed enclosures are now thought to have functioned as centres for seasonal gatherings, exchange of commodities and ritual enactments. At Hambledon Hill the occurrence of human remains suggests that the enclosures may have been used for the exposure and excarnation of bodies, linked to ancestor rites. Finds at Maiden Castle were more domestic in nature, but included exotic items brought from afar. Some 300 years later, c. 3300 B.C., a long mound and causewayed enclosure (Alington Avenue and Flagstones, Dorchester) aligned on the ridge-crest overlooking the River Frome, were constructed NE of Maiden Castle. Human remains in the ditches indicate that these two monuments were primarily concerned with the disposal of the dead. Also built in this period was the DORSET CURSUS (Gussage St Michael etc.), two parallel banks with external ditches running across Cranborne Chase for more than six miles, the longest cursus in Britain. It was built in two main phases, and was integrated with several long barrows. It probably functioned as a processional way for ritual ceremonies.

In the LATER NEOLITHIC period, 2750–2500 B.C., stone and timber circles and large henges were built to enshrine religious belief and to enclose ceremonies. HENGES, a class of monument of many different forms, were circular with circuits of deeply cut pits or ditches and banks, and one or more entrances. Large henges were built near the earlier long barrow concentrations in south Dorset at Dorchester, and on Cranborne Chase at
6   Knowlton. These, built to impress, provided new ceremonial spaces and centres for seasonal gathering, trade and communal endeavour. Henge earthworks are buried below Maumbury Rings (Dorchester), and others enclose Knowlton church. Still traceable in a ploughed field at Mount Pleasant (West Stafford) is a large henge enclosure of twelve acres. Smaller post- and pit rings have also been discovered, and a huge timber-post setting buried below Dorchester town centre. In south Dorset are sarsen stone circles; the best preserved stands beside the River South Winterborne (Winterbourne Abbas).

Some henges continued in use for many centuries. During their lifespans, c. 2500 B.C., new pottery types known as Beakers, and the first copper knives, were introduced from Continental Europe. This CHALCOLITHIC PERIOD, or Copper Age, 2500–2250 B.C., also saw the construction of many small ditched ROUND BARROWS, tumuli or burial mounds, which contained inhumation burials associated with Beakers and grave goods such as knives, stone archers' wristguards, flint arrowheads and a few ornaments made from amber or gold.

In the EARLY BRONZE AGE, 2250–1600 B.C., many hundreds of ROUND BARROWS were constructed on the chalk downs, carefully sited on ridges and hill-slopes, sometimes singly but more often in groups. Recorded in most downland parishes, they are often ploughed away and survive only as cropmarks. The

arrangement and proportion of barrow mound, ditch and bank
have been used to describe the final earthwork profile (sometimes inverted), such as pond, saucer and bowl barrow. Most are
enclosed by a ditch or bank; the bowl profile is the most common.
Excavations have shown long periods of use, with re-interment
and replacement of primary burials, and the insertion of new secondary burials, frequently associated with phases of enlargement.
Over time the practice of inhumation was replaced by cremation;
both were sometimes accompanied by offerings and grave goods,
made of flint, bone and bronze, often with distinctive pottery
urns. Large numbers of round barrows were built in the areas
around the henges at Dorchester and on Cranborne Chase. One
of the largest concentrations in southern Britain is along the
South Dorset Ridgeway. A particularly long and complex group,
including the massive Culliford Tree Barrow (Whitcombe), was
aligned with the bank barrow at Broadmayne; a single barrow
seals the nearby Whitcombe long barrow. The linear group along
Bronkham Hill (Winterborne Stickland) is particularly conspicuous. Clusters occur at intervals on wider Ridgeway hilltops and
on spurs to the N. Close to the source of the South Winterborne
at Poor Lot (Winterbourne Abbas) is the core of a very large
cluster, well preserved in pasture. Near to the henge monuments at Dorchester are two particularly large barrows, Conquer
and Lawrence barrows. Round barrow mounds, placed at the
centre of earlier monuments, such as at Flagstones Enclosure
(Dorchester), on Ridge Hill (Upwey and Winterborne St Martin)
and to the NE of Eggardon (Askerswell), appear to have claimed
and reserved the shared sacred spaces of earlier times for special
burials, perhaps those of an aristocracy or religious élite.

In the MIDDLE BRONZE AGE, 1600–1000 B.C., a sedentary
society was established with the construction of small SETTLE-
MENTS and major field systems. Settlements usually contained
two or three round timber structures, comprising a main house
and ancillary huts for animals, storage or crafts. Key examples
have been excavated at Shearplace Hill (Sydling St Nicholas) and
Rowden (Winterbourne Steepleton). The theory that each farm
was occupied only briefly was confirmed at Bestwall (Wareham),
where four successive houses were dated by radiocarbon. Bronze-
work included tools, often axes or spearheads, and especially
ornaments for the neck, wrist or finger. Most BURIALS were
cremations, often deposited inside urns of bucket or globular
shape. Some were interred within existing round barrows, or
newly built ones, which tended to be small; others were buried
in 'flat' cemeteries. Burials tended to be near settlements, and
the small numbers of individual burials in each cluster suggest
that the cemeteries served families or small social groups. The
'flat' cemetery at Rimbury (Preston) and the burials within the
Deverel Barrow (Milborne St Andrew) have given their names
to the Deverel–Rimbury culture.

p. 14

The earliest FIELDS, commonly named 'Celtic' fields, were
often laid out in a regular (coaxial) manner, cutting across the
topography. Such fields were common on the chalk in central

Milborne St Andrew, Deverel Barrow.
Engraving, 1826

Dorset and also occurred at Bestwall (Wareham), where they
were initiated in the C16 B.C. Other field systems grew more
organically. Fields would have been used for both arable farming
and stock. Ploughing on slopes gradually caused the downhill
movement of soil, which collected behind the boundary banks
to form deep lynchets. The field system on Grimstone Down
(Stratton) is especially well preserved.

Associated with the fields were DYKES consisting of substantial
banks and ditches. Some of these extended across large areas
and may have functioned as boundaries between territories, or
between zones designated for arable or pasture. Other dykes
were built across prominent ridges. A fine set of such cross-
dykes survives on the hill spurs S of Nettlecombe Tout, surrounding Lyscombe Bottom (Cheselbourne, Melcombe Horsey,
Piddletrenthide).

Small SETTLEMENTS of two or three round structures were
also characteristic of the LATE BRONZE AGE, c. 1100–600 B.C.
At Tinney's Lane, Sherborne, settlement was associated with
extensive pottery production in the C12 to C11 B.C.; other settlements include the three successive units at Bestwall (Wareham).
Some of these lasted into the earliest Iron Age, and those on
Purbeck, such as Gaulter Gap (Kimmeridge) and Eldon's Seat
(Corfe Castle), have produced evidence for the production of
shale bracelets and salt. Throughout the Bronze Age, metalwork was highly prized for ornaments and tools. By the C9 B.C.
networks of manufacture, exchange and recasting distributed
new products between regions. Two bronze axe types are named
after Blandford and Portland. Buried HOARDS, often found near
settlement sites and close to water sources, can be identified as
votive offerings; a few may have been the hidden stock of craft
metalworkers. Bronze axe hoards are frequent, while gold objects
were rare and deposited separately. The pair of gold neck rings

from Fleet Common, discovered on a spring line below a settlement, must have been of great value. The massive hoard of socketed axes from Langton Matravers, the largest in Britain, was deposited at the beginning of the Iron Age.

Throughout the IRON AGE, from 600 B.C., field systems continued to be developed, respecting older land allotment and barrow cemeteries. Earliest Iron Age SETTLEMENTS have been excavated in Purbeck, as at Eldon's Seat and Rope Lake Hole (both Corfe Castle), and many others may be identified by the occurrence of distinctive red-coated haematite pottery. These open settlements are associated with field systems, later buried below Roman successors, as at Kingston. Small enclosed settlements were also built within and across field systems, often on hill-slopes facing s and e, as at Ringmoor (Turnworth). Distinctive enclosure types expressed local identities, power and purpose. Those on Cranborne Chase were particularly large and distinctive. The enclosure excavated at Sovell Down (Gussage All Saints) remained in occupation until the Roman period.

HILL-FORTS were built from *c.* 400 B.C., at a time when a new regional pottery style, Maiden Castle–Marnhull, begins to identify a distinct Iron Age community in Dorset. Twenty-nine Iron Age hill-forts are recorded in Dorset, all surviving as earthworks, although some are now much reduced by ploughing. They vary in size from a few hectares, as at Abbotsbury, to one of the largest and most magnificent in Britain, Maiden Castle (Winterborne St Martin). All were built on and around hilltops, often associated with earlier cross-ridge dykes, well sited above water courses and river valleys. All were built to impress. The defensive banks and ditches have one or more entrances, often designed with outer protective banks, sophisticated ramps and passageways to control and limit access. Hill-forts commonly occur in pairs, of which one is sometimes smaller and has less complicated ramparts and entrances, such as Maiden Castle and Poundbury (Dorchester), Hambledon Hill (Iwerne Courtney) and Hod Hill (Stourpaine). These pairs may have fulfilled complementary roles rather than serving competing groups. Dispersed farming groups must have contributed a great deal to the construction of these places, which may at times have functioned as small towns and villages. At Maiden Castle a sequence of occupation can be understood in some detail, and the settlement visualized with its planned hut groups, streets, working areas, stock enclosures and grain-pit storage. The plan of the occupation at Hod Hill, urban in scale, has been discerned from geophysical survey.

By the later Iron Age, pottery made around Poole Harbour was being traded over the whole of Dorset and bronze coinage was in use, providing a new regional identity to the communities, identified by the Romans as the *Durotriges*. They adopted a burial practice of inhumation accompanied by rich goods for both female and male interments. In south Dorset small cemeteries were attached to unenclosed settlements. Bronze mirrors, their backs engraved with sophisticated swirling designs, were particular to a concentration of female burials centred on Portland and the Dorset coast. Trade across the Channel from Gaul,

5

p. 572

to villages around Poole Harbour such as Ower (Corfe Castle),
is represented by ceramic imports, including Roman wares and
amphorae, used in the transport of wine.

Dorset in the Roman and post-Roman periods, to A.D. 700

The ROMAN period began in 43 or early 44 A.D. when Vespa-
sian, commanding the Second Augustan legion, fought his way
through Dorset. Suetonius refers to thirty battles, the subjec-
tion of two tribes and the capture of *oppida*, fortresses. These
fortresses must have been hill-forts, some certainly within the
territory of the *Durotriges*. Their capture is dramatically illustrated by the construction of a Roman fort within the hill-fort
p. 572 at Hod Hill (Stourpaine). Other hill-forts were no doubt occupied for short periods. Evidence of warfare has been found in a
mass-burial pit at Spetisbury Rings and in the trauma injuries
recorded in the Durotrigian cemetery at Maiden Castle (Winterborne St Martin). A half-legionary fort was also built at Lake
Gates Farm (Corfe Mullen), s of Badbury Rings, supplied by a
road constructed from a fort at Hamworthy (Poole) on Poole
Harbour. A supply road from Weymouth Bay to a road junction
NW of Maiden Castle is also likely. Further to the w is the fort
at Waddon Hill (Stoke Abbott), above Marshwood Vale, near the
hill-forts of Lewesdon (Broadwindsor) and Pilsdon.

In the aftermath of the conquest, the road network was consolidated along legionary supply routes and ancient trackways
between hill-forts and settlements. This network can be traced in
linear stretches of present roads, and in earthworks, none more
impressive than Ackling Dyke (Gussage All Saints), running
into the county from Old Sarum (Salisbury) to Badbury Rings
(Shapwick). After Badbury the road heads for Maiden Castle,
with a fine stretch at Puddletown. A walled Roman town, built
at the road junction NW of Maiden Castle, has been identified
in the Antonine Itinerary as *Durnovaria* (Dorchester) on the
London–Exeter road, and the Durotrigian settlement at Crab
Farm (Shapwick), w of Badbury Rings, as *Vindocladia*. *Durnovaria* was one of two walled towns in the *Durotriges* territory,
the other being at Ilchester (Somerset), *Lindinis*, on the Roman
road to *Isca Dumnoniorum* (Exeter). Both would have been *civitas*
capitals for governance, trade and markets within a productive
urban and rural economy.

Pre-Roman settlements continued to farm the 'Celtic' fields
on the chalk downs, such as Grimstone (Stratton), and to
make pottery, salt and stone products on Poole Harbour and in
Purbeck, as at Bestwall and Worgret (Wareham) and at Norden,
Ower (both Corfe Castle) and Redcliffe (Arne). From the C2
A.D. Romano-British settlements across Dorset adopted rectangular buildings, including houses with central porches and workshops, as at Norden, around and within *Durnovaria*, and on the
downs, such as on Tolpuddle Ball. Many-roomed villas were
built on certain settlements, often next to springs and streams,

probably at the centre of prosperous estates. In the C3 to C4 these became increasingly complex, with added wings and corridors, bath houses, heated rooms and mosaic pavements. The style of a number of fine figurative mosaics identifies a highly skilled group of mosaicists working at the villas N of *Durnovaria* in the C4, notably at Frampton (Maiden Newton) and Hinton St Mary, where Christian elements were included. The designs of this Durnovarian Group were otherwise characterized by hunting scenes, fleshy beasts and sea creatures, and busts of the Four Seasons. Aspects of religious belief are also frequently encountered in the deposition of votive objects in pits, linked to the dedication of boundaries, buildings and sometimes particular rooms, perhaps household shrines. Pagan and Christian cemeteries have been identified, such as those on the settlement sites around Dorchester (*Durnovaria*), often located with reference to pre-Roman burials, structures and enclosures, as were the temples constructed on Jordan Hill (Preston), at Maiden Castle and at Norden.

p. 323

The mineral wealth of Dorset was exploited throughout the Romano-British period. Purbeck and Portesham were the sources of building stone, to be seen in *Durnovaria* and in the C3–C4 villa buildings. The early success of pottery production on sites around Poole Harbour, reaching Hadrian's Wall along military supply routes in the C1 to C2, and more local regional supply until the C5, was accompanied by the production of salt. Products worked from Purbeck stone were made at the large settlement at Norden: a large-scale workshop production of limestone mortars, chalk and mudstone tesserae, and polished marble panels. Here and elsewhere in Purbeck, Kimmeridge shale was worked on an industrial scale, making lathe-turned bracelets and vessels, carved table legs, table tops, platters and trays. Many Purbeck products were traded out of the region.

In the C5, with Roman Britain outside the Empire, the monetary economy, commodity production and regional trade all collapsed. In the POST-ROMAN period the character of the settlement around Dorchester continued, but by the end of the century its extra-mural settlements were reorganized, with new buildings and cemeteries. New cemeteries are also recorded into the C6, W of the settlement at Tolpuddle Ball, at Ulwell (Swanage) and elsewhere. A Saxon presence is revealed by burials with weapons, in and around barrows as at Maiden Castle, and in the far W at Hardown Hill (Whitchurch Canonicorum). The reinforcement of the ancient boundary of Bokerley Dyke (Pentridge) and the severance of the Roman road known as Ackling Dyke (*see* Gussage All Saints) may be seen as a response to the perceived threat of Anglo-Saxon settlement along the Avon. Perhaps this represented the defence of a BRITISH KINGDOM, organized by an aristocracy centred on *Durnovaria*, and on *Vindocladia* at Badbury Rings (Shapwick), where ramparts were also strengthened. Gildas, a British scholar possibly resident in Dorset and writing sometime between the mid C5 and mid C6, records among many defeats a famous victory of the British at *Mons*

Badonicus, identified by many as Badbury Rings. This may have held back any Anglo-Saxon advance for some time. However, by 700 A.D. settlement patterns had shifted. Many sites were abandoned, including those at Dorchester, villas were left as ruins, and new boundaries were established in an Anglo-Saxon land allotment. In 789 A.D. *The Anglo-Saxon Chronicle* recorded a royal palace at *Dorceastre*, the successor to *Durnovaria*.

ANGLO-SAXON DORSET

Clear indications of major ANGLO-SAXON development in Dorset do not occur until the three *burhs* listed in the Burghal Hidage of the reign of King Alfred (871–99): Wareham, Shaftesbury and Bridport. At Shaftesbury the *burh* occupied land to the N and E of the abbey founded at about the same time. At Bridport, the scanty evidence suggests a town centred on present-day South Street. Only in Wareham is there a clear plan of defensive ditches and road layouts. Another indicator of significance came fifty years later, when mints were set up under King Athelstan (925–39) at Bridport, Dorchester, Shaftesbury and Wareham. Sherborne and Wimborne are not on this list, but settlement at each seems already to have grown up around the major churches, founded *c.* 705 at Sherborne under King Ine, and at Wimborne at about the same date. Sherborne was the cathedral for a new see, formed from the w half of the Anglo-Saxon diocese of Winchester. Under Ine (*c.* 688–726) and his predecessor, Caedwalla (*c.* 685–*c.* 688), a system of minster churches was also created, each serving a wide area as well as being the nucleus of settlement.

Lady St Mary at Wareham, probably the earliest Anglo-Saxon church in Dorset, was obliterated during its rebuilding in 1841–2. Descriptions and drawings suggest that this was a major priory church, dating from the C10, and that it possessed a long, narrow and high nave with arcades of six bays to the N and seven to the S. Above these were tall and narrow round-arched windows. What survives is a series of Saxon inscriptions from the C7 to the C9, more than for any other English building, unearthed during the demolition. That they are cut on Roman architectural fragments indicates a continuity of occupation, although there is little other Roman evidence here.

Enough fabric survives from the Anglo-Saxon cathedral at Sherborne to reconstruct much of its form, and excavations at the w end indicate a w tower with *porticūs* to N and s.* These are indications of a possibly more extensive 'westwork', such as at Centula, or St Riquier, near Abbeville. The whole building appears to date from the mid C11 (probably the rebuilding carried out for Bishop Ælfwold between 1045 and 1058), with the lost w

---

* *Porticūs* (singular: *porticus*) were side chapels developed for burials. These were prohibited in the main body of the Anglo-Saxon church.

Wareham, Lady St Mary prior to rebuilding.
Engraving by John Bayly, c18

tower having been retained from an earlier phase. Its main body includes much of the structure of an 'extruded' central tower that is wider than the original nave, transepts and choir, such as that at Stow, Lincolnshire, of about the same date, and in Dorset at Wimborne Minster. [13]

At Wimborne too there is evidence that at least the inner parts of the transepts are contemporary with the crossing structure. As a result the minster represents the most substantial standing structure of this period in the county. However, the small c11 church of St Martin, Wareham (if one imagines away the N aisle) provides a more complete experience of a church of this [7] date. Its chancel arch is nearly complete, with a roll moulding that would have extended alongside the jambs towards the floor. Here too are the tall nave proportions one would expect of an Anglo-Saxon church.

We are left with more fragmentary indicators of earlier structures. Herringbone masonry, taken to be an indicator of Anglo-

Saxon construction (although also found as late as the early C12), is generally absent in Dorset, the chief exception being some of *c.* 1080 at Corfe Castle. Long-and-short work also betokens Anglo-Saxon fabric, and there is much at the w end of Sherborne, some at Winterbourne Steepleton and at St Martin, Wareham. Many Anglo-Saxon churches have *porticūs* rather than aisles. None survives in Dorset, although their large entry archways (similar to transept arches) may be seen in the chancel at Canford Magna. Fragments of another *porticus* arch are in the NE corner of the nave of Bere Regis, where long-and-short work may also be found. Lastly, a doorway in the nave N wall at Loders church has the proportions and detailing to suggest Anglo-Saxon origin.

Of Anglo-Saxon SCULPTURE there is rather more to report. There are sections from about eight crosses, all seemingly from the shaft. All have interlace decoration of some kind, such as on the piece at Gillingham church, probably C9. At Whitcombe, because of the incompatible types of interlace, the stones can be taken as from two different shafts. A more elaborate piece is at Melbury Osmond, where the interlace enmeshes a beast, probably of the late C9 or early C10. By the late C10 the increasing influence of Continental decoration causes the interlace to become more scrolly, as seen on the fragments at Todber. Perhaps also later is the interlace combined with rope banding at Yetminster church. More rewarding are the fragments of FIGURATIVE SCULPTURE, the most significant of which is now inside the church at Winterbourne Steepleton: a flying angel, thought to be of the C10 or C11 (similar but superior to the pair at Bradford-on-Avon, Wilts.). Less well preserved is the St Michael at Stinsford of similar date, likewise recently brought into the church. His wings are spread and he is striding to the l. More mysterious is the primitive-looking figure at Buckland Newton church, now thought to be from Continental North Europe or to be British Celtic, and to date from any time from the C8 to the C11.

As a tailpiece it is worth mentioning FONTS. Late Anglo-Saxon and Early Norman fonts are practically indistinguishable. Examples are at Toller Fratrum, where the crudeness of the figure carving and the presence of interlace may indicate an early C11 date, and at Melbury Bubb, with similarly rough treatment of animals in relief combined with rope mouldings. The decoration is inverted, and the shape of the font suggests that it may have been a capital, later inverted and hollowed out.

ECCLESIASTICAL ARCHITECTURE,
C11 TO C16

Monastic foundations

We have already mentioned Shaftesbury Abbey and Wimborne Minster, both Anglo-Saxon foundations. The earliest datable

ruins at Shaftesbury suggest structure of no earlier than the late
CII. Under the Benedictines, it became the richest nunnery in
England (although its eventual wealth fell far short of Glastonbury, Somerset). Wimborne had communities of monks and
nuns, but by the Conquest it had become a secular college, as
re-founded by Edward the Confessor. Anglo-Saxon Benedictine
foundations from the second half of the CIO include Milton,
Cranborne, Cerne and Sherborne. At Sherborne the cathedral
came under Benedictine rule in 998, but ceased to be the centre
of a diocese in 1075 (when the new see of Sarum was created).
In addition to these, Abbotsbury was founded *c.* 1044.

After the Conquest, new Benedictine cells were set up at
Frampton, Povington (near Tyneham), Stour Provost, Spetis-
bury, Loders, Horton and Piddletrenthide. In building terms
nothing remains of these smaller foundations. There was also a
Benedictine priory of St Mary at Wareham of *c.* 1100, just s of
Lady St Mary church; there are no standing remains on this site
earlier than the CI6. All that survives of the Cluniac priory at
Holme is the chancel arch, re-erected at Creech Grange. Of the
Cistercians, there were two monasteries and one nunnery. The
monasteries were at Forde (founded 1141) and Bindon (founded
near Lulworth in 1149 and transferred to its site near Wool 1172).
At Forde, still standing are the vaulted chapter house, the CI3
dormitory, some parts of the frater, part of the early CI6 cloister and the lavish early CI6 Abbot's Hall. Bindon has standing   48
ruins and some architectural features. Only ancillary agricul-
tural buildings remain at Tarrant Crawford, the location of the
Cistercian nunnery. The story of monastic communities where
nothing survives is completed by the Franciscans of Dorchester (founded before 1267), the Carmelites of Bridport (before
1266), the Austin Friars of Hermitage (probably late CI3) and
the Dominicans of Melcombe (1418). In contrast to this loss are
the great survivals: the abbey of Sherborne, bought for the town
at the Dissolution by Sir John Horsey and retained but with the
loss of the adjoining late CI4 town church; Milton Abbey, purchased by Sir John Tregonwell in 1540 after he had assisted in
its submission in the previous year; and the monastic buildings
at Forde, converted to a house firstly by Sir Richard Pollard and
more magnificently by Edmund Prideaux in the mid CI7.

Norman architecture and sculpture

The earliest NORMAN CHURCHES – those built before *c.* 1135
– are few in the county. Indications of several are to be seen in
surviving and often re-set features, such as the intersecting arcading at Tarrant Gunville of the early CI2, improbably relocated
high above the N aisle arcade. At Worth Matravers the nave, w
tower and chancel are of *c.* 1100, but the chancel arch is clearly
later (*c.* 1170) and was brought in from elsewhere. Although the
aisles of Gussage St Michael were rebuilt in the CI3, changing
the character of the nave, its vertical proportions and plain w

tower are all typical of the earlier Norman phase. The nave is probably late CII, the tower early CI2. Also the small church at Winterborne Tomson is of the first half of the CI2 and exhibits the decorative simplicity of other buildings of this period. Stud-

11   land is the most complete example, however, its nave of the late CII and cross-vaulted chancel of the early to mid CI2. This is contemporary with a multi-shafted chancel arch, with decorated scalloped capitals and chip-carving on the imposts and arches. The most significant Early Norman work is without doubt the

13, 14   rebuilt crossing tower at Wimborne Minster (c. 1135–40). Here there are more blank intersecting arches, also found at Sherborne Abbey (although now only visible in the two N chapels there). Both these works mark the beginning of rebuilding campaigns carried on through the CI2.

When we enter the later Norman phase, around the mid CI2 onwards, more elaboration of detail is seen, especially on S door-ways and CHANCEL ARCHES. That at Studland is typical, as are

16   the chancel arches at Powerstock (of before 1150) and Worth Matravers (re-set, as mentioned above). These are both of mul-tiple orders, the outer two arches at Worth of chevron. Power-stock is the more sophisticated in its ornament, with two orders outside the square responds and one within. Each column shaft also carries decoration of various forms. Similar arches at Creech Grange and Hinton Parva (the first brought in, the second re-set) are of the mid century.

This later period also saw the most impressive large-scale REBUILDING PROJECTS. At Sherborne Abbey, rebuilding started from the E end and reached the S porch only by c. 1170. At about

14, 25   this time work started on the new nave, choir and upper parts of the tower at Wimborne Minster (1170–90), of which the nave was probably completed last, with its pointed TRANSITIONAL arcade. Pointed arches and arcades are also found in the naves at Charminster and Bere Regis, and in the S aisle at Whitchurch

21   Canonicorum, although here they are of very irregular widths.

17   There is also a pointed arch on the S doorway of Milborne St Andrew church. The later CI2 S arcade at Canford Magna has round arches, however, with roll mouldings combined with scal-

7   loped capitals, and at Wareham, St Martin, the central pier of the two-bay arcade has four slender corner colonnettes and a capital of early crocket variety. More curious is St Aldhelm's

12   Chapel – a square late CI2 building with a mid-pier and four square rib-vaults.

In rebuilding Norman churches in later centuries, doorways and fonts appear often to have been venerated and retained. The more elaborate DOORWAYS tend to be on the S side of the nave, the N pairing usually lacking decorative features. Starting with the simplest and most typical mid-CI2 arrangement, the doorway at Maiden Newton has one order of columns with scal-loped capitals, a plain tympanum and an arch of a roll, chevron and a hoodmould of fillet section. Here the headstops have been removed. Even simpler is that at St Catherine's Chapel, Milton Abbas where the chevron is omitted (and the capitals are of foliate type, suggesting a slightly later date). The S doorway of

Whitchurch Canonicorum is again similar, no chevron but an inner billet-decorated moulding, and animal headstops. At Sherborne Abbey (*c.* 1170) there is the most elaborate arrangement in the county. Two orders of columns, the capitals with fanciful beast-heads; an outer arch with chevrons at right angles to each other; an inner arch with flat chevrons between two roll mouldings; and a billeted hoodmoulding with beast-head terminals, here turned outwards to follow the line of a linking string course.

Of SCULPTURAL TYMPANA, the earliest in the Norman sequence is the oddly shaped St George at the Battle of Antioch with soldier figures in the style of the Bayeux Tapestry at St George, Fordington (Dorchester), thought to be no later than 1100. There are two affronted bird monsters and the signature '*Alvi* me fecit' at Wynford Eagle; at Worth Matravers in the tympanum of the s doorway is the only Coronation of the Virgin in Dorset, very eroded but once very fine, in an entirely Norman setting. In France this subject does not occur in sculpture before *c.* 1190, at Senlis. But Dorset has few tympana, and those that survive are generally plain.

As mentioned before, FONTS, especially those of the CII, are hard to date with precision. Those likely to be C12 are of more organized design, such as Puddletown, with a grid of palmette motif, their stems interlaced; Stoke Abbott, where below a tier of arcading with figures are flowers in linked hexagons; and the lead font bowl at Wareham, with figures in an architecturally legible arcade. A curious example is at Pimperne: cauldron-shaped, with leaves in chains of large scrolls.

The survival of SCULPTURAL PANELS is generally fortuitous, often found during rebuilding, reversed or buried in later walling. There are three very small panels of Christ in Majesty (Buckland Newton, Maiden Newton, Sixpenny Handley), a small panel with winged figure thought to be St Kenelm (Hinton Parva), and – far superior – the fragment at Toller Fratrum of the Magdalene washing Christ's feet, work very close to the great Chichester reliefs. Also four small hoodmould stops of *c.* 1200 re-set in the chancel of Wimborne. The Christ in Majesty at Maiden Newton is in a small roundel. Its better-preserved twin, by the same hand, has a rider on a horse. Finally, in the porch here are two highly elaborated capitals seemingly from a multi-shafted chancel arch. They deserve to be better known.

A few CHURCH MONUMENTS of the Norman period survive. The best two are of ecclesiastics: Abbot Clement of Sherborne (*c.* 1180), although only the head in its arched surround is preserved, and the complete slab of Philip the Priest at Tolpuddle (mid-C12), both of polished Purbeck marble. At Shillingstone there is an incised slab of *c.* 1200 depicting a naked man.

Early English to Decorated

The replacement of short, often apsed, Norman chancels with the longer square-ended type occurred in Dorset from around 1200 onwards. By this date Transitional forms of C12 design

had given way to the new EARLY ENGLISH GOTHIC. Its chief
characteristics may be seen in the chancel at Wimborne Minster
(*c.* 1230). Especially fine is the triplet E window, the lancets
having either a quatrefoil or a sexfoil roundel above. The lights
are defined by groups of three shafts of polished Purbeck marble,
while the central light is emphasized by dogtooth ornament.
The remainder of the chancel has wall bays defined by single
shafts, also seen in the rebuilt chancels at Buckland Newton,
Loders, Long Bredy, Winterborne Whitechurch and Whitchurch
Canonicorum. At the last, E.E. started earlier (*c.* 1200) in the
rebuilding of the N arcade. One may observe here in the capitals
the transition from trumpet-like leaf carving to the full stiff-leaf
of the E.E. (In the Norman S aisle here, the transition is initiated by a capital of the waterleaf type, the most developed of C12
types.) Especially in the rebuilt chancels, decoration is confined
to the interior; externally there is little to see apart from spaced
lancet windows, often with a linking roll moulding. Also of the
early C13 E.E. is the Lady Chapel at Sherborne, of which only
one bay survives. The chancel of Yetminster was consecrated only
in 1312, and yet is still E.E. and not Dec. At Stinsford there is
a good, although somewhat restored, early C13 E.E. S arcade.
For a complete example of an E.E. church, Church Knowle
(*c.* 1225 onwards) has small windows with a mixture of plate
and Geometrical tracery. E.E. tracery is otherwise scarce in the
county, a sole example on the larger scale being the Geometrical
tracery of the four-light N transept window at Wimborne Minster
(*c.* 1260–70).

From the evidence of Yetminster, it looks as if DECORATED
GOTHIC developed late in Dorset, and the county was very rarely
tempted into the dizzy world of flowing tracery. The S chapel at
Glanvilles Wootton (founded in 1344) has two such windows,
but even though we are here in the mid C14, one looks no later
than 1300. Also slow to engage in the possibilities of Dec was the
master mason for the first phase of rebuilding at Milton Abbey
after the fire of 1309. There are no ogee lights in this work, and
the quadripartite vaults of the presbytery and aisles seem Late
E.E. rather than Dec. Reticulated tracery was introduced only in
the later C14 S transept great window. Reticulated tracery is also
found in the E windows of Lady St Mary, Wareham, and at Bere
Regis, but otherwise is missing from Dorset. The most complete
Dec church is Gussage All Saints (except for the rebuilt chancel).
Its re-set E and *in situ* W windows are of the triple lancet form
under a single arch, with cinquefoil cusping, as used at Milton
Abbey, with which it is contemporary. Here too a rare use of
ballflower ornament in this county, on the tomb-recess. Ballflower also appears on the capitals of the arcade to a N chapel at
Gillingham, but this is minor, another indication of the paucity
of Dec in Dorset. By the time we reach the mid-C14 arcades of
Tarrant Hinton and Netherbury, the piers have resolved themselves into the four shafts and four hollows that become the
Perp standard, but the bases are round and the arches remain a
sunk quadrant. Somewhat more inventive, although small-scale,

examples of Dec are the tracery with straight diagonals and no curves at Poyntington, and the highly inventive stone grilles to the squints at Tarrant Rushton.

Nationally, it was with the Decorated style that TOWER and SPIRE building adopted the distinctive English forms so beloved of Victorian architects. Examples in Dorset are few. The finest spire is at Trent (formerly in Somerset), of the early CI4. Here the S tower parapet of pierced quatrefoils has a trefoiled corbel table below, immediately datable to the period; also windows with Y-tracery, and flowing Dec tracery in its S window. Beside this, the heavily buttressed early CI4 tower at Winterbourne Steepleton, with its recessed spire and four spirelets, seems crude. The spire at Iwerne Minster (third and last of the county's medieval spires) has two bands of quatrefoil decoration, but is misshapen after it was rebuilt at a reduced height in 1853. The tallest spire in the county sat on the central tower of Wimborne Minster. Thought to have been built in the CI3, it collapsed in 1600.

Perpendicular churches

The PERPENDICULAR STYLE was slow to arrive in Dorset. Bridport may be the earliest church rebuilding in Perp, 'in hand' in 1397 and largely complete by 1403. This is a full sixty years after the Early Perp work at Gloucester Cathedral, and fifteen years after the rebuilding of Yeovil church in Somerset, the nearest and probably most influential example. The designer of the latter was William Wynford, the key figure in the introduction of the style into the West Country. The closest link with him in Dorset is *Robert Hulle*, known to have worked in Sherborne 1442–4, and likely to have been previously involved in the rebuilding of the choir of Sherborne Abbey (*c.* 1425–50). Hulle took over the rebuilding of the nave of Winchester Cathedral after Wynford's death, and no doubt continued in much the same vein stylistically. At Sherborne the county makes its major contribution to the history of church design. Here a full-sized fan-vault was used that proved to be the model for similar vaulting elsewhere. Work on rebuilding Sherborne was interrupted by the fire of 1437, so it was not until *c.* 1450 that the upper part of the central tower was reconstructed, and the nave was completely refashioned only by *c.* 1490. The designer of the nave and the fan-vaults of the N transept and Bow Chapel may have been *William Smyth*, since they match work known to be by him at Wells. Fan-vaults were continued westwards, but in the aisles they remained of the lierne type.

In parallel with Sherborne, progress in rebuilding Milton Abbey following the 1309 fire was sporadic. A pause had already occurred from *c.* 1344 to the later CI4, probably owing to the Black Death. Soon after 1481 (under Abbot Middleton) a concerted effort was made to vault the transepts, the tower having been completed *c.* 1450. The towers of Sherborne and Milton are

26

p. 148

34

27, 31

therefore contemporary and indeed very similar. In both cases the upper part is subdivided by a central stepped buttress, and at the corners the buttresses are set back. Each buttress is topped by a slender crocketed pinnacle and, since there are double buttresses at the corners, here two pinnacles add to the lively effect. At Milton the parapet is pierced with quatrefoils; at Sherborne it is plain, but surely was intended to have had the same treatment. The tall two-light bell-openings under two-centred arches have a transom and typical Perp tracery.

In the later Middle Ages many abbeys planned a great w tower, and for parish churches of this period WEST TOWERS became the most common type. A full uninterrupted height, with no more than a secondary w doorway to incorporate, allowed masons to develop a rich range of architectural and ornamental effects. Broadly, in Dorset, towers fall into three design categories.

TYPE 1 is the earliest: plain, usually diagonally buttressed walls, with the doorway and w window treated as separate elements and with the stair-turret handled modestly, usually positioned in one of the E tower angles. A datable example of the type is at Cranborne (1440 indulgence). East Lulworth (late C15) is elaborated with a panel of three bell-openings, and pinnacles rising from the buttresses.

TYPE 2 seems to be found mostly in SW Dorset. Similar design principles apply, with the exception of the stair-turret. This forms a key element in the display, often at the centre of the N or S side and rising above the tower parapet with its own embattled crown. Buttresses are always of the set-back form, either stopping short of the parapet, as at Askerswell, or rising the full height of the tower with double corner pinnacles, seen most clearly at Whitchurch Canonicorum. Similar examples are at Litton Cheney (early C15), Broadwindsor and Bere Regis (late C15), the last with flattish four-centred arches to its bell-openings. A variation here is that the set-back buttresses fall well short of the top, but have pinnacled terminals. Another variation on this type has a pair of bell-openings to each face. Piddletrenthide is the most useful example as it is dated to 1487. St Peter, Dorchester and St George, Fordington (also Dorchester) are of similar design and date. Marnhull (c. 1470) is something of a hybrid: set-back buttresses, but topped by a single stout pinnacle; single bell-openings to the N and S faces, two on the E and W faces, framed by diagonal shafts with crocketed pinnacles. Also pinnacles rise from the first reduction of buttress size, and there are pinnacled image niches, unconnected with other openings.

TYPE 3 takes its cue from the great Perp towers of Somerset. But the display in Dorset never quite reaches the Somerset heights, and the number of this type are far fewer. Essentially there are four. In rough date order they are Bradford Abbas (late C15), Cerne Abbas (c. 1500), Beaminster (c. 1503) and Charminster (early C16). Starting with buttresses, on this type they are of either the set-back type (Beaminster and Charminster) or octagonal (Bradford Abbas and Cerne Abbas). In both of the octagonal cases the buttresses reduce in girth at each tower stage, and each carry a panelled corner pinnacle. A forerunner of the octagonal buttress is found on the tall W tower at Wimborne Minster (1448–64). Image niches are introduced at Bradford Abbas and Beaminster to enrich the W tower front. At Beaminster these are linked by quatrefoil banding and weather-courses at each stage. The elaboration becomes profuse as a result of further hooded image niches attached to the faces of the buttresses and tower corners. Also here there are triple pinnacles at the tower corners and a central one to each face.

30

At Whitchurch Canonicorum the tower arch was modified in the later C15 to a panelled type. Indeed PANELLED ARCHES, whether on towers or elsewhere in the church, appear from c. 1420 and continue in use throughout the Late Perp period. At St Peter, Dorchester the arches to the S chapel are panelled, as is the chancel arch at Buckland Newton. At Silton there is a pan-elled arch to the N chapel of c. 1500. In each case the panelling consists of either one or two sets of trefoil-headed arches, one above the other in blank panels. They are set within slender roll mouldings. The idea may have come from St Cuthbert, Wells, Somerset, completed c. 1420.

The addition of W towers from the late C14 onwards was often linked to the rebuilding of the nave, or the addition of aisles. Building programmes were frequently incremental, such as at Loders, where a new W tower was added in the late C14 and the S aisle (incorporating a porch) added some sixty years later. At Marnhull the process was more complicated. A C12 N chapel was adapted to become part of a N aisle in the late C14. Then this was incorporated more fully c. 1470, when a new S aisle was also added. Finally the N aisle was rebuilt at a greater width in the early C16. Buckland Newton had a new nave with spacious aisles erected in the mid C15 (at the same time as the W tower), and at Lyme Regis the new church (c. 1500, described by Pevsner as the 'Perp *beau idéal*') was built on the site of the chancel of a much earlier building, the nave and crossing base of the latter being retained as a long W porch, or ante-nave.

New PERPENDICULAR CHURCHES are at Bridport ('in hand' 1397, dedicated 1403), Wyke Regis (dedicated 1455), Sydling St Nicholas (mid-C15) and Mappowder (late C15). These take full advantage of the possibilities of the new style. Light is brought into the church more effectively through large windows and high aisle arcades. At the larger churches such as Bere Regis, Charminster, Puddletown, Abbotsbury and Cerne Abbas the nave roof was raised to allow for a clerestory. Clerestories were of course provided during the rebuilding at Sherborne and Milton abbeys, and even on the small church at Gussage St Michael. Nave and aisle roofs were usually of slight incline, lead-covered and concealed behind battlemented parapets. The lower-pitched roofs normally required access for maintenance and so extra stair-turrets were provided on the aisles, giving opportunities for yet more embellishment. A good example is the S stair-turret at Loders: octagonal in plan, with a battlement crown enlivened

p. 148

by small crocketed pinnacles at each apex, and with gargoyles
on a string course below. There are two similar stair-turrets at
Bradford Abbas.

PERPENDICULAR WINDOWS are at once distinguishable from
earlier forms. First, especially at the E and W ends of churches,
or as the major windows of a transept, they are of many lights.
Very large windows are at Sherborne (E and W, nine wide)
and the N transept of Milton Abbey (eight wide). The main
lights usually have cinquefoil heads, although the Milton Abbas
window combines narrower lights with trefoils and wider ones
with cinquefoils. The upper row at Sherborne (E and W) has
ogee-headed lights; these flow into a subdivision of lights in the
tracery zone where the major divisions are centred on the main
lights below, a process that is repeated again above, causing
the main divisions to realign with the main window lights. The
process is obviously an elaboration of reticulated tracery from
which the idea was developed, but in Perp work the proliferation of tracery lights has a clear vertical emphasis. In both of
these cases the window is further divided vertically into three,
with major mullions rising their full width. A variation on this,
first seen in the S transept of Gloucester Cathedral (1331–6),
is for these vertical subdivisions to arch across the upper parts
of the window, forming, as it were, two windows in one. A
much later Dorset example is the N cloister walk of Forde Abbey
(early C16).

Throughout this period a standard type for ARCADE PIERS was
adopted (and is referred to as such in the gazetteer): that is, four
shafts and four hollows in section. Capitals may be a band all
round, sometimes with leaf decoration, or just small capitals to
the shafts. At Beaminster both varieties occur. The pier section
can of course vary. At Lyme Regis triple shafts replace the single
shafts; at Bridport straight diagonals replace the hollows; at St
Peter, Dorchester the pier is a square with demi-shafts; and at
Bishop's Caundle and Maiden Newton the shafts are three sides
of an octagon. Only at Sherborne Abbey are wholly different
piers developed, broad with a giant panelled order in the choir,
broad and panelled all over in the nave, the former c. 1420–35,
the latter c. 1510–20. In Perp work the capitals become small.
However some are enriched by angel busts (Holwell and Marnhull, later C15, Stalbridge, c. 1500), and angel busts also appear
on the apexes of arches, for example at Sherborne. The arches
themselves, either panelled or just moulded, increasingly take
a four-centred form as the C15 progresses. Wide and low four-
centred arches are certainly the hallmark of Late Perp work,
especially so for the early C16.

There are relatively few examples of STONE-VAULTED churches
in the county other than at Sherborne and Milton abbeys. While
FAN-VAULTING seems to have been first developed in the cloisters of Gloucester Cathedral (1381–1412), its use over major
spaces is not known until the building of the choir of Sherborne
Abbey (c. 1425–50), perhaps designed by *Robert Hulle*, as already
mentioned. Walter Leedy sets out a number of reasons why the

Sherborne vault was new in conception.* What one sees is a seamless flow from the mouldings of the lower arches and wall face into the spreading of ribs from the springing points. It was a pattern repeated in the crossing of Milton Abbey (some time after *c.* 1450). On a smaller scale, fan-vaults were used in the N chapel at Silton, and on the porch to the Abbot's Hall at Cerne Abbas, both of *c.* 1500. Otherwise lierne or tierceron-vaults were the norm, such as in the late C15 porches at St Peter, Shaftesbury, or Buckland Newton (lierne), or the W tower of Wimborne Minster (tierceron-star). A more unusual type is the cross-ribbed TUNNEL-VAULT of St Catherine's Chapel, Abbotsbury (*c.* 1400). This heavy vault created the requirement for strong external buttresses, the tops of which have a brattished enrichment (also found on the contemporary tithe barn there).

TIMBER ROOFS of the period are more common, usually the low-pitched compartment type with carved bosses at the intersections. At Yetminster (mid-C15) a panelled wagon roof was built over the nave, with compartment roofs on the aisles, a not infrequent combination. Both have bosses, some with their original painting. Bere Regis nave has a fine hammerbeam roof (late C15), the best timber church roof in the county. It is elaborated with tracery and carved figures attached to the ends of the hammerbeams. Another such roof is at the Abbot's Hall of Milton Abbey (dated 1498), but here the structural components and decorative additions combine into a satisfyingly complicated whole. It is accompanied by a contemporary screen that, in its modelling and ornament, is typical of the Late Perp architecture in the region, with a lively cresting of crocketed pinnacles and cusped and crocketed ogee arches. There are also fine roofs with arched collars and wind-bracing over the Guesten Hall of Sherborne Abbey (part of Sherborne School) and at the frater of Forde Abbey, both C15. Perhaps the most lavish is the compartment ceiling over the Abbot's Hall at Forde, created for Abbot Chard (1528).

Churchyard crosses, parsonages and monastic buildings

All that remains of the CHURCHYARD CROSSES of the period in the county are bases and parts of the shaft. Two are especially noteworthy, however. At Trent the shaft has leaf motifs on the angles. At Rampisham the cross base is a good indicator of how richly ornamented the whole must have been. The base includes carved figures (including a St Thomas Becket) and a black-letter inscription, now eroded, with the date 1516. While not a churchyard cross, the late C15 MARKET CROSS at Stalbridge is unusually intact. There are carved scenes on the base and a shaft with half-buried pinnacles on the diagonal faces. On one side of the shaft there is a figure under a canopy. Only the head is a C20 copy.

---

* Fan Vaulting: A Study of Form, Technology and Meaning (1980).

Next parsonages (or priest's houses) and almshouses. The earliest of the PARSONAGES is The Chantry at Bridport, probably first built in connection with the navigation of the River Brit in the late C13 (or early C14); it was adapted in the late C14 to become a priest's house. The Chantry at Trent is later, probably of *c.* 1500, well appointed with handsome contemporary fireplaces. At Pimperne, all that remains is a doorhead on which the date 1503 was once legible. Abbey House, Witchampton is a special case, most likely built *c.* 1530. It is a noble building in diapered brickwork with stone-dressed window surrounds and bold chimneystacks. Equally fine is Senior's Farm, Marnhull (*c.* 1500), probably dating from the remodelling of the church next door. There are also two cases where chantry priests had lodgings within the church. One is again at Marnhull (late C14), the other at Tarrant Hinton (early C16), both built over N chapels. ALMSHOUSES before the Reformation are rare in Dorset; even those at Poole, the St George Almshouses founded before 1429, are a later rebuilding. This leaves Sherborne Almshouse of 1438–48, probably designed by *Robert Hulle*. It is unusually complete, styled in the manner of a monastic infirmary (the obvious medieval model), with access from two levels to a chapel at the E end of the range.

Finally MONASTIC BUILDINGS. From references above, it will be clear that the abbeys at Forde, Milton and Cerne all embarked on major architectural campaigns in the late C15 and early C16. First came Milton, its chief survival being Abbot Middleton's hall of 1498. Then no doubt similar accommodation was provided for Abbot Sam of Cerne, although all that survives is the porch-tower of *c.* 1500. This has a fine oriel window over the main entrance archway, but not as fine as that built for Abbot Chard at Forde Abbey. The porch-tower at Forde justly prefigures the richness of the abbot's accommodation within, with a two-storey oriel, much ornamented with Late Perp tracery, and inscriptions making clear that it was built for Chard in 1528 (only eleven years before the abbey's surrender to Henry VIII's commissioners). Although resited in the town centre, the former lavatorium of Sherborne Abbey is of similar date; hexagonal in plan with uncusped tracery panels, typical of Late Perp.

Church furnishings, sculpture and monuments

We concluded the brief discussion of FONTS in about 1200 (p. 23). By that date a standard type had emerged, of which many may still be found: a square bowl (in Dorset usually of Purbeck marble), with slightly recessed arch motifs on each face, supported on a central columnar stem and four colonnettes. There are many variations of carving on the bowl, such as at Walditch where one side has radiating arrows. The type seems to have held sway until *c.* 1300 when octagonal fonts became more common. An early example is at Gussage All Saints (early C14) where the bowl has plain splayed sides and is supported on a

plain cylindrical pillar. Also Dec (mid-C14) is the octagonal font at Burton Bradstock. Again splayed sides, each with trefoil- or cinquefoil-headed blank lancet panels. By the end of the C14 a standard Perp type was almost universally in use: octagonal with straight sides, each with a quatrefoil, often with a shield at its centre – no doubt once painted with the arms of its donor. C15 examples may be found at Fordington (Dorchester), Lillington, Long Crichel and Purse Caundle. The fonts at Wool and Yetminster are built into an adjoining pier. An individual design is at Wyke Regis (c. 1455), where the octagonal bowl has a shallow moulded rim and a splayed stem with roll mouldings that have colonnette bases. Finally two quite exceptional designs. At Winterborne Whitechurch the mid-C15 font has a shallow octagonal   36
bowl with a splayed underside on a similarly octagonal stem, with additional (but structurally unnecessary) square pillars at the corners rising to shields. All is elaborated with the most delicate carving. Bradford Abbas has an equally elaborate later C15 variant with statuettes in place of shields at the corners.

Medieval SCREENS are rare in Dorset. Many were removed without record during the C18 and C19 when the need for visual separation between chancel and nave was no longer paramount. Indeed our view of the spaciousness of Perp churches is anachronistic. The late medieval church was divided by screens and filled with stalls and benches, subsidiary altars with reredoses and so on. So the furnishings must be seen as part of the intended effect. Stone screens were, however, more resistant to disposal, and a group of them are still to be found in the NW part of the county. The best is at Bradford Abbas (mid-C15), with four cinquefoil-headed openings either side of a multi-foiled central doorway. The late C15 screen at Nether Compton has traceried openings with small quatrefoils above ogee-headed openings, and is asymmetrical in layout. At Batcombe a screen of similar date (although simpler and symmetrical) has required some cutting out of the jambs of the chancel arch for its fitting: was it brought in from elsewhere? Thornford has another late C15 stone screen, very similar. Apart from the minor screen at Winterborne Came (early C16 with linenfold panelling), the only wooden screen is at Trent. A gorgeous piece, it is quite up to the standard of the   35
very best Devon screens. There is elaborate Perp tracery to the openings, a pair of doors to match, and rib-vaulted coving and carved foliage bands above. At Trent too is a C15 FONT COVER with pierced tracery, while at Winterborne St Martin the late C15 cover has crocketed corner pinnacles matching those on the church tower. More unusual is the pierced stone cover at Pimperne, probably C14 (but said to have been found only in the early C19).

The few medieval BENCHES that survive are to be found in the NW of the county. Trent and Bradford Abbas have major sets of c. 1500, both with ends with straight tops; the best, at Trent, decorated by tracery, the Instruments of the Passion, and initials. The earlier type with poppyhead ends is found at Yetminster and at Buckland Newton, where some have foliate finials.

No medieval CHOIR STALLS survive in Dorset, although Sherborne Abbey still has MISERICORDS of the C15. For PULPITS the situation is equally bleak. There are only four to note, the earliest, of *c.* 1400, at Cranborne; circular in plan with arches and tracery. Also circular, but of stone, is the ornate pulpit at Okeford Fitzpaine, of the C15. Its side has many ogee-arched niches separated by pinnacle-topped mini-buttresses. (The statues in the niches are a plausible mid-C19 restoration, as are the painting and base.) The niches match those made in wood and used singly on each face of the hexagonal pulpit at Winterborne Whitechurch. By the early C16 there was a trend towards the incorporation of linenfold panelling, such as in the lower panels at Stourton Caundle; the upper ones here have blank tracery arches however, and crocketed pinnacles are fitted at the corners. Two remarkable survivals are the C15 PYX-SHRINE at Milton Abbey (one of only four in England) and the even more unusual C13 stone TOMB SHRINE of St Wite at Whitchurch Canonicorum. The REREDOS of Milton Abbey is also a major Late Perp feature (of 1492), with three tiers of niches with canopies. Although brought in, the remarkable reredos at Hammoon with its image niches still filled with contemporary figures is of the late C14 or early C15.

To complete the furnishings, the wall surfaces and windows of any medieval church would have been covered with religious images. There are around twelve places in the county where WALL PAINTINGS may be seen (in varying states of legibility), and many more where fragmentary survivals of decorative schemes are found, usually on aisle arcades or timber roofs. The earliest good example is at St Martin, Wareham, where a succession of murals commences with the C12 horsemen scenes in the chancel. Late C12 lining-out survives at Gussage St Andrew with late C13 figures imposed upon it. At Whitcombe there is late C13 painted arcading, and the best C15 piece in the county, a St Christopher. Another fine set is at Tarrant Crawford, taking advantage of the windowless nave N wall (it faced the adjoining nunnery): many scenes from the legend of St Margaret of Antioch; also the allegory of the Three Living and the Three Dead, and an excellent Annunciation. All are of the first half of the C14. There are many well-preserved scenes of about the same date above the S aisle arcade at Cranborne. The most distinctive is the Tree of the Seven Deadly Sins growing out of the head of a woman. Finally, Hilton preserves a set of PAINTED PANELS of the Apostles of *c.* 1500, removed from a screen at Milton Abbey in the late C18. Much more may survive under later layers of paint elsewhere.

Only one complete medieval STAINED GLASS window survives in the county, at Sherborne Almshouse. It has been dated to *c.* 1475 but is re-set and poorly served by the restorers. This leaves two good C15 panels at Melbury Bubb, and at Abbotsbury a panel with the figure of the Virgin from a late C15 Crucifixion scene. There are many smaller fragments, often re-set, and many pieces remain *in situ* in tracery lights.

There are also a number of SCULPTURAL PANELS, by far the most important that on the w face of Abbotsbury tower. Probably mid-C14, thought to have been moved from the abbey, it depicts the Throne of Grace. Also of note is the small C15 panel of St Eloy shoeing a horse at Durweston. To conclude church furnishing, two free-standing pieces: the late C15 TRIPTYCH ALTARPIECE in Sherborne Almshouse chapel (North French); and a TAPESTRY at Lyme Regis, Flemish of c. 1490.

So to CHURCH MONUMENTS. From the later E.E. period there is an abbot's effigy with heavy chasuble folds at Abbotsbury, c. 1300. Far more numerous are the knights' effigies. These begin in the middle of the C13 and are often represented with crossed legs. There are examples of Purbeck marble (e.g. two at Wareham and another at Horton) and of other stone. The earliest is probably that at Seaborough. Of the early C14 more survive than can here be listed. A miniature one (perhaps a heart burial) is at Mappowder. Other than knights, two ladies are at Puddletown and Horton, civilians at Glanvilles Wootton and Trent. Late C14 knights are also well represented. The low belt and the shape of the helmet indicate the date. Two, at St Peter, Dorchester, come in for special mention because both are not strictly recumbent but rather a little turned to one side, so that the crossing of the legs is an attribute of ease rather than a formula.

In the Perp period there are chiefly two types to be followed: alabaster tombs and Purbeck marble tombs. The former, made in the alabaster centres in Derbyshire, Nottinghamshire and Staffordshire, are in their complete form tomb-chests with statuettes against the sides and effigies on top. The only complete or nearly complete examples are at Puddletown c. 1470–80 and Netherbury some thirty years later, the latter with a canopy presaging the Purbeck type. Both have angels holding shields against the tomb-chest. But alabaster effigies only are more frequent (Melbury Sampford †1467 and another, Marnhull, Puddletown, Stourton Caundle, Wimborne †1444). Of stone effigies the only interesting one is at Stalbridge, which has a cadaver on top of the tomb-chest (c. 1500).

That leaves the Purbeck type. This is, and not only in Dorset, a type consisting of a tomb-chest, a backplate and two detached shafts or colonnettes or pillars carrying a canopy. The canopy usually has a straight soffit on two quadrant curves rather than an arch, and a frieze generally of quatrefoils and a top cresting. The soffit is decorated with quatrefoils or panelling and often also pendants. The backplate may have kneeling figures of brass, or the tomb-chest may have brasses. There are two of the type at Bere Regis, two at Charminster and others at Lytchett Matravers, Milborne St Andrew (†1527), Milton Abbey and Puddletown. The type died hard. It still went on – though in stone not in Purbeck marble – at Bere Regis in 1596 and at Church Knowle in 1572.

The tomb at Church Knowle includes some very minor RENAISSANCE details. They were of course not the first such occurrences in the county. At Tarrant Hinton is a classical Easter sepulchre with the initials of a rector who was in charge from 1514 to 1536; on the Abbot's Hall at Forde (dated 1528) there are Renaissance or near-Renaissance panels.

As an addendum to the monuments, we should note that BRASSES are very rare and almost all humdrum. The best, to Sir Thomas Brook (and his wife) of Holditch Court, is at Thorncombe (†1419), but the marginal inscription is restored and the stone in which the brasses sit is of *c.* 1870. Most tantalizing are three slabs with indents for what would have surely been exceptionally fine brasses. The first is a slab in two pieces (one part at Askerswell, the other at Whitchurch Canonicorum), dating from *c.* 1300 and thought to have come from Abbotsbury Abbey. The indents indicate foliate crosses with hoods and a marginal inscription to Thomas de Luda and Alianore his wife. Next an

Scale

Brass to Thomas de Luda and wife.
Now divided between Askerswell, St Michael and Whitchurch Canonicorum, St Candida and the Holy Cross

early C14 slab at Bindon Abbey with indents indicating Abbot Richard de Maners. Finally that at Lytchett Matravers where a grid is stretched over the whole slab. It was probably for John, Lord Matravers †1364 (the possible co-murderer of Edward II). There are also several brass figures, such as that with fine inscription scrolls at Compton Valence to Thomas Maldon, c. 1440. Apart from the Thorncombe brasses, the largest figures in brass are those at Rampisham to Thomas Dygenys †1523 and wife; they are 19 in. (48 cm.) long.

MEDIEVAL SECULAR BUILDINGS

We must begin with CASTLES, and the iconic Corfe Castle. This was erected from 1080 onwards, with an inner bailey (complete by 1100) to which a fully fortified W bailey was added, enclosing an C11 hall, and then an outer bailey to the SE, added 1201–c. 1215, so that Corfe could be referred to as 'the most secure of English castles'. Apart from the early date of its late C11 great tower, what makes it especially significant is that, by 1205, a royal residence for King John (known also as the Gloriette) had been erected just to the E. This included a hall and presence chamber raised above an undercroft, reached by a staircase that combined defensive and ceremonial functions. In terms of architectural style (being roughly contemporary with the nave at Whitchurch Canonicorum), it was one of the first buildings in the county to use the E.E. style, and certainly its most developed domestic use there. In 1377–8 Edward III extended the residence by a five-storey chamber tower at the SE corner, called the Gloriette Tower.

The second major castle was built at Sherborne in 1122–39 by Bishop Roger of Salisbury, Henry I's trusted advisor and regent. The area enclosed by the mainly ruined curtain wall of this substantial episcopal palace occupies some 3 acres. Standing at its centre is a grandly appointed residence, a hybrid building type incorporating the typical medieval hall-house layout, but also with chapels on two levels in a N range and, at its SW corner, a great tower. The architectural treatment here (where any detail survives) is Early Norman, with fragments of an arcade of intersecting arches on the inner wall face of the upper chapel. After Bishop Roger's demise during the reign of King Stephen, Sherborne Castle reverted to the Crown. Castles that were Crown property were also at Wareham and Dorchester, but apart from their identifiable sites there is nothing standing.

King John was a frequent visitor to Dorset to enjoy the hunting, and for that purpose built four HUNTING LODGES. The largest was King's Court Palace at Gillingham, begun in 1199 and extended for Henry III in the 1250s. Here only the earthworks of moats are now to be seen. At Cranborne was a small hunting lodge in the form of a fortified house of 1207–8. There were also royal lodges at Bere Regis and Powerstock, both

9
p. 220

p. 225

p. 550

10

p. 234

lost. The significance of Lodge Farm, Pamphill (near Kingston Lacy) has only recently been recognized: it is a late C15 hunting lodge associated with the medieval Kingston Hall, with its hall on the upper floor, indicated by mullioned windows with arch-headed cusped lights.

The lists of licences to crenellate, where the Crown granted permission for defensive structures to be erected by private individuals, indicate a number of FORTIFIED RESIDENCES throughout the county. At Chideock and Holditch (Thorncombe) licences were granted in 1380 and 1397. Part of the tower at Holditch survives as a ruin, but for Chideock one has to rely on Buck's p. 207 1733 engraving of the gatehouse. At East Chelborough (Lewcombe) there are two castle sites, not mentioned in the list of licences, and there are other unlisted sites at Cranborne and Marshwood, the latter a fortified manor of which little survives. The more substantial ruins of Rufus Castle, Easton, Portland, perched above a cliff face, appear to belong to the C15. The most 42 significant surviving FORTIFIED MANOR is Moignes Court at Owermoigne: its licence was granted in 1267, but building was restricted to the strengthening of the house 'with a good dyke and stone wall, but without making crenellations'. The dyke largely survives, as does the main range of a new house of that date with a first-floor hall. On its w front are three E.E. windows with plate tracery.

There were also two MAJOR HOUSES in the county, owned by the nobility but not used as main residences. The Lacy Earls of Lincoln possessed what Leland later described as a 'fair maner place' in the grounds of the present Kingston Lacy house. Archaeological investigations indicate a large establishment arranged around inner and outer baileys. Hutchins recorded a large medieval manor house at Canford Magna that stood until 1765 to the NE of a surviving kitchen range (confusingly called 'John of Gaunt's Kitchen'). The greater part of its structure may relate to a house built for the Earls of Salisbury of the 1337 creation. The sketch reproduced by Hutchins indicates fabric of the C12, with successive adaptations, the last of which appears to have been a large C16 oriel window.

Hutchins (writing in the mid C18) recorded some thirty-five major houses of the medieval period built for families with significance in local affairs. Two of the late C15 survive at least in 49 part. Athelhampton Hall was erected for Sir William Martyn, p. 103 who was granted a licence in 1495 to 'enclose and fortify' his manor 'with walls of stone and lime, and to build towers within the said manor and crenellate the same'. Almost contemporary p. 196 is Wolfeton House (Charminster), just NW of Dorchester, rebuilt for John Trenchard around a courtyard. At Clifton Maybank John Horsey built a substantial and partially fortified house, much of 43 which was lost in a Tudor rebuilding. Woodsford Castle, another fortified manor, is of the early C14, built for William de Whitefield who had been sheriff of Somerset and Dorset from 1327 to 1331. p. 702 It is a long range (later thatched) with tower projections along the sides, one of which was later adapted as accommodation.

Most of the houses described incorporated a HALL, the centre of domestic life, from which a solar and parlour led off at the 'upper' end, and service rooms, usually beyond a screen and cross-passage, at the 'lower' end. Halls were often substantial spaces: that at Purse Caundle Manor (c. 1460–80) was 26 by 20 ft (8 by 6 metres). At the upper end of the hall was an oriel, or bay window. Unusually, its solar was at the lower end. It resembles a small hall with a high open roof and an ornate oriel overlooking the passing lane. An earlier first-floor hall is at Barnston (Church Knowle; c. 1300), and we have already mentioned that at Moignes Court of 1267. A larger hall was at Fiddleford Manor (c. 1340), 30 by 19 ft (9 by 5.8 metres). Hall and solar both have fine roofs of   45 cusped wind-bracing, and in the hall an arrangement of quatre-foils and trefoils in the roof-truss apexes. At Woodsford, the four-bay-long hall was on the first floor, as befitted its semi-fortified intent, while the largest hall constructed for a private residence is at Athelhampton, 38 by 21½ ft (11.6 by 6.6 metres).   47

As at Fiddleford, the HALL ROOF provided an opportunity for elaboration. That at Purse Caundle Manor is typical: four bays long with two tiers of wind-bracing, the lower tier arranged as quatrefoils. Athelhampton Hall takes its elaboration further: the three major trusses have astonishingly large projecting pierced cusps.

None of these halls matched the great monastic halls in scale or display. The largest were those built for the abbots of Milton   46 (1498) and Forde (1528). The former is 53½ by 26½ ft (16.3 by 8.1 metres); before subdivision, that at Forde was a monumental 85 by 28 ft (26 by 8.5 metres).

Several of the houses described above were arranged around a courtyard. This implies some form of GATEHOUSE, protecting entry. A simple gatehouse (probably C15) is indicated at Font le Roi, Folke, although this is little more than a barn-like structure with a carriage arch and pedestrian arch alongside. At Bingham's Melcombe (Melcombe Horsey; early C15) and Poynting-ton Manor (c. 1500) the carriage openings are in two-storey ranges with accommodation above; at Wolfeton a full expression   p. 196 of defence was achieved by twin pyramid-roofed towers flanking the gate opening. All of these gatehouses produced only an illu-sion of fortification, an indication perhaps of less turbulent times, especially by the start of the C16.

Most of the halls described had CHIMNEYS, the normal loca-tion being on one side at about a mid-point. There are only a few cases where original fireplaces remain in situ. The earliest were relatively crude and devoid of decoration, such as those in 'John of Gaunt's Kitchen' at Canford Manor. An earlier alternative was to vent a central fire through louvres in the roof. Construction relating to a smoke louvre is found over the hall at Fiddleford Manor, but such evidence is rare in buildings of higher status. For WINDOWS there are few survivals from the earlier period, the chief examples being the hall windows with E.E. plate tracery at Moignes Court (1267) and the remains of the N-facing solar   42 window at Fiddleford Manor. This has two trefoil-headed lights

flowing into a central ogee quatrefoil above; Dec, exactly as one
might expect for the *c.* 1340 date. By the time of Athelhampton, a
Perp polygonal oriel was built at the upper end of the hall. STAIR-
CASES throughout the Middle Ages tended to be of the masonry
spiral type, incorporated in the thickness of walls or projecting
as turrets. By the Early Tudor period a new form had emerged,
as incorporated in the W front of Winterborne Clenston Manor,
c. 1480. Entry is through a side door and the staircase is within
a turret on an octagonal plan, above which is a gable corbelled
out in an elaborately moulded way over the canted corners. A
turret of about this date was also at Wolfeton, although its upper
part was later altered. There is also one at The Castle, Bridport
(early C16), although here the doorway was set in the front face.

CHAPELS were routinely incorporated in major houses. Evidence for them survives at Cranborne and Mappercombe (*see*
Powerstock) manors and at Woodsford Castle. At Chantmarle
a rear range was adapted from a C15 chapel, while at Wolfeton
a chapel was incorporated in the N range of John Trenchard's
courtyard house. WALL PAINTINGS not infrequently embellished
the more significant houses. By far the most important survival is
the late C14 Annunciation in the solar at Fiddleford. The painting
on a screen at Senior's Farm, Marnhull (*c.* 1500–30) depicts St
Catherine of Alexandria.

Surviving TOWN BUILDINGS of the medieval period are scarce.
While most were built at the street end of narrow burgage plots,
indications are that, for larger houses, confined sites almost
inevitably led to a courtyard plan. Scaplen's Court, Poole is a
merchant's house of *c.* 1500 with its hall alongside the street,
and with parlour and service ranges running back on either side
of a courtyard. Here the main range was two-storeyed from its
inception, with the solar above the hall. Another such building
(although not for a merchant) is the Manor House, Newland,
Sherborne. Although much remodelled, it has an oriel of *c.* 1500
overlooking the street. Lesser town dwellings are also to be
found in Sherborne and in Cerne Abbas. A number of buildings
of *c.* 1500 or just after stand in Cheap Street, Sherborne, and its
N extension Higher Cheap Street. Many of these are TIMBER-
FRAMED, typical examples of which are the shops just above
Abbeylands. Both have a jettied upper floor, one plastered (as
it would have been originally), the other with its square framing
exposed. The original timber-framed front of The Julian, a medieval inn given to Sherborne Almshouse in 1437, is clearly implied
by the shape of its stone flank walls. A four-centred carriage arch
immediately adjacent (now part of an adjoining inn) may also
be C15. Again at Sherborne the abbey built a tenement row (in
Half Moon Street) *c.* 1532–4. This is of stone: a long and plain
building, its chief feature the Late Perp mullioned windows
on the first floor. Cerne Abbey built a similar tenement row in
Abbey Street (Cerne Abbas) of about the same date, but this
is timber-framed. Some good details survive, especially on The
Pitchmarket, where an ogee-headed doorway has pierced quatrefoils in the spandrels.

47, 49

p. 682

55

Three MONASTIC TITHE BARNS survive (the roof structure
of a barn at Winterborne Clenston may come from a fourth).
The finest, although no longer roofed along its full twenty-three-
bay length, is that at Abbotsbury, of *c.* 1400. Some degree of   44
decoration was applied outside, such as the buttresses with their
brattished tops (matching the buttresses of the contemporary St
Catherine's Chapel). Internally it has a C17 roof with diminutive
hammerbeams at the eaves. Abbey Grange, Sherborne is of about
the same date but heavily truncated when converted to a house,
while Cerne Abbas tithe barn, also converted in the late C18, is
smaller and earlier. There are also two medieval DOVECOTES
(although those thought to be C17 may turn out to be earlier).
These are the two-cell rectangular one at Abbotsbury, probably
of the C15, and the early C16 circular dovecote at Athelhampton.
This type, with its conical stone roof, set the pattern for the
remainder of the C16 and C17.

Finally BRIDGES. All those of the medieval period have been
subject to rebuilding and modification (especially widening). The
most complete is White Mill Bridge, Shapwick, perhaps largely of
1341. Its eight arches are all rounded, while the late C15 or early
C16 Town Bridge at Sturminster Newton has six pointed arches.   50
Pointed arches too at Cornford Bridge, Holwell, built over the
Caundle Brook *c.* 1480. Crawford Bridge, Spetisbury is mostly of
1505 and the longest of this period, with nine segmental arches.

TUDOR AND STUART DORSET,
c. 1540 TO *c.* 1714

Secular architecture to c. 1640

Late in Henry VIII's reign, a series of CASTLES were constructed to protect the south coast. Three are in the county. One,
Brownsea Castle, was a mere rectangular blockhouse, in course
of completion as late as 1547–8, and now wholly hidden within
the castle's later growth. Of the pair built in 1539–41 to guard
Portland Harbour there is more to see of their full layout. Henry's
castles reflected recent developments in artillery, for they were
designed as platforms for cannon, and no longer as a refuge
for large numbers of individually armed defenders. Hence their
compactness and squatness, and the provision of no more living
space than for a small garrison. Hence too the polygonal plans
of many of them, allowing wide and overlapping arcs of fire. At
Sandsfoot Castle, Weymouth, all this can hardly be appreciated,
as nothing stands but the ruinous walls of the guardroom: the
octagonal gunroom seaward of it has fallen to coastal erosion.
Portland Castle is a happy contrast, one of the most complete   52
survivors of the series. Its gunroom is fan-shaped, as it was
intended to cover a single direction.

The DISSOLUTION OF THE MONASTERIES under Henry VIII
was, for land and buildings, the key aspect of the Reformation:

the most significant event in national history since the Conquest. It not only marked the end of a medieval land controlled by Church and Crown, but initiated a new age of private owner-ship and private opportunity. For Dorset, 1539 was the year when all of the remaining county monasteries were surrendered, their land and buildings passing to people with a wide variety of motives. What most concern us here are those purchased with the intention of adapting the buildings for use as a country seat.

p. 405

ADAPTING MONASTIC BUILDINGS in this way started in Dorset at Milton Abbas, where Dr John Tregonwell, as one of the King's Commissioners, had overseen its dissolution. In 1540 he purchased the abbey, immediately adapting the buildings as his house. More surprising was his retention of the (still incomplete) abbey church, which then continued in use as both the parish church and the Tregonwell private chapel. The changes to the monastic buildings were considerable, but the architectural style employed was a continuation of that in use in the latter days of monastic improvement. Since virtually all of this work was swept away in the mid C18, we must rely on Hutchins's description and the 1733 Buck view. Here we see a range running to the N ending in a gable flanked by octagonal buttresses, and with these and the gable apex crowned by carved figures, no doubt partially armorial in intent. So the detailing found on Abbot Chard's additions at Forde Abbey continued at Milton after it fell under secular control. Similar work may be found in South Somerset, at Brympton D'Evercy (*c.* 1534) and Barrington Court (1552–9), built just before and just after the Dissolution. And it has been shown that the centre for such distinctive craftsmanship was the stone quarries just w of Yeovil at Hamdon Hill; indeed many Early Tudor houses were constructed in the ochre Ham Hill stone so characteristic of the cross-county zone.

48
pp.
294–5

Since the work at Forde Abbey was comparatively new, its post-Dissolution owner, Richard Pollard, concentrated on creat-ing good dwelling rooms in the private chambers at the w end of Abbot Chard's great hall. But here the church itself was demol-

p. 122

ished.* At Bindon Abbey the buildings were left as a partial ruin until their incorporation in a new mansion for Viscount Howard from 1555 onwards. Also here, from *c.* 1560 to *c.* 1580, a series of elaborately planned water gardens were adapted from monastic fish ponds, one of the earliest Elizabethan gardens of this type in the country.

Monastic estates also provided land for NEW HOUSES. From 1540 onwards we see these arising, generally (at least in the w half of the county) adopting the distinctive designs of the Ham Hill centre. One can trace them almost year by year as each owner took advantage of the availability of craftsmen. First came

53

the two largest: Melbury House (Melbury Sampford) for Sir Giles Strangways (1540), and the rebuilding of Clifton Maybank (*c.* 1545–50) for Sir John Horsey. Next four smaller projects: the

49

new w wing at Athelhampton Hall (*c.* 1545–9); Sandford Orcas

---

*The abbey churches were also demolished at Shaftesbury, Tarrant Crawford, Abbotsbury and Cerne Abbas.

Manor (*c.* 1551–4); a new wing at Mapperton Manor (*c.* 1550); and, last of the group, the new hall range at Bingham's Melcombe (1554–8). All have similar details that will be described shortly. But first more needs to be said about the two major houses. Melbury has a formality of planning that is quite unexpected outside the highest circles. A regular quadrangle is formed, with two of its ranges presenting gable-ends. At the mid-point of one side, above the original main staircase, rises a prospect tower, hexagonal in plan at the top, much like those at Oatlands Palace, Surrey (of 1538) and the Spye Tower of Warwick Castle. Within, the formality breaks down as the usual late medieval hall arrangement is squeezed into the pre-determined layout. Of Clifton Maybank all that survives is a large fragment, with a major section re-erected (not necessarily in its original configuration) at Montacute, Somerset (*c.* 1786), and other components appearing at the Manor House, Beaminster, and Compton House, Over Compton, after their late C18 sale. All we are left with are the Late Perp components.

On all these houses buttresses are frequent: octagonal in plan, usually with concave facets, and always diminishing in girth at each string course. (The w tower of Cerne Abbas church of St Mary, *c.* 1500, is the true local harbinger of this type.) Each buttress has a spiralled pedestal at its top, crowned either by a finial (diagonally set) or a heraldic beast. Gables could be crocketed for a more elaborate silhouette still, and the centre of an oriel gable or porch was a further opportunity for ornamental heraldry. There could be lozenge-shaped panels as at Athelhampton or Sandford Orcas, or the larger panelled displays at Bingham's Melcombe and Montacute. Tellingly, since this is the last house in the series, the panel at Bingham's Melcombe is framed by two classicizing attenuated pilasters, set at forty-five degrees to the wall face, rising to frame a window above and breaking the gable-line at the top. Also at Bingham's Melcombe the oriel corner buttresses have a primitive form of superimposed order, at least on the second and third stages. So the RENAISSANCE had arrived, integrated into a Late Perp design framework. Classical detailing had appeared earlier at Wolfeton House on a range completed in 1534. In a purely Perp context, putti serve here as finials and window surrounds, and hoods are carved with scrolls and fruit such as must have been copied from some North Italian design.

After this burst of activity there appears to have been a lull until the 1590s. With the exception of a wing at Stafford House, West Stafford, of *c.* 1560–70, and the expansion of the now-disappeared Tyneham House in 1583, the new phase starts with Sir Walter Raleigh and his conversion of Roger of Salisbury's p. 550 medieval episcopal castle at Sherborne into a country house. From 1592 onwards this was slowly given the features required of an Elizabethan 'prodigy house', the most obvious of which was a large window in the s front of Bishop Roger's great tower. This mirrored, on a smaller scale, the more considerable improvements made to Kenilworth Castle, Warwickshire by the Earl of Leicester (*c.* 1570).

Later in the 1590s Raleigh's emphasis moved to the building
60   of a HUNTING LODGE (partly incorporating a late C15 structure)
to the S of the Castle. In this he seems to have been encouraged by Robert Cecil, the younger son of Lord Burleigh, and it
p. 553 was no doubt through Cecil that a plan for the lodge was pro-
cured from *Simon Basil*. The tower-like lodge (at the centre of
the present house) has four storeys but only a small rectangular
59   plan. Lulworth Castle (East Lulworth; *c.* 1608–10), also built as a
hunting lodge (for Viscount Howard of Bindon), has something
of the same plan and also came about largely at Cecil's behest. At
Sherborne the corner towers are hexagonal, at Lulworth they are
circular. Both had provision for viewing the chase from rooftop
leads, and the turrets of both rose higher than the roof-line and,
accessed from the roof, could be used as small banqueting houses.
61   In fitting out Sherborne, both in Raleigh's ownership and in
the resumption of work under Sir John Digby from 1617, CLAS-
SICAL FEATURES became increasingly common. Elsewhere, a
56   frontispiece dated 1586 was erected at Waterston Manor with an
especially academic demonstration of the three superimposed
orders. The great-chamber fireplace of *c.* 1600 at Wolfeton also
has superimposed orders, but with panels of Flemish-inspired
strapwork. More generally, the porch or entrance provided the
obvious position where the minimum of elaboration could most
effectively update a house. So at Hammoon Manor the porch is
entered through an order of attached, rusticated Tuscan columns
of *c.* 1600; Hanford House (1604) has a frontispiece of superimposed orders, probably added just before completion; while even
the otherwise vernacular Almer Manor has a curious two-storey
porch (*c.* 1620–30), the classical orders barely fitting its canted
sides. Classical features abounded in the otherwise typically Jacobean mansion at Stalbridge Park of 1618–20, and existed in a
64   curious fusion with vernacular forms at Warmwell House (begun
probably in 1618).

The hand in charge of Warmwell, and no doubt also responsible for its Y-plan, was almost certainly *William Arnold*. Arnold
was connected to the later generation of Hamdon Hill-based
craftsmen who themselves were no doubt employed at Longleat
House, Wiltshire (*c.* 1572–80). He may have been responsible for
the classical features at Wolfeton, Hanford and Sherborne Castle,
especially the gate screens enclosing the N and S courtyards at the
last. These have strapwork cresting and shell-hood niches of the
63   type also seen at Cranborne Manor, where Arnold was certainly
the architect from 1609 until Robert Cecil's death in 1612. Here
the old King John hunting lodge was adapted internally, extended
by two balancing wings, and given a cloak of exotic Jacobean classical ornament. One of the 'signature' features of Arnold's work
is a shell-hooded niche with the gadrooning radiating from the
crown of the arch, rather than rising from the centre at the back.
Such niches line the porch walls at Poxwell Manor of *c.* 1610
(where the porch arch has bold, typically Arnold detailing), and
are also found at Lulworth Castle (where the mason-in-charge

was Arnold's brother *Godfrey*) and at Hanford. As idiosyncratic as some of Arnold's work, but built after his death, is the curious s wing at Waterston Manor, added probably in 1641 for Sir John Strangways. Tall cross-windows are combined here with classical pediments, arched openings are placed at eaves level between the three gables, and at the centre there is a balustrade-topped half-round bay.

Two curious buildings should be mentioned at this point. The first is the riding house at Wolfeton House of *c*. 1610, a barn-like building, similar to that built for Prince Henry at St James's Palace between 1607 and 1609. The second curiosity no longer exists: it was the gatehouse at Clifton Maybank of *c*. 1600, which, to judge from its detailing, was almost certainly designed by *William Arnold*. It had a chequerboard arrangement of windows and panels with niches, and two odd pepperpot turrets. Unfortunately it was dismantled *c*. 1800 for re-erection at Hinton St George, Somerset, something that appears never to have happened.

Another marked tendency was towards SYMMETRY of composition, even where the building failed to incorporate any overtly classical features. The original frontage of Edmondsham House, dated 1589, has a balanced grouping of three shaped gables, the central porch gable brought forward. Similarly, the five-gabled front at the Old Manor, Kingston Maurward (1591) is arranged symmetrically around the central gabled porch. Even four-gabled Wraxall Manor (1610) has a gabled porch set centrally (and somewhat awkwardly) between gables two and three in order to maintain balance. Look at the back elevation of such houses, however, and a more utilitarian jumble persists. At Tomson Manor (Winterborne Tomson; *c*. 1600) the four-bay symmetrical front contrasts with the back, which has an off-centre gabled porch-turret with, in its angle, a massive chimneystack with multiple, diagonally set brick shafts. Symmetry within a composition of vernacular elements on the large scale is found at Chantmarle, built for Sir John Strode in 1612 to a design by *Gabriel Moore*. Here we learn from Strode's written explanation that the house was to an E-plan because the 'E' referred to Emmanuel. An *p. 188* elaborate chapel was in one wing of the house, since lost, also fully described by Strode. Symmetry too seems to be the key to the remodelling of Stafford House, West Stafford (1633), hampered to a degree by the need to incorporate a mid-C16 wing.

Chantmarle had a spreading, spacious plan, but a trend towards more compact forms also emerged, presaging the DOUBLE-PILE houses of the mid C17 onwards. Anderson Manor (1622) is the first in Dorset with such a plan, combined with some sophistication in the layout of its front elevation (gable, window bay, porch gable, window bay, gable), the window bays with multi-stack chimneys set behind. Wynford Eagle (1630) is more compact, originally with two gables to each face and a gabled porch between them at the front; a similar arrangement at the Manor House, Dewlish is of about the same date. Wyke,

Bradford Abbas (1650) has a double-pile plan but no main-elevation gables, and it is the same with Tolpuddle Manor (1656).

In this period the WINDOWS on major houses are the same as one would find on contemporary cottages and farmhouses. This is less surprising on Parnham House (Beaminster) of c. 1559, where no symmetry is attempted, the windows being of the multi-light, hollow-moulded or cavetto type, with depressed-arched (or Tudor-arched) heads. The hall position is fully expressed in the medieval manner. Even at the highly formalized Chantmarle we see the same window form, by this date (1612) almost an anachronism, but used in an entirely symmetrical arrangement. Arch-headed lights were, however, soon abandoned in favour of square heads, and window proportion gradually becomes significant too. Wynford Eagle and Benville Manor, Corscombe have mullioned-and-transomed windows of more vertical than horizontal proportion; at Anderson Manor CROSS-WINDOWS, that is a window two lights wide and two high with a transom set between halfway and two-thirds of the way to the top, are standard. Becoming increasingly common and spreading down the social scale, cross-windows are to be seen at Lower Farm, Kington Magna and the New Inn, Cerne Abbas (both late C17). Over the same time the preferred window moulding changed from hollow-chamfered to the more bulbous ovolo, but this is never a reliable dating feature.

Generally from the medieval period masonry windows had individual HOODMOULDS. An increasingly common alternative was to group windows together under a single hoodmould, and with symmetry, including a doorway at the centre. By the end of the C17 continuous drip-courses had become the norm, but exceptions remained, such as Wych Farm, Bothenhampton, where a house with individual hoodmoulds is dated 1705. Mullioned windows continued in use well into the C18, such as at Sydling St Nicholas, dated 1733, and on a series of houses in Stoke Abbott dated 1748, 1751 and 1762.

All of the above buildings are of stone with occasional use of roughcast render. BRICK arrived in Dorset as a building material as early as c. 1530 at Abbey House, Witchampton, and the now fragmentary Tudor house at Woodlands, both with diaper patterning. It becomes more common on gentry houses in the early C17, at Bloxworth House (1608), the lodges s of Cranborne Manor (1620) and gatehouse at Poxwell (1634), and at Wimborne St Giles on the stables of St Giles's House (c. 1620) and the almshouses (c. 1624). A special brick bond of one course of headers to two of stretchers was used at Anderson Manor (1622) and repeated at Blandford St Mary and Muston (Piddlehinton) manors (c. 1630 and c. 1670 respectively). The s wing of Waterston Manor (1641) combines brick, stone and render in a highly individual way, and an equally distinctive use is found on Woolbridge Manor (Wool; 1635). Dutch influences in Dorset brickwork are rare, but one link is at the Old Rectory, Hamworthy of c. 1635. Here the shaped gables are topped by alternative triangular and segmental pediments, and the façade has giant Ionic engaged columns with terracotta capitals. It is in the tradition of SE English brickwork, with the Netherlands as the ultimate source.

One room type in particular during this period afforded opportunities for high levels of ornament: the GREAT CHAMBER. These were sited on the first floor and usually reached by an equally great staircase. Few survive in the county. One of the most impressive, at Wolfeton House of *c.* 1595–1600, was stripped of its elaborate plasterwork ceiling during later alterations. It is entered through a fine classical doorcase (probably by *Allen Maynard*), pedimented with Corinthian pilasters, and reached by a contemporary staircase with an arcaded stone balustrade. A similar room known to have existed at Upcerne Manor was destroyed in 1840. So at Herringston (Winterborne Herringston) we are fortunate in the survival of a panelled great chamber with PLASTERWORK of considerable distinction. The ceiling is coved, and panelled with wide, enriched ribs. Among other designs it encloses (as useful dating features) the Prince of Wales's feathers and initials CP, so it was completed after 1616 and before 1626. Along the centre are five pendants, including three large ones with openwork on metal armatures. At the new Sherborne Castle, the two principal rooms have ribbed plaster ceilings installed for Raleigh (*c.* 1600), one elaborated with Tudor roses, the other with acorn pendants, fleur-de-lys and cartouches of the Raleigh arms. Earlier examples of elaborate plasterwork are at Mapperton Manor, where one plaster frieze of *c.* 1540–50, installed when the N wing was completed, is accompanied by a ceiling of *c.* 1570–90 with ribs and pendants. Two rooms at Court House, Corfe Mullen (a fragment of a much larger house) also have good rib-and-pendant ceilings of *c.* 1600, with the ceiling compartment beams given plaster mouldings and enrichment on their lower face, typical of more vernacular usage.

STAIRCASES include one of 1609–12 at Cranborne Manor, of wood, with Tuscan columns rising from each newel post to the underside of the post above, the stairs themselves rising in short flights. A version of this is also found at West Hall, Folke and Folke Manor, both of *c.* 1600. The staircase at Warmwell House (*c.* 1618) is unusually monumental for its status; it is of stone, with bulbous classical balusters and thin Tuscan posts rising to the ceiling.

Some early WATER MILLS survive from this period, although most would have been rebuilt as they expanded in the C18 and C19. Usefully dated 1566 is a long inscription on the small stone mill next to Fiddleford Manor. There are also fragments of a mill of this period built into the later work at the Old Mill, Fordington (Dorchester; of 1590–1607). The earliest part of Sturminster Newton Mill (of *c.* 1650) is also of stone. In red brick, however, is the Mill House at Wimborne St Giles of the 1620s, built as a paper mill.

Finally ALMSHOUSES, a building type that proliferated in the early C17. The most accomplished architecturally are those at Wimborne St Giles (1624), Milton Abbas (*c.* 1674, re-erected at the model village in 1779) and the Ryves Almshouses at

58
62
61
57

Blandford Forum, dated 1682. Each is formally composed, those at Wimborne St Giles and Milton Abbas with a central gabled hall. At the centre of the Ryves Almshouses there is a gable with a plaque below. One should also mention the Old School Room at Sherborne School (1606–8) by *Roger Brinsmeade* (and *John Reape*, carpenter). It was the first purpose-built SCHOOL BUILD- ING there after re-founding as a secular establishment in 1550.

Jacobean and later Stuart churches

No CHURCH BUILDING can be identified for almost the entire Tudor period after the Dissolution. Churches existed in plenty, so in Dorset we do not have one Elizabethan church, and the only major works carried out on a church were those at Sherborne Abbey in 1560, to convert the Lady Chapel to school premises (*see* above). Even during the Early Stuart era, only six major church-building projects took place. But they are an interesting group, characterized by three- or five-light windows with the heads of the lights uncusped, the middle light taller than the others, and a hoodmould stepped up to it and down from it. This is all a development from Late Perp, as found at, for example, Lytchett Matravers of *c.* 1500, simplified and unornamented. The four main churches are Leweston (1616), the N chapel at Mint-erne Magna (*c.* 1615–20), the tower, porch and refenestration at Ryme Intrinseca (probably *c.* 1620), and Folke (1628). The aisles at the last show some stylistic invention. The curious combina-tion of octagonal piers, boldly fluted, and pointed arches with fleurons, is a revival, rather than continuance, of Gothic, and a highly individual revival at that. Can we involve *William Arnold* with this work? It certainly has his creativity (and Mark Girouard has made the attribution).

A more thorough adoption of Gothic happened at Iwerne Courtney in 1610, the windows having the three stepped lancet lights under one arch of Milton Abbey, for instance. The work was commissioned by Sir Thomas Freke, also the patron for a chapel in much the same style added to his house at Higher Melcombe, Melcombe Horsey. There is a scholarly thoroughness in this work, especially in the convincing C15-Perp arcades at Iwerne Courtney. The S aisle at Abbotsbury has the odd combi-nation of round-headed windows but a sort of Late Perp tracery. It takes its likely date of 1636 from the S chapel doorway. Inside is a lovely stucco chancel vault, installed for Sir John Strangways and dated 1638.

The choice between Gothic Survival and Gothic Revival was no longer topical when church building began again about 1700. The tower of Frampton, which is of 1695, illustrates the attitude well. It is at first sight a plain Perp tower, and in that would be taken as Survival, but at the angles instead of clasping buttresses are two tiers of Tuscan columns – a motif of the day. The mason (or the client) was not up in Wren towers yet, but in his elemen-tary way he wanted his tower to be of his own day.

Church furnishings and monuments, c. 1540–c. 1714

The seventy Elizabethan and Jacobean years and the years immediately following were a time of busy CHURCH FURNISHING.
The first impulse was the Elizabethan Settlement, the second
Archbishop Laud's care for ritual. The earliest post-Reformation
PULPIT, at Broadwindsor, is undated but must be late C16; with
its pinnacled angles it remains in the Perp tradition. Elaboration of detailing then becomes the theme, starting with Iwerne
Minster (1610) which has a knotted cable pattern, through the
arabesques and strapwork at Leweston (*c.* 1616), until a more or
less standard type is reached with tiers of arched blank panels
at Winterborne Came (1624), Charminster (1635) and Cerne
Abbas (1640). At Shillingstone (mid-C17) the treatment of the
panels is more classical, as is the pulpit at Puddletown (*c.* 1635)
with its tall arched panels and tall Tuscan columns at the angles.
Here too a backplate, and a TESTER or sounding-board, the most
elaborate of which are to be found at Lyme Regis (dated 1613
on a splendid inscription) and – somewhat less florid – at Cerne
Abbas (1640), which nevertheless has pendant arcading. Three
more dated pulpits worth recording are Chickerell (1630), with
arabesque-stylized trees in the panels and crudely classical fluting
to the posts; Hammoon (1635), with guilloche decoration with
rosettes; and Oborne (1639), with lozenges, that most typical of
Jacobean motifs. With pulpits come HOURGLASS STANDS. There
are two: one at Folke of iron, the other at Spetisbury of wood.

COMMUNION RAILS played an important part in the Laudian
arrangements ('one yard in height and so thick with pillars that
dogs may not get in'). A dated example is at Winterborne Came
(or rather the pulpit, with which it appears contemporary, is
dated 1624), and also from after the Restoration at Burton Bradstock (1686). Of course they are present at the highly Laudian
Folke, and at Puddletown of *c.* 1635 where they are around
three sides of the altar, with an indication that they once also
ran behind to complete the quadrangle. In design, one sees
more elaboration in the early C17, in common with pulpits, and
an increasing standardization as the century progresses, vertically symmetrical balusters giving way to the more familiar vase-
shaped type. SCREENS of this period are rare. Two good dated
examples are those at Iwerne Courtney of 1610, dividing off the
Freke Chapel, and the slightly less elaborate one at Melcombe
Horsey of 1619, also, it seems, installed for Sir Thomas Freke.
The most thorough arrangement is at Folke (1628), where the
screens not only formed an entrance into the chancel but also
marked off the family pew in one of the aisles. While the arched
openings in them are pointed, the cresting is of typical Jacobean
strapwork.

From the later Tudor period onwards, many ROYAL ARMS may
be seen, mostly on painted panels. The earliest is probably the
Tudor arms in Wyke Regis church, but this is said to have come
from Sandsfoot Castle. There are royal arms of James I at West
Stafford, and more unusually those of Henry, Prince of Wales in

Sherborne Abbey, dated 1611 and signed by *Charles Rawlings*. Many were no doubt removed during the Commonwealth but, following the Restoration (when they once were again required by law), a flurry of royal arms installation took place, many of them dated. First, and not surprisingly, Corfe Castle (1660), followed by Bishop's Caundle and Winterbourne Abbas (1661), Longburton (1662) and Todber (1663). Several of these include a loyal motto, the best of which is at Longburton: 'Curse not the King, noe, not in thy thought'.

Two FONTS are of this period, at Folke and Swanage (St Mark). The former, no doubt dating from the 1628 work on the church, is as individual in design as one might expect from *William Arnold*. It has a cover with inturned volutes. However in Swanage the 1663 font is simply a replica of the C13 Purbeck type. There are numerous C17 FONT COVERS. They tend to fall into two types: the pyramidal cover, usually with a knob final, such as at Chideock and Puddletown; and those with a central turned finial, often accompanied by supporting volutes, as at Purse Caundle and Sandford Orcas. The pyramidal one at Ryme Intrinseca is dated 1637; an apparently earlier one is at Tarrant Crawford (late C16, pyramidal type).

BENCHES are rare in this period. However, there are two good dated examples, both of 1547, at Affpuddle and Bere Regis. The latter have ends entirely in a Late Perp mode, while those at Affpuddle have Renaissance motifs. A similar undated set, surely by the same hand, is found next door at Turners Puddle. Thoroughly in the Jacobean style are the fine CHOIR STALLS at Wimborne Minster of 1608, although they would be better still if they retained their canopied back-screen. Also at Wimborne Minster is a brass eagle LECTERN of 1623.

Finally WALL PAINTING. From the mid C16 onwards this was usually scriptural lettering rather than images. There are numerous survivals, e.g. Charminster, Hilfield, Marnhull, Upwey, Wareham (St Martin), West Stafford and Winterbourne Steepleton. A good example is that at Puddletown of *c*. 1635.

68

Tudor and Stuart church monuments

We have already seen how the canopied Purbeck type of monument was continued well into the C16, the last being at Church Knowle in 1572. Likewise, the monument to the Marchioness of Exeter (†1558) at Wimborne Minster, could equally have been made a century beforehand. And decidedly Late Perp is the black marble monument to Sir John Arundell (†1545) at Chideock, although the tomb-chest has balusters, a Renaissance indication. More classical still is the monument to Sir John Horsey (†1546) and his son (†1564) at Sherborne, although the detailing is Tudor and the mood undoubtedly a development from the Purbeck type. So one has to go beyond 1550 to see the new style fully accepted, and as one examines ELIZABETHAN MONUMENTS, one will then at once realize that the Italian Renaissance had but a small contribution to make. The source of direct inspiration was the Netherlands. Dorset is not the most useful county to argue this out, for there are few major Elizabethan monuments. But wherever strapwork is found and canopies on columns and obelisks, there the Netherlands have had their effect. The best Elizabethan monuments are at Sixpenny Handley (†1579) with no effigy and typical for a certain Early Elizabethan type, at Sherborne (John Leweston †1584, probably by *Allen Maynard*) and at Spetisbury (†1599 – still with black-letter). Specially interesting is an early C17 monument at West Chelborough with a lady in bed under a blanket and the blanket as it might really lie. Also worth noticing are two brass plates †1594 and †1596, because they are signed (respectively) *Edmund Colepeper* (Pimperne) and *Lynil Brine* (Marnhull). The next signature is again a brass, at Chilcombe, with the date of death 1662 and the engraver *Richard Meadway*.

JACOBEAN MONUMENTS and those of the 1630s in Dorset show no change of type or style, but a great increase in numbers: Sir Edmund Uvedale †1606 at Wimborne, alabaster, and the deceased on his side; Longburton †1609 and earlier with six columns; Winterborne Came †1611 with the family kneeling frontally against the tomb-chest; Whitchurch Canonicorum †1611 with particularly intricate strapwork and ribbonwork; Gillingham †1625; Longburton †1625 with six columns and a gruesome display of bones; Frampton †1627; Wimborne St Giles †1628 with an elaborate canopy; Motcombe †1627; and so on. Other types current in these decades are kneeling effigies, singly or two facing one another (specially elaborate †1617 St Peter, Dorchester, where they kneel under a columnar canopy and the centre is a fancifully decorated arch; Preston †1614; Puncknowle †1616; Charminster †1636; a whole family at Sandford Orcas †1607), and frontally placed figures, either demi-figures, usual for divines (Hampreston †1630, Maiden Newton †1635) or a whole figure seated (Cranborne †1641) or kneeling (Stourpaine 1670). Changes towards the Inigo Jones–Christopher Wren type begin to appear about 1650–60, e.g. the Hanham Monument †1650 at Wimborne. This last also highlights a trend towards the use of boldly contrasting black and white stones. The Hanham monument has white figures against a black ground, while the earlier John Cole monument (†1636) at Witchampton still includes obelisks in the Jacobean manner.

In LATER STUART MONUMENTS from 1650 to 1700 the development of classical forms and detailing continues, but two telling backward glances in design are worth noting at this point: Rachel Sutton at Winterborne Stickland and Sir Thomas Freke at Iwerne Courtney, of 1653 and 1654 respectively. The Sutton monument is no effigy but a column with a piece of entablature and the epitaph carved on the column. 'Statua sepulchri' ('image of the grave') it calls itself, and it has the new simplicity and at the same time the conceitism of the age of Donne and Nicholas Stone. The Freke monument has no effigy either, but is very large and stands on the floor. The motifs are partly already classical. Then there are those monuments that altogether shake off their typological fetters. At Glanvilles Wootton (†1679) two of the conventional kneelers are raised to the top of the tablet. At Wimborne, Anthony Etricke (1693) has a black shrine with heraldic shields and no figure at all. But the type most characteristic of the moment about 1700 is that with standing life-size figures against a kind of reredos architecture – a claim to the grandiose which in architecture is paralleled by the works of Vanbrugh and Hawksmoor. We have in Dorset Sir Hugh Wyndham at Silton by *John Nost I* (1692) – a judge in his garb and wig and two mourning women and two twisted columns – and Lord Digby (†1698) at Sherborne, also by *Nost*, with three figures, and Thomas Strode at Beaminster (also †1698 and again by *Nost*). As for other types, Lord Holles (1699, probably by *Grinling Gibbons*) at St Peter, Dorchester reclines; Sir Nathaniel Napier at Minterne Magna (1725, by *Thomas Bastard II*) has standing allegorical figures; and General Churchill (†1714), also at Minterne Magna, has a display of military trophies and no effigy. The 3rd Earl of Shaftesbury, the philosopher (†1712), at Wimborne St Giles has one standing figure in a niche. But the most frequent type of the late C17 and early C18 is the cartouche, and the percentage of aesthetic success is exceptionally high among them.

In the W part of the county, substantial CHURCHYARD MONUMENTS become numerous during the C17 (as they are across the border in south Somerset). They are usually of the chest type, clearly a development from the medieval tomb-chest, but evolve only slowly from Jacobean forms into the late C17, long after they would be thought too old-fashioned within the church. The most notable groups are at Portesham and Powerstock, one at the latter very eccentric in shape with bulbous ends, tapering-panel sides and standing on moulded feet like a piece of furniture – a development from the increasingly common balustered-corner type.

Stuart country- and town-house building after the Civil War

The end of the Civil War brought opportunities for rebuilding or replacement of damaged property. For COUNTRY HOUSES, a new architecture, highly influenced by the work of Inigo Jones and John Webb, was adopted from the outset. So we see a more austere classical appearance, illustrated in the W wing of 1647 at Cranborne Manor by *Richard Ryder* for the 2nd Earl of Salisbury. The key elements of the new style are there: symmetry; a hipped roof; bold window and door surrounds; windows of a tall proportion, especially on the main storey; quoining at the corners; a platband (as opposed to a string course); and cleanly detailed eaves, here with large modillions. Variations on these precepts are found on a larger scale at Charborough Park (1650) for Sir Walter Erle, one of the Parliamentary commanders. Here the house has a centrepiece where ornament was concentrated, and a symmetrical arrangement of dormer windows and strong chimneys.

Erle's house was of brick with stone dressings, materials also used
in the E wing of St Giles's House, Wimborne St Giles (begun   71
1651) for the 1st Earl of Shaftesbury, in sharp contrast with the
rambling accumulation of the existing house. Edmund Prideaux,
Cromwell's Attorney General, restricted his external changes
at Forde Abbey (purchased in 1649) to fenestration changes
to the abbot's former lodgings, and to a new saloon. However,   48
these additions could hardly be described as austere or Puritan,
even less so the interior. Two grand rooms were made at the W
end of Abbot Chard's house, one taken out of the huge great
hall. Fine plasterwork and tapestry-hanging decorated these and
other rooms, especially the new staircase and first-floor saloon.   70
To accompany the Flemish tapestries there is boldly executed
plasterwork.

Country houses of the RESTORATION continued much in
the same vein. The chief Jonesian example is Kingston Lacy of   100
1663–70 by *Sir Roger Pratt* for Sir Ralph Bankes, a returning
Royalist. Here perhaps some of the restraint of the Commonwealth houses was lost through more dramatic modelling of the
exterior, especially of the roofscape, with its balustraded lead-flat
and cupola, and of the N façade, where a pedimented centre
allowed an armorial display in its tympanum that would have
been frowned upon some ten years earlier. A smaller version is
the nearby High Hall, Pamphill (*c.* 1670), perhaps by the same
building contractor as Kingston Lacy, *Sir Thomas Fitch*. Another
example is Stepleton House, Iwerne Stepleton (*c.* 1660), built for
Thomas Fownes with the expected hipped roof and windows of
a tall proportion. Two sets of STABLES of this date are unusually fine. The dated example is the pair of ranges of 1670 facing
each other at Mapperton Manor. Here we see the use of cross-
mullioned windows with moulded architraves, bolection friezes
and triangular pediments, a variation of the form that became
standard over the next fifty or so years. A near-identical set is at
the Manor House, Beaminster.

Smaller MANOR HOUSES were updated in the new style by
more modest works, such as the E range of Puncknowle Manor
(*c.* 1665), symmetrical and compact under a hipped roof but
still with arch-headed stone-mullioned windows. Fontmell
Parva (Child Okeford), a house of *c.* 1680, has a hipped roof   72
also combined with stone-mullioned windows, but without the
archaic arched heads. Finer proportions and detailing are found
at Waddon Manor, Portesham, its new wing of 1695–1700 having
much the same proportions as Belton House, Lincolnshire
(1685–8). The latter is a larger H-plan house, where the centre
has a double-pile plan, but this type was not adopted in Dorset,
probably as entirely new houses on this scale were not then
required. The nearest, at least in plan, is Ilsington House, Puddletown (*c.* 1680), but here the elevations imply a *piano nobile*
over a basement but no attic storey, so the overall effect is rather
squat. At Melbury House an attempt was made in the 1690s   53
to classicize the Tudor fabric, the chief element of which was a
remodelled E façade. Designed by the otherwise unknown *John*

Watson, the work resulted in eleven bays with three at the centre emphasized by the use of superimposed attached orders under a pediment. But curiously the pediment falls short in width, making a structural and visual nonsense of its centrepiece.

Finally to TOWN HOUSES. The Old House, Blandford Forum (*c.* 1650–60) is a demonstration piece of cut and moulded brickwork, symmetrical about a projecting two-storey porch, but curiously grouped with an extra r. bay under an all-encompassing hipped roof. The Manor House, Wareham (1712) and West End House, Poole (*c.* 1716) show the way to the standard Georgian town house, of which there will be plenty to describe.

TRADITIONAL DORSET RURAL HOUSES
BY BOB MACHIN

Building materials

Traditional Dorset buildings are predominantly of STONE. The great variety of local stones is covered in the Geology and Building Materials sections (pp. 3–10). Transport costs were high, so apart from stone mullioned windows and other quality dressings the stone usually originated in the parish. Several manorial customs mention the tenants' right to get stone from designated quarries on the 'waste' (common land). For example at Yetminster one can still see the pits dug in the 'Quarr Closes' to the W of the village. The exceptionally detailed building accounts for Mapperton rectory make no reference to the transport of stone and it must have come from a large, unnatural depression in the garden.

Where there was no suitable stone – as on the Chalk – builders used flint or cob. FLINT was readily available, but required large quantities of expensive lime mortar and imported dressings for corners and wall openings (from the C18, predominantly of brick). COB, which is basically mud with a fifty per cent admixture of small stones and straw, was cheap but the labour involved was intensive. This was an advantage for self-built structures, particularly for the poor, and the occasional survival of cob within the stone regions suggests that it was formerly more widespread. There are still a few cob farm buildings in Marshwood Vale, and earlier parts of several farmhouses in west Dorset have cob walls – visible in the gable-end of a house almost opposite the shop in Chideock and in the original half of Lavinces Farm, Netherbury.

TIMBER FRAMING is restricted to the N, NE and extreme E of the county. Rare survivals such as the splendid barn at Lower Stockbridge Farm, Lillington suggest that timber framing was formerly more widespread. However, very large panels in the framing – as in the gable-end of Dominey's Farm, a C15 openhall house at Fiddleford – indicate economical use of a material that was in short supply.

Except in Purbeck, where stone roofs predominate, the traditional roofing material was THATCH: not the smooth, neat
modern reed version, but the unkempt straw-bundle technique
seen in early photographs that always looks as if the building
needed a visit from the barber. Anyone who could thatch a rick
could thatch a house – but he had to return every twenty years
or so to repair it. This was offset by the cost advantage, that straw
could be laid on rafters that were little better than beanpoles.

If there was no chimneystack, Dorset gable-ends were hipped
or half-hipped. If there was a gable stack, the thatch was wrapped
around the gable-end – unless, for status reasons, the owner
chose expensive gable tabling (large slabs of stone terminating
on shaped kneelers).

Even in stone houses, the majority of CHIMNEYSTACKS above
ridge level are brick. This is so commonplace that one might
describe it as a local tradition. But what was used before bricks
became readily available in the C19? Around half-a-dozen internal
timber-framed stacks have been identified. Were these formerly

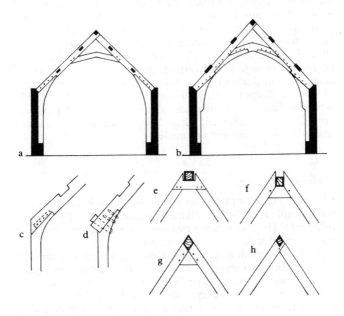

Farmhouse roof construction.
Drawings by Robert Weston

a. Jointed cruck truss with through purlins and cranked collar
b. As above with arch-braced cranked collar and trenched purlins
c. Mortice and tenon jointed cruck, side-pegged
d. Free (or slip) tenon jointed cruck, face-pegged
e. Early apex: saddle with square-set ridge
f. Early apex: yoke with square-set ridge
g. Apex with block, ridge set on edge
h. Jointed apex, ridge set on edge

more common – and did the smoke issue from a wickerwork opening in the thatch?

All these features are visible from the outside. The following internal features can only be seen inside.

ROOFS were usually carried on cruck trusses until the early C17. True crucks are comparatively rare. Like Devon and Somerset, Dorset was a jointed-cruck region. Open-hall houses usually had crucks with two soffit pegs and a lower slip tenon. This was not an efficient joint, and from the early C16 edge- or side-pegged joints were adopted. By the early C17, jointed crucks were succeeded by simple A-frames. A house called The Bricks at Broadwindsor shows the sequence. It was built in 1519 as the church house, with edge-pegged jointed crucks. When, after a century or so, the cruck posts decayed, they were simply removed, leaving the principal trusses standing on the stone walls as an A-frame.

Other quality INTERNAL WOODWORK is largely restricted to partitions and ceiling beams. Plank-and-muntin partitions were standard in the C17. Muntins were stout vertical timbers with side grooves into which planks with feathered edges were slotted. A few plank-only partitions, with C15 shouldered door-heads, reveal an earlier tradition. Occasionally ground-floor ceiling beams with complex mouldings were set in a grid to give a panelled effect, but most ground-floor beams have simple forty-five-degree flat chamfers. The earliest examples have 6-in. (15-cm.) chamfers, but during the C17 they diminished to 2 in. (5 cm.) or less. The fashion in the C18 was to hide the beams by nailing plastering laths to the underside. Modern owners prefer exposed beams, but nail-holes and ghost-lines of removed laths reveal where this improvement was made.

Traditional plan types

765 surviving pre-C18 Dorset farmhouses have been studied in some detail (RCHME, National Trust surveys and the author's fieldwork). They have either two or three ground-floor rooms in line. Original lean-tos or wings are rare.

Analysis of room-naming in C17 probate inventories provides useful statistics. Everyone had an all-purpose living room, called the hall, and a ground-floor bedroom called the chamber, or 'the chamber within the hall' (known as the parlour by the late C17). Twenty-five per cent had no more ground-floor rooms. Another thirty per cent had a third room, which was either a buttery (storeroom) or kitchen (for baking and brewing rather than cooking). The remaining forty-five per cent had four or more rooms that were always additional service rooms such as a pantry, larder, scullery or dairy. To fit these 'extra' rooms into two- or three-room plans, one of the outer rooms had an axial partition giving two rooms, one behind the other. Thus at Corfe Castle we read about 'the buttery against the street' and 'the buttery against the backside', or at Spring House, Longburton, 'the chamber within the hall' and 'the chamber within that'.

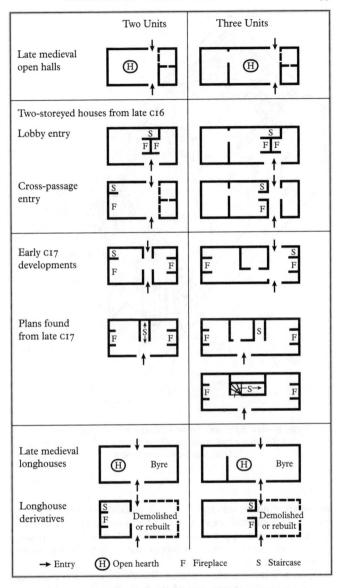

Comparative house-plan types

Almost all of these axial partitions have disappeared, but their former frequency explains why these plans are described as two- or three-units rather than rooms in line.

Eighty-six (eleven per cent) of the sample were originally OPEN-HALL HOUSES, identified by internally smoke-blackened roofs. Occasionally – as at Upbury Farm, Yetminster – a tall

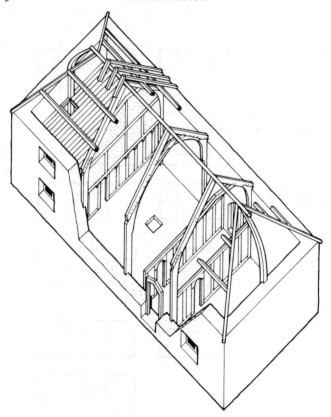

Partly floored open-hall farmhouse, the roof of jointed crucks,
with centre hall truss arch-braced, and end crucks.
Drawing by Robert Weston

open-hall window survives, but that usually indicates manorial
status. Most examples can be identified externally only by awkwardly contrived upper-floor windows. Most open-hall houses
had an upper storey over the adjacent unit(s), but this was usually
no more than a loft.

Open-hall houses were entered directly by opposed doorways
in the long walls at one end of the hall. This standard form of
entry was known as 'betwixt doors' in Dorset, but we will use
the modern term, CROSS-PASSAGE. Draughts defined this as
the inferior or 'low' end. The adjacent lower-end unit was often
axially divided with a pair of doorways side by side and a loft
over. In THREE-UNIT EXAMPLES the 'chamber within the hall'
was accessed by a single doorway at the upper end of the hall.
At Longburton and perhaps elsewhere, this chamber was also
axially divided and might have a loft over.

When, from the mid C16, halls were ceiled over – requiring chimneystacks and staircases – these two simple medieval plans evolved into six common plan types, distinguished by the location of the entry, stack(s) and staircase.

The primary distinction is between cross-passage and lobby-entry plans.

The LOBBY ENTRY originated in Kent, spreading N as far as East Anglia and W as far as Hampshire. But after a few miles across the county boundary into Dorset it struck a cultural barrier, so that most of Dorset is cross-passage territory.

Until the middle of the C17 STAIRCASES were of winder type, always placed in line with the principal stack, and rising from the hall. But in the second half of the C17 even the principal bed was moved upstairs, and straight flights of stairs became desirable. It proved difficult to fit this feature into traditional plans, and a CENTRALLY PLANNED STAIRCASE HALL plan became the national norm.

The introduction of stacks into traditional cross-passage houses led to a remarkable divergence between two- and three-unit plans. In the latter, the hall stack always backed on to the cross-passage and was set against the front wall, so that visitors had to walk along most of the cross-passage before making an indirect entry to the hall. But if indirect entry (implying a greater degree of privacy) was the objective of lobby-entry plans, this was not the case in two-unit plans. Broomhill Farm, Rampisham is the only surviving two-unit house with a hall stack backing on to the cross-passage. In every other case, the stack and adjacent spiral staircase was built against the gable at the upper end of the hall. In a few cases the cross-passage had partitions on both sides, but usually the cross-passage was treated as part of the hall and one walked directly into it.

Gable-end stacks were a novelty. In the other three plan types the stack rose from somewhere in the centre of the house, and gable-ends were either hipped or half-hipped. But the idea caught on, and from the last decade of the C16 we find two new plan types with a stack on both gable-ends.

The two-unit version is found throughout the county, of which fifty-seven (eight per cent of the total of surveyed houses) are pre-C18 examples. There are probably many more, but the diagnostic feature of a winder staircase requires internal access. The three-unit version of the two-gable stacks plan is more easily identified from the façade. It has the revolutionary concept of an unheated central room (abbreviated as the UCR PLAN.) This became the standard C17 plan for larger farmhouses in Dorset and no central-hall houses are found after 1650.

With 132 (nineteen per cent) examples, we can establish an evolutionary sequence for the UCR plan. Initially there was an off-centre cross-passage, and if there was only one spiral staircase, it rose from the gable-heated room adjacent to the cross-passage, indicating that this was the hall. Access to the other gable-heated room (parlour) was via a corridor alongside the unheated central room – one of the earliest examples of the corridor in vernacular planning. After 1650, when straight flights of stairs became desirable, this novelty was introduced transversely across one end of the unheated central room. Somewhat surprisingly, the new type of staircase was not initially used as a display feature but was hidden behind a doorway that balanced the entry to the unheated central room from the corridor. At the same time, the front doorway was moved to the centre of the house, giving a symmetrical façade. Finally, around 1700, the staircase was made a display feature by placing it parallel to the front wall. The effect was overwhelming, and the unheated central room was soon replaced by a staircase-hallway with a framed staircase set further back so that it could be appreciated properly. At which point, the plan became indistinguishable from the C18 'centrally planned house'.

This brief survey of common Dorset plan types would be incomplete without reference to a curious uncommon type. Excavations show that a common medieval plan was the LONG-HOUSE, in which the family and animals lived under the same roof with direct internal communication between the two halves of the house. Over a hundred surviving examples have been recorded in Devon, and it would be surprising if there were none in Dorset. The RCHME found only one – Charity Farm, Osmington – but the author has identified another seven. These are enough to suggest that the medieval longhouse was formerly more common in Dorset. In eighty-one of the 193 three-unit central-hall houses, the cross-passage and third (lower end) room have been rebuilt. The clues are a vertical straight joint, different ridge heights, and/or different wall thicknesses. Surely these are former longhouses with the byre end rebuilt? The same features are found in several UCR plans. Did the unusual UCR plan evolve from a two-unit longhouse tradition?

GEORGIAN AND REGENCY ARCHITECTURE,
c. 1714 TO c. 1840

Country houses

The ENGLISH BAROQUE arrived in Dorset as a jolt to provincial classicism, nowhere more effectively than at Chettle House, commissioned c. 1715 by George Chafin and designed with flamboyant inventiveness by *Thomas Archer*. What we see today is a diluted version, still with Archer's round-cornered end bays and a giant order with odd, wedge-shaped, inward-tapering capitals. But the E façade is missing the two great triangles of broken pediment (derived from the late C16 Villa Aldobrandini at Frascati) with, between its arms, a cupola. Kingston Maurward of 1717–20 for George Pitt, almost certainly by *Archer*, has more conventional Corinthian pilasters but an entablature that is bracketed. Engravings show that this too was once a much more lively composition with an extraordinary roofscape equal to that of Chettle. It, like Chettle, was of red brick with stone dressings, but was simplified and encased in Portland ashlar in the late c18, when its roofscape was stripped of all eccentricity.

We also have little to see at Eastbury, designed on a palatial scale for George Dodington by *Sir John Vanbrugh* and built *c.* 1716–38 (completed by *Roger Morris*). A sequence of designs was prepared, some reproduced in *Vitruvius Britannicus,* that show all of Vanbrugh's theatrical flair in the composition. All we are left with is one service range and the court behind it, entered through a monumental archway. From them one can appreciate Vanbrugh's massive severity and unexpectedness, though not the mastery of dramatic grouping which the house itself would have displayed, if it had been built fully in accordance with his plans, and if it still stood.

The project must have drawn in many local craftsmen, especially masons and joiners, and its location only some five miles from Blandford Forum meant that the craftsmen in that town would certainly have been involved. So when Blandford town was largely consumed by fire in 1731, this new learning informed its resurrection (*see* p. 125), and new country-house building in the county thereafter. The Vanbrugh style was highly influential on the amateur architect *John Pitt,* brother of George Pitt of Kingston Maurward. He built two houses for himself in this vein: Encombe House (from *c.* 1734) and West Lodge, Iwerne Minster (a remodelling of *c.* 1740). Encombe is that very rare thing, a creation that is wholly original within an adopted idiom. The Vanbrughian vocabulary and compositional method, binding disparate masses together by a single appearing and disappearing order, are used by Pitt to create a low-lying, reposeful and undemonstrative house perfectly suited to its site before a horseshoe of

76

86

87

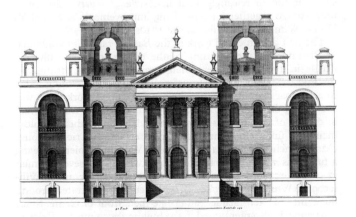

Eastbury, design for entrance front.
Engraving by Henry Hulsbergh, 1717

hills. The Vanbrugh mode was also used to update the otherwise minor East Melbury Farm, Melbury Abbas, in the mid C18.

Before mentioning those especially connected with Blandford, we should note the PALLADIAN influences that emerged in the house that *Sir James Thornhill* appears to have designed for himself near Stalbridge after 1727 (called Thornhill House), a style that soon superseded the Archer–Vanbrugh Baroque for new country houses. Of the two house projects that are documented as being by *Francis Cartwright* of Blandford St Mary, the second, Came House (1754) at Winterborne Came, is decidedly Palladian in its N façade, while its S front has a more provincial character, similar to Cartwright's S façade at Creech Grange (1738–41). Both have a pedimented centre with a window in the tympanum (a lunette at Came, segmental-headed at Creech). Similar to the Came N front, but of brick, is the W façade of the wing added to Edmondsham House (*c.* 1740), presumably also by *Cartwright*. The Palladian W façade at Kingston Russell House (*c.* 1740) has more in common with the N front of Came, although Kingston Russell has bold Ionic pilasters and plain window surrounds (in the Vanbrugh mode) rather than the giant Corinthian columns and keyed moulded window architraves of Came. A likely source for Cartwright's earlier, less Palladian work is *Nathaniel Ireson*, who had worked with Thomas Archer at Hale Park, Hampshire (*c.* 1717), before becoming an increasingly independent architect. His first country house in Dorset was probably Spetisbury House (*c.* 1735, demolished). It had the Borromini-style inturned volute capitals that Archer used on several of his projects; a small Venetian window in its pediment tympanum; and a bracketed entablature similar to Archer's at Kingston Maurward. Ireson's work became in time more Palladian, no doubt owing to working under *Henry Flitcroft* at Redlynch House, Somerset (1750s). The Palladian wings added to Stepleton House (1758) must surely be a product of this association. Flitcroft was probably also responsible for the increasingly Palladian style of Cartwright, since they worked together on classicizing improvements at St Giles's House, Wimborne St Giles in the 1740s.

The first documented work of the *Bastard* family of craftsmen of Blandford is the re-fitting of the dining room at Lulworth Castle in 1727. They were then retained to work throughout the mid C18 at the castle, transforming it from a hunting lodge to a compact country house; their last recorded work there was *c.* 1770. By the 1740s the brothers *John* and *William Bastard* were in charge of the business. The first indication of their employment in a full architectural capacity elsewhere is Crichel House (More Crichel), rebuilt 1744–6 for Sir William Napier following a fire. This was a compact house of five bays by seven, similar in character to Moreton House (1744) and Whatcombe (Winterborne Whitechurch 1750–3), with detail concentrated around the centre of each façade, rather like the S front of Came. Since *Cartwright* is also mentioned in the building accounts for Crichel, it seems likely that they worked together, and no doubt Ranston, Iwerne Courtney (1753) and Merly (1752–60) were by this loose

88

partnership, Cartwright responsible for the exterior, the Bastards for the interiors. Many identifying features of houses designed wholly by the *Bastards* may be seen on the fully attested town house at Poole, designed and built for Sir Peter Thompson by *John Bastard* in 1749, and he was almost certainly the architect for the additions at Smedmore of 1761.

If Cranborne Lodge was started *c.* 1730 it is unlikely to have involved the Bastards. As first built this was an extremely compact house, to a square plan with front and back façades both with full-width pediments. *Cartwright* may have been its architect, since it has the telling tympanum window employed by him. The architect of Dean's Court, Wimborne Minster (1725) is harder   75
to identify, although improvements to the interior in 1758 were almost certainly by the *Bastards*. *Benjamin Bastard*, a younger brother, appears to have been based in Sherborne from at least 1749. Sherborne House (*c.* 1720) is often wrongly credited to him, but the stables at Sherborne Castle (1758–9) are a documented work.

Two major projects signal the arrival in Dorset of the NEO-CLASSICAL generation of national architects. Of these the most important and proficient was *Sir William Chambers*, first seen in the county at Duntish Court, Buckland Newton (1764, demolished). This was a compact and carefully proportioned block with pedimented centrepieces and pavilion wings. Classical ideas of this nature were first offered in Dorset by *John Vardy*, *c.* 1754, at the second and more significant project, Milton Abbey House. In a modest initial proposal here, he had offered a Gothick scheme as an alternative to a classical one, but it was *Chambers* (Vardy's successor in 1769) who took the Gothick idea further in the large new building. This retained only the Abbot's Hall and swept away   94
Tregonwell's 1540s adaptations. The result is a memorable fusion of Gothick detailing and classical forms, best seen on the w and N elevations, incorporating also the octagonal buttresses of mid-C16 Somerset and Dorset Tudor houses. Building ran from 1771 to 1775, when Chambers was dismissed, and replaced by *James Wyatt*, who saw the interior through to completion. *James Wyatt* and his brother *Samuel* were also employed at Crichel (1772–80) to provide state rooms within the house then undergoing enlargement for Humphry Sturt, using the *Bastards* as architects. And at Bryanston (1778), *James Wyatt* designed a new compact classical house to replace its rambling predecessor.

Achieving a classical exterior at Sherborne Castle, as extended   60
in the C17, posed a challenge. Schemes by *Robert Adam* (*c.* 1761) were left unexecuted, as was a design for a Neoclassical gateway with Egyptian features by *Chambers*. In 1779 a classical orangery was added while landscaping improvements under *Capability Brown* were in progress, its likely architect being Brown's son-in-law *Henry Holland*. Holland, or perhaps *Thomas Leverton*, may also have designed Downe Hall, Bridport (1789), since its refined Adam-like façade has much in common with their other work. A more austere approach is found at Sadborow, Thorncombe by *John Johnson* (1773–5), an architect normally associated with

Essex; and near Melbury Bubb (on the fringes of the Melbury estate) a Neoclassical house was designed by *John Crunden* (1770–2, demolished *c*. 1820). Still standing is Crunden's Bel-
95 field House, Wyke Regis of *c*. 1780, one of the first villas built in the Weymouth suburbs following George III's association with the emerging maritime resort (*see* p. 64). The austere Neoclassical style may also be found at Leweston Manor (*c*. 1800) with an insistent use of round-headed windows. Lesser examples of later C18 houses are Frome House, Frome St Quintin (1782), a brick house with a particularly delicate two-storey ashlar porch with Adam-style detailing, and Belmont, Lyme Regis (after 1784), especially interesting as it was embellished for *Mrs Eleanor Coade*. Its façade incorporates many examples of *Coade* stone as a piece of self-advertisement.

Early C19 architectural style became a matter of choosing from a variety of possibilities, while Neoclassicism continued in the hands of architects such as *C. R. Cockerell*. At his Langton House, Langton Long Blandford (1826–32, demolished), a refined Italian-classical style was employed, seen in greater severity on
98 the surviving stables and brewhouse. Refinement is also present in the work of *John Tasker*, especially Chideock Manor (*c*. 1810), assuming that the executed design was his.

The chief alternatives to classicism were Gothick and Tudor. Initially these styles were used mostly on garden or landscape buildings (*see* below) rather than residences, with exceptions such as Chambers's Gothick at Milton Abbey. GOTHICK of a pictur- esque, fanciful kind is seen on houses from *c*. 1800 onwards, e.g. a façade at Herringston, Winterborne Herringston (*c*. 1803 by *Thomas Leverton*) and especially at Pennsylvania Castle, Port- land (*c*. 1805 by *James Wyatt*). Parnham House (Beaminster) was provided with a Gothic treatment by *John Nash* (1807–11), incorporating battlements, pinnacled buttresses and a kind of Perp tracery to the windows. Another example is the small house by *Tasker* in the grounds of Bindon Abbey (1794–8), where the windows are pointed Gothick, and the principal room has an E.E.-style vault.

103 TUDOR is best seen at Canford Manor (1826) by *Edward Blore* for Lord de Mauley, less apparent in the composition than the use of gables with tall finials, battlemented parapets and tall, octagonal-shafted chimneys. *P. F. Robinson* in his various books provided designs including 'Old English', 'Castellated' or 'the style of building in Tuscany'. Bridehead, Littlebredy (*c*. 1822, extended 1831–3) shows his version of Tudor, with attenuated corner turrets as well as the usual castellations. From *c*. 1840 Tudor became the most common country-house style, with examples more sedate (and perhaps more satisfying) than Rob- inson's at e.g. Upwey House; Compton House, Over Compton (by *John Pinch Jun.*); Chedington Court; Fryer Mayne, Broad- mayne (all of these of *c*. 1840); and the E front of Creech Grange of *c*. 1844. A curiosity was Woolland House of 1833 by *W. J. Donthorn* (who designed Highcliffe House, Christchurch, Hants,

c. 1830): picturesque Perp that was neither Tudor nor medieval in any way. It was demolished in 1962.

Country houses through the Georgian era were increasingly accompanied by LANDSCAPED PARKS of some distinction, complete with garden buildings. The most significant extant parklands are at St Giles's House, Wimborne St Giles, where avenues laid out c. 1740–50 radiate from the house, and at Sherborne Castle, where in 1753 and 1774–8 *Capability Brown* altered the formal landscaping, incorporating a lake and bringing the ruins of the Old Castle into the composition. For its date, the land- 10
scape designed by *Vanbrugh* and *Charles Bridgeman* to accompany Eastbury (c. 1725) was advanced in its thinking, with earthworks and peripheral planting of a new type. The buildings there were also redolent of Antique Roman references, especially the Praeneste complex used as the basis for the raised temple at the far end from the house. LODGES first mirrored the styles of the houses to which they formed an entry, such as the Higher Lodges at Milton Abbey by *Chambers* (c. 1774) or the North Lodges at Lulworth Castle (1785, probably by *Tasker*). But lodges, like other garden buildings, provided the ideal opportunity for romantic fantasy, as at Gaunt's House (c. 1803), a *cottage orné* with an 96
umbrella thatched roof. It was probably by *William Evans* and is contemporary with his Neoclassical main house. A shell-lined GROTTO of some complexity was built (by *Mr Castles* of Marylebone) at St Giles's House (1745–52), and a very elaborate one of similar date stands in the garden of Harper House, Hound 89
Street, Sherborne. At Encombe is a primitive ROCK ARCH (built by c. 1780), and there are also arches at St Giles's House (1748 and castellated) and Creech Grange (before 1746), here an eye- 77
catcher on the hill-crest.

Building in a GOTHICK STYLE happened earlier on garden and landscape buildings than elsewhere, e.g. the dairy probably by *Capability Brown* at Sherborne Castle (1753–5) and the garden turret at Melbury House (c. 1762). Gothick windows were incorporated in the tower at Horton (1726, probably by *Archer*), the first of the series of TOWERS in Dorset parks. Later examples are the Charborough Park tower (1790, rebuilt higher 1840), and – on a cliff top rather than in a park – the Clavell Tower, Kimmeridge (c. 1830). A forerunner to this series is the Philosopher's Tower at St Giles's House (c. 1700), really a tall gazebo. Standing apart is the curious building at Duntish, Buckland Newton, where classicism was taken to a fundamental level in a 'primitive hut' (probably by *Chambers*, c. 1765). Here columns and entablature are formed from half-logs, an idea derived from Marc-Antoine Laugier and illustrated by Chambers himself in his *Treatise on Civil Architecture* (1759).

A corollary of a landscaped park was often the demolition and rebuilding of a village that stood in its way. The best-known example of a model ESTATE VILLAGE is at Milton Abbas, the 93
cottages designed by *Chambers*, the layout by *Brown* (c. 1780). It has a curved street of matching cottage pairs, each with a thatched roof. Another is Newtown at More Crichel, although

only one C18 cottage survives. The expansion of the park at Charborough (after 1841) involved re-routing a major road. This was
accompanied by a long and very plain brick wall, punctuated by
a series of entrance archways, one of which celebrates the gift
of the new road.

Town and public building

The development of architectural styles may also be traced
through URBAN CONSTRUCTION. Much was triggered by the
need to rebuild following fires (Sturminster Newton, 1729; Cerne
Abbas, 1740; Beaminster, 1781; Bere Regis, 1788; Lyme Regis,
1844). However, rebuilding in these places was patchy and had
no consistent quality. In contrast, at Wareham after the 1762 fire,
and especially at Blandford Forum after the great fire of 1731,
attempts were made to impose architectural order on the new
street scene. At Blandford the local craftsman family of *Bastard* is
associated with most of the work, which gave a great opportunity
to use their joinery in most new interiors of quality. At least three
of the new TOWN HOUSES, however, were designed by *Nathaniel
Ireson*. Coupar House (*c.* 1735) is a safe stylistic attribution, as is
p. 130   No. 75 East Street/No. 26 Market Place and the former Red Lion
Inn, although the latter was commissioned and fitted out by *John
Bastard* for himself. Of this period too are Joliffe's House (*c.* 1730,
possibly by *Francis Smith* of Warwick) and Sir Peter Thompson's
House (1749 by *John Bastard*), both in Poole. In that town also a
simpler, more refined style occurs later in the C18 at the Mansion
House (*c.* 1790) and Beech Hurst (1798).

p. 645   At Weymouth, given impetus by the visits of George III and
his occasional occupation of Gloucester Lodge from 1789, The
Esplanade developed from the centre of old Melcombe Regis
northwards. Here the middle-sized houses, intended for the
boarding of visitors, were grouped together into TERRACES. The
first was Gloucester Row (*c.* 1790 by *James Hamilton*), followed
by the Royal Crescent (*c.* 1801), Royal Terrace (*c.* 1816 and 1818),
and so on until Victoria Terrace of 1855–6. The first were simpler,
of brick or stucco, with a first-floor balcony, and symmetrically
composed. Later terraces gained in scale and in grandeur of
façade treatment. In Weymouth and elsewhere, VILLAS became
the fashionable alternative to a terraced house. These are found
throughout the coastal towns, e.g. at Lyme Regis. A particularly
fine group is Hill Side in Charmouth, a row of three matching
stucco villas of 1827 by *Joseph Wilson*.

In contrast with the quality of the new domestic architecture
in towns, TOWN HALLS and GUILDHALLS could be prosaic,
such as Poole's Guildhall of 1761. Employment of a London
architect does not seem to have helped either, witness *William
Tyler*'s Town Hall, Bridport, 1785–6, and *Thomas Hardwick*'s
Shire Hall, Dorchester, 1796–7. In some ways the Guildhall at
101   Weymouth (1836–8) hits the note (although still provincially);
it is by the otherwise unknown *George Corderoy*. Typical official

nautical building can be found at Poole on the harbourside: the
Custom House of 1813, with its jaunty pedimented porch, and   *p. 456*
the nearby Harbour Office of 1822, stucco with its upper floor
above a colonnade. PUBLIC MONUMENTS of the period are few.
The most notable is that to George III at Weymouth, erected in   97
1809. It is of *Coade* stone and was designed by *James Hamilton.*

With increasing mechanization, most CORN MILLS greatly
expanded from their Tudor or Stuart size. This expansion was
almost always in brick and usually involved ranks of similarly
detailed windows on each floor. Typical is Sturminster Newton
Mill, with a large block of *c.* 1800 extending over the River Stour.
Likewise, the Old Mill at Fordington (Dorchester) was enlarged
in 1841. However, the large FLAX-MAKING operation at Pymore
Mills, Bradpole was new-built (of local stone) in the late C18, and
later much expanded. This was part of a major flax and hemp
industry that had grown up in and around Bridport from the
medieval period. Associated buildings include Court Mills, West
Street (developed from the mid C18 onwards), the Priory Mills
group in Priory Lane (of 1838), and North Mills, where a long
ROPE WALKS building of the late C18 survives. The picturesque
White Mill at Shapwick (corn) is a new building, no doubt on   92
an old mill site; it is dated 1776.

Road-building under the various turnpike trusts accelerated
towards the end of the C18 and beyond, often associated with
BRIDGES. The best examples in the county cross the River
Stour, at Blandford Forum (1783 and 1812, by *William Moulton*
and *William Bushrod* respectively), Durweston (1795 by *Joseph
Towsey*), and Canford Bridge, Wimborne Minster (1813, by *John
Dyson Jun.*). Also, in two places it was thought advisable to make
TUNNELS in order to ease the gradients of roads on improved
alignments. They are both of the early 1830s, that at Horn Hill
N of Beaminster by *Michael Lane*, the other N of Charmouth
on Thistle Hill. Finally, on the subject of transport, mention
should be made of the extraordinary COBB at Lyme Regis, a
sickle-shaped breakwater and jetty, mostly of 1756, but altered
thereafter and incorporating work dating back to the C16.

Georgian and Regency interiors

The best EARLY C18 INTERIORS are staircase halls. The finest is
undoubtedly *Archer*'s at Chettle House, where the staircase rises
theatrically in the two-storey hall. The highest quality joinery is
at Charborough Park (1718) and Sherborne House, Sherborne   74
(*c.* 1720). Both have the added attraction of surrounding walls
painted by *Thornhill*, who from 1720 was a local man (having
returned to his family estate). The Charborough paintings are
signed, the Sherborne ones confidently attributed. They are in
a far higher class than the paintings by *Lanscroon* at Melbury
House, Melbury Sampford, dated 1701.

Later in the century taste turned to inset paintings. Those by
Casali at Ranston, Iwerne Courtney, date from the 1750s. The

Casali ceiling painting at the Manor House, Beaminster, was brought in from Alderman Beckford's Fonthill Splendens, Wilts., as was the splendid marble fireplace (probably by *J. F. Moore*) with scenes from the Trojan War.

By far the most common form of interior elaboration was PLASTERWORK, and much remains in Dorset houses, mostly in a semi-naturalistic Rococo style. A good example is the dining room at Eastway House, Blandford Forum (*c.* 1750), with flowing fronds and vine trails. Otherwise, little is of first-rate quality, and one can mention only *Flitcroft*'s interiors at St Giles's House, Wimborne St Giles (1740–4), and the outstanding Rococo ceilings at Came House, Winterborne Came (by *Vile & Cobb* of London) and at Merly House, both executed late in the 1750s. For JOINERY, work by the *Bastard* family is found over much of the county, especially in Blandford Forum itself. A tell-tale is the staircase handrail terminated by a widening or claw rather than the more usual spiral wreath. They were also responsible for plasterwork, but this, although distinctive, is highly provincial in character. The mention of two locations in Blandford may suffice: Coupar House and No. 75 East Street/No. 26 Market Place, the latter John Bastard's house, both of *c.* 1735. Fine NEOCLASSICAL INTERIORS are at Milton Abbey House: several on the ground floor by *Chambers*, and the magnificent ballroom on the first floor by *James Wyatt* after he had taken over in 1775. As mentioned before, the suite of state rooms at Crichel is by *Samuel & James Wyatt* (1772–80). There is a fine interior at Sadborow, Thorncombe by *John Johnson* (1773–5), centred on a top-lit staircase in a round well, and a permutation of this arrangement is at Belfield House, Wyke Regis by *Crunden* (*c.* 1780). GOTHICK INTERIORS are less common: an early example is the library at Sherborne Castle of 1757–8 by *William Ride*, with Jacobean-style ceiling plasterwork by *Francis Cartwright*.

Churches, chapels and church furnishings

By the early C18 Gothic was no longer locally considered a viable alternative to classical for church building. That is, with one somewhat puzzling exception: the new church at Castleton, Sherborne of 1715, reputedly by the *5th Lord Digby*. If the church was indeed designed by him, he was either so conservative a designer as to not have noticed current trends, or was a truly advanced thinker in architectural matters, presaging the arrival of Georgian Gothick. Its windows have Y-tracery and the pointed arcades have octagonal piers. More typical of the new church style is St Mary, Charlton Marshall of 1713–15, fitted out internally by the *Bastard* family. The chief characteristics are regularly spaced round-arched windows with architraves, keystones and imposts; low-pitched roofs with plain parapets; and a short, undemonstrative E end. Similar work is found in the remodelled naves at Almer (*c.* 1720) and Winterborne Stickland (1716). After the fire

at Blandford Forum, the new church (1733–9) was inevitably   86
a showcase of the latest ideas as well as the centrepiece of the
town. So it has the features just mentioned, but carried out with
a panache beyond anything else of its date in the county. Its
architect is unrecorded, although the *Bastard* family were clearly
involved with more than its furnishing. The designer was most
likely *John James* (who stayed with John Bastard when in Blandford), probably with *Nathaniel Ireson* and *Francis Cartwright* as
local executants. Certainly the slight polychromy in its materials
is also found on other work by *Ireson*, while the two frontispieces,
in the W front and in the centre of the S front, have decidedly
Baroque passages. The Blandford tower design has similarities
with that at Wimborne St Giles of 1732, suggesting that this too
was by *Ireson*. Quite apart from the above narrative stands the
Vanbrughian tower added to Horton church by *John Chapman*
in 1722–3 and the curiously old-fashioned Stuart Baroque of St
George, Reforne, Portland, built in 1754–66 by the Portland-   83
based *Thomas Gilbert*. This is a monumental building with a W
tower in a Wrenian style, but with other features that owe more
to Hawksmoor and Vanbrugh.

From this point new Church of England churches in the C18
turn Gothick (*see* below). To maintain the classical thread one
must follow NONCONFORMIST CHAPELS and Roman Catholic
church building. The best of the former are the two Congregational chapels of 1745–55 and 1777, at Lyme Regis and Poole
respectively. Lyme has a Doric entrance, round-arched lower   p. 369
windows and *œil de bœuf* above; Poole has a curvy gable but
windows that are just slightly pointed. A pure late C18, almost
domestic style is found in the Unitarian chapel at Bridport (1794,
now the Chapel in the Garden), while the stuccoed Neoclassical
of the early C19 is most apparent at Wareham Unitarian church
of 1830 and at Bridport Wesleyan Methodist church of 1838 by
J. Galpin.

Two ROMAN CATHOLIC CHURCHES deserve special notice.
The first in date and significance (as the first Catholic free-
standing chapel erected in England since the Reformation) is
Lulworth Castle Chapel, of 1786–7 by *J. Tasker* for Thomas Weld.   85
This was built prior to the Roman Catholic Relief Act of 1791,   p. 273
so a special dispensation was given by George III. It has a quatrefoil plan with two porches, W and E (ritually), and the altar
end encased in rooms on two floors so that from some angles
the whole looks like a house – or perhaps a garden temple or
mausoleum, meeting the condition that it must not look like
a church. The interior with the four segmental arches and the
shallow dome is beautiful and peaceful. The second church, at
Lyme Regis and by *H. E. Goodridge* (1835–7), illustrates the return
to Gothic. In the former Congregational church at Sherborne
(1803, altered 1821) one also finds an example of the increasing
use of Gothic in Nonconformist chapels.

GOTHIC became the style of choice for Church of England
churches and chapels from the 1770s onwards. We see this at the
private chapel to Charborough Park (1775), at Moreton church

(1776, probably by *John Carter*) and at the new parish church at
Milton Abbas by *James Wyatt* (1786). Three later examples are
99   St James, Poole of 1819–21 by the local architects *John Kent* and
Joseph Hannaford; Fleet, by *William Strickland*, 1827–9; and Charmouth, of 1835–6 by *Charles Fowler*. However, the last has the
plain lancet style associated with Commissioners' Churches (i.e.
those funded by the Church Building Commission from 1818
onwards), also seen at Lytchett Minster (1833–4) and Holt (1834–
6), both by *John Tulloch* of Poole. Gillingham, by *Henry Malpas*
(1838–9), lumpily incorporates elements of classical composition
into the mix. Perp gets an early revival at Sturminster Newton
(1825–8), designed by an otherwise wholly classical architect,
William Evans of Wimborne. NEOCLASSICAL CHURCHES were
built in parallel with the lancet Gothic type, notable examples
being at St Mary, Weymouth by *James Hamilton* (1815–17), with
giant quatrefoil piers, galleries and plaster tunnel-vault, and St
Swithun, Allington, Bridport by *Charles Wallis* (1826–7).

   Most of the churches listed above retain their original FUR-
NISHINGS, well worth seeing at St George, Reforne, Portland,
with its two opposing pulpits, and the complete mid-C18 installation at Chalbury. For individual pieces, the most splendid classical REREDOS (with Commandment boards, the Lord's Prayer
82   and the Creed) is at Charlton Marshall, probably by the *Bastards*.
The contemporary Castleton, Sherborne reredos is more in the
Wren style, while that at St Mary, Weymouth is supplemented
by *Thornhill*'s Last Supper of 1721, hung above. The seating in
Blandford Forum church is by the *Bastard* company, including
the fine mayor's chair of 1748, while in that church, at Charlton
Marshall and in other churches refurnished in the 1740s are a
series of stone BALUSTER FONTS, many by the *Bastards*. By the
late C18 there was increasing awareness and respect for medieval
Gothic, a typical response being *Wyatt*'s stucco restoration of the
great medieval reredos at Milton Abbey (*c.* 1789).

Georgian church monuments

There are any number of Georgian MONUMENTS, mostly tablets.
79   A selection must start with Sir Richard Newman at Fifehead
Magdalen, who died in 1721. He has a monument still in the
spirit of the magnificence of 1700, by *Sir Henry Cheere*: an
obelisk, with his whole family depicted on three busts and oval
medallions. A monument at Seaborough (†1738) has a bust, the
tablet to Ann Browne at Frampton (†1714) a lively and elegant
medallion. The 1st Earl of Shaftesbury at Wimborne St Giles
has a bust too (by *Rysbrack*) and an obelisk. That monument
80   dates from 1732. Frances Dirdoe (†1733) at Gillingham, probably designed by *Nathaniel Ireson*, has three standing figures
in relief and is uncommonly fine. Back at Wimborne St Giles,
James Stuart as late as *c.* 1771 repeated the properties of the 1st
Earl for the 4th (in a monument made by *Thomas Scheemakers*). The more famous *Peter Scheemakers*'s Brodrepp monument

at Mapperton of *c.* 1740 has again an obelisk and in addition two medallions. His much grander Strode monument (†1753) at Beaminster on the other hand has two reclining effigies and two allegorical figures. Also of note here is Mary Bancks at Milton Abbas of *c.* 1725, with an awkward reclining effigy. The tablet to the architect Francis Cartwright (†1758) at Blandford St Mary is remarkable because it shows his tools and his design for the N front of Came House, Winterborne Came. But monuments can appear grand without any figures. Thomas Strangways †1726 (by *William Goodfellow* of Salisbury) at Melbury Sampford has just reredos architecture, and the designer of the monument for Robert Browne †1734 at Frampton included in his reredos as its centre a real, large, arched window.

GOTHIC, whether revived or continued, makes little appearance in church monuments in the late C18 or early C19, but something of it can be seen in *Robert Adam*'s design for the monument at Milton Abbey to Lady Milton who died in 1775. The admirable effigies are by *Carlini.* Adam's tomb-chest is Gothic and charming. But otherwise the best monuments have nothing to do with the Gothic Revival and continue in the urn-and-obelisk tradition with the same mourning female standing or sitting. In one of the largest and best, even the Baroque Roubiliac tradition continues, the monument to Elizabeth Smith †1811 (by *King* of Bath) at Sydling St Nicholas. Another equally large one with obelisk and medallion is at Sherborne Abbey, †1784, by *Thomas Carter*. Not all, even of the best, are signed. *John Bacon* signed three tablets at Canford Magna (1788–99); *Richard Westmacott* did three (at Burton Bradstock, Charborough and Frampton), that at Charborough very fine with two seated allegorical figures; *Chantrey* also three, the best that to the Countess of Ilchester at Melbury Sampford (1821). But the excellent true-to-life statue of Robert Goodden at Over Compton (1825) is unsigned, as is the excellent classical relief to John Gould at Fleet (†1818).

81

VICTORIAN AND EDWARDIAN ARCHITECTURE

Church and chapel architecture, c. 1840–c. 1920

The period from *c.* 1840 was a great age of church building, rebuilding and restoration. For the CHURCH OF ENGLAND, funds became available from a variety of sources, especially the Incorporated Church Building Society. One corollary was the need for competent architects, well versed in ecclesiastical construction and, more importantly, with detailed knowledge of historical styles. So we see fewer schemes by local surveyors or even builders, and more by national and local architects. For Anglican projects there was a choice between Gothic and NEO-NORMAN (classical or Italianate having too many Catholic associations). So we see *George Alexander* designing East Stour and Enmore

Green (both 1842) in Neo-Norman, a style also selected for
Creech Grange chapel (1840) and Hinton Parva (*George Evans*,
1860), where genuine Norman fabric was incorporated. Melplash
by *Benjamin Ferrey* (1845–6) is also Neo-Norman, a surprising
choice for the first biographer of *Pugin*. A later example is at
Grove, Portland, where *Sir Edmund Du Cane* designed a very
substantial church in this style, built 1870–2.

For churches in GOTHIC, the initial examples continue the
Commissioners' Gothic of the early C19. We see this in the plain
lancets or in anything more than the shortest of chancels at, e.g.,
Swyre (1843–4) and the estate church at Winterborne Clenston
by *Vulliamy* (1840), although here the handling of an E.E. style
is more accomplished. This is also the case with *Scott & Moffatt*'s
Holy Trinity, Shaftesbury (1841) and *Alexander*'s Sutton Waldron
church (1847), although all three just mentioned have fine towers.
Those at Winterborne Clenston and Sutton Waldron also have
good spires, the first E.E., the second more Dec. The key to this
period is the choice of E.E. or Dec, both of which seem equally
allowable, and both are applied in a well-informed manner. What
is significant is the influence of well-researched and thoroughly
illustrated books on medieval church architecture, such as those
by Thomas Rickman (1817 etc.) and J. H. Parker (1836 etc.). For
French Gothic influence, the *Dictionnaire* by E. Viollet-le-Duc
(1854–68) was the key text.

Matters of style were brought to a head by the highly polemi-
cal publications of *A.W.N. Pugin*, promoting the Middle, or
Second, Pointed Gothic specifically: that is, the architecture of
c. 1300, Dec before the tracery became flowing or the ideas more
fanciful. For the Church of England, the works of the Cambridge
Camden Society were also influential. A more ARCHAEOLOGI-
CALLY CORRECT GOTHIC ensued not only in the churches by
Pugin himself – for in Dorset we have two Anglican churches by
him, the chancel of Rampisham and the whole of Halstock (both
1846–7) – but also those by his closest followers, *Benjamin Ferrey*
and *T. Talbot Bury*. While *Bury*'s work is consistent and pure in
its Puginian Gothic, e.g. Askerswell (1858) and the two chapels of
ease at Eype (1864–5) and Broadoak (1865–6), and especially the
large church of St John, Weymouth (1850–4), *Ferrey* could adopt
a more flexible approach. His Compton Valence (1839–40) is
Dec externally, pioneering this style in C19 Dorset, but the arcade
within is more Perp, to harmonize with the arch of the retained
genuine Perp tower; also the Neo-Norman of Melplash (already
mentioned) illustrates his less strict approach. In contrast, his All
Saints, Dorchester (1843–5) is purer in its Middle Pointed. The
dates of Pugin's publications may be important here: *Contrasts*
came out in 1836 (a year after his conversion to Catholicism),
while the more detailed architectural arguments of *True Principles*
are of 1841. In that year too the Cambridge Camden Society
started publication of its journal *The Ecclesiologist*, the chief non-
Catholic disseminator of Gothic Revival ideas.

Pugin was clearly a key influence on *R.C. Carpenter* (the
'Anglican Pugin'). His work is much in evidence in the county,

chiefly in Sherborne. Of new churches, Monkton Wyld (1848–9) demonstrates Pugin's Middle Pointed to great effect in a large church for a small community. His partner *W. Slater* did Pentridge (1855–7) and his son *R.H. Carpenter* thoroughly restored Thornford church (1865–6) and added the chancel at Mappowder (1868). *Sir George Gilbert Scott*'s practice had fully developed by the time he returned to Dorset to build Woolland church (1855–6), where the style is *c.* 1280 rather than *c.* 1300, and hence more powerful in its features. The same characteristics apply at Cattistock (1857), where the church was almost completely rebuilt (with further major work by Scott's elder son nearly twenty years later). *T.H.Wyatt* was involved nationally in almost as many new churches and restorations as Scott. In Dorset he was diocesan architect from 1836 until his death in 1880 and so was involved, either directly or indirectly, in most church building in the county. His own work varies in quality according to budget, but is best seen at St James, Shaftesbury (1866–7), West Orchard (1876–8) and Winterborne Zelston (1865–6). Stylistically he was flexible, responding to the circumstances of the case and often conjuring an illusion of growth through time. So, e.g., at Shaftesbury he used Dec and Perp, while Winterborne Zelston is E.E. and Perp.

Of LOCAL ARCHITECTS, the key figures are *George Evans* of Wimborne, *John Hicks* of Dorchester and *George Rackstrow Crickmay* of Weymouth. *Evans* worked in a bold, generally E.E. style. His churches at Compton Abbas (1866–7), Melbury Abbas (1851–2) and Fontmell Magna (1862–3) are particularly effective.* All three churches were commissioned by the Glyns of Gaunt's House. Evans's E.E. was not far removed from Wyatt's own work, and features perceived by the Low Church faction of the Church of England as Catholic, such as screens, were avoided. Matters proved more divisive in the county with those churches commissioned by (or restored for) the Tractarian Rev. Thomas Sanctuary of Powerstock with *J. Hicks* as architect. The results of this collaboration are very fine, best seen in the restoration at Powerstock (started by *R.C. Carpenter* and completed by *Hicks*, 1854–9) and the new church at North Poorton in *Hicks*'s preferred Early Dec style (1860–2). (Oddly enough, despite being unashamedly 'High', they both lack screens.) *Hicks*'s second finely furnished new church is East Holme (1865–6): E.E. style, for the Bond family of the adjacent Holme Priory. After Hicks's death in 1869, his practice was taken over by *G.R. Crickmay*, who became diocesan architect ten years later, succeeding Wyatt. His churches are indeed sub-Wyatt in style, typical examples being Southwell, Portland (1879) and Lytchett Heath (with his son *G.L. Crickmay*, 1898). The last is more idiosyncratic, absorbing many emerging Art and Crafts ideas about vernacular style. As a footnote, we should briefly mention the novelist and poet *Thomas*

---

*Evans entered the Lille Cathedral competition of 1855 in partnership with R.P. Pullan, William Burges's brother-in-law. Evans's work at Fontmell Parva, Child Okeford, is especially suggestive of that sort of connection.

Hardy, who worked for Hicks before moving to London, and later returned to assist Crickmay. He helped *Hicks* at St Peter, Dorchester (1856–7) and designed the Early French Gothic foliage capitals for *Crickmay* at Turnworth (1869–70). In the w of the county, several churches were rebuilt by Somerset-based architects, such as *R.H. Shout* of Yeovil at Evershot (1852–3 and 1863), *J.M. Allen* of Crewkerne at Thorncombe (1866–7) and Corscombe (1876–7), and *Carver & Giles* of Taunton at Holy Trinity, Beaminster (1849–51). Compared with their Dorset rivals, their designs seem pedestrian.

Of the NATIONAL ARCHITECTS working in the county, *J.L. Pearson* and *G.F. Bodley* (with *T. Garner*) are most noticeable. *Pearson*'s best church is a gem: Catherston Leweston of 1857–8, by its position virtually the private chapel to the manor house next door. Less richly finished is his s chapel at Iwerne Minster (1880); much larger is St Peter, Parkstone, Poole (1881–92), a church of cathedral monumentality, the construction of which saved an unstable earlier church by *Frederick Rogers* (1876–8). *Bodley & Garner*'s new churches are later, the most idiosyncratic being Woodlands of 1892 with a double nave. More representative of their Perp-inspired style is St Aldhelm, Branksome, Poole (1892–4), a large church sadly lacking its splendid s tower and 107 spire (not executed owing to lack of money). *G.E. Street*'s Kingston church (1873–80) is one of his masterpieces, on a scale to match Pearson's Parkstone. It is strongly E.E., dramatic from the E, of a calm perfection inside, economic in its effects, yet sumptuous throughout.

LATER GOTHIC STYLES, especially Late Dec and Perp, became more influential from the 1870s, at least with the most progressive architects. We have already mentioned Branksome in this 106 respect. The tower and other additions to Cattistock by *G.G. Scott Jun.* (1874) are fully Perp, but seem to work in harmony with his father's Early Dec. Also more Perp than anything are Bryanston by *E.P. Warren* (1896–8) and Westham by *G.H. Fellowes Prynne* (1894–1913). The latter is especially advanced with its double-gabled transepts, an idea repeated at All Saints, Easton, Portland (1914–17) in the Temple Moore-like church designed by *G.L. Crickmay*, a fine building which deserves to be better known. Lastly there is *C.E. Ponting*'s *magnum opus* of St Mary, Dorchester (1910–12), although like Branksome also doomed to never receive its projected tower.

So to the ARTS AND CRAFTS MOVEMENT. Its main representative in Dorset is *E.S. Prior*. At Bothenhampton (1887–9) 108 in the cross-arches spanning the nave interior, Prior tested out forms that he would later use at Roker, Sunderland (1906–7, with A. Randall Wells). The altar at Bothenhampton was designed by *Lethaby*, who used the same cross-arch idea at Lower Brockhampton, Herefordshire (1901–2). Stylistically flexible, *Prior* adopted a more Byzantine language for St Osmund, Parkstone (1913–16), which, appropriately enough, is now an Orthodox church. Externally, Bothenhampton has much of the massing of a tithe barn, and this interest in secular forms may also be found at Colehill by *W.D. Caröe* (1893). Here he combined timber framing with mechanical red brick, materials unfortunately conveying a West Midlands suburban flavour. Much better are his Lady Chapel at Sherborne (1921) and chapel at Gillingham church (1919–21). Finally, *Ponting*'s St George, Gillingham of 1921, with a rustic, rolling thatched roof, is a poignant war memorial for the lost son of a local family.

CHURCH RESTORATION was possibly the most important architectural activity in early to mid-Victorian church history in Dorset. The three great medieval churches in the county were each subject to thorough restorations of varying degrees of sensitivity. Perhaps least responsive to existing fabric and fittings was *T.H. Wyatt* at Wimborne Minster (1855–7), where he removed the canopied backs of the C17 choir stalls and reconstructed the nave roof and clerestory to a different bay pattern. *Sir G. G. Scott* at Milton Abbey (1864–*c.* 1870) added much that was appropriate by way of furnishings while hardly interfering with the structure. His chief addition is the small W porch, curiously scaled against the sheer, incomplete W end. The most assured sequence of restorations was at Sherborne Abbey. Here, in three phases, the structure was stabilized while the interior was re-furnished with fittings of the highest quality. *R. C. Carpenter* was architect for work on the nave and transepts (1849–51), his partner *Slater* restored and re-fitted the choir (1856–8), and Slater with *R. H. Carpenter* repaired the tower (1884).

Restoration also affected smaller churches. We have already mentioned the restoration of Powerstock church by *R. C. Carpenter* (followed by *Hicks*). *Hicks* was also in charge of work at St Peter, Dorchester (1856–7), where the Georgianized E end was rebuilt in Gothic form, and he did much the same at St Mary, Bridport (1858–60). At Bradford Abbas, *William Newbury*, a Sherborne carpenter, took out a wall inserted above the stone choir screen to create a new chancel arch (1858); and in 1902–3 *Bodley* carried out a delightful redecoration at Shillingstone (including a choir screen, regrettably removed in 1977). But *T. L. Donaldson*'s rebuilding of Lady St Mary, Wareham (1841–2), while retaining the chancel, tower and chapels, was wholly destructive of the most important Anglo-Saxon church in the county.

The building of new ROMAN CATHOLIC CHURCHES gained pace after the Emancipation Act of 1829. With the conversion of Pugin to Catholicism in 1835, archaeologically correct Gothic in his mode became available for the new buildings. In Dorset these were by *C. F. Hansom* (Stapehill, 1847–51) and *J. A. Hansom* (Grove, Portland, 1868). Later Gothic churches were by the prolific Canon *A. J. C. Scoles*, son of the architect J.J. Scoles. Typical are the former St Michael, Wareham (1889, re-erected in Dorchester), Sacred Heart and St Aldhelm, Sherborne (1893–4) and Holy Spirit and St Edward, Swanage (1902–4). Unlike the Puginian work of the Hansoms, Scoles's Gothic is more dilute and less stylistically specific. The change to Perp-inspired Gothic is also reflected in Catholic churches by *E. Doran Webb*, e.g. Holy Name and St Edward, Shaftesbury (1909–10).

For NONCONFORMIST CHAPELS, the plain, round-arched window style of the earlier C19 initially continued unabated (e.g. West Bay and Kington Magna Methodist chapels of 1848 and 1851). A more overt classical pediment was provided by *William Gollop* for the façade of Longham Congregational church (1841). *Poulton & Woodman* of Reading introduced a more rigorous Gothic in their Congregational churches at Dorchester (1856–7) and Bridport (1859–60), although a full classical treatment remained an option, such as on the Congregational church at Shaftesbury (1859 by *A. Trimen*) or the façade added to the Baptist church at Weymouth in the same year. From this time onwards, lancet Gothic with varying degrees of elaboration became the most common choice,

Dorchester, Congregational church.
Engraving, 1856

especially for Methodist churches. A number were designed by
T. Hudson of Gillingham, including Motcombe (1870), Gillingham (1877) and Iwerne Minster (1879), and the Baptist chapel
at Gillingham of 1892–3, although the last is more Perp-inspired.
A free Gothic based on Perp became more popular towards the
turn of the century, as seen at Underhill (Portland) Methodist
church by *Robert Curwen* (1898–1900), the Congregational church,
Swanage by *Thomas Stevens* of Bournemouth (1901–2) and the
Baptist church, Upper Parkstone (Poole) by *Lawson & Reynolds*
(1907–8). Finally two curiosities: the odd Neo-Baroque of *Sydney
Jackson*'s Dorford Baptist Church, Dorchester (1912–14) and the
E.E.-cum-Art Nouveau of Easton Methodist church, Portland   117
by *La Trobe & Weston* of Bristol (1906–7), a large church with a
blend of styles combined theatrically, and continued with fine
craftsmanship within.

In 1855, in response to the overcrowding of churchyards, an
Act was passed allowing municipal authorities to build public
CEMETERIES. These were invariably landscaped, often with
meandering driveways, and usually had two chapels: one Church
of England, the other for Nonconformists and Roman Catho-
lics. The earliest in Dorset date from 1856, such as Dorchester (chapels by *G.J.G. Gregory*), Wimborne Minster (chapels
and lodge by *R.H. Shout*), and Bridport (chapels and lodge by
Henry Hall). At Sherborne, where the chapels, lodge and receiving house are by *William Haggett* of that town, the highlight is
the Digby Mausoleum of 1862–77 by *William Slater*, in French   p. 541
Gothic with fine craftsmanship. In most cases the chapel architect was also responsible for the landscaping, as at Poole of 1857,
by *Christopher Crabbe Creeke* of Bournemouth.

Church furnishings and monuments

The period saw the introduction of furnishings in revived medieval styles, either to supplant older fittings that were deemed
un-ecclesiastical, or for entirely new churches. So as well as
pulpits and fonts, screens, reredoses and stained glass completed
the revived Gothic picture. The best work was by craftsmen
from outside the county, such as *James Forsyth*, who provided
an elaborate reredos (to *Slater*'s design) at the high altar of Sherborne Abbey (1858). During a later phase of work (for *B. Ingelow*)
he made an equally elaborate pulpit (1899), and the family
connection continued there with a screen of 1909 by his son,
J. Dudley Forsyth. Forsyth was also the chief contributor to the
rich refurnishing of Melbury Sampford church, for the 5th Earl
of Ilchester (*c.* 1876). Again, the reredos is especially elaborate.
Equally proficient was *Thomas Earp*, whose pulpit at Wimborne
Minster (1868) is the finest feature of the refurnishing carried
out under *T.H. Wyatt*. Fonts attracted the highest level of design
and craftsmanship. Especially fine is that at Rampisham of 1844,
designed by *A.W.N. Pugin* and surely inspired by the Late Perp
cross base in the churchyard.

Local architects not infrequently brought in the best crafts-men, especially when they had the budget. So the most fully
16 furnished churches by *John Hicks*, at Powerstock (1854–9), North Poorton (1862) and East Holme (1865–6), have carved work by *R.L. Boulton* of Worcester, on the pulpit at the first, the figures on the pulpit at the second, and on the font and roof corbels at East Holme. A particularly fine example of this combination of architect and craftsman is the restoration of 1865–6 at Okeford
37 Fitzpaine, where the medieval pulpit was elaborated with a new base and its niches given figures. Also a truly Wagnerian-Romantic chalice-like font was made. The sculptor *Benjamin Grassby*, who probably trained with Earp before moving to Power-stock in 1862, is often as proficient as Boulton, and is equally accomplished in stone or wood. He was frequently brought in by *Hicks*, e.g. North Poorton roof corbels, pulpit and font, all 1862. He also carried out much of the carved work at Framp-ton (under *Ferrey*, 1862), although the reredos and font were by *Earp*. In 1892 *C.E. Ponting* was made diocesan architect for the Dorset archdeaconry (in succession to *G.R. Crickmay*). His frequent involvement in church restoration has a notable legacy in a number of fine, Perp-style chancel screens. The best are at Netherbury (1911), Stalbridge (1912), Beaminster (1913) and Sturminster Newton (1919). He also provided a similar screen for his own St Mary, Dorchester (1910–12). The richest fitting out of the period immediately before the First World War was that of 1910 by *Sir Ninian Comper* at Wimborne St Giles. Here he designed an extravagant screen to accompany his 'English' high altar and stained glass.

The great revival in STAINED GLASS is also a key to the character of Victorian churches. All of the major firms are repre-sented in the county. In date order, the highlights begin with the chancel windows at Trent by *William Wailes* of Newcastle (started in 1842). Another early window in the county by *Wailes* is in the s aisle at Lyme Regis (1843), to which a matching set was added by the successor firm, *Wailes & Strang* (*c.* 1880). Rampisham has windows in the chancel designed by *Pugin*, with *J.H. Powell*, and made by *Hardman* (1847–8); Pugin's greatest single window is
113 in the s transept of Milton Abbey, designed with *F.W. Oliphant* (1848), part of what would have been an extensive scheme. The earliest window by *Clayton & Bell* is at Cattistock (1858); at Silton (1869–70) a complete scheme by them is accompanied by deco-rative painting. The best example of their early, more original style is at Tolpuddle (*c.* 1860), designed by *R.T. Bayne*, who joined *Heaton & Butler* in 1862. This firm's most impressive work is at the chapel of ease at Eype; colourful and well composed, avoiding the formulaic character that this maker – and others – descended into as the century progressed.

A new style, based on later medieval glass, emerged especially under *Burlison & Grylls*. An early scheme of theirs is in the bap-tistery at Cattistock (1874). Since *Bodley & Garner* instigated the setting up of this company, it is not surprising to find their work at Shillingstone (1903) and St Aldhelm, Branksome (1911), both by those architects.

A freshness of purpose entered stained glass work through designers versed in the ideas of the ARTS AND CRAFTS MOVEMENT. The key national firm is of course *Morris & Co*. Their best window in the county is also at Cattistock (1882), partially designed by *Burne-Jones*. Two windows at St George, Fordington (Dorchester) are later (1903 and 1913). Several windows in Dorset were made by *Christopher Whall*, the best being those in the cemetery chapel, Dorchester (1891), and the E windows at West Stafford (1913) and Iwerne Minster (1914). Finally, two unusual works: the window at Symondsbury designed by *W. R. Lethaby* (1885) with strongly medievalizing figures, and the Art Nouveau-influenced window at Bourton by the Dane *Baron Arild Rosenkrantz* (†1910).

The WALL DECORATIONS at Silton by *Clayton & Bell* have already been mentioned. There is also a significant scheme by *Owen Jones* at Sutton Waldron (1847). This leaves Victorian and Edwardian CHURCH MONUMENTS, of which there are many, chiefly Gothic wall tablets and recumbent effigies. The best of the latter are at Milton Abbey – the monument to Baron Hambro (†1877) with an elaborate canopy of carved openwork designed by *J. O. Scott* – and that to Canon Reginald Southwell Smith †1895 at West Stafford. Here the architectural setting was by *Ponting* and the sculptor was *Harry Hems* of Exeter. Also worth seeking out are *Hems*'s fine (and usually small-scale) tablets. The best are at St Peter, Dorchester (†1885), Melcombe Horsey (†1908) and West Stafford (†1913). Finally, the most prominent PUBLIC MONUMENT of the period is that on Black Down, Portesham to Admiral Sir Thomas Masterman Hardy, 1844. But it is only a chimney-like tower with what John Newman described as 'crinoline base-mouldings'. Its architect was *A. D. Acland-Troyte*.

Victorian and Edwardian public architecture

With the 1835 Municipal Reform Act, the building of TOWN HALLS spread from the old boroughs to those with new civic status. Those in Dorchester (1847–8 by *Benjamin Ferrey*), Wareham (1869–70 by *G. R. Crickmay*) and Lyme Regis (1887–9 by *George Vialls*) were all Gothic, although in the last case of a curious Free-Style fusion. HOSPITALS also reflected this stylistic trend, and were often designed by the same (non-specialist) architects. So those at Dorchester (1839–41) and Sherborne (1866) are by *Ferrey* and *Slater & Carpenter* respectively. The construction of ALMSHOUSES was also revived, on the medieval model architecturally. Especially fine are the extensions to the Sherborne Almshouse, 1858 by *William Slater*. Much the same mood is found at the Turners Almshouses at Trent (1845–6, perhaps by *R. J. Withers*) and the Home of the Homeless, Frampton (1868 by *Ferrey*). The same architects also designed SCHOOLS, such as Tincleton (*c.* 1840 by *Ferrey*), Beaminster (1868 by *Slater & Carpenter*) and Powerstock (1848–50 by *R. C. Carpenter*). This last architect initiated a major expansion of Sherborne School from 1855, starting with the adaptation of the monastic Guesten Hall

115
114
3
104
p. 537

and Abbot's Hall, to form a library and chapel respectively. The
work was continued by *Slater* and *R.H. Carpenter*. From 1894 the
continuing programme was in the hands of *Sir Reginald Blomfield*.
At the nearby Sherborne School for Girls, the first architects
were *John Harding & Son* (from 1902), with *W.D. Caröe* taking
over after Harding's death in 1910, and providing a clock tower
of considerable distinction.

The Victorian era also saw a proliferation of building types,
often designed by architects and surveyors who were national
specialists in their field. Of the many WORKHOUSES established
under the 1835 Poor Law Act, Dorchester (1836) was by *George
Wilkinson*, a national specialist; Weymouth (1836) by *T. Dodson*
and *T. Hill Harvey*; and Bridport (1837) by *H.J. Whitling*. Of
well-known national architects, *Lewis Vulliamy* designed Sturminster Newton workhouse in 1836, while the Dorchester-based
Charles Wallis did that at Cerne Abbas, 1836–7. PRISONS established through reforms in the penal code in the treatment of
convicts were, however, normally in the hands of specialists. So
the early Grove Prison, Portland (1848, now an adult and young
offenders' establishment) was by *Joshua Jebb*, a key figure in the
prison-design improvements of the time.

Commercial and industrial building was rarely Gothic, and in
the case of BANKS (also proliferating through the C19), a Renais-
sance-based classicism was desirable. This is most clearly demonstrated by the former Williams Bank, Dorchester by *Charles
Wallis* (1835), and the series built for the Wilts. & Dorset Bank.
Many in Dorset were by the Wimborne-based practice of *George
Evans*, succeeded in 1874 by *W.J. Fletcher*. An exceptional building is that at Weymouth, built for Stuckey's Bank, of 1883 by
Bonella & Paull in a florid French Renaissance style with Dutch
gables.

Large INDUSTRIAL BUILDINGS of the period are rare in this
predominantly rural and maritime county. The most architecturally expressive are BREWERIES, of which the largest groups are
at Dorchester and Weymouth. At the first, the main buildings are
of 1879 onwards (partly rebuilt after a fire in 1922), designed in
heavy Renaissance-influenced polychrome brick by *Crickmay &
Son*. Groves Brewery in Weymouth (1903–4) is in a red brick,
Dutch Mercantile style, designed in this case by the brewery
specialists *Arthur Kinder & Son*. The same firm also designed the
Hall & Woodhouse Brewery at Blandford Forum (1899–1900).
The process of replacing craft skills with fully mechanized operations at MILLS continued, together with the introduction of
steam power. This is illustrated at Pymore Mills, Bradpole, where
large flax warehouses, weaving sheds and an engine house with
a tall chimneystack were added from the mid C19. Here too
accommodation for the workers was provided on site, together
with a school, making a self-sufficient community. Corn-milling
machinery of the mid C19 survives *in situ* at Sturminster Newton
Mill.

The new phenomenon of the age was the railway. Several early
RAILWAY BUILDINGS survive in the county, chiefly associated

with the Salisbury & Yeovil Railway, on which the stations at Gillingham (1859) and Sherborne (1860) are by *Sir William Tite*, and with the Great Western line to Weymouth. Along this route are Dorchester West station and the Grimstone viaduct, both by *I.K. Brunel*, and Maiden Newton station by *R.P. Brereton*, all of 1857. Dorchester West station is Italianate, that at Maiden Newton relatively styleless. The styles used by different companies could indeed vary widely. Those on the Salisbury line were cottagey, as were those constructed at a later date on the Swanage branch (1885), designed by *W.R. Galbraith*. In complete contrast is the red brick, Dutch-gabled Wareham station of the following year, architect unknown.

More florid BUILDING STYLES in opposition to the Gothic Revival became more common in the two last decades of the c19. The Edwards' Homes, Weymouth (1894 and 1896 by *Crickmay & Son*) are in an ornate Tudor revival style. Two buildings by *Sir George Oatley* for Stuckey's Bank (Dorchester 1899–1902, Gillingham 1900–2) interpret classical forms with more stylistic freedom than hitherto, heading towards Edwardian Baroque. More freedom and ornate interactions of materials are found at the POST OFFICES designed by *John Rutherford* at Dorchester (1904–5) and Weymouth (*c*. 1905). The trend continued in the BANKS by *Whinney, Son & Austen Hall* at Weymouth (1923–4), and that at Poole (*c*. 1922), probably also by them.

Finally the ARTS AND CRAFTS MOVEMENT. This is more generally associated with domestic buildings, but examples by architects best known for houses are to be found in the public field. So Wootton Fitzpaine village hall by *F. W. Troup* (1906) is a full expression of traditional building materials, while St Ann's Hospital, Canford Cliffs, Poole by *Robert Weir Schultz* (1910–12) is a powerful and idiosyncratic exercise, combining Scottish features with English Georgian.

Domestic building, c. 1840–c. 1920

From *c*. 1840 the predominant choice for COUNTRY-HOUSE STYLE was between Italianate classical, Tudor Revival and Gothic Revival. The master of the first was *Sir Charles Barry*, although his remodelling of Kingston Lacy (1835–55) was highly respectful towards the Jonesian classicism of the original house. The picturesque qualities possible in Italianate were more fully expressed in Barry's enlargement of Canford Manor (1847–50), although the detailing was Tudor Revival, to match Blore's earlier house. Clyffe House, Tincleton (1842–4) by *B. Ferrey* exhibits Gothic Revival, a style rarely attempted on a large scale in the county, the only other instance being Iwerne Minster House by *Alfred Waterhouse* (1878). A Tudor–Jacobean style was often preferred in the county, so *Ferrey*'s alterations at Stafford House, West Stafford (1848–50) were in a c16 vernacular style, with only the loggia with a classical arcade. *Salvin*'s library at Melbury House (1872) took the form of an early c16 collegiate building,

100

103

53

also in a Tudor style to blend with the original building. As a continuation of the enthusiasm for Tudor in Dorset, by the last decades of the C19 an elaborate Elizabethan–Jacobean blend became the alternative to classical. Of the former we see *George Devey*'s extensions at Melbury House (1884–5) and the new Motcombe House (1892–4) by *Sir Ernest George & Peto*, while a Wren-ish Renaissance was used by *Norman Shaw* in his Bryanston of 1889–94. The classicism of South Lytchett Manor by *W.D. Caröe* (1900–4) is more eclectic in its sources and more eccentric in its combinations. Equally original in its free combinations of historic elements and details is Minterne House, Minterne Magna by *Leonard Stokes* (1904–6), but here all is handled with aplomb, producing the great house of its age in the county. Finally, in the Free Style, the house that *Thomas Hardy* built for himself at Max Gate, just outside Dorchester (1883–5).

After the turn of the century the stylistic choice moved on to that between Neo-Georgian and Arts and Crafts. A typical NEO-GEORGIAN example is the Lutyens-inspired Horn Park, Beaminster by *T. Lawrence Dale* (1911). Much the same approach may be seen at Crendle Court, Purse Caundle by *Walter Brierley* (1908–9), and Marsh Court, Caundle Marsh by *Macpherson & Richardson* (1910). In the ARTS AND CRAFTS mode are Hill Close, Studland by *C.F.A. Voysey* (1896), in his typical white-walled style with a big roof and prominent chimneystacks; and Thistlegate House, Charmouth (1911) by *F.W. Troup*, exhibiting the same care for craftsmanship as his contemporary village hall at Wootton Fitzpaine, previously mentioned. It is perhaps best to note here two houses built well after 1920: Ashley Chase by *Sir Guy Dawber* (1925) and Weston, West Lulworth (1927) by *Sir Edwin Lutyens*, each a typical exercise by its architect. Ashley Chase is more Neo-vernacular, built in local stone; perversely for Purbeck, Weston is of brick and in a free interpretation of Early Georgian.

It was at a smaller scale that the Gothic Revival was best utilized in a domestic context, especially in PARSONAGES. This was demonstrated by *Pugin* in his Rampisham rectory of 1845–7. Equally successful is the rectory at Monkton Wyld by *R.C. Carpenter* (1849) and the much smaller rectory at Tarrant Hinton by *Ferrey* (1843). At Beaminster *William White* designed a typically bold vicarage (1859–61), while a more conventional Gothic may be seen at the two rectories designed by *J.E. Gill* of Manners & Gill, at St James, Shaftesbury (1860) and Buckhorn Weston (1861). *G.R. Crickmay* also designed many clergy houses (such as the main part of Compton Valence House, 1872; the Old Rectory, Owermoigne, 1882; and Folke House, 1884), but rarely built more substantial dwellings. Two exceptions are Purbeck House, Swanage of 1875, designed in an eclectic and highly individual assemblage of elements for George Burt, and Holmwood Park, Longham of 1897, where the mixture of timber framing and pargetting is in an Arts and Crafts mode.

The development of Swanage as another of Dorset's SEASIDE RESORTS, started c. 1823 by William Morton Pitt, was continued by Burt from 1862. Here are a number of terraces and villas built for visitors and new residents (chiefly those retiring there). A particular oddity was his introduction of older features. Some are in the garden of his Purbeck House; others include the façade of Mercers' Hall, London (incorporated in the town hall by *G. R. Crickmay*, 1881–4) and the Wellington Testimonial Clock Tower of 1854 by *Arthur Ashpitel*, also from London, re-erected in 1868.

Many of the new buildings at Swanage (by either *Crickmay & Son* or *Clifton & Robinson*) took West Country vernacular as their inspiration. This was also the case in resorts elsewhere, especially on Pier Terrace at West Bay by *E. S. Prior* (1884–5), its source undoubtedly the Nunnery, Dunster, Somerset. A more diverse range of architectural treatments was used in the maritime suburbs of Poole at Branksome Park and Canford Cliffs, the former developed from *c.* 1860, the latter from *c.* 1900. These were on much the same lines as Bournemouth, with an informal layout and much landscaped space around the buildings. The earlier and more elaborate houses, ranging in style from Scots Baronial to Wagnerian Gothic, have mostly been demolished, although two Gothic Revival houses of the 1880s survive (Clieveden and Park Manor, both in The Avenue, Branksome Park, the latter by *J. Dixon Horsfield*). The Royal Hotel, Weymouth, florid Free Renaissance by *C. Orlando Law* (1897–9), is the only large purpose-built HOTEL of the period in Dorset.

Lastly, ESTATE BUILDING was carried out on a large scale by patrons concerned with improving their tenants' accommodation. More numerous than others are the many cottages in various locations on the Canford Estate, designed in a Tudor Revival style by *Banks & Barry* between *c.* 1860 and *c.* 1890. As well as at Canford Magna, they may be seen at Hampreston, Hamworthy, Longham and Poole. At Iwerne Minster, the office of *Waterhouse* provided plans for many of the village buildings in a red brick and timber-framed Home Counties style (*c.* 1880), while in a more picturesque vein *Ferrey* built or altered a number of cottages at Littlebredy (*c.* 1840–50). The estate cottage story concludes with those at Briantspuddle and the Bladen Valley hamlet, by *Halsey Ricardo* and *MacDonald Gill* for Sir Ernest Debenham (1914–*c.* 1920).

ARCHITECTURE IN DORSET SINCE *c.* 1920

Churches, church furnishings and memorials

It is appropriate to start with the best of the WAR MEMORIALS commissioned from notable designers. The first, and the most original, is that at Bladen Valley, Briantspuddle, by *Eric Gill* (1916–18): a stylized market cross with a Virgin and Child on one face, made more powerful by avoiding any overt period reference. After this many seem pedestrian, although those in Gothic Revival mode by *Sir Giles Gilbert Scott* at Iwerne Minster and Bridport are well worth a close study. Typically medieval is the Wimborne Minster memorial by *Sir Ninian Comper*. *F.C. Eden* did one at Hinton Martell, while that at Maiden Newton is by *E.S. Prior*, both highly individual, especially the latter.

There is nothing significant to report on interwar CHURCHES, apart from the simple lines of St John, West Bay by *W.H. Randoll Blacking* (1935–9). Its low-lying roughcast form is entirely appropriate for the maritime site. For the Church of England, the key new church after the Second World War is St George, Oakdale, Poole, by *Potter & Hare* (1959–60). It is of brick externally, with a tall tower; white-walled within, with green granolithic piers. Its only challenger in the Modern style is St Joseph (R.C.) at Wool, by *Anthony Jaggard* of *John Stark & Partners* (1969–71). The exterior hints at its qualities within: open and well lit, its intricate space-frame roof structure contrasting with plain areas of pale brick in differing shades. In the church context, mention should be made of Faith House, Holton Lee, Wareham. This is a multi-functional congregational building by *Tony Fretton Architects* (2002). Its simple Miesian forms and fine-lined details speak of the spiritual use intended.

After 1920 and into the 1960s, STAINED GLASS makers continued to explore both traditional styles and those in a more free Arts and Crafts mode. Of the former kind are *Sir Ninian Comper* (e.g. the E window at Colehill, 1957) and more numerous examples of glass by *Christopher Webb* (who was articled to Comper). Webb's best window is in the Randoll Blacking church at West Bay (1958). For the Arts and Crafts, there is a highly personal window at Sturminster Newton by *Harry Clarke* (1921), and the beautifully coloured Thomas Hardy memorial window at Stinsford by *Douglas Strachan* (1930). Glass engraving was the specialism of *Laurence Whistler*, and the key location for his work is Moreton church, carried out between 1955 and 1984. Of this later period too are a number of Modern Expressionist windows, the best being those by *Alan Younger* at Fifehead Magdalen (1973); two windows by *L.C. Evetts* at Alton Pancras (1955 and 1963); and the E window in Milton Abbas church by *Lawrence Lee* (1969–70). The more traditional style evolved considerably in the hands of *H.J. Stammers* (e.g. his windows at Preston, 1949). The W window of Sherborne Abbey (of 1996–7, controversially replacing a *Pugin* and *Hardman* one of 1851) gave *John Hayward* the opportunity to produce a work that is Expressionist in detail, while building up a figurative coherence derived from the more traditional approach.

Public, commercial and domestic architecture

After 1920, classically based styles dominated PUBLIC BUILDING. POST OFFICES designed in the *Office of Works* were carefully proportioned Neo-Georgian buildings with fine detailing. Three in Dorset are by *David Dyke*: the earliest, at Parkstone, Poole (1927), Adamesque, the later pair at Blandford Forum (1935) and Wareham (1936) on an earlier C18 model. More convincingly c18 in style is the Post Office at Sherborne by *Archibald Bulloch* (*c.* 1930). As for CIVIC OFFICES, a Civic Centre was constructed at Parkstone for the enlarged borough of Poole, by *L. Magnus Austin* (1931–2). Stripped classicism was employed here, otherwise rarely seen in the county. The follow-up building for the police by *E. J. Goodacre* (1940) had more in the way of Art Deco influences, a stylistic trend cut off by the return of war. When work on this site resumed in 1960 (with the *Farmer & Dark* Central Clinic), the style was modern functionalism of some elegance. The Brutalism of the adjoining Law Courts of 1967–9 (by *G. Hopkinson*, Borough Architect) was in contrast quite ungainly. Spanning the war years, the new County Hall, Dorchester (1938–55), was designed in a modernistic style to a cruciform plan by *H. E. Matthews*, the County Architect. LIBRARIES also saw opportunities for the architects of public bodies to show their allegiance to Modernism. The most extreme (in an otherwise highly traditionalist setting) is Swanage library, by *J. R. Hurst* (Matthews's successor as County Architect), 1965. It is a glazed dodecagon. Hurst's library at Shaftesbury (1971) is octagonal. More sensitive to the historic environment, and yet not traditional in any way, is Wareham Library of 1976, highly successful in its reticence. Equally sensitive is *Hurst*'s library at Blandford (*c.* 1963), again Modern, but proportioned responsively to the Georgian architecture of the town.

Hurst also designed many SCHOOLS in the county, few of which survive unaltered. That at Beaminster (1960–5) is typical in its loose grouping of low buildings, the roofs (of two different types) running in different directions on each block. Much the same spirit may be seen at Hurst's Bovington Primary School, Wool (1966–7) and Lady St Mary Primary School, Wareham (1969–70). The most significant collection of new school buildings in the private sector is at Bryanston, where there are fine examples by *Piers Gough* of *CZWG* (1987–8 and 1994–5) and *Hopkins Architects* (2007 onwards), many of these replacing earlier buildings (of 1952–62) by the *Architects' Co-Partnership*.

COMMERCIAL ARCHITECTURE in the county between the wars rarely achieved anything of architectural consequence. For its impressive sweep and sheer size, mention should be made, however, of the Riviera Hotel, Preston (just outside Weymouth), by *L. Stuart Smith*, 1937. It is Art Deco, with a long curving colonnade of two tiers and, at its centre, the all-important tower. In the 1950s any buildings of consequence were of the Modern Movement, a late local flowering perhaps, since little was built in this style in Dorset before 1939. Although it has been badly altered, many of the Modernist precepts of the Loewy Robertson factory at Branksome, Poole by *Farmer & Dark* (1953–5) are still detectable. They are more obviously intact at the concrete Brutalist Freshwater Biology Laboratory, East Stoke, by *Ronald Sims* (1964), and at the former Dorset Water Board Head Office, Poole by *Farmer & Dark* (1969), of brick. The divergence in recent architecture can be demonstrated by

comparing the Lutyens–Vernacular shell of Tesco, Dorchester
(1991, by *William Bertram & Fell*), built on Duchy of Cornwall
128   land, and the Modern Expressionism of the RNLI College and
Museum, Poole (2004 by *Poynton Bradbury Wynter Cole*). The
first is accompanied by an axial pond, with a pair of classicizing
lampposts, both on a 1920s–30s model; the second avoids all
historical allusions in its three quite different linked solids, the
most conventional being a waterside rotunda.

   For DOMESTIC BUILDING three overlapping styles competed
through the 1930s: *moderne*, Art Deco and the purer International
Style. Maritime building on the coast near Poole attracted the
more commercial *moderne*, a superficial Expressionist Modernism redolent of ocean liners and aircraft. The key architects
were *A.J. Seal & Partners* of Bournemouth. Much of their work
has been replaced, but the Harbour Heights development at
Canford Cliffs of 1935–6 largely survives, the rectangularity of
each building contrasting with curved expressed stair-turrets. In
122   the International Style are Landfall, Poole (1936–8) by *Oliver
Hill*, one of his purest exercises, and the less well-known No. 18,
Maiden Castle Road, Dorchester (1937) by the local architect
121   *C.W. Pike*. More strongly Art Deco is the Y-plan Yaffle Hill,
Broadstone (1930) by *Sir Edward Maufe*, built for a director of
the *Poole Pottery Co.* and incorporating many of its products,
especially the peacock-blue pantiles. Of similar date are the interiors at Leweston Manor, as remodelled by *Maxwell Ayrton*, with
murals and ceiling paintings by *George Sheringham*. Throughout
this period, a more dilute Arts and Crafts style, often integrating
Art Deco motifs, also continued to be popular, e.g. the houses
around Weymouth by *E. Wamsley Lewis*.

   When domestic building revived in the post-war period the
choices became more polarized. Traditional styles continued for
the remodelling of Ranston, Iwerne Courtney by *Louis Osman*
(1961–3), and Neo-Georgian for the new country houses by
Anthony Jaggard of *John Stark & Partners* (Lulworth Castle
House, East Lulworth, 1975; Bellamont, Long Bredy 1995). In
contrast, individual houses in a Modern Movement style
continued to be built, such as two by *Richard Horden*, one in
Branksome Park (1975), the other at Salterns (2003), both in
the Poole suburbs. Another in the same vein was built in Parkstone, Poole by *Rebecca Granger* (2004). As the larger Victorian
and Edwardian villa sites of Branksome Park were redeveloped,
new owners sought houses in a variety of modern styles, ranging
from recreations of the International Style to others in a fantasy
Expressionism (e.g. Moonraker by *Steve Lyne* of *KL Architects*,
2005, and Thunderbird by *Eddie Mitchell* of *Seven Developments*, 2006). A creative approach, fusing modern ideas with
historical elements (or Postmodernism), is rarely handled
successfully. However, a recent country house by *Robert Adam*
126   of *ADAM Architecture* near Bere Regis (2004) achieves this, as
does Brownsword Hall (*c.* 2000) by *John Simpson*, at the centre
of Phase One of the Poundbury development, near Dorchester.

At one level POUNDBURY, started in 1993, is an exercise in   125
contextualism, one of its aims being to use styles indigenous to
Dorchester town. At a smaller scale, this approach had proved
successful in e.g. Abbotsbury, under a masterplan by *William
Bertram & Fell* (1973). At Poundbury, on a scale much larger than
previously tried (under a masterplan by *Leon Krier*), any attempt
to replicate the architectural achievements of the main Victorian years (*c.* 1840–*c.* 1890), or those post-dating the First World
War, is avoided. This makes the building mix highly personal in
appearance, distinctively 'Poundbury', and objectively arbitrary.
What is one to make of Queen Mother Square, at the centre of
the project? Its three main sides have classical buildings of an
architectural stature seemingly equal to those in the government
quarter of the capital of a minor European state. This must surely
distort its relationship with historic Dorchester. Poundbury is
neither a suburb nor a quarter (in the European sense), but a
rival town, bolted on to Dorchester's western approach. An alternative is displayed in the Brewery Square redevelopment (2009
onwards), s of the town centre: vibrant modern architecture (by
CZWG Architects and *Conran & Partners*) such as one may see in
any major British city, but no specific references to Dorchester
or Dorset building.

FURTHER READING

The beginning for all historical work in Dorset is the COUNTY
HISTORIES. The earliest is the brief account of *c.* 1625 known
as *Coker's Survey of Dorsetshire*. Published in 1732, it was once
thought to be by Thomas Coker of Mappowder, but Thomas
Gerard of Trent actually wrote it. Much more comprehensive
are the four volumes of John Hutchins's *History and Antiquities
of the County of Dorset*, first published in 1774. Its third edition
of 1861–74 is the most useful (although several engravings from
the earlier editions were omitted). A more modern overview is
Cecil N. Cullingford, *A History of Dorset*, 1980. More detailed
articles, occasionally touching on building, are to be found
in the *Proceedings* of the Dorset Natural History and Archaeological Society (*PDNHAS*, 1877 to the present). The *Victoria
County History* has yet to publish any topographical volumes for
Dorset.

The GEOLOGY of Dorset has been mapped by the British
Geological Survey (BGS) at the scale of 1:50,000, and may be
viewed through OpenGeoscience at *www.bgs.ac.uk*. The maps'
descriptive sheet memoirs (1898–1999) are also available to view.
A valuable overview is R.V. Melville and E.C. Freshney, *British
Regional Geology: Hampshire Basin and Adjoining Areas*, 4th edn,
1983. A general account written for the layman is P. Ensom,
Discover Dorset – Geology, 1998. For a wider context there is

P. J. Brenchley and P. F. Rawson (eds), *The Geology of England and Wales*, 2nd edn, 2006 (Geological Society of London). W. J. Arkell, *The Jurassic System in Great Britain*, 1933, is a classic work on these strata (including the Purbeck Limestone Group, now mostly considered of Cretaceous age). For the coast see J. C. W. Cope, *Geology of the Dorset Coast*, 2012, with a series of excursions from east to west, and P. C. Ensom and M. Turnbull, *Geology of the Jurassic Coast: The Isle of Purbeck – Weymouth to Studland*, 2011. The *Bibliography and Index of Dorset Geology*, 1989, compiled by J. Thomas and P. C. Ensom, including references to building stones, can be accessed at *http://research.dorsetcountymuseum.org/gbibcontents.html*. In addition to these web links, Dr Ian West's invaluable site *The Geology of the Wessex Coast of Southern England – the World Heritage Jurassic Coast – and more* provides a wealth of geological information at *www.soton.ac.uk/~imw*.

Turning to ARCHITECTURAL HISTORY, Dorset is fortunate indeed as being the subject of the last completed county inventory published by the Royal Commission on the Historical Monuments of England (RCHME). It is in eight books (five volumes, some with multiple parts), published from 1952 to 1975. Coverage is best in all except the early vol. 1 (West). Nothing like this is likely to be published in print today, and so for further lists of buildings one must rely on the internet. For LISTED BUILDINGS, the source is *www.historicengland.org.uk/listing/the-list*, the National Heritage List for England. At present, while it has useful location maps, there are no illustrations. For these (in most cases) one must turn to the Images of England website at *www.imagesofengland.org.uk*. Both have advanced search facilities of varying degrees of usefulness. In complete contrast, the *Shell Guide to Dorset*, 2nd edn, 1966 (by Michael Pitt-Rivers) is a delight to look through, even if it is highly opinionated (and at times decidedly anti-Victorian).

The best background to the ARCHAEOLOGY and early history of the region is Barry Cunliffe, *Wessex to A.D. 1000*, 1993. A useful guide to prehistoric sites is John Gale, *Prehistoric Dorset*, 2003. The Late Iron Age is covered by M. Papworth, *The Search for the Durotriges*, 2011. Other books and monographs, many of which are published by the DNHAS, include H. C. Bowen, *The Archaeology of Bokerly Dyke*, 1990; R. T. Hosfield and C. P. Green, *Quaternary History and Palaeolithic Archaeology in the Axe Valley at Broom*, 2013; S. Palmer, *Culverwell Mesolithic Habitation Site, Isle of Portland, Dorset*, 1999; R. Mercer and F. Healy, *Hambledon Hill, Dorset, England*, 2008 (Neolithic causewayed enclosure); N. Sharples, *Maiden Castle*, 1991; R. J. C. Smith *et al.*, *Excavations along the Route of the Dorchester By-pass, Dorset, 1986–8*, 1997 (Neolithic and Bronze Age sites); P. J. Woodward *et al.*, *Excavations at Greyhound Yard, Dorchester, 1981–4*, 1993 (Neolithic timber enclosure and an *insula* within the Roman town); and P. J. Woodward, *The South Dorset Ridgeway: Survey and Excavations 1977–1984*, 1991 (Neolithic and Bronze Age settlements and Bronze Age barrows). The reconstructed town house at Dorchester has been published in E. Durham and

M. Fulford, *A Late Roman Town House and Its Environs*, 2014. For the internationally important extra-mural cemeteries and settlements at Poundbury, see C. S. Green, *Excavations at Poundbury, Dorchester, Dorset 1966–82, vol. I: The Settlements*, 1987, and D.E. Farwell and T.I. Molleson, *Excavations at Poundbury, vol. II: The Cemeteries*, 1993. S.R. Cosh and D.S. Neal, *The Roman Mosaics of Britain, vol. II: South-West Britain*, 2006, illustrates all the mosaics found in the county for which records survive. The post-Roman and Saxon periods are covered in D.A. Hinton, *Discover Dorset: Saxons and Vikings*, 1998. The RCHME inventory volumes also have much detail on archaeological sites, and the Schedule of Ancient Monuments may now be consulted online as part of the National Heritage List, mentioned above.

The earliest standing buildings are MEDIEVAL CHURCHES. For the Anglo-Saxon period the best overviews are *The Architecture of the Anglo-Saxons*, 1983, by Eric Fernie, and the more detailed work by H.M. and Joan Taylor, *Anglo-Saxon Architecture*, 3 vols, 1965 and 1978. The *Corpus of Anglo-Saxon Sculpture* covers Dorset in its vol. 7, *South-West England*, by Rosemary Cramp, 2007. Eric Fernie has provided the best account of Norman architecture in *The Architecture of Norman England*, 2000, and of Europe as a whole in *Romanesque Architecture*, 2014 (*Pelican History of Art* series). For the Decorated style we have the studies by Jean Bony and Nicola Coldstream, respectively of 1979 and 1994, and Paul Binski's *Gothic Wonder*, 2014; for the Perpendicular style, John Harvey's book of 1978. The last subject is badly in need of a fresh approach. On the county specifically, the various editions of *Dorset Churches* by Sir Owen Morshead, 1975 etc., provide a useful illustrated introduction. Two books by F.P. Pitfield are more thorough, although his survey was left incomplete. *Dorset Parish Churches, A–D*, 1981, was the only book of a projected four-volume work to be published. His *Purbeck Parish Churches*, 1985, in the same format, is at least complete for that area.

Several of the books already mentioned also deal with SECULAR MEDIEVAL BUILDINGS. The best overviews are John Goodall, *The English Castle*, 2011, with much of the latest thinking about castles, and Margaret Wood, *The English Mediaeval House*, 1965, reprinted 1983. For specific studies, *Sherborne Old Castle, Dorset*, 2015, by Peter White and Alan Cook, is as detailed an analysis as one could wish for. It is a pity that Corfe Castle has not received an equivalent modern treatment. Many of the same buildings are covered in Anthony Emery, *Greater Medieval Houses of England and Wales*, vol. 3, 2006. Studies of smaller or vernacular houses are few for Dorset (unlike its more fortunate neighbours). All we have is R. Machin, *The Houses of Yetminster*, 1978, although there is much information throughout the RCHME volumes.

For COUNTRY HOUSES the starting point is *Country Life*, with its excellently illustrated articles on specific houses, often in multiple parts. Arthur Oswald wrote many of these and collected his thoughts in *Country Houses of Dorset*, 1935, revised edn 1959. Michael Hill's more recent two-volume survey expands and updates this work – *East Dorset Country Houses*, 2013; *West Dorset Country Houses*, 2014 – and extends the survey more thoroughly through the C19 and up to the end of the C20. A very personal survey is David Cecil, *Some Dorset Country Houses*, 1985. One should also add here Mark Girouard, *Elizabethan Architecture*, 2009, covering 1540–1640. It represents his latest views on a period dealt with previously by his *Robert Smythson and the Elizabethan Country House*, 1983. Mention should also be made of *The Manor Houses of Dorset*, 2007, by Una Russell and Audrey Grindrod, useful for its anecdotes and illustrations. Another valuable source, especially for the locations of illustrations, is Michael Holmes, *The Country House Described: An Index to the Country Houses of Great Britain and Ireland*, 1986. Finally for country houses, the Victorian and post-Victorian history is covered by Mark Girouard, *The Victorian Country House*, 2nd edn, 1979; Clive Aslet, *The Last Country Houses*, 1982; and John Martin Robinson, *The Latest Country Houses*, 1984, this last bringing the story more or less up to date.

GARDENS have been covered less thoroughly, so we must turn to general surveys for an overview. Two books by David Jaques take us through the C17 and C18: *Gardens of Court and Country: English Design, 1630–1730*, 2017, and *Georgian Gardens: The Reign of Nature*, 1983, continuing the narrative to 1830. Thereafter, reference should be made to Brent Elliott, *Victorian Gardens*, 1986, and Tom Carter, *The Victorian Garden*, 1984. For the C20 the two best references are David Ottewill, *The Edwardian Garden*, 1989, and Jane Brown, *The English Garden in Our Time*, 1986. Specific to Dorset is Tim Mowl's idiosyncratic but informative *Historic Gardens of Dorset*, 2003.

Returning to CHURCHES, a number of general studies provide useful background on those built after the Reformation. For the C18, what must be the ultimate study is Terry Friedman, *The Eighteenth-Century Church in Britain*, 2011. Also for churches before the mid C19, Mark Chatfield, *Churches the Victorians Forgot*, 1979, includes four Dorset churches. Continuing into the Victorian period, the most useful are C. Brooks and A. Saint (eds), *The Victorian Church*, 1995, and C. Webster and J. Elliott (eds), '*A Church as it Should Be*': *The Cambridge Camden Society and Its Influence*, 2000. The records for CHURCH RESTORATION (from 1849 onwards) are held in the faculty archives of the Diocese of Salisbury at the Wiltshire and Swindon History Centre in Chippenham, Wilts. The online catalogue may be consulted via the National Archives website. Also online are the plans for churches that received grants from the Incorporated Church Building Society, at *http://images.lambethpalacelibrary.org.uk/luna/servlet/*. For STAINED GLASS, the few medieval windows in the county are listed on the Corpus Vitrearum Medii Aevi website (*www.cvma.ac.uk*). For Victorian and later glass, the best general references are Martin Harrison, *Victorian Stained Glass*, 1980, and Peter Cormack, *Arts and Crafts Stained Glass*, 2015. Useful too for comparison are the photographs in the copiously illustrated *Stained Glass from Welsh Churches*, 2014, by Martin Crampin. An essential local source is Joan Brocklebank, *Victorian Stone Carvers in Dorset Churches, 1856–1880*, 1979.

For ROMAN CATHOLIC CHURCHES, apart from the overview in Christopher Martin, *A Glimpse of Heaven*, 2006 (which includes the chapel at East Lulworth and Chideock church), there is nothing much apart from the reports for the Diocese of Plymouth by the late Nicholas Antram. Two exceptions are the article on the Lulworth Chapel by Anthony Jaggard in *PDNHAS* 120, 1998, and the entry on St Joseph, Wool in Elain Harwood and James O. Davies, *England's Post-War Listed Buildings*, 2015. NONCONFORMIST CHAPELS are dealt with in Christopher Stell, *Inventory of Nonconformist Chapels and Meeting-Houses in South-West England*, RCHME, 1991, although many later C19 and early C20 buildings are not covered.

The RCHME, and its successors English Heritage and Historic England, have surveyed BUILDING TYPES not covered by many other publications: *English Hospitals, 1660–1948*, 1998; *The Workhouse*, 1999; *English Prisons*, 2002; and the more esoteric *England's Seaside Resorts*, 2007. With James Douet, *British Barracks, 1600–1914*, 1998, these provide much background, and detailed information, on buildings in Dorset. Further essential studies are T. Brittain-Catlin, *The English Parsonage in the Early Nineteenth Century*, 2008, and Colin Cunningham, *Victorian and Edwardian Town Halls*, 1981. Specific to the county is the useful *Discover Dorset* series published by the Dovecote Press. Most relevant are *Bridges, Castles and Forts, Farmhouses and Cottages, Railway Stations* and *Towns*. A good introduction to the county's railways is D. St John Thomas, *Regional History of the Railways of Great Britain, vol. 1: West Country*, 4th edn, 1973.

Books on specific TOWNS and PLACES are numerous, many of very high quality. The most useful in terms of architecture are G.H.D. Pitman, *Exploring Sherborne*, 1966, and two in English Heritage's *Informed Conservation* series: Mike Williams, *Bridport and West Bay: The Buildings of the Flax and Hemp Industry*, 2006, and Allan Brodie, Colin Ellis and David Stuart, *Weymouth's Seaside Heritage*, 2008. Also essential reading for Dorchester is the extended article on the buildings in the town by David Lloyd in *PDNHAS* 89, 1968. An archaeological background for Dorset towns has been usefully set out in *Historic Towns in Dorset* (1980) by K.J. Penn. For more general town histories, there is the Barracuda Press *The Book of…*, series, covering Beaminster, Bridport, Dorchester, Sherborne and Wimborne Minster; and the well-illustrated Phillimore Press books, *Blandford Forum: A Pictorial History*, 1995; *Bridport Past*, 1999; *Dorchester Past*, 2001; *Ferndown: A Pictorial History*, 1997; *Poole: A Pictorial History*, 1994; *Swanage Past*, 2004; and *Wareham: A Pictorial History*, 1994. More detailed histories are Stuart Morris, *Portland: An Illustrated History*, 1996 edn; Brenda Innes, *Shaftesbury: An Illustrated History*, 1992; and Maureen Boddy and Jack West, *Weymouth: An Illustrated History*, 1983.

For BUILDING MATERIALS the best single source is Jo Thomas, *Dorset Stone*, 2008. VERNACULAR ARCHITECTURE in the county is discussed in a national context by Pamela Cunnington in *How Old Is Your House?* (1980, and later eds).

Studies of individual ARCHITECTS become more common once the C17 is entered. The starting point is Sir Howard Colvin's *Biographical Dictionary of British Architects, 1600–1840*, 4th edn, 2008. Less detailed, and without any lists of works, is the *Directory of British Architects, 1834–1914*, RIBA, 2 vols, 2001. More useful for its period is A. Stuart Gray, *Edwardian Architecture: A Biographical Dictionary*, 2nd edn, 1988. For Dorset, the most useful monographs are Kerry Downes, *Sir John Vanbrugh*, 1977; C. Ridgway and R. Williams (eds), *Sir John Vanbrugh and Landscape Architecture*, 2000; John Harris, *Sir William Chambers*, 1970; Dorothy Stroud, *Capability Brown*, 1975; John Phibbs, *Capability Brown*, 2017; John Martin Robinson, *James Wyatt*, 2012; Jill Allibone, *Anthony Salvin*, 1988, and *George Devey*, 1991; Anthony Quiney, *John Loughborough Pearson*, 1979; Michael Hall, *George Frederick Bodley*, 2014; Andrew Saint, *Richard Norman Shaw*, 2nd edn, 2010; Jennifer M. Freeman, *W.D. Caröe*, 1990; and Sarah Whittingham, *Sir George Oatley*, 2011. Especially relevant for Dorset is T.P. Connor's short monograph, *Thomas Hardy's Master: John Hicks, Architect*, 2014. For Hardy there is Claudius J.P. Beatty, *Thomas Hardy: Conservation Architect*, 1995, and *The Architectural Notebook of Thomas Hardy*, 1966, introduced by Beatty.

The equivalent source to Colvin for MEDIEVAL ARCHITECTS is John Harvey, *English Mediaeval Architects: A Biographical Dictionary down to 1550*, 1984 edn, although such a work is obviously constrained by the paucity of sources for the period. For SCULPTORS, the standard resource is Ingrid Roscoe *et al.*, *A Biographical Dictionary of Sculptors in Britain, 1660–1851*, 2009, structured on the Colvin model. Also useful on this subject are Margaret Whinney, *Sculpture in Britain, 1530–1830*, 2nd edn, 1988, and Benedict Read, *Victorian Sculpture*, 1982. For BRASSES see W. Lack, H.M. Stuchfield and P. Whittemore, *The Monumental Brasses of Dorset*, 2001.

GAZETTEER

ABBOTSBURY 5080

A village of long rows of thatched cottages that has grown around
the ruins of the Benedictine abbey, founded before the middle of
the C11. After the Dissolution both the abbey and its lands came
to Giles Strangways of Melbury Sampford. The Ilchester Estate
continues to own much of the place, no doubt accounting for its
continued homogeneous character and avoidance of unattractive
change. Remarkably, for such a small settlement, a branch line
serving Abbotsbury was opened in 1885 (closed 1952).

ABBEY. Very little remains of the abbey buildings (English Heritage) and nothing at all spectacular, if we leave out the barn.
The identifiable remains are either C14 or C15. The CHURCH
lay immediately s of the parish church (i.e. in the present
churchyard). Of its N wall a little has been exposed, with
grouped Perp wall-shafts and a seat along the wall. E of this
a thicker wall was found, and this appears to have been the N
transept E wall. The nave s wall is also identified. The nave was
54 ft (16.5 metres) across. Of the cloister, apart from its location, nothing at all is known. The buildings further s, all parts
of ABBEY HOUSE, are of comparatively little architectural
interest. PINION END, the high gable, was the E end of a major
monastic range s of the cloister. The remains of the OUTER
GATEHOUSE are across the E–W road leading to Abbey House.
There was a pedestrian as well as a cart entrance. The same
is true of the INNER GATEHOUSE, now included in a house
(ABBEY DAIRY HOUSE) on the w side of Church Road. The
arches are four-centred, and an upper two-light window with
ogee-headed lights survives. (The second window is a modern
copy.) Its s end has a good display of buttresses with the gable
above slightly set back (cf. the Abbey Barn).

ABBEY BARN. A tithe barn 272 ft (83 metres) long with 44
closely set buttresses and two porches, the rhythm to the N
being 7–porch–6–porch–7. This is what one clearly sees in the
plan, but not all is easily taken in looking at the building. Only
about half is roofed and thatched; for the rest there is a gap

in the wall, and one porch is missing. It is one of the largest barns in England and seems to date from *c.* 1400. The roof is of the C17 and has small hammerbeams at the eaves. Notable too are the remains of architectural embellishments, chiefly surviving on the W gable. Here there is a continuous mould-ing at eaves level (suggestive of a moulded parapet around the whole barn), the central end buttress spanning this and rising to a castellated finial. The corner buttresses also rise above eaves level to castellated tops – cf. the similar arrangement on St Catherine's Chapel nearby (*see* below). No doubt all of the side buttresses were also finished in this manner, creating what must have been a very rich effect. The porch that remains was rib-vaulted – cf. the corbels and the springers – and has diagonal buttresses and a four-centred arch. Above this a moulded parapet behind which the gable is set back.

DOVECOTE, 50 yds E of the Abbey Barn. A two-cell pigeon house, C15. The louvres are on the roof ridge. Also pairs of unglazed dormers.

SWANNERY. The swannery lies ¾ m. S. It is mentioned in 1393 and is a roughly square pond, largely artificial.

ST NICHOLAS. A perfect oblong except for the W tower and the N porch of two storeys. This and the N aisle are early C14 Dec – cf. the tall two-light windows in the latter. The W tower is late C14 Perp. Three stages with diagonal buttresses and an embattled parapet. Tellingly, the octagonal NE stair-turret has the same mini-battlements (or brattishing) as the tithe barn and St Catherine's Chapel. This pins its date to *c.* 1400. Later still the early C16 S aisle, its six-bay arcade of standard Perp elements repeated in a rebuild of the N arcade at the same time. The S chapel doorway has the date 1636, and it is certainly tempting to explain the extremely strange round arches of the windows with the Perp tracery below them by considering that the whole S wall is a reconstruction of *c.* 1636. The clerestory windows are typically Henry VIII and the clerestory itself looks oddly blocky against the gabled roof of the chancel. With this one expects some clear architec-tural break within, but there is no structural division between nave and chancel. Nave ceiling flat and of 1823, when the N and the still-remaining W galleries were inserted. In 1638 Sir John Strangways, descendant of Sir Giles, who had bought the abbey estate in 1543, put a decorated plaster tunnel-vault over the two E bays. It has angels and cherubs down the centre and shields of the family in the widest sense either side. Contemporary with this is a plasterwork achievement of arms over the tower W window. – REREDOS. 1751. A fine classical piece with Corinthian columns, a vine frieze and a pediment. Given by Mrs Horner of Melbury Sampford. – TILEWORK in the sanctuary by *Minton*, from the restoration by *Sir Arthur Blomfield*, 1885–6. – PULPIT. Early C17. Octagonal; oak. Two tiers of blank arches set architecturally between fluted corner pilasters. Strapwork enrichment to the entablature and arab-esque to the base. Similar elaboration to the backplate. Small

69

tester also treated as an entablature. – FONT. C15. Octagonal, with arched panels. – WEST GALLERY. 1823. Carved Hanoverian ROYAL ARMS mounted on the front. – PEWS. Finely detailed; by *Blomfield*. – SCULPTURE. Panel over the tower W doorway. Probably mid-C14. An important and unusual relief depicting the Resurrected Christ, an inventive adaptation of the Throne of Grace. It is in a hooded niche with delicate figure-stops of angels swinging censers, and includes a miniature Crucifixion at Christ's feet. Also a dove representing the Holy Spirit. Square fitting holes at the base suggest that it may have formed part of a larger structure, probably originally in the abbey. – A small relief of a Crucifixion over the N doorway, C15. – CHANDELIER of brass, in the usual Baroque shape; C18. – STAINED GLASS. In a S chapel window a good demi-figure of the Virgin from a late C15 Crucifixion. Also many C18 fragments. S chapel E window by *R. Anning Bell*, 1911. Two S aisle windows by *Clayton & Bell*, †1920 and †1922. Another by *M.C. Farrar Bell*, †1952. – MONUMENTS. In the N porch, effigy of an abbot, Purbeck marble, *c.* 1300. Heavy chasuble folds. – Maria, Countess of Ilchester †1842. Tablet with Gothic surround by the *Marble Works* of Westminster. – Giles Digby Robert Fox-Strangways †1827. Grecian tablet by *Reeves & Son* of Bath.

ST CATHERINE'S CHAPEL. On the very top of a bare grassy hill, *c.* 250 ft above, and *c.* 700 yds SW of the church. Of *c.* 1400. The chapel is under 45 ft (13.7 metres) internal length but extremely substantially built. The might of the buttresses and the thickness of the walls find their explanation in the totally unexpected provision of a stone tunnel-vault, pointed and with eight major transverse ribs. Between each pair are three panels in two tiers, each panel trefoil-headed. The N porch also has a pointed tunnel-vault with cross-ribs. Stone tunnel-vaults are foreign to the south of England. The nearest parallels to St Catherine's Chapel are in Scotland (e.g. Rosslyn Chapel, Lothian). The chapel has Perp windows and a NW stair-turret and the buttresses end instead of pinnacles bluntly in square turrets or pedestals, with the same mini-battlement (or brattishing) detail as elsewhere on the monastic buildings. Heavy stone-slab roof draining through arched outlets in the parapets.

CONGREGATIONAL CHAPEL (former), Back Street. 1870 by *R.C. Bennett* of Weymouth. Lancet Gothic.

OLD MANOR HOUSE, W of the church, across Church Street. A haphazard growth of the late C16 and C17. The S gable and its fellow at right angles, partly obscured by a later staircase projection, are work of some quality, ashlar-faced and with gable kneelers moulded in a refined way. These two blocks were joined in the early C17 by a linking block. Many hollow-moulded mullioned windows. At the back an unusual external stone staircase brought from Kingston Russell House.*

*This house, at one time the vicarage, was probably the first Strangways residence in Abbotsbury until the new mansion on Chesil Beach.

The village street is very attractive, having a faint air of formality in the raised pavements and continuous stone cottage
terraces in Rodden Row and Market Street, distinguishable by
the shapes of the windows as of the C18 or earlier. Thatched
cottages continue more loosely for a considerable way to the
w. Where the road bends in the middle the demonstrative
Gothic former SCHOOL (now Strangways Hall) of 1858 faces
the dignified classical front of the ILCHESTER ARMS HOTEL
of 1768, the builder *Stephen Carpenter*. The local buff ashlar
with Portland stone angle strips make a good colour contrast
on the latter.

Three exemplary housing developments of the early 1990s,
all mimicking the local vernacular.* In BACK STREET, two
groups, the first on the l. by *Clive Hawkins* ease up the hill
with their stepping thatched roofs. Another on the r. by *William
Bertram & Fell*. At the E end of the village, GLEBE CLOSE by
Ken Morgan Architects also succeeds in its unobtrusiveness.

ABBOTSBURY CASTLE, 1¼ m. WSW. A 'fair mansion house'
(Coker) for Sir John Strangways was erected in this unlikely
location just above Chesil Beach around 1600. This was
destroyed in a Civil War battle in 1644 and replaced by a
castle-style house by *Charles Hamilton* (of Painshill, Surrey)
for Countess Elizabeth Ilchester, complete by 1766. This in
turn was destroyed by a fire in 1913. Its replacement by *Ernest
Newton*, left incomplete in the 1920s, was finally pulled down
in 1935. Nearby are the well-known sub-tropical GARDENS,
created from the mid C18 onwards.

RODDEN HOUSE, 2¼ m. ESE. Nice small house of c. 1760,
probably for Isaac Sparks. Faced with Portland ashlar. Just a
three-bay formula: hipped roof and a little pediment containing a lunette over the central bay. Big quoins, keyed window
architraves, and a doorcase designed still in a Baroque way.
On the sides the sashes mingle with a more irregular, stone-
mullioned fenestration.

ABBOTSBURY CASTLE, 1½ m. NW. A HILL-FORT covering
10 acres. Single ditch with cross-ridge ditches and enlarged
banks at the w and SE, an original entrance alongside the SE
ditches, and postern in the middle of the NW rampart. Inside,
a mound and hut hollows are visible, E of the old parish
boundary running from the SW to the NE corner. On the w
inner rampart a ditched enclosure, c. 65 ft (20 metres) square,
excavated in 1974; probably Roman or later in date. It has an
eastern entrance.

CHAPEL HILL, ½ m. SW, is almost surrounded by strip lynchets.

ASHLEY CHASE and ST LUKE'S CHAPEL. *See* p. 100.

---

*Following a study of Abbotsbury by *William Bertram & Fell*, commissioned by the
Ilchester Estate in 1973.

AFFPUDDLE

A linear village alongside the River Piddle. Cob and thatch cottages are interspersed with modern houses and bungalows.

ST LAURENCE. A church of many medieval phases blending harmoniously together. One enters by an uncommonly fine mid-C13 S doorway. The arch is pointed-trefoiled and above it is a blank pointed arch. In the spandrels a symmetrical stiff-leaf motif. Also a continuous keeled roll. Hoodmould on headstops. This provides the earliest date for the nave, otherwise much rebuilt c. 1400 and later in the C15 in chequerboard flint and ashlar. Of this latter period the Perp W tower with rectangular SE stair projection, higher than the tower and with its own pinnacles of golden Ham Hill stone. Set-back buttresses and grotesques on the top set-off. The chancel is c. 1400 (e.g. the chancel arch of three moulded orders, and a blocked N doorway), with C15 Perp windows in the S wall, especially the three-light window under a low-pitched head. Just W of this a re-set mid-C14 window of two cusped lights. Chancel E wall rebuilt c. 1840 when its Early Dec-style window was inserted. Good C15 N arcade piers, square, with wide double-wave diagonals – like a printer's bracket. Of this date the large squint in the chancel arch N jamb. Rood-loft stair on the S side of the chancel arch, lit by a small lancet of c. 1400. The roofs are from the restoration of 1875–6 by *T.H. Wyatt*, whose work here is unintrusive. – Brightly coloured REREDOS and ORGAN GALLERY FRONT, both by *Loughnan Pendred* of Cambridge, 1952 (the reredos frame designed by *S.E. Dykes Bower*). – SCREEN. In the N aisle but presumably moved from the chancel arch. C15, of 3:4:3 divisions, each light ogee-headed. – BENCHES. A set dated 1547 (by one in the N aisle). Rustic Renaissance motifs. The ends have small poppyheads, and a moulding scrolls to form the arm-rests. Some matching pew-fronts, taller and narrower. – PULPIT. With small figures and also some Renaissance decoration; hence probably also 1547. – FONT. Late C12 square bowl with blind arcading on each face. C19 base (probably c. 1876) with colonnettes. – STAINED GLASS. W window (obscured by the organ) by *Powell & Sons*, 1880. – MONUMENT. Edward Lawrence †1751. Classical with side scrolls.*

WAR MEMORIAL. A roofed shrine containing a crucifix by *Pendred*, c. 1950.

HURST BRIDGES, 2 m. S, taking the B3390 across the several branches of the River Frome, are part of a causeway constructed in 1834. *William Evans*, County Surveyor, designed the bridges, of many shallow segmental brick arches on

---

*The arms (Lawrence quartering Washington) are said to have provided the source for the flag of the United States of America. George Washington's mother was a Lawrence.

snub-nosed Portland stone cutwaters, more easily appreciated by anglers than motorists.

WADDOCK FARM, just to the N, where the ground rises, red brick and thatched, is worth a look. Built in the early C18 to face N, in 1797 it was turned about: hence its muddly front and formal back.

ALDERHOLT

Originally a scatter of cob and red brick cottages. Major post-war housing development at Charing Cross, 1 m. E.

ST JAMES. Of dark brown heathstone rubble. Completed in 1849 for the *2nd Marquess of Salisbury* and probably designed by him. The style is almost Celtic in inspiration, a studied attempt at ancientness. Crowstepped gables to the W end and W porch, with stone slabs creating triangular tops to the nave windows instead of arches; primitive buttresses. Small spired W bellcote. Goodhart-Rendel wrote: 'Looks like the latest thing by E. S. Prior'. Conventional chancel by *W. Marshall* of Hatfield, 1922, with trefoil-headed lights and an E triplet of plain lancets. Simple nave interior with utilitarian trussed roof. – PULPIT. From St Osmund, Parkstone, Poole. A very attractive piece of *c.* 1915 in the Gimson style by *Prior & Grove*: an open grid with excessive chamfering, originally black-stained but now stripped.

CONGREGATIONAL CHURCH, Hillbury Road. 1923. Neo-Romanesque, with diaper brick and ashlar on its W gable. Large extension by *Pro Vision Planning & Design*, completed 2011.

ALDERHOLT PARK, ½ m. N of Charing Cross. Mostly of *c.* 1841, incorporating a house reported as new-built in 1810. Asymmetrical and vaguely Italianate. Red brick. Contemporary LODGE on the E park entrance.

ALMER
Sturminster Marshall

No village; just a church, manor and house off the A31.

ST MARY. Heathstone with some ashlar banding, especially on the unbuttressed Perp W tower with its battlemented parapet and small crocketed pinnacles. C12 nave with S wall, rebuilt *c.* 1720; C14 N aisle, presumably a replacement for a C12 predecessor; late C19 chancel. Restored by *Forsyth & Maule*, 1908, when it was refurnished. Mid-C12 S doorway with stop-chamfers and a simple roll moulding to its segmental arch. Two large arched early C18 nave s windows with moulded architraves. The N arcade of three bays is mid-C12: base spurs, round piers, scalloped capitals, square abaci, unmoulded round arches. Inelegant two-centred chancel arch of 1908 on partly medieval responds. Two moulded orders to the tower arch, continuous with its jambs. The nave roof was raised when the tower was added. – FONT. C13, Purbeck marble, octagonal, with two flat pointed arches each side. The base of the font is another, reversed, font. (The font originally had a hexagonal stem with six shafts around it. The original base, indicating this, is in the churchyard.) – ROYAL ARMS. Of 1800, above the s doorway. – STAINED GLASS. Re-set in the chancel N window a very small Last Judgment, Swiss, 1610; Mannerist in style. Fine late C19 and early C20 memorial glass by *Powell & Sons*, mainly to the Ernle-Erle-Drax family of Charborough Park (q.v.). Chancel s window, 1931, by *William Glasby*.

ALMER MANOR, ⅛ m. NE. Late C16, of flint with limestone bands. NW-facing two-storey range, the original hall to the r. of the entrance, indicated by a fine two-storey, five-sided window bay, with parlour beyond. Projecting contemporary wing at the back creating an L-plan. The porch, with weedy Corinthian upper columns and entablatures at both levels, also five-sided, appears to be an addition, perhaps of *c.* 1620–30. Thus, with the addition of the porch, near-symmetry was achieved, although this was later disturbed by an inserted ground-floor window at the l. end. A transomed hall window (renewed) is squeezed between the bays.

ALTON PANCRAS   6000

A linear village on the River Piddle, its cottages mainly of cob and thatch.

ST PANCRAS. The chancel is by *Ewan Christian* (E.E. style), the nave by *G.R. Crickmay* (getting more Perp), both 1874–5. Flint with stone banding. Only the W tower is medieval; C15, embattled with crocketed corner pinnacles. – FONT, *c.* 1500, but looking very restored. Octagonal, with quatrefoils. – FUR-NISHINGS. Plainish, but a complete scheme of 1875. *Crick-may*'s oak pulpit is on a dumpy stone pillar base. – STAINED GLASS. E window by *Lavers, Barraud & Westlake*, 1875. Also by them the adjacent lancet and a nave s window. Chancel s window by *Horace Wilkinson*, 1916. Nave N window, and another in the tower, both by *L.C. Evetts*, the former of 1963, the latter, depicting St Francis, of 1955. These are fine Expres-sionist windows of the period.

One approaches the church through two tall rusticated GATEPIERS of *c.* 1740. Gadrooned urn finials.

MANOR HOUSE, immediately s (for which the gatepiers were
built). The five-bay E front is the best part, of purple brick
with red dressings, and yellow ashlar for the even angle quoins,
the aprons of the windows and the moulded string course – a
somewhat startling colour scheme. It must belong to the
remodelling between 1730 and 1744 mentioned by Hutchins
(for Thomas Haskett). The N return is rendered and has a
gigantic blank niche in it. This relates to an early C19 expansion of the house to the w, creating a symmetrical N front.
This front was recessed twice in the middle, and there was
a round-headed staircase window in a w wing, to which the
niche replied (as illustrated in an early C19 view). Modest
mid-C18 interiors, with in the NE room a classical chimneypiece flanked by ogee-headed, i.e. Gothick, recesses with a trail
of olive leaves round the ogee.

AUSTRAL FARM, immediately N. Large rectangular early C19
stucco farmhouse. Next, a long mid-C19 range of FARM
BUILDINGS, flint with brick banding. On the opposite side
of the yard, an earlier BARN (perhaps c. 1800) of the same
materials, with further long SHELTER-SHED ranges beyond.

ANDERSON

Typical gathering of manor house, church and farmstead.

ST MICHAEL (now a private chapel). C13 in origin but extensively rebuilt, following the old plan. Nave with double bellcote
and chancel. Flint and bands of carstone. The chancel is largely
of c. 1622, refenestrated by *W. J. Fletcher* in 1889, when the
nave was rebuilt. The s chapel of 1755 (banded flint and
brick) was rebuilt above the window line as part of Fletcher's
work.

ANDERSON MANOR, 80 yds N. The house stands, facing s,
close by the church but almost invisible from it. A new,
formal approach from the s was made c. 1911, to pass down
an avenue, through wrought-iron gates and across the stream
into a balustraded forecourt (a route since abandoned). Such
formality perfectly suited Anderson Manor, which, though
a manor house of no great size or ambition, has a façade of
delicate sophistication. Rainwater heads give the date 1622 and
the initials of John Tregonwell, for whom the house was built.
After 1910 it was restored for Mrs Gordon Gratrix.

The plan forms a rectangle with rooms on the double-pile
principle, the earliest recorded double-pile house of the region.
The central porch however leads into the lower end of the hall
in the old way. The upper end of the hall grows out to form
the r. wing of the façade, and the dining room (originally the
kitchen) is similarly L-shaped to form the l. wing. Further
service rooms and two staircases to the rear. Two storeys, and

a third in the roof, lit by the gables of the wings and those on the sides. These have (restored) ball finials at their bases and tips. The porch, three-storeyed, and forming five sides of an octagon, ends in a flat top, behind which rises a central, broader gable. The splendid spine of lozenge-shaped chimneystacks, four plus four, places crowning stresses over the intermediate bays of the façade, establishing a simple rhythm of gable, stack, gable, stack, gable. The other three, flat fronts are not thoroughly organized: the entrance façade was the one that mattered. In details too the entrance front is differentiated. Round-headed entrance arch, with a keystone. Other doorways (and fireplaces inside) of Gothic outline. On the front all the main windows are of classical proportions, with stone cross-mullions and transoms. Hollow-chamfer moulding; continuous drip-courses. This applies also to the windows in the canted porch. No transoms in the gable windows, but hoodmoulds with labels. At the sides some windows are of three lights, with a transom; at the back there are no transoms at all, which makes e.g. the staircase window in the NE corner look very peculiar. At the back and on the W side all windows have hoodmoulds.

Anderson Manor is a beautiful colour, plum red with white dressings. Brick (by no means common in Dorset in the early C17) is used in an unusual bond, two rows of stretchers and one of vitrified headers, creating the banded effect so popular hereabouts. The dressings, of white Purbeck limestone, are generous, especially the flat alternating quoins.

Externally the house remains wonderfully unaltered. Even the window fastenings survive. The NW wing is either of c. 1646 or much later C17, added corner-wise, with raised brick quoins, and in the E wall a classical doorcase of c. 1700. Inside, however, almost no original C17 feature remains. The Jacobean-style panelled rooms are of c. 1910, replacing long-neglected C18 interiors.

COMBS DITCH. See Winterborne Whitechurch.

ARNE

A tiny village on a Poole Harbour peninsula, reached over heathland.

ST NICHOLAS. Nave and chancel in one, c. 1200. Some E.E. lancets, including an E triplet. Also a N priest's doorway. Restored by *John Belcher*,[*] 1856, when huge E buttresses were added. Major repairs by *E. Wamsley Lewis*, 1949–50, following war damage. – Simple interior with FURNISHINGS mostly of c. 1856. – Late C17 COMMUNION RAIL, reconstructed in 1940.

[*] Father of the better-known architect of that name.

– FONT. C14, octagonal, with a quatrefoil to each face. – PAINT-
ING. Above the doorway, early C16 stencilling in red, perhaps
representing pomegranates.

ICEN HOUSE (formerly Rodwell), 3½ m. WSW. A large Lutyens-
style house of *c.* 1920. Classical porch; a two-storey arcaded
loggia facing E.

ROMAN POTTERY KILNS and production sites at REDCLIFFE
FARM, ½ m. SE of Wareham church, on the slopes to the NE
next to the River Frome and ¼ m. SW on NUTCRACK LANE.

DYKES, 2¼ m. W of Wareham church on Worgret Heath and
Wareham Common, to E of BATTERY BANK (*see* East Stoke).
Date uncertain.

KING'S BARROW, Stoborough, 1 m. S of Wareham church. Now
in a garden. Excavated in 1767. A central inhumation, without
skull, was wrapped in stitched animal skins, some with 'gold
lace', laid in a hollowed oak trunk and accompanied by a
Kimmeridge shale cup.

ASHLEY CHASE

1¾ m. NNW of Abbotsbury

Built in 1925 by *Sir Guy Dawber* as a shooting lodge for Sir
David Milne-Watson, the Scottish governor of the Gas, Light
and Coke Co. The house stands in an astonishingly lonely
position. Neo-vernacular with much use of local materials.
Cotswold-style entrance front, not admitting to the high jinks
that go on towards the garden. There the l. part extends
obliquely, struck through by a big chimney-breast, and in the
angle stands a bow becoming a turret with a naughtily curved
cap. The service wing in the NE corner was built to a reduced
scale, and not as indicated on the drawings exhibited at the
Royal Academy in 1925 (as Dawber's diploma submission for
associate membership of the Academy). By the 1930s its height
had been raised to match that of the main range. – BATHING
PAVILION, in the garden. Of the late 1960s, by *John Rouse.* An
Italian Renaissance loggia.

ST LUKE'S CHAPEL, ½ m. WNW of the house. Fragment of a
C15 chapel, 32 by 18 ft (9.75 by 5.5 metres). The fragment
marks the NE angle. In the W wall the opening of the W
window. Stabilized in the 1930s by the Milne-Watsons by the
addition of rubble buttresses.

ASHMORE

A high-lying village grouped about a big round duck pond. There
is a rich combination of flint, greensand and mellow red brick on
the houses, together with the occasional thatched roof.

St Nicholas. Deceptively large. Rebuilt by *C. F. Edwards* of Exeter, 1874, with ashlar blocks scattered within flintwork – not an attractive effect. Nave with bellcote; chancel; style of *c.* 1300. (A C13 former chancel arch is said to be that reused as the vestry opening.) Chancel arch of 1934 by *Marshall Sisson*. The interest of the church lies in the internal corbels by *John Skeaping*, carved in 1949 for Geoffrey Howard. Skeaping was asked for deer scenes, since Ashmore is located in the Cranborne Chase. They are stylized in the Eric Gill tradition. – REREDOS. In the Comper style, by *W. H. Randoll Blacking*, 1949. – FONT. C12 cauldron-shaped bowl on an C18 baluster. COVER probably also by *Randoll Blacking*. – ROYAL ARMS, 1816, on a hatchment-like panel. – STAINED GLASS. E window by *Powell & Sons*, 1917. Chancel S window engraved by *Simon Whistler*, †1994. Effective, yet simple. Nave windows with grisaille decoration by *J. Drake & Sons* of Exeter, 1874.

Wesleyan Methodist Chapel (former). 1855. Plain oblong of brick and flint bands; lancet windows.

Manor Farm, beside the church. Remodelled in the early C19. It has a band of corbelling across the SE gable-end that is undoubtedly a trophy from *Vanbrugh*'s demolished Eastbury.

Old Rectory, facing the pond. Early C18. Windows in a rhythm 2:1:2. Stone doorway with an open segmental pediment. Enlarged at the back by *W. J. Fletcher*, 1871.

Manor House, ½ m. SE. 1925 by *Curtis Green* for A. L. Sturge. Cultivatedly wayward Neo-Georgian. Both the central hipped roof instead of a pediment and the mere single-storey side parts (but raised by *Curtis Green* to two storeys in 1934) suggest a certain scrupulous restraint. On the garden front, the first-floor balcony with its fine wrought ironwork is also part of the 1934 enlargement. The large *œil de bœuf* dormer over the entrance was added by *Marshall Sisson*, *c.* 1965.

Roman road, ½ m. E of the village. This is part of the road from Badbury Rings to Bath.

ASKERSWELL   5090

A picturesque gathering of cottages, some thatched, interspersed with artificial-stone-faced bungalows.

St Michael. 1858 by *Talbot Bury*, except for the tower. The church is Perp, not Second Pointed: no doubt Bury's response to the high, early C15 W tower. This is battlemented with a higher SE stair-turret. Three stages with set-back buttresses. W doorway with shields in the spandrels. Panelled arch to the nave. – The FURNISHINGS by *Bury* are of high quality and complete. – FONT. C12. Bowl with intersecting arches. Cylindrical stem; square base with spur ornaments. – SCULPTURE. On the tower W wall, small, poorly carved (and very eroded) relief of the Crucifixion; C15. – STAINED GLASS. N aisle window in the *Burlison & Grylls* style, *c.* 1880. – MONUMENT. The larger part of a brass indent (for the rest *see* Whitchurch Canonicorum) with an elaborately foliated cross of *c.* 1320. The inscription is in French and refers to Thomas de Luda and Alianore his wife and to the gift of a manor to 'ceste mesun', meaning Abbotsbury Abbey.

p. 34

ASKERSWELL HOUSE (formerly the rectory), 100 yds NE. Dated 1851. Tudor Gothic, perhaps by *Talbot Bury*. Alterations by *John Hicks*, 1868.

SOUTH EGGARDON HOUSE, ¾ m. NNE. A rear part, forming the S end of the main range, is C16, perhaps for Thomas Eggardon. Also at the back a kitchen wing adapted from a medieval house. The reused late medieval windows in the SE wing may be from this part. The S front is quite a regular affair (refacing the gable-end of the C16 house), not much before 1642 one would say, the date scratched on the inner door of the porch. Windows of four lights upstairs, three lights downstairs. Ovolo mouldings. Continuous hoodmould to the r. of the gabled porch projection, entered at the side.

EGGARDON HILL, 1½ m. NE, partly in Powerstock. Iron Age HILL-FORT, multivallate, covering 20 acres of the spur, with entrances at NW and SE. The ramparts have been lost to a landslip on the S, later reinstated to some degree. Within the enclosure are two BARROWS and linear BANKS of Bronze Age date, and many hollows and hut rings, contemporary with the hill-fort occupation. On the ridge spur to the SW, the Roman road from Dorchester turns eastwards, route beyond unknown.

7090

ATHELHAMPTON

49   ATHELHAMPTON HALL. As seen from the S* the Late Perp hall, with porch and oriel, and the mid-C16 parlour wing make a superb show. Both are of excellent quality and boldly, not fussily, enriched. The earlier part is all of creamy limestone ashlar from Portesham, the later has golden Ham Hill stone dressings against the cream of the walls.

Athelhampton ('the very name intimates nobility', wrote Coker) was built – or rather rebuilt, since there was a house here before – for Sir William Martyn (†1504), a man of considerable local importance who had held a key tax-collection post at Poole since at least 1485. Naturally he demanded the best that money could buy in rebuilding his family home, for which he received a licence to crenellate in 1495. As left by him it must have been the *beau idéal* of the late medieval manor house. It has battlements throughout, for the hall, its

---

* Really SW. The cardinal points are used throughout this account, as being less confusing than more accurate directions.

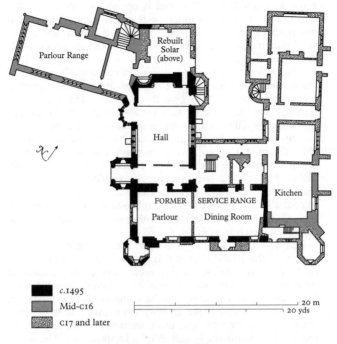

c.1495
Mid-C16
C17 and later

20 m
20 yds

Athelhampton Hall.
Plan

oriel bay to the l. and the porch to the r., and further r. the
(former) service end rounded off by the polygonal turret at the
SE corner. Continuous string course crowning the plinth and
another below the battlements. The porch is oddly detailed,
its angles chamfered, and thin round shafts, hardly more than
a roll moulding, up all four corners thus produced. Two-
centred entrance arch broadly moulded with a wave and
hollow, and given a hoodmould on worn headstops. Quatrefoil side windows down here. Two-light window to the upper
room in the porch. This has two-centred-arched lights, like
the hall window.

The hall window itself is set high, of two-and-two lights
divided by the thin upper part of a buttress more decorative
than necessary. Rectangular window surround outlined by a
roll moulding, and sunk into the depth of the wall by a hollow.
Identical window and buttress round on the N side of the hall.
The hall oriel is four-sided and rises nearly but not quite to
full wall height, so that it has its own battlements. The plinth
moulding here shifts slightly from the established level; so
it looks as though the oriel is an afterthought. The fact that
its design is unrelated to the rest of the front can hardly be
taken as supporting evidence, as in the last years of the C15
houses still tended to be designed feature by feature, not as

a whole. Each face of the oriel is opened for almost its full height by a two-light window with a two-centred head and two transoms. Simple cuspless tracery in the heads and below the lower transom. A thin shallow buttress with two set-offs against each angle.

The gable to the r. of the porch set insouciantly on top of the battlements goes with the reorganization of the SERVICE END in the early C17 to give three storeys. Three-light and four-light windows here, with ovolo-moulded mullions and hoodmoulds. The extent of the original house can be worked out by following the plinth moulding round to the E front. Here the modifications have been many, but the S two-thirds are in their walling of the earliest period, as the plinth mould shows. That gave a long, rectangular service range. Towards the W, the solar end is greatly extended, for the square room W of the hall as rebuilt in the C20 shows a little early walling towards the W and corresponds with a smaller room shown on Buckler's sketch plan of 1828.

49 The PARLOUR RANGE was added at an angle to the SW corner of the hall *c.* 1545–9.* It is two-storeyed with gabled dormers to the attics, a lively profile and rhythm, quite at odds with the robust simplicity of Sir William's house. So, we have seen, is its colouring. Its handling is also fairly strong, so that it does not make an easy companion. It is of three evenly spaced bays by one, the E windows of four lights, the lower ones slightly the longer. All the lights arched. The upper windows have individual hoodmoulds, the lower are linked by a first-floor string course dropping vertical projections l. and r. of each window in lieu of hoodmoulds. Two gabled dormers placed without regard for the windows below. The S gable-end has a similar arrangement, with room for a four-light window in the gable. First-floor six-lighter, ground-floor four-plus-four-lighter with a transom and arched lights below it. As this window rises higher than the E ground-floor windows, the string course does a decorative leap up round the angle buttresses.

The buttresses are one tell-tale sign that this range belongs to the group of C16 buildings for which design as well as stone seems to have come from Hamdon Hill, Somerset. They are octagonal, the faces concave, and support short twisted finials and the heraldic monkey of the Martyns. The apex finial turns into a series of volutes, a semi-Renaissance form found also e.g. at Bingham's Melcombe, Melcombe Horsey and Sandford Orcas Manor. The other piece of pure decoration is the lozenge panels below the gable windows, with carved surrounds and tufts of leaves at the angles (cf. Sandford Orcas for that too).

* Set in an alcove behind cupboard doors is the achievement of arms from the demolished gatehouse. This has the initials RM EM, for Robert and Elizabeth Martyn. The shield, however, is that of their son Nicholas, who took over Athelhampton after the death of his father in 1548. These facts lead to the fairly precise dating of the parlour wing given in this account. (Information kindly sent by Sir Mervyn Medlycott.)

The diagonal SE buttress on the parlour range is mid-C19, marking where a wall originally linked this corner to the gatehouse already mentioned (*see* e.g. Buckler's view of 1828 in the British Museum). This stood to the E of the parlour range and was aligned on the main porch. Early views show that it was in the same style as the parlour range. It was demolished in 1862. The W side of the range is irregular, for here is the chimney-breast, and a gabled projection for a closet at each level, beside the gabled staircase, projecting less far.

The NORTH RANGES are largely modern, of c. 1895 for A. E. Cart de Lafontaine (probably by *H. Inigo Thomas*) and 1920–1 for G. Cockrane, carrying on a Tudor style. The roughly symmetrical rounding off of the E front, with gable and turret at the r., is of the earlier date. At the back of this turret early C17 brickwork, in connection with an extension of the service range. The bonding, of more than one row of stretchers to each header row, is a speciality of Dorset at that period. Yet the brickwork includes a diagonal buttress. The service range was widened at about the same time, as can be seen towards the W, within a late C19 one-storey corridor. These ranges replaced irregular parts that formed a courtyard N of the hall.

INTERIORS. The HALL has two splendid sights: the roof 47 and the interior of the oriel. The roof's normal structure of collar-beams on arch braces with cusped wind-braces is barely appreciated because of the astonishing cusps given to the arch braces of the major trusses. The cusps extend upwards to form a curved collar at the apex. In effect the hall is spanned by three giant trefoils. Abnormally deep upper purlin, moulded and carved with two rows of square flowers. The gadrooned corbels that give rest to the trusses are a modification of the late C17. They are of plaster, as are the rafter feet; the lower sections no doubt suffered from decay at some point, hence the replacement. It seems likely that the original arrangement was of rafters rising from an enriched wall-plate, similar to that in the Abbot's Hall of Milton Abbey (q.v.). As for the oriel, it is vaulted, with cusped vault-ribs, and shafts up the deep entrance arch and a shafted super-arch as well. A doorway is ingeniously incorporated into the panelled arch, leading into the C16 range, so the latter must have had a predecessor of some sort. The regular doorway to the solar undercroft is in the hall's W wall, r. of the fireplace; and the N doorway leads to a staircase to the solar, rebuilt, together with the solar, c. 1920. At the E end the front and back doorways to the screens passage keep their original doors. Two service doorways. Three-light window in the gable, blocked by the early C17 creation of a two-storey E range. The screen itself however is not native to the hall,* but is nonetheless basically a Late Perp piece, brought in from St Donat's Castle, Glamorgan, by de Lafontaine. The hall panelling is also of this provenance. George Wood, owner from 1848 to 1867 (who also demolished the gatehouse), installed

---

* *See* the engraving in Nash's *Mansions of England in the Olden Time* (1841).

the main gallery structure in the mid C19. Some of the armorial stained glass is C16.

Elsewhere in the house there is less to record. The best room is the upper room in the C16 range, occupying its full length. More armorial stained glass; but the panelling is dated 1893 and the plaster ceiling is of that time, Arts and Crafts Jacobean, with knob-like pendants and roses and lilies in the fields. In the room below a slavishly copyist Jacobean ceiling of 1905, and some re-set panels of mid-C16 carving, with heads in relief. E of the hall, the upper room called the STATE BEDROOM has a C15 chimneypiece, with square moulded opening and deep stone lintel decorated in a favourite way: roses and shields alternately in quatrefoils, in ogeed almonds rather than the usual circles.

DOVECOTE, SW of the house. Early C16. Circular, of rubble stone, buttressed all four ways. Conical tiled roof and louvre.

FORMAL GARDENS, SE of the house. Laid out after 1891 by *Inigo Thomas*, and one of his finest surviving schemes. Three separate enclosed gardens, making much use of architecturally trimmed topiary. With its pool aligned on the centre of the E front, the Private Garden. To its S a linking *rond-point*, known as the Corona: circular, with a cresting of obelisks to its scooped-topped wall. Between this and the main road, the Great Court: a large square parterre, with a raised terrace along its S side terminated by a pair of pyramid-roofed pavilions. Further landscaping to the W by *Thomas Mawson*, 1904.

ST EDWARD (Christian Orthodox), formerly St John, opposite the E entrance to Athelhampton. After the house, the church is inevitably a disappointment. Goodhart-Rendel describes it unkindly as 'a pert little nave and chancel with an ugly bell-cote'. It is by *John Hicks* of Dorchester, of 1861. As is typical of Hicks, the cleanly executed style is characterized by E.E. plate tracery; its proportions are also pleasing, and the bell-cote robust and integrated into the whole. Chancel arch with naturalistic flowers in its giant cusping. Well-designed foliage corbels, carved by *Henry Burge* (perhaps drawn by *Thomas Hardy*). – Plain stone PULPIT projecting from the wall. – TILES around the altar by *Godwin*. – FONT. By *Hicks*. Circular bowl with carved water-lily and bulrush enrichment. – STAINED GLASS. E window and three chancel side windows by *Heaton, Butler & Bayne*, 1892–3. Nave N window by *J. N. Comper*, 1917–18.

BATCOMBE

No village centre; just a scattering of farms and the isolated church.

ST MARY. At the end of the village and with bare green hills rising on W, S and E. A flint-and-rubble, three-stage, early C15 W tower;

stately. Battlemented parapet with crocketed corner pinnacles and gargoyles. Polygonal N stair-turret. Panelled arch to the nave. Nave and chancel low in comparison with the tower. The nave is late C15. Perp three-light windows with thin shafts inside (one, nave N wall, the old E window re-set); wagon roof. Major restoration and reconstruction by *John Hicks*, 1864, including the rebuilding of the chancel. – PILLAR PISCINA. C12. Moulded base and cushion capital, the latter scooped out. – Sanctuary TILES by *Godwin* of Hereford. – SCREEN. Late C15, but heavily restored by *Hicks* after damage caused by the collapse of the chancel arch during the works of 1864. Of stone, with single-light divisions, each trefoil-headed. The chancel arch was cut back to make it fit. – FONT. C12, but made from two separate components, seemingly not intended to fit together. Circular bowl with cable moulding making four corners. Square-section stem with chamfered corners and a crude volute capital. – BENCH-ENDS. Two carved ends from Hilfield church (q.v.). – The other furnishings are most likely by *Hicks*.* – MONUMENTS. Three within the tower: John Minterne †1592. Plain but with black-letter carving. – Frances Minterne †1648. Classical surround with Corinthian columns and an anthemion-enriched entablature. Strapwork-like scrolls above and below. – John Palmer †1702. Richly carved frame. – Nave: George Harris †1804. By *E. Gaffin*. Sarcophagus-shaped.

CHURCH FARM, ⅛ m. N. Mid-C17. Thatched roof, the eaves later raised. Its chalk-block (or clunch) walls are an indication of the nearby chalk downs.

NEWLANDS FARM, ¾ m. N. Early C19. A typical villa-style farmhouse with wide sashes and a hipped slate roof. More remarkable is the GATEWAY. Ham Hill stone. Pedimented; dated 1622 in the tympanum. Three tall tapering finials. Round arch with roll moulding. It must relate to a previous house.

CROSS AND HAND, Batcombe Down, 1 m. E of the church. A stone shaft with a rough capital. Possibly pre-Conquest.

BEAMINSTER

4000

Sited at the confluence of several streams, and at the head of the River Brit, Beaminster is one of the most attractive small towns in Dorset. By the early C16 it was the 'praty market town' seen by Leland. A series of town fires with ensuing rebuilding changed its architectural character. There are only one or two buildings that survived the first of these in 1644, when the whole town was burnt except for East Street and Church Street. In 1684 the market house burnt down, and in 1781 fire destroyed all of the

---

* Some reseating was carried out by *Jesse Gane* of Evercreech, 1844. The PEWS may be by him.

Beaminster, Shadrack Street.
Drawing by H.W. Colby.

houses in Shadrack Street and on the w side of The Square. All of
the larger merchants' houses on the fringes of the town escaped
damage, as did the church.

Access to Beaminster was comparatively tortuous until new
turnpike roads to Bridport and later to the nearby Somerset
towns were constructed in the late C18 and early C19. Despite
these, the failure of any railway scheme to reach fruition, and a
decline in the local flax industry through the earlier part of the
C19, led to a fall in population. There are few buildings of the
later Victorian period, and until the arrival of the motor car in
the C20 the town was described as 'sequestered'. Lack of later
development has fortuitously preserved continuous frontages of
C18 and early C19 cottages and houses, while a notable number
of early shopfronts remain.

30   ST MARY. The w tower is no doubt the most spectacular of
     Dorset, up to the standard of the proudest of Somerset. A

legacy indicates that this piece of unrestrained display can almost certainly be dated to 1503. A full description is called for, starting from the quatrefoil base band and the set-back buttresses and wandering up the two tiers of niches on the buttresses and then the (typically Somerset) detached buttress-shafts with their pinnacles. They even grow out of the angles of the tower. The top with a higher stair-turret is a stockade of pinnacles. The w side moreover has a display of sculpture. A pity only that the large w window is of 1863, a precursor to the major tower restoration by *William White* for the Rev. Alfred Codd, 1877–8. The large quatrefoil at the top seems out of character. The project included the restoration of the many missing pinnacles, especially those above the top line of the parapet. Three niches are above the w window; in the middle one the Virgin (badly weathered). Another frieze of quatrefoils etc. at that level. Above the niches a relief of the Crucifixion, and above that two small scenes in relief framed by diagonally set buttress-shafts, the outer two with crocketed pinnacles. Niches with figures l. and r. of them, on the same level. Finally, the bell-openings are pairs of two lights, each with a transom. Six of the niches have replacement statues by *Harry Hems* of Exeter, installed as part of White's restoration.

After the tower the rest of the church exterior inevitably seems ordinary. The flat buttresses are an indication that the E part of the N aisle is C12 or C13 in origin, and formed the N transept to a cruciform church. However all changed during a campaign of rebuilding through the C15. So the aisles have Perp windows, and the s aisle is embattled. N chapel with a four-centred arch to the N window, its parapet not quite lining up with that of the N aisle. It was built in 1505 for John Hillary. Chancel with a five-light E window. Embattled Gothick N porch of 1830. The whole church was in a very poor condition by the mid C19, and the first part of a major restoration programme was carried out by *White*, 1861–3. (The second was on the tower, 1877–8, mentioned above.) On the s side of the tower the C14 MORT HOUSE (on C13 foundations), originally free-standing until the tower was built against it, when it was reconstructed. It was linked to the main body of the church only when an existing arch was opened between it and the s aisle as part of White's scheme.

Now inside. The arcades are of five bays with standard elements. The E bays have moulded capitals, the w bays leaf bands. Also the E bays are narrower than the w bays – a change of plan no doubt. In fact w seem to be earlier than E, the latter perhaps built only once the old crossing tower had been taken down. s of the tower is the w bay of the s aisle. The N chapel connects with the chancel and the N aisle by wide four-centred arches. Panelled chancel arch, panelled tower arch, panelled arch between tower and s aisle, all indicative of a date *c.* 1500. The nave roof was part of *White*'s first restoration, with carved corbels by *Burge & Allen*. The aisle roofs are C17. Also boldly shaped SEDILIA, typical of *White*.

FURNISHINGS. ALTAR. All that survives of *White*'s stone
altar is a decorative strip below the E window. – CHOIR
STALLS. Also part of *White*'s restoration, the details matching
the sedilia. – SCREEN. In a Perp style; by *C.E. Ponting*, made
by *Herbert Read* of Exeter, 1913. – PULPIT. Early C17. Two
tiers of elaborated arches; splayed linenfold plinth. A now-
disappeared sounding-board was apparently dated 1619.
– FONT. Late C12. Square, of Purbeck marble, with four
round-headed panels on the E face. Stem, colonnettes and
base of 1921. – STAINED GLASS. E window by *Wailes*, 1862.
Wailes also did the W window in 1863. Chancel S window by
Hardman, †1896 (designed by *D.J. Powell*). S aisle E also by
Hardman, but earlier, of 1878 (and designed by *J.H. Powell*).
S aisle windows of 1884 and 1931, by *C.E. Kempe* and *Kempe
& Co.* respectively. N aisle window by *A.L. Ward*, 1911; very
colourful. – MONUMENTS. The finest piece by far and one
of the finest of its time in Dorset is *Peter Scheemakers*'s to
George Strode †1753. Simple black sarcophagus and on it the
couple reclining, he in a kind of toga, she pointing something
out to him in a book. The figures stand out against a black
obelisk. To l. and r. two standing allegorical figures. – It is all
so much more refined than Thomas Strode, Serjeant-at-Law
†1698 by *John Nost I*. He stands a pompous figure in a wig,
of unshakable self-confidence, and no doubt agreeing with the
inscription calling him 'juris prudentia, pietate, consilio insig-
nis' ('distinguished for his understanding of the law, loyalty
and wisdom'). Reredos background with pilasters. Weeping
putti l. and r. – Henry Samways †1706. Corinthian pilasters,
segmental pediment; winged cherubs' heads in the entablature.
– Daniel Cox †1778 and others to 1801. Standing female figure
with a staff by an urn.

HOLY TRINITY, Shortmoor (now a dwelling). 1849–51 by
Carver & Giles of Taunton.* Quite large for the second church
of so small a town. Nave and lower chancel. Paired lancets in
the S aisle, round windows in the clerestory. Bar tracery in the
W window, stepped triplet of lancet lights in the E window.

CONGREGATIONAL CHURCH (former, now BEAMINSTER
MUSEUM), Whitcombe Road. Founded 1662, built 1749, enlarged 1825. Front of four bays, entrances and round windows
in bays one and four, large arched windows between. These
windows have a curious C17 flavour: two lancet lights and a
lower round-arched light between, with a vertical connecting
the apex of this with the apex of the whole window.

ALMSHOUSES (now the Strode Room), beside St Mary's churchyard. The gift of Sir John Strode and dated 1630. Very humble.
They were converted to a meeting room in 1977. Beside these
a LIFT TOWER giving disabled access to the church. Low-
pitched pyramidal roof. A good piece of streetscape of *c.* 2000.

OLD VICARAGE, Clay Lane, 250 yds NW. 1859–61 by *William
White* for the Rev. Alfred Codd. Tough High Victorian Gothic,

*Giles called it 'a small church of cheap order'.

a rarity in Dorset. Bold asymmetry on the SE (garden) front
with some tile-hanging. Gables of two sizes on the entrance
front, and an arched plate-tracery window over the main
doorway.

NATIONAL SCHOOL FOR GIRLS (former), Hogshill Street. 1868
by *Slater & Carpenter*. Bold E.E. in style, with two gables facing
the road. One has a tall plate-tracery window, the other a pair
with Geometrical tracery. Carved crosses to each gable apex.

BOYS' ELEMENTARY SCHOOL (former), East Street. 1875 by
J.M. Allen of Crewkerne. Mildly Gothic, the tall chimneystacks unfortunately now shortened.

BEAMINSTER SCHOOL, Newtown, ½ m. N. 1960–5 by *J.R.
Hurst*, County Architect. An excellent example of the quiet,
sensitive, all too ephemeral style associated with the 1950s.
Loose grouping of lowish buildings, their roofs some pitched,
some elliptically curved. Four hues of buffish-brown, brick,
stone and pebble facing, generating a chequer pattern on large
surfaces. Several later buildings of lower architectural quality.

PERAMBULATION

Starting at THE SQUARE (triangular in plan). The ROBINSON
MEMORIAL, on the site of the market cross, loosely modelled
on e.g. the Conduit, Sherborne, was built in 1906 by Vincent
Joseph Robinson of Parnham House in memory of his sister.
The surrounding buildings are modest in scale. No. 4, N, on
the corner with Hogshill Street, is of the later C17 with mullioned windows on the upper floor, replaced on the ground
floor by C19 shop-window bays. More mullioned windows
with ovolo mouldings on the rear wing. The attic was altered
to its present configuration after damage in the 1781 town
fire. At the SW end of this row, at the start of Church Street,
the former LLOYDS BANK, built for the Dorsetshire Bank
in 1872. Typically commercial Free Style, changing on each
floor: Romanesque-cum-Gothic on the ground floor, vaguely
Italianate on the first, but plain at the top with a modillion
cornice. On the opposite corner, the CO-OP is early C19 with
a good double-bowed shopfront of that date. At the SE corner
of The Square, the RED LION HOTEL. Brick and stone commercial Jacobean of 1892, its name in stone lettering in the
three otherwise blank dormers with side scrolls.

Leaving along HOGSHILL STREET heading W, first on the r.
is the WHITE HART of *c*. 1850. Italianate, with a low-pitched
gable and balcony over the carriage arch. Next, set back from
the road, is THE ELMS, an early C19 ashlar refacing of a late
C17 house. At the back the windows are mullioned; on the
front large sashes with thin architraves and a doorway with
Tuscan pilasters. In contrast DEVONIA, further along the road
on the opposite side, is entirely of 1783, with an ashlar façade
and rubble stone elsewhere. Owing to the earlier date, the
sashes are smaller with keyed architraves. It is of only four bays
(the doorway is at the back). After Shadrack Street on the l.,

DANIELS HOUSE, c. 1840, with two-storey bay windows and a Greek Doric porch. Here the sides are of brick, with only the front in stone.

Returning to The Square, we turn N into FLEET STREET. On the r. the BEAMINSTER INSTITUTE, in the style of an C18 town house but actually of 1902. The next building of note is THE PINES (now NFU Mutual), opposite. A pair of plain late C18 ashlar-fronted houses (probably of 1780) with a good early C19 double-bay shopfront. Further on the l. the former WESLEYAN METHODIST CHAPEL (1854), its ground floor opened out to provide entrances to flats made within. Further on the r. BARTON END. What we first see is the brick-built front block of five bays, c. 1730, the sashes with moulded and keyed architraves. Also a pedimented doorway and chamfered quoins. All of the details are in stone. Around the corner and stone-built is the C17 rear range, at right angles to the street.

Back to The Square and then NE into NORTH STREET. After about 100 yds on the l. is a group of stone-mullioned cottages, probably built almost immediately after the catastrophic 1644 fire. Further, still on the l., the MANOR HOUSE. Plain late C18 house. This is seen on the rougher E front. Enlarged in 1822 by *G.A. Underwood*; the ashlar entrance and remaining façades are his. Reduced in size 1967. Its linear LANDSCAPED PARK, created for Samuel Cox in the late C18, is graced with a sickle-shaped lake to the N, a GROTTO behind, a rocky CASCADE in the style of *Josiah Lane* (late C18) and a garden GATEWAY made up from octagonal buttresses and finials of the C16, gleaned at the dismantling of Clifton Maybank (q.v.). Inside the house are two splendid pieces from Fonthill Splendens, Wiltshire (dem. 1807), the predecessor to William Beckford's Gothic Fonthill. They are a CEILING PAINTING by *Andrea Casali* of the Feast of the Gods, and a really remarkable CHIMNEYPIECE. This is of white and a little mottled marble, carved on the lintel with great virtuosity with scenes from the Trojan War. The large figures up at this level l. and r. must be Odysseus in hiding, and Ajax committing suicide. It is probably by the Hanoverian sculptor *J.F. Moore*. The STABLES alongside the road are of c. 1670, and in their eared and pedimented windows an almost exact match with the stables at nearby Mapperton, which bear that date.

Back again to The Square, to leave via PROUT HILL towards the SE. At the bottom of the hill on the l., BRIDGE HOUSE, of the early C17, the windows mullioned and with hoodmoulds (but made to look earlier with Tudor-arched timber window inserts). Round the corner in WHITCOMBE ROAD the early C18 front of FARRS hides behind bulging yew hedges, beyond the Congregational chapel. Ovolo mouldings to the windows, those on the ground floor tall in proportion. Again, at the centre a pedimented doorcase. A little further along on the r. the C17 stone front of HITTS HOUSE, again with ovolo-moulded mullioned windows, and the delightful C18 additions of a big shell-head canopy to the doorway, and big ball-topped

gatepiers. Finally, on the l. EDGELEY COTTAGE. Yet another
stone house, this probably mid-C17, for the three-light windows,
hollow-moulded and regularly spaced, are linked at the lower
level by a single stretched hoodmould.

OUTLYING BUILDINGS

THE LODGE, Clay Lane, 250 yds NW. 2012 by *Western Design
Architects*. Single-storeyed with vertical boarded cladding.
Curved corners, the whole structure raised on decking. The
organic design was generated by the need to work around the
mature trees.

THE LODGE, Tunnel Road, ⅓ m. NW. A villa of *c.* 1820, set back
in its own grounds. Five-bay front with a Tuscan-columned
porch at the centre.

PARNHAM HOUSE, ¾ m. SSW. A mid-C16 mansion built for
Robert Strode and completed by his son John Strode (whose
name and the date 1559 appear on a panel of armorial glass in
the Hall). The precise date of the start of work is unknown, but
Strode's grandson called the house 'reedifyed and enlarged,
tempore Hen. 8'. It was intensified in its Gothick between
1807 and 1811 by *John Nash* for Sir William Oglander. Further
transformations, largely of the interior, were made *c.* 1900 for
Vincent Joseph Robinson, and between 1910 and 1915 for Dr
Hans Sauer.

   The original form of the house and its evolution can be
taken at one view of the E-facing ENTRANCE FRONT. Local
golden-brown stone, ashlar-faced. E-plan, but the N stroke of
the letter projecting less far than the S and faced in a wider
gable. No doubt many of the pre-Nash features are renewals

Beaminster, Parnham House, prior to C19 alterations.
Engraving by James Basire, C18

of C17 work, probably from the time of Sir Robert Strode
(†1623). Typically, grouping and fenestration are controlled
by need, not by a desire for symmetry. So one can deduce
from the front that the Hall lies to the l. of the porch and was
one-storeyed from the start. The lower part of the projecting
chimney-breast here was removed by *Nash* and substituted
by a more elaborate window. The chimney (as one might
expect) originally went down to the ground, with a window
l. and r. Two-storey solar range to the s, served by a generous staircase projecting in the re-entrant angle. This had
gables on its re-entrant side originally: its battlemented top is
a *Nash* alteration. Similar staircase projection r. of the porch,
also originally with a gable facing the front and also later
battlemented by Nash. Windows of many shapes and sizes,
the largest mullioned with transoms. All have arched lights,
and are sunk within typical square surrounds, deeply hollow-
moulded. (Since such windows were used on Chantmarle for
Sir John Strode in 1612, it is impossible to distinguish the
mid-C16 work from those added in the early C17.) The E
windows of the s wing come in a canted projection, giving
1:6:1 lights with a transom to both storeys. This must be early
C17. Similar canted porch oriel, on many-moulded corbelling,
the windows of 1:3:1 lights, without transoms. The armorial
cartouche here is also of the C17: see the leathery surround.
Four-centred entrance arch with continuous mouldings. The
C17 N range gets in three storeys below the gables, and has
regularly placed mullioned windows, two or four to a hoodmould. These are probably mid-C16, as that on the ground
floor fits neatly into the base-mould. Nash re-profiled the
main gables and added the spiky finials (resembling coolie
hats).

The SOUTH FRONT is largely *Nash*'s work of 1807–11, but
the rather thinly detailed mullioned-and-transomed windows,
their hoodmoulds drooping down each side, are of 1910–15
by *Harry Lindsay*, replacing Nash's Gothick traceried ones.
By Nash too the Dining Room doubling the depth of the Hall
towards the w, and masking the C16 hall windows and w porch
to the screens passage. N of the w porch, two storeys of C16
windows, visible inside the house. Regularly spaced buttresses,
topped by the same finials as on the E front. More battlements.
At the w end a wider bay with a canted window projection.
The s and w fronts seen together certainly group well, and
looked much more distinctive before watering down (*see* the
Country Life photographs of 1908).

The SERVICE COURT to the NW is basically of the C17,
wholly renewed and recast in the early C20. The FORECOURT
of 1910–15 for Dr Sauer reinstates the 'wall about the base
court' erected for Sir Robert Strode in the early C17 but swept
away in C18 landscape improvements. Ball finials to the main
stone piers, obelisks with tiny ball-finial tops to the secondary
piers. Also for Sauer and, together with the forecourt, clearly
inspired by the gardens of Montacute, Somerset, the SOUTH

TERRACE. Balustrading with obelisk-topped piers and termi-
nating summerhouses with openwork ogee strapwork tops.
These are all by *Lindsay*, perhaps assisted by his wife *Norah
Lindsay*. The gardens have been further elaborated to the S for
Michael Treichl from *c.* 2002 onwards.

The INTERIOR* has also undergone a succession of
changes. In the HALL, Nash's Gothic ceiling was removed by
Sauer, opening it to the roof once again. The screen was also
brought in at this time, and the fireplace surround made up
with parts of another C15 screen. However, the armorial glass
in the E windows is native to the house. The best ensemble is
the OAK ROOM, largely a creation of Robinson, 1898–1910.
This is downstairs in the N range. Linenfold panelling said to
come from West Horsley Place, Surrey, and a deep frieze of
Early Renaissance scrollwork and roundels enclosing armorial
devices, i.e. mid-C16 joinery. The only early interior is the
LIBRARY SW of the Hall, of the late C17. The memorable
part is the overmantel, an inset portrait surrounded by carved
fruit and flowers. In the room above, a re-set chimneypiece of
the early C17, executed with unusual crudity. Central relief of
Joseph and Potiphar's wife. Elsewhere, the DRAWING ROOM
is of the Sauer period, fitted up in the Caroline style. The
DINING ROOM was refitted with a Jacobean-style pendant
ceiling and late C17 fireplace at the same time.** In the E part
of the house is a substantial staircase by *William Bertram*,
c. 2002, its spiky-finialled newel posts and Gothick balustrading echoing Nash's detailing. Here also a Jacobean-style plaster
ceiling.

HORN PARK, 1½ m. NW. One of those pure Neo-Georgian
country houses designed just before the First World War by
followers of Lutyens. Of 1911 by *T. Lawrence Dale* (then aged
twenty-six, a former pupil of C.E. Ponting, the diocesan architect), for J.A. Pinney. Horn Park is only a five-bay villa in
size, but has great presence in the continuity of its stone
walls, hipped roofs and dormers, and great white cornice.
Segment-hooded stone porch on coupled columns. Inside this,
the segmental barrel-vaulting of the central corridor prepares
the way for the capital space, the drawing room at the far
end of the house, which brilliantly combines a Soanic groin-
vault with pretty, Gimson-ish foliage-trailing plasterwork.
Some Jacobean panelling brought in from Parnham House
(*see* above).

ROAD TUNNEL, 1¼ m. NW. A remarkable foretaste of railway
engineering. *Michael Lane*, engineer (who had assisted Mark
Brunel on the Rotherhithe Tunnel in 1825). Constructed in
1831–2 at the behest of Giles Russell, a Beaminster solicitor,
for the Second Bridport District Trust. It takes the Crewkerne and Yeovil to Beaminster road through the ridge of
Horn Hill.

*Tragically gutted by fire, April 2017. This account was written prior to the fire.
**These three rooms were initially completed by *Nash* in a full Gothick style.

BEER HACKETT

ST MICHAEL. Mostly 1881–2 by *G.R. Crickmay*. The plain
C15 tower largely rebuilt by *C.E. Ponting*, 1897. Several C15
windows re-set by Crickmay in the chancel and nave. C15 N
porch doorway with leaf spandrels. Much reused masonry
in the tower also, including the Perp W window (but with
renewed tracery), upper tower windows, gargoyles and the
weather-stones on the E wall indicating the original nave roof
profile. The panelled tower arch is Ponting's. – FONT. C15.
Octagonal, plain, but against the underside nice leaf patterns
and simple traceried panels. – The other FURNISHINGS are
mainly of the *Crickmay* phase. – ORGAN in fine Gothick case,
by *Bates & Son*, *c.* 1869. Moved from Thornford Methodist
Chapel, 2003. – STAINED GLASS. E window by *Clayton &
Bell*, 1882.

BELCHALWELL
Okeford Fitzpaine

ST ALDHELM. Small and Perp, apparently C15, but a length of
nave S wall (rendered on the exterior) survives from a late C12
predecessor. Ruinous by 1905, when it was carefully restored
by *C.E. Ponting*. Short two-stage S tower to which the porch is
attached as a lean-to on the W side. This is of the same large
ashlar as most of the nave. Inside the porch is a doorway of
c. 1190, a good example of the Transitional style. It has one
order of colonnettes, a pointed arch, chevron at right angles
to the wall surface, and a dogtooth hoodmould terminated
with carved heads. No chancel arch, perhaps lost when the
church was ruinous. Later C15 N aisle with a Perp three-bay
arcade of standard elements and some surviving colour. The
tower arch is panelled. Windows generally square-headed with
cinquefoiled lights. The E windows are heavily restored, probably based on C15 originals. – PULPIT. C17, hexagonal. Oak,
with arabesque panels at the top.

BERE REGIS

Once a small market town, Bere Regis was badly affected by
a fire in 1788, its rebuilding having little architectural distinction. A few terraces of plain brick Late Georgian cottages along
West Street. North Street has more of a village character with
many cob and thatch cottages. The town is on the former main
turnpike road (of 1841) between Dorchester and Poole. It was

bypassed in 1981, accounting to some extent for its present character as a backwater.

ST JOHN THE BAPTIST. A large and interesting church. Its history began at some point in the mid CII (i.e. either before or shortly after the Conquest, the period known as Saxo-Norman). Externally, however, what one sees is CI5 and CI6 Perp work; it is inside where the earlier phases are more immediately apparent. The indications of this first church are largely confined to the N jamb of the chancel arch and the first pier to its W in the N aisle, the two structures suggesting a wide opening. In Saxon terms this would have been a *porticus*. This arch is also out of line with the remainder of the aisle, indicating that the first nave was out of alignment with the chancel. The presence of a similar S *porticus* can be assumed in the matching wide spacing of the present E bay of the S arcade. Next comes a late CI2 S aisle, originally only three bays long, hence the survival of two columns midway in the present arcade. The piers are round, the bases have spurs, the capitals are multi-scalloped (two of them with heads at the angles), the abaci are square, the arches single-stepped, pointed and with nailhead on the hoodmould. An early CI3 N aisle of similar length came next. The capitals here are flat and moulded, and there are no hoodmoulds. There follows to the E the narrow 'porticus' arch, in its present form, with two single chamfers, also early CI3. The aisles were extended to the W *c.* 1300, with wider arches having two chamfered orders. They did not link up with the present tower, which is of the late CI5.

We now return to the exterior to see further developments. First, in the CI4 both aisles were rebuilt to a greater width, the fenestration being partially of that date, e.g. the three-light window with reticulated (Dec) tracery just E of the porch. The large five-light E window of the S chapel (Turberville Chapel) was rebuilt in a similar style, 1873–5, part of a major restoration and refurnishing by *G.E. Street.* (Inside, next to it, an ogee-headed PISCINA.) The S aisle has banded flint and ashlar, rebuilt after a fire in its upper parts in 1760 with brick bands in place of the ashlar. In the early CI5 the chancel was rebuilt, and around 1500 the N chapel (Morton Chapel) was reconstructed.* Its two windows have uncusped lights under straight heads, typical of the last phase of Perp. These two operations took away the last substantial remains of CII structure. Taking the chancel next, this has three-light arched Perp windows with tracery typical of *c.* 1430 on the N and S sides. A plate-traceried E window of *c.* 1300 was retained (the tracery itself renewed in 1873–5). Mid-CI4 PISCINA in the SE corner, of double width under a cinquefoiled arch. The N aisle was given flat-headed

*The two transeptal chapels have specific dates related to them. The Morton Chapel, N, was built under the will of Cardinal Morton (proved in 1500), who founded a chantry here. The Turberville Chapel was built under the will of John Turberville, 1535.

three-light Perp windows in the late C15. Brick-banded s porch by *Street*. Finally the w tower, also late C15. Of three stages and one of the most imposing of this period in the county, it is a substantial piece, of flint and stone chequer. The w doorway has leaf spandrels, there are niches l. and r. of the w window, and set-back buttresses continued in triangular pinnacles at the height of the bell-openings. The latter are of three lights and have two transoms and Somerset tracery, but they are blank below the lower transom. The arch towards the nave is panelled. The nave clerestory is probably contemporary with the tower since its windows remain cusped, rather than the plain work of *c.* 1500. Of *c.* 1535 in the s chapel is a Perp window of five lights with reticulation units but under a segmental arch, which leads to curious shapes. There is moreover a square hoodmould over the segmental arch. Inside, the reveals are panelled, suggesting that the opening is late C15.

33   So returning within to see the late C15 nave roof. It is the finest timber roof in Dorset. It seems to have hammerbeams, and the carved figures at the ends of the hammers are a joy, but in fact the roof structure – based on tie-beams – and the *soi-disant* hammerbeams are no more than a decoration of the arched braces. These are cusped and sub-cusped, the tie-beams have big bosses, there is tracery above them between crown-posts and queenposts, and finally longitudinal arched braces help to stiffen the purlins and the ridge-piece. It is worth studying so ingenious a system.

FURNISHINGS. Low stone CHANCEL SCREEN and PULPIT both by *Street*, the last intended to harmonize with the bench-ends. – The CHOIR STALLS and CLERGY DESKS (two incorporating C15 linenfold panelling) are typical of the bold Gothic Revival work of *Street*. – Encaustic FLOOR TILES with green slip bands between, by *Godwin* for *Street*. The designs were based on medieval tiles found in the church and those at Bindon Abbey. – BENCH-ENDS. A superb set. Motifs are mainly tracery-based but include a big Pelican in piety, a merchant's mark and an inscription referring to the church-warden, 'ION DAV WARDEN OF THYS CHARYS'. Another gives the date 1547, which is the same year as the bench-ends at Affpuddle, but here they have rectangular panels. – PANELS of early C16 linenfold and of the C17 with arcaded decoration, reused in the N aisle vestry screen. – FONT. A good late C12 piece. Big, of cauldron shape, with intersecting arches. Flower roundels in a band above. C19 fluted stem and moulded base. – STAINED GLASS. An extensive scheme by *Hardman* for *Street*, 1875–7. Very typical of the firm's style at this date. Elongated figures, pale faces, white clouds. In the Turberville Chapel s window, an armorial window restored from that recorded in 1600. – MONUMENTS. In the s chapel are two of the familiar early C16 Purbeck monuments with cusped and sub-cusped quatrefoils on the tomb-chest, and a canopy on detached shafts, the canopy having a straight panelled underside on quadrant arches, a quatrefoil frieze and a top cresting. – Also the mutilated remains of a similar Purbeck monument in the N aisle. – In the chancel another such monument, but not of Purbeck stone, and in the details of shafts and canopy underside rustic Renaissance. Against the back wall brasses to John Skerne (†1593) and wife (†1596). – S aisle, a cusped TOMB-RECESS and part of another. – Also Anna Maria Radclyffe †1854. Gothic tablet by *Raggett* of Weymouth.

UNITED REFORMED CHURCH (formerly Congregational), Butt Lane. Built *c.* 1871 as a school. Converted to a chapel 1892–3. Brick. Four large Gothic windows facing the street, interrupted by a matching doorway.

DRAX HALL, North Street. Built as a Congregational chapel, 1829. Converted to a village hall in 1893. Brick. Plain façade with large sashes.

The more urban appearance is to. be found in West Street, beyond the church and THE OLD VICARAGE, on the opposite side of the road. This is of *c.* 1820, extended l. by *John Turnbull* of Windsor, 1865. It is set back behind a high brick wall. Stucco. Hipped roofs. Further on the r. the DRAX ARMS, C18 in origin, but mostly a mid-C19 rebuilding. Bay windows and a tall lateral chimneystack. Next, Nos. 85–85A (POST OFFICE), early C18, thatched, with a central chimneystack. No. 72 is a C19 brick thatched cottage, creating a picturesque corner at the junction with Butt Lane. Lastly, Nos. 52–54, dated 'DRAX 1904', with the appearance of almshouses.

In NORTH STREET many pre-fire cob and thatch cottages. Much of the town must have had this appearance before the fire.

SITTERTON, a hamlet ½ m. WNW. A tightly packed grouping of mostly cob and thatch cottages, much like North Street, Bere Regis. It leads up to the big early C18 red brick SITTERTON FARM at the W end, also thatched.

HYDE HOUSE, alongside the River Piddle, 3 m. SSE. A replacement country house, completed in 2004 by *Robert Adam* of *ADAM Architecture*. Stucco with low-pitched slate roofs. Nash-like elements composed in a picturesque manner (almost creating an Arts and Crafts butterfly plan). 126

HUNDRED BARROW, ¾ m. E. Perhaps the site from which Barrow Hundred was named.

WOODBURY HILL, ½ m. E. Iron Age univallate HILL-FORT enclosing 12 acres, defences much broken down. The site of an annual sheep fair from *c.* 1267.

BETTISCOMBE 3090

ST STEPHEN. Rebuilt in 1862 by *John Hicks*, including the unbuttressed Perp-style W tower. The chancel windows are *c.* 1400 Perp, reused from the previous church; also the tower W window. A chancel S window has a shield as a hoodmould stop. N aisle with its own gabled ends. Good roof corbels carved by

H. Burge. – High-quality CHOIR STALLS and CLERGY DESKS
by *Hicks.* – TILES by *Godwin* in the sanctuary. – Typically
High Victorian stone PULPIT and stone FONT, both carved by
B. Grassby. – STAINED GLASS. Rather purple E window by *Cox
& Son*, 1864. Three chancel side windows by *Hardman*, 1862
and 1884. Nave S window by *Goddard & Gibbs* (designed by
A.E. Buss), 1954. W window of *c.* 1910.

BETTISCOMBE MANOR HOUSE, ¼ m. NE. When imported classicism met vernacular tradition at the end of the C17 the result
was often a building of attractively unsophisticated dignity.
Bettiscombe is a case in point. It is of 1694 for the Rev.
John Pinney, rector of Broadwindsor. Brick walls, red brick
with vitrified headers, were a novelty on the Dorset–Devon
border then, and so were windows with rubbed brick heads.
Stone angle quoins to the house and to the chimneystacks
too. Continuous string courses. But in plan an old fashion is
followed, the front range and the two back ranges of equal
importance, and gable-ended too. The chimneystacks are
set on the gable-tops, as fashion-conscious houses had had
them *c.* 1620. At the back the upper string course steps up
and over the windows, a sure sign that hoodmoulds were
not forgotten. The windows appear to have been sashes from
the beginning, an unusually early example in the county.
However those on the main front were all altered *c.* 1800,
probably the same date as the Doric pedimented door hood,
although the support brackets seem mid-C18. Original shell-
hood over the back door.

Even more sophisticated (in this rural context) is the panelled hall with its screen of three arches. This is of *c.* 1720–30
for Azariah Pinney (grandson of John). The walls and compartment ceiling are also of this date: see the way the arch keys
are taken up over the beam mouldings. Bolection-moulded
doorcases and fire-surround. Also a good early C18 staircase in
the E range, unexpectedly classy with its three turned balusters
per tread and its fluted Doric-column newels.

RACEDOWN, 1 m. NNW. Red brick chequer, and for the Pinney
family, like Bettiscombe. Of *c.* 1790, enlarging and refacing
a house of 1758. Three broad bays and three storeys below
a parapet. Chimney-slabs rise high l. and r. Big hipped roof.
Tripartite ground-floor windows. Round-headed windows at
the back (N). Otherwise there is nothing special about it (apart
from it being let to the Wordsworths, 1795–7). Enlarged on
the N side, *c.* 1910.

BINCOMBE

No more than an out-of-the-way hamlet of farms, the church
among them, perched on the slope of the chalk downs.

HOLY TRINITY. Nave and chancel of *c.* 1150, but partly rebuilt
and refenestrated when the tower was added in the C15. This

is plain and lacking the top of its parapet. Also of this later date the raising of the roof. So the exterior is Perp, except for the blocked N doorway (*c.* 1150) and the C17 S porch. In the nave S wall a blocked rectangular rood-loft or gallery window. Chancel E wall rebuilt in 1865, when there was a thorough restoration. At this time the segmental responds to the double-chamfered chancel arch (an early C13 alteration) were heavily re-tooled. The bases have spur ornament. – STAINED GLASS. E window by *Charles Gibbs*, 1865. Nave N window almost certainly by *Lavers & Westlake*, 1909.

On DAIRY HOUSE, 170 yds NW of the church, are re-set two corbels supported on figures, one a standing man with sword and shield, the other a seated woman. They were originally of quite good quality, perhaps mid-C14. What did they come from? A monument or shrine, one would say, rather than a full-scale building.

BINCOMBE DOWN, 1 m. NW. ROUND BARROWS, clustered and linear groups, spread W to RIDGEWAY HILL (*see* Upwey), where many have been reduced by ploughing.

BINCOMBE HILL, ¼ m. NE. ROUND BARROWS. A tight linear group, SE–NW immediately above the village, including a triple bowl and bell barrow, lie at the S of a sweeping arc of bowl barrows running N to Came Wood (*see* Winterborne Came). In the centre is a well-preserved BANK BARROW, aligned E–W.

CHALBURY, ¾ m. SE. Iron Age univallate HILL-FORT enclosing 8½ acres. Original entrance at the SE. Quarry pits, hut circles and storage pits are visible inside the defences. Excavations in 1939 revealed a rampart with external and internal stone walls retaining a soil-and-stone core. Stone outcrops are incorporated within the defences. On the ridge to the SW is Rimbury (*see* Preston).

BINDON ABBEY
½ m. E of Wool

8080

Bindon Abbey was founded as a Cistercian house at West Lulworth (q.v.) in 1149 and transferred to Bindon in 1172. As for this and the whole monastic establishment, a plan tells one more than the site, though the site is more enjoyable. The plan is the traditional Cistercian one, with the church on the N side of the cloister, the chapter house on the E and the frater on the S. The W end of the CHURCH, where a substantial masonry angle stands some 25 ft (7.5 metres) high at its NW corner, had solid walls instead of arcading in the westernmost bay between the nave and aisle. After that one recognizes the arcade by the base of one round pier. Five arches of the N arcade survived in 1733, as indicated by a Buck engraving, but only three and a half in 1760, as illustrated in Hutchins. The Transitional character of the arches suggest a date of *c.* 1200. Further E is the base of the broad pulpitum which went across,

Bindon Abbey, north arcade.
Engraving by James Basire, C18

then the rood screen and the crossing and transepts. E of each
transept were two straight-ended chapels. In one of them is
a Purbeck marble slab with indent for a large brass. This
was the MONUMENT to Abbot Richard de Maners and dates
from the early C14. It has a border with indents for individual
letters. These read: ABBAS : RICARDUS : DE : MANERS : HIC :
TUMULATUR : AD : PENAS : TARDUS : DEUS : HUNC : SALVANS :
TUEATUR. (Abbot Richard de Maners is buried here. May God
who is slow to punish protect him as his saviour.) The straight-
ended chancel projected further than the chapels. While piers
and column positions are generally only indicated by their
footings, rather more of the external walls stand, mostly at
about 4 ft (1.2 metres) in height. This equally applies to the
building on the E side of the cloister. Immediately S of the S
transept here was the tunnel-vaulted sacristy, and to the S of
that the CHAPTER HOUSE with two bays of rib-vaulting on
wall-shafts. Those in the middle are oddly sunk in the wall (cf.
Forde). The narrow W bay was arched and carried the passage
to the DORMITORY, which was always on the upper floor. Its
two-naved UNDERCROFT is well discernible. The walls of the
S and W ranges stand only slightly above their footings.

After the Dissolution the abbey property passed to Sir
Thomas Poynings. His brother sold the estate to Viscount
Howard of Bindon in 1555. Howard adapted the claustral
buildings to become his country house, although physical evidence of those adaptations has disappeared. Associated with
these works are the WATER GARDENS located to the E and S
of the abbey ruins. These were laid out c. 1560–80, slightly
pre-dating similar gardens at Theobalds, Hertfordshire. Their
origin was as monastic fish ponds, but their redesigned layout
is characteristically Elizabethan. That to the E has a rectangular

island within a surrounding canal, and at its centre a circular mount with its own surrounding canal. A similar arrangement of a canal-enclosed island within a larger canal-enclosed area (but without the mount) is to the sw of the abbey. Here the central island is lozenge-shaped.

In 1641 the abbey ruins came into the possession of the Welds of Lulworth Castle (q.v.), notable for their success in erecting buildings for R.C. worship before it was again legal to do so. At Lulworth they had put up the earliest post-Reformation church for such worship (*see* East Lulworth). At Bindon in 1794–8 Thomas Weld built immediately w of the ruins a villa-like house of retreat, and a gatehouse to the precinct.

GATEHOUSE. Probably by *John Tasker* (architect of the Welds' R.C. church at Lulworth). This sets the right medievalizing mood, with its pointed entrance arch, pointed window l. and r., filled with wooden tracery, and battlements. Ironstone walling, red brick for the battlements and the arches.

HOUSE (known as BINDON ABBEY). Also by *John Tasker*. It is of Purbeck stone, the porch alone of ashlar, and continues this innocent, un-archaeological Gothic, but to serious purpose. The gable-ended block is orientated W–E, and the pointed upper windows with intersecting tracery are in a much loftier upper storey than the hoodmoulded lower ones. The upper windows were restored to their original form before 2000. The clues are easy to interpret: the upper storey is a three-bay chapel-like room (but only registered as a chapel in 1885). Plaster groin-vault inside, carried on groups of four elongated E.E. shafts projecting from the side walls. The house was clearly intended to receive but a few at any time, and has only four rooms in the low ground storey (two in a rear lean-to), and two at the level of the eventual chapel. Central staircase running up, from a groin-vaulted hall passage, in a higher projection at the back. Thin pinnacles on all gables, and Gothic detailing throughout the interior of the house.

BINGHAM'S MELCOMBE
see MELCOMBE HORSEY

BISHOP'S CAUNDLE   6010

A linear hilltop village, much affected by post-war development. At its centre a string of stone-built former farm buildings and cottages.

ST PETER AND ST PAUL. Nave and chancel of *c.* 1300, both largely rebuilt in 1863–4 by *W. Slater*, preserving (and no doubt enhancing) the E.E. character. The E window has three

stepped, cusped lancet lights under one arch, the side windows
have Y-tracery. Of the *c.* 1300 date the E part of the S aisle,
but this otherwise enlarged in the later C15. Of this date also
the three-stage, battlemented Perp W tower. This has a N stair
projection, rectangular becoming octagonal and rising slightly
above the main parapets. Two-light belfry openings with Somerset tracery. Nave N wall completely rebuilt in 1864. The
extent of the restoration is clear within, the chancel arch, the
E aisle arcade bay and the chancel being largely rebuilt by
Slater. The remainder of the S arcade is genuine Perp, four
chamfered shafts per pier. – REREDOS. With luscious High
Victorian vine carving by *James Forsyth*, 1864. This is set below
an E.E. blank arcade. – PULPIT. Unconvincing Perp style. By
Forsyth, 1864. – FONT. C15, octagonal, with quatrefoils. Trefoil-
headed panels on the pedestal; similar panels to the splayed
bowl base. – ROYAL ARMS. Of Charles II, dated 1661. A good
example, with the added motto 'Fear God, Honour the King'.
– STAINED GLASS. E and other chancel windows by *Clayton &
Bell*, 1864. S aisle E end, two good windows by *Joseph Bell* of
Bristol, 1897. – MONUMENT. Daubeney and Herbert families,
1815 by *King* of Bath. This is large and very ponderous, and yet
he could be so elegant. Shrouded urn. Tablet with side scrolls.

3000

BLACKDOWN
Broadwindsor

HOLY TRINITY. 1839–40 by *E.L. Bracebridge*. Nave and
chancel in one. Simple lancet Gothic. A transparent conical
spire of mild steel rods, 1963, added during rebuilding after a
fire. – FONT. Featureless cauldron, C12 or C13. Nicely placed
on a simple black metal stand, also 1963.

BLACKDOWN HOUSE, ¼ m. S. An earlier C17 farmhouse,
enlarged and refaced. Over the S doorway – which has arched
head, hoodmould and pediment (the last an C18 addition) – the
date 1697. Also the initials P M I for one of the Pinney family.
Roughly symmetrical five-bay façade; three dormers above.
Mullioned windows with ovolo mouldings, and linked hoodmoulds for the lower storey. A scatter of windows of various
dates at the back. Large Neo-Tudor block added at the W end
c. 1840 for J. A. Pinney.

RACEDOWN. *See* Bettiscombe.

9000

BLANDFORD CAMP
Tarrant Monkton and Tarrant Launceston

Completely rebuilt in 1964–71 for the Army School of Signals,
in two phases, to designs by the *Architects' Co-Partnership*

(appointed 1961). Much of this work survives as the core of the present base. Blackish-brown brick with horizontal concrete panels, hence a horizontal window emphasis. ALL SAINTS' GARRISON CHURCH, on a hexagonal plan, with roof composed of pentagons to the E, is part of this scheme. Much later replacement building in a variety of styles, breaking up the original unified effect.

BLANDFORD FORUM   8000

The centre of Blandford forms one of the most satisfying Georgian ensembles anywhere in England; not only was it rebuilt in a single campaign, but there is a distinct architectural flavour about the whole, the basic uniformity of design and materials being relieved just enough by spirited individual touches. The passing of the last two centuries has marred the picture really remarkably little.

Blandford grew up at an important crossing of the River Stour. Defoe called it a 'handsome well built town, but chiefly famous for making the finest bonelace in England'. Its name comes from Blaen-y-ford, meaning 'the place near the ford'. The Latin 'Forum', as an alternative to the more usual 'Chipping' to indicate a market, is found from 1540. No Roman connections may be implied from this, however. A minor fire affected the town in 1713, but much more significant was the great fire of 1731, which consumed almost the whole of the town's centre. A survey of the town was carried out by *William* and *John Bastard*, who were also the chief sufferers from the fire, losing their extensive joinery workshops. The rebuilding provided them with an opportunity to expand their joinery trade, with all of the more important new buildings having interiors designed by them. As clients for the reconstruction of their own property, as churchwardens and as bailiffs to the borough council, they also exerted great influence on the whole reconstruction programme, including the selection of architects, masons and other craftsmen. There is no evidence, however, to support the notion that they acted as architects in the strict sense, at least before the mid 1740s.

Perhaps the most influential of the architects invited by the Bastards was *John James*, who may well have provided initial designs for the new church. (John Bastard later wrote that James was 'often at our house'.*) *Nathaniel Ireson* is a significant West Country master mason known to have worked in Blandford at this time, and it was probably he who was responsible for the Archer-esque flourishes on the buildings facing the church. (Ireson seems to have acted in a subsidiary capacity for Thomas Archer between 1716 and 1719.) And there is documentary

---

*Letter from John Bastard to Sir Peter Thompson dated 6 July 1752, transcribed in D. Beamish, J. Hillier and H. F. V. Johnstone, *Mansions and Merchants of Poole and Dorset* (1976).

evidence that *Francis Cartwright* (of Bryanston) worked on the church, so he may also have been responsible for other buildings in the town.

The Somerset & Dorset Railway of 1863 made little impact on the architectural character of Blandford. Expansion in the C19 and C20 has been to the E or N. The water meadows of the Stour to the S and W continue to provide a relatively undeveloped sharp boundary, with new development on this side away from the centre, around Blandford St Mary (q.v.).

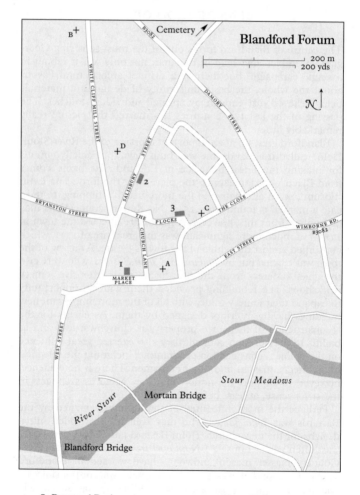

A St Peter and Paul	I Town Hall
B Our Lady of Lourdes and	2 Ryves Almshouses
St Cecilia (R.C.)	3 Post Office
C Methodist church and	
Sunday School	
D United Reformed church	

CHURCHES

St Peter and St Paul. Rebuilt in 1733–9, tower completed   86
1749. Most likely by *John James*, probably with *Nathaniel Ireson*
as executant. *Francis Cartwright* is recorded as working at the
church in 1742–3. Joinery and plasterwork by *John* and *William
Bastard*. A sum of £3,200 was raised, although this was over-
spent. It is a large church to demonstrate the self-confidence of
the smitten town. As a Georgian church it ought to have been
placed axially, but that could not be done without abandon-
ing the old site. So, although the site at the end of the wide
Market Place was ideal, the tower does not face it, nor is even
the Fire Monument (*see* p. 129) placed at the end of the middle
axis of the street.

The church is a noble and eminently interesting building.
It has a high w tower with a top cupola, finished in 1749 (the
latter cost £500). The Bastards maintained that it was their
intention to have a spire. (William Bastard's drawing of the
tower completed with a spire is undated, but is in a bundle
of drawings by him and his brother, one of which is dated
September 1749.) The tower was probably one of the *Bastards'*
earliest building works. The w portal has Doric pilasters and
the window over it has side volutes at the foot. The tower rises
just behind a big broken pediment. The side views are typically
Georgian in that they introduce a nave mid-frontispiece into
the longitudinal flow from w to e. On the n side this is plain;
on the s side it has Doric pilasters. Both sides have pediments.
The window feature above is less classical and indeed rather
Baroque. To its l. are three large arched windows, and to its r.
the same. Blank attic panels above the windows, balustraded
parapets and French quoins. Originally at the e end was only
the apse. In 1895–6 *Charles Hunt* (of Blandford) interpolated
a chancel, a skilful job rebuilding the original apse further e.
The building is mildly polychromatic, of greensand ashlar with
dressings of pale Portland and ochre Ham Hill stone (the latter
perhaps reused from the old church). On the n wall, as a cost-
saving measure, roughly dressed greensand rubble is used with
flint in place of Ham Hill stone.

The interior is exceptionally fine. Giant Portland stone
columns, unfluted and with Ionic capitals, carry a straight
entablature, a motif found in England from the 1640s (e.g. at
the demolished Broadway Chapel, Westminster, of *c.* 1640).
The transeptal axis has a wider intercolumniation. To its e
are three bays, and to its w it could be the same if the tower
did not fill the w bay. The transeptal extensions faced by the
frontispieces just mentioned were originally entirely open to
the aisles. The vaults are groin-vaults with decorative groins,
square over the 'crossing', oblong over the nave bays. In 1896
the e end was made more Cinquecento than Georgian, largely
by colouring and the coffered tunnel-vault of Hunt's chancel.
But the apse vault and the reredos aedicule are original,
although re-erected. The west gallery with its nicely

convex front and its fluted Ionic columns is of 1794. In 1819
it was extended across the w end of the aisles. Galleries along
the length of the aisles (by *John Tulloch* of Wimborne) followed
in 1837. Their removal in 1968 has been a visual blessing.

FURNISHINGS. REREDOS. Gilded Corinthian tabernacle
with mosaic added after 1896. – CHOIR STALLS by *Hunt*,
also post-1896, in a curious Jacobean-inspired style. – PULPIT.
From Wren's St Antholin in London, demolished 1874.
Nicely restrained. Columned base and stairs added *c.* 1895.
– Original BOX PEWS, reduced in height in 1880. – Richly carved
MAYOR'S CHAIR, dated 1748, almost certainly by the *Bastard*
workshop. – FONT, *c.* 1739. Elaborately decorated square baluster with octagonal bowl. Wooden COVER. – ORGAN. 1794
by *Richard Seede* of Bristol; panelling and ornamental pipes
by *G. P. England.* – ROYAL ARMS, w gallery. 1794. – STAINED
GLASS. Chancel windows by *Powell & Sons*, 1896–8. Three aisle
windows on each side, 1904 and *c.* 1920. The latter by *Jones &
Willis*, who may also have done the earlier windows. – MONU-
MENTS. Many tablets, several erected as post-fire replacements.
John Gannett †1778, topped by a half-shrouded urn. – Retro-
spective tablet to the Creech and Bastard families. Dated 1731
but erected *c.* 1770. This notes that John and William Bastard
'rebuilt this Church, the Town Hall, with several other Publick
& Private Edifices'. – William Wake †1705, an urn against a
large obelisk ground. – William Pitt †1730, a scroll-bordered
Baroque cartouche. – Richard Pulteney †1801, tablet with
urns and arms. – In the churchyard, the Bastard family tomb
with, at the head of the tomb-chest, a nicely decorated obelisk,
dated 1769.

OUR LADY OF LOURDES AND ST CECILIA (R.C.), White Cliff
Mill Street. 1934. Red brick with Gothic stone dressings.

WESLEYAN METHODIST CHURCH and SUNDAY SCHOOL, The
Close. At the r. end, Gothic brick chapel of 1874 with its short
tower. To its l. a church hall of 1892, and beyond, further l.,
schoolrooms of 1905, both in roughly matching styles.

UNITED REFORMED CHURCH (formerly Congregational),
Salisbury Street. Dated 1867. By *W. J. Stent* of Warminster.
Pale brick with red brick and stone dressings. Franco-Italian,
with a wheel window over the entrance. To its l. the JOHN
ANGELL JAMES MEMORIAL BUILDINGS of 1904, by *J. T.
Thomas* of *Aldridge & Thomas* of Bournemouth. Also pale
brick. Arts and Crafts-influenced.

CEMETERY. Salisbury Road. Laid out in 1856 by *J.B. Green*
of Blandford. Two near-identical E.E.-style CHAPELS of that
date at its centre.

PERAMBULATIONS

1. The Market Place and Salisbury Street

Beginning at the w end of the church one can see the full length
of the MARKET PLACE, and appreciate that the post-fire

rebuilding made no change in the street pattern, except for somewhat widening the Market Place. Here too is the FIRE MONUMENT, erected (and doubtless designed) by *John Bastard* in 1760 (see the inscription on the back: 'In grateful Acknowledgment of the DIVINE MERCY, that has since raised this Town, like the PHAENIX from it's Ashes, to it's present beautiful and flourishing State'). Crisply detailed tabernacle of Portland stone, with Doric columns carrying an entablature and triangular pediment. Its practical purpose was as a head for a water supply, should fire-hoses be needed in the town in future.

The N and S sides of the Market Place establish the full range of the post-fire style. In the centre of the former, the TOWN HALL, a suitably municipal three-bay façade, with an overall triangular pediment and pedimented first-floor windows with enriched pulvinated friezes, the central one incorporating the date 1734. Ground floor open as an arcade on piers. Designed by *Sir James Thornhill*, despite the inscription 'BASTARD ARCHITECT' in the pediment over the central window.* In its Palladianism the design has much in common with his Dorset house (Thornhill House, q.v.) of *c.* 1720.

The rest of the Market Place was redeveloped throughout with three-storey façades, but not altogether uniformly. In general façades are four or five bays wide, the walls faced with vitrified bricks laid all as headers, the dressings of rich crimson brick, especially rubbed window heads, and in the centre of each window head a white keystone. On the N side no further comment is needed, except to notice the Neo-Georgian HSBC BANK of *c.* 1920 (possibly by *Whinney, Son & Austen Hall*) beside the Town Hall, and to add that, although many shop-fronts have been modernized, some quite tastefully, several C19 and early C20 fronts survive and are worthy of study in themselves.

The S side is distinguished by three more grandiloquent façades. No. 75 East Street/No. 26 Market Place, and the former RED LION INN, at the E end, are two versions of the same design, stylistically attributable to *Nathaniel Ireson*, who appears to have been heavily involved at Blandford after the fire. Central carriage entrance with giant pilasters framing the central bay of each, crowned by a small open pediment with a round-headed window pushing up into it. Timber modillion cornices to both. Hereafter the details between the two differ. The pilasters of Nos. 75/26 have Corinthian capitals (but with unorthodox volutes), the windows are heavily rusticated on the first floor and given keyed and eared architraves and shaped aprons on the second, while the façade is framed with stone quoining. On the Red Lion Inn the capitals have

*A drawing of an earlier version of the design is in Sir John Soane's Museum. The Borough Chamberlain's accounts indicate payments to the *Bastards* for internal fitting out and secondary work only. There is no evidence that they were builders at this time, despite their later claims.

86

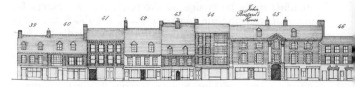

Blandford Forum, south side of Market Place and East Street.
Elevation drawing, 1966

more pronounced incurving volutes, a form taken from Rossi's engraving of a Borromini capital. Otherwise a less demonstrative building, with plain brick detailing to the windows. Nos. 75/26 was built as a trio of houses, in the l. one of which John Bastard himself lived. A lease dated August 1732 (granted to John and William Bastard) indicates that it was swiftly built following the fire. The first-floor room at the back is very completely decorated and a showpiece, typical of the work of *Bastard*. A carved pedimented doorcase, a frieze carved with masks and drapery, and scrollwork firmly controlled within panels, i.e. decidedly pre-Rococo. The chimneypiece with an open pediment on scroll-topped pilasters is flanked by two doorcases (one false), formerly with a bust set in the rectangular niche over each. The third imposing building, the OLD GREYHOUND INN (now Greyhound House) of *c.* 1735, at the far w end, takes façade decoration to Bavarian extremes. Built for the Bastard brothers, who owned it at the time of the fire. Seven bays, the centre four with Corinthian pilasters through two storeys, carrying a pediment. All the window frames very much enriched, the top ones with elaborately shaped aprons too. The rear is entirely vernacular in character, its long wing (perhaps kitchens or the tap room) part of the *c.* 1735 rebuilding. Two doors to the l., the intrusion of Ham Hill stone is LLOYDS BANK of *c.* 1880, possibly by *C. C. Creeke* of Bournemouth (built for the Wilts. & Dorset Bank).

WEST STREET continues the w side of Market Square with more post-fire façades on both sides. The vista is very successfully closed by the Neo-Georgian CROWN HOTEL, of 1937–8 by *L. Magnus Austin*, built as a facsimile of the previous building, intending to deceive and succeeding, except at close inspection. (Set of contemporary MURALS by *Osbert Lancaster* in the former assembly room, now covered up.) Round the corner the town abruptly stops, with water meadows and the river, and the wooded cliff of Bryanston beyond (q.v.). Also, on the l., sadly but predictably, a car park and the rear of a supermarket.

SALISBURY STREET, which runs from the NW corner of the Market Place, was rebuilt in a more modest way, and is much altered. However, at the corner with Market Square on the r. late C18 shopfronts survive at No. 9. Just beyond, two good late C19 shopfronts with classical detailing. At the junction where WHITE CLIFF MILL STREET forks away to the l.,

the multi-gabled, tile-hung former CORNER TEMPERANCE HOTEL, Queen Anne of *c.* 1895, closes the view. Up White Cliff Mill Street, opposite the United Reformed church (p. 128), on the l., EAGLE HOUSE, a fine building of the 1730s, standing free. Five-bay E front, blue brick and red dressings. Plain pilasters divide the façade 2:1:2, the central pair topped by an open pediment. Beyond, on the same side, Nos. 21–25, three sharply detailed suburban villas in fine brickwork, of *c.* 1830. No. 23 has Gothick-shafted porch columns.

Returning and continuing up SALISBURY STREET, first on the r. No. 38, a typical post-fire house (now a shop), notable as the birthplace of Alfred Stevens (1817–75), 'Sculptor, Painter, Architect'. Near the brow of the hill, i.e. beyond reach of the fire, the one-storey RYVES ALMSHOUSES, or 'Gerontocomium' as the inscription on the building has it. 1682. Brick. U-plan open towards the road. Central gablet with a shield of arms and flamboyant mantling over it. Prominent panelled chimneystacks. Also on the r. Nos. 76–88, a group of late C18 houses, some singles, others in pairs. Brick or stucco. Opposite and just beyond these are suburban houses. First DALE HOUSE (No. 79). Two red brick houses with stone dressings and coved eaves of a pre-fire type. That at the rear has a re-cut date of 1684 on a pedimented doorcase on its S front. It was reportedly moved here in 1930 from the E front of the slightly later adjoining house. This faces the street and has windows 2:1:2, with a steep-pedimented central projection. The S bay windows are later C18 and early C19. LANGHAM HOUSE (No. 81) is three-storeyed, of three wide bays, perhaps as late as *c.* 1780. Red brick. Wooden canted window bays l. and r. and a doorcase with fluted Composite pilasters. Beyond the crossroads the former BADGER, a red brick pub by *Crickmay & Son*, opened in 1899, and a nice example of the neatly witty picturesqueness of the turn of the century.

2. *Church Lane, The Plocks, The Close and East Street*

From the Market Place, a second rewarding sally begins up CHURCH LANE, from the W end of the church. First, on the r. OLD BANK HOUSE, a plain five-bay house, post-1731 but with vestiges of the pre-fire house in the lower parts of the

W end wall. Beyond it, along CHURCH WALK to the r., the pedimented triple entrance to the (demolished) ALMSHOUSES, of greensand, rebuilt in 1736. On the l. on Church Lane an unfortunate gap with a car park and Neo-Georgian telephone exchange.

Then on the r. COUPAR HOUSE, the finest post-fire house in Blandford. Of c. 1735, in the style of *Nathaniel Ireson*, with fitting-out by the *Bastards*. It has the advantage of generous bowed forecourt walls, with panelled ashlar gatepiers and stone urns on top. Stable court to the S with rusticated brick piers. The house itself has a five-bay front, faced with bricks laid all as headers, purple brick in the centre, red at the sides. This centre bay is defined by Ionic pilasters of Portland stone carrying an entablature with a bulgy frieze, and has in the third storey a round-headed rusticated window breaking up into a triangular pediment. Channelled angle quoins. Pedimented Doric doorcase, and a window over with very fanciful side scrolls. The design then is essentially the same as No.75 East Street/No.26 Market Place but elaborated another way. Central vestibule with a staircase rising out of it. Turned balusters with under-turning handrail scrolls of the distinctive Bastard type; carved tread-ends. Restrained pre-Rococo plaster ceiling above it. Ground-floor rooms l. and r. with original panelling and pedimented overmantels. Similar first-floor rooms, one retaining the *Bastard* chimneypiece.

Opposite, at the top, LIME TREE HOUSE (Blandford Fashion Museum), a modest five-bay, two-storey front, purple brick with red dressings including vertical chains of brick between the windows. The blue plaque on the side wall dates it 1760. The vista up the street is closed by the symmetrical front of OUTHAYS HOUSE, 'new-built' in 1759 (but its wide sashes look early C19).

Now r. along THE PLOCKS. On the l. a Neo-Georgian POST OFFICE of 1935, by *David Dyke* of the *Office of Works*. On the opposite side of the triangular space, the COUNTY BRANCH LIBRARY, Blandford's only attempt at a Modern style close to the Georgian centre. For its date it is sympathetic to its surroundings. By *J.R. Hurst*, County Architect, c. 1963.

Going further E, the street becomes THE CLOSE. Beyond the Methodist church (p. 128) one soon comes to THE OLD HOUSE on the r., a highly remarkable survivor of the fire, and a *tour de force* of cut and moulded brickwork. It was probably built c. 1650–60 for Dr Joachim Frederick Sagittary, a German. However, the architecture suggests links with the Home Counties, where such games with brickwork were freely indulged in the mid C17. The front is of four bays, the three l. bays symmetrical about a boldly projecting porch. The whole surface here is rusticated. Round-headed entrance, with two rows of radiating voussoirs; where the two systems leave odd spaces, little hearts and mouchette wheels in cut bricks are popped in. Also a blank panel flanked by gouty balusters. Side windows of three lights, mullioned and transomed. The r. bay is plain, with small two-light windows, and houses the kitchen, but must be an afterthought. Yet the second thoughts came quickly, for the huge hipped roof, on far-projecting timber brackets, is clearly unaltered and includes everything. The crowning glory is the pair of short polygonal chimneystacks, set on square bases, and ringed by colonnettes, each bearing a piece of entablature. All this is brick too. (The wide oak staircase went to Wilsford Manor, Wilsford-cum-Lake, Wilts. in 1904–6.)

Back down to the church and then l. into EAST STREET, where C18 houses catch the eye. This part of the town was unaffected by the fire of 1731, having suffered from an earlier one, in 1713. On the l. the most complete front is that of LYSTON HOUSE, c. 1730. Good contemporary front room, perhaps by the *Bastards*, with a Palladian chimneypiece, panelling and ceiling plasterwork. The principal house to deserve comment is EASTWAY HOUSE, c. 1730, near the far end on the r. The five-bay brick façade, with its shaped top parapet, going up by a curve, a step and a pedimental gable, with two types of urn upon it, has a flavour not quite like the rest of Blandford's architecture. The house is set back a pace or two behind railings, with urns to match those on the parapet. Back dining room of c. 1750 with a spectacular Rococo chimneypiece, with   90 a curvaceous fireplace opening, doubly curvaceous plaster lintel and a completely wild plaster overmantel, perhaps by *Francis Cartwright*. The Rococo also continues in the ceiling plasterwork and on the opposite wall to the fireplace around an original buffet niche with marble shelf and bowl. The niche is embellished with waterfowl and plants in relief and a vine trail over. The room was probably made for John Ayliffe, a land agent who was hanged at Tyburn for deception and forgery in 1759. At the end of the long garden, a small GAZEBO of c. 1755.

OUTLYING BUILDINGS

St LEONARD'S CHAPEL, ¼ m. E at the end of the town, behind St Leonard's Farmhouse, Wimborne Road. Perp. Probably built as an infirmary. Flint walls with thin bands of stone. Three-light E window with panel tracery, traceried N window and a S doorway with two-centred head and sunk wave moulding. Originally the side walls were symmetrical in design.

BLANDFORD BRIDGE, West Street (but S of the town centre). A handsome stone bridge over the Stour, mainly of two dates, 1783 and 1812. The surveyors were *William Moulton* and *William Bushrod* respectively.

MORTAIN BRIDGE, E of the above. 1996–2000 by *Mike Coker* of *North Dorset District Council*. A steel-framed suspension footbridge.

HALL & WOODHOUSE BREWERY, 250 yds SE of Blandford Bridge. Substantially of 1899–1900 by *Arthur Kinder & Son*. Two large red brick blocks with an office building in front. The latter in a vaguely French style, with an angled corner turret topped by a tall pavilion roof. Also several more recent buildings.

At the road junction beyond the bridge (in Blandford St Mary parish, q.v.) an informal group of C18 COTTAGE ROWS, forming an L. They stand on one side of the roads to Dorchester and Poole, facing the grand entrance to Bryanston (q.v.).

BLANDFORD ST MARY

A village in two parts: a scattered settlement grouped around the church, rectory and manor house and a suburb next to Blandford Bridge (*see* Blandford Forum, above).

ST MARY. Unbuttressed four-stage W tower of *c.* 1350, partly faced in bands of dark heathstone and flint. C15 Perp chancel of flint and greensand chequer. Perp nave. Chequerwork also to the S aisle of 1837, but its windows are of the same date as the N aisle and transept by *T.H. Wyatt*, 1863–4. S arcade of 1919 by *C.E. Ponting*, replacing two iron pillars of 1837. – FURNISHINGS largely by *Wyatt*, 1863, except the panelling on the E wall of the chancel, added in 1931. – TILES by *Minton* on the sanctuary step. – STAINED GLASS. E window by *Lavers, Barraud & Westlake*, 1893; chancel S window by the same, †1884. S aisle E window by *Ward & Hughes*, 1887. S window W of the doorway also *Lavers, Barraud & Westlake*, 1901. Two windows at the N aisle W end by *Heaton, Butler & Bayne*, 1863, both losing their paint. – MONUMENTS. Rev. John Pitt †1672 (but dated 1712). Slightly bowed, with winged skull in apron below gadrooned base. – Francis Cartwright †1758, the builder-architect. Charming tablet with still-life of T-square, dividers and a half-rolled-up design of an elevation, representing the N front of Came House, Winterborne Came.

CLERKENWELL HOUSE (the former manor farm) goes visually with the church. Early C18, the walls broadly banded in red brick and flint. The same livery for the farm's BARN (now a dwelling) and the wall along the road.

THE OLD RECTORY, 100 yds N. Simple five-bay Early Georgian front. Red brick laid all as headers; white keystones and brick aprons to all the windows: such details connect it with the post-fire architecture of Blandford. So the date 1732 on the staircase is just what one expects. Turned balusters. Under-(not outward-)curling scroll to the handrail, an indication of joinery by the *Bastards*. Extension of 1870 to the NW in a different brick bond, lower eaves height and with a scatter of more vertically proportioned sashes. Also of this date two large canted bays at the rear.

THE MANOR HOUSE, ¼ m. N. Two ranges at right angles, each with an unaltered façade showing neatly the break-up of medieval building traditions. The SW range is of *c.* 1630, probably for Francis Chettle. Of pale pink brick, laid with three rows of stretchers to one of headers, an odd bond (but cf. Bloxworth House of 1608 and Anderson Manor of 1622 for something similar). Big non-projecting quoins of Portland Purbeck stone. Symmetrical front, two-storeyed with three mullioned windows at each level, of four, then two, then four lights. Hollow-chamfered mullions, hoodmoulds, i.e. the early C17 standard. Central doorway now converted to a window. In the SE end wall an upper four-light window and a broad late C17 doorway, classically moulded. A wing of c. 1700 for another Chettle (replacing an older wing in the same position) continues to the SE, r., and here the brick is the typical russet red, the bonding normal English, the dressing a local ochre stone, the windows mostly of four lights, with hollow-chamfered mullions, but instead of hoods a band of bricks laid as voussoirs, projecting in three places and rendered to look like key blocks. Coved eaves. The greater regularity and resource of the brickwork are the telling things. Pedimented timber Doric porch. Mid-C18 addition in the rear angle, including a fine oak staircase of this date with vase and Tuscan-column balusters. Wreathed handrail termination. Here fine mid-C18 plasterwork, including the landing soffit. Similar plasterwork in the two main rooms. Wreathed roundels with busts in the corners of the drawing room ceiling.

LITTLETON HOUSE, ⅓ m. SE. Hidden by a high brick wall on the Poole Road. Brick. Five-bay centre of c. 1735. Porch with Ionic columns. Further two bays added at each end, c. 1780.

HALL & WOODHOUSE BREWERY. See Blandford Forum, p. 133.

SAXON or EARLY MEDIEVAL VILLAGE, 2 m. W of Littleton. Rectangular platforms in some of the fifteen closes, first mentioned in 1086.

BLOXWORTH

8090

A village and two hamlets each with a scattering of cob and thatch cottages, many recently restored after a period of neglect in the 1960s and 70s. Bloxworth village itself is most affected by new development.

ST ANDREW. Much successive rebuilding. The earliest feature is the re-set C12 S doorway. Moulded imposts with nailhead ornament. Two-stage Perp W tower (of brown heathstone) and some nave structure, C14. Nave largely reconstructed and ashlar-faced on the S, c. 1680, the same date as the Savage Pew, the former N chapel. The result is an assortment of nave windows, including the odd S one of three stepped arched lights and two nave N windows of two arched lights. The stuccoed N chapel has three keyed oval windows, and other openings with classical architraves. In contrast the chancel is Gothic Revival of 1870 by *George Evans*. Here flint walls with scattered ashlar and heathstone blocks. Two filled image niches on the E wall. Wide nave with plastered wagon roof. Tower arch with a continuous chamfered order. – Rich FURNISHINGS to Evans's chancel. Here also carved corbels, a REREDOS and sanctuary floor, both with TILEWORK by *Maw & Co*. The PULPIT is also *Evans*. – FONT. C13, of Purbeck marble. Circular bowl, moulded with just one fleur-de-lys. – PAINTINGS. Over the tower arch late C16 text in decorative framing, largely faded. Several heraldic paintings in the N chapel, Savage family, *c.* 1680. – STAINED GLASS. E window and one chancel S by *Heaton, Butler & Bayne*, 1870. They probably also did the tower window, †1875. Two more chancel windows, one perhaps by *Ward & Hughes*, †1861, the other by *Clayton & Bell*, †1881. Nave S window also by *Clayton & Bell*, †1880. – MONUMENT. Cartouche to Sir John Trenchard †1695. Attributed to James Hardy (GF) – Also in the N chapel many tablets to members of the Trenchard, Pickard, Pickard-Cambridge and Lane families, successive owners of Bloxworth House.

BLOXWORTH HOUSE, ¼ m. N. An early brick house, dated 1608 in the topmost room in the porch. Built for William Savage. It shares with Anderson Manor (q.v.) the unusual bond of two rows of stretchers to one of headers. However, compared with Anderson the symmetrical gabled frontage is conservative – a typical E façade, with a central three-storey gabled porch and gabled wings. Originally one small stair projection, spoiling the symmetry, in the l. re-entrant angle. This is now balanced by a similar projection in the r. angle, added *c.* 2000 for Martin Lane Fox. Gables, each topped by a square chimneystack, a typical arrangement in Dorset (cf. Hanford House, etc.), but given no special value. No quoins. Stone windows, of three and four lights, mullioned, with hoodmoulds. Splendid expanses of clay-tiled roofs with large Purbeck slabs at the eaves. The C18 infilling of the recesses of the N front was removed *c.* 2000, making the most of what the building has to show. Early C19 two-storey bay window on the r. gable, its parapet topped with ball finials (restored). W addition (also with a two-storey bay) shortly after 1848. The S elevation has gable roofs brought through from the front but is otherwise undemonstrative.

The OUTBUILDINGS are more strongly characterized than the house itself. The STABLES to the E, dated 1649 and 1669, are remarkable for conscious gothicisms. What else does one make of the fact that the doorways have flattened four-centred heads, the windows hoodmoulds and the brick walls a prominent diaper?

The BREWHOUSE, just S of the house, is undated but must be later C17. It is one of a group of Dorset buildings which exploit the bold effects possible in cut and moulded brick. Rusticated window heads and round-headed door surround. Quoins even in length but made of one whole block and two

half-blocks alternately. All this is of brick and the whole building makes a splendidly strong effect.

Former RECTORY (now BLOXWORTH LODGE), ¼ m. SE. Of
1818 for the Rev. George Pickard-Cambridge. Square block.
Stuccoed. Windows set chequerboard-style on the S front.
Gabled N addition of 1845.

WOOLSBARROW CAMP, 1½ m. SE. A single bank with inner
ditch encloses 2¼ acres, with a simple gap entrance at the SE,
surrounding a flat-topped, bag-shaped gravel knoll, rising 20 ft
(6 metres) above a low spur. Undated.

BOTHENHAMPTON

4090

An outlying hamlet to the SE of Bridport, now swamped by
suburban development.

HOLY TRINITY (Churches Conservation Trust), ¼ m. E of the
new church. The nave has disappeared, except for a little of
its NW angle. So the large single-chamfered W arch inside the
church is the arch of the C14 chancel. Re-set C15 W doorway.
The chancel windows are straight-headed Dec. C15 S tower.
Two stages without buttresses, but with an embattled parapet
with corner gargoyles. C15 E window, blocked by the REREDOS.
First half of the C18. Ionic pilasters with a pediment open
over the centre part. Matching panelling on either side, swept
down to the COMMUNION RAIL, also C18, with turned balusters. – FONT. Probably C13. Plain circular bowl with splayed
underside. Late C19 stem.

HOLY TRINITY (new church). By *E. S. Prior*, 1887–9, built by
Thomas Patten of Bridport. Externally nothing special. All the
more impressive is the interior. The outside is just nave, chancel
and S porch, rock-faced, with lancet windows. However, there
are outside clues that there is more to this church. First, the
buttresses are over-wide with gables. Second, the bellcote over
the nave E gable has an interesting treatment, its gabled roof
in line with the church, a pair of small lancets with trefoil
above E and W, and the corbelling so that it overhangs the
chancel roof without touching it. The S porch has sides with
trefoil windows in very deep inner reveals, also an overture
to the interior. Here Prior did already what he was going
to do over fifteen years later at Roker in County Durham,
namely to articulate the nave by three sweeping single-chamfered transverse arches. The idea probably came from the great
hall of Norman Shaw's house at Adcote, Shropshire, 1875–81.
The chancel has the same motif, but less powerfully handled,
with steep arched braces. More strength from the chancel
windows. These, including the SEDILIA, are in excessively deep
reveals, and above, just below the springing of the roof and on
each side of the chancel, six corbels carry blank arches with

108

the same deep reveals. Rere-arches and colonnettes to the E triplet window. The church ought to be known much more widely. – ALTAR. Designed by *Prior* (made by *Lethaby* and *Augustus Mason*), shown in the Arts and Crafts Exhibition of 1889. Arcaded, below a frontal of gesso. – Simple arrow-head and chevron TILEWORK in the sanctuary. – CHANCEL SCREEN. 1910. Of wrought iron by Bridport craftsmen. A bit delicate against the power of Prior's masonry. – PULPIT. 1904, made by *E.H. Gilbert* of Bridport. Linenfold panels on a taper-ing stone base, cantilevered out from the l. jamb of the chancel arch. Entered through a forty-five-degree trefoil-headed mural doorway. – FONT. By *Prior*. A circular marble bowl on a cluster of nine polished granite colonnettes. – STAINED GLASS. E window by *Christopher Whall* (with *Britten & Gilson*), 1896. It was commissioned by Prior and made from his thick, hand-made glass. Chancel N window by *A.L. Moore*, 1908. Two W lancets by *Jones & Willis*, 1923. Nave N window by *W.G. Rich*, †1900.

LYCHGATE, *c.* 1910. Timber-framed with big curving side-braces.

WYCH FARM, ⅝ m. SSW of the old church. The front to the road has a complete array of mullioned windows and the surpris-ingly late date 1705 on the doorway.

BOURTON

Bourton is at the N tip of Dorset, one mile NW to Somerset, one mile NE to Wiltshire. An early industrial area, with flax mills to the N of SANDWAY, the loose hamlet to the E, and linen weaving in the stone cottages.

ST GEORGE. A complicated evolution. First a new church of 1810–12. An enlargement in 1837–8, adding the W tower, S transept and porch, was by *R. G. Festing* of Stourton. Much was retained in the major remodelling by *Ewan Christian*, 1876–7, e.g. the S transept and much of the nave walling including the buttresses. The tower (much wider N–S than E–W) was given its fine upper stage in Dec style by *C.E. Ponting*, 1902–4. It is two bays wide at bell-stage level facing E and W, a single bay facing N and S. With its distinctive pinnacled silhouette and higher stair-turret, it is the best feature of the church. Wide and high buttressed nave with five tall Perp-style windows on the N side, the S interrupted by the refenestrated, low-pitched transept of 1838. Spacious interior with a broad chancel arch and equally broad polygonal apse. – FONT. Perp style, by *Christian*. – STAINED GLASS. In the apse seven single lights of *c.* 1879. Two are by *Burlison & Grylls*, the others by *Clayton & Bell*. W window by *Clayton & Bell*, *c.* 1886. Art Nouveau-influenced S window (†1910) by *Baron Arild Rosenkrantz* (PC), made by *Lowndes & Drury*.

CHAFFEYMOOR HOUSE, ½ m. w, has two-light mullioned
windows towards the N, and a datestone of 1700 at the back;
so here the medieval tradition goes on remarkably late. Several
early C19 additions including the bay windows on the s front.

CHAFFEYMOOR GRANGE, 50 yds N of Chaffeymoor House, is
a C17 farmhouse with a gabled, mullioned-windowed s front
of c. 1910.

BULLPITS, ¾ m. NE. A former cloth mill of c. 1720, adapted to
a house c. 1820. Symmetrical stucco front. Its central Italianate
porch and the matching extension on the E side are mid-C19.

BOVERIDGE

Cranborne

_0010_

ST ALDHELM (now a dwelling). 1838, in an odd, very idiosyncratic, debased Georgian, probably by the _2nd Marquess of
Salisbury_, who commissioned it. Flint and brick bands; bold
and vigorous projecting, alternating quoins; arched windows.
Its finest feature is the NW tower. Slender, rising through an
Italianate stage to an open arcaded canopy of four columns
and an ogee dome. Converted to a dwelling in the 1980s,
retaining the open space of nave and chancel and the archway
to the former family pew (now the kitchen). Two CARTOU-
CHES, one dated 1708, the other, matching, 1838.

BOVERIDGE HOUSE, ½ m. w. Originally a five-bay villa of
c. 1820 by _William Evans_ of Wimborne for Henry Brouncker,
on the site of a Tudor mansion. Light brick with ashlar dressings. An additional bay added at each end (providing new
E and W fronts), probably in 1887, as the tetrastyle Doric W
portico, retained from the villa and re-erected, is thus inscribed.
Further additions after 1919 by _E. Guy Dawber_, including a
large drawing room on the E end and an arcaded garden loggia
attached to the SW corner. Formal terraced GARDENS, also
after 1919, by _Thomas Mawson_, perhaps to planting plans by
Gertrude Jekyll.

BRADFORD ABBAS

_5010_

A village of scattered cottages, a few villas and a major church.
It seems to have grown to the N in the C17, but was split in two
by the Salisbury & Yeovil Railway in 1860. Much later housing
added to the N in the 1960s.

ST MARY. A C15 church with a splendid late C15 four-stage W
tower. It has polygonal clasping buttresses, diminishing in girth
at each stage (cf. Wimborne Minister W tower) and a higher
octagonal NE stair-turret. Battlemented parapets with a single

crocketed pinnacle at each corner, but a whole set of smaller pinnacles creating a coronet top to the stair-turret. The w face has a shallow porch within the thickness of the wall. It has a cusped arch and an ogee gable (probably once topped by a figure) and is flanked by small polygonal buttresses, topped with what look like pedestal bases for statues. To the l. and r. of the doorway, paired image niches with canopies, while above these, either side of the four-light w window, two pairs of larger single-image niches, one pair above the other. Above these a row of three niches, two of them still with their figures, and each flanked by smaller niches. In all there would have been twenty sculpted figures on this tower face, a very rich effect. Pairs of two-light bell-openings with a transom and Somerset tracery. Panelled arch to the nave.

The aisles have battlements and three-light Perp windows, except for the middle one on the N side above a blocked doorway. This is Dec with squashed reticulated tracery in its head, presumably re-set. The Perp tracery E of that window differs from that of the two to the w; these have ogee-headed lights. This is suggestive of a prolonged building campaign running from, say, 1450 to around 1500. On the S side there are also a short aisle and a chapel to the E (formerly a vestry). At its SE corner an octagonal stair-turret. The corresponding N chapel was built as an organ chamber in 1911–14, by *C.B. Benson* of Yeovil. The aisle arcades have five bays N, two bays S. The elements are standard. To the S chapel a wide and very deep panelled arch opens, intended no doubt for a monument. Its w respond has a passage at an angle, doubling as a squint. The archway to the N chapel is a copy (but without the passage). The chancel has C14 and C15 Perp fenestration, but is modified from an earlier structure, perhaps as early as the C12. Its arch is a restoration of 1858 by *William Newbury* (a carpenter of Sherborne), replacing a blank wall that had oddly been inserted above the stone screen (*see* below). In the S wall a pretty priest's doorway with a small, steeply gabled porch. On its front face another canopied image niche. Stone ceiling inside with three roundels. Good Perp roofs of nave, tower, N aisle and S aisle. In the latter a corbel angel carries a shield with the initials of the Abbot of Sherborne who ruled from 1459 to 1475. Three angel corbels resited in the S chapel. Here the E roof bay retains C15 painted decoration. In 1865 and 1890 the walls were regrettably stripped of their plaster, and *c.* 1960 two good early C18 monuments were taken from the chancel.

FURNISHINGS. SCREEN. A C15 stone screen of one-light divisions, with solid wall below instead of a dado. Cinquefoiled lights, pierced above, with a multi-foiled central archway (cf. the tower w doorway). – PULPIT. Oak. Dated 1632. Much carved elaboration, with one tier of blank arches. Radiating gadrooning above the top tier of panels. – FONT. An elaborate C15 piece, somewhat re-tooled. Octagonal, with four square pillars in front of the diagonals (cf. Winterborne Whitechurch). Statuettes (of St John the Baptist and three bishops or abbots) in angled niches at the top of each pillar; quatrefoils against the bowl. Moulded cornice with running foliage. – BENCHES. A fine set with ends of c. 1500 in a variety of designs. Some incorporate intricate foliage, others animals or traceried compositions. Two ends with a griffin and a St Paul. A few removed from redundant benches and resited on the E side of the chancel screen. Two especially elaborate and shaped ends (with poppyheads) reused to provide clergy seats w of the screen. – STAINED GLASS. In the s chapel several tracery fragments. Some also in a chancel s window, C15. E window by *O'Connor*, 1867. Also some fragments of C15 glass in the tracery lights above. s aisle window by *Powell & Sons*, 1896. w window by *Clayton & Bell*, 1890. – In the churchyard the remains of a late C15 CROSS. High base with quatrefoils. Against the shaft formerly statuettes under canopies, all much eroded.

WAR MEMORIAL, Church Street, just E. 1917 by *C.B. Benson*. An open-fronted gabled shelter. Dry-stone walling forming an alcove.

VICARAGE, Church Street, ⅛ m. E. Of c. 1828. Weak Tudor Revival. Low-pitched gables. Refronted 1870 by *Charles Trask* of Norton. Two octagonal battlemented turrets.

COOMBE (originally The Villa), ½ m. N. Of c. 1860. Tudor Revival. Stone with tall decorative brick stacks.

TOLL HOUSE, Yeovil Road, 1⅓ m. NW. Dated 1854. Tudor Revival. Turret set on the diagonal with a pyramidal roof. Decorative ironwork casements.

WYKE, 1 m. E. A stately mid-C17 stone manor house for Eliab Harvey, surrounded by a moat. There is a date 1650 on the N doorway. It is instructive to see that at that date strict symmetry was still not considered necessary. Two-storey fronts, with double gables at the ends. That means rooms set two deep, a C17 advance in planning. N front of seven bays, the two- and three-light windows not quite regularly spaced. s front as wide, but six bays only and more regular, though the staircase window (in line with the N doorway) breaks the pattern, set squarely between the storeys. Windows of roughly square form, but without transoms. Hollow-chamfered mullions. Continuous string courses, an important aid to organizing the façades. Chimneystacks set on the gable-ends in the Dorset way. – BARNS, to the NNW. Two in one, both C16. The s longer, of thirteen bays with two gabled porches on the E side. The N one with only one porch and only seven bays. Curved principals to the collar-truss roof, with curved wind-bracing. The whole buttressed range is an impressive sight.

BRADFORD PEVERELL

6090

ST MARY. 1849–50 by *Decimus Burton* for H.N. Middleton (cost £1,850). A big church for such a small village (replacing

Bradford Peverell, St Mary.
Photolithograph after J. H. le Keux, 1863

a more humble medieval predecessor). W steeple, the spire
with broaches and two tiers of lucarnes. Nave and chancel.
Archaeological Dec, with hints of Commissioners' Gothic.
Spacious aisleless nave. Wide chancel arch with a big Caen
stone PULPIT alongside. Mural entry to the latter via the
vestry. Above (over the chancel arch) lettering in scrolls
by *J. Pouncy* of Dorchester. – Most of the FURNISHINGS
designed by *Burton* remain *in situ*. – Encaustic TILES in
the chancel. – ROYAL ARMS of Queen Victoria. Woodcarv-
ing. – STAINED GLASS. In the chancel N window four re-set
C15 panels, including a small Coronation of the Virgin and a

small Annunciation. E window designed by *N.J. Cottingham*, *c.* 1850, said to incorporate some late medieval glass from New College, Oxford. It was probably made by *C.A. Gibbs*. Two chancel S windows probably also by *Cottingham*, *c.* 1850. One of the nave N windows has some armorial glass relating to William of Wykeham (said to come from New College) re-set, probably by *Cottingham* and *Gibbs* also. Next in date are three memorial windows, nave S, all *c.* 1860 and almost certainly by *Hardman*. That to Hastings Nathaniel Middleton (†1824) and his wife Emilia (†1859) has a fine brass sill plate, shaped to fit, again most likely by *Hardman*. Nave N window by *Lavers, Barraud & Westlake*, †1885. Finally a nave S window probably by *Percy Bacon Bros*, †1890.

BRADFORD PEVERELL HOUSE, 1 m. SW. Design of 1850–1 by *Decimus Burton*, executed by his nephew, *H.M. Burton*, 1863–7, for H.N. Middleton. Stuccoed, with a number of gables and bays. Built around a courtyard.

BARROW GROUP, Seven Barrow Plantation, Penn Hill, ¾ m. SW. A small bank barrow, with a round barrow at the S end and one to the N, to which are set two short alignments of round barrows to the SW. A short long barrow to the S, other round barrows distributed N and SW. No excavation records.

BARROW GROUP, N and NE of Highfield Plantation, 1 m. SE. A linear arrangement of round barrows, running NE from a bell barrow in the woodland, along a spur to a long barrow above the River Frome; bell excavated by Cunnington (1887), long barrow (1881) and four others (1881–7); Early Bronze Age grave goods included a food vessel, beakers and a Wessex dagger.

ROMAN AQUEDUCT. *See* Dorchester, p. 264.

BRADPOLE

4090

Bradpole was a small village until later C20 development engulfed the centre. However, much of the historic character (including a few thatched cottages) can be appreciated on a circuit of lanes to the E and SE of the parish church.

HOLY TRINITY. A sizable rebuilding, of 1845–6 by *Richard Cornick* of Bridport. Inelegant spire added to the NW tower, 1863. Nave and chancel and a N aisle. The bulk of the tower caused it to project beyond the aisle and the nave W front. Lancet windows, octagonal arcade piers (five bays). The fanciful junction of pier and arches shows the date. Much more competent in its Gothic is the N addition (for the organ and a vestry) by *C.E. Ponting*, 1897, treated externally as a chapel. Against the W wall inside the head of a C15 three-light window. The PAINTINGS over the chancel arch, and those either side of the E window, are of 1897 by *W.G. Rich*. – ROYAL ARMS. Metal; Hanoverian. – STAINED GLASS. Chancel windows by *Rich*,

1894. Also by him one of the nave s windows, 1897. Another by *Heaton, Butler & Bayne*, †1877. The windows towards the W end of the nave are probably all *c.* 1850. – MONUMENT. Frances Way †1823. Grecian with side scrolls and an urn. By *Gibbs* of Axminster.

OLD VICARAGE, across the road to the E. Of *c.* 1830. Tudor Revival. Sashes with hoodmoulds and marginal panes.

PYMORE MILLS, ¾ m. WNW. Late C18 self-contained mill complex built jointly by several Bridport flax merchants. Many of the mill buildings have been demolished in C20 redevelopment. At the N end of the site, two mid-C19 three-storey FLAX WAREHOUSES. Between them the long and low late C19 steam WEAVING SHEDS and ENGINE HOUSE with brick chimneystack. In the S corner the former workers' HOSTEL, C19 red brick, looking like a terrace of houses, and mid-C19 Gothic SCHOOL. To the W a long row of terraced WORKERS' COTTAGES, mid-C19, and in the centre of the site the early C19 three-storey red brick MANAGER'S HOUSE.

WOOTH MANOR, ¾ m. NW. A typical early C17 stone house, just a single range. Five- and four-light stone-mullioned windows. Ovolo mouldings. The best-preserved part is a staircase projecting at the back. Three-storeyed, with windows of five, four and three lights on the way up. The S end of the house rebuilt in brick in the late C18 after a fire. Mid-C19 red brick Gothick tower at the N end.

BRIANTSPUDDLE

There is much to delight and amuse at Briantspuddle. It is a village of dumpy white-walled cottages with thatched roofs, and intermingled with them a number of C20 cottages, all trying to keep in tune, but not all succeeding equally. Beginning at the W end, as the cottage idiom establishes itself, notice on the r. the Disneyland eaves of Nos. 15–16, one of Sir Ernest Debenham's estate cottages of the 1920s by *Halsey Ricardo* with *MacDonald Gill* (elder brother of Eric, *see* below). Ricardo had designed Debenham's London house of 1904–7 at No. 8 Addison Road, Kensington; Gill, who lived locally, was appointed in 1914 to act as executant architect. On the other side No. 27, a bungalow faced with rough-hewn Portland stone, quietly making its own individual contribution. By *R. R. Jones*, 1960. Further on the picture is spoilt by the half-hearted attempt of 1960s COUNCIL HOUSING to partake in the character of the place. In shape and size each house is right, and one accepts the purplish pantile roofs; but the slack layout in a standard cul de sac is most unhappy.

At THE RING, beyond, still on the r. by *Ricardo* and *Gill*, 1915, for Sir Ernest Debenham, there is greater sensitivity in siting a linked group. Two-storeyed with a one-storey centre, round an oval green planted with walnut trees. The rather studied symmetry and the self-conscious brick-trimmed turrets with their caps of thatch, if typical of the time, are just what is needed in the way of personal expression. The walling, surprisingly, is of concrete blocks, made of local gravel. Though cottages now, The Ring was first built as a dairy, the earliest of a series on Debenham's estate to be run on model lines that would demonstrate the greater productivity of efficient farming methods, and ultimately – and this was the point – reverse the drift of farm workers to the towns. To its rear are the main DAIRY FARM buildings, started in 1914, by *Ricardo* and *Gill*.* These include SILAGE TOWERS with pyramidal, oast-house-like roofs, and STABLES of 1917.

Opposite, CRUCK COTTAGE is long and low, of the late C15. Thatched, with cob walls much rebuilt in rubble. It incorporated four cruck trusses, of which three survive. Chimney and fireplace inserted in the hall in the late C16, when an upper floor was created. Along the lane to the W (on the N side), the VILLAGE HALL. Early C19 barn of cob and thatch, converted *c.* 1920, probably by *Ricardo* and *Gill*. Alongside it a GRANARY. Early C19. Brick walls carried on small arches. Sensitively altered to become a Post Office.

MOOR LANE HOUSE, ⅓ m. N. Of *c.* 1920, probably also by *Ricardo*. White-walled, hipped tiled roofs and a high cob wall surrounding the S garden.

BLADEN VALLEY, the hamlet ¼ m. W, is wholly Sir Ernest Debenham's creation. It has been suggested that the layout is in imitation of Nash's Blaise Hamlet, but the gentle curve of the street has more in common with Milton Abbas. The thatched idiom also lacks Nash's picturesque sense of fun, and the result is redolent of the more practical Great War period. The aim, though, was characteristically idealistic, each having a quarter-acre garden, pigsty and indoor lavatory. Building began soon after 1914, again to designs by *H.Ricardo* with *MacDonald Gill*. The COTTAGES stand either singly, in pairs or in terraces, each symmetrical in composition. Any picturesque quality comes from changes of roof level and the bringing of thatch down over porches. With the tree planting now mature, the scene is largely bucolic, seemingly (and intentionally?) unresolved by the open S end facing over meadows.

At the N end, where Bladen Valley joins the lane, the mighty WAR MEMORIAL, a major work by *Eric Gill*, 1916–18. It is modelled on such a medieval market cross as Stalbridge cross (q.v.), but is un-medieval in being of Portland stone and in eschewing period reference in the details. Low on the S face of the shaft a Virgin and Child placed under a canopy; high on the N face a draped Christ displaying the stigmata in his hands as he holds a reversed sword – unusual iconography. Round the base run Julian of Norwich's words, in every way appropriate:

119

---

* Sir Ernest Debenham bought the 3,500-acre estate from the Frampton family of Moreton in April 1914.

It is sooth that sin is cause of all this pain
But all shall be well and all shall
be well and all manner of thing shall be well.

4090

BRIDPORT

Bridport is one of the best towns in Dorset, and for a continuously sustained urban feeling perhaps the best of all. At the
junction of the T formed by the three main streets stands the
Town Hall, the focal building of the town. All three streets are
unusually broad, their broadness the result historically of Bridport's medieval prosperity, the even breadth of the streets no
doubt inhibiting the encroachment of island buildings, with the

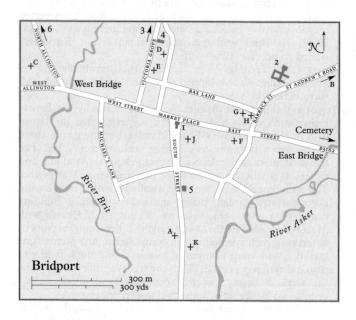

A	St Mary	I	Town Hall
B	St Andrew (former)	2	Bridport Union Workhouse
C	St Swithun		(former)
D	St Mary and St Catherine (R.C.)	3	St Catherine Primary School
E	Baptist church	4	Foresters' Hall
F	United Church	5	County Library
G	Chapel in the Garden	6	Bridport Community
H	New Meeting House		Hospital
J	Wesleyan Methodist chapel		
	(former)		
K	Friends' Meeting House		
	and almshouses		

exception of the Town Hall itself.* East and West streets slope
gently downwards towards the rivers Asker and Brit, respectively,
so that the urban vistas end in distant views of green hills. It
seems that the earliest settlement was concentrated in South
Street, around the church, although excavations have found no
trace of Anglo-Saxon activity, despite the town being on the list
of *burhs* in the Burghal Hidage of *c.* 880.

Today, South and East streets have for much of the way Georgian frontages of unusual unity. These speak of the wealth generated from Bridport's chief historic activity, the production of
rope and netting. The manufacture of such goods from flax and
hemp can be traced back to the early C13, but its chief architectural consequence is the associated mill buildings, the houses of
its proprietors and, in between, those built for the outworkers
from the industry: twine spinners or net-makers. Only from
the late C18 were mill-owners' houses built outside the town
(e.g. Downe Hall and The Hyde, Walditch, q.v.). Another consequence was a large number of Nonconformist chapels, typical
of settlements with a heavy reliance on craft activity. Bridport's
prosperity received a boost in 1857 with the opening of the Great
Western Railway branch from Maiden Newton (later extended
to West Bay, but closed in 1975).

CHURCHES

ST MARY, South Street. The church is essentially C13 E.E. and
    C15 Perp, with the E.E. confined to the transepts. These are
    all that survive of a cruciform church (with E chapels flanking
    the chancel). One would expect the crossing to participate
    in the style, but the four arches form part of the great C15
    rebuilding, providing the tower and an aisled nave of four
    bays. To judge by the fact that there was a dedication in 1362,
    work in progress in 1397 and further dedications in 1403 and
    1486, rebuilding seems to have been carried out over a long
    period.** Since much of the Perp looks quite early, it seems
    likely that it was complete by the first of the C15 dedication
    dates. E.E. the shallow transept buttresses without set-offs, the
    lancet windows and the rich responds to former E chapels, the
    arches multiform and with fillets, the capitals streaked verti-
    cally – an odd feature – and one reeded. Perp on the other
    hand the most prominent features. The high crossing tower
    has a higher NW stair-turret. Battlemented parapets with (no
    doubt restored) corner pinnacles, and angle buttresses on the
    lower two stages. A two-light bell-opening to each face. The N
    and S transept end windows are of five and six lights respec-
    tively; the arcades, their piers with four shafts and four flat
    diagonals, are all of a refined Perp. The small capitals also of

*And shambles to the N of it – gone by the early C19 – and a market house to the
S, demolished in 1947.
**The 1362 date may refer to a S chapel leading off the chancel. This appears in
early views but disappeared during the mid-C19 restoration.

Bridport, St Mary.
Engraving by B. Howlett, C18

the crossing arches with leaves or fleurons. *John Hicks* was the
architect for the two nave w bays, 1858–60, copying the detailing of the C15 work and (to judge from early C19 illustrations)
virtually rebuilding the old w front in its new, more westerly,
location. He similarly copied the Perp work in his rebuilding
of the chancel and chapels. They look fine with their three
gables right on the street. Next to the s porch, which is two-
storeyed, is a sw chapel, also C15. The upper porch room has
a charming oriel window.

FURNISHINGS. PULPIT. Caen stone, with a relief scene
of The Sermon on the Mount. Probably by *Boulton* of
Worcester, 1860. – FONT. C15. Octagonal with quatrefoil bowl
and panelled stem. – SCULPTURE. A defaced relief outside
the s transept. Angled sides with a pointed top. This may
have been a reliquary or a heart shrine. At the bottom a
shield-holding angel, C15 in style. An inscription reads: 'Formerly part of the chapel of St Andrew at the High Cross,
which was consecrated in 1262. Demolished AD 1786'. Probably erected here in 1860. – STAINED GLASS. E window by
Lavers & Barraud, *c.* 1855, re-set 1860. s chapel: E by *A.L.
Moore*, 1907; s by *E.Baillie*, dated 1851. s transept E window
by *Joseph Bell* of Bristol, 1865; N transept E by *Moore*, 1908.
Three N aisle windows: *Moore*, 1908; *Powell & Sons*, 1909;
Cox, Sons, Buckley & Co., †1884. sw chapel window possibly
by *Heaton, Butler & Bayne*, †1893. Nave s window by *Powells*,
1912. – MONUMENTS. Effigy of a cross-legged knight of Ham
Hill stone, late C13. The face has been replaced. – Many other
tablets and brasses. Of note is Samuel Bull †1777. Obelisk
slate surround with garlanded urn. – Harriett Templer †1905
by *Eric Gill*, 1907. Marble and alabaster. – In the churchyard,

obelisk to the Roberts family, 1830. With relief of the Good Samaritan.

WAR MEMORIAL, immediately N. 1920 by *Sir Giles Gilbert Scott*; sculpture by *Frances Burlison*. Tapering column with gabled top. Gothic detailing. On the E face St George and the Dragon in a canopied niche. Wing walls with inscription panels.

CHURCH HOUSE, just N. By *F. Cooper* of Bridport. Foundation stone 1925. Gothic. Built for community use but now partly converted to flats.

ST ANDREW (now an organ repair workshop), St Andrew's Road. 1860 by *Talbot Bury*. Local rubble with ochre Ham Hill stone dressings. E.E. style. Set of five lancets at the w end over the doorway. Bellcote above. Otherwise plate tracery; buttressed. Steep roof.

ST JOHN, West Bay. *See* West Bay.

ST SWITHUN, North Allington. 1826–7 by *Charles Wallis* of Dorchester. A delightful front, the best of the date in the county. White rendering, a portico of two pairs of stubby, rather French, Tuscan columns carrying a pediment, and one arched window l. and r. of the portico. Circular turret or cupola. The church is on a reverse orientation, i.e. the altar recess is at the w end of the wide rectangular room. Fanlight on w wall visible only externally, with original coloured glass. – WEST GALLERY on slender cast-iron columns. – ROYAL ARMS of Queen Victoria. – Large fixed CRUCIFIX and ALTAR by *Francis Stevens* of *Faith Craft*, 1959. The crucifix is carved, painted and gilded, the altar with bulbous baluster corners. – Original BOX PEWS, adjusted by *C.E. Ponting*, 1901.

ST MARY AND ST CATHERINE (R.C.), Victoria Grove. 1978, architect unknown. Extended towards the road, 2016, by *Grainge Architects*. Polygonal plan; low-pitched roofs. Cross at the apex. – STAINED GLASS. Re-set from the previous church of 1845–6, demolished 1977. – PRESBYTERY to the r., 1846 by *William Fry*.

BAPTIST CHURCH, Victoria Grove. 1841. Stucco. Three-bay front with a three-bay pediment. The excessive length of the windows shows that Georgian pattern-book correctness has lost the battle.

UNITED CHURCH (formerly Congregational), East Street. 1859–60 by *Poulton & Woodman*. The previous edition described its style as 'shrill Dec'. In its gabled and pinnacled N front there is an excess of emphasis on its gothicness, but the design commands respect, especially for the anchoring of the façade by a pair of porches. Polygonal s apse. Inside a gallery around three sides; hammerbeam roof. Organ recessed within a great Dec arch. Reordered in 2015.

CHAPEL IN THE GARDEN (formerly Unitarian), East Street (opposite the above). Architecturally quite a different mood. Of 1794, lying back from the road beyond a garden lined with tombstones. Painted brick. Modestly classical with its round-headed windows and Ionic columns for the semicircular porch.

The painted lettering 'UNITARIAN CHAPEL' on the platband was added in 1821. Complete interior of 1794, the galleries round three sides on Ionic columns, the pulpit against the N wall, within the communion rail.

NEW MEETING HOUSE (now the LYRIC THEATRE), Barrack Street. Mostly 1837 (incorporating a building of 1776–7). It became a Liberal Hall in 1886 (indicated by a plaque). Stone. Tall round-arched windows.

WESLEYAN METHODIST CHAPEL (now BRIDPORT ARTS CENTRE), South Street. Stucco, set back behind matching stucco houses. All of 1838 by J. Galpin of Bridport. The best of Bridport's Nonconformist chapels. Three-bay front with three-bay pediment. The middle bay has two fluted giant Ionic columns in antis. Windows l. and r. in two tiers: segmental-arched below (with lugged architraves), round-arched above. Gallery around three sides on cast-iron columns.

FRIENDS' MEETING HOUSE and ALMSHOUSES, South Street. Rubble stone. From the street only the tall windows of the meeting house give it away. The property came to the Society of Friends in 1697. The meeting house was converted from a barn, c. 1707. Tiny internal quadrangle, the N, E and W ranges of various earlier dates, given at the same time to be alms-houses. In the NE corner a stair projection entered via a simple four-centred arch.

CEMETERY, Dorchester Road, ¾ m. ENE. Opened in 1856. Two chapels and an entrance lodge by Henry Hall, who also designed the layout. The chapels Gothic; buttressed. Doorways in their gable-ends. Bellcotes. The Church of England chapel (E of the drive) has a polygonal apse; the Nonconformist big cusping on the doorway.

PUBLIC BUILDINGS

TOWN HALL, Market Place. 1785–6 by William Tyler. It cost almost £3,000.* The clock and small cupola, so prominent in one's memory of the Town Hall, were added about twenty years later. Red brick block with stone dressings, three by three bays, with a narrower projection to the S. The N front is very broad, the centre bay really three in one, pedimented and displaying the borough arms below the first-floor Venetian window. Three-bay arcades of rusticated ashlar below. The open arcade continues round three sides of the building, but in brick. Rubbed brick niches on the W side. The COUNCIL CHAMBER has a panelled dais at the W end of 1897, elaborated by Francis Newbery, 1924–7. In the spandrels of its coved recess, murals depicting Bridport industries. Also several hanging paintings by Newbery on similar historical themes.

BRIDPORT UNION WORKHOUSE (now flats), St Andrew's Road. 1836–7 by H. J. Whitling. Laid out on the recommended

*Design exhibited at the Royal Academy in 1786. The mason in charge was James Hamilton, the Weymouth-based architect.

cruciform plan with four separate courtyards (as also formerly at Dorchester). The main block faces s. This has a severe façade of Purbeck stone with a 2:1:3:1:2 rhythm. A hint of a pediment over the central three.

ST CATHERINE'S CATHOLIC PRIMARY SCHOOL, Pymore Road. Nice crisp small school of *c.* 1966–8 by *Peter Falconer & Partners.* s extension by *Grainge Architects,* 2009.

FORESTERS' HALL (now Royal British Legion Hall), Victoria Grove. 1875–6. Red brick. Gothic with bold and idiosyncratic detailing, e.g. the triangular-headed porch and windows.

COUNTY LIBRARY (formerly police station), South Street. 1861–3 by *Hicks.* Mild Italianate detailing.

BRIDPORT COMMUNITY HOSPITAL, Hospital Lane, North Allington, 1 m. NW. 1996 by *Kendall Kingscott Architects.* Yellow brick with concrete tiles. Informal grouping centred on a tower-like block. Window by *Tom Denny,* 1997.

PERAMBULATION

Starting at St Mary's church in SOUTH STREET, one may at once recognize the uniform quality of the extensive Georgian street-scape. First, though, heading some way s downhill towards the River Asker, on the r., THE CHANTRY. This is a highly remarkable and puzzling building, small, of stone and now more clearly seen after the widening of the adjacent road. Late C13 or early C14, perhaps as a municipal building.* Adapted in the late C14 as a chantry priest's house. The appearance from the street is, disregarding the sash windows, of a semi-fortified tower house. Rectangular, quite tall, with a porch projection and two-centred doorway at the front, and a chimney projection at the back. Its plan is also highly individual. At the centre a newel staircase (probably part of the mid-C14 adaptation) with a C19 staircase alongside. Facing the street two rooms quite unaligned on the two rooms of the parallel rear range. What appears on the front as a possible stair-turret proves to be nothing of the kind. The small first-floor room of the porch has an ogee-headed recess with a drain. This was most likely a priest's oratory; it is entered through a two-centred arch.

Further on, after crossing South Bridge, PALMERS BREWERY (Bridport Old Brewery), West Bay Road. Established in 1794. The ORIGINAL BUILDINGS form an L-plan block facing Skilling Hill Road. At the W end an extension of 1841 with a single undershot waterwheel of 1879 (made by the *Thomas Helyear* foundry in West Street). Facing the main road, the twin gables of two thatched BEER STORES (*c.* 1796 and 1833). Former STABLES (now offices) s of the front building, on the further side of a carriage arch. Beyond these a brick-built OFFICE of 1890. At the s end the multi-gabled WINE

* See K. A. Rodwell in *Medieval Archaeology* 34, 1990. Here it is suggested that the initial function of the building was to carry a beacon in connection with maritime navigation.

STORE by *David Oliver*, 1985. To the rear of this, facing the River Brit, a MALTINGS, dated 1857 (modified by *H. Stopes*, 1884). To the N of the main block (across Skilling Hill Road), the red brick MINERAL WATER PLANT (built as a beer store, 1865).

Returning up South Street, on the W side after St Mary's church, No. 64A is an ALMSHOUSE by *J. Galpin*, 1834–6. A curious combination of Tudor and classical detailing. Continuing further, on the E side, ELECTRIC PALACE (Cinema). Of 1926, Art Deco and a gem, behind a typical 1920s shop frontage. Small foyer with original murals by *George Biles* depicting garden scenes. More classically detailed auditorium with curved ceiling. Art Deco light fittings. Still on this side, THE CASTLE (now Bridport Museum). It has a fine early C16 street front of stone. The porch is five-sided, open below by a Tudor entrance arch, with a wave and a hollow, and above by a mullioned window of 2:4:2 arched lights. Above that there is multi-moulded corbelling to allow for a normal gable, similar to that at Winterborne Clenston Manor (q.v.). To the l. a three-light window on both levels, the lower with remains of cusping to the arched lights. To the r. the five-light hall window, below a two-lighter and a three-lighter also with cusping. All the windows have square, deeply hollow-moulded frames. Bold string course. The generosity of all the detailing is typical of the date. The main structure behind was rebuilt after a fire in 1876. Finally the stucco former Wesleyan Methodist chapel, and its attendant blocks (*see* p. 150).

So to the Town Hall (p. 150) and the choice of directions. WEST STREET requires less in the way of detailed description. Here only do late C19 and very recent replacements intrude (e.g. SUPERDRUG on the S side with its slit windows, and WAITROSE further on, with a blocky oversailing upper storey). Halfway down on the N side GRANVILLE HOUSE (the Post Office), a typical mid-C18 town house. Brick, of five bays with a handsome early C19-looking doorway with baseless Doric columns. Window above with a Gibbs surround. (Gutted in 1971 during conversion.) The previous POST OFFICE was the building next door (on the corner with Victoria Grove). This has every appearance of a later C18 town house, but is in fact of 1913 by *C. B. Smith*. Very fine brick detailing. The pair of bay windows flanking the central doorway continues the illusion. Opposite, W. FROST deserves more than a glance for its upper part, a five-bay composition of *c.* 1780, with a central Venetian window. Further on, N side, No. 33 is another fine town house of the late C18, this time in two colours of brick. At the bottom, on the N side, THE COURT (part of Court Mills). This is an imposing multi-storey stone building, extended 1838 and largely rebuilt in 1844 (datestone for the latter), a reminder of Bridport's staple rope manufacture.* The factory

---

*This was Joseph Gundry & Co., a company established in 1665. A building is shown occupying this site on the 1773 Hutchins map.

behind dates from the mid 1860s. After crossing the River Brit (on West Bridge) into the suburb of ALLINGTON, on the N side at the junction between North and West Allington, ALLINGTON VILLA, a stuccoed box of *c*. 1830, the doorway graced by recessed Greek Doric columns. Several more villas of about that date as the main road continues westward, but nothing to single out. A short detour up NORTH ALLINGTON, passing St Swithun's church on the W side (p. 149), after 150 yds reaches REFORM PLACE on the E side. A stuccoed terrace of six cottages. The paired doorways have hoods on decorative cast-iron brackets. Dated 1835 on a panel, and with the text 'Vox Populi, Vox Dei'.

EAST STREET can offer much more, and its early C19 items are of considerable character. First, almost opposite the Town Hall, comes the splendid early C19 shop façade, formerly of BEACH & CO. (currently Cancer Research UK). Everything is there, the two bowed shop windows, the two bowed windows of the shopkeeper's apartment, and the name-board all across the top, arching up to a point in the middle, and with big openwork side scrolls. It was opened as Roberts' Chemists in 1805. A C17 structure behind, the George Inn, dating from at least 1651 (when it was used by Charles II). Late C18 uniformity continues, interspersed with mid-C19 commercial buildings such as the GREYHOUND HOTEL next to the Town Hall. Stucco with its arched windows multiplying into a lively rhythm on the ground floor. On the N side, after Downes Street, a typical Neo-Wren bank building of *c*. 1920 (now HSBC), and further, S side, the Soanic pedimented front of BARCLAYS BANK, built *c*. 1855 for Edward Gill Flight (a solicitor). Yellow brick with bold stone details, such as the pilasters and first-floor balconies. In contrast the somewhat hyperactive façade of the stuccoed BULL HOTEL (raised and refronted 1877), with canted bay windows and vigorous panelling. Inside a mid-C19 ballroom with a wrought-iron balustraded orchestra balcony in a raised alcove. Then, just before the United Church (*see* p. 149), the Barryesque Italianate ashlar façade of No. 36, 1847, quietly insisting on its superiority. (It was originally a savings bank.) On the opposite side of the road the equally fine lofty façade of the former LITERARY AND SCIENTIFIC INSTITUTE, classicism typical of the 1830s, probably by *J. Galpin*. Opened in 1833, built as the Mechanics' Institute. Portland ashlar, rusticated below, forming an arcade of upper windows. Doorway in the r. bay, an oddly diminutive and Ledoux-like composition of recessed Greek Doric columns and a pinched semicircular arch. Former Reading Room (ground floor) with a bas relief of Minerva uniting Art and Commerce by *John Gibson*.*

No. 74, some way further along on the S side, is Bridport's most swagger C18 front. It must date from *c*. 1760. Five-bay composition plus a carriage-arch bay to the r. Red brick header

Bridport News, 15 October 1864. Information from T. P. Connor.

bond with Portland stone dressings, i.e. for the eared window frames and their keystones, the central Ionic Venetian window and its supporting consoles, and for the bullseye window within the almost bottomless top pediment. Pedimented doorcase on Ionic three-quarter columns. Last on the N side No. 115. Of 1768, built for James Rooker, Independent Minister (according to a building lease), and for a Dissenting Academy, as well as for the home of its founder. Five-bay front with broad pilaster strips at the angles. Opposite, Nos. 124–128, a towering row of a similar date, built as the Marquis of Granby Inn (opened in 1769); given a new stucco façade c. 1830; reconstructed as a Masonic Hall (opened in 1926), resulting in the blocking of the second-floor windows. Hiding behind it is a C16 building at right angles, said to have been the Hospital of St John the Baptist. It is built of stone and can show a very humble oriel window, of 1:2:1 arched lights. Beyond, across the stream, Bridport's first eastward suburb, four stuccoed villas of c. 1840.

A final detour N of East Street, along Barrack Street to ST ANDREW'S ROAD, is worthwhile to see typical mid-C19 suburban development. Nos. 78–80 and Nos. 82–84 on the r. are of c. 1863 by *John Hicks*. Vaguely Gothic semi-detached pairs.

OUTLYING BUILDINGS

DOWNE HALL, ⅓ m. N, reached from Barrack Street. Close above the town, secreted in a miniature park. 1789 for William Downe, a London merchant. Palladian, its refined town-house design worthy of a London architect such as Henry Holland or Thomas Leverton. Five bays, two-and-a-half storeys, Portland ashlar, rusticated below, with a three-bay pediment above on Ionic pilasters running through a storey and a half. Top balustrade. Balustrade also for the low wings. If these are not original, they were certainly in place by 1815. Also an addition the small semicircular porch of c. 1807, now glazed in. Major remodelling, mostly at the rear, of 1893 by *E. S. Prior* for A. W. H. Dammers. Some fine chimneypieces within, and further fittings imported by Prior. Now divided into flats, with houses built in the parkland.

STABLES and FIRE-ENGINE HOUSE, 75 yds SE. Also 1893, by *Prior*. Brick.

CONYGAR VILLA, just E of Downe Hall's park. Of c. 1860 for E. G. Flight. Rambling Italianate.

RAX, Rax Lane, ¼ m. N. 'Lately erected' in 1786. Remodelled c. 1835 for Mrs Colfox. Of this last date the stucco W front with ashlar quoins, banding and cornice. At its centre a Venetian window below a pediment. Tripartite sashes. Also early C19 the brick single-bay end additions, each with sashes in an arched recess. Plainer E front of the earlier date. Some Grecian detailing. Also in the pedimented DOORWAY in the garden wall facing the street.

VILLAS, Nos. 46–52, West Allington, ½ m. NW. 1836–7 by *John Knight* of Lyme Regis. A set of four matching stucco villas.

Wide bracketed eaves. No. 48 has two late C19 ashlar bay windows.

PORTVILLE, West Bay Road, ½ m. S. 1836 by *J. Galpin*. A row of four detached stucco villas. Differing detail to each. Behind them is BELMONT HOUSE, *c.* 1840 by *Galpin* for himself. Picturesque Tudor with bold curvy bargeboards.

PRIORY MILLS, Priory Lane, 250 yds NW. Of 1838, built as a steam-powered flax-spinning mill for Stephen Whetham & Sons. Three-storey stone-built block with a steam engine house built into the structure at the N end. Parallel three-storey WAREHOUSE alongside the lane. Larger three-storey WARE-HOUSE with its S gable-end on Gundry Lane, 100 yds NE.

NORTH MILLS, North Mills Road, ½ m. N. Mid-C19 warehouse. The main survival from the large flax-milling and net-making complex of William Hounsell & Co. Also here a long, low ROPE WALKS building. Early C19. The largest of its type surviving in Bridport.

BROADMAYNE   7080

At the centre of the village a group of cob and thatch cottages. Otherwise its character is overwhelmed by recent housing development.

ST MARTIN. C13 nave and chancel. At the E end is an E.E. triplet of lancets. Two Dec nave S windows, the larger extensively restored. C13 S tower; top stage of *c.* 1500. Plain parapet. Late C15 W doorway with window above. Major restoration 1865–6 by *John Hicks*, adding a N aisle. Fine E.E.-style chancel arch and aisle arcade with naturalistic corbels and capitals, these by *Boulton* of Worcester. Re-set PISCINA of *c.* 1300 in the chancel. – FONT. C15; octagonal. The panelled stem is of 1866. – STAINED GLASS. E window, †1859, possibly by *Charles Gibbs*. Two chancel S windows no doubt also by him.

WESLEYAN METHODIST CHAPEL. Dated 1865, by *William Hammett* of Tolpuddle. Round-arched windows.

FRYER MAYNE, ⅝ m. E. A fragment of a house of *c.* 1600, probably built for John Williams of Tyneham. Mullioned windows under continuous string courses. The impressive part is the three-storey porch, with a gable on shapely kneelers. Round-headed entrance arch. This has dogtooth enrichment. The remainder *c.* 1840, lively Tudor Revival, for Thomas Cockeram.

This site was a property of the Knights Hospitaller, and some C14 fragments from this were incorporated in a yard wall including a PISCINA.

BANK BARROW, 1½ m. SW. Neolithic monument, 600 ft (180 metres) long, along the crest of the South Dorset Ridgeway. It provides a focus for the Bronze Age ROUND BARROW

GROUP on the spur to the NE: a ditched bowl on the W end, and a linear group continuing to Culliford Tree Barrow (*see* Whitcombe) and into Came Wood (*see* Winterborne Came). Altogether there are twenty-six round barrows of all types visible.

BROADOAK
Symondsbury

ST PAUL. 1865–6 by *Talbot Bury* for the Rev. Henry Rawlinson. Brown rubble stone. Nave with bellcote and short chancel. E.E. style with lancets and plate tracery. – STAINED GLASS. Several panels painted by *Mrs Rawlinson*, 1866.

BROADSTONE

The impetus for the development of Broadstone came from railways. The Southampton & Dorchester Railway arrived in 1847, followed in 1872 by a branch to Poole; and in 1885 a spur of the Somerset & Dorset Railway was added. The station closed in 1966. Rapid growth took place between the wars, and the NE area, on the rising ground of Canford Heath, soon became a fashionable suburb.

ST JOHN THE BAPTIST, Macaulay Road. 1887–8 by *W.J. Fletcher*. White brick, Geometrical tracery, no tower. N aisle, 1909 (by *Fletcher, Son & Brett*), continuing the original style. Lady Chapel, S, 1929–30, by *W.D. Caröe*. This is of rock-faced rubble with Doulting facings, Arts and Crafts-influenced, with a cross-shaped E window. Internally the chapel has a complex, but highly successful, relationship with the older parts: a wide segmental arch to the chancel and a narrower pointed arch to the nave. – FONT. Octagonal, on a multi-marble-shafted stem. – STAINED GLASS. E window of 1888 by *Powell & Sons*. Also by them the chancel S window, 1907. A nave S window by *Comper*, 1935. Several by *J. Wippell & Co.*, 1951–62. Bold W window of 1920 by *Martin Travers*, a fine example of his work.
ST ANTHONY OF PADUA (R.C.), York Road, ¾ m. S. 1959, by *Peter A. Burne*. Brick hall with round-arched windows. Niche with statue of St Anthony at the NW corner.
METHODIST CHURCH CENTRE, Lower Blandford Road, 150 yds SW. 2003 by *Saunders Architects*. Brick, with expressed 'Glulam' arch structures of timber.
UNITED REFORMED CHURCH (Congregational), Higher Blandford Road, ¼ m. NW. 1928 by *George Baines & Son*. Perp. Adjoining and contemporary MANSE.

CREMATORIUM, Gravel Hill, ¾ m. E. 1986 by *Poole Borough Architects' Department* (*R. Warmington*, project architect). Brick with spreading hipped plain-tile roofs, swept up to integrate the chimney.

BROADSTONE FIRST SCHOOL, Dunyeats Road (opposite St John's church). 1872 by *Banks & Barry* for the 1st Lord Wimborne. Gothic; yellow brick. Now much extended.

YAFFLE HILL, ½ m. E, in Water Tower Road. An Art Deco period piece among the pine trees: 1930 by *Sir Edward Maufe* for Cyril Carter, a director of the Poole Pottery Co. The plan is three sides of an octagon to trap the maximum sun, the walls white-rendered over brick, the hipped roof covered with the shiniest of shiny peacock-blue pantiles. Oyster-grey faience tiling bands emphasize the horizontality of the composition. Several areas of mosaic work within, all products of *Poole Pottery*. Reflecting pond on axis with the centre.   121

WATER TOWER, 50 yds NW of Yaffle Hill. 1894 for the Poole Water Co. Three-stage tower of decorative multicoloured brick. Panelled cast-iron tank.

WAR MEMORIAL, Broadstone Park, 300 yds W of Yaffle Hill. 1920 by *Gilbert Bayes*. A tapered Portland stone pillar topped by a winged angel in mourning (Memory). Fine bas reliefs of men and officers of the Army, Navy and Royal Flying Corps on the base.

Substantial remains of the ROMAN ROAD survive, on the boundary with Corfe Mullen on the W. The course can be traced s from the Roman military base at Lake GAtes Farm (*see* Corfe Mullen), along the W side of Holes Bay, down Almer Road, and thence SE from the local crest past the S side of St Michael's church at Hamworthy (q.v.).

BROADWEY   6080
3 m. N of Weymouth

The old village on the Dorchester Road was, by *c.* 1940, largely absorbed into a linear suburb extending N from Melcombe Regis (*see* Weymouth).

ST NICHOLAS. A curious church, quite big, where nothing goes harmoniously with anything. This is the product of successive C19 and early C20 enlargements. Details, no longer *in situ*, have been retained from the C12 and early C15. First the C12 S doorway with segmental head, one order of colonnettes, very lively capitals with a face, entwined monsters and a quadruped, and chevron and nailhead in the arch. N aisle of 1815; windows with intersecting tracery and starved octagonal arcade piers. W end rebuilt further W, 1838 by *Roper* of Upwey, incorporating an early C15 Perp window, apparently originally from the S wall. External niche with canopy in the S jamb of the (re-set)

W window. Chancel rebuilt 1862 and enlarged eastwards 1896, re-setting the earlier features. Insistent Neo-Norman by *G.R. Crickmay*. Smooth Perp S aisle and Neo-Norman choir S aisle of 1901, incorporating the C12 doorway, also by *Crickmay*. – PULPIT. Early C17, with two tiers of panels; the upper panels have leaf carving. – FONT. Low bowl with fluting; C12. – STAINED GLASS. Two-light E window by *Lavers, Barraud & Westlake*, c. 1877. Two W windows by *Clayton & Bell* (†1897 and 1918); the other W window perhaps by *Lavers, Barraud & Westlake*. – HEADSTONE. In the churchyard, the artist Thomas Henry Nicholson †1870 and his niece †1870, aged eleven. By *N.N. Burnard*. They are heads in profile hieratically facing one another. His palette is between them. The child was Burnard's daughter.

At NOTTINGTON, ¾ m. SW, the tall, gaunt octagonal house, rendered, with a vaguely Soanic treatment of the wall surfaces, was built as a spa over a sulphurous spring, and accommodated baths and a pump room. 1830, by *Robert Vining*.

BROADWINDSOR

Quite a large village. At its centre a cluster of early C19 houses with wide sashes and good contemporary shopfronts.

St JOHN THE BAPTIST. Quite a large church. Externally, but for the late C15 tower, nearly all of 1867–8 by *J.M. Allen* of Crewkerne. The N aisle entirely by him; the S C15, extended to the E by Allen. Also his the S clerestory. Big W three-stage tower, embattled with bold, set-back buttresses. Octagonal N stair-turret, raised above the tower by *Allen*, also embattled. Panelled tower arch. The chancel is E.E. to Dec in style, without parapets. Inside a S arcade of c. 1180 and a N arcade of the early C13, both lengthened by Allen. The S piers are round, the capitals scalloped, the abaci square, but the arches, though single-chamfered, are already pointed. The N piers are round with moulded capitals, and the N arches are pointed and double-chamfered. – PULPIT. Late C16. Oak (on an 1868 stone base). Seven-sided with pinnacled angles. Enriched upper panels, the lower plain, separated by a scrolled rail. – FONT. Late C12 or early C13. Square, of Purbeck marble, with simple geometrical motifs. Multi-shafted stem of 1867–8. Moved here from Burleston church. – ROYAL ARMS. Dated 1783. Painted and framed. – STAINED GLASS. E window by *Hardman*, †1868. S aisle W window by *F.C. Eden*, 1919. The other aisle windows (†1902 and †1899) probably also by *Eden*. – MONUMENT. Edmund Hall †1839 *et al*. By *Wilkins* of Beaminster. Clustered flanking columns and a relief of a dragoon beside his horse.

BROADWINDSOR HOUSE, ¼ m. E, in its own grounds. Built as the vicarage, 1838, by *J.H. Good* for the Rev. G. Denison. Tudor Revival; large. Symmetrical with two end gables on the

E and S fronts. More picturesque assembly of gables of various sizes on the W (entrance) front. Tall brick chimneystacks in clusters.

(THE BRICKS, 100 yds NW. Of 1519, built as the church house. Much rebuilt in the C19. Rubble stone wall on which sit the decayed remains of cruck construction, visible only internally.)

LEWESDON HILL, ¾ m. S. Hilltop ENCLOSURE of *c.* 3¾ acres, above steep scarp slopes with entrance and cross-ridge dyke on the W; much damaged by quarrying.

BROWNSEA ISLAND

The thrill of Brownsea is the island's forested survival in full view of busy Poole. In the C16 its S tip was made defensible, and garrisoned during the Civil War; but from the early C18 onwards the island became a retreat for a series of owners who adapted the castle to that purpose. Of these, Colonel William Petrie Waugh, who bought the island in 1852 intending to exploit his find of china clay, built more than any, but was soon forced to sell when the clay qualities proved illusory. The castle became a centre of high society after its purchase by the industrialist Charles van Raalte in 1901, a phase sharply contrasted by that of the reclusive Mrs Bonham-Christie, who was the last private occupier. During the Second World War the W end of the island was the site of one of the 'Starfish' bombing decoy sites, its flares drawing enemy attention away from Poole and Bournemouth. In 1962 it was passed to the National Trust.

ST MARY. A new church of 1853–4 by *Philip Brannon* of Southampton, for Col. Waugh. W tower, nave and chancel, the tower looking Perp, nave and chancel late C13. S mortuary chapel, 1908. The church is fitted out extensively with elaborate furnishings brought in by George Cavendish-Bentinck of Brownsea Castle, who died in 1891. First the C16 SCREENS to the family pew under the tower, SW chapel and N vestry. Said to come from Crosby Hall in London; the family pew ceiling also (reportedly parts of the ceilings of Parlour and Great Chamber). Also under the tower a FIREPLACE with *Minton* tilework. – The brass CHANDELIER in the tower is English, C18. – The parchemin PANELLING in the chancel may be English or Netherlandish. – Much else is certainly from the Netherlands, notably the two good pieces of SCULPTURE of *c.* 1500 l. and r. of the fireplace (Faith, and a man holding a shoe and a knife), the extremely intricate canopies above the overmantel, the two canopied groups of the early C16 l. and r. of the overmantel (the Entombment and the Presentation) and the two coloured reliefs (the Annunciation, and the Adoration of the Shepherds) of *c.* 1600 on the nave N wall. But the best pieces are Italian Renaissance, a Quattrocento marble relief of the Madonna with a putto head below (placed as a memorial to

William George Cavendish-Bentinck †1909) and two beautiful standing Angels from a Venetian group of the Mourning of the Dead Christ. – STAINED GLASS. The E window and others are by *E. Baillie & G. Mayer*, 1854. – MONUMENTS. Charles van Raalte †1908. Recumbent effigy in his mortuary chapel. – A late C15 Italian POZZO (well-head) in the form of a Corinthian capital outside the church. Its elaborate iron gear supports a bronze plaque inscribed to George Cavendish-Bentinck †1891.

BROWNSEA CASTLE. The castle, now stylistically somewhat chaotic, is the result of a number of building campaigns, not all brought to a conclusion. The first impression is of battlements everywhere. It began as a blockhouse, built by Henry VIII as an afterthought in his system of South Coast defences. This was being completed in 1547–8. The blockhouse survives in the basement, a square (43 by 44 ft, 13.1 by 13.4 metres) with a battered plinth. The site of the contemporary gun platform is on the SE side, polygonal in plan. This was rebuilt by *William Benson*, the notorious supplanter of Wren as Surveyor of the Works and the first owner to exploit Brownsea as a retreat. From 1724 he built a four-storey belvedere tower over the Tudor blockhouse. By 1774, Hutchins shows, there was a four-storey castellated block with Venetian windows. The print also illustrates low wings with more Venetian windows added to three sides. That facing NW was by *Benson*, as his great hall. The others were added either for Benson or Humphry Sturt (of Crichel House), the owner after 1765. A new NW front was added *c*. 1820 for Sir Charles Chad. This is of brick, in a rambling turreted style. Three bold projections (round, rectangular, round) produce a symmetrical front, upset at the l. end by a skewy addition of *c*. 1840 in a similar style (for Sir Augustus John Foster). The windows, all in broad flat Portland stone surrounds, are rectangular cross-mullioned or, where there is space, Venetian with the arch pointed, a very odd form designed to match Benson's belvedere windows. The other fronts are either of stone, *c*. 1853 by *Philip Brannon* for Col. Waugh, in a rich Tudor style,* or of bright red brick, partly a refacing after a fire of 1896 (possibly by *R. S. Balfour* for his cousin Major Kenneth Balfour), in no consistent style. Further changes including a raised loggia on the SW side for Charles van Raalte, *c*. 1902.

Inside almost everything is post-fire, and quite successful in its varied vaulted spaces. Balfour and the van Raaltes refitted the main rooms in a largely early C18 style, especially the STAIRCASE HALL and MUSIC ROOM. A mighty C16 Italian stone CHIMNEYPIECE is in the NE room, very classical, except for the typical motif of the imposts descending to gigantic paws. This may be a survivor from before the fire.

With the island, the castle is a property of the National Trust (currently used by John Lewis Partnership as a staff hotel).

---

*A painting of the Brannon scheme is in the RIBA Drawings Collection (incorrectly catalogued as by 'Philip Brown'). The scheme where executed is less elaborate than indicated on this view.

The QUAYSIDE BUILDINGS are clearly all of the mid C19, of brick and rendered. To the l. the FAMILY PIER, of *c.* 1854 (not built as elaborately as indicated in Brannon's view), fronted by a pair of white stuccoed turrets, octagonal, the windows pointed with hoodmoulds. The pier has a covered walk lit by arrow loops, housing a collection of Venetian armorial panels and other minor structural pieces brought in by George Cavendish-Bentinck. Battlements here, and on the various buildings further r. The pier was linked to the castle by a series of conservatories in the walled garden, removed by 1901. To the E of the pier, the CHIEF COASTGUARD OFFICER'S HOUSE (called 'The Villano'), with octagonal corner turrets, a BOAT-HOUSE and ENGINE HOUSE, a terrace of four COASTGUARD COTTAGES, and the 'WARDEN'S HOUSE', another more sub-stantial house, all of *c.* 1842 for Sir Augustus John Foster. Between the pier and the castle, a buff brick GATEHOUSE (*c.* 1854) and garden enclosure walls. The GARDENS them-selves were largely the creation of Charles and Florence van Raalte after 1901.

THE VILLA, ¼ m. NW of the church. Built as a vicarage, *c.* 1854, probably by *Brannon.* Tudor Gothic. Symmetrical.

BRYANSTON

8000

The great mansion is now the centrepiece of an extensive private school 'village', with estate church, farms and cottages, and ancillary buildings to the earlier mansion, all (except for the Portman Chapel) in school use.

BRYANSTON SCHOOL. Built by *Norman Shaw* as a country house for the 2nd Viscount Portman, the owner of large tracts of the West End of London and a major estate in Dorset. The contract drawings are dated 1889, rainwater heads bear the date 1891 and completion was in 1894. Its cost was enormous: the final payment alone was £200,000. The builders were *Holland & Hannen* of London.

105

The entrance from the SE is through a GATEWAY, built *c.* 1778 by *James Wyatt* to go with his new house of that date for Henry William Berkeley Portman, demolished apart from the service buildings (*see* below) in 1890. Lofty arched entrance, with Doric half-columns l. and r. and a pediment on top. Low lodges attached on each side. This puts one in the right frame of mind, and so does the mile-long drive through the woods with a steep bank down to the river (known as 'The Cliff') on the r. The drive at last sweeps round, cuts through the hillside and suddenly emerges before the colossal geranium-red and white mansion.

In style the house is loosely Neo-Wren, the Wren of Hampton Court, but freely introducing un-Wren-like details, and nothing like Wren in the panache with which the various forms are juggled about. Shaw, however, had a second frame of reference, Château Menars on the Loire (especially for the handling of the SE front, where the terracing is also influenced by that at Vaux-le-Vicomte). Yet this mode was not a new style for Shaw but a revival of his early partner Nesfield's style at Kinmel Park, Denbighshire. Finally, the Franco-Wren style was chosen because it enabled interiors to be created where reuse of fireplaces, doors and other fittings was stylistically possible, even if the Wyatt fireplaces sit oddly under heavily detailed late-C17-style plasterwork ceilings. The style that emerged at Bryanston, although puzzling contemporary critics used to, and in awe of, Shaw's 'Old English' and 'Queen Anne' revival work, came to influence later designers such as Sir Edwin Lutyens and Sir Albert Richardson, and in many ways Bryanston may be seen as the first Neo-Georgian showpiece.

It was certainly at this time a curious decision to demolish a fine (although reportedly somewhat damp) Wyatt house and replace it with something twice the size and in a more commanding position. Perhaps the comparatively modest Wyatt building (and with Wyatt then at the nadir of fashionableness) no longer met the family's appreciation of its own dignity. This certainly seems to have been the case with regard to Mary, Viscountess Portman, used to the scale of her ancestral home, Wentworth Woodhouse, Yorkshire; at 600 ft (183 metres) it had the longest front of any in England. Andrew Saint has fittingly summarized what the Portmans achieved at Bryanston as allowing them to join 'the great club of European aristocracy, unaware that its days were numbered'.

On the ENTRANCE FRONT, the centre block, of 2:3:2 bays, is surmounted by a hipped roof and prominent chimneystacks. Windows with Gibbs surrounds, long ones in the centre, and short ones at the sides, are played off against extra-long pairs of first-floor windows at the sides, seemingly marking staircases (although that to the l. does nothing of the kind). Two-bay links, continuing for one bay round the corner, take one to the service wings, which come forward at right angles enclosing the *cour d'honneur*. A busy rhythm of windows here too, the main part of 1:5:1 bays with a big segmental pediment *à la française* over the wide centre. The materials are brick and Portland stone, the quoins introducing even rubbed brick to alternate with the bulging cushions of stone.

105   The GARDEN SIDE is basically the same, though the main block is brought forward, and the wings lie back in line with it, so that the whole mass is extended on the crown of the ridge, looking over the trees to the expansive view of the Stour valley. The detailing here is less restless and less emphatic, though one is startled by even such an apparently innocent motif as the mighty scrolls that support the window architraves. The gardens descend by a series of terraces and steps, handled in a way that unites them visually with the house. Prior, however, who admired Bryanston intensely, wrote of these: 'Unfortunately the layout of the domain was taken out of the architect's hands, and so the conception remains an incomplete one.' This

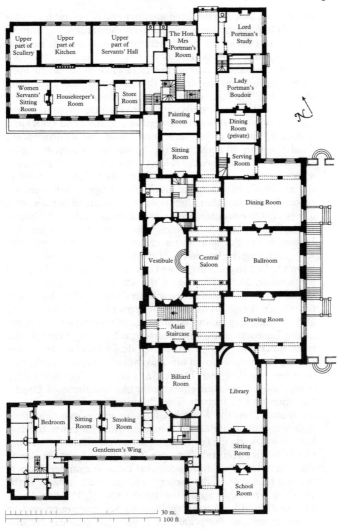

Bryanston.
Plan

would also explain the very utilitarian service blocks added to the NE end of the house after Shaw's work had ceased.

There is also some sophistication in the PLANNING, as one would expect from Shaw. In general terms, the gentlemen's rooms (Billiard and Smoking rooms) are in the NW wing with male servants' accommodation in the basement and attics. To maintain separation of the sexes, Lady Portman's Boudoir is in the opposite wing (with Lord Portman's Study next door), likewise with female servants' areas in the basement and attic. To achieve this, while following Palladian planning, Shaw successfully adopted the conceit of long wings set at right angles to the main block, articulated at either end to resemble smaller units. When the house is viewed from the garden, the impression is therefore of near-detached side wings styled as smaller-scale versions of the main block.

At its formidable centre, the INTERIOR is yet more overwhelming, both in size and by the way Shaw uses great areas of very fine Portland stone. The front door leads into a vestibule apsed at both ends, out of the centre of which steps rise through a mighty stone doorway into the great CENTRAL SALOON. This is at the same time a hall and a corridor, the focal point for all activity in the house, and is a room organized with brilliant panache. Giant Ionic columns carry curved upper balconies, beyond which light enters from windows in the end walls of the main block. These upper balconies are reached by broad, short flights of steps in the upper corridor, a very effective arrangement. Central dome. Below, the broad, straight, groin-vaulted corridor runs far this way and far that. However, the Portland stone ceases at two rusticated archways, defining the boundary of the central, semi-public areas. Beyond, the materials are more conventional oak panelling and plasterwork. Main staircase on the NW side, a straightforward late C17 type – balusters copied from Cobham Hall, Kent. The three main rooms on the SE front seem vast, often uncomfortably so. Late C17 plaster ceilings, except for Wyatt-style work in the Ballroom and some bedrooms. The side rooms in the main block each have a projecting alcove (that to the former Dining Room now closed off) and the ceiling is supported here on a free-standing pier. In the BALLROOM, which has a deep cove, this produces an effect more like the Baths of Diocletian than an C18 interior. The chimneypieces in these rooms are reused from the Wyatt house and seem a little delicate in detailing and under-scaled when measured against the big, bold Shaw work, except perhaps in the Ballroom, where they match its architectural character. That in the Drawing Room, with caryatids, is a fine Neoclassical piece. A number of doors are also reused from the earlier building. The LIBRARY in the SW wing, retained in that use by the school, has fine *Shaw*-designed fitted bookcases, including a set running around an alcove at one end. Here, and occasionally elsewhere in secondary rooms, the ceiling plasterwork is more eclectic in style.

Throughout, the materials and workmanship are of the highest quality, so that even now, when the main rooms are classrooms and hundreds of pairs of feet tramp daily over the parquet, the interior gives one a sense of euphoria. The house adapted easily to its new use, with the loss of the upper level of the former double-height (and top-lit) Billiard Room as the only significant alteration. Between the service wings of the house, a DINING HALL by *Richard Horden* (1986), greatly remodelled and expanded by *Conran Architects*, 2010.

The highest standard of servicing was provided. The main rooms have conventional fireplace heating, but hot air is ducted to grilles in the circulation areas. Coals and luggage were conveyed from the basement to the upper floors by hydraulic lifts.

Structural steel was incorporated, freeing up the upper-floor planning above the big rooms. Like Shaw's Cragside, Northumberland, the house was lit throughout by electric light.

The Portmans lived in the new house for thirty years, but multiple death duties brought the need to sell.* The contents went in 1925 and the house and grounds in 1927. The purchaser was J. G. Jeffreys, the founding headmaster of Bryanston School. Initially modest Neo-Georgian additions were made on the NE side. These expanded to a series of buildings stepping down the hill on the same side in an uncompromisingly modern style. Since the 1980s a new confidence has led to the erection of a string of buildings, as architecturally impressive as they are varied.

Of the three school houses of the earlier period (1931–2) by *Sir Edwin Cooper*, one, FOUR WINDS, 250 yds W, survives unaltered. Brick, with bullseye windows flanking the central doorway. Mansard roof. Since all of the *Architects' Co-Partnership* buildings of 1952–62 have been superseded and demolished, this takes us to the bold wedge shapes (in plan as well as elevation) of the COADE THEATRE, 100 yds NE, of 1964–6. Monopitch roofs, slabs of fine brickwork and ground-to-roof fenestration. Deliberately arbitrary in the total effect. By *Frank Gollins* (of *GMW Architects*), consultant architect *L. Magnus Austin* of Poole.

Postmodernism arrived in 1987–8 with a CRAFT, DESIGN AND TECHNOLOGY BUILDING by *Piers Gough* of *CZWG* immediately NE of the house. Its brick and cast stone make humorously bold references to the Shavian language of the main house, against which it holds its own. Oversized screw columns (with the screws reversed from usual) speak of the building's function. The courtyard it creates is spectacularly completed by the crescent of the SANGER CENTRE FOR SCIENCE AND MATHEMATICS, 2007 by *Hopkins Architects*. Handmade Michelmersh Brick and minimal detailing, contrasting with its neighbour. Its rationalism is more effective as a result, while the placement is highly sensitive to the main house. The MUSIC SCHOOL of 2014, by the same architects and in a similar idiom, completes this square on the S side. N of this, the circular-ended first phase of BRAMWELL, 2011–12, classrooms around a central area with an air-assisted roofing fabric, also by *Hopkins*. This is planned to expand to the W. Beyond and 80 yds to the SE of the Coade Hall, the BOARDING HOUSES of 1994–5 by *CZWG* are another variation, two Y-plan houses joined end-to-end at the base by an archway. In the N angles, with windows spiralling around them, are circular towers containing toilets, showers and bathrooms. Also of interest is CRANBORNE HOUSE (next to Four Winds) by *David Morley Architects*, 1998–9. Two monopitches on a curve, the framing either lead-clad or with brick-stack infill. The BOATHOUSE, ½ m. E, of 2011–12 by *Rob Adams* (of *Adams*

124

---

*The 2nd, 3rd and 4th viscounts Portman died in 1919, 1923 and 1929 respectively.

& Collingwood Architects), continues the expressive modern trend with steel-framed balconies contrasted with horizontal timber boarding.

The rest of Bryanston is in the nature of grace-notes. The *Wyatt* house lay ¼ m. SE, further down the hill. It replaced a previous house of 1580 to 1610 (remodelled and extended at various dates). Here also stand two churches on either side of a green.

PORTMAN CHAPEL (formerly church of St Martin). Built in 1745, replacing the previous church of *c.* 1550. Declared redundant 1976. Nave and chancel in one, with quoins of alternating blocking and a W cupola. The somewhat oversized priest's doorway with attached Ionic columns must be a reused *Wyatt* feature. An ugly, entirely plain late C19 S attachment. The chapel has a W front with a steep broken pediment – rather a gable – and a doorway with a proper pediment on unfluted Ionic columns. To the E and N Venetian windows. Inside, the ceiling has a big coving. Charming altar surround with trophy-like pendants l. and r. of the pediment reredos. Fine wooden surround of the W doorway. – PULPIT and COMMUNION RAIL, *c.* 1745. – MONUMENTS. Many Portman tablets, e.g. an inscription plate starting with Henry Portman †1796, by *Nollekens*. The best is Henry William Portman †1761, with an obelisk; white and light-brown marble.

ST MARTIN (now owned by Bryanston School). 1896–8 by *E.P. Warren*, best remembered for his college and town buildings at Oxford. A large church of smooth greensand ashlar, in an effective and expressive free Perp style, clearly inspired by Bodley, to whom Warren had been articled. Fine, stately W tower with two two-light bell-openings each side. S arcade of piers whose arches die into them. The interior has a number of calculated contrasts of S against N – rather like Paley & Austin. – ORGAN. By *George Lhôte* (built by *Nigel Church*), 1980. Large, dramatically and surprisingly placed under the chancel arch (blocking views of the E end). – FONT. Hexagonal, with sides convex in plan and elevation. In grey and white marbles. – STAINED GLASS. The E window (behind the organ) is worth seeking out. By *R. Anning Bell* (executed by *A.J. Dix*), 1899. Richly coloured Crucifixion. S aisle, central S window, 1902 by *Powell & Sons*. S aisle, W end (†1900) and main W window (Viscountess Portman †1899) both by *E. Frampton*.

Between the two churches a SERVICE BLOCK of *Wyatt*'s house of 1778–80. Greensand ashlar (reused in part from *Vanbrugh*'s demolished Eastbury). Nine bays, one storey. Pedimented centre with three arched openings. Round-headed windows in the wings. No moulding anywhere. Beyond and above, the STABLES, red brick, mid-C18, i.e. built for the yet earlier Bryanston, in three ranges round a square court. Round-headed windows. Pedimented centrepiece with a round-headed rusticated stone entrance in the W range.

BRYANSTON HOME FARM, ¼ m. S of the School. Of *c.* 1850, on a large scale. Two parallel red brick ranges, arranged N to S, with open yard between. Many elliptically arched openings. Former ENGINE HOUSE and ESTATE COTTAGES, E side of

the lane. Contemporary HOME FARMHOUSE immediately N.
Stucco with wide sashes.

BUCKHORN WESTON   7020

ST JOHN THE BAPTIST. A church of medium size, basically
C14, but with additions. C15 porch with a multi-moulded,
four-centred-headed arch. Perp image niche in its gable with
pinnacled canopy. The badly weathered effigy within (brought
in from elsewhere and originally recumbent) from its small size
may suggest that its original purpose was to indicate a heart
burial. The low W tower was rebuilt in 1861 by *Thomas Richards* of Wincanton under *T.H. Wyatt*'s direction. The N aisle is
a replacement of 1870–2 by *G.R. Crickmay*, who reconstructed
the two-bay arcade as three, with other rebuilding. Most of the
windows are also of this date. – Oak LECTERN. Given in 1696.
Yet the baluster is still of Jacobean type. – FONT. Octagonal;
Perp. – PAINTINGS. Six very poorly painted panels of the late
C17, including two angels, King David and the Nativity. These
came from the gallery front. – STAINED GLASS. E window
probably by *Alexander Gibbs*, *c.* 1870. Two chancel S windows
perhaps by *Wailes* (†1868 and †1874). – MONUMENT. Recumbent effigy in civilian dress. Late C14: see the low belt purse
and dagger belt.
Beside the church *Crickmay*'s little brick and stone SCHOOL,
designed in 1877. Typical of the date the combination of
chimney and bell-gablet.
OLD RECTORY, just up the hill. Dated 1861, Gothic. Probably by
J.E. Gill of *Manners & Gill*. Gabled with a scatter of lancets on
the entrance elevation. Altered in 1877 by *Crickmay*.

BUCKLAND NEWTON   6000

The old village, including the church, former vicarage and manor
house, is built around meandering lanes at the head of the River
Lydden. From the mid C19 a new village grew up at a crossroads
to the E.

HOLY ROOD. The external character of the church is somewhat marred by smooth render, probably first applied in the
early C19. Only the interior now brings out its best, spacious
and light and homogeneous, though of two distinct periods.
The chancel is early C13 and has widely spread single lancets
N and S, shafted inside. The E triplet fits with this, but is
an 1870 replacement by *T.H. Wyatt*, complete with Purbeck
marble shafts and rere-arches.* The nave is C15 and has wide

---

*What it replaced was a Perp-style window of 1841.

aisles, large three-light windows with ingeniously treated transoms (depressed arches carrying reversed depressed arches),
and slender arcade piers of standard section and two-centred
arches. Panelled Perp chancel arch, very wide. Excellent Perp
head corbels in the chancel, dating from when the roof was
raised to its present profile. The w tower is c15 too. Apart from
its w window it is strangely plain, with c16 square-headed belfry
openings. Two-storey Perp s porch, again with later (perhaps
c16) upper window. Wide porch doorway with quatrefoil- and
dagger-enriched spandrels. Within the porch a stone lierne
vault. In the N aisle the head of a central arched doorway
projects into the window above. – ALTAR and REREDOS.
Of 1927 by *A.R. Mowbray & Co*. Both elaborate, the latter
with hooded image niches and fretwork cresting. – CHOIR
FURNISHINGS. Part of *Wyatt*'s first restoration programme
(of 1869–70). – Sanctuary TILES by *Minton*. – PULPIT. C18, oak.
Simple panelling with some marquetry. – FONT. C15. Octagonal, with big leaf motifs, differing on each face. – BENCHES.
Late c15 or early c16 (but restored in 1878). Mostly straight-
topped ends with linenfold panelling. Some bench-ends with
foliate finials and the initial 'w' with a stylized crown on the
reverse. One has an appreciably older section (said to have
come from Glastonbury Abbey). – TOWER SCREEN of 1930 by
Ernest Emerson. – ORGAN GALLERY, 1937 by *George Osmond
Ltd* of Taunton. – POOR BOX. C16, square, of oak. Boldly
carved corner balusters, with scrollwork between. Diagonal
banding on two sides of the post. – SCULPTURE. Above the s
doorway outside a small c12 Christ in Majesty. It was formerly
in a niche on the w tower face, much weathered. – Inside, a
yet smaller relief of an extremely primitively treated figure,
probably a warrior. It has been attributed either to North
Europe or Celtic Britain, and dated c8 or c11. Found in the
vicarage garden in 1926. – STAINED GLASS. Chancel windows
by *Lavers, Barraud & Westlake*, 1870. The fine w window is by
Kempe & Co., 1916. – MONUMENT. Fitz(walter) Foy †1781,
but erected after 1806. By *King* of Bath. Mourning standing
woman by an urn.

PRIMITIVE METHODIST CHAPEL (former), ½ m. E. Brick,
dated 1876. Crudely fitted with a shopfront.

CONGREGATIONAL CHURCH (former), Duntish, ¾ m. NNE.
Dated 1867. Round-arched style, stuccoed. Sunday School
attached at the N end.

BUCKLAND NEWTON PLACE (formerly the vicarage), down the
hill E of the church. Characterful and not small, as is so often
the way with c18 parsonages in Dorset. Of 1729, for the Rev.
Timothy Collins, with a symmetrical red brick E front. Seven
bays wide, but the centre three brought forward like a pavilion.
Broken top pediment here, all of brick, and a round window
in it. Segment-headed windows on both storeys, with white
keystones. Doorway with white channelled pilasters. The sides
and rear wings stuccoed and in part early c19.

MANOR HOUSE, w of the church. Dated 1803 on a rainwater
head, an early date for the revival of Tudor detail in this

fairly educated way. Mullioned-and-transomed windows with hoodmoulds, gables with finials. Tall, symmetrical front, rendered walls and, final incongruity, a mansard roof between the gables. At its core however is a genuine Tudor house, probably that built for Robert Hyde in 1596.

DUNTISH COURT, 1 m. NNE. The fine villa built in 1764 for Fitzwalter Foy by *Sir William Chambers* was sadly pulled down in 1965. Only part of one ruined wing survives, including the square arcaded lantern, which in the later C19 was given a folly-like look by taking up an octagonal battlemented chimneystack through the middle of it.

PRIMITIVE HUT, in the wood, 100 yds W. Probably also by *Chambers* and probably contemporary with the house. Brick and rubble stone with half-round rough logs tacked on as columns and entablature. Diocletian window at the E end. A remarkable survival of a building type based upon the writings of Marc-Antoine Laugier.*

DUNGEON HILL, 1¼ m. N. An Iron Age HILL-FORT, univallate, occupies the hill-crest. The rampart encloses 9 acres.

BUCKLAND RIPERS

Church and manor house, happily placed in a fold of the downs.

ST NICHOLAS. Small, and mostly of 1655, rebuilt after a fire (which reportedly destroyed much of the village). The chancel is early C14, but with no obviously datable features. Its arch (widened later to become an ellipse) has a pendant, which is something one would not find often. – COMMUNION RAIL. Mid-C17, balustered.

MANOR HOUSE, just to the NE. Of two phases. Gabled mid-C17 core (as rebuilt after the mid-C17 fire). The NW part early C19 with sash windows and a hipped roof.

TATTON HOUSE, 1½ m. W. Stuccoed villa of *c.* 1830. Surprisingly formal. Square plan with a hipped roof and chimney at the centre. Two windows per wall, the lower ones Venetian on the front façade.

BURLESTON

CHURCH. Very little can now be examined, in the trees, the undergrowth and the climbers. All but the chancel was demolished *c.* 1860 when a new church was built, ½ m. away, at Athelhampton. The chancel too is roofless, but retains a C15 E window.

*Timothy Mowl, *Georgian Group Journal* 13, 2003.

BURSTOCK

ST ANDREW. E.E. S doorway with continuous roll moulding. Early C15 the W tower, chancel arch and N chapel arch. The tower is embattled, of three stages with diagonal W buttresses. Gargoyles on a string course and crocketed corner pinnacles. C16 nave windows. Major restoration of 1877 by *P. H. Peters* with windows with Y- and intersecting tracery. The chancel is of this date. Medieval STOUP in the porch, re-set. – FONT. Of *c.* 1200. Tub-shaped, with a rope moulding.

MANOR FARM, at the NW end of the village. Standard C17 front, long, low and not regular, the windows mullioned. The raised gable-end coping shows that it was originally thatched. C18 gatepiers with ball finials. Also C18 a rear wing and staircase.

BURSTOCK GRANGE, ⅜ m. SSE. Partly C15, remodelled in the early C17 to present a standard front.

4080

BURTON BRADSTOCK

The cottages come in picturesque and varied clusters, especially the thatched cottages around the network of lanes near the church. There are more rows alongside the main road from Bridport to Abbotsbury. A large C20 expansion to the N, avoiding spoiling the older part of the village.

ST MARY. The church is entirely Perp, the nave late C14, the transepts and central tower early C15. Chancel rebuilt in the C16. Its most interesting feature however is the S aisle. There is first broad central tower, with embattled higher SW stair-turret. Bold gargoyles at the tower corners; smaller ones on the turret. The turret appears to have lost its own battlements at some point (or perhaps they were never completed). The whole rests on high Perp arches which include a panelled order – a more sophisticated arrangement than e.g. Symondsbury (q.v.). Wooden ceiling to the crossing, on four angel busts. The chancel N windows have uncommonly deep reveals, going right down to the ground. Wagon roofs in the transepts and the nave. The S aisle is a surprise as soon as one sees it. When and by whom can the window heads have been designed? They have lintels with a very low-pitched triangular underside. The roof is as original, at least in the way it meets the outer wall. And the arcades have three-centred arches and concave-sided capitals. It presupposes a designer of developed idiosyncrasies. He is indeed *E. S. Prior*, and it was done as part of a full restoration in 1894–7. As the church is not far from Bothenhampton, one ought to have guessed. – COMMUNION RAIL. Dated 1686 and yet still entirely Jacobean. Strange knob-like finials. – FURNISHINGS. Much by *Prior* and typically original. Good CLERGY DESK with carved leaf trails; the PEWS have shaped arms at the ends like park benches. PULPIT of 1935, more conventional. – FONT. C14, Dec. Octagonal, with flat blank arches. They alternate between trefoil-headed arches in pairs, and single panels with either trefoil or cinquefoil heads. Cylindrical shaft and base with spurs, late C12. – PAINTING. Delightful frieze of vine trails on the N wall of the nave, painted by *Mrs Templer* and ladies of the parish (*c.* 1900). – STAINED GLASS. First two chancel windows and those of the S aisle by *Prior*, using his thick handmade glass. All have small coloured slips, but to differing patterns, those in the aisle more Art Nouveau. Nave N window by *Christopher Whall*, 1923. – MONUMENTS. Elizabeth Best †1747. Rather primitive broken pediment. A panel with symbols of mortality, much as one might expect on a chest tomb. – William Daniell †1823. Grecian pediment and urn in relief with laurel-leaf wreath surround. By *Richard Westmacott Jun.*

PUBLIC LIBRARY (former WESLEYAN METHODIST CHAPEL), facing the village green. Dated 1825. With the large sashes of that time.

READING ROOM (former), High Street. Dated 1879. With two round-arched windows, and looking like a chapel of fifty years earlier.

In CHURCH STREET, at the E end behind trees, THE ROOKERY. Large house, the earliest part of *c.* 1640, extended to the E later in the century. Just opposite the church, THE MAGNOLIAS is typical of the later brick houses that have enlivened the texture, its wide sashes indicating an early C19 date. In SHADRACK, a lane towards the N of the village, GIRT HOUSE. A larger brick-fronted house of the mid C18. Five sashed bays with a rudimentary Venetian window above the front door.

NORBURTON HALL, Shipton Lane. ⅓ m. NE. Main range of *c.* 1640, considerably enlarged and remodelled in 1902 by *R.A. Sturdy* for E.T. Sturdy. Arts and Crafts, with many multi-light stone-mullioned windows. Canted, S-facing porch where an angled wing was added at the E end in 1902. Tudor-style stair hall with much stone carving.

CANFORD BRIDGE *see* WIMBORNE MINSTER

CANFORD MAGNA   0090

Prior to the late C18 the village was no more than the ancient manor and more ancient church, together with a scatter of cottages. All of this changed in 1826 with the erection of a new mansion for the Hon. William Ponsonby, later 1st Lord de Mauley. Further additions from 1847 for the Guest family (later Lords Wimborne) made this one of the largest country houses in the county. The work was accompanied by a model village, whose cottage and school designs were repeated in various locations throughout the extensive Canford estate.

Canford Magna, church.
Engraving by B.J. Pouncy, 1813

CHURCH (no known dedication). This is without any doubt
one of the most interesting churches of Dorset – which is
emphatically not the same as saying one of the most beautiful.
Externally its evolution is difficult to read. Inside, it becomes
apparent that there are at least three phases of Norman, and
possibly Anglo-Saxon, work. The church consists, broadly
speaking, of a chancel which was the nave of an earlier church
whose chancel has disappeared, a short Norman nave to the w
and a Norman N tower in a curious position, N of the w end
of the chancel. Also a noble w end which looks like an E end.
    The earliest features of the CHANCEL are the opposed broad
round arches at the E end, formerly leading N and S, into
what may have been Anglo-Saxon *porticūs*. Further w is the
familiar Norman arrangement of roughly central opposed processional doorways and plain, narrow and high, round-arched
window openings, later altered, all part of a second phase.
(The arches were lined during one of the C19 restorations,
with a consequent loss of evidence for their original detailing.
The westernmost arches may even be C19.) A small arched
window in the s wall (only visible from the chancel s aisle), set
centrally above a dividing pier, may be of the first phase. The
Norman N doorway, although narrow, has moulded imposts
and a semicircular tympanum typical of post-Conquest work.
An indication of the first wall arrangement is to be seen in
the chancel N wall, where the arch of an earlier window, with
alternating polychrome chamfered voussoirs, is cut into by one
of the later arches. There is also a rood-loft stair in the s pier
of the chancel arch.
    It is recorded that a church was founded here by Canute
c. 1030. Could the earliest fabric of the present chancel be
of that date? H.M. Taylor found no Anglo-Saxon indicators, although, after A.W. Clapham, the RCHME suggested
that the irregular angles of the planning are a pre-Conquest

characteristic. Furthermore, the RCHME saw the *porticūs* as suggestive of a cruciform plan, typical of a minster church, and postulated that the chancel is CII, possibly *c.* 1050.

The aisled NAVE post-dates the gifting of the church by William, Earl of Salisbury, to the Augustinian canons of Bradenstoke Priory, Wilts. between 1190 and 1196. Built when the old nave was converted to a chancel, this nave is unusual too. The two bays are divided by a chunk of solid wall so that there is no pier – only responds. The capitals are of the trumpet-scallop type but with variations in detailing. Roll-moulded round arches to the E and SW bays with roll-moulded hoods and turned-up stops. The two-centred arch of the NW bay with chamfered orders was rebuilt in the early C14. In the 1870s the walls were enlivened by two N and two S circular openings with sexfoiling. Several Norman windows survive in the aisles, and a decidedly Late Norman S doorway with a rounded-trefoiled arch. The capitals of the colonnettes here are decorated. The Norman N doorway is simpler but has decorated capitals too. A Transitional two-centred arch, over an opening with Norman colonnettes, leads E from the N aisle into the tower, which was added soon after completion of the nave. A second archway facing S into the chancel (and that further E into the later vestry) is also two-centred. The tower is of four stages and has twin bell-openings of a familiar Norman type in the third. Plain parapets.

Alterations in the C14 removed traces of the earliest fabric, especially when the two-centred chancel arch was installed. The S chapel is of the C14, together with the chancel S aisle. The nave aisles were widened and raised in height (see the external evidence at their W ends) and three-light side windows installed at their E ends. Soon after 1828 *Edward Blore* designed a western extension to the church. This was rebuilt by *David Brandon* during his restoration of 1874–8.* It is of carstone ashlar with Purbeck marble-shafted lancets and a stepped group of three in the W wall. The Dec E window is also his, as are the porches and the NE vestry. The ORGAN and WEST GALLERY are of 1973, by *Kenneth Wiltshire* of the *Brandt Potter Hare Partnership*.

OTHER FURNISHINGS. ALTAR SURROUND. *Salviati* mosaic of two large angels, 1876. – COMMUNION RAIL. Of wrought iron; probably C18. – A fine set of oak STALLS by *Brandon*, supplied by *Michael & J.C. Buckley* (made in Bruges). Theirs also the PULPIT and the PEWS. – FONT. Octagonal, C13, of Purbeck marble, with two foiled arches on each side. – STAINED GLASS. Mostly commemorating members of the Guest family, particularly Sir Josiah John (†1852) and Lady Charlotte Guest (†1895). Three-light E window by *Hardman*, *c.* 1855. Two W window lights, †1862, by *Clayton & Bell*. Three-light N aisle W window, 1908, and two small windows at the W end of the aisles, 1896, all probably by *Burlison & Grylls*. – MONUMENTS.

---

*There is a tradition that in Brandon's time the foundations of the Saxon chancel were found.

An unusually fine set. Starting in the s chapel, Thomas Mac-namara Russell, Admiral of the White †1824, by *H. Harris* of Poole. Marble tablet with naval trophies at the top and shield of arms on the apron. – Catherine Willett. Standing woman by a book on a pedestal. By *John Bacon Sen.*, 1799. – Choir s aisle. Bust of William Rodney, mid-C20; good quality. Artist and date unrecorded. – Nan Guest †1918. Free-standing young woman with young child. – Montague John Guest †1909. Tablet in a Florentine Renaissance style. Two angels and some baluster framing. – John Willett Willett †1815, by *Peter Turnerelli*. Woman holding an urn with a portrait in profile. – Nave s aisle. Henrietta Mary Wilkie †1790, by *Bacon*. Mourning seated woman. – Samuel Martin †1788. *Bacon* again. Profile medallion in an obelisk. – N aisle. Richard Lloyd †1732. Cartouche.

CHURCHYARD. Several monuments to the Guest family, including one to their relative, the antiquary Sir Austen Henry Layard †1894, who discovered and excavated Nineveh in 1845 (*see* below). Of Scottish granite, in the style of an C18 chest tomb.

CANFORD MANOR (Canford School). A mighty C15 kitchen and a mighty C19 mansion. That the latter is Dorset's Victorian mansion *par excellence* is due almost entirely to *Sir Charles Barry* in the 1840s; but Canford is not only a spectacular composition, it is as pretty an archaeological conundrum as the enthusiast of C19 architecture will find anywhere. The facts are these.

A major medieval house, probably built *c.* 1400 for the Montagu earls of Salisbury, was demolished in 1765, but not before it had been recorded for the first edition of Hutchins's county history. Of this, the fortress-like kitchen wing (known as 'John of Gaunt's Kitchen') is all that survives. A successor house (perhaps retaining some medieval fabric) was also swept away, when *Edward Blore* was commissioned by Lord de Mauley in 1826 to build a replacement, Tudor Revival house. This and the 17,400-acre estate (that reached the sea beyond Poole) were bought in 1846 by Sir Josiah John Guest of Merthyr Tydfil, the ironmaster, and his wife, Lady Charlotte, Welsh scholar and editor of the *Mabinogion*. The next year they called in *Barry* to turn it into a mansion,* with porch-tower at the NW, great hall in the former courtyard, monumental staircase and extensive service ranges. This work, executed by *Thomas Cubitt & Co.*, was completed in 1850 and presented a fairly compact, although large-scaled, composition. Its present, more sprawling character cannot be fully blamed on Barry. In 1851 he was commissioned to add a conservatory and exhibition room to the NE (the so-called Nineveh Court) for Guest's Assyrian reliefs. In 1873–6 *David Brandon* did a bit of remodelling for Guest's son, the 1st Lord Wimborne, and in 1888 *Romaine-Walker & Tanner*'s long Smoking Room and Billiard Room wing extended from the w side. At the same time they elaborated the principal interiors. Buff local brick and pale stone dressings, Caen, Portland or Bath, were used by both Blore and Barry, giving a disappointingly pallid tonality to the

---

* *Thomas Hopper* was initially consulted but he failed to impress.

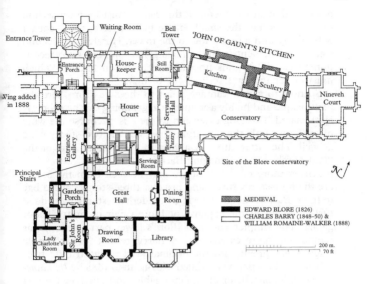

Canford Magna, Canford Manor.
Plan

building; the style veered between Tudor, Perp and Dec. With
the family concentrating their efforts on Ashby St Ledgers, the
Northamptonshire house altered by Lutyens in 1904 and 1909,
Canford declined in use. The 2nd Lord Wimborne sold the
property in 1923, which is when Canford School was founded.

The mansion stands in flat grounds on the S side of the
Stour, land that never lent itself to bold garden design. Around
the fringes of its S prospect, school buildings are scattered,
generally respectful of its setting, while other concentrations
of school buildings stand to the E and W.

To do justice to the EXTERIOR one may begin by approaching from the W, passing between the churchyard and the Stour,
to arrive at the front door on the N side. At the approach
then the house begins with the one-storey range of 1888 by
Romaine-Walker & Tanner, in a flowery Dec style – fancy cresting to the bay windows and so on. This pales before *Barry*'s
gigantic entrance tower. This is one of the best things Barry
ever designed, Perp of course, and unmistakably an echo of the
Victoria Tower of the Houses of Parliament, in its sheerness
and squareness.★ Square turrets rise from broad, low angle
buttresses, the SE turret octagonal and the highest. Over the
entrance arch a three-storey full-height oriel, also rectangular
not canted. Tracery only at the top. The N front of the service
court is also Barry's but keeps quiet, and with its small gables
and mullioned windows is hard to distinguish from Blore's
parts, which we shall see on the garden elevations. The coarse

★The Guests visited the Palace of Westminster then under construction from which,
according to Lady Charlotte's diaries, they took 'hints'.

oriel window at the E end of this range must be an insertion of *Brandon*'s; but the small square bell-turret at the E corner is by *Barry* and a pretty foil to the tower. Heraldic beasts and stepped battlements round an octagonal top part. Curvaceous domed cap. This joins up with the medieval kitchen, which must be separately described (*see* below).

So now to a new vantage point to the SW. From here the picturesque and highly asymmetrical grouping can be properly appreciated. The long extension to the l. is of course the wing of 1888, not only the one-storey part but the two-storey wing as well. The latter cuts out a view of the bottom part of the great porch-tower, damaging Barry's intentions.

Rather more of *Blore*'s house may be seen from the S. His are the four-storey turret and broader three-storey canted bay to the r. *Barry* echoed these in a broader two-storey bay added further r. but at the expense of Blore's pair of pretty Tudor gables. The simpler Tudor of Blore's lower part to the l. was remodelled more extensively by Barry, rebuilt forward of its original alignment, and the original oriel replaced by a two-storey bay. This part was fiddled with again in 1888 by *Romaine-Walker & Tanner*, being given fancy gables and a pierced parapet to match the Dec of their long W wing. What *Barry* also did was to develop Blore's composition into depth. The steep roof of the Great Hall rises behind Blore's turret, and leads one's eye back to the porch-tower, which Barry intended to stand at the far l. corner of the group in the way well-nigh obligatory for Early Victorian mansions (but compromised by the long W wing, as already mentioned).

Further back to the E, on the site of Barry's conservatory, is a long Perp screen wall like a cloister wall, its last bay open to the NINEVEH COURT. This last pavilion is a Greek cross in plan, with a boarded stencilled roof and Egyptian motifs on the doors, built in 1851 to house the magnificent Assyrian reliefs from Nimrud, presented by the archaeologist Sir Henry Layard to his father-in-law. The reliefs, sold in 1932 and 1959, are now in the Metropolitan Museum, New York, and else-where. A remaining relief, thought to have been a plaster cast, was in 1992 found to be an original and subsequently sold. A plaster-cast copy of this last panel is in its place. Still surviving are the decorations in a Ninevite style, designed to accompany the reliefs, with stained glass and cast-iron grills also incor-porating Assyrian motifs. Externally there was a curious two-tiered roof lantern at the crossing, since removed.

The so-called JOHN OF GAUNT'S KITCHEN, lying N of the screen wall, is the medieval survivor. It has Perp features, so far as there are any: two four-centred-arched N doorways and a string course on the S wall with grotesque heads. Walls of squared grey limestone blocks, with dark local brown stone used low down and high up. Vast projecting chimney-breasts. Also, a rare survival, the original louvred chimneys. Internal division into a larger W room, where the large fireplace opening in the cross-wall is at right angles to the monumental fireplace opening in the N wall. A third fireplace in the E room. Why were all three needed? Hutchins's plan of the manor before its demolition *c.* 1765 shows the main house, not unusually large, to the NE, attached corner-wise to the kitchen, not an unusual arrangement; but as for multiple fireplaces Margaret Wood only mentions South Wingfield, which had two.

The INTERIOR of the house was arranged by *Barry* so that Blore's service wing became a long entrance gallery from the entrance tower at the N to the reception rooms at the S. Plaster rib-vault. The elaborate terracotta chimneypiece in a Quattrocento style is by *Romaine-Walker & Tanner*. Barry's carved stonework is excellently executed, Sir John's and Lady Charlotte's initials appearing everywhere. In the garden porch an exceedingly naturalistic display of stone carving on the chimneypiece and overmantel, dead game, signed by *Salesio Pegrassi*, 1866. This is the vestibule to the Great Hall, of *c.* 1850, Barry's second set-piece, and a sop to Lady Charlotte's yearnings for medievalism. Placed within the body of the house and thus lit only from the expansive Perp windows in the end gables, its use as a central concourse is signified by the prominent fireplace in the far wall. Many doorways, not all of them able to be opened. Timber roof of elaborate arch-brace and wind-brace construction, now painted in primary colours. Stained glass in the end windows, mainly heraldic, designed by *Pugin* and made by *Hardman*.* Mosaics below, of kings, under tabernacle work. The W gallery and panelling in an Early Renaissance style is *Romaine-Walker & Tanner* of *c.* 1888. That is also the date of the staircase in its present remodelled and oppressively over-timbered form, following a fire that badly damaged this part of the house in 1884. Barry however had established its plan, starting in one flight, wide at first, then narrowing, and returning in two. The staircase window is also by *Pugin* and *Hardman*, apart from the lower panels of *c.* 1888 (note the Golden Jubilee portrait of Queen Victoria). Of the S rooms the former Drawing Room, with two window bays, has a Pompeian-style painted ceiling (probably of 1873–6); the present Headmaster's Study, W of it, a gilt ceiling in the Louis Quinze manner of *c.* 1888.

SCHOOL BUILDINGS. After Canford became a public school, first the block to the E of 1930, by *H. Tomlins* of *Reynolds & Tomlins* of Bournemouth, copying the house, in an inappropriately matter-of-fact way. ASSEMBLY HALL, similar in style and date, further E, also by *Reynolds & Tomlins*. Further to the SE is the MUSIC SCHOOL, 1974, by *Reid & Seal*. Brick with monopitched roofs in a faintly Aalto style. To its N the LAYARD THEATRE, 1998, by *NVB Architects*. Pale brick, exposed blockwork and metal-covered roofs arranged around a central polygonal pyramid.

SW of the house are two earlier school buildings, both designed by the art master, *Robin Noscoe*. In the PAVILION-CUM-OPEN-

---

*The glass at the E end appears to be a replacement of the 1950s. *Pugin* also made designs for metalwork at Canford.

AIR THEATRE, 1965–7, he used a fashionable butterfly roof in a way that gives it meaning. Black brick walling. Concrete relief by *Geoffrey Clarke* over the entrance to the theatre. The ART SCHOOL, 1970, consists of a central pavilion, the studio, glazed at both ends, set beyond a huge tree and a formal pool, and lower study rooms l. and r. Again the directness of the design is highly successful.

LODGE at the main entrance. By *Barry*, c. 1850. A proper preludium to the house, as lodges rarely are. Archway with gable over and an ogee-domed turret. Enlarged a little. – RAILWAY BRIDGE over the private drive, ¾ m. W. 1853 by *Banks & Barry*. Four-centred pointed arch. Much heraldic carving to the stonework. – At the end of the drive, 200 yds further W, WIMBORNE LODGE. Of c. 1853 by *Banks & Barry*. Tudor. Wrought-iron GATE SCREEN with pedestrian turnstiles (explicitly intended to prevent the passage of cyclists). – SOUTH LODGE, Magna Road, ¾ m. S. Also *Charles Barry*'s, and dated 1850. To the SE C18-style wrought-iron GATES with overthrow, moved from near to the house in 1936.

The VILLAGE is a very complete example of the Victorian model estate, meticulously, if not stiflingly, philanthropic. Buff brick and terracotta cottages. Two rows dated 1870 and 1872 by *Banks & Barry*, and several pairs of cottages along Oakley Lane. Former SCHOOL, 1876 by *Banks & Barry*.

At CANFORD HEATH, 3½ m. S, the MEDICAL CENTRE, Mitchell Road. 1998 by *Stephen Sherlock*. Wave- and mono-pitched roofs intersecting. An elegance and economy of detailing.

CANN *see* SHAFTESBURY

CASTLETON *see* SHERBORNE

CASTLETOWN *see* PORTLAND, p. 484

CATHERSTON LEWESTON

Monster rock-faced GATEPIERS guard the approach to church and house.

ST MARY. Rebuilt in 1857–8 by *J. L. Pearson* for R. C. Hildyard, QC, Lord of the Manor and M.P. for Whitehaven, Cumberland. In the grounds of his manor house. In the style of a chapel of ease, richly detailed. Nave and chancel of the same height, but divided. Walling of Chert in crazy-paving pattern and with careful elimination of all black and dark grey. Instead light grey, white, beige. W bellcote. All of crisp masonry, in the style of c. 1300. Especially fine is the W doorway with delicate leaf carving; big cinquefoil to the door arch. Shafted chancel windows. Roofs with wind-braces and carved corbels. – FURNISHINGS. All very high quality, especially the pulpit and font. – TILEWORK by *Minton*. – STAINED GLASS. By *Clayton & Bell*, 1858. A good set.

MANOR HOUSE. 1887. What one sees from the church is a rich and scholarly evocation of the Early Tudor style: not exactly what those gatepiers had prepared one for. This is a major remodelling for Major J. B. Symes Bullen. Behind lies a house of the late C16, visible especially at the far E. Here a late C16 porch, rebuilt. Two-storeyed; quite simple. Inside, earlier alterations made in the mid C18, especially the staircase.

CATTISTOCK   *5090*

The village is quite large and unusually coherent, with streets of continuous houses, varied in date and character, winding about, so that the church tower can be admired from many angles.

ST PETER AND ST PAUL. This is a Victorian masterpiece among   106
Dorset churches. Parts of the outer walls of the N and S chapels are partly C15 and C17, but what matters here is the thrilling combination of the works of *Sir George Gilbert Scott* and his son *George Gilbert Scott Jun.* These parts are highly illustrative of the development of Gothic Revival church architecture, showing the changed enthusiasm from that of the Middle Pointed to the acceptance of the value of Perpendicular as an equally authoritative source. Scott Jun. was the leading figure in this changed Gothic aesthetic, joined by Bodley and later by Temple Moore. Here we see the implications of that change, and a renewed interest in the virtues of letting the style of the building be influenced by the locale. So in Scott Jun.'s work the use of Ham Hill stone contrasting with Belgian sandstone creates a two-tone effect as found, for example, on nearby Chantmarle (q.v.).

To deal with the earlier parts first, the N chapel is said (by Hutchins) to date from 1630, but has a Perp N window and a wagon roof. The S chapel has a Perp E window. In 1857 *Sir Gilbert* added a S aisle of two bays with a round pier and, more importantly, a polygonal apse (similar to that of his contemporary church at Woolland, q.v.). This is built of flint with Ham Hill banding, the materials used throughout Scott's restoration. The apse (said to be following the foundations of a medieval apse) is late C13 in style (of perhaps *c.* 1280). Polished Purbeck marble colonnettes to the rere-arches and chancel arch. The nave W end and much of the S aisle were also rebuilt at this time. Carving, especially fine on the capitals, by *Farmer & Brindley*. The 1857 work cost £1,900, at the expense of the Rev. H. Still.

Scott Jun. in 1874 tackled the job in a different spirit and, thanks to the family of the Rev. K. H. Barnes, on a different scale. (The costs were also on a different scale, rising from an estimate of £2,700 to a final price of £6,046 12s. 6d.) He pulled down the existing N tower and replaced it by a two-bay arcade, with its arches dying into pier and responds, challenging his father's faith in the Middle Pointed. The *tour de force* here is of course the new TOWER, for which he chose a NW location where the falling ground adds to the impressive height, especially as seen from the w. Its models are to be found across the border in Somerset at e.g. St Cuthbert, Wells, or St Peter, Evercreech, where the bell-openings are extremely tall and are subdivided by a prominent central rib or mullion on each face. In the Somerset examples these have pointed tops; here Scott provided similar tracery heads but set back under strong flat hoods, more in tune with Charminster. However, the slender proportions of the tower, reinforced by the original effect of the corner buttresses only reaching the lower part of the bell-openings, are unparalleled in the county. The bell-openings are in pairs of two lights with two transoms. Scott's drawings, and the blank raised panels, indicate that further carved elaboration was intended but left unfinished, such as above the bell-openings and around the w doorway. A fire in 1940 caused considerable damage, requiring much rebuilding by *J. Sydney Brocklesby*, 1948–51. No doubt for some structural reason, he heightened the corner buttresses, weakening Scott's well-judged tower profile.

Stretching across the w end of the nave are vestries, equally challenging to the Middle Pointed Goths in their use of overtly Tudor detailing, such as the pair of oriel windows. These have flint banding to harmonize with Sir Gilbert's exterior masonry. A baptistery is placed in the base of the tower, separated from the w side of Scott Jun.'s porch by a screen, and with another opening through into the w end of the nave. Combined with the opening out of the w side of the N chapel, the interplay of spatial experiences here is of the highest order. Finally to the porch itself, Perp with a low-pitched gable, and open also on the w side to allow access from stone steps leading up from the lower w ground level.

FURNISHINGS. Fine TILEWORK by *Minton* in the chancel. – Here also good wrought-iron GATES, made by *L. Curtis* of Maiden Newton to *Sir Gilbert Scott*'s design. – Low chancel SCREEN and matching CHOIR STALLS, all by *Scott*. – PULPIT. By *Scott*. Entered through the pier of the chancel arch. Richly carved (by *Farmer & Brindley*) from Ham Hill stone with Caen stone figures of St Paul and the Evangelists. Raised on polished stone colonnettes. – The plainish granite FONT was given an extremely high COVER, *c.* 1904, by *Temple Moore*. It has an ingenious inner part that is raised to reveal the bowl. – WALL DECORATION with a large painting of St George, stencilled foliage and two tiers of standing figures, by *W. O. & C. C. Powell* of London and Lincoln, 1901, in the style of Burlison & Grylls. – SCULPTURE. A small piece of Saxon interlace in the chancel N wall, C9 or C10. – STAINED GLASS. As one might expect, a highly representative selection of the best designers. Part of Scott's 1857 scheme the chancel windows and a large 'Tree of Jesse' w window made by *Lavers & Barraud*, with *Alfred Bell* as designer. s chapel E probably also by them; the adjoining s window by *Kempe & Co.*, 1917. s aisle, a window by *Hardman*, 1880, and, to its W, an exquisitely beautiful one by *Morris & Co.*, 1882. Two lights and just six angels in gorgeous red and white robes against a glowing dark blue background. The uppermost two angels were designed by *Burne-Jones*. s aisle W window, stamped quarries by *Powell & Sons*; another such in the N chapel. Baptistery windows by *Burlison & Grylls*, 1874. N chapel E window by *R. Anning Bell*, 1923.

HOLY WELL in the churchyard. Mid-C19, with an arch in a Transitional style.

SAVILL MEMORIAL HALL, Duck Street, ⅛ m. NE. Dated 1926, perhaps by *E.P. Warren*. It takes its cue from Chantmarle (q.v.).

CHALMINGTON, 1 m. N. A long range of *c.* 1770 incorporates a small C16 portion. The house was enlarged and rendered in 1867 (date on rainwater heads) when picturesque gabled blocks were added at either end. The little LODGE (presumably also of *c.* 1867) and the big STABLES across the road make a characteristic group.

HOLWAY FARM, 1 m. NNW. Very complete early C17 small stone house, spoilt only by the slate roof. Rectangular plan. For dating the telling feature is that the windows, of three and four lights, have no hoodmoulds. Continuous string course instead. (In one room a C17 plaster ceiling with vine-scroll ornament to the main beams; semicircles of palmettes in the compartments. Another has a plaster overmantel with two seahorses and a central lion's-head mask.)

THE CASTLE, Castle Hill, ½ m. NE of the village. A terrace around the hilltop forms an ovate enclosure, with two ramped entrances. Undated.

CAUNDLE MARSH

6010

ST PETER AND ST PAUL. Rebuilt in 1857 by *R.H. Shout* of Yeovil. A pleasant small and low church. Bellcote at the nave E end. E.E. with twin windows on the sides, Geometrical at the ends. – FURNISHINGS. The E end was given some solid stone fittings in 1920. These include the ALTAR, EASTER SEPULCHRE, PISCINA and PULPIT. – FONT. Octagonal, Perp, with quatrefoils. C15 bowl, restored on a base *c.* 1857. – STAINED

GLASS. E window by *N. W. Lavers*, 1857. W by *Lavers & Barraud*, †1860. – MONUMENT. John Brit †1587. Tomb-chest built into chancel wall. Simple lozenges and shields in panels. No effigy. – Mrs St Lo †1846. Gothic tablet.

MANOR FARM, beside the church. In origin late medieval. There is a cross-passage doorway on the N front with a C16 pointed head, and the traces of its fellow in the S wall. The range running N from the W end is of the C16: see the windows with arched lights in its E wall. Through passage here into the churchyard. The S windows of the early part are of the C17, three-light and four-light. E range running S, also of the C17, but with refenestration its age can now be deduced only from the inside.

MARSH COURT, ⅓ m. N. Mainly craftsmanly Neo-Georgian of 1910 by *Macpherson & Richardson* of Derby, for the Hon. L. J. O. Lambert. But the central chimneystack has the re-set date 1731. This indicates the date of the earlier house that was remodelled, retaining a few features, such as the stone centrepiece of the W front. This includes both the doorway with a hood on well-carved brackets and the window above, with decorative side scrolls but the two window lights arched, an odd combination. That can hardly be believed until one learns that mullioned windows are re-set round the side and at the back.

6000

CERNE ABBAS

For the Middle Ages Cerne Abbas was no doubt primarily the abbey of Cerne; for us it is the parish church with its prominent tower. Historically Cerne was a town. Decline to its present status came after *c.* 1840, when local industries (silk working, brewing and tanning) died. But the way it grew up in relation to the abbey is still very clear. The two main streets are quite different in character. Long Street, running E–W, has a typical mixture of buildings from the late C16 to the early C20. Architectural changes were probably prompted by two town fires, in 1644 and 1740. These do not seem to have affected Abbey Street, leading from the former market place at its S junction with Long Street to the gateway of the abbey itself.

ST MARY. What one sees today appears to be a large church of Late Perp unity. Its evolution is far more complex, starting with a late C13 building of which only the chancel N and S walls survive. The aisles, or at least their arcades and the walls E of the S porch, are mid-C15. The aisles W of the porch, and the W tower, are of *c.* 1500; the clerestory was added *c.* 1530. Even the chancel E wall is later, as this is of 1639, its six-light window in a panelled surround presumably re-set (and said to have been brought in – perhaps from the abbey).

The tower, embraced by the aisles and of Ham Hill stone, is one of the finest in the county. Three tall stages with octagonal corner buttresses of diminishing girth, and a quatrefoil-enriched band between the second and third stages. Three-light bell-openings with a transom and Somerset tracery, and a higher stair-turret on the NW corner, this a wider version of a corner buttress. W doorway with quatrefoil-and-dagger spandrels; flanking angled shafts. Four-light W window with hooded image niches in the reveals; an early C16 statue of the Virgin above it, heavily draped in a cloak with sagging rounded folds, in a more elaborate niche. Central spirelet to each tower face just below the bell-openings.

As for the rest, some stone and flint banding. Embattled S porch and N and S chapels continuous with their aisles. Clerestory with typical three-light Tudor windows. Against all this the chancel stands out as Late E.E.: see the small pointed-trefoiled lancets. The interior is as rewarding as the outside, or more so, but largely cleared of historic furnishings. The wall paintings (*see* below) were conserved as part of a careful restoration by the *Brandt Potter Hare Partnership*, completed in 1967. An earlier restoration by *T.H. Wyatt*, 1870, put back a chancel arch and took out galleries. The most interesting feature is the stone SCREEN, C15. It has a solid wall instead of a dado, and above it, until 1870, there was no chancel arch but again solid wall.* So, while the wall was in place, one looked into the chancel through the openings in the screen only. They are two lights, four lights, the doorway, four lights, two lights. No tracery at all. The screen's crenellated top is of 1870 and part of the restoration. Other features to note are the very high, panelled tower arch and the lower (also panelled) arches from the tower into the aisles. Arcades of four bays plus one to the chancel chapels, of standard elements. In the chancel a C14 PISCINA. Elaborated ogee trefoil head.

OTHER FURNISHINGS. COMMUNION RAIL. Early C17. Turned balusters and a thin moulded handrail. – PULPIT. Dated 1640 on a shield. A fine piece but highly provincial for its date. Two tiers of highly elaborated arched panels. A single arched panel on the backplate with different detail. Tester with pendant arcading. – FONT. Plain. Tapering octagonal bowl. Perhaps C14. Painted COVER with a conical top, 1963. – TOWER SCREEN. Dated 1749, yet still C17-looking. Curious barley-twist balusters alternating with plain. Shaped top. – CHANDELIER. Large, undated, but probably later C18. – PAINTINGS. In the chancel on N and S window reveals, late C14 wall paintings. A female saint in a S window reveal, four scenes from the life of St John the Baptist in the NE corner. Some touching up. Also many inscriptions of verses from the Bible, 1679 and later. These are principally above the aisle

---

*The wall paintings indicate that this upper wall was in place by at least the mid C17. However, it is hard to believe that this, and the one at Bradford Abbas, were not replacements for earlier chancel arches.

arcade. The tops of some remain above the restored chancel arch. – STAINED GLASS. In the E window C15 shields, re-set. A window in the S aisle by *N.H.J. Westlake*, 1910. – MONU-MENTS. Two John Notleys †1612 and 1626. Simple brasses in the nave aisle. – William Cockeram †1679. Painted wooden panel. It describes him as a 'Practicioner in physick & Chir-urgery'. – Thomas Cockeram †1862. Gothic tablet signed by *W. Osmond* of Salisbury. – Major Thomas Davis †1855. Gothic and even more elaborate (but hidden by the organ). Also signed by *Osmond*.

CONGREGATIONAL CHAPEL (former), Abbey Street. Of *c.* 1870. Gothic, with polychrome brickwork to the arches; also a diaperwork band.

CERNE ABBEY, 250 yds N. A monastery existed here in the late C9. It was re-founded before 987 as part of the Benedictine impetus of the C10. Very little is known of the buildings. The present graveyard, orientated E–W, is the probable location of the abbey church. As a result of this use, no excavations have been made, and the plan of the abbey has not yet been recovered. The abbot's lodging and guest house appear to have been in the SW corner; their remaining standing structures are now in the garden of Cerne Abbey.

'CERNE ABBEY', at the N end of Abbey Street. Partly late C15, but incorporating late C16 and C17 features. Mostly rebuilt *c.* 1750 after a fire. A substantial house. The central gabled pro-jection, on which Abbey Street is aligned, must have formed the main gateway of the abbey – see the angle buttresses, and in particular the springing of the entrance arch (double-chamfered) now embedded in the wall. For the rest, it appears, old walling and windows were employed to reconstruct the building after the fire. The central window of the gateway projection amusingly proclaims the date, a four-lighter given a pointed central head to make it Gothic Venetian. Just r. of this a round-arched doorway, early C17. At the rear a lozenge panel of *c.* 1600.

Across the path to the E, the detached GRAVEYARD of the church, entered through a small early C17 GATEWAY crowned with three obelisks. Here some fragments of the ABBEY WALLS still stand. There are also small fragments built into various houses. Just NW of the graveyard are three more substantial remains.

Entry is through a gate alongside 'Cerne Abbey'. Just r. is the so-called GUEST HOUSE, perhaps built as an earlier Abbot's Lodging. Probably *c.* 1460 (a fireplace now in 'Cerne Abbey' has the initials of John Vanne, abbot 1458–70). It is of two storeys with banded flint and chalk. In the N wall its best feature, an oriel with a two-light transomed window to each face, the upper lights with trefoiled heads. Four further first-floor windows, with transoms and cusping missing but originally matching. On the ground floor, part of a doorway and further two-light windows.

PORCH to the ABBOT'S HALL, N of the Guest House. Built for Thomas Sam, abbot 1497–1509. A sumptuous piece, comparable with that of Forde Abbey (q.v.) and only slightly less elaborate. Four-centred arch with multi-moulded jambs; label moulding with beast-stops. Above this a two-storey oriel, two by three lights, these with cinquefoil heads, the lower row with tracery. Below the windows rows of shields. The porch has diagonal buttresses and an embattled parapet. Inside a damaged fan-vault with bosses. The doorway inside towards the hall has shields in the spandrels. Above it are shafts connected with the hall, although here much later rebuilding.

A BARN stands NNW of the porch. C15; not large. Above a doorway a stone with E.E. foliage.

The church stands in ABBEY STREET, *ante portas*. Along the other side of the street runs a range of early C16 timber-fronted houses, originally forming a continuous row of seven abbey shop-tenements, probably built as a speculation. Two storeys with a jetty. Nos. 3 and 5 (THE PITCHMARKET and   55 ABBEY COTTAGE) have been stripped down to the timbers, and the former has a pretty decorative timber door lintel, quatrefoils forming an ogee doorhead. Broad stone party walls, with moulded corbelling at the overhang, and stone backs. There is little else like this left in the county now; though even in stone areas builders in the late Middle Ages often preferred timber for fronts because of the flexibility this gave in the matter of window openings. Nos. 7 and 9, adjoining, retain their plaster. No. 7 was refenestrated in the early C19, including a sashed bow shop window. A similar transition has occurred to No. 9, but here an early C19 half-dormer with sashes in a canted bay. (Built into the back wall of No. 7 an elaborate Perp BRACKET, a fragment from the abbey church, of, it may be, sedilia or reredos.) Beyond the former Congregational chapel (*see* above) and a row of 1960s houses (fitted out as if they were jettied), No. 15, another early C15 house, jettied with early C19 casements.

Abbey Street also has some fine early C18 houses. The best on the W side, adjoining Nos. 3 and 5, is No. 1 (THE OLD HOUSE). Painted brick, with new windows of the early C19. The telling feature is the platband, set at the same level as the bressumer of the adjoining timber-framed buildings. Good shell-hooded porch with Doric columns.

Abbey Street makes a T with LONG STREET, the main street of the village. The mixture here of orangey stone and flint, red brick and colourwash is extremely attractive. The most significant building is the NEW INN, to the W (on the S side). Late C17 but seemingly remodelled from something earlier. The removal of its early C19 stucco illustrates the degree of rebuilding. The windows, of seven bays regularly spaced, are upright, not horizontal any longer. Those on the ground floor to the l. of the early C19 carriage arch (in bay five) are the earliest: stone-mullioned and transomed with hoodmoulds. To the r. these have wide sashes installed *c.* 1800. The two-light mullioned

first-floor windows are a later change, indicated by the rebuilding in brick around them. A large area of banded flint and
stone at the l. end (mirrored in a shorter length at the r.) indicates early construction, but the banding between the ground-
floor windows does not match. In complete contrast, set back
on the N side is THE OLD MANSE (to the Congregational
chapel). Of *c.* 1740. Brick (Flemish bond with burnt headers)
and early C19 wide sashes, these no doubt contemporary with
the mansard roof. Pedimented doorcase. Opposite this, on
the S side, No. 20 (formerly the Old Bell Inn) has banded flint
with mullioned windows. Probably *c.* 1600. Does this give us a
probable original appearance of the New Inn? Two doors E of
this, the former Red Lion (now THE GIANT INN). Red brick,
incorporating three Ipswich windows on the ground floor. It
was rebuilt in 1898 after a fire (as stated on the sign).
    There are also a number of good early C19 SHOPFRONTS sur-
viving in Long Street. The best are at the junction with Duck
Street, to the W. No. 1 (THE OLD SADDLER), an early C19
stuccoed block, has a near-symmetrical arrangement taken
around the corner. Also fine is that on the opposite corner
(No. 2, CERNE ANTIQUES). Here too an early C19 wrought-
iron-fronted balcony. Finally, opposite this group, on the S side
of Long Street, the former POLICE STATION and MAGIS-
TRATES' COURT of 1859 (now cottages). Chequerboard stone
and flint and a row of half-hipped gables, striving at picturesque grouping.
    TITHE BARN, 440 yds SW. Mid-C14; the S end converted to a
house, late C18. A very fine monastic barn. Walls of knapped
flint, deep-set ashlar buttresses, stepping in high up with three
set-offs. Segment-headed arch to the two wagon-porches.
Gothick pointed windows at the S end belonging to the conversion. In the S gable there are two tiers of three, set between
the buttresses. The barn, now nine bays long, was originally
longer at the N end.
CERNE UNION WORKHOUSE (now CASTERBRIDGE MANOR),
    ⅓ m. NW. 1836–7 by *Charles Wallis* of Dorchester. Stucco. Cru-
    ciform plan with main block on the E side.
CERNE GIANT (National Trust), ⅓ m. N. He is a turf-cut figure,
    200 ft (60 metres) high and 165 ft (50 metres) wide, holding a
    knobbed club 120 ft (37 metres) long in his r. hand. His l. hand
    is empty but outstretched. It is generally agreed that the figure
    represents Hercules. It was first recorded in detail in 1763; the
    engraving of that date differs little from that seen today. A soil
    resistivity survey in 1980 revealed traces of a cloak over his
    l. arm, reinforcing the Hercules notion. In date the figure is
    probably no earlier than the mid C17; the earliest documented
    reference to it is in 1694.
THE TRENDLE, above the Giant. A rectangular EARTHWORK
    ENCLOSURE, undated, possibly prehistoric. Evidence for later
    uses, including maypole dancing.
BLACK HILL, ¾ m. SSE. ENCLOSURES and 'CELTIC' FIELDS
    across the hilltop, some unploughed, including hut circles,

pit hollows and mounds; Bronze Age, with some Roman occupation.

CHALBURY

A scattered settlement on a hill. The main village, still very small and no older than the late C18, is ½ m. E at Chalbury Common.

ALL SAINTS. A small church of flint rubble and ashlar, neatly whitewashed, concealing a degree of brickwork rebuilding. Features of several dates include a blocked C13 N lancet (with a residue of original painting in the head), a group of early C14 E lancets, traces of Perp N windows and a most prominent C18 W window. C13 nave (C16 N wall and windows) and chancel, but with much work in the nave walls of the C18, when it was largely refenestrated. Plain boxy bellcote with a hipped roof at the W end.

Chalbury has the most completely preserved mid-C18 INTERIOR of any Dorset village church. How lucky that such a place should have escaped the Ecclesiologists. There they all are, the elements of Georgian worship: the baluster FONT, the modest three-decker PULPIT, the SQUIRE'S PEW with a balustraded front, the BOX PEWS, the WEST GALLERY and a depressed chancel arch which, like a veranda screen, has depth as well as width and height; this is supported on thin separating columns, creating a rustic Venetian-window effect. Two square compartments (one used as a tiny pew) flank the arch. – COMMUNION RAIL. Oak, by the *Brandt Potter Hare Partnership*, with turned balusters. Installed in memory of Sir Owen Morshead (†1977), first chairman of the Dorset Historic Churches Trust.
DIDLINGTON LODGE, ½ m. NW. 1871 by *William Eden Nesfield*. Old English, with timber framing above red brick. It is the E lodge to Crichel House (*see* More Crichel).

CHALDON HERRING

A gathering of farms and cottages with a triangular village green at its centre.

ST NICHOLAS. Late C14 Perp W tower of two stages, battle-mented, boldly buttressed and with a stair-turret in the SE corner. C15 N porch. The remainder rebuilt by *G.R. Crickmay*, 1879, reusing the Perp chancel windows. Traceried E window reportedly C14, but it seems heavily restored. Nave roof largely retained in the rebuilding. Heavy S arcade by Crickmay. – All of the FURNISHINGS are of 1879. – FONTS. Late C11. Tapering cylindrical bowl. Also one by *Crickmay*, with supporting colonnettes. – E window by *Clayton & Bell*, †1885. S aisle window perhaps by *Heaton, Butler & Bayne*, 1897.

OLD VICARAGE, diagonally opposite. Of 1874, probably by *Crickmay*. Brick. Vaguely Gothic.

THE MANOR (formerly Chaldon Grange), just SE. Late C16 but refronted in the early C18. Long range with sash windows 2:3:2. Hipped stone roof.

FIVE MARYS, ¾ m. N. Six ROUND BARROWS in a linear group along the ridge. Two contained adult inhumations with stag antlers.

'CELTIC' FIELDS cover The Warren, into West Lulworth and to the sea. Part of a 340-acre field system, including Newlands Warren (West Lulworth).

HOLWORTH, 1½ m. W, is a deserted MEDIEVAL VILLAGE, with seven house platforms (tofts) and narrow banked fields (crofts) behind them. Excavation of one house in 1958 demonstrated use from the C13 to C15.

CHANTMARLE
Cattistock, ⅝ m. SW of Frome St Quintin

When it still remained complete, Chantmarle must have been one of the classic statements of the E-plan manor house. It is most regrettable that the end strokes of the E are lopped off. Such a plan was the standard Late Elizabethan and Jacobean ordering of the medieval plan, with its hall and porch between solar wing one way and kitchen wing the other (chapel wing at

Chantmarle, principal front prior to demolition of the wings.
Engraving, 1774

Chantmarle); but here the plan was given symbolic significance.
On the keystone of the porch doorway, with the date 1612, is
the word EMMANUEL, and Sir John Strode, the owner, gives the
explanation in his diary: the plan was 'in forma de littera (E),
per Emmanuel, id est Deus nobiscum in Eternum' ('in the form
of the letter E, for Emmanuel, that is God is with us for ever').
1612 is the beginning date for the rebuilding. The chapel, started
in 1612, was 'finished and covered before the rest of the dwelling house'. The building was completed in 1623. It is entirely of
Ham Hill ashlar. The chief masons were *Joseph & Daniel Rowe*
of 'Hamdon' (i.e. Ham Hill), and the surveyor whom Strode
employed, *Gabriel Moore* – 'a skilfull architect' – was also connected with that area. As to Moore's responsibilities, Strode, in
a way typical of his time, records that he employed him 'only to
survey & direct the building to the forme I conceived & plotted
it'. The house cost Strode £1,142.

What then is the personal vocabulary of Chantmarle? First the
    pedantic stress on symmetry. The entrance front faces E, two-
    storeyed, and the higher central porch is flanked by three
    bays of windows, all large and with transoms, but arranged
    in the sequence two-light, four-light, two-light at both levels.
    The extension to the l. is of *c*. 1907–10 by *Arthur Stratton*,
    reusing in the r. bay windows from the demolished N wing.
    The windows are without hoodmoulds, except for the porch
    gable window. The hoods over the upper four-lighters must
    have been inserted when the gables l. and r. of the porch
    were removed – *see* Hutchins's print of 1774. Continuous
    string course at first-floor level. What is remarkable is that
    the lights are all arched, an archaizing form deliberately
    chosen here (cf. Puncknowle and Herringston, Winterborne
    Herringston).
        Other rounded forms are the first-floor oriel of the porch,
    the porch doorway in a square surround and the niches beside
    it, and the steps up to the doorway; also a small wreathed
    roundel in the gable. On the wing ends there were two-storey
    bows, striking this note the loudest. If Strode insisted on the
    E-plan, it was surely *Moore*, the professional, who united the
    whole façade by this touch of artistry. Straight gable to the
    porch, with finials. The other six gables of the front have gone.
    A final comment is that the decorative features – oriel, finials,
    niches – are all too small and timid, a common fault in Jaco-
    bean façade design.
        The N wall is irregular, although part of the C17 work. The
    Gothic window with two ogee lights tells of the C15 chapel
    which Strode embodied in the house. To the S the extension
    of *c*. 1907–10 takes in a two-gabled block, of Strode's building,
    originally standing free, and an C18 addition to its rear. Same
    details as the main house. It is at the back however that one
    can read most clearly both the layout of Strode's house and
    the extent of the pre-existing building. This, the W front, has
    a big chimney-breast towards the r. marking the hall, lying
    in the S half of the main block; and towards the l. the gabled

stair projection. Two-light windows with a transom, extending to a third light where the hall is. The oblong range running off obliquely to the NW is clearly older. It is of flint and stone in bands with irregular windows of two or three arched lights plus hoodmoulds.

The interior has no C17 features of note, but many Jacobean-style plaster ceilings and fireplaces of *c.* 1910. The best of the new ceilings is in the hall, where it has ribs and pendants, and where the walls are partially panelled. The additions of this date were made when the house was rescued from dereliction by F. E. Savile. A further large kitchen wing to the N is by *E. P. Warren*, 1919, for Charles St John Hornby.

The terraced GARDEN to the E is of *c.* 1910 by *F. Inigo Thomas*. Balustrading around the pond at the centre of the SOUTH GARDEN. Also a canal-like pond running along the E boundary, below the terrace. The retaining wall on its upper side has small obelisks at the corners, a pair either side of a niche (marking a cross-axis of the garden) and another pair flanking a projecting and curved balustraded balcony, lining through with the main porch.

BLOCKS further W for a Police Training Centre, *c.* 1965.

COTTAGES, ⅓ m. E at the road junction. Two by *Alfred Powell*, for Hornby. Arts and Crafts; L-plan. Thatched with expressed flint and brick highlights. Waney-edged weatherboarding to the lean-tos.

CHARBOROUGH*

CHARBOROUGH PARK. Built *c.* 1655–62 for Sir Walter Erle, the Parliamentarian. The C17 house was of the up-to-date hipped-roofed type, seven bays by five, of local carstone (red) with ashlar dressings. It was extended in the C18 towards the E, and about 1810 *John Nash* homogenized the whole by means of stucco, a new hipped roof and, on the N front, a central five-bay pediment carried on Ionic pilasters.** This makes a house eleven bays long, two storeys high. Small SW water-turret of *c.* 1850 in a Vanbrugh style added for J. S. W. Sawbridge-Erle-Drax. An Ionic-columned porch was added here a little later. Long one-storey library, C18, remodelled *c.* 1810, coming out at right angles at the same place. It is behind a high screen wall. Bowed middle. Roof reconstructed and SE corner remodelled *c.* 1970 by the *Brandt Potter Hare Partnership*.

Inside, the spine corridor goes back to Sir Walter's time. Of the features to consider, the finest is undoubtedly the

---

*Access was refused, and the account is based on published sources, including John Newman's text following his visit for the first edition.
**J. B. Burke, *A Visitation of Seats and Arms*, vol. II (1853).

STAIRCASE HALL of 1718 for General Thomas Erle in the centre of the s front. This represents high fashion of that moment, and is a room of first-rate quality. The stairs rise in a rectangular well, three slim tapered balusters and carved ends to each tread. Newels in the form of fluted Corinthian columns, with a very elaborate arrangement at the bottom, where, at the under-curling handrail's end, a lion crouches, and a further piece curves round to carry a big vase. Doorcases with eared and ramped-up surrounds. The walls and ceiling of the well are all painted by *Thornhill*: see his signature and the date; also the dates, 1840 and 1953, of restoration. Grisaille putti and trophies below, mythological scenes in full colour above. Thornhill unites walls and ceiling in the Baroque way, but somewhat timidly. The subject is also a unity: the Judgment of Paris and the Rape of Helen, signifying the Triumph of Love. Also on the s front, in a projecting corridor added *c.* 1850, the ARMOURY, fitted out with much elaborate Gothic joinery. Its purpose was to provide a passage to a double-height, top-lit gallery beyond, of the same date, since demolished.

The landscaped PARK is the most splendid in Dorset, the clumps and belts of trees majestically mature. No landscaper's name is attached to it. It is also fully equipped with the appropriate features, of which the church is among the least conspicuous. Much is as late as *c.* 1850.

ST MARY (private). A Gothick toy behind the house, at the foot of a staircase up to a terrace. The church was built by Thomas Erle Drax in 1775. Two bays only, an obelisk bell-turret and obelisk pinnacles. Un-medieval angle pilasters, windows with cusped Y-tracery and a cottagey open w porch. This has clustered shafts and battlements. Before entering one expects a dainty white stucco interior. Instead one is stunned by big dark wooden spoils from Continental countries everywhere. They hardly leave you enough space to take them in individually. In 1837 the walls were heightened and a new roof constructed, a transformation made by J. S. W. Sawbridge-Erle-Drax. Of the items brought in then, the best is an ALTARPIECE from Antwerp, typical of *c.* 1520–30 in its curvaceous outline and crowded carving. It is on a side wall, above STALLS with dates 1626 and 1651 and with pieces both English and Continental. – The PULPIT is a bumper piece with decorative figures from the C16 to the C18, and relief scenes. It is a two-decker. The scenes are excellent, Mannerist work probably from the Netherlands.* – ALTARPIECE (at the e end). A pedimentally shaped Last Judgment, again *c.* 1600, again probably Netherlandish. – COMMUNION RAIL. Later C17. Wooden. – CHANDELIER. This may well be Neo-Baroque of the 1830s (French?). – STAINED GLASS. e and

*They may correspond to the panels recorded in 1858 as being in Drax's possession, and described as carved by *Berger* and brought from the Abbey of Pare near Louvain, Belgium. *See* Charles Tracy, *Continental Church Furniture in England: A Traffic in Piety* (2001).

W windows both no doubt also 1830s. In the W window the Christ from Raphael's Transfiguration, in the E window three large figures. – MONUMENTS. Richard Drax Grosvenor †1819. By *Sir Richard Westmacott*. White marble tablet with large seated figures of Faith and Charity. – Mrs Sawbridge-Erle-Drax †1853. With profile medallion. By *M.W. Johnson* of London.

Also close to the W side of the house, the GROTTO, perhaps late C18 in origin, rebuilt *c.* 1840, with a curvy shaped gable. A plaque above its entrance records it as the place where the plan to place William III on the throne was hatched. Further up the hill, the handsome kidney-shaped CONSERVATORY, of *c.* 1810.* Portland ashlar piers between full-height sash windows. The STABLES lie beyond, to the SW. Early C19, red brick, unhappily proportioned, with four very long arched windows under the central pediment. At the entrance to the stable yard unusual early C18 openwork iron GATEPIERS.

Further away, SE of the house, on a hilltop, the TOWER, that Late Georgian essential. This one is exceptionally high, octagonal, Gothic, of five storeys, with lancets and balustraded battlements, as it were. Rendered. Round the bottom two stages of pinnacled buttresses. The tower was built in 1790, but struck by lightning in 1838 and rebuilt higher in 1840. Circular stone staircase with Gothic cast-iron balustrade. Triumphal way from the house between big pedestals which await their statues.

Finally the sequence of GATEWAYS around the perimeter, interrupting the brick park wall that runs the full length of its boundary with the present A35. Fortunately, three may be viewed from the public highway. However, the earliest, PEACOCK LODGE, is far inside the park (and hence inaccessible). This must be of *c.* 1790. Ashlar-faced. Cubical lodges l. and r. with bullseye windows. Elliptical entrance arch with a deer on top. In 1841 Mr Sawbridge-Erle-Drax succeeded in getting the main Wimborne–Dorchester road re-routed to give him a much enlarged park.** He celebrated his success with three mighty gateways along the new road. They are the LION GATE, 1 m. NE, a straightforward stucco-faced triumphal arch with coupled Ionic columns, surmounted by a lion; STAG GATE, 1 m. N, a single lofty brick arch bearing a stag; and EAST ALMER LODGE, 1 m. NNW, also stucco, with two lodge blocks linked by an archway topped by a pediment. Also, ¾ m. WSW, a polygonal, conical-roofed thatched LODGE COTTAGE, of perhaps twenty years earlier. The roof edge is supported on slender timber posts. It was originally circular with porthole windows.

---

*Recent aerial views suggest that this is now roofless and derelict.
**He was also a Parliamentary Commissioner for Highways (Anthony Jaggard). On EAST ALMER LODGE an inscription panel celebrates the building of the diverted road.

CHARLTON MARSHALL   *9000*

A long main-road village, grown steadily southwards away from
the church.* The church once formed a group with Charlton
House, a villa of 1810 on the opposite side of the road. This was
demolished in 1979 and replaced by housing.

St MARY. Flint and stone, for nave and chancel in chequer. Late
C15 two-stage W tower. Its distinctive top with obelisk pinnacles and four little pediments between is a mid-C18 enrichment. The church is entirely of 1713–15 (although the three
chancel buttresses may reuse medieval material), rebuilt at
the expense of its rector, Dr Sloper, and costing 'near £1,000',
according to Hutchins. For the fitting-out, he used the *Bastards* of Blandford. Nave and chancel in one, arched windows,
gabled S porch. N aisle arcade of square piers with sunk panels,
round arches with keystones. Some rebuilding to this aisle
c. 1820. – REREDOS. A splendid piece, filling the whole E wall   82
and surrounding the E window. Giant pilasters separate the
centre from the side parts with the Ten Commandments.
The centre below the window has the Lord's Prayer and
the Creed under an open scrolly pediment. – COMMUNION
RAIL. Balusters include fluted Doric columns. – CHANCEL
S DOORWAY. Elaborate wooden architectural framework,
bow-fronted inscription panel above. – PULPIT. With excellent marquetry, a fine backplate and a tester. – FONT. An
ornately decorated square baluster (cf. Blandford). Domed
timber COVER. – ROYAL ARMS. Of Queen Anne, but with
monogram GR for George I. – STAINED GLASS. E window 1932,
W window 1956, both by *Powell & Sons*. – MONUMENTS. Dr
Charles Sloper †1727, possibly by *John Bastard*. A good tablet
with a skull in half-profile and putto heads. – Henry Horlock
and others, † to 1741 (including Bastard connections). Dainty
relief in an oval at the foot. – Thomas Bastard (IV) †1791. By
R. Cooke. Putto by an urn.

   The VILLAGE STOCKS (ironwork perhaps C18) have been
repositioned on the S side of the tower under a roof of 1930.
CHARLTON BARROW, ½ m. SE (just in Spetisbury parish). A
cottage orné-type house of *c.* 1845, by *George Evans* for himself.
COMBS DITCH. *See* Winterborne Whitechurch.

CHARMINSTER   *6090*

The River Cerne flows through the low-lying centre of the village,
with more substantial villas to the E and humbler thatched cottages to the W.

---

*The previous edition called the culs de sac of bungalows at the S end '*suburbia in
rure* at its worst'.

St Mary. At the core of this church is a substantial nave of
c. 1100 with late C12 aisle arcades. But outside, it is the w
tower that arrests attention. Of the early C16, with a monogram
on each stage of the w buttresses alluding to its builder, Sir
Thomas Trenchard of Wolfeton. The monogram is an inter-
woven pair of stylized Ts. The tower has set-back buttresses, a
five-light w window, bell-openings in pairs of two lights each
with two transoms and straight tops, and pinnacles in triplets
at the corners. The aisles embrace the tower and their windows
are Perp too, though mostly a little earlier. The chancel is low
and poor in contrast with the bold Perp work. It is of *c.* 1838
(perhaps by *John Barnes* of Dorchester, who wrote a report),
but incorporates a C17 Perp e window with tellingly incorrect
tracery, placed the wrong way round. The higher roof-line of
the medieval chancel is visible. Higher up, one also notices
the clerestory, and there, alternating with the square-headed
two-light late C15 windows, are four small round-headed ones
of *c.* 1100, two on each side.

And indeed the prevalent impression inside is Norman. Both
arcades are late C12, and as the clerestory windows do not
tally with the arcades the clerestory could be older than the
aisles. The arcades are of five bays with round piers carrying
much-scalloped capitals and square abaci; but the arches are
already pointed. Also their hoodmoulds have nailhead decoration. Two N capitals have small volutes, and the bases differ
N from S, which has spurs. Plain responds at the E end of
each arcade, probably of *c.* 1100. The chancel arch goes with
the arcades, so is part of the C12 rebuilding, but presumably
came first, as it is round with slight chamfers. The responds
have scalloped capitals and the middle member is keeled. To
the l. of the arch a large plain C16 squint. The width of the
original C12 aisles is given by the strikingly narrow w part
of the s aisle. In the rebuilt, wider e section three re-set late
C12 corbels, one with a bull's-head carving. The tower has
a panelled arch towards the nave of ochre Ham Hill stone,
used throughout the tower on decorative work. In the lower
panels are shields with the T monogram. This is repeated in
the same position on similar panelled arches to the w bays
of the aisles. The s chapel (really the e continuation of the
aisle) is much wider. Wider still is the N aisle, but that is
of 1875 (by *G.R. Crickmay*), though the re-set windows are
genuine late C15 work. The pews that remain in the nave and
s aisle date from a careful restoration and refurnishing by *C.E.
Ponting,* 1895–7. – PULPIT. Dated 1635 on an internal panel.
Two tiers of round-arched panels. – FONT. Probably C12 in
origin, but re-cut in the C15 to fit an octagonal stem. – ROYAL
ARMS. Of George II, on a wooden panel. Dated 1757. – PAINT-
ING. The arcade piers have the residue of a medieval scheme.
On the spandrels of the w tower arch a C16 painting of the
Tree of Life, very faint. On the nave N wall a fragment of a
pretty strawberry all-over pattern, probably early C16. Also late
C16 verses above the arcades, partly obliterated. – STAINED

GLASS. S chapel E window by *Burlison & Grylls*, 1912 (considered 'Florentine-looking' by Pevsner). Large W window by *C.E. Kempe*, 1896. – MONUMENTS. The S chapel was the Trenchard Chapel. The two anonymous Purbeck monuments are no doubt Trenchard tombs, dating from the second quarter of the C16. They are very similar. Tomb-chests with elaborate quatrefoils, no effigy, canopy with an arch, flat on segments, and a cresting. One has a panelled underside to the canopy, the other has a pendant there and indents of brasses on the back wall. – Grace Pole †1636. Kneeling figure between columns. Putti in clouds above her. Open pediment with crest at the centre. The monument was re-coloured in the mid C20.

CHURCHYARD CROSS. By *C.E. Ponting*, 1919. Elegant.

CHARMINSTER HOUSE, almost opposite the church. Partly of 1706; but the main S-facing part of this long house (with its back directly on the village street) is of the early C19. Stucco S front with a cast-iron veranda and French doors.

LITTLE COURT, ½ m. SE. Of 1909 by *P. Morley Horder* for K. Thruston. L-plan, with a third wing (together with a tall water tower) added between 1925 and 1929, completing the W-facing forecourt. Roughcast render with stone details and areas of red brick. Some stone-mullioned windows. Integral compartment garden to its E and S.

CHARLTON DOWN, 1¼ m. N. Here the former HERRISON HOSPITAL forms the core of a new-built village. Originally the County Lunatic Asylum, of 1859–63 by *H.E. Kendall Jun*. A central block with four long L-plan wings. Those to the S stucco-faced. At its centre a polychrome brick CHAPEL, raised up over a high undercroft. Large multi-bay-windowed and turreted hospital extension to its E of 1895–6 by *G.T. Hine*, also brick. This became the female half of the hospital, the original section being given over to male inmates. NE of this the original MORTUARY CHAPEL, *c.* 1860 by *Evans & Fletcher* of Wimborne (with banded flintwork), became the chancel of a new chapel by *Hine*, *c.* 1895 – a rather dull red brick affair. HERRISON HOUSE for private patients, 1904–14, also by *Hine*, was added to the NW in landscaped grounds. Elaborate Dutch-gabled style in brick with stone dressings. Much internal panelling, conveying the atmosphere of an Edwardian country house.

FORSTON HOUSE, 2 m. NNW. Square five-bay house of *c.* 1720 for Robert Browne. Red brick with stone window surrounds. Front and back the façades are made to rise boldly in a concave quadrant to support a flat top with urns. Thus the double gable-ends are hidden and an effect achieved of Baroque display. A long range was added to the N side in 1832 when Forston became a Pauper Lunatic Asylum. This was demolished *c.* 1900. Its existence explains why Herrison Hospital (*see* above) is on the hill to the SE.

WOLFETON HOUSE, ⅜ m. S. The Trenchards of Wolfeton were in the C16 a leading Dorset family. Between *c.* 1490 and 1534 Sir John (†1505) and his eldest son, Sir Thomas Trenchard (†1550), built themselves a compact courtyard house in an

Charminster, Wolfeton House.
Drawing, early C19

unusually festive style, and Sir George Trenchard enlarged it
c. 1580 in an unusually classical style. The enlargement remains
pretty nearly intact; but it is a grievous loss that only the gatehouse and the sw corner of the original house have survived.
The first range of the house, on the w side, was complete by
1506; the gatehouse in the opposite range may be contemporary, or may be associated with a second phase of work, completed for Sir Thomas in 1534, the date on a plaque recording
the completion of the house, resited on the gatehouse in the
mid C19.

This GATEHOUSE faces E, and here a study of Wolfeton
must begin. Either of the first phase (completed by *c*. 1506) or
forming part of Sir Thomas's building campaign, it is built of
coursed limestone rubble. Two round towers of unequal size
project diagonally from the E angles of the rectangular block
of the gatehouse, through which the entrance, with its broad
four-centred arches, is pierced off-centre. All is kept quite low,
two-storeyed although, to judge from early views, the conical
roofs were originally to a much steeper pitch and had tall
finials. So this is no flamboyant display piece. On the other
hand it is a mere nod towards defence, for which suffices an
arrow loop in each tower to cover the entrance. What does
call for attention is the finesse and elaboration of the details.
Windows with arched lights, bits of foliage in the spandrels,
and elegant mouldings carried down on to minuscule pedestals. The complex mouldings of the outer entrance arch are
brought down on to pedestal bases which return to form
the plinth moulding of the whole gatehouse. The arch-hood
ends on labels carved as a wild man and a satyr. The towers
themselves (intended as dovecotes) have a simpler moulding
to the plinth. The w entrance arch is more boldly moulded,
but has a similar relationship to the plinth moulding, which in
its turn carries round until it meets the tower on the N side.
The question arises whether the towers were built earlier than
the rest of the gatehouse; but the continuous string course at

first-floor level round the whole building seems to confirm that the discrepancy is without significance. Original internal newel stair of wood. The N chimney-breast here bears a date panel of 1534 recording completion. Completion of what? The panel is said to be re-set and to have come from the destroyed part of the s range of the house. Yet the early C19 drawings in the house which record the s range before demolition show the datestone already in its present position, supporting the proposition that the gatehouse was part of Sir Thomas's scheme to complete a quadrangular house. Stylistically the most significant details are the tiny shield-bearing putti at the apex of the W entrance arch and as hoodstops. They come from a Renaissance context and suggest that the carver took a North Italian engraving as his pattern.

The gatehouse now stands free of the house except for a C19 link corridor; but in the C16 its SW angle, now neatly mended to heal the scar, joined the s range of the house, and it thus formed the E range of the house around a remarkably tight little courtyard. Almost all of that house has gone: the N range (which contained a chapel) was demolished at some point before 1774 by William Trenchard, the last of the family to own Wolfeton. The remainder, including the N half of the W range and the whole of the s, went just after 1811, as part of a scheme to reduce the size of the house for Trenchard's solicitor, Robert Henning, who acquired the property in 1807 in dubious legal circumstances.

This left only the SW corner, just enough to give the flavour of the EARLY TUDOR HOUSE. Its short s end is the one to study, the other faces having been rebuilt to cover the demolition scars. In its walling it matches the gatehouse, and in the arched lights of its large windows and the mullions springing from little pedestals. But these windows are most curiously cramped between a broad polygonal staircase tower to the r. sharing a base-mould with the s wall, and a garderobe projection at first-floor level to the l., canted, under a candlesnuffer roof, and set on a thick square buttress. Similar base-moulding to this, but at a different level. No agreement at all about the level of the first-floor string course. The windows here must have been rearranged, the lower r. one inserted and lowered, cutting through the plinth frieze; but from the start the design was disorganized. Yet this was no despised back-side of the house. The details show that, being of greater elaboration than any others which remain. The upper five-light window and the lower two-lighter with a transom are set in square surrounds bordered with grooved scrolls and have heavy hoodmoulds carved on the undersides with bulging fruit, motifs which tell the same tale as the putti on the gatehouse, of Renaissance influence, from North Italy most probably, creeping into an otherwise purely Late Perp scene. Semicircular, not four-centred, arches to the lights, the slender mouldings carried down the sides of the mullions to pedestal bases. The third window, replacing presumably a twin of the two-lighter, has more elaborate pedestal-mouldings, stepping up and out

across the deep reveals in an effect of perspective. The same
effect on the square-headed w doorway to the octagonal stair-
turret. Embattled turret-top of *c.* 1830, added for Henning's
son James, and replacing a corbelled-out gable.* The E elevation of that range is of that date, although a nearly matching
turret was added to its NE corner between 1862 and 1875 for
Dr William Weston.

The Great Chamber is on the first floor of the three-bay
ashlar-faced continuation of the s front towards the W. This
wing was added *c.* 1580 for Sir George Trenchard (or rather it
was a thorough remodelling of a lower, earlier service range).
Trenchard moved in the highest circles, this no doubt explaining the stylistic links between the classicism in this phase of
work and that at Longleat. Two storeys, rising slightly higher
than the earlier elevation, with four-light windows lofty enough
to need a transom. No hoodmoulds, just a plain but correct
entablature carried across above each storey. Before 1798 the
centre bay projected as a half-octagon, hence the slight irregularity in the window spacing. Two charming concessions are
made to the existing house: the window mullions rise from
pedestal bases below and also above the transom, and have a
delicate wave moulding; and the upper entablature projects l.
and r. of the first and third window, hoodmould-like.

The INTERIOR reveals the whole purpose of the late C16
range, with features even more remarkable. A shorter staircase
range lies to the N, in the angle with the rear of the earlier W
range, the staircase rising beyond a stone archway from the
narrow ENTRANCE HALL. This, entered now as in the C16 from
the N, has a two-bay stone groin-vault, and an archway that
looks *c.* 1600 in style and has much in common with *William
Arnold*'s work. Fat soffit roll with upright leaves across it, key
blocks decorated with hyphens, all rather elephantine. Another
such arch leads into the hall, and the plasterwork here, in a
purer style, is also of *c.* 1600. The STAIRCASE appears to be
earlier and part of the first phase of work in this part of the
house of *c.* 1580. It is of stone, rising in one broad, long flight
to a half-landing, and returning in a second flight to first-
floor level. Monumental arcaded balustrade and square panelled newels (possibly in part a reconstruction for Dr Weston,
c. 1865). Both the staircase and the doorway to which it leads
have been attributed by Mark Girouard to *Allen Maynard*, the
French mason and colleague of Robert Smythson at Longleat.
The doorway, which leads into the Great Chamber on the
first floor, is of unusual classical purity. Triangular pediment
to the doorway, finely carved frieze of palmettes and acanthus fronds, Corinthian pilasters on tall pedestals flanking the
square door opening. Original landing window here. To the
r. of the doorway a caryatid figure, as if to start some superstructure at the head of the staircase. The staircase carries
scratched dates of 1732, 1745, etc. but Mark Girouard has

58

* Like the porch gable of *c.* 1480 at Winterborne Clenston Manor.

pointed out its affinity with Longleat, where there was a stone staircase, swept away by remodellings in the early C19. The whole sequence is unique in a C16 English house, paralleled only at Hardwick Hall. Another room reached from the top of the staircase, now the GREEN ROOM, was no doubt formerly part of the L-plan Long Gallery. This appears originally to have occupied much of the first floor above the hall, and that of the demolished Tudor s range. (Hutchins reported that its windows faced N, E and S.)

The GREAT CHAMBER has lost its tunnel-vaulted plaster ceiling and only the giant stone chimneypiece remains. Its coupled superimposed columns, Composite above Corinthian, are normal enough, but the strapwork in an overmantel surround of egg-and-dart, and the strange half-panel of strapwork below, show it to be a product of a workshop active in the West Country c. 1600, and it has similarities with the work of *William Arnold* (as mentioned above in connection with the entrance hall archway). There are similar chimneypieces at Montacute and Wayford in Somerset and Stockton in Wiltshire, as well as at Herringston, Winterborne Herringston. The overmantel panel has small figures: Charity in the middle, reclining in her own frame, then floating naked figures in among the strapwork. A source for the design has been identified by Anthony Wells-Cole as being a plate from Cornelis Bos's French proverbs of the 1550s. So it is possible that, upon completion of Maynard's work c. 1595, the fitting-out was carried out by *Arnold*, perhaps under Maynard's direction. In the main rooms downstairs rich and less sophisticated wooden chimneypieces and doorcases of c. 1610, further enriched and elaborated by the Victorian addition of C16 and C17 carved woodwork. The plaster overmantel in the WEST DRAWING ROOM, with strapwork, swags and terms, is another contact with Montacute. It is based on a plate of the Judgment of Paris by the Flemish designer Jacob Floris, taken from his *Compertimentorum* (1566) – a source much used by Arnold. In the EAST DRAWING ROOM the most noteworthy motif is the giant Corinthian columns, of wood, attached l. and r. of chimneypiece and doorcase. The way the fluting on the doorcase columns is reinterpreted as bootlaces knotted here and there is extremely peculiar. Also in this room a ceiling with strapwork decoration, also based on designs by Floris.

Re-set in an upper room of the gatehouse, a CHIMNEY-PIECE of the same design spirit as the landing doorway. Beautiful gadrooned border and side pilasters with enriched Ionic volutes.

RIDING HOUSE, 125 yds N of the house. This is not an unusually large and well-made barn, but may be the earliest surviving riding school in England, identified as such by its similarities with two Smythson drawings: the plan of Prince Henry's riding school at St James's Palace, built between 1607 and 1609, and the elevation for the riding school at Welbeck Abbey, 1622. However, with a width of only 24½ ft

(7.5 metres), the late Giles Worsley pointed out that it would have been uncomfortably narrow for the turning of a horse. An alternative suggestion (by Paul Drury) for its use is that of multi-purpose recreation, such as at the contemporary building at Ansty Manor, Wiltshire. Perhaps also by *Arnold*, it is ashlar-faced (except on the N side), seven bays long with end gables. Slim buttresses divide the s front, making an extra-wide E bay, where the doorway is. Large square three-light windows, under pieces of string course, in alternate bays. Similar windows in the end gables, under hoodmoulds. So there were two storeys inside, the lower lofty and well lit, the upper almost all within the roof-space. Small round windows low in the E wall. For its dating one must rely on style. The combination of string courses and hoodmoulds suggests the C17 rather than the C16, and the s doorway, round-headed with a round-headed hood-mould over, reminds one of Lulworth Castle; sure enough, above it is a small lion mask very like those that dot the walls of Lulworth. So a date *c.* 1610 seems indicated.

3090

CHARMOUTH

Charmouth still has the character of a Regency or Early Victorian resort, with some typical stucco villas. The straight, steeply climbing street gives it a properly formal air. In contrast the seafront is an architectural disappointment, as is the suburb between it and the town proper.

St ANDREW. Rebuilt in 1835–6 by *Charles Fowler*, the market specialist (cf. e.g. Exeter). Fowler is not at his best here. w tower with long lancets. Nave, aisles and short chancel with lancets and thin buttresses. Big interior with w gallery. A general reordering of the nave took place in 1860–1, and the E end was further reordered in 1936 by *W.H. Randoll Blacking*. – REREDOS. Gothic, with Commandment Boards etc., 1861. The text panels are covered up by curtains. – Encaustic TILEWORK in the sanctuary, probably related to the 1861 work – PULPIT. Of 1885. Stone with open trefoil-headed openings and green marble colonnettes. – SCULPTURE. Statuette of an abbot against a cross; C15. – STAINED GLASS. E window by *Christopher Webb*, 1936. Most of the large nave lancets are by *Lavers & Barraud*, 1861 onwards. From 1868 the firm was *Lavers, Barraud & Westlake*. The first from the E on the s side (dated 1878) is different and may be a Continental import. Another by *Webb*, 1938, under the gallery. – MONUMENTS. Anthony Ellesdon †1737. Pedimented tablet with Ionic columns by *M. Sidnell* of Bristol. – Joseph Hodges †1835. He rises in his bed. Death with his spear stands behind, a woman kneels at his feet.

UNITED REFORMED CHURCH (formerly Congregational), 200 yds E. Dated 1815 (with 'restorations' of 1866 and 1963). Stuccoed with round-arched windows. Pedimented N front with cupola.

ABBOTS HOUSE HOTEL (formerly THE QUEEN'S ARMS), beside the United Reformed church. At first sight the usual early C19 stuccoed hotel. But the doorway is of stone, and has the characteristic early C16 shape, four-centred head and deep hollow moulding. The stone heads of two apparently C19 windows to the r. also have C16 mouldings. Inside, the whole plan of the Early Tudor house can be made out, a single range without projections. The doorway led to the screens passage, naturally, with a single-storey hall to the r. and the kitchen down a passage to the l.; the present doorway takes one to the upper end of the hall, and the room on the r. is the former solar, with a four-centred fireplace arch and a small blocked window of two arched lights r. of it, marking the end wall of the house.

HILL SIDE, opposite the church and just NW of it. Three matching villas of 1827 by *Joseph Wilson*. Stucco with hipped slate roofs. The sashes are graded in width on the first floor, five panes wide, four panes, five panes. Ground-floor windows in elliptical-headed recesses.

LOOK-OUT HUT, ⅓ m. S, on the seafront. Of *c.* 1804 for the Revenue Service. Cement-rendered stone. Octagonal, with a hipped roof.

THISTLEGATE HOUSE, 1 m. NW. Built in 1911 by *F. W. Troup* for Mrs Capper Pass (*see* Wootton Fitzpaine). Lutyens-inspired. Red brick. Late Stuart style, broadly and comfortably proportioned, and without strict symmetry. Arts and Crafts detailing internally. Studded plank-and-muntin doors; heavy turned balusters on the oak staircase.

ROAD TUNNEL, 300 yds NW of Thistlegate House, on the original line of the Axminster to Charmouth road. Built 1830–2 for Bridport First District Trust. Intended to ease gradients on Thistle Hill.

CHEDINGTON

4000

The village – just the little church and a few substantial houses – is very beautifully situated, contouring round the wooded hillside.

ST JAMES (now a dwelling). 1840–1 by *Richard Carver*. Of the Commissioners' type. Nave and short chancel. Tall two-light Perp 'lancets' and shallow buttresses between. Of 1898 (by *George Vialls*) the low W baptistery and the SE vestries.*

---

*The church that this replaced was to the N. The STAINED GLASS by *Herbert Bryans* (E window 1899, two others 1901 and 1904) has been removed.

RECTORY (former), 80 yds W. Of *c.* 1850. Probably by *R.C. Carpenter*. Pinwheel plan. Many-gabled, asymmetrical elevations. Bold gable-mounted chimneys. Trefoil-headed mullioned windows with polychrome relieving arches.

CHEDINGTON COURT, 120 yds NNE. Of *c.* 1840 for William Hody. Much remodelled *c.* 1895 by *Harold Peto* for his elder brother, Sir Henry Peto. The original block was in a simple Tudor Revival style. Peto's elaborations are best seen on the N-facing entrance front. Tall shaped gables crowned with spiky Jacobethan finials. Also a two-storey porch in the same vein. Large great-hall wing added at the W end by *Sir James Dunbar-Nasmith*, just after 1997.

MANOR FARM, 80 yds NE. Dated 1634 (for Thomas Warren). A long range, with an off-centre porch towards the road. Four- and five-light mullioned windows. Ovolo mouldings. Hoodmoulds.

7090

CHESELBOURNE

ST MARTIN. Much flint, banded on the S aisle and lower stages of the tower. Starting from the S side, first an E.E. S aisle – see one window with plate tracery. Early C14 Dec chancel – see the N lowside window with transom and the E window, both with pointed-trefoiled heads to the lights. The remaining windows are part of a C15 refenestration that goes with the Perp W tower and the N aisle with one big Perp window. Since the upper part of the tower is plain stone rubble, it suggests a slightly later completion. Inside the evidence is less simple. First the S arcade with, as its centre, one round pier and the W respond of the C13. They have beautifully moulded Purbeck capitals and two double-chamfered arches, that to the E widened and heightened. Was there a plan to build a transept? To the W a Perp arch resting on a grotesque figure as its W corbel. The N arcade is C15, but with a narrow, early C16, triangular-headed opening between the E respond and the E nave wall. As a result, there is no alignment between the two aisles, the breadth of which makes the body of the church wider than it is long. Cinquefoil-headed PISCINA in the chancel, C15. Another smaller PISCINA in the S aisle, *c.* 1500. Here also a Perp image niche next to one of the two plain squints.

The FURNISHINGS mostly date from an otherwise light restoration by *G.R. Crickmay*, 1875. – PULPIT. Octagonal, *c.* 1630. The upper panels with strapwork decoration. – FONT. Octagonal, of Purbeck marble, *c.* 1200. Two lancet-headed recesses to each face, the sides slightly tapering. C15 octagonal stem. – TOWER STAIRCASE. Of timber, late medieval. Very steep and not quite reaching the floor. Solid oak steps. – STAINED GLASS. E window by *Joseph Bell*, 1956. – MONUMENTS. Hugh

Kete †1589. Three brasses re-set on the E wall of the N aisle.
Each has a shield of arms, the largest plate also with a long
inscription. – CI5 CROSS in the churchyard. Base, steps and
part of the shaft, with roll mouldings up the angles.

OLD RECTORY, 300 yds N. Of *c.* 1600. Banded flint with hollow-
chamfered mullioned windows. E extension, *c.* 1800. Mid-CI9
two-storey half-octagon porch with hipped roof.

CROSS-DYKES. Two in the NW of the parish, on a spur SW of
Nettlecombe Tout (*see* Melcombe Horsey), projecting SE from
Lyscombe Hill.

KINGCOMBE and WEST DOWN, 'CELTIC' FIELDS. *See* Puddletown.

CHETNOLE   6000

A straggling village on the W bank of the River Wriggle. Several
crossing points, two of them fords.

ST PETER. Early CI5 W tower (said to have been rebuilt 1580).
Three-stage, with embattled parapets, crocketed corner pinna-
cles and bold corner gargoyles. Angled buttresses, those on the
E face carried on large internal head corbels (perhaps reused).
Two-light bell-openings with Somerset tracery. Good four-
light W window; doorway with continuously moulded arch
below. Both have the string courses carried up over them. Late
CI3 nave – see the one S lancet – re-windowed in the CI5. New
chancel, 1859–60 by *W. Slater*; new N aisle, 1865 by *Slater &
Carpenter*. Good Perp-style arcade and CI3-style chancel arch.
However the interior walls have been scraped of their plaster
(reportedly in the early 1960s), spoiling the appearance. Wagon
roof in nave, CI5. – REREDOS. Five mosaic circles inlaid in
marble. By *Salviati*, *c.* 1860. – PULPIT. Made up using 'old
materials', 1860. – FONT. By *Slater*, 1860. – STAINED GLASS. E
window and three of the four chancel side windows by *Clayton
& Bell*, 1860. N aisle E window perhaps by *Alexander Gibbs*,
†1885. – MONUMENT. W. G. D. Wingfield Digby †1907. Marble
with mosaic inlay, perhaps by *Powell & Sons*.

CHETNOLE HOUSE, 120 yds NE. Well-proportioned red brick
house of *c.* 1760, with the character of a rectory. Five bays.
Pedimented porch on Doric columns. Hipped roof, early CI9,
contemporary with two flat-roofed side wings. Late CI9 alterations to rear (S) façade for W. G. D. Wingfield Digby. Panelled
dining room with chimneypiece of two superimposed Doric
orders and open Baroque pediment. Flanking alcoves with
Doric columns and pulvinated frieze.

Chetnole House faces out over a field to two vernacular thatched
stone houses with mullioned windows, a telling contrast.
MANOR FARM appears early CI8. Regularly spaced two-light
mullioned windows. Its asymmetrical plan indicates that it is

a remodelling of a late C16 house. FORD MEAD COTTAGE is earlier. Original open hall r. of the cross-passage, C15. Major rebuilding *c.* 1600 with hollow-chamfered mullioned windows.

NAPPERS, 200 yds s of the church. Typical of *c.* 1820. Ashlar-faced. Three very wide bays divided by pilaster strips. Tripartite ground-floor windows under round arches. Greek Doric porch. Low roof on deep eaves.

CHETTLE

73   CHETTLE HOUSE. The plum among Dorset houses of the early C18, and even nationally outstanding as a specimen of English Baroque. Built *c.* 1715 for George Chafin, who held the post of Ranger of Cranborne Chase. For his architect he chose – there is no doubt in the matter – *Thomas Archer.** The builder is likely to have been *Francis Smith* of Warwick. So Chettle is the only domestic building of Archer's maturity to survive relatively unspoilt. However, a watercolour at the house shows an attic storey, topped on the E garden façade (the original entrance front) by a giant broken pediment, based on that at the Villa Aldobrandini, Frascati, Italy (*c.* 1600), and a central domed cupola (or 'lantern room'). The latter was reportedly struck by lightning in 1816 and it was shortly thereafter that the cupola and pediment were taken down. The upper storeys of the wings were also dismantled after its purchase in 1846 by Edward Castleman. The end bays were rebuilt, higher than originally, with detailing matching the centre block, by Major E.W.F. Castleman in 1912.

The house is built of red brick, like most others of any pretension in NE Dorset, with dressings of Chilmark stone. It is a seven-bay block plus round-cornered end bays, of two very tall storeys, set on a high, vaulted basement, and rising in the three-bay centre for a further attic storey. Top balustrade on a deep bracketed cornice, the balustrades originally returned to exclude the curved ends. Giant brick pilasters articulate both façades, a cluster of them used to mark the angles. They have exceedingly odd capitals, grooved and tapering upwards. Lofty segment-headed windows, the upper with raised brick aprons. The basement windows reuse C17 stonework from a previous house, with a step and a hollow chamfer. But in the centre the façades are sharply contrasted. On the w, where the entrance now is, a big round-headed doorcase, with a cornice above it raised high by consoles; and curved corners to the centre projection. The E front has a slight projection only of the centre, but it is broken up into superimposed arcades, the piers between the windows banded with stone, the arches moulded

---

*This is confirmed by a plan in the RIBA collection, and anecdotal family records.

and given bold keystones. That handling of a centrepiece is a favourite of Archer's and his alone.

The great thrill of the INTERIOR is the entrance hall on the E side. Two-storeyed, containing the staircase. This rises in two flights against the l. and r. walls, turns and joins at a balcony. From there a single flight of only a few steps, and then a second division, to lead through the spine wall of the house and re-emerge as a balcony l. and r. Originally, and even more dramatically, a central flight returned high across the room to balconies on the opposite wall. This arrangement was altered, probably after 1846. Flat ceiling on groin-vaulting. The central flight ends at a doorway, with a tunnel-vaulted ceiling above. Three turned balusters per tread, and fluted Doric columns as newels. The room in the centre of the W front has bowed ends, and huge pilasters carrying Doric entablatures to frame the doorcases, an original feature. Lunettes over the doorways with bas reliefs by *Alfred Stevens* (whose father was employed as a decorator when the house was altered). S drawing room of that time in a typical Louis Seize style, designed by Mr *Blake* of Wareham.

ST MARY, in the grounds. Battlemented early C16 two-stage W tower of flint and greensand ashlar bands. Nave, chancel and 'transepts' (the last a vestry and family pew), with the same bands, 1849–50, by *John Morris & C.G. Hebson* for Edward Castleman. Finely detailed in Perp style, with a bellcote over the nave E gable. Interior FURNISHINGS as completed in 1850, with *Minton* TILES in the chancel. – PULPIT. A curious heavy rectangular stone box with Perp detailing. – FONT. Another quaint attempt at Perp. – STAINED GLASS. A contemporary scheme (perhaps by *William Miller*) includes a pictorial E window. – MONUMENTS. Two set on either side of the chancel arch. The more elaborate is Thomas Chafin †1691 and wife by *John Friend* of Canterbury, a cartouche erected in 1708. – Also George Chafin †1766. A simpler tablet with small cartouche above.

CASTLEMAN HOTEL (formerly Chettle Lodge), ⅓ m. N. Early C18 main block, incorporating earlier fabric. Enlarged in Tudor style to E and S *c.* 1850, for Edward Castleman. Staircase with similar detailing to that in Chettle House. Two C19 rooms, one with extensive use of imported Jacobean joinery, including an elaborate chimneypiece.

CHETTLE LONG BARROW, 1 m. W. Part was dug away for a grotto before 1767. The barrow is aligned SE–NW.

THICKTHORN BAR, ⅓ m. S. The barrow is aligned E–W.

CHICKERELL   6080

A village of C17 cottages, swamped by the westward expansion of the Weymouth suburbs.

St Mary. The nave and chancel are late C13, with the continuous hollow chamfer of the chancel arch and the group of three stepped E lancets with pointed-trefoiled heads. In the nave S wall a large C15 window and, above it to the r., a small C14 ogee-headed window, probably lighting a rood loft. Also C14 a two-light window to the W of the porch, and the mid-buttress with double bellcote at the W end of the nave. S porch dated 1722. In 1834 a N aisle was added (dated on a panel at the W end), but with three cast-iron pipe-columns in lieu of arcade piers (cf. Farnham, 1835). It has windows with intersecting tracery. The two ochre-stone Dec windows in the chancel S wall are of 1865. Further restorations (with no architect recorded) in 1875 and 1896. These retained the WEST GALLERY of 1834, also on cast-iron columns. – PULPIT. Inscribed 1630 RWIM. Three tiers of panels, the lower two with carved arabesque-stylized trees in each. Also crudely classical fluting to the posts. Vernacular rather than polite. – FONT. C12, with bands of fluting, bead and interlace decoration. C19 stem and step. – STAINED GLASS. E window possibly by *Alexander Gibbs, c.* 1865. Nave S window by *C.C. Townshend,* 1927. – MONUMENT. C15 incised slab to a young rector in academic dress.

METHODIST CHURCH, just down the lane to the S. By *John Dyne,* 1865. Of red and yellow brickwork (rendered on one side). Segmental-arched windows. – STAINED GLASS. Central S window by *G. Maile & Son,* 1957.

EVANGELICAL CONGREGATIONAL CHURCH, East Street. 1883. Brick. Lancet style.

    Adjoining it on the W the former PETO MEMORIAL READING ROOM (now Library) of 1890, possibly by *George Vialls.* Queen Anne style with a Dutch front gable.

Opposite the church, No. 6 is an early to mid-C17 cottage with hollow-chamfered mullioned windows.

CHIDEOCK

4090

The village, of thatched stone cottages and barns lining the A35, is worth stopping to appreciate in spite of the traffic pounding through.

St Giles. The earliest part of the church is the C14 Dec N transept, with an E window having cusped intersected tracery. Next comes the early C15 W tower, three stages with a higher octagonal S stair-turret. Set-back buttresses. The battlemented parapet, gargoyles and belfry openings were put back in 1851. Following soon after the tower, the Perp S aisle, S porch and S chapel, built as one item with continuous battlements. A major restoration in 1880 by *Crickmay & Son* saw the rebuilding of the nave N wall with one C15 window re-set. C19 paintings in

the church show that the chancel was under-scaled against the
Perp rebuilding, a situation remedied only in 1883 with a new
chancel by *Crickmay*. Four-bay s arcade of standard elements,
the details somewhat *recherché* for the C15. The tower arch has
one continuous moulded order. Above, the weatherings for the
line of an earlier nave roof. – Complete scheme of FURNISH-
INGS of 1880–3 by *Crickmay*. – FONT. C15. Octagonal, a big flat
bowl with quatrefoils. Trefoil-headed panel to each face of the
octagonal stem. C17 pyramidal oak COVER. – STAINED GLASS.
s aisle window by *Lavers, Barraud & Westlake*, 1889. Another
by *Horace Wilkinson*, 1919. Nave N window by *Lavers, Barraud
& Westlake*, 1880. (Behind the organ, three more windows by
the firm, *c.* 1880.) – MONUMENT. Black marble monument
probably to Sir John Arundell (†1545). Tomb-chest already
with balusters, i.e. a Renaissance motif. The effigy in typical
Henry VIII armour. Four-centred back arch.

MAUSOLEUM. Just N of the churchyard, the Weld Mausoleum.
Dated 1852. Designed and built by *Charles Weld* in the form
of a Greek cross with a raised centre crowned by a pyramid
roof. Very random rubble (really fine-textured crazy paving).
At the w end a boldly and very individually carved crucifix in
relief. In the equivalent position in the E gable a cross of inlaid
glazed tilework. In the E and N gables a mandorla window, the
w a mandorla with Y-tracery and the s an encircled quatrefoil.
(Four pointed arches at the crossing within. Walls richly decorated with FRESCOES and TILEWORK. Further painting to the
underside of the roofs.)

On the higher ground to the NE, ditches mark the site of the
CASTLE of the de Chideock family. Roughly square moated
enclosure. No masonry now, though Buck's view of 1733 shows
a mighty gatehouse (destroyed in 1741). This view, and documentary evidence from licences to crenellate, suggest that the
castle was built *c.* 1370–80.

Chideock Castle.
Engraving by Nathaniel Buck, 1774

Former CASTLE INN, just E of the church. Late C19. Tudor
Revival front in rich ochre-coloured stone. Red brick sides.

CHIDEOCK MANOR, ⅜ m. N. A puzzling house of *c.* 1810, built
for Humphry Weld, sixth son of Thomas Weld of Lulworth
Castle, who purchased the property for him in 1802.* Ashlar
block, of four even bays towards the road, but on the entrance
(E) front an apparently deliberately asymmetrical composition,
with a square projecting full-height porch and shallow full-
height bow, and round the corner to the S another bow. The
parapet climbs up steps in the oddest way and incorporates at
the N end a window surround in an unlikely place. The alterations at the N end are of the 1950s (when an early C20 three-
storey block was demolished), and undoubtedly effective.
Battlemented rough-stone walls to the kitchen garden. Several
older features re-set, many from Chideock Castle. Mullioned
windows and fireplace lintels, outside and in, especially the
monumental dining-room chimneypiece of *c.* 1500 with a row
of sub-cusped quatrefoils bearing shields and roses and a band
of paired mouchettes. The final surprise is the Roman Catholic CHAPEL where the stables are expected, looking, from the
garden side, like an orangery.

OUR LADY OF MARTYRS AND ST IGNATIUS (R.C.). Built in
1870–2 by *Charles Weld* to his own design. The façade has a low
narthex and the nave is indeed Early Christian or Byzantine in
character. Above the narthex a roundel with smaller enamelled
roundels within and with an enamelled Our Lady at the centre
in front of a vesica. Nave and aisles and an unorthodox clerestory, more Early Renaissance in character. On the E exterior
of a former barn, at its centre, a gable with image niches and
some elaboration below the gable coping. The church was
extended into the barn in 1884 by *J. S. Hansom*, creating a
domed sanctuary.

A richly decorative and intricate interior. Over the sanctuary,
an octagonal lantern and low dome are carried on tripartite
arches in all four directions, the arch groups being of the Venetian type, i.e. with two pillars and a flat entablature between
them and the wall, but an arch – oddly a pointed arch – in the
middle. Pointed arches too at forty-five degrees on plan over the
L-sections of entablature. The latter carry Latin inscriptions.
While the combinations are surprising, the increase in decorative intensity towards the E end is compelling. The capitals etc.
incidentally are carved by *Charles Weld* too (with the assistance
of *B. Grassby*). Above the arcades are framed paintings of the
English Martyrs and Sir John Arundell. Decorative painting to
the pointed ceiling vault (also by *Weld*). Organ loft at the W
end over. At the E end of each aisle an apsed side chapel. In
front of the sanctuary arch, two free-standing COLUMNS with
Cosmatesque inlay within fluted spirals, each topped by an
Italian marble statue (of Our Lady and St Joseph). Either side

*The design for the house by *J. Tasker*, among the Weld papers at the Dorset Record
Office, was not the one executed.

of the sanctuary, running N and S like transepts, two sections
of the former barn, converted to a chapel by Humphry Weld in
1810–15. These parts include the SACRISTY and LOFT CHAPEL
beyond, containing rich FRESCOES, covering the entire walls
and ceiling. Those in the latter chapel are probably C18 and
therefore pre-Emancipation in date. – ALTAR and REREDOS.
A fine Gothic piece with much painting (by members of the
Weld family) and gilding. – FONT. An elaborated bowl with an
oak pyramidal COVER. – PAINTING of the Chideock Martyrs
by *Francis Newbery*, 1929. – MONUMENTS. Humphry Weld
†1852. Large brass by *Gawthorp* of London. – Sir Frederick
Aloysius Weld †1891. An even larger brass, set in the floor,
also by *Gawthorp*.

CHILCOMBE   5090

CHURCH. A small building. Chancel and nave S wall C12 in
   their masonry: indeed the arched S doorway still has two
   scallop capitals, although the columns are missing. Late C14
   Dec chancel arch, placed asymmetrically. Nave N and W walls
   rebuilt, probably C15. Of this date the W bellcote. Blocked Perp
   N doorway. – FONT. C12 bowl with a scalloped underside; herringbone cable decoration just below the lip. – ROYAL ARMS.
   Gilded wood; Hanoverian, before 1801. – STAINED GLASS.
   Some C15 fragments in the tracery lights of the E window. S
   window perhaps by *Joseph Bell* of Bristol, *c.* 1840. W window
   of *c.* 1896. – MONUMENTS. Henry Michel †1662. Small stone
   surround with broad rusticated pilasters; crucifix and shell
   motifs. Set in it a beautifully engraved inscription brass, signed
   Jo. Bishop Capitan fecit, *Richard Meadway* sculpsit. Beneath
   another panel with a skull-and-crossbones inscribed Memento
   Mori. – John Bishop †1682, a cartouche. The Bishops were
   lords of the manor.
CHILCOMBE MANOR, just W. The courtyard house, built in
   1578 for John and Eleanor Bishop, was demolished in 1936.
   The present three-storey block is of *c.* 1770 for Edward Foyle,
   added to older buildings.
CHILCOMBE HILL, ¼ m. N. Iron Age HILL-FORT, univallate,
   enclosing 19 acres, with three possible entrances: E, NW and,
   more doubtful, S.

CHILD OKEFORD   8010

A straggling village with a strength of gathering at The Cross.
The church is ideally situated at the upper end of a lane leading
E, beyond which is the avenue to the Manor House, with the
great bare ridges of Hambledon Hill as a backdrop.

ST NICHOLAS. Tall late C15 or early C16 W tower of big blocks of greensand. Embattled parapet with crocketed corner pinnacles. The rest by *T. H. Wyatt*. The S aisle is of 1850 (with *David Brandon*), the remainder of 1878–9, adding up to a satisfying whole, especially internally. Flint with bands of stone and Dec-style tracery. Wide nave and aisles. Sculptural group in the gable over the S porch doorway. The chancel window rere-arches, N arcade and S arch all have polished granite colonnettes. This richness was increased when the chancel walls were faced with marble panels in 1911, by *Wippell & Co.* – FURNISHINGS. A high-quality set designed by *Wyatt*, 1879, including the reredos with a little gold mosaic. – PULPIT. Made by *Earp & Co.*, again above average, incorporating alabaster and polished granites. – FONT. C13, circular. – STAINED GLASS. An extensive set of late C19 and early C20 windows, many of high quality. Chancel E and first S windows, and the S chapel E window by *Henry Hughes*, 1879. Other S aisle windows by *C. E. Kempe*, 1888; and three by *H. T. Bosdet* (one signed and dated 1920). Tower W window and another in the N aisle, also by *Bosdet*, 1920. Bosdet's are unusually lively and colourful.

WAR MEMORIAL, 1919. Medieval-inspired, possibly by *Ponting*. Finely sculpted cross-head.

MANOR HOUSE, ¼ m. E. Late 1880s, for Lord Portman of Bryanston. Arts and Crafts style with diaper-patterned brickwork. Curious Perp-style main doorway taking its inspiration from Berkeley Castle, Gloucestershire.

The older cottages in the village are thatched with some timber framing. MONK'S YARD, at THE CROSS, is early C16 in origin, although this is hard to tell from the front. More comprehensible is THE OLD COTTAGE, High Street, perhaps C15, displaying timber-framed rubble masonry and banded brick and flint areas of walling. Just behind Monk's Yard is the former rectory, now CHILD OKEFORD HOUSE, C17 and C18. Two gables on to the lane and a stuccoed garden front with a two-storey bay window of the mid C19. The entrance to MILLBROOK HOUSE, ¼ m. NW, has a pair of early C18 greensand ashlar gatepiers that may have come from Eastbury.

FONTMELL PARVA, 1¼ m. NNW. A characterful small house of *c.* 1680 for Edward St Loe, and super-characterful enlargement of *c.* 1850 and 1864–9, the first for Col. Malet, the second for the Rev. H. T. Bower. The *tout ensemble* is one of the most enjoyable sights in Dorset. Square, double-pile block, facing E, two-storeyed on an unusually high basement (giving ten steps up to the front door). Stone-slated hipped roof. Projecting central porch of three storeys. Red brick, English-bonded and generous ashlar dressings. The style is unmistakably classical, if interpreted with provincial gusto. Thus the windows have classically moulded frames but, being short for their width, have a mullion but no transom. A key block links each window to the square-sectioned string course. Deep coved eaves. Doorway with an open triangular pediment, taking a handsome coat of arms. The house's eminently effective crown is a great rectangular spine of chimneystacks, brick, with blank arcading, set at right angles to the façade. At the back, as so often in C17 Dorset, vernacular traditions reassert themselves: there are two gables and a central projection carrying another chimneystack, and probably housing a staircase originally.

The Victorian additions, by *George Evans* of Wimborne, were, oddly, built in two phases. The s wing, to the l. of the old block, was the first, followed after a change of ownership by the N wing and the roof enrichments.* Same materials, red brick and much stone, but very Victorian motifs: triangular gablets closed below by a semicircle, each wing with one gablet to the front and three at each side. In the centre of the s front a chunky bowed oriel. The one interference with the Stuart façade is another gablet to crown the porch.

Inside only one feature of note. The porch leads into a mahogany-lined lobby ending in a splendid shell-headed niche. Here there are two principal doorways, one l. and one r. This was a modification of *c.* 1700 for Rear-Admiral St Loe, who brought the materials back from Honduras.

WALLED GARDEN at the back, entered by unusually fine wrought-iron GATES, with an overthrow, and lyre-shaped panels at the sides. Early C18. Big Victorian STABLE BLOCK, also by *Evans.*

HAMBLEDON HILL. *See* Iwerne Courtney.

CHILFROME   5090

Low-lying village set on the edge of River Frome water meadows, the church standing among huge yews. An unusually large number of substantial early C19 villas.

HOLY TRINITY. Small, of nave with bellcote and chancel. C14 nave with some C15 fenestration, probably re-set. The chancel was rebuilt in 1852 by *John Hicks.* He gave the priest's doorway a characterful projecting surround. *Hicks* was also responsible for a major restoration of the nave, 1864. The chancel arch with continuous chamfers may be of *c.* 1300. – Complete set of FURNISHINGS by *Hicks* of the two dates. – Encaustic TILES in the sanctuary. – Angled stone PULPIT with mural entry. – Good, bold roof CORBELS in the nave, carved by *Grassby.* – SCULPTURE. Small medieval relief of the Virgin in a quatrefoil outside the gabled vestry (by *Hicks*, 1864). – STAINED GLASS. E window and the two chancel side windows by *William Wailes*, *c.* 1864.

*Designs in the Dorset History Centre are unsigned, but an estimate refers to the fee of *Mr Evans*, architect, and a payment to G. Evans Esq. is recorded.

Former RECTORY just w of the church. Four-square villa of
c. 1840. Sash windows. A larger version of about the same date
is CHILFROME HOUSE, 350 yds NW.

CHURCH KNOWLE

A linear settlement of Purbeck cottages, mostly with heavy stone
roofs.

ST PETER. Much of the church is early C13, the date made patent
by the use of plate tracery, and plate tracery uncusped. First
to be built was the chancel, c. 1225; the transepts and nave followed shortly thereafter. So it is in the chancel where we find
the best examples of E.E. plate tracery: an E window, two on
the N side and one on the S (its twin replaced by a C15 three-
lighter). Each has two trefoil-headed lights and a continuous
roll moulding surrounding these and the circular tracery light.
Here the E light is a cinquefoil and the side lights quatrefoils,
a nice distinction. The windows on the transepts are simpler,
i.e. without the roll mouldings or cusping. Two tall lancets in
the nave S wall are C19 alterations. Inside, the triple opening
into the chancel may be of the early C13 too (two continuous
chamfers). Its side openings were no doubt originally closed
and probably held reredoses for side altars. Next to them are
good SQUINTS, cut through in the C15. The w tower with
pyramid roof was rebuilt in 1741 but retains typical Purbeck
proportions. A slightly jarring note is the N aisle, added in
1833–41. With it came WEST and NORTH GALLERIES, the
latter filling the aisle, and no doubt the decidedly funny roof
tracery: a series of very applied cusped circles jammed into
fake hammerbeam trusses. The original PEWS survive in the
gallery. – PAINTING. Pretty leaf decoration in the framing of
the chancel arch and recesses and the E window, partly C16
but mostly C19 overpainting. – STAINED GLASS. E window and
two chancel side windows by *Heaton, Butler & Bayne*, 1891. A
later window (1932) by the same firm, chancel N. S transept E
and a window in the N aisle by *Marion Grant*, 1956 and 1957
respectively. – MONUMENT. John Clavell †1609, but erected in
1572. Yet still the Purbeck type of the early C16 (cf. the monuments in Bere Regis church and that to Sir John Tregonwell in
Milton Abbey, †1565). Of fine Purbeck stone. Tomb-chest with
cusped quatrefoils, the canopy with a panelled underside, and
a distinctive quatrefoil frieze and cresting suggesting that the
same craftsman was involved as at Bere Regis. The shafts try
to show off a little of Renaissance detail, and the same is true
of the underside. Three BRASSES on the back are also placed
much as the other examples.

BARNSTON MANOR, ¾ m. WSW. An almost complete house
of c. 1300, built for John Estoke, remodelled in the mid C16

for Roger Clavell. Rubble walling, the s refronting of ashlar blocks. The *c*. 1300 evidence is in the central cross-wing and w wing. The N gable of the former has a plate-traceried two-light window, i.e. a quatrefoiled circle over two lancets, with inside a window seat, a rebate for shutters and a vertical stone rib with slots for the shutter-bolts. The w wing has two lower lancets and one upper blocked one to the s, and an upper N window of two lancet lights. What was the function of these two parts? The answer is largely concealed in the rebuilt mid-C16 and C17 E block, for this was the likely site of an open hall with a cross-passage at its E end and service rooms beyond. To confirm this, there is evidence in the E wall of the hall of the chamfered jambs and relieving arches of the screens doorways to N and s. However, rebuilding of the E end has removed any further evidence of this layout. (The huge C17 buttress here speaks of later subsidence.) So if this was the hall – and indications of C13 masonry exist at the base of its N and s walls – the cross-wing to its w would have been the solar, with its fine window described above. The narrow wing beyond (i.e. further w) was probably a wardrobe, with a garderobe beyond it, now largely gone. This is the type of layout described throughout the building writs of Henry III, and is a development from the arrangement found at Old Soar, Plaxtol, Kent, of *c*. 1290. Access to the solar from the hall may have been by an internal staircase. If so, two otherwise inexplicable corbels beneath the ceiling in the w wall of the present hall would have supported its landing. The mid-C16 hall was ceiled from its inception, with moulded beams, and has a big s fireplace with a moulded four-centred opening. The N projection here, with a lean-to roof, contains a stone newel stair, also dated to the C16.

The C16 remodelling was intended to give greater light to the solar wing, hence the two-storey bay to the s, giving one light in the canted parts and three plus three to the front. Quite elaborate moulded plinth and for the windows a deep hollow, a roll and chamfered mullions. The C13 former wardrobe to the w had two four-light mullioned windows inserted on the s side, one on each floor, at the same time. Its eaves level was also raised.*

CREECH BARROW, on Steeple parish boundary, 1¼ m. WNW. A bowl barrow originally containing five inhumations.

CLIFTON MAYBANK

5010

The mansion built by Sir John Horsey, probably *c*. 1545–50, was the most spectacular of the group of houses on the Somerset–Dorset

---

*R. Machin, 'Barnston Manor, Dorset and Aydon Castle, Northumberland', *Archaeological Journal* 134, 1977. I am grateful also for his further thoughts, revising the original conclusions.

border built for the most part in the second quarter of the c16. Melbury House (*c.* 1540) came first, then Clifton Maybank, followed by the group that includes the parlour range of Athelhampton, Sandford Orcas Manor, the wing at Mapperton Manor and Bingham's Melcombe, Melcombe Horsey. All these houses are built of Ham Hill ashlar and show such similarity in detail that they must be, or depend upon, the designs of a single master mason, no doubt based at the Ham Hill quarries. What makes them of great historical importance, even in a national context, is the versatility shown in matters of planning. This makes it all the more regrettable that the greatest part of Clifton Maybank was dismantled in 1786 by the Earl of Uxbridge. No view of the house is known as it was before the dismantling, nor have excavations ever been undertaken to recover the plan.* A gatehouse, probably by *William Arnold* (*c.* 1600), which stood to the w of the house, was dismantled *c.* 1800, allegedly for sale and re-erection by Earl Poulett at Hinton St George, Somerset, although this appears never to have happened.

What we have are one corner of the mansion to full height, converted and enlarged in 1906–7 for Francis Daniel to form a house; an independent building of the early c15, clearly a fragment of something larger, probably built by Thomas Horsey; and the brick-banded walls that appear to be part of an entirely independent building campaign – perhaps the 'greate foundation' started by James Ormond, Earl of Wiltshire, who (illegally) took possession of the house, probably in the 1450s.

Of the main building only the s front gives any adequate idea of the mid-c16 character. Two unequal bays of two very lofty storeys divided by a delicately moulded string course and crowned by a parapet pierced with a frieze of lozenges enclosing quatrefoils. Behind the parapet two unequal-sized gables in which are the only surviving untouched windows. They are mullioned, of three and two lights, the moulding a wave and hollow. Hoodmoulds. The lights are not arched. The memorable motif of Clifton is the octagonal buttress-shafts, at the angles and between the bays. They rise, with a moulding ranging with the house's moulded plinth, through four stages, marked by shaft-rings, at each of which the profile of the octagon's faces changes, from hollow to wave to roll-on-hollow to syncopated wave. Perp panelled top at parapet level. The finials are lost. The detailing has much in common with Abbot Chard's enlargements at Forde Abbey (q.v.), dated 1528, with the merest hints of the coming Renaissance, as in the gadrooning on the finial-base at the tip of the l. gable.** To the r. a lower addition of 1906–7 as part of the remodelling of the house.

---

*The decorative components of the entrance front are preserved, rebuilt as the N front of Montacute, Somerset. Minor fragments are at the Manor House, Beaminster, and Compton House, Over Compton.
**Also, the elements taken to Montacute have outstandingly well-understood Renaissance details in the armorial panel over the doorway.

The w front is wider, but was given an extra bay in 1906–7 to make a four-bay façade; here the doorcase (which became central with the extension) had already been given a segmental pediment, and the windows keystones, in the c18. Big central gable, with a canted oriel window re-set, absurdly high, in it. The oriel is quite an elaborate Perp piece, on a moulded corbel and with a deep frieze of sub-cusped quatrefoils. The lights – one, three, one, with a transom – confirm that at Clifton the arched light-heads of the early c16 are abandoned. Many of the remodelled windows reuse original mouldings, of a deep hollow and a chamfer or double chamfer. Inside there are two doorways, four-centred-arched and deeply hollow-moulded. Horsey crest in the spandrels.

Internally, the chief surviving feature of the Horsey era is a heavily built oak staircase, rising through four storeys. Probably of c. 1600 (to judge by the turned balusters). Elaborate carved finials on the newel posts, presumably intended to reflect those outside. Several rooms with panelling of the early c18; fireplaces with bolection-moulded surrounds of this date too.

The SOUTH-EAST BUILDING is much humbler. It has the same plinth moulding as the main house but is of rubble, not ashlar. It has a polygonal turret at the NW angle, and mullioned windows with arched lights. Two doorways with simple Perp mouldings. From the NE corner project two parallel walls, perhaps of the 1450s. These are the beginnings of a more important building, probably aborted since they come out and are at once snapped off. Jamb of an inserted c16 window in the front wall, a small three-lighter in the back. What is really remarkable is that these walls are faced with broad bands of ashlar and of red brick. It is clearly the original facing, and not only of memorably early date for brick, but an astonishing one to use when fine facing stone was so readily available. It suggests that the decorative value of brick was already appreciated.

Associated either with the Ormond phase or with Sir John Horsey's house are the earthworks of a TERRACE WALK around four sides of a lawn to the E.

COLEHILL

Before the c19 a scatter of cob and thatch cottages. Thereafter, a fashionable suburb on the hillside E of Wimborne, consisting of large villas; two of these are now schools.

ST MICHAEL AND ALL ANGELS. By *W. D. Caröe*, 1893. Of red brick with timber framing in a NW English style, thought appropriate 'to the landscape surrounding the site'. A blend of ecclesiastical muscularity with domestic asymmetry, not wholly comfortable in effect, except in the interest provided by the detailing. Here Caröe shows his characteristic inventiveness, even if the results seem a little wilful. From the E the chancel is all brick, except for a little timber-framed gable, and the central tower is brick up to the bell-stage, with a bold pyramid roof interrupted by tall louvred dormers facing N and S, and an even steeper pyramid over the N stair-turret. Linked dormers in the S aisle roof, the latter overlapping the transept gable to make a porch. The nave and S aisle have brick only for the dado, and the rest timber-framed, patterned on the N side. On the S side a timber porch. Spacious interior with a lot of dark-olive-stained wood, including the S arcade posts. (Over-)complicated timbering of the nave dormers, and a very weird arrangement for the S chancel chapel: two bays of unmoulded brick arches and on them smaller brick arches. Odder still, above these, and in the sanctuary arch, brickwork lines pick out vaguely Gothic mouchettes and quatrefoils. The tracery, where windows have any, is flowing. – Most of the FITTINGS are *in situ*. However, Caröe's CHOIR STALLS have been stripped of their original finish. – ALTAR. Four niches along the front with openwork carved tracery heads containing embroidered angels, thought to be from *William Morris*'s workshop. – STAINED GLASS. E window by *Sir Ninian Comper*, 1957.

Former VICARAGE adjoining to the w in Smugglers Lane, also by *Caröe*, 1903.

The largest surviving Victorian villas are BEAUCROFT, ½ m. S, and WOODLEAZE at FURZEHILL, ¾ m. NW, both *c.* 1885. Picturesque in composition, of red brick. The latter is now the offices for East Dorset District Council.

WILKSWORTH FARMHOUSE, 1¼ m. NW. Brick, *c.* 1700. Irregularly gabled S front concealing a structure of *c.* 1500, altered *c.* 1600. Segmental-arched sashes.

8010

COMPTON ABBAS

Two villages, West Compton on the main road, where the Victorian ensemble of church, rectory and school were built; and East Compton, where the tower of the demolished medieval church stands among C17 and C18 farm buildings. (For West Compton alias Compton Abbas West *see* p. 635.)

ST MARY. 1866–7 by *George Evans* of Wimborne, for Sir Richard George Glyn. Built by *A.H. Green* of Blandford. S tower with broach spire and lucarnes, its big side buttresses, flush with the S face, creating a distinctive effect. Nave, narrow S aisle, chancel, polygonal apse. E.E. lancets, those to the aisle with gables. The chancel and apse have stone rib-vaulting, rich capitals and marble colonnettes. – Good PULPIT and READING DESK, both no doubt by *Evans*. – FONT. C12, but probably re-cut 1866. Cauldron shape. The bowl is decorated with

long trails, quite lucidly arranged. Base with spurs. – STAINED
GLASS. Central E window by *Powell & Sons*, 1908. The other
apse windows 1950 by *J. Wippell & Co.* W window by *W.T.
Carter Shapland*, 1957. S chapel E quatrefoil by *Francis Skeat*,
1959.

Completing the group, to the E the former RECTORY of 1866
by *Evans* and the SCHOOL and SCHOOL HOUSE of 1849, N.
TOWER of the original church, ½ m. ENE. Late C15, of two stages.
The church itself was demolished in 1867.

COMPTON VALENCE   *5090*

After the bare downland landscape, the valley here is full of trees
of startling luxuriance. They envelop the Gothic Revival grouping of the church and former rectory.

ST THOMAS OF CANTERBURY. Only the tower is medieval. C15,
of two stages with an embattled parapet and big buttresses.
Plain chamfered tower arch with imposts, the whole looking
early C13. The buttresses and W window are mid-C19 and
go with the rebuilding of the church by *Benjamin Ferrey* for
Robert Williams I and the Rev. W.H.P. Ward, 1839–40. Some
assistance was provided by *A.D.H. Acland*. It is remarkable
that Ferrey chose Dec as his style for the body of the church
at this date, although local architects had already started to
build apsed E ends (cf. nearby Wynford Eagle). Now the point
is that Dec as a choice, a polygonal apse as a choice, and the
more general tendency to let a village church appear 'real',
i.e. a real medieval village church, is usually connected with
Pugin and Scott. But neither did this sort of thing before 1840
(although the short apsed sanctuary is exactly what one would
expect for the date). So here is an advanced guard of proto-
Ecclesiological church architecture, carried out by a group
highly influenced by the Oxford Movement. Compton Valence
is therefore of more than local significance.

Apart from the use of Late Dec windows, the buttresses are
unnecessarily wide (compared with the W angled buttresses of
the tower). Those to the apse have gabled set-offs with delicate
cusping. Random rubble walling, very similar to that used by
Hicks and then Pugin at Rampisham. Simple stone vaulting to
the porch and most tellingly in the chancel. Also inserted in the
tower (and the reason for the additional buttressing). Otherwise Ferrey's openings are more Perp than Dec, especially the
chancel arch and his big N arcade. – REREDOS. Three Gothic-
framed panels with flattish Dec crocketed hoods. This, by
Ferrey or *Acland*, was accompanied by a stone ALTAR, replaced
by another in wood, probably by *Ferrey*, 1871. – PULPIT. Bath
stone. By *Ferrey* and integral with the overall design. Mural entry
through an arched doorway set at forty-five degrees. – FONT.

C15, octagonal, with paterae on the splayed underside. Plain stem. Base with shield-shaped decoration. – A complete set of FURNISHINGS by *Ferrey, in situ*. The clergy seats, choir stalls and pew-ends all have bold fleur-de-lys finials. – The ORGAN CASE has a bold Gothic treatment. – Boldly lettered INSCRIPTIONS on the walls, e.g. those over the chancel arch and above the built-in ALMS BOX. – STAINED GLASS. The apse windows have grisaille decoration, *c.*1840, probably by *Willement*. – MONUMENTS. Brass to Thomas Maldon, rector, *c.*1440. Demi-figure, 11½ in. (29 cm.) long, with two symmetrical inscription rolls. – Mary Thistlethwayte †1720. Slate tablet with a plain classical surround. – Ann Best †1740. A conservative tablet. Pedimented, with bold side scrolls.

COMPTON VALENCE HOUSE (former rectory), 200 yds W. A building of *c.*1800 was added at the E end of an otherwise plain early C19 villa by *Ferrey* in 1839 for the Rev. W.H.P. Ward. Of this date the gabled porch with its oriel window set above a pointed-arched opening. The remainder was rebuilt in 1872 by *G. R. Crickmay* for the Rev. Septimus Hobbs. Less obviously Gothic. Gabled with multi-shafted chimneystacks.

COOMBE KEYNES

8080

A cluster of farmsteads and thatched cottages.

HOLY ROOD (declared redundant in 1974, now a community hall). 1860–1 by *John Hicks*, E.E. to match the retained C13 W tower. This has clasping buttresses (added by Hicks) and lancet bell-openings. C13 chancel arch of two continuous chamfered orders (reused from the demolished aisle). A C13 lancet in the E wall of the tower, above a doorway, but no tower arch as such.*

CORFE CASTLE

9080

The starting point was the castle on its own hill at the N end of the village. It was a notable place in Saxon times, and was associated with the death of King Edward the Martyr, recorded in the *Anglo-Saxon Chronicle* as taking place at Corfe Gate in 978. The village developed throughout the Middle Ages, and

---

*Goodhart-Rendel was not impressed by this church. He considered the design 'inexperienced' and wrote that there was 'a maddening little row of ninepin buttresses all down the smooth side'. He added that the 'whole thing looks as if it was designed by somebody's aunt who was clever with a pencil'.

was dependent upon the castle. As the Purbeck stone industry grew in the C13, the village also became the base for the marblers' yards and their houses. This does much to explain its homogeneous character, almost all the buildings being constructed of the local stone, and most with stone-slate roofs (although much thatch survives also).

Corfe Castle was incorporated as a town borough in 1576, and sent two members to Parliament until 1832. Notoriously, after the Restoration they were nominated by the Bankes and Bond families, the local landowners. The diminutive size of the C18 Town Hall (see below) shows how Corfe's importance had dwindled. Today it keeps an essentially medieval urbanity, unaffected by whatever later rebuilding there has been (although strangled by traffic, especially in the tourist season). The shape of the place is a V pointing from the S towards the castle, with, at the junction of the arms, the short, slightly bowed square.

CORFE CASTLE

The castle occupies an extraordinary natural position, a steep-sided hillock at the base of a cleft in the spine ridge of the Purbeck Hills. On the summit stand the silvery slabs of the Norman *magna turris*, deliberately shattered by mines and explosives after its long resistance to Parliament during the Civil War. Down the slope to the S cascade the walls and towers of the bailey in ghastly disarray.

Corfe was a classic example of a late C11 great tower, later reinforced with stone walls and bastions surrounding inner and outer bailey, the system developed at the end of the C12 at Dover and at Château Gaillard in Normandy. In spite of such extensive destruction, the system can still be readily appreciated at Corfe. But whereas at Dover the castle is essentially the creation of a single extended campaign, Corfe's defences grew stronger stage by stage, beginning probably with a pre-Conquest fortress.

By the time of Domesday (1086) Corfe was held by the king. It remained a royal possession throughout the next two centuries, which saw its full construction, and well beyond. Domesday states that William the Conqueror built a castle here (Domesday's 'Wareham Castle in the Manor of Kingston' is generally agreed to refer to Corfe), and of that a good deal remains: a lofty stone wall round the crown of the hill, forming an inner ward, and a fragment of a hall to the W at a somewhat lower level, placed no doubt against the timber palisades which would have surrounded the bailey. The Great Tower could be William's as, stylistically, it is likely to be as early as *c.* 1080. With the building of the tower Corfe became virtually impregnable, so long as no weapon had the firepower to touch it from the higher ridges to E and W. A timber outer bailey wall seems to have accompanied the Great Tower on the S and W sides, rebuilt in stone in the early C13. In 1139 Corfe was called 'unum omnium Anglorum castellum tutissimum' ('the most secure of all English castles'). The next big royal expenditure on the castle was in 1201–4, when

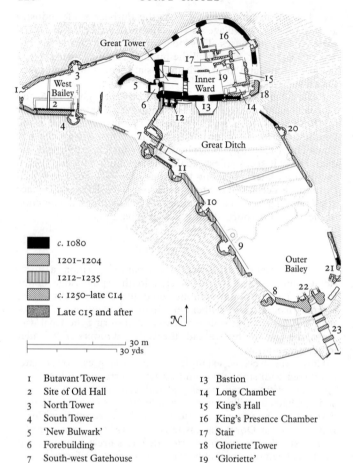

Corfe Castle.
Plan

<table>
<tr><td>1</td><td>Butavant Tower</td><td>13</td><td>Bastion</td></tr>
<tr><td>2</td><td>Site of Old Hall</td><td>14</td><td>Long Chamber</td></tr>
<tr><td>3</td><td>North Tower</td><td>15</td><td>King's Hall</td></tr>
<tr><td>4</td><td>South Tower</td><td>16</td><td>King's Presence Chamber</td></tr>
<tr><td>5</td><td>'New Bulwark'</td><td>17</td><td>Stair</td></tr>
<tr><td>6</td><td>Forebuilding</td><td>18</td><td>Gloriette Tower</td></tr>
<tr><td>7</td><td>South-west Gatehouse</td><td>19</td><td>'Gloriette'</td></tr>
<tr><td>8</td><td>First Tower</td><td>20</td><td>Plukenet Tower</td></tr>
<tr><td>9</td><td>Second Tower</td><td>21</td><td>Horseshoe Tower</td></tr>
<tr><td>10</td><td>Third Tower</td><td>22</td><td>Outer Gatehouse</td></tr>
<tr><td>11</td><td>Fourth Tower</td><td>23</td><td>Bridge</td></tr>
<tr><td>12</td><td>South Annexe</td><td></td><td></td></tr>
</table>

building that cost £752 was carried out. Part of that went on strengthening the defences, enclosing the w triangle of the bailey with walls. Here came the first of Corfe's mural towers. With the rest King John built an unfortified courtyard house – the 'Gloriette', not large but elegant, immediately E of the Great Tower. Throughout the rest of the C13 attention was devoted to strengthening the castle towards the SE, where alone the ground sloped gently, down to the flat where the village grew up. Miners were employed in 1207 and 1214, and excavated a great ditch s of the inner ward, thereby isolating the inner ward and inner bailey from an outer bailey. The next step was to provide the inner bailey with a gateway and to surround the outer bailey by an enceinte with mural towers. This was achieved in two stages, 1212–c. 1215 and c. 1250–80. With that Corfe Castle was finally fortified.

Corfe was sold into private ownership in 1407, although it later reverted to the Crown. The final break with royal ownership occurred only in 1572, when it passed to Sir Christopher Hatton. He improved the accommodation within the Great Tower, referred to as the 'King's Tower' at that time. (The Gloriette was inaccurately called the 'Queen's Tower'.) Hatton also improved the defences by adding the New Bulwark for cannon to the w of the tower. A further change was made before the Civil War by the construction of the Bastion, on the s side of the inner ward.

After capture by Parliamentary troops in 1646, when its command was under Mary, Lady Bankes, widow of Charles I's Lord Chief Justice, the castle was 'slighted' by undermining and placement of charges. As a postscript, its restoration as a residence was mooted by William John Bankes of Kingston Lacy, whose 'Blank Book' of 1835 contains his record drawings of the castle, together with proposals for rebuilding. From an archaeological point of view, it is fortunate that these schemes were never carried out, and that the castle, crowned by the slabs of its tall Great Tower, remain a Purbeck symbol. After the death in 1981 of its last private owner, H.J.R. Bankes, Corfe Castle formed part of his bequest to the National Trust, with Kingston Lacy.★

Detailed description begins with the latest parts, for those are the first encountered by the visitor. The BRIDGE across the artificially deepened ditch between village and castle is of four unequal arches on rectangular piers, a massive structure, largely ashlar-faced, but of such basic functionalism that it gives no clue to its date. The piers are dated to c. 1250–80 and the semicircular arches to the late C16 or later. The bridge leads straight to the OUTER GATEHOUSE, building c. 1250–80 and now much ruined at the top and the back. It must always however have been relatively modest, not presenting an intimidating appearance, but relying on more practical deterrents. Ashlar. Round-headed entrance arch between two round towers, which rise from sloping plinths. Inner arch with a double chamfer, set beyond a machicolation-slot and a portcullis groove. Segmental vault. Signs that there were arrow loops in the towers at first-floor level. At the back just the

★This account depends principally on the complex deductions set out in full in the RCHME inventory volume covering Corfe Castle (*Dorset*, vol. 2 (1970), part I); John Goodall, *The English Castle* (2011); his article on 'The King's Tower' in *Country Life*, 14 June 2012; and the revised phase dating in the National Trust's guidebook (2005).

wall-stubs of guardrooms, and traces of a semicircular vault springing from chamfered string courses. A defensible gateway at this point would certainly have been needed from the earliest period, even if the defences on either side were only timber palisades.*

The fall of the ground makes it hard to see much of the mural towers to l. and r. of the outer gatehouse, but also perhaps explains why the outer bailey was encircled with stone defences so slowly. Towards the NE, i.e. to the r. of the outer gatehouse, the HORSESHOE TOWER belongs to the c. 1250–80 build: see the plinth mould in common with the outer gatehouse. Then comes a straight joint, telling of a pause in construction. The pause was not a long one, for – beyond the very ruined tower-less stretch** – the PLUKENET TOWER, high to the E of the great ditch, is datable 1269–70. Alan de Plukenet, Constable of Corfe Castle in those years, had his shield of arms carved on its E face, held up by two hands. The Plukenet Tower joins the C12 bailey wall directly. Remains of a newel stair and evidence of the wall-walk to which it led, NW of the tower.

Starting again at the outer gatehouse and working towards the l., one finds a much more substantial series of wall towers, towers more substantial and twice as numerous in a similar distance of wall. Even the wall itself is thicker, for this was naturally the more vulnerable direction, and it was on this side that the route up to the inner bailey needed guarding. Undermining in 1646 has tipped and dislodged the masonry, but for the most part not destroyed it. These towers, like those described already, are ashlar-faced, the outward faces rounded, the backs open, the only frontal openings being arrow loops. The S tower of the series, of c. 1250–80, is closely similar to the outer gatehouse in details, except for the more widely jointed ashlar. The other three, and the intermediate wall, are earlier: see especially the longer and narrower arrow loops. These belong to the first phase of remodelling the outer bailey, 1212–c. 1215. At that time the entire outer enclosure below the inner ward was undivided by stone walls. So the SOUTH-WEST GATEHOUSE, set at the end of a cross-wall linking it to the forebuilding of the Great Tower, is later and in style goes with the latest defences. The cross-wall, of rubble stone, was built in 1235, and at first an undefended doorway opened in it at this point.

Altogether the development of the outer bailey strikes one as casual, bright idea after bright idea, not a coherent plan. That of course is striking only on reflection; immediately so is the astonishing cleavage of the gatehouse, whereby the l. half stands intact several feet lower than the r. The gatehouse is reached across a bridge of two arches and is itself ashlar-faced and of

---

* Excavation of the W guard chamber in 1986 revealed the outline of a building and flight of steps to the top of the curtain wall to the W, as shown on Treswell's survey of the castle of 1586.
**Where Treswell's plan shows that a stable was built against the wall.

the usual form, two round towers for guardrooms flanking the entrance passage. Segmental entrance arch, double-chamfered. The passage was defended by portcullis and machicolation at the front end, and at the back by two portcullises and a door: see the rebating of the rear arch. The towers were probably three-storeyed, and have radiating channelling at the top for the timbers of a projecting gallery, similar to the arrangement surviving at Stokesay Castle, Shropshire (1290s). Also cross-loops (for crossbows) at second-storey level. Square rooms inside. Doorway with shouldered head into the NE room.

With that a higher level is reached, a level which formed a separate WEST BAILEY, naturally protected on two of its three sides by precipitous slopes. This was walled in 1201–4 and given a NORTH TOWER and a SOUTH TOWER, both projecting with a semicircular face, and on the far W point of the promontory the polygonal BUTAVANT TOWER. That is an early date for experimentation with something more impregnable than the standard rectangular plan. All the towers were open-backed, and polygonal internally; but only the North Tower remains reasonably intact, as does the wall here almost to its full height. W of the North Tower patching of the wall where there was a postern gateway, and W of that traces of a recess in the wall for a garderobe.* Much more worthy of close inspection however is the wall beside the South Tower, where carefully laid herringbone masonry remains as evidence of the HALL in the bailey of c. 1180. Excavation has recovered the dimensions of the hall, or rather of its undercroft, 72 by 17 ft (22 by 5 metres). Three original blocked windows, square-headed and suitable only to an undercroft.

So to the highest level, by a route which is almost a piece of mountain scrambling. The present pathway into the INNER WARD at its narrowest NW point passes close to the site of the original gateway, but of that there is nothing except some footings to be seen. Immediately to the r. however a piece of rough rubble enclosure wall rises to a height of about 15 ft (4.6 metres). This, although quite different from the herringbone walling in the W bailey, must be of the same date, i.e. c. 1080, for the S annexe of the Great Tower is built on top of a continuation of this wall further E. The wall originally enclosed the entire inner ward, and round the NE side quite a long stretch survives to give still a feeling of enclosure.

The GREAT TOWER stands in part to full height, but its N wall and all but a narrow stack of its E wall lie prostrate. It is an extraordinarily tattered effect, but if one tries to discount it one can feel the Early Norman style in its full power. This structure was uncompromisingly a tower, 43 by 48 ft (13.1 by 14.6 metres) on plan, but c. 70 ft (21 metres) high. The W forebuilding and the annexe to the S built over the earlier wall, though structurally separate from the Great Tower, must have

---

*As Treswell's plan shows. In 1989 three further posterns were discovered.

been planned with it, as they are both essential to circulation around the Tower. In all parts the walling is of rather roughly squared ashlar blocks, i.e. earlier in technique than Roger of Salisbury's finely jointed ashlar at e.g. Sherborne Castle, which set new standards. Decoration and mouldings hardly appear, so that the Tower, which, one must remember, was the fortifiable dwelling place of the king, not a mere fortress, has an air of stark and uncompromising bareness. No external string courses, just slight, chamfered set-offs at three levels. Pilaster buttresses, dividing the tower into four bays by five. The only external decoration is blank arcading, large scale but of the most primitive sort, at the level of the top storey. No wall chambers, no wall piercings except round-headed windows cut straight through the wall, without inward splays. The passage arch through the s annexe is similar.

The Great Tower originally had only two floors above a basement (the top storey enclosed a double pitched roof, the central valley resting on a spine wall). With the help of Treswell's late C16 plans preserved at Kingston Lacy, it may be deduced that the Tower itself, divided by an E–W spine wall, had public rooms on the ground floor, the great hall occupying the whole of the s half, and the king's apartments above. One telling detail remains of these: half of the doorway in the E stump of the cross-wall. Round-arched head outlined with a roll decorated with billet and set on a long jamb shaft, of which the capital has primitive leaf volutes; one may represent the image of a pelican. The tympanum was originally solid. The s annexe and the forebuilding also show that it was at first-floor level that a display was needed. The former, beside the passage arch, has a guardroom and a garderobe; but above, inaccessible now except by ladder, not only evidence of another garderobe but a doorway decorated similarly to the upper doorway in the Great Tower, which means that there must have been an important room in the annexe here, perhaps the ante-room to the king's appearance doorway. The forebuilding housed the staircase to the first floor, approached through a N doorway, and from which a third enriched doorway led into the royal apartments. Traces of C13 pentices with flights of steps up to the passage through the s annexe from E and W. Some C16 fenestration high in the Great Tower.

By 1201–4, the date of the GLORIETTE, which stands in ruins to the E of the Great Tower, it was realized that the curtain walls made the fortification of the royal dwelling an over-timid precaution. So the Gloriette, built in four ranges round a small courtyard, was attached to the C11 s wall of the inner ward, but given no defences of its own. The N, s and W ranges are reduced practically to rubble, but the walls which stand show that the Gloriette was designed in an E.E. style of stylish restraint. The hall, four bays long, raised on an undercroft which had a groin-vault, is faced with ashlar of the most exact workmanship. The windows, lancets of unusual breadth, were no more than double-chamfered outside, under

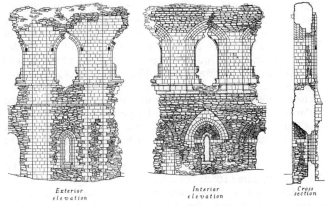

Exterior
elevation

Interior
elevation

Cross
section

The East Wall of the King's Hall and Undercroft

Corfe Castle, Gloriette, elevations and section.
Drawing, 1970

a hoodmould brought down to little stops of stiff-leaf foliage,
and had double-chamfered rere-arches. Double-chamfered
lancets to the undercroft. Shallow pilaster buttresses divide
the bays. The hall was entered through a porch at the NW
corner, broad enough to shelter besides the hall doorway a
doorway to a small but elaborately treated room to the N.
Porch approached up a straight flight of steps, now reduced
to a ramp. Part of a large window to light the porch, and the
hall doorway reasonably intact. This has a continuous outer
roll moulding, and a chamfer. The SW angle within the small
N room has evidence of a recessed Purbeck marble shaft to
carry vaulting, so the room was one of importance. Continuous roll l. and r. of it.

With the help of Treswell's plan it can be said that the S range
had a solar stretching its entire length, and that the service
rooms were in the W range with the kitchen beyond. The
foundations at the SE angle are of the GLORIETTE TOWER,
constructed for Edward I c. 1280, to link the Gloriette with
the CII wall.

THE VILLAGE

ST EDWARD, KING AND MARTYR. By *T.H. Wyatt*, 1859–60,
and surprisingly large for so small a town. The scale is set
by the early CI5 three-stage W tower. Ashlar, with a doorway
with an almost straight-shank arch, tracery and shields in the
spandrels, and image niches l. and r. Big gargoyles below
the battlements. From the old church also the CI4 chancel N
doorway and a CI3 lancet, and in the chancel S wall inside a
CI3 arch on a shaft with moulded capitals. Wyatt's church is
E.E. style, but with several CI5-style windows responding to

the tower. Broad N porch retained from the previous church, its C12 colonnette jambs heavily restored. E window of 1947 (by *Martin Travers*) replacing Wyatt's. On the E gable a STATUE of St Edward by *Francis Newbery*, 1931. The piers of the arcades have French Early Gothic foliage capitals, those of the chancel arcades clustered Purbeck shafts. The E pier of the S arcade has a genuine E.E. capital, reused. Early C16 roof bosses re-set on the chancel roof cornice. – PISCINA in the N chapel. C13. Sexfoiled Purbeck marble bowl with three-lobed underside. – FONT. C15, of Purbeck marble. The stem panelled, the octagonal bowl with vesica-shaped quatrefoil panels each making a square. – In 1940–7 *Martin Travers* supplied the bold mid-C17-style FONT COVER and the N chapel SCREEN.* – ROYAL ARMS. Of Charles II, dated 1660. – STAINED GLASS. E window by *Clayton & Bell*, 1864, re-set in new tracery by *Travers*. N chapel E window by *Travers* (completed by *Lawrence Lee*), 1948. Several other windows by *Clayton & Bell*, 1857–82. – MONUMENTS. Two early C15 inscription tablets in the N chapel, to Robert Rynkyn recording a contribution to the building fund, and to the same recording a benefaction to the church.

EVANGELICAL CONGREGATIONAL CHURCH, East Street. 1835. Round-arched with Neo-Norman triplet at the E end.

PERAMBULATION. We must start at THE SQUARE with, on the N side, THE GREYHOUND INN as its main accent. C17, with a porch dated 1733, when the building was a pair of houses, projecting over the pavement on Tuscan columns. Unusually for Corfe, where one expects bare stone, it is limewashed. The BANKES ARMS HOTEL on the E side, on the other hand, despite its use of the correct materials, is a false note. It is all too obviously of the 1920s, the giveaway features being its proportions and exposed rafter ends at the eaves. N of it, round the corner, is UVEDALE'S HOUSE, what remains of a once-important late C16 house. Two six-light windows, one per floor, towards the road, with hollow-chamfered mullions, the lower window having a hoodmould. Hutchins mentions glass in the house dated 1575. On the S side of The Square the late C18 TOWN HOUSE (now Post Office), three bays, ashlar-faced, the centre bowed out strangely with a round-headed window in the upper part of the bow, jammed against a half-hipped roof. A very curious plan for what was originally a pair of cottages, part of the upper floor of each being taken by the mayor's diminutive robing room, entered separately from the churchyard. This has a coved ceiling. Also on the S side the VILLAGE SIGN by *Francis Newbery*, 1927. (Its painting of St Edward the Martyr is a copy by *Robin Pearce*, 1952. The original is in the museum.) The TOWN HALL, round the corner in WEST STREET, is another little oddity, just a red brick room at churchyard level, built shortly before 1774.

*A REREDOS by *Travers* has been removed from the chapel.

Here begins the most characteristic part of the village, WEST STREET, which deserves to be explored when one is feeling receptive to every twist and turn, every widening and narrowing, every shift in roof level. The cottages (for nothing approaches a town house in scale here) are mostly late C17 to early C19, with little to distinguish their date apart from window forms. In many cases they appear to have been rebuilt (or at least refenestrated) *c.* 1800. Special mention need only be made of No. 30, the cottage on the r. at the sharp corner. C17 but possibly of C15 origins. The section of quatrefoil panel over the doorway is re-set, but within is a large and somewhat rustic Perp chimneypiece, perhaps removed from the castle. If it is *in situ*, the implication is that the cottage is a fragment of a larger house. Much further down the street is a small group of vernacular-style houses by *Western Design Architects*, 2003, built using natural materials (two with large Purbeck stone slates, one thatched), showing what can be done to fit into the historic street scene.

Back to the Square and directly s into EAST STREET. After the first 150 yds it becomes less urban in character (and is affected significantly by through traffic). The first accent on the l. is a pair of cottages (once a single house) with an C18 brick porch built out like the porch of the Greyhound Inn, on monolithic Tuscan columns, clearly a Corfe Castle speciality. Then, after *c.* 100 yds on the l., MORTON'S HOUSE, of the early C17, probably for Edward Dackham. Free-standing and grand enough to have an E-plan front towards the street, even if a somewhat constricted one. Long wings, short porch. Only one storey, plus gabled dormers. Two-light windows symmetrically arranged, the mullions, as usual, hollow-chamfered. Round head to the porch arch, but Perp mouldings. The central block was extended to the rear in the later C17 to create a double-pile plan. Diagonally opposite, THE OLD FORGE is partly C15 and has a subdivided former hall with two raised crucks, although externally nothing of this is discernible. Thereafter cottages continue, none singling itself out for comment; but there are several happy groups, extending altogether for more than a quarter of a mile. Two items of note, further along on the l: the Perp-style WAR MEMORIAL GATEWAY to the cemetery, 1922 by *Francis Newbery*, full of Dorset references; and the C18 former ALMSHOUSES, modest architecturally but with a long straight flight of steps up to the front door. Just beyond, on the r., ABBOTS COTTAGES, sensitive vernacular-style infill by *Ken Morgan Architects* for Corfe Castle Charities, 1995–7.

Two last detours. From The Square, up STATION ROAD to the e, the RAILWAY STATION, 1885 by *W. R. Galbraith* for the London & South Western Railway (now part of the preserved Swanage Railway). Two-storey cottage style. Purbeck rubble stone, similar to that at Swanage. Also of 1885 (dated on a cartouche), on the e side of the road N from Corfe, a graceful four-arch VIADUCT, spanning the Studland road.

OUTLYING BUILDINGS AND ARCHAEOLOGY

REMPSTONE HALL, 2 m. E. Late C16, but much remodelled (see the bay windows and pedimented doorcase). Long brick addition of c. 1790 creating a house terrace effect.

THE RINGS, ¼ m. SSW of the castle. Earthwork remains of a ring-and-bailey CASTLE, probably of a siege-castle built by King Stephen in 1139 when he unsuccessfully besieged Corfe. They were reused by the besieging forces during the Civil Wars.

BLASHENWELL, 1 m. SW. The MESOLITHIC SITE produced flint implements and animal bones. Iron Age and Roman SETTLEMENT REMAINS above.

NINE BARROW DOWN, 2¼ m. ESE. A compact nuclear group of seventeen ROUND BARROWS and a focal long barrow.

REMPSTONE STONE CIRCLE, 2¼ m. E. Twelve stones, five standing, set in an arc of a circle 80 ft (24 metres) in diameter. Possibly Early Bronze Age.

CORFE COMMON, ¾ m. S. Eight BOWL BARROWS along the spine of the ridge.

ELDON'S SEAT AND ROPE LAKE HOLE, 2½ m. SSW, S of Swyre Head. Excavated Bronze Age and Iron Age SETTLEMENT TERRACES, with hut structures, shale working and salt production.

NORDEN, ½ m. NW of Corfe Castle. ROMANO-BRITISH SETTLEMENT of 15 acres, much quarried. Excavations identified houses and workshops producing Purbeck stone mortars on an industrial scale; also a temple and enclosure.

OWER PENINSULA, 3½ m. NE of Corfe Castle. Late Iron Age and Romano-British ENCLOSURES and TRACKWAYS over 7½ acres to Cleavel Point, with workshops and pottery kilns.

BUCKNOWLE, ¾ m. SW, on the W side of Corfe River. On the site of a Neolithic enclosure and Middle Bronze Age cemetery barrow, an IRON AGE SETTLEMENT of several phases of circular buildings, including possible shrines. Of the early Roman period a series of stone structures, including a BATH HOUSE. From the C4 the site was dominated by a wealthy courtyard VILLA, and the bath house was enlarged.

CORFE MULLEN

Church and Court House straddle the Wimborne to Dorchester highway. Post-war development has created a large village centre ½ m. SE, along the Blandford and Wareham roads.

ST HUBERT. Nave and chancel C13 – see the E lancets, the chancel S doorway and the pointed-trefoiled nave and chancel lancets. Stout early C14 W tower of heathstone. Three stages with a plain parapet. Two-light early C16 W window with cinquefoiled heads. Long S transept of brick and short contemporary N transept (adapted from the N porch of *c.* 1400), of 1841 by *George Evans* of Wimborne. – INTERIOR. Largely as in 1841, with galleries at the W end of the nave and S end of the S transept. Nave re-pewed in 1865, when a S vestry was added. Late C15 plastered wagon roofs to nave and chancel with timber bosses at the intersections of moulded timber ribs. One boss has three hares sharing just three ears. Matching roof in the S transept. – FONT. Octagonal, of Purbeck marble, with two pointed-trefoiled flat arches each side. – STAINED GLASS. Fine three-light E window, 1893, by *Clayton & Bell.* – N transept, two by *George Cooper-Abbs*, 1947 and 1949. – BRASS. Chancel N wall, Richard Hirt †1437, civilian, 12 in. (30 cm.) long.

ST NICHOLAS OF JERUSALEM, Wareham Road. 1997 by *Christopher Romain* of the *Sarum Partnership*, incorporating an earlier church hall of *c.* 1964. Geometrical plan to the church, brick with spreading hipped roofs and slit windows between expressed buttresses; roof topped by a spirelet. Chapel in matching style attached with multi-functional narthex behind.

MORTUARY CHAPEL, Blandford Road. 1922 by *Fletcher & Brett* of Wimborne. Brick. Well-judged Arts and Crafts, with raking buttresses and a hipped tiled roof. Tower with pyramidal roof at the N end, large lunette window at the S.

CHAPEL IN THE VALLEY (Baptist), Newton Lane, just S of the above. 1879. Buttressed brick, plain pointed-arched windows. Engulfed in an expansion of 1986 by *Jack Keelan.*

CORFE MULLEN FAMILY CHURCH (Evangelical Free), Wareham Road. 1932. Insistent banded brick and ashlar, with crowstepped gables and battlements. Matching banded walling to the adjacent MINISTER'S HOUSE, an otherwise typical detached dwelling of the period.

COURT HOUSE, ⅛ m. N of St Hubert's church. The Phelips family had a manor house here, and this seems to be part of it. Small two-storey rectangle, gabled at the short ends. The N end is made up, and the surviving fragment represents the centre and S arm of an originally cruciform plan. W wall ashlar-faced, so this must have been an important front. One three-light upper window. Mullions with an ovolo moulding, not typical of Dorset, but suggesting an early C17 date. Hoodmould. Big projecting S chimney-breast with three lozenge-shaped brick stacks. First-floor string courses round both fronts including the chimney-breast. The E side, of rubble stone walling, seems to be largely C19 in its openings. The corbelling of the upper oriel here is genuine. Good plaster ceilings in the lower S room, and in the upper, both *c.* 1600. Re-set C17 staircase with turned balusters and turned finials on the newels.

KNOLL HOUSE, ½ m. S of St Hubert's church. Two sash-windowed blocks, one of *c.* 1800, the other of *c.* 1860, linked by a tower and angled porch. Now Castle Court School.

POTTERY KILN, 1 m. E. Claudian (C1 A.D.), providing pottery for the Roman army. Excavated in 1932. Related to the Roman fortress at Lake Gates Farm (*see* below).

ROMAN FORTRESS, 1¼ m. ENE of St Hubert's church, N of Lake
Gates Farm. Roman legionary fort, with roads N to Badbury
Rings and S to the Roman military base at Hamworthy (q.v.).

CORSCOMBE

A straggle of stone cottages with some C20 infill development.
The most significant buildings noted below are well to the E and
SE of the village.

ST MARY. Unbuttressed C15 W tower. Three stages and an
embattled parapet with crocketed corner pinnacles. Elaborate
Perp N doorway with niches l. and r. and three niches over.
The lower niches have corbels on shafts. Also the three W
bays of the Perp S arcade (with columns of standard type) are
original. Otherwise, the church was rebuilt and slightly enlarged
by *J. Mountford Allen* of Crewkerne in 1876–7. Perp except for
the chancel, where the architect permitted himself Second
Pointed. – PULPIT. Elaborate, with small pink and green
marble shafts. Given in 1883. – FONT. C15. Octagonal, with,
on each side, two cusped blank arches. – STAINED GLASS. E
window by *Hardman*, 1877. W window by the same firm.

CORSCOMBE HOUSE (formerly the rectory), immediately NE.
C17 E–W range with hollow-chamfered mullioned windows.
To the E of this, facing the lane and at right angles, a wing of
the early C19. The Gothic porch on the E front is of this date.
Second rear wing added by *R.H. Shout*, 1855.

CORSCOMBE COURT, ⅜ m. NNE. An L-shaped house within an
L-shaped moat. The earliest part is the longer N range, adapted
in the C20 but retaining a two-centred-arched doorway facing
W. This appears late C13 or early C14 but may be re-set. Also
probably no longer *in situ* a small blocked lancet in the N gable
wall. Owing to its date, this wing has been associated with
the grange of Sherborne Abbey at Corscombe. The S cross-
wing, with its three uniform bays of three-light windows with
hoodmoulds, *c.* 1700 (although it may be as late as 1775, the
date on one of its chimneys). Of this date too the E windows
inserted in the medieval range in simple classical surrounds,
but with a single mullion. – BARN with a deep stone porch,
the arch segmental and with diagonal buttresses, and with a
crocketed pinnacle at its gable apex. Of the C15 presumably.

BENVILLE MANOR, 1 m. SE. Also on a moated site. The S
front has a fine appearance, symmetrical about a central gable
crowned by a chimneystack (cf. Little Toller Farm, Toller
Fratrum). Despite this apparent unity, the house, of H-plan,
has undergone considerable evolution. The S range is C17 in
origin, but gained its symmetrical layout (and modest Tuscan-
columned porch) in the early C19. The canted two-storey bay
windows to l. and r. may be C17 also, but acquired small hipped

roofs in the late C19. The lights on the bays are arranged 1:4:1 on both storeys. Chamfered quoins to the corners of this range and elsewhere. Behind the façade everything is thoroughly remodelled. On the N side is a staircase projection and a secondary wing, the usual early C17 arrangement. However, much of this was rebuilt in brick, presumably in the C19 to judge by the tall-proportioned and simply moulded stone-mullioned windows. This wing has a W return, seemingly contemporary with the S front. The E part of this wing has been pulled down, probably in the early C19. A window in the SE corner of the house has heraldic stained glass of *c.* 1500 (re-set *c.* 1880): it includes the arms of the Arundell family, known to have owned Benville at that date.

CORTON

6080

2¼ m. E of Portesham

Simple chapel and imposing farmhouse, as spectacularly sited as Waddon Manor nearer Portesham.

St Bartholomew. Early C13 chancel (see one S window) and C16 Late Perp nave. Dec E window; late C19 W window. C13 PISCINA. The building was rescued from dereliction in 1897 by *T.G. Jackson*. – ALTAR. Impressive. A great stone slab carried on cross-walls. Early C13. – TILES. Medieval, re-set in the chancel floor.

Corton Farm. The farmhouse has unexpectedly sumptuous C16 windows in the W wall. Below are a pair of three-lighters under a common hoodmould. The upper window has five lights and a hoodmould. Arched lights moulded continuously with the mullions. Elaborately stopped jambs. Other more normal C16 and C17 windows. It appears that the house began, in spite of its windows, quite simply as a two-storey range with three rooms in a row.

Friar Waddon Farm, ½ m. NE. Excellent and picturesque farm group with thatched roofs. An C18 COTTAGE alongside the road has a re-set C16 mullioned window with three arched lights. At right angles to this, a C16 cottage with a lateral chimneystack. Also a long BARN, to the E, probably C17 but with a roof reconstructed in the C19.

CRANBORNE

0010

The village has always been dominated by Cranborne Manor and the church, but until the C19 Cranborne was a small market town on the narrow River Crane. Bypassed by a new road in 1757, its market began to fall out of use. The Crane was culverted in 1841. Many elegant brick houses and cottages of the C17 and C18, most of which probably date from after a major fire in 1748. A large number of estate cottages erected in the 1890s and 1900s by the Cranborne and Edmondsham estates.

ST MARY AND ST BARTHOLOMEW. The church was attached to a Benedictine abbey founded *c.* 980. Tewkesbury was subordinate to it. In 1102 the relation was reversed, and Cranborne remained a cell of Tewkesbury. At the Dissolution it had only two monks. None of the monastic buildings survives and none of the structure of the present building is earlier than the C12.* Built of flint and rubble with stone bands. It has a correct E.E. porch of 1873 and a spacious E end of 1874–5, both by *David Brandon*. The nave of *c.* 1300 with, on the N, a re-set mid-C12 doorway. This has a single order of colonnettes with chevron decoration at right angles to the wall outside the shafts. Two orders of arch, the inner plain, the outer of two sets of chevron, at right angles and parallel to the wall, with an outer band of nailhead ornament. The two-centred inner arch was most likely originally segmental. The clerestory above the lead low-pitches of the N aisle is largely blank, save for two small C15 three-light windows at the E end. The S aisle is incorporated under the main nave roof. Original windows of *c.* 1300, mainly two lights under flat hoodmoulds, with ogee-headed lights. Towards the E end of the S aisle a C15 four-light window. Powerful Perp W tower (indulgence for its erection granted in 1440), of five stages with battlemented parapets, diagonal offset buttresses and two-light traceried belfry openings. Brown heathstone and pale greensand to the lower levels, mostly banded flint above. Large five-light Perp W window with distinctive straight diagonal tracery, above a two-centred-arched W doorway under a bold flat hoodmould. Expressed S stair-turret in two sections, the lower almost central, the upper smaller and further E. Six-bay arcades with two-centred arches, looking of *c.* 1300, with piers alternating between octagons and quatrefoils in section. The latter have Purbeck marble cores. One exception to the pier alternation is l. of the N entrance: here the pier base indicates that it originally fitted the general pattern, i.e. it was of quatrefoil section. Westernmost bay cut into by the C15 tower. C15 wagon roof to the nave. Broad chancel arch with attached Purbeck marble columns, part of *Brandon*'s 1874–5 alterations. Purbeck marble also for the colonnettes supporting the rere-arches of the five-light E window. Re-set in the chancel N wall is a Perp TOMB-RECESS.

FURNISHINGS. REREDOS, S aisle. A heavily wood-carved Victorian piece with characteristic leaves and flowers. It is, as well as the ALTAR and the SCREEN, the work of the *Rev. F. H.*

---

*An Anglo-Saxon carved panel, probably from a C9 or C10 cross, was found close to the church in 1935. It may be related to a predecessor building.

Fisher, vicar 1888–1910. – PULPIT. Perp, circular, oak, with blank arches and blank tracery. The initials TP may refer to Thomas Parker, Abbot of Tewkesbury and Cranborne (1389–1420). Stone pedestal of *c*. 1875. – FONT. Of Purbeck marble, C13, octagonal, with two shallow blank pointed arches to each side. – PAINTINGS, nave S wall. Early C14. From the E, allegory of Three Living and Three Dead, much defaced; St Christopher, partially obliterated; the Tree of the Seven Deadly Sins growing out of the head of a woman and with naked girls climbing about; the Tree of the Seven Virtues. Over the chancel arch, Christ in Majesty with the Twelve Apostles, *c*. 1880. – ROYAL ARMS. Above the N doorway, Queen Anne, 1709. – STAINED GLASS. C15 fragments in a S window. Otherwise, except for the E window of 1990 by *Alan Younger*, many are late C19 and early C20, generally of high quality. Three by *Percy Bacon Bros*: two in N aisle, one E end of the S aisle, †1910. More colourful, although not necessarily finer, in the N aisle by *H. Ramburt*, 1886. Four-light window in the S aisle, 1886 by *Mayer & Co*. The large W window in the tower, by *Cox, Sons, Buckley & Co.*, 1885, commemorates Edward Stillingfleet, Bishop of Worcester †1700. – MONUMENTS. Purbeck marble chest tomb to John Hawles †1571. Cusped front panels. – The next three monuments were removed from the chancel in 1875. Canopied monument with two recumbent effigies and three columns carrying nailhead-ornamented arches, the middle one in front of the effigies, probably of John and Elizabeth Chafin (Hooper), *c*. 1600. Strapwork top with achievement. – Ann and Katherine Hooper †1637 and Katherine's husband, Thomas †1638. Wall monument, not correctly reassembled. Three inscription plates, no effigies, but two badly carved allegorical figures, naïvely painted, on the shanks of a wide open pediment. – Wall monument to John Elliott †1641, a schoolboy who, according to the Latin inscription, died suddenly while at school. Small frontally seated figure, the head pensively supported by one hand. The elbow rests on a skull. – Mrs Susanna Stillingfleet †1647. An elaborate tablet. – HEADSTONE W of the church tower by *Eric Gill*, Michael Charles James Cecil †1937. Its companions were designed to echo *Gill*'s work.

CRANBORNE MANOR, just W of the church. Externally the aspiring but delicately fantastic house created by the 1st Earl of Salisbury early in the reign of James I remains almost unaltered, the S front rising above its gatehouses and walled garden, the N front above its terrace and walled garden. Only the wings W and E have changed, the former rebuilt in quite another form as early as 1647, the latter pulled down without trace in 1716.

The story starts, however, in the C13. In 1207–8 a royal hunting lodge in Cranborne Chase was rebuilt by King John. What survives of the medieval structure conforms precisely to a surviving detailed survey of the building carried out by John Norden for Robert Cecil in 1605 (the year in which Cecil was created Earl of Salisbury by James I). Externally, the surviving

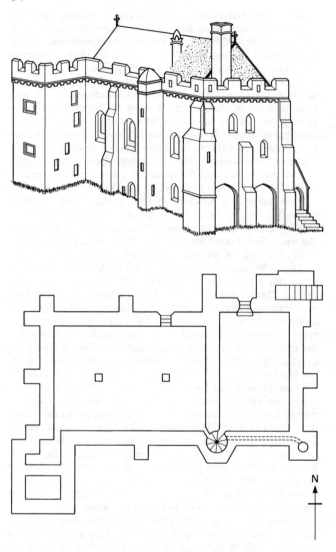

Cranborne Manor, view from the south-east and plan.
Drawing by Anthony Emery, 2006

rubble walling of this rectangular building is rendered, with its
ashlar dressings largely left exposed. Angle buttresses with two
shallow set-offs rising the full height at the NE and NW corners.
Intermediate buttresses divide the N wall into three bays. On
the s front there is one buttress and a polygonal stair-turret,
dying away at the top where the battlements rise to protect

it. Battlements on the s side, with arrow-slits in the merlons, set upon a table of moulded corbels; the last also found on the three other walls, interrupted by later inserted fenestration. The sw tower was a part of the original hunting lodge, rising, according to Norden's survey, to the same height as the main block. That survey also shows large round-headed window openings in the upper part of the s elevation, one of which remains detectable to the r. of the stair-turret; a lancet in the e wall also conforms with Norden's record. At the nw end is a blind arch low down which shows that the building was set on an undercroft, indicated in the 1605 drawing at the e end. Internally however the crucial evidence is in the ne corner. The lancet was the e window of a first-floor chapel. Mutilated piscina, and a large cupboard in the e wall, with a well-moulded bell capital above. In the n wall the moulded rere-arch of a window, more evidence of high-class workmanship. Traces of a se projection, which must have been for garderobes. The cross-wall that divides the main building into a small e part and a large w one belongs to the original fabric, and the stair-turret projecting from the s wall serves both parts.

Robert Cecil in his turn needed a hunting lodge; it was probably in 1604 that he purchased the medieval lodge to add to other lands previously granted him by Elizabeth I. At Cranborne Cecil entertained James I, and his remodelling of the c13 house, by that time semi-derelict, had to take these functions into account: Cranborne would never be a permanent residence but it must have splendour worthy of a king. Work on the house and n forecourt was carried out in 1609–12, and is one of the better-documented commissions undertaken by *William Arnold*. Arnold appears to have worked on Montacute (Somerset), *c.* 1595–1601, probably built a gatehouse at Clifton Maybank (illustrated by Hutchins), since demolished, and was based at Oxford in 1610–12, designing and building Wadham College for Dorothy Wadham. He later (from 1617) went on to remodel Dunster Castle (Somerset) for George Luttrell. At Cranborne, the s forecourt and brick lodges were complete by 1614.

The old building was gutted and given grand big windows, mullioned and transomed, with small hoodmoulds. Two lofty storeys to the s, three to the n. The sw tower was heightened to out-top the main block, and a se tower was built to match. Against the short sides wings were added, each containing a room on the first floor which had a bow window front and back. These are the wings that have disappeared. The plan then was symmetrical, compact but complex, an embodiment of the Jacobean love of conceits. The silhouettes too are contrived with an eye to dramatic effect, the s front with its twin towers projecting at the corners, the n front with lozenge-shaped chimneystacks shooting up beside a central gabled dormer. The buttresses here are prettified by paired pilasters in three tiers, Tuscan, Doric, Ionic. But the prettiest features are the little – too little – arcaded loggias projecting

63

in the centre of each front. The s loggia's two storeys (the upper storey of which was 'the Prince's study' according to contemporary drawings) reach the main first-floor level. Doric columns carry banded segmental arches, a strange variation of a Doric entablature, and a top storey crowned by semicircular merlons, the centre two carved with roundels of Libra and Virgo, brilliant in design and execution, which can be said very rarely of Jacobean sculpture. The columns with their lower shafts rusticated, and the use of the niches, l. and r. of the window, are derived from Serlio. A blank roundel below the window, a motif picked up by the discs punched in the main block at first-floor level. The N loggia has a purer Doric arcade but is otherwise fussier, with plenty of strapwork and cresting, though only one-storeyed. Gargoyles, big-nosed lion heads, in the spandrels.

The WEST WING, rebuilt in 1647–50 following Civil War damage, is completely different in character and scale to its predecessor: an advanced example of mid-C17 design, with a deep, steep hipped roof, bold eaves consoles and raised, over-sized classical quoins. The designer of the wing, which consists of one room per storey, was *Richard Ryder*, who was at that time working at Wilton (Wilts.) under John Webb. The roof caused comment at the time, for the master mason, *Thomas Forte*, jus-tified it both on aesthetic and practical grounds, pointing out how it echoed the pitched roofs of the towers and explaining that it was better 'for the defence of the weather, for as fast as the weather cometh up, it flyeth off every way'. Its original fenestration was cross-windows with full architraves and triple keystones, replaced by the present mullioned-and-transomed windows in 1863, dulling the contrast with the remainder of the building. This was the first of a number of changes made when the 2nd Marquess of Salisbury decided to take over the house for his own use (it having been used as a farmhouse since *c.* 1700).

The INTERIORS are therefore largely post-1863. A number of made-up chimneypieces in a Jacobean style are probably of the *2nd Marquess*'s own devising. Apart from the C13 features mentioned already, comment is needed only on the fine Jaco-bean staircase in the SW tower: timber, rising in short flights round a tight rectangular open well. Stout Tuscan columns spring as supports from the newels. Between them angled fretted arches with central pendants, presumably by *Arnold*, or at least in a convincing Arnold style. Vertically symmetrical turned balusters. The LIBRARY in the W wing was fitted out in a classical style by *T. Dalton Clifford, c.* 1960.

An elaborate GARDEN SETTING was conceived as part of Arnold's scheme, but carried out no doubt under *Mountain Jennings* and *John Tradescant* (Cecil's garden designers at Hat-field, Herts.). The N approach was down a tree-lined avenue from the Salisbury road, crossing the stream and entering a formal walled garden through a gateway. To the s, the approach

through woodland ends at another walled forecourt entered
between two lozenge-plan LODGES, brick, conical-roofed and
with a single chimneystack rising l. and r. of the entrance arch.
The garden to the E, heading towards the church, included an
orchard and mount, the latter now lost, while to the W were
hedged gardens. These were all much restored from the C19
onwards. In the S courtyard a WATER SCULPTURE, La Source
by *Angela Connor*, 2001.

CRANBORNE LODGE (No. 10 Castle Street). A striking and
powerful Early Georgian house. Central block of *c.* 1730–40,
for Samuel Stillingfleet; quite out of the ordinary run. Designed
on a square, double-pile plan, it was as tall as it was wide. Red
brick with lavish stone dressings. The N front has a four-bay
centre with a huge Ionic entablature and a pediment that
spans the original width of the house. The outer main windows
have gigantic triple keystones; the inner pair, with smaller but
still bold keystones, replaced what was originally a central
Venetian window, the outline of which is just detectable in the
brickwork. Slabs of rustication on the window imposts. Round-
headed windows in the later recessed bays l. and r. relate to a
substantial enlargement of *c.* 1755 for Thomas Drax, possibly
by *Francis Cartwright*, making it a viable country house. On the
S front the extensions are more obvious, lengthening the façade
from three to nine bays. Its central pedimented breakforward
(three bays as opposed to the four on the N) has similarities
with the work of *Nathaniel Ireson*: a central rusticated, round-
arched window above a pedimented doorcase in the rendered
base. The giant Ionic pilasters were added *c.* 1790 for Lewis
Tregonwell. Fine Rococo plasterwork ceiling in the principal
first-floor room of the W wing: an eagle with radiating lightning bolts and billowy clouds, very similar to plasterwork at
Came House, Winterborne Came (dated 1754). Here also an
elaborately scrolled Rococo chimneypiece. An enriched entablature in the Pillar Room relates to the original phase, its
Ionic-columned screen marking the end of the house before
expansion. The N hall chimneypiece is also of the earlier date.
    Facing S on the W end, a GARDEN LOGGIA by *Marshall
Sisson*, *c.* 1960. A simple brick arcade.
On the E side of the churchyard the VICARAGE, Tudor Revival
brick of 1828. Opposite, on the N side of CHURCH STREET,
a row of thatched cottages, possibly C15, but refronted in the
early C19. On emerging from Church Street, THE INN AT
CRANBORNE, Wimborne Street, is opposite. At the back a S
gable shows evidence of an unusual C16 roof structure. One
scissor truss. Kingposts in the N–S range. Its main frontage
is the result of late C18 remodelling. Further N along Wimborne Street the POST OFFICE, retaining a fine early C20
shopfront. On the opposite side a rather incongruously bulky,
suburban-looking, brick and half-timbered house of *c.* 1900.
Several more C18 red brick cottages in HIGH STREET and
SALISBURY STREET, presumably erected after the fire. The

widened E end of High Street, known as THE SQUARE, has
an early C18 house (No. 14) that is typically transitional in its
features: polite platband and segmental-arched window openings; vernacular raised parapet gables on kneelers, suggesting that it was once thatched. More early cottages to the E
along WATER STREET, several still thatched. Together with the
houses in CASTLE STREET, these are interspersed with pairs
of picturesquely gabled early C20 red brick estate cottages, one
dated TM 1908. Modern development is at the E end of the
village.

CASTLE, ½ m. SE. A perfectly preserved MOTTE AND BAILEY.

BOKERLEY DYKE. *See* Pentridge.

CREECH GRANGE

CREECH GRANGE. The story starts in the mid C16 with a U-plan
house for Sir Oliver Lawrence. To this a three-storey gabled
block was added in the NE corner, *c.* 1600. However everything of architectural significance belongs to two later periods:
1738–41 and *c.* 1844. The E (entrance) front is of the C19 date,
built for the Rev. Nathaniel Bond, and to a distant view makes
quite a convincing show of being an Early Elizabethan front,
now that the Portland stone ashlar (anachronistic material) is
lichened over. In fact one feature only has precise historical
justification: the two-storey window bay at the l. end, canted,
with 1:4:1 lights at both levels. The old stonework inside is
the proof of that.

The C18 s front was designed by *Francis Cartwright* of
Blandford (according to the building accounts and his signed
drawing), for Denis Bond. This too is of Portland ashlar, as
one would expect, and has the sobriety which this material
seems to have encouraged. Seven bays, two storeys. Central
pediment, balustrades l. and r. of it. Quoins, even at the ends,
alternating to mark the centre. Doorcase with Tuscan pilasters
and triglyph entablature. There are some individual touches:
the deep banded architrave, which gives the façade a heavy-
lidded look. This must have been in the way of an adjust-
ment to the Tudor gable behind, though the present gable
arrangement is altogether of the C19. Also the group of three
chimneystacks on the pediment (one on the apex). These are
not shown on Cartwright's drawings so may be later additions.
Facing w, Cartwright's windows recur with their moulded
frames and keystones; but the façade is rendered and gabled
at the ends, clearly a façade without pretensions.

Two interiors deserve further comment: the LIBRARY and
the DRAWING ROOM, both in the s block. Originally they
had a passage to the front doorway between them, but this
was later split between the rooms and the doorway blocked.

Both have mid-C18 fitting-out, the Drawing Room with a fine Palladian chimneypiece. Here too a mid-C16 bay window, retained during the C18 remodelling, with ARMORIAL GLASS of the C17. In the HALL, more GLASS, C19, probably that supplied by *Thomas Willement* in 1835. The mid-C19 STAIR-CASE was built in a new top-lit hall formed in the C16 central courtyard.

ST JOHN THE EVANGELIST. A chapel was built here in 1746 to house the Norman chancel arch of Holme Priory, 5 m. away (*see* East Holme). The mid-C12 arch is an exceptionally fine piece, because it is not overdone. It has two orders of Purbeck marble shafts with capitals either of decorated scallops or of big, streaked leaves, chevron, chevron at right angles, and chevron combined to form lozenges. Then in 1840, for John Bond, a solid Neo-Norman church was built around this Norman relic, with a N transept and a W tower whose top has more of the Italianate villa than of the Normans. This replaced the C18 chapel. The chancel and vestry-cum-organ chamber in a matching style are of 1868. – FURNISHINGS. Screens and a pulpit in a robust Neo-Norman style. – STAINED GLASS. The earliest is the central E window of 1844 by *Thomas Willement*. Two flanking lights probably by *Clayton & Bell*, *c.* 1868. The transept window is another by *Willement* (1849), in a Holbein-Germano-Swiss-Renaissance mood. Three chancel side windows by *Powell & Sons*, 1892.

NW of the house a set of three rectangular LAKES, part of a garden layout not swept away in the later C18 passion for landscaping. The GRANGE ARCH however, appearing above the wooded hillside on the skyline to the S, is an example of the other C18 mania, for follies. Erected before 1746, of Portland stone ashlar, but a rugged composition: three openings making a Venetian motif, the centre battlemented, the sides with pyramid finials.

77

DEWLISH

7090

A village of farmsteads, largely rebuilt after a major fire in 1859.

ALL SAINTS. Built of stone-banded flint with a stone tower. Brick C18 porch with an early C19 brick-banded flint vestry to its W. C12 N doorway with chevron, also at right angles to the wall. Hoodmould with nailhead on the headstops. The doorway arch looks as if it was later rebuilt to a pointed profile, with smaller chevron stones inserted at the apex. Good headstops representing a king and queen. Re-set C12 doorway with continuous chevron; now the W entrance to the partly rebuilt S aisle. Early C14 lower part of the W tower – see the W window with cusped Y-tracery – but a late C14 Perp upper

part. Tower arch with continuous chamfers. The two-bay N
aisle (later serving as the Michel family pew) is of *c.* 1500,
as indicated by the panelled arches. Later C16 uncusped
straight-headed windows here. An earlier S aisle was modified
by *T.H. Wyatt* in 1872, when it was refenestrated and given
a new, typically robust arcade. Choir aisle also by *Wyatt* (or
more likely by his son Thomas Henry Jun.), 1880, when the
chancel itself was refenestrated. At the same time an earlier C19
window (with reticulated Dec-style tracery) was repositioned
here. – PULPIT. Early C17, with one tier of blank arches with
enriched framing. – STALLS. With reused C17 PANELLING.
More C17 panelling in the chancel with enriched top rail, some
reused in the CHOIR STALLS. – FONT. A plain bowl, probably
early C13. On a C19 pillar. – Panelled oak GATE into the N
porch, C18. – STAINED GLASS. E window by *Warrington*, 1844.
Chancel S window by *Clayton & Bell*, 1900. In the N aisle a
window of *c.* 1860 filled with military badges associated with
Field Marshal Sir John Michel (†1886). His MONUMENT is to
the l. A large assemblage. At its centre, a medallion with a seated
angel on the l. with a trumpet, and a cherub on the r. This is
set beneath a cinquefoil arch. The inscription panel is below,
and a relief depicting a scene from the Indian Mutiny of 1858–9
below that. The whole is odd mixture of Empire Baroque and
Christian Gothic. – Another MONUMENT to Elizabeth Moore
†1722. Open pediment on top; skull at the bottom.

WESLEYAN METHODIST CHAPEL, ⅛ m. NE. Dated 1859. Brick
front (of 1905), stucco sides. Gothick, and rather out of date
for its time.

MANOR HOUSE. Built *c.* 1630 for Arthur Radford. Squarish
plan, two rooms deep, essentially a double-pile layout. Originally it must have had two gables to each face (cf. Wynford
Eagle, dated 1630). These still exist on the almost symmetrical N front. Four bays, but with the gables uneven-sided and
the windows below out of alignment with them. Three-light
windows with hollow-chamfered mullions, and hoodmoulds
not yet discarded for the more architectural continuous strings.
Chimneystacks on the gable apexes. No porch, modest four-
centred-arched doorway. Since the present eaves of the E
elevation (facing the churchyard) squash the hoodmoulds of
the upper windows uncomfortably, this provides support to
the idea of missing gables. There are also traces of the gable
kneelers. (C17 plaster friezes in some rooms. Also a bedroom
window with arabesque-enriched Ionic pilasters.)

MODEL FARM, *c.* 1860, on axis across the road. Flint banded
with brick and diapered on the gable-ends. It stands on the
original formal approach to the Manor House, its entrance
arch aligned precisely. This is C17, of stone, incorporated in the
later building. Round-headed, with continuous hollow chamfer
and wave. Barn behind (now converted) and other lower buildings alongside.

OLD PARSONAGE FARMHOUSE, ¼ m. NE. Of *c.* 1700, and sufficiently on the edge of the village to have survived the mid-C19
fire. Brick with boldly coved eaves and platband. Oddly asymmetrical S front, presumably a result of early C19 refenestration. The blank arched window (cf. Puddletown Vicarage) just
above and r. of the (later) porch hints at a lost formality.

DEWLISH HOUSE, ½ m. SW, in extensive parkland. Late Stuart
hipped-roofed nine- by four-bay house, beautiful for its patina
and for the relaxed simplicity of its design. Built in 1702 for
Thomas Skinner (but incorporating a C15 house); his arms
are incorporated in the open arms of the porch pediment.
The N front has a prettily shaped and prettily carved central
pediment. This side is of Portesham ashlar. Raised quoins, of
even length, rather tentatively applied. The projections of end
pairs and centre trio of bays are also tentative. Doorcase on
attached Doric columns. Round the corner the colour changes
from grey to the ochre of Ham Hill ashlar; but the same plinth
moulding continues. This part is of *c.* 1760 for David Michel,
built to unify the E end of the house after the S-facing range
was added *c.* 1730. The S front, of eleven bays to the width of
the N front's nine, represents a doubling of the house depth to
make it a double pile. It is of brownish-red brick. The pedimented central feature, installed on this front *c.* 1760, has a
round-headed window (lighting the main staircase) linked by
an apron to a pedimented doorcase, both with big keystones.
Keystones and bright red rubbed heads to the windows under
the three-bay pediment. At the sides the windows maintain a
slightly forced rhythm, of three plus one at each level, a posi-
tioning left over from the original, eleven-bay (3:5:3) façade
arrangement. The plinth moulding is cut short at the corners,
and the r. quoin starts with alternating blocks, but quickly
reverts to the system of the N front. The S centrepiece has a
mere suggestion of rustication, the recessing of one brick in
every five courses.

Fine mid-C18 staircase with balusters, twisted, fluted, twisted,
set three per tread. Half-landing supported on Ionic columns.
Kentian chimneypieces and overmantels of good quality, one
downstairs, one upstairs. All this goes with the *c.* 1760 centre
of the S front. In plan, the rooms in the N and S halves of the
house do not align, and those in the N range suggest a hall
with cross-passage plan, the original parlour being at the E end
of the house. In the room immediately W of the entrance hall
is a fireplace incorporating fragments of a C15 traceried
window.

'CELTIC' FIELDS, on the downs W of Chebbard Farm, ¾ m. W.
See Puddletown.

COURT CLOSE, E, S and SW of the church. Earthwork remains
of a MEDIEVAL SETTLEMENT.

DORCHESTER

Dorchester, the *Durnovaria* of the Romans, lies within an area of rich archaeological interest. These prehistoric and Roman remains are best understood as a group, and as such are described in a separate section beginning on p. 260. This also includes an account of the history and topography of the Roman town itself, and what remains of its monuments.

From the C8 a royal palace, mint and mother church were established within and around *Durnovaria*, recorded as *Dorceastre* in 789. The medieval parishes, *Dorcestre* and *Fortitune*, were established by 1086. Domesday also recorded that Dorchester was a royal borough, although almost entirely surrounded by the parish of Fordington. The medieval town was bounded by the circuit of the Roman town walls, s of the River Frome. The walls were not kept in repair, and those surviving were demolished to create the tree-lined Walks in the C18. By the later Middle Ages Dorchester was a cloth town of some importance, and by 1525 had become as populous as Bridport, Shaftesbury and Sherborne. In 1610 and 1629 it received two new borough charters (renewing those first granted by Edward II in 1324). With its growing significance as the county town, by the mid C17 Dorchester was the largest inland town in Dorset. By 1801, together with Fordington, it had a population of 3,290. Much rebuilding took place after a major fire in 1613, and two more in the C18: one in 1725 affecting the South Street area, another in 1775 destroying houses in High East Street. The chief exception to the predominantly late C18 and early C19 character is the centre of the town, where the grouping of three churches (one medieval, two mid-C19), together with a mid-C19 town hall and late C19 county museum, with their towers, spires and pinnacles, provides a memorable Gothic centrepiece at the crossroads.

In 1847 the town was given a boost with the arrival of the Southampton & Dorchester Railway. Large suburbs developed beyond the line of the town walls, on the E, W and S sides, partly on land owned by the Duchy of Cornwall; the natural constraint of the Frome valley prevented such growth on the N side. Further development in the W followed the opening of a second railway line (Wiltshire, Somerset & Weymouth Railway) in 1857, a trend that resumed some 150 years later with the building of an entirely new quarter on the Bridport Road at Poundbury, commissioned by the Duchy itself.

CHURCHES

3   ST PETER, High West Street. Now the main Anglican town church. It lies right in the middle of Dorchester, on the crossroads. There is hardly any space around it, and in that respect also it is a typical town church. With one exception it is Perp in style. A will by Robert Grenelefe dated 1420–1 left 20 marks 'to the fabric of the new construction' of the church. Everything

is of that date or slightly later apart from the re-set S doorway. This is late C12, and probably in the process of re-setting converted from round into pointed. The arch has horizontal pieces of chevron and chevron arching at right angles, producing half-folded lozenges. The church is of white Portland stone, with some ochre Ham Hill used in (restored) tracery and other elaborations. On the three-stage W tower, the bell-openings are long pairs of two lights each with straight tops. The upper parts of the bell-openings have Somerset tracery; the lower have stone louvres. Battlemented tower parapet with crocketed triple corner pinnacles and a central pinnacle to each face. The stair-turret projects quite subtly from the NE corner. The S aisle and chapels also have battlements and pinnacles. The windows are large, of three lights. The chancel E wall and the N vestry (an extension of the N chapel) are by *John Hicks*, who carried out a restoration in 1856–7. *Thomas Hardy* worked in his office at the time and a plan signed by him hangs in the church. The interior has arcades with piers not quite of the Perp standard. They are here a square with four demi-shafts. The chancel arch is of the same type. The tower arch is very high, the arches to the S chapel are panelled. Contemporary roofs in the nave and aisles, wagon and lean-to.

FURNISHINGS. Re-set in the chancel is an EASTER SEP-ULCHRE. An inserted tomb-chest with quatrefoils is undatable, but its ogee arch is C14 Dec. – REREDOS and ALTAR SURROUND. With Leonardo's *Last Supper* in relief. Designed by *C.E. Ponting*, who carried out a restoration in 1902–5. The arcading was filled with mosaic panels by *William Glasby*, 1922. The SEDILIA are probably from *Hicks*'s 1856–7 restoration. – TILEWORK by *Minton* in the sanctuary and choir. – The CHOIR STALLS are better than average with good leaf terminals. They are probably by *Ponting*. – S DOORS and their ironmongery by *W.D. Caröe*, 1902. – PULPIT. Early C17. A fine piece, with two tiers of blank arches and plenty of arabesque work. – FONT. C15, octagonal, on a C19 Perp-style stem. – HATCHMENTS. Two mid-C18 lozenge panels, one of the Bertie family, the other Williams. – ROYAL ARMS. Three in the tower. The oldest of Charles II, from All Saints' church; another, also Stuart, carved in the round (from Holy Trinity church); and a third, C19, also in the round, set above panelling. – STAINED GLASS. E window by *A.L. Moore*, 1898. A set of five S windows (in the chapel and aisle) also by *Moore*, 1890–1901, and another by him in the N aisle, †1903. N aisle window by *Goddard & Gibbs*, 1957.

MONUMENTS. For the tomb-chest in the Easter sepulchre, *see* above. – In the S chapel two eminently interesting late C14 effigies. They are a mirrored pair and were presumably set either side of an altar or together on a tomb-chest. Both are knights, each wearing a bascinet with their heads resting on great helms. Both not strictly recumbent and not strictly cross-legged. The heads and busts are a little turned to one side, and the legs cross easily and naturally. It is this naturalism which is so remarkable, though one ought to expect

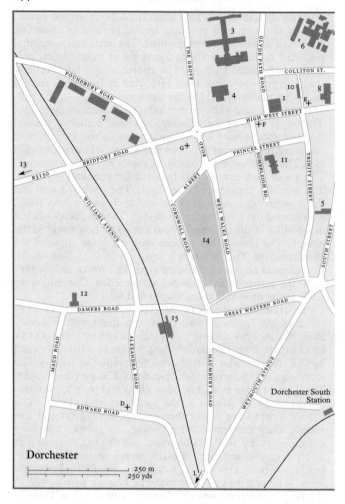

A   St Peter
B   All Saints (former)
C   St George
D   St Mary
E   Holy Trinity (R.C.)
F   Our Lady Queen of Martyrs
    (R.C.) (former)

G   Dorford Baptist Church
H   Baptist chapel (former)
J   United Church
K   Primitive Methodist
    chapel (former)
L   Cemetery

it in the age of Chaucer and in comparison with events in sculpture in France and Germany. – The next two monuments, both repositioned in 1856, stood facing each other on opposite sides of the chancel. Sir John Williams †1617 and wife (completed in 1628). A large monument in a dark corner of the N chapel, shamelessly crowded out by the organ. The centre is a black shrine with roof, and helmet, gauntlets, etc. arranged

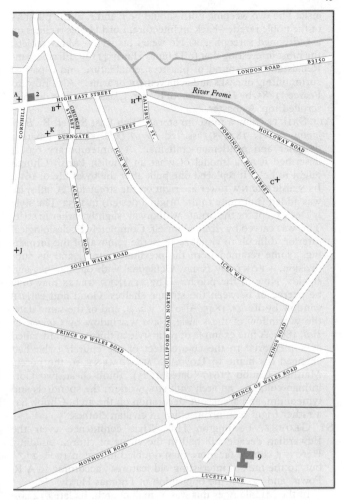

1 Shire Hall
2 Town Hall
3 County Hall
4 County Library (former)
5 Post Office (former)
6 Prison (former)
7 Barracks (former)
8 Dorset County Museum
9 St Mary's Catholic First
   School
10 Holy Trinity Infants' School
   (former)
11 Dorset County Hospital
   (former)
12 Damer's Hospital (former)
13 West Dorset General
   Hospital (former)
14 Borough Gardens
15 Dorchester West Railway
   Station

on it. To its l. he kneels, she to its r. Both are within columned
structures with a column in each corner. These columns carry
a highly elaborated arch whose underside has the typical Elizabethan motif of a chain of circles and squares. – Denzel, 1st
Lord Holles, †1679/80, but made in 1699, probably from the
workshop of *Grinling Gibbons*. A large standing monument,
moved to its new location, squeezed in at the w end of the N

aisle. The two weeping putti should be l. and r. of the pilasters of the noble reredos-back architecture. Lord Holles reclines on a gadrooned sarcophagus. He wears his wig. – Many tablets, the most interesting that to Thomas Hardy †1599. Elizabethan-Renaissance surround of pilasters, entablature and a pair of surmounting obelisks and achievement of arms. – Also Edward Pearce †1885, by *Harry Hems* of Exeter. Classical with a double-scrolled top. Alabaster.

ALL SAINTS (now a museum store), High East Street. By *Benjamin Ferrey*, 1843–5, assisted by *A.D.H. Acland*, amateur designer and gentleman-craftsman. A contemporary report described it as a 'model of what an English Parish Church ought to be'.* It replaced one built after the town fire of 1613. Its N aisle and NW tower are right on the streetside. A tall spire was added (not quite to the original design) in 1852. The style is Dec except for the ornate W doorway, slightly earlier in style. This was carved by *Acland* himself. Completely Ecclesiological interior, difficult to visualize since the removal of the furnishings (some retained from the previous church) and its subdivision. – FONT. By *Ferrey*. Octagonal with ogee arches and shields. Now in the porch. – The STAINED GLASS may only be peered at between the storage shelves. Good and early E window by *Wailes*, 1845. Also by *Wailes*, and of the same date, the W window of the S aisle. Nave W window by *Clayton & Bell*, 1862. A fine example of their style of this period. Installed as a memorial to the co-architect of the church (who had changed his name to Troyte). – MONUMENT, in the porch. Matthew Chubb †1617 (dated 1625). Tomb-chest, two Corinthian columns, an arch with strapwork in the spandrels and tympanum, and arabesque decoration on the arch. Chubb has a rather frigid recumbent effigy in civilian clothes.

ST GEORGE, Fordington Hill. What confidence even the Edwardian decade still had in the virtue of church building. Here is a church far more than doubled in size in 1906–27,** but 'to the hurt of interesting old features', according to A.R. Powis, and against the opposition of Thomas Hardy.

In the Middle Ages this was a small church. Its late C12 size is determined by the three-bay S arcade, but the S doorway must then have been re-set as it is a hundred years older. The tympanum is odd in shape and exciting in representation. It follows the three-sided profile of the doorhead, the lower edge incorporating the roll moulding of the doorway. In the middle part is St George at the Battle of Antioch, his spear intervening in the scene on the r. In the l. panel two soldiers are praying, having leant their spears and shields against the wall. In the r. panel the battle is raging. The style is remarkably close to that of the Bayeux Tapestry, i.e. hardly later than 1100. The S arcade is not very consistent in its detailing. There are round piers (but with different masonry) and abaci, one

---

*T.P. Connor, 'Three Dorset Churches: Early Tractarian Architecture in West Dorset', *PDNHAS* 132, 2011.
**Datestone at the E end of the S chapel.

capital with scallops, and double-chamfered arches. A Perp
bay was added when the s transept was built in the C15 (and
much rebuilt later). The E opening to the former s transept
with tracery above the arch is part of the early C20 campaign.
It is matched by a similar arch in the N aisle. In the late
C15 an ambitious three-stage W tower was built. It has set-back
buttresses, a four-light W window with a transom, and pairs
of two-light straight-topped bell-openings with a transom and
Somerset tracery. Turret top by *W.D. Caröe*, 1902, intended
as the beginning of a scheme for remodelling and enlarging
the church. This included rebuilding the N aisle, added in
1833 and as long as the s aisle. It has the drab big lancets
and thin buttresses of the Commissioners' churches, and its
designer was the vicar, *H.J. Moule*. Regrettably, Caröe was not
in the end employed on further improvements and it was not
until 1906 that the local architect *Jem Feacey* was given his
head; his client was the new vicar, R.G. Bartlett (who changed
his name to Bartelot). This resulted in three more bays of
nave, a long chancel, a large s chapel and then a halt – the
N chapel was not built. This *novum opus* is all Perp. In the
chancel on the N wall a Dec-style sepulchre and on the s
sedilia, both *c.* 1910.

FURNISHINGS. ALTAR in the s chapel. Of stone, *c.* 1390,
with large blank Perp two-light panels. Brought in in 1958–9
from Salisbury Cathedral, where it had been adapted by *James
Wyatt* as the high altar. – PULPIT. Octagonal, of stone, with
panelled sides. Many initials and dates, the oldest '1592 ER 34'.
Is this the earliest known stone pulpit from after the Reformation? – COMMUNION RAIL. From Milton Abbey. The strong
outline of the vase-shaped balusters indicates *c.* 1700. – FONT.
C15. Octagonal with shields in quatrefoils. – A second very
small FONT in a niche by the s entrance. Gadroon-like ornament. It is probably C12 or earlier. – TOWER SCREEN. Heavy
double doors, with Rococo ornament, *c.* 1750. From Bavaria,
re-set here in 1935. – GALLERY. W end of N aisle. 1833. Panelled front. – STAINED GLASS. When the church was visited
for the previous edition it had two *Morris & Co.* windows that
Pevsner described as 'excellent'. One survives in the s transept,
of 1913, using older *Morris* and *Burne-Jones* cartoons. The
figures glow against a patterned blue background. The second
window (of 1903, in the tower, entirely from *Burne-Jones* cartoons) has been destroyed, or rather the figures taken out and
distributed within clear glass in the E and chapel E windows.
They now appear dingily coloured and out of context. The
work received a faculty in 1969. Chancel s wall, lancet by
William Glasby, *c.* 1920. One in the nave s aisle by *Wippell &
Co.*, 1962. N aisle, small single figures of Apostles. Are they
of *c.* 1833? – ROMAN TOMBSTONE, set against the N jamb of
the tower arch. It was discovered under a corner of the porch.

Outside there are the toothings for the N chapel, but in contrast a hipped-roofed MEETING HALL by *Stephen Hebb*, 1989,
occupies this position. Its pale brick and dark boarding do not
read well against the silvery Portland stone.

St Mary, Edward Road. By *C.E. Ponting*, 1910–12 (costing £10,000, exclusive of the tower). Ponting was Diocesan Architect of Salisbury and lived at Marlborough. This is his *magnum opus*. It is Gothic still – i.e. not liberated yet, as Prior and Lethaby and Lutyens (Hampstead Garden Suburb) were – but free Arts and Crafts Gothic: largely Late Perp in inspiration but with Dec features to liven things up. The building is large and lavish, with transepts and clerestory and a flèche, the last alas taken down in 1998. External decoration is concentrated on the s porch, which was meant to be the base of a tower. Funds ran out and the unfortunate consequence is a lean-to roof. But the most attractive, because most original, feature is the priest's doorway further e. Inside, the porch leads into a kind of transeptal space, i.e. not simply the aisle with its arcade, and the n aisle opposite has a normal arcade, but it carries the richest decoration. Similarly the architecture of the organ chamber n of the chancel differs from that of the chapel s of the chancel. Here Ponting, on the precedent of Pearson, has interjected a narrow aisle between the chancel and the apsed chapel. – The FURNISHINGS are largely as completed by *Ponting*. In the sanctuary Perp sedilia with a Dec piscina adjoining; a typically well-detailed ensemble of ROOD SCREEN and PULPIT; and a plain square FONT with polished Purbeck columns. – SCULPTURE of the Pietà by *Herbert Palliser*, 1940. – STAINED GLASS progresses from the e end of the s chancel aisle, along the s until the w end, with one in the n aisle. First a small window by *Kempe & Co.*, 1912. A set of five by *George Parlby* with *Curtis, Ward & Hughes* in the s chapel, *c.* 1912. The large window in the s transept is by *Parlby*, 1943. A row of three brightly coloured four-light windows in the s aisle, all also by *Parlby*. In the n aisle a window by *Francis Skeat*, 1961. Plain glazing still to the e window.

Holy Trinity (formerly Anglican; R.C. since 1976), High West Street. Rebuilt by *Ferrey*, 1875–6. The s aisle right along the High Street. Hence an entrance from the w into the s aisle which starts further e than the nave, but the main doorway at the w end. The church is E.E., and has bar tracery. The aisles are of differing treatments. The shorter s aisle is narrow, gabled at each end; the n broad under a lean-to roof. Transeptal vestry at right angles on the n side, forming a cloister-like garden. The restoration for R.C. use was by *Anthony Jaggard* of *John Stark & Partners.** – REREDOS. High, of wood, gilt, with much figure carving. Made in Oberammergau and installed in 1897. – PULPIT. Brown marble with inlet stone angel, presumably late c19. – FONT of similar materials and date. – Many FURNISHINGS transferred from the former church of Our Lady Queen of Martyrs (*see* below), including the onyx marble ALTAR. – STAINED GLASS. In the s chapel and s aisle a set by *C.E. Kempe*, 1901. Earlier than these, a single light by *Kempe* in the chancel, 1897. Nave s window by *Burlison & Grylls*, 1911.

* In 1906 *Thomas Hardy* produced a sketch plan 'in an idle moment' for the addition of a tower.

Two windows in the N aisle, one by *Herbert Bryans*, 1905, the other by *A.L. & C.E. Moore*, 1925.

OUR LADY QUEEN OF MARTYRS (formerly R.C.), High West Street. This is the church of St Michael at Westport, Wareham, by *A.J.C. Scoles*, 1889. It was re-erected here in 1906–7 under the supervision of *Reginald Jackson*. Lancet style. Rose window at the N end. Since 1968 it has been in use as an exhibition hall.

DORFORD BAPTIST CHURCH, Bridport Road. 1912–14 by *Sydney Jackson*. Brick and stone dressings. The façade frankly independent of the body of the church. Baroque motifs, freely composed. Awkwardly named around an oculus (with the 'F' of Dorford on a keystone!).

BAPTIST CHAPEL (former), at the junction of Fordington High Street and High East Street. 1830. Stucco. Convex three-bay front with a convex pediment. Round-headed upper windows.

UNITED CHURCH (formerly Congregational), South Street. *p. 74* 1856–7 by *Poulton & Woodman* of Reading. Rock-faced limestone. Rather like Bassett Keeling, i.e. what Goodhart-Rendel used to call rogue architecture. A large late C13 style window, a spiky steeplet to its r. and, supporting it, buttresses with crazily steep set-offs. Polygonal E end with a pointed-arched organ recess behind the pulpit.

PRIMITIVE METHODIST CHAPEL (former), Durngate Street. 1875 by *Samuel Jackson* of Weymouth. E.E. Gothic. Brown brick with ashlar dressings. SUNDAY SCHOOL of 1892 in matching style alongside.*

CEMETERY, Weymouth Avenue, ¾ m. S of St Peter's church. With two identical CHAPELS by *G.J.G. Gregory*, 1856. Rock-faced. The N chapel was Nonconformist (now disused), the S Church of England. Bellcote above the W gable of each, with a projecting porch below. Dec-traceried windows. – STAINED GLASS. In the E window of the S chapel a fine work by *Chris-* 114 *topher Whall* (with *Britten & Gilson*), 1891.

PUBLIC BUILDINGS

SHIRE HALL, High West Street. 1796–7 by *Thomas Hardwick*. Austerely dignified classical façade of Portland ashlar, sited with surprising modesty in a streetline. Two storeys, where neighbouring houses take three. Seven bays, the centre three with the entrances as a rusticated arcade. Pediment over the centre. The Crown Court remains almost in its original state, preserved as the place of the 1834 trial of the Tolpuddle Martyrs. The cells, extended later in the C19 (by *W.J. Fletcher*), survive below the courtroom. On the r. corner of the façade are inscribed the distances to Hyde Park Corner, Blandford and Bridport.

TOWN HALL, High West Street. Built in 1847–8 by *Benjamin Ferrey* to house the Town Hall proper above, the Corn Exchange below. Buff Broadmayne brick with diaper patterning on the

*The Methodist church in South Street (1875 by *W.S. Allardyce*) was demolished in 1983.

w gable; Bath stone dressings. Tudor windows over an arcade of four-centred arches. Two-storey oriel round the side. The clock turret at the angle, on its corbel decorated with rank mouchettes, is an addition, by *Ferrey* also, of 1864, the portal with incongruous Romanesque foliage capitals an addition of 1876. At the rear, the former NEW EXCHANGE and POLICE STATION of 1865–7 by *Henry Hall*. Buttressed. Half-domed roof over the market hall.

COUNTY HALL, Colliton Park. Foundation stone laid 1938, completion 1955, by *H.E. Matthews*, the County Architect. Unexpectedly big and cruciform behind the entrance block. Brown brick. Modern style with modernistic overtones. Circular central feature, not really noticed from ground level. Some later and lower additions with hipped roofs.

COUNTY LIBRARY (former), to the S of the County Hall. 1966 by *Fred Pitfield* of the County Architect's department (under *J.R. Hurst*, County Architect). Mildly fashionable, with its recessed top storey and picture windows, and quite agreeable.

POST OFFICE (former), South Street. 1904–5 by *John Rutherford*. Baroque. Lively in red brick and white stone, successfully taking the architecture around a street corner. Extended along New Street by *David Dyke*, 1929.

PRISON (former), off North Square (currently being redeveloped for housing). Built on the site of the medieval castle. The present buildings are of 1879–80 in hot red brick. This was the first prison to be built after the Prison Commissioners took over responsibility for prison design across England. However, it was also the last to utilize a radial layout for the blocks, parallel blocks subsequently becoming the norm. On the N side of the perimeter wall the rusticated Portland stone PORTAL of the previous prison, designed in 1787 by *William Blackburn*, a collaborator with John Howard the prison reformer. Built in 1790–2.

BARRACKS (former), Bridport Road. A monumental gatehouse of 1876–7 (now the DORSET MILITARY MUSEUM), always standing separately from the other buildings. Two round towers to the front, the archway between. Three storeys of long slit windows. Rock-faced with a vengeance. The designer was probably *Major H.C. Seddon* R.E., head of the War Office design branch at the time, who is known to have worked in this vein. (More commonly Seddon's designs were executed by district engineers, but this, possibly unique, gatehouse is unusually bold and is more likely to be of Seddon's own design.) Several barrack buildings behind survive, completed in 1879. Those on the r. side of Barrack Road are brick with round-arched windows. Further NE, a symmetrical set in rock-faced stone. Central three-storey block with battlemented top. Low wings with two-storey pavilions.

3 DORSET COUNTY MUSEUM, High West Street. 1881–3 by *Crickmay & Son* of Weymouth, lavish Perp towards the street (carving by *B. Grassby*), with a two-storey bay window of 1:5:1 lights and a bowed angle oriel. Inside, the main exhibition hall

has cast-iron columns and arches supporting a glazed roof, all spindly and busily detailed, and very effective now that Crickmay's intended scheme of bright primary colours has been restored. Gallery added in 1903. Fine main staircase with a mid-C18-style ironwork balustrade. Crisp, unpretentious addition of 1968–70 at the back, by *Michael Brawne*. The museum extends over the adjoining shop to the w. On the upper floor is a panelled room from the demolished Tyneham House. Early C17, brought here in the 1960s.*

ST MARY'S CATHOLIC FIRST SCHOOL, Lucetta Lane. Well-composed school by *Jackson & Greenen* of Bournemouth, 1966. Sympathetic new building with bold flat and vertical planes by *Genesis Design Studio*, 2006.

HOLY TRINITY INFANTS' SCHOOL (former), Grey School Passage. Dated 1857, probably by *E. Mondey*. Gothic, in part now roofless.

DORSET COUNTY HOSPITAL (former), Princes Street. Basically quite a handsome building of 1839–41, by *Benjamin Ferrey*. Yet to design a hospital to look like a gabled Elizabethan mansion, a Loseley in Portland stone, is really to run away from the design problem. It was not the solution Pugin was at that moment formulating (or William Slater, see e.g. his almshouse extension at Sherborne). Symmetrical E-plan grouping, the former chapel in the SE wing (added by *Ferrey* in 1862). Notice the piquant LODGE opposite: 1885, by *Crickmay & Son*. Cut brickwork of the Queen Anne style popular then.

DAMER'S HOSPITAL (former), Damers Road. Built as a workhouse by *George Wilkinson*, 1836. Largely demolished apart from the E wing. Attached at the S end, alongside the road, the ASHLEY MEMORIAL CHAPEL by *Jem Feacey*, 1899. Brick with stone banding. Buttressed with an E.E. eaves detail. – STAINED GLASS. E windows by *Swaine Bourne & Son, c.* 1899.

WEST DORSET GENERAL HOSPITAL, Bridport Road. By *Percy Thomas Partnership* (assisted by *Barry Payne* of the South-West Regional Health Authority), completed in phases, 1983–7. Rectangular block with nodal pavilions, not unlike workhouse architecture. Brown brick with red brick features and post-office-red windows – a not wholly successful colour combination. Many triangular-ended bays breaking up the massing.

BOROUGH GARDENS, West Walks Road. Opened in 1896, layout by *William Goldring*. Serpentine paths. – CLOCK TOWER. Dated 1905. Cast iron. Ornamental (somewhat similar to the Weymouth clock tower). – BANDSTAND of 1898. Cast iron. Built to commemorate Queen Victoria's Diamond Jubilee.

DORCHESTER WEST RAILWAY STATION, Great Western Road. 1857 by *I.K. Brunel* for the Wiltshire, Somerset & Weymouth Railway. Italianate, with grouped round-arched windows; projecting hipped roof. This is a type repeatedly used by Brunel

---

*A scheme of extensive enlargement by *Carmody Groarke*, retaining the Victorian buildings but replacing those by Brawne, is likely to start in 2018.

(as an alternative to a Tudor Revival style). Glazed platform
awning of 1934.

PERAMBULATIONS

1. The High Street, from Grey's Bridge to Top O'Town

The one essential is to walk the length of the HIGH STREET,
which has a truly urban feeling at its centre. In appearance,
really very little has changed since the late C19. The visual
climax comes halfway along with the pinnacled grouping of
the former All Saints' church, the Town Hall and St Peter's
church.

We start at the junction with FORDINGTON HIGH STREET,
where the main road becomes HIGH EAST STREET (and
alongside the Baptist chapel, *see* p. 249). At this point it starts
its climb towards the town centre and various houses and terraces are passed, brick and *c.* 1845 on the s side, ashlar and
c. 1795 on the N. No. 6, on the s side, is the first Early Georgian
town house. Mid-C18. Brick; of five bays, with a fine pedimented porch and fluted Ionic pilasters. It was savagely eaten
into by an entrance to rear car parking. The first Victorian
accent is No. 44 on the N side, a startling mixture of red brick
and terracotta of the late C19. Free Renaissance, probably by
Crickmay & Son. Further on, the early C19 rusticated ashlar
archway formerly leading to 'PALE ALE BREWERY', as is pro-
claimed over the arch. Industry in Dorchester was often down
short narrow lanes off the main street. A truly urban scale is
reached with UNITY CHAMBERS (built for the Wilts. & Dorset
Bank), also on the N side. Italianate, of Bath stone, *c.* 1860.
Opposite is All Saints' church (p. 246), its long side and spire
beside the street, as all three of the High Street's churches are
placed, making the maximum contribution to the long vista.
A detour past the E end of the church, down Church Street
and Acland Road, takes us to WOLLASTON HOUSE, the most
eloquent of the C18 free-standing town houses. Dated 1786
(on a foundation stone in the cellar), a brick box with a five-
window N front and an Ionic-columned porch.

Back to High East Street. The KING'S ARMS HOTEL diagonally opposite the church has a fine expansive early C19
stuccoed front, a symmetrical composition at its centre about
a generously glazed window bow. This sits on a square-plan,
very broad porch with Doric columns. Extensions of differing lengths on either side, also stuccoed; that to the l. with
the canted bay window of an assembly room. To the rear a
coaching courtyard. Facing the Town Hall is the early C19
shopfront of No. 24 with attached Greek Doric columns (the
fascia altered). Above, the Grecian style is continued in the
detailing of two broad tripartite sashes.

This is the halfway mark. At the junction with Cornhill
(*see* below), the street becomes HIGH WEST STREET. This

3
p. 254

begins on the N side with the town's major group, St Peter's
church (p. 242), the Town Hall (p. 249), the County Museum
(p. 250) and Holy Trinity church (p. 248). It is worth looking
back from a little higher up the street to see how well the
Victorian buildings compose themselves with the medieval
church. Part of the reason is that they do not all keep strictly to
the streetline. In front of St Peter, a bronze STATUE of William
Barnes, the dialect poet, signed by *E. Roscoe Mullins*, 1888. The
sequence on the other side begins with LLOYDS BANK. Its
symmetrical and pedimented w block was built first in 1835
(probably by *Charles Wallis*) for Williams' Bank. The extension to the l., taking it around the corner into Cornhill, was
added in 1902. Two doors up, the Cinquecentesque front of
No. 5, also built as a bank (Elliot, Pearce & Co.), *c.* 1875. Next
door comes JUDGE JEFFREYS' LODGING, a characteristic
timber-framed town front of *c.* 1600, with jetties at two levels.
Ground storey modern. Stone flank walls and rear wing, the
latter with stone mullioned-and-transomed windows. Nothing
else like it survives in Dorchester now, except its neighbour
No. 7, which may have lost an upper storey. Rectangular bay
windows to both houses, of six or eight mullioned lights, with
a transom. The structure at No. 7 is also of stone for the party
and rear walls. In complete contrast, next on the S side are a
pair of late C18 houses (Nos. 8–9), and a further, later corner
block (No. 10). All are in brownish brick with red brick dressings. Here we reach TRINITY STREET (opposite Holy Trinity
church, p. 248). No. 15 is just beyond, bringing a Late Georgian
character to the street with its pair of two-storey bow windows.
Next the OLD SHIP INN, similar in date to Judge Jeffreys'
Lodging, but of stone, and almost wholly reconstructed. Original upper windows, of four and five lights, not in projecting
bays. A little further on, the street becomes more continuously
Georgian, with No. 23, dated 1735 on the rainwater heads,
deserving comment. Originally only two-storeyed, of five bays,
the centre wide enough to have a tripartite first-floor feature,
of a round-headed window breaking up into a pediment, and
niches l. and r. between Ionic pilasters. It looks as if it would be
more at home in Blandford Forum, and one can only suspect
the involvement of one of that town's architects.

Meanwhile the N side has a grander and more consistent
character. After the church, two smaller Georgian houses
of differing heights and of differing brick colours. The first
(No. 63) is mid-C18 with early C19 inserted tripartite sashes;
the second (No. 62), early C19 with a handsome bow window
above the later C19 shopfront. Next, AGRICULTURE HOUSE,
which was built as late as 1883, by *G. R. Crickmay*. Buff brick;
classical with Neo-Greek detail, and window surrounds of a
Victorian broadness. It was built as a town house. After the
Shire Hall (p. 249), a detour N down GLYDE PATH ROAD (or
Shire Hall Lane, as is inscribed in the stonework), passing on
the l. COLLITON HOUSE. Handsome, if irregular, built on
an L-plan in the C17, extended to the SW *c.* 1700, and much

Dorchester, High West Street.
Drawing by Hanslip Fletcher, 1939

remodelled *c.* 1740. Stone-faced. The N gable shows the earliest date, the gable on kneelers. Blocked hoodmoulded window
high up. The N front, lying back, was made into a symmetrical
composition at the latest date, with windows in plain surrounds, the centre one round-headed. E windows earlier, with
moulded surrounds. The S side is the most memorable, for its
trio of fine brick chimneystacks with arcading, *c.* 1700. Behind
County Hall (p. 250) the ROMAN TOWN HOUSE in Colliton
Park (p. 265).

Back to HIGH WEST STREET. On the S side, after passing
Alington Street, a sequence of stucco-fronted houses. The first
pair (Nos. 28–29) are mid-C19, with an elaborate wrought-iron
balcony at first-floor level. The next two (Nos. 30–31) have
early C19 fronts, but are early C17 in origin behind. A similar
rebuilding happened to the larger block next, the WESSEX
ROYALE HOTEL, but more comprehensively, in the mid C19.
No. 45 is the last town house on the N side. Of the mid C18.
Ashlar front of two bays and a pedimented attic storey. It was
later widened by one bay to the E. Thereafter, the main theme
becomes that of a general falling off in architectural stature.
And so up to the roundabout, today's way of marking the end
of the town. On the way we may glance at Nos. 43 and 44,
a humbler, cottage-scaled row on the r., enlivened by bow
windows.

Facing us at the roundabout is TOP O' TOWN HOUSE of
c. 1835–40. Stucco with taller sashes on the first floor than
those below. On the S side of Bridport Road, opposite, the
Dorford Baptist Church (p. 249). Turning r. here we reach the
STATUE of Thomas Hardy by *Eric Kennington*, 1931, as an old

man, hat on knee, seated on a flowery tree stump. The striking
tapered plinth is by *Verner O. Rees*.

Back to the roundabout and straight over into ALBERT
ROAD, where on the l. there is the only visible fragment
of the Roman town wall (*see* p. 264). Further on, into the
WEST WALKS that runs along the E side of Borough Gardens
(p. 251), where an avenue of trees forms part of the planting
by which in the C18 the line of Dorchester's town walls was
marked, and which still so agreeably defines the Roman size
of Dorchester. Here some typical stuccoed villas of *c.* 1840.
An about-turn, then r. into PRINCES STREET. On the N side
the stuccoed MASONIC HALL of *c.* 1860. Classical with a
pediment and pilasters. The street is otherwise a backwater
that reaches, on the r., SOMERLEIGH ROAD. This passes the
former Dorset County Hospital (p. 251) on the l., while opposite, seen down a short lane, is the former HOLY TRINITY
RECTORY by *John Hicks*. Of 1850, it has steep stone gables and
a quaint timber-framed centrepiece. At the S end of the road,
SOMERLEIGH COURT (now a nursing home, much extended
on the S), 1860 for the banker Edward Pearce, perhaps by
B. Ferrey. It became somewhat rambling when two additions
were made in the 1880s.

2. From the centre to the South Walks and Brewery Square

Back to the centre of town to follow the town's second main
street, leading into the residential suburbs and towards the
first railway to arrive in Dorchester. The start is in CORNHILL
(as the street is named for its initial short length), next to the
Lloyds Bank extension of 1902. This is followed by the former
HOWE'S BAKERS (now also part of the bank), also of 1902,
and by *Jem Feacey*. Elizabethan, getting more Baroque at the
top. In the centre of the street a banded OBELISK with ball
finial, erected in 1784 as the town pump. On the E side the
street starts with Dorchester's most consistent run of C18 red
brick fronts, one (No. 3) with a nice unspoilt Georgian shop
window. The last on this side before Durngate Street is early
C19 stucco-fronted with a tall late C19 shopfront, another fine
survival. The ANTELOPE HOTEL, opposite, has for its façade
a very happy composition of *c.* 1815. A shallow two-storey
bow l. and r. of the carriage entrance, buff brick walling, the
whole composition governed by broad stuccoed pilaster strips
with sunk panels. At this point the road becomes SOUTH
STREET, and from here on there is much post-Second World
War rebuilding in among older survivals. On the l., dark red
brick and lead sheeting on an over-scaled corner shop, built
in the mid 1980s as a replacement for the Methodist church
(*see* p. 249), is one of the worst of the newcomers. Just after
this is the entrance to a shopping arcade leading to WAITROSE
SUPERMARKET. At the entrance to the shop, MURALS depicting Dorchester history by *John Hodgson*, 1986.

Back into the main road and further on, standing side by side on the r., two banks illustrate contrasting commercial styles of the early C20. The first was built in grey Portland stone as the NATIONAL PROVINCIAL BANK *c.* 1912. Contrasting in colour and mood, the NATWEST BANK (built for Stuckey's Bank) exhibits the Free Baroque of Norman Shaw in ochre Ham Hill stone. It is of 1899–1902 by *(Sir) George Oatley* of Bristol. Facing these is another good group of C18 façades, one of them, now BARCLAYS BANK, with an unmistakable air of superiority. It is not just that it is set back from the building line. It is faced with nothing but vitrified headers; though it can't be before *c.* 1780, when that practice was beginning to go out of fashion. Red brick dressings. Windows in a simple, but real, composition. The porch, an open pediment on brackets, has a round-headed window l. and r. and another above. Re-erected at the E end of the shopping arcade is a four-centred Perp ARCH, which came from a house in Greyhound Yard, South Street. The last building of note in South Street, oppo-site the Post Office (p. 250), is NAPPER'S MITE, now a minute shopping precinct, but built as almshouses for ten poor men in 1616 under the will of Sir Robert Napper of Middlemarsh. The street front is of 1842, but repeats the original arcading of the ground floor. Behind lies a tiny courtyard with one-storey rubble-stone ranges round. The chapel was in the SE corner, with a three-light window in the E wall, its lights arched. Plain two-lighters elsewhere.

At the s end of the street, and just round the corner to the E, the DORCHESTER CENOTAPH of 1921 by *Grassby & Son*. Next to it a *Penfold* hexagonal PILLAR BOX. These were made between 1866 and 1879. Further along on the l., in SOUTH WALKS, SOUTH LODGE, a plain house of *c.* 1760, its brick being covered with stucco *c.* 1820, so that it looks later. Five-bay façade with a Roman Doric porch. Two significant items within of the earlier date. The staircase has the strutted balustrade commonly known as Chinese Chippendale, with a turned-over handrail end, typical of the *Bastard* company. In the SE room Rococo plasterwork, wall decoration of unhackneyed generosity. Continuing along South Walks, which follows the line of the Roman s town wall, on the opposite (s) side SUN-NINGHILL PREPARATORY SCHOOL, built as South Court, a house for Alfred Pope of the brewing company in 1892–4. Credited to *G.R. Crickmay*, although he copied a design by *William Wilkinson* of Oxford.* At the end of the road on the l. three bronze statues commemorating the DORSET MARTYRS. A highly effective work by *Elizabeth Frink*, 1986. Two represent the martyrs in loincloths, the third the hangman. They stand on the site of the Dorchester gallows.

Return the way we came, but at the s end of South Street continue SW along WEYMOUTH AVENUE. To the l., incor-porating the former Eldridge Pope Brewery, the BREWERY

---

* *See* plates 9 and 10 in Wilkinson's *English Country Houses* (1875).

SQUARE development, under a masterplan by *CZWG Architects* in association with *Conran & Partners*. The first we see of this is the ATRIUM HEALTH CENTRE of 2009 by *CZWG*. Its façade is of three white curved planes overlapping and diminishing in size towards a centrally placed entrance. It contrasts almost as completely as is possible with the former BREWERY OFFICES for Eldridge Pope of 1880 by *G.R. Crick-may*. A square house-like block in clashing contrasts of red and cream brick, with bracketed eaves. Behind the offices the BREWHOUSE itself, again of the same date and by *Crickmay*. The main block has its elevations divided by giant arched bays. A wing to the NE has gables with Venetian-style brick detailing. Further SE the MALTINGS of 1879. In the same polychrome brickwork with, at one end, a row of multiple slit windows grouped under a wide arch. (These last two buildings were rebuilt by *Crickmay & Son* after a major fire in 1922.) Back to Weymouth Avenue and next the former BONDED WAREHOUSE and BOTTLING STORE, of the same date, also by *Crickmay*. A large building in the same materials but more monumental, with a run of nine little arched windows with huge fanning voussoirs. Beyond, still on the l., a small square formed by the end of the warehouse and two boldly contrasting new buildings, both by *CZWG* and completed in 2012. Set back, a block of flats incorporating the ODEON CINEMA. On the w side of the square, FAIRFIELD. More flats with a restaurant below, all set behind a dramatic steel grid of giant intersecting two-centred arches. Next, after the former STATION PUBLIC HOUSE (now the Brewhouse and Kitchen), the entrance to Brewery Square itself, a gathering of large-scaled, mainly residential blocks around the Dorchester South railway station. Two matching blocks by *CZWG*, forming the entrance to the new Pope Street, have curved ends, a modernist interpretation of Roman Baroque streetscape. They were still under construction at the time of writing, but the block on the l. has a sea-green end façade with, along Pope Street, a powder-blue elevation above curvy low-level canopies. The DORCHESTER SOUTH RAILWAY STATION is a rebuilding of 1986, echoing Brunel's Italianate Dorchester West station (p. 251).

111

OUTLYING BUILDINGS

FORDINGTON HOUSE, Icen Way, Fordington, ½ m. SE. Of the mid to late C18. Main S-facing front. Stuccoed, the windows 1:3:2, the centre pedimented. Large early C19 W wing.

THE OLD MILL, Fordington, 130 yds NE of Fordington church. Some structure of 1590–1607, when it was rebuilt by William and John Churchill. Of this date a four-centred arch. Major rebuilding in brick of 1841. It became housing in 1940. Remodelled and enlarged (on a bridge over the river), 1986 by *John Stark & Partners*.

GREY'S BRIDGE, London Road, ½ m. E. The bridge is of 1748, built of silvery Portland ashlar. When opened this allowed

direct access to the E end of the town for the first time, prior
to which there was a complicated route through Fordington.

MAX GATE (National Trust), Alington Avenue, 1 m. SE. *Thomas
Hardy*'s house, designed by him and built in plum brick by the
building firm run by his brother, *Henry Hardy*. Two phases, the
first of 1883–5. The main front has tall, square corner turrets.
That on the r. corner was added during a second phase of work
in 1895–6. Each of the towers is topped with a pyramidal roof.
Off-centre a gable, more conventionally Queen Anne, crowned
by a small chimneystack. The rear range was lengthened as
part of the enlargement, providing a first-floor study for the
author, and an attic workspace for his wife, Emma.

Hardy had left architectural practice in 1872 and was established as a novelist when the house was built. Its style is eccentric and highly original. Once on the edge of the town, the
house's setting has changed considerably since the building of
the by-pass, adjacent overbridge and nearby suburban housing.
The house itself is shrouded by trees, as Hardy intended.

MAIDEN CASTLE ROAD, ¾ m. SW. No.18 is of 1937 by *C.W.
Pike* of Dorchester. White-rendered International Style, with
Crittall windows. A wedge-shaped plan with the flat end
towards the road.

TESCO SUPERMARKET, Weymouth Avenue, 1 m. S. Opened in
1991. Exterior by *William Bertram & Fell* of Bath. Built on
Duchy of Cornwall land. A broadly classical cloaking, one's
arrival trumpeted by fountains and a pair of obelisks.

POUNDBURY

A new suburb on Duchy land *c.* 1½ m. W of the centre of Dorchester, commenced in 1993. The area was designated for expansion
of the town by the planning authority, but the Duchy estate
chose to carry out the development itself. The principles adopted
follow those advocated by the Prince of Wales in his book *A
Vision of Britain* (1989). Based on a masterplan by *Leon Krier*, its
key features are high-density building; fully integrated affordable
housing (intended to be indistinguishable from owner-occupied
dwellings); businesses, shopping and leisure facilities intermingled with residential buildings; and priority to the pedestrian,
reducing the impact of vehicles on the daily lives of its residents.
In addition, on a technical level, it incorporates environmentally
responsible energy systems. Buildings throughout use a mixture of
brick, stone, stucco, tile and slate, based on the mixtures found in
Dorchester itself. Even more significantly, only traditional (non-
Victorian, non-modern) designs are permitted, as produced by a
wide variety of architects designing in these styles.

As one walks around Poundbury – and walking is recommended to appreciate its finer points, of which it has many – one
sees time and again well-composed groups of houses and terraces
where the sense of scale and detailing is often delightful. What
seems more unnerving is when the scale is ratcheted up, as in
Queen Mother Square, or on those larger blocks visible from

the roundabout at the W end of the development where traffic is diverted on to the relief road. One, a fire station, has a thinly classical cloaking that fails to hide its ugly proportions. The sheer size of the place is also unsettling. To walk through such a large settlement and meet no reflection of anything that has happened, architecturally, through the Victorian years, or after, say, 1914, is to experience a profound sense of displacement.

PHASE ONE. The first of four phases was completed in 1999, immediately W of the western edge of the town and separated from the later phases by a new relief road. The first hint of the use of historic styles (as permitted by a Building Code) is the buildings flanking BRIDPORT ROAD, as Poundbury is approached. On the l., the FLEUR-DE-LIS flats by *Robert Taylor*, centred on a four-storey pyramid-roofed tower that has a distinctly Continental character. On the r., in a Neoclassical mode, the ST JOHN'S AMBULANCE STATION by *Lionel Gregory Architects* (2000), with beyond it a housing group in a Voysey-inspired style by *Francis Roberts Architects*. All of these approach buildings form MANSELL SQUARE, a fore-work to Phase Two straight ahead. First we turn l. into Phase One proper, down MIDDLEMARSH STREET, where the low-rise but tight-knit planning of the residential areas is immediately apparent. The buildings are either interpretations of local vernacular or, at key points, blocks following more C18 or early C19 modes. At the centre, in PUMMERY SQUARE, two buildings of note. On the r., BROWNSWORD HALL by *John Simpson* develops a mixture of rustic classical and vernacular elements, e.g. the dumpy columns to the arcade and the steeply gabled upper-floor meeting room. At its corners visual strength is provided by the wide raking buttresses. This fusion represents the most effective of the architectural treatments in Poundbury, heavily influenced by Postmodernism. On the l., the VILLAGE STORES by *Ken Morgan Architects* repeats the dumpy columns, below an Arts and Crafts-influenced superstructure.

PHASE TWO. A larger development area to the W of Phase One, started in 2000 and at the time of writing near completion. It stands on either side of the Bridport Road with a large-scale centrepiece, Queen Mother Square, to the N. There are large enclaves of lower-height, generally vernacular-based housing as in the first phase, but a ramping up of architectural stature appears at several locations. The approach to this 'District Centre of Poundbury' is along Peverell Avenue East, heading NW from the Bridport Road. Two contrasting sentinel blocks ahead. To the l., MANSELL HOUSE by *Craig Hamilton Architects* (2002) takes Marble Hill House by Colen Campbell as its source, and recreates its N façade in a provincial manner. To the r., CASTLE VIEW, a residential nursing home by *James Gorst Architects* (2000), a chunky blend of vernacular and classical design. Turning r., PEVERELL AVENUE EAST heads towards the centre of the entire Poundbury settlement. An

indication of a rise in architectural hierarchy is the replacement of the Neo-vernacular cottage groups by Neo-Georgian
terraces. This reaches its apogee at QUEEN MOTHER SQUARE
itself (commenced 2014), set back on the r. Ahead, forming
the W side of the square, the first of the Neoclassical blocks
by *Quinlan & Francis Terry*, forming the two long sides of
the square. As with all of the buildings, this houses a mixture
of uses: broadly shopping and offices on the lower levels;
flats above. Facing it, on the E side, are two buildings.
STRATHMORE HOUSE, a palace-like block, perhaps takes its
typological origin from the elder John Wood's terrace on the
N side of Queen Square, Bath. On the corner with Peverell
Road East a block in the distinctive Terry stucco style, housing
a pub on the ground floor (The Duchess of Cornwall). At
the N end of the square, ROYAL PAVILION by *Ben Pentreath*.
Here the sources are perhaps C.R. Cockerell for the main
block and Thomas Archer for the Neo-Baroque tower. With a
STATUE of H.M. the Queen Mother by *Philip Jackson* (a copy
of the one on The Mall, London), the whole square is due for
completion in 2017.

Returning to BRIDPORT ROAD, passing W between the
sentinel buildings mentioned above, scales and styles vary,
again increasing in density towards a secondary centre,
THE BUTTER MARKET. This has as its centrepiece an
125   octagonal turret (THE BUTTERCROSS) by *Ben Pentreath*, 2014.
This road follows the Roman road into Dorchester from the
W, yet surprisingly, little is made of its significance and alignment. Around the Buttercross, pleasing terraces with an early
C19 simplicity by *George Saumarez Smith*.

PHASES THREE AND FOUR. These are under construction at
the time of writing. Their stylistic mix will be the same as
the earlier phases, drawing on local vernacular and (generally
English) classical sources, in date up to around 1840, and Arts
and Crafts styles of *c.* 1890 to *c.* 1910.

PREHISTORIC AND ROMAN REMAINS

This regional centre, surrounded by the barrows of South Dorset,
has one of the densest concentrations of prehistoric monuments
in southern Britain, comparable to that of the Stonehenge area.
Within the boundary of present-day Dorchester is a wealth of
sites and monuments from the Neolithic onwards, between
the Maiden Castle ridge, the confluence of the rivers Frome
and South Winterborne, and the ridgeway running WNW to
Eggardon. On the W–E Dorchester Ridge to the S of the historic
centre, for 2¾ m. between the Poundbury Belvedere and Frome
Hill, West Stafford (q.v.), three monumental enclosures were
built: Maumbury Rings, Flagstones and Mount Pleasant, West
Stafford, as well as smaller henges and barrow groups. To the N,
in the central combe, is the Dorchester Henge, probably built
across an ancient route crossing the Frome to the southern ridge.
Many more barrows were constructed on the three ridge spurs

to the N. On a NW spur above the Frome is Poundbury Camp, a hill-fort built over a sequence of earlier enclosures and cross-ridge dykes. Neolithic and Bronze Age settlement remains have also been recorded in some density in recent years across this chalkland, and also on the northern Poundbury ridge.

Durnovaria, the Roman town of Dorchester, was built in the central coombe at the junction of Roman roads, constructed in the CI A.D. along ancient routes towards the surrounding hill-forts. It was the *civitas* capital of the *Durotriges*, covering *c.* 80 acres. Established by 70 A.D., it was a thriving Roman town with extra-mural settlements in a rich farmland. This continued into the C5, with two of the outlying farmsteads in operation into the C7. Its later history is described on p. 242.

POUNDBURY BELVEDERE, 1¼ m. WSW of St Peter's church. Built for the Millennium, 2000. From here is one of the best vistas across the prehistoric landscape s and w of Dorchester, including Maiden Castle (*see* Winterborne St Martin). To the w are a Bronze Age enclosure and dyke, and to the NE were small fields and round-houses. To the E, along the southern Dorchester ridge, are round barrows excavated at the Rugby Club and at Thomas Hardye School. Preserved below a sports-field terrace at the latter is a linear group of four barrows with conjoined ditches, aligned W-E. Along Coburg Road are several mini-henges, and further E, 1 m. from the Belvedere, is the massive henge at Maumbury Rings (*see* below).

MAUMBURY RINGS, on the E side of Weymouth Avenue, ½ m. S. Successively a Neolithic henge, a Roman amphitheatre, and a C17 gun emplacement. It was excavated by St George Gray in 1908–13. As constructed *c.* 2400 B.C., the henge had a single N-facing entrance, a bank originally about 11 ft (3.4 metres) high, and an internal ring of conjoining shafts dug up to 36 ft (11 metres) into the chalk. The Romans adapted the henge for use as an amphitheatre by removing nearly 12 ft (3.7 metres) of material from the interior to make a floor for the arena. They cut back the chalk bank to form the wall of the arena, which was revetted with timber. Around the inside of the arena there was a safety barrier, and a timber corridor was provided for performers. A gate 12 ft (3.7 metres) wide closed the entrance. Three rectangular chambers were cut into the bank at floor level on the s, w and E sides. Although Gray thought that the s room may have been used as a pen for wild animals it is more likely that all three were designed to house perform-ers or shrines. All three had structures above them, possibly boxes for important spectators. Probably constructed in the later CI, the amphitheatre had gone out of use by the mid C2. It was reused in the C3 and C4 but the nature of this activity is unclear. In 1642, in the Civil Wars, the Parliamentarians holding Dorchester fortified Maumbury to guard the Wey-mouth road. The prominent internal terraces belong to this period. At the same time a sunken trackway linking the site to the town's defences was dug from the entrance of Maumbury to the s gate of the town.

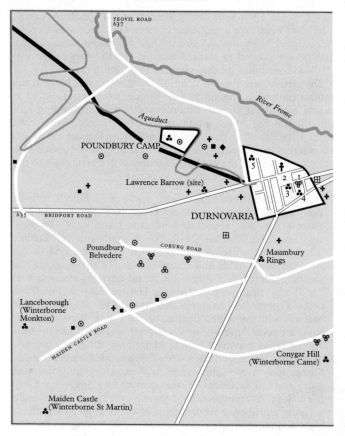

DORCHESTER HENGE, ¼ m. SE of St Peter's church. First
discovered at GREYHOUND YARD, now marked in Waitrose
basement car park. An arc of 6½-ft (2-metre) deep pits, cut
2400 B.C., to hold massive oak posts some 3 ft (1 metre) in
diameter: part of a circle *c.* 1,000 ft (300 metres) in diameter.
This has been recorded S to an entrance facing that of Maumbury Rings henge, and N towards High East Street.

ALINGTON AVENUE, traffic roundabout ¾ m. E from Maumbury Rings, W for ¼ m. A linear group of barrows, now all
destroyed, along the ridge-crest. They included two barrows
aligned to a Neolithic long mound with two massive parallel
ditches 40 ft (12 metres) apart and 230 ft (70 metres) long,
constructed *c.* 3300 B.C. Close to the long mound were Iron
Age burials. An enclosure, cemetery and stone-footed buildings have been found dating from the CI A.D. through to
the C5, followed by timber-post buildings and fenced enclosures, contemporary with a probably C7 cemetery to the N of
the road.

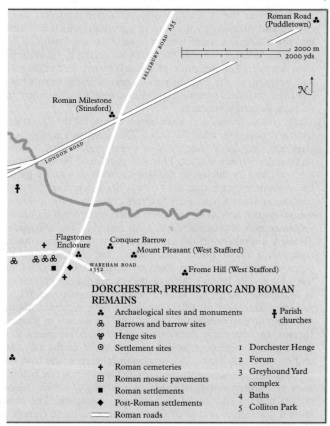

SALISBURY ROAD A35

Roman Road
(Puddletown)

2000 m
2000 yds

N

Roman Milestone
(Stinsford)

LONDON ROAD

Flagstones
Enclosure

Conquer Barrow

Mount Pleasant (West Stafford)

WAREHAM ROAD
A352

Frome Hill (West Stafford)

DORCHESTER, PREHISTORIC AND ROMAN REMAINS

- Archaelogical sites and monuments
- Barrows and barrow sites
- Henge sites
- Settlement sites
- Roman cemeteries
- Roman mosaic pavements
- Roman settlements
- Post-Roman settlements
- Roman roads

- Parish churches

1 Dorchester Henge
2 Forum
3 Greyhound Yard complex
4 Baths
5 Colliton Park

FLAGSTONES ENCLOSURE, 270 yds E of Alington Avenue. Half of a circular causewayed enclosure, constructed *c.* 3300 B.C. Uncovered in excavations on the by-pass route; destroyed in the cutting, but the eastern part is preserved, but not visible, surrounding Max Gate (*see* p. 258). Ditch segments, some with chalk-cut pictograms (the largest now displayed in Dorset County Museum), formed the western arc of a circle some 330 ft (100 metres) in diameter. Two SARSEN STONES from ditch segments can be seen at Max Gate and Louds Piece, outside the southern circuit.

CONQUER BARROW, ¼ m. E of Flagstones Enclosure, is a massive barrow mound on the western bank of the Mount Pleasant henge enclosure (West Stafford, q.v.). One of the largest in the area, and a marker point on the Dorchester municipal boundary of 1836, as was the massive Lawrence Barrow, now destroyed, ¼ m. w of St Peter's church.

POUNDBURY CAMP, ¾ m. NW of St Peter's church, above the River Frome. A HILL-FORT covering 13½ acres. It is bivallate apart from at the N scarp, where the outer ditch has been eroded and cut away by the Roman aqueduct (which also cuts into the E ditch). A single barrow mound has survived plough-ing of the interior. Outside the defences on the E, excavations have uncovered a sequence of PREHISTORIC SETTLEMENT and fields up to the Roman period, one of the Roman CEM-ETERIES outside *Durnovaria*, and evidence for continuity to C6 post-Roman settlement.

ROMAN TOWN. *Durnovaria* was a *civitas* capital for the *Durotriges* territory, covering some 80 acres. The town was established after A.D. 70, on a roughly N–S street grid, within a sub-rectangular banked circuit. This was reinforced by walls after A.D. 130, and by ditches in the late C2, with W, S and E gates. Excavations indicate that the FORUM lies below Cornhill and that the BASILICA lies under St Peter's church to the N. Exca-vations to the S, at GREYHOUND YARD, uncovered an urban sequence now reconstructed in a tile mural in Tudor Arcade. To the E are preserved the excavated parts of a Roman baths complex, a major public undertaking fed through conduit pipes alongside the streets from an aqueduct constructed in the C1 A.D. (*see* below). Also of the C1 are the amphitheatre at Maumbury Rings (*see* above) and the Roman roads. Exca-vations within and outside *Durnovaria* have recorded about sixty mosaic pavements, the largest total for a town in Roman Britain. In large-scale excavations, other building plans and development sequences have been uncovered in the SW, NW and SE town quadrants. Urban growth faltered in the later C2 to early C3, recovering in the C3–C4. Cemeteries (*see* below) were established along the roads, in locations of earlier Duro-trigian burials, and in the extra-mural settlements. The only known gravestone is that of Carinus, C2 A.D., in St George's church (p. 247).

ROMAN ROADS of the C1 A.D. can be traced to the S and W gates of the town, and from the E within the town, aligned towards the S gate.

WALLS and GATES. Near the Top o' Town roundabout, S of the W gate, a fragment of the ROMAN WALL survives. The outer counterscarp banks of the infilled defensive DITCHES can be seen below Nos. 17–18 Great Western Road, and at the South Walks junction with Acland Road.

BATHS. Preserved in the centre of the coombe, and originally cov-ering perhaps 1¼ acres. The SW suite of baths was uncovered S of a palaestra (gymnasium), or perhaps a temple precinct. The aqueduct supply failed in the later C2, with the baths out of use by 320. Structural alterations followed, with continuing occupation into the C5.

AQUEDUCT, running from the W gate for *c.* 4½ m. to the NW. It can be seen in places as a terrace, following the contours on the S of the Frome valley. It was probably supplied by a reservoir constructed across the mouth of Church Bottom, Frampton. Excavations at several locations showed a timber-box channel construction that failed in the later C2.

MOSAIC PAVEMENTS. All but two are assigned to the C4, of which only one is figurative, a Four Seasons mosaic at Colliton Park (*see* below). The C4 mosaicists belonged to the Durnovarian Group responsible for the fine figurative work in the villas N of Dorchester, notably at Frampton (Maiden Newton) and Hinton St Mary, where Christian elements were included. Of the mosaics in Dorchester, the C2 pavement of Oceanus from outside the E gate and two of the finest examples of C4 geometric work, from Olga Road and Durngate Street, are re-set in the floor of Dorset County Museum.

ROMAN TOWN HOUSE, in Colliton Park, behind County Hall. Excavated 1937–8. Standing in the NW angle of the defences, it is the only Roman building on view in the town, and has the distinction of being the only such complete town house visible in Britain. Three C3 houses, each with three rooms, were extended in the C4. The two western houses were connected by a new E–W room and all the rooms were provided with mosaic floors. The original eastern house was also extended and, with ovens and a hearth, appears to have included a kitchen and/or workshop. Both properties had one room with a heated hypocaust floor, and the properties were linked by a corridor. Between the two properties a well-shaft, 33½ ft (10 metres) deep, had been infilled and blocked in the post-Roman period with several column shafts, of which only one now remains on site. All the MOSAICS were uncovered prior to the construction of the new superstructure and can be viewed through the glass walls. Protective SUPERSTRUCTURE with Purbeck stone slates (replicas of those found on site) by *Anthony Jaggard* of *John Stark & Partners*, 1997–8.

CEMETERIES. Many hundreds of burials are recorded around the town, within large cemeteries on High Street Fordington to Fordington Green, along Weymouth Avenue, at Albert Road, the barracks and N of Bridport Road, and outside Poundbury Camp. The last is the most extensively excavated cemetery of Roman Britain. Perhaps best known are the E–W grave rows, plots, pathways and mausolea of the C3–C4 cemetery, some with Ham Hill stone and lead-lined coffins and identified as Christian. An exceptional survival is a painted Christian scene from the E wall of a mausoleum, with a chi-rho monogram and purple-robed figures, identified as Apostles, now in Dorset County Museum.

EXTRA-MURAL SETTLEMENTS. Excavations around *Durnovaria* have uncovered extensive Iron Age and Romano-British settlements and fields, at Poundbury, Poundbury Camp, Alington Avenue, a VILLA with mosaics at Olga Road, with a trackway SW to a three-quarter-mile-long settlement NW of Maiden Castle Road and on to Lanceborough (*see* Winterborne Monkton) and at Fordington Bottom. Post-Roman buildings and cemeteries into the C7 are extensive at Poundbury Camp and Alington Avenue; single buildings are recorded at others.

DRIMPTON
Broadwindsor

ST MARY. 1867 by *J.M. Allen* of Crewkerne. Nave with bellcote and chancel. Lancet Gothic; a triangular W window with bar tracery. Poor W porch, *c.* 1965.

WESLEYAN METHODIST CHAPEL, Netherhay, ½ m. NW. 1838, the bargeboards, pottery finials and porch added 1898. Simple round-arched windows.

OLD NETHERHAY, ⅜ m. NW. Dated 1638 on the front wall. So here are dated mullioned windows with ovolo mouldings and hoodmoulds; and the typical plan with a gabled staircase projection at the back.

OLD SANDPITS, ½ m. SE. S range of *c.* 1500, built as an open hall. (Collar-beam roof with arch braces and wind-braces.) Ceiling inserted *c.* 1600, the date of the main range to the N. The external appearance is all post *c.* 1600, with two storeys of mullioned windows with hoodmoulds. Thatched.

CHILDHAY, 1 m. SW. A late C15 manor house, probably built for the de Crewkerne family. The whole house of that date presents itself on the E front. At the centre the least altered part: a two-storey porch with an array of sportive grotesques, a single diagonal buttress and big battlements. Four-centred porch arch, and above, a two-light window to the front, and a singleton to the side, both with carved labels to the hoods. The same base-moulding vouches that with the porch goes the whole E front, the long hall range lying back to the l. and the gabled service range touching the porch to the r. Sadly, no other Perp features, except one screens doorway inside, explaining the plan. The solar, since gone, was presumably at the S end of the hall. An alternative (seen e.g. at Purse Caundle Manor) is that it was in the upper floor of the service range. With the exception of the porch, the exterior was heavily rebuilt in the late C16 for Sir Arthur Champernon of Modbury, Devon, hence the much later pattern of mullioned windows.

DURWESTON

Durweston is the first village above Blandford in the valley of the Stour. As one comes from the S across the bridge, it appears handsomely, crowned by the church, above the flat meadows, surrounded by the generous curves of the downs.

ST NICHOLAS. Lively C15 three-stage W tower with three image niches. Rectangular NE stair projection ending beneath the bell-stage. The tower is greenstone ashlar, the church flint and blocks of stone. The architect of the rebuilt church was *P. C. Hardwick*; the date is 1847. Hardwick re-set over the S

doorway an inscription referring to William Dounton, rector,
and ending in the date 1459. Some other Perp details reused
inside as well. It is noteworthy that Hardwick made the s aisle
Perp, but chancel and N side E.E. Chancel extended eastwards
by a bay in 1913–14 by *E.P. Warren*. The large, flat-roofed N
vestry and organ chamber are also of this date. – FONT. The
base slab for five supports is C12 or C13. – SCULPTURE. Small
C15 panel over the s door of St Eloy shoeing a horse. The saint
is busy with a detached leg; the cow-like horse meanwhile is
standing on three legs, supported by its rider.* Two statues in
the s-facing tower niches by *Donald Potter*, 1990. – STAINED
GLASS. Large E window installed for Lord Portman, perhaps
by *Lavers & Westlake*, 1914. s aisle E window (Viscountess
Portman †1899) by *E. Frampton*.

PORTMAN LODGE, in the main street. Early C19 dower house.
Stucco and slate. Large tripartite sashes on the ground floor.

DURWESTON LODGE to Bryanston, a few yards further E. Probably by *P.C. Hardwick*, c. 1850. Tudor lodge. Late C18 pedimented GATEPIERS.

BRIDGE, ¼ m. E, over the Stour. Of stone, with triangular cutwaters and refuges. Dated 1795, designed by *Joseph Towsey*, and
built at the expense of H.W.B. Portman of Bryanston.

KNIGHTON HOUSE, ¼ m. S. Large stucco house of c. 1830 for
the Portman family. Now a school.

WEBSLEY FARM, I m. SSW. A model farm group, 1850, for Lord
Portman. Banded brick and flint. Slate roofs. Contemporary
stucco-fronted farm COTTAGES.

EAST BURTON
8080

BURTON CHURCH (now WOOL CORNERSTONE CHURCH).
Small. Built in 1836–40. The architect was one *J.T. Parkinson*
of Jersey who, as a newspaper put it, furnished gratuitously
the plan of this 'elegant, chaste and cheap church'. *Culme
& Mondey* of Dorchester were local executants. Three bays
only, windows with Y-tracery. W porch, blank E window, low-
pitched roofs. Interior now subdivided.

EASTBURY
9010
Tarrant Gunville

Eastbury was *Sir John Vanbrugh*'s biggest country house, except-
ing always Castle Howard and Blenheim. The first designs
p. 59

---

*Brian and Moira Gittos point out that the rider is dressed in the fashionable gentry
costume of the second quarter of the C15.

were made *c.* 1716 for George Dodington, a nouveau riche, who died in 1720 leaving the estate to his nephew George Bubb (Dodington), son of a Weymouth apothecary, together with £30,000 to complete the house. Its completion was not until 1738, *Roger Morris* succeeding as architect a few years after Vanbrugh's death in 1726. The main block was completed to a modified, Palladianizing design, although the monumental outer works erected first were entirely to Vanbrugh's design. The house is said to have cost £140,000;* for Bubb Dodington developed into a flamboyant eccentric, determined to use his money to maximum effect. In the few surviving descriptions of the interiors it is clear that they were very richly decorated and furnished. At his death in 1762 (a year after he had been raised to the title of Lord Melcombe) the house became an incubus, and twenty years later was largely dismantled. The present house consists of the original stable court, somewhat curtailed. Thus its arcade formed the N side of a huge forecourt, some 150 ft (45 metres) across, balanced by an identical arcade and kitchen court on the s side, with the house towards the E. Cellars survive under the site of the E range of the kitchen court, and also a domed half-octagon below the site of the detached octagonal eating room in this range.

Eastbury is built of greensand ashlar, sombre in colour. Since what survives was intended for subordinate parts, the impression of Vanbrugh's austerity and impatience with mouldings is overwhelming. Behind the nine-bay arcaded loggia rises a cubical block, with first-floor windows forming an upper arcade, and an attic storey below a plain modillion cornice and a blank parapet. Lower side parts with bullseye windows. The ends of the range were adapted for Thomas Wedgwood (younger son of the pottery manufacturer) to form it into his house, *c.* 1800. The stable court behind is entered through the much-photographed ARCHWAY upon which grow a pair of pine trees. Here Vanbrugh's design plays off the square-section imposts, arch moulding and coping against the barely less elemental corbel table, giving a quicker rhythm, and the surprisingly richly carved scrolls l. and r. Within the court all is quite simply handled and not altogether in its original state. The octagonal chapel in the E range of the stable court, as Vanbrugh's published plan of 1725 shows it, was radically altered and all that survives is a canted bay facing into the court. The E side of the court is one-storeyed, with an irregular arrangement of oval and round-headed windows l. and r. of a three-bay arcade. Under the main arcade and in the stable court large stone eggs on leaf bases, presumably originally finials.

The PARK was laid out by *Vanbrugh* and *Bridgeman*, to a complex, almost diamond-shaped design. It was advanced in its thinking, combining formality at the centre with an early version of c18 romantic landscaping around the edges.

---

*That is to say, twice as much as Castle Howard, and about half the cost of Blenheim.

It included earthworks and peripheral planting of a new type. Also compartment planting but with axes extending to intersect with the boundary works, including a stepping arrangement of woodland planting focusing on the W façade of the house. Its chief building, the Great Temple at the far (E) end, took the Praeneste complex as its main Antique Roman source, but with a more conventional temple at its summit. Much of the park layout and beech planting can still be traced, as well as mounds and banks, especially two octagonal mounds 20 ft (6 metres) high and 40 ft (12 metres) across on the N side of the main E–W axis.

GATEPIERS, beside the road. Square, banded piers bearing balls, unexpectedly small considering the scale of the house. Subordinate piers l. and r. mark out an area beyond the one-arch BRIDGE over a rivulet. Mighty voussoirs to the bridge arch. More stone eggs here.

EAST CHELBOROUGH see LEWCOMBE

EAST COMPTON see COMPTON ABBAS

EAST HOLME   8080

A village little more than the church, priory house, farm and a cottage terrace. It stands alongside water meadows with a ford at its centre.

HOLME PRIORY was founded c. 1107 as a Cluniac cell from Montacute, Somerset. Nothing remains of it *in situ*. The chancel arch is at Creech Grange (*see* p. 239). Some masonry reused in the rear wing of the present HOUSE. Of c. 1770 for Nathaniel Bond. Stucco. L-plan. Five-bay S front, an arched window at the centre above a blocky porch. W elevation extended by two bays, c. 1835.

ST JOHN THE EVANGELIST. By *John Hicks*, 1865–6. Rock-faced ironstone. Tenders were for about £1,500, although the actual costs (met by the Rev. Nathaniel Bond) exceeded this. Nave with bellcote and chancel, the windows mostly lancets. From the Priory probably the loose stone fragments and the two Purbeck shafts of the S doorway. Carved angel corbels in the chancel by *Boulton* of Worcester. – The richly carved chancel FURNISHINGS (by *B. Grassby* of Powerstock) appear untouched since the church was completed. – Sanctuary-floor TILEWORK by *Minton*. – FONT. By *Hicks* (and probably also carved by *Boulton*). Bowl on a central pier of pink Irish marble. Four green Purbeck marble colonnettes. Carved marble medallions depicting the Evangelists let into the bowl. – PAINTINGS. Of 1866–91. The texts and leaf scrolls were painted by *Lady Selina*

Bond of Holme Priory. – STAINED GLASS. A complete contemporary scheme by *Clayton & Bell*. – MONUMENTS. Nathaniel and Lady Selina Bond, 1912 by *Powell & Sons*. Alabaster tablet.

HOLME BRIDGE, ¾ m. NW. Largely of stone, with much brick rebuilding. The centre three of its six round arches are medieval, perhaps C14.

EAST LULWORTH

A typically West Purbeck village of stone, cob or brick cottages, mostly thatched. It is overshadowed by Lulworth Park to its N and w. The village was moved to its present position as part of the laying out of the castle grounds in the C18.

LULWORTH CASTLE. A Jacobean fantasy castle, in much the same mould as the Little Castle, Bolsover, Derbyshire (1612) and Ruperra, Glamorgan (1626, with which Lulworth has a marked resemblance). Thomas Howard, 3rd Viscount Bindon, was the builder; his cousin, made 1st Earl of Suffolk in 1603, the intended occupant. Howard had his main seat at Bindon Abbey, a few miles away, and Lulworth was what was in Jacobean parlance called a lodge, i.e. a compact house for occasional use or subsidiary to a major house. Sir Walter Raleigh's Sherborne Lodge and the 1st Earl of Salisbury's Cranborne Manor were both of this type. A letter from Lord Bindon to Lord Salisbury dates the probable completion of building at Lulworth to *c.* 1608, and proves that Lulworth was really Salisbury's idea.★ But Cranborne was classically detailed, though medieval in origin. Longford, Wiltshire, was the Elizabethan castellated house *par excellence*, and must have inspired Lord Bindon.

Lulworth's plan is a square battlemented block, of three storeys above a basement, with big round battlemented angle towers. These are four-storeyed, but were not intended to give access to the flat roof since this is achieved by a central core tower. The E front is faced with Purbeck ashlar, the other sides with coursed rubble. Besides the towers and battlements, Lulworth sports windows with arched lights, in pairs and unexpectedly long. These may seem archaic but, in Dorset, such windows of this elliptical-arched sort are found at Chantmarle (1612), and Herringston, Winterborne Herringston (*c.* 1610). Hollow-chamfered mullions. The windows are symmetrically arranged in three storeys, with a fourth in the towers. Continuous string courses running over their heads deprive them of the need for hoodmoulds. On the E (entrance) side an

★What Lord Bindon wrote was: 'If the little pile in Lulworth park shall prove pretty or worth the labour bestowed on the erecting of it, I will acknowledge as the truth is, that your Lordship's powerful speech to me at Bindon, to have laid the first foundations of the pile in my mind.'

Ionic triumphal-arch arrangement round the doorway, added
c. 1700. Mounted upon it c18 statues of Julius and Augustus Caesar, based on Antique originals. Over the doorway
(between the statues) a sort of rose window. Its tracery of six
circles round a seventh was added in the mid c19 (replacing
radiating spokes). The circular windows with hoodmoulds l.
and r. were there by c. 1800, and the Gibbs surround to the w
doorway must be of the c18 too. So there was just one classical
motif from the start, the shell-headed niches, very small and
lost-looking at first-floor level. Also lion heads dotted along at
this level, on the E side and on the w.

So who was its architect? Similar shell-headed niches occur,
one remembers, at Cranborne and other buildings associated
with *William Arnold*, so he was most likely the executant architect here. It is known that *Godfrey Arnold*, identified by Mark
Girouard putatively as William's brother, was principal mason
at the castle, 1603–5. Girouard has also pointed out that the
plan owes much to one by *John Thorpe*.

The initial ground-floor plan involved entry through an
enclosed porch into an ante-room, l., and thence (via a pair of
matching archways) into a hall running the remainder of the
length of the s side. The NW corner, beyond a main staircase,
was occupied by a chapel. Its Jacobean interiors were classicized by 'Mr Bastard' (most likely *John Bastard*) in two phases
(1727 and 1738). Further replanning took place c. 1770 by the
two *Thomas Bastard*s. On the first floor a grand dining room
was completed by *John Tasker*, c. 1780. But none of this is to
be seen since the fire that gutted the house in 1929, leaving
only a masonry shell. Stone and brick vaulted ceilings survive
in the basement, in part supported by Tuscan columns (much
as at Bolsover).

Abandoned after the fire (and with an ensuing period unpro-
pitious for reinstatement), the castle shell continued to decay
and by the 1970s its loss seemed possible. However, throughout the 1980s and 90s a major campaign re-roofed and stabilized the shell, after earlier ideas of reinstating it as a country
house proved impractical.

The balustraded TERRACE was constructed on the E side
first, probably in the early c18 but before 1721, and extended
round the N and s sides before 1765. All reconstructed 1776.
Margaret Weld's 1721 bird's-eye view shows a heavily formalized LANDSCAPE. This was swept away in the late c18 (at the
same time as the removal of the village) and a vaguely Brownian scheme created.

Together with the former stable courtyard and 1970s house
(*see* below), in the grounds are two churches: the parish church
of East Lulworth and the Catholic chapel of the Weld family.

STABLE COURTYARD, to the SE. Largely of 1777, incorporating c17 masonry. Remodelled c. 1900 with timber-framed
gables and dormers.

ST ANDREW. 1863–4 by *John Hicks*, except for the formidable
late c15 w tower. It is of grey stone, with big diagonal carstone

buttresses with many set-offs, ending in pinnacles below the bell-stage. The bell-openings are three square-headed lights each side, set in deep reveals with two tiers of trefoil-headed openings. Battlemented parapet with crocketed corner pinnacles. Triangular tower arch, rounded at the springing, with very broad mouldings on the E side, within which are niches with crocketed canopies. Springings with traceried pendants indicate that the tower was intended to have a stone vault. Hicks's nave and chancel are Perp. – FONT. C15. Octagonal with a quatrefoil on each face. Panelled stem and roundels on the bowl. – ROYAL ARMS. Dated 1785. Painted wood. – HATCHMENT. William Baring, 1820.

85 LULWORTH CASTLE CHAPEL (ST MARY, R.C.). Built in 1786–7 by *John Tasker* for Thomas Weld, at a cost of £2,380. Various alterations, including Neo-Byzantine decoration and minor window adjustments (executed under *J.A. Hansom*, 1865) were reversed by *H.S. Goodhart-Rendel* in 1951–3. The story is that George III gave Thomas Weld permission to build a Catholic church only on condition that it should not look like a church. The architect fulfilled that condition and produced the first free-standing Roman Catholic church to be built in Britain since the Reformation. From a distance the building looks like an uncommonly large garden temple, from nearby like a house, especially from the (ritual) NE, where the two-storey fenestration and the big bow tell. The plan is a quatrefoil with a rectangular tail behind the altar. To the W (ritually) the entrance is a simple porch of Tuscan columns; to the E however there is a proper three-bay façade with a Tuscan porch flanked by niches with elegant vases of *Coade* stone. The portal is set in a blank segmental arch with an urn on the entablature of the portal. Behind this E façade are the sacristy and priest's rooms. The W porch is set in an apse; the N and S apses are also visible externally, but the E or altar apse is not.

The INTERIOR is wonderfully serene: the four apses, three with galleries on Tuscan columns, the fourth with the altar space, short diagonals with Ionic pilasters facing the apses, a dome above, its PAINTING depicting the Assumption of Our Lady by *Sarah Janson*, 1988, and a light-giving lantern. Terry Friedman points out the close similarity of Lulworth to James Wyatt's Pantheon, Oxford Street, London (1769–72), itself derived from the Hagia Sophia, Istanbul.* The pavement has in black on grey a large and a small circle, and convex lobes from the former inward. – ALTAR. Of *c.* 1770 by *Giacomo Quarenghi*, made in Rome, and intended for the English College in Bruges. Purchased by Mr Weld, *c.* 1786. Of various marbles with bronze enrichment, including two kneeling angels on the front. – SANCTUARY SEAT and LAMPS by *Anthony Jaggard*, 1986. – Fine COMMUNION RAIL with S-motifs. – ORGAN. By *Richard Seede* of Bristol, 1785. – HATCHMENTS. Of the Weld

---

*Friedman, *The Eighteenth-Century Church in Britain* (2011).

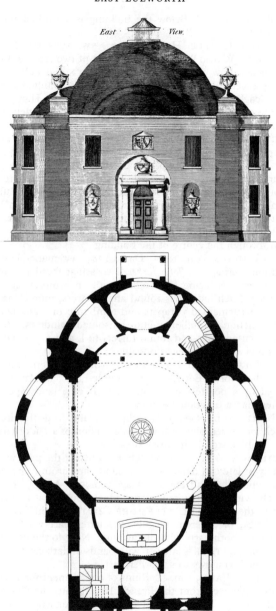

East Lulworth, Lulworth Castle Chapel, elevation and plan.
Engraving, 1803

family, mainly C18. Below the building is a vaulted funeral CRYPT.*

LULWORTH CASTLE HOUSE, ⅛ m. SW. 1975 by *Anthony Jaggard* for Wilfrid Weld. Neo-Georgian of two storeys. Brick. Full-height bow windows, two to the main N and S elevations, a single central one to the E. Top-lit barrel-vaulted central hall. Scagliola columns reused from The Grange, Hampshire. C18 marble fireplaces imported from Ince Blundell Hall, Lancashire.

WAREHAM GATE LODGE, ½ m. NE. Of *c.* 1608–10 (i.e. contemporary with the castle), taken down in 1753 and re-erected here in 1808, hence the prominent datestone on the W side. It first stood just E of the castle, providing an axial entrance to a forecourt, all swept away in later landscaping. Rubble stone, rendered. Three-bay block, of two storeys and a half. Battlements, and windows like the castle's but of timber. The undercut string course is clearly original, but not the carriage arch through the centre of the building.

NORTH LODGES, ⅞ m. NNW. Dated 1785. A remarkable composition, perhaps by *John Tasker*. Two ashlar-faced triangular lodges, apexes facing each other, with an armorial gateway between. Each lodge has round angle towers, mimicking the castle, battlemented parapets and a mixture of blank lancets and functional mullioned-and-transomed windows. Rough battlemented walls and round turrets to l. and r., to make as extended an eyecatcher as possible.

CLARE TOWERS, 1 m. NW. Late C18 (probably contemporary with the North Lodges). Two rubble-built circular towers linked by a pointed arch. The effect is of a landscape folly rather than a functional entrance.

THE FORT, 1¼ m. NNE, on the edge of a lake. Mid-C19 circular mock fort, resembling a small-scale version of a Tudor coastal fort. Rubble stone with brick dressings.

The VILLAGE, ¼ m. ESE of the church outside the park wall, is largely of late C18 date, when the landscape around the castle was remodelled and the old village removed. Mostly cob and thatch, with a particularly picturesque grouping at its centre. Just N, the thatched LITTLEMORE COTTAGE is half-cob and half-brick, of different heights, the latter part with a platband, and both parts with tile-hanging. Near to the park wall, MANOR COTTAGE is late C16 with bands of dark carstone and mullioned windows to its earlier part, r.

MONASTERY FARM, 1 m. SE. Ruins of a settlement for Trappist monks, refugees from the French Revolution. Built in 1795, partly of cob, they represented the first monastic establishment in England since the Reformation. Now in the Lulworth military firing range.

---

* In 1790 John Carroll, first Bishop of Baltimore, was consecrated in the chapel. Latrobe's Baltimore Cathedral of 1805–18 is also centrally planned with four segmental arches and galleries in the arms of the cross.

FLOWERS BARROW, 1¼ m. SE of the village. An Iron Age HILL-
FORT, formed of two enclosures, partly eroded into the sea.
Presently covering some 15½ acres. An original entrance survives on the SE. Occupation platforms are visible within the
interior. E of the hill-fort is a CROSS-RIDGE DYKE.

EASTON *see* PORTLAND, p. 485

EAST ORCHARD   *8010*

ST THOMAS. By *Evans & Pullan*, 1859. Plain lancet-windowed
Gothic in Todber greenstone with Bath dressings. Nave with
bellcote and chancel. Five graduated thin lancets in the W
gable. Plain moulded chancel arch. Original pitch-pine FUR-
NISHINGS. – Late C12 or early C13 bowl FONT.
Two former WESLEYAN METHODIST CHAPELS, Bleax Hill,
¼ m. NE. The older is of *c.* 1800, enlarged 1824. Round-arched
windows with Y-tracery. A contemporary cottage at the N end
under the same roof. Now converted to a house, as is its successor of 1876, adjacent.

EAST STOKE   *8080*

ST MARY (declared redundant in 1985, now three dwellings). Of
1828 by *Thomas E. Owen* of Portsmouth. Lean proportions,
especially noticeable on the W tower doorway. Thin buttresses
and pointed windows, those to the four-bay nave with cusped
Y-tracery. Chancel rebuilt in 1885 by *John Colson & Son*. The
whole was rendered some time after it was converted in 1994.
FORMER CHURCH, ⅓ m. SW. C15. Ruinous. Parts of the nave S
wall and S porch. Perp window. (Good STOUP in the porch.)
BINNEGAR HALL, ¾ m. E. 1868 by *David Brandon* for O.W.
Farrer. Rock-faced Ham Hill stone. Jacobethan. Gabled.
Heavily detailed on the N entrance front. More successful on
the S elevation: broadly symmetrical, with square bay windows
and a spired turret in the SW angle.
HETHFELTON (or Heffleton), 1½ m. NW. Neo-Georgian mansion
of 1929 on the site of an earlier house. Stuccoed. Hipped roofs.
Seven-bay S front arranged 2:3:2 with a pedimented doorway
at its centre. Informal side elevations.
FRESHWATER BIOLOGY ASSOCIATION RIVER LABORATORY,
Stoke Mill, ¼ m. S. 1964 by *Ronald Sims*. Undemonstrative,
but a characterful group, laboratory and wardens' cottages,
of brown brick. Many little monopitch roofs and the glazed
sawtooth N wall of the laboratory establish its character. A little

coarsely detailed. Concrete FLUVARIUM, 1970, built straddling the stream, so that the water flows through two glass aquaria, to allow research into river plants and animals.

BATTERY BANK, ½ m. NE. Stretches of a discontinuous dyke over 2 m., to the W of Worgret Heath dykes (*see* Arne). Date uncertain.

WOOLBRIDGE MANOR. *See* Wool.

EAST STOUR

CHRIST CHURCH. By *G. Alexander*, 1842. Neo-Norman to a £200 budget. The style was popular in the 1840s, especially with this architect.* Chancel, transepts, broad crossing tower and nave. The crossing has thick pseudo-Early Norman responds. Transept galleries remain *in situ*, as do most of the rather thinly detailed Neo-Norman PEWS. The W gallery has been removed. – PULPIT. By *Ponting*, 1903. – FONT. Of the Purbeck table type, with shallow-sunk round-headed arcading, three arches to the side, C12. – LECTERN. The top is a fine C18 wooden pelican. – STAINED GLASS. E window of *c.* 1882 and nave N window (†1887), both probably by *Hardman*.

EDMONDSHAM

Small village to the SE of the house and church, of C18 brick houses and late C19 estate cottages.

ST NICHOLAS. Small and simple. C12 nave, chancel. C14 replacement N aisle. Nave and chancel are of brown heath-stone. Diminutive three-stage NW tower of flint and greensand blocks, added in the C15 when much rebuilding was carried out. Further extensive rebuilding and reordering in 1863 by *George Evans*, including the S porch. Many restored Perp two- and three-light square-headed windows with trefoil-headed lights. An arched two-light in the N aisle is a C15 original. Two-bay C12 N arcade with square piers and minimum imposts. Later pointed arches, probably of 1863, as is the pointed chancel arch (replacing the C12 original) springing from carved foliage capitals. Niche canopy re-set at the E end of the N aisle; elaborate Perp carving. – FONT. Octagonal with quatrefoil panels, C19. – ROYAL ARMS. Dated 1788. – STAINED GLASS. All of *c.* 1865–70. – MONUMENTS. The E end of the N aisle is dominated by a set of heraldic grey stone panels from the Hussey

---

*This and the church at Enmore Green (q.v.) were both built for the Rev. Henry Deane.

vault, dismantled in 1863; earliest inscription †1684, but most mid- and late C18.

EDMONDSHAM HOUSE, immediately N. A Late Elizabethan or Jacobean house not of the ordinary run, with wings sympathetically added c. 1740–50. The date 1589 and Thomas Hussey's initials on the topmost finial of the porch must have been cut in the C19; but it is not clear whether they were based on evidence. Hussey bought Edmondsham in 1563 and died in 1601.

The details – the prettily shaped gables, with finials, and the refined mouldings of the square window mullions, sunk panels and ingeniously arranged recessed panels round the angles of the window bays – are idiosyncratic, and certainly without local parallel. The windows – large, transomed and the major ones carried round all three sides of the bay – make one think of Longleat (Wilts.) or Montacute (Somerset). No hoodmoulds, but continuous string courses linking the window heads. For the gables however one would feel happier with an early C17 date. The house is built of brick, though rendered in the early C19. Stone dressings, stone lower part of the porch and cartouche of arms. The S front is absolutely symmetrical, with slightly projecting wings and a more boldly projecting porch. The whole house, including the porch, is three-storeyed, and strikingly tall and compact, giving room between the projections only for chimney-breasts, the stacks – now replaced – no doubt intended to partake in the composition. All of this is typical of early C17 designing, not unlike Anderson Manor. The back has four uneven straight gables, and no system to the fenestration. The C18 wings are possibly by *Francis Cartwright* (note their similarity to his S front at Creech Grange of 1738–41). They have the tact not to project far, and are even given semicircular gables to screen the roof pitches, a sensitive touch. Windows in broad frames, the upper ones round-headed. Round the side the W wing takes up a different refrain, the standard mid-C18 one of projecting centre, with a pediment. 2:3:2 bays, normal fenestration. Just one accent, the very emphatic rusticating blocks round the door and continued up round the window above. The E façade of the E wing is a simplified version of the W one. Sturdy staircase of c. 1660 with dumb-bell balusters and balls on the newels.

STABLES, NE. Dated 1864, brick. U-plan. Central gabled pavilion with spired roof lantern.

ENCOMBE HOUSE

9070

2½ m. SSW of Corfe Castle village

At Encombe one can for once see the grandly austere Vanbrughian idiom being used by another architect in an independent-minded and intelligent way. The architect is likely to have been *John Pitt*, to whom Encombe came in 1734. He had

a reputation as an amateur architect, also working at Stratfield
Saye, Hampshire, for his elder brother George. What was pro-
duced is a powerful composition, exceptionally so for an amateur.
No doubt Pitt learnt much about Vanbrugh from watching the
erection of Eastbury Park for his acquaintance George Bubb
Dodington. One sign of its power is that the early C19 GARDEN
TEMPLE and STABLES to the SW, erected for Lord Eldon, the
Lord Chancellor, who bought Encombe in 1807, and *Anthony
Salvin*'s alterations of 1871–4 to the house for the 3rd Earl of
Eldon, closely follow the C18 style. Everything is built in the finest
silvery Purbeck ashlar.

The NORTH (ENTRANCE) FRONT consists of a centre block, with
wings not related to it and lying further back, the product of
an uncompleted plan. Wide, low two-storey centre, of nine
bays, the middle five close-set, then a gap so that bays two and
eight read with the slightly projecting end bays. The ground-
floor windows have arched tympana, and are linked by impost
mouldings which create a system which resembles blank arcading. The square pedimented dormers with side scrolls however,
which give further stress to ends and centre, and the broad
central chimneystack, arched through its middle, are *Salvin*'s,
added when this became the entrance front.* A hint of arcading is continued on the E return front. The windows here
form three arcaded bays at both levels, under an overall open
pediment. Shades of Hawksmoor – of, say, his N front of St
George, Bloomsbury. An C18 plan shows wings projecting at
right angles here to form an open-ended court, but only the
S wing was ever built. In the three-bay glazed loggia here the
arcade finally materializes fully.**

87   The SOUTH FRONT (the original entrance front) is less
elaborate but more unified, an extraordinarily spreading
composition which rises above two lowish storeys only with
the central pedimented dormer. All the horizontals – string
courses, cornices and blank panelled parapet – lay emphasis
on the lowness. The far projection of the wings adds to this
effect. Only Vanbrugh's Claremont (1715–20) had achieved
such a result, and Claremont was, like Encombe, set in front
of a hillside. As a composition too Encombe is worked out in
a Vanbrughian way, controlled, as the N front of Blenheim is
controlled, by an order that appears and disappears. Here the
order is Tuscan, employed in a single scale on the doorcases
of the centre and wings, and for the open columned loggias l.
and r. The arcading that is so important for the N front is here
a subordinate theme, stated by the wide-spaced ground-floor
windows in centre and wings. The outer wings l. and r. are
too austere to take up either theme, and give as it were the

*A pedimented Tuscan porch, adapted from a garden loggia and attached here in
1959, was removed during a partial restoration of 2005 by *William Bertram*. The
rather tight forecourt walling is also of that date.
** Clearly the N front was never considered satisfactory. An unexecuted 1841 scheme
by *G.S. Repton* exists for refacing the entrance front, unifying the composition.

mere rhythm, in which the tune of arch and column is played. Hutchins's engraving of 1774 shows battlements over the projecting centres of these wings.

But one must still ask why the long low mass seemed desirable. There are really two points. First, that the three-bay centre has unusually low storeys, which can be explained by the retention of earlier walls and floor levels belonging to the old house (built c. 1600 for the Culliford family) incorporated in the central block. This controlled the levels of the window openings. Second, that the house's position, embraced from the N by hills, made a horizontally stressed house seem right. House and hill, as seen from the S, interlock. S of the house a lake and beyond a glimpse of the sea like an extension of the lake.

The INTERIOR is a product of several periods. *Salvin* was responsible for much. Hall and Drawing Room in the centre were both given big white marble chimneypieces, probably of c. 1812, Neoclassical in style (brought in from elsewhere). The Hall now has a richly grained Vanbrughian fireplace, installed as part of a major restoration for James Gaggero, 2009–12. In the Morning Room, on the E side, a Kentian plaster ceiling that seems to belong to the original period. Good Neoclassical chimneypiece of c. 1800, its central panel depicting a priest pouring a libation on an altar. Also in the E wing a fine Library, created by Salvin from two early C19 rooms. It has two matching Neoclassical fireplaces, one original, the other a copy. Main staircase in an early C18 style, but clearly of C19 workmanship. Surprisingly it is by *Salvin* and a svelte piece, not at all what one expects of the 1870s. The major room of the W wing is the Dining Room, a later C19 double-height space in a Neoclassical style, with a fine late C18 marble chimneypiece returned here from the entrance hall as part of the recent improvements. The best in the house, this has fluted Corinthian columns and an entablature with masks and figures copied from the Choragic Monument of Lysicrates.

OBELISK, ⅓ m. NE. Put up in 1835, in honour of Lord Stowell, brother of Lord Chancellor Eldon, who had bought Encombe in 1807.

ROCK ARCH, ¼ m. S. Cyclopean blocks haphazardly laid form a bridge with a labyrinth and an alcove underneath, whence, before the trees grew up, a vista could be had of the sea. Paintings originally in the house make it clear that this *jeu d'esprit* was in existence before tricorn hats went out of fashion, i.e. by c. 1780.

ELDON SEAT, ⅔ m. SW. A simple stone seat of 1835, inscribed 'ELDON SEAT' in large letters.

ENMORE GREEN

8020

A scattered W suburb of Shaftesbury centred on a crossroads. It became part of the borough in 1933.

ST JOHN THE EVANGELIST. 1842–3 by *G. Alexander*. Neo-Norman (cf. East Stour nearby, also by Alexander). Apsed chancel, transepts, crossing tower and nave. Shafted windows. Wheel window in the w gable. The original galleries survive in the transepts and nave. – FONT. C15. Square top, chamfered, with incised fleur-de-lys motifs. Curious oak boss, probably also C15, at the centre of the COVER. – STAINED GLASS. Three armorial windows of *c.* 1843 in the apse.

PRIMITIVE METHODIST CHAPEL (former), Breach Lane, ¼ m. SE. Italianate, dated 1868.

5000   EVERSHOT

Formerly a small market town, as is evident from the wide village street (Fore Street), its raised pavements and occasional shopfronts imparting a degree of urbanity. The C19 architectural character comes from phases of rebuilding and improvement by the earls of Ilchester of the nearby Melbury Park estate.

ST OSMUND. Almost wholly rebuilt by *R. H. Shout* in two phases, 1852–3 (nave, s aisle and upper part of tower) and 1863 (chancel), apart from the N aisle and w tower, both C15. So the exterior is full of Shout's mild eccentricities, e.g. the angled doorway at the SW corner of the tower and the almost domestic porch hood at the s doorway. Also the dome-and-pinnacle stair-turret-top incorporating a clock face on one side. More elaboration on the chancel, with an arcaded parapet, crocketed pinnacles and rock-faced masonry. The s arcade is Perp to match that of the N aisle. Late C12 chancel arch with shafted responds and scalloped capitals re-set at the E end of the N aisle. C12 responds to the tower arch with chamfered imposts; C15 pointed arch. The most Perp of Shout's internal features is the tracery screen between the chancel and organ loft. – The chancel FURNISHINGS (1863) are rich, with encaustic tilework by *Godwin* at the sanctuary and brass candleholders on the STALLS. (– SCULPTURE. In the vestry a Norman capital with a figure holding a key.) – STAINED GLASS. E window by *Hardman*, 1864. A Crucifixion, with some paint loss. Two chancel side windows by *Clayton & Bell*, 1864 and †1878. The aisle windows have stamped quarries by *Powell & Sons*, 1853. – BRASS to William Grey, rector, †1524, an 18½-in. (47-cm.) figure.

THE MANSION, nearly opposite the church. Seven-bay front of *c.* 1725, with the central three windows grouped together. Presumably it was rendered (covering the brick parapet). Continuing on the r., some cottage terraces have good early C19 shop windows. THE OLD RECTORY, beyond, is early C17 with a two-storey canted window bay, the windows of 2:2:2 lights. Square-headed lights. Further down on the l., a pair of later c19 Melbury ESTATE COTTAGES. Opposite, and set back from the road, SUMMER LODGE (now a hotel). Stuccoed. A central hipped-roofed block of 1789, built for the 2nd Earl of Ilchester as a dower house. Extended and an extra floor added in 1893 by *Thomas Hardy* for the 5th Earl.

EYPE

Symondsbury

ST PETER. 1864–5 by *T. Talbot Bury* at the behest of the Rev. Henry Rawlinson. £3,000 for its building was a bequest from Rawlinson's predecessor, the Rev. Gregory Raymond. Nave, chancel, transepts, N aisle and W bellcote. Local brown rubble stone. Dec window tracery including rose windows (of differing patterns) to the transepts. The porch is a lark, its walls being projecting (unnecessary) buttresses. Well-proportioned but sparingly detailed Dec-style transept and N arcade arches. Slightly more detail in the chancel arch. The church became an arts centre in 2004 with the nave cleared of all furnishings except for the font, and the N transept divided off. – TILE-WORK. *Minton* diapered majolica unglazed tilework on the E wall (the pattern based on the St Dunstan shrine, Canterbury). *Minton* floor tiles in the sanctuary. – PULPIT. A high-quality piece carved by *R.L. Boulton* of Worcester. Trefoiled niche-arch to each face with marble corner colonnettes. Figures of Christ and the Four Evangelists in the niches. – FONT. Another fine piece by *Boulton*. Perp style. Octagonal with richly carved sides. Stem and four marble colonnettes. – STAINED GLASS. An excellent set by *Heaton, Butler & Bayne* in the chancel. All of 1865. Rich in purples, reds and blues, they are some of the finest produced by this maker. S transept window by the same firm, 1878. They also made the panels in the N aisle windows.

FARNHAM

A village of cob and thatched cottages, many aligned gable-end to the road and evenly spaced. Some c19 brick estate cottages.

ST LAURENCE. Nave of the C12 (see one shallow W buttress), S tower of *c.* 1500 over the porch, N aisle 1835–6 by *Edward Haskell* (builder), chancel 1886. The tower has flint and stone bands; battlemented parapet. C18 pointed windows to the nave. Instead of an arcade, the N aisle has just two thin iron columns to the nave – take it or leave it (cf. Chickerell). There is a weird recess under the nave W window, probably intended to get light into the space below the former W gallery. – PULPIT.

Early C18. – FONT. Probably Perp, but very eroded. It replaced an C18 baluster font (now in the porch). This is almost a joke; the bowl is so small. – WALL PAINTING. On the w wall two cartouches; 1733. – STAINED GLASS. Nave s window by *Arthur J. Dix*, 1922. – MONUMENT. Philip Rideout †1834. Gothic, but simply a high square pedestal.

Opposite the entrance to the church a WELL HOUSE, designed like a lychgate, late C19.

WESLEYAN METHODIST CHAPEL (former), ¼ m. N. Dated 1865. Brick with lead-latticed Gothic windows.

PITT-RIVERS MUSEUM (former), ⅜ m. S. Main block of 1847, built as a 'Gypsy School and Orphan Asylum' by *L. G. Butcher* for the Rev. John West. Converted and enlarged, 1889–90, by General Pitt-Rivers, the pioneer archaeologist, as a 'Peasant Museum'. This displayed his ethnographical collections together with excavated finds from his estates around Rushmore, Wilts. The multi-gabled building has a Tuscan four-column porch and gablets, added *c.* 1930. The main museum areas were in large sheds to the rear. It is now subdivided into houses. The big banded ashlar GATEPIERS (inscribed 'ARP 1894') look as if they began life a few miles off at Vanbrugh's Eastbury. The museum was designed as an adjunct to General Pitt-Rivers's pleasure grounds, the Larmer Grounds, 2 m. N across the boundary with Wiltshire. In 1899 there were over 12,000 visitors, and 40,000-odd went to the Larmer Grounds. The collections were dispersed *c.* 1975, with the most significant local items passing to the Salisbury and South Wiltshire Museum.

FARRINGTON
2 m. NW of Iwerne Courtney

ST PETER. Rebuilt in 1856. Nave and chancel in one; bellcote. Now a house.

CHURCH FARM, a few yds s. Early C17 (with a recent addition). The older part, N, has two attic gables facing the road. Ovolo-moulded stone-mullioned windows, one a four-light, the others three. Hoodmoulds.

FERNDOWN

Hardly more than a cluster of cottages in 1920, Ferndown is now the fifth largest settlement in the county in terms of population. It becomes immediately apparent on entering the town (so designated in 1977) that there has been no overall design to the growth. As a result, beyond the church, there is little of

architectural note, although in the 1980s a shopping centre was
created at the crossing of Ringwood, Victoria and New roads.

St Mary. 1932–4 by *Herbert Kendall*. Chancel and sanctuary
by *L. Magnus Austin*, 1938–40. N transept, 1964; s transept
and w battlemented tower, 1971–2, by *James George Morley*
all largely to Kendall's intentions. Rock-faced and bulky; Dec-
and Perp-traceried windows. Moulded stone arches to the
chancel, transept and aisle arcades, but plain arch into the
tower. A curiosity, largely ignoring c20 architectural developments. – STAINED GLASS. An aisle window by *Morris & Co.*
of Westminster, 1934.

FIDDLEFORD
¾ m. E of Sturminster Newton

8010

FIDDLEFORD MANOR. Fiddleford has the most spectacular
medieval manor house interior in Dorset. The main part, after
purchase by the Ministry of Works in 1956, is now a property
of English Heritage. The house was formerly thought to have
been built for William Latimer, sheriff of Somerset and Dorset
in 1374 and 1380, although recent dendrochronological dating
of roof timbers suggests construction *c.* 1340. What remains is
the two-storey solar wing and half the Hall to the E of it; and
what makes both spectacular is their open timber roofs. The
trusses are basically of the standard West Country construction,
collar-beams on arched braces, with two tiers of wind-braces
against the rafters. Bold cusping of wind-braces and decorated
panels above the collar, boldly cut out in trefoils and quatrefoils,
elaborate the system. Many ogee curves. The Hall has a variant
apex for the louvre truss. The Solar is yet more elaborate, as suits   45
a room where the roof is not so far overhead. The wind-braces
are sub-cusped, longitudinal braces spring from the collars,
and there are horizontal braces too, all arched and cusped.
As a design the Solar roof is a triumph, creating a complex
spatial effect but not spoiling it by an abundance of decoration:
every member has an unmoulded upper side. Only one original
window, the E (blocked) window of the Solar, restorable as two
trefoiled lights with an ogee quatrefoil in the head. Transom
and an internal seat. A late c14 wall painting at this E end was
discovered in 1990. Although incomplete, it can clearly be seen
as depicting the Annunciation. There is also an inscription: 'Ave
Maria Gracia Plena' ('Hail, Mary, full of grace').

In the c16 the solar wing was much extended to the N and
the Hall remodelled. The latter work is of high quality, the
stonework creamy Marnhull limestone, and recurring initials
prove it to be the work of Thomas White (†1555). It is still
entirely Gothic in character. Ashlar facing of the N wall of the
Hall. Octagonal shafts, with moulded bases and moulded caps

that continue as a string course, flank a blocked window, with a similar window to its r.

Inside, a screens passage was contrived at what had been the Solar end of the Hall. Presumably the Solar undercroft now came into use as service rooms. Fine four-centred doorways here, two W and one S, with wave mouldings for the arch and for the square surround. Some stones for this were reused; one shows C14 carvings on the rear side. The solar was given a fireplace with moulded jambs jutting out two-thirds of the way up. Its plaster overmantel, incorporating the initials of White and his wife in a central cartouche, is not currently *in situ*. The upper room N of the Solar (now part of the adjoining property) has a plaster ceiling of *c.* 1580, similar to that removed from the Hall (and installed at Hinton St Mary Manor) in the mid 1960s. Moulded ribs make geometrical patterns, and fleur-de-lys bud out into the fields. The longitudinal sides of the ceiling are gently coved. On the other two walls a contemporary frieze also with fleur-de-lys incorporated.

The N range was continued further N in the C17, and has nothing to show but mullioned windows of that date (mostly renewed in the C20).

On the free-standing MILL HOUSE further N a pair of re-set black-letter inscription panels dated 1566. The text is an exhortation to the miller, and worth quoting in full:

> He thatt wyll have here any thynge don
> Let him com fryndly he shal be welcome
> A frynd to the owner and enemy to no man
> Pass all here frely to com when they can
> For the tale of trothe I do alway professe
> Miller be true disgrace not thy vest
> If falsehod appere the fault shal be thine
> And of sharpe ponishment think me not unkind
> Therefore to be true yt shall the behove
> [To] please god chefly [that liveth] above.

DOMINEY'S FARM, ½ m. SE of Fiddleford Manor. C15 open-hall house, with large timber-framed panels in the E part. A jointed cruck is visible in the N gable-end. Stone refacing on the road frontage, with a S extension of the C18 also in stone.

FIFEHEAD MAGDALEN

7020

Sited on Fifehead Hill on the W bank of the Stour, opposite the twin hill of Stour Provost.

ST MARY MAGDALENE. Nave, chancel, and two-stage S tower, all small in scale. Basically C14, see e.g. the S windows. The N chapel was built *c.* 1750. Restorations of 1884 and 1905 (the latter by *E. Doran Webb*) seem unobtrusive. – FONTS. Two: an early C18 fluted baluster with a small octagonal bowl, and a new-looking, more standard Perp-style font. – DOOR. Oak, of two folding leaves, dated 1637 and with individual letters (WTB, OIT) within shield-shaped recesses, rather like hallmarks. – Four CHANDELIERS of brass, C18. Of two tiers each. – STAINED GLASS. Expressionist W window by *Alan Younger*, 1973. Nave N window (Good Shepherd) by *Percy Buckman*, 1905. – MONUMENTS. Dominating the chapel, Sir Richard Newman †1721, wife †1730 and son †1747 by *Sir Henry Cheere*. Also three daughters who died later. Large hanging monument. At the top an obelisk with three busts in front, his a little higher up than those of the wife and son. Below, the busts of the daughters in oval medallions. White, brown, grey and black marble. – Two more large tablets to Thomas Newman †1649, and Richard Newman, 1683.

79

Adjacent to the church the entrance gateway to FIFEHEAD HOUSE of 1807 (pulled down in 1964).

Three well-executed vernacular-style ESTATE COTTAGES of *c.* 1925 to the W of the church, along the main village street.

FIFEHEAD NEVILLE

7010

ALL SAINTS. Only the C14 chancel arch with continuous cham-fered mouldings survived a remodelling of the nave in 1736. This has arched windows, like those of Blandford, and a square-headed S doorway. Awkward W bellcote, erected after demolition of the tower in 1736. N aisle of *c.* 1500, also with C18 windows; Perp arcade with piers of standard section. The abaci have small lozenge motifs, but the E respond has an angel (cf. Marnhull), partly defaced. Chancel rebuilt in 1873. – COMMUNION RAIL. Oak, late C17, with turned balusters. – PULPIT. C18 with fielded panelling. – FONT. C14, octagonal. Bowl of Purbeck stone on a greensand stem and base. – STAINED GLASS. E window of *c.* 1880, almost certainly by *Clayton & Bell*. – MONUMENTS. Robert Ryves †1658. With an open pediment and a thick garland over it. – William Salkeld †1715. A cartouche.

In the churchyard to the N a brick MAUSOLEUM, in the form of a large chest tomb. Headstones clamped around the sides, the earliest to Charles Brune (†1703).

The MANOR HOUSE backs on to the W boundary of the church-yard. Late C17, but most visible features are C18 and early C19.

THE OLD RECTORY, ⅛ m. E. 1863 by *Edward Mondey* of Dorchester. Pointed windows, but hardly Gothic.

PACKHORSE BRIDGE, ¼ m. E. Possibly medieval. Two pointed arches crossing the River Divelish alongside a ford.

LOWER FIFEHEAD FARM, Fifehead St Quintin, ½ m. SE. Enthusiasts may want to make a pilgrimage to see the two early C16 upper windows in a block set back from the road. Three arched lights each, with hoodmoulds carved, and this is the unusual thing, to look like ropes. A C17 wing projects forward. – BARN alongside the road with the date 1881 in the brickwork.

ROMAN VILLA, ⅜ m. E. In a field called Verlands two wings of an extensive Roman villa were uncovered in 1881 and in 1902–5. About 1850 nearly twenty cartloads of worked stone were dug out of this field to be used in buildings in the village. The wing with rooms containing mosaics was orientated E–W, and measured over 120 by 50 ft (37 by 16 metres). At the W end a room measuring 13 by 12 ft (4 by 3.7 metres) had a mosaic with a design of a two-handled chalice set in a circle within two concentric borders, the inner border containing seven fishes, the outer four dolphins. This design was set in a square with stylized leaves in the four corner triangles. On the N and S were strips of dentil pattern, the whole thing surrounded by a crowstep border. To the S of this room was a rectangular plunge-bath, and to the W the remains of a hypocaust system. At the E end of the same block a mosaic floor of a room 19½ ft (6 metres) square had a design with a female bust, and a staff or spear, in a central roundel, surrounded by geometrical designs. In another room of the same size to the E, fragments of mosaic survived. In a room to the S, measuring 19 by 17 ft (5.8 by 5.2 metres), was a damaged mosaic floor with 'heads in a circle' carried on a hypocaust. One of the rings had a chi-rho monogram, the other a dove with olive branches and a chi-rho monogram. The other wing, of 160 by 24 ft (49 by 7 metres), ran N–S from the E end of the main block. It appears to have contained two barns.

FIFEHEAD ST QUINTIN
see FIFEHEAD NEVILLE

3090

FISHPOND
Whitchurch Canonicorum

ST JOHN THE BAPTIST. 1852; the name of the architect seems unrecorded. A chapel of great simplicity (visually crushed by the huge electricity pylon next to it). Lancets. W bellcote. Well-chosen sanctuary FLOORING of rough and polished slate squares by *John Stark & Partners*, 1963. Also very good PEWS of the mid C20. – STAINED GLASS. E window by *Arthur E. Buss*, 1967. Semi-abstract.

6080

FLEET

The village hardly has a coherent centre, although it is memorably placed beside the eponymous waters trapped by Chesil Beach.

OLD CHURCH, ¼ m. SSE of the new. Medieval of uncertain date. Only the chancel remains after the sea swept away the rest in 1824. – MONUMENTS. Two brass plates with kneeling families in stone surrounds with nearly semicircular open pediments. Also a slate tablet in a similar surround. All of the inscriptions are in Latin. The brasses commemorate Margaret Mohun †1603 and Maximilian Mohun †1612; the slate tablet is for Francis Mohun †1711/12. The earlier surrounds must be of about 1670; the later copies the style but with early C18 detailing, e.g. the scalloping and winged cherub's head.

HOLY TRINITY. 1827–9 for the Rev. George Gould by *William Strickland*.* The Commissioners' type, but with a nice personal touch inside. Outside is its w tower (with a delicate quatrefoil band on the W face), nave with long two-light Perp windows and buttresses between, and a short chancel with polygonal apse. But inside the nave has a low-pitched plaster roof with long thin arched panels starting from the walls and meeting the apexes of their arches at the ridge. In the chancel the scale is smaller and the arrangement prettier. Three shafts in the angles between the chancel and the polygonal apse and little plaster vaults with Dec motifs over the apse and over the oblong spaces on the N and S sides of the chancel. – PEWS of 1892. – FONT. Neo-Norman in an early C19 way. – ROYAL ARMS. Of either George IV or William IV. A carved stone panel. – STAINED GLASS. E window by *Powell & Sons*, 1886. The nave windows are also by *Powell* and of this date, using their patent stamped quarries. In the high W window fragments of the original, rather vibrant, enamelled glass scheme. – MONUMENT. John Gould †1818. An excellent piece, unsigned. A young man, looking Roman, supports a mourning young woman by an urn. On the r. an allegorical female with a bible.

MOONFLEET MANOR HOTEL (formerly Fleet House), 1 m. W. E-facing block of *c.* 1720 for Robert Mohun. Seven bays of sashes with architraves and keystones. Central Ionic porch with a bay above, later enclosed. Enlarged for John Gould, 1806, when the roofs were made hipped. Minor internal alteration by *Lutyens* for Lady Noble (the granddaughter of I. K. Brunel), 1931.

FOLKE   6010

The centre of the village, at the end of a lane, has little more than the church, manor house and rectory.

---

*This may have been the American architect of that name who was visiting England at that time.

ST LAWRENCE. Rebuilt in 1628 and fully furnished at that time. Perhaps by *William Arnold* (and so attributed by Mark Girouard). As for the architecture, the dominant motif is triplet windows: two little, the middle one taller, the heads with uncusped depressed arches, and a hoodmould stepping up and down. It is exactly the same as at Leweston in 1616 and very similar to St Katherine Cree in London of 1628–31. The church certainly wants to appear Gothic. It is e.g. embattled, and has a W tower which, though the semicircular stair projection is incorrect and has a half-domed top, could pass with many as Perp.* But the crocketed corner pinnacles are too diminutive, and the belfry openings have stone grilles of a diagonal grid. The arcades inside on the other hand are more Jacobean than Perp. Octagonal piers with big flutes (almost round-headed niches) to each face. Billeted capitals and bold mouldings to the pointed arches. Their soffits have fleurons. Restoration of 1875–6 by *William Farrall*, probably working under *Carpenter & Ingelow*. – COMMUNION RAIL. Heavy turned legs. Some elaboration of the upper and lower rails. – SCREENS. Wholly Jacobean, with big strapwork. Even so, however, the arches are pointed. So is the archway in the N arcade, also with big strapwork, which may once have led to the family pew. – LECTERN. Just a desk attached to the screen. Elaborated with fluting, reeding and a floriated pattern. – PULPIT. Octagonal. A fret design to the upper panels; reeding to the lower (cf. Holnest). An old photograph in the church shows that it was originally canopied. – HOURGLASS STAND by the pulpit. Metal frame. – FONT. A strongly detailed piece, very much in the *Arnold* mould. Twisted stem; octagonal bowl, fluted and gadrooned. Vitruvian-scrolled edge. COVER with inturned volutes, decorated. – STALLS. Two sets. Those in the choir early C17. The ends have elegant scrolls and shell finials. Elsewhere of 1875–6, taking up the round-topped theme, again with shell motifs, and with knob finials. – HATCHMENTS. One, dated 1658, an achievement of arms of Henning. – STAINED GLASS. E window by *W.F. Dixon*, 1878. A window in the N aisle is probably by *Heaton, Butler & Bayne*, †1883. – MONUMENT. Thomas Chafe (†1701) and others, dated 1730. A fine cartouche against a drapery background.

MANOR HOUSE, opposite the church. Rubble stone to a dog-leg plan, the main range running N–S, a S cross-wing, and an E range linking with the slightly lower NE wing. This last is thought to represent the original manor house, dating from *c.* 1500. This cannot be readily discerned externally, since its fenestration consists of mullioned or mullioned-and-transomed windows, largely of the early and late C17. One feature of the earlier date (if indeed it came from here) can be seen on the exterior of the main range of the house, which is structurally of *c.* 1600. This is a re-set window of two lights and

---

*The tower appears to be of a different build to the main body of the church. Is it somewhat later? A blocked N doorway looks C18.

a transom, each of the lights with two-centred-arched heads. This is positioned above a C17 arched doorway, itself re-set (in the early C19). At the centre of the E range is a compartment ceiling in the location of the hall. It is unclear whether this was a later C16 insertion, or whether the hall was originally ceiled. To its W, i.e. in line with the gabled porch of *c.* 1600 in the nook of the wings, was a screens passage. Indications of this are found in the beam at this point, and the survival of a triangular-headed doorway (although this could equally be part of a refit *c.* 1600). A solar was to the E, now subsumed into later service rooms. The main N–S range has internal features that are more consistently *c.* 1600. Its two-storey gabled porch (mentioned above) has a round-arched doorway with a carved keystone. In the SW corner of the hall are a pair of oak-framed, triangular-headed doorways, one leading to a contemporary staircase rising through three storeys. This – almost identical to the staircase at West Hall (*see* below) – has newels with turned columns set upon them and turned balusters that are symmetrical vertically, and is housed in a W-facing projection. At the S end of the range, a cross-wing contains the principal rooms: drawing room below with early C17 panelling, main bedchamber above. Both have fireplaces with four-centred moulded stone arches. The S side has an off-centre, two-storey canted bay window, probably also early C17.

To the NNE of the church, a MOATED SITE may represent the location of an even earlier manor house.

FOLKE HOUSE (former rectory), ⅛ m. N. Late C17. Extended W by *G.R. Crickmay*, 1884. Much of the S-facing fenestration is of this date. Also the tall diagonal-shafted chimneys.

WEST HALL, ½ m. SW. Rubble stone. Over-restoration and a big N addition of 1924 (for Thomas Eccles) somewhat undermine its historic character. Nevertheless, there is much to enjoy. As with Folke Manor, the NE range seems to be the earliest, of the C15 for the Hymerford family: see its lower roof-line and, inside, the arch-braced collar-beam roof with cusped wind-braces. Otherwise all is early C17 for Sir Thomas Mullins: a range at right angles, with the porch, typically, in the nook between the old range and the new, and, towards the W, wings coming forward, that on the r. for the staircase, that on the l. cross-gabled and meant for downstairs private rooms. Hollow-chamfered mullioned windows with hoodmoulds, the lower windows in the cross-gabled wing mullioned-and-transomed crosses. In *c.* 1700 (for Thomas Chafe) the SW angle was filled in and given another gable to the W, with a hoodmoulded two-lighter in the gable. As built, the main windows would no doubt have had timber mullions and transoms with leaded casements in moulded stone surrounds with little keystones. These were converted to sashes in the mid C18, nine panes over nine.

The porch leads into a C17 cross-passage, with the HALL extending to its l. The most memorable feature of the house comes here, where from the SW corner two big stone arches lead to parlours downstairs and upstairs. The arches are round-headed and have huge faceted keystones. They are not unlike other work attributed to *William Arnold*. Perhaps he worked here while rebuilding the church, i.e. *c*. 1630. The STAIRCASE seems earlier, *c*. 1600, a fine piece of stout Jacobean joinery (cf. Folke Manor, above). Vertically symmetrical turned balusters. Newel posts shaped as tapering Tuscan columns. The stairs rise the full height of the house in short flights round a narrow rectangular well. Inside the SW wing of *c*. 1700 a fine room with bolection panelling.

FONT LE ROI, ¾ m. ENE. Rubble stone, and more delicately repaired than Folke's other two houses, so that one can see what beauty of texture they have lost. Here too there is a C15 and an early C17 part. C15 gateway range, the main entrance merely with a baulk of timber across the top, the blocked arch for pedestrians l. of it two-centred, with a big chamfer. This must have led to an earlier house, since lost. Attached to its S corner an early C17 house. Facing NW a handsome gabled bay of perhaps the second quarter of the C17. Its lower room has a plaster ceiling with thin ribs and sprigs of flowers (repaired in 1938), and to light it a splendid window encompassing the bay with six lights, the outer two blocked, under a single hoodmould. Ovolo-moulded mullions. Above, a three-light window, *en suite*. Also a small three-light window to the gabled wing adjoining l.

FONTMELL MAGNA

A large village mixing low-eaved thatched cottages with Early Victorian brick-and-flint estate buildings. Its centre, at the crossroads with the A350, is almost industrial in character, dominated by the former brewery.

ST ANDREW. Mostly rebuilt 1862–3 by *George Evans* of Wimborne, for Sir Richard Plumptre Glyn of Gaunt's House. Large and lavish, of greensand ashlar with rusty-orange Mapperton freestone dressings. C15 four-stage W tower with a rectangular SE stair-turret and pinnacled battlemented parapet. Its upper stage and silhouette are entirely Evans. Another distinguishing feature of the church is the parapet of solid quatrefoils with openwork panelling over. It runs right round the building and is developed from a length which is genuine Perp, dated 1530 (Hutchins saw the date). This was on the S porch but is now on the N aisle. It has many different motifs in the quatrefoils. The interior has arcades with standard piers, but Evans's capitals have High Victorian angel busts and naturalistic foliage. One base (NE) is genuine Perp. Also fine are the carved roof corbels. – The CHOIR STALLS are *Evans*'s typical Gothic type (carving by

B. Grassby); the nave PEWS are plainer (and later?). – SANCTUARY FLOOR of *Minton* encaustic tiles. – PULPIT. Richly carved in Todber stone by *Blentham* (with figures by *Boulton*). Entered through the N chancel arch pier. – FONT. Mid-C12 (reinstated in 1958), of cauldron shape. The bowl has rather irregular trails and eight birds. – SCREEN. First half of the C16, re-set under the tower arch. Dado with linenfold panelling. One-light divisions with pretty tracery. – ROYAL ARMS of George III. Framed canvas. – STAINED GLASS. E window and two chancel s windows by *Clayton & Bell*, *c.* 1868. Beautifully coloured W window by *O'Connor & Taylor*, 1874. A window in the N aisle by *Francis Skeat*, 1960. S aisle E window by *E.J. Dilworth*, 1969.

WESLEYAN METHODIST CHURCH (former), Church Street. The older part is of 1831, ashlar, with round-arched windows. The later part, l., is of 1874, brick and Gothic.

The key buildings in the VILLAGE are grouped around the triangle formed by the junction between Crown Hill, Lurmer Street (A350) and The Knapp. From the W, along Crown Hill, CROSS HOUSE stands out as an assertively symmetrical house of the late C16; three gables, echoed by the later porch. It was extended to the r. in the early C19. Next a gabled brick building dated 1846, presumably once part of the adjacent brewery. It has a Gothic niche-hood re-set high in the gable, no doubt salvaged from the medieval church. The main part of the BREWERY, dated 1876, is next, overshadowing the stucco-fronted terrace of the early C19 former CROWN INN.

On the E side of Lurmer Street, alongside the Fontmell Brook, COACH HOUSE, a housing development of 2005 by *Peter Thompson Architects*. This is an effective exercise in fitting sensitively into the historic streetscape, mixing classical and vernacular features (as at Poundbury, Dorchester). Just to its N, also on Lurmer Street, Nos. 27–29, a C15 timber-framed house (later subdivided) with, at its core, three cruck bays of a former hall. Undulating thatched roof with a central gable.

FONTMELL HOUSE (former vicarage), Parsonage Street, ¼ m. SE. 1871, probably by *Evans*, for the Rev. George C. Glyn. Large, in extensive grounds. Brick with a bell-turret and some Gothic windows.

There are two minor pleasures to be found further out: WOODBRIDGE MILL, 1½ m. NW, early C19 with a mansard roof; and MANOR FARM, ⅝ m. N, a perfect farmhouse group. Here the long ashlar farmhouse is of the C17, with four-light mullioned windows with hoodmoulds, supported on the l. by a stone barn and on the r. by a black tarred barn (both alas now converted to dwellings). Above them rises the abrupt slope of Fontmell Down.

FONTMELL HILL HOUSE, 1½ m. E. 1929–30 for *Balfour Gardiner* the composer, to his own designs, helped by *Basil Sutton*. Roughcast. In a style based on, say, the early Baillie Scott.

CROSS-DYKES on Fontmell Down, 1 m. NE. Prehistoric.

FORDE ABBEY

Forde Abbey was founded initially at Brightley, Devon, as a Cistercian house from Waverley, Surrey, in 1136. It was transferred
to Forde in 1141. At the Dissolution, when the establishment
had declined to the abbot and just twelve monks, the abbey was
granted to Sir Richard Pollard (son of the Lord Chief Justice of
the Common Pleas). Either Pollard, his son, or William Rosewell
(the owner from 1581 to 1593) is likely to have demolished the
abbey church itself, which lay in the standard position on the
s side of a cloister of which only the N walk remains. In 1649
the abbey was bought from Sir Henry Rosewell by Edmund
Prideaux, Attorney General under Cromwell. When Prideaux
acquired Forde, certain of the monastic buildings had already
been converted to dwelling rooms, although precisely what was
done is lost in later alterations. The work seems also to have
included the creation of a private chapel in the former chapter
house (Sir Henry Rosewell was investigated for holding a private
Puritan chapel here in 1634). Prideaux continued the process,
incorporating more of the monastery into his mansion. He possibly employed the London surveyor *Edward Carter* as architect.
(Carter worked on the Inner Temple when Prideaux was Treas-
urer there, also in the 1650s.) Further work was carried out for
Francis Gwyn and his successors in the C18. So the building as
we see it now combines the Middle Ages – chiefly the mid to
late C12 and early C13 – and the early C16, with Prideaux's work
of *c.* 1650–60 and various C18 changes. The quality of the early
C16 and the Prideaux parts is among the highest in the country,
and the blend is a happy one.

Standing in front of the principal, s-facing façade, one stands
where the abbey church has been. To the r. of the centre, one
faces the N range of the cloister, a Late Perp rebuilding, and, continuing r., the chapter house in the former E cloister range, later a
private chapel; while to the l. is a block of mid-C17 domestic work
instead of the former cloister W range. To the W of that, the magnificent abbot's house, its W end converted in the mid C17. The
back of the house is more irregular, or rather less picturesquely
irregular. The most prominent feature is the former monastic
dormitory reaching out to the N from behind the chapter house.

Now all this must be looked at in detail, internally as well
as externally, and the monastic parts are in the following taken
chronologically.

EXTERIOR. The story begins with the CHAPTER HOUSE (now
the chapel) of the mid to late C12. The E window is an early
C16 alteration: five lights under a four-centred arch. The spandrels include the letters Tho Char for Thomas Chard, the last
abbot, who ruled from 1521 to the Dissolution in 1539 and of
whom we shall soon hear more. The W façade is Prideaux and
introduces the characteristics of his style instructively in an

arched doorway and a large circular window over. The cupola
is probably early C18.

For the early C13 the best evidence is the DORMITORY
RANGE (or dorter) extending N from the chapter house, 168 ft
(51 metres) long. It has an undercroft of eleven bays. (Two
further bays at the S end were altered in the early C16.) A
row of slender octagonal piers runs down the centre line.
Single-chamfered ribs extend seamlessly from them without
any capitals. The dormitory itself was on the upper floor. Its
thirteen small lancets are fully preserved to the W. To the E a
series of two-light windows were inserted in the late C16, and
any remaining C13 lancets were blocked. The gabled part at the
S end is an early C16 alteration. Also C16 is the roof, though
not visible to the public. It has arched braces up to collars and
wind-braces. The centre of the N range was the REFECTORY
(or frater), originally open to the roof, but horizontally divided
in the C14 to create a separate meat-eating area, after the Cistercian rule on that point was relaxed. It was also originally
longer, but shortened at the N end in the C15. W of the refectory
is the KITCHEN, projecting to the N as far as the refectory, but
originally shorter. The big chimney is C17, but in the W wall is
a tall C15 mullioned window.

The Dec is in fact missing from the abbey chronology, and
the C15 is weak, but the Perp – the latest and most elaborate Perp – without any doubt dominates. This is owing to
the ambition of Abbot Chard, who commenced a programme
of rebuilding, curtailed by the Dissolution, beginning on the
grandest scale with his own accommodation. His princely
Great Hall, intended for the lavish entertainment of lay guests
(on whom the monastery's patronage depended) as well as for
his own luxury, is preceded by a PORCH of equal pretence. It is   48
a tower so elaborate that it must be described motif by motif.
An entrance with a three-centred-arched head leads into a fan-
vaulted lobby. Above is a two-storey oriel, each tier on the front
face with six narrow lights above a transom and three below
(the last as simplified by Prideaux). Lozenges, shields, etc.,
in the two sill zones, buttress-shafts at the angles, a top frieze
and battlements. The shields in the lower panel are those of
donors, probably of the Redvers and Courtenay families; those
in the upper panels relate to Chard himself. That in the parapet
includes the inscription: 'Anno Dni millesimo Quingentes-
imo vicesimo octavo a domino factum est Thomas Charde
Abbate' ('made by Abbot Thomas Chard, master, A.D. 1528').
The porch leads into the E bay of the GREAT HALL, a hall of
five bays (but originally seven) with large four-light windows
with transoms and very slightly segmental tops, originally to
N as well as S. Again a top frieze and battlements. In the frieze
one notices certain Renaissance motifs. So this is when the
Renaissance comes in, i.e. c. 1525–35. The pedimented sundial
is an addition of c. 1700.

Chard's work continued to the w. Here were his private rooms, but they have been totally remodelled. Also, the three window bays to the r. here represent two original bays of Chard's hall, as remodelled for Prideaux. Chard is however picked up in the concave-sided polygonal angle buttress at the sw corner (there was most likely a similar buttress on the se corner of this tower-like w section) and one more four-light upper window around the corner. Above the latter a carved panel and a blocked opening. At the back of this w end of the range more single Renaissance panels, some no doubt displaced.

Once work on his own lodgings was complete, Chard began to re-do the CLOISTER. He started with the N range, but even this was not completed. The bays each have a large four-light window with a transom. The storey above was added c. 1655, with an embattled parapet of the early c18. Windows each with moulded architraves and an entablature with a pulvinated frieze. The sashes with polygonal lights are mid-c18.

Now for Prideaux. Externally his, apart from the chapterhouse front, is the centre of the s front, where the cloister w range once was, though the one-storey loggia projecting s is early c18, altered in the early c19. Behind and above this is Prideaux's SALOON, its front with two straight-headed windows flanking a higher arched one, and above the straight-headed

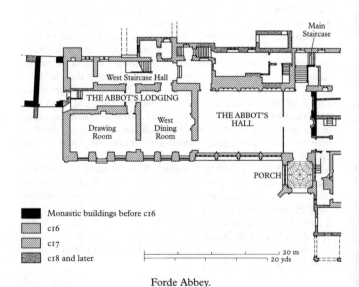

Forde Abbey.
Plan

windows horizontally placed ovals. The battlements are continued. The bays W of the great hall are also Prideaux's. They
have simple architraves and plain aprons. The central window
of the three on the top floor to the l. has a segmental arch,
making a crude Venetian-window motif.

INTERIOR. First the GREAT HALL. As built, this would have
been some 85 ft (26 metres) long, making it one of the largest
abbatial halls in England (perhaps the largest). It was originally
lit on the S by six large windows (of which four survive) and on
the N by seven, but that over the chimneypiece is a blank. When
the W two bays were taken out of the hall in the mid C17, the

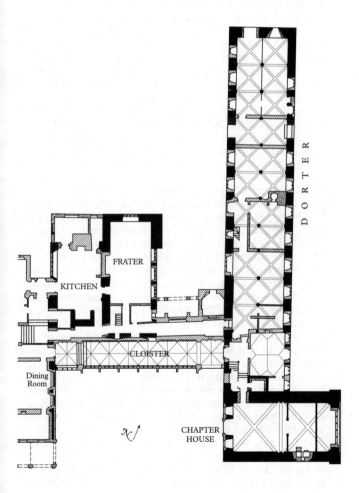

original chimneypiece was moved one bay E to remain nearly central. The elaborately panelled ceiling is curiously unaligned on the wall divisions and, to confirm its original extent, it continues in the roof-space above the bedrooms at the W end. Nevertheless, it is a design of some subtlety. Low-pitched and subdivided into bays, cross-ribs making compartments, each with further diagonal ribbing and a central boss. Also bosses at the rib intersections but not along the main transverse ribs, to preserve the line. In the cellar below the Hall W end, evidence that the Hall had a s-facing oriel window, while parts of a dais panel are visible in a bedroom above the West Dining Room.

Prideaux's rooms have outstanding woodwork and outstanding plasterwork. The main rooms are the WEST DINING ROOM and DRAWING ROOM, both W of the Great Hall, and the SALOON, constructed in the first floor of the stub of the former cloister W range. Also the main STAIRCASE. They represent two stages: so-called Artisan Mannerism and Wren classical. Of the first stage the two rooms w of the Great Hall. Both are panelled with pilasters, and have overmantels that display characteristics of Artisan Mannerism: pilasters growing out of volutes or of claws, and wholly broken pediments. The bunchy garlands on the Ionic capitals of the West Dining Room fireplace are typical. This room also has fluted Corinthian pilasters between wall panels that are divided by a strange criss-cross at mid-height, while the Drawing Room has plain pilasters setting off its late C16 Flemish tapestries and a simpler, bolection-moulded fireplace. Plasterwork in both of these rooms also belongs to the earlier phase: it is all post-Jacobean – no ribs or bands but wreaths, no all-over design but single geometrical schemes of round, oval, oblong panels. The principal features are close garlands of fruit, flowers and leaves – big, fat, juicy leaves – and decidedly rustic figures.

The STAIRCASE of course has its own type of woodwork. The telling feature is the pierced luscious foliage panels instead of balusters and the carved vases of flowers upon each newel. In the ceiling is a date, 1658. These openwork leaf panels were in fact the height of fashion in the 1650s (cf. Ham House, Richmond, London 1638, Thorpe Hall, Peterborough c. 1655, and Durham Castle 1665). Here and in the adjacent SALOON, the plasterwork has foliage trails that are thinner and more elegant, although the ribs in the Saloon have anachronistic Jacobean pendants at the intersections, combined with a modillion cornice and classical frieze. Otherwise, in the Saloon the games have stopped, and a noble restraint reigns. The walls have giant Corinthian fluted pilasters, and both overmantel and doorcase have segmental pediments. The walls here are hung with Mortlake tapestries, given by Queen Anne to Francis Gwyn c. 1713, when he was her Secretary at War. Prideaux also introduced a suite of rooms adjacent to the Saloon, and above the cloister N walk. Most were later redecorated by the Gwyn family in the C18, but one, the OAK ROOM, retains its mid-C17 plaster ceiling.

Next, two interiors from the monastic phase. First the N walk
of the CLOISTER, where the tracery pattern of the large four-
light Perp windows is repeated as blank panels on the N wall
within. That is except in one place, where the C13 arcading of
the LAVATORIUM has been exposed. The vault is of plaster and
must be early C19. Secondly the upper floor of the REFECTORY
was made into a LIBRARY in the early C19. However one can
still see the C15 recess in the NE angle which belonged to the
reading pulpit and also the fine roof with arches formed by
braces up to collars, and wind-braces as saltire crosses.

So this leaves the CHAPEL, built in the mid to late C12 as
the chapter house. Two spacious rib-vaulted bays, the responds
oddly recessed in the walls and with scallop capitals, the transverse arch with two rolls, the ribs triplets of thinner rolls. The
W and E arches have chevron. It has a SCREEN of c. 1655 with
bunchy garlands on its pulvinated frieze and, above the door,
a length of pierced foliage. Above this is a segmental pediment
broken by a panel of the Prideaux arms. – PULPIT. Of c. 1710.
A curious arrangement with panelled pilasters and the reading
desk front raised up. Recessed, with a half-projecting tester.
A circular window gives it back-light. – ORGAN. Early C19,
Gothick. – MONUMENTS. Edmund Prideaux †1659 (but of
1704). Pedimented with urn and cartouches of arms. – Francis
Prideaux †1677. Tablet with scrolled pediment. Also a small
figure of a woman and a skeleton at the top. – Mrs Gwyn
†1808. By R. Blore. With a sad angel.

The GARDENS were first laid out for Francis Gwyn in the early
C18. There were a series of formal avenues of which the LONG
WALK, running parallel and to the S of the house, is the chief
survival. Also incorporated into the scheme were the series of
monastic fish ponds, one of which acts as a reflecting pool to
the SW of the house. In the second half of the C19 the layout
was softened with more colourful, typically Victorian, 'Garden-
esque' planting.

FORDINGTON see DORCHESTER

FRAMPTON   6090

Frampton has unmistakably the air of an estate village. The cottages are not uniform, but they line up along one side of the road,
hidden from the park by a belt of trees. Around 1840 the landowner, Richard Brinsley Sheridan (grandson of the playwright),
demolished the cottages on the parkland side of the road.

ST MARY. Here is an odd W tower indeed: Perp at first sight,
but how did the two tiers of fat big Tuscan columns get to the
angles above the ground stage? Whoever was responsible for

this tower wanted to do it Perp yet modern. The responsible
man was Robert Browne of Frampton Court, and his tower is
dated 1695. Also not really Perp are the square-headed bell-
openings and the obelisk-like pinnacles. In the s wall a re-set
Perp doorway of *c.* 1500. What embraces the tower is more
Gothic, but just as easily recognizable as not the real article.
The wide aisles, wider than the nave, are early C18, remodelled
1820 (N), and 1871 by *Benjamin Ferrey* (s). What gives the
date away is the pretty and showy openwork parapets and
pinnacles, and the placing of the s porch in the middle of
the aisle. Big w windows with archaeologically correct Perp
tracery. The early C18 date for the N aisle is hidden by the later
remodelling (except for the central round-headed window).
The chancel was rebuilt in High Victorian Gothic in 1862 by
Ferrey (having been previously rebuilt, 1747–8). The aisle
arcades have standard elements. The s arcade is essentially
C15, with its capitals with carvings of men and rope quoits. The
chancel arch too is convincing standard Perp. Leaf capitals.
The N arcade is an alteration of 1878–9 intended to match
the s.

Inside one notices the lavish spaces and rich furnishings.
Much of 1820, with many exceptionally good tablets of earlier
dates, generally concentrated in the N aisle. Richer still the rebuilt
chancel by *Ferrey*. Polychrome banded masonry. – REREDOS by
Ferrey, 1868. A gabled niche triplet, with flanking arcading.
Much stone inlay and mosaic (including Maltese stone). The
carving here is by *Thomas Earp*. – Chancel encaustic TILE-
WORK by *Minton*. – Two MOSAIC ANGELS above the chancel
arch by *Powell & Sons*, 1879. – PULPIT. Sculptural panels
set into a Ham Hill framework. Three of the panels may be
C15, but they are much reworked. The others are of 1862 by
Grassby. – FONT. An elaborate piece by *Earp*, 1862. – Extensive
set of well-detailed BOX PEWS, their carved ends by *Thomas
Champion*, son of the Frampton Estate foreman. – STAINED
GLASS. The church was thoroughly fitted out with glass over
the second half of the C19. First the E window and four chancel
side windows by *Lavers & Barraud*, 1862. Also by them the
central round-arched window in the N aisle. In the s aisle
a window by *Powell & Sons*, 1871, and another to the E of
the doorway reportedly of German manufacture, *c.* 1871. Two
large w windows by *Clayton & Bell*, †1888 and †1890. Another
smaller window by them in the N aisle, †1884.

MONUMENTS. Set in gabled recesses in the side walls of
the chancel upon C19 tomb-chests (with carving by *Grassby*)
the following effigies. Rear-Admiral Sir John Browne †1627
and his wife. Two recumbent effigies and some saved pieces
from the dismantled monument. – Joane Coker and her son
William Coker †1653. Small effigy of an infant in a winding
sheet. – Then, chronologically, the principal piece, the memorial to Robert Browne of the tower, who died in 1734. It is a
reredos in type and is placed in the middle of the N aisle wall

so that two pairs of large Corinthian columns and a coffered arch frame not a painting or a relief but an arched window. There is no effigy, but the long inscription praises the deceased and refers to his having built the tower, the 'Isle' and Frampton Court. – Ann Browne †1714. Small tablet with a lively bust in a medallion, rather like a portrait in a Second Empire Paris salon. – Frances Browne †1740. White urn against an obelisk-shaped grey marble background. – John Browne †1750. White and grey marble with free-standing bust. Columns l. and r., and outside them palm branches growing out of volutes. Broken pediment with two putti and a shield. The long inscription ought to be read. – Frances Browne, 1751. Obelisk and urn. – Robert Browne †1772. By *John Ford* of Bath. Marbles of several colours. Relief of a woman seated by an urn. – John Browne †1771. Also by *Ford*. With a similar scene, but here she sits in a churchyard. – Frances Browne †1806, signed by *(Sir) R. Westmacott*. No figure, but a marble tablet. – Francis John Browne †1833. Similar, but more Grecian. By *William Croggon*. – Finally, by *E. Fuchs*, 1902, Richard Brinsley Sheridan, portrait in a medallion, with an architectural surround.

FRAMPTON COURT, the seat of the Brownes and Sheridans (*see above*), of 1704 with two later phases of enlargement, was demolished in 1932–5. Its loss removes the obvious focus of the riverside park. However the PEACOCK BRIDGE, ⅜ m. SE, remains, taking the E entrance drive over the River Frome. It is of stone, three segmental arches with a top balustrade, elegantly expensive but a standard mid-C18 design. – SAMWAYS BRIDGE, 300 yds W of the church on the W drive. Late C18. Brick with chinoiserie timber railings. – Also surviving, two sides of the former COACH HOUSE and STABLES, *c.* 1780. Converted to houses *c.* 1950. These include a pedimented carriage archway, now blocked.

HOME OF THE HOMELESS, an almshouse by the church, dated 1868. By *B. Ferrey*. Rock-faced, with gables and plate tracery.

HYDE CROOK, ¾ m. N. 1936 by *John Proctor*. A large, two-storey flat-roofed block. Brick, later rendered.

ROMAN AQUEDUCT. *See* Dorchester, p. 264.

FROME ST QUINTIN   *5000*

A single street with only two buildings of note, the church – approached over a meadow – and Frome House.

ST MARY. Nave and chancel late C13 with C14 Dec and C15 Perp alterations, i.e. one lancet, one pointed-trefoiled lancet, one window with reticulated tracery, one straight-headed Perp window. C14 Perp NW tower of rendered flint with stone bands.

An 1881 restoration saw the external refacing of the S and
W nave walls and unfortunately the scraping of the nave
interior as well. – FURNISHINGS. A complete set of, presumably, 1881 (although the PULPIT is 1899). Many brass
candleholders and oil lamps. Also the Caen stone ALTAR with
polished granite top and its matching REREDOS. The former
incorporates a sculpted panel, the latter a mosaic Crucifixion. Less happy is the shiny-tiled chancel dado. – FONT. C13.
Octagonal, Purbeck marble, each side with two shallow blank
pointed arches. – SCULPTURE. A C12 corbel carved with a
muzzled boar's head, re-set above the pulpit. – STAINED
GLASS. E window by *Heaton, Butler & Bayne*, 1896. – MONU-
MENT. George Baker †1803. White marble oval with blank
shield, by *T. King* of Bath.

FROME HOUSE. A house of 1782 for George Baker, a rare
period in these parts, and of rare distinction. Originally no
more than three bays wide, the walls of red brick laid all
as headers, the windows with fluted keystones. Fluted string
course with paterae. Against this plain background is set the
canted porch, all of Portland ashlar. The lower storey is open
on Doric columns with fluting below the caps and fluting in
the frieze of the entablature (interrupted by rosettes in place
of triglyphs). Doorway flanked by rather pinched niches. The
upper storey is almost as open, just one large window each side,
with a little rusticated wall below and yet more fluting. So it
is the Adam vocabulary, with no loss of refinement, just of a
little urban polish. Big three-bay addition of 1913 to the l. for
Major A. Ritchie (and another to the rear of the same date).

FROME VAUCHURCH

½ m. SSE of Maiden Newton

ST FRANCIS. Small, of flint, rubble stone and roughcast render.
Nave with bellcote and chancel. Both parts are late C12.
The chief indicator is the nave N doorway (now a window)
with a solid tympanum concave on the underside and with
dogtooth on the hoodmould. Several windows also (notably
two in the chancel), and the imposts of the chancel arch
with half-dogtooth. Much C16 rebuilding, e.g. the area of
banded flint at the E end of the nave N wall, together with
refenestration. E triplet from an 1879 restoration. In the C17
the responds of the chancel arch were widened in a curious
way. Also a second pointed arch was cut through alongside,
presumably to enter the pulpit. The nave roof corbels date
from 1879; Pevsner called them 'excellent Victorian studies
in the E.E.' They have fine undemonstrative stiff-leaf decoration. – ALTAR. Stone, mid- to late C19. Three big quatrefoils
on the front. – Encaustic TILES in the sanctuary, probably by

Godwin of Hereford. – PULPIT. Early C17. Elaborate, with two tiers of enriched arched panels. – FONT. Early C13. Square bowl with chamfered corners. The base with spurs. – PEWS. With bold fleur-de-lys ends, presumably mid-C19. – STAINED GLASS. E window with stamped quarries by *Powell & Sons*, *c.* 1880.

FROME VAUCHURCH HOUSE (formerly the rectory), diagonally opposite at the crossroads. Of *c.* 1798 with major additions, *c.* 1873 by *G.R. Crickmay*. Tudor Revival. A rambling picturesque gathering. Various gables. Mullioned windows.

GAUNT'S HOUSE
Hinton Martell

0000

Large brick mansion of 1884–91 by *George Devey*, standing in a fine park with a serpentine lake. It encases, at the r. end, a five-bay villa of *c.* 1803 by *William Evans* of Wimborne. This was Devey's last country house and the outcome, partly dictated by a restrictive brief from Sir Richard George Glyn, was largely the work of his assistants. After Devey's death (1886), they formed themselves into the partnership of *Williams, West & Slade*. Hack detailing, mixing Italianate (on the broad tower near the l. end) and Dutch gables on the remainder, including the refaced villa. A few classical features, particularly the porch of paired Greek Ionic columns, reused from the villa. Unlike the present house, the villa had some refinement. Internally, the cantilevered stone staircase with its delicate wrought-iron balustrade are further indications of its quality.

STABLES, 200 yds E. Of *c.* 1888 to *Devey*'s design. Diaper brickwork.

LODGE, on the B3078 at Hinton Parva, 1 m. SW of Gaunt's House. The complete *cottage orné*, of *c.* 1803, presumably also by *William Evans*. Absurd thatched roof and thatched porches with umbrella eaves. The plan is an L with angled corners (where the porches are placed) facing the drive entrance.

96

GILLINGHAM

8020

For a small town Gillingham is (with a few exceptions noted below) singularly devoid of architecture worth noticing. This may be due in part to a destructive fire of 1694. Apart from the chancel of St Mary's church, there is nothing standing from before 1700. At that time Gillingham was one of the six most important wool-producing towns in the county. It seems then to have been a compact settlement arranged tightly around the church. Many buildings with C18 origins can be seen in that area, often with mid- to late C19 refronting or refenestration. Trade and wealth seem to have expanded after the opening of the Salisbury & Yeovil Railway in 1859. Newbury, a suburb with medieval origins on the E side of the Shreen Water, was rebuilt and grew further eastwards, with a new street heading S towards the railway station. Within ten years a brickworks, bacon-curing factory and dairy had all opened; the less-than-attractive salmon-red brick made by the first may be found throughout the town.

Of all of the small market towns in Dorset, Gillingham's architectural heritage has been least appreciated. The loss of notable local buildings, especially the Town Mills (and the Royal Hotel, Newbury), through fire damage and demolition respectively, has been followed by relatively bland redevelopment.

ST MARY. Remarkably large for its environment. The chancel, five bays long, is C14, but completely refenestrated and buttressed in 1840–1. That was just after the rebuilding of the remainder (aisled nave, N chapel and W tower) in 1838–9 by *Henry Malpas*.[*] Malpas's tower was remodelled in 1908–9 by *C. E. Ponting* and a S chapel (of the Good Shepherd) was added in 1919–21 by *W. D. Caröe*. The latter, with its ornate façade inside towards the S aisle, is the best piece of the church. Ponting's tower with its pretty doorway and Somerset tracery in the bell-openings comes second, the rest is indifferent. The pedimental gables of the two-storey porches, with huge kneelers, are as uninformed as any Georgian Gothic and heavier, and the N chapel exterior is an ugly block. This chapel replaced a C14 chapel – see the responds of the two-bay arcade with their ballflower capitals, an unusual motif. Ballflower also on the string courses outside the chancel. The Purbeck pier of the chapel arcade is of 1840–1 (but the base and capital appear reused). The CHAPEL OF THE GOOD SHEPHERD is an intense work by *Caröe*, commissioned by Carlton and Emily Cross (of Wyke Hall) as a memorial to their son, who died in the First World War. A Perp-style archway with figures in niches and carved lettering leads down steps into the chapel. Perp again the roof and a fine REREDOS with figures carved by *Nathaniel Hitch*. Hitch also did the enriched canopy terminated by winged angels. Flanking Perp stone doorways complete the composition.

MAIN REREDOS. 1925–6. Large relief of the Virgin with the Magi and the Shepherds. Designed by *H. P. Burke Downing* and carved in Nailsworth stone by *Hitch*. – PEWS. A block of C16 Perp pews at the front of the nave. Straight-topped ends; also some poppyheads. – FONT. Perp, C15. Octagonal and

---

[*] Malpas, 'Architect & Surveyor', signed the drawings and completion certificate. He took over the project from *William Walker* of Shaftesbury, who made the initial designs.

of Purbeck marble, with weathered paterae motifs. – ROYAL
ARMS in the N aisle. A splendid piece, probably of 1618. Carved
in the round and painted. – SCULPTURE. Loose on a sill in the
N aisle, a piece of Anglo-Saxon CROSS-SHAFT, C9. Fine interlace on one side; more eroded on the other two faces, although
here further traces of interlace. – STAINED GLASS. Figurative
E window of c. 1850. Seven rather dark chancel side windows
mostly of decorative and armorial glass, possibly by *Ward &
Hughes*, c. 1865. Window over the S chapel entrance, by *Powell
& Sons*, 1930. W window by *J. Dudley Forsyth*, 1910. – MONU-
MENTS. A very curious memorial tucked ignominiously behind
the organ, the Rev. John Jesop †1625 and Dr Thomas Jesop
†1615. Probably not in the original state. Two recumbent effigies (holding hands), a wall arch above the one, a totally
free-standing arch above the other. Four obelisks, illustrated
by Hutchins, have gone. Several other detached components
are stacked on Dr Jesop. – Henry Dirdoe †1724 (chancel). By
John Bastard of Blandford. Large, with three putto heads at
the top below a curved pediment. – Frances Dirdoe †1733.   80
Pedimented standing monument with a large relief panel of
three standing figures representing, according to the inscription, Mrs Dirdoe and her sisters. Probably designed by Nathaniel Ireson. – Edward Read †1779. By *Francis Lancashire &
Son* of Bath. Another large tablet.

ST GEORGE, Langham Lane, 1 m. W. A delightful thatched   118
building of 1921 by *C.E. Ponting*, for the Manger family of
Stock Hill House (in memory of their son, another who died
in the First World War; cf. St Mary, above). Arts and Crafts in
character, with the thatch rolling over the gables and around
the apsed E end and miniature N transept. Timber bellcote at
the W end and a timber-framed porch. Simplicity rules the
interior, the only show being the carved timber bosses of the
timber-ribbed plaster roof.

CEMETERIES, Cemetery Road. LODGE of c. 1865. Gothic, of local
brick, with an earlier-looking stone carriage archway leading
into the cemetery. A second cemetery, 150 yds further on, was
opened in 1890. Its Nonconformist MORTUARY CHAPEL is a
simple buttressed building.

BAPTIST CHAPEL, Newbury. A Gothic replacement of 1892–3 in
local brick by *T. Hudson*, for a stone Romanesque-style building of 1858–9 that stood next door.

PRIMITIVE METHODIST CHAPEL (former), Queen Street.
Dated 1876. Round-arched style, with a pair of towers topped
by pyramid roofs.

WESLEYAN METHODIST CHURCH, High Street. Dated 1877, by
T. Hudson (and costing £2,920). Gothic, rock-faced Mendip
stone, with a prominent spire on the SW corner balanced by a
staircase projection.

A PERAMBULATION need go no further than ST MARTIN'S
SQUARE, past the E wall of the churchyard, and a brief look
at the HIGH STREET, which becomes Newbury as it heads
E towards the railway. The former VICARAGE (now part of

Rawson Court), of 1883, on the corner opposite the church, is quite a strong design, by *E. Swinfen Harris*, with memories of Street and Webb in its half-hipped gables. It incorporates stained glass by *Gibbs & Howard*. The one-storey OUTBUILD-INGS along St Martin's Square, adapted *c.* 1820 for a Sunday School, are probably medieval in the walling. Next comes LIME TREE HOUSE, a nice, very typical, house of *c.* 1720. Stone. Five windows wide, two high, with a hipped roof. The windows in moulded stone surrounds with key blocks. The doorway slightly stressed by having ears and an entablature. The next house, *c.* 1885, is typical of the post-railway building of Gillingham. In a hard salmon-red brick. Mixed style with some terracotta details. Opposite, the square is neatly closed off by the s-facing BROADHAYES of *c.* 1840, with its low-pitched hipped roof and wide sash windows.

Returning s, turning r., HIGH STREET has a group of early C17 buildings with mid-C19 refenestration (e.g. the RED LION), as it leads into THE SQUARE, with the view closed by a shaped-gabled brick house of *c.* 1880. Wyke Street, beyond, was cut off by the by-pass *c.* 1995.

From The Square, SOUTH STREET runs e and passes the early C19 town LOCK-UP (a simple pitched-roofed building with a vestigial pediment over the doorway) before turning N into HIGH STREET. Turning r. and heading e towards the station, over the COUNTY BRIDGE (dated 1800) across the Shreen Water, we enter uninspiring post-railway expansion. In the car park, the WAR MEMORIAL of 1920 by *W. Morrish* of Gillingham, moved here from its original position in the High Street. Ham Hill stone with a crocket-enriched niche head.*
In NEWBURY the sole item of more than local note is the splendid Baroque former NATWEST BANK, on the corner of Station Road, s. 1900–2 by *Sir George Oatley*, originally built for Stuckey's Bank (and costing £4,449). Local limestone with red pointing – the last an Oatley characteristic – and Ham Hill dressings. Advantage is taken of the corner site, with an angled entrance portico-porch. The RAILWAY STATION itself, ⅓ m. SE of St Mary's, is a standard design by *Sir William Tite*, largely as erected by the Salisbury & Yeovil Railway in 1859. Across the car park the former SOUTH WESTERN HOTEL of *c.* 1860, now missing its decorative bargeboards.

KNAPP HOUSE, ¼ m. SW. Probably late C17 in origin, refronted in ashlar in the mid to late C18. An early C19 wing projects forward, somewhat spoiling the long informal façade.

WYKE BREWERY, ¾ m. w. Of *c.* 1860. Looming over the road, an incredible affair that manages to look ecclesiastical while being Italianate in the details. Now converted to flats.

WYKE HALL, 1 m. w. A late C17 farmhouse core, much expanded in several phases. First, *c.* 1820 for John Farquhar in Tudor-esque style; second, at the s end and dated 1853 on rainwater

---

*The TOWN MILLS that stood back on the N side beyond the memorial were burnt down in 1981.

heads, in a more *cottage orné* style for George Whieldon; and third, just after 1913 at the N end, for Carlton Cross. Some original mullioned windows survive on the E front at the centre of the house.

STOCK HILL, 1¼ m. W. Of *c.* 1870, for Major Matthews, owner of the Wyke Brewery. In an informal, vaguely Italianate style in its small parkland. Matching LODGE.

BAINLY HOUSE, 2½ m. WNW. A stone house by itself in a dip. A C17 shape, a narrow gabled range, with a central projection towards the road. But the big raised quoins and the finely detailed Venetian window to the S show that the shape was still being repeated in the mid C18.

HIGHER LANGHAM HOUSE, 2¼ m. WSW. Central block dated WB 1770 on the tall brick chimneys. Three bays under a hipped roof. Central pedimented doorway on the S side. Later, lower wings.

SANDLEY HOUSE, 2⅓ m. SW. An ashlar-faced villa of *c.* 1855, originally symmetrical in its W-facing frontage. Extended *c.* 1880 and again in 1998, resulting in a more informal arrangement.

KING'S COURT PALACE, ¾ m. E, just in Motcombe parish. Dry moats and banks only are visible of the hunting lodge, begun in 1199 by King John and for which two chapels and a hall chamber were commissioned in 1250; demolition was ordered by Edward III in 1369.

LONGBURY or SLAUGHTER BARROW, 1¼ m. WNW. A long barrow, aligned E–W.

GLANVILLES WOOTTON   *6000*

ST MARY. Perp W tower of *c.* 1400; battlemented with corner pinnacles; square stair-turret on the N side. The nave N side and the chancel by *G.R. Crickmay*, 1875–6. The main interest of the church is the heavily buttressed S chapel with the C15 porch attached to its W side. The chapel was founded in 1344 by Sibyl de Glaunvyll, and it is purely Dec. Two bays, two windows with flowing tracery, one still rather 1300- than 1344-looking. The windows are shafted inside. An equally good chapel E window. Wide depressed arch to the nave, a small doorway to its W, a bold squint to its E. The corbels of the wide arch also look rather 1300 than 1344. The arch itself starts with a short vertical piece. In the S wall two TOMB-RECESSES and an ogee-headed PISCINA. – BENCHES in the S chapel; High Victorian by *Crickmay*; good. – Also re-set TILES, mid-C14. – FONT. Early C13, octagonal, of Purbeck marble. Two lancet panels per face. Central stem support and eight Purbeck marble colonnettes. – STAINED GLASS. Many fragments re-set in the S chapel S windows, C15 mainly. Chapel E window by *Lavers, Barraud & Westlake*, 1878. Chancel E window and S side window by the same, *c.* 1890. – MONUMENTS. One of the two tomb-recesses is empty; in the other is a mid-C14 effigy of a man in surcoat, probably the founder's husband. He has a sword and a tool, perhaps for testing the quality of wool. – Large tablet to John Every of Cothay in Somerset †1679. At the top two kneeling figures with an open semi-circular pediment between. The whole framed by Corinthian columns. – Rev. Humphrey Evans †1813, by *T. King* of Bath. Pedestal supporting an urn.

WESLEYAN METHODIST CHAPEL (former), ⅛ m. NW. Polychrome brick Gothic, 1869.

MANOR HOUSE, ⅓ m. NNE. Vernacular range of *c.* 1640 for James Dale. Main block of 1804 with mansard roof. Doorways with reeded architraves within.

ROUND CHIMNEYS FARM, ⅞ m. N. A Late Elizabethan manor house, incorporated into an early C17 house of some style for John Churchill, ancestor of that eminent family. In 1662 it had eleven hearths. Reduced in height and altered in other ways in the early C19, after having been recorded by Hutchins. He noted the date 159– on one of the chimneys, since lost. Mullioned-and-transomed windows of two and three lights, with ovolo mouldings, not the usual hollows. No hoodmoulds, but string courses that rise hood-like over the windows. Cylindrical chimneys, mostly re-set from the former multi-gabled, three-storey house. Inside, an attempt at a classical vocabulary in two round-headed archways, with ovolo and wave mouldings and jewelled imposts and key blocks.

GOATHILL

6010

ST PETER. The nave is late C13 – see one pointed-trefoil-headed lancet – but otherwise rebuilt in 1804. Commissioners' church-style lancets. W bellcote. The chancel of 1873 matches the lancet style. Very plain interior with a narrow chancel arch, probably also of 1804. – FONT. C12. Tapering cylindrical bowl. – STAINED GLASS. C16 fragments in the E window.

GOATHILL LODGE. *See* Sherborne, p. 557.

GODMANSTONE

6090

Linear village on the A352. A few thatched cottages.

HOLY TRINITY. Banded flint and stone. C15 W tower and nave; early C16 S aisle and N chapel, and some refenestration. Major restoration of 1848, when the chancel was rebuilt. Three-stage but short W tower; diagonal buttresses. Square-headed belfry

openings; the w window traceried, however. Two big, square-
headed but traceried five-light windows (E window and N
chapel, N); a smaller version in the nave, N. S doorway, palpably
Neo- and not genuine Norman, presumably c. 1848. It has a
tympanum with fish-scale decoration above two bands of small
saltire crosses. But genuine C12 chancel arch responds. They
are very unusual. Four demi-shafts separated by ridges – in
places like spurs. Scalloped capitals of thin long scallops. The
arch itself is C16. At the base of the S respond a ROMAN
ALTAR, cut down by the Norman builders. Perp S arcade and
N chapel arch. Standard pier and respond section. Simple leaf
capitals. Four-centred arches. PISCINA with cinquefoiled head,
C15. – PULPIT and CLERGY SEAT. By *E. Wamsley Lewis*, 1966
and 1967. Vertical-ribbed designs. – FONT. C15, octagonal, but
re-cut with crosses in lancet panels, mid-C19. – STAINED GLASS.
Chancel windows by *A. K. Nicholson*, 1931 and 1932. – MONU-
MENTS. The Revs G. C., M., and M. Vicars, †1844, 1850, 1852.
With a fine small relief of a clergyman seated by a dying man,
a woman at the latter's head. – Frances Helen Wainewright
†1852. Plaster relief in the style of Flaxman.

MANOR HOUSE, 100 yds E. Of c. 1830. Stucco villa. Pilaster bay
divisions with capitals. Veranda on E front.

OLD RECTORY, 150 yds SE. Mid-C18; roof raised and rear additions, mid-C19. Brick-banded flint. Panelled attic stage. Two
C15 quatrefoils re-set above the doorway.

Former SMITH'S ARMS, 150 yds E. Converted from a C15 smithy
in the mid C17. Flint and thatch. Reputed to have been the
'smallest pub in England'.

GROVE *see* PORTLAND, p. 488

GUSSAGE ALL SAINTS   9010

A linear village with some cob, timber-framed and thatched cottages at right angles to the street.

ALL SAINTS. A surprising church. Standing as it does and being
as uniform as it is, one would take it for the Victorian estate
church of a prosperous estate, whereas it is in fact a genuine,
ambitious early C14 building. The date is indicated by the
nave windows: plainish Dec tracery, three of two lights to N
and S walls, three lights for the W window. The chancel was
rebuilt by *Ewan Christian*, the nave restored by *John Hicks*,
both 1864–5. Spacious, aisleless nave. Good roof corbels carved
by *R. L. Boulton*. S tower (upper stages C15) with porch under
it, its entrance of two continuous chamfers. All the windows
have cusped rere-arches, repeated in the new chancel. In the
nave a richly carved Dec TOMB-RECESS with a depressed,

crocketed ogee arch and buttress-shafts. The cusps are pierced and studded with ballflower. The organ-chamber arch is said to incorporate material from the original chancel arch, although this is not obvious. Three PISCINAE, two at the E end of the nave, in the N and S walls: C14 with trefoil heads. Another in the chancel with a cinquefoil head, heavily restored. – PULPIT. Of timber on a stone base; by *Boulton* (to *Christian*'s design), 1865. – FONT. Early C14, Dec. Octagonal of Purbeck marble with splayed sides. Plain cylindrical pillar. Something of a transitional form between the E.E. shapes and Perp. – STAINED GLASS. E window by *Bell & Beckham*. Pevsner wrote: 'It would be fine if it were 1875, but it is 1909 . – MONUMENTS. Touching tablet to Nicholas Tyser †1962, six years old. By *John Skelton*.

GUSSAGE HOUSE. Small late C17 hipped-roofed house, of red brick with big stone quoins, considerably altered and restored. Fine original staircase, *c.* 1700.

DORSET CURSUS. *See* Gussage St Michael.

ACKLING DYKE, 3½ m. NNE on Wyke Down, and running N across Oakley Down (Wimborne St Giles). Part of the Roman road from Old Sarum to Dorchester (*Durnovaria*), via Badbury Rings and Crab Farm (*Vindocladia*) at Shapwick. This stretch, perhaps the best-preserved part of a Roman road in southern Britain, forms the parish boundary with Wimborne St Giles and Gussage St Michael.

IRON AGE FARMSTEAD, ½ m. S, on Sovell Down. Early to Late Iron Age sub-circular enclosure, 3¾ acres, with a single entrance with curved external ditches flanking the approach from the SW. Continuous occupation. Circular houses and re-cut ditches, with internal enclosures for stock and a single house in the final phase. A typical farmstead on Cranborne Chase (*see also* Gussage St Michael).

9010

GUSSAGE ST ANDREW

Sixpenny Handley

ST ANDREW. A very elementary flint-walled structure. Nave and chancel in one and a small louvred W bell-turret. The nave is C12 – see one N window and the blocked S doorway – but may be an adaptation of an earlier structure: see banded herringbone masonry at the base of the nave W wall. Three-light early C16 W window with trefoil-headed lights. The chancel lancets date from restoration in 1857. Dec chancel S window with a PISCINA in the E reveal. – COMMUNION RAILS. Oak, early C18, with turned balusters. – PULPIT. C17. Panelled. – FONT. C12, on a moulded stem. – CHANDELIER. C18, brass. Given in 1920. – WALL PAINTINGS. Uncovered in 1951. Two tiers, late C12 lining-out with figures superimposed upon this, probably in the late C13. Not enough is recognizable for enjoyment, but it is a blessing all the same that they were preserved and not repainted. The top scene is the Betrayal of Christ. Below the Scourging, the Crucifixion, the Deposition. Also the Suicide of Judas. Black-letter texts added, probably in the C17. – STAINED GLASS. In the nave S window a C15 roundel. – FLOOR SLABS. Beneath the altar, William Williams †1725 (aged 100). Coffin-shaped inscription surrounded by skull, crossed bones and flaming urns. Similar slab in the nave to John and Mary Lush †1722.

GUSSAGE ST MICHAEL

A scatter of farmsteads. Much C20 building in the village.

ST MICHAEL. The church is of flint. Early C12 lower stages of the W tower, at first recognizable by the W buttress but then also inside by the low arch towards the nave. The arch itself is entirely unmoulded. A tall narrow nave, perhaps C11 in origin. The two-bay arcades are early C13. They have round piers, simply moulded round capitals and double-chamfered pointed arches. One S pier has a little dogtooth ornament. Rounded corbels above the piers originally supported the roof, the former profile of which can be seen on the E face of the tower. Two narrow C13 lancets high above the chancel arch. The aisle and clerestory windows are C15 Perp, added when the nave and aisle roofs were raised; also the battlemented top tower stage and similarly battlemented N porch. The N aisle originally continued into a chapel, hence the two-centred E arch, now leading to *Ponting*'s vestry of 1896. The chancel and its arch were rebuilt by *G. E. Street* in 1857 (who had previously added a vestry). The E window with its blunt plate tracery is typical of him, and the REREDOS of 1870 even more so. Its powerful, almost over-scaled shapes are typical. – CHOIR STALLS by *Street*. – Nave and aisle FURNISHINGS of 1896 by *Ponting*, who carried out a major restoration. – ROOD SCREEN also by *Ponting*, 1918. – FONT. C13. Circular bowl on a stem, both heavily moulded. – TOWER STAIRCASE. Early C17 with turned balusters. – ROYAL ARMS of Charles II, high over the tower arch. – STAINED GLASS. In the chancel, probably by *Wailes*, c. 1857. – MONUMENTS. Defaced Purbeck marble coffin-lid in N aisle, probably C13.

    LYCHGATE, 1923 by *Ponting*.

WESLEYAN CHAPEL (former), 1907 by *W. T. Chinchen* of More Crichel. Brick. Round-arched windows.

RYALL'S FARMHOUSE, ¾ m. NNW. C16 rubble and flint, probably timber-framed originally between the gables. Central front doorway leading to projecting stair-turret at the rear. Paired diagonal-set chimneystacks on the gable-ends. Front rebuilt in brick, late C18, when a rear wing was added making an L-plan.

PACKHORSE BRIDGE, adjoining to the SW. C18. Single arch, brick.

DORSET CURSUS. The longest CURSUS MONUMENT in Britain runs for 6¼ m., from Thickthorn Down to Martin Down. It consists of two parallel banks about 270 ft (83 metres) apart, and was constructed in the earlier Neolithic period. Excavations of 1982–4 showed that the W ditch was 6–10 ft (2–3 metres) wide and 4 ft (1.2 metres) deep. The bank may have been revetted and nearly 6½ ft (2 metres) high. The monument was built across hills and valleys in two main phases, with the first, SW section terminating on Bottlebush Down. Midway along this section is a LONG BARROW which is sited on Gussage Down such that the midwinter sun sets behind it. Further long barrows were integrated with the monument in both phases.

The SW end is well preserved, with two LONG BARROWS to the SE, and long barrows are also visible at the NE end. It is best preserved between Wyke Down, SW of where it is cut by Ackling Dyke, and Bottlebush Down. It probably functioned as a processional way used during ritual ceremonies, and later became the focus for many round-barrow cemeteries.

LONG BARROWS. Two on Thickthorn Down, 1¼ m. NW, two on Gussage Hill, 1½ m. NNE, and one S of Gussage Hill. The last, aligned ESE–WNW, is much reduced by ploughing. The other four are aligned SE–NW towards the Dorset Cursus, one being incorporated within the bank.

On Gussage Down, 1½ m. NNE, an IRON AGE AND ROMANO-BRITISH SETTLEMENT, associated with boundary dykes and 'Celtic' fields. One of the largest native occupation sites in Dorset, extending for nearly a mile NW–SE. The central part overlies the Dorset Cursus, now much ploughed, to the N of the trackway.

5000

HALSTOCK

Gathered around the triangular village green are cottages typical of the local mix. The church, school and rectory are all along a lane to the N.

ST MARY. C15 embattled W tower of three stages. This appears to have been thoroughly restored when the church was rebuilt in 1846–7 by *A.W.N. Pugin*. (It had previously been rebuilt in 1773.) After 1872 the chancel was also rebuilt to Pugin's plans, enlarging it from its C18 size to something approaching its medieval length.* Typical Pugin Middle Pointed style. N aisle with its own gables and bold buttresses. Wide, three-light nave and aisle windows. Label stops and roof corbels

---

*The executant architect was one *Thomas Stent* of Yeovil.

lacking their intended carving, presumably owing to a restrictive budget. – ALTAR. Stone, with a pierced trefoil. – PULPIT. A stone box; plain. – TILES in the sanctuary by *Minton*. – STAINED GLASS. E window probably by *Heaton, Butler & Bayne*, c. 1875. Nave S window by *G. Maile & Son*, 1960. Colourful W window by *Sally Pollitzer*, 2012.

GLEBE HOUSE (formerly the rectory), Church Lane, 80 yds N. 1870 by *William Chick* of Hereford. Gabled, with big mullioned-and-transomed windows.

In the village three houses worth a glance. NEW INN FARM-HOUSE is of late C18 height but has two good C17 ovolo-moulded windows, re-set. OLD HOUSE and the adjoining cottage have stone-mullioned windows of the same horizontal shape, but in simple classical surrounds, establishing an C18 date though not yet C18 proportions. By way of contrast, next to it, HALSTOCK HOUSE has the upright proportions and wide sashes of the early C19.

HAMLET HOUSE *see* YETMINSTER

HAMMOON   8010

The grouping of the manor house and church, very low-lying beside the River Stour, is one of the most memorable in the county.

ST PAUL. Nave of late C12 or early C13; mid-C13 chancel, when there was much rebuilding to the S side of the nave also. Incongruous timber and tile-hung bell-turret of 1885, added when the W end of the nave was rebuilt (in an ugly grey stone) and the chancel arch installed. Inside it is immediately obvious that the chancel is strikingly out of axis with this nave. One explanation may be that a narrow S aisle was formerly taken off the nave, but there is no obvious evidence for this. The nave N wall is where the earliest masonry is to be found, and at the junction with the chancel are indications of a possible rood-stair-turret. – REREDOS of stone with six small statuettes in niches and the Crucifixion in the centre. The style indicates late C14 to early C15 and English provenance. It was installed in 1946. – COMMUNION RAIL. C17, oak, with turned balusters. – STALLS. Of 1946, the fronts incorporating early C16 parchemin panels. – PULPIT. Inscribed 1635 C.P. With two tiers of narrow panels. Guilloche decoration with rosettes. – FONT. Octagonal, C14. It seems to have been hollowed out from a pier base. – STAINED GLASS. Brightly coloured three-light E window by *Hugh Powell*, 1960.

MANOR HOUSE. A simple L-plan stone house with an air, in spite of a classical porch, of simple innocence under its

thatched roof, and the big sycamore tree overhead. The building history however is a complex one, the result of piecemeal
enlargement and changes of mind. It was just at the moment
when Gothic forms were being overtaken by classical that Sir
Thomas Trenchard, proprietor of Hammoon, decided to make
a modest show. First he built a two-storey addition at the SE
corner, giving it a full-height bay with windows of 1:3:1 lights,
their heads arched and a hoodmould over all. Round the side
two-light windows on each level. All these have deep hollow-
moulded surrounds. Thin polygonal SE angle shaft, its fellow
almost obscured by the porch. By its features then one would
date this part to *c.* 1540–50 (but it may have been imported from
elsewhere).* Not so the porch, with its shaped gable and simple
strapwork-and-obelisk cresting. That looks more like *c.* 1600. Yet
the two parts share plinth and string course of the same moulding. And the porch window matches the others. The handsome
entrance however, of Purbeck limestone, must be an insertion,
or at any rate a feature separately ordered. Its round-headed
entrance arch, stout banded Tuscan columns, and the roundels,
with crisp gadrooning and egg-and-dart, are convincingly
classical; though the entablature with frieze of hyphens con-
vinces less. The W parts of the S front are rude work: a refronting of an early C16 timber-framed wing, probably of the early
C19, trying to keep in style. The rubble stone W gable-end is
original. The long NE range however is a C17 rebuilding – see
the ground-floor windows with hollow-moulded mullions but
straight-headed lights.

HAMMOON HOUSE (formerly East Farm). A blocky, hipped-
roofed villa of *c.* 1880, starkly out of sympathy with the character of its water-meadow setting, but inescapable on the E
approach to the village.

0090

HAMPRESTON
Ferndown

Linear layout: brick houses, mostly C18, farms and estate cottages leading towards the meadows of the River Stour.

ALL SAINTS. Brown heathstone with limestone dressings. The
re-set N door arch indicates a C12 church. The W tower is C14
Dec below (see the very weathered W window), C15 Perp above,
with two-lighted pointed-arched belfry openings and a battlemented parapet. The staircase projection is oblong, at the NE
corner, and carries a small ogee-headed niche. The church is
quite large, though not high. Much of what one sees from the
N is by *Romaine-Walker & Tanner*, 1896–7. Theirs is the N aisle,

---

*Richard Jones suggests Fiddleford Manor as the source, when it was partially
dismantled in the C17.

the porch and the rebuilt s nave wall, all in Dec style, to match the c14 chancel. Two-light Dec windows here with cinquefoil-headed lights, three per side originally. One was removed on the N when the organ loft was created; another was blocked on the s in 1823 by a vestry with a Y-traceried s window. Early c15 three-light E window with trefoil-headed lights. Rood-loft stair-turret on the s. The corbels for the chancel roof of 1896–7 are specially enjoyable: a set of c12-style grotesques. – COM-MUNION RAIL. c18. Turned balusters and newels with later spiky finials. – FONT. Late c12 or early c13. Primitive octag-onal Purbeck stone bowl. – STAINED GLASS. A fine set of chancel windows by *Mayer & Co.* of London and Munich, all 1890s. Three by *C.E. Kempe*: tower (1892), and nave NW and s (1898, 1903). – MONUMENTS. Miles Brownes, rector, †1630. Flat frontal half-figure in a classical surround with two black columns. – Edward Greathed †1803, signed by *Nollekens*.

SCHOOL, 1875, and adjacent pair of CANFORD ESTATE COT-TAGES, 1872, by *Banks & Barry*.

EAST LODGE to Canford Manor (q.v.), Little Canford, ¾ m. NW. Picturesque red brick and half-timbering, *c.* 1860, probably by *Banks & Barry*. Gate screen removed but piers retained. Beyond is a BAILEY BRIDGE, re-erected *c.* 1950 over the Stour.

HOLMWOOD PARK. *See* p. 364.

HAMWORTHY
1½ m. NW of Poole

When the first bridge to cross from Poole was built in 1837 the village became an industrial suburb. Two pottery works were established, together with shipbuilding. The industrial character has survived the closure of the potteries and the demolition of a large power station (built 1945 onwards) in 1993. A new cross-Channel FERRY TERMINAL was constructed in 1973.

ST MICHAEL. 1958–9 by *Allner, Morley & Bolton* of Poole.* Red brick. Bulky, with a square-topped (ritual) N tower. Flat-roofed aisles. Spacious, although unsophisticated, interior. – REREDOS. Fanlight-shaped faience work by *Carter & Co.* – PULPIT with carvings by *F.J. Fisher.* – STAINED GLASS. E window by *Goddard & Gibbs* (designed by *A.E. Buss*), 1959.

OLD RECTORY, ½ m. SE. A complete and remarkable brick house of *c.* 1635, with very close parallels to the Dutch House at Kew (1631) and Barnham Court, West Sussex (*c.* 1635), but of a type quite unexpected in Dorset.** Also an early use of the

---

*It replaced a church of 1825–6 by *John Tulloch* of Poole.
**Nicholas Cooper (*Houses of the Gentry*, 1999), suggests that the craftsmen, and possibly even the bricks, may have travelled to Poole by sea from London.

double-pile plan. It faces SE, and the front consists of two-and-a-half bays each side of a deeply projecting porch. The telling features are the giant Ionic pilasters, rather thin and tapering, and set on high pedestals, between each bay and on the porch; and the three big Dutch gables, their S-curved sides, and the pediments, triangular, segmental, triangular, deeply modelled in moulded brick. Two storeys of casement windows and a third in the gables. Big projecting chimney-breasts against the short ends of the house, and at the back three straight gables.

Several pairs of gabled brick CANFORD ESTATE COTTAGES by *Banks & Barry*, from 1871 to 1875, are in Blandford and Lake roads. The former SCHOOL, also by *Banks & Barry*, 1869, at the corner of Blandford Road and Tuckers Lane (½ m. SE), has been converted to dwellings. The RAILWAY STATION, ½ m. NW (originally known as Poole Junction), is a relatively unaltered brick structure for the Southampton & Dorchester Railway, 1847.

THE BOAT HOUSE, Lake Drive, ¾ m. SW. 1935. A concrete-framed, flat-roofed Art Deco house with whitewashed red brick cladding. Remarkable interiors largely reconstructed from *Harold Peto*'s second-class drawing room salvaged from the Cunard liner *Mauritania*, 1907.

POOLE BRIDGES. *See* p. 457.

ROMAN MILITARY BASE, ⅔ m. SE, below Broomhill Way. Constructed during the Claudian campaigns of the CI A.D. as a supply base for the fortress 4 m. N, at Lake Gates Farm (*see* Corfe Mullen). The connecting Roman road can be traced N with remains along the W side of Holes Bay and on the Corfe Mullen parish boundary.

8010

HANFORD

HANFORD HOUSE (now Hanford School). A major Jacobean house, externally almost unaltered. It was built for Sir Robert Seymer and is dated 1604 (although this date panel, on the staircase, is C19). Sir Robert's father bought the manor in 1599. Two rainwater heads on the N front have the date 1623. This front is of finely jointed ashlar, and the five bays of windows are arranged with the three straight-sided gables to form a precisely symmetrical design. There is a rusticated central arch, flanked by fluted Doric pilasters, above which rather puny Corinthian pilasters carry a triangular pediment. The window thus framed has an eared surround with classical mouldings and a shaped apron below. *William Arnold* may have been brought in to deal with this façade, perhaps after construction had begun (and perhaps *c.* 1623). The shell-headed niches that line the porch walls (*see* below) are also typical Arnold features. All this then makes a classical frontispiece contrasting with the standard vernacular mullioned windows elsewhere, of four and three lights with a transom. Mullioned windows in the gables with hoodmoulds. Standard early C17 mouldings, a step and a hollow chamfer.

The other show front faces E, though here there is no classical reference and symmetry is not quite achieved. But it is the stronger composition of the two, with five-sided polygonal window bays at the ends, denoting that the major rooms lay on this side, and four gables sprouting at their apexes paired round-shafted chimneystacks with thin slab caps, a feature typical of this county at this date, but used here to particular effect. These may have drawn their inspiration from the similar chimneys at Longleat, Wilts. Crisply moulded string courses link the two façades. At the base of each of the bays a half-submerged and blocked two-light mullioned window – an indication of changed ground levels. On the S and W fronts gables, and chimneystacks similarly placed; but the windows come much at random, and the stone walls are here not of ashlar but of coursed rubble.

The PLAN of Hanford is interesting, for the arrangement of four ranges round a small central courtyard is unmistakably a modernized version, affected by the new desire for regularity and compactness, of the medieval arrangement whereby the hall lies on the far side of a court, approached through a gatehouse opposite. The small size of the courtyard (30 by 40 ft; 9 by 12 metres), however, would have made turning a carriage rather awkward. Sir Christopher Hatton's Kirby Hall or Holdenby Hall, Northants, may have been the inspiration for the courtyard plan, albeit here executed on a tiny, almost impractical scale.* The archway in the N front opens into a passage, lined with shell-headed niches (matching those by *Arnold* at Cranborne Manor and Lulworth), two plus two, and this leads straight into the courtyard, where a projecting three-storey porch stands on axis opposite. This has Ionic pilasters flanking the round-headed entrance, with not quite classical mouldings, and a splendid coat of arms with mantling above, and strapwork to l. and r. The hall must have lain in this S range, possibly with a bay window in its end wall. Large mullioned-and-transomed windows towards the courtyard in all directions (N window blocked out). The courtyard was always an impractical space in which to bring carriages, so it was inevitably a Victorian owner – H. Clay-Ker-Seymer, *c.* 1870 – who roofed it over to create a central SALOON so desirable since Barry's day. This has top lighting, a mixture of Renaissance-style and more Jacobean-style woodwork, especially on the giant fireplace, an upper gallery resting on Ionic columns along the N side, and panelling to the lower parts of the walls with tapestries above. With new doorways leading into the E and W ranges off the saloon, the hall on the S side became somewhat stranded and redundant. It was therefore

* Seymer served at the Court of the Exchequer, while Hatton was Lord Chancellor and owner of Corfe Castle. The house may therefore be some kind of personal tribute to Hatton.

subdivided into smaller rooms, providing a new library and study. A staircase had already been taken out of the W end of the hall, c. 1700, this having twisted balusters and a scrolled handrail.

All the remaining C17 INTERIORS are in the NE corner. Here is the main staircase, going up in straight flights. Sturdy turned balusters and large turned urn-like newel finials. On the upper floor two rooms have ceilings with narrow ribs and motifs in the fields, heads mostly in the N room, fritillary-like flowers in the NE room. This latter was a major chamber, for the ceiling ribs grow into pendants, and there is a mighty stone chimneypiece, with caryatids, strapwork and a top hamper of demi-figures of knights and niches flanked by colonnettes. It is a great piece of Jacobean vulgarity. The drawing room below was enlarged c. 1700 by removing a wall and introducing a set of slender cast-iron columns. Here too a pedimented doorcase of c. 1750 and a marble chimneypiece of c. 1780, also with caryatids and not of high quality.

ST MICHAEL. Small, and tellingly the chapel of the house (and now of the school). Dated 1650 on the parapet of the W porch, but seemingly of medieval origin. Late Perp end windows; C18 Y-tracery side windows. The porch is very curious, with what look like parts of a classical door surround (with lugs) and continuing with a bulgy frieze and a bulgy cornice and a depressed rounded arch. – PAINTING round the E window of 1930, by *Lucy Buckler* (Mrs Seymer). She had been a pupil of Puvis de Chavannes. – WEST GALLERY, 1990 by *Hugh Harrison*. – STAINED GLASS. One S window by *Warrington*, c. 1865.

STABLES, W of the house. Formed in the C19 from a fine, probably early C17, barn. Brick, in English bonding, on stone footings. The two deep E projections, part of the original arrangement, were probably porches.

Hanford House became a school in 1946. NE of the house, FANS HOUSE of c. 1965, by the *Architects' Co-Partnership* (job architect *Michael Powers*). A sympathetic modern building, reticent in character. Largely one-storeyed, of dull brown brick. Each section has a very low-pitched metal-sheet roof.

HAMBLEDON HILL. *See* Iwerne Courtney.

HAYDON

A once complete Victorian grouping of church, school and vicarage. A glaring gap between has been left by the loss of the school (by *P. C. Hardwick*, probably 1857), demolished c. 1975.

ST CATHERINE (now a house). By *R.H. Carpenter*, 1883. A replacement church on a new site. Goodhart-Rendel called it 'humble and respectable'. Nave with bellcote and chancel.

Plate tracery, but also some genuine C13 features: one N lancet
by the former rood-loft stairs, the E triplet and two S lancets.*
VICARAGE (former), rock-faced and gabled. By *P. C. Hardwick*,
1857 (estimate for £1,473). Set back behind a continuous stone
wall. To the N, in front of the school site and the church, the
boundary becomes railings.

HAYDON LODGE (to Sherborne Castle, q.v.), just N. Of *c.* 1850.
Gothic windows in a canted bay. Fine contemporary ironwork
SCREEN and GATES.

HAZELBURY BRYAN   7000

A collection of hamlets with the main settlement at Wonston, the
church, manor farm, school and almshouses at Droop, and much
modern development at Kingston.

ST MARY AND ST JAMES. A large mid-C15 church with a
sturdy four-stage embattled W tower, the tallest in this part
of the county. W doorway with traceried spandrels. Four-
light window above with niches l. and r. Higher oblong stair-
turret. Chancel rebuilt in 1827 and restored in 1895. The
remainder sensitively restored by *C. E. Ponting* in 1902–4.
Further redecoration by *Sir Charles Nicholson* in 1935. The S
aisle and S porch have battlemented parapets and low-pitched
roofs. Three-light windows in the N aisle, slightly later in date
than the tower (and nave). Four-bay arcades of standard elements, but the N arcade with round abaci to the piers and the
S arcade with polygonal abaci. The N arcade has fleurons in
the abaci. Panelled tower arch. One-bay S chapel, the responds
and arch with square leaves. The nave has a wagon roof, and so
does the N aisle, but the S aisle, S chapel and S porch have ceilings with moulded beams of the late C15. In the S chapel two
very fine Dec capitals, re-set. In the N aisle two small canopied
niches and a wide image niche with a crocketed ogee gable. This
is now fitted with a carved CALVARY by *Nicholson*. – REREDOS.
Of 1893 with cinquefoil-headed niches at the centre. Polished
green and pink granite colonnettes. Panels of coloured terracotta by *Carter* of Poole. – PULPIT. Inscribed Ben Lidford
1782; plain. Handsome, concave cone-topped sounding-board
supported by a chain. – FURNISHINGS. Mostly dating from
Ponting's restoration. – FONT. Octagonal, C12, of Purbeck
marble with two shallow arches on each side (cf. Lydlinch).
The COVER is late C17, simple and handsome. It was made up
from part of the pulpit sounding-board. – WALL PAINTINGS.
Late C16. In the nave above the S arcade. A triangular panel

---

*The BENCHES were to an early C17 style with shell-tops (cf. Folke). They were
reportedly removed from Sherborne Abbey during R. C. Carpenter's restoration,
and are now at Rollestone, Wilts.

and a cartouche with angels. – ROYAL ARMS of Queen Anne, but lettered GR; dated 1715. – STAINED GLASS. Many small C15 pieces in several windows, especially angels in N windows. The angels have shields bearing symbols and monograms, one of which seems to carry the initials of John Tonkee, the rector of 1426–42. – Late C15 or C16 fragments in the upper part of the E window, which is otherwise of 1919 by *William Morris & Co.* of Westminster.

High-quality LYCHGATE of 1954 by *H.A.N. Medd.*

Plain-looking ALMSHOUSES of 1841 (restored in 1939) alongside the churchyard.

PRIMITIVE METHODIST CHAPEL, between Wonston and Pidney, ¾ m. NW. Dated 1863. Two colours of brick.

HERMITAGE

6000

Named after a former hermitage (Blackmoor) loosely connected with the Augustinians. Its site is now represented by Church Farm.

ST MARY. The building is puzzling. Possibly C14, but most of what is seen follows a major rebuilding. This is dated 1682 (datestone on W gable); also dated a later repair of 1799. Big bell-turret and gargoyle below with l. and r. in the W front two lancets, these perhaps of the later date. The Perp windows, especially those in the nave S wall, look C17 in their tracery. The E window is similar. Barrel-vaulted and ribbed ceilings, probably *c.* 1800. The vault reduces in width at the chancel, the 'arch' on short entablature lengths, probably late C17. Restoration and refurnishing by *Crickmay & Son,* 1889. – COMMUNION RAIL. Turned balusters and moulded handrail, early C18. – FONT. Late C17. Round bowl cut back to an octagon. Octagonal stem.

ALMSHOUSE FARM, ¾ m. N. Dated 1849, by *R.J. Withers.* Jacobean style with mullioned-and-transomed windows.

HIGHER BOCKHAMPTON
see LOWER BOCKHAMPTON

HILFIELD

6000

ST NICHOLAS, in an isolated hillside location. Early C14 origin, extensively rebuilt in the C15, and again by *R.J. Withers,* 1848; the chancel appears wholly of this date. Nave with bellcote on the E gable. Banded stone and flint. Many old features reused by Withers, e.g. the C17 N and S nave windows and the Dec W window. Two C15 brackets at the W end, presumably to support a gallery. – PULPIT. By *Withers*, incorporating some C15 carved work. – BENCHES and STALLS. C17, with the elaborate ends carved by *William Halliday* of Chilton Polden (Somerset), 1848.* They have religious scenes and figures of Late Perp and Baroque inspiration. – TILES in the sanctuary by *Minton*. – FONT by *Withers*, 1848. – WALL PAINTING. A small area of black-letter text in English; probably C17. – STAINED GLASS. Two chancel side windows by *Powell & Sons*, 1848. Scrolled design.

HILFIELD MANOR, 1 m. N. Late C19. Octagonal tower built as a shooting lodge for the Bide family. Tudor style. Flat-roofed addition of 1901 for T.W. Dampier-Bide.

HILFIELD FRIARY, ½ m. SW. Of *c.* 1913, by *R.G. Spiller* of Taunton. Three cottages and a bell-tower. Flint with brick dressings; originally with thatched roofs, now mostly tiled. Initially a self-governing community for children called The Little Commonwealth, set up by the educational reformer Homer Lane and the 8th Earl of Sandwich. It became the Home of St Francis in 1921. Several later buildings. FLOWER'S FARM adjoins. Late C19 with bell-tower of *c.* 1913.

HILTON

7000

The village is best viewed from the SE. Then the thatched buildings of Lower Farm and nearby cottages make a picturesque composition and the church tower rises behind, silhouetted against woods.

ALL SAINTS. A substantial Perp church, except for one Dec S aisle window. It took its present form after the widening of the S aisle in 1569 (three initialled datestones below the parapet) and the building of a N aisle at about the same time. The latter is the Perp climax, with five closely set splendid four-light windows with panel tracery, and buttresses with gargoyles (one a bagpiper). Slightly narrower blind arches at either end result in six bays overall, a stately effect. The masonry most likely came from the cloisters of Milton Abbey. Here they are set higher, with the internal colonnette bases well above floor level (and with vault springings between each window internally). A further four-light window of the same type is at the E end of the aisle. A re-set C15 five-light E window is in the S aisle. In the late C15 battlemented W tower there is a window of four lights with a transom. The higher stair-turret is also battlemented. The piers of both arcades are standard, but those of the N arcade are materially earlier, e.g. the capitals and the two-centred arches. The chancel arch goes with the S arcade and the S chapel N arch; the N arcade has the spirit of Milton

*Information from Julian Orbach.

Abbey, as does the panelled tower arch. A rood-loft stair is embedded in the s chancel arch pier, doubling as a squint. The late c15 s porch is very oddly pushed half into the s aisle, a sign that, when it was built, there was still a much earlier, narrower aisle. It is elaborately vaulted, and in its E wall is a little vaulted niche. Are these features also introductions from the abbey?* – PULPIT. Late c16 diaper panels assembled into a mid-c17 piece. – FONT. c12, Purbeck marble, square, with four shallow blank arches to each side. Modern base. – PAINT-INGS. Twelve 7-ft (2.1-metre) panels of the Apostles on painted plinths (divided into two sets of six each), the figures badly done and probably of *c.* 1500, but heavily repainted. They were removed from a screen in Milton Abbey during *Wyatt's* late c18 restoration there. – At the w end of the N aisle, early c16 CARVED STONEWORK. Perhaps part of a parapet. – STAINED GLASS. E window of 1908 by *Henry Holiday.* Small s aisle window by *Horace Wilkinson,* 1930.

To the NW of the church, one first passes a row of eight POOR COTTAGES, 1812, built for Lady Caroline Damer of Milton Abbey. Plain apart from the paired Tudor-arched porches. Beyond, the former SCHOOL and SCHOOL HOUSE, Gothic, 1863 by *St Aubyn.* Banded red brick and flint walls.

At LOWER ANSTY, 1 m. w, quite a big mid-c19 group, all banded flint – pub, farm and a U-shaped terrace of cottages, and among it the VILLAGE HALL, which is something a little out of the ordinary. It is a large, one-storey stone range with big modern windows, and was built in 1777 as a malthouse. The materials are said to have come from Higher Melcombe, Melcombe Horsey. Converted to a hall in 1946. To its s, three blocks of the former BREWERY, converted to housing in 1997. STRIP LYNCHETS cover *c.* 60 acres around the village.

HINTON MARTELL

A few brick and cob thatched cottages, interspersed with later c19 and c20 houses. The fountain in the centre of the village is a surprise.

ST JOHN THE EVANGELIST. 1868–70 by *John Hicks* (completed by *G. R. Crickmay* after Hicks's death in 1869), possibly assisted by *Thomas Hardy.* Banded ashlar and flint. Battlemented w tower with octagonal NE stair-turret. Nave, N aisle and chancel. Reused early c14 two-light window in the chancel, various Perp windows in nave and tower. Dec window also reused at the w end of the N aisle. Fine figured roof corbels. – PULPIT. Stone front, typical of *Crickmay.* – FONT. Octagonal, Purbeck

---

* One of the bosses carries the arms of Milton Abbey.

marble. C13, but re-cut, with two flat blank arches each side. – STAINED GLASS. Nave S window by *W.G. Taylor*, 1888.

WAR MEMORIAL, *c.* 1920 by *F.C. Eden*. Pillar with a miniature carved Pietà in a gabled niche.

Former SCHOOL SW of church, 1847, given by the Countess of Shaftesbury. Brick with broad pointed windows.

GAUNT'S HOUSE. *See* p. 301.

HINTON PARVA
(*or* STANBRIDGE)

0000

A picture of a mid-Victorian village in miniature. Its three elements (church, rectory and cottage row) were all built for the Glyn family of Gaunt's House.

ST KENELM (now redundant). A lavish estate church of 1860 by *George Evans*, at the expense of Sir Richard Plumptre Glyn. Neo-Norman tower with broach spire and transepts; Neo-E.E. nave and chancel. The Norman was chosen because of some original C12 fragments retained from the previous building: the roll-moulded and chevron-decorated chancel arch and two column shafts facing the nave, one spiral-fluted, the other with a scale pattern, both with their capitals. Also over the door a piece of genuine Norman SCULPTURE, a relief of St Kenelm(?), with a cross r., a palm tree l. The church is of flint with stone bands and very finely built, but now neglected. The chancel and W windows are Purbeck-shafted. Rich fitting-out including a tiled chancel dado and Neo-E.E. arcading in chancel with Purbeck marble shafts. Also a Neo-Norman arcade dividing off part of the N transept. – STAINED GLASS. Five chancel windows by *Powell & Sons*, the E of 1897, the others later. W window by *A.L. Moore*, 1912. – MONUMENT. Harriet Muller †1825. A standing woman by an urn.

Former RECTORY and SUNDAY SCHOOL (now STANBRIDGE HOUSE) opposite the church. Early C19 core, greatly enlarged *c.* 1860 by *Evans*. Banded brick and flint, with picturesque grouping of gables with ornamented bargeboards and finials.

STANBRIDGE COTTAGES, 100 yds NW. These must be by *Evans* as well. Of *c.* 1860. Diaper brickwork with Neo-Norman stone porches and windows.

GAUNT'S LODGE, ⅛ m. SE *See* Gaunt's House, p. 301.

HINTON ST MARY

7010

Pretty, trim village of mostly thatched houses. The church and fine manor house dominate.

ST PETER. 1846 by *William Oborne*, in a Late Perp style. Two-stage C15 W tower with battlements and crocketed pinna-cles. – 'English' ALTAR with carved angel finials to the posts, by *C.E. Ponting*, 1911. Part of an otherwise unexecuted scheme to elaborate the chancel. – PULPIT. C18. Fielded and enriched panels (brought here from Blandford Forum church). – FONT, C12. Tub-shaped, with heavy scallops along the bottom rim. Quite extensive remains of colour: red and green. – ROYAL ARMS above the chancel arch. C19, cast iron. – STAINED GLASS. E window of *c.* 1870 by *Clayton & Bell*. Chancel S window by *Mary Lowndes*, 1893. Central panel to each of the four nave windows by *Tom Denny*, 2001. – MONUMENT. Thomas Freke, 1655. A skull at the foot, black columns l. and r. carrying an open pediment.

MANOR HOUSE, immediately E of the church. Mostly a house of *c.* 1630, for Thomas Freke, but incorporating as its central block a remodelled medieval hall, possibly C13 in origin, perhaps the 'retiring place' recorded here for the nuns of Shaft-esbury Abbey.* The hall is represented by the recessed centre of the main SE front. To its l., overlapping the cross-passage, the early C17 wing presenting a gable-end, with a smaller gable over the porch. This carries a carved panel with the arms of Thomas Freke over the upper window. At the r. a later cross-wing, probably of 1695 (datestone), which is also when the building was given its unmedievally large mullioned windows with hoodmoulds. A long wing runs back facing the church, and here the C17 windows remain largely intact. The lower windows of four lights, with hoodmoulds, the upper of three lights, too near the eaves to be hooded. Gabled dormers. Tall chimneystack above the l. angle, a typically striking piece of *c.* 1900 composition when the house was enlarged, mainly to the rear. Inside, a two-centred-arched opening, now blocked, in a passage at the rear of the former hall may be the remains of a medieval window. The staircase has a late C16 plaster ceiling brought from Fiddleford Manor (q.v.), in the mid 1960s. A similar type of ceiling has been created in replica in the drawing room. Also panelling brought in from King John's House, Tollard Royal, Wilts.

From the 1890s until the 1930s, Alexander Pitt-Rivers (son of the archaeologist) and George Pitt-Rivers turned the manor house into a miniature country seat, also laying out the formal GARDENS. A panoramic view now opens towards Bulbarrow Hill.

By the gateway SE of the forecourt a TITHE BARN, late C15 or early C16, much altered and adapted as a theatre in 1929–39, having been converted to a village hall in the 1890s; and at right angles the stone STABLES, also originally a barn, a building of great charm. Towards the road it has an unwindowed side wall of lemon-yellow stone, with tilted stone eaves, and nine short,

---

* Mr Pitt-Rivers believes the house to have been part of a lay brothers' settlement.

Hinton St Mary, Roman villa, mosaic.
Painting by David S. Neal

stout, stepped buttresses, very satisfyingly spaced. A timber-framed late C19 ESTATE OFFICE, on the driveway from the centre of the village, completes the picture.

DALTON'S FARM, ⅛ m. N. The most imposing of the smaller village houses, set back in its railed garden. Of c. 1740, five bays, two storeys, it has upright stone-framed windows with key blocks, and an open segmental pediment to the doorway.

HAIMES FARMHOUSE, just N of the above, is late C17 with a five-light hollow-chamfered and mullioned window below, with a hoodmould, and a four-lighter above. Thatch.

CASTLEMAN'S FARMHOUSE, ¼ m. NW. Dated 1685 but seemingly earlier. A timber-framed wing projects on the r. Thatched roof dropping to a lean-to.

ROMAN VILLA, ¼ m. WSW. Discovered in 1963, part of more extensive building ranges. These include a double room resembling a *triclinium*, with a C4 mosaic pavement of the Durnovarian Group (*see* Dorchester) measuring 28 by 19½ ft (8½ by 6 metres), one of the best figurative mosaics in the country. It was lifted in 1965 and is now in the British Museum (sadly, only the central roundel of the E square room is presently displayed). This roundel contained the bust of a man with a chi-rho monogram behind the head, and pomegranates on either side. Certainly with Christian symbolism, it has been interpreted as a representation of Christ. In the other eight surrounding panels, further Christian symbolism has been inferred in a single tree (of life), below the central roundel, four male corner busts (the Evangelists), and, in the w room the central roundel of Bellerophon riding Pegasus and spearing the Chimaera (Triumph of Good over Evil). Seven scenes of the chase (with dog, stag and doe) surround the schemes.

p. 323

6000

HOLNEST

ST MARY. On its own – a nice picture with its variety of roofs. Short w tower, nave and chancel, and s aisle. Nave probably earlier than *c.* 1400. Of that date the Perp tower. Three stages with an embattled parapet. Perp nave windows and s aisle. s porch dated 1656. Major restoration of 1855, the likely date of the chancel. The curiously plain s arcade is an C18 remodelling. – PULPIT. Early C17, hexagonal. A fret design to the upper panels; reeding to the lower (cf. Folke). Similar panels forming the back. Sounding-board missing. – BOX PEWS. Late C18, plain. They have C19 arched wrought-iron hoop candleholders. – FONT. C13. Cylindrical bowl. – C19 encaustic TILES in the sanctuary. – STAINED GLASS. Tracery lights only of the E window, probably by *Wailes*, 1869.*

HOLNEST PARK, ½ m. S. Central pedimented block of *c.* 1780 for Mark Davis. Its nine bays remodelled and extended by four-bay wings *c.* 1850, for J.S.W. Sawbridge (by then Sawbridge-Erle-Drax). Italianate, the later wing with an 'Osborne' tower. The E front of the original nine-bay block pedimented; off-centre bowed window to the w front. N wing demolished by 1900. Expensive interiors, e.g. the

---

*MONUMENT. A large mausoleum for J.S.W. Sawbridge-Erle-Drax was erected E of the church, *c.* 1866–72 (he died in 1887). Neo-Byzantine and elaborate. Demolished in 1935.

marble-balustraded staircase. In the grounds several FOUN-
TAINS, said to have come from the Great Exhibition.*

HOLT

A scatter of mostly cob and thatch, with later brick cottages,
in various hamlets surrounding Holt Heath. Restrained C20
development, preserving the heath's distinctive bleak character.
Uddens House, a stucco-faced, bow-windowed country house
of *c.* 1800 (added to an earlier block of *c.* 1747), was largely
demolished in 1955.**

ST JAMES. 1834–6, by *John Tulloch* of Poole. Refurnished in
1875 by *T.H. Wyatt* (who removed the galleries). Chancel and
transepts added 1889. Brick. The work of 1834–6 is a low-
pitched nave, tall plain lancets. Oddly, the E.E. w window
(and bellcote) are original. The otherwise unknown *Rolfe &
Coggin* of London were probably the architects of the remarkably personal chancel and transepts.*** The windows are particularly distinctive: the lights – three in the short transepts,
five at the E end – are separated by blank vertical strips or
panels of brick. The transept windows have straight tops, the
E window is arched. Internally, the transepts are divided from
the sanctuary and nave by lancets. – REREDOS. 1902 by *Percy
Bacon Bros.* Oak. – PULPIT. From Wimborne Minster. Early
C17, with very elongated blank arches and detached Corinthian
angle columns. – STAINED GLASS. E window of five lights,
1889, by *J. Jennings.* Two nave windows, 1912, by *Joseph Bell
& Son* of Bristol.

HOLWELL

The present village of Holwell (or Crouch Hill) is a hamlet of C17
origin, ¾ m. S of the old village known as The Borough. Here
are the church and rectory, a farm and a few thatched cottages,
standing on a medieval N–S route at an abandoned crossing of
the Caundle Brook.

ST LAURENCE. A complete late C15 church of golden Ham Hill
stone. Nave, w tower, N aisle and S chapel (the latter together

---

*A 9-ft (2.7-metre)-high bronze STATUE of Drax on a tall pillar, erected by himself,
was later removed to Kent.
**For the *cottage orné* LODGE, *see* Stapehill.
***They unsuccessfully applied for a grant for this work from the Incorporated
Church Building Society in that year, according to Dr Brandwood.

with the porch an addition of *c.* 1500). Chancel and large organ chamber of 1885 by *G.R. Crickmay*, who also carried out a restoration. The three-stage embattled W tower has a S rectangular stair projection, gabled at the top. Embattled aisle, S porch and continuous chapel with big gargoyles and three-light windows. The N arcade piers have very handsome capitals with angel busts (cf. Stalbridge), their wings interconnecting. Some carry inscription scrolls, deeply undercut and linked. One has a running lion. The S chapel is attached to the S porch. The arch into it from the nave has standard responds, as does the tower arch. The E bay continuing the chapel is of the 1885 restoration. The nave has a ceiled wagon roof, the aisle a ceiling with moulded beams and bosses, these also well carved and in harmony with the aisle capitals. The chancel is of 1885 (Perp style), but the chancel arch is genuine C15 Perp, although strangely low in comparison with the aisle. – PULPIT. Oak, late C17. Panelled with fretwork elaboration. – FONT. Octagonal and Perp style, but no doubt by *Crickmay*. – ARCHITECTURAL FRAGMENTS re-set in the chancel on the N wall. – ROYAL ARMS of George III, 'the gift of Henry D'Aubeny', 1804. – STAINED GLASS. N aisle, two windows by *Clayton & Bell*, 1892 and 1895.

WESLEYAN METHODIST CHAPEL (former), Crouch Hill, ¾ m. S. Dated 1903. Red brick, E.E. style.

OLD RECTORY, just S of the church. C18, with rusticated quoins. Hipped tile roofs with stone-slate verges. Walls later stuccoed, probably early C19. Recessed balcony on the S front of this later date.

At BARNES CROSS, ½ m. W, a PILLAR BOX. Of 1853, made by *John Butt & Co.* at Gloucester. Cast-iron, octagonal plan. Vertical letter slit. Said to be the earliest pillar box still in public service.

BUCKSHAW HOUSE, ¾ m. WSW. Quite a handsome seven-bay façade, of *c.* 1740 for John Herbert. Pedimented attic storey, added in 1894 for the Hon. E.C. Digby. This is a Baroque curiosity. At the same time a red brick wing was added to the r., unbalancing the symmetry. The main block is two-storeyed. Rendered with ashlar dressings. Slightly projecting centre three bays, the alternating quoins giving further emphasis. The central window has a moulded surround and side scrolls above the segmental pediment of the doorway. All the other upper windows have the Early Georgian embellishment of raised stone aprons.

CORNFORD BRIDGE, ½ m. W. Bridge of *c.* 1480 over the Caundle Brook (much repaired). Three pointed-arched spans. Cutwaters between.

MANOR HOUSE, 1¼ m. SW. Late C16 in its N wing, but otherwise a major rebuilding of 1889 for M.S. Yeatman. The whole *c.* 1600-style S front is of this date, with a three-storey gabled porch and gables to l. and r. A three-storey canted bay facing W is also of this date, but reusing some earlier masonry features. The whole looks convincingly Jacobean from the end of the long S driveway.

NAISH FARM, ⅝ m. SSE. C15, an almost complete late medieval farmhouse. Perhaps the steepness of the hipped thatched roof might make one suspect the age of this rubble-stone cottage, although otherwise there is nothing external to suggest so early a date. There is a hall between the two-storey solar end and the addition to the l., partly replacing a one-storey service end beyond the through passage. Inside, two timber partitions (those between the cross-passage and service end, and between the hall and solar) are original C15 work. Even the later out-buildings are thought to occupy the site of original buildings, and to illustrate the layout of a medieval farmstead.

WESTROW HOUSE, 1 m. SSW. Of c. 1840. Stucco. A square block with a veranda along the S front.

HOOKE

ST GILES. The exterior is dominantly Victorian, with *G.R. Crick-may*'s rock-faced W tower of 1874–5 coinciding with a thorough restoration, and the chancel largely of 1840 by *J. Spinks* of Charminster. But the interior has a great surprise – the entry arch from the nave into a former chantry or funeral chapel: a wide arch panelled and with lively leaf bands either side of repeating (blank) shields, a swagger display. By the shape of the chapel windows it can be dated 1510 or 1520. But the nave is earlier, of the mid C15. Of this date in the N wall a fine canopied niche on an angel bust. Another, flatter one in a N window reveal. – The FURNISHINGS are completely by *Crick-may*, including his characteristic stone-fronted PULPIT. – In the nave niche a SCULPTURE of St Giles by *B. Grassby* of Powerstock.* – FONT. C15. Quatrefoils on each face, with an oddly elongated hexagonal shape so that it fits against the wall. Now in *Crickmay*'s specially made niche. – STAINED GLASS. E window by *Francis Skeat*, 1964. – MONUMENTS. Edmond Semar †1523. Brass inscription. – Samuel Rawlins †1847. Tablet with Gothic surround.

HOOKE COURT, ⅜ m. NW. The size of the rectangle marked out by the moat suggests that there was a substantial mansion here. The E wing, demolished c. 1965, was probably of the C15. Only its simple Perp plinth moulding remains.** Footings of a SE wing have also been found, defining a courtyard. What is left is a late C17 S wing of rubble stone, three-storeyed, five windows wide, as orderly as a warehouse. At its S end, two bays in the W front appear to be earlier, and may represent part of the range built for William Paulet, 3rd Marquess of Winchester, who inherited Hooke in 1576. Around and above the masonry

---

*He won a silver medal for this at the Dorset Industrial Exhibition, Weymouth, in 1878.
**Perp canopy-work was found built into the S wall. The N wall had a row of three pointed-arched openings, later blocked.

is clearly a rebuilding, but retaining three-light arched windows on the ground and first floors with continuous string courses passing over the window heads. A rebuilding is known to have taken place in the later C17 to repair Civil War damage, and the ashlar E front and S end must be of this date (see the windows with mullion-and-transom crosses). At this stage the block was no doubt gabled. It was made more orderly and given an extra storey and hipped roof in the later C19 by the 7th Earl of Sandwich. The porch and N addition are of this date, as are the canted bay windows (although the turret-like bay at the S end is earlier). Inside an early C16 Perp chimneypiece with a deep lintel carved with sub-cusped quatrefoils, the centre bearing the Paulet arms. The Paulets inherited the estate only in 1559, so the chimneypiece may have been brought in.

Hooke Court is now a residential study and event centre. Various buildings around the main block of the 1960s. These were built for St Francis School (closed in 1992).

HOOKE PARK, 1 m. SW. Among the trees a training centre was started here in the 1980s by the furniture designer John Makepeace. Of this date a WORKSHOP by *Frei Otto* and *Ahrends, Burton & Koralek*, 1989. Organic forms using spruce thinnings to form a series of compression arches. Also WESTMINSTER LODGE, a four-lobed dormitory of timber construction with a low-domed, grass-topped roof by *Edward Cullinan*, 1995. After 2002 the site was taken over by the Architectural Association School of Architecture in London as the base for their Design & Make courses. The chief outcome of this is THE BIG SHED, 2012, a workshop designed by the students under *Martin Self*. Cross-braced trusses of timber in the round, organized to create an angular, cedar-boarded exterior. Further student-designed buildings in progress.

CENTRE POINT FOUNTAINS. Of *c.* 1965 by *Jupp Dernbach-Mayen*, originally alongside the Centre Point tower by Richard Seifert & Partners, in Central London. Removed in 2010. Re-erected at Hooke Park, 2016. Abstracted flower forms in rough concrete. They were originally arranged in a blue-mosaic-lined pool.

HORTON

A village of timber-framed, brick and thatch cottages and one or two more substantial late C18 brick houses. Its setting is dominated by the nearby Horton Tower.

ST WOLFRIDA. Substantially a Georgian church, perhaps on the foundations of a Benedictine priory church, a cell of Sherborne, founded *c.* 970. Some C12 or C13 fabric remaining exposed in the N wall of the chancel; otherwise this is faced in brick. Brick too on the W and S walls of the nave, the latter

also partly concealing earlier masonry. Arched windows. In
1720 the church was recorded as being ruinous and rebuilding took place shortly thereafter. The long N transept of 1755
reuses much old stone, including buttresses. The transept has
a doorway with Tuscan pilasters and no pediment; the initials
IC in the gable may refer to the mason, *John Chapman*. He
was responsible for the earlier tower of 1722–3 in the angle
between the transept and nave. It is a memorable piece: its
spire, which is rather a pyramid, has pedimented dormers
as lucarnes – an inventive job on a small scale, by someone
who must have known Vanbrugh or Hawksmoor. The interior spreads without clear directions. Hutchins characteristically called Horton church 'a very ugly edifice'. – REREDOS.
Rococo, but with Ionic fluted pilasters and a pediment.
Unusually, it is all of plaster. – PULPIT. C18, the stairs of iron,
probably from 1869. – CHOIR STALLS and ORGAN. An incongruous attempt to impose Victorian chancel arrangements
(1891). – BOX PEWS. Mid-C18, probably contemporary with
the N transept. They were accompanied by galleries and, until
1925, faced the pulpit, then sited at a mid-point on the S wall
of the nave. – MONUMENTS. Knight and lady, he of Purbeck
marble, she of Ham Hill stone, both early C14. He crosses his
legs, she wears a wimple. A pity they are so weathered.

ABBEY HOUSE. The surviving reminder of the mansion of the
Uvedales built on the site, and possibly incorporating fragments, of the Benedictine priory. It was enlarged for Sir
Anthony Sturt in 1718 but the main block had largely gone by
the late C18. What survives was a service range. It incorporates
a timber-framed structure of *c.* 1500 with an opening – possibly a gateway – in the middle. Red brick E front made up
in the later C18 into a two-storey, seven-bay composition, the
centre three bays slightly projecting. In the end bays nothing
but a single overgrown arched mezzanine window. Extra S bay
with a blocked archway.

HORTON TOWER, on a hill ½ m. S. A megalomaniac folly of
1726, erected for Humphry Sturt of Horton. Probably by
Thomas Archer.* It was later called an 'observatory'. This six-
storey brick tower, a hexagon with three-quarter-round turrets
against alternate faces for two-thirds of its height, allowing for,
say, eighteen rooms, seems over-large for that purpose. Pointed
windows. Domes for the turrets, pediments against the flat
faces of the tower. Originally a larger dome roofed the central
hexagon, topped by a lantern; these collapsed in the early C20.

STANBRIDGE MILL BRIDGE, ⅓ m. NW of Horton Inn. Medieval with four pointed arches. Rebuilding dated 1666.

---

*Archer lived at Hale Park, 12 m. away in Hampshire, 1715–43. Sturt's brother-in-
law, George Chafin, employed Archer at Chettle *c.* 1720. *See also* Edward Marsden
in *Country Life*, 13 April 1978.

7000

IBBERTON

A scattered gathering of mainly modest cottages climbing up towards the church.

St Eustace. A small C15 church, halfway up the steep hill. It was in ruins and the E end roofless when *Ponting* carefully restored it, 1901–9. Embattled two-stage W tower with higher stair-turret, the stair projection rectangular. Nave and chancel and a N aisle, the two-bay arcade with piers with four chamfered projections. N chapel arch and chancel arch of standard section, the latter restored by Ponting. Curious Gothic E window tracery, perhaps early C17 (cf. Low Ham, Somerset). – FONT. C15, octagonal, Perp, much worn. – TOWER SCREEN. Jacobean; elementary. – STAINED GLASS. C15 fragments in several windows. In one N aisle window a beautiful Elizabethan oval royal arms, yellow and brown. Next to it another Elizabethan piece with a Tudor rose and the letters E R.

Wesleyan Methodist Chapel (former). Brick, dated 1884.

Below the church the very modest MANOR HOUSE, just a typical C17 cottage, banded in stone and flint. The dates on the porch, 1666 and 1686, presumably go with the three- and four-light windows lacking hoodmoulds. An early C19 extension at the W end with sashes hardly affected the original symmetry.

There are two CROSS-DYKES, one, 315 yds (290 metres) long, on Long Down, ½ m. NE of the church, the other, almost ploughed out, on Ibberton Hill, S of the village.

IWERNE COURTNEY
(*or* SHROTON)

8010

A picturesque straggle of a village on a loop off the A350. At the N end farms and cottages; at the S, beyond the church, the parkland walls and estate buildings belonging to Ranston.

St Mary. The church is of greensand ashlar, quite large and has one eminently interesting feature: the alterations and additions made by Sir Thomas Freke in 1610. They are Gothic and have a type of window current about 1300: three stepped lancet lights under one arch. The N aisle and chapel have them, and the E bay of the S aisle. This style was continued when the S aisle was extended westwards by *T.H. Wyatt* in 1873 (except for its W window, which is standard Perp). The chancel, however, has C14 features on its N and S sides. They may not be too trustworthy as it was fully refaced in 1873; the E window is of this date. The W tower is C15, of three stages with crocketed pinnacles. Curiously sited 1873 vestry in the angle between the W end of the N aisle and the tower. Inside, Freke's

N arcade is perfectly correctly West Country Perp standard. This is copied, but with more correct arch geometry, in the two bays of *Wyatt*'s S arcade. The tower arch is genuine Perp. It dies into the imposts. – FONT. Perhaps late C12. Octagonal, of Purbeck marble, with one large blank arch-head to each side. If this is Transitional it is totally re-tooled. – REREDOS. 1889, of Dalton Ware terracotta, with corn ears, grapes, the bust of Christ and two angels. Made in a local pottery managed by *Lady Baker*, who was her own designer. – SCREEN to the Freke Chapel. A charming piece of 1610. One-light divisions with colonnettes and dainty small-scale strapwork tracery. On top heavier strapwork. – TILES by *Minton* on the stepped sanctuary floor. – STAINED GLASS. Three chancel windows by *Warrington*, c. 1870. The N one is plain and mostly grisaille. Three in the S aisle by *Clayton & Bell*, 1872–7. – MONUMENTS. Sir Thomas Freke (†1633), erected 1654. Classical. A very large standing monument, too large for the church and especially for the chapel in which it stands. Also the figural sculpture is inept if lovable. So it may be just as well that there is no effigy. The centre is a long inscription flanked by vertical bands of coats of arms. The top is an open segmental pediment with coat of arms and flanking putti. Trumpeting angels are either side of the swagged base. – In the S chapel several enjoyable tablets to the Baker family of Ranston.

As one turns off the A350 (at the S end of the loop), the view of the church, with a shoulder of the downs behind, looks inviting as it appears over long red-tiled barns. Anticipation is further roused by the road running along between high walls, until it suddenly emerges at the church proudly standing between stone cottages of c. 1800 and a group of thatched barns incorporating a C17 DOVECOTE.

SHROTON HOUSE, at the far NW end of the village. Datestones of 1728 and 1736. Mildly classicized c. 1780, when the four giant Doric pilasters and a bow window were added. Further extension c. 1925 at the SW end, in matching style. Opposite, WILLIS'S SHROTON FARM, a townish three-storey red brick house of c. 1800.

RANSTON, ¼ m. SE. W front of 1753 by *Thomas Ryves* (of the notable Blandford family) for himself, probably assisted by *John Bastard* or perhaps *Francis Cartwright*. Five bays, two storeys upon a basement. Pediment over the centre three bays, carried on fluted Corinthian pilasters. Twin flight of balustraded steps, intended from the start (*see* below) but only reinstated c. 1963. It is then a standard formula of a façade, executed without overtones of provincialism. This was originally attached to a Jacobean house, demolished when a smaller house was built in its place. The other three fronts belong to this replacement, which is of 1961–3 by *Louis Osman* for Selina Gibson Fleming. Osman was better known as the creator of the Prince of Wales's investiture crown than as an architect. He did a very intelligent job of reduction, forming a square block, rendered and quite unadorned, except for raised quoins and a blocky, Vanbrughian front doorway on the E, with a Venetian opening over it. Osman also removed a pair of wings added in 1808 for P. W. Baker, the Portman Estate property agent (who is commemorated in Baker Street, London).

Inside, the staircase, with the date 1753 on the reverse of a crest, has a wrought-iron balustrade and mild Rococo plaster-work on walls and ceiling, of the type found in many houses in the Blandford area. Pairs of columns, Ionic downstairs, Corinthian with incurving volutes upstairs. The ceiling paint-ing however is by *Andrea Casali*, a London-based artist. Other paintings by Casali, including a set of four symbolizing the Arts. The figure of Architecture holds a scroll with the design for the W front of the house. All these features, introduced in the 1750s, have been skilfully reassembled into new relation-ships as part of Osman's remodelling.

The LANDSCAPING, including two ornamental lakes W of the house, and a classical balustraded BRIDGE of *c.* 1785 between them, was carried out for Peter Baker, who purchased the estate in 1781. This has been recently fully restored for James Gibson Fleming.

HAMBLEDON HILL (National Trust, also in Child Okeford and Hanford), ½ m. W. A complex of Neolithic causewayed enclosures and dykes, two Neolithic long barrows, and an impressive Iron Age hill-fort. The Neolithic features, mainly levelled in the 1960s, were investigated by excavations 1974–82 and re-surveyed in the 1990s. The hill-fort remains largely unexcavated. The hill is an outlier of the NW escarpment of Wessex chalk: a central dome with four spurs radiating out to the N (the hill-fort), E (Shroton spur), S (Stepleton spur) and W (Hanford spur, W of Stepleton spur).

The site is best approached by the steep track ascending from Shroton village. The summit of the hill, near the trig. point, is in the centre of the main Neolithic CAUSEWAYED ENCLOSURE, covering 20 acres. To the SW of the fence-line the earthworks are visible; to the NE they are ploughed away. The ditch segments were 6½ to 16 ft (2 to 5 metres) wide, and 2½ to 7½ ft (0.8 to 2.3 metres) deep below the chalk. Prob-able entrances lay E, NW and S. The enclosure was enhanced by double outer cross-dykes running across the Shroton and Stepleton spurs. The main enclosure contained more than seventy pits. Between the main ditches and the Stepleton cross-dykes was an oval LONG BARROW aligned NNW–SSE, 85 ft (26 metres) long and, until the 1960s, 3 to 6½ ft (1 to 2 metres) high; now rebuilt after excavation. A second LONG BARROW occupies the high point of the northern spur, within the ram-parts of the hill-fort. This, aligned N–S, is 240 ft (73 metres) long, nearly 6½ ft (2 metres) high, and has parallel side ditches.

To the S, past Coombe Wood, the Stepleton spur was the site of a second CAUSEWAYED ENCLOSURE, now ploughed away, of about 2½ acres. The ditches were up to 6½ ft (2 metres) deep, and the enclosure was strengthened by double outworks. This enclosure contained more than eighty pits. Linking the two causewayed enclosures, and probably enclosing the entire hill and all the spurs, were outworks, sometimes double or triple, which survive as an EARTHWORK along the W side of the hill (the Western outwork).

Construction of the Neolithic complex began in the C36 or C35 B.C. (calibrated radiocarbon dates), and continued over 300 to 400 years. The main enclosure was built first. The Neolithic ditches and pits contained rich deposits of pottery, stone axe-heads and grinding equipment, flint tools, food remains (especially of cattle) and human bones, many of which were disarticulated, gnawed and weathered. Some of the pots and axe-heads came from distant regions. People gathered here for short periods during which feasting and earthwork construction took place. Some dead bodies were exposed on the hill, and selected bones deposited deliberately in pits and ditches. Men, women and children were represented. Some of the ramparts were burnt, and a few victims of arrowshot indicate that attacks had occurred.

Returning N along the Western outwork, the HILL-FORT is reached. The outline, following the contours of the northern spur, covers 30 acres. There are two main ramparts, a quarry zone inside the inner rampart, and two cross-ramparts. The N section was probably the earliest, with a single rampart. This was extended S as far as the second cross-rampart, enclosing the large Neolithic long barrow and further Neolithic outworks. Finally the whole spur was enclosed by double ramparts, and on the S side massive outworks comprising twin banks and ditches were constructed across the spur. There are entrances on the N, SW and SE. Within the interior are 207 hut platforms.

IWERNE MINSTER

8010

The village shows many signs of a wealthy and patriarchal lord of the manor (for whom *see* below). However, the fact that *Waterhouse*, or his office, was responsible for much of the estate building, and that a loud red brick with prominent half-timbering was adopted, creates an appearance more typical of the Home Counties than the West Country.

ST MARY. The most important and interesting church in its neighbourhood. At its core, mid- and late C12 fabric; early C13 N transept; C14 Dec chancel and W tower, the latter of three stages with an original spire, short and recessed. One of only three medieval spires in the county, this was reduced in height in 1853 when it was somewhat inelegantly rebuilt.* In the C14

*The others are at Trent and Winterbourne Steepleton.

much external rebuilding of the aisles was carried out. Three restorations: the first of 1870–1 by *T.H. Wyatt*; another of 1880 by *J.L. Pearson*, who added the fine S chapel and rebuilt much of the S transept S wall in banded flintwork; and a third by *C.E. Ponting* of 1913–14, when a new E window was installed and the organ resited on a new W gallery. The story begins with the N arcade, which is of three bays, uniform Late Norman work, with round piers, round, much-scalloped capitals and round single-step arches – say 1170. The arcade presupposes a Norman nave of some size. N transept in origin of the early C13, although the two Norman windows are re-set and separated by a detached Purbeck shaft with a stiff-leaf capital, i.e. a C13 feature. Furthermore, this part of the church was heavily rebuilt in 1870–1, which may have confused matters. The arch from the aisle is a typical aisle-to-transept arch. The S arcade of the nave, which was originally only of two bays, has motifs of *c.* 1200 (round piers, heavily moulded capital, chamfered responds with a demi-shaft, double-chamfered pointed arches). The reason why it was not made to tally in length with the N arcade, and why the heights of the S piers and their bases and arches do not tally with those on the N side, may have been the presence of a S tower. The transeptal third (E) bay of the S arcade is further W than the N transept. It has an awkward, lop-sided arch, probably erected when the putative tower was removed in the C15. (Externally, masonry in the SW corner, including a C12 buttress, remains largely *in situ*.) The C14 tower arch to the nave is of three continuous chamfers. The chancel is Dec, though the flowing tracery of the E window is of 1913–14. In the aisles are Late Perp windows with straight tops. *Pearson*'s fine S CHAPEL, with its stone lierne vault, has a typical Dec three-bay arcade (piers of eight shafts, the diagonal ones of Purbeck marble) and Dec windows; the two S windows are re-set originals, with the E window designed by Pearson to match.

Many FURNISHINGS by *Wyatt*. The best are the CHOIR STALLS and clergy seats. – REREDOS. Of *c.* 1920 by *Sir Giles Gilbert Scott*. – PULPIT. Dated 1610, with panels of knotted cable pattern. – FONT. C15, octagonal, with slightly tapering quatrefoil sides. – ROYAL ARMS on canvas, 1814–20. – HATCHMENTS. Three, all with shields of arms of Bower, first half of the C19. – STAINED GLASS. One of the glories of the church, following Ponting's alterations, is the fine E window of 1914 by *Christopher Whall*. The easternmost of the other chancel windows are by *Alexander Gibbs, c.* 1870; another, S side, is signed W.W. for *William Wailes*, 1847. S chapel, all by *Clayton & Bell*, 1890. E wall of the N transept, 1926, by *Powell & Sons*. S transept window by *A. Gibbs*, †1871. – MONUMENTS. Good tablet to Robert Fry †1684 (S aisle W). – Two *opus sectile* panels, S aisle, 1917 and 1931, by *Powells*.

EBENEZER BAPTIST CHAPEL (former, now Abingdon Memorial Hall), The Chalk, ⅛ m. SW. 1810, enlarged 1860. Round-headed windows. Rendered brick.

West Lulworth, Durdle Door, from the W (p. 637)
Shaftesbury, Gold Hill, looking S (p. 518)

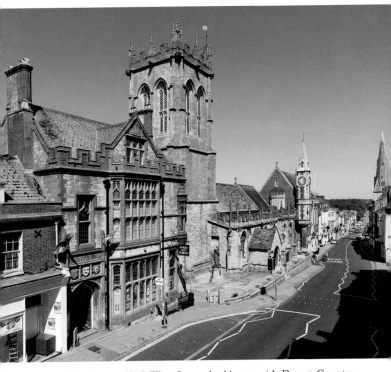

3. Dorchester, High West Street, looking E, with Dorset County Museum by Crickmay & Son, 1881–3, and St Peter's church, mostly 1420–1 (p. 252)

4. Weymouth, Trinity Road (old town), from the N (p. 654)

Winterborne St Martin, Maiden Castle, c36 B.C. to CI A.D. (p. 688)
Knowlton Rings and Barrows, c. 2750–2500 B.C., and church ruin,
mostly CI2 (p. 348)

7. Wareham, St Martin, C11, interior, N aisle *c.* 1180 (p. 625)
8. Winterbourne Steepleton, St Michael, sculpture, C10 or C11 (p. 697)

9. Corfe Castle,
Great Tower,
c. 1080, and
part of w
bailey, mostly
1201–4, from
the sw (p. 219)

10. Sherborne,
Old Castle,
sw gatehouse,
1122–39,
altered late
C16–early C17
(p. 550)

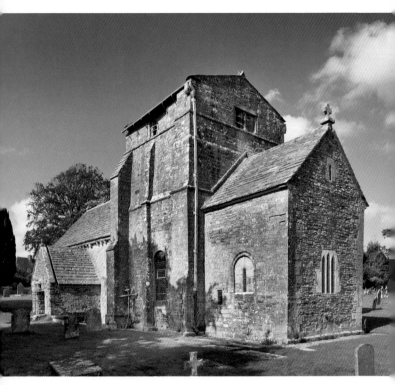

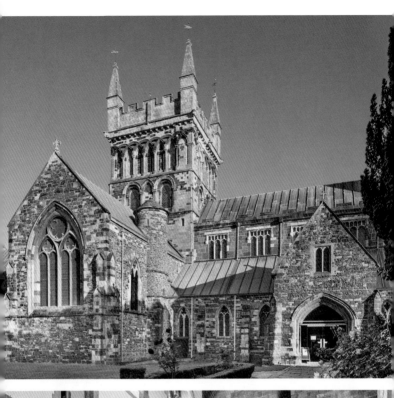

18
19
20

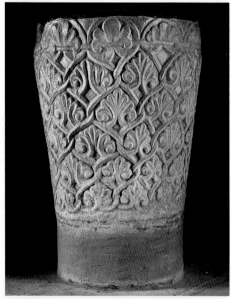

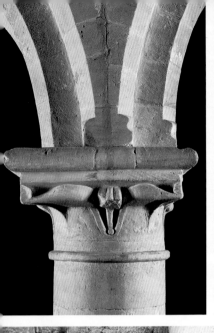

4. Sherborne Abbey, Lady Chapel, early C13, extended by W.D. Caröe 1921–33, interior (p. 529)

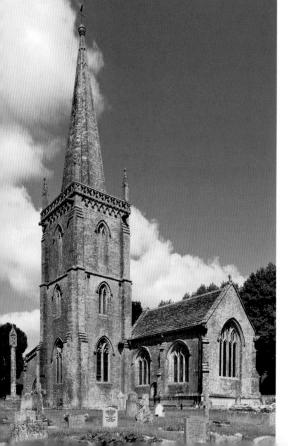

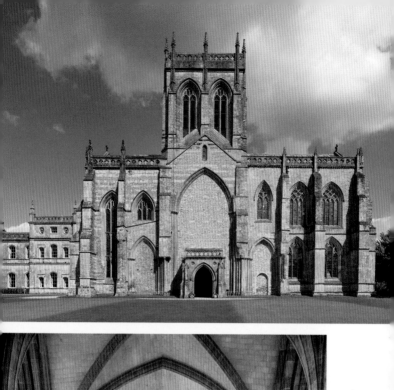

29. Abbotsbury,
St Catherine's
Chapel, *c.* 1400,
from the SW
(p. 93)

30. Beaminster,
St Mary,
W tower, 1503,
1877–8 (p. 108)

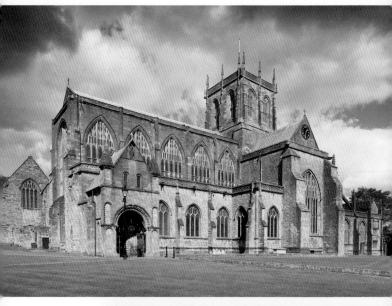

1. Sherborne
   Abbey, largely
   c. 1425–*c.* 1490,
   from the sw
   (p. 523)
2. Charminster,
   St Mary, w
   tower, early
   C16 (p. 194)

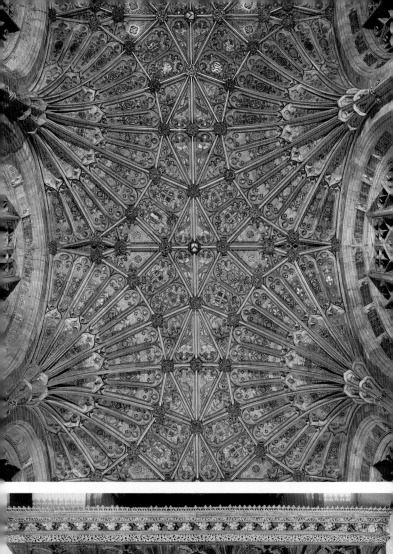

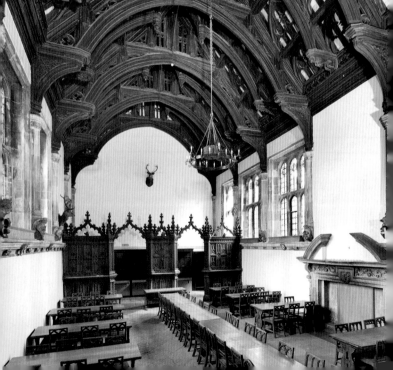

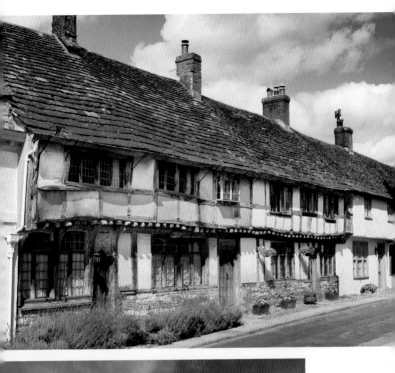

61. Sherborne Castle, Green Drawing Room, *c.* 1600 (p. 555)
62. Winterborne Herringston, Herringston, Great Chamber, plasterwork between 1616 and 1626 (p. 684)
63. Cranborne Manor, 1207–8, remodelled and extended by William Arnold 1609–12, N front (p. 235)
64. Warmwell House, S front, possibly by William Arnold, *c.* 1618 (p. 630)

61 | 63
62 | 64

65. Wimborne St Giles, monument to Sir Anthony Ashley †1628 and wife (p. 672)
66. Leweston, Holy Trinity, probably by William Arnold, 1616, from the sw (p. 353)

67. Wimborne Minster, monument to Sir Edmund Uvedale †1606 (p. 666)
68. Puddletown, St Mary, wall painting, 1635 (p. 499)
69. Abbotsbury, St Nicholas, chancel vault plasterwork, 1638 (p. 92)

70. Forde Abbey, Saloon, *c.* 1650–60 (p. 296)
71. Wimborne St Giles, St Giles's House, E range, 1651–9 (p. 673)

2. Child Okeford, Fontmell Parva, *c.* 1680, E front, wings by George
   Evans, *c.* 1850 and 1864–9 (p. 210)
3. Chettle House, by Thomas Archer, *c.* 1715, W front (p. 204)

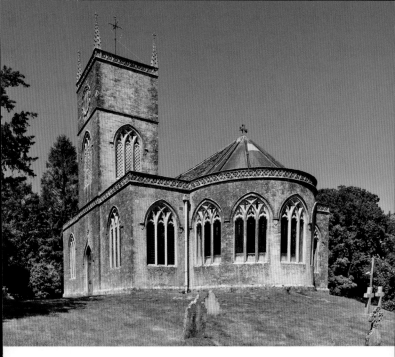

90. Blandford Forum, Eastway House, dining room, plasterwork attribute
    to Francis Cartwright, c. 1750 (p. 133)
91. More Crichel, Crichel House, State Drawing Room, by Samuel &
    James Wyatt, ceiling, 1772–80, paintings by Biagio Rebecca (p. 424)

2. Shapwick, White Mill, 1776, from the s (p. 521)
3. Milton Abbas, model village, by Sir William Chambers and Capability Brown, c. 1770–90 (p. 415)

102. Rampisham, Pugin Hall (former rectory), by A.W.N. Pugin, 1845–7 (p. 508)

103. Canford Magna, Canford Manor (Canford School), by Edward Blore 1826, enlarged by Sir Charles Barry, 1847–50, and by Romaine-Walker & Tanner, 1888, from the SW (p. 174)

104. Sherborne, Almshouse of St John the Baptist and St John the
Evangelist, 1438–48, enlarged by William Slater, 1858 (p. 540)

105. Bryanston (Bryanston School), by R. Norman Shaw, 1889–94, s front
(p. 162)

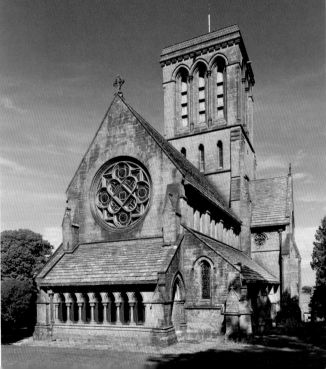

6. Cattistock, St Peter and St Paul, enlarged by Sir G.G. Scott, 1857,
tower by G.G. Scott Jun., 1874 (p. 179)

7. Kingston, St James, from the w, by G.E. Street, 1873–80 (p. 339)

8. Bothenhampton, Holy Trinity, by E.S. Prior, 1887–9, interior (p. 137)

109 | 111
110 | 112

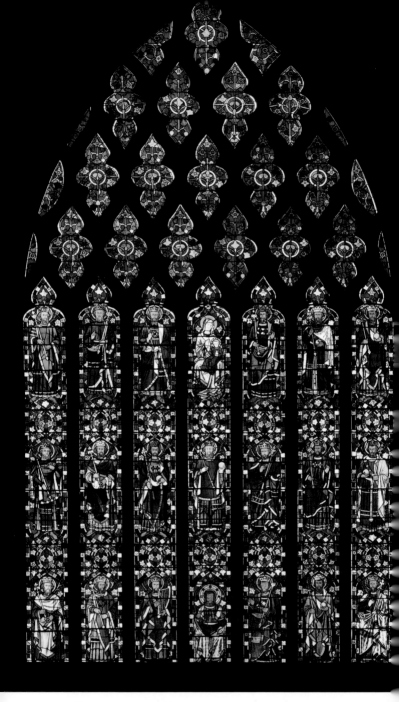

113. Milton Abbas, abbey church, s transept, stained glass showing Tree of Jesse, by A.W.N. Pugin with F.W. Oliphant, 1848 (p. 410)

117. Portland, Easton Methodist Church, by La Trobe & Weston, 1906–7, interior (p. 487)
118. Gillingham, St George, by C. E. Ponting, 1921, from the NE (p. 303)

19. Briantspuddle, Bladen Valley war memorial, by Eric Gill, 1916–18 (p. 145)

120. Preston, Riviera Hotel, by L. Stuart Smith, 1937 (p. 497)
121. Broadstone, Yaffle Hill, by Sir Edward Maufe, 1930 (p. 157)
122. Poole, Parkstone, Landfall, by Oliver Hill, 1936–8 (p. 479)

23. Wool, St Joseph (R.C.), by Anthony Jaggard of John Stark & Partners, 1969–71, baptistery (p. 704)
24. Bryanston School, Craft, Design and Technology Building, by Piers Gough of CZWG, 1987–8, Sanger Centre for Science and Mathematics, by Hopkins Architects, 2007 (p. 165)
25. Dorchester, Poundbury, The Buttercross, by Ben Pentreath, 2014 (p. 260)
26. Bere Regis, Hyde House, by Robert Adam of ADAM Architecture, 2004 (p. 119)

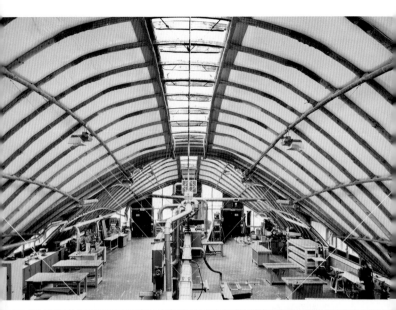

127. Hooke, Hooke Park, workshop, by Frei Otto and Ahrends, Burton & Koralek, 1989, interior (p. 328)

128. Poole, RNLI Lifeboat College, by Poynton Bradbury Wynter Cole Architects, 2004 (p. 463)

WESLEYAN METHODIST CHAPEL, ¼ m. SW. By *T. Hudson* of
Gillingham, 1879. Red and white brick with a wheel window
in the front gable.

Immediately S, on the opposite side of the lane to the church,
comes THE OAK HOUSE (formerly The Homestead), by *Baillie
Scott & Beresford*. Built as a village club, the gift of James Ismay
in 1921, and converted to a dwelling in the early 1930s. Coyly
complicated, with a half-timbered porch and a big tiled projection nudging your shoulder as you walk up OLD SCHOOL
LANE. On the W garden front more timber framing and a long
window under the projecting eaves. It is a Surrey not a Dorset
idiom. Just to its W (and glimpsed from the lane through a
gateway), THE CHANTRY, in contrast, is pure Dorset. Three-
storey S-facing front, two-storeyed behind. Banded flint and
ashlar with tall, diagonally set chimneystacks. Tall, compact,
symmetrical front, with three-light mullioned windows, even
in the central projecting porch. This is surprising as, in the
Dorset way, the porch houses the staircase. The house probably belongs to the first half of the C17. Along CHURCH ROAD
(running E from the church), on the r., DEVINE HOUSE (the
former vicarage). Dated 1836. Crowstepped gables.

Going W from THE CHALK, towards the main road, beyond
the Methodist chapel on the l. is a block of brick and half-
timbered COTTAGES, a former COACH HOUSE and the TALBOT
ARMS (facing the A350). All probably by *Waterhouse*, c. 1880.

At the upper end of the village, the WAR MEMORIAL,
1920, by *Sir Giles Gilbert Scott*. Finely carved (in Doulting
and Hopton Wood stones) in the form of a medieval market
cross. Triangular-section shaft. E, along HIGHER STREET, a
gabled SHELTER (known as The War Office), with a sculpture
of Mercury over the opening, also by *Scott*, for James Ismay.
Earlier than these, the adjacent PUMP SHELTER is dated
'W. 1880' (for Lord Wolverton). Beyond this, the PRIMARY
SCHOOL of 1884, most likely by *Waterhouse*.

CLAYESMORE SCHOOL (formerly IWERNE MINSTER HOUSE),
¼ m. W. The most ambitious High Victorian mansion in the
county, built for George Grenfell Glyn, 2nd Lord Wolverton,
the banker and politician, by *Alfred Waterhouse*, at a cost of
£80,240. Dated 1878 on the porch. Rubble stone with Bath
stone dressings, not creating a strong contrast of colour. Otherwise everything is typically emphasized and perhaps more
effective on the garden front. Entrance front facing N, the main
block to the l., with two uneven gables and a polygonal bay.
Steep roofs and emphatic chimneystacks of course. Projecting
porch with a cusped entrance arch. Big staircase window. The
service wing ends in another big gable and a tourelle growing
out beside it. The windows have cusped arched lights. Low
Tudor-style addition of 1908 at the l. end for James Ismay
(probably by *J. Francis Doyle*, who worked for the Ismays and
the White Star Line in Liverpool). Ismay purchased the estate
in that year. The garden front is a more casual composition of
three gables, two paired with bay windows. To the r. of these a

canopied veranda. To the l. the secondary wing, at a lower level, with its own cross-gable and multiple-shafted chimneystack.

Inside, Waterhouse's main space is an entrance hall combined with the spine corridor and staircase-well. Staircase balustrade with characteristic struts and geometrically pierced timber panels. Huge fireplace, salvaged from the dining room of *Norman Shaw*'s Dawpool, Cheshire, of 1882–4, installed here *c.* 1930. Mosaics underfoot throughout the ground floor. The other rooms remodelled *c.* 1908, with Quattrocentesque chimneypieces here and Neo-Adam ceilings there. Jacobean interior to the annexe.

In the STABLE COURT, E of the house, Waterhouse really lets himself go. Red brick now; and the clock tower over the entrance is built up with tourelles and buttressing forms as a *tour de force* of geometrical fun and games. To the N of the stables, the curious TROPHY ROOM, *c.* 1880 and presumably also by *Waterhouse*.

WEST LODGE, 1¾ m. NE. Few houses in the south of England can be so spectacularly sited as West Lodge. The house stands on the crest of the downs with a view of vast extent to the SE; and it stands here for the very good reason that at first this was a lodge of Cranborne Chase, which begins at the foot of the downs. The present rather melodramatic house is a remodelling of *c.* 1740 by *John Pitt* of Encombe of a house *c.* 1600, for himself. White-rendered. Facing SE, the centrepiece is a giant attached portico of four stone Tuscan columns, carrying a proper Tuscan timber pediment. Circular upper windows here, originally lighting a single room as wide and high as the portico, and a lunette in the pediment. The sides of the pediment are taken down for a further bay each side, creating a prodigious slope. The three-bay SW wing is contemporary with this, although altered in the numerous later recastings. Of these, the balancing NE wing incorporates structures of several dates. The W (entrance) front is similar, without the portico. Internally, fittings are generally *c.* 1830, *c.* 1860 and of the 1930s, reflecting various attempts to make a hunting lodge into an independent country residence. The process continues, with an entrance court formed between matching brick wings by *Tim Reeve*, under construction in 2014. Also an extensive landscaping scheme is under way.

ROMAN FARM BUILDING, 1 m. SW. Excavated in 1897. An aisled villa was succeeded by a rectangular C4 building with a tower granary attached.

IWERNE STEPLETON

Only the house and its private church, hidden behind planting and high walls alongside the sharply cornered A350.

STEPLETON HOUSE. A four-square house of fine ashlar, not large. Six bays by five, two-storeyed, with a hipped roof. The house is of *c.* 1660, for Thomas Fownes, who purchased in 1654. As first built (and as preserved on the N and W fronts), Stepleton had upright, classically proportioned windows throughout. The window mouldings are of the familiar step-and-hollow-chamfer variety. Moulded first-floor string course; two-light mullioned windows in the basement. Sashes replaced the assumed original mullioned-and-transomed crosses, improvements made after Julines Beckford bought Stepleton in 1745 (for £12,600). The E front received new window surrounds and a central emphasis by a one-bay broken pediment on brackets, and a round-headed central window above the channelled door surround. The S front however has the entrance, and here the central part is remodelled into a three-bay composition of considerable delicacy and charm. A central round-headed niche breaks up into a pediment, and fluted pilasters flank it in a Venetian composition. The doorway hood and flanking windows are so close to those at Sir Peter Thompson's House, Poole, as to suggest that *John Bastard* was the designer.*

In 1758 (date on rainwater heads) rectangular wings were added l. and r., probably by *Nathaniel Ireson*. The builder was *Richard Kittermaster* of Yeovil, Ireson's son-in-law. These are Palladian in their design and detailing and are clearly in a different hand from the main block. Ionic loggias on the S side, doorways with Gibbs surrounds and pediments on the N.

Inside there are mid-C18 plaster ceilings in most ground-floor rooms, none needing special artistic notice. One room has the Fownes arms, dating it to before 1745. The central top-lit staircase (filling an earlier light well) has a bravura display of Dorset Rococo plasterwork on the walls. Wrought-iron balustrade. Both date the work to *c.* 1755 (cf. the hall and staircase at Ranston), an alteration probably also by *John Bastard*. Upper arcade on piers, opening to the landing. Work may have remained incomplete in 1762, for in that year Edward Gibbon wrote that Stepleton was 'unmeaning, expensive and unfinished'. His comments may relate partially to the landscaped surroundings, then in the course of development.

The PARKLAND to the E of the house was largely the creation of Peter Beckford, owner from 1765. To provide an uninterrupted view from the house, a turnpike proposed in the late C18 was diverted to the W, resulting in the tortuous route now taken by modern traffic.

ST MARY. The church is embedded in the grounds of the house. It is of *c.* 1100 and consists of nave and chancel, at present roughcast. The present chancel has very thick walls and may originally have formed a tower base, with an earlier (demolished) chancel further E. Narrow, round-arched windows formerly lit the nave, one of which has been partially revealed. There

* Cf. also Moreton House, of 1744–6.

must have been an apse or a square altar space originally, for the only decorated piece is the E arch (to the original chancel), now just framing a Perp window. The imposts have friezes of saltire crosses. The similar enrichment of the arch is mid-C19. A Perp niche l. of this arch, and a Perp PISCINA. – STAINED GLASS. A set by *Clayton & Bell*, c. 1890. W window also theirs, c. 1901. – MONUMENT. Martha Cameron Lindsay †1918. By *François-Léon Sicard*, 1921.* Large, immaculately white marble relief with her seated figure in very shallow Donatellesque relief. The style is more French than English. – Many other family tablets.

Simple early C18 brick STABLES W of the house. Round-headed Gibbs surround to the doorway in the central, pedimented pavilion.

KIMMERIDGE

A village of bleached grey limestone and thatched cottages with the church, parsonage and farm forming a group at the top end.

ST NICHOLAS. All that remains of the earlier church is the simple C12 S doorway with moulded imposts and the curious arrangement of windows on two levels at the W end, presumably C18 and linked to a now removed gallery. The remainder of 1872, probably by *Crickmay*. Broadly C16 Perp style, with a blank N wall. Buttressed W bellcote. – FONT. Plain C12 bowl. – FURNISHINGS. Of 1872 and unremarkable apart from their completeness. At the W end a raised platform with pews and an organ console. – TILEWORK by *Minton* in the sanctuary. – STAINED GLASS. Fine E window by *Kempe*, 1904. – MONUMENT. Crisp tablet to William Clavell †1817 by *Tyley* of Bristol.

MUSEUM OF JURASSIC MARINE LIFE, just below the church. By *Kennedy O'Callaghan Architects*, 2015. Neo-vernacular of Purbeck stone and blue slate, counterbalanced by timber boarding and glazing. Two ranges at right angles.

KIMMERIDGE FARM, W of the church, took its present three-gabled form in 1829 (according to a datestone on the back wing).

THE OLD PARSONAGE, E of the church (probably by *Mondey* of Dorchester), with its steep gables and grouped diagonal-set chimneystacks, is dated 1837.

Although the village has an immemorial air, the row of cottages below the church only came in 1848. Another cottage pair is dated 1854.

---

* Sicard did many monuments in France, and also the Apollo Fountain in Sydney, Australia.

CLAVELL TOWER (Landmark Trust), 1 m. SSW, is a circular three-storey look-out tower on the promontory above Kimmeridge Bay. A scholarly mixture of motifs, as befits a folly: round the bottom a colonnade of Tuscan columns of the primitive type favoured by French painters such as David for their backgrounds, and round the top false machicoulis and a parapet pierced with quatrefoils. The Rev. John Richards Clavell of Smedmore built the tower c. 1830. The whole tower was taken down and rebuilt some 25 yds inland of its original location, 2006–8.

GAULTER GAP, ¾ m. SW, spreading to the W. An Early Iron Age shale-working and salt-boiling site next to the coast; also inhumation burials. The pottery from this site has provided the name of the Kimmeridge Early Iron Age style.

KING'S STAG

7010

Lydlinch

MEMORIAL CHAPEL. 1914 by *Arthur E. Bartlett.** Timber-framed with a matching bellcote. Buttressed stone W doorway. Built in memory of Lady Barbara Yeatman-Biggs of Stock House. Thatched MISSION ROOM of 1836, a few yds N. Tudor.

PRIMITIVE METHODIST CHAPEL, ⅓ m. S. Dated 1854. Stuccoed, with round-arched windows.

KINGSTON

9070

The ridge-top village is dominated by *Street*'s church. Its tower is all that can be seen on approach above the increasingly mature tree planting. The village is also mainly of the mid to late C19. Several cottages have picturesque Gothic Revival features, such as bay windows and buttresses.

ST JAMES. A replacement for the then relatively recent building by *G. S. Repton* at the other end of the village (*see* p. 341), far exceeding it in size. Its builder, the 3rd Earl of Eldon, evidently regarded the project as an act of Christian duty, as well, no doubt, as considering such a large edifice as commensurate with his own means and dignity. The cost is estimated at £70,000. Stone was from Eldon's Purbeck estate, roof timbers and stone slates from his Gloucestershire estate. The earl was twenty-eight when the new building was started and, as the grandson of a Lord Chancellor, he naturally went to *Street*, 107

*A pupil of Sir Reginald Blomfield. Information from John Worth.

who at the time was building the Royal Courts of Justice in the Strand (also of Portland stone). Eldon undoubtedly gave Street the opportunity for his grandest church in the country. It rose between 1873 and 1880. And it rose high. The central tower is visible on its ridge for miles, and it is equally impressive from nearby, especially from the E, where apse, short transepts – the r. one with a round stair-turret partly inspired by Christchurch Priory, Hampshire – and tower form a vigorously steep group. So the church has nave and aisles, a lower narthex at the W end, transepts, crossing tower and apse. Street kept a strict economy on window shapes. It is all his characteristic E.E. lancets, in pairs or groups, except for the great W rose and one little S transept window. The rose also is the only piece where Street stakes a claim to originality. He inserts a square in the circle and a quatrefoil overlapping the centres of the sides of the square, and a smaller inner quatrefoil, and a smaller square in that set diagonally.

One enters by the narthex and is faced by a tripartite composition like the entrance to a chapter house. In the portal there is more small-scale decoration than anywhere else in the church; for the church is economical with motifs inside as well, though the motifs are richer than outside. The arcades have as their piers Purbeck clusters with stiff-leaf capitals (with carving here, as elsewhere by *G.W. Milburn* of York); the aisles have Purbeck shafting too. So has the clerestory, but here used more sparingly. In materials the E end could not go beyond: so it achieved its climax by stone vaulting. The nave has an open timber roof; crossing, transepts and apse are rib-vaulted.

The church, in all but size, stakes a cathedral claim. The sedilia and piscina group in the chancel press home that claim. Street, as in the contemporary Great Hall of the Law Courts, is equal to the demand. He is discriminating and admits only the best. Harmony, symmetry, nobility are the qualities he aims at. Passion, if expressed at all, is expressed through the insistent build-up of shafting and vaulting at the E end; it is not expressed through elaboration of decoration or profusion of colour. It is a perfect interior, and one that is extremely well preserved in its initial state, perhaps owing to the small size of the community and the lightness of use.

Street loved to design for wrought iron. So the ironwork to the WEST DOOR, in the openings alongside and on the PULPIT and ALTAR RAIL is his (made by *James Leaver* of Maidenhead); also the high CHANCEL SCREEN (made by *Thomas Potter & Son* of London). – Sanctuary TILEWORK by *Craven, Dunnill & Co.* – STAINED GLASS. Street gave it all to *Clayton & Bell*. A coherent set of figurative windows fill the sanctuary, aisles and W rose, while the clerestory windows are purely decorative. – MONUMENT. 1st Earl of Eldon, 1839. Designed by *G.S. Repton*, portrait carved by *Sir Francis Chantrey*. White tablet with profile medallion below the inscription. – Matching adjacent panel to the first Countess. Both moved from the old church.

Approach paths to the church have distinctive pitch-stone PAVING, with small local slabs set diagonally around the entrance.

Opposite, a stone WATER PUMP with E.E. detailing. It must be by *Street, c.* 1880.

Former CHURCH (now a dwelling), 250 yds E. By *G.S. Repton* (builder *John Tulloch* of Wimborne), 1833. Repton was the son-in-law of the 1st Earl of Eldon. Repton's is a simple, though not a small church. It has a N tower and much solid wall. The windows are straight-headed with ogee arches to the lights. Repton liked to use this pattern also for single-light openings. No structural division of chancel from nave. S transept with entrance added between 1841 and 1861. Reused doorway masonry from the C12 chapel embedded in the W wall. Diaperwork arch.

KINGSTON HOUSE, 100 yds SW. Built as the parsonage, 1878–80 by *Street.* Range with gabled cross-wings at the ends. Gothic Revival features confined to the arched porch entrance, buttresses and cylindrical-ended chimneyshafts.

SCOLES MANOR, ½ m. NE. Modest early C17 farmhouse facing E with a two-storey porch. Round-headed entrance arch. Panel above with a carved rope circle. Three-light windows with hoodmoulds. Pair of C18 buttresses. Attached to the NW corner a small independent HALL of *c.* 1300 with a two-light S window, lancets united by the filleted hoodmould. C18 bee boles built into the W wall. – Adjoining OUTBUILDING with pointed-arched doorway, also *c.* 1300.

'CELTIC' FIELDS AND SETTLEMENTS. On Kingston Down, 1 m. S, 'Celtic' fields and earthworks covering about 150 acres and set around two adjacent settlements with a boundary between.

Kingston House, principal front.
Photo lithograph, 1878

KINGSTON LACY
Pamphill

After the loss of Coleshill (Berks.) in 1952, Kingston Lacy is the most important surviving work of that most discriminating gentleman-architect *Sir Roger Pratt*. Before *Barry*'s alterations of 1835–55 it was the epitome of the Restoration house, although it had already by that date undergone a slow erosion of original features. Built in 1663–5 for Sir Ralph Bankes, it made a complete contrast to Corfe Castle, the no-longer-habitable home of his father, the Attorney General Sir John. There survives unusually good documentation of the house: Pratt's original design for the N front, and much detail of the building operations in Pratt's notebooks, including the names of the master mason, *Goodfellow*, the executant mason, *Joseph Godfrey* (of Sherborne), and the contractor, *Sir Thomas Fitch* (or Fitts) of Farnham in Surrey. The last stresses the most important fact about the house: that, when constructed, it was alien to Dorset. Together with the W wing of Cranborne Manor of 1647, St Giles's House, Wimborne St Giles, of 1651, and Charborough Park of 1655, it was one of a group of houses to introduce a new metropolitan style into the county. Gone now are the excited conceits of a Lulworth or a Sherborne, and a reposefully harmonious formula takes their place. Compact planning was another aspect of this innovation, setting the whole under a hipped roof without recourse to cross-wings at the ends.

As seen today, the exterior and much of the interior is the result of *Sir Charles Barry*'s extensive remodelling project, and all the more interesting for that. Since 1982, together with a large estate including Corfe Castle (q.v.), Kingston Lacy has been a property of the National Trust.

EXTERIOR. The house is of nine bays by seven, two-storeyed on a semi-basement, and appears unexpectedly small as one comes upon it in its park. Hipped roof on a cornice with big blocky dentils. Central balustraded flat and a small cupola. Angle quoins, alternating in size, and similar quoins to mark the slightly projecting centre three bays of the N (entrance) front, which have the duty to support a pediment with Sir Ralph's coat of arms and the date 1663. The other fronts have merely a closer spacing of the centre three windows as a stress-mark.

So much of what is seen today, however, is a result of *Barry*'s Jonesian restoration-amplification for W.J. Bankes, the Italophile friend of Byron who had harvested in Italy an unusually choice collection of paintings. What Barry did was at one and the same time to restore the house's original character and to take the project further by a typically Victorian and Barryesque heightening of that character, on the mistaken, although fortuitous, understanding that Kingston Lacy had originally been designed by Inigo Jones. Pratt's house was of brick with Chilmark stone dressings. Barry left it faced with Chilmark stone and Portland stone dressings. At the entrance front the

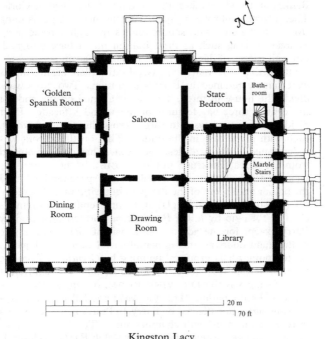

Kingston Lacy.
Plan

ground was lowered to turn the basement into a full storey. Towards the garden, false quoining laid more than Pratt's almost undetectable stress on the centre trio of windows, and the triple dormer above took matters a step further. To the E a loggia was opened up with a trio of arches, heavy entablature and applied columns with banded rustication; to the N a *porte cochère* was added. Barry introduced variety to the window frames, giving ears to some, architraves to others, driven, no doubt, by various Jonesian examples. As a homage, the W front was refenestrated, much as it would have appeared initially with mullioned-and-transomed cross-windows. (The other windows had been altered to sashes in the late C18.) Finally, after re-profiling the roof and reinstating the balustrade and cupola, the skyline was enlivened with busily shaped surrounds to the dormers, and Barry's favourite chimneystacks, placed at the four corners of the house *à la* Coleshill.

100

In the INTERIOR Barry remodelled the circulation and much else, contriving in a small space a remarkably majestic approach to the main rooms on what had been Pratt's ground floor. From the entrance vestibule (in the C17 basement) one goes up a few steps, turns l. and enters the ashlar-faced stairwell, in which short flights rise round a solid square core. Tunnel-vaults in the Italian Renaissance way. At the half-landing, in three large niches, life-size statues by *Marochetti* of Charles I, Sir John

Bankes and Lady Bankes, the heroine of the siege of Corfe. Their blackened bronze is highly effective here. Upper landing (to the first floor) with saucer domes through a triple arch. Staircase ceiling such as Pratt himself might have designed, but wall friezes of dancing putti, Italianism again.

Other than the new staircase, Pratt's plan arrangements were largely retained in Barry's alterations. Two cross-walls divide the house in three, these walls aligned on the ends of the central three-bay features of the N and S façades. Pratt divided the outer bays into three across the E and W fronts, each with a staircase in the middle. That on the E front was redeveloped by Barry as described above (having been altered from the 'Great Backstair' in the late C18). In the central bay facing N are the SALOON, a double-height space retained from the hall or ante-room of the C17 plan but without the 'pergolo' (or two-storey internal loggia) at its inner end. It was remodelled in 1784–90 by *R.W.F. Brettingham*, and left unaltered by Barry except for the addition of a pair of niches either side of the main doorway. Its segmental barrel-vaulted ceiling has contemporary 'alla grotesca' painting by *Cornelius Dixon*; the Carrara marble fireplace is by *John Flaxman*. The equivalent room facing S is the DRAWING ROOM, occupying the same space as Pratt's parlour. This too was remodelled by *Brettingham* and again not affected by Barry. In Pratt's plan the corners were each taken up with chamber suites. The LIBRARY now occupies the SE corner, originally Sir Ralph Bankes's closet. It has bookshelves from its refitting by *Brettingham*, and an early *Guido Reni* ceiling painting (*c.* 1596–7) of the Separation of Day and Night, from the Palazzo Zani, Bologna.

In Pratt's house dining occurred in the Great Chamber, located on the first floor. (There was also a gallery running the full length of the attic.) The late C18 changes saw this move into the ground-floor suite in the NW corner, originally a bedchamber. This room was spectacularly remodelled as the SPANISH GOLDEN ROOM, W.J. Bankes's *chef d'œuvre*. Here an imported Italian gilt beamed ceiling: a typical mid-C16 design, said to be from the Palazzo Contarini degli Scrigni, Venice. The square central painting of The Creation of the Elements is in the style of *Paolo Veronese*. This left the problem of where to create a large DINING ROOM.* This was made by taking out the late C18 W staircase so that the room now occupies just over half of the length of the W front. It has a relatively sober late C19 decorative scheme, a replacement following a fire. Its ceiling by *Barry*, modelled on those at Coleshill, survives however.

---

* Henry Bankes, who commissioned the *Brettingham* improvements, subsequently sought ways in which to achieve a larger dining room. In 1779 he had asked *John Soane* to produce designs that were never followed up. One of many schemes by *Thomas Cundy Jun.*, made in 1819, 1824 and 1827, included wings, one of which would have housed a dining room. And in 1821 *Sir Jeffry Wyatville* proposed something similar but with a portico entrance on the E front. *See* Anthony Cleminson, 'The transition from Kingston Hall to Kingston Lacy', *Architectural History* 31, 1988.

Many other rooms are quite unaltered from their C19 state, the colours mainly browns and golds, beautifully mellowed.

STABLES and COACH HOUSE to the W. Brick with stone dressings around a courtyard. Italian-classical. Dated WRB 1880. Just S an Egyptian SARCOPHAGUS, C14 B.C., brought here by W.J. Bankes. E of the house, an ITALIANATE GARDEN by *C.E. Ponting*, 1899.

The PARK is a very beautiful one, the part to the N of the house devoted to specimen trees. Facing the S front the pink granite Egyptian OBELISK of 116 B.C., removed from Philae and set up here in 1829–37. Inscriptions (in Egyptian hieroglyphics and Greek) record that it was erected by the priests of Philae as a perpetual memorial of their exemption from taxes. A second OBELISK to the SW is dated 1887.

The site of an EARLIER HOUSE, 250 yds NW, has been excavated. Courtyard plan, perhaps from part of the house recorded in 1252 as suitable for a visit by Henry III. By 1535 Leland reported that the 'fair maner place' had largely been destroyed.

WIMBORNE EAST LODGE, ⅝ m. E, probably by *Barry*, *c.* 1850. Italianate.

BLANDFORD LODGE, ½ m. NW, dated 1912, probably by *Ponting*. Intended to match.

ST STEPHEN. *See* Pamphill.

KINGSTON MAURWARD

7090

OLD MANOR HOUSE. The Late Elizabethan E-plan manor house refined to a point of perfection. Hutchins saw a date 1591 on armorial glass in the hall, in which case it was built for Christopher Grey. The house's effect is entirely derived from its massing and multiplicity of gables. Also the distinctive balance between plain wall and the large mullioned-and-transomed windows. The W front has five straight gables, one over each stretch of wall, with gables also to the inner re-entrants of each wing, and to the sides of the porch. These were restored in the extensive but sensitive late 1960s repairs by *R.A. Sturdy*. Four-light windows, with a single transom, on both main storeys. Continuous undercut string courses, so no hoodmoulds except to the small attic windows in the gables. There is still no sign of interest in Renaissance forms, except the round-headed entrance doorway, although here the moulding is still continuous in the medieval way. (Over the doorway a carved stone achievement of arms dating from *c.* 1630.) Nor indeed is decoration of any sort employed, except the plain knob-topped gable finials and, charming motif, elaborate base-mouldings on every window mullion. This must be imitated from Wolfeton House, Charminster, nearby, a sign that the early C16 style was still admired right at the end of the century.

Early in the C17 a wing was added to the SE, and the back is now largely a reconstruction. There was evidence for the central staircase projection as now restored. Big chimney-breast N of it, suggesting that the service parts were in the N end of the house, and that the hall lay to the S, with a cross-passage between. But inside all is now remodelled, after years of dereliction following mid-C19 subdivision.

KINGSTON MAURWARD COLLEGE. The last Grey heiress, Lora Grey, married George Pitt, who built in 1717–20 a new house on the next rise to the W of the Old Manor House. The two houses are linked by an avenue that lays proper emphasis on their relationship. Kingston Maurward House, a substantial mansion of Portland ashlar, is also the ghost of something else. The ashlar is a casing in 1794 for William Morton Pitt of a red brick house, which, to judge by Hutchins's tantalizingly small engraving of 1774, had the dramatically eccentric look which only *Thomas Archer* was master of. Had it survived in its naked glory it would have been a fitting companion for Chettle. The casing was not just a casing but a simplification, especially of the busy skyline; but the early C18 character remains. So the house is still a lofty block of two storeys with a third above the cornice, nine bays by six, and the long narrow windows cannot have been much altered in shape. Arcaded chimneystacks, the last vestige of Archer's roofscape, survived until 1912. The banded angle pilasters correspond to what Hutchins shows, and so do the richly carved Corinthian pilasters across the centre three bays of both N and S fronts: Archer's Portland dressings. On the N side there is more, for the entablature over the pilasters, with characteristic upright consoles, undoubtedly belongs to the original build. Service wing to the E of c. 1870, as is the broad porch on the N side, and steps in it up to the two-storey hall. This too is Baroque in effect, though largely of c. 1914 for Sir Cecil Hanbury, with its superimposed half-columns all round, its giant yellow marble chimneypieces l. and r., and the copious plasterwork. The plasterwork of the ceiling, and so the two-storey height, may be original.

GARDEN TEMPLE, SE of the house. Mid-C18. Ashlar. The Doric temple front flanked by carved side walls with niches and angle pilasters.

The GARDENS themselves are largely the creation of Lady Hanbury, c. 1918–30. These lie alongside the River Frome, which provides the S boundary. A sinuous lake was made here in the C18.

KINGSTON RUSSELL HOUSE

2½ m. N of Abbotsbury

A house with two façades of distinction, both of Portland ashlar. Its history is more complicated than one might at first imagine.

In *c.* 1670 John Michel added a new w block to a straggle of earlier buildings running to the E. This block had a symmetrical E façade, compromised at the r. end by a link to older structures. So, looking at the present E front there are six regularly spaced windows, tall, classically proportioned, with a mullion and two transoms, an unusual type unknown elsewhere in Dorset. Normal enough mouldings, just a step and a hollow chamfer. These are on each floor to the l. of a scar, or change in the masonry. Here is where the connection with the previous house was made. The new block is of two storeys, with a balustraded skyline. The central doorcase with a slightly swan-necked open pediment is presumably contemporary; the string courses between the storeys and below the balustrade have profiles of copybook classicism.

The w façade is clearly not contemporary. First, the cornice moulding comes round from the w front, disappears from view and then appears at the SE angle, where it can easily be seen to differ from the E front's cornice. Second, in style it is typical of the work of local architects in the early 1740s: a straightforward Palladian statement delivered in Vanbrughian tones. Two storeys. Seven bays, the centre three marked by broad steps up to them and giant Ionic pilasters carrying a pediment that breaks through the balustraded skyline. In the centre, round-headed windows punched straight through the walls; at the sides, segment-headed windows with broad flat surrounds. Brackets for all their sills. It has much in common with two façades by *Francis Cartwright* of Blandford, the s front at Creech Grange (1738–41) and the N front of Came House, Winterborne Came (1754), and is probably of *c.* 1740.

Next the short, one-bay wings. These were added by *Philip Tilden* for George Gribble, 1913–14. At the time the house was derelict. In carrying out a thorough restoration, the aim was also to achieve a larger house and remove the cottagey older wing at the rear. Here, on the E front, Tilden is at his least successful with a jumble of windows at the r. end where the old wing connected. This was in part owing to the placing here of a new staircase. While making the façade proportions over-long, the new wings are however successful in their reticence.*

Inside, a fine Early Georgian staircase, with three twisted balusters per step, brought in by Tilden. Further interior reconstruction using panelling removed from the house in the late C19 by the Bedford Estate, and bought back from Woburn by Gribble. Also interiors of 1939 by *Felix Harbord* in a Gibbs style, including the hall with its elaborate plasterwork.

88

---

*Before Tilden's work, the ends of the building had only rough stone suggestive of a C17 or C18 plan for wings. *See Country Life*, 28 December 1951.

KINGTON MAGNA

ALL SAINTS. A major rebuilding by *Charles Turner* of Southampton, 1861–2. He left the low but massive late C15 W tower. This has a broad, rectangular stair-turret ending below the tower top with a lean-to roof. Also the aisle arcades of *c.* 1400 were retained. Nave, aisles and chancel (raised up following the lie of the land) with somewhat archaeological Dec fenestration. Re-set Perp PISCINA (s aisle). – ROYAL ARMS of Charles II. – STAINED GLASS. E window, an early (i.e. *c.* 1862) work by *Clayton & Bell.* W window, 1878 by *Heaton, Butler & Bayne.* Sir Owen Morshead considered the window by *Shrigley & Hunt* (1914) at the E end of the s aisle 'unusually good'.

    LYCHGATE of 1914, possibly by *Ponting.*

PRIMITIVE METHODIST CHAPEL (former), Chapel Hill, ¼ m. SW. Dated 1851, by *T. Tanner*, mason, according to the stone in the gable.

MANOR FARM, E of the church, has a stone N front of the mid C17. One notes that the windows, four-light below, three-light above, are without hoodmoulds. Central projection, with a window at half-height, that shows there is a staircase inside.

LOWER FARM, ¾ m. SW. Late C17 five-bay front of mullioned-and-transomed cross-windows. A string course touches the heads of the lower ones, and is bent up in the centre to clear the central doorway. Gabled ends. Porch incorporating a possibly re-set doorway with classical details of *c.* 1720.

KNOWLTON
Woodlands

6

KNOWLTON RINGS AND BARROWS, 1 m. SW of Wimborne St Giles church. Three Later Neolithic henge monuments (*c.* 2750–2500 B.C.), of varying sizes, in a straight line NW–SE, the outer ones destroyed by cultivation. The central circle, with the medieval church built within it, has a definite entrance on the SW and a doubtful one on the NE. 200 ft (60 metres) E is a round barrow covered with trees, its mound 138 ft (42 metres) in diameter and 20 ft (6 metres) high. It is surrounded by its own ditch and by a concentric ditch 100 ft (30 metres) from the foot of the barrow, with a possible outer bank. All but the central mound has been ploughed out. Other barrows, mostly levelled by ploughing but visible from the air, are set close by the three henges.

    In the middle of the central circle stands a CHURCH ruin, mostly of flint. Why it was built here is unclear, as the settlement of Knowlton, now gone, lay ⅓ m. to the NW. C12 nave and chancel. C15 N chapel. The N aisle was rebuilt *c.* 1730. The unbuttressed C14 W tower with bands of flint and stone and a

double-chamfered arch of continuous mouldings to the nave
is still complete. The nave s wall has a simple C12 doorway
similar to the chancel arch.*

NEW BARN FARM, ¼ m. s. An unaltered group, farmhouse and
a quadrangle of farm buildings, of c. 1800. Plum brick house
with a little pediment.

LANGTON HERRING   6080

A tight cluster of cottages and terraces, hunched on a ridge
against the sw winds.

ST PETER. C14 Dec, but much repaired in the C17 after a fire.
Unbuttressed w tower with lancets, probably of 1827. The s
aisle with its Perp window is of 1837 by *Philip Dodson*, a builder
of Weymouth. His is the monstrous round pier of the s arcade
with its chunky capital. Perp windows inserted in the nave N
wall, one blocking a C14 N doorway. The C13-looking chancel
arch must be a C19 installation. – COMMUNION RAIL. With
short turned balusters; of the second half of the C17. – PULPIT.
Plain; oak. Cut down in the C19. – FONT. C15. Octagonal
with a quatrefoil to each face. Trefoil-headed panels to the
octagonal stem. – The FURNISHINGS are mostly the result of
a later restoration of 1858. – STAINED GLASS. E window with
stamped quarries by *Powell & Sons*, c. 1858. – MONUMENT.
William Sparks †1829. Tablet with laurel-leaf wreath. By *John
Chislett* of Beaminster.

NATIONAL SCHOOL (now VILLAGE HALL), opposite the church.
1856. Large Gothic windows with intersecting glazing bars.

THE OLD RECTORY, 150 yds NW. Stucco villa of c. 1820. Hipped
roof with two chimneys grouped at the apex. Enclosed N porch
with slender Doric pilasters.

LANGTON CROSS, ⅔ m. E. Medieval. A crude stone cross with
its top arm missing.

LANGTON LONG BLANDFORD   8000

A small former estate village, noticeably lacking the mansion
formerly at its centre.

ALL SAINTS. 1861 by *T. H. Wyatt*, for James John Farquharson
of Langton House. Largish and competent, flint and stone,
with transepts, a N aisle and a battlemented w tower. The style
is Perp. – *Wyatt*'s FURNISHINGS are complete. – Extensive

* Ruins stabilized and repaired by the *Ministry of Works* in 1965.

TILEWORK by *Minton* in the sanctuary. – STAINED GLASS. An extensive, consistently high-quality set. E window, 'the principal events in the life of Our Lord', by *Heaton & Butler*, 1862.*
By the same the armorial W window, two chancel S windows and two windows in the S aisle. The successor firm (i.e. with *Bayne*) probably made the N transept N window, *c.* 1890. Two S transept windows by *Clayton & Bell*, 1874. Two in the N aisle (†1890 and †1898) no doubt by *Lavers & Westlake*. – MONUMENTS. Brasses to John Whitewod and two wives †1457 and 1467. The figures are 18 in. (45 cm.) long. – A number of tablets, notably James Farquharson †1795. Small relief of the dying man seated between Faith and Father Time. – Keith Frazer †1826 by *Samuel Manning*. Round tablet with wreath and crossed swords. – Anne Farquharson by *J. Browne* of London, 1840. Greek Revival. – Frederick Farquharson †1841 by *W.G. Nicholl*, depicting a sword.

LANGTON HOUSE, ⅜ m. SE. *C.R. Cockerell*'s Italian-classical house of 1826–32 for J.J. Farquharson (with landscaping by *W.S. Gilpin*) was pulled down in 1947. What is left is part of the service wing and two free-standing buildings with small cupolas, the brewhouse and the stables. All are of finely cut ashlar. Architecturally the STABLES are the memorable thing. Octagonal, with lunette windows in round-headed recesses, and an internal courtyard shaded all round by hugely projecting eaves. Front and back entrance through a mighty round-headed arch under a broken pediment. The arch is chamfered. That shows the hand of the advanced architect in the early C19, who chooses the simplest of mouldings, even non-classical ones for a classical context. Sensitively converted to dwellings by *Peter Thompson Architects*, 1989. The BREWHOUSE, SE of the main block site (and also now dwellings) is more demonstratively Italianate in character, its S loggia having paired columns supporting an arched arcade.

LANGTON FARM, W of the church. Unusually substantial. Ten-bay façade to the house, and a handsome C18 pedimented stone porch on Doric columns, brought from the predecessor to Cockerell's Langton House.

LANGBOURNE (formerly Langton Lodge) 1½ m. N. Three wide bays. Stucco. Of *c.* 1840 with older wings at the back.

LANGTON MATRAVERS

Two settlements, one grouped around the church, the other around the Methodist chapel. Much later cul-de-sac development.

ST GEORGE. Short Perp three-stage W tower with battlemented parapets. The S stair-turret was altered when the church was

---

*This was exhibited in the 1862 International Exhibition in South Kensington.

rebuilt by *Crickmay* in 1876. Within, two sets of roof-line marks on the E side indicate a narrow C13 nave built into the C15 tower, and a later wider nave (associated with an 1828 rebuilding) not axial with the tower. The 1876 church, in a vaguely Dec style with rock-faced rubble walling, was intended to be capacious, and its bulk sits awkwardly against the medieval tower. Since the nave has a clerestory, its roof rises higher than the tower; the broad aisles also add to the dramatic change of scale. These have flattish lean-to roofs in contrast to the steep gables of the E chapels. Inside, the squat arcade piers, made so by high tapering pedestals, are not the happiest of Crickmay's ideas. From the chancel arch eastwards, full-height polished Purbeck columns and colonnettes have a much more successful effect. – STAINED GLASS. Bold E triplet and two more sober S chapel lancets by *William Morris & Co.* of Westminster, 1910. W end of the aisles, two war memorial windows, the first by *Percy Bacon Bros*, 1920, the other by *G. Cooper-Abbs*, 1949. – MONUMENT. Ruth Hopwood †1910, by *Powell & Sons*. Renaissance-style alabaster surround with figure on mosaic ground.

WESLEYAN METHODIST CHAPEL, ⅛ m. W. Of 1875, replacing an earlier building dated 1842 alongside (dem. 1988). Bold Gothic gable with corner pinnacles.

LEESON HOUSE, ½ m. ESE. C17 core. Three heavily pinnacled gables of a remodelling of *c.* 1800 face E. At the S end a more ornate *cottage orné*-style addition of *c.* 1850 for John Bingley Garland. Many Italian and Flemish carvings elaborate the main interiors, all brought in by Garland.

LEIGH

A village with several stone-built farmhouses and cottages of late C16 and early C17 date, many thatched. Much post-war infilling, so that the vernacular buildings rarely form a coherent group.

ST ANDREW. Mid-C15 W tower with rectangular NE stair projection. Battlemented parapet with crocketed corner pinnacles and bold corner gargoyles. W doorway with shields and foliage in the spandrels. One spandrel has the initials TM, perhaps the donor. C15 also the nave, but with mixed fenestration, including a small rectangular window lighting the former rood loft, s. Chancel C15, but heavily rebuilt 1849–51 by *R.H. Shout*. N aisle added at the same date. Major restoration of 1889–90 by *Crickmay & Son*. Small N extension in the shape of a porch by *Chris Romain Architecture*, 2016. C15 PISCINA in nave S wall. N arcade with broad arches; octagonal columns. Broad arch also to the chancel, all by *Shout*. – PULPIT. By *Shout*. – FONT. C13 bowl; C19 stem. – Some encaustic TILES in the sanctuary, probably by *Godwin*. – PEWS. Generally 1889–90 but with some reuse of ends. Several with whorl tops instead of poppyheads; probably C16. One more elaborate end with a carved St Andrew and poppyhead is from Hilfield church (q.v.). – STAINED GLASS. E window by *Hardman & Co.*, 1855. N aisle E window by *Percy Bacon Bros*, 1908.

VILLAGE CROSS, ¼ m. E. C15. Ham Hill stone base and shaft, so worn that one can only say that there was sculpture here once. Early C20 cross-head.

NATIONAL SCHOOL (former), just S of the Cross. By *Rawlinson Parkinson* of London. Dated 1861. Brick and Ham Hill stone.

CROMWELL COTTAGE, W of the Cross. Dated 1628. Rebuilt from a mid- to late C16 cottage, perhaps with an open hall. To the r. of the cross-passage a lower range. Eaves raised 1726 (a second datestone).

ROOKERY FARM, ⅔ m. SSE. Of *c.* 1600. Thatched and picturesque. Extended at various dates. Confusingly dated IW 1665 on a re-set heraldic panel on E front. Below this a round-arched doorway, its head made up from gadrooned and enriched stonework. These are re-set features, perhaps from a house at Stalbridge Weston, near Stalbridge. (The 'IW' refers to James Weston, who probably moved here in 1665.)

MIZ MAZE, ¼ m. SSE. Hexagonal bank, ploughed but visible. No sign of the maze upon it. Medieval to post-medieval.

5000

LEWCOMBE
(*or* EAST CHELBOROUGH)

Just a church, cottage and former rectory in a very secluded location, but only 1 m. W of Melbury Osmond. However, there is no road from there.

ST JAMES. The parish church of East Chelborough. The building is 38 by 15 ft (11.6 by 4.6 metres). It seems to be of the early C16 and early C18. Of the latter date the W front with doorway and a circular window over; bell-turret on the top. The remainder is C16: side windows straight-headed and with uncusped lights. But what is one to make of the E window? It is large and circular and has tracery of Second Pointed character: two interlocked triangles and daggers and trefoils in the interstices. The glass (*see* below) records a death in 1893. However the tracery looks earlier, perhaps *c.* 1835 for the Rev. Blakley Cooper, who built the Gothick rectory. In the C18 the window would have been subdivided differently. The size of the circle is C18. That is proved by the handsome sanctuary PANELLING. The smaller C18 circular W window has similar tracery and glass. – Remaining FURNISHINGS all C18: PULPIT and READING DESK in one. COMMUNION RAIL with turned balusters. Complete set of PEWS; plain. – FONT. C18. Moulded octagonal bowl on baluster stem. – STAINED GLASS.

The E and W windows (†1893 and †1890) are probably both
by *Clayton & Bell*. – MONUMENTS. Charlotte Mary Crockett
†1849, Charlotte Mary Cooper †1846. Plain tablets let into the
sanctuary panelling.

LEWCOMBE MANOR (formerly the rectory), 200 yds SW. Of
1832 for the Rev. Blakley Cooper. Gothick; stuccoed. Refaced
on the W side and greatly extended to form an L, 1902 for the
Hon. G. F. Digby. Rock-faced Arts and Crafts style.

OAKLANDS HOUSE, ⅓ m. SW. 1973. Large Neo-Georgian block.
Courtyard buildings added *c.* 1990.

CHELBOROUGH HOUSE, 1¼ m. SSW. Early C17 farmhouse;
early C19 refronting with wide sashes and arched door hood.
Thatched. To its N, MANOR FARM. Early C19 with decorative
cast-iron glazing bars to the slightly arched windows. The main
range is seemingly abandoned.

CASTLE HILL, ¼ m. SSW of Chelborough House. A MOTTE-
AND-BAILEY EARTHWORK. A lower earthwork may be the
site of an earlier castle.

LEWESTON   *6010*

HOLY TRINITY. Built in 1616 for Sir John Fitzjames, replacing   66
a chapel on the same site. Its architect was most probably
William Arnold.* The windows are typical of the date, a triplet
of stepped lights under uncusped depressed arches with a
hoodmould stepping up and down (cf. Folke). There are two
of these to the S, one to the N. The buttresses are also arranged
differently: three on the S, the centre higher, two on the N.
The church is no more than a chapel by the house, with no
structural chancel. Externally, the decoration is concentrated
on the W porch, its pitched roof in line with the chapel (but
just off-centre). Doorway on the S side. This has a four-centred
arch, label mould and stepped panel above with the Fitzjames
arms in a cartouche above the words 'Trinte Chappel'. An
eaves string course has 'Sir Io. F.' incorporated in its strapwork
enrichment (above a line of dogtooth), and above this is a
near-semicircular pediment, slightly pointed in profile – this
form copied in the profile of the barrel-vaulted roof within. In
the pediment a lozenge panel. Within, a timber-ribbed barrel-
vaulted roof with carved bosses.

The chapel retains its contemporary FITTINGS. – PULPIT.
In the SE corner. A splendid two-decker. Hexagonal pulpit with
an upper tier of strapwork-elaborated panelling; the same to
the rectangular clerk's desk. The lower panels to the former
are arched; those to the clerk's desk have fluted and arabesque-enriched pilasters, with two more low tiers of panelling
below and boldly carved feet. – PANELLING. Throughout, but

*According to Mark Girouard.

elaborated at the E end with Ionic pilasters (matching those on the clerk's desk) and an entablature with lozenge panels and a boldly carved rose and thistle between. – BENCHES. The ends have rounded shoulders with circular heads, each with a roundel, with a further roundel and lozenges below. – FONT. In the porch; C13. Circular, on a short stem with moulded capital and base. – GALLERY with clock mechanism in the porch. – STAINED GLASS. A band containing a running inscription from window to window: 'Johannes Fitz James me struxit in honorem Sanctae Trinitatis pro antique capella dilapidate per moltos annos huic domui pertinenti' ('John Fitzjames erected me in honour of the Holy Trinity for the demolished old chapel that belonged for many years to this house'). Much of this has evidently been renewed.

LEWESTON MANOR. The late medieval house of the Lewstons ('much beautified with Buildings and other Ornaments' by John Fitzjames, †1625) had been demolished by 1774. The present house is of *c.* 1800 for William Gordon (†1802). For its date it is unusually direct and bold in design. Ashlar. Two-storeyed, seven bays by four. Large round-headed windows on all sides, the lower ones descending almost to the ground. The centre three bays of each front are brought forward uncompromisingly; the N and S projections have pediments. Continuous parapet and top balustrade with finials like cannonballs. The parapet runs rudely up and over the pediments. Ground-floor bow windows, of wood, one E and two S, of *c.* 1930. Neo-Georgian, for E. Hamilton Rose. These and the Art Deco interiors of this date are by *Maxwell Ayrton*. The chimneypiece in the hall intensely typical of its date: low and with a swoopy surround of polished Travertine. Painted map of the estate above by *George Sheringham*, incorporating a working clock and weathervane. The corridor between the hall and dining room has a circular space, the 'Parrot Cage', decorated as a bird cage by Sheringham. He also did the murals and ceiling paintings in a tunnel-vaulted small drawing room at the E end of the house. Here too an Art Deco Travertine fireplace. Ayrton's top-lit staircase hall has a metal gridwork balustraded staircase with a handrail of reeded green glass by *Powell & Sons*.

Church and manor now belong to LEWESTON SCHOOL. The most significant new buildings are to the N. First the CHAPEL by the *Brandt Potter Hare Partnership*, of 1968–70. The plan is two pentagons set at an angle to each other. Basement assembly hall. Above, in the chapel itself, the altar stands beneath a high N tower, triangular in plan. It lets light in from a window on its S side which is reflected down to the altar. Linking this with the manor house an ENTRANCE AND RECEPTION AREA by *Brian Watts* of *Philip Proctor Associates*, 2010. A glazed refronting of an earlier building.

To the E of the house a formal walled garden, and to the SW the ITALIAN GARDEN, both by *Thomas Mawson* for G. Hamilton Fletcher, 1906–10. The latter has, as its most distinctive feature, the GLADE, a 200-yd-long, narrow grassed avenue cutting through woodland. Its SW terminal, where one emerges from the woodland, is an oval space, the BELVEDERE, centred on a Venetian well-head. Entry is down steps between a pair of pineapple-topped columns. At the lower level a pair of quadrant-plan, colonnade-fronted pavilions.

WATER TOWER, 250 yds W. Of *c.* 1930 by *Maxwell Ayrton*. Converted to a dwelling by *Saxon Architects*, 1997. A concrete octagonal cylinder. Open viewing platform with a pyramidal copper roof.

LILLINGTON

6010

A memorable combination of church with bold Somerset-scaled tower, and adjoining barn, on the edge of a hill. Just one or two cottages and farmhouses in addition.

ST MARTIN. Dominant W tower, datable *c.* 1529 by a bequest from William Newman. Three stages with a rectangular stair projection at the NE. A battlemented parapet runs around this and the main body at the same level. Crocketed pinnacles. Gargoyles at the corners. Four-centred arch to the W doorway. Three-light Perp window above. Two-light belfry openings with Somerset tracery. Late C13 nave – see one S window with plate tracery. One large C15 N window. Opposed doorways, that on the S now a window. Perp too the C15 chancel. Windows here with cinquefoil-headed lights in square-topped openings. C18 S chapel with a hipped roof. Its S window with peculiar cusping looks C19. Plastered wagon roof with bosses. C18 chancel arch. Restored and refurnished by *R. J. Withers*, 1848. The Perp-style E window is probably of this date. – FONT. Late C15. Octagonal, with shields and flowers in quatrefoils. C17 COVER. Scrolled supports to a central turned spindle. Small turned knobs at the corners. – Tower GALLERY of 1763 (dated on an adjacent board). Altered in 1848. – ROYAL ARMS in the gallery. Stuart. – STAINED GLASS. E window by *Curtis, Ward & Hughes*, 1920. – MONUMENTS. Samuel Whetcombe, probably *c.* 1742. Open pediment with cartouche of arms on apron. – Thomas Gollop †1793. Tablet with side scrolls on a figured marble ground, obelisk-shaped at the top.

The BARN of Manor Farm, *c.* 1600, is a fine companion for the church (now converted to a dwelling). Buttressed walls. The square-headed openings to the N and S porches have jambs and timber beams with wave-and-hollow mouldings. Robust roof of collar-beam trusses with two tiers of arched wind-bracing.

Former SCHOOL, just W of the barn. Of *c.* 1850. Very small and very simple.

LOWER STOCKBRIDGE FARM, 1¼ m. SSE. FARMHOUSE of the
first half of the C17, enlarged in the C18 to the N. Behind it
a large timber-framed BARN of *c.* 1600, a rare survival of this
form of construction in this part of the county.

5080

LITTLEBREDY

The perfect estate village in a perfect setting, the major house
nearby in an exquisite landscaped park with exotic planting
alongside a lake.

ST MICHAEL. Of the medieval church, all that can clearly be
identified is the late C13 chancel and the C14 S tower. This
is Dec – see the porch entrance and small Dec window. The
chancel lancets are also original, although their Purbeck
marble colonnettes and dogtooth-enriched rere-arches within
look too good to be true. They must be part of *Benjamin Ferrey*'s restoration of 1850 for Robert Williams II. Surely the
adjacent E.E.-style PISCINA is his rather than late C13. Ferrey
added the delicate recessed spire with lucarnes on the cardinal faces; also the plate- and bar-traceried windows in the
rebuilt nave and aisles. Confident and characterful detailing,
e.g. the two diagonal W flying buttresses (done to allow access
beneath). The square-headed S aisle window of four trefoiled
lights hints at a Perp addition, but this too is by Ferrey. Strong
arcades of unequal length, the S given a more decorative treatment. Unless otherwise described, the FURNISHINGS are by
Ferrey. – ALTAR with open arcaded front. – STALLS with pop-
pyheaded ends. – PULPIT. Stone, with only the most minimal
of decoration. – FONT. In a C13 style. Leaf trails on the bowl.
Centre and four outer supporting columns. – STAINED GLASS.
E window and others in the chancel by *Thomas Willement*,
1836; grisaille. N aisle E window by *Lavers, Barraud & Westlake*,
c. 1875.

PARSONAGE (former), just W. Of *c.* 1830. Stucco. Oval window
above the front door. Two large square bay windows.

BRIDEHEAD, ¼ m. SE. Evidence for the late C16 house built by
Sir Robert Mellor can be found in the N range, especially some
windows and a pointed-headed doorway that appear to be *in
situ*. Another contemporary doorway and two fireplaces of this
date have been relocated into the E part of the later house. This
was completed in phases by *P. F. Robinson* for Robert Williams
I, the E part of *c.* 1822, another range to its W of 1831–3 and
then a large domed conservatory by *Ferrey*, *c.* 1840. Stucco, in
the Tudor Gothic style illustrated by Robinson in his *Designs
for Ornamental Villas* (1827). John Newman described it as
'Tudor of excruciating awkwardness'. The additive effect along
the long S front, moving from the more picturesque E block to
the sudden symmetry of the 1831–3 range, is not easily likeable

when viewed square on. But with its spectacular setting in the
bowl of the valley, especially when seen from the hills above,
or reflected in the oval lake, the result is far more pleasing.
Also more effective is the E elevation: four bays, the doorway
at the centre having a porch with thin columns. Battlemented
parapets, and mini-battlements to the Gothic-panelled spindly
corner turrets. These also delineate each element of the house.
The domed conservatory, affected by further changes at the
W end c. 1900, was replaced by a simpler glazing arrangement
in the early 1970s.

Around 1840 *Ferrey* (with *A.D.H. Acland*) made internal
changes, including the furnishing of the library, with Gothic
bookcases, a powerful chimneypiece and other Perp fittings.
The adjoining corridor was also altered then to make a small
chapel or 'prayer room'.

The VILLAGE is a delightful essay in Picturesque estate housing,
owing much to Nash's Blaise Hamlet, but more complex and
diffuse. Rough irregular green at the top, not normal for
Dorset, and a magnificently contrived view from it down the
Bride valley to the W. Some of the cottages are C18 or early
C19; many either new-built or enhanced c. 1850 by *Ferrey*. The
entry from the W is marked by stumpy octagonal gatepiers and
WEST LODGE by *Ferrey*, its upper floor mostly timber-framed.
Ornate bargeboards and glazing patterns.

Splendid Gothic FARMYARD, 150 yds N of Bridehead. Undoubtedly by *Ferrey*, c. 1840, adapting earlier buildings. It stands
around three sides of a courtyard.

KINGSTON RUSSELL STONE CIRCLE, 1 m. SW. On Tenant's
Hill, an irregular oval arrangement of eighteen recumbent
conglomerated sarsen stones, 79 by 92 ft (24 by 28 metres).

ENCLOSURE on Tenant's Hill, some 380 yds N of the stone circle.
Sub-rectangular, with SW entrance. Adjacent HUT CIRCLE and
BANK. Probably Bronze Age.

BARROWS, ½ m. N and NW on the South Dorset Ridgeway.
Some twenty-two round barrows on both sides of the Kingston Russell parish boundary, in clusters and linear groups
above Poor Lot; also two bank barrows. Most much reduced
or removed by ploughing. On White Hill a further group of
five, ploughed flat.

POOR LOT, 1 m. N. For the Bronze Age BARROW CEMETERY
see Winterbourne Abbas.

'CELTIC' FIELD SYSTEM. One of the best preserved in the
county is at the E end of the Bride valley, including Crow
Hill, Black Down and the Valley of Stones. The latter is named
after a spread of sarsens. The whole covers about 450 acres,
including a section to the NE above Loscombe (*see* Winterbourne Steepleton). Bronze Age, with enclosures and field
development of later periods.

OLD WARREN, ¼ m. SW, is an unexcavated ENCLOSURE formed
by bank and ditch, variously referred to as an Iron Age defensive site and as Alfred's *burh* at Brydian.

LITTON CHENEY

A small, scattered, and secluded village. Several cottage rows to the E of the church, some thatched. These intermingle with farmsteads.

ST MARY. The church stands high above the village. Stately early C15 W tower of three stages. Battlemented with a higher and also battlemented octagonal SE stair-turret. Set-back buttresses, two-light Perp bell-openings and good gargoyles. Of this date too the nave and chancel arch. Large Perp nave windows. Perp panelled arches to both the tower and the chancel. But the chancel is late C14 and Dec – see the ogee-headed side windows. A major restoration of 1878 by *Richard Cornick* of Bridport, who stripped out the box pews, high pulpit and gallery, together with much of the character, while adding the N transept. Behind the 1878 pulpit a cinquefoil-headed niche, and a cinquefoil-headed PISCINA alongside; both C15 and re-set. Also two re-set carved brackets. – ALTAR. Of 1856–7 by *William Butterfield*, moved here from Balliol College, Oxford, in 1937. Geometrically elaborate openwork front. – COMMUNION RAIL, c. 1700, with thin turned balusters. – FONT. Perhaps C13. Circular bowl with two bands, the upper scalloped, the lower more unusually of leaves. – ROYAL ARMS. Framed painting dated 1719. – STAINED GLASS. E window by *Powell & Sons*, 1927. Two nave windows by *F. C. Eden*, presumably c. 1920. Re-set in plain obscured glass. – MONUMENT. George Dawbney †1612. A large stone armorial tablet; painted.

PRIMITIVE METHODIST CHAPEL (former), 300 yds SW. Dated 1873. Stuccoed with round-arched windows.

COURT HOUSE, in grounds opposite the chapel. Ashlar villa built c. 1850 for Benjamin Legg. Sophisticated detailing. Three-bay front, the centre projecting and pedimented. Tall tripartite sashes with conventional sashes above.

LODERS

Loders had a Benedictine priory founded c. 1106 as a cell of Montebourg. It was dissolved as an alien house in 1411, and none of the premises survive. The village has a proper street, like a minor version of Abbotsbury, running along a typical Dorset close-sided valley.

ST MARY MAGDALENE. At first this appears to be a largely late C14 Perp church with a C15 S aisle. The fine W tower of three stages, battlemented with a SE octagonal stair-turret, is typical of others in the area (e.g. Askerswell and Litton

Cheney). Set-back W buttresses. The S porch is contemporary but appears all of a piece with the later S aisle, having the same embattled parapets. An octagonal stair-turret to the r. of the porch gives access not only to the room over the porch (with its small Perp window) but also to the flat lead roof over the aisle. It thus rises higher than the parapets, with a grotesque-enriched string course and crocketed pinnacles. Buttresses to the aisle with good gargoyles above and larger crocketed pinnacles enlivening the parapet. From the outside the chancel seems earlier (but with some C15 rebuilding and refenestration on the S side). Its E wall probably goes with the 1899 restoration by *C.E. Ponting*.

The complications reveal themselves within. The first problem is the blocked main N doorway. Its proportions and its masonry point to an Anglo-Saxon date, yet it is unacknowledged by any of the standard references on the subject. More secure is the C12 dating of a chancel N window. Did the blocked doorway below it lead into the priory? Its lintel appears to be the upturned and reversed top of another C12 window. This is problem number two. Problem number three is the Norman shaft and scalloped capital E of the window. Does it tell of former rib-vaulting? In the same chancel N wall a C13 E.E. lancet. So perhaps the explanation, as far as the chancel is concerned, is that it was originally near-square in plan with a cross-vault. The reused window head may be from the pair of the *in situ* window in the N wall. The elongation of the chancel beyond the C12 shaft is a typical C13 modification. C14 ogee-headed TOMB-RECESS in the chancel N wall. Also a Purbeck marble COFFIN-LID with a relief cross; probably C13. Perp two-bay S arcade with piers of standard section. Here a cinquefoil-headed PISCINA, early C15. Tower arch with an outer chamfered and inner moulded order.

FURNISHINGS. ALTAR in the S aisle with four panels of *c.* 1400 with carved tracery re-set in its front. – PULPIT. 1899 by *Ponting*. What is more interesting is the curious access arrangement as a branch of the rood-loft stair. – FONT. Of *c.* 1200. Square, of Purbeck marble, each side with four of the standard flat arches. Circular stem with four attached shafts. – PAINTING. Time and Death, very faint against the W wall. Probably C17. – SCULPTURE. Part of a small Crucifixion relief in the S transept; C14, perhaps rescued from the priory. – Another Crucifixion in the blocked N doorway. From the dress, probably late C14, thus dating the tower. It was removed from the ogee-headed niche to the l. of the W door. The panel includes small figures possibly representing the donors. – STAINED GLASS. Various fragments in the tracery lights, especially in the S aisle. Some C15, others later and re-set. Interesting small figures. E window in the style of *Wailes* but more likely by *Francis Oliphant*, *c.* 1850. Two chancel N windows by *W.G. Rich*, both 1900. – MONUMENTS. John Sampson, vicar. Purbeck marble ledger slab. Probably late C14. Black-letter inscription in Latin.

The initial letters are highlighted in red paint. – Sir Evan
Nepean †1812. Draped altar with the profile head of Sir Evan.
WESLEYAN METHODIST CHAPEL, Uploders, ⅞ m. ESE. Dated
1827. Stucco with a steep slate roof. Round-arched windows.
E porch with Roman Doric columns. Bellcote on the W gable.
LODERS HALL (formerly the vicarage), E of the church. Mainly
of 1861 by *John Hicks*, but incorporating an early C16 house
in its E part. Two single-light windows in the N wall. The
main survival is a room with moulded ceiling beams and very
wide fireplace, its opening four-centred, giving room for small
encircled trefoils in the spandrels. Two S windows light the
room, each of three lights with depressed ogee heads. The W
part has gables and pointed windows.
LODERS COURT, immediately N. Its grounds surround the
church, providing a memorable sylvan setting. Of 1799 for
Sir Evan Nepean, possibly on the site of the priory buildings.
Stucco, with a hipped roof. A plain block, made plainer by the
loss of its balustraded parapet and wrought-iron W veranda in
the mid C20. Two-bay N porch with Roman Doric columns,
paired at the centre.
UPLODERS PLACE, 1¼ m. ESE. Of *c.* 1820. Stucco-walled villa.
E front with upper windows in segment-headed recesses.
Wrought-iron veranda with a flared roof.
UPTON MANOR FARM, 1½ m. ESE. Thatched stone farmhouse,
and thatched and pantiled barns, a splendid group as one looks
down from the road. The thatched roof of the farmhouse drifts
down the hill. At its centre a C16 dwelling, extended into a byre
dated 1655 at the rear.

LONG BREDY

A village in two parts: the cluster of church, former school and
rectory at the N end under Long Barrow Hill; a straggle of cottages to the S, separated by some 400 yds of open lane.

ST PETER. Smooth grassy hills form the immediate background
of the church. The chancel is so long that one guesses the C13
at once. It has indeed a handsome stepped triplet of lancets,
shafted with Purbeck marble inside, and a N lancet. But more
memorable is the interior, with wall-shafts carrying extremely
depressed segmental arches. *Benjamin Ferrey* carried out what
seems to have been a delicate restoration of the chancel in
1842. The plain W tower is early C15 with narrow two-light
bell-openings. Earlier than the tower was the nave, and later
the C18 S transept. Both were thoroughly restored in 1862–3
by *John Hicks*, who added the S aisle between the porch and
transept. His, then, the leaf corbels in the nave and the leaf
capitals of the chancel arch (both carved by *B. Grassby*). – The
chancel FURNISHINGS are no doubt by *Ferrey*; elsewhere they

are by *Hicks.* – FONT. Of 1863. Square Purbeck marble bowl
with alabaster medallions by *Grassby* of the Evangelists on each
face. Green serpentine marble colonnettes around a central
column stem. – STAINED GLASS. Chancel windows with two
varieties of grisaille decoration, *c.* 1850. W window with scrolls,
†1871. – MONUMENTS. Joseph Symes †1830. Octagonal tablet
by *Edward Lester* of Dorchester. – Thomas Samson †1849, and
others up to 1912. Gothic tablet by *R. Brown* of London. – In the
porch, Mary [...] †1697. Classical with detached side-columns.

LANGEBRIDE HOUSE (formerly the rectory), 120 yds SW, above
a long boundary wall. Mid-C18, remodelled and enlarged in
the early C19. Stucco. Porch with slender columns on the NE
front; two-storey bow window off-centre on the SW front.

BELLAMONT, ½ m. SE. 1995 by *Anthony Jaggard* for Anthony
Sykes. Classical block with wings; rigorously battlemented
parapets. Additions by *Stuart Martin, c.* 2000.

WHATCOMBE HOUSE, ¾ m. SE. 1939 by *E. Wamsley Lewis*
for C. Foster Symes. Neo-vernacular with bold tapering
chimneystacks.*

On MARTIN'S DOWN, ⅓ m. N, a Neolithic BANK BARROW,
650 ft (200 metres) long and aligned NE–SW. It stands in the
middle of a group of eight round barrows, marking the western
end of the great concentration of barrows along the South
Dorset Ridgeway. To the SE on the Ridgeway a LONG BARROW
120 ft (36 metres) long, aligned E–W.

GREY MARE AND HER COLTS, 1⅓ m. S of Littlebredy church.
The remains of a megalithic chambered long barrow, 80 ft
(24 metres) long. A stone burial chamber has been exposed
behind the surviving stones of a NW façade of crescentic plan at
the wider end. The barrow was opened early in the C19, when
'many human bones and some pottery' were found.

LONGBURTON   *6010*

A linear village, slowly descending to marshy land at its S end.

ST JAMES. Mid-C13 W tower with an early C17 battlemented
top. The gargoyles may have been re-set at that time. Bold
diagonal buttresses. C14 Dec W doorway. The arch to the nave
has boldly moulded, characteristically E.E. capitals with short
shafts above corbels. Three lancets, one per face (except the
E), each with a trefoiled rere-arch. C15 nave and chancel. C17
N chapel, still Perp, added for Leweston Fitzjames before 1638.
Respectful, gable-ended N aisle added by *William Farrall* of
Sherborne, 1873–4. Panelled chancel arch. A good Perp-style
N arcade by Farrall. The plain blocky capitals and keystones of

*Illustrated in *Ideal Home*, December 1949.

the two C17 arches to the chapel seem like the work of *William Arnold*. – FONT and REREDOS, both by *Farrall*. – SCREEN. There were two early C17 sections filling the N chapel arches. One is resited in the tower arch. Arabesque enrichment and radiating gadroon ornament. Railings fill the upper open panels, and are continued upwards with spikes. – FONT. C15. Octagonal with quatrefoils and rosettes. – ROYAL ARMS. Dated 1662. A large panel with a pointed top. It includes a text from Ecclesiastes 10:20, 'Curse not the King, noe, not in thy thought'. – ARCHITECTURAL FRAGMENT. A stone with C12 chevron (N aisle E). – STAINED GLASS. Fragments and panels re-set in two N aisle windows, probably C15. Many windows by *Heaton, Butler & Bayne*. Three, including the E, of 1874. Another chancel S window, †1887. N aisle W window, 1884. An earlier chancel S window is perhaps by *Lavers, Barraud & Westlake*, †1869. – MONUMENTS. In the N chapel two large, nearly identical monuments, both standing and both with a canopy on six Corinthian columns and big achievements of arms on the top. The l. one is to Sir Henry Winston †1609, his wife, and his father, Thomas Winston. The father's effigy is of alabaster, the other two effigies are of stone. The father's is earlier than the son's and daughter-in-law's and was reportedly made for Standish church, Gloucestershire. He lies below in an area between the floor and the slab for the other two. The space is low. The similar space below the r. monument to Sir John Fitzjames †1625 and his wife has a gruesome display of bones. The effigies are all recumbent and realistically painted. The monument structure itself is painted and gilded. – Large slab to Sir John Fitzjames †1670.

WESLEYAN METHODIST CHURCH, ½ m. S. 1878 by *Thomas Farrall*. Triplets of shafted lancets in the gable-ends. Plain lancets elsewhere. The road gable also has a circular window with Star-of-David tracery.

VICTORIA TEMPERANCE HALL, opposite the Methodist church. 1907 by *Walter W. Hayward* of Longburton. Simple lancet style. Rock-faced walling.

VILLAGE. Longburton has a number of characteristic examples of the local vernacular styles, these being either of stone with stone roofs, or of cob with thatch. With two exceptions, the best buildings are S from the church. Heading S, on the r. the former SCHOOL (now VILLAGE HALL). 1852 for J.S.W. Sawbridge-Erle-Drax of Holnest. Mullioned windows, with transoms to the school hall. On the l. at the narrowing in the road, the S-facing OLD DAIRY HOUSE. Early C17 with two four-light mullioned windows, one re-set in a canted bay, and two thatched dormer windows. Next S, the Italianate GLENWOOD HOUSE of *c.* 1850. Four-bay S-facing range with a round-arched first-floor window and balcony overlooking the road. N from the church, after 200 yds, on the l., down Spring Lane, SPRING HOUSE is C15 in origin, with an open hall. Upper floor and hall chimney inserted in the late C16. The pair of eyebrow dormers in its thatched roof are of this date.

BURTON HOUSE, ½ m. N. 1908–10 by *M.H. Baillie Scott* for
E.W. Bartlett. Set back from the road behind high hedges,
apart from the slightly later LODGE. A typically Arts and Crafts
L-plan with the staircase at the join. Stone vernacular style with
gables of various sizes. Stone-mullioned windows, some reused
from Court Farmhouse, Batcombe. Also from there fireplaces
and oak partitions. Other details copied from Folke Manor
(q.v.). Various compartment GARDENS to the S and E of the
house, also designed by *Baillie Scott.*

LONG CRICHEL

A linear village with farmsteads at the key points and estate cottages between.

ST MARY (Friends of Friendless Churches). C15 W tower, main
W part of nave C16, the remainder of 1852 in Perp style by
P. C. Hardwick for H.C. Sturt, and costing £4,000. N transept added *c.* 1875, possibly by *Macvicar Anderson.*[*] Flint with
ashlar bands, matching the retained tower. Nave without aisles
and apsed ashlar chancel with crocketed pinnacles and openwork parapet. Two transepts, the N longer, plainer and with
more Gothic fenestration, the S for the squire's pew. Hardwick was hardly the most up-to-date of church architects and
his work here is defiantly un-Ecclesiological. As rebuilt, the
nave is really a Georgian space in Perp form, long, uniform,
well lit – it might be a schoolroom. Moreover, the windows
are large and square-topped, of Georgian proportions, though
with panel tracery. Nave ceiling with square panelling resembling the framing of a conservatory. The E end is an apse with
a ceiling of wooden reticulated-tracery panels between radial
arched braces. The tower is Perp proper and has a rectangular stair-turret and image niche on the N side; battlemented
parapet. Inserted moulded two-centred-arched S doorway of
1852 with gabled stone hood on brackets, oddly placed on
the S side of the tower. – SCULPTURE. Delightful depiction
of the Ark in its own ogee-headed recess in the N wall of the
nave at the E end. – FONT. C15, Perp, of Purbeck marble.
Octagonal; quatrefoils with set-in shields as decoration.
– STAINED GLASS. Three sanctuary windows may correspond
with a payment to *Barraud & Co.* in 1851. The W window
appears *c.* 1860. – BRASS. The earliest un-robbed brass in the
county. Just a two-line inscription in French, to John Govys;
c. 1360. Re-set in a medieval-style granite coffin-lid at the time
of the rebuilding.

LONG CRICHEL HOUSE, to the SE. Dated 1786 above the former
doorway location. Built as the rectory. Banded brick and flint

[*] See *Kelly's Directory* and payments in Sturt's bank account archives.

with ashlar dressings. Pedimented N doorway, moved from the W elevation and re-set below a Venetian stair window.

MIDDLE FARM, ½ m. NW. Of *c.* 1820. Post-enclosure square-plan house, brick with hipped roof. Sash windows, those to the S front with ashlar architraves. Contemporary FARM BUILD-INGS to the NW.

HIGHER FARM, ⅛ m. further on. A later (*c.* 1860), plainer version, with a courtyard of earlier farm buildings on the opposite (NE) side of the road.

LONGHAM

Ferndown

UNITED REFORMED CHURCH (formerly Congregational). Dated 1841 on its pedimented façade. By *William Gollop*, builder, of Poole. Large for the village, owing to the mistaken expectation that an estate village was to be built here. Grey brick, with yellow brick dressings. Flanking Ionic pilasters. The windows are arched and, on the side elevations, divided from each other by pilasters. White clock turret with slender spire. Tuscan porch. Original GALLERY, PULPIT and SEATING, as adjusted in 1892.

Three pairs of CANFORD ESTATE COTTAGES dated 1869, 1870 and 1888, to *Banks & Barry* designs, along the road southwards.

HOLMWOOD PARK, ¼ m. NE. 1897 by *Crickmay & Son*. Brick, half-timbered and pargetted Old English style. Reduced in size in the 1950s and savagely shorn of most of its features.

LONGHAM BRIDGE, ¾ m. S. Rebuilt in brick, 1792, by *Anthony Sergeant* of Wimborne Minster. Segmental arches. What remains of the 1728 bridge (by *John Wagg* of Ring-wood, who was paid £2,000) are the stone piers with pointed cutwaters.

LOWER BOCKHAMPTON

Stinsford

A group of thatched, mainly early C19 estate cottages associated with Kingston Maurward.

HARDY'S COTTAGE (National Trust), at Higher Bockhampton, 1 m. N. Of two dates, detectable by the change in ridge height. The l. part of *c.* 1800, the r. *c.* 1840. Thatched with brick walls increased in height in cob. The birthplace of Thomas Hardy.

LYDLINCH

St Thomas a Beckett. Early C15, with a two-stage W tower. Its battlemented parapet has corner and intermediate crocketed pinnacles. N stair with a C14 circular window. Porch dated 1753; sundial on its gable. Major alterations of 1838, when the nave roof was raised, chancel arch rebuilt and a new two-bay N arcade provided for the C16 N aisle. A GALLERY (also of 1838) installed at the W end. Chancel almost completely rebuilt in 1875 by *G. R. Crickmay*. The arcade has tall piers and continuous mouldings. – FONT. Octagonal, late C12, of Purbeck marble with inscribed shallow arches each side. Supported on a central pillar and corner colonnettes (cf. Hazelbury Bryan). – ROYAL ARMS of James II, dated 1686. – HATCHMENT. Charles Brune, *c.* 1650, over the clergy doorway. Two others in the nave. – STAINED GLASS. In one S window four C15 feathered angels. E window of 1920. – MONUMENT. Nicholas Romayne †1702. Cartouche with swags and a skull. – Two LEDGER SLABS with architectural surrounds, of 1661 and 1668, just E of the font.

At the S end of the village street the early C18 symmetrical MANOR FARM faces on to a small village green. Two-light mullioned windows and a hipped roof.

PLUMBER MANOR, 2 m. SE. The house illustrated by Hutchins had been simplified to a farmhouse on an L-plan by the mid C19. This was extended *c.* 1938 for the Prideaux-Brune family, retaining the C18 core. Idyllic setting next to the River Divelish.

LYME REGIS

Lyme's existence depends upon The Cobb, a breakwater creating a tiny artificial harbour. The town, incorporated as a borough in 1284, grew up a quarter of a mile to the E, where it could find a foothold along the bank of the River Lim, and up the ridges of the flanking hills. (Lyme has always been plagued by erosion of the friable Blue Lias clay.) Defoe found it a 'town of good figure', but it was Jane Austen (staying here in 1803 and 1804) who wrote of it in its heyday. The prevailing character even today, in spite of a serious fire in 1844, is of a Late Georgian resort, though as different from Weymouth as chalk from cheese. In many cases Regency rebuilding is only skin deep, especially so on Broad Street, whose character was transformed during the more genteel phase of Lyme's growth as a tourist resort.

The older part of the town is found along Coombe Street and in the block formed with Church and Monmouth streets. George's Square, a triangular public garden, is thought to have been the site of the earliest market, although this later moved to the lower end of Broad Street. Here a typical 'island' incursion

had occurred by the C17, built around a timber-framed shambles structure. Sea bathing brought with it, in the 1770s, Marine
Parade, known locally as The Walk, a promenade extending westwards from Broad Street. In the C20 mass tourism, initially
driven by the arrival of a railway branch line in 1903, resulted
in typical esplanade architecture, linking Lyme proper with the
Cobb hamlet.

CHURCHES

ST MICHAEL. The parish church of Lyme Regis is more an
architectural puzzle than an architectural success and, with
its low-lying nave and aisles, has more of Devon in its character than Dorset. Its position is superb, on the Lias cliff and
turning its chancel to the sea. As for the architecture, it is two
churches in one, the older not having been pulled down, as
was the custom, for the new church to be built. So we have
now a prosperous, spacious Perp town church with a w tower,
and w of this a w porch, the former nave. In its lower structure
the tower is a C12 crossing tower, retaining its E and W arches,
the E arch having responds and an arch of one step and one
thick half-roll. To the w a C13 arch, blocked when the tower
received a stair-turret at the time when it became the w tower.
The porch N wall incorporated a C13 arcade of two bays with
round pier and round abacus and double-chamfered arches.
The porch was shortened by about 10 ft (3 metres) in 1824.
The N lancet was re-set when the arcade was blocked. On
the s side also traces of an arcade. The new church was built
c. 1500. There is much here in common with, say, Marnhull

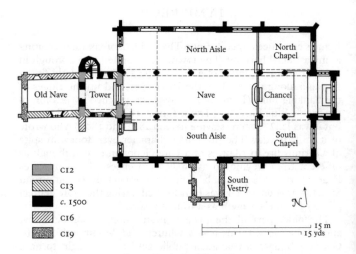

Lyme Regis, St Michael.
Plan

of a similar date. It is a uniform job of wide nave and wide aisles, of six bays, no chancel arch and only slightly projecting chancel. Large Perp two-light windows. Piers with triplet groups of shafts and hollows in the diagonals. Capitals only to the shafts, with leaves and shields. Plastered wagon roofs. Several restorations, the most significant being that of 1885 by *Crickmay & Son*, when the side galleries were removed, the church re-seated, the porch-like s vestry added and doorways inserted in the aisle w windows. Chancel restoration by *Ewan Christian* of the same date; another restoration of 1933 by *Sir Harold Brakspear*, when the w wall of the porch was rebuilt.*

FURNISHINGS. PULPIT. A splendid inscription around the tester dates it: 'To God's Glory Richard Harvey of London Mercer and Marchant Adventurer, 1613. Faith is by Hearing'. Cornice with pendants, pinnacles and cresting. The pulpit itself has two tiers of blank arches. Early C18 handrail to the steps, perhaps by the *Bastards* of Blandford. – SCREEN. 1889 by *George Vialls*, intended to match the pulpit. – WEST GALLERY. In the same spirit as the pulpit and equally well inscribed: 'John Hassard built this to the Glorie of Almightie God in the eightieth yeare of his ago Ano. Domini 1611'. The parapet rests on pillars and has the usual short blank arches. Further galleries were installed in 1825, probably when the two large N windows were replaced with smaller ones. – FONT. Of *c.* 1880. Quite out of place in its Norman setting but almost more spectacular as a result. Alabaster with pink granite colonnettes. Elaborate spired COVER in a C15 style dated 1846. – TAPESTRY on the N wall. A museum piece, Flemish, *c.* 1490 (restored by the National Trust in 1977). – WALL PAINTING over the chancel screen, *c.* 1850. – STAINED GLASS. A very assorted collection dating from the 1840s onwards, much of good quality. Starting at the E end and working clockwise, the E window itself, together with its two accompanying side windows, is *Thomas Willement*, 1843. s aisle window by *William Wailes* of Newcastle, central two lights dated 1843, the others added to match, *c.* 1880 by *Wailes & Strang*; and a First World War memorial by *Powell & Sons*, 1920. Across in the N aisle, interrupted by the gallery, a memorial to Mary Anning by *Wailes*, 1847; next a window by *Clayton & Bell*, 1918; and further E one by *Powell & Sons*, 1921. The N aisle E window is of 1888 by *Bell & Beckham*. In the baptistery (under the tower) another by *Wailes*, 1843, and a single light in the N wall by *Kempe & Co.*, 1913. Finally, in the w porch a triple light of 1842 probably by *Willement*, and a single light opposite of 1930 by *Alexander Strachan* (PC), commemorating Thomas Coram. – MONUMENTS. Robert Fowler Coade †1773 (the uncle of Mrs Eleanor Coade of *Coade* stone) and other family. A column in relief bearing an urn. By *D. Gibbs* of Axminster. – Arthur Raymond †1789 and others. With a

---

*This scheme included an unexecuted proposal to rebuild the old nave aisles, for which only the toothing exists on the w corners.

seated genius. By *T. Gaffin*. – Elizabeth Emmitt †1817. With a
standing female figure. – Many more tablets.

St Michael and St George (R.C.), Uplyme Road. 1835–7
by *H.E. Goodridge*. Lancet style, rendered with Ham Hill
stone dressings. Octagonal buttresses with pinnacles at the
(liturgical) w end; the doorway here is a skilful piece of E.E.
imitation. The octagonal belfry tower connects with the
PRESBYTERY, 1838–9 by *A.W.N. Pugin*. A tall slender spire
was intended. The present shorter spire is of 1855 (rebuilt
in 1936). Flint and stone transept (which serves as the Lady
Chapel) of 1851–2 by *C.F. Hansom*. The nave has a plaster
rib-vault inspired by Salisbury Cathedral. – REREDOS. 1844
by *George Goldie*, originally painted and gilded, but since 1972
left plain. – STAINED GLASS. E window by *Lavers, Barraud &
Westlake*, 1883.

Peek Memorial Chapel (former), Pound Street. Built as a
private chapel for the Rev. E. Peek. By *G. Vialls*, 1884. In the
kind of half-classical, half-C17 which T. G. Jackson was popu-
larizing at that moment. Built as a chapel of ease.

Baptist church, Silver Street. Probably late C18 white-
rendered hall with a red brick late C19 porch.

Congregational church (now Dinosaurland Fossil
Museum), Coombe Street. Built 1745–55 as a Presbyterian
chapel. A fine, stately façade of five bays, arched windows
and round windows in the attic. Broad doorway with Doric
pilasters and a metope frieze. Two fluted pillars supporting the
roof. Gallery on smaller fluted pillars.

cemetery, Charmouth Road, ⅓ m. N. Laid out by *Henry
Osborn* of Lyme Regis, who also designed the two CHAPELS
and LODGE, 1856. Neo-Norman.

PUBLIC BUILDINGS

Guildhall, Bridge Street. 1887–9 by *George Vialls*. Jammed up
against the road, the porch and oriel huddled together against
a circular tower. This rises to become an octagon topped by
a concave roof. Grey stone, the dressings now painted white.
Refacing with arcading alongside the road. At the back externally an C18 part (but early C17 features within) with an upper
Venetian window at the back and re-set on the front.

Museum and Art Gallery, Bridge Street. 1903–4 by *Vialls*.
Grouped with the Guildhall, but in quite another style: C17
Dutch, with stepped gables and the red brick and stone
banding that go with the style. At the back a purely Victorian
tower with protruding stair oriel, polygonal top and cupola.
The arcade that forms the back of the tiny open square looks
really convincing as wildly provincial English classicism of
c. 1600, especially now that the stone is so crumbled.*

---

*Above the distinctive shell-hooded machicolation were a pair of Flemish-inspired
gables with, set in them, an almost Arabian perforated stone screen.

South Elevation

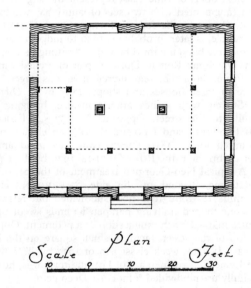

Plan

Scale   10   0   10   20   30   Feet

Lyme Regis, Congregational church.
Elevation and plan, 1952

PERAMBULATIONS

The starting point for the perambulations is Cobb Gate, an opening in the almost continuous frontages of buildings next to the sea.

1. Broad Street and the western part of the town

BROAD STREET, heading w, has the most worthwhile runs of buildings. As it climbs, the first encounter on the s side is MIDDLE ROW, an island block built on the space of the medieval market. One house has an upper overhang, suggesting late C16 timber framing behind. The Late Georgian resort expresses itself a little further up with the bows and bays of its inns. The ROYAL LION HOTEL on the r., of stucco, with enlarged windows in conspicuous rusticated surrounds, rebuilt after the fire of 1844. The former BOROUGH OFFICES of *c.* 1790 next door, of Blue Lias, represent the slightly earlier moment (augmented with two sets of jaunty bay windows in the C19). Opposite, the former THREE CUPS HOTEL, also of Lias rubble, is later, probably *c.* 1830 to judge by the wide sashes, of three bays, the third bowed and resting its weight on columns which are Roman Doric. A pair of arched windows on the ground floor. The rear altered at various stages.* Next a terrace of three houses and shops, 1825 by *S. Osborn* of Lyme. Stucco, with sashes graded in size, bringing some uniformity to the street. Opposite, Nos. 53–54 (FORTNAM SMITH BANWELL and LLOYDS BANK), an elegant pair of houses in red brick, *c.* 1810. The doorways have good fanlights. Further up on the r. the POST OFFICE, 1929 by the *Office of Works*. A typical Neo-Georgian treatment of the period with good detailing. Beyond, on this side, SHERBORNE HOUSE with a mid-C18 front. It is now subdivided but retains the *Coade*-stone-topped unifying parapet, its ends swept up and the centre marked by the suggestion of a pediment. Opposite, at the top of the street, facing a small square on the l., the REGENT CINEMA, weak classicism of 1937 by *W.H. Watkins* for the Lyme Regis Cinema Co. The auditorium is, however, a mercifully un-subdivided minor Art Deco gem.

At this point the road forks. The l. fork is POUND STREET with, after the Peek Memorial Chapel (p. 368), set back on the l., the HOTEL ALEXANDRA (formerly Poulett House), a much-altered town house of six sashed bays, built *c.* 1730 as a retreat for the earls Poulett of Hinton St George, Somerset. Two stuccoed, semi-detached pairs of houses, of the early C19, are further up on the l., the second set with TIVOLI COTTAGE attached, an early C19 octagonal folly-villa in the style of a toll house.

---

* One of the best buildings in the town, it has been disgracefully left unused for many years.

Next on the l. a real historical curiosity. This is BELMONT (Landmark Trust), *c.* 1770, with a handsome later C18 façade. Two-storeyed, of five bays, profusely decorated with enriched string courses, vermiculated quoins and vermiculated Gibbs surrounds to the round-headed ground-floor windows and doorway. Masks on the keystones, dolphins on the impost blocks. The explanation for this frenzy of decoration is that it is all executed in *Coade* stone for *Mrs Eleanor Coade* herself, who was given Belmont by her uncle in 1784 and used it as her maritime villa until her death in 1821. With her acute sense of publicity, she made sure that the house was her own best advertisement, displaying many stock items from her catalogue. Extended in the 1880s with two large wings (since demolished) and a LOOK-OUT TOWER, now free-standing. The tower retains winding gear for its revolving roof, with telescope hatch. Thorough restoration of the house and tower, including reinstatement of the original pink colour on the house, was completed by the Landmark Trust in 2015.

The most vehement expressions of the Victorian aesthetic in Lyme come next on the other side of the road. CORAM TOWER, rich in Blue Lias with Ham Hill stone dressings, rises abruptly from the pavement, a tower house with a pyramid roof, 1903–4 by *Vialls*. Also on the r., CORAM COURT makes a display of half-timbered gables. Built 1851 by *Hicks* as a 'new vicarage house'. Enlarged (and dated) 1889 by *Vialls* for the Rev. Edward Peek as part of St Michael's College, a school for sons of the clergy. In masonry to the l. of the timber-framing, a sculpture of St Michael by *Thomas Earp & Co.* A little further, on the crest of the hill, placed where the view to the sea could be had, the most intensely characteristic Late Georgian buildings. HIGH CLIFF, on the same side of the road, lies back and is quite large, a broadly proportioned version of the classical front with bows l. and r. Opposite, the early C19 UMBRELLA COTTAGE, built as a lodge to Upper Cobb House (*see* below). Its polygonal body and huge thatched roof coming down umbrella-like on posts make it as ebullient as a house like High Cliff is reserved. Behind this is UPPER COBB HOUSE itself (formerly Little Cliff), a typical three-bay early C19 villa but with interiors and a large 1922 addition by *Arnold Mitchell* (who may also have enhanced the picturesque qualities of its lodge).

2. A short circuit to the east and north

Starting from Cobb Gate again and turning E, BUDDLE BRIDGE, which takes Bridge Street over the river, is partly C14. Next the Guildhall and Museum (p. 368). Behind these, GUN CLIFF WALK. An area of protective sea wall and esplanade by *Rainey Petrie Design*, 1995. This, including an odd oblong turret, partly obscures sea walling of the late C18. Above and to the NE, CHURCH CLIFFS, 2000 by *Boon Brown Architects*. A jaunty

maritime terrace, each house with a curved roof leading to
the next. On one corner a circular Art Deco-inspired turret.
Returning to the main street, after the bend into CHURCH
STREET there is only the MERMAID SHOP AND GALLERY
(formerly the Old Tudor House Hotel) that is worth a line
or two. The hoodmoulds to the lower windows and the string
course above are evidence that here is a late C16 or early C17
house heightened. Stone chimneypiece with moulded fireplace
opening in the S room, which also has a moulded compartment ceiling. In the entrance hall a mid-C18 staircase. (In an
upper room at the back, a thin-ribbed plaster ceiling of the
same date has been removed. Its decorative frieze, still *in situ*,
is dated 1601.)

At the church it is worth turning l., directly opposite, into
the near-pedestrian precinct of MONMOUTH STREET and
COOMBE STREET. In the former, No. 4 (facing the small
public garden) has a mid-C18 stucco façade and doorcase
with Ionic pilasters worth a glance; in the latter is the pretty
shopfront of No. 14, of just after the 1844 fire, opposite the
former Congregational church (p. 368). To return to the town's
centre, a route may be taken over the bridge at the W end of
Coombe Street, then l. up SHERBORNE LANE. Here, on the r.
side, several of the cottages remain thatched. This emerges on
to the top of Broad Street, next to the Baptist church (p. 368).

3. An esplanade walk to the Cobb

Turning SW and following the seafront, MARINE PARADE is
engagingly modest, bordered by cottages and slate-hung Victorian villas, with here and there a Regency bow or veranda.
Of note are MADEIRA HOUSE and MADEIRA COTTAGE,
the former genuine Regency, the latter a rebuilt imitation
of the mid 1930s by *J. B. S. Comper* (son of Sir Ninian) for
Sir Maurice Abbot-Anderson. These form part of a picturesque pink-washed thatched row. Next, LIBRARY COTTAGE,
early C19, also thatched and with an accumulation of French
antique leadwork added in the 1920s, and THE SUNDIAL, a
stone and flint tower house of 1903 by *Arnold Mitchell*.

The esplanade leads to THE COBB hamlet. This, the maritime quarter of Lyme, has been developed on land reclaimed
from the sea since the breakwater to the W was built. Simple
marine-vernacular architecture of *c.* 1800–20, weatherboarded
houses and the former BONDED WAREHOUSE, 1830, of worn
Blue Lias. Beyond this the plain classical CUSTOM HOUSE of
1845–6 in Cobb Road.

THE COBB itself, principally built of large cobbles or Cow-
stones, has its origins in a breakwater known to have existed
in 1539 (although a timber structure here is first recorded in
1294). It is sickle-shaped in plan, splitting at its E end where the
landward arm was extended (as VICTORIA PIER) in 1842–52.

A connection with the shore was made only in 1756. Much reconstruction in Portland stone in 1824, after storms. Enclosure of the harbour was completed by the NORTH WALL in the early C19 (partially reconstructed in 1849). On the Cobb is a row of former cottages and warehouses, probably late C18, although much adapted.

LYSCOMBE
2 m. NW of Cheselbourne

7000

A thatched-roofed flint cottage here was a CHAPEL. Its chancel is of c. 1200. The chancel arch and the E window, a C13 lancet, are preserved. The chancel arch has segmental responds, scalloped capitals and a single-step pointed arch. In the C15 and C16 the nave was rebuilt. Sensitively repaired in 2005 by *Architecton*. The adjoining COTTAGE, in part C16, is now a ruin.

LYTCHETT HEATH

9090

ST ALDHELM. 1898 by *Crickmay & Son* for Lord Eustace Gascoyne-Cecil. An idiosyncratic building, but one of the best examples of what this local firm could do when given their chance. They started by rock-facing the building and then decided, about 8 ft (2.4 metres) up the walls, to change to golden ashlar, and the ashlar is extended down to encompass the windows. The W tower, however, is rock-faced and battered with a W buttress across its full width; bold corbelled cornice. Upon this sits a very squat bell-stage, and on that follows an Italian pyramid roof with very deep eaves. The whole is very effective and compares with some of the best Arts and Crafts church work nationally. Simpler and more typically Late Gothic Revival interior, well fitted out. – STAINED GLASS. The E window is by *Kempe*, 1899. Five nave windows by *Jude Tarrant*, 2001.
   Fine setting in a circular clearing of the forest with a stone wall and a LYCHGATE.

LYTCHETT HEATH, ¼ m. NW. 1875–9 by *David Brandon* for *p. 374* Lord Eustace Gascoyne-Cecil. A large mansion concealed by trees among rhododendrons and wellingtonias. Jacobethan. Diapered red brick, Bath stone dressings. Pinwheel plan with an elongated service end, now truncated. Nearly symmetrical entrance front but otherwise a studied asymmetry, with a mix of canted and square bay windows. Shaped gables. Some alterations after 1921, somewhat disrupting Brandon's intended effect.

Lytchett Heath.
Engraving by A. Betty, 1879

LYTCHETT MATRAVERS

A largely modern village now, located well to the SE of the church, manor house and former rectory. Interspersed are some cob and brick cottages, many with thatched roofs.

ST MARY. Two-stage W tower of *c*. 1200, the lower stage heavily buttressed. Early C16 pinnacled parapet. Inside, the pointed tower arch has chamfered imposts as does the chancel arch, both *c*. 1200. The remainder of the church, apart from the chancel as rebuilt *c*. 1400, is of *c*. 1500, dated by a brass inscription to Margaret Clement †1505, who is called 'generosa benefactrix reedificacionis huius ecclesie' ('generous benefactor of the rebuilding of this church'). This is close to the entrance. Of this date, therefore, is a thorough rebuilding of the nave and S porch, and a new N aisle. One chancel S window has bar tracery (a quatrefoiled circle) of *c*. 1280. The bars are enforced by thin rolls inside. Another to its W of *c*. 1400. Nave windows with curious blank tracery. Open wagon roof in the nave. – The chancel FURNISHINGS date from a restoration in 1873. – FONT. Octagonal, of *c*. 1500. Panelled stem and pointed, diagonally placed quatrefoils on the bowl. – ROYAL ARMS of George IV. Painted panel. – HATCHMENTS. Several of the Trenchard family. – STAINED GLASS. N aisle, some arms of *c*. 1500. Also in the W window a figure of St Anne flanked by two male saints. – BRASSES. On the N aisle floor a large slab with a most unusual brass indeed – simply and impressively just a version of the Matravers fret stretched to fit the shape of the slab: two diagonals and a lozenge. Only the indents for the now lost brasses survive and only a short length of marginal inscription *in situ*. Probably for John, Lord Matravers

†1364 (the possible co-murderer of Edward II). – Chancel, Thomas Pethyn, rector, *c.* 1470. A 15-in. (38-cm.) figure with tonsure. – MONUMENT. A Purbeck wall monument of the usual type (with no brasses indicating its dedicatee), but smaller and flatter than most, e.g. with no detached shafts for the canopy. Probably *c.* 1500.

WESLEYAN METHODIST CHAPEL, Wareham Road, 1 m. SE. Simple heathstone and stucco round-arched building of 1853. Higher section of brick facing the road, 1910.

MANOR HOUSE, adjoining the church on the N. Partly C17. The Italianate house of *c.* 1850 was demolished *c.* 1960 and a smaller Neo-Georgian block built in its place.

Former RECTORY (now called Lytchett St Mary), ¼ m. SE. Mainly *c.* 1830. Stucco, of five bays. Tuscan portico.

LYTCHETT MINSTER   9090

A scatter of cottages alongside the old A35, concentrated around the church, school and park wall of South Lytchett Manor.

CHURCH. 'Rebuilt in a plain manner', 1833–4 by *John Tulloch* of Wimborne, except for the battlemented two-stage W tower, which is C15. This is of brown heathstone, the church of buff brick. The windows originally had Y-tracery. In two cases, where stained glass has been fitted, more elaborate tracery has been inserted, the effect adding to the incongruity of the whole. The chancel is the typical short one of the period. There is a WEST GALLERY with an early C19 ROYAL ARMS.* – FONT. C15, octagonal. – STAINED GLASS. E window by *Heaton, Butler & Bayne*, 1898. One window on each side designed by the painter *Percy Buckman* of Lewisham, 1912. Another S window by the same, 1917. The three were made by *A.J. Dix.* – MEMORIAL. NW of the church, Mary Styring †1857. Gothic chest tomb with colonnettes to the sides. Panels between with *Minton* tiles.

UNITED INDEPENDENT AND BAPTIST CHAPEL (now United Reformed), ¼ m. SW. Dated 1824. Brick with round-arched windows on the front and very large square-headed sashes on the sides.

WESLEYAN METHODIST CHAPEL, Upton, ¾ m. E. By *J.B. Corby* of Stamford. Dated 1865. Gothic, with a Geometrical traceried (liturgical) W window. Brick.

PARISH HALL (disused and falling into disrepair), ⅛ m. S of the church, beside the main road. A nice example of its date, 1900. Low roughcast walls, buttressed, under a mansard roof. Two large windows on the W side in segmental half-dormers (one

---

*The fine panelled mahogany DOORS probably came from the original (1807) South Lytchett Manor.

altered). The chimney wittily provided for in its own gabled
projection.

SOUTH LYTCHETT MANOR (Lytchett Minster School), ⅜ m. N.
A house of 1807 called Sans Souci, completely reconstructed
in a loud Baroque style by *W.D. Caröe* for Sir Elliott Lees; one
of his more wayward designs. The builder was *Parnell & Son*
of Rugby. Of mustard-coloured Ham Hill ashlar. The scheme
was published in 1900, and the building bears the date 1904.
The entrance (w) front has to be seen to be believed. Symmetry was intended, but Caröe seems intent in destroying its
impact by the informal massing of the building behind. First
a pedimented *porte cochère*, unfortunately interfering with the
great niche behind *à la* Belvedere Courtyard, Rome. This
is crowned by a composition of broken pediment, dormers
and a curvy attic. The w front towards the garden is more
restrained, an almost Caroline centre block (influenced by
Barry's Kingston Lacy?), open on an arcade below, and lower
side pavilions, one built as a conservatory, the other a library.
Rustication, Gibbs surrounds, etc. pep it up, while the pavilions are in themselves satisfying compositions. According to
the design, the main s block was due to be crowned by a balustraded lead flat roof and a cupola. Their absence is sorely
felt. Inside, a top-lit hall, also by Caröe, *c.* 1892, added to the
earlier house and incorporated in the later project. Stained-
glass-domed entrance lobby. In the library a heavy grey stone
Baroque fireplace of typical Caröe invention.
    LODGE and GATES on the main road, ½ m. E. By *Caröe*.
Of 1905. Pyramid roof rising to a central chimney. Elaborate
wrought-iron gates. The whole C17 in character.

POST GREEN HOUSE, ⅓ m. NW. A surprisingly large three-
storey, five-bay, late C18 house. This is N-facing with an early
C19 lower enlargement facing S, built back to back. The latter
has bay windows and is more informally disposed.

HARBOUR VIEW WOODLAND BURIAL GROUND, 1 m. NE.
2005 onwards. A landscaped burial site. It includes the non-
denominational ISLAND CHAPEL, by *Western Design Architects*,
under construction in 2016. Built into a bank or berm, glass-
sided where exposed. Surrounded by a linear pool to represent
the River Styx.*

BULBURY CAMP, 2 m. WNW. A single-banked Iron Age ENCLO-
SURE of 8½ acres. Possible entrances on the E and S; now
almost entirely reduced by ploughing. Material found in 1881
during cutting of field drains included two small cast-bronze
horned bulls with curved tails ending in flowers (possibly
chariot fittings), an iron anchor with some yards of chain,
two sledgehammers, an iron axe, andirons and fragments of a
tankard, snaffle-bit, dagger, sword and mirror, all of bronze.

---

*REST HARROW nearby, by *Sir Hugh Casson*, 1956, no longer has its original 'small
and quiet' appearance owing to alterations.

MAIDEN CASTLE
see WINTERBORNE ST MARTIN

MAIDEN NEWTON   *5090*

A small market town on the banks of the River Frome.

St Mary. Central tower, a s transept and a s aisle. The base of
the stout tower is mid-C12, but this can only be seen inside.
Externally it is mid-C15. Small (for the tower width) two-light,
trefoil-headed bell-openings with Somerset tracery. Battlements to the tower and mid-C15 aisle and transept. The N side
of the nave is much more revealing. The whole wall is C12, with
an off-centre N doorway and corbel table. Here small double
arches between each of the corbels. Some C15 rebuilding to the
r. of the doorway when the two large Perp windows went in.
To the l., adjoining the tower, a tall C12 round-arched window,
later extended downwards. The doorway itself has one order of
colonnettes with scallop capitals, chevron in the arch, a hoodmould and a plain tympanum. Good early boarded DOOR. In
the nave W gable an early C14 window with reticulated tracery
but no hoodmould. No battlements to the chancel, which is of
c. 1400, its E wall rebuilt in striped flint and ashlar in the later
C15 (to match the transept and aisle).
  Inside, of the mid C12 the E tower arch. This has triple
responds with scalloped capitals and a double-chamfered
pointed arch. The much wider W arch has a C13 segmental
respond. The arcade is Perp, of three bays, the piers quatrefoil
but with chamfered projections (three sides of an octagon). At
the apex of the nave N doorway a very small carved medallion
with Christ in Majesty. Another, in crisper condition, re-set
over the s doorway. This depicts a man on horseback. Both are
late C12. – Most of the FURNISHINGS from a major restoration by *B. Ferrey*, 1850, were removed after a 2011 fire. (The
chancel had been largely cleared before.) The chief survivals
are the very fine ALTAR and REREDOS. – FONT. Late C12,
Purbeck marble. Octagonal, plain, on nine supports. Mid-C19
Gothic COVER, perhaps by *Ferrey*. – SCULPTURE. In the porch
a short column with unusually elaborate capital and base, C12.
Perhaps from the original s doorway. – STAINED GLASS. Small
C15 fragments mainly in the s windows. E and two chancel side
windows by *Lavers, Barraud & Westlake*, 1881. – MONUMENT.
John Whetcom †1635, rector. Frontal demi-figure between
black columns.
Wesleyan Methodist chapel (former), Dorchester Road.
Formerly dated 1871. By Mr *Bush* of Sydling St Nicholas.
Neo-Norman. Rock-faced stone. Tall, round-arched windows,
iron-framed with decorative borders.
the town. Apart from the buildings described separately, the
best street of Maiden Newton is CHURCH ROAD. Here, just
s of the church, MAIDEN NEWTON HOUSE, a substantial

former rectory. Dated 1842. L-plan. Tudor Revival, with buttresses. Secondary range facing the churchyard, probably earlier. Banded flint but with some mid- to late C19 detailing. Further s, the WAR MEMORIAL, *c.* 1920 by *E. S. Prior.* A hexagonal obelisk rising from a triangular plinth. Further along, the former SCHOOL. 1841. Gothic. Wilfully rough rubble and flintwork. Projecting cast-iron CLOCK over the porch doorway commemorating Queen Victoria's Golden Jubilee (1887). At the s end of the street a once fine C15 MARKET CROSS. Lias stone. Square base, squarish stem, with weatherbeaten figures on the w face. At this point we reach the congested A356, Dorchester Road.

Former CORN MILL by the bridge over the Frome. Of *c.* 1800. Red brick. An imposing three-storey range, reducing to two, but maintaining the ridge height, to the w end. Here the stone-built mill house with sash fenestration.

RAILWAY STATION, Station Road, 250 yds E. 1857 by *R. P. Brereton* for the Great Western Railway. Flint with Ham Hill dressings. Low-pitched roofs to both the main (up line) building and the shelter (down line). Largely unaltered. Both have original canopies (although the approach-side canopy to the main building has been removed). Refreshment room, 1860–1, added to the s end of the main building.

CRUXTON MANOR, West Cruxton, 1 m. SSE. An unusually characterful house, built of flint banded with thin stripes of stone. There are buttresses at the NW gable-end, on a SW-facing turret and at a mid-point on the wall to the r. of the porch, suggestive of an early C16 date. The three-storey gabled porch, with a flattened four-centred arch under a jumped-up hood, and the sets of arch-headed mullioned windows (hollow-chamfered with no hoods) tell of *c.* 1600. It was even more characterful before *c.* 1950, when the walls of the range l. of the porch were raised to make the roof-line through with the r. part, and the thatch was replaced by tiles. Some later refenestration.

FRAMPTON ROMAN VILLA, 2 m. SE. The L-shaped earthwork in the water meadows of Throop Dairy House is all that remains of the villa discovered in 1796. The mosaics recorded then by Lysons, of the Durnovarian Group (*see* Dorchester, p. 264), are some of the most elaborate in Dorset.

HOG CLIFF HILL, 1½ m. ESE. A Bronze Age ENCLOSURE of *c.* 25 acres with bank and internal ditch. In the interior a series of round-houses lasting into the earliest Iron Age.

MANSTON

The church, manor house and family mausoleum form a group s of the village on the Stour river bank.

ST NICHOLAS. Mid-C15 battlemented w tower with an inserted w doorway dated 1534. Diagonal buttresses on the w side only.

The bell-stage has Somerset tracery, the window on the s side half-obscured by the polygonal stair-turret. Panelled arch to the nave. E.E. chancel with long lancets. The N aisle has two lancets too, probably *c.* 1300–10, and the arcade of three bays has arches with two continuous chamfers – a Dec motif. The E window of the N aisle on the other hand is later C14, i.e. it has flowing tracery just congealing into Perp. In 1870 it was blocked by the vestry. The W arcade bay was also blocked when, in 1780, the W bay of the aisle was demolished. The three Y-traceried nave s windows are probably late C17 insertions. A curious triplet above the chancel arch was inserted in 1885–7, when the chancel was heavily restored, the whole church refurnished and the plaster removed. However, the N aisle was largely left alone in its early C19 condition with limewashed window surrounds and tracery. Squint, C14 on the N side of the chancel arch. C13 PISCINA with a trefoil head in the chancel E wall. – Rich TILES on the sanctuary and chancel floors, all of *c.* 1885. – FONT. Also *c.* 1885. Perp style, with Somerset alabaster panels inlaid to each face. – STAINED GLASS. E window with Crucifixion and much grisaille decoration (†1869), possibly by *Charles Gibbs.* Similar glass fills two chancel side lancets. – MONUMENT. Grace Morris †1689. By *Nicholas Mitchell* of Shere Lane, London. It cost £21 (T.P. Connor). The inscription on a convex, semi-cylindrical surface. Foliage and a putto head at the foot, an urn at the top.

WESLEYAN CHAPEL (former), ½ m. NW. Dated 1864. Lancet Gothic in unusually fine masonry. Now derelict.

The church belongs to a typical, if very humble, manorial group. MANSTON HOUSE looks early C19, but was in fact rebuilt after a fire of 1857 for Capt. Thomas Hanham. Three-bay front, rendered, with a pediment over the centre bay.

On the other side of the church, family MAUSOLEUM of *c.* 1876, by *James Soppitt* of Shaftesbury. With a Neo-Norman doorway and a low dome. – STAINED GLASS. Circular armorial window, 1879.

Just visible above the churchyard wall, to the rear of Manston House, a small classical private CREMATORIUM, first used in 1882. Public cremation became available in Britain only after 1885, to a degree following Capt. Hanham's example here.

OLD RECTORY, ⅛ m. N. Of *c.* 1880, probably by *Waller & Son* of Gloucester. Tudorish, of rock-faced stone. Tile-hanging in the gable apexes.

In the village, opposite the turning for Sturminster Newton, a Tudor Revival TOLL HOUSE of *c.* 1840.

MAPPERTON   5090

There can hardly be anywhere a more enchanting manorial group than Mapperton. Part of the charm lies in the vagueness about what is public and what private. The U-shaped group, open to the w, includes the modest church connected to the house as its s range. It is all railed off from the road and seen beyond early C17 gatepiers off which lead eagles are about to flap. Across the road, a pair of stable blocks continue the arms of the U. Detailed description must begin, historically, with the church.

ALL SAINTS (private chapel). The chancel is medieval, the w tower C15. The tower hardly reads as such since its roof is now continuous with the nave. It was repaired with new pinnacles as late as *c.* 1770, so was most likely reduced during the 1846 restoration.* The nave was rebuilt at an earlier date with two-light windows having round heads in a framing surround. One might take them for *c.* 1670; they are in fact 1704 (see the plaque above the doorway recording the rebuilding by Richard Brodrepp). Of the earlier existence tells a handsome trefoil-headed E.E. doorway and the C15 E window, although the latter was largely remade in 1846. Of this latter date also the Dec w window. – COMMUNION RAIL. Mid-C18 with turned balusters. – Other FURNISHINGS largely from 1846. – Two RELIEFS either side of the E window by *Cecil Thomas*, 1928. A memorial to Charles Labouchere †1926. – FONT. C12. Cylindrical bowl. Plain above, scalloped below. – STAINED GLASS. A collection of small pieces, the earliest date 1509, the latest 1632. Mostly heraldic roundels. The glass is mainly brought in, although mostly local in origin. w window probably by *Wailes*, †1850. Two panels in the vestry by *Caroline Swash*, 2001. – MONUMENT. Richard Brodrepp, a son and a daughter. Last death recorded 1739. By *Peter Scheemakers* and very fine. Standing monument with the usual grey obelisk. Against it one portrait medallion. Below two free-standing putti not at all symmetrical. They hold another portrait medallion.

MANOR HOUSE. The house forms an L. The N range must on style be dated to the middle years of the C16. The E range is in its bones of the same date, for it contains the hall, where in the C18 Hutchins saw an inscription referring to Robert Morgan, builder of the house, probably *c.* 1550. This E range wears an aspect however that is of the mid C17, in this case most likely of the 1660s as the first of a series of improvements for the second in a line of successive owners named Richard Brodrepp. In both parts all the carved stone dressings come from Ham Hill. The style of the N range allies it to the mid-C16 group of buildings connected with the Ham Hill quarries, of which Clifton Maybank was in its day the most spectacular. Polygonal angle buttresses rising to twisted pedestals for carved armorial finials. Towards the courtyard there are windows of three and four lights, with hoodmoulds and arched lights, the topmost window a gabled dormer, with twisted shafts on corbels up the sides of the gable. This same configuration can be seen on the lesser gables of Barrington

*A bellcote was substituted but this too has been removed.

Court, Somerset, also of the 1550s and certainly by the same group of craftsmen. The N side of the wing was sashed *c.* 1750, and the centre brought a little forward to make a classical composition, but the angle buttresses survive, as do the plinth and string course.

Coming round again now to the front one can follow this plinth and string course from the N range across the polygonal l. bay, the main front and the polygonal r. bay of the entrance façade, but they are not to be seen on the porch. This was altered in the mid to late C19, when it was fitted with its Tudor-arched doorway.* The inner porch doorway however is mid-C16, with a four-centred head with Morgan griffin-heads in the spandrels. So it seems that Mapperton began as two-thirds of a composition of the type which Barrington Court most relevantly represents: that is to say, the centre range and l. wing were built of a U-plan house with extruded corners, three-sided in Mapperton's case, whereas at Barrington they are square. The classicizing entrance front then represents a remodelling, substituting a top balustrade and dormers, where there had no doubt been gables, putting in new classically pro-portioned windows, with mullion-and-transom crosses, which fit the polygonal bays especially happily, and replacing the porch completely. In the porch the date 166–, cut haphazardly in the wall, most likely dates this work. Still the r. bay looks as if it hopes for a r. wing to join on to, and this was no doubt the intention at the time. The C17 buildings that lie E of the church are quite irregular, and have only been joined to the main body of the house in the C20.

On entering the PORCH, there are shell-headed niches, two per side. These have their shells inverted, i.e. with the scallop-ing widening from the top, an indication of the likely involve-ment of *William Arnold*. So the porch was an addition of the early C17, externally remodelled with the rest of the range later in the century. It leads into the screens passage, and, l. through the made-up screen, into the HALL. Here the plaster ceiling is of the 1920s; the gargantuan plaster overmantel with the arms of James I in the centre and large pieces of strapwork scrolls l. and r. came in 1909 from Melplash Court (q.v.). The date on it, 1604, is C20 but must be about right.** In the NW corner of the Hall is a boldly detailed arch (described in the previous edition as an 'ignorant attempt at classicism'). Its round head, keystone and the two semicircular soffit rolls are also typical of the Manneristic invention of *Arnold*. It contrasts strongly with the graceful restraint with which the mid-C17 exterior is handled, and has strong similarities with arches like this at Herringston, Winterborne Herringston, datable *c.* 1612, and

*It had previously had a flat-topped opening, as shown in a drawing of 1828 by John Buckler.
**It is likely to be by *Robert Eaton* of Stogursey, Somerset. *See* John and Jane Penoyre, *Decorative Plasterwork in the Houses of Somerset* (1994).

in the NW wing of Sherborne Castle, c. 1630, also likely to be by Arnold.

The NORTH RANGE contains two rooms down, and two up, divided by the STAIRCASE. This is mid-C18, with a handrail curling under itself at the bottom. Simple Rococo ceiling here, and in the LIBRARY, all typical of the work of the *Bastard* company of Blandford. The library has another chimneypiece brought from Melplash, with the arms of James I in a fairly restrained surround. The plaster ceilings of the DRAWING ROOM and the room above it are a pair. Of c. 1570–90, their ribs making a geometrical pattern; fleur-de-lys in the fields. The upper ceiling has the extra distinction of pendants. But the UPPER ROOM was already in the earliest period important, for the plaster frieze of heads in roundels held by putti, and the plaster overmantel, with a broad border of judiciously spaced foliage and a fat foliated baluster l. and r., speak the language of c. 1540–50 and are therefore contemporary with the building of this wing. Similar, more fussy, overmantel in the WEST UPPER ROOM, the indispensable balusters used to form a lozenge in the centre.

The STABLE RANGES to the W are a pair, one-storeyed, having large classical framed cross-windows, bolection friezes and triangular pediments. That is an extension of Mapperton's mid-C17 vocabulary, and the date 1670 on the S range is what one expects. Carriage entrance to the S range only, this incorporating an earlier barn.

In the formal GARDENS, first completed in the valley to the E in 1927 by Mrs Labouchere, there is a tiny two-storey building, quite plain, but probably of the C17, presumably a summerhouse. The garden layout was modified in the 1950s and 1960s by Viscount Hinchingbrooke (10th Earl of Sandwich), harmonizing its appearance.

RECTORY, 100 yds N. Dated 1701 inside. Symmetrical with seven-window front, all two-light except for an inner pair either side of a projecting two-storey gabled porch. Ovolo mouldings to the stone mullions. (Inside on a door lintel the date 1701 and initials IP for John Powell, the rector.)

MAPPOWDER

Several pairs of early C19 estate cottages, interspersed with older cottages, farms and modern bungalows.

ST PETER AND ST PAUL. A very complete late C15 church, except for the chancel of 1868 by *R.H. Carpenter*, and in its uniformity very satisfying. W tower with Somerset tracery in the bell-openings; plain parapets. Nave and chancel and S aisle with three-light windows. An elaborately panelled parapet to the N (repeated on the chancel), battlements to the S. The church is of mellow Ham Hill stone and the three-bay arcade of standard details is of the same. The E respond has a Green Man. This pier has a squint, neatly set beneath rood-loft stairs. – PULPIT. Jacobean style with perforated decoration. Presumably *c.* 1868. – Decorative TILEWORK on the chancel floor. – The other FURNISHINGS are appropriately unimposing. – Good C12 FONT, of uncommon design. Purbeck marble, of table type with five pillars on a matching moulded base. Eight of the usual shallow arches on one side, chevron on another, a chain of lobes running horizontally and meeting at their apexes on yet another, and leaf squares on the fourth. – SCREEN under the tower. Prettily Flamboyant. It looks Victorian, but is of 1926, by the *Rev. G.A. Coleman* and his friend *Mr Ringrose.* – REREDOS. Also by *Coleman* and *Ringrose,* 1929. – MONUMENTS. In the S aisle a mini-effigy of the late C13 or early C14. Knight with crossed legs, the hands clasping a round object. This may indicate a heart burial or some other type of viscera burial. The niche has two re-set Norman heads. – Under the tower two matching tablets, †1644 (N below) and †1648 (S), each with paired Corinthian colonnettes and a spiky Jacobean top. A third (†1636, N top) is somewhat simpler.

MAPPOWDER COURT, ¼ m. SE. All the big gatepiers, especially the biggest with C17 stone busts on top, suggest that there was once quite a grand house here; but the mansion of the Coker family was demolished soon after 1745. What one sees is an L-plan C18 vernacular stone building (reusing some earlier structure), achieving a symmetrical E front. This alone is rendered, of three bays, the outer windows being four-lighters above, five-lighters with a transom below. C18 pedimented doorcase.

MARGARET MARSH

8010

A scattering of farmsteads, several with late medieval fabric, in an area very prone to flooding.

ST MARGARET. Mid-C15 ashlar battlemented W tower, similar in many respects to that at Manston. Diagonal buttresses, but turning shallow pilaster-strip (i.e. really rather thin embracing buttresses) at the bell-stage. Bell-openings with Somerset tracery. The church itself is a replacement of 1872–3 of the Perp original, also Perp in style, by *G.R. Crickmay,* reusing some stonework. Competent but uninspiring. – FONT. C13 bowl on a contemporary cylindrical shaft. C18 base.

HIGHER FARM, ¼ m. NE, a pretty thatched cottage of rubble-stone walls, with a higher part and a lower part, built with a hall open to the roof in the C15. Wind-braces, and trusses probably of cruck construction.

GORE FARM, 1½ m. NE, appears similar (although no longer thatched). The lower part to the l. is C16, with walls raised in height in brick in the C18. Of the late C18 or early C19 is the higher portion to the r.

MARNHULL

Marnhull is a large village made up until recently of a number of hamlets centred at road junctions. Of these, Kentleworth (at the junction between New Street and Church Hill), has the church, rectory and a major house. The others, such as Burton and Pillwell, have cottage rows, or groups of late C19 villas. Scattered throughout are some larger gentry houses, from when Marnhull was a centre for the Blackmoor Vale hunt. Dotted about among all this, houses with the mullioned stone windows of the C16 and C17, small sash-windowed C18 and C19 ashlar villas, and mid- to late C19 stone terraces. Several Nonconformist chapels are interspersed, some now converted to dwellings. The two more architecturally imposing are noted below. A number of housing estates have infilled the open pattern of the village since 1972, something to be regretted but perhaps inevitable.

QUARRYING of Todber freestone took place at Gannetts, with smaller quarries at the E end of Crown Road opposite New Inn Farm, and on Great Down Lane.

ST GREGORY. A large Perp church. However, inside in an unexpected place, halfway down the N arcade, is one late C12 pier, square with keeled semicircular projections and a capital with scallops and masks. So the church has an earlier and more complicated history than was evident outside. It is mainly of three Perp phases: the late C14, another of c. 1470 and further work of c. 1520. Also there are Victorian works in several phases by different architects. The major restoration and enlargement was in 1852 by *George Alexander*. The S wall and S arcade are of this date, in a style intended to match the chancel arch of c. 1470. At this time several C18 round-arched windows were replaced with traceried Gothic, and a vestry was added. The chancel itself is a rebuilding of 1882. The N chapel was restored in 1898 by *C.E. Ponting*, who added an organ chamber in the following year. (*Ponting* replaced Alexander's vestry in 1921.) The remainder is Perp, climaxing at the three-stage W tower of c. 1470 with its divers canopied niches and its odd variety of bell-openings. To the E and W there are two bell-openings with transoms, to the N and S one long opening, that to the N with a transom, the lower part of the S one blocked by an C18 clock face. According to Hutchins, the tower collapsed c. 1718, although rebuilding appears to have been confined to the S face of the top stage, where the detailing was simplified. The N aisle of c. 1520, remodelled chapel and rood turret (which

is thought to have originally served as a late C14 lodging for a
chantry priest, removed in the early C16) are best viewed from
the N. Within, the N arcade, apart from the Norman pier, has
late C14 octagonal piers. The S arcade has one pier of *c.* 1470,
which, with the chancel arch responds, is of standard section.
Capitals with small leaves and delicately carved angels supporting blank shields, the carving taking full advantage of the
fine local stone. Nice contemporary arch from the N arcade
into the N chapel, again with fine angel carving on the capitals.
In the chapel an ogee-headed PISCINA, C14. To its N a stone
SCREEN of two lights, installed when the N aisle was widened
c. 1520. Of this date the nave roof of moulded coffering. The
panels have various quatrefoil decorations, some with Tudor
roses, one with the Carent arms. A similar, although simpler,
ceiling in the N chapel. The N aisle ceiling is of the wagon type.
In the chancel a re-set corbel with two angel busts.

OTHER FURNISHINGS. REREDOS. Ceramic tilework of
c. 1910. – PULPIT. 1852. – FONT. An enormous, uncouth
square block with top spurs, perhaps originally a cross base.
Low Perp stem, panelled, probably intended to carry the 'spare'
octagonal font bowl loose in the church. – ROYAL ARMS. On
a lozenge panel over the S doorway. Stuart arms, but the 'C'
altered to a 'G' when the date 1732 was added. – Here and in
the N aisle a number of HATCHMENTS on lozenge boards, the
earliest dated 1631. – WALL PAINTINGS. Three layers above
the chancel arch, the first a Doom, overlaid by three panels of
C16 Decalogue; this overpainted by an early C18 Lord's Prayer
and Creed in an architectural framework. More C16 lettering
elsewhere. N and S of the tower arch a skeleton and a naked
man, C15 or C16. – STAINED GLASS. E window depicting the
Crucifixion, 1911 by *Morris & Co.* to a *Burne-Jones* design.
Chancel N window by *W.G. Taylor*, †1897. Chancel S and N aisle
E windows both by *Alexander Gibbs*, 1882 and †1894 respectively. S of the latter, one by *Mayer & Co.* of Munich, †1903.
S aisle, a window also by *Gibbs*, dated 1889. – MONUMENTS.
On a panelled C19 tomb-chest under the N chapel arch, three
alabaster effigies, husband and two wives; *c.* 1480, thought to
be the twice-married John Carent of Silton, †1478. The effigies
are exceptionally well preserved with much colour remaining.
– Adjacent, on the chancel arch, a brass to Robert Sidlin, 'Alyas
Warrin', with a verse. Set on an Early Renaissance-style carved
panel, inscribed on the lower moulding: 'Anno Domini 1596
by me *Lynil Brine*'. – N aisle, John Pope, 1681. Open scrolly
pediment surmounted by an armorial cartouche.

Just SE of the chancel, WAR MEMORIAL, 1922 by *Ponting*.
Pillar with medieval-style crocketed top containing four miniature figures.

OUR LADY (R.C.), Old Mill Lane, 1 m. N. Nave of 1832. Lancet
Gothic. Similar chancel of 1884. Adjoining, the former PRIORY
AND COLLEGE OF ST JOSEPH of 1886. A plain three-storey
block.

WESLEYAN METHODIST CHAPEL (former), New Street, ¼ m.
w. Dated 1904. With rock-faced rubble and a wheel window
in the gable-end.

PRIMITIVE METHODIST CHURCH, Pilwell, ¼ m. N. Dated
1899. Rock-faced rubble; buttressed, with a pair of curiously
chunky kneeler finials on the w front. Gothic tracery in round-
arched openings.

SENIOR'S FARM, just over the w wall of the churchyard. Built
perhaps as a grange of Glastonbury Abbey (or as a priest's
house). Ashlar-faced two-storey rectangular range of c. 1500;
C18 wing to the rear. The evidence is of work of outstanding
vigour and quality, sadly mutilated at many dates. To the E
blocked and reopened windows suggest that there were as
many as six bays on the ground floor with four above, the splendid doorway in the third leading to an original cross-passage.
This has a two-centred arch with a double-wave moulding,
and a square hood brought down a long way to handsomely
carved lozenge-shaped labels. Foliage in the spandrels. It is
somewhat mutilated to admit a square-headed door. Just two
original principal windows, both on the upper floor: upright
in shape, square-headed, of two lights with ogee heads and
a little tracery above. The last ground-floor window (on the
r.) is C16, with arched lights, while that at the l. end is a C19
copy. On the upper floor the two square-headed windows on
the r. are C17 substitutes. There is a miniature original trefoil-
headed stair light above and to the l. of the doorway. The w
front has a doorway with a wave and a hollow moulding, and
another original window above it. Plank-and-muntin partitions
within, including a section with trefoil-headed panels facing
on to the (much later) staircase. (On the screen a painting of
St Catherine of Alexandria, dated by Professor David Park to
c. 1500–30.)

OLD RECTORY, s, on the opposite side of New Street. Dated
TCM 1695 on a roundel re-set in the E front. Ashlar elevations
with sashes of c. 1780, the upper parts remodelled c. 1860 for
the Rev. R. B. Kennard, when it was given a symmetrical s front
with a gable at either end. That at the E end since demolished.

CHANTRY FARM (formerly Pope's Farm), ¾ m. WSW. A most
satisfying group of farmhouse, barn at right angles in front,
and enclosing walls, all stone. Both house and barn have
the windows which, in Dorset at least, one recognizes as no
earlier than c. 1620, with hollow-chamfered mullions and no
hoodmoulds, and with a continuous drip-course over the
ground-floor windows. But the doorways are still of flattened
four-centred-arched outline. The farmhouse roof has a hip
to the l. and a gable on kneelers to the r. The barn, with two
four-centred-arched doorways and windows that suggest that
one part was meant to be lived in, has gables on kneelers at
both ends.

NASH COURT, Nash Lane, ⅝ m. N. The 4-ft (1.2-metre)-thick
walls of the E-facing gabled front, although largely late C19,
indicate possible structure of pre-Dissolution date, when this

may have been another property of Glastonbury Abbey.* This, and additions of the late C16 or early C17, were incorporated into an E wing in 1836 for the Hussey family, who had owned it since 1651. W wing of the early C18, much altered in 1885 for the Rev. R.B. Kennard. He also created the present twin-gabled E front with its central bell-turret. Subdivided in 1979 into three dwellings.

LOVELL'S COURT, Burton Street, ½ m. NW. A large suburban-looking villa of 1902. Part stone, with red brick bay windows at the S end, one with a conical roof. Half-timbered gables. Ill-related two-storey W Tudor porch.

KING'S MILL, King's Mill Road, 1½ m. SW. Of c. 1830. Big, two-storey stone block. To its S, KING'S MILL BRIDGE of 1823 by *G.A. Underwood*.

ALLARDS QUARRY, Gannetts, 1¼ m. NE. Iron Age and Romano-British SETTLEMENT. The Middle Iron Age pottery gives the name to the Maiden Castle–Marnhull style.

MARSHWOOD

3090

ST MARY. Rebuilt in 1883–4 by *G. Vialls*, replacing a smaller chapel of ease of 1840–1. The W tower, with high lancets and a quatrefoil as a bell-opening, is said to be of 1841. It was evidently remodelled to harmonize with the rest of the church after 1884. Yet, externally at least, the church looks more 1841 than 1884. Flint and brown stone. Pairs of small lancets. Nave, short S aisle and chancel. Curious sedilia arrangement in the chancel. – Some encaustic TILES by *Maw & Co.* in the sanctuary. – FONT. Octagonal. Thin Gothick. Quatrefoil to each face. It must be of 1841.

MARSHWOOD CASTLE, 1¾ m. SE. Most likely a fortified manor, built for the de Mandeville family, who owned it in 1205–64. A large, nearly square, moated enclosure, not readily appreciable. Also a stone SW tower, although nothing left standing but rubble core of walls.

MARSHWOOD MANOR, ¾ m. E. Dated 1853, for J.B.T. Tatchell Bullen. Brick. Asymmetrical, with differing-size gables, one with a small bellcote. Tall, slab-sided chimneystacks. Pointed windows. It resembles a vicarage.

NASH FARM, ½ m. SW. A late C16 remodelling of a C15 hall house, this probably built by William de Carent. A single range with hollow-chamfered mullioned windows and a lateral chimneystack, midway along the S front. Inside two C16 plank-and-muntin partitions, dividing a central cross-passage from the former solar at the W end and the hall at the E. Arch-braced collar-truss roof. One original timber window in the W end.

---

*This may equally be of *c.* 1600.

LAMBERT'S CASTLE, ¾ m. WSW. Iron Age HILL-FORT, univallate, covering some 15 acres.

MARTINSTOWN
see WINTERBORNE ST MARTIN

MELBURY ABBAS

A scattered village with several Glyn estate cottages, some brick,
others of local greensand stone.

ST THOMAS. 1851–2 by *George Evans* of Wimborne, one of his
best churches. A sizeable building, costing £2,500, commissioned by Sir Richard Plumptre Glyn (of Gaunt's House). Dec
in style, with a varied skyline. SW tower with higher, spired
stair-turret and a baptistery inside. Nave, S aisle, transept and
chancel. The roof braces form a diagonal cross over the crossing reminiscent of the ribs of a square rib-vault. Finely carved
stone angel corbels. – TILES. Rich *Minton* encaustic tilework
in the sanctuary and baptistery. – FURNISHINGS. A complete
Gothic set, no doubt by *Evans*. – His FONT is octagonal, with
ornate Gothic carving. – STAINED GLASS. Several windows of
c. 1852 inscribed with *Thomas Willement*'s monogram. His are
in the chancel, including the fine E window, and in the vestry.
W window probably also by *Willement*. Nave N window (†1915
and †1920) by *Heaton, Butler & Bayne.*
  Timber LYCHGATE of 1920, neatly formed over the gabled
entrance piers.
    RECTORY (former), just N of the church. Of *c.* 1800 (appar-
ently around an early C18 core). Greensand ashlar walls and
a hipped slate roof.
      SCHOOL (former) across the road. Tudor style, dated 1844.
PRIMITIVE METHODIST CHAPEL (former), Cann Common,
½ m. N. Dated 1846. Round-arched openings.
EAST MELBURY FARM. At East Melbury, a sequestered downland hamlet, ½ m. ENE. A typical C17 vernacular stone front,
with hoodmoulded mullioned windows, four-light below,
three-light above, symmetrical plus an extra S bay, transfig-
ured by mid-C18 attention to the centre bay of the design.
Big shaped gable with a round-headed keystoned window in
it, a Venetian window below, and a doorway with architrave
on brackets. Broad, flat mouldings; so this is a quiet echo of
Vanbrugh's style at Eastbury a few miles away.
WINTERFIELD, ¼ m. E. 1923 by *E. Turner Powell* for F.W. Ste-
phenson in a Lutyens-inspired style. Rubbly local masonry,
especially so on the chimneyshafts.

MELBURY BUBB

Just the church, manor and former rectory, with farm buildings at a discreet distance. Nearby (¾ m. s) the site of Wool-
combe Hall, demolished *c.* 1820. The HOUSE was classical, by
John Crunden, 1770–2, the landscaping by *William Eames*, 1782.
No traces visible, especially since the Yeovil to Weymouth railway
drove through the site in 1857.

ST MARY. Beautifully set against a leafy hill. s tower, nave and
   chancel. Late C15 tower, probably of *c.* 1466–80 as it carries
   the initials of Walter Bokeler in a quatrefoil band between the
   second and top stages. The mid-stage also has a triangular
   buttress-shaft standing on an angel bust, while the embattled top has a crocketed pinnacle at each centre. Somerset
   tracery. Most of the windows re-set in the 1853–4 rebuilding
   by *R.H. Shout* of Yeovil* are also late C15. – REREDOS. No
   doubt of *c.* 1854. Very fine. It depicts the Adoration. – Flanking the E window two IMAGE NICHES of probably the same
   date. – SCREEN and other FURNISHINGS. By *Shout*, very
   respectful to the Perp character. – FONT. A significant although
   puzzling piece. Probably early C11 and therefore pre-Conquest.
   Boldly cut carving, a scheme involving animals (a stag, wolf,
   horse and lion), their tails forming a kind of interlace. This is
   upside-down, suggesting that the piece was not made as a font
   originally. It may have formed the head of a column or cross-
   shaft – see the beginnings of fluting around the rim, and the
   moulding at the base.** – STAINED GLASS. In two N windows
   some very good C15 pieces including two panels: an Annunciation with Christ showing his wounds, and the Sacrament of   40
   Ordination. Also smaller fragments in the tracery. Restored in
   1887. Of the C19, the chancel N window is by *Hardman*, 1856.
   E and W windows both by *Clayton & Bell*, 1886, both with C15
   pieces re-set in the tracery lights. One fragment in the E refers
   to Walter Bokeler, the probable builder of the tower. Chancel
   s window by *Heaton, Butler & Bayne*, 1888.
MELBURY BUBB MANOR HOUSE, immediately NW. Early C17,
   possibly C16 in origin (indicated internally by the roof of the
   N end). No great formality on the exterior. The E front projects two wings. Between these wings a mullioned window of
   3:3 lights; a doorway to its r. with a two-centred-arched head,
   marking the cross-passage. A continuous hoodmould above
   these, but separate elsewhere. All of the dressings of Ham
   Hill stone, ochre against the grey local rubble. Towards the
   W a two-storey gabled porch, the doorway in one side. This
   projects off-centre from the gabled hall chimney-breast. With

---

* *The Ecclesiologist* incorrectly credits R.J. Withers with the work.
** This interpretation follows the RCHME, H.M. Taylor, *Anglo-Saxon Architecture*
vol. 3, 1978, and Rosemary Cramp (ed.), *The Corpus of Anglo-Saxon Stone Sculpture*,
VII: South West England (2006).

a tiny gabled outbuilding alongside this presents a picturesque centre to the whole. Some renewed fenestration (the deeper mullioned windows) and later rebuilding at the s end, raising the eaves level. Inside, the hall has a plank-and-muntin partition to the cross-passage and a broad, square-headed moulded stone fireplace.

MELBURY BUBB HOUSE (formerly the rectory), 100 yds NE. Early C19 block. Ashlar under a pyramidal slate roof. Large addition to the N, 1861 by *James Davis* of Frome. Brick with gables and canted bay windows.

5000

MELBURY OSMOND

The village is worthy of a picture book, the thatched cottages set all ways on the slope southward down to a ford.

ST OSMUND. C15 w tower. The nave and chancel rebuilt in 1745 at the expense of Mrs Susanna Strangways Horner of Melbury House (*see* Melbury Sampford). Chancel altered 1873. The nave has round-arched windows with Y-tracery. On the s side in the middle is the portal (later blocked) with a Gibbs surround; a keyed circular window above it. Another plainer circular window in the s wall of the tower. This was refaced in ashlar at the same time as the 1745 rebuilding, cf. also the Y-traceried window above and the inserted circular Gothick windows on the other tower faces. E.E.-style chancel arch, 1888; part of a restoration and refurnishing by *Sir Arthur Blomfield*. – REREDOS. Incorporating early C17 carved panelling, perhaps from a pulpit. – SEATING. Adapted in 1888 from C18 box pews. – FONT. Perhaps C13; round and plain. – FRAGMENT. The weird beast seen from the top and enmeshed in interlace (chancel N) may be from an Anglo-Saxon CROSS; late C10 or early C11. The subject has been interpreted as Abraham's ram caught in the thicket. – STAINED GLASS. E window by *Clayton & Bell*, 1873. This firm also did the two smaller chancel windows, *c.* 1880. – Nave circular window perhaps by *Heaton, Butler & Bayne*, †1888. – MONUMENTS. The Rev. John Jenkins Matthews †1855. By *J.S. Westmacott*. A Neo-Renaissance tablet, which is interesting. Two marble statuettes, an angel in the tympanum. – Opposite, the tablet (in the style of a memorial) commemorating the rebuilding of the church in 1745. Broken pediment, side scrolls and bold console brackets. – In the nave several tablets to members of the Perkins family (dates 1791 to 1867). One signed *Hellyer* of Weymouth. Mostly Grecian. – More tablets in the tower.

OLD RECTORY, immediately SE. s cross-wing dated 1641, perhaps recording the raising of this part to two storeys. Stone-mullioned windows. Range running N, later C17. Early C18 staircase.

Of the village cottages, the OLD POST HOUSE just down the hill
on the l. is worth noting. Early C17. Doorway with depressed
arch in a square head. Hollow-chamfered mullioned windows
to the ground floor. C18 leaded casements above, probably
when the roof was raised.

MELBURY SAMPFORD   5000

MELBURY HOUSE. 'Mr Strangeguayse hath now a late much   53
buildid at Mylbyri *quadrato*, avauncing the inner part of the
house with a loftie and fresh tower.' So wrote Leland after visiting in 1542. The lofty and fresh tower remains, with much else
of Giles Strangways's remarkable house, tantalizingly obscured
by a remodelling at the end of the C17.* The house, built of
Ham Hill ashlar, is an early member of the group of architecturally inventive houses in Somerset and Dorset designed
by a master mason or masons based at Hamdon Hill. That is
revealed by the octagonal angle shafts, their faces hollowed,
and the barley-sugar finials. At Melbury, what is left of the first
work is all Perp, with nothing in the way of Renaissance details.
Crockets up the straight slopes of the gables, windows with
uncusped arched lights and square, deeply hollow-moulded
surrounds. Two-storey window bay facing W in the wall S of the
tower. Plinth moulding and moulded string course at first-floor
level. These are the motifs which one picks out as one tries to
establish the extent of the early C16 house. The gable-ends of
the N and S fronts show that the main block, a square of 100 ft
(30 metres), has not been enlarged. So Leland's '*quadrato*' must
refer to the plan, highly unusual for its day in its regularity,
a regularity taken up into the elevations, to judge by the four
identical gables that survive. W of the main block a short full-
height projection, ending to the W in a gable and having the
only original chimneystacks, tall, octagonal, decorated with a
raised chevron pattern. But this is the part called by Leland
'the inner part of the house'. The tower and its substructure
make it impossible that the hall was here in the W range. So
where was the hall, and where the entrance range? And what
function was served by the S range? What we do know is that,
according to Leland, 3,000 loads of Ham Hill freestone were
used in its construction.
    The TOWER, raised well above the house, a hexagon,
crowned with battlements and finials, contains at the highest
level a room glazed on five sides with full-width windows,
six lights with a transom. Against the sixth side a hexagonal
stair-turret rises higher. Small fireplace. Here then is a room
devoted to the pleasure of viewing the distant countryside.

---

*There is no clear evidence that anything of the earlier house of the Browning
family, whatever form it took, was integrated into the new building.

There are prospect towers elsewhere equally early, e.g. the Spye Tower at Warwick Castle and that at Oatlands Palace, erected in 1538 (and also hexagonal).* Leland's words suggest that Melbury's was thought a novelty, perhaps because in both of the above examples the tower was added to an existing building rather than incorporated in the original concept. It is at any rate without a peer for prominence. The substructure has a certain air of the improvisatory. It can be described from the top downwards. The hexagon rests on the square by means of squinches, complicatedly moulded. The room where they are visible is entered by a four-centred-arched doorway with Giles Strangways's initials in the spandrels, one of a trio on a half-landing above the main first-floor landing. Fireplace here too with 'G.S.'. Both levels are lit from the E by a pair of three-light windows, i.e. they look into the courtyard, the lower set further E, to give a rooftop balcony for the room with the squinches. This means that at landing level there is a broad four-centred internal arch, to support the E wall of the tower above. Doorways to N and S here. The most remarkable part comes below, the staircase, straight stone flights set within the walls that support the tower, covered by a tunnel-vault of four-centred section, and lit at the half-landing by a long one-light window with a transom. This is the window one sees outside from the SW. At ground level two doorways towards the S, the l. one leading into a corridor that ran around the courtyard. For a contemporary courtyard corridor one can point to Hengrave Hall, Suffolk, begun in 1525. To the N however not a doorway but a lofty arch, four-centred, on sheer unmoulded imposts. According to normal planning this would suit the link from the dais end of the hall to the staircase, and so would imply that the hall was situated in the N range. This location is reinforced by the fact of the historical route to the house coming from the N, causing the entrance to be in this position, and that the kitchens were originally located in a building attached to the W side. The E range may have provided the solar function, with perhaps a doorway similar to that between the tower and assumed hall, since lost.

The LATE C17 WORK, to consider it for itself, and no longer as the destroyer of the Tudor house, was done for Thomas Strangways, who employed a certain Mr *Watson*: his portrait is in the house, a fact worthy of note, and on it the date 1692 is given. Accounts indicate that the architect was *John Watson*, an otherwise obscure West Country architect, and that the work cost £3,031 2s. 6d.; it was carried out between 1693 and 1699. He created an entirely new E (entrance) front and remodelled the N and S fronts, although a painting in the house by Thomas Hill (*see* below) shows the house with all three frontages given complete classical façades, and the tower removed. What was actually achieved on the S and N fronts

* Mark Girouard suggests that the original purpose of the prospect room was for banqueting.

was a five-bay channelled centrepiece, against which pilasters
of superimposed orders (Tuscan below, Corinthian above) sit
happily enough, the centre bay getting a semicircular pediment
at the top. These are of two storeys, flat-faced and flat-topped,
in so far as the C16 gables that flank them allow them to be.
Balustrades and pedimented dormer windows. Tall rectangular
chimneystacks, with channelled angles. The gables themselves
are remodelled as two bays l. and r. Where, on the E front,
Watson had a free hand to compose an eleven-bay façade, the
problem proved somewhat too hard. He expanded the pediment to a three-bay width and made it triangular, but stopped
it short of the outer half-columns so that it makes little structural or visual sense. The channelled walling extends for five
bays to make a centre wider than the plain walling l. and r.
of it. Quoins frame the plain walls, not the channelled, which
throws further doubt on what is meant to be stressed and
what not. The careful distribution of the dormers only adds
to the delightfully provincial confusion. Windows throughout
with keystones but no surrounds. The sashes themselves are
late C18 replacements. What redeems all of Watson's work is
the colour contrast between the ochre of the Ham Hill stone
walling and the white of the Portland stone for orders, quoins
and keystones.

INTERIORS. The only significant earlier interior is an early
C17 ensemble in the SW room on the first floor. It has the
usual elaborate overmantel, above a C19 chimneypiece, displaying in particular a shield of arms with many quarterings,
in a strapwork surround where little figures are seated holding
further shields with further quarterings. Flat ceiling decorated
lavishly with quite broad beams, vine-scrolled on their soffits,
and scrolly flower motifs in some of the fields, and in others
birds and beasts amusingly paired, e.g. tortoise with lobster,
dove bearing an olive branch with heron bearing an eel.

Otherwise much internally is of the *Watson* period. The main
changes were the creation of a five-bay HALL in the centre
of the E front, which has two marble fireplaces with Grinling
Gibbons-style naturalistically carved woodwork overmantels.
This is flanked by two smaller rooms, both with most of their
original fittings, that in the NE with a painted ceiling of swags
of flowers, and birds flying free. This is possibly by *Andien de
Clermont*, and of c. 1730. In the SE room, silk hangings of 1735
brought from Redlynch House, Somerset, in the late C18.

The main late C17 work is the STAIRCASE, built in a thicken-
ing of the E range into the space of the courtyard. Two turned
balusters per tread, issuing from foliage bulbs. Big round-
headed archways open from the first-floor landing. Walls,
ceiling (depicting The Council of the Gods), and the soffits of
the staircase itself are painted, allegorically, by *Lanscroon*, who
dated his work 1701. Large canvas painting on the N wall by
Thomas Hill showing a group of Thomas Strangways and his
family standing in the grounds of Melbury (with Lion Gate
shown in its original position, *see* below).

Late in the C19 the 5th Earl of Ilchester found that the house lacked a room large enough for entertainment. In 1872 *Anthony Salvin* added the LIBRARY (cost £4,000) to the W, single-storeyed like a great hall (or a conservatory) and in a Tudor style to fit the Tudor parts. It doubled as an entertaining room. Two canted bays, battlemented. Floor-to-ceiling windows all across, with many mullions and two transoms. Chimneypiece carving by *Harry Hems*.

In 1884–5 *George Devey* made Melbury house-party-sized by means of a RETURN RANGE to the W, linking up with a massive battlemented TOWER to the S, and the extensive stable court to the N. Devey's tower and Salvin's Library are a handsome pair and create a S front which taken together is of an eminently Victorian grouping, with its planes moving backward and forward, and its great tower at one end set off against its subsidiary tower somewhere near the middle. In the tower Devey goes beyond the style of the C16 house with three-storey window oriels and bold bands of quatrefoils. Clearly the porch of Forde Abbey was in his mind.

The STABLE AND SERVICE COURT on the other hand, especially its entrance-archway composition (based on that at Montacute Priory, Somerset), blends well with Giles Strangways's house. Devey had to make the link, as the door to his new entrance hall to the house is under the arch. The E range of the stables, however, is a late C17 piece, long and low, with a small central pediment, and classical windows with moulded surrounds, i.e. not like Watson's style. Battlements and other Tudor trimmings, by *Devey* no doubt. Further ranges of the stable courtyard behind are dated 1801–2 and possibly by *R.W.F. Brettingham*.

THE TURRET, W of the house. Hexagonal, of coursed rubble stone, revealed as of the C16 by its plinth moulding and string course, in spite of the pinnacles, Gothick entrance doorway, and plaster vault inside. These embellishments, complete by 1762, fitted it up as a summerhouse. What was it before? Just a summerhouse? It seems to have had a twin to the N, gone by the early C19.

ST MARY. The church lies SE and below the house, dwarfed by Devey's tower. Yet it is not really a small church. It is all C15 except for a W extension of the nave, and a major remodelling and refurnishing of the interior, 1874–6 by *J.K. Colling* for the 5th Earl of Ilchester. The church consists of nave, transepts, crossing tower and chancel. The chancel is wider than nave or transepts, with a higher roof. Battlemented parapets and carved figure finials at all of the corners, the latter no doubt part of Colling's enrichments. All the crossing piers have typical Perp details except for the E where the inner orders are taken on carved shield-bearing putti. Hammerbeam roof to the nave and a curious wooden internal cupola under the tower, all by Colling (made by the Norfolk builders *Cornish & Gaymer*). – The ornate REREDOS (all of *c.* 1876 and by *James Forsyth*) has at its centre a Last Supper in relief. Its side compartments run across the whole E wall and have crocketed canopies of Caen stone with, beneath, emblems of the Evangelists in alabaster. The enriched cresting carries around to the N and S walls, interrupted by windows, as does the coloured marble inlay. – Carved chancel STALLS, returning on to the W wall by *Forsyth*, who also did the wooden PULPIT with its pierced and carved tracery, and the nave PEWS. – Floor TILE-WORK by *Minton, Hollings & Co.* – FONT. C15, octagonal, with quatrefoils. On a panelled trumpet-stem, partly built into the adjoining crossing pier. – STAINED GLASS. A large number of heraldic pieces, including a bishop of Wells of 1425–43 and a bishop of Salisbury of 1438–50. That fixes completion to c. 1440. Also, in the W window, C17 heraldic glass. This extensive scheme was arranged by *Willement* in 1839. The E window is heraldic of 1938,* reportedly 'entirely designed' by the *6th Earl of Ilchester* himself. A figurative window facing W in the S transept, probably by *Shrigley & Hunt*, †1886.

MONUMENTS. Few places in Dorset are as rich in monuments as Melbury. We must start with the two canopied tomb-chests in grey Purbeck marble either side of the crossing. Each contains a recumbent alabaster effigy of an armoured knight. In the N transept William Browning †1467. The tomb-chest has lozenges, the canopy four-centred arches and a panelled underside. The other (S transept) is identical but for an inscription to Sir Giles Strangways †1547. It no doubt represents a Browning and was appropriated by the Strangways. – Many other monuments; the selection is listed by location. Chancel. Caroline Leonora, Countess of Ilchester (†1819), 1821 by *Chantrey*. Neoclassical. Large kneeling young woman in the round. – Lord Stavordale †1845. Gothic tablet with enriched canopy. – N transept. Thomas Strangways †1726. Supplied by *Nathaniel Ireson* and costing £200. Execution attributed to *William Goodfellow* of Salisbury (GF). Noble reredos architecture of white and mottled grey marble. Pedimented Doric order, without any effigy. – Denzil Vesey Fox-Strangways †1901. White recumbent effigy on a Perp tomb-chest. – S transept. Brass of Sir Gyles †1562, 25-in. (63.5-cm.) figure. – Nave, four cartouche tablets, the two older the least elaborate: Thomas Strangways's children, 1706, and Thomas Strangways †1713. – Also Susanna Strangways Horner †1758, and Stephen, 1st Earl of Ilchester †1776, almost identical with the previous and erected by a daughter of Mrs Horner. – W end of the nave, large brass plaques in matching designs to Brig.-Gen. Thomas Fox-Strangways †1854 and the 3rd Earl of Ilchester †1858, both by *Waller* of London.

GARDEN and LANDSCAPE. This was formalized as part of the late C17 classicization of the house. The most prominent feature was an approach aligned axially on the E façade, where the avenue crossed over a widening of the stream by a six-arch bridge. It was swept away by more flowing mid-C18 landscaping, in the

*Replacing one of 1876 by *W.M. Pepper & Co.*

Brownian mode. Broad grassed areas finish some 150 yds to the s of the house at Melbury Lake, a remodelling of more formal ponds of the earlier c18. Also, ¾ m. to the NW, a circular clearing in the Great High Wood, with radiating avenues. This dates from after 1742.

LION GATE, ½ m. s. Late c17. Ham Hill stone piers, rusticated with niches. Topped by Portland stone standing lions, each bearing a shield. Moved here from the E front of the house in the mid c18.

CHETNOLE LODGE, ½ m. NE. Dated 1870, perhaps by *Salvin*. Rich local rubble with Ham Hill highlights. Slightly Scots Baronial.

7000

MELCOMBE HORSEY

The church stands in the grounds of Bingham's Melcombe, yet the parish takes its name from the owners of the other medieval manor, Higher Melcombe.

ST ANDREW. Not a large church. The stout and embattled W tower stone, the rest flint. Mostly mid-c14 Dec. The tower and E windows have reticulated tracery, but most of the windows are straight-headed with ogee arches to the lights. Two chapels (representing the two medieval owning families), the s with a gable-ended roof extending over the porch. The windows here are c15 Perp, part of an extensive rebuilding of the chapel. In 1844 the chancel E wall was rebuilt in banded flint (with the window re-set). In the E jamb of the s doorway, a STOUP with an ogee-arched cinquefoil head, c14. The E wall inside the s porch has a big flat niche with an ogee arch. There are indications that this may once have had a more elaborate surround. – COMMUNION RAIL. Of *c.* 1630, with widely spaced vertically symmetrical balusters. – PANELLING. Probably of the same time. – PULPIT. Simple with fielded panels. By the *Bastards* of Blandford, it cost £10 in 1723. – SCREEN. To the s chapel, with vertically symmetrical balusters. Guilloche enrichment on N side, fluted on s. Dated STF 1619, probably for Sir Thomas Freke. That to the N appears c20 but in an early c17 style. (Probably of 1929, since this is the date on the similar TOWER SCREEN.) – FONT. c12 circular Purbeck marble bowl, installed in 1956. – HATCHMENT. Bingham, on a c19 panel in the N chapel. – STAINED GLASS. Two c14 panels in the N chapel E window. Further fragments in tracery lights of s chapel, c15. Also a gathering of pieces in the s window, c14 and c15. W window probably by *Lavers, Barraud & Westlake*, 1882. – MONUMENTS. John Bingham †1735. Tablet with a round-headed pediment and scrolled sides. By *P. Scheemakers*, 1750. – Reginald Bosworth Smith †1908. Alabaster classical

tablet by *Harry Hems*. Touching wreathed tablets beneath to
the daughters, †1919.

BINGHAM'S MELCOMBE. A completely irregular small courtyard house of many dates from *c.* 1400 onwards. It was started
by one Robert Bingham and continued by another and was
completed by 1561, according to an inventory drawn up after
the death of the second Robert in that year.

The outstanding part architecturally is the HALL ORIEL,
closely allied in style with Sir John Horsey's Clifton Maybank
(q.v.). Higher Melcombe was Horsey property in the C16, so
this looks like a neighbourly recommending of architects by
Horsey to Bingham. Stained glass in the Hall oriel window
refers to Philip and Mary, which would give a very acceptable
building period 1554–8. The oriel bay is built of silvery limestone ashlar, the carved parts all golden, of Ham Hill stone.
The latter freely introduce Renaissance motifs: that is Bingham's Melcombe's historical significance. The coat of arms at
first-floor level is held by vigorous putti (very like those in a
similar position on the re-set frontispiece of Clifton Maybank,
now at Montacute) and its surround involves scrolls, acanthus
leaves and voluted corbels and finials to the side-shafts. These
are carried up, framing the window above, to project higher
than the gable, forming a composition with the octagonal
angle shafts. The shafts have volutes and leaf-bulbs and shafts
which change their section at every stage, a *jeu d'esprit* that
can be seen at Clifton Maybank too. The large windows, sunk
deeply in the wall by means of a surround with chamfer and
slight hollow, are a six-lighter below, a four-lighter above. The
decoration spotlights the upper window, though the window
lights only a small chamber.

The oriel began the transformation of a modest manor house
into a spectacular one. The ashlar walling and base-moulding
continue to the r. across the face of the Hall, and the moulding starts to return at the point where the porch projects. Just
enough room for a four-light window. That is all; and perhaps
work was abandoned altogether at that point, for the porch is
made up of earlier material, using mid-C16 moulded stones as
the jambs for the outer and inner entrances. Further r. there
is an apparent two-bay Early Georgian continuation, banded
with stone and flint, in place of the expected service parts.
Round the corner the walling is C16, so the Georgian work is
really a refacing.

The Hall range stands on a terrace, raised picturesquely
above the humbler w and gatehouse ranges that form the
courtyard. The earliest part is the commodious GATEHOUSE
RANGE. It is most likely contemporary with the remainder of
this range running w. Here there are indications that this was
the site of an earlier open hall, perhaps with lofted areas at
either end. This part has been dated to the C15 and may be
as old as *c.* 1400. So, with its bold triangular-headed entrance
arches and continuous moulding of a big wave we have a

plausible date for the gateway itself. Walling of squared limestone blocks. Early Georgian windows, somewhat weakening
its appearance of defensive strength, contemporary with those
in the later Hall range (*see* above). A casual non-alignment
with the Hall, and the fact that walling and mouldings do not
correspond with the mid-C16 parts, both confirm the piecemeal progress in the evolution of the house. The medieval
hall became the service wing in the C16 when its functions
were superseded.

The WEST RANGE (linked to the gatehouse range) is, on
the contrary, contemporary with the oriel, as will be explained
below. Towards the courtyard its lower storey is hidden by a
much later one-storey corridor; but the gabled dormers are
two of them of the mid C16, the l. one, with ovolo-moulded
mullions, being a century or so younger. The corridor masks
two C16 two-light windows and a re-set Perp doorway.

It remains to trace the extent of the MID-C16 HOUSE. Lying
back to the l. of the oriel is a gable checked with squares of
Ham Hill stone and knapped, squared flints. That is a new
motif; but structurally the gable belongs with the oriel, for the
apex chimneystack connects with the oriel's upper fireplace.
Likewise the low projection in front, linking with the W range,
houses the staircase that serves the oriel. Small windows with
arched lights here. In structure then, if not in design, all is
one; and in fact the chequered gable belongs to a parlour wing
described in the inventory of 1561. So the mid-C16 building
campaign did indeed continue beyond the oriel, but in a different style. The N end projects slightly beyond the Hall (the
N side of which was rebuilt by *Evelyn Hellicar* for the last
Bingham owner in 1893–4). Also here is the entrance doorcase
from Tyneham House (*see* p. 616). This was re-set *c.* 1967 in a
one-storey, flat-roofed porch. Doorway dated 1583, and naïvely
classical. Round arch, and a shallow pediment pushed well
up above it on strip brackets. Wave and ovolo mouldings. On
the N side the wall pattern is not checks but stripes. Six-light
lower window, four-light upper with a hoodmould. Mullions,
and no arched lights. The windows are of Ham Hill stone and
set in deeply hollowed surrounds, i.e. different in material and
mouldings from the oriel windows.

The W front continues, largely re-windowed. Original doorway and window r. of it, and the base-moulding. Further S
comes a gabled garderobe projection, doubled in width and
given round-arched windows in the C18. The SW angle of the
range is clear enough, in a straight joint with what we now
believe to be the original hall range.

Inside, the body of the HALL is all of 1893–4; but the one-
storey oriel, opening off the Hall by a wide, very depressed
four-centred arch, keeps all its original openings. They are
given consistent mouldings throughout. The entrance arch
rests on moulded shafts and capitals with foliage that matches
the external details of the oriel (and with the foliage on the
lozenge panels at Athelhampton and Sandford Orcas). From

the E shaft grows a fireplace, and in the opposite wall two doorways open: the lower l. one leading through the wall and so out into the later corridor, linking with the kitchen; the higher r. one to the parlour wing and the stone newel stair that gives access to the upper storey of parlour wing and oriel. Plain tunnel-vaulted plaster ceiling and a fireplace in the upper oriel room. The DINING ROOM that occupies most of the ground floor of the parlour wing has a plaster ceiling of c. 1600, cut short at the S end. Moulded ribs and tufts of foliage. The colossal overmantel with numerous coarsely carved figures is of the same date, but the chimneypiece itself is mid-C18, going with the windows, and with the original Rococo mirrors and side tables fixed to the wall between them.

PANELLING elsewhere is just worth mentioning. There are rather crude C16 Renaissance panels in the 'Oak Bedroom' in the W range, perhaps from the Hall. In the gatehouse, early C17 panelling in a bedroom with an enriched frieze. Here too an elaborate fireplace overmantel of the same date. And of the Georgian period, the early C18, bolection-moulded panelling of the Library, r. of the porch. Behind this is the main STAIRCASE of c. 1725, with turned balusters.

The GARDENS are a remarkable survival. *G.A. Jellicoe*, who restored them for Lady Grogan in the 1930s, called them the best example remaining of the 'Stonehenge of English gardening'. He called the garden compartments 'flowered rooms'. One, a ladies' garden, is the flower garden N of the house. The lawn to the W was a bowling green for the men. Wonderfully swelling aged yew hedge here, and at the far end a semicircular brick ALCOVE built in one with a wall dated 1748. It has a basket arch and an original curved fitted seat. Circular DOVECOTE of rubble stone, late C17.

HIGHER MELCOMBE, 1½ m. w. Built for a Sir John Horsey in the mid C16 but a great disappointment. No trace of the Horsey style of Clifton Maybank or the tomb in Sherborne Abbey, although the house of that date is embedded in the main domestic range. The buff stone and flint banded walling here is mainly a later C16 refacing.

However, the real interest of Higher Melcombe attaches to the CHAPEL added at the N end of the house by Sir Thomas Freke (cf. Iwerne Courtney) before 1633. This is purely Gothic, though not purely debased Perp, which is what one might have expected. It is also large and lofty for a domestic chapel. Three bays, the N windows Perp, the S windows Dec rather, three lancets under a pointed arch (the same pattern used by Freke in the N aisle at Iwerne Courtney, dated 1610). Nicely profiled W buttress on this side, and a facing of grey stone and flint bands. Internally the windows have uniform ashlar reveals, and the chapel roof has moulded ribs and small restored bosses, a tunnel-vault in section. – STAINED GLASS. Two chapel windows by *Stephen Bowman*, 1988 and 1992.

The E front of the HOUSE RANGE is much altered. Its various mullioned windows and blocked doorways obscure rather than reveal the fact, suggested by Buckler's drawing of 1828, that the front was approximately symmetrical, crowned by a pair of gabled dormers, an addition of the time of the chapel. By the mid C19 some windows were sashes. These were refitted with mullioned windows *c.* 1900; a canted bay window also added to the E front at that time. The SE projection is ashlar-faced, perhaps an C18 change. The S and W walls, partly red brick of *c.* 1840, now all rendered and uninformative. There is evidence, in a blocked cellar doorway, that the house went further S originally. Its moulding, a big hollow chamfer, also suggests a date earlier than anything above ground.

(The upper room in the main range has a plaster ceiling datable soon after 1603, by the rose and thistle growing off the same stem in the fields between the broad ribs. Linenfold panelling re-set in the NW room.)

NETTLECOMBE HOUSE, ¾ m. S of Higher Melcombe. New country house of 2003 by *Nigel Anderson* of *ADAM Architecture*, for George Bingham. Neo-Georgian. Five-bay central block. A pair of single-storey pavilion wings.

NETTLECOMBE TOUT, 1 m. NW of Higher Melcombe. A massive DYKE, defending the hill-crest, of about 30 acres. Surely related to the extensive SETTLEMENT and 'Celtic' fields with cross-dykes which lie immediately S and around Lyscombe Bottom. One of the dykes, on Bowden's Hill, has been excavated; it produced sherds of the Late Bronze or Iron Age in the secondary silt of the ditch (*see also* Cheselbourne and Piddletrenthide).

Remains of MEDIEVAL SETTLEMENTS, each covering about 10 acres, S of the church at Bingham's Melcombe and in Chapel Close, immediately NW of Higher Melcombe.

MELPLASH

Netherbury

CHRIST CHURCH. 1845–6 by *B. Ferrey*. At first one can hardly believe it, Ferrey having been a convert to Pugin's faith in the Second Pointed. Yet here he is putting up a complete and almost wholly convincing major Norman church – with a high crossing tower, an apse, transepts, one with an E apse, shafted windows, chevron in appropriate places, twin demi-shafts for all the crossing responds, and so on.* Only the hammerbeam roof is un-Norman. The church must have cost a great deal. It was built by James Bandinel, Senior Translator to the Foreign Office, in memory of his father, at one time vicar of Netherbury. The interior was divided in 1976, the nave stripped and made available for community use, the crossing, transepts and apse remaining in church use. Reordering moved the

---

*Ferrey had used neo-Norman before, at St James, Morpeth, Northumberland of 1843–6.

altar to the N transept and made the apse a baptistery. This function is reinforced by decorative glazed TILEWORK on the floor and around the apse walls (although intended for the sanctuary). – FONT. A copy of that at Whitchurch Canonicorum. – STAINED GLASS. Three apse windows by *Lavers, Barraud & Westlake*, †1878.

SCHOOL (former). 1849. Next to the church, yet gabled Tudor. Also built by James Bandinel and probably by *Ferrey* too.

MELPLASH COURT, ½ m. N. From the road Melplash looks a gabled manor house of considerable size; but by thinking away the SW range with its big gable at the r. added in 1922 by *E.P. Warren* (for Mrs Gundry of Bridport), one can appreciate that the original house was a tall and compact single range of *c.* 1600. This must in turn have replaced an earlier building from which a doorway (*see* below) is the sole surviving feature. At this point it was owned by the More family, but was lost by Sir Thomas More *c.* 1532. It was probably George or William Paulet who built the house *c.* 1600.

The NE gable-end is in order, with a central chimney-breast projecting for the full height, and standard three-light mullioned windows l. and r. of it in both storeys. Old photographs show that the NW gable-end before Warren's addition was like this too. The entrance (NE) front is not so straightforward. There are three gables, a three-storey porch set against the l. one, a projecting chimney-breast running up the centre of the centre one, and the r. coming forward somewhat and with the present doorway here. So, in the l. gable, three-light hoodmoulded windows, in two and three storeys, transformed to sash windows in the C18 but later restored. Earlier reused features in the porch, the doorway of *c.* 1500 – see the four-centred arch with a wave mould – the traceried spandrels and the hoodmould with big square labels; and a SE window with arched lights. Later features in the r. gable. The doorway with semi-classical mouldings, and the string course above, and the top pair of windows sharing a hoodmould. That looks as if the whole projecting gabled bay is an enlargement later in the C17. So it may be that the front started flat, with three even gables, and the chimney-breast as the central feature. The unusually tidy short ends make one expect an equally tidy façade. On the SW side the five-light lower window for the hall, and the two windows above, are all that is original.

Warren's addition is respectfully recessed from the earlier r. gable on the NE front. Its mullioned fenestration is also suitably reticent. The secondary wing to the rear is presumably intended to look like an early C19 addition.

Nothing of the C17 interior remains except for the ruggedly moulded early C17 hall screen, introduced for Richard Brodrepp of Mapperton, *c.* 1700. Of this date too the staircase with big turned balusters. Two monster Jacobean overmantels are now at Mapperton, moved there in 1909 by H.F. Compton.

C17 circular stone DOVECOTE close to the SW corner of the house.

MERLY HOUSE
1½ m. w of Canford Magna

A swagger but conventional house for Ralph Willett, F.S.A. and West Indian nabob, who bought the estate in 1751. Dated 1756 on rainwater hoppers and completed four years later, it is possibly by *Francis Cartwright* (with the *Bastards* handling the interior work), although Willett claimed to have designed the house himself. Seven bays by four. Red brick N front, rendered S front. Bitty sides: two supporting pavilion wings, added in 1772, were demolished in the early C19. The N front makes a show with a three-bay centrepiece of Portland stone. Ground-floor podium for giant Ionic half-columns carrying a triangular pediment. Round-arched upper windows here, and lower ones in Gibbs surrounds. Otherwise there are two-and-a-half storeys, and the size of the ground-floor windows and their surrounds shows that the important rooms are at this level. Stone angle quoins, and top balustrade. The S front is simpler and has the end bays brought forward slightly in pairs.

It is the INTERIOR which has real splendour. Throughout the ground-floor rooms there are mid-C18 plaster ceilings of outstanding quality, possibly by *Thomas Stocking* of Bristol.* They show very well the style of that moment, the nearest England approached to a true Rococo. The HALL, in the centre of the N front, is appropriately more restrained, and indeed Palladian, with a Doric frieze. Next the DINING ROOM, the only interior with wall decoration (possibly C19 replica work) of matching richness to the ceiling. This has a central oval with (appropriately) Bacchus and Ceres. A special ceiling is also found in the DRAWING ROOM, with the Judgment of Paris in the centre. The ceiling of the SALOON, longways in the centre of the S front, is in the fully luxuriant Rococo manner, with a central sunburst and brilliant naturalistic angle vignettes. The chimneypiece is in an Adam style, like those in other rooms, but seems to have been brought in. The STAIRCASE HALL has a similarly fine plasterwork ceiling. Its staircase of two turned balusters per tread has a veneer of *lignum vitae*.**

STABLES, E of the house. By *G.S. Repton*, c. 1796, while working under *Nash*. Entered through a round-headed brick archway set in a semicircular brick wall.

* Cf. Stocking's plasterwork of c. 1760 at The Cedars, Wells, Somerset, also done for a West Indies slave-owning family.
** One of the demolished wings was fitted up as a library and had plasterwork of a yet more ambitious character, by *Thomas Collins*, favourite craftsman of Sir William Chambers.

The landscaped PARK, probably contemporary with the stables, is referred to by Nash's partner *Humphry Repton* in his *Observations*, published in 1803. It is a shame that the splendour of its maturity is compromised by the caravans parked around the house.

In Ashington Lane, ½ m w, several pairs of CANFORD ESTATE COTTAGES to *Banks & Barry* designs, dating from 1868 to 1902.

MIDDLEMARSH *see* MINTERNE MAGNA

MILBORNE ST ANDREW   *8090*

A cluster of red brick and cob cottages (some thatched), rather more built up towards the crossroads on the Blandford to Dorchester road.

ST ANDREW. Flint and ashlar. Of the late C12 church, first the s doorway, with an order of colonnettes with decorated scallop 17 capitals, a tympanum with a segmental underside, chevron, also at right angles to the wall, and a hoodmould with nailhead. Chevron also up the jambs l. and r. of the colonnettes. Then the nave s quoins and the chancel arch (re-set at the E end of the N aisle), which again has decorated scallop capitals and chevron at right angles to the wall, but also a pointed (Transitional) arch. C15 w tower of banded flint, battlemented, with an angle-sided N stair-turret. Open wagon roof of the C15 to the nave. The church was restored and enlarged by *G.E. Street* in 1878–9. His are the chancel with lancets, the vestry and the N aisle with his beloved plate tracery in the windows and with an arcade of round piers. A further two-bay arcade leads into a long N transept (incorporated by Street but built in 1855 by *J. Wellspring* of Dorchester). – REREDOS. By *Street*. Tiled, with arcading on either side. – TILES. By *Minton*. – PULPIT. A typically well-judged *Street* feature; stone. – FONT. Tubshaped, C12, with simple cable-decorated bands; scalloping at the base. – CHOIR STALLS and PEWS. By *Street*. – ROYAL ARMS of George III. – CHANDELIER, N aisle. Of brass, dated 1712. – STAINED GLASS. E window of 1883 by *Burlison & Grylls*. Two chancel side windows by the same. – MONUMENTS. A good series to follow developments over nearly 150 years, and a reminder of the lost Milborne House (*see* below). John Morton †1527 (nephew of Cardinal Morton). Purbeck marble monument with tomb-chest decorated by cusped quatrefoils and a canopy on concave-sided shafts with an arch, straight on quadrants, a panelled underside and a cresting. Indents for kneeling brass figures. The inscription plate is a C20 copy. – Also fine tablets, notably, in the vestry, Sir John Morton †1698, Edmund Pleydell †1726, Edmund Morton Pleydell †1754 and Mary

Sophia (Pleydell) †1827, by *J. Harris* of Bath. – Either side of
the tower arch, John Morton Pleydell †1705, Edmund Morton
Pleydell †1794 and Elizabeth Margaretta Pleydell †1825, by
Tyley of Bristol. – In the tower, Judith Gould †1684 and John
Cole †1790, by *E. Coffin* of London.

WESLEYAN METHODIST CHAPEL (former), Chapel Street. Of
1867. Polychrome brickwork; Gothic.

MANOR FARM, ¼ m. SSE. The mansion house of the Mortons
stood here until 1802. Nothing shown in Hutchins's engraving
of a multi-gabled, H-plan house (probably of *c.* 1620) remains
identifiable, except the large WALLED GARDEN to the E. The
present HOUSE is clearly on the site of the old one, yet it does
not look like a C19 rebuilding: rather it must be part of the
old house remodelled to form a U, two-storeyed, with a heavy
hipped roof.

The big stone GATEPIERS, alone in a field to the N, ringed
with broad bands of rustication, suggest the one-time pretensions of the Mortons. The piers are certainly of the late C17,
for the armorial trophies that crowned them are datable, and
now at Winterborne Clenston Manor (q.v.).

WEATHERBY CASTLE, ¾ m. SSE. Iron Age HILL-FORT, covering 15 acres. Two concentric enclosures with an original outer
rampart and inner entrances on the NW. The stuccoed brick
obelisk set up here in 1761 by Edmund Morton Pleydell, was
intended to be seen from Milborne House.

DEVEREL HOUSE, MILL HOUSE and MILL, ¾ m. N, are a
happy group, framed below the wooded hillside, nicely varied
in colour and material. The central part of the white-painted
mill house was built in 1781. Behind, the early C19 red brick
mill. To the r. the mid-C19, vaguely Italianate and much larger
replacement.

On DEVEREL DOWN, 1 m. NE, is a group of eight ROUND
p. 14   BARROWS, including the Deverel Barrow, a bowl barrow. Inside
the Deverel Barrow, which was excavated in 1824, was a
semicircle of sarsens, enclosing Middle Bronze Age cremation
burials, many in bucket and globular urns of a type named
Deverel–Rimbury, so named with the urns from Rimbury (*see*
Preston, p. 498).

STABLE BARROW, 1 m. NNW. Surviving in the parish boundary
hedge. It is probably 'Bagber' Barrow, where cremations in
twenty-three urns, nearly all of Middle Bronze Age bucket and
globular type, were found.

8000   # MILTON ABBAS

In the map of Dorset there is a certain emptiness at its centre.
It is not just that the highest hills are here, for there are plenty
of settlements among them. What is missing is a focus of settlement, and this is because between 1771 and 1790 the 1st Earl of

Milton Abbey.
Engraving by Samuel and Nathaniel Buck, 1733

Dorchester swept away the market town of Milton Abbas, which
in the Middle Ages had grown up beside the abbey. Dr John
Tregonwell, a king's commissioner who oversaw the dissolution
of the monastery in 1539, was also its purchaser one year later.
He took the unusual step of saving the abbey church by taking
it over for his and his tenants' use. William Woodward's map of
1769–71 shows the town stretching s of the church's e end, with
Market Street running away from the Precinct, then High Street,
Newport Street, Broad Street and the rest.* Today what we see
is the fruit of an C18 landowner's not unusual possessiveness,
his mightily magnified private chapel and former abbots' great
hall the only – but inescapable – reminders of Milton Abbas's
monastic past.

MILTON ABBEY was founded about 933 by King Athelstan
as a house for secular clerks. It became a Benedictine monastery in 964, and later had forty monks, though there were only
thirteen at the time of the Dissolution. A larger church was built
in Norman times, but of this, apart from loose fragments (*see*
below), only ashlar blocks remain, reused in the present building.
The Norman church was destroyed by fire ('totaliter inflam-
mavit' with even 'columnis decrustatis' ('totally burnt', 'spalling
columns') in 1309, and rebuilding as a new church to a cruciform
plan must have begun soon after. We have no dates for progress,
which, owing to the relative poverty of the monastery, was less
than swift and continued for around 200 years. The nave was
not built, since work had only reached the w arch of the crossing
by the Dissolution. One corner of the cloister leant against the
N transept. The church and the great hall of Abbot Middleton
(1481–1525) are all that is left of the monastic parts. The hall is
now part of the house.

John Tregonwell was knighted by Mary I in 1553 (an indication
perhaps of his equivocal position with regard to the Dissolution).

---

*A plan of 1773 in the RIBA, prepared in connection with Capability Brown's visit,
shows few houses standing along these streets. The town must by then have been
almost completely cleared away.

The ultimate heiress of the Tregonwells married Sir Jacob Bancks, whose heir sold Milton in 1752 to Joseph Damer, a local man who married a daughter of the Duke of Dorset. Damer was created Lord Milton in 1753, and forty years later Earl of Dorchester. Architecturally, his is the ownership that now matters, virtually all traces of Tregonwell's and Bancks's adaptations of the monastic buildings having been lost. From 1852 to 1933 Milton belonged to the Hambros; in 1954 the house became a boys' public school.

ABBEY CHURCH OF ST MARY, ST SAMSON AND ST BRANWALADER

27　The CHURCH lies s of the house and consists of presbytery, crossing and transepts only. It is like a huge Oxford college chapel. The total length is 136 ft (41.5 metres). The architecture outside as well as inside is singularly limpid and harmonious. What little there is of differences in style does not detract from the clarity.

Construction started at the E end around 1310, under Abbot Walter de Sydeling. By the time the work paused in 1344, the chapels and presbytery were complete, with the transepts and crossing raised to around the level of the clerestory window sills, but missing their w walls. The onset of the Black Death no doubt delayed resumption, but when work restarted the sequence seems to have been this. In the later C14 the walls of the s transept were raised to full height (but it was not then vaulted). The tower is early to mid-C15. Under Abbot Middleton after 1481 a concerted attempt to finish the work at least to the w of the crossing was made, with the vaulting of the s transept, completion of the N transept and installation of the crossing vault, probably the last work done before the Dissolution. However, despite evidence of some footings having been started, and vault springings being incorporated, the nave was left undone. The earliest parts of the rebuilding were demolished at the Dissolution, these being the retrochoir or ambulatory, the Lady Chapel and the chapels N and s of the Lady Chapel. Excavations have proved these to have been straight-ended, with the Lady Chapel longer than the others.

James Wyatt restored the church in 1789–91. *Sir George Gilbert Scott* carried out a major restoration between 1864 and *c.* 1870.

Exterior

Approaching from the village, the first thing one sees is the E wall of the church with five blocked arches and simple wall-shafts and springers of an ambulatory rib-vault. The presbytery with its aisles follows, of seven bays, very uniform in style and hardly possible later than, say, 1325. All the windows of the aisles as well as most of the clerestory are of three stepped lancet lights, cusped, under one arch with the spandrels pierced. Oddly, the second and fourth of the clerestory from the E are of two lights.

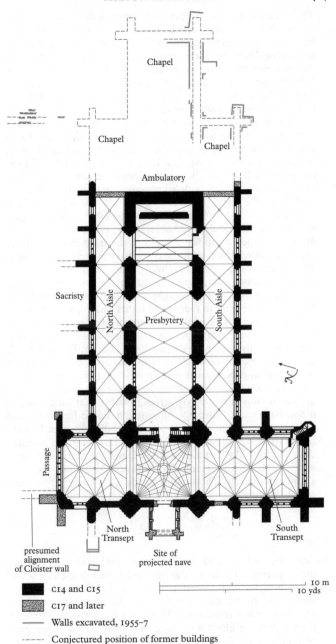

Chapel

Chapel

Chapel

Ambulatory

Sacristy

North Aisle

Presbytery

South Aisle

Passage

North Transept

Site of projected nave

South Transept

presumed alignment of Cloister wall

■ C14 and C15

▨ C17 and later

—— Walls excavated, 1955–7

---- Conjectured position of former buildings

10 m
10 yds

Milton Abbey.
Plan

The aisle parapets have openwork quatrefoils. The E window of the clerestory, above ambulatory and chapels, is of seven stepped lancet lights. Buttresses carry two sets of pinnacles and carry down the thrust from elegant flying buttresses. In the transepts there are two radical changes in window tracery. It is flowing, i.e. Late Dec (*c.* 1370), in the S transept and Late Perp in the N transept, completed *c.* 1500. The great S window is of seven lights and thoroughly reticulated in the tracery. The S transept side windows are as in the presbytery at lower level (where work was probably complete by 1344), but above either simply flowing when of two lights, or reticulated when of three. This work must then have been built on the already complete earlier walls, hence the change in fenestration. The tower was next to be built after completion of the S transept wall. It is of *c.* 1450, and has to each side two long two-light bell-openings and three buttresses topped with crocketed pinnacles (i.e. with double pinnacles at the corners). Quatrefoil-pierced parapet, as on the W walls of the transepts. The tower has much in common with the contemporary crossing tower at Sherborne Abbey (q.v.). Finally the Late Perp of Abbot Middleton's building campaign. The N transept is shorter than the S transept and has one eight-light N window with standard Late Perp tracery, similar to that found on its two tall side windows.

Against the N wall of the transept are the remains of four bays of a passage, with springers for fan-vaults. So this probably represents one of the ranges of the cloister. But which? We can't say, as nothing is known of the cloister. It does not appear in Samuel and Nathaniel Buck's view of 1733, and what we know of it are the four windows and two blank bays re-erected at Hilton church (*see* p. 319). It is possible that little more of it had been built. Normally of course it would have stretched along the nave. But no nave was ever built, yet clearly work had started, i.e. the arches from the transepts into the aisles, the E jambs of the first aisle windows, and the first N clerestory window, all Perp in detail. The springers of the vault are also at once noticeable. The small W porch is by *Scott*, but replaced one of about the same size built between 1733 and 1774.*

Interior

28   Inside, the early C14 vaults of AISLES and PRESBYTERY are quadripartite without a ridge rib, and have bosses. The whole effect is quiet and powerful. The piers have strong attached shafts and round moulded capitals, the arches the typically Dec sunk wave mouldings. There are from the W two bays, then a piece of blank wall, then one more bay, another piece of wall, and another bay. This is reflected in the curious exterior window-width changes, the narrower clerestory windows

---

*No porch is shown on the 1733 view by the Bucks, although something similar to Scott's is indicated on the 1774 view by Edward Rooker.

sitting above the plain wall bays. The crossing continues the same system, although the crossing piers have to each side four, not three, shafts. Between the two W presbytery aisle arches is cinquefoil-decorated low-level arcading, intended to provide a backing to the monks' stalls. Three open SEDILIA to the S aisle; to their E a PISCINA forming part of the composition. Typical early C14 Dec, with cusped and sub-cusped arches and crockets and finials.

The treatment of the lower window arcades in the SOUTH TRANSEPT continues the same detailing as the presbytery, but the higher-level fenestration is Late Dec, as mentioned before. There is further elaboration of *c.* 1500 through the introduction of a passage at the level of the clerestory windows with diagonally set pointed quatrefoils. This is in ochre Ham Hill stone, as are the vaulting ribs and the architectural detailing of the transept W side, another indication that this part of the building was completed at a later date.

The NORTH TRANSEPT is Middleton's. Here the Late Perp departs further from the presbytery detailing, e.g. the thin colonnettes with small bases, much smaller than the Dec ones. He was also responsible for the lierne vaults of both transepts (one N transept boss refers to a bishop of Winchester who died in 1501) and the crossing tower fan-vault, the last part of the building to be completed in the early C16, perhaps to the designs of *William Smyth*.*

Furnishings, stained glass and monuments

The church is exceptionally rich in FURNISHINGS, enhanced especially by *Gilbert Scott*'s 1860s restoration. This included a great deal of internal work, setting much of its character as we see it today.

PRESBYTERY. REREDOS. A large image wall with three tiers of niches with canopies, and a small Latin inscription across referring to Abbot Middleton and Thomas Wilken, vicar of Milton Abbas, and giving the date 1492. This sets the collegiate tone of the interior. Upper part restored in stucco, using moulds from New College, Oxford, by *Francis & Bernato Bernasconi* under *Wyatt*'s direction. – STALLS. Some parts original, including five C14 or C15 MISERICORDS. The remainder by *Scott*, include two very fine CLERGY DESKS. – PYX-SHRINE. C15, of wood, reassembled 1958. It would have contained the pyx and been suspended over the high altar. One of only four such shrines to survive in England.** Square and then hexagonal with a spire. – TILEWORK. By *Godwin* of Hereford,

---

*John Harvey, *English Medieval Architects* (1984 edn) compares Smyth's known work on the Camery Lady Chapel at Wells Cathedral with the nave vaulting at Sherborne Abbey and the crossing vault here.
**The others are at Dennington (Suffolk), Tewkesbury (Gloucestershire) and Wells Cathedral (Somerset).

c. 1865, replicating medieval tiles elsewhere in the building. – PULPITUM. A solid early C14 structure with a rib-vaulted passage in the middle, decorated by a big leaf boss. Staircases lead up to the loft. The responds of the passage are triple Purbeck shafts. Heightened *c.* 1500. In the loft floor medieval TILEWORK re-set during Scott's restoration. – PAINTINGS. On the pulpitum, two incredibly bad panels from a late C15 screen: King Athelstan and Queen Egwyma. Repainted in the C19. – STAINED GLASS. E window, some C15 and later fragments. – MONUMENTS. Purbeck marble floor slab; broken with indents for figure brass and individual inscription letters. Probably Abbot Walter de Sydeling †1315. – Between the chancel and N aisle. Baron Hambro †1877, designed by *J. O. Scott.* Recumbent marble effigy on a richly detailed alabaster chest. Elaborately cusped and pinnacled canopy with filled image niches.

PRESBYTERY NORTH AISLE. STAINED GLASS. Hambro memorial window probably by *Shrigley & Hunt,* 1906. – MONUMENTS. Sir John Tregonwell †1565. Purbeck marble monument (dwarfed by the Hambro tomb adjoining). It is the standard type: tomb-chest with cusped quatrefoils, twisted shafts carrying a canopy. Instead of an arch two quadrants and a straight top. Panelled underside. Quatrefoil frieze and cresting. Tregonwell's is a kneeling brass figure. – Mary Bancks †1704 and others to 1725. Standing monument with awkwardly reclining effigy. She holds a book and a skull. Reredos with inscription on drapery and three putto heads in clouds over. Detached Corinthian columns and a partly segmental top. – John Artur, 'monk of this place'. C15 inscription brass.

PRESBYTERY SOUTH AISLE. ALTAR by *Wyatt.* Alabaster, with shield-bearing pointed quatrefoils and a short frieze of carved drapery above. – SCULPTURE. Upper half of a St James, *c.* 1500. – Probable MONUMENT. Niche missing its decorative outer structure (but still outlined in red paint). Above, the elaborately carved rebus for Abbot William Middleton.

TRANSEPTS and CROSSING. FONT. Of 1860 by the Danish sculptor *Adolf Jerichau.* Two life-size white angels, one with a cross, the other with a palm branch. A rock between them and below an insignificant basin. – SCREEN. Remains of a closely panelled early C16 screen wall in the S transept, retaining some colouring. – ARCHITECTURAL FRAGMENTS. A number of Norman and later ones on a rack in the S transept. There also is the fragment of an Anglo-Saxon CROSS-SHAFT with interlace. – TILES. Some are collected in the S transept. – STAINED GLASS. The gorgeous S transept S window is by *A.W.N. Pugin* (and *Francis W. Oliphant*) for Lord Portarlington, made by *John Hardman,* 1848. Tree of Jesse; typically brilliant colouring. The only window executed of a complete scheme that would have cost £3,890. The price for this window was £400. Late C18 armorial glass in the N transept N window (inscribed *J. Pearson* 1775). – MONUMENTS. Lady Milton †1775, wife of the builder of the house. Designed by *Robert Adam* and carved by *Agostino Carlini*. White marble. Daintily Gothick tomb-chest. Lady Milton is represented recumbent, Lord Milton pensively contemplates her, his head propped by his elbow. – Two contrasting Gothic panels: Caroline, Countess of Portarlington †1813, Tudor Gothic style with a broad arched surround; Henry Dawson-Damer †1841, bronze, Italian Gothic surround.

MILTON ABBEY HOUSE*

The monastic buildings lay to the N of the abbey church, as has already been mentioned. After the Dissolution they were converted to be the mansion of Sir John Tregonwell, purchaser of the abbey lands. *John Vardy* was employed by Joseph Damer, Lord Milton, to prepare alternative Gothic and classical schemes *c.* 1754, and he was no doubt also the designer of the quadrangular house illustrated in Hutchins's *History* in 1774. This involved the demolition of all but the Abbot's Hall. However little progress was made and, beginning again in 1769, *Sir William Chambers* was brought in to construct the new mansion (1771–5). As first proposed by Vardy, it was built around four sides of a quadrangle, and is entered from the N. Historical considerations, though, make it natural to describe first the monastic survival on the s side of the courtyard.

The ABBOT'S HALL at Milton, together with that at Forde, speaks of the wealth, pride and heady sense of display felt in Dorset, as indeed in other counties too, by the monastic orders even in the last decades before their dissolution. Forde's display is primarily external; at Milton it is the interior of the Hall which receives the weight of decoration. Outside, almost everything is restored, but a small part of the original wall surface remains to the l. of the doorway, banded flint and rubble stone. The windows are of three arched lights, with a transom and arched lights below it. There are two of them, with a buttress between. The dais bay to the l. is broad, deep and square, but the big square-headed s window here has tracery which does not look medieval and is part of *Chambers*'s scheme to make the s elevation symmetrical (*see* below). Entrance doorway to the screens passage with a four-centred head.

The date of this Late Gothic work is given inside: 1498 appears on the string course of the W wall and on the timber screen, and the rebus of William Middleton, abbot at the time, turns up several times among the copious heraldry. The Hall is designed on the principle of increasing decoration with increasing height. Thus the lower part of the walls is quite plain, the upper part is occupied by the grid of windows, and

46

*There is no public access to the school buildings, of which this forms the principal part.

above the elaborately moulded wall-plate and cornice springs
an open roof of almost unbelievable denseness of timberwork.
It is of six bays, the principal trusses resting on moulded wall-
shafts that come down between the windows to end in shield-
bearing demi-angels. These trusses are arch braces which
spring from hammerbeams, and rise in a very widely spread
two-centred curve, to collar-beams with panel tracery in the
space above. Intermediate trusses in each bay play a variation
on this system, and introduce pendants high up and music-
playing grotesques on the hammerbeams. Against the rafters
are four tiers of arched wind-braces, all cusped and arranged
in different ways, and with purely decorative finial forms. The
top tier has cusps overlapping two deep, though one is hardly
aware of that in the gloom high up. Basically then it is a much
enriched version of the standard West Country roof, the hammerbeams introduced to cope with the Hall's great width.

The roof is matched by the open timber SCREEN. Its three
entrances are marked by many-moulded uprights set lozenge-
wise and bearing cusped finials, each surrounded by four subsidiary finials. The panelling below, divided halfway up by a
cusped cove and crowned by another, is completely covered
with panel tracery of two repeating patterns. The cusped and
crocketed ogee arches which form a cresting and span the three
openings are oddly weak and under-scaled. They are of the C15,
but probably tampered with in the C18. Altogether, however,
the design of the screen lacks discretion and discipline and is
not in the same class as the roof.

The hall has a large stone chimneypiece of c. 1670 or so,
with open segmental pediment and finely carved acanthus
scrolls on the lintel. The oriel bay, large enough to be a room
in its own right, has a flat ceiling divided by beams in groups
of four square panels, with an extra-large field in the centre,
where an extra-large pendant displays Abbot Middleton's
rebuses. – STAINED GLASS. C16 and C17 armorial roundels in
Hall and oriel windows, representing many Dorset alliances.
Brought-in Continental roundels, also C17, in the modern
corridor N of the Hall.

It remains to say that the Hall was originally approached
from the N, and here, as the central feature of the courtyard,
remains the PORCH of 1498. It is two-storeyed and ashlar-
faced, but the upper parts were altered in the C18.* The two-
centred entrance arch has a square frame above it, giving
here too space for heraldry, among it the initial and rebus
of Abbot Middleton. Pierced top parapet. Upper traceried
window with straight-sided head. Elaborate C18 wrought-iron
bell and bell-pull.

Swept away by the C18 house were new works carried out by Sir
John Tregonwell soon after his purchase. Dr Pococke, visiting
in 1754, mentions a Star Chamber, to the w of the Abbot's

---

* Buck's engraving of 1733 shows octagonal buttresses and twisted finials, favourites
in Dorset in the early to mid C16.

Hall, and that Lord Milton was encasing the buildings 'in a beautiful modern taste', presumably a reference to the *Vardy* scheme that had at least been started by that date.

NEW HOUSE incorporated the Hall as the centrepiece of its S range, but the S was not the show front. The façades that mattered were to the N, where the entrance was, and to the W, overlooking the broad valley. *Chambers*, more than most of his contemporaries, was antipathetic to the half-hearted Gothic of the time. So it is not surprising to find that when he carried the Gothic style round to the show fronts his gothicism was used as part of an underlying classical composition, synthesizing Gothic features as a sub-scheme to the more classical whole. Both fronts are of beautifully cut Portland ashlar, now lichened (although his iron cramps have burst the stone on a regular pattern). Even the minuscule carved string courses have retained their crispness. The resultant compositions are bold. N front with a central gatehouse feature of canted bays (originally with ogee domes) flanking the entrance arch. This is three-storeyed. Two-storey links lead to three-bay, three-storey pavilions. The windows have flattened four-centred heads and hoodmoulds. Bullseye windows in the top storey. The W front is basically similar, but with a flat centre part of 2:3:2 bays, with quatrefoil attic windows and triangular gablets (or pediments with Gothic detailing) over the side parts here, a peculiar, although classical, feature. Polygonal angle buttresses, hinting at the C16 architecture of Tregonwell's day. Pierced top parapet and small finials, the skyline's only punctuation, the parapet repeated from the church.

Even so to our eyes there is still a glaring disparity between the two buildings. The pinkish-grey of the house is a flat contrast with the church's ochre hues. The horizontality of Chambers's Palladian composing is clearly at odds with the verticality of the lofty church. The window–wall relationship is quite different in the two buildings. Finally, the bulky mass of the house, which should dominate, and did dominate in the context in which a Neoclassical architect normally worked, is here inevitably trumped by the church's greater mass. So in normal terms, despite the Gothic references, the buildings do not sit well together.* With such an impossible brief, Chambers himself despaired: 'this vast ugly house in Dorset' was what he called it, although his attitude may have been influenced by the appalling treatment he received from his client.

The greatest curiosities are to be found on the S side, where Chambers had to work in the genuine Early Tudor Gothic of the Abbot's Hall. He repeated the motifs of the Hall in an

94

---

*John Harris, noting the discrepancies between Hutchins's print, made when the house was barely complete, and the house today, makes the attractive suggestion that Chambers was merely modifying a design forced on him by his patron, who had it from *Vardy*. We know that Chambers was given the Vardy plan. The N front, as Mr Harris points out, is basically a Kentian design, very reactionary for the 1770s, but what one would expect of Vardy, the publisher of William Kent's designs.

arbitrary way, masking a C17 dining room (burnt out in 1957 and reconstructed as a kitchen) with an answering, although functionally redundant, oriel bay, and ending the composition with rectangular pavilions of three storeys, which come further forward and are given battlements and corner turrets, more or less falsely contrived. The banding of the walls is continued, in flint and Portland stone. So the choice of materials and of style is here governed by the desire to match existing work.

Inside the courtyard pointed windows continue, with tentative tracery here and there, and the attic windows of the gatehouse are given fanciful ogee outlines.

For the INTERIOR, however, Chambers reverted to his normal mode. The W range contains suites of state rooms on both main floors. The STAIRCASE between the medieval hall and this range is in a large square well. Wrought-iron balustrade with a lyre-shaped motif. From here one enters a square room with minor plasterwork. Apart from the staircase, Chambers only completed three rooms before he was supplanted by *James Wyatt* at the end of 1775. The first, the grand KING'S ROOM or Dining Room, lies S of the staircase (or immediately W of the Abbot's Hall). It has inset full-length portraits, and a ceiling with deep beams creating a central square field, surrounded by lozenge-shaped coffers. Fine white marble chimneypiece with Doric columns and a central panel with a sacrificial ram's head. The S room (in the SW pavilion) has a ceiling decorated with roundels all over, a design taken from Wood's *Ruins of Palmyra* of 1753. Three rooms to the N of the King's Room occupy the centre of the W range. The DRAWING ROOM is the largest and most important. This similarly has an architectural ceiling, with a great central oval of ostrich plumes, another design from Wood (also used by Robert Adam at Osterley). A finely restrained marble chimneypiece here. The original Neoclassical bookcases must be by *Wyatt*. The final room in the suite is the LIBRARY, installed by *Wyatt* in 1776. It also has original bookcases, between coupled Ionic pilasters and a delicate, typically Wyatt, ceiling. Chambers brought in *Joseph Rose* as his plasterer, and no doubt Wyatt continued to use him throughout the remainder of the long campaign to complete the fitting-out. If the sharpness of Chambers's interiors is contrasted by Wyatt's inimitable and more delicate style, the transition between the two is curiously successful.

Apart from the library, *Wyatt*'s key interiors were upstairs. The three S rooms here formed a bedroom suite. In the centre portion of the house (facing W) is a groin-vaulted ANTE-ROOM and the great segmental tunnel-vaulted GALLERY, both with reticent, and much less architectural, ceiling plasterwork in Wyatt's typical style. Marble chimneypiece with acanthus scrolls, carved by *Richard Westmacott Sen.* to Wyatt's design (drawing of 1793 in the RIBA). Several more rooms further N, also with Wyatt ceilings.

Buildings in the grounds

Various SCHOOL BUILDINGS to the E and N, none especially distinguished.

St CATHERINE'S CHAPEL, on the hill, 300 yds E of the church and exactly in line with it. Built of flint and consisting of nave and chancel. The building is late C12 – see the two Norman windows and two Norman doorways with tympana character-ized by the segmental curve of the underside. The S doorway is more elaborate. It has one order of colonnettes with foliate capitals and an inscription on a jamb stone promising a 110-day indulgence to pilgrims. This is carried over more than one stone, so must have been carved *in situ*. Late C12 chancel arch with triple responds, the middle one keeled, waterhold-ing bases (already), scallop capitals and a pointed unmoulded arch with a continuous outer roll moulding. Late C18 Gothic refacing of W end (probably by *Wyatt*), i.e. to be viewed at a distance from the abbey below, and an ogee-headed three-light E window of similar date. – C13 to C15 TILES in the chancel and at the W end of the nave. These were transferred from the abbey in the C19.

The GROUNDS were landscaped in two phases (1763–70 and 1774–83) by *Capability Brown*, the second phase concentrating on work associated with the erection of the new settlement. Today, with school playing fields in the foreground, one sees a bowl of undulating green sward and field, and the surrounding hillsides clothed in dense wood.

GOTHIC 'RUINS', ⅓ m. SW. Early C19, but not before 1811. Made to seem a Gothic chapel front, incorporating a Perp corbel and ceiling boss. Increasingly broken down by tree growth.

The entrance of *c*. 1774 was from the upper road to the E, and this is marked by the HIGHER LODGES, ¾ m. NE, probably by *Chambers*. A pair of pedimented boxes of the finest ashlar, the windows to both floors in shallow arched recesses. Linked to ball-finial-topped gatepiers by slightly curving walls.

At LOWER LODGE, ⅔ m. SSE, a pair of fine late C18 GATEPIERS, probably by *Wyatt*. Each has a frieze with swags above Greek-key fretting and vermiculated quoins.

THE VILLAGE

The MODEL VILLAGE, ¾ m. SE, seems to have been one of Lord Dorchester's last enterprises. Obliterating the town was delayed by having to await the termination of a number of ten-ancies. *Chambers* made designs for the cottages, but building in accordance with his plan was carried out only *c*. 1780. *Capabil-ity Brown* however received payment of £105 for his plans for the village in 1773, so the picturesque curving layout can best be credited to him. The pert white thatched boxes that line the long street look charming behind broad mown verges and with the wooded hillside at the back on each side (although the

93

clutter of modern-day parked cars detracts from the Georgian arcadia considerably). Windows making one-and-a-half storeys in a Palladian way. Accommodation was very limited however, for each box is a pair of cottages, just a room front and back on each floor, and a midget communal vestibule. Many have now been combined into a single dwelling, a largely undetectable change.

ST JAMES, halfway up on the r. Church of 1786 by *James Wyatt*, perhaps following an initial *Chambers* design. Unfortunately in 1888–9 *W.J. Fletcher* built a new chancel and a new s aisle so that the interior no longer has the Wyatt character. However, when viewed from the street, what one sees is very much as Wyatt intended. The w tower and the N side along the street, in their rich ashlar and with their Y- and intersecting tracery, represent the orderliness of Late Georgian Gothic. Internally the nave is dominated by Fletcher's clumsy N arcade. – FONT. Octagonal, of Purbeck marble, with two pointed-trefoiled blank arches to each side; late C13. Central stem and outer pillars are unusual in that they are hexagonal in section. Quatrefoil-decorated sub-base of Ham Hill stone, C15. – STAINED GLASS. The highly effective E window is by *Lawrence Lee*, 1969–70. The first impression is of an abstract design. In fact there are figures easily recognizable and even pieces of architecture.

ALMSHOUSES, opposite. For six. One-storeyed, with a higher central room fronted with a centrepiece of three arched openings on crude Tuscan columns between two larger, but also crude, Corinthian columns, carrying an entablature. Top gable with bullseyes. The almshouses were first built *c.* 1674 in the old town, and so show a backward rusticity in grasping the classical vocabulary. They were re-erected here in 1779.

The view down the street here is magnificent, to *Brown*'s artificial LAKE with woods behind, and to the lowest house, the VICARAGE, 1771,* with a large central lunette window. Just E, VICARAGE COTTAGE has two small Gothick windows and is mildly *cottage orné*. At the top end of the street some alien ESTATE HOUSING of *c.* 1865; a typical red brick and flint SCHOOL, 1853; a former COTTAGE HOSPITAL (opened 1873) and the former WESLEYAN METHODIST CHAPEL of 1896.

One admires the exhilarating situation of the village, yet there is something pathetic about Lord Dorchester's desire to have his tenantry housed totally out of sight in a side valley. In the 1950s the completeness of the village was carefully respected when COUNCIL HOUSING was pushed away beyond the hilltop woods to the N.

DELCOMBE MANOR, 2 m. N. Some medieval fragments from Milton Abbey, including windows and a datestone of 1515, are made up into a house with a triplet of gables, designed initially as an eyecatcher in the mid C18. In the early C19 it was rebuilt

* By *Chambers*, according to *Kelly's Directory*.

as a secondary house on the estate. A slightly smaller C19 brick
COTTAGE, also presenting three gables, stands to its r.
MILTON MANOR (formerly Hill House), 1 m. E. By *E. Turner
Powell* for Sir Edward Hambro, 1911. Tile-hung gables. It
incorporates a mid-C19 house at the rear.

MILTON-ON-STOUR

Gillingham

A hamlet on the Mere road with two large houses, to which a
prominent spired church was added by the family who owned
both of them.

ST SIMON AND ST JUDE. 1868 by *Slater & Carpenter*, commissioned by the Matthews family of Milton at the behest
of the Rev. Henry Deane, vicar of Gillingham.* E.E. style,
built in fine Tisbury ashlar. Prominent W tower with a slender
broach spire (Pevsner considered it 'a little thin') not completed until 1892, well detailed and with a good rectangular
staircase projection ending below the tower top in a saddleback
roof. Lean-to aisles and no clerestories, making the interiors a
little dark. Polygonal apse. Interior with round piers carrying
stylized capitals. Detached mid-shafts in the two-light aisle
windows. – PULPIT. Added c. 1885, by *A.W. Blomfield*. Pierced
front with green Connemara marble colonnettes. – CHOIR
STALLS. 1904 by *Ponting*. – FONT. Circular bowl on a ring
of colonnettes, presumably c. 1870. – STAINED GLASS. Two
extensive schemes. The first in the sanctuary and choir by *Ward
& Hughes* comprising seven windows, including the E window
of the S aisle, all of 1867. The second, of nine aisle windows of
c. 1885, probably by *Clayton & Bell*. Porch windows by *Daniel
Bell*, 1904.
MILTON LODGE. Opposite the church, in its small parkland.
Rather severe classical house of c. 1855 for Thomas Matthews.
THE KENDALLS, ⅓ m. S, of c. 1870, has a picturesque grouping
of hipped roofs, battlemented bay windows and a pedimented
emphasis to the entrance front. Matching LODGE of c. 1890.

MINTERNE MAGNA

An estate village in a fine landscaped valley setting, dominated
by Minterne House and the church.

---

* It was built on land given by Thomas Matthews, who had acted as local surveyor
for the building of the Salisbury & Yeovil Railway.

St Andrew. Banded flint. C15 nave and chancel, thoroughly restored in the mid C19 and 1894. w tower, rebuilt in 1800 by *Admiral Robert Digby** and heightened 1894. Of this date its traceried openings, part of the re-gothicization carried out then. w door and window united under a plain pointed arch, this repeated on the N and S faces. S bell-stage opening with Somerset tracery and an inscription below: 'Le temps passe, l'amitié reste' ('Time passes, friendship remains'). Upper stage with plain corner pilasters. Embattled parapet with double-stepped merlons. Crocketed pinnacles and bold gargoyles, all of 1894. Elaborated nave S buttresses. Of *c.* 1615–20 the N chapel (cf. Leweston, not far away). The N window of five lights with the middle one taller and the hoodmould stepped up for it is a safe indication. – FONT. C15. Octagonal with quatrefoils. – Much of the FURNISHING is of 1897 by *Nathaniel Hitch*. Especially elaborate are the pew-ends. – STAINED GLASS. Apart from one, the windows are all by *Heaton, Butler & Bayne*. Dates are from the E window of 1875 to the middle nave S window, †1896. The best is the large N chapel window, the memorial to Almarus Kenelm Digby †1886. Another nave S window by *A.K. Nicholson*, 1933. – MONUMENTS. The N chapel was no doubt commissioned by Sir Robert Napier, who died in 1615 as it was under construction. He has no monument to himself, though he heads the inscription on a cartouche tablet, *c.* 1685, attributed to *James Hardy* (GF). Flower garlands. – Also in the chapel, Sir Nathaniel Napier †1708. By *Thomas Bastard II*, 1725. Large standing monument of reredos type. Wide, open segmental pediment on detached Corinthian columns. Two allegorical figures, *c.* 4 ft 3 in. (1.3 metres) tall, on the l. and r. – Countess of Gainsborough †1693. Segmental pediment with achievement of arms; side scrolls and gadrooned at the base; boldly carved apron. – Nave. General Charles Churchill †1714, attributed to *Thomas Bastard I* (GF). Trophy at the foot, trophies on the top. Long inscription. Three putto heads and bones above the inscription. – Admiral Sir Henry Digby (†1842) and Jane, Lady Digby (†1863). Large brass tablet by *Waller* of London. Gothic. – At the E end of the nave two floor slabs. Slate. John Churchill †1659; Ellen Churchill †1673.

Church of Our Lady and St Lawrence (R.C., formerly Wesleyan Methodist), Middlemarsh, 1¾ m. NNE. Of *c.* 1860. Brick. Lancet Gothic but elaborated on the front gable. Stone corner pinnacles; pinnacles to the gabled porch too.

Minterne House. Built in 1904–6 for the 10th Lord Digby, who thus gave *Leonard Stokes* his only large country-house job. Stokes responded with a beautifully sophisticated design, executed throughout in Ham Hill ashlar. In its mixture of

---

*An amateur architect who had previously designed Pinford Bridge at Sherborne Castle (q.v.).

forms of many periods, the traceried windows of the Hall, the mullioned window bays of the s front, the idiosyncratic battlements and blocky rustication, the house is a late flower of the all-embracing ideal by which from the 1870s onwards architects hoped to produce a style for their time.

It was the third house on the site. A C16 gabled brick house was rented by John Churchill in the early C17, and from the late C17 this was rebuilt piecemeal for successive Churchills. Its freehold was purchased outright by the 9th Lord Digby, who added a domed tower, probably by *E. B. Lamb*, c. 1865.* By the late C19 this (by then) rambling house was suffering from dry rot, drainage smells and an infestation of rats.

Sweepingly long and low proportions for both main fronts. The N front (entrance) is irregularly U-plan, with a low central porch, given a typical deep curved hood. Stylistic curiosities here are the broad buttresses that fail to reach the ground, and the battlements-cum-triglyphs of the parapet. The s front is more Jacobean in character. Symmetrically arranged with alternating polygonal bays and gabled dormers, it is further extended to the l. by the billiard-room wing canted forward. Here, though, the odd triglyph feature continues on the parapets. The short E end, where the land drops, rears up with a two-storey bow, and a broad tower above, providing a visual stop to the main fronts.** The bow was a feature which had to be copied from the earlier house, with the Tapestry Room of the previous house reconstructed inside it.*** The allegorical ceiling painting, moved from the staircase ceiling of the previous house, is said to be by *Thornhill*. Throughout, the foundations of the old house were largely followed. One can criticize the sw wing for being too small, or the tower, which houses the water tank, for being too bulky, but Stokes's verve and freshness in the end silence criticism.

The interior is an epitome of Edwardian mansion planning. The porch leads in below the stairs, and a l. turn presents the two-storey HALL. In spite of the Gothic windows, there is a plaster tunnel-vaulted ceiling with penetrations and, for support, coupled Ionic pilasters. Balcony at the w end, so that there is a view down from the stairs. White marble chimneypiece made for the first Eaton Hall, Cheshire, of 1675–83. The overall effect is a Wren style which, when combined with the Gothic window tracery, recalls the atmosphere of one of the great European Baroque monastic interiors. Vaulted spine corridor on both floors, *à la* Bryanston, the Hall opened to it

112

---

*Drawings surviving at the house appear to be signed by the otherwise unknown L.B. Lamb.

**Stokes used similar stocky towers at All Saints' Convent, St Albans (Herts.); Inholmes, Hungerford (Berks.); and especially Downside School, Stratton-on-the-Fosse (Somerset).

***Some of the TAPESTRIES (by *Judocus de Vos*) were given to General Charles Churchill in the late C17 by the States of Holland.

at the lower and the upper level. The main living rooms face
s, and here too, regardless of the Elizabethan windows, the
decoration is Baroque or Adamish. One or two reused late
C18 chimneypieces.

Some up-to-date TECHNOLOGICAL INNOVATIONS were
incorporated, such as the fixed vacuum cleaning system. A
pump in the basement was linked to points upstairs where flex-
ible-tubed cleaners could be 'plugged in'. Also electric lighting
and an electrically powered luggage hoist. More surprising is
the minimal original bathroom provision – a particular foible
of Lord Digby. Stokes nevertheless supplied the plumbing for
later bathroom installation. The house was also one of the first
to be built around a steel frame, with floors of *in situ* concrete
on corrugated-iron arched shuttering.

GARDENS and LANDSCAPE. The first phase of work in a
Brownian style (tree clumps and lakes on the River Cerne) was
carried out for Admiral Robert Digby, *c.* 1770 onwards. *Capability Brown* may have become involved as he was working in
1776–9 at Sherborne Castle (for Digby's brother). His advice
was certainly sought. Richly coloured planting of azaleas,
rhododendrons and magnolias was added to this layout by
Admiral Sir Henry Digby, *c.* 1820–30, and further developed
in the late C19 and C20.

Entrance GATEWAY and LODGE, probably by *Stokes*, *c.* 1908.

STABLES, w of the house, by *R.H. Shout*, 1843. Two parallel
ranges. Broadly Tudor style.

In the village a number of ESTATE COTTAGES, mid- to late C19.
Tudor Revival. Some may be by *Shout*.

SCHOOL (former), ½ m. NNW. Dated 1860. Probably also by
Shout. Tudor Revival. Mullioned windows with ornate cast-
iron casements.

DOGBURY, ½ m. NNE. EARTHWORKS of a cross-dyke or unfinished hill-fort.

3090

MONKTON WYLD

Two great Early Victorian buildings by the 'Anglican Pugin',
high on the wooded hillside to the N of the main Axminster to
Charmouth road.

ST ANDREW. Built in 1848–9 by *R.C. Carpenter* for Mrs Elizabeth Hodson. As one would expect from Carpenter, the style
is an archaeologically knowledgeable Dec. Of flint, with a
central tower with a Northamptonshire broach spire (with two
tiers of lucarnes), the spire completed in 1856.* The chancel

---

*A reduced version of the spires that Carpenter designed for St Paul, Brighton,
East Sussex and St Mary Magdalene, Munster Square, London, neither of which
was built. (Information from John Elliott.)

is nearly as long as the nave – an effect of the teaching of the Ecclesiologists. The S porch is of wood with open sides with Dec colonnettes. NE sacristy in matching style by *J. Hayward & Son*, 1887. The interior is fully Victorian, made sumptuous by the later elaboration (for the Rev. J.B. Maher Camm). This all reads well against Carpenter's bold Dec handling of the crossing arches and aisle arcades. Stencilled chancel roof and painted foliage on the chancel E wall.

FURNISHINGS. Brass COMMUNION RAIL. – Good carved STALLS, 1886, by *Hayward & Son* (made by *E.L. Luscombe & Son* of Exeter). – Excellent SCREEN of wood, painted and gilded, by *F.C. Eden*, 1888. The brass GATES are by *Hardman*. – PULPIT. Of 1887, also by *Hayward & Son* (and made by *Luscombe*'s). Carved oak with figures in niches, on a base of Mansfield stone with green Devon marble colonnettes. – FONT. By *Carpenter*. Octagonal, with a quatrefoil to each face. – STAINED GLASS. Four chancel windows by *Wailes*, *c.* 1855. Five excellent windows in the aisles of *c.* 1875 by *G.E. Cook*. Central window at the W end and W aisle windows by *Ward & Hughes*, 1871.

LYCHGATE. Perhaps also by *Carpenter*, *c.* 1850. Bold side framing. Gambrel roof.

WAR MEMORIAL, just beyond the lychgate. Of *c.* 1920. Broken column on a pedestal with a bronze wreath.

MONKTON WYLD COURT, 120 yds E. Built as the rectory by *R.C. Carpenter*, 1849. An elaborated version of the grave and restrained E.E. used by Carpenter on e.g. Sherborne School (q.v.). Two parallel ranges with sharp gable-ends. Two front-facing gables, a two-storey bay on the l., single-storeyed on the r. The entrance hides in the secondary W gable.

MORCOMBELAKE

4090

A network of rambling lanes facing the sea, high around Hardown Hill. Its twin, Ryall, to the NE, faces inland.

ST GABRIEL. This is the parish church of Stanton St Gabriel, though it is on the A-road at Morcombelake. It was built in 1840–1, by *T.H. Wyatt & D. Brandon*. Nave with bellcote and chancel in one; W porch. The chancel is a rebuilding of 1856. Simple interior with its FURNISHINGS much as completed in 1841 and 1856. – TILEWORK by *Minton* in the sanctuary and a square around the font. – ROOD BEAM. C15, with some C19 make-up. Fleurons. Removed from Stanton St Gabriel church. – FONT. Probably late C12, but re-cut. Tub-shaped, with a band of interlace. C19 stem and base. – STAINED GLASS. Various arrangements of coloured glass. Also a nave S window with stamped quarries and diagonal text-bands. All by *Powell & Sons*, 1857.

MORDEN

Three farming hamlets, the largest being East Morden, where the church and rectory are located.

ST MARY. Rebuilt in 1873 by *Joseph Sellers*, surveyor to the Charborough Estate. Brown heathstone. An upright church, made the more so by its position on a small hill. Everything about it suggests a date of, say, 1840. Sellers, it seems, was a carpenter-cum-builder who eventually was given his head here.[*] The faculty drawings are very primitive and the design treatment quite dated. The proportions of the three doorways alone and the treatment of the abaci are evidence enough of the early C19 style. Equally the short nave and aisles, the height of the clerestory, and the use of identical straight-headed three-light windows with Dec, but incorrect Dec, tracery. The same window type is used even in the vestry. Only the E window is different, but just as unlikely. Long, two-light, Perp. The chancel arch is correspondingly steep. The arcades have five bays to the three bays of windows. The piers are quatrefoil, the capitals rather mechanical leaf bands. – FONTS. One C12, re-cut and made octagonal from a square original. Stem and corner colonnettes of 1928. – Another C14 Perp. Octagonal but with stem missing. – HATCHMENT. Drax family, C19. – STAINED GLASS. E window probably by *Ward & Hughes*, *c.* 1873. – MONUMENT, dated 1597. Thomas Earle kneels N of the tower arch; three dummy-like members of his family seem to be rising from a pedestal, S of the tower arch. Both sub-pedestals are identical and each carries an inscription brass set into a recess with gadrooned surround. The kneeling figure is portrayed incidentally in the attitude of homage not of prayer.

CHURCH VILLA, ⅛ m. SW. Of *c.* 1830. Stucco. Two storeys with a hipped roof rising to a row of Tudorish brick chimneystacks. The windows have marginal panes.

(MORDEN PARK COTTAGE, 1¾ m. SSW. Deep in the woods, but like a lodge. One room up, one down, beneath a pyramid roof. Each has a Venetian window facing NE. Red brick. Late C18.)

MORE CRICHEL

Nothing of the village remained after Humphry Sturt moved its occupants to Newtown to the S when he created his park after 1765. It is now no more than the house, the former parish church and various outbuildings.

---

[*] *Sellers* (1804–79) is recorded as a carpenter in the 1841 census and a builder in 1861, but by 1871 he calls himself 'architect'. In the faculty application he is described as surveyor to J.S.W. Sawbridge-Erle-Drax of Charborough Park.

CRICHEL HOUSE. A fire destroyed the early C17 house in 1742. Its replacement by *John Bastard & Francis Cartwright* was a three-storey, five-bay brick-built block with ashlar dressings (cf. Whatcombe House, Winterborne Whitechurch, before its enlargement), of 1746 for Sir William Napier.* Humphry Sturt inherited Crichel in 1765 and, between 1768 and 1780, engulfed the earlier work with three ranges, rendered, with Portland stone dressings. These match the height of the 1740s block but, by having double-height rooms on the ground floor, are of two storeys, not three. The silhouette of the whole was made consistent by a continuous balustraded parapet, interrupted only by pediments at the centre of the s and e fronts. Sturt is said to have been his own architect for the new work, but payments to *John & Thomas Bastard IV*, between 1768 and 1773 (totalling £2,245), indicate that, together with handling the building work, they were probably its true architects. The centrepiece of the e façade, for example, in its gauche combination of classical elements, is highly suggestive of other work by the Bastards. *Samuel & James Wyatt* were employed on the interiors of the two finest rooms between 1772 and 1780. The w (entrance) front was remodelled in 1869 by *William Burn & Macvicar Anderson* for Henry Gerard Sturt (later 1st Lord Alington), when enlarged service offices on the N side were also erected. Further remodelling of the interiors occurred *c.* 1905 for the 2nd Lord Alington (perhaps by *Harold Peto*, who laid out an Italian garden at this time).

Examining the EXTERIOR, front by front, commencing at the w, the wall of the 1742–6 block is seen flanked by the projecting wings of Sturt's enlargement. (That on the l. – with three expressed storeys – is slightly wider as it needed to incorporate a service wing retained from the 1740s house.) The r. wing is the end of the s range. It has two keyed-arched Venetian windows set side by side on the ground floor (and matching the 1760s windows on the s front), installed in a former blank wall in 1869. *Porte cochère* of 1869 and alteration of the windows on the w side by *Burn & Macvicar Anderson*. A pair of Venetian windows flanks the five-bay recessed Ionic-columned portico of the s front, above which the first floor is treated as a classical attic with sashes between short Corinthian pilasters supporting the main pediment. The elevations of the 1740s house, obscured by later work, can be glimpsed within the s portico (where there is a 1743 datestone). Moulded window frames, the centre one with scrolled side-pieces, above a pedimented doorcase. The pilasters came later: they are merely the responds to the columns of the portico. As the ground is lower here and on the e elevation is exposed, it is of rusticated Portland ashlar, as are the curved perron-type staircases. The seven-bay 1760s e front has pedimented sashes on the ground

*Payments totalling just over £2,000 imply that Bastard and Cartwright were also the builders. *See* John Cornforth, 'The Building of Crichel', *Architectural History* 27, 1984.

floor and a three-bay pedimented centre. Another Venetian window forms the central garden entrance with an open pediment above, raised on scrolled brackets; a rusticated panel links this with the first-floor band, and with a smaller Venetian window above (which has a depressed arch to allow it to fit under the main pediment). The projecting perron, with curved staircases, runs the width of the pedimented centre. A basement entrance, with scroll-topped architrave, is flanked by niches. To the N all is a refacing after 1960, needed after the 1869 service wing had been taken down. Little domed pavilions and a balustraded area, a neat arrangement, by *E.F. Tew* of Bath.

(The INTERIOR* has some of the most spectacular c18 rooms in Dorset. So it should, for they after all were the reason for the enlargement. Work of two c18 periods, the earlier in a Kentian style, the later in precisely the style one associates with *Wyatt*. They represent before and after 1772, for in that year the first of a series of payments to *Samuel & James Wyatt* were made which eventually totalled £183 9s. 6d. The earlier style comes in the vestibule into which the w entrance leads, originally the staircase hall of the 1740s house. This has plasterwork, pedimented doorcases and an Ionic screen across its inner end, all contemporary with the first new house. One of Sturt's alterations was to move, and very cleverly enlarge, the staircase, so that it stood top-lit in the centre of the expanded house. The staircase is a fine typical Early Georgian piece, with a twisted, a fluted and a turned baluster to each step. Framed wall panels by *Cipriani*, moved here from Arlington Street, London. Good Kentian chimneypieces in two N rooms. The best chimneypiece, however, is in the Library, the post-1768 room in the sw corner of the house, where it has a fine contemporary overmantel. This may have been moved from Redlynch House, Somerset (after this was demolished in 1913). It is accompanied by a ceiling combining *c.* 1740 and *c.* 1770 elements, probably by the *Bastards*. On the s front, behind the loggia, the Long Drawing Room (or Mirror Room) was made *c.* 1905 by combining two rooms. Less Kentian and more Neoclassical in character is the post-1768 central room of the E front, a square, with monumental pedimented doorcases. The ceiling has painted fields. For the two major rooms on this front, dining room and drawing room, Sturt, to his credit, abandoned the local team and brought in the *Wyatts*. The State Dining Room, in the NE corner, has a ceiling on a deep cove, with fluted corner-pieces. On the walls painted ovals by *Biagio Rebecca* with classical subjects, in delicate plasterwork frames. The SE State Drawing Room is more monumental, with a segmental barrel ceiling, inset paintings by *Rebecca* in the style of Angelica Kauffmann, and a wall treatment of arabesqued pilasters. (Rebecca was paid £147 17s. in 1779.) The

---

*Owing to lack of access, the description is based on published accounts and illustrations.

Venetian window in the s wall is very mighty with its scagliola columns (reinstated 2014–15, *see* below). Both rooms have fine classical fireplaces, probably by *John Devall Jun.*, as a payment of £100 to 'J. Devall' is recorded in 1779. Both of the Wyatt rooms were restored to their original appearance, 2014–15, by *Peregrine Bryant* (with *Patrick Baty* as consultant), for Richard Chilton Jun.)

ST MARY. SE of the house on the lawn and near the lake, replacing a medieval building. The church is small, of nave and chancel with a N and a S chapel. There are quatrefoil parapets, and picturesque turrets at the SE corner of the nave and on the S chapel, the latter turret larger. The side windows are Perp, the arcading around the W doorway is E.E., the window above is Dec. The E wall window between roof and the much lower chancel has curious tracery surrounding a central circle. All this is of 1850 and cost £10,000; probably by *Thomas Hopper* and completed by *P. C. Hardwick*. (*George Alexander* has also been suggested as another possibility.) In 1886 the *Rev. Ernest Geldart* made ambitious elaborations of the chancel for Lord Alington. His also is the hammerbeam roof of the nave, startlingly high up. But if the chancel is low, it is as a recompense fan-vaulted: two bays with gilded ribs. The walls of the chancel are stencilled, the doorway to the vestry has an elaborate surround, the N transept blank stone arcading along the E wall. – STAINED GLASS. Six chancel windows by *Cox, Sons, Buckley & Co.*, 1886–9 (who also executed *Geldart*'s decorative scheme). All fittings were stripped after the church was declared redundant in 1973. (A brass of Isabel Uvedale †1572 was moved to Witchampton church.)

STABLES, NW of the house. Brick, probably by *John & Thomas Bastard IV*. This seems to have been Humphry Sturt's first work after 1765. Grand, if muddled, façades. Three-storey S entrance tower, with a pyramid roof; three-bay links to pyramid-roofed end pavilions, each with a Venetian window under a sunk relieving arch. The disorder of disparate motifs in the centre tower needs to be seen to be believed: the Neoclassical vocabulary used without discretion. The E range has as its centrepiece a shaped Dutch gable.

Brownian landscaped PARK, with a great sickle-shaped lake, and woods coming right down to its further margin. The gardens to the S and E of the house were elaborated *c.* 1908 with Italianate gardens by *Harold Peto*. These have since disappeared. Many ESTATE BUILDINGS designed by *P. C. Hardwick*, *William Burn* and *Macvicar Anderson*, *c.* 1854 to *c.* 1880.

ENTRANCE ARCH and LODGE, 1 m. S. Dated 1874, by *Macvicar Anderson*. Rock-faced stone. A bold Neo-Norman tower with battlements, corner turrets and machicolations above carriage archways. Matching single-storey lodge attached.

NEWTOWN, 1 m. SSE. The new settlement created by Humphry Sturt beyond the borders of his park. Only one C18 house is left.

MANSWOOD, ¾ m. W. THE BUILDINGS. A remarkably long row, originally of twelve cottages. Probably C18. Cob and thatch with late C19 brick lean-to additions to the rear. Former SCHOOL. Mid-C19, extended 1892. Brick. Picturesque half-timbering above and conical-roofed turret.

MORETON

Very much an estate village, with the house and church away on the E side in parkland.

ST NICHOLAS. A gem of Georgian Gothick externally, refitted internally in the mid C19. Built in 1776 (so dated on the label stops of the S doorway), replacing a medieval church. Probably by *John Carter*,* for James Frampton of Moreton House. N aisle and W porch added 1848 by *Joseph Barnes* of Dorchester. The display side is the S. Here, in the middle is a tower, and l. and r. of it are side chapels. Their windows and the three windows to the N are of three lights and have cusped intersected tracery. The E end is an apse with five such windows. The N windows belong to an aisle, an exemplarily tactful enlargement. The date is lucky: five years later and they would probably have Gothicized seriously. As it is, the wide C18 nave dominates with its plaster rib-vault (installed in 1842–3, presumably replacing something similar) and the fairly correctly Perp aisle piers blend in well. – The FONT of *c.* 1848 stands in the middle of the nave. – REREDOS, PULPIT and BENCHES show more clearly the heavier hand of this date, but even these are relatively sensitive installations for the period. – An extensive scheme of encaustic TILES by *Minton,* also of *c.* 1848. – GLASS. In 1848 *Willement* installed a scheme in the apse windows. These were blown out when the church was seriously bomb-damaged in 1940. The great gain from this is the engraved glass installed in the five three-light apse windows in 1955 by *Laurence Whistler,* who continued to add similar windows throughout the church until 1984. They are a stroke of genius, having the elegance and the lightness of the building. Those in the apse represent the symbols of Christ's Passion, a Christmas tree, a young ash in bud, six medallions, and in all the outer lights candles with ribbons wound loosely round them. Four in the N aisle (1974–5) include the Seasons and the Dream of the Rood, windows also serving as memorials to the Findlay family. In the Trinity Chapel a memorial to a wartime pilot (1982), while that in the vestry (1984) makes reference to the local rivers. All of these are three-light windows. For the larger four-light W window (also 1984) Whistler depicts a spiral galaxy. – MONU-MENTS. In the Trinity Chapel (the Moreton family pew), Mrs

---

* Proposed by the late Terry Friedman.

Moreton, St Nicholas, engraved glass.
Photograph by James O. Davies

Frampton †1762. Inscription in a very pretty frame, sprinkled
with flowers. The inscription reads:

> She was a rare example of true Conjugal Affection,
> and of those amiable qualities on which alone are
> founded the Charms of Domestic Happiness. The
> Advantages She enjoyed of a very ample Fortune,

an engaging Manner and pleasing Form, were far surpassed by the inestimable Endowments of her Mind, by her Modesty and Gentleness of Manners, Chearfulness and Sweetness of Temper, Good Sense and unaffected Piety, with a most exemplary Patience and Resignation under the severe Trial of a lingering painful Illness: These Virtues endear'd her to all Ranks of People, and render'd her during an Union of Sixteen Years, the Comfort and delight of her Husband Who truly sensible of her uncommon Merit and his own Unhappiness in the Loss of so excellent a Person whom he most highly esteem'd and dearly loved, Erected this Monument as a Testimony of his Affection, Grief and Gratitude.

The monument is by *Thomas Carter Jun.* and *P. M. Vangelder.* – Also a brass with kneeling figure: Jamys Framton †1523. – William Frampton †1755. Tablet framed with Ionic colonnettes and a broken pediment.

MORETON HOUSE. Built by *John Bastard* for James Frampton in 1744. Of fine Portland ashlar, two-storeyed and with a hipped roof. Cultured but unassuming W front, of three broad bays. Centre brought forward slightly under a pediment, just suggesting the Palladian villa formula. Round-headed doorway flanked by small windows in channelled surrounds, so that a Venetian motif is formed (cf. Bastard's use of this feature at Stepleton House, Iwerne Stepleton and Sir Peter Thompson's House, Poole). The windows cut straight into the wall surface, those below given a big keystone, those above a small one. The three-bay depth was extended by a fourth in 1779–81 and the E front formed. This carries on the sparing motifs already established, and introduced a seven-sided central bay, with windows in every other facet. The service wing to the N was the part first built, in 1742.

Inside, the entrance hall has modest plasterwork of the first period, and the drawing room a plaster ceiling of the second period (in a Wyatt style, with a central relief of a Roman sacrifice). Also of the later period the dining room, with an excellent marble chimneypiece (*c.* 1760) that may have come from Fonthill House, Wiltshire.*

At the gates to house and church the buttressed brick wall of the early C19 SCHOOL, and behind, the brick GLEBE HOUSE, built *c.* 1750 as the rectory.

LYCHGATE to the cemetery, 100 yds SW of the church. Classical, which is startling. The four Ionic columns, however, and the pedimented roof started life *c.* 1800 as the entrance to the kitchen garden of Moreton House. They took on their new role *c.* 1950. Within the cemetery, the GRAVE of Lawrence of

---

*It would in that case be by *J. F. Moore*, one of his 'caryatic' chimneypieces, dispersed in the sale of 1807. A similar but better example is at the Manor House, Beaminster.

Arabia (†1935). Headstone and inscribed open book, carved
by *Eric Kennington*.
OBELISK, ½ m. s. 1785–6 by *James Hamilton* of Weymouth.
Raising an Adamish urn above the trees. Erected as a memorial to James Frampton.

MOSTERTON

ST MARY. 1832–3 by *Edmund Pearce*, surveyor. Plain w tower,
wide nave with lancets, short chancel with a stepped triplet
of lancets, i.e. the Commissioners' type. – WEST GALLERY on
fluted columns. – PULPIT. By *Sir Harold Brakspear*, 1933. Suitably plain. – STAINED GLASS. E window by *Geoffrey Robinson*,
1975. Christ in Majesty with tractor.

MOTCOMBE

A large former estate village. Farmhouses and cottages of various
estate vintages, from Picturesque greensand ashlar to mildly
Gothic red brick. Interspersed are a few C17 and early C18 vernacular cottages, some with thatched roofs. The centre of the
village is unusually verdant, although much recent infilling and
housing culs de sac have in places introduced a suburban note.

ST MARY. Rebuilt in 1846 by *G. Alexander*. Archaeological Perp,
of greensand ashlar, with battlemented w tower and end-
gabled aisles. Octagonal arcade piers. – PULPIT. 1907. Of Caen
stone with alabaster enrichments by *Wippell & Co*. – FONT.
C13. Circular bowl; plain. Stepped pedestal. – A curiosity is the
Perp-style cinquefoil-headed niche, said to have been removed
from the previous church and re-set internally over s doorway.
It appears, however, more likely to be mid-C19 in date. This
houses a fragment of C15 SCULPTURE, thought to be the lower
half of a statue (possibly representing St Catherine of Alexandria trampling on the Emperor Maximian). Alternatively it is a
complete piece, perhaps representing a visceral burial. – To its
r. ROYAL ARMS of Charles II; to the l. a HATCHMENT of Whitaker, 1816. – Behind the organ, the very large canvas ROYAL
ARMS dated 1773. – STAINED GLASS. The E window retains
its original plain glazing with coloured margins. Two chancel
s windows, one by *Henry Hughes*, 1871, the other by *Clayton
& Bell*, †1897. E window of s aisle, 1914, by *Paul Woodroffe*
of Chipping Campden, Glos. – MONUMENTS. Elizabeth
Webbe †1627. Large tablet with columns l. and r. – Elizabeth,
Marchioness of Westminster, of Motcombe House, †1891. By
G. Maile & Son, Euston Road. Already Neo-Georgian. – Hon.

Hugh Raufe Grosvenor †1930, s aisle. Bronze sculptural tablet by *L. S. Merrifield*, 1936.

In the churchyard a CROSS BASE with part of the shaft; C15. – Also an enclosed MONUMENT to the Marchioness of Westminster †1891. Edwardian in character. A surmounting urn is missing. Scrolled wrought-iron railings.

WESLEYAN METHODIST CHAPEL, The Street, ½ m. N. Gothic. Dated 1870, by *T. Hudson* of Gillingham.

SCHOOL, just w of the church. Two buildings, both Tudor Gothic with high-quality detailing. The larger dated 1839. Attached former school house at right angles to the classroom block. To its w a matching former boys' school of 1874.

In the VILLAGE a good group of four cottages in CHURCH WALK, 100 yds E. Three late C18 brick (two joined to form one house) and thatched, one symmetrical Tudor Gothic in greensand ashlar with a hipped slate roof. w of the school, MOTCOMBE HALL, a classical rectory-style house of 2000 by *Jeremy Nieboer*. A successful exercise of keeping-in-keeping. ½ m. N, in THE STREET, beyond the Methodist chapel, RED HOUSE FARM. Late C18 ashlar with a late C19 cross-wing and a red brick parallel range facing w.

NORTH END FARM, 1¼ m. N. Fine symmetrical ashlar front, probably of the early C17. Three-light lower windows under a continuous string course, upper windows of the same size with hoodmoulds, and two bold gabled dormers.

Many of the estate-built FARMS are of high quality. The best is MANOR FARM, ½ m. SW. Dated 1836, of greensand ashlar in a Regency Tudor style. Three-bay front block with a parallel, longer range behind. Central canted two-storey porch with a hipped roof.

MOTCOMBE HOUSE (PORT REGIS SCHOOL), ½ m. s. A large mansion built for the 1st Lord Stalbridge (who was a Grosvenor) by *Sir Ernest George & Peto*, 1892–4. (Dated 1893 on a rainwater head of the N front, 1894 on the staircase ceiling.) It was the successor to a somewhat rambling house sited some 200 yds NW, comprising a villa built *c.* 1800 for William Whitaker, extended *c.* 1820 for Robert, 2nd Earl Grosvenor. Red brick, with dressings of Ham Hill stone. The style Tudor to Elizabethan: broad and lofty mullioned-and-transomed windows, some with arched lights, some without. Frontispieces detailed with scholarly reference to Early Renaissance models and to Jacobean ones. But what matters about a house like this is the highly professional picturesque grouping. One approaches from the SW, so the finest composition is shown to this aspect, with a stout, low, battlemented tower prominently placed, and the main house running away beyond, a row of five even gables above two rectangular projecting window bays. The spreading, reposeful grouping is characteristic of the 1890s. The entrance is to the N, where the main block lies back with lower wings l. and r. in a half-H-plan. Two-storey stone porch with all the emphasis. The short E front is the most piquant, the two big gables and the big polygonal window bay weighted against nothing but a very showy chimneystack. After this the garden front, so impressive from a distance, seems a little pedestrian. The main interior space is finely managed. One enters a vestibule out of which rises a spacious staircase, open through an upper arcade to the two-storey great hall, which is lit at the far end by the polygonal E window. Chimneypiece of ashlar, sparingly detailed, though it rises to the ceiling. Similar restrained chimneypieces in other rooms. They reinforce one's feeling that Sir Ernest George was a designer of quality, if not a particularly original one.

Motcombe House became a school in 1947. Two notable SCHOOL BUILDINGS, both by *BTA Architects* and of 2003. W of the mansion, the DINING HALL. Red brick, with a mono-pitch roof sloping to the N, against which is planted a great glazed S-facing swoop, a nicely judged counterpoint to the rectangularity of George & Peto's house. Behind, 150 yds NW, standing with a reflecting lake in the foreground, the FARRINGTON MUSIC SCHOOL. Octagonal central pavilion glazed on three sides, the glass outward-leaning above a base of sharply battered buttresses. A wrap of lean-to red brick around the remaining five sides.

NETHERBURY

4090

An intricate village nestling among a confluence of streams and steep-sided hills.

ST MARY, set against the hillside and above the village. High Perp W tower with a higher, octagonal SE stair-turret. Battlemented with gargoyles at the corners, and all around the stair-turret top. This, the S aisle and the chancel are all part of an early C15 rebuilding. The refenestration of the N aisle at the same time gives the church an overall Perp character, that is until one enters. Fine interior, here decidedly mid-C14 Dec, although the arcade piers have already the standard Perp section of four shafts and four hollows. But bases and capitals of the shafts are round, and the arches have the Dec moulding of the sunk quadrant. The Dec chancel arch is contemporary with and matches the aisle arcades; the tower arch is clearly later, but its capitals seem intended to respect those of the Dec arcades. Also Dec the (blocked) N aisle E window. The N doorway with the smaller window over it are 1850 by *C.E. Giles* of Taunton, who carried out a major restoration. It is a nice conceit that the doorway and window are just off-centre to each other. Prior to this (in 1848) Giles replaced the S porch in a bold Perp style. Several niches in the nave and aisle E walls. Three of these have STATUES, that of the Virgin and Child by *Wippell & Co.*, 1953. – TILEWORK by *Minton* in the sanctuary. – SCREEN. A fine Perp-style piece by *C.E. Ponting*,

Netherbury, St Mary.
Engraving by Bartholomew Howlett, 1819

1911. – PULPIT. Early C17 and unusually fine. Corinthian
columns at the angles and two tiers of blank arches filled with
inlaid decoration. Tapering fluted stem on a short post. – The
other FURNISHINGS are mostly by *Giles* and lacking in any
Ecclesiological enthusiasm. The scheme is largely complete,
however. – FONT. Late C12. Square, of Purbeck marble, very
shallow in height. Against the sides either scalloping or rows
of blank shields, all badly preserved. Leaves in the spandrels
of the top surface. On a stout central stem with colonnettes at
the corners, still on its original base. – ROYAL ARMS. C17 Stuart
arms on a panel with moulded frame. – STAINED GLASS. The
large E window with the Evangelists is signed by *Wailes*, 1844.
Chancel S window by *Francis Skeat*, 1944. *Skeat* also did the
S aisle W window, 1947. Brightly coloured S aisle E window
by *Taylor & O'Connor*, †1877. N aisle W window by *Wailes*,
†1845. N aisle window over the doorway by *Christopher Webb*,
1945. – MONUMENT. Alabaster effigy of a late C15 knight,
damaged. The tomb-chest has alabaster angels holding shields;
similar to that at Puddletown. However here also a canopy
with spreading ogee arches. Openwork cusped and sub-cusped
with an openwork quatrefoil frieze and brattished octagonal
colonnette corners. In the frieze, one of the shields has the
arms of More of Melplash. – Humphrey Saunders †1673. Latin
tablet with Ionic columns and an entablature with a primitive
Baroque pediment. – Robert Conway †1837, with many other
family members. Marble tablet in a stone Gothick surround
by *Evans* of Bristol.

CONGREGATIONAL CHAPEL (former), 150 yds SW. Of *c.* 1840,
with three pointed windows.

OLD RECTORY, opposite the church. At the r. end, two C16 windows on the ground floor, one four-light the other three-light, both with arched heads. The house appears to have expanded l. in the C17 to just beyond the gabled porch. Several C18 alterations, the sash windows of this date changed to stone cross-windows in 1886. This phase of alterations, by *G.R. Crickmay*, also added the Tudor-style chimneystack on the front elevation.

NETHERBURY COURT, 200 yds N. Of *c.* 1912. Art and Crafts stone house in grounds, for the Misses Shaw. Enlarged in the 1930s when the extensive gardens were laid out.

SLAPE MANOR, ⅝ m. S. Main block with pedimented centre on the N side of *c.* 1740. Two storeys and hipped roof. Two bays l. and r. of the centre, this breaking forward a little and marked by quoins. An arched entrance porch was added in 1871 for F.W. Gundry by *G.R. Crickmay*. The W wing was extended to provide a new drawing room at this date; designs by *Thomas Hardy* survive for this. Somewhat incongruous Jacobean gable at the W end also of this date. A more considerable enlargement and remodelling by *E.P. Warren* for B.K. Ronald took place in 1931; the narrow arched windows with bullseyes above are of this period, as is the large service block in broadly matching style to the l. On the garden front are small hipped-roofed blocks in the re-entrants, given arched windows and again bullseyes by Warren, livening up this side.

STRODE MANOR, 1½ m. W. 1828 by *Joseph & Frederick Galpin* of Bridport for George T. Gollop. Ashlar villa. Five bays on the S façade, three, somewhat irregularly disposed, on the entrance front, E. Low-pitched hipped roof with deep eaves. Doric porch.

NETHER CERNE

6090

The church and manor house form a memorable group in the landscape, set against the dark trees of the hill behind.

ALL SAINTS (Churches Conservation Trust). A small church of banded flint and stone. C13 with a short late C15 W tower. This is of three stages, battlemented with eight crocketed pinnacles, each coupled with a bold gargoyle below. Polygonal N stair-turret. Tower arch of one continuous chamfer. Small carved angels at the springing. Nave and chancel in one and a late C13 S chapel (to St Etheldreda). The chapel has an E lancet window shafted inside, and with a cinquefoiled rere-arch, and a three-light S window of very characteristic late C13 tracery design, the middle light lower so that there is space for a large top circle filled with three spherical triangles. Also a trefoil-headed PISCINA. – FONT. C12, of cauldron shape, fluted with

alternatingly broad and narrow flutes. C14 base and octagonal
stem. – Several other FURNISHINGS from a restoration by
B. Ferrey, 1876–7. – STAINED GLASS. E window *c.* 1877. A
Christ with much grisaille work (and paint loss). Chancel N
window by *Jones & Willis*, 1897. Nave N window by *Cox, Sons,
Buckley & Co.*, 1889.

NETHER CERNE HOUSE, immediately N. Banded flint and
stone. Late C17 range facing the church. Taller, early C19 block
facing W. Stone-mullioned windows with hoodmoulds to the
former; sashes, those on the ground floor larger, to the latter.
'CELTIC' FIELD SYSTEM. *See* Piddletrenthide.

5010

NETHER COMPTON

A stone village, and one which, rarely for Dorset, has some sense
of formality. A small green opens N of the church, but the houses
stay on the main village street rather than gathering round it.
Some C17 cottages with late C19 estate building in between.

ST NICHOLAS. C13 nave and chancel, the former with late C15
refenestration. The chancel retains a single N lancet, made
up from fragments during a heavy restoration by *F.E. Smith*,
1885–6. The chancel was enlarged, but the E window is C15,
re-set with a cinquefoiled rere-arch within. Late C15 three-
stage W tower with a battlemented parapet, corner pinnacles
and an octagonal N stair-turret (cf. Over Compton). Other
windows are Perp, retained and re-set during the restoration;
the wagon roof to the nave is, however, genuine Perp. Its S
porch is C13, but the arch itself must be C19 (although *c.* 1300
in style). The arch to the N chapel is Perp and the tower arch
is panelled. – SCREEN. Late C15. Of stone (cf. Bradford Abbas)
but asymmetrical in layout. – PULPIT. Early C17. Lower tier
of blank arches. Upper panels with arabesques. – C14 canopied NICHE in the N chapel. – FONT. C14. Crudely octagonal without decoration. – BENCHES. C17, but one end in the
chancel is early C16 and has blank Perp tracery and a fleur-
de-lys poppyhead. – STAINED GLASS. E window perhaps by
Heaton, Butler & Bayne, 1909.

HALFWAY HOUSE CHAPEL (formerly Congregational), ¾ m.
SSE, on the A30. Built *c.* 1750. Symmetrical S front. Two large
mullioned-and-transomed windows flanked by two four-
centred-arched doorways. Pyramidal roof. Side walls punc-
tured with new windows when converted to a house, *c.* 1976.

DISSENTERS' BURIAL GROUND, Stallen, ½ m. SE. The heavy
classical GATEWAY is of 1732. Pedimented with paired pilasters. Small side scrolls. All rather eroded.

NATIONAL SCHOOL (former), just S. Dated 1843. Perp style.
Set back behind wrought-iron railings.

NORTH POORTON

St Mary Magdalene. 1860–2 by *John Hicks*. The perfect small church by Hicks, for the Rev. Thomas Sanctuary of Powerstock (cost £1,400). Nave and chancel, and a turret with a nicely judged spire in the angle of the porch and N chapel. Windows simple, of early C14 type. Big cusps to the porch arch. Elaborate leaf corbels for the roof and elaborate capitals for the chancel arch (with short columns of red Mansfield stone). This all carved by *Benjamin Grassby* of Powerstock. – Enriched stone PULPIT incorporating an ogee-headed niche with a figure of Christ. Carving by *Grassby*, with the figure by *R.L. Boulton* of Worcester, 1862. – TILEWORK by *Minton* in the chancel, becoming more elaborate in the sanctuary. – FURNISHINGS by *Hicks*, complete and *in situ*. Made by *Thomas Champion* of Frampton. – FONT. Perp style with Purbeck marble colonnettes around the stem. By *Grassby*. – STAINED GLASS. E window by *Hardman*. The remaining grisaille windows by *Joseph Bell* of Bristol, all 1862.

The ruin of the OLD CHURCH is to the N. No walls higher than *c.* 2 ft (60 cm.).

Manor House, 50 yds NE. A vernacular combination very common in many counties far from London, but rare in Dorset. Mullioned windows with hoodmoulds, and decorative ovals on their sides, l. and r. of one door, and above the other. L-plan. The ovals and the window configuration suggest a late C17 date. Thatched. The S wing has a symmetrical E front, the door in the centre, and a long hoodmould embracing both the ground-floor windows and hopping up over the doorway. The second doorway is in a canted piece between the two wings.

NORTH WOOTTON

OLD CHURCH. Demolished about 1883, leaving the W tower of *c.* 1400. Pointed tower arch with chamfered reveals. Diagonal W buttresses. Hipped roof.

St Mary Magdalene (now a house), ⅛ m. SE, on the main road. By *R.H. Carpenter*, 1883. It may at first seem surprising that the church is Perp (one would expect E.E. or Dec from them). However, the architects re-set late C14 and C15 windows from the old church. Nave and chancel; no bellcote. A W tower was planned but never built; as a result the old tower was retained to hold the bells.

OBORNE

St Cuthbert (Churches Conservation Trust), on the A30. Only the chancel of the former church. It was built in 1533, according to a Latin inscription over the N window. Two shield-panels flank the head of the E window with another above. They commemorate John Myer, the then abbot, and John Dunster, sacrist of Sherborne Abbey. Typical Henry VIII windows. The two earlier Perp window heads in the W front come from the nave.* – COMMUNION RAIL. C17. Turned balusters. Enriched top rail. – PULPIT. Dated 1639. Lozenges and some other motifs. – Some C14 or C15 TILES collected and re-set in two panels.

ST CUTHBERT. New church by *W. Slater*, 1861–2. Nave with bellcote, chancel and apse. Slater & Carpenter's typical twin lancets (set singly around the apse) with pointed-trefoiled cusping. Polished marble shafts to the chancel arch with good leaf carving (by *Poole & Sons* of London). The arch itself has alternating coloured stone voussoirs. – FONT and PULPIT are of stone and patently of the 1860s. Fine decoration to both. – STAINED GLASS. The three apse windows are by *Christopher Webb*, 1932.

Former RECTORY to the NE. Also by *Slater*, 1858. Very similar to his work at Sherborne School.

OKEFORD FITZPAINE

The village is unusually coherent, with almost nothing out of scale or in other ways striking a false note. Thatch is the predominant roofing material, on cottages of banded stone or timber framing. A few new houses have conformed successfully to the established palate.

ST ANDREW. A large aisled C15 church in origin, but substantially rebuilt in 1865–6 by *John Hicks* for the Rev. Robert Price, who replaced a chancel of 1772 (itself a replacement). The feature which will be remembered is the curious way in which a three-stage C15 W tower replaced a C14 one. Of the C14 the two free-standing piers in the nave carrying the tower arch and connected by small arches to N, S and W. C14 also the W window with its reticulated tracery. But the C15 thickened, strengthened and no doubt raised the tower, broadening the E halves of the N and S walls to reach the width of the nave. The S extension holds the tower staircase. The N aisle is in its N wall Perp, otherwise rebuilt; the S aisle is 1865–6. Hicks's N porch is helpfully dated 1866. Several Perp windows were re-set, such as the small square-headed two-lighter above the S doorway; also two niche heads, re-set in the N aisle. The arcades are by Hicks, of four bays with standard Perp elements, probably repeating the original.

*Displayed inside, copies of Buckler's sketches of the church when the nave still stood in 1802.

The FURNISHINGS incorporate two Victorian highlights. PULPIT, a remarkable confection with a genuine C15 Perp circular stone body with many narrow ogee-arched niches separated by pinnacle-topped mini-buttresses.* The statuettes are of course mid-C19, as is the medieval-style painting. *Hicks* designed the foliage base (carved by *Boulton*), the steps and the lancet-pierced stone balustrade. – FONT, in a *Minton*-tiled baptistery in the tower. High Victorian, of Caen stone, also carved by *Boulton*. Triangular in plan and chalice-like in appearance, with kneeling angels at the corners and a central red alabaster support. Utterly romantic. – *Minton* TILES also in the sanctuary. – BENCHES in the N aisle, late C17, very simple and very attractive. – The CHOIR STALLS are by *Hicks*, more Gothic in character than his PEWS. – STAINED GLASS. The chancel E window and two side windows are by *Mayer* of Munich, 1874. A good early example of their work, although with an insensitively placed trade inscription in the fifth light of the E chancel window. E windows to N and S aisles by *Heaton, Butler & Bayne*, 1921 and 1922. W window by *Henry Payne*, 1914. A few C15 and C16 fragments in the N aisle. – MONUMENT. Rev. Duke Butler †1779, and other family. Adamesque, urn finial.

WESLEYAN METHODIST CHAPEL (former), Lower Street, ¼ m. NW. Dated 1830. Brick front with Gothic tracery to the round-arched windows.

The church is at the S end of the village, on a hummock. It faces GREENHAYES, a large mid-C18 rectory. Built, says Hutchins, by the Rev. Duke Butler, a name with the right connotations for this stately five-bay façade. Centre bay wider than the rest. Two-storeyed. Hipped roof with rendered walls. The road curves away to the NW between a row of thatched timber-framed C17 COTTAGES upon a raised walk on the l., and on the r. ST LO HOUSE, thatched also, and a happy mixture of shapes and materials. The timber-framed r. end is the earliest part, an early C16 hall with cross-passage. Later this was extended to the l. in stone (see the end wall), and in 1638 this part was thickened front and back, the walls banded in flint and stone. Five-light mullioned window here, and round the corner the datestone that was set above the C17 front door (now masked).

Beyond this is the centre of the village, and the stepped stone base of a C15 CROSS. To the W, HIGH STREET, lined with cottages and long garden walls that maintain the village texture. To the N LOWER STREET, with *J.B. Green*'s miniature brick SCHOOL of 1872–3, exactly in scale, with a bellcote and decorative brickwork on the porch. On the opposite corner the ROYAL OAK INN, early C19 brick mercifully clear of modern signing. Further W on the l. another small house (YEATMANS), with a stone and flint banded part, datable to the early C17 by the windows, three-lighters with hollow-chamfered mullions and hoodmoulds.

---

*In 1772 this was removed from the new chancel, built for the Rev. Duke Butler, and converted for use as a font.

BANBURY HILL CAMP, 1¼ m. NW. A small univallate Iron Age HILL-FORT, now ploughed, with its entrance on the W.

OSMINGTON

A village of thatched cottages in a dell.

ST OSMUND. C15 W tower, two stages with corner buttresses and a battlemented parapet. Canted N stair-turret with a conical top. To this a new church was added by *B. Ferrey*, 1845–6. Perp, taking his cue from the tower and ignoring the *c.* 1300 style that progressive architects, such as himself, were preaching for. Inside the style is indeed *c.* 1300, Ferrey's S aisle convincingly matching the genuine *c.* 1300 of the N. The chancel arch is earlier, of *c.* 1200, with a double-chamfered pointed arch, the outer order springing from engaged shafts with scalloped capitals. – SCREEN. Timber, in a Ferrey style, but of 1897 by *J. Arthur Reeve*. – PULPIT. Stone, of 1884. A fine bold piece. E.E. with trefoil-headed panels, each with pink polished colonnettes. – FONT. C13, square. Purbeck type, with four pointed arches each side and four plain corner columns. – STAINED GLASS. E window, probably by *Alexander Gibbs*, †1857. At the E end of each aisle, windows almost certainly by *Burlison & Grylls*, *c.* 1879. Fragments in a S window, given in 1966. The most complete piece is a fine small figure of a bishop. E of this a window by *William Aikman*, 1936. – MONUMENTS. Monument to a Warham, *c.* 1620. The poorly worked inscription on a strapwork tablet with curving-forward rim, set within a classical surround. Another poor inscription on the frieze. Pevsner thought that originally there would have been a tomb-chest. – Chancel E wall, Rev. John Fisher, Canon of Salisbury, Constable's friend, †1832. A plain tablet by *S. Osmond*.

On the N side of the churchyard the remains of the C17 MANOR HOUSE. The E part is thought to have been a hall with, to its l., a low doorway beneath a solar. Hollow-chamfered mullioned windows set at various levels.

SCHOOL (former), on the A353. Dated 1835. Perp-ish windows either side of a gabled porch.

THE LONGHOUSE (formerly part of Charity Farm), at the N end of the village, was built as a longhouse, familiar from Devon, i.e. the dwelling-house and cow byre in a single range (*see* Introduction, p. 58). Late C16 but rebuilt at the NW end in the C17. The hipped thatched roof will be C18. In the same group a number of converted farm buildings. On the A353, EAST FARM is of the C17, with an extension to the N. Mullioned windows with hoodmoulds in both parts, those to the N taller. The main doorway is inscribed 1697, probably the date of the extension. S of the church, THE WHITE HOUSE hints that Weymouth is near. Stuccoed symmetrical three-bay front of *c.* 1830 with two buxom full-height bows, in fact quite unlike the shallow bows of Weymouth.

OSMINGTON HOUSE, ¼ m. NE. Italianate villa for Edward Atkyns Wood, *c.* 1850. Two gables with ground-floor colonnade between on the main façade.

WHITE HORSE, 1 m. NNW. The figure of George III on horseback, cut in 1808 in the chalk of the downs. The very shape of the horse gives the date away.*

Five BARROWS are in the mostly ploughed out East Hill group in Preston (*see* p. 498).

OVER COMPTON

5010

A memorable grouping of church and spikily Tudor country house, both of glowing Ham Hill stone, and with a mighty cedar of Lebanon and macrocarpa between them. A few cottages and a lodge on the w approach driveway.

ST MICHAEL. A C15 church. Good three-stage w tower with battlements, and octagonal N stair-turret, and small corner pinnacles. Somerset tracery in the bell-openings. Of this date too the nave with a consistent set of four three-light windows (two per side) under square heads. The remainder is Perp in character but later in date. The N chapel was built in 1776 by *Robert Goodden*, who was patron and acted as his own architect. He made it Perp in 1821–2 when the s baptistery was added (or converted from a porch). Of this date also the N vestry, looking like a porch. The chancel is of 1876–7. C15 wagon roofs in the nave and baptistery. – PULPIT. A splendid early C17 three-decker. The upper deck hexagonal with arabesque-enriched panels above a lower tier of arches. Similar enrichment to the middle and lower decks. – FONT. C15. Octagonal with quatrefoils, yet dated on the rim 1620 (perhaps a date when it was moved). Splayed pedestal. – STAINED GLASS. In the chancel and the N chapel N window, four by *Kempe & Co.*, 1906–7. – HATCHMENTS. Five to members of the Goodden family; C18 and early C19. – MONUMENTS. The starting point has to be the spectacularly lifelike statue of Robert Goodden, dated 1825 – he died in 1828. It seems to be unsigned but is possibly by *Flaxman* or *John Bacon Jun.* It stands in a niche in the chapel he designed. – Also in the N chapel Robert Goodden †1764, an oval tablet set within a classical surround, and Wyndham Goodden †1839, Grecian, possibly by *W.H. Burke & Co.*, who signed a second Grecian tablet to Ann Goodden †1862. Many other Goodden tablets

---

* *The Western Flying Post or Sherborne and Yeovil Mercury*, 10 October 1808, reports that the White Horse on Osmington Hills was 'lately' cut on land owned by Mr Wood, at the expense of John Rainer, brother of the late Admiral.

in the chapel. – Nave. Mary Goodden (†1812) and her brother (†1813) by *Reeves & Son* of Bath. With a kneeling mourning woman. – Isabella (†1720) and Charles (†1726) Abingdon. With drapery surround and achievement of arms above. Set at an angle behind the chancel arch.

COMPTON HOUSE, immediately SW. Built of Ham Hill rubble and ashlar, by *John Pinch Jun.* of Bath for John Goodden, after 1839. In an exaggerated version of the local Tudor style, making a vigorous show of gables and gabled dormers, two-storey window bays with buttresses and quatrefoil friezes, and tall octagonal finials. Symmetrical on the NE front. An C18 rear wing was retained.

LODGE, ⅛ m. W. Dated 1891, by *E. Hellicar*. In a more subdued Tudor style. Just in front of it a PINNACLE from Clifton Maybank, a house which must anyway have been in Pinch's mind when he designed the new block.

Opposite a WALLED GARDEN. Late C19, with a re-set (and heavily restored) boldly cusped C14 doorway.

DRIVE COTTAGE and GABLE END, just W of the lodge. Pair of estate cottages in a good late C17 style. Dated 1892, no doubt also by *Hellicar*.

ROUND HOUSE, ¼ m. E. Early C19 *cottage orné*. Circular with a conical thatched roof and a lower veranda roof, also thatched, on rustic timber posts. Greatly extended in a matching style but on a rectangular plan, 1985, by *T. A. G. Macbean*.

OWERMOIGNE

Some thatched cottages among former farms, their buildings converted and land around built upon.

ST MICHAEL. Rebuilt in 1883 by *Samuel Jackson* of Weymouth in a finely judged Perp style. Cost £756. The two-stage early C15 W tower was retained. Rounded N stair-turret stopping short of the bell-stage. Three C16 side windows in the chancel were re-set. – Most of the late C19 FURNISHINGS survive, apart from in the chancel. – FONT. C18, columnar. – ROYAL ARMS. Late Hanoverian. – STAINED GLASS. E window by *Heaton, Butler & Bayne*, 1883. Of the same date, W window almost certainly by *Lavers, Barraud & Westlake*.

OLD RECTORY, 200 yds SE. Mainly of 1882 by *G. R. Crickmay*. It incorporates a section of late C16 jettied-out timber framing along the N front. Also the E stone wall against the lane with its small Perp window is probably of this date.

MOIGNES COURT, ¼ m. N. Another rarity, one of far greater significance. Where else would you find a more perfect secular set of E.E. traceried windows? The house was built under a licence granted to William le Moyne by Henry III, dated 25 February 1267. Interestingly, the grant allows the strengthening of the house 'with a good dyke and stone wall, but without making crenellations'.* What one sees today on the W front is the first-floor hall of the C13 house on the l., its former service end at the centre, and a gabled addition of the 1890s to the r. Two chimney-breasts project, that on the l. cut short at the central of the three E.E. windows. This window then was clearly inserted when the chimney was cut down. It is slightly taller than the others and seems likely to have come from the N gable (where there are indications of shiftings of this kind). Other mullioned windows are mainly late C19. The E.E. windows have steep two-centred heads enclosing an encircled quatrefoil of plate tracery over two pointed-trefoiled lancets, every element outlined with delicate mouldings. Inside, the windows have shafts with moulded bell capitals and bases not of the water-holding variety, and there are shutter rebates. One window has an internal hoodmould too. The second chimney-breast, to the r., is broader and suggests that this was the original location for the kitchen. Also signs of opposing doorways, E and W, of a through passage at the S end of the hall. On the E side a blocked upper doorway with more complex mouldings and hoodmould. This is likely to have been the main entrance to the hall, reached by an external staircase. The solar wing has disappeared, but the late C19 NE wing must be on its site.

The DYKE mentioned in the grant survives as a water-filled moat, roughly 170 ft (52 metres) long on each side. The best length is to the S, but sections to the N and W are traceable; a length to the E has recently been restored. Also further E indications of a disappeared VILLAGE and what was probably the platform for a predecessor house.

PAMPHILL

The estate village of Kingston Lacy but without the character of such. A remarkably large number of cob cottages, all thatched.**

ST STEPHEN. 1907 by *Charles E. Ponting.* The estate church for Kingston Lacy (q.v.), built by a bequest from Walter Bankes. Portland limestone speckled with heathstone. Solid square W tower. Bold gable buttressing, that at SW corner with carved figures by *Herbert Read* of St Stephen and the young Ralph Bankes (son of Walter) in a niche. Perp-traceried windows. Arts and Crafts leaf carving to the S porch entrance. Transepts attached to chancel. Richly furnished chancel and FAMILY

---

*The only other recorded example of this restriction is a licence for Haddon Hall (Derbyshire) of *c.* 1194.
** One of these, in Cowgrove, was rebuilt by *St Ann's Gate Architects* for the National Trust in 2012 after a major fire, using straw-bale walling in place of cob.

PEW, W end. – FONT. Alabaster with a square bowl, supported on a central shaft and shield-bearing angels. A fine piece. Elaborate REREDOS, LECTERN, PULPIT and STALLS. – STAINED GLASS. Armorial W window, using re-set C16 glass from the N transept of Wimborne Minster, removed c. 1890. E and S transept windows by *Horace Wilkinson*, 1907–10. These include likenesses of the Bankes children, Ralph, Viola and Daphne – a typical Edwardian conceit.

MONUMENT to Walter Bankes †1904, in the style of a medieval cross, also by *Ponting*.

The walk that begins at Pamphill church is entrancing. The road runs SE, lined with oaks, across a big rough green. Almost entirely hidden on the r., PAMPHILL MANOR, rebuilt around an older core for Matthew Beethall, the former Bankes estate steward, in the late C17. Of great charm. Seven bays in a rhythm two, three close-set, two. Brick, with a big stone-slated and clay-tiled hipped roof. Hipped dormers, and a Dutch-gabled centre. This has a central opening with an eared brick surround and balustraded apron. C18 urn finial. The windows especially typical of the years before 1700, on the first floor keeping their mullion-and-transom crosses. The lower windows with C18 sashes set in blank arcading. Carved acanthus-scrolled keystones. Two rear wings, the NW late C18, the SW early C20.

At the far end of the green, where the ground slopes down (and the vastly over-scaled pylons striding by must, if possible, be ignored), GILLINGHAM'S SCHOOL AND ALMSHOUSES (now Pamphill First School), built in 1698. This too is a composition of delightful insouciance. For the young, the upstanding centre – the 'free Writing School' – of dark red brick, with two big windows l. and r. of the doorway. Broken segmental pediment. A stone tablet above states that this was the gift of Roger Gillingham of the Middle Temple. Roundel in the pedimental gable. For the old, the almshouses extending long and low each side. Brighter brick. Eight doors. Two-light windows, too low to sport a transom.

ST MARGARET AND ST ANTHONY, 1 m. ESE. The chapel of a former leper hospital and still the chapel of adjoining almshouses. Heathstone rubble with ashlar dressings. Nave and chancel in one, early C13. Flat NE buttress and S window of two pointed-trefoiled lights; two-light C15 N window. Otherwise heavily restored. Several single-storey ALMSHOUSES nearby, one attached to the chapel, dating from no earlier than the C16.

CEMETERY CHAPELS (Anglican and Congregational), Cemetery Road, 175 yds NE of the Chapel of St Margaret and St Anthony. A pair, 1855–6. By *R. H. Shout* of Yeovil. Rock-faced limestone. Gothic, mirror-imaged, each with a spired bellcote on the buttressed outer end gable. S porch; short chancel at the inner end. – LODGE, dated 1856 over the adjoining pointed carriage arch.

LODGE FARM, 1¼ m. NW. A rare survival, carefully restored in the 1980s. The late C15 hunting lodge associated with the medieval manor of Kingston Lacy. A simple rectangular building of dressed heathstone with Chilmark dressings. Its first-floor hall is indicated externally by a set of windows of the standard Perp type with cusped arched lights, two two-light with a quatrefoil above, one single-light. The ground-floor casements are later insertions. Although altered, the four-centred-arched central doorway is thought to be original, leading to a cross-passage. To its l., within, a recess in the front wall contained a spiral staircase that gave access to the hall. A solar occupied the northern third of the upper floor. Arched wind-bracing survives in most bays. The central truss to the hall has moulded arched bracing. The present C17 rear outshut replaced a garderobe.

HIGH HALL, 1½ m. NE. A hipped-roofed box, a Kingston Lacy in little, typical of c. 1670. Five bays, two storeys on a high basement, dormers in the roof, and a pair of stout chimneystacks, with recessed faces. Built originally of brick, even the raised angle quoins, but later rendered. The pedimented stone doorcase however has a classical purity which makes one recall more seriously Pratt's work at Kingston Lacy, two miles away. High Hall was built for Samuel Gilly, brother-in-law of Sir Ralph Bankes, Pratt's patron, most likely by the same contractor, *Sir Thomas Fitch*, or perhaps by his brother *John Fitch* (who bought High Hall in 1691). S windows grouped 1:3:1, and altered c. 1750 (when it was rendered), making the lower ones round-headed; N windows evenly spaced. Lower additions, that to the W by *Crickmay & Son*, designed in 1885, with a bowed end. The two-storey pavilion block to the E is a scholarly piece of keeping-in-keeping by *Gotch & Saunders*, 1909–10. Early C18 dining room with two heights of bolection-moulded panelling. Also a chimneypiece with a pulvinated frieze. Later staircase by the *Bastards* – see the under-curling handrail terminal. Other interiors Adamesque, by *Waring & Gillow*, contemporary with the Crickmay work.

Handsome red brick STABLES to the E, with a pedimented central projection and clock turret. (A date of 1751, scratched in the plaster inside, has been recorded.) Behind this is a tall WATER TOWER of c. 1910.

LODGE, ½ m. E of High Hall, on the B3078 (in Colehill parish). Early C19 brick *cottage orné*. Three gables with decorative bargeboards. Gothicized windows.

STONE PARK, ¾ m. ESE. A compact yet imposing Regency house, 1809, for George Garland. White stucco and low-pitched hipped slate roofs. Three-storey centre, two-storey bow-fronted wings.

ROMAN ROADS. N of Badbury Rings (*see* Shapwick) is the junction of the Roman roads from London to Exeter and from Hamworthy through Lake Gates Farm, to Bath.

ROMAN ROAD, NW of the Roman fortress (*see* Corfe Mullen).
The agger or road embankment stretches for some 650 ft (200
metres) by a backwater of the River Stour, across Eye Mead.

PARNHAM HOUSE *see* BEAMINSTER

PENTRIDGE

One village street with thatched cob cottages and farmsteads.
Some C19 brick Shaftesbury estate cottages.

ST RUMBOLD. Rebuilt 1855–7 by *William Slater* in Dec style.*
This was one of Slater's earliest churches after the death of
his master, R. C. Carpenter. Flint and stone blocks. Short W
tower with angle buttresses and low broach spire. Timber-
framed S porch. Fine Geometrical tracery to the three-light E
window. – Simple original FURNISHINGS including an octagonal stone FONT. – STAINED GLASS. E window, 1865 by *Clayton
& Bell*. Two others by the same, 1877.

SCHOOL (former), 100 yds N. Of *c.* 1850, given by the Countess
of Shaftesbury. Brick with broad pointed windows. A smaller
version of a standard design (cf. Hinton Martell).

BOKERLEY DYKE is a defensive earthwork running 4 m. across
the downs, along the county boundary. It may originally have
had thick scrub at each end. In its final form it was a post-
Roman frontier work, protecting the Dorset side from Saxon
settlement expansion. It was, however, developed on the line
of a prehistoric boundary, established since the Middle Bronze
Age, which formed the W limit of the Wessex linear ditch
system. The Roman road (Ackling Dyke) very probably passed
through an existing break in the dyke. An Iron Age settlement next to this crossing (which is known as 'Bokerly Junction') expanded in the Roman period and extended SE of the
crossing by the C4. In the late Roman period a 'Rear Dyke',
slightly to the W, blocked the road, but it was later reinstated.
Massive heightening of the dyke on Blagdon Hill may also have
occurred at this time. A further 'Fore Dyke', E of the main
line and N of the 'Junction', is very possibly post-Roman, and
intended to defend against Saxon intruders from the E. The
dyke was subsequently slighted.

DORSET CURSUS. *See* Gussage St Michael.

LONG BARROWS, ¾ m. NE. All aligned SE–NW, towards the NE
terminal of the Dorset Cursus. A pair on Bokerly Down is
sited similarly to the pair at the SW terminal (*see* Gussage St
Michael).

PENBURY KNOLL, ⅔ m. SE. Iron Age HILL-FORT, univallate,
damaged by gravel digging, with 'Celtic' fields on the NW side
of the hill.

---

* *The Ecclesiologist* 16, 1855.

PIDDLEHINTON

Long and quite strung out on the E bank of the River Piddle; many cottages of cob or banded flint with thatched roofs.

ST MARY. An all-Perp church, the S tower and aisle of the later C15, the chancel and N aisle early C16. In 1867–8 *Ewan Christian* carried out a major restoration, rebuilding the N aisle and extending the church by a bay to the W. Bold three-stage S tower with higher stair-turret and crocketed pinnacles in each corner. Chancel of brown and white stone; some banded flint elsewhere, especially on Christian's rebuilt N aisle and W end. Arcade piers and responds of the common standard. The chancel vault is of plaster and looks *c.* 1800. Its walls however have had their plaster stripped. SEDILIA of the late C15, re-set. Two seats with arm-rests and a hood like a set-tle's. The coarse back-panelling runs into the underside of the hood. – The chancel FURNISHING is of 1930 by *Newborn & Smith.* – Complete nave and aisle PEWS by *Christian.* – FONT. Octagonal, Perp style, by *Christian.* – STAINED GLASS. E window by *E.R. Suffling,* 1902. Another in the chancel by *Horace Wilkinson,* 1915. – BRASSES. A good collection in the chancel, all re-set. – Part of a brass figure, 12½ in. (32 cm.) long. – Thomas Browne †1617, parson. A plaque with a Latin verse and a small effigy with beard and hat. – MONUMENTS. John Clavering †1644. Painted wooden panel with crude pediment and shield of arms. – Jane Iles †1828 and other family. Reeded pilasters and top urn. By *Gray* of Weymouth. – Several other tablets, e.g. Henry Allen, early C18, and Mary Kellaway †1712.

SCHOOL (now VILLAGE HALL) and SCHOOL HOUSE. On the village crossroads. 1852 by *John Hicks.* Flint banded with brick. Gothic window in the end gable.

GLEBE COURT, 100 yds WSW. Built as the rectory on the substantial scale so favoured by Dorset incumbents, and dated PM 1753 (for the Rev. Phillip Montague) on the S doorway. This has a moulded surround flaring out at the bottom, and goes with a five-bay two-storey façade, the walls of banded flint and stone. C19 two-storey canted bay window to the l. In the N front, brick replaces stone in the banding, three bays occupy the width of five, the sashes segment-headed. Central round-headed stone doorcase with a Gibbs surround. This parallel range is an addition, probably of *c.* 1770. The way that the side elevations manage the chimney is typically Early Georgian, linking parapets disguising the various roof pitches.

MUSTON MANOR, ⅞ m. SE. Quite modest, of *c.* 1670 for William Churchill. Of brick, which makes it worthy of note. The bonding is of one row of headers to two of stretchers (as e.g. at Anderson Manor). The front was heightened in the late C19, but the two-storey porch, with round-headed but Perp-moulded arch, and the four-light mullioned windows of the lower storey are original. In the hall a CEILING PAINTING, brought from Colliton House, Dorchester, and said to be by *Thornhill*. Also a fireplace brought from Waterston Manor, *c.* 1965.

WHITE'S DAIRY HOUSE, in a good farm group by the roadside at the N end of the village, is dated 1622 on a stone just below the eaves of the N part. Banded flint and stone; thatched roof. A piece of re-set Perp tracery in the wall of the later S part. To its S a substantial brick and thatched C18 BARN, with triangular vents.

'CELTIC' FIELDS at Druce Hangings, Bourne Hill and Dole's Hill in the E of the parish (*see also* Puddletown).

PIDDLETRENTHIDE

The village is strung out along the upper Piddle valley, historically subdivided into three tithings. In the Upper Tithing, the church; the Middle has the manor house and its parkland; in the Lower is the hamlet of White Lackington. Many flint and brick cottages with thatched roofs, a few with cob walls.

ALL SAINTS. The core of the building is C12. That is proved by the S doorway and the S respond of the chancel arch. The doorway has a order of chevron at the jambs, parallel with one order of colonnettes. Its arch (no tympanum) is segmental and has two orders of chevron, the inner at right angles to the wall surface. The chancel arch has a respond of a half-round and two smaller three-quarter shafts. Scalloped capitals with small-scale chevron ornament above. The rest of the church is Perp, of three closely dated phases. Of the first half of the C15 are the chancel, vestry and S porch. This is rougher work compared with what followed. Next came the W tower (dated 1487, *see* below) and the aisles, *c.* 1500, all now in ashlar. So the C15 was taken up with a more or less continuous building programme. Otherwise there is a heightening of the walls by *John Hicks* in 1852–3 as part of a major restoration for his brother, the Rev. James Hicks. The stately three-stage W tower has two two-light bell-openings with a transom, prominent gargoyles and a liberal supply of pinnacles: three each at three corners, more on the higher octagonal stair-turret, and four intermediate ones. The W doorway has leaf spandrels, and above, between the buttresses, runs a Latin inscription dating the tower to 1487. The W window is of five lights (but with mid-C19 mullions and tracery). The tower is embattled, as are the aisles, which have three-light windows and one of four lights. They are also boldly buttressed. Within, the arcade piers have standard elements. N chapel of two bays with octagonal piers and simple details, an oddity being the way in which the W pier is set back N of the chancel arch N respond. – HATCHMENTS. Three lozenge panels, the earliest of Newman, C18. Two others to members of the Bridge family, both C19. – STAINED GLASS. One of the first things one notices is the number of large Victorian stained-glass windows in the church. These all post-date Hicks's restoration. The tone is set by *W. Wailes* of Newcastle, *c.* 1854. His are the chancel E and one S window; also two later windows in the S aisle (†1862 and †1863). A chancel S window by *Lavers, Barraud & Westlake* (†1885) and another probably by the same firm at the E end of the S aisle. Two war memorial windows by *Clayton & Bell*, 1915 and 1918, one in each of the aisles.

MONUMENTS. An exceptional number of tablets, the most interesting being that in the chancel to John Bridge †1834. It was designed by *C. R. Cockerell* and carved by *W. G. Nicholl*, and it looks as if it might be of 1884. White marble with a portrait medallion in profile and two allegorical statuettes l. and r. The detail is Gothic, handled remarkably freely – see e.g. the segmental arch. (It was originally on the S side, but was moved to the N in 1880 during a restoration.) – A particularly fine group in the N aisle includes Robert Albion Cox †1790 by *Ford* of Bath, with a mourning woman and an urn on the ground; Louisa Bridge †1841, by *Nicholl*, a praying woman in a heavy cloak; William Cox †1802 by *P. Chenu* of London, with a draped urn; Robert Bridge †1836 by *Nicholl*, with an angel by a mourning woman; Robert Bridge †1858 by *J. S. Farley*, with his shield of arms against military banners and a sword; Thomas and Mary Bridge †1792 by *W. Theed*, 1816, a double portrait medallion with above, in an oval-topped alcove, a reclining woman in Grecian dress; and, behind the organ, William Cox †1799, a woman in mourning beside an urn. – Elsewhere cartouches to William Collier †1708 and William Constantine †1723; and Thomas Bridge †1826 by *F. A. Legé*, a Grecian sarcophagus with a weeping child above.

ST JOHN'S BAPTIST CHAPEL (former), 1¾ m. S, at White Lackington. Dated 1876. Stucco with Y-traceried windows.

WESLEYAN METHODIST CHAPEL (former), 1 m. S. 1894. Flint; vaguely Gothic.

SCHOOL (former), ½ m. S. 1848, with alterations of 1999. Brick and flint. Gothick. The gift of John Bridge of Rundell & Bridge (and of the Manor House here), of the Royal Goldsmiths to George III.

PIDDLE VALLEY FIRST SCHOOL, ⅛ m. S of the above. By *Madin Partnership*, 1997–9. Long and low with walls of banded brick and flint in the local manner. It has at its entrance the GATES moved from the previous school. They came from Bridge's collection of antiquities and were originally from Peterborough Cathedral, being re-set in Westminster Abbey *c.* 1605. Early C16, matching the railings of the monument to Lady Margaret Beaufort in the Abbey. Spearheaded railings, and finials of two openwork stages. Bridge acquired them when they were turned out of the Abbey in 1826.

MANOR HOUSE, ½ m. S. Of *c.* 1780 for Robert Albion Cox. A square block, E-facing, originally of two storeys over a basement. Five-window front façade, the upper storey with a

Venetian window with squashed arch. Two tripartite windows on each side above mullioned windows, probably re-set from the earlier house. Upper floor and blocky central porch added in 1832.

The house with its twin-entranced forecourt is on the w side of the road. The PARKLAND is to the E, climbing a sinuous valley to Plush. GAZEBO on the N side of this valley, some 200 yds NE of the house. Early C19, octagonal. Stucco. (Six plaster casts of bas reliefs by *John Flaxman* inside.)

(DOLES ASH FARM, 1¼ m. E. Largely early C19, but incorporating on the NE front a C17 basement. Flint banded with brick on this side; more formal SW façade of stucco. Re-set wooden chimneypiece of the early C17, quite elaborate. Caryatid pilasters in the form of bearded figures holding serpents, with between them a pilaster representing a dancing woman in a short skirt.)

On WELL BOTTOM DOWN, 1½ m. SW, is part of a 'CELTIC' FIELD SYSTEM traceable over 800 acres into Charminster, Piddlehinton and Nether Cerne. There are more on WEST HILL, Plush (where there is also a prehistoric or Romano-British settlement), and on HOG LEAZE and WHITCOMBE HILL, 2 m. ESE (*see* Puddletown).

CROSS-DYKES. A concentration in the far W of the parish, SW of Nettlecombe Tout, above Lyscombe Bottom (*see* Cheselbourne).

4090

PILSDON

ST MARY. Late C14 Perp, with drastic restorations of 1830 and 1875. The five-light E window is Perp, as are some corbels inside. W bell-turret with spire of 1875. Big stepped buttresses at the E end and midway on the sides. The straight-shank porch arch looks C16. – STAINED GLASS. E window by *Percy Bacon Bros*, 1924.*

PILSDON MANOR. An unusually fine C17 manor-house façade, this S range being all that survives of the quadrangular house of *c.* 1630 for Sir Hugh Wyndham. The comparison to make is with Wyke, Bradford Abbas, dated 1650. No gables to the S front, but end gables W and E. Large mullioned windows with a transom. Symmetrical arrangement of the windows, but not of the doorway, the pattern somewhat arbitrary: six four-lighters in pairs below, and six three-lighters in pairs ranged above them, leaving space for two small intermediate windows of two lights. Hollow-chamfer moulding throughout. The string course between the storeys retains a memory of the outmoded

---

* Pevsner wrote: 'Who would believe that the glass in the E window could commemorate a death in 1918 – twenty-two years after the death of William Morris? The artist was even so ill advised as to sign: *Percy Bacon*, London.'

hoodmould, in its turned-down ends like an all-embracing hoodmould.

PILSDON PEN, 1 m. N. Iron Age HILL-FORT, bivallate, enclosing 7¾ acres. Original entrances to the NE, SW and halfway down the SW side. At the N the inner rampart covers earlier defences and an entrance. Fourteen round-houses have been excavated, below a square ENCLOSURE made for a post-medieval rabbit warren. To the S are five ROUND BARROWS.

PIMPERNE

A former farming village, once on the Bryanston estate, hence the many estate cottages and farmyards. The latter are now mostly converted to dwellings.

ST PETER. A large church, built at the expense of Viscount Portman of Bryanston. Only the mid-C15 three-stage W tower (except the crowning feature) is genuinely Perp. The architect of the church, which dates from 1873–4, was *J.B. Green* (carving by *Boulton*). Goodhart-Rendel wrote: 'A remarkable church, though an ugly one. Arcades of obtuse two-centred arches, the mouldings dying into octagonal continuations of the piers, above coarse flower capitals....Windows with very strange tracery...divided into many small lights with odd transoms here and there....The woodwork is horrible but shows the same idiosyncrasy as the stone work....But oddly enough its particular freakishnesses are in advance of their time – the sort of thing that was generally done in the nineties.' The church incorporates two Late Norman piers, the S doorway, and the former chancel arch, now leading into a N chapel. They have chevron, also at right angles to the wall surface, meeting the normal chevron to shape folded lozenges. Fine fancy capitals with small volutes. – Stone REREDOS together with the sanctuary walling and PULPIT, designed by *W. Tranah* of Blandford (who took over after Green died). – FONT. C12, of cauldron shape, with large leaves in chains of large scrolls. Delightful stone COVER of pierced tracery, called 'modern' in 1861, but a genuine medieval piece, probably C14.* – STAINED GLASS. E window and a N aisle window, both of 1874, in all likelihood by *Burlison & Grylls*. – BRASS. In the vestry, Dorothy Williams †1694. Signed by *Edmund Colepeper*, a rarity on a brass. Skeleton recumbent on a half-rolled-up mat and small kneeling figure. Scroll with 'Death where is thy sting' etc. *p. 450*

LYCHGATE by *J. Hatchard-Smith & Son*, 1946. Timber-framed on brick and flint side walls.

---

* It was reportedly found close to the church in the early C19.

Pimperne, St Peter.
Brass to Dorothy Williams †1694

The stepped base of the late medieval VILLAGE CROSS remains, and the stump of its octagonal shaft: more than one generally finds.

THE OLD RECTORY. Flint and brick, hipped-roofed house, dated 1712, but surely thoroughly remodelled in 1862–3. The interesting parts however are the carved stone fragments set into the middle of the façade. The doorhead, with a straight hood on lozenge-shaped labels, has the remains of a black-letter inscription, which in Hutchins's day included the date 1530 and the name of Thomas Wever, then rector of Pimperne and Tarrant Hinton. Above is a niche with the arms of Henry VIII on the base, and an Early Perp window, three ogee-headed lights, under a wide two-centred traceried arch, all set in a rectangular surround. A high cob wall hides the house from the village street.

LETTON HOUSE, 1 m. S. 1855, for Edward Castleman of Chettle. Vaguely Italianate villa. Curiously miniature parkland (now redeveloped with housing).

LONG BARROW, 1 m. NE. Neolithic. 330 ft (100 metres) long, 140 ft (43 metres) wide, and 9 ft (2.8 metres) high, aligned SE–NW. The side ditches do not run round the ends and are separated from the mound by broad berms.

Pimperne Down, 1 m. w. Iron Age univallate ENCLOSURE
of 11 acres, C5 B.C. Excavations (1959–63) uncovered a large
round-house, some 52 ft (16 metres) in diameter, the record
of which was used in experimental reconstruction of the 'Pimperne type' house.

PLUSH   7000
1¼ m. NE of Piddletrenthide

A hamlet of cob and thatch cottages in the upper part of one
of the most delectable and unfrequented valleys in Dorset. This
valley climbs from the Manor House in Piddletrenthide.

St John the Baptist (now privately owned). 1848 by *Ferrey*,
  but not in the new archaeologically faithful idiom of his friend
  Pugin. Nave and chancel, the chancel still short, the nave
  impressively buttressed but un-aisled within. Windows Perp,
  not Second Pointed. Hammerbeam roof in the nave. Substantial w bellcote. – STAINED GLASS. E window by *Wailes*, 1848.
  w window by the same firm a year or two later.
Manor House, just w. At its centre a stuccoed Regency house,
  three bays wide but deeper in plan. This of 1785. Two balancing wings with canted bays added in a matching style, c. 1950
  and c. 1970.
Little Platt, at the s end is of white brick, sensitively handled
  for its date. By *Colin Metters*, of *Roydon Cooper Associates* of
  Yeovil, 1969.

POOLE   0090

The earliest reference to the existence of Poole is in a document
of c. 1180. By 1224 the settlement had developed sufficiently to
become a major southern port. It soon took over this role from
Wareham because the River Frome and the upper reaches of
Poole Harbour became increasingly prone to silting. Poole grew
quickly, and by 1248, when the town was granted a degree of
independence from the lord of Canford, Sir William de Long-
espée, it had become urban in character, although confined to
the sw tip of its peninsula. Naturally sluiced by the tides, the
quay at Poole grew in use and by the C14 trade had outstripped
any Dorset rivals, the town becoming the largest port between
Southampton and Cornwall. In 1433 Poole became a staple port,
and shortly afterwards the town was granted a licence 'to wall,
embattle and fortify' itself.
    When Leland visited c. 1540 he reported that Poole was 'much
encreasid with fair building and use of marchaundise'. By this

date the town walls were complete; entry to the town across a dyke on its landward side required passage through 'an embatelid gate of stone'. Leland also noted 'a fair toun house of stone by the kay', which may be a reference to Scaplen's Court (*see* p. 456). Poole gained further status in 1568 when it was made a county corporate by Elizabeth I.

The great age of prosperity for the town followed international recognition of Newfoundland as a British territory in 1713, after which Poole merchants invested heavily in the Newfoundland trade. This consisted principally in the development of cod fisheries on that island and the import of dried and salted fish to Europe. Daniel Defoe, writing after his visit in 1723, called Poole 'the most considerable sea-port in all this part of England'. The wealth this brought was expressed in fine civic buildings such as the Guildhall, and the many grand merchants' houses. Business declined sharply after 1812, when Britain lost her monopoly over the Newfoundland fisheries. With the arrival of the Southampton & Dorchester Railway at Hamworthy in 1847, reached from Poole by a bridge across the harbour erected in 1834, coastal shipping also declined.* Other industries that developed in the town and its surroundings, especially brick- and tile-making and potteries, compensated to a limited degree for the loss of shipping and trade.

During the 1840s and 1850s Parkstone and then Bournemouth, across the county boundary in Hampshire, became fashionable resorts. The latter grew so that by the turn of the C20 it had three times the population of Poole and had become a county borough in its own right.** (Meanwhile, as if to symbolize its further decline, Poole lost its equivalent status in 1888.) Throughout the C20 the suburbs of Poole continued to expand, so much so that when a new Civic Centre was built between 1931 and 1940 it was located about halfway between the old town and Parkstone.

In the old town itself, post-war development was unusually destructive to historic road alignments and buildings, despite the designation of a 'special precinct' in 1963 and a conservation area in 1974. To a great degree development was driven by the common challenges for towns at the time: road improvements, the provision of car parking (two multi-storey car parks are particularly insensitive) and the need to meet housing shortages, including slum clearance in several areas. Improved road access to Poole Bridge was also required as part of the revival of shipping. By 1972, following the RCHME's recording of buildings from before 1850, fifteen out of forty-six pre-1714 buildings had gone, while 150 of the 329 post-1714 structures were demolished. In addition, the centre of focus of the town was drawn N in 1969 when the Arndale Centre was opened, followed by Barclays House in 1975 and a major arts centre in 1978. With the advent of comprehensive listing in the early 1980s, the pace

*The London & South Western Railway arrived at the centre of Poole only in 1872.
**Population figures for Poole: 1866, 10,021; 1901, 19,463; 1931, 60,196; 2001, 138,288.

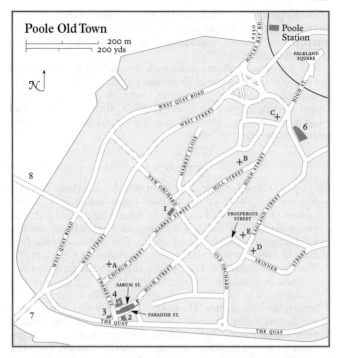

Poole Old Town

200 m
200 yds

A	St James	1	Guildhall
B	Baptist church	2	Custom House
C	Wesleyan Methodist church	3	Harbour Office (former)
D	United Reformed church	4	Scaplen's Court Museum
E	Friends' Meeting House (former)	5	Poole Museum
		6	Free Library and School of Art (former)
		7	Poole Bridge
		8	Twin Sails Bridge

of destruction slowed, and further conservation areas in the old town were designated in 1981 and 1986. Positive contributions since then have included housing schemes sensitive to the special character of Poole in Thames and Market streets, and repairs to the Town Cellars and Scaplen's Court.

Re-established as a unitary authority in 1997, Poole has regained much of its independence. By 2000 the port was considered the second busiest in the South-West after Avonmouth. Nevertheless, at the time of writing, substantial dangers to the historic townscape remain. A vacant site at the W end of The Quay, near Poole Bridge, has only just avoided a scheme as visually damaging as that at the E end, completed in 2004. On a positive note, expressive modern buildings at the RNLI College illustrate that, on appropriate sites, Poole is able to accommodate the architecturally bold and contemporary. Also, the spread

of development over Canford Heath, seemingly unstoppable in
1972, has slowed, thanks to the protection of large areas under
international nature conservation legislation and the designation
of planning green belt.

The following account deals with the old town, followed by
the suburbs of Branksome; Branksome Park; Canford Cliffs and
Sandbanks; Longfleet; Parkstone, Salterns and Lilliput; and
Upper Parkstone, Newtown and Oakdale. Broadstone, Canford
Magna, Hamworthy, Merly House and Upton House have their
own separate gazetteer entries.

CHURCHES

St James, Church Street. The right size for the Poole of today
and for the Poole of the Middle Ages. But it is a church
neither of today nor of the Middle Ages. The medieval church
was pulled down in 1819 and replaced in 1819–21 by this
solid, capacious, ashlar-faced edifice. The architects were *John
Kent* of Southampton and *Joseph Hannaford* of Christchurch.
The first estimate was for £5,600, although the final cost was
£11,740. Restored and refurnished 1892, by *W.J. Fletcher*. The
church has a w tower and nave and aisles. The tower entrance
betrays the date at once. Those high, relatively narrow doorways
are unmistakable. Equally unmistakable are the windows of
three stepped lancet lights or with Y-tracery and their arrangement in two tiers. That represents galleries inside, and they
are indeed still there. The arcades have giant quatrefoil piers
made up of whole trees or maybe masts, apparently brought
here from Newfoundland. Nave and aisles are all rib-vaulted in
plaster. – REREDOS. A fine piece of 1736, retained from the previous church, given originally by Richard Pinnell. Pedimented
centre. Corinthian pilasters. Panels containing the Commandments, Creed and Lord's Prayer. – The N aisle REREDOS
includes Early Renaissance panels. – CHOIR STALLS, with
canopies. From Canford church (possibly by *Blore*), installed
here by *Ponting & Crickmay*, 1914. – PULPIT. Oak, Jacobethan.
By *Fletcher*, 1892. – FONT. Of *c.* 1820. Mahogany, with dainty
decoration partly classical, partly Gothick. – ROYAL ARMS of
1821 on the w gallery. – Large set of BENEFACTORS' BOARDS
on the E wall of the inner vestibule. The earliest date is 1612.
Presumably entirely *c.* 1820, with later additions.

  STAINED GLASS. E window, 1897 by *Cakebread Robey & Co.*
Four in the lower s windows, from l. to r.: *Goddard & Gibbs*
(designed by *A.E. Buss*), 1957; *Heaton, Butler & Bayne*, 1912
(adapted when transferred from St Paul, Poole, 1958); *Gordon
Webster*, 1960; and *Jon Callan*, 1999. – MONUMENTS. Many
of high quality. The most noteworthy are: N aisle, William
Spurrier †1809 by *J.S. Hiscock* of Blandford. Standing woman
by an urn. s aisle, Alderman Francis Lister †1738 and others to
1780 by *Robert & Benjamin Shout*. Seated woman in relief near
the top of an obelisk. – Galleries: Thomas Gregory Hancock
†1848 by *J. Chapman* of Frome. – Large standing woman.

– Thomas Parr, Deputy Provincial Grand Master †1824. An odd shape, a kind of ogee-sided obelisk. An angel on clouds and below Masonic tools and emblems. – James Seager †1808, by *William Whitelaw* of London. Also with a standing woman. – George Lewen †1718. A boldly modelled cartouche. – Mary Slade †1816 by *Hiscock*. Sarcophagus-shaped.

BAPTIST CHURCH, Hill Street. 1815. Red brick, the front rebuilt 1886. Pediment with matching porch below. Terracotta enrichments.

WESLEYAN METHODIST CHURCH, High Street and Chapel Lane. 1880 by *Charles Bell*. Rock-faced masonry. A pair of large Gothic windows under a single (liturgical) W gable, flanked by hipped-roofed staircases. Buttresses, turrets and an octagonal NW tower crowned by a spire. A predecessor of 1843, behind, has been replaced by a bland grey box extension by the *Intelligent Design Centre*, 2016.

UNITED REFORMED CHURCH (formerly Congregational), Skinner Street. A fine church of 1777. The cost was £1,400. It has a front five bays wide and not high but with a very stretched shaped gable across. The windows have Y-tracery. A cartouche carries its date. The elegant porch (with Tuscan columns) is an addition of 1833. Fine galleried interior with elliptical arches on slender columns, somewhat similar to St James's; altered *c.* 1823. Further furnishing changes in 1880.

FRIENDS' MEETING HOUSE (former), Prosperous Street. 1795–6 by *M. Searle*, enlarged in 1820, and now part of the POOLE OLD TOWN COMMUNITY CENTRE. Three round-arched windows on the NW wall survive. Disgracefully disfigured by additions.

PUBLIC BUILDINGS

GUILDHALL, Market Street. Built in 1761, the gift of John Gulston and Col. Thomas Calcraft, the town's M.P.s (see the inscription in the E wall). Seven bays by three, only the SW end pedimented. The arcaded ground floor was never open fully and is now glazed. Brick with alternating stone quoins, keystones, and impost and platbands. Central domed lantern. Typically functional, as befitted a trading town, mainly memorable for the charming way in which the entrance to the Council Chamber is managed: at the S short end two semicircular flights of steps swing up to a big Tuscan porch set on rusticated walling. Large clock face in the main pediment. The former COUNCIL CHAMBER occupies most of upper floor. Pedimented Doric doorcase at the SW end; platform entered, somewhat comically, through a central pedimented doorcase at the NE.

CUSTOM MOUSE, The Quay. Rebuilt in 1813, supposedly as a replica of a predecessor of *c.* 1788. Brick, three-storey, and wedge-shaped in plan. Central pedimented projection at the entrance front, W; *piano nobile* a full storey above street level, entered up a pair of curved stone steps similar to those on the

Poole, Custom House and Harbour Office.
Drawing, *c.* 1822

Guildhall. Flat-headed Tuscan porch. Round-arched basement windows.

Standing in its forecourt, the much-restored medieval TOWN BEAM, or wool scales.*

HARBOUR OFFICE (former), now H.M. COASTGUARD, The Quay, just W of the Custom House. 1822, stucco. Four-bay Tuscan colonnade carrying the upper storey. Central sundial dated 1814. On the E side, high up, re-set relief signed by *J. Awbrey* of a half-length gentleman in full-bottomed wig and a chain of office, a portrait of the mayor of 1727. Both sundial and relief were salvaged from earlier buildings.

SCAPLEN'S COURT MUSEUM, Sarum Street. Built *c.* 1500 as a wealthy merchant's house, when the quayside was much nearer. Originally L-plan with a parlour wing leading back from the l. end of the street-facing hall range. Soon a kitchen building was added at the rear of the courtyard; in the later C16 a narrower fourth range completed the quadrangle. Extensively adapted thereafter, including an C18 brick refronting. Heavily restored in 1928–30 for *H.P. Smith*, the local archaeologist, and the Society of Poole Men (when many historic features were imported from elsewhere and others removed); between 1950 and 1959 (with major reconstruction of the rear block); and most recently in 1986 by *Poole Borough Architects' Department* (*Michael Gooding*, project architect) with *Graham Smith*, the Curator of Museums. In use as a museum but with its structure clearly displayed.

*Last restoration in 1947.

Purbeck rubble-stone. Facing the street a large two-storey, lead-clad hall bay window and two restored four-centred-arched doorways in partially rebuilt walling, products of the 1986 restoration. Prior to this the front range was roofless (although stabilized), with much of the front wall missing. The stumps of a suggested projecting porch may be bogus. Entry here is straight off the street into a passage. To the l. the main ground-floor room, a ground-floor hall, lit principally by the large bay window. Both imposts of the hall doorway are heavily restored although one has an original trefoiled head to the panelled reveals. These have a double-wave inner moulding. To the r. of the passage a store with separate access from the street, lit by a small, single-light window. At the far end of the hall a restored cross-wall closes off another small room lit in its far wall. Also from the hall a four-centred-arched doorway, with the standard moulding of wave and hollow, leading to a parlour. This has an intersecting beamed ceiling and a muti-lated fireplace opening with a narrow relief border of flowers. On the first floor a similar arrangement of major rooms. A courtyard staircase and gallery, which presumably originally gave access to the upper rooms, have been reconstructed. This allows one to pass through the surviving upper doorway into a large front chamber, with a smaller chamber at right angles over the parlour, where the roof timbers, moulded arch braces, and wind-braces decoratively strutted in four levels, show that this was an important room. Above a restored doorway leading into the parlour from the courtyard is a carved shield of arms of Poole with an inscribed date, WP 1554. This was found in the garden of Sir Peter Thompson's House (*see* p. 461) and installed here in 1931.*

POOLE MUSEUM, High Street. Formerly an early to mid-C19 warehouse and subscription library of 1830 (the latter demol-ished when offices for the Poole Harbour Commissioners were built in the mid 1960s). Front facing up the High Street rebuilt, 2007, by *Horden Cherry Lee Architects*. Glazed gable with a forebuilding in steel expressing the gable shape.

FREE LIBRARY and SCHOOL OF ART (former; now The Lord Wimborne pub), Lagland Street. 1887 by *Lawson & Donkin*. It cost £2,500. Victorian Baroque in brick, stone and terracotta. Elaborate entrance with an oriel breaking through above a scrolled pedimented arch.

POOLE BRIDGE, Bridge Approach. 1927. Reinforced concrete and iron. Two raising spans. The third successive bridge in this location.

TWIN SAILS BRIDGE, Poole Harbour, 2012 by *Gifford & Part-ners* with *Wilkinson Eyre Architects*, after a design competi-tion. The 20-metre-wide central span has elongated triangular lifting arms. When raised these resemble ships' sails.

* Report by Keystone Historic Buildings Consultants, 1996.

PERAMBULATIONS

1. From the Quay to the Guildhall and Sir Peter Thompson's House

We start at the historic and symbolic heart of Poole, where one
can appreciate the great landlocked harbour, with the Purbeck
hills beyond and in the middle distance Brownsea Island, that
surprising, wooded punctuation mark. A most memorable
grouping of the Custom House, the former Harbour Office
(*see* Public Buildings, above) and TOWN CELLARS, now the
Local History Centre. A storage building, resembling a tithe
barn (historically known as 'The Wool House' or King's
Hall'). Of *c.* 1300, the front rebuilt and roof replaced, CI5.
Of stone and partly buttressed, originally 120 ft (37 metres)
long. A vivid indicator that trading flourished enough in the
CI5 to make this extremely substantial warehouse necessary.
The building was divided into two *c.* 1798 when Thames
Street was driven through. One can see only the six-bay E
part, and the matching pair of brick gable-ends across the
street, where the cut was bound up. The original centre is
marked by the big arched opening in the W bay. Two other
doorways on the S side, one square-headed (altered from a
window), another with a two-centred arch. Small square-
headed windows front and back, one remaining entire in the
S wall, with two cinquefoiled lights. Corbelling for a possible
turret at the E end of the front wall. Collar-beam roof with
arched wind-braces. Floor inserted as part of conversion to
a local history centre in 1976.

On THE QUAY itself, Poole's maritime heritage is celebrated
by Sea Music, 1991 by *Sir Anthony Caro*. A large steel SCULP-
TURE incorporating viewing platforms. The W end of the Quay
frontage is very effectively terminated by the BARBERS WHARF
development of houses and flats, 1991, by *MWT Architects*. A
vernacular-inspired combination of warehouse-like blocks in
brick. The vacant site immediately to its E begs for something of a similar quality. Returning E along The Quay, we
pass the mixture of four- or five-storey CI9 warehouses (now
mostly flats) and two-storey houses and taverns that make up
the waterfront character of Poole. Some sensitive warehouse-
style infill, such as Nos. 15–19 of 2002. The POOLE ARMS,
early CI7 in origin, is remarkable for its late CI9 green-glazed-
tile gable front. Then more warehouse-scaled buildings, two-
storey shops and public houses. Next E a shock: the DOLPHIN
QUAYS mixed-use development of 2004 by *SMC Charter
Architects* of Bournemouth, on the former Poole Pottery site.
Its seven storeys dwarf the historic frontage, and the glazed,
prow-ended glitz is entirely out of keeping.

Returning once again W along The Quay and entering Castle
Street we reach an area of almost complete 1960s redevelop-
ment. A lone survival is No. 10 on the SW corner with Strand
Street. Early CI9 brick with arched ground-floor windows set
in semicircular-headed recesses. Continuing N along Castle
Street, to the r. a late 1960s multi-storey car park, and ahead,

on the corner with the High Street, ORCHARD HOUSE, another large mixed-use development. Of 2008 (remodelling early 1970s offices), by *Terrence O'Rourke*. A lower block faces the High Street; the corner with Old Orchard incorporates a twelve-storey tower. Turning l. down the HIGH STREET, the buildings are generally of two storeys with late C18 or early C19 frontages. These occasionally conceal a much earlier building behind, such as Nos. 12–14 on the N side. Of the mid to late C16, with a stuccoed, sash-windowed elevation of *c.* 1830. On the first floor of No. 14 what may have been a Great Chamber, with a ceiling of quartered squares within quatrefoils. Double-headed eagles within foliage bosses at the intersections carry the merchant's mark of Thomas Bingley, mayor in 1555.

Continuing into SARUM (or SALISBURY) STREET, between Scaplen's Court and the Poole Museum (*see* p. 457), one passes the rear of the Town Cellars. Attached as a lean-to the ashlar LOCK-UP, dated 1820 over its doorway. Closing the view at the end, THE KING CHARLES. Late C16, timber-framed, but much restored. Turn r. into THAMES STREET. Here, on the r., an imaginative housing scheme by *Nigel Clark Associates*, *c.* 1975. Brick. Modern detailing but carefully scaled. Opposite No. 4, a short detour down the alley called St Clement's Lane will reveal a short length of surviving C16 TOWN WALL.

Continuing along Thames Street, at the end on the l., the first we see of Poole's swagger C18 mansions, THE MANSION HOUSE. Red brick. In style hardly before *c.* 1790, probably built for Benjamin Lester, one of the richest of the Newfoundland traders. The attempt to impress is somewhat naïve, with blank arcading enormously high, framing the semi-basement and the round-headed ground-floor windows as well. Semicircular porch on unfluted Doric columns in front of the slightly projecting central bay. Here not only a Venetian window and a lunette above,* under the little pediment, but quite different window levels, a hint that the front door opens on to a grand staircase hall. The staircase keeps up the tone, going up in one flight, returning in two, the landing between two tiers of coupled columns, the lower excessively lofty, with Tower of the Winds capitals. In the dining room a marble chimneypiece carved with nothing but two fillets of dried cod, frank admission of what all this ostentation was based upon.

The churchyard is lined with lime trees and maintains its Georgian urbanity, though there is little space to spare and the houses crowd in round it. On the W side the façade of POOLE HOUSE, reconstructed in 1965–6, but the design typical of *c.* 1730. Brick. Top parapet with urns. The three bays divided vertically by chains of Portland stone. Windows with broad eared surrounds, the central upper one round-headed and with a Gibbs surround. Beyond, Neo-Georgian houses complete the BARBER'S GATE development, 1992 by *MWT Architects*.

*The sequence borrowed from Sir Peter Thompson's House, Market Street, of some forty years earlier.

At the NW corner WEST END HOUSE, St James Close, said to have been built as early as *c.* 1716 for the Slade family of merchants.* Five bays, two storeys, the top parapet balustraded and with pineapples as well as two sorts of heavy urns. Windows on brackets, with moulded surrounds and keystones. The central climax this time is scrolls added to the upper window surround, and a pedimented doorcase on Ionic pilasters banded with squares of vermiculated rustication. (Some minor Rococo plasterwork inside, and a staircase of the same style as that at Sir Peter Thompson's House. RCHME) Forecourt railed, with the C18 overthrow and lamp socket over the gate surviving.

St James Close was, before a major realignment of roads, West Street. To reach the remainder of WEST STREET, one has to continue NW from Thames Street along Barbers Gate (formerly a lane called Barbers Piles). To the r., stranded on the opposite side of West Street, about 100 yds further on, is JOLIFFE'S HOUSE, *c.* 1730 for William Joliffe, possibly by *Francis Smith* of Warwick.** Three-storeyed. Plain, with the usual quoins and moulded window surrounds. Porch on Tuscan columns, with an entablature of idiosyncratic design. Formerly it had two projecting wings of *c.* 1835, creating a forecourt. Only that on the r. survived road widening. Staircase with two turned and one twisted baluster per step.

Back to the church close. On the SE side the buttressed brick Gothic-windowed CHURCH HALL, built as a Sunday School by *Creeke & Parken* of Bournemouth, 1862. On the opposite side of the road, up an alley squeezed past the E end of the church, THE RECTORY, a plain red brick front of 1786. Returning and going l., CHURCH STREET is now the most complete old street in Poole, retained when so much was lost elsewhere in the town. The funnel shape, widening out to give a full view of the end of the Guildhall with its flights of steps, makes it especially attractive. Past fine C18 town houses, three-storeyed on the l., two-storeyed on the r. Further on the r., ST GEORGE ALMSHOUSES, founded before 1429 (see the plaque of 1904 on the l. chimney gable), but successively altered. Two broad brick gables towards the street carrying pairs of chimneystacks set lozenge-wise, a curiously homely orientation for the building. The street's funnelling is really done under the name of MARKET STREET. On the l., Nos. 6 and 8 are a mid-C18 brick refronting of a large, stone-and-timber-built house of the late C16. ST AUBYN'S COURT on the r. is another housing scheme (also *c.* 1975) by *Nigel Clark Associates*. It sensitively retains the all-important building line. No. 20, *c.* 1740, is a plain but eye-catching merchant's house. Tripartite keystones to the windows. Staircase with one turned, one twisted baluster per step, and an under-curling end to the handrail, suggesting *Bastard* company involvement.

Country Life, 27 February 1958.
**Andor Gomme, *Smith of Warwick* (2000).

Continuing NE, Market Street splits in front of the Guildhall. To reach its continuation one must take the l. fork and cross the by-pass, NEW ORCHARD. To the l., some straightforwardly designed three-storey blocks of flats, 1968–9, by *Geoffrey Hopkinson* (the Borough Architect) and *Michael Gooding*. N of New Orchard the street name changes, first to Dear Hay Lane, then (after turning l.) to MARKET CLOSE as it regains its original alignment. After about 50 yds on the r. is SIR PETER THOMPSON'S HOUSE, the finest house in Poole. Built 1746–9 (and dated 1749) by *John Bastard* of Blandford.* He was certainly both its architect and in charge of construction (according to his letter to Sir Peter Thompson of 6 July 1752). In many ways it is an admirable design. Three storeys with a top parapet. H-plan, the centre bay only slightly recessed, but differentiated by being stuccoed to imitate ashlar; for the two-bay wings are of brick. They are kept plain, the topmost windows only segment-headed and with apron-pieces, but all with key blocks. In the broad centre however there is almost a feeling of overcrowding. Hooded doorway in one composition with narrow windows l. and r. given rusticated imposts. Full-scale Venetian window above, and at the top a lunette. At the back an answering Venetian window. These windows light the most remarkable of the rooms, a through room on the first floor. It has a Kentian chimneypiece and an unsuitably effete plaster ceiling in the local Rococo manner. Similar ceiling in the N room downstairs, similar chimneypiece, and the original panelling, with an elaborately framed panel on the W wall. One must imagine the house on the edge of the town 'bleak, and much exposed' (as so described in John Bastard's letter), but facing a garden and an ornamental canal (as indicated on the town map of 1756).

2. From the High Street to the new town centre and RNLI buildings

This perambulation takes in much that is new in Poole, at the NW end of the old town.

Starting from where Old and New Orchard cross the HIGH STREET, we first look down OLD ORCHARD for a view of the major housing renewal of the 1960s for the Borough Council. On Lagland, Skinner and East streets a mixture of four-storey low-rise and eleven-storey tower blocks. These followed almost total clearance of historic housing, although in places early C20 (two-storey) terraces have been retained, such as opposite the United Reformed church, Skinner Street.

Returning to the HIGH STREET, turning NE, most surviving older buildings have mid- to late C18 frontages (altered by successive shopfronts). None is especially noteworthy except

*D. Beamish, J. Hillier and H.F. V. Johnstone, *Mansions and Merchants of Poole and Dorset* (1976).

Nos. 73–75 on the SE side, formerly the BULL'S HEAD INN, a single early C16 structure, refronted in the early C19. There is a two-light stone-mullioned window in the rubble-stone rear of No. 75. (Inside No. 73 a decorative early C17 plaster ceiling on the first floor. RCHME) Also of note No. 87, a three-storey merchant's mansion of 1704, set back from the road and partially concealed behind a later building to the l. Where HILL STREET joins from the l. a wedge-plan former MIDLAND BANK of c. 1922, probably by *Whinney, Son & Austen Hall.* Classical. Brick with semicircular rusticated ashlar entrance. Further on, angled back at the junction with Lagland Street, the NATWEST BANK of c. 1800 has some refinement in its brickwork. Arched sashes within semicircular recesses to the ground floor. Next on the r., over the road crossing, BEECH HURST is the other really magniloquent merchant's house. Built for Samuel Rolles, and dated 1798. It stands free, set back and above the street by a flight of steps. Red brick, of three storeys and five broad bays, bays one and five set back slightly, the rest crowned by a big pediment containing a shield of arms embraced by splendid palm fronds. Otherwise no enrichment except that, as so often at this date, the ground-floor windows in the central three bays are round-headed and set under blank arcading. Semicircular porch, the Tuscan columns carrying pieces of entablature – not a happy arrangement. Inside, the staircase has had its lower flight removed, but its well occupies the centre of the house, with a cantilevered first-floor landing all round.

Across the railway level crossing FALKLAND SQUARE is entered, an informal shopping area of 1976–8, added to the ARNDALE CENTRE of 1963–9 by *W. Leslie Jones & Partners.* The latter is best viewed from KINGLAND ROAD. Its blocks, from l. to r., are the bus station, sports centre, library and shopping parades, the last now the DOLPHIN SHOPPING CENTRE. Of the blocks, the only one with a significant architectural presence is the CENTRAL LIBRARY, of three storeys with some elegance in proportion and refinement in detailing. On its flank wall, contemporary lettering and a large Poole coat of arms. Opposite, THE LIGHTHOUSE arts centre, a partial remodelling by *Short & Associates* in 2002 of an ugly 1978 complex clad in pre-cast concrete by *D.W. Hills*, Deputy Borough Architect.

To the NW, alongside the RAILWAY STATION of 1988 (the third on this site), BARCLAYS HOUSE, Wimborne Road. 1972–5 by *Wilson, Mason & Partners.* Bulky and dominant. Three octagonal nine-storey towers arranged around a slightly higher square core. Pre-cast concrete vertical strips, splayed at the base, alternating with bronze-coloured glazing. High above the entrance the backing to a large metal Barclays eagle. This was taken down in 2007, apparently because it was deemed too Teutonic. On the opposite side of the main N approach into Poole, in contrast, a slender and not inelegant twelve-storey residential tower by *Mason Richards Partnership*, 2005. This is attached to a corner of ASDA, designed by the same architects. Behind, a rather overstated waterfront housing block (crudely hinting at the jazz-modern of A.J. Seal of Bournemouth) by *BCA Architects*, 2008.

The best thing in Poole to be built so far in the C21 is the RNLI LIFEBOAT COLLEGE, West Quay Road, SW of the railway station. By *Poynton Bradbury Wynter Cole Architects*, 2004. Three main elements. One, nearest to the entrance, is conventionally rectangular with low overlapping barrel-roofs. This is linked by an angled bridge to the second part, which has more bravura: L-plan with forty-five-degree corners, banded grey and brown brick walls. Nautical porthole windows on the outer walls. A glass-brick outer corner turret rises to express the roof structure. Finally, lower in height and facing the harbour, a rotunda with outward-splayed glazed sides. Oval GATEHOUSE, also with outward-splayed walls, and a tilted flat roof.

At the road entrance, the RNLI MEMORIAL by *Sam Holland*, 2009, for the RNLI Heritage Trust. Stainless-steel boat frame with two figures. Angled plinth carrying inscribed names designed by *Ellis Belk*.

Opposite the entrance, in WEST QUAY ROAD, another competent exercise in much the same mood as the RNLI College, the RNLI SUPPORT CENTRE, 2004 by *Ellis Belk*.

SUBURBS*

BRANKSOME

An artisan suburb that grew up in the mid C19 on the Poole to Bournemouth road. Its main industries were a pottery and large gasworks, to the N, contrasting sharply with genteel Branksome Park to the S.

ST ALDHELM, St Aldhelm's Road. 1892–4 by *Bodley & Garner*, and a very typical example of their later years, graceful and refined. Long, low, Portland ashlar West Country exterior with three gables and no clerestory. W end completed in 1911–12 by *Cecil G. Hare*, Bodley's last partner. The intended SW tower and spire were not built.** NE bellcote added in 1916 by *F.C. Eden*. Elaborate Dec tracery in the E window. Wagon-roofed interior with long even arcades. Only six bays originally completed. A further four (the last shorter, due to the road frontage) added at the W end in 1911–12, in accordance with Bodley & Garner's intentions. No chancel arch. – ROOD SCREEN. Across the full width. Fine Perp work in oak. By *Bodley & Garner*, 1894. – FONT by *Eden*, 1918. Chalice-shaped, with a

---

*The original author of this section (1972) was Nicholas Taylor.
**A perspective produced by *Hare* shows that it would have been similar in design and placement to Bodley's at St Chad's, Burton-on-Trent, Staffs. (1903–10).

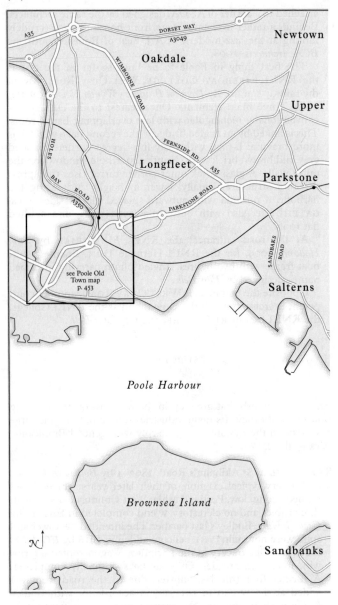

gilt Laudian CANOPY by *W.H. Randoll Blacking.* – STAINED
GLASS. Good E window, 1911 by *Burlison & Grylls.* They also
did the Lady Chapel windows at about the same time. Central
w window, 1922, and s aisle w window, 1925, both by *Kempe
& Co.* The church was one of those founded by Alexander
Morden Bennett of Bournemouth.

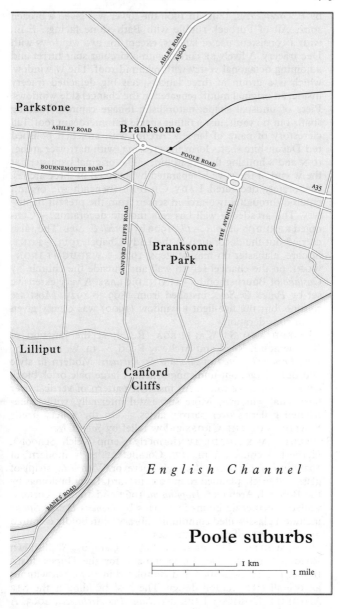

Poole suburbs

├─────────────── 1 km
├─────────────── 1 mile

ST JOHN THE EVANGELIST, Surrey Road, ½ m. E. A large
church in a fashionable suburb. Erected for Miss Durrant,
owner of the Branksome Estate. Built in stages. The W part of
the nave and aisles by *Thomas Stevens* of Bournemouth, 1889.
The remainder of the nave, transept-like S chapel, chancel
and first 50 ft (15 metres) of the N tower, in matching style,

by *E. Greenleaves*, 1898. In 1906 the tower was given a broach spire. All of Purbeck rubble with Bath stone facings. E.E., with a consistent use of lancets, except for two windows with Dec tracery. A lively SE corner with a circular stair-turret and adjoining octagonal vestry with pyramid roof. The W window, which is a group of three lancets, has big detached tracery inside, an original motif, repeated in the chancel side windows. Piers of unusual shape, naturalistic foliage capitals. Vaulting shafts but no vault, just a rather sparse hammerbeam roof. Tall clerestory of pairs of lancets. Arches with attached polished red Devonshire shafts form the crossing, with narrower arches to N and S housing the organ pipes. The original baptistery at the W end of the nave is separated by a screen of three arches. Elaborately decorated LADY CHAPEL (beneath the organ), entered through a two-arched screen from the present baptistery. The arcaded E wall has rich mosaic decoration. – Canopied REREDOS of *opus sectile*, 1909 by *Powell & Sons*. They also carried out the decoration in the Lady Chapel, 1913. – FONT. Square, alabaster on marble steps, 1923. – WROUGHT IRONWORK on the chancel screen wall and outside the church, by *Caslake* of Bournemouth. – STAINED GLASS. A very extensive set by *Powell & Sons*, installed from 1899 to 1929. Most are routine, but the five-light E window (1900) was clearly given more consideration.

ST JOSEPH AND ST WALBURGA (R.C.), at the junction of Bournemouth Road and Archway Road, ¼ m. W. 1960–2 by *P. N. Lamprell-Jarrett* of *Archard & Partners*. Modern in style and quite large, but undistinguished. A large pale brick block with a slender SE tower. An insistent pattern of vertical over horizontal windows. More successful internally, with stone-fronted galleries over narrow aisles. – On the gallery fronts STATIONS OF THE CROSS in low relief by *John Green*.

ST ALDHELM'S ACADEMY (formerly Kemp-Welch Schools), Herbert Avenue, 1¼ m. NW. Competent 'early modern' of 1938 by *E. J. Goodacre*, Borough Surveyor. With long strips of glass and brick, planned round a courtyard. Later buildings by the Borough Architect, *Hopkinson*, 1967 and 1970–1, curtain-walled. Further additions in 2004–5 by *Genesis Design Studio* include a glass-walled community library, with boldly coloured giant transverse fins or buttresses.

BOURNEMOUTH UNIVERSITY, Talbot Campus, Wallisdown Road, 1½ m. NE. Developed initially for the Dorset Institute of Higher Education and completed in 1976, but without an overall architectural design. The best building is the SIR MICHAEL COBHAM LIBRARY, *Saunders Architects*, 2003. A four-storey octagonal extension linked to two earlier octagons. Adjacent a SCULPTURE by the Japanese artist *Koichi Ishino*, 2008. The polygonal plan motif is continued in the FUSION BUILDING at the SE corner of the campus. Large, by *BDP Architects*, completed in 2016. It has a higher polygonal central block with attached lower blocks, either polygonal or circular in plan. The lower polygonal blocks have a horizontal rhythm of strip glazing, integrating with the central block. In contrast, the lower circular blocks are grey with horizontal marking out and the minimum of glazing. Inside a large top-lit, as well as side-lit, atrium. At its centre a pillar splitting into branches to support the high flat roof.

To the S, in the adjoining ARTS UNIVERSITY BOURNEMOUTH campus, DESIGN STUDIO by *CRAB Studio* (*Sir Peter Cook* and *Gavin Rowbotham*, architects), 2016. Organic form in blue-coloured steel-sheet cladding. Large N-facing oval oculus and a smaller north-light worked into the design as principal external features.

The approach to Branksome from Bournemouth along Poole Road opens with COUNTY GATES HOUSE, begun in 1970, a long nine-storey slab by *Scott, Brownrigg & Turner*, cleanly detailed in plum-coloured brick, with the usual glazed stair-case clipped to the gable-end. Its purity of form is in con-trast to the nautical-flavoured extensions at lower level by *Trinity Architecture*, 2006. Opposite is FRIZZELL HOUSE, 1968–72 by *Patrick Holden & Associates*, a long and lower office block which pioneered in Britain the large-scale use of GRP (glass-reinforced plastic) as a facing material. The big bulgy 'pilasters', cream-coloured, are an attempt to indicate the sculptural freedom of plastic, but seem closer in spirit to the old-fashioned 'streamline-modern' of suburban factories. Mushroom-columned pilotis to the basement car park; spiky hexagonal staircase tower at the centre of the N elevation. Excellent concrete FOOTBRIDGE spanning Lindsay Road, on openwork clusters of struts.

If Branksome can be said to have a centre, it is in the area of the (largely rebuilt) railway station. Opposite is the brick and half-timbered BRANKSOME RAILWAY HOTEL of 1894, with a machicolated water tower and, adjoining the hotel, the gabled ST ALDHELM'S TERRACE of about the same date, curving round the corner. Two converging RAILWAY VIADUCTS, ½ m. to the E, cross high above the Bourne valley. Dating from 1888 and 1893, they were built by the London & South Western Railway.

DISCOVERY COURT (formerly Loewy Robertson Engineer-ing Co.), Wallisdown Road, 1½ m. NNW. 1953–5 by *Farmer & Dark*, enlarged in 1961–2, but drastically rebuilt *c.* 2000. The inspiration for the two-storey offices, a classic 'hollow square' of curtain walling on stilts, was undoubtedly American, from Mies van der Rohe's Illinois Institute of Technology and especially from the office blocks of the early 1950s by Skidmore, Owings & Merrill. They have been entirely re-clad and given a pitched roof. Gone too is most of *Brenda Colvin*'s landscaping, replaced by car parking. However, the abstract MURAL, of aluminium extrusions amid Chesil Beach pebbles, by students of Bournemouth College of Art led by *Gillian Rowbotham*, remains in place on the E side, a reminder that fine art and design once found a place in a more optimistic industrial world. In Loewy Crescent, 200 yds w, the accompanying DRAUGHTSMEN'S HOUSING survives, also by *Farmer & Dark*.

BRANKSOME PARK

Branksome Park was purchased by C.W. Packe M.P. (of Prest-wold, Leics.), in 1852. His plain stone Tudor house of the following year, Branksome Tower, designed by the great Scots Romantic *William Burn* (who was also Packe's architect at Prest-wold), stood in the SE corner of the park. Later it was expanded as a hotel, tricked out in 'joke oak', *c.* 1920, but retaining Packe's rambling cliff-top gardens. It was finally demolished in 1973, and replaced by the most unromantic of blocks of flats.* Following Packe's death in 1859, the estate was sold to Henry Bury, who proceeded to create a series of building plots, chiefly in its western half. He also built the church and vicarage. By *c.* 1900 a new formal approach drive to Branksome Towers, THE AVENUE, was laid out leading from County Gates (*see* Branksome) to the mansion. This part of the estate attracted larger detached houses, such as Cerne Abbas (also demolished; *see* below). These have been replaced gradually by blocks of flats, although in the southern part of the park many more of the original houses remain. Throughout, the pine trees are a blessing, planted by Packe and Bury on this previously open heathland, and screening both the smaller houses and their more mundane flat-block replacements.

ALL SAINTS, Western Road. 1877 by *H.M. Burton & T. Stevens* of Bournemouth for Henry Bury (*see* above). Simple buttressed bellcoted chapel, Dec, with a polygonal apse. The form somewhat compromised by the organ loft and vestry added by *Edgar H. Burton* to the N side in 1882, intended as part of a tower. Central W porch of 1927 by *S. Tugwell*. Gracefully proportioned interior retaining original fittings. – REREDOS. Fine Last Supper carved from Caen stone, 1884. – Low CHOIR SCREEN of stone and wrought iron by *E.H. Burton*. – PULPIT. Carved stone with polished red Devonian marble corner colonnettes. – FONT. Octagonal C13 bowl with two trefoil-headed panels to each face (from St Edmund, Salisbury, redundant in 1973), on a C19 stem. – STAINED GLASS. Apse windows by *Powell & Sons*, 1884–9. Further *Powells* windows of 1894 in chancel, s. Nave s window also *Powells*, 1900. Nave N window by *Leonard A. Pownall*, 1916. – Tall CHURCHYARD CROSS (NE of the church) in memory of the Bury family. – GRAVESTONES. Several of high quality, including James Simpson †1907, a granite cross with a pretty Art Nouveau bronze of a soul being received into heaven, by *Grassland McClure*. – Henry Shoosmith †1918, by his son *A.G. Shoosmith*, Lutyens's chief assistant at New Delhi.

---

*A greater loss was HAILEYBURY, Martello Road South (for a time The Oratory Preparatory School), an excellent early work of *Basil Champneys*, 1878.

Contemporary brick and half-timbered VICARAGE, also by *Burton & Stevens*, immediately S of the church.

PERAMBULATIONS

1. From County Gates to the Parke Mausoleum

At County Gates, there is now nothing to see of *Burn*'s lodge, swept away by the County Gates Gyratory. As one proceeds S down THE AVENUE, it is immediately apparent that nondescript blocks of flats, such as WESTERNGATE of 1969–72 by the *Wyvern Design Group*, have replaced most of the large houses. One typical original house survives: No. 36, CLIEVE-DEN, brick Gothic of *c*. 1885, now extended and converted to flats.* At the crossroads with Tower Road and Tower Road West are the GATES to the now demolished Cerne Abbas, a Wagnerian fantasy of *c*. 1890 in bright red brick Gothic, with a high château-roofed tower. The replacement Postmodern courtyard of flats, by *Plincke, Leaman & Browning*, 1988, has chunky classical detailing. Below, on the lower side of Tower Road West, No. 12, WHITEHOUSE PARK is a severe Voysey-ish house typical of the second phase of house building, with a strong group of gables. Probably by *R. Heywood Haslam* (cf. The Teak House, below), who published a very similar design for a 'house at Branksome Park' in 1908. Next down The Avenue, on the r. side, No. 48, EDEN HOUSE, in the more aggressive style derived from *R.A. Briggs*, with mansard gables and streamlined oriels. *Haslam* certainly designed No. 52 (formerly Narrow Water), on the corner of Dalkeith Road (1902). Other pleasant Edwardian houses in Dalkeith Road, Ettrick Road and Tower Road West. Continuing down The Avenue towards the sea, on the l., No. 31B, MOONRAKER, a curving house of fantasy Expressionism by *Steve Lyne* of *KL Architects*, 2005.

THE TEAK HOUSE is concealed up a curving driveway. Now converted to flats, it is one of the major houses of Branksome Park, on a large plot between The Avenue and Westminster Road. By *A. Wickham Jarvis* and *R. Heywood Haslam*, 1899–1900, in Voysey's earlier roughcast and half-timber manner.** What makes the exterior memorable is the five-storey tower added at the E end in 1914, bare, roughcast and flat-roofed, with thin stone oriels to give relief. (In 1972 the interior had Art Nouveau glass and a brick-arched alcove in the entrance hall. The drawing room had stained glass, teak panelling to three-quarter height, and a vigorous ceiling, with teak beams and the plaster between them roughened into waves like an Art Nouveau storm at sea. The best detail was the dining-room chimneypiece, framed to ceiling height by

---

*Another survivor is PARK MANOR (formerly Gablehurst), St Aldhelm's Road, a large brick house now much extended. By *J. Dixon Horsfield*, 1884.
**Haslam was apprenticed to Voysey between 1895 and 1898.

Mackmurdo-style pilasters and faced with teak, with recesses for china.)

The Avenue leads down to the delectable pine-wooded BRANKSOME CHINE (gardens of 1930 by *E.J. Goodacre*, Borough Surveyor). Jaunty white BEACH-SIDE BUILDINGS of the 1920s, one block, a SOLARIUM of 1932, with intense blue-glazed pantiles and a *Carter & Co.* faience panel over the entrance. As first built, segregated accommodation provided ultra-violet radiation rooms, one of the first buildings in the country to do so.

BRANKSOME DENE CHINE to the E was also landscaped by *Goodacre*, in 1928. BATHING HUTS by the Borough Architect, *Hopkinson* (cf. Canford Cliffs). On the cliff to the E is the romantic Portmeirion-style eyrie of VIEWPOINT HOUSE (No. 25 Sandbourne Road), built in 1931: white walls, splayed wings, and a bow under a spreading roof of subtly mottled grey-green tiles. It may be by *Philip Hepworth*, who certainly designed No. 37 (1932; demolished) further E, just across the boundary with Hants.

Climbing back up r. into Westminster Road, then r. again into Pinewood Road, another turning to the r. (signed to Branksome Dean Chine), past a lodge of belated Edwardian prettiness (1928 by *Goodacre*), takes us to the PARKE MAUSO-LEUM, 1869 by *Burn*, the last surviving architectural evidence of the original Towers estate. Romanesque, with arcading along the sides.

2. From All Saints' church to Canford Cliffs

Heading W along Western Avenue, climbing past several large houses of spreading proportions, we reach, on the l., the most zestful of recent houses: No. 16, THUNDERBIRD, 2006, by *Eddie Mitchell* of *Seven Developments*. More fantasy Expressionism, curving with a dramatic swept corner, copper roofs and horizontal fins offsetting the white-rendered walls. A more rectilinear, International-Style house is opposite at No. 25, INSPIRATION, with horizontal louvres used as a foil to glazing expanses. Adjacent to Thunderbird is the entrance to a major house, No. 18, BRANKSOME PARK HOUSE (originally Grey-stones), *c.* 1912. An L-plan, Portland stone manor-style house with a roof of Westmorland slates, tall octagonal-shafted chimneys and an angled porch at the centre. It is now almost completely obscured by trees, as is No. 12A, WILDWOOD, a work of more serious modern intent by *Richard Horden* for his parents, 1975. Inspired by the Californian Case Study Houses (those of Craig Ellwood in particular), its minimalist frame and fully glazed walls with flat roofs are laid out as a rectangle, with an entrance through a walled courtyard and past a pond.

Returning to the l. down Bury Road, set back high to the l., and concealed behind other houses is No. 23, BEL ESGUARD, 1939. Whizzing 'early modern' with Mendelsohnian flourishes,

by *A. J. Seal* of Bournemouth. Its horizontal emphasis is counterbalanced by two vertical incidents: a two-storey semicircular
bay window and a circular stair-turret.

Turning r. at Western Road we pass, on our l., No.20,
BERKELEY TOWERS, *c.* 1890, an example of the larger earlier
mansions with the characteristic cone-roofed corner tower.
Opposite the junction at the s end of the road is the neat
former LODGE of *c.* 1913, by *J.H. Brewerton*, to another large
mansion of *c.* 1900, MARTELLO TOWERS, subsequently a
hotel.* The lodge, now a public library, is roughcast with
arched window recesses and segment-headed dormers. Similar
COTTAGE behind.

CANFORD CLIFFS AND SANDBANKS

The CANFORD CLIFFS estate was developed from *c.* 1900
onwards on cliff-top former heathland. The centre is Haven Road,
now a built-up shopping street. By 1910 the main streets were
complete, a large number of the detached houses having been
designed by *Sidney Tugwell* of Bournemouth. Most of these have
been demolished.** The Canford Cliffs Hotel (burnt down in
1941) dramatically overlooked the Canford Cliffs Chine. Further
SW is Flaghead Chine, a second deep inlet. Beyond, in the 1930s,
the Harbour Heights estate was developed. Here the architect *A. J.
Seal* introduced a curved-cornered, white-walled architecture that
also became the norm for the first post-war decade.

Forming the NE arm of Poole Harbour entrance, the low-lying
SANDBANKS peninsula was, except for some coastguard cottages
and the Haven Hotel, developed after 1920. The first houses were
modestly scaled, generally in Arts and Crafts mode, but these
were soon joined by larger Art Deco structures. From the 1960s
the pace of demolition and replacement accelerated, generating
in the process residential projects in a wide variety of modern
styles, many derivative, some quite idiosyncratic. Sandbanks is
now famed for having some of the highest property values outside
the capital.

THE TRANSFIGURATION, Chaddesley Glen, is a bungaloid
church of 1962–5 by *Lionel E. Gregory*, the exact ecclesiastical equivalent of Dunromin and Thistledo, with crazy-paved
walling and sawtoothed dormers. The squat N tower with
pyramid roof, which set the style for the rest of the church, was
built as early as 1957. Timber framing inside from the mission
church of 1911 by *H. Kendall*, around which the present church
was built. – ENGRAVED GLASS. W window, 1998, by *Sally Scott*.

ST ANN'S HOSPITAL, Haven Road, 300 yds NE. A remarkable
and severe building of 1910–12 by the Scottish Arts and Crafts
architect *Robert Weir Schultz*, one of Lethaby's circle. It is

---

*Demolished 1971. It was Scottish Baronial, with crowstepped gables and bulbous
tourelles.
**A survivor is LEES COURT (No.39 Cliff Drive).

boldly composed on the cliff top, with splayed wings and long balconies on brick piers. Dark red brick with shaped gables, Georgian windows and much balustrading of pierced brick. The dormers have a slightly Scottish flavour. On the entrance side there is a separate forebuilding with a cupola. The hospital was the seaside branch of Holloway Sanatorium in Surrey. The inevitable modern extensions (of 1988 and 2013) are placed sensitively to one side. *Schultz*'s contemporary tile-hung LODGE stands at the site of the former hospital entrance.

Between Haven Road and Chaddesley Glen, on the hillside over-looking Poole Harbour, 50 yds N, is a brave and enterprising group of 'early Modern' buildings, the HARBOUR HEIGHTS estate of 1935–6 by *A.J. Seal & Partners* of Bournemouth (with *Jasper Selway*). Of the three original larger buildings, the Harbour Heights Hotel has had a mansard roof added, while nibbling changes have affected Harbour Court (for-merly The Haven). Conning Tower has been updated and a second block added at right angles: an exemplary scheme by *David Quigley Architects* of 1999, now called Conning Towers. Below these are two rows of single-storey flat-roofed terrace houses (Harbour Close). The buildings are admirably sited, with prominent glazed staircase curves derived from Mendel-sohn; but the detailing everywhere degenerates into what John Betjeman called the Tel Aviv style.

Also in CHADDESLEY GLEN, 300 yds SSE, is No. 29, an Art Deco house of 1939 by *L. Magnus Austin*. Y-plan with a tiled conical roof at the centre.

From the N, the first section of promenade along the foreshore of Poole Harbour is earlier than the nearby buildings; the dolphin LAMPPOSTS (Thames Embankment-style) are inscribed with the engineers' names, *James Lemon* and *John Elford*, 1895.

COMPTON ACRES, Canford Cliffs Road, ½ m. N. The famous gardens created by the owner *T. W. Simpson* from 1919, restored and remodelled by the London architect and property devel-oper *J. Stanley Beard* (†1970). It continues to develop and is becoming more populist, although this seems to have been the original intention.

HAVEN HOTEL, Banks Road, 1¼ m. SW. From *c.* 1880 this was the North Haven Hotel. Rebuilt as the present hipped-roofed main block *c.* 1920, with several phases of later large additions.

LONGFLEET

Longfleet grew as the first suburb of Poole from *c.* 1850. Now visually a continuation of the new town centre.

ST MARY, Longfleet Road. Complicated development. Nave by *Edward Blore*, 1833, chancel by *G.E. Street*, 1864 (extended E in 1893), NW tower and spire by *Crickmay & Son*, 1883–4. In 1915 the nave was replaced by *Herbert Kendall*, remov-ing all trace of Blore's work. Most of the church is E.E., with rock-faced masonry. Crickmay's high spire is a major landmark. Unremarkable interior, although spacious and stylistically homogeneous. Square piers with arches dying into them. Largely stripped of C19 furnishings. – STAINED GLASS. A wide variety of designers and dates. Those that can be identified include the w window by *Clayton & Bell*, 1920. One in the N transept, r., by *William Morris & Co.* of Westminster, 1932. Four windows in the w baptistery, now entrance foyer, by *Cakebread Robey & Co.*, 1893. In the aisles several by *Reginald Bell*, 1937–46.

ST MARY (R.C.), Wimborne Road. 1971–3 by *Max Cross & S.A. Kellaway* of Bournemouth. An irregular hexagonal plan with a pyramidal metal-sheet roof. Walls of brick and textured concrete. The roof is interrupted by two wedge-shaped projections with monopitches rising outwards, giving hints of Liverpool Metropolitan Cathedral. Open interior with benches orientated on the sanctuary. Odd triangular roof-grid treatment.

POOLE HOSPITAL, Longfleet Road. 1959–69 by *Stewart Kilgour* for the Wessex Regional Hospital Board. A large and varied group, built over a long period. Like the other public buildings of this period in Poole, not of outstanding architectural value. The main block, parallel with Longfleet Road, has a layered frontage, each floor introducing a new mixture of materials. An L-plan block at the sw end is taller and, yet again, treated differently. Immediately behind is the main seven-storey block, while further back, adjoining Parkstone Road, is a thirteen-storey Y-plan nurses' accommodation tower. Additions include the red brick PHILIP ARNOLD UNIT at the s end, 2008.

Two pairs of gabled, pale brick CANFORD ESTATE COTTAGES of 1870 by *Banks & Barry*, ½ m. NE in Ringwood Road.

PARKSTONE, SALTERNS AND LILLIPUT

From 1833 PARKSTONE began as a separate town from Poole. It was in that year that the parish was established and the predecessor to the present parish church begun. Until the railway arrived in 1874, houses w of Ashley Cross tended to be smaller, with larger villas for the merchant families of Poole standing in extensive grounds to the E. The latter were concentrated in the Castle Hill area, below the promontory of Constitution Hill. A grid-plan of more intensive housing had expanded on to land E of Parkstone by *c.* 1910, particularly to the s of Bournemouth Road. By the 1930s many of the larger villas had found institutional uses, and in the 1960s and 1970s development pressure led to their demolition and replacement with housing, a process that is dwindling owing to lack of sites to redevelop.

SALTERNS, an area of later development around a house of that name, grew along the road southwards from Parkstone to Sandbanks. It is adjacent to the Blue Lagoon, a bay that in the mid C18 was the site for salt extraction. The South Western Pottery, to the s of Parkstone, built Salterns Pier in 1867 for the import of coal and export of pottery products. This was developed as an artificial peninsula with housing and a boat marina in the 1980s.

When its church was built in 1874, LILLIPUT was hardly a village. A position elevated above Poole Harbour made it, from the 1880s, an attractive location for larger villas, a characteristic retained to this day, despite incursions of blocks of flats and bungalows.

CHURCHES

ST PETER, Church Road. Even though the 212-ft (65-metre) spire on the N side was not built, this big stone church appears at first sight to be a complete replacement by *J.L. Pearson* of the original chapel (1833–4 by *John Tulloch*). It is in Pearson's favourite blend of Early English and Early French, with a high roof ridge and lavish internal shafting; yet it lacks the serenity of St Stephen, Bournemouth, the main vault being only timber. The explanation is that Pearson had to salvage someone else's work: one *Frederick Rogers* designed the chancel, crossing and transepts (1876–8), ambitious in their three-storey interiors with a bold square-piered triforium. The chancel is straight-ended in a North Country way, with a trio of arches behind the altar and a lancet triplet above. Pearson was brought in to add the vestries and organ chamber in 1881, but evidently found that he had to prop up Rogers's work, doubling the arches in the triforium in an alternating pattern. Rogers's narrow stone-vaulted ambulatory was retained. Pearson commenced the nave in 1891, largely in the same style as the chancel, the western bays being completed by his son *F.L. Pearson* in 1900–1. The main vault runs without a break from E to W, with crossing arches to the transepts only. The clerestory windows have plate tracery. The aisles are stone-vaulted, the arcades having the same clustered piers with lavish stiff-leaf capitals as in the chancel. S porch by *F.L. Pearson*, 1933. Canon *Ernest Dugmore*, the vicar, is said to have largely designed, as well as paid for, the Chapel of the Holy Name (E of the S transept), 1877. This was extended W in 1926 by *Ponting*.

FURNISHINGS. HIGH ALTAR with carved figures by *Zwincke* of Oberammergau, 1893–4. – REREDOS of the Holy Name Chapel by *Zwincke*, 1904, to the designs of *G.A. Bligh Livesay*. – ROOD SCREEN of wrought iron, said to be by *Pearson* (given in 1877), but executed exactly as shown on *Rogers*'s drawings of 1876. – PULPIT by *F.L. Pearson*, 1909. – SANCTUARY LAMPS, seven of them, said to be C17 Florentine, from the Cavendish-Bentinck collection at Brownsea Island (*see* p. 159). – FONT. Alabaster, with an elaborate, two-tiered oak Gothic canopy, *c*. 1900. – STAINED GLASS. E window by *James Bell*, 1879. Holy Name Chapel, by *Kempe*, 1904. Two central lights of the W window in S aisle by *Percy Bacon Bros*, 1908; outer and tracery lights added by *Horace Wilkinson*, 1936. Three lights of the W window, N aisle by *Joseph Bell & Son* of Bristol, 1927 (to match a 1911 single light). – MONUMENTS. William Parr

†1863, Gothic marble tablet. – Henry Rose †1902. Pretty Arts and Crafts-influenced triptych.

St Luke, Sandecotes Road. 1907–8 by *J. Henry Ball* (with *T.J.B. Holland* of Parkstone), for Lady Wimborne. A depressing Dec church in cheap buff brick, with aisles but without a tower, and without the inspiration of which Ball was capable (cf. St Agatha, Portsmouth, Hants). Long, cool, and well-proportioned interior with boarded roofs. Paired aisle windows in arched recesses. – STAINED GLASS. Many windows by *Powell & Sons*, 1926–60.

St Dunstan's Orthodox Church (formerly St Osmund), Bournemouth Road. Professor *E.S. Prior*'s last work, 1913–16, designed in partnership with *Arthur Grove*. As rich and strange as anything by Prior. The Byzantine vocabulary had been fixed by the earlier chancel of roughcast and terracotta, 1904–5 by *G.A. Bligh Livesay* of Bournemouth; and Prior's balancing of a low central dome by two Greek-looking w turrets is conventional. But the w front is a riot of colour and texture, prophetic of the Expressionism of the 1920s. The brick, mottled from red to brown to yellow, was specially handmade near Wareham. Its flickering texture is picked up by the bustling arcades of two galleries and by the elaborate geometry of the great rose window, with its spider's web of leading. The triangular-headed arches of the lower gallery and the criss-cross tile patterns in the gable are an Anglo-Saxon echo (Earls Barton, Northants) . The portal below is a superbly decisive segmental arch of terracotta, broad and low, spanning from turret to turret and moulded with a trailing vine. The turrets consist of clustered brick shafts; similar shafts, like brick drainpipes, alternate with round-headed windows along the aisle walls, disappearing abruptly under a kind of Lombard frieze along the eaves. Circular windows in the clerestory and vestries. Particularly attractive the Chapel of the Incarnation at first-floor level to the SE, where the ground falls away, with a loggia under the apse.

The interior is a surprise, cool and pure, with greyish roughcast surfaces and buff terracotta dressings; the capitals, with bold foliage, are splashes of red terracotta, with winged angels soaring above them in the crossing. Nave arcades round-headed on square piers; nave roof of timber between diaphragm arches. The aisles are very wide and barrel-vaulted in reinforced concrete,* with further barrel-vaults at right angles over the outer passage aisles, supported alternately by circular piers and pierced buttress walls. The N aisle, N transept and vestries were completed in 1927 to Prior's original design. His concrete however proved faulty; the dome was rebuilt in 1922 by *Sidney Tugwell* and the s aisle in 1950 by *L. Magnus Austin*, with external flying buttresses in ordinary red brick. *Livesay*'s

---

* It seems likely that Prior knew Anatole de Baudot's Saint-Jean-de-Montmartre, Paris, completed 1904. The brick façades have similarities, as well as the concrete structure.

sanctuary is raised high over a crypt with a ciborium based on that of San Clemente in Rome and arcades on fluted Ionic columns of red terracotta. Prior's transept has a Lady Altar of marble and onyx, separated from the Chapel of the Incarnation (to its E) by a marble-lined wall with an openwork grille (*see* below) filling the arch above. The chapel altar and apse are also faced in marble.

FURNISHINGS. LECTERN by *W. Bainbridge Reynolds*, 1926, excellent. Reading desk and twin candlesticks form a thin and elegant cage of hand-beaten bronze.* – FONT, a fluted bowl from Sturminster Marshall, probably C13, on a base by *Prior*. – RAILINGS to the ambulatory, good C18 work from St Mary-le-Bow, London. (Railings in the crypt originally enclosed the tomb of Thomas Newton, Bishop of Bristol, †1782, in the same church.) – GRILLE between the two chapels decorated in gold, black and white, with a painting of the Annunciation, by *MacDonald Gill*. – His brother *Eric Gill* did the INSCRIPTIONS on the altar of the Incarnation Chapel, and over the sacristy door. – STAINED GLASS. The most notable internal detail, designed by *Prior* himself in the thick handmade 'Prior's Glass' he had patented. Wholly abstract patterns, mostly in pale pinks, blues and greens, but in the S transept rose window deep red and blue. Three windows in the apse of the Chapel of the Incarnation by *A. K. Nicholson*, 1932. – STATUE of St Osmund (over the NW door), 1924 by *Alec Miller*. – WAR MEMORIAL in the S aisle with a statue of the crucified Christ as High Priest, 1920 by *MacDonald Gill*. – MEMORIAL to the church's first architect, G. A. B. Livesay, in the ambulatory. He died while serving at sea in 1916.

HOLY ANGELS, Lilliput Road, Salterns. Nave 1874, N aisle 1881, chancel 1891, S aisle 1898. Further E extensions of 1965–6 by *Allner, Morley & Bolton*. Externally a simple chapel in cheap buff brick. Internally, the openness and light predominate. – ROOD SCREEN. Typical Perp of 1906 by *Bodley*, as are the CHOIR STALLS and the prettily stencilled ORGAN CASE. – REREDOS. By *G. Baden Beadle* of Faithcraft, 1956. – SCULPTURE. A fine group of Art Nouveau bas reliefs, signed by *A. G. Walker*.** Triptych in a wooden frame, with a white marble Pietà in the central panel and a gleaming silver angel in each side panel. The mixture of materials is restless, the execution in each of them graceful and delicate. – STAINED GLASS. An extensive scheme, including five-light and three-light W windows, by *Clayton & Bell*, 1916–17.

UNITED REFORMED CHURCH (formerly Congregational), Commercial Road. 1892–3 by *Lawson & Donkin*. Hot red brick with a polygonal tower at the corner, formerly capped by a short spire (dem. 1981).

---

*The original PULPIT is now at Alderholt (q.v.).
**'A good New Sculpture man of the second generation' was the collector Lavinia Handley-Read's description of him.

PUBLIC BUILDINGS

CIVIC CENTRE, Parkstone Road. 1931–2 by *L. Magnus Austin*, working under *E. J. Goodacre*, Borough Surveyor. Stripped classicism, as favoured on the Continent at that moment. Portland ashlar. The angle site well handled, with a pedimented centrepiece on the corner frontage in which a giant recessed arch is made the main feature. Hipped pantile roofs.

POLICE STATION, Sandbanks Road. 1940, probably by *Goodacre*. Stripped Art Deco. The L-plan repeats, but with less confidence, Austin's angled corner motif in much plainer Portland masonry.

LAW COURTS, Sandbanks Road. 1967–9 by *G. Hopkinson*, Borough Architect. Short block towards the road interlocking with a long, low range behind. Ungainly Brutalism, not improved by minor alterations. A mixture of Portland stone, plum brick and some leadwork. Four main storeys, paired and raised over the brick basement. The set-back brick penthouse block has lost its original brise-soleil.

CENTRAL CLINIC, Sandbanks Road. 1960–2 by *Farmer & Dark*. Simple in its functionalism (in contrast to the Law Courts), and more successful as a result. Two-storeyed, the upper storey slightly projecting on pilotis.

CROWN OFFICES, Park Road. An eight-storey tower slab of 1962 to the rear of the Clinic.

BOURNEMOUTH AND POOLE COLLEGE, North Road. By *Enrico de Pierro*, built from 1956 to 1966 in phases, initially for Poole Technical College. The fashionable grey brick and concrete facing used in a satisfactorily straightforward way, creating, in the 1966 phase, a long classroom block at the r. with windows in continuous bands, and a hall block at right angles to the l. The first block is at the NE end of the site. The KUBE (formerly the Study Gallery) is a glazed multi-storey cube at the s end, 2000 by *Horden Cherry Lee Architects*.*

ST PETER'S SCHOOL (former), Parr Street. 1833. Stucco-covered cob. Three Y-traceried arched windows, a fourth made into a doorway. A battlemented screen wall with the original doorway at either end.

RAILWAY STATION. 1874 for the Poole & Bournemouth Railway. Two-storey station house with polychrome window arches and banding.

PERAMBULATION

From Poole, Parkstone is entered along Parkstone Road, passing the Municipal Buildings (*see* above) on the r. Reaching Commercial Road, to the l. an Art Deco-influenced former bank of *c.* 1935, now Poole Car Centre. Stuccoed villas of *c.* 1830–40 originally ran continuously along the l. side but, apart from a

*The gallery itself closed in 2010.

short row and No. 45, TOWER HOUSE, with its amusing battlemented belvedere, these have been replaced by office blocks.
To the l. at Ashley Cross (the centre of mid-C19 Parkstone),
Parr Street leads to St Peter's church (p. 474). At the fork
between Britannia and Salterns roads, to the r., PARKSTONE
LIBRARY of 1899 (originally Parkstone Municipal Buildings)
makes picturesque use of its wedge site. Brick and stone with
timber-framed gables and a battlemented tower. Further E
along Commercial Road, PARKSTONE PARK on the r. was
laid out in 1890, centred on a fountain pool. Opposite its top
corner, LLOYDS BANK (originally the Wilts. & Dorset Bank) of
1896, in a lively Victorian Baroque mixture of brick and stone.
Next l. POST OFFICE PARADE is a typical run of two-storey,
vaguely Art Deco shops of c. 1930, leading to the three-storey
Adamesque block of the POST OFFICE of 1927 by *David Dyke*
of the *Office of Works*.

By the late C19 a number of small mansions and villas had
been built in the area N of Commercial Road. The main survivor is HIGHFIELD HOUSE, at the end of Courtenay Road.
It is good Italianate of c. 1835, stucco, with pediments on three
sides and wide Tuscan eaves on thin brackets. Gothick glazing
bars, slim openwork timber porch and elegant balustrading to
the terrace and steps, the house being raised on a high basement for the views to the Purbecks. Worth a detour, ¼ m. N
of the church, is No. 11 Gervis Crescent, OLD HARRY HOUSE
by *Rebecca Granger*, 2004. Minimalist, almost a pure rectangle,
with a defining white frame, the glazing set back. In terraced
gardens.

On Sandbanks Road, ¾ m. SE from the Municipal Offices,
Nos. 215–217 on the l. are a pair of CANFORD ESTATE COT-
TAGES of 1873 by *Banks & Barry*.* In complete contrast
Nos. 223–227, flat-roofed, white-walled houses of the late
1930s, of which the first is the least altered. On the r., ¼ m.
further, SALTERNS COURT is jazz-modern flats of that vintage,
possibly by *A.J. Seal*. Its chief features are the entrance tower
at the centre of the frontage and curved-cornered window
strips.

In Alington Road, a turning to the l. ½ m. beyond Salterns
Court, is a group of buildings by *John Birch*, a prolific writer
of architectural pattern books. LILLIPUT HOUSE (1891), brick
with picturesque timber-framed gables, derived from George
Devey, has similar stables of 1889 (now called LITTLE COURT).
The lodge has witty triangular windows on the side, and recent
extensions by *Western Design Architects*. SHORE LODGE across
the road, with a little cupola, may be by *Birch* too. Sharply
contrasting again is EVENING HILL, next but one to Shore
Lodge, and almost completely concealed behind hedging. It is
a modern design of 2003 by *Richard Horden*. Fully glazed walls

*More pairs by *Banks & Barry* are in Constitution Hill and Fernside Road.

with living spaces on the upper floor to take advantage of views over Poole Harbour. The plan is a parallelogram.

In contrast to the locally popular 1930s Art Deco, LAND-FALL, No.19 Crichel Mount Road (500 yds N), is a truly Modernist house, announced by a curving white garden wall with steel letters. This delicious design of 1936–8 was by *Oliver Hill* for W.D. Shaw Ashton, a documentary film director and fellow admirer of Alvar Aalto. It was originally set in a pine forest, with a stark counterpoint of transparency and foliage.* While suburbia has since encroached on its surroundings, many of the pine trees have been retained. The solid-walled entrance front, its curving staircase bay pierced by portholes, is the backcloth for the almost wholly glazed, and carefully proportioned, garden side, which has continuous balconies on tubular steel posts connected by an elegant spiral stairway of concrete at one corner. To the l., a more solid area of walling with two more portholes. Inside, the three main living rooms can be thrown into one, a sinuous timber staircase leading around the circular hall to the sun-room on the roof. Much contemporary fitting-out still *in situ*, including a radiogram. The client had had discussions with Mendelsohn, Lubetkin and Wells Coates before fixing on Hill; he took them all to see the buildings of Seal (*see* Canford Cliffs and Sandbanks) as examples of what to avoid.**

122

UPPER PARKSTONE, NEWTOWN AND OAKDALE

A settlement midway between Branksome and Constitution Hill on Ashley Road, to the NE of Parkstone. UPPER PARKSTONE (also known as Heatherlands) first emerged in the early 1880s. NEWTOWN was developed on heathland in the angle between Ringwood Road and Old Wareham Road, to the N of Parkstone, at about the same time. OAKDALE, about 1 m. W of Newtown, grew from the 1920s around Poole Cemetery (opened in 1855, *see* below).

ST JOHN THE EVANGELIST, Ashley Road, Upper Parkstone. 1902–3 by *Romaine-Walker & Besant*, costing £5,260.*** Red brick with Bath stone dressings. Nave with aisles each present-ing gables at the ends. Chancel with large N vestry addition of 1931 by *H. Kendall* (who also added the N aisle to complete the original design). Amputated bellcote on the W gable. Windows in an odd mixture of Perp tracery under round-headed arches, perhaps strangest in the large E window (mostly filled with hor-rible 'Cathedral' glass). Unexpectedly showy interior in full-blooded Romanesque, more stone than brick. The capitals to

* It so happened that the client, an asthmatic, was allergic to flowers.
** HEATHSIDE, No.355 Sandbanks Road, and WAYFOONG, No.17 Crichel Mount Road, the first remodelled, the second new-built, both by *J.J. Joass*, have been demolished.
*** According to Basil Clarke, who also commented that it was 'horribly low'.

the six-bay nave arcades have beasts at the corners, over drums of basketwork. Spandrels with wreathed medallions interrupting continuous vertical ribbing. Two-bay chancel arcades with clusters of detached columns. Barrel-vaulted roofs. LECTERN to match.

CHURCH HALL (the previous church). 1880–1, by *Horner & Adams* of Bournemouth. Buff brick with angled buttresses and a timber-framed porch.

ST CLEMENT, St Clement's Road, Newtown. 1889 by *Romaine-Walker & Tanner*. Given by Viscount Wimborne and originally an isolated heathland chapel; now enveloped by bungalows and overlooked by the megalithic Ryvita silos. Competent Dec, aisleless, in Purbeck stone, with a timber bellcote and shingled spirelet over the chancel arch. Utilizing an original arcade, the N aisle of 1986 by *Read, Loveless & Morrell* strikes a more modern note, with windows rising into dormers and a mansard roof. – PULPIT. Cylindrical, with grey granite colonnettes and polished red Devonian inlay.

ST GEORGE, Trigon Road, Oakdale. 1959–60 by *Potter & Hare*. A very fine example of its date. Canted red brick side walls under a spreading, gabled, low-pitched copper-sheet roof. Cruciform plan. Beautifully detailed, widely spaced, leaded-light windows running the full height of the walls. Green granolithic concrete panels fill the lowest openings of the pre-cast concrete window grids. Thin strip windows above, under the eaves. Large convex-plan windows of similar detailing at the E end and on the S transept. Tall campanile with parabolic roof at the W end. Highly effective open-plan interior, with plenty of natural light reflecting off the white-painted walls, the polished black-tile floor and the varnished timber ceiling. Very slender faceted columns of green burnished granolithic concrete, flared at top and base. The altar is brought forward, leaving a LADY CHAPEL (lit by the large E window) behind. W gallery with fluted panels to its balustrade. It is reached by a circular staircase which winds elegantly around a baptistery sited on the main E–W axis in its well. Some of the FURNISHINGS are equally fine, including the ALTAR and PULPIT. – FONT. Stone, shaped like an upturned bell. Elegant burnished steel COVER.

BAPTIST CHURCH, Ashley Road (corner of Loch Road). 1907–8 by *Lawson & Reynolds*, in the usual red brick free Gothic.

WESLEYAN METHODIST CHURCH, Ashley Road (corner of Wesley Road). 1902, red brick. Gothic, with Dec-style tracery. Buttresses with finials.

POOLE CEMETERY, Cemetery Avenue, Oakdale, ¾ m. SE of St George's church. Layout and the two identical CHAPELS of 1857, by *Christopher Crabbe Creeke* of Bournemouth. Rock-faced, buttressed, with a W bellcote and circular end windows. Many fine mid- to late C19 monuments. Glazed pottery plot-markers.

MASONIC HALL, Ashley Road, ½ m. E of St John's church. Built 1895 as a Baptist church (known as 'The Tabernacle').

Refronted 1926, when it became a Masonic hall. Roughcast Gothic, with a corner turret.

WATER TOWER, Mansfield Road (250 yds SW of St John's church). Dated 1884, for Poole Water Co. Almost identical to that at Yaffle Hill (*see* Broadstone).

To the N of Oakdale and the A35, the six-storey office block of HAMWORTHY ENGINEERING, 1968–9 by *Young & Purves*, makes a full stop to Poole, much as it did in 1972.

Nearby, the former DORSET WATER BOARD, HEAD OFFICE, Nuffield Road. 1969 by *Farmer & Dark*. A refined building for its date. The walls, reduced to thin shafts, single or coupled, between the windows, rise to support a deep far-projecting cornice. All executed in dusky red brick.

PORTESHAM

6080

Quite a large village, of good Portesham stone cottages and a red brick C19 terrace. However, new bungalows and houses generally misjudge their proportions and spacing.

ST PETER. At its core this is a late C12 building, as revealed by the blocked N arcade. This includes (visible inside) a round pier with scalloped capital, a square abacus and a pointed arch. Further W some more C12 details. Next in order of time the E.E. W extension to the nave, the three-stage W tower and the chancel. The tower has high up on the S side a small window with a continuous roll moulding, and a contemporary tower arch of two chamfered orders. Its top stage is *c.* 1500 Perp, with a battlemented parapet and crocketed corner pinnacles. The stair-turret in the S angle with the nave is also Perp. Returning to E.E., the chancel has a charming N doorway with a trefoiled head and again a continuous roll mould-ing. Here also two early C14 Dec windows and a late C15 E window.

The evolution of the nave N wall provides a happy mixture of C12 and *c.* 1500 inside. The arcades have panelled arches, the piers with niches and brackets; the chancel arch goes with the arcades, and there are more brackets. In the nave one Perp and one large C17 window. The restoration of 1872 by *G. J. G. Gregory* of Dorchester was mercifully minimal. – PULPIT. Early C17. One tier of blank arches with enriched arcading; above and below this, panels with close geometrical pattern. Just behind the pulpit, a rood-loft staircase. – SCREEN. Of *c.* 1500, with single-light divisions. Traceried openings. – FONT. Prob-ably C13 but quite featureless. – SCULPTURE. Small Virgin and Child in the N aisle W wall. Also a bracket inside, in the N aisle. – HATCHMENT, N aisle. Of Sir Andrew Riccard, 1672. – ROYAL ARMS. Of George II, painted by *Thomas Iron-side*, 1754. – STAINED GLASS. E window probably by *Alexander*

Gibbs, *c.* 1872. – MONUMENTS. s porch, tablet †1682 and 1695. Only crudely classical. – Mary Weare †1675, s aisle. A crudely lettered plain tablet. – More refined, a tablet to the wives of Harry Chafin, †1701 and †1721 (with Mr Chafin added †1726), e end of N aisle. Classical with small flaming urns and cherubs in the spandrels. – John Callard Manfield †1808. Topped by a flaming urn on a black marble ground. By *Lancelot Wood* of Chelsea.

CHURCHYARD MONUMENTS. Quite a number in the west Dorset and south Somerset tradition here, mainly of the chest-tomb type. In the early C17 they are plain, with only an inscription; later they have a rather archaic Jacobean arcading, still used in the 1670s and 80s. One, built against the s wall, to William Weare †1670 (although the tablet is C20). Chest tomb and backplate with columns.

METHODIST CHURCH, 150 yds NW. Dated 1867 but plain-rendered, the walls subdivided by pilaster-like strips. To its l. its twin: a SCHOOLROOM dated 1906.

TEMPERANCE HALL (former), just s of the above. Dated 1882, by *Mark Hopson*. Plain rubble walls with an end porch.

A brief walk along the lane to the w of St Peter's will reach PORTESHAM MANOR, a piece of early C17 vernacular with considerable character. Low lower storey with many three-light windows; high upper storey with few three-light windows, with hoodmoulds. Near the centre a minimally Gothic doorway flanked by Perp niches, the latter surely C19 additions. The string course leaps up over the deep doorway lintel. Various additions at the back, one hipped and early C19. On round the lane to the s a row of cottages (now TUDOR HOUSE) with walls obviously raised in height. Good early C17 doorway and hollow-moulded mullioned windows. Extensions at both ends, the larger of *c.* 1830 in buff Abbotsbury stone. At the end of this lane a small village green on the s entry to the village with, opposite, the KINGS ARMS HOTEL of *c.* 1910. In a Home Counties style that has a certain snugness of appearance that suits Portesham among its downs. On the road w, PORTESHAM HOUSE, a trim C18 house turned into a villa with early C19 refronting.

WADDON MANOR, 1¼ m. E. In a splendid situation on the side of the downs looking across to the sea, but a curiously restricted site for such a large house. Before a fire in 1704 the house was larger, its main part extending to the w – see the patching of the present w wall. What is left is a main two-storey range seven bays by two, set end-on to the hill. This, built for Harry Chafin, dates from between 1695 and 1700 and has all the features – windows with mullion-and-transom crosses (moulded surrounds with very small keystones), alternating quoins, flat string course between the floors, hipped roof on a dentil cornice, dormers and crowning chimneystacks – which characterize the second half of the C17. Also blank upright ovals flanking the basement doorway in the s wall. At Waddon the features are very satisfyingly combined.

The principal rooms are arranged in enfilade, with the doors at the E end of the cross-walls. Fine bolection-moulded panelling in the parlour at the S end. Paired pedimented doorcases also.

To the E two lower ranges form a service court open to the S. These are in the same style at an earlier stage in its development. One-storeyed, the cross-windows very large, the hipped roof and chimneys seeming extra tall. The comparison to make is with Ashdown House, Berkshire, of *c.* 1660, and it is historically of some importance that this part of Waddon was built probably soon after 1651, for one Bullen Rymes.

BARNS to the SE, not maintaining this advanced style. The thatched barn beside the road is dated 1702, yet it still has two-light windows with hoodmoulds, and chamfered jambs to the doorway.

Fine C18 GATEPIERS to the W garden, and, to the E, an C18 GARDEN HOUSE with a pyramid roof.

HARDY MONUMENT, 1¼ m. NE, on the summit of Black Down. 70-ft octagonal chimney-like stone tower built in 1844 to the design of *Arthur Dyke Acland-Troyte*. Unmistakably Victorian with its crinoline base-mouldings, and bulging-out top. The Hardy commemorated is Admiral Sir Thomas Masterman, Nelson's flag-captain, of 'Kiss me, Hardy' fame (†1839).

BLACK DOWN, 1¼ m. NE. A group of five BARROWS cluster on the hill-crest at the Hardy monument. One, a bell barrow cut away by a gravel pit, contained four Middle Bronze Age urns.

HELL STONE, ½ m. SSW of the Hardy monument. Nine upright stones supporting an oval capstone, the incorrect rebuilding in 1866 of the chamber of a Neolithic long barrow.

HAMPTON HILL STONE CIRCLE, ½ m. NW. Excavation in 1965 showed that this circle consisted of nine stones, with narrow V-sectioned ditches on the E and W sides.

PORTLAND

6070

To anyone following the history of building in England, what matters about Portland is that it is a quarry, or rather a series of quarries. The excellent properties of the white limestone, soft enough to carve but exceedingly durable, were first widely appreciated in the early C17. This was not the beginning, as much stone was exported from the island in the medieval period, when Portland stone was used on Exeter Cathedral and Christchurch Priory. From *c.* 1630 Charles I operated a royal monopoly, managed by Inigo Jones with great rigour. Stone was shipped off the island at the King's Pier, a stone jetty on its E side. At the end of the century, Wren's St Paul's Cathedral was faced throughout with Portland stone, and it must have been this which created a countrywide demand. Until the post-war advent of industrialized building materials, with only minor fluctuations (caused mainly by shipping and labour difficulties), the demand rarely slackened. In the C19 convicts were introduced to produce the large quantities of stone required for the Portland Harbour Breakwater (*see* below), and the prison, together with military fortifications, has remained a feature of the landscape ever since.

Though geologically Portland is related to Purbeck, it feels like coming to a far part of the country as one crosses the bar from Weymouth to this rock with its largely treeless heights, the ground pitted everywhere with quarries. Signs of medieval cultivation appear further s, with significant survivals of earthen baulks subdividing strip fields. The isolation was ameliorated by the completion of a bridge in 1839, and with the coming of the Weymouth & Portland Railway, opened in 1865 (and closed in 1965). Housing has also rapidly increased from the 1960s onwards with settlements expanding out of all proportion to their previous size, transforming the quarry-dominated world.

There is no full-sized town in Portland, and certainly not one that could claim to be the centre. Each settlement is treated one by one alphabetically.

CASTLETOWN

The castle (*see* below) was the only structure here until *c.* 1790, when a small quay and cottages were built to the E. These were linked to the ever-expanding stone quarries on Tophill in 1826, when the Merchants' Railway was opened. Construction of the breakwater from 1849 to 1872 saw additional railways built for stone transport, and after completion the Royal Navy dockyard was developed. This, together with the adjacent Air Station, closed in the 1990s, the former becoming a commercial port. The settlement was therefore largely bereft of what had become its main reason for existence. However, facilities created for the sailing events of the 2012 Olympic Games, together with the development of the port and new industry, have changed the character of the place considerably.

52 PORTLAND CASTLE (English Heritage). A link in the chain of castles built by Henry VIII from Kent to Cornwall in his fear of a French invasion. Among them it is perhaps the best preserved of all. The Portland stone ashlar has remained wonderfully crisp, a happy foil to Sandsfoot (Weymouth) across the bay. The castle was built probably in 1539–40, and cost £4,964 19s. 10¼d. In plan it is simpler than many of Henry's castles, like an open fan, the curved face presented towards Weymouth Bay. What is typical is its squatness, the low outer walls hardly surmounted by the inner. All that was needed were fortifiable platforms for cannon and garrison quarters. Curved outer faces to the merlons with embrasures between. In the curved outer wall, deep gun embrasures with slightly pointed heads. Above this was a flat roof (probably removed in the early C19) supporting further cannon. A roof for cannon was also above

the accommodation areas. As a result guns could be mounted at three levels. Cruciform arrow-slits to the landward side, some converted to hoodmoulded windows in the C19, when the castle was inhabited. The only decorative feature is the string courses running round at three levels. Wing walls of unequal length on either side provide a further terrace for guns.

Entrance is down a dog-leg passage from a doorway in the E wall. Internally there is an octagonal central space of two storeys, divided by timber-framed partitions to form three rooms below and five above. Below is the castle's only refinement, a central octagonal post with elaborately moulded cap and base. All the rooms have fireplaces. Doorways with flattened four-centred heads. Further, larger, rectangular rooms NE and SW, the latter identified as the kitchen.

Immediately W the MASTER GUNNER'S LODGINGS. Of the C17, converted from a brewhouse in the early C19. L-plan. This has battlemented parapets and an outer battlemented wall attached. A gateway (with the arms of Charles II over) leads through into a yard. Beyond this, to the E, the walled GOVERNOR'S GARDEN, landscaped in 2003 by *Christopher Bradley-Hole*.

PORTLAND HARBOUR BREAKWATER. In four sections, the first two of 1847–72, by *J.M. Rendel*, succeeded by *(Sir) John Coode* after Rendel's death in 1856. The contractor was *J.T. Leather*. Two further N sections finally completed in 1905. An immense undertaking, eventually spanning the 2½ m. from Portland to Bincleaves, Weymouth. The actual length is longer owing to the curved layout. When complete it provided the largest area of man-made harbour in the world. Built using large blocks of stone from the quarries on the Verne, for which a special railway was constructed. At its S end on its own jetty, the former VICTUALLING STORE of *c.* 1850. A long two-storey stone-built structure. On the S side of the central breakwater opening or East Ship Channel, BREAKWATER (or 'CHEQUERED') FORT, of 1879. A large circular structure, 200 ft (60 metres) in diameter, of granite and Portland stone with reinforced concrete and armour plating, modified at various dates to incorporate more advanced guns and steam power for their operation. On the N side of this entrance, at the SE end of the North Eastern Breakwater, PORTLAND HARBOUR LIGHTHOUSE of 1851. A tapering metal lattice tower, 26 ft (8 metres) high.

OFFICERS' FIELD, Victory Road, ¼ m. S from Portland Castle. Major housing development by *HTA Design* for ZeroC Holdings, 2009–13. Simple repeated domestic forms. Natural Portland rubble stone and roughcast render; pitched slate roofs. A highly effective scheme on this open hillside site overlooking Chesil Beach.

EASTON

In effect a small town, centred around a trapezoidal 'square'. Two wide main streets, heading N and SE. The latter, Wakeham,

includes a number of late C17 and early C18 cottages in a continuous run, interspersed with the occasional, more elaborate, late
C19 house. It ends with *Wyatt*'s embattled gateway to Pennsylvania Castle (*see* below).

ALL SAINTS. 1914–17 by *G.L. Crickmay* of *Crickmay & Son*. A
large and prosperous-looking church, which Pevsner thought
'untouched by all the new developments in early C20 church
architecture'. However, Crickmay seems to have been aware of
such contemporary architects as Temple Moore, whose work
may very well have been influential here. Finely tooled ashlar,
Late Perp, with a planned but unbuilt SW tower. Aisle with
cross-gables. Graceful four-bay arcades, the last only slightly
higher in response to the transepts. – Original FURNISHINGS
complete. Typical of their date are the PULPIT, CHOIR STALLS
and CLERGY SEATS. – STAINED GLASS. The E window and
windows in the SE chapel by *Clayton & Bell*, *c.* 1920.

ST ANDREW (old), Church Ope Cove, ½ m. SSE. Down a footpath, about 100 yds from Church Ope Road. Of C12 origin
with C14 rebuilding after a fire. Abandoned in the mid C18 after
a landslip. Of the earlier date, the chief datable survival is the
N respond of the chancel arch with two continuous mouldings.
There are also two openings into a S aisle. The ruin, further
damaged by a Second World War bomb, has been consolidated
during more recent archaeological investigations.

83 ST GEORGE (Churches Conservation Trust), Reforne, ½ m. W.
The most impressive C18 church in Dorset, owing partly to
its solitary position on the top of Portland, partly to the fine
Portland ashlar work, and partly to its singular architecture.
It is by *Thomas Gilbert*, a liveryman of the London Masons'
Company and a member of a local masons' family.* Designed
and built by him, 1754–66. His conception has true grandeur.
St George is a large church with a W tower, a nave, transepts,
an apse and a kind of abortive dome over the crossing. The
plan owes something to Wren, the exterior no doubt more to
Hawksmoor. There are two tiers of windows, all with simple,
broad raised frames without any moulding. The result makes
a masculine show, to quote Vanbrugh. The tower top has four
aedicules of Tuscan columns with straight entablatures – no
pediments anywhere – and a concave-sided top stage with
a finial, Wren-ish and decidedly suggestive of the St Paul's
Cathedral towers. C19 pedimented N porch.

The INTERIOR has segmental plaster vaults throughout
and a shallow unlit dome. – FONT. A baluster with a fluted
bowl. – PULPIT AND READING DESK. A matching pair either
side of the main aisle, just E of the crossing. Part of an early
C19 refurnishing. The remarkably unaltered set of BOX PEWS
are also of this date, although the COMMUNION RAIL appears
of *c.* 1700 and may therefore have been brought in. – Three

---

*The inscription in the dome of the vestry in the W tower reads: 'Thomas Gilbert
of this island architect and builder of this church A.D. 1758.'

GALLERIES, at the W end and in each of the transepts, accessed separately. They are carried on iron columns. – TILES by *Minton* in the sanctuary. – STAINED GLASS. E window by *Alexander Gibbs*, 1878. – MONUMENTS. In the churchyard good mid-C18 tombstones. Also several more elaborate C19 monuments, taking full advantage of the fine stone. As elsewhere locally, the masons have allowed themselves a high degree of invention.

LYCHGATE. 1935, by *Ravenscroft & Rooke*. A heavyweight Portland structure.

EASTON METHODIST CHURCH, Easton Square, ⅛ m. W. 1906–7 by *La Trobe & Weston* of Bristol, costing £7,000. Fanciful for its date, a Free Style blend of E.E. and Art Nouveau. Two corner turrets, with pepperpot cupolas. Two plate-traceried windows above the central porch, its French-looking gable growing out of the wall-plane. Over the doorway (arched in chevron and dogtooth) a carved Christ in Glory. Also freely handled the long sides, but treated as a nave and transepts. Apsed 'E' end (actually W). Spectacular interior, a gallery on three sides supported on cast-iron columns with leaf capitals. Gallery front of cast plaster with tree and wheatfield emblems. Its colour matches the stone pulpit and reading desk set forward of the pointed arch to the apse. The pulpit has a carved Last Supper on its bowed front. Behind more carved panels, then behind again and set back in the apse, the organ, crowning the whole composition. The other FURNISHINGS and FITTINGS are exceptionally complete. Note particularly the curvaceous detailing on the pulpit stair handrails.

WESLEYAN SCHOOL (former), just l. of the church. Dated 1878. Chapel-like but with inventive detailing.

SALVATION ARMY CITADEL (former), Easton Street, ¼ m. N. Dated 1926. Vaguely Dutch-shaped gable.

CLOCK TOWER, Easton Gardens, 100 yds W. Of 1907. A blend of classical and Gothic features. The focal point of the gardens of 1904.

ST GEORGE'S CENTRE, Reforne, ¼ m. W. Built as a school. Tudor Revival. Opened 1857. H-plan, the linking range arcaded. School hall, c. 1880, l.

DRILL HALL (former), Easton Street, ⅓ m. N. Of 1868 by *G.R. Crickmay*, for the Portland Volunteer Artillery Corps. Castle style, of rock-faced stone. Towers added by *Crickmay*, 1884 and 1900.

RUFUS CASTLE, Church Ope Road, ½ m. SE. A castle here is mentioned as early as 1142. What stands today on the cliff edge is a late C15 replacement. Built of large smooth blocks of island stone. An irregular pentagon in plan, the thicker angled sides with circular first-floor gunports, deeply splayed within. These face inland. On the SE cliff edge a thinner blank wall that has partially fallen away. This may have been an internal wall originally, exposed owing to cliff collapse. (Jamb of a doorway in it.) Of architectural and datable details there are the entrance gateway in the SW wall with a four-centred Perp arch; some

shaped corbels for a machicolated parapet; and an early C19
gateway cut into the N wall, approached by a contemporary
arched bridge over the sunken lane.

PENNSYLVANIA CASTLE (now an event venue), Pennsylvania
Road, ½ m. SSE. Built *c.* 1805 by *James Wyatt* for John Penn, the
Governor of Portland (and grandson of the founder of Pennsylvania). It stands on the brink of the drop down to the sea
above Church Ope Cove. Just a villa in accommodation, but
at that date such a situation seemed naturally to call for cas-
tellation. This one did not, however, call forth Wyatt's higher
powers (cf. the more theatrical Norris Castle, Isle of Wight, of
1804). The irregular grouping which was then just beginning
to be sought he achieved by merely tacking a round tower on
to the NE corner of a rectangular block with four square corner
turrets. Not much differentiation by height of the different
parts. Similarly with the Portland stone, ashlar in some parts,
rubble in others, but to no special effect. Entrance loggia on
the short N side, of three pointed arches. Lancets on this side.
Big round-headed windows in the tower, and pointed windows
to light the corridor along the E front. Low later additions to
the SE turret and on the S side have not helped the composition. No original interiors.
    Castellated GATEWAY, also by *Wyatt*.

GROVE

Mature trees, together with the fine Portland ashlar buildings,
initially suggest a well-appointed suburb. However, apart from
modern housing the core of the hamlet is connected with the
convict prison, originally built here in 1848.

ST PETER (disused). 1870–2, by *Sir Edmund Du Cane* of the
Royal Engineers, late Chief Administrator of all H.M. Prisons,
and built by convict labour. In its own way as surprising and as
bold in scale as St George, Reforne, Easton. It is also of ashlar,
Romanesque not Norman in style, has a dwarf gallery under
the eaves, large apsed transepts, a low, wide E apse with small
windows, and no campanile. Wheel window set in a blind
pointed arch at the W end, above a colonnaded lean-to narthex-
porch, the latter oddly off axis. The roof is open timbering with
hammerbeams and arched braces and the crossing marked by
pairs of diagonally set arched braces. – The PAVEMENTS are
mosaic work by female convicts from other prisons. – PULPIT,
LECTERN and FONT. All strong Neo-Romanesque masonry
compositions, no doubt by *Du Cane*. – STAINED GLASS. A
mixed set in the nine apse windows, mostly by *Clayton & Bell*,
c. 1875 to 1921. The outer two by *Mayer & Co.*, 1890.
OUR LADY AND ST ANDREW (R.C.) (disused). 1868, by *J.A.
Hansom* for Fr George Poole. Chancel and sacristy added,
1881. The façade is rock-faced and in the style of *c.* 1300. Plain
interior with a hammerbeam roof.

A fine ashlar WALL with bold GATEPIERS lines the roadside from the VICARAGE (1885), past the church to beyond the former SCHOOL. The latter is a boldly detailed Neo-Romanesque composition of 1872, probably also by *Du Cane*. Matching addition in the l. re-entrant of 1898.

Next along the road heading SE is ALMA TERRACE. A long Portland stone cottage terrace built for prison officers, 1854. Two parallel-roofed ranges. The original six houses are now twelve cottages.

H.M. PRISON AND ADULT/YOUNG OFFENDERS' ESTAB-LISHMENT, ¼ m. SE. Erected as a convict prison in 1848 by *Joshua Jebb*, using convict labour. This was a new departure in the treatment of convicted felons. Previously they were either transported or imprisoned in hulks. Enlarged N, 1910, when the cell blocks were rebuilt. (As first built the cell blocks were partially timber-framed, with external boarding.) Two parallel four-storey blocks, that to the W with a long side wing. Substantial, but architecturally inexpressive, GATEHOUSE on the S boundary. Its main feature is a carved royal arms above the parapet.

Opposite, the former GOVERNOR'S HOUSE (now visitors' centre), *c.* 1850. A plain two-storey block, extended at each end *c.* 1870.

Along the coastal section of the road, two SEWER VENTILATORS. Of *c.* 1870. Portland stone, 24 ft (7.3 metres) high. Octagonal shafts on high pedestals.

PORTLAND BILL

OLD UPPER and OLD LOWER LIGHTHOUSES. Two, of uniform design but different height, built 1866, on the site of 1716 structures (rebuilt 1789). Both replaced by the NEW LIGHT-HOUSE, near to the Bill itself, 1906, by *Wakeham Bros* of Plymouth. The cost was £13,000; height 115 ft (35 metres).

OBELISK, on the Bill. Dated TH (for Trinity House) 1844. Three-sided, of Portland stone; 30 ft (9 metres) high.

SOUTHWELL

The most southerly village on the island. In its barren location, it has similarities with Cornwall.

ST ANDREW. 1879 by *G.R. Crickmay*. The church was paid for by a national fund, including contributions from the relatives of those lost in the wreck of the *Avalanche* off Portland, 1877. Nave and chancel; rock-faced, with tiled roof. The baptistery is placed as if it were a S porch. W bellcote. Unusually complete interior with more interest than often with Crickmay. Large cusps to the baptistery arch. High-quality FURNISH-INGS, especially the choir stalls and clergy desks. – Wrought-iron TORCHÈRES. – Cylindrical PULPIT typical of *Crickmay*, and bowl FONT, both with four polished stone colonnettes. – CURIOSA. Glass-fronted cabinet in the porch containing artefacts salvaged from the *Avalanche*. – STAINED GLASS. An extensive scheme by a sequence of makers. The E, W and baptistery windows by *Lavers, Barraud & Westlake*, 1879. Most of the side windows are by *Alexander Gibbs*, 1879. His is only the centre light to one on the S side, the others by *E.R. Suffling & Co.*, 1884. A pictorial window by the pulpit, possibly also by *Suffling*. Finally, a bold blue S window by *Jon Callan*, 1981.

WESLEYAN METHODIST CHAPEL (former), ⅛ m. SE. Dated 1849. Simple front with porch and sashes.

MARITIME HOUSE, SOUTHWELL BUSINESS PARK (former Admiralty Underwater Weapons Establishment), ½ m. W. 1948–52 by the department of the *Civil Engineer in Chief, Admiralty*. Very large Progressive Modern block, the windows in long bands divided by fluted panels. Big bowed projection, keeping the typical strongly asymmetrical massing. Faced with Portland ashlar.

To the N and S, large areas of STRIP FIELDS of medieval origin, subdivided by earthen baulks, survive over about 150 acres. These vary greatly in length, with groups abutting each other at right angles. C19 mere-stones, usually inscribed with capital letters, are also occasionally found.

CULVERWELL, ½ m. S, on the N side of the road to Portland Bill. Mesolithic WORKING FLOORS and MIDDEN.

UNDERHILL

A small town sited between Verne Hill and Chesil Beach. It was in existence by the late C17, and consisted of four distinct settlements: Chiswell (also known as Chesil or Chesilton), Maidenwell, Mallams and Fortuneswell. By the early C19 it was the chief village on the island. Its main street, Fortuneswell, is the most urban on Portland. The mixture of cottages at Chiswell has a unique character, brought about by their position under the ridge of Chesil Beach. At various dates storms have swept through Chiswell, flooding houses and streets, thence bringing about campaigns of rebuilding. The most destructive case was in 1824.

ST JOHN THE BAPTIST. 1839–40 by *Edward Mondey* of Dorchester. Ashlar, of the Commissioners' type, W tower, nave with big wide lancets. Short chancel with an E wheel window, added by *Crickmay*, 1877. Simple interior with W gallery. – STAINED GLASS. E window by *Clayton & Bell*, 1920. Two S windows by *A.L. Moore*, 1906. Two more recent N windows, one by *C.D. Williams* and *K. Batty*, 1968, the other by *Colwyn Morris* for *G. Maile Studios*, 1972.

ROYAL MANOR THEATRE (former Primitive Methodist chapel), ⅛ m. NW. 1869, by *James Kerridge* of Wisbech, Cambs. Gothic, with rusticated pilaster strips above buttresses.

UNDERHILL METHODIST CHURCH, ¼ m. SE. 1898–1900 by *Robert Curwen*. Perp, with a big traceried W window. Corner pinnacles, those flanking the 'nave' more elaborate.

CONGREGATIONAL CHAPEL (former), High Street, Maiden-well, ¼ m. WSW. 1858, by *James Cheney*, the minister. Lancet Gothic.

WAR MEMORIAL, Yeates Road, ⅓ m. S. 1926. Stone obelisk on two-stage base. Wreath above the main inscription panels.

SCULPTURE, New Road, ⅓ m. S. The Spirit of Portland, 2000 by *Joanna Szuwalska*. Figures of a stone mason and fisherman.

QUEEN ANNE HOUSE, ¼ m. SE. Of *c.* 1730 by *Thomas Gilbert*, architect and quarry merchant, for himself. Five bays wide. Gibbs surrounds to the ground-floor windows and doorway. Plainer architraves above, these with aprons. A demonstration piece.

H.M. PRISON (now an immigration removal centre), ⅓ m. E. This occupies the VERNE CITADEL, terraced fortifications cut into the hillside in 1852–67, by *Captain W. Crossman* of the Royal Engineers. Its purpose was to guard Portland and Weymouth harbours. The works consisted of batteries and an artificial ravine, 120 ft (36.5 metres) wide and up to 70 ft (21 metres) deep, with brick-arched, earth-covered ramparts. The chief external feature is a bold arched gateway with carved royal arms over the arch. The prison within opened in 1949. A new wing was added 1972–5.

PORTLAND BILL *see* PORTLAND, p. 489

POUNDBURY *see* DORCHESTER, p. 258

POWERSTOCK

5090

The church tower crowns the village on the side of a knoll among knolls, sharp-sided and wooded. Mostly Victorian houses, but of local materials and so spaced about that one gets many pleasant diagonal views among them.

ST MARY. The most elaborate Norman chancel arch in any Dorset parish church. Three orders of sturdy columns, rudely and variously decorated capitals, arch with rope, dogtooth and chevron orders. The shafts of the two outer columns are decorated too: horizontal strips of chevron, lozenges and a delicate loose interlace. No motif would make a date after 1150 necessary. (A hoodmoulding was removed at some point.) Late C14 Perp W tower, incorporating several C12 fragments within. Early C15 top stage, the bold buttressing added at this date. Embattled parapet with small gargoyles on a string course. The Dec W window is part of a major restoration carried out by *R.C. Carpenter* for the Rev. Thomas Sanctuary, 1854–9, completed by *John Hicks* after Carpenter's death in 1855. Polygonal S stair-turret with a small bay window at its

head, added by *C.E. Ponting*, 1915. Genuine Perp the W and
S doorways, the former with side pinnacles, the latter quite
ambitious, with statuettes l. and r. and three niches over. All
of these with crocketed-pinnacled hoods. Continuous mouldings to the tower arch. Within the W doorway arch, cross-ribs
with bosses (cf. St Catherine's Chapel, Abbotsbury). Early
C14 S aisle arcade with round piers and double-chamfered
arches. The N aisle arcade a copy, the aisle itself of 1854–5
by *Carpenter*. S aisle remodelled by *Hicks*, who repositioned
the porch one bay to the W. Also by *Hicks* the chancel. It is
in an Early Dec style and has inside triple shafts to the roof
and leaf corbels. The complicated S squint, also Early Dec, is
mostly a contrivance by Hicks, but so authentic-looking as to
have confused earlier writers.* It has to the chancel two shafts
and two pointed-trefoiled arches. Nave roof corbels carved by
Seymour of Taunton.

FURNISHINGS. REREDOS. 1917 by *C.E. Ponting*. Stone,
with an image niche and crocketed pinnacles. – Good CHOIR
STALLS, CLERGY SEAT (by *J. Wellspring*) and PEWS (by *Carpenter*) with poppyhead ends. The PEW FRONTAL is probably
an addition by *Hicks*. – FLOOR TILES by *Minton* throughout
the chancel, including a set in the sanctuary depicting various
figures, designed for Minton by *Pugin*. Either side of the
reredos, diapered majolica unglazed tilework, also by *Minton*
(the design based on tiles from the shrine of St Dunstan,
Canterbury). – PULPIT by *Boulton*. Of the 1850s; Caen stone.
Elaborate in a Dec style with figure-niches to each face. – FONT.
Rectangular bowl with chamfered corners, early C15. Multi-
shafted stem, perhaps C13. – WALL PAINTING. Nave arcade
spandrels by *Harland & Fisher*, also 1850s. Running foliage in
orange-red. Also leaf trails around the chancel windows and
within the reveals of the E window. – STAINED GLASS. Chancel
E, N and S windows by *Hardman*, 1859. Very good, freshly
detailed with strong, pure colours. W window by *Hardman*,
1892. S aisle W window by *Tom Denny*, 1991. – MONUMENTS.
In the tower a medieval coffin-lid with a carved foliate cross.
– Thomas Larcombe †1610. Arched tablet with putti in the
spandrels. – Rev. Thomas Sanctuary †1889. Large brass by
T. Pratt & Sons. – Also a good group of CHURCHYARD MONU-
MENTS, including one very eccentric in shape with bulbous
ends, tapering-panel sides and standing on moulded feet like
a piece of furniture.

LYCHGATE, *c.* 1858. Of stone. Strongly built, with carved
eagles at the corners.

The PRIMARY SCHOOL, of 1873 by *G.R. Crickmay*, is built of
materials from the chapel of St Mary Magdalene, West Milton.
The most obvious feature is the two-light Perp window in
the S wall. At the bottom of the hill a SCHOOL of 1848–50 by
R.C. Carpenter. Very typical with its bald plate-traceried semi-
dormers. At the top of the village, N of the church, GLEBE

---

*A plain squint opening is all that is shown on *Hicks*'s survey drawing of 1855.

HOUSE, of two parts, the l. dated 1669, which is a helpful guide to vernacular usage. Windows with hollow-chamfered mullions and hoodmoulds, i.e. no change yet in inherited tradition. Further N the former VICARAGE of 1843. Wide sashes and a low-pitched central gable.

MAPPERCOMBE MANOR, ¾ m. SSW. The house has grown clockwise, the earliest part at the SE corner. Here in the E wall a Perp upper window, of two sub-cusped arched lights in a square surround. Inside a trefoil-headed S recess, suggesting that this was a chapel when the house was a possession of Cerne Abbey. C17 S block, well windowed to the S, with mullioned windows of 4:5:4 lights, not quite evenly spaced, on both storeys. But the centre bay is of 1905 by *Crickmay & Son* (in place of a two-storey gabled porch), when the house was considerably enlarged for Capt. H.B. Nicholson by the addition of a gabled block at the NE corner. The tall brick chimneys are also of this date. Round to the NW comes a long wing dated 1699 for Nicholas Browne (indicated by his initials).

CASTLE, ⅜ m. SE. Motte and bailey. King John bought the manor in 1205, but of the lodge which he erected here nothing can be seen.

EGGARDON HILL. *See* Askerswell.

HENGE, 220 yds E of Eggardon hill-fort. Circular ditch and outer bank, 100 ft (30 metres) in diameter. It incorporates a ditched BOWL BARROW on the SW side, and surrounds a central BARROW MOUND.

POXWELL

7080

5 m. SE of Dorchester

Now without its church, the village centre is the manor house, with the farm and cottages further along the road.*

POXWELL MANOR HOUSE. The house illustrates lucidly the state of major manor-house design in the earliest years of the C17. It is probably of *c.* 1610, built for John Henning, son of a Poole merchant, and county sheriff in 1609. There is no exact date, just a casually scratched 1618 in the porch to give a *terminus ante quem*. The entrance front, of Purbeck ashlar, faces E and may have been intended to be symmetrical, with gabled wings projecting to l. and r. and a stretched-out centre of four bays, with a central porch. But in the event the S wing was never built. Ample four-light mullioned windows, with one transom, those in the N wing C20 replacements. No hoodmoulds, one notices, but continuous string courses linking the window heads. The porch is oddly weak, its gable rising only to the eaves level of the main range; but it introduces new motifs,

---

*The medieval church (whose crypt remains in the burial ground) was replaced in 1868 by one on a different site by *G. Evans*. This too was demolished, in 1969.

both vernacular, the upper window with a hoodmould, and of the local classicism. Round-headed entrance arch and inner arch, the latter with rustication round it; shell-headed niches l. and r. of the entrance, and a pair each side within the porch. The niches are of the Montacute (Somerset) and Cranborne variety, slightly coarsened, and the porch arch similar to one in a wing at Sherborne Castle. This is suggestive of the involvement of *William Arnold* or his Hamden Hill colleagues, at least in the porch.

What strikes one altogether about Poxwell is its limpness as a design. Beyond its detailing, nothing architectural is made of the porch, or of the gables or chimneystacks. No bold silhouette is achieved. And the back (w) elevation is a vernacular jumble of rubble stone, as to a lesser degree is the N front. The N front has one plus three gables, with apex chimneys, and a further W extension of *c.* 1850. W doorway to the screens passage with a double-wave moulding. The result of this is a T-plan, the main range one room deep, the hall opening to the r. of the porch. Two doors from the screens passage to the l., where service rooms might have been expected. Yet the kitchen fireplace, part of the original build and now the dining room, occurs in the W arm of the N wing, so perhaps a S wing was not in fact planned. To add to the asymmetry, there is a small block built in the re-entrant between the hall and the NW wing. This is ashlar-faced, though at the back of the house, and was clearly intended to give an additional comfortable chamber on each floor. In 1634 the façade was declared complete, when the brick-walled front garden was built, the charming brick gazebo-gatehouse aligned on the porch. Round-headed entrance arch, with the date, the arch mouldings still Gothic. The gatehouse is hexagonal in plan, with a pyramidal roof, and round angle buttresses capped with bell-shaped finials; it gives the house just the spark of fantasy it needs.

Internally there is nothing more to mention except the hall chimneypiece (said to have been moved from an upstairs room). It has coupled Corinthian columns, an awkward arrangement of pediment and entablature above, with a cherub's head, and tiny figures of a putto, an old man and Diana. It is certainly too crude to be a piece by Arnold. The Jacobean plasterwork in this room seems much later, while the semicircular-headed doorway into the N wing (continuous mouldings) is re-set.

At MANOR FARM, just to the N, is a late C16 stone BARN, not large but of unusual grandeur. Large porch on each side. In the S wall the window has a piece of reused Perp tracery. Roof trussed with crucks springing from the tops of the walls.

PUMP on the roadside. Dated 1843, built for John Trenchard. A gabled ashlar niche. Wing walls.

TRENCHARD COTTAGES, further along the road to the N. Four pairs of estate cottages, also dated 1843. Fine Purbeck rubble. Thatched. Nos. 5 and 6 are distinguished by a front gable.

CAIRN RING, ½ m. SE. A continuous ring of stones, exposed from within a destroyed barrow mound.

POYNTINGTON

A loose gathering around a triangular central area, the church up the hill to the SW.

ALL SAINTS. An early C14 Dec church, except for the C12 N doorway and the chancel. The doorway has one order of columns with free volute capitals and a solid, blank tympanum. The most likely date is the early C12. The chancel with its apse is of 1863–6 by *Henry Hall*. It is E.E. in style with a polygonal S vestry. Dec two-stage W tower, the lower stage very high. W window with reticulated tracery, but no W doorway. Upper stage of *c.* 1400, therefore Perp. Higher stair-turret. The tower arch has continuous mouldings. Dec nave (with a C16 three-light window l. of the porch) and S aisle (nave and aisle restored 1896 by *Thomas Farrall*). Here a Y-traceried window at the W end and a square-headed S window with ogee tracery. Also a typically perverse S window: the tracery bars are two saltire crosses forming a lozenge in the middle. Flat-headed four-light E window; C16. The aisle arcade has fat octagonal piers with moulded capitals and an arch with fillets. In the S wall are two cusped TOMB-RECESSES and a PISCINA, all early C14-looking. – REREDOS. 1860s. A row of four *Minton* tile-filled quatrefoils, set in leaf carving by *T. Earp* and *B. Grassby*. – Encaustic TILEWORK in the sanctuary, probably also by *Minton*, copying old tiles found in the church. – PULPIT by *Farrall*, 1896. – FONT. C12. Of Ham Hill stone. Circular bowl and stem in one, of tapering shape. The bowl has a rope moulding at its bottom. – BENCHES. Plain C17 work. – STAINED GLASS. E window by *Lavers & Barraud*, 1866 (designed by *M.F. Halliday*). Chancel N window by *Lavers & Barraud*, *c.* 1860–70. – MONUMENTS. Knight, late C14 – see the basinet helmet, the low belt and the head resting on a great helm. – George Tilly, wife and daughter, all kneeling; early C17. Painted alabaster. – Two wooden panels to Baldwin Malet †1646 and Thomas Malet †1665. Each with well-painted achievement of arms.

COURT HOUSE. Beside the churchyard. Very restored late C14 Dec stone house. The E front seems to be basically in order, a recessed centre, with screens-passage doorway at its l. end, and two renewed two-light windows with a quatrefoil in the pointed head. The doorway has a trefoiled rere-arch. The S cross-wing projects somewhat, and here is a solar window, much restored (the label mould running along the transom is distinctly odd). Two lights and a quatrefoil above. Re-set C14 corbel carved as a bearded head.

Poyntington, National School.
Engraving by J. S. Heaviside, 1848

OLD RECTORY. 1837 by *W. Kendal*, surveyor. Just a box, but a
shape, especially the hipped slate roof, typical of its date.

NATIONAL SCHOOL (former), just W of the above. 1848 by *R. J.
Withers*. Dec style with reticulated tracery.

POYNTINGTON MANOR HOUSE, at the foot of the hill. The
most fully surviving Late Perp courtyard house in the county,
c. 1500. Architecturally it can never have made a great show.
Today it makes even less, largely re-windowed as it was in the
C17 (probably for Sir Thomas Malet, †1665), and deprived of
the patina of age in the mid C20. Even so, the plan remains
unblurred. The N is the entrance range. High four-centred
archway, the arches front and back moulded with a broad
double wave, and the N arch slightly elaborated from that.
Square window above with a hoodmould on carved heads
and two cinquefoiled lights. The gable, like all the rest
of the roof, is modern. At its W end what seems like an original arched doorway, set very low down. Above it a three-light
window with arched lights, probably early C17. The E range
both towards the courtyard and on the outer side has windows
that may be of the C17, but many must be C20. So we cannot
say anything definite about the intermediate range linking
gateway and hall. The S range, lower than the others, belonged
to an open hall. Staircase projection at the SE junction, i.e.
access from hall to private apartments, which then must have
occupied the E range. Here is the best sequence of original
windows, three cinquefoiled two-lighters under square heads
with hoods. The only remaining window of the hall is much like
them, but is hoodless and has a transom and a wave-moulded
surround. Hollow-chamfered mullions. Buttress to the r. of the
hall window, but nothing else to comment on.

PRESTON

A village on the Wareham road, 2½ m. from Weymouth, but now
a suburb. Sutton Poyntz to the N still has village characteristics,
but to the S the slopes to the sea are covered with a large static
caravan settlement.

ST ANDREW. The C14 Dec nave was much altered in the C15,
when the chancel and porch were added, and in the early
C16 upon the building of the W tower and S aisle (although
the Dec tower arch was retained). Two-stage battlemented
and buttressed tower. The N and S windows have depressed
two-centred arches, i.e. later C15, those in the S aisle reused.
S arcade of four bays with four-centred arches and piers of
standard section. Major restoration by *T.H. Wyatt* in 1855, when
the church was thoroughly refurnished. – FONT. Purbeck bowl,
c. 1200, square with tapering sides, and the familiar four blank
arches each side. C15 octagonal stem and base. – STAINED
GLASS. Distinctive E window by *H.J. Stammers* of York, 1949.
By the same, a Pilgrim's Progress window (nave N). The Art-
Nouveau-influenced chancel S window (moved from Weymouth
College Chapel, 1940) is by *Catharine Ewbank*. W window by
Kempe & Co., 1908. – MONUMENT. William Lockett †1614.
Kneeling figure in academic dress in a box-like recess. The
inscription below reads: 'The Vicar here intombed lyes, whose
patron him doth eterniz'.

   LYCHGATE. Of 1911, said to incorporate moulded C15
timbers from Sutton Poyntz court house.
WESLEYAN METHODIST CHAPEL (former), Sutton Road,
300 yds N. Of *c*. 1817. Brick, with a pair of Gothic windows.
Sandwiched in a cottage terrace.
At SUTTON POYNZ, ½ m. N, in Plaisters Lane, four small
pre-war houses by *E. Wamsley Lewis* of *Trent & Lewis*, best
known as the designers of the New Victoria Cinema in
London (1928–30). Portland rubble stone and thatch, i.e. local
materials, still in the Arts and Crafts tradition. Going NW,
on the l. they are VALLEY COTTAGE, 1937 (but with a large
later addition), SPINNEYS, 1936, STADDLES, 1933–4 (the only
one to be published and still much as first built), and on the
r. RUSSETT COTTAGE, 1936. Also much altered but retaining
thatch, COB COTTAGE, White Horse Lane, of 1939. They
are interspersed with more recent houses and concealed by
mature planting.
WATER WORKS, Sutton Road, Sutton Poyntz. Robust Neoclassical pavilions with linking range, 1856. Portland ashlar.
RIVIERA HOTEL, Bowleaze Coveway, ⅔ m. S. 1937, by *L. Stuart   120
Smith*. White-plastered Art Deco. A long arched-colonnaded
sweep with bedrooms on two floors leading off open-air
walkways. At the centre an administration block with communal facilities, highlighted by a high square-topped tower.
Built of reinforced concrete using the *Mouchel-Hennebique*
system.

ROMANO-CELTIC TEMPLE. On Jordan Hill, 1 m. SW. The stone foundations of a square temple. The finds are predominantly of the C4, but include earlier Roman material.

EAST HILL, 1 m. NE. Two groups of ROUND BARROWS, the most easterly on the South Dorset Ridgeway. Others in Osmington parish (q.v.).

RIMBURY, ½ m. NW, 400 yds SW of Chalbury hill-fort (*see* Bincombe). An URN FIELD which produced nearly 100 Middle Bronze Age urns of Deverel–Rimbury type, so named from this site and from the Deverel Barrow (*see* Milborne St Andrew); most were destroyed on discovery. Many contained cremation burials. There were also earlier inhumations in stone cists and a Beaker burial. The site is in part destroyed by a water reservoir.

7090

PUDDLETOWN

A tight-knit former market town (originally called Piddletown) on the S bank of the River Puddle (or Piddle). From the mid C19 it grew S to include the main Dorchester to Poole road, since bypassed. Many cob and thatch cottages, to which the C18 added brick and the C19 stone.

ST MARY. Evidence of a C12 building exists, but it is not impressive: a flat buttress on the W side of the W tower pointing to a much smaller C12 W tower, the S respond of the chancel arch, and some fragments outside the E wall of the N aisle. Two C13 transeptal chapels originally, the N mostly demolished and incorporated in the N aisle. The S (Athelhampton) chapel is still *in situ* but with Perp windows. After that the tower arch of the present tower: late C13 or early C14. The greater part of the tower with the higher, octagonal stair-turret and the many pinnacles is C15, as are the big windows to the S chapel, and that to the former N chapel, re-set in the later N aisle. This and much else is of a later phase of Perp work, probably of *c.* 1530. Also the panelled arch into the chapel. Recent investigations indicate that this arch post-dates the installation of the Martyn monument which largely fills the opening (*see* below). The N arcade of standard elements with small leaf capitals is typical of the 1530s, as is the clerestory and nave roof, this of the low-pitch type with ribbed panels. Cusped cross-bracings to each panel. Later Perp windows are square-headed and the final ones (e.g. the clerestory windows) uncusped. There was in fact a re-dedication in 1505, perhaps indicating a pause in the Perp remodelling. The chancel and N chancel chapel are by *C. E. Ponting*, of 1910–11, correctly Perp, and highly sensitive.

FURNISHINGS. The church was refurnished in 1635. Much of this scheme remains *in situ* and is remarkably complete. If no other dates are given below, the items are of that scheme. – COMMUNION RAIL. A Laudian arrangement. Three-sided (but with indications of a missing fourth, cf. Lyddington, Rutland), with vertically symmetrical balusters. – PULPIT. A three-decker with one tier of unusually elongated blank arches and tall columns at the angles. Back-panel and tester. – BOX PEWS. Two towards the front have low balustrades suggesting family pews. – FONT. A very fine C12 piece, with an all-over palmette motif, their stems interlaced. The font is tumbler-shaped. Octagonal pyramid COVER with a ball finial. – WEST GALLERY, with vertically symmetrical balusters and a deep carved frieze, the latter dated 1635. At the centre too a carved shield of arms of France and England. The same widely spaced balusters on the gallery staircase. – PAINTINGS. Several exceptionally bold inscriptions, including one (on the nave S wall) in black-letter, with an open bible held by two hands. This no doubt dates from the 1635 refurnishing. – STAINED GLASS. E (re-set) window by *Campbell & Christmas* of London, 1906. S chapel S by *A. O. Hemming & Co.*, 1905. An elaborately armorial display. Next to it, facing W, a window by *Comper*, 1906.

MONUMENTS. In the S chapel an exceptionally good set of effigies, many to members of the families who owned Athelhampton Hall (q.v.), the best in the county.* Cross-legged knight and lady, *c.* 1320–30 (in the corner with the Nicholas Martyn monument built over them). – Mid- to late C14 knight in an ogee-arched recess. On a tomb-chest with trefoil-topped arcading, each bay with a (very eroded) small figure. – Alabaster monument, *c.* 1470–80. Restored to a free-standing format and placed in the centre of the chapel, 2013 (*Sue & Lawrence Kelland*, conservators), having stood in the NE corner since at least 1774 with two of the tomb-chest panels fixed to the wall above. These panels have been repositioned as part of the free-standing arrangement. Arcading to the tomb-chest, more elaborate than for the late C14 knight mentioned above. Some retained colouring, especially the light blue background. Two recumbent effigies, a knight and a lady, somewhat damaged. – Forming a screen between the S chapel and nave, Sir William Martyn †1504. Purbeck marble monument with a canopy consisting of a big arch of quadrants and long flat top and a top cresting. The underside of the canopy is panelled in a form of flattened fan-vaulting. The fine alabaster effigy is a generation earlier, perhaps depicting Sir Thomas Martyn †1485. It is unusually well preserved and includes a shield. – Christopher Martyn †1524. Brass with kneeling figure with the Trinity to the l. Older Gothic stone surround, cut away to allow the fitting of the brass. – Nicholas Martyn †1595. Kneeling figures on brass plates fixed to the back of a stone monument with Ionic columns, an arch still like the one of the Purbeck monuments, and strapwork at the top. – Sir John Brune †1639 and others to †1645. Big tablet with Tuscan columns set diagonally and an open segmental pediment. – In

*See Brian and Moira Gittos, *The Monuments of the Athelhampton Chapel, Puddletown*, 2014.

the chancel, Roger Cheverell †1517, a 10½-in. (27-cm.) brass partial figure. – James Lukyn †1671. Tablet with Corinthian columns, a full entablature, and armorial cresting.

CHURCH HALL, in the SW corner of the churchyard by *David Illingworth Architects*, 2012. Suitably reticent vertical boarding. Only small areas of stonework.

VILLAGE. The church lies N of the main road, and it is here that Puddletown's best part can be found, all quite humble and villagey. A colourwashed row of cob and thatch cottages presents to THE SQUARE a return face of the early C19, with a bowed glazed upper part, the centre of it treated as a Venetian window, all carried on thin Tuscan columns. TUDOR COTTAGE stands opposite, banded flint and stone, and dated 1573. Three-light mullioned windows with hoodmoulds. Hollow chamfer. Central doorway with flattened four-centred head. From here S along MILL STREET to the main road, fearsome Victorian terraces take over, the gift of John Brymer, of Ilsington House (*see* below), bearing dates between 1864 and 1870. Some are of brick, the better rows of Purbeck stone with multiple gables, e.g. the Tudor Revival row dated 1864 on the N side of the main road. On the corner with Mill Street the READING ROOM of 1870, its best feature the two-storey bay on the end. After two stone sets of cottage pairs (one dated 1870), the former SCHOOL of 1864. They were all designed, it seems, by a firm of surveyors, *Wainwright & Heard* of Shepton Mallet.* One is not surprised to discover that.

Former VICARAGE, E of the church. Early C17 and irregular on the E side. A hipped-roofed block projects W from this in quite handsome brickwork of *c.* 1722 (for the Rev. Henry Dawnay). Chequer brick with red dressings. Shaped aprons below all windows, the upper windows with segmental heads. Coved eaves and a panelled chimneystack. On the W end four blank arched recesses.

ILSINGTON HOUSE (now the Old Manor), E of the vicarage. Rendered *c.* 1835 (but originally brick), with other C19 modifications, muffling the effect of what must once have been an unusually handsome house of *c.* 1680.** Hipped roofs. Prominent panelled chimneystacks. Quoins, and broad windows in two storeys. The N front has three-bay wings projecting l. and r. of a centre in a 2:1:2 rhythm. A segmental pediment over the central bay. The S front, oddly long and low, has giant Tuscan pilasters breaking the bays into the rhythm 2:1:1:1:2, the centre bay being much the narrowest (also with a segmental pediment). The upper windows longer than the lower. Former ballroom at the E end added *c.* 1865 for John Brymer. A mid-C18 oak staircase inside.

*Brymer papers in Dorset History Centre.
**The central range may incorporate the late C16 hunting lodge built by the 3rd Earl of Huntingdon.

BARDOLF MANOR, ¾ m. NE. Of 1895 for George Wood Homer, by *Thomas Pike*, builder, of Mudeford-on-Sea, Hants. Gothic at times. Rock-faced stone with a battlemented corner tower and pyramid top.

BARDOLFESTON. Earthworks ¾ m. ENE, exceptionally well-preserved remains of a deserted MEDIEVAL VILLAGE. A hollow way up to 40 ft (12 metres) broad runs SW–NE across the site, flanked by at least eleven house sites with yards behind.

RAINBARROWS, 2 m. SW. Three bowl barrows on the edge of Duddle Heath.

PUDDLETOWN DOWN, in the northern corner of the parish. 'CELTIC' FIELDS, now much reduced by ploughing. Part of a field system, including barrows and enclosures, covering over 2,000 acres, for some 2½ m. northwards to Kingcombe on both sides of a winterborne valley, in Cheselbourne, Piddle-trenthide, Piddlehinton and Dewlish parishes.

ROMAN ROAD, 2 m. SW. Earthwork remains of the approach road to Dorchester from Badbury Rings can be traced for 1¼ m. across to Thorncombe Wood.

PULHAM

7000

St THOMAS BECKET. C15 w tower and chancel. C16 aisles and two-storey S porch. Both aisles largely rebuilt during a major restoration of 1870–1. The N aisle retains its square-headed windows; the S has windows to the designs of the Rev. *F.C. Hingeston-Randolph* of Ringmore in Devon (reportedly copies of the previous windows). At this time bold C16 gargoyles were re-set in the C19 parapets. Good C16 four-bay arcades, the piers of standard Perp section, with capitals only to the shafts. The capitals carry elementarily stylized leaves. The W responds have shields carried by little figures. That on the S side has just the slightest hint at Renaissance gadrooning. The easternmost bays are of *c.* 1400 with crude figurehead corbels (evidence for lost transepts). In the chancel a gorgeous canopied niche such as appear frequently on the outside of towers. But can this one ever have been outside? – Extensive TILEWORK in the sanctuary. – FONT. C12, tub-shaped, of Purbeck marble, with the familiar shallow blank arches. C15 base. – STAINED GLASS. E window by *Powell & Sons*, 1853. Further windows by *Powells* to match, 1871.

Close by the church, the OLD RECTORY, a rectory such as few parsons could boast of.* The three-bay main block is late C18 and has a NW front developed into a full Palladian composition of centre block with low wings, all translated

---

* It is said to have been designed by the rector himself, based on Milton Abbey House (Roger White).

into skin-deep Gothic of the Milton Abbey variety. Rendered walls and brownish stone dressings. Slightly recessed centre; two-and-a-half storeys, the windows pointed Venetian below, then four-centred with, illogically, straight hoods, and ovals on their sides for the half-storey. Arrow crosses in the links, and in the side pavilions hoodmoulded lancets and another oval. Battlements all across, the littlest, oddly, in the middle. Nor is it just a façade. The house has an unusual plan, a Greek cross of corridors, meeting at a circle supported on pendentives. This followed early C19 enlargement to the SE. Circular S room with four niches. Bowed porch with Greek Doric columns at the centre of a more modest elevation. Further mid-C19 addition in the S corner.

Late C18 Gothic GATEPIERS to the NW.

PUNCKNOWLE

The village shelters from the sea by the Knoll to the S. Puncknowle (pronounced Punnoll) has at its centre a village street with church and manor house behind high walls to the S, and a continuous run of thatched cottages to the N.

ST MARY. The most interesting church in its neighbourhood, especially as regards furnishings. Concerning architecture there is a C12 chancel arch with plain imposts and the arch just one-stepped, and the C12 W tower with an unmoulded, later heightened, arch to the nave. The S stair projection is semicircular with a stone-slab sloping top. Alterations were made in 1678 (date on the tower arch), when it was raised in height and given its present hipped roof. Its pointed-arched N doorway and plain lancet W window are probably of that date. Heavy C19 restoration of the nave and chancel windows. The S chapel is of 1660, but also heavily restored. It replaced the chapel of St Giles at Bexington on the coast, destroyed by the French during a raid in 1440. The N aisle is entirely of 1894 by *J. Houghton Spencer* of Taunton. A proposed organ chamber and vestry to its E were never executed (see the masonry toothings). – FONT. Two, one above the other. The upper is C12. A very large bowl with stars of bold rope moulding. The lower is late C12. It came from Bexington and has a big head and palmette-like motifs. Late C17 pyramidal oak COVER. – PAINTING above the chancel arch, perhaps C16. Not easy to read. It consists of three panels with roses in the borders. The l. panel has traces of a figure. – ROYAL ARMS. Wooden panel and frame dated 1673. – HELM of a Napier; early C17. – MONUMENTS. William Napper †1616. Brass of a small kneeling figure in a crudely classical stone surround. The date of death is left blank. Above the figure, a brass achievement of arms and shield. Beneath, a tablet with a Latin inscription referring to the presentation of the rectory by William Napper to William Carter, 1597. – Sir R(obert) N(apier), shortly before 1700. Inscription in Greek, Latin and English and the signature '*Johannes Hamiltonus* Scoto-Britannicus fecit'. Big classical surround with a shield above the inscription and an open segmental pediment and an urn in it. – Sir Robert Napier's father, mother and mother-in-law; 1691. The inscription says no more than RN AN KN MN. Surround with detached Corinthian columns, palm branches outside them growing out of volutes, an open segmental pediment at the top, a skull at the bottom.

PUNCKNOWLE MANOR. What one sees, on looking over the churchyard s wall, is the compact, symmetrical E wing added to an earlier house *c.* 1665 for Robert Napier. Stone eaves, suggesting that the hipped roof may be original. Its form is therefore right up to date, but its fenestration not at all so. At the centre a broad projecting porch, only slightly lower than the main block, also with a hipped roof. The round arch (leading into a tunnel-vault) has above it a blank panel and above that a three-light window with its own hoodmould. This is a scaled-down version of the windows used as a standard type on this block. The oddity is that they all have arch-headed lights, already somewhat *recherché* when they were used at Chantmarle in 1612 and even more so at this later date. At a mid-point, either side of the blank panel, are two single-light versions of the same window type, also scaled down. An earlier house ran back from this block to the w (recorded as having thirteen hearths in 1662). This was replaced *c.* 1850 by the present block, for M.G. Mansel. It has a row of gabled dormers on the s side and on the N a curious castellated extension, perhaps *c.* 1900. Inside the porch a staircase of remarkable elaboration, going up in two flights which merge for the final flight to the upper floor. Two fine rooms on the upper floor of the E block. Both have panelling in large fields, of *c.* 1700, intended to be painted from the start. The s room has grisaille genre scenes of fanciful classical buildings. (The N room, coloured pink and green, mostly a background for crude cherubs' heads.)

To the E a pair of rusticated classical GATEPIERS, also *c.* 1665. They have pulvinated friezes and bold ball finials. Another GATEWAY to the churchyard has the initials RAN (for Robert and Ann Napier) and a defaced C17 date.

LOOKE FARM, ⅞ m. E. Dated 1700 on the door lintel. Just three bays wide on its formal sw front. 'Look' is what it seems to say, with its four eccentrically shaped chimneystacks pricked up from the outer corners of the hipped roof, and the semicircular stone pediments to windows and to door, the latter having fat swags of fruit dangling over it to l. and r. and an urn above. Its windows were originally mullions and transoms (one side window survives).

PURSE CAUNDLE

Rambling village, its two highlights centrally located.

St Peter. All Perp, but not all of one date. C15 W tower with
rectangular SE stair projection up to the second stage only. Battlemented top with corner pinnacles. Early C16 N chapel under
its own gabled roof. Perp windows here too, copying the C15
ones. But, although not obvious, the chancel is a 1731 rebuilding, retaining in its S wall two different C15 Perp S windows,
one especially nice. Nave rebuilt in 1883 by *W. J. Willcox* of
Bath, with replica Perp windows: a sensitive job. S porch (also
1883) with a re-set C15 four-centred arch. Within, the panelled
chancel arch is C15, but the highlight is the chapel. This is
separated from the chancel by one bay and a MONUMENT
under an arch. The arch is cusped and sub-cusped, is panelled
inside and has leaf spandrels. Top cresting with angel busts
l. and r. To the chapel the tomb-chest has quatrefoils, large
and small. There is no effigy. A Perp DOOR leads from the
SW into the chapel. – COMMUNION RAIL. C17, with turned
balusters and an interesting leaf enrichment to the rails and
posts. – PULPIT. Early C18, oak. Hexagonal with fielded panelling and matching sounding-board. – FONT. C15. Octagonal,
with shields in quatrefoils. COVER with scrolled supports to a
central handle, probably C17. – HATCHMENT. Hoskins impaling
Seymer, dated 1694. – ALMS CHEST. Mid-C16. Plain. – BIER.
Dated 1733. – STAINED GLASS. Perp fragments in three
windows. E window by *Kempe & Co.*, 1907. Chancel S window
by *W. G. Taylor*, 1883. – BRASSES. Knight, *c.* 1500, a 26-in. (66-
cm.) figure. – Elizabeth Longe †1527; 13 in. (33 cm.). – Richard
Brodewey, rector, †1536. A headless 8½-in. (22-cm.)
figure. – Large brass to Henry Huddleston †1858, probably by
Hardman. – MONUMENT. Peter Hoskins †1682. Latin inscription on a brass plate set into an oak frame. Pedimented, with
twisted side-columns.

Purse Caundle Manor. The slender oriel window overlooking the road proclaims at once that the house is essentially
of the late C15, built for John Long. Four long cinquefoiled
lights, canted 1:2:1, with shields in a frieze for heraldry below.
The oriel rests on simple corbelling and a buttress. Diagonal
buttress (now very weathered) meant to mark the angle of the
house, but sunk into a contemporary wall extending further to
the l. This gable-ended range was clearly the original solar end,
projecting some way from the line of the Hall. At the N end of
the E front the same rubble walling appears. So that was the
service end, with a chimney-breast in the N wall. The ashlar-
faced intermediate projection, with its two even gables towards
the E, and the four-light mullioned windows with hoodmoulds
represent a C16 development of the E side of the Hall, rather

more than a mere porch, as we shall see inside. Round on the
w side the Hall is made obvious by the large five-light window
with two transoms and cinquefoiled lights. However, this was
installed in the 1920s by Lady Victoria Herbert, and is certainly
not a faithful representation of what was there.

Inside the Hall there is a puzzle. Which was the upper end
originally? As it stands there is a NE oriel, entered through
a four-centred arch with a simply panelled soffit, and two
service doorways at the S end, also four-centred-arched and
merely chamfered. The porch opens from the E into a screens
passage in a perfectly normal way; but the doorway N of this,
with in the spandrels WH (for William Hannam †1576), leads
to the intermediate space behind the ashlar E front, where
there was a well behind the Hall chimney-breast. All of this
is self-consistent, but contradicts the solar-oriel and kitchen
chimney-breast, which tell perfectly clearly that the upper end
of the Hall was at first the S, not the N. So Hannam must
have turned the house completely round, in spite of the fact
that further development took place at the S end under James
Hanham, creating, c. 1600, a whole symmetrical E-plan S front,
the three projections all with doorways. Oddly this mainly
contained service rooms, required here following the turning
around of the Hall.

So, to return to the HALL itself, William Hannam maintained a simplified Perp style, and indeed the doorway bearing
his initials is four-centred-arched and has a wave and a hollow.
C15 hall roof, its tie-beam trusses with upright and raking
struts, collar-beams and, between them, two tiers of wind-
bracing. The lower tier of these last is formed into quatrefoils within lozenges, the upper into arched pairs. There is
a much-restored frieze of quatrefoils below them. The roofs
of the upper rooms in the SE and NE gables (including the
former SOLAR or GREAT CHAMBER) are tunnel-vaulted, with
crudely moulded timber wall-plates and thin beams making a
pattern of squares. STAIRCASE with stout turned balusters, of
c. 1670, in the NW wing.

To sum up, then, Purse Caundle is stimulating as an
archaeological puzzle, and reveals a purpose of its later
owners (the Hannams especially) to respect its relatively
humble late medieval origins. It has a rambling aesthetic, no
doubt typical of many such houses before they were tidied up
in the C18 and C19, and as such is an extremely important
survival.

CRENDLE COURT, ¾ m. NNW. Large and reposeful Neo-
Georgian house by *W.H. Brierley*, built in 1908–9 for the Hon.
Mrs Alfred Ker. Banded rubble in the local way, with local
ashlar and rubble stone. H-plan with a lower service court
attached at the N end. The principal rooms have plasterwork
by *G.P. Bankart*.

RADIPOLE

1¾ m. NW of Weymouth

The village, on the River Wey, at the head of Radipole Lake, remains surprisingly rural. This despite major interwar suburbs of Weymouth close by.

ST ANN. A simple C13 nave with one lancet in the N wall. Of the C14 are the chancel and N chapel. The chancel has a Dec arch to the nave, with continuous chamfers, and Dec also are a lancet and priest's doorway, both ogee-headed; the E window is mid-C15 Perp. In the N chapel two windows with, in their tracery, arches upon arches, a motif of c. 1300 (cf. the Lady Chapel, Wells Cathedral). A narrower but contemporary S chapel was rebuilt in 1735, retaining its arch. Its S window has curious lancet-based tracery. A datestone carries the initials of the churchwardens. The porch is dated 1733. Rough tie-beam roof in the nave. The church will be remembered for its early C16 triple bellcote, one arched opening above two, the whole supported externally by a massive stepped W buttress, and on a tower-like arch within. – COMMUNION RAIL. Incorporating stubby C16 balusters salvaged from No. 4, North Quay, Weymouth. – PULPIT. Carved oak. Part of the restoration by *G.R. Crickmay*, 1864. – PEWS. Also of 1864, unremarkable apart from being painted white. – FONT. C13 bowl, formerly square but re-cut to an irregular semicircular shape. New stem and columns, 1980. – WEST GALLERY. An 1864 replacement. Front beam supported on a pair of C14 head corbels. – ROYAL ARMS. Canvas, of William IV. – PAINTINGS. Set of four biblical scenes on the nave ceiling by *Ann Tout*, 1987–2009. – STAINED GLASS. Various, of mixed quality. The best are the E window (1887), N chapel, behind the organ (1899), and two single lights in the chancel (1894), all by *Powell & Sons*. – MONUMENT, in the churchyard. Robert Herbert Dominy †1864. Spirelet hood on six pink granite colonnettes. Hexagonal.

RADIPOLE OLD MANOR, hard up against the E wall of the church. Not small, but using the vernacular style of c. 1600 without pretension or even any attempt at symmetry. It was rebuilt for Richard Watkins, whose initials are in the very tentative pediment over the main doorway. Mullioned windows with hoodmoulds, all sizes from five-light to two-light. Two identical gables, with finials and three storeys of windows. The main front faces E and is L-shaped, with the porch in the crook of the L. On the W side, placed in relation to the porch (and screens passage), a projecting stair-turret, with a small blocked outer doorway into it. A fragment of an earlier building was retained as a cross-wing at the N end.

Completing the group, opposite, former SCHOOL of 1840. Two classrooms, one entered from a central gabled porch. Moulded Gothic doorway.

St Aldhelm, Spa Road, ⅓ m. E. Core of 1939–41 by *W.H. Randoll Blacking*. Brick with a Perp window at the N end, bellcote over. Enlarged by *K.C. White* of Chelmsford, 1982, when the internal orientation was reversed. – STAINED GLASS. Intensely blue *dalle-de-verre* chancel window by *Jon Callan*, 1985. Others in the W aisle by *Powell & Sons*, 1908–22, brought here from Weymouth College Chapel in 1949.

Large PARISH CENTRE at the back by *John Stark & Crickmay*, 2012. Two colours of brick with curved metal-sheet roofs.

Corfe Hill House, ¼ m. NW. Square yellow-brick block of 1821 for Edward Balston. Symmetrical E front. Doric porch. Large sash windows. Hipped roof with central stack. Lower service range, W.

RAMPISHAM   *5000*

A scatter of cottages of various dates but with two excellent Gothic Revival buildings: the church and former rectory.

St Michael. Three-stage Perp tower on the S side, unbuttressed. Of two dates, the lower two stages early C14, the top C15. While this is typical of the area, the chancel is not, being a fine example of *A.W.N. Pugin*'s work, unusually for the Church of England; of 1846–7, costing £742 2s. 8d.* Ecclesiological in the extreme, it was commissioned by the Tractarian-leaning Rev. Frederick Rooke (who became rector in 1845). So one finds a stone ALTAR, SEDILIA to the r., fine CHOIR STALLS, TILEWORK by *Minton* and painted decoration to the sanctuary ceiling. Externally it has crazy-paving masonry, an odd choice having no local precedent. The body of the church is by *J. Hicks*, 1858–9, and in the Dec style, with crazy-paving stone to match. This phase cost £1,179 8s. 1d. Less demonstrative, it acts as a perfect foil for Pugin's E end. – FONT. A magnificent piece by *Pugin*, 1844. Octagonal and richly carved, depicting Apostles and Evangelists, and surely inspired by the cross base in the churchyard. – STAINED GLASS. Three fine windows in the chancel designed by *Pugin* (assisted by *J.H. Powell*) and made by *Hardman*, 1847–8. Two further chancel windows and another in the S aisle by *Hardman*, †1856 and 1857, equally good. In the N aisle two by *Clayton & Bell*, †1882 and 1891. Large W window by the same, 1907. – BRASS. Thomas Dygenys †1523 and wife. The figures are 19 in. (48 cm.) long.

CHURCHYARD CROSS. Reportedly dated 1516, this having since eroded. Only the base survives, sufficiently indicative of a richly ornamented monument. Also a portion of the shaft. The base is square with carved figures (e.g. the Martyrdom

*One of only six Anglican churches worked at by Pugin.

of St Thomas Becket on the NW side) and scenes. A black-letter inscription runs around the angled sub-base, recorded by Hutchins as reading: 'Fili Dei miserere mei et sic dicit Porter in nomine Ihu Amen Obiit A.D. M.D.X.V.I.' ('Son of God have mercy on me and thus says Porter in the name of Jesus amen died A.D. 1516'). Each word is separated by a small flower from the next.

MANOR HOUSE, next to the church. Dated (on a sundial) 1608. Originally gabled but altered in the C19. Two-storey gabled porch facing the road.

102   PUGIN HALL, ⅓ m. NW. The former rectory of 1845–7 by *Pugin*, built for the Rev. F. Rooke by *G. Myers* (cost £1,926). Pugin's 'best, most fully realised house' (Rosemary Hill), fully Gothic Revival in its handling, rather than Tudor Gothic. A fine design in Forest Marble rubble with Ham Hill dressings. Pinwheel plan, projecting an asymmetrically placed, steep-pitched gable to the two main elevations, with a second smaller gable alongside over the (SE) entrance. Here a stepped hoodmoulding over a two-centred Dec arch and a small Dec-traceried window above. Otherwise the fenestration is mainly mullioned and transomed. Tall, octagonal-shafted chimneys. Also remarkably unaltered, complete with many original fittings by Pugin.

SCHOOL, just SE of Pugin Hall. Dated 1846, perhaps by *Pugin* (but more likely by *Myers*'s men in a Pugin style), for Rooke.

(BROOMHILL FARMHOUSE, ⅓ m. NE. Of the later C17. Built as a two-unit house, with ovolo-moulded mullioned windows.)

RINGSTEAD

A deserted MEDIEVAL VILLAGE in a cove close to the sea. The bumps in the grass marking its site are S of Glebe Cottage, which contains the chancel arch of West Ringstead church. The remains of houses, yards and enclosures cover 10 acres in all, with a deep hollow way on the w.*

RYME INTRINSECA

A structureless street mixing old cottages with small-scale new development.

ST HIPPOLYTUS. Recorded as a chapel in 1297. Late C13 nave and chancel. w tower of *c.* 1620, together with refenestration and a N porch of the same date. Restoration by *F. W. Hunt*,

*The 'radar shields' mentioned in the previous edition were in fact part of a US 'tropospheric scatter' communication system, linked with Gorramendi, Spain. They were removed in 1974.

1885. Of the C13 the narrow chancel side lancets, and a pair of wider lancets in the nave S wall. The N doorway is early C15. The windows of *c.* 1620 include two of the three-light type with the hoodmould stepping over the higher central light, as at Leweston, 1616, Minterne Magna, *c.* 1615–20, and Folke, 1628. One is in the chancel E wall, the other in the nave N wall. A large trefoil window in the N wall lighting the pulpit, also *c.* 1620. The tower is Perp, but its late date is indicated by the two-light belfry openings (with Somerset tracery) and the W window. It is battlemented, of two stages, with a square stair-turret on the N side. This has a conical roof. Diminutive crocketed corner pinnacles. – Many FURNISHINGS from the *Hunt* restoration. – FONT. Late C15, octagonal on a splayed stem. COVER dated 1637. Conical with a knob finial. – ROYAL ARMS. Dated 1793, by *John Williams* of Yeovil. – ORGAN. Early C19. White and gold. – MONUMENT. John Elford, rector, †1664. Tablet with enriched surround. – WEATHERVANE. Dated 1799. Opposite the church, LILAC COTTAGE and THE LILACS, 1928, probably by *Petter & Warren* (with *Lt-Col. P. N. Nissen*). They are under a Nissen-hut type of roof. Next, the OLD SCHOOL HOUSE. 1875. Gothic. Further E, MANOR FARM has a mid-C17 W range, but is much altered. Going W, on the r., the POST HOUSE is dated 1772. Brick with replacement casements in segmental-arched openings. On the l., COURT HOUSE. Late C17, with ovolo-moulded mullioned casements to the ground floor; later C18 casements above, under a raised thatched roof.

ST ALDHELM'S HEAD

Worth Matravers

ST ALDHELM'S CHAPEL – if it was built as a chapel. There was a chaplain in the C13, and the building belongs to the late C12, yet the plan seems so unsuitable for a chapel.* The building is a square, about 25 by 25 ft (7.6 by 7.6 metres) inside, and has a central pier and four square rib-vaults. The pier is a square with four oblong attachments. The ribs and transverse arches are heavy and pointed and have slight stop-chamfers. Stop-chamfers also in the pillar attachments. There is a late C12 round-arched doorway in the NW side, and there is no indication of an altar or a piscina. Of other original features one clasping buttress and one small window survive. On the SE side a length of late medieval string course at a height to suggest structure rising higher than at present. The building is covered with a pyramid roof with a short cylindrical base on top. The big battered buttresses come from one of the two C19

---

*One suggestion is that it was built as a seamark. If so, did it have a superstructure?

restorations for the earls of Eldon. – STAINED GLASS. A lancet
is filled with glass of varying shades by *Alan Younger*, 2000.

SALWAY ASH
Netherbury

HOLY TRINITY. At Kingsland. 1887–9 by *Crickmay & Son*.
Rather Home Counties in the tiled roofs and the bell-turret
of timber with tile-hanging. – REREDOS. Carved oak with
some inlay. – TILEWORK by *Minton* in the sanctuary. – FONT.
A square tub with rounded corners, on coloured marble colonnettes, typical of *Crickmay*. – STAINED GLASS. E window by
Lavers, Barraud & Westlake, 1895.

ST SAVIOUR. At Dottery. 1881–2 for the Rev. Dr Alfred Eders-
heim. Corrugated iron. Timber-lined. Rudimentary W bellcote.

SANDFORD ORCAS

A string of cottages, many still thatched, in a winding valley N
of Sherborne. At its centre the fine grouping of the church and
manor house.*

ST NICHOLAS. Early C14 Dec chancel, mid-C15 W tower, nave
and S chapel and porch. N aisle of 1871–2 by *Henry Hall*, in
a reasonably convincing Perp style. C15, but much restored,
chancel arch with standard-section, but still round, not polygonal, capitals. Also three windows show reticulation (two S,
one N) and one is a lancet. The E window is Perp but retains its
trefoiled rere-arch within. The S chapel has a straight-headed
four-light window under a curious straight string course. Inside
a good Perp compartment roof. Two-stage battlemented tower;
rectangular stair-turret with sloping top. Typically mid-C15 W
doorway with two-centred arch and leaf carving in the spandrels. An ogee-headed C14 lancet re-set above the Perp W
window. – FURNISHINGS generally of 1871–2 and Perp in
character, including the stone REREDOS by *Thomas Earp* and
encaustic TILEWORK in the chancel and chapel. – FONT. Early
C13. Tub-shaped with big flutes. C17 oak COVER with a central
spindle and four scrolled brackets. – TOWER SCREEN. C15, with
narrow one-light divisions and many blank, cusped ogee gables
(cf. Trent). Was it once part of the chancel screen? – STAINED
GLASS. A number including the E window by *Clayton &
Bell*, mainly of 1872, but one chancel S window of *c.* 1880.**

---

*Until 1896 it was in Somerset.
**Fragments of mid-C15 glass from the chapel are now in a staircase window at the
Manor House (*see* below). Two depict the device of Edward IV.

– MONUMENTS. Tablet to William Knoyle †1607. Painted alabaster. The small kneeling figures include his two wives, four
swaddled infants by the first wife, and three sons and four
daughters by the second. – John Hutchings †1774. Nice tablet
with an urn in an open, scrolly pediment. – Mrs Hutchings
†1869. Small white marble tablet with a Quattrocento frame.

In the churchyard C15 CROSS BASE and part of shaft. Also
an unusually early plain CHEST TOMB dated 1587.

METHODIST CHAPEL (former), ⅝ m. SE. 1864. Plain, brick-
lined lancets. Circular window in the gable.

SCHOOL (former), ¼ m. S. 1859. Bold Tudor Gothic, also by *Hall*.

MANOR HOUSE, next to the church. A complete small manor   54
house of the mid C16, a fine piece of architecture in itself, and
very little altered. There was a house recorded here in 1501,
although little of it is evident in the rebuilding for Edward
Knoyle, carried out probably *c*. 1551–4. Knoyle was an infant
when he inherited in 1533, and reached his majority only
in 1550. He married Katherine Martyn of Athelhampton
the following year and it seems likely that this prompted the
rebuilding. Considerations of style and planning also indicate a
mid-C16 date, especially the similarities with the parlour range
of Athelhampton, built *c*. 1545–50.

The GATEHOUSE introduces the style, and is in its position
the main peculiarity of plan. It adjoins the N wall of the house,
in such a way that to enter the E-facing porch one must pass
under the entrance arch and then turn through 180 degrees.
At first sight the gatehouse is all Late Perp, yet the windows
are mullioned without arched lights, a slight advance from
the Athelhampton type. Ham Hill ashlar. Rooms over the
entrance way and a small garderobe projection. Four-centred
carriage arch flanked by small decorative buttresses with foliage
capping. Four-centred arch for pedestrians. Wave-and-hollow
mouldings. Bold plinth moulding, and string course carried
up over a small window in lieu of a hoodmould. Lozenge
panel over the archway, meant for a shield of arms, its angles
clasped by bunches of Late Perp leaves, the bottom bunch
overlapping the string course too. There are identical panels
at Athelhampton. One detail only tells of a post-Gothic idiom,
the chimneystack capped by volutes.

The EAST (ENTRANCE) FRONT is quite irregular, and after
the taking down of the two gables at the SE corner was more
so. These were rebuilt for Hubert Hutchings in 1873 as part of
a careful restoration by *Henry Hall*. At the l. end a splendidly
glazed two-storey bay, canted, the lights arranged 1:3 plus 3:1,
the lower window of double height and with a transom. Round
the corner to the S a second canted bay of the same height,
and even broader, enough for eight lights across the front face.
From the angle, this area of glazing is quite impressive, presaging the later great windows of the Elizabethan period (e.g.
Hardwick Hall). So here must be the Hall, but a one-storey
Hall, carrying a Great Chamber above it. The so-called SOLAR
WING that continues the S front in a plane further forward

is only one-storeyed and very humble, perhaps reflecting the height of the previous house.

At Sandford Orcas then the medieval hall–solar arrangement is given up, and the SW wing is really a closet wing that provides a small intimate room off the Hall. The end-lighting as well as side-lighting of Hall and Great Chamber, a bonus which this arrangement allows, is here gloriously exploited. Yet, to repeat, this important planning development is not accompanied by greater formality on the main front; the gabled, two-storey porch is not central, and the gabled bay to the r. has a window of four lights over one of three, not even at the same level as the two-lighter l. of the porch. The details noted on the gateway are more prominent on the E front: the flat-topped lights, the window surrounds deeply hollowed, the mullions with wave and hollow, and the string courses bending up and over the windows. The porch however adds something more: octagonal angle shafts, with foliage where the strings cross them, and voluted caps, referring once more to knowledge of an Ionic capital. Obelisk finials. Over the simple porch arch another lozenge with foliage knobs. The armorial cartouche remains, one half Knoyle, the other left blank with only drill-holes indicating where later arms were attached. It may have been made just prior to Knoyle's Martyn marriage and installed two or three years later. At the back (W) the ground falls, and here is a secondary CROSS-RANGE, linked at both ends now to form a tiny internal court. Here rather more alterations were made in 1873.

The INTERIOR merely confirms what one might expect of a house of this type, although several features are later installations. The HALL has a screen with strapwork cresting, which must be early C17. It has similarities with cresting on a screen in the chapel of Wadham College, Oxford (built 1612–13, the screen made by John Bolton). The wooden overmantel here is C19, but made up with some early C17 panels and framing; the stone fireplace below is mid-C16. Mid-C16 armorial glass in the S window. From the screens passage a stone newel stair leads to the upper floor, and another goes up from the dais end of the Hall to the Great Chamber. The former stair may be from the earlier house, although it is unclear whether it is *in situ*. In the upper NE room an OVERMANTEL with a flamboyant achievement of arms of James I. It is said to have come from Joiners' Hall, Salisbury. Several other minor pieces brought in, timberwork and glass.

JERARDS, ⅜ m. SSW. The rubble-built range facing E is guaranteed as late medieval in origin by the SE buttress, with one set-off. N cross-wing of the early 1920s. C17 mullioned windows, and a one-storey porch, ashlar-faced, dated 1616. Round entrance arch decorated with a band of rectangles and lozenges. Similarly decorated string course above, with the date. The lozenge panel in the gable has the arms of the Jerard family. Probably at the same date the back received a pair of three-storey projecting bays, also ashlar-faced, gabled and with mullioned windows, all hollow-chamfered and under hood-moulds, but not all transomed. Also a continuous moulded plinth and first-floor string course. The architectural effect of the chimney-breasts projecting from the inner side of each bay is spoilt by the C20 infill that engulfs them.

Late C16 BARN, W. Also a STABLE to the S. Late C17. Stone cross-windows; doorway with eared architraves. Both buildings are thatched.

SEABOROUGH

St John. By *G.R. Crickmay*, 1882, except for the N chapel, which was built in 1729 (but refenestrated during the general rebuilding). Nave and chancel in one with a double W bellcote. Inside only the slightest division between the chancel and nave: a double cross-rib supported on marble double colon-nettes, the carving here by *Harry Hems*. Complete scheme of FURNISHINGS. – Encaustic TILES in the sanctuary by *Maw & Co.* – STAINED GLASS. E window by *Clayton & Bell, c.* 1895. N chapel window by *Horace Wilkinson*, 1928. – MONUMENTS. Small effigy of a knight, cross-legged, but wearing a C13 great helm. The date is probably the mid C13, which is very early for effigies of knights altogether and for cross-legged knights in particular. Its base chest was added in 1928. – Adam Martin †1738. With an excellent, fully convincing portrait bust.

Old Rectory, 50 yds sw. Of 1784 for the Rev. John Wills. Tall and narrow. Rather gaunt sash fenestration.

Seaborough Court, 200 yds w. 1878–9 by *T. H. Wyatt* for Lt-Col. T. Goff.* Jacobethan mansion in a spectacular loca-tion. Picturesque grouping towards the E front and at the S side. Square-topped porch-tower with openwork parapet. Large mullioned windows, and window bays. Straight gables with some strapwork elaboration. Panels of four-petalled flowers, a Dec motif, over the entrance. This is in an Early Tudor-style framework. To the l. of this an oriel, rather than a bay. Prominent chimneystack clusters. Notice how one chimneystack grows from the root of a gable. This mixture is typical of Wyatt's domestic work – cf. Orchardleigh, Somerset (1856–8). Classical orangery added 1907 by *Harold Peto* for W. R. Mitchell.

Higher Farm, ¼ m. NW. The vernacular vocabulary of three- and four-light windows, the lower ones with hoodmoulds, the mullions hollow-chamfered. Ashlar walling; thatched. Dated 1628 on a re-set chimneypiece inside.

*An earlier house nearby burnt down in 1877.

SHAFTESBURY

'Vague imaginings of its castle, its three mints, its magnificent apsidal abbey, the chief glory of South Wessex, its twelve
churches, its shrines, chantries, hospitals, its gabled free-stone
mansions – all now ruthlessly swept away – throw the visitor,
even against his will, into a pensive melancholy.'* Thomas Hardy
was easily thrown into pensive melancholy, but these are the right
thoughts with which to approach Shaftesbury. This commanding
spur over 700 ft (210 metres) high, probably already inhabited
owing to its natural defensibility, was the site of a *burh* created
by King Alfred *c.* 880. The abbey, founded a little later, stood
to the E of the *burh*. This Anglo-Saxon *burh* occupied only the
western half of the promontory, with its market street in what is
now Bimport, a Saxon name. On the E side, the site of the town
wall is marked by the present N–S line of the High Street. So
most of medieval Shaftesbury grew initially as a suburb, along the
pilgrimage routes to the abbey. Early medieval Shaftesbury had
twelve churches, only one of which survives, and there were five
market crosses.** A castle, dating from the reign of King Stephen,
stood at the far W end of the spur. With the loss of the abbey and
most medieval buildings from within the burgh perimeter, it is a
poignant view that one gets approaching from the S or W, of an
almost untenanted hilltop.

From 1820, however, when the Grosvenor family purchased
about three-quarters of the town property, little more was lost
and much of architectural merit added. Two major churches
were rebuilt (in 1838–40 and 1841), that of Holy Trinity con-
tributing a landmark tower to the hilltop silhouette; a third
was rebuilt in 1866–7. All three were largely funded by the
Grosvenors, whose main motive was the control of votes in this
notorious pocket borough. They also built the, for Shaftesbury,
impressive Grosvenor Arms hotel (combining three smaller inns
on that site). Little further of note was done until the arrival in
1932–3 of the Savoy Cinema in Bimport. The first edition of this
work found the Savoy 'deplorable'; it was demolished in 1986 and
replaced by unobjectionable housing.

By virtue of the town's precipitous hilltop location, post-war
expansion of Shaftesbury has been largely confined to its eastern
side, where it makes little impact on the finest views of the town.
While four churches have become redundant in recent years, all
still stand in new uses.

CHURCHES

ABBEY CHURCH OF ST MARY AND ST EDWARD. The foundation charter has been dated to the years 871–7, although

---

* *Jude the Obscure* (1895), part 4, ch. 1.
** St Mary's Cross, removed *c.* 1790; Gold-Hill Cross, removed 1827; the Fish Cross,
removed *c.* 1783; the Butter and Cheese Cross, taken down 1727. For St John's
Cross *see* p. 516.

it seems more likely that the foundation actually occurred somewhat later, in 888. Alfred's daughter Æthelgeofu is said to have been the first abbess. Shaftesbury became the wealthiest Benedictine nunnery in England and had as an equal in the West Country only Glastonbury, the richest monastery in the country.* The most precious possession was relics of Edward King and Martyr, murdered in 979, brought from Wareham. In 1218 it was decreed that there should be no more than 100 nuns, in 1326 that existing numbers must be reduced to 120. At the Dissolution, when the abbess attempted to avoid closure by offering 500 marks to Henry VIII and £100 to Thomas Cromwell as bribes, there were still fifty-six. Little survives above ground. The church we can at least follow partially in plan, but the cloister and the domestic parts round the cloister have entirely gone. If they stood to the S, they would have had very little space because of the steep fall. Excavations have proved inconclusive and, given the lack of space, it is more likely that the cloister was to the N (as at Sherborne). The building whose footings were located to the S of the S transept would therefore not have been the chapter house, as once thought.

THE CHURCH. Of the Saxon church no major evidence has yet come to light, though in the museum are fragments with interlace and also a steep column base. These have been sufficient to allow a tentative reconstruction of its interior, however. For the Norman church we have no dates, but excavations have told us of its plan as far W as the crossing. The date seems to be the late CII and the early CI2. The E end was of the type of Durham, i.e. with staggered apses – chancel, chancel aisles and one short chapel E of each of the two transepts. The apses of the chancel aisles ended externally straight. Chancel and aisles were separated by solid walls. The crossing had massive piers, one of them (the SE pier) with a semicircular N respond. The nave had aisles, but the pier locations are largely conjectural. That they were round, supporting semicircular arches, is indicated on a drawing of 1548. The nave went further W than the wall to Abbey House, now marking the close of the area. A precise location for the W termination of the nave, and plans of the presumed W towers, remain unknown.

Of post-Norman additions the following need mention. First, E of the N transept was the Chapel of King Edward. The CRYPT beneath it survives. It is early CI4 work and was rib-vaulted, as indicated by springer-stones. Second, the S chancel aisle was replaced in the CI4 by a wider and longer straight-ended chapel, probably the Lady Chapel. It had vaults, their ribs springing from floor level – see the SE corner. Third, screens seem to have run between the arcade piers to separate the aisles from the nave. Maybe this had something to do with the separation of clerics from laymen. In the nave are foundations

---

*A contemporary saying was 'If the abbot of Glaston could marry the abbess of Shaston, their heir would hold more land than the king of England.'

(from E to W) of the pulpitum, the rood screen and, W of it, the lay altar. The FLOOR TILES are poorly preserved in patches (crumbling from frost). Those in the museum are in a much better condition and date from the later C13 and C14. – CROSS. In the place where the high altar stood. The cross (St John's Cross) is secular and comes from the S end of Angel Lane. The shaft was decorated with four alabaster panels of familiar types of the late C14 and early C15. These have been removed from their sockets and displayed in the museum.

ABBEY MUSEUM, by *Philip Proctor Associates*, 1999. A suitably deferential structure hidden behind the abbey precinct wall. A new gable in the wall marks the entrance. Flat-roofed timber structure behind, glazed where it faces the abbey footings. Apart from the tiles and the Saxon fragments already referred to, it displays many Norman fragments, both Early (volutes of capitals) and Late (three-dimensional chevron, twisted shafts, a double capital no doubt from the cloister), and even more Gothic fragments (one stiff-leaf capital of the C13, C14 vaulting bosses, parts from a reredos, etc.).

ST PETER. Next to the Town Hall in the High Street, the N side facing right on it. Earliest of all is the low, three-stage Perp W tower of the C14, presumably for an earlier building, since the church is of the second half of the C15. It has large arches to N and S as if for aisle bays to embrace it. But they were not built (or were removed in the C15 rebuilding), and instead in the S wall blocking the arch is a blocked lancet window, either not *in situ* or a survival. Many alterations of the C16 to C18, such as the S aisle windows with straight heads, the S clerestory windows, the central mullions of the arched N aisle windows, and the W window in the tower. The tower is preceded by a late C15 W porch, its entrance with a four-centred head. Within a fine stone lierne vault. In the church proper, the arcades are Perp with standard elements to the piers, but the capitals remain in the raw and uncarved – except, that is, for those of the tower arch, planted against the earlier tower structure. Here the capitals carry carved angels (cf. Marnhull). The arches have mouldings not fitting the piers, but also Perp. A series of NICHES in the N aisle E wall of the C15 probably relate to chantry chapels. One or two of the niches are C14 and therefore not *in situ*. Some original paint survives. Under the whole S aisle is a crypt. The church has no chancel proper. Restoration of 1889 by *Crickmay & Son*. The handsome parapet with pinnacles and quatrefoils on the N wall, facing the street, was regrettably removed *c.* 1980. Reordering in 2007–8 removed most of the historic furnishings. – CREED and COMMANDMENT BOARDS. Mid-C18. At the E end, obscured by curtains. – FONT. C15. Octagonal, with blank tracery on stem and bowl. – ROYAL ARMS. One over the W door, dated 1780. A second, W end of the S aisle, Queen Anne, *c.* 1710.

ST JAMES, at the bottom end of the town. 1866–7 by *T.H. Wyatt*, a typical and harmonious blend of Dec and Perp. It cost

£3,350, yet is quite big. W tower with tall, elegant finials, nave and aisles, pseudo-transepts and a lower chancel. The S aisle E window is genuine C14,* the aisle parapets are C15, and the two C14 aisle W windows were also retained from the previous church. These are all identifiable, as they are of Greensand. Inside ornate naturalistic leaf capitals and leaf corbels, the latter supporting a robust roof in the nave. – Wyatt's FURNISH-INGS are mostly intact. The best are the READING DESKS and CHOIR STALLS. – FONT. A C12 base with trumpet-scalloped widening; the bowl inscribed 'John Monde Churchwarden 1664'. Moved from St Rumbold's church, 1975. – TILES in the chancel by *Maw & Co.* – ROYAL ARMS. Stuart, late C17. – STAINED GLASS. Fine E window by *Clayton & Bell*, 1884. Three others by *Lavers & Barraud*, 1867.

ST RUMBOLD (former), Salisbury Street. Originally Cann parish church, now part of Shaftesbury Grammar School. Lancet style, 1838–40 by *William Walker* of Shaftesbury.** Ashlar-built, of W tower, nave and chancel. Elaborate steep roof. Restored by *Ponting*, 1909–10, when a vestry was added. – STAINED GLASS. E window by *Alexander Gibbs*, *c.* 1870. Chancel S window by *Powell & Sons*, 1909; another by *T.H. Lea* of *Weaste Stained Glass*, Salford, 1931.

HOLY TRINITY (former), Bimport. In various uses. The church preceding the present one was a chapel adjoining the abbey walls. The present church is a substantial building (costing £3,230) and an early work of *Sir George Gilbert Scott* when in partnership with *W.B. Moffatt*. The date is 1841, and there is indeed still much of the Commissioners' type and nothing yet of the Pugin type. Lancet windows in pairs and triplets. Its best feature is the W tower with big pinnacles (and a higher stair-turret). The lower chancel is of 1908 by *Doran Webb*, replacing Scott & Moffatt's apse. Arcades with octagonal piers. Clerestory. Thin roof timbers. Now subdivided with an inserted floor.

HOLY NAME AND ST EDWARD (R.C.), Salisbury Street. 1909–10 by *E. Doran Webb*. Tower completed 1925. Convincingly Perp, the Tisbury stone now well weathered to a medieval hue – STATIONS OF THE CROSS carved by *Peter Watts*. – STAINED GLASS. E window by *Henry Haig*, 1999.

CONGREGATIONAL CHURCH (former), Mustons Lane, now a restaurant. 1859, by *A. Trimen*. Italianate, with a Corinthian portico of two pairs of columns. Top pediment and pedimented doorway. The chapel cost £1,300.

UNITED CHURCH (formerly Wesleyan Methodist), Parsons Pool. 1907 by *Gordon & Gunton*, noted architects of Nonconformist

*An early photograph in the church indicates that it was the medieval chancel window.
** *Walker* designed the town WORKHOUSE of 1838 on Castle Hill, demolished in 1949.

chapels. Arts and Crafts Gothic with an attractive façade, the
main elements set in a giant arch.

For ST JOHN THE EVANGELIST and the former PRIMITIVE
METHODIST CHAPEL, *see* Enmore Green.

PUBLIC BUILDINGS

TOWN HALL, High Street. Built in 1826–7 at the instigation
of the 2nd Earl Grosvenor. In the minimal Tudor style of
that period. It was designed as a two-storey market (with an
enclosed room above), the lower floor accessible from Gold
Hill, where it incorporated a lock-up. Symmetrical front, not
at all grand, or even dignified. Arcaded ground floor, now
glazed, and an upper arched balcony in the projecting porch.
Porch heightened to take a clock in 1879. At the back, where
the ground falls, the loggias, one above the other, were originally open.

POST OFFICE, Coppice Street. Dated 1946, perhaps by *Henry
Seccombe* of the *Office of Works*. Neo-Tudor. Ashlar-faced,
with a blue-grey Westmorland slate roof. On a grand scale for
Shaftesbury, especially surprising so soon after the war. The
corner site very competently managed.

ABBEY PRIMARY SCHOOL, St James's Street. By *James Soppitt*
of Shaftesbury. Dated 1873. Two gables with, between them,
two Gothic doorways for the boys and girls.

PERAMBULATION

From the two main monuments, St Peter's church and the Town
Hall, one should first turn down GOLD HILL, undoubtedly
the most spectacular and evocative place in Shaftesbury. On
the r. the mighty buttressed retaining walls of the abbey precinct, on the l. a row of modest stone cottages, some still
thatched, stepping down the steep slope, and beyond, the vast
green expanse of the Dorset landscape. Underfoot are stone
cobbles. Set back at the top of the hill, on the l., a cottage has
been converted to GOLD HILL MUSEUM. Curved extension
at the rear by *Proctor Watts Cole Rutter*, 2011.

Back to the HIGH STREET, which is more characteristic of
Shaftesbury in its patchiness. The most urban buildings are
in the N arm, which includes a triangular space called THE
COMMONS. On the l. (w) side, note need only be taken of
the GROSVENOR ARMS, built in 1826, with very thin detailing. Three-storeyed, the centre of the five bays coming forward
under a small pediment, the ground floor open over the street
on Tuscan columns. On the opposite side, No. 14 appears to
be a town house of *c.* 1740, with four big Doric pilasters and a
central pediment. It is said to have been rebuilt, so how much
do we believe?

Back towards the Town Hall. In the angle, on the r., KING
ALFRED'S KITCHEN, Shaftesbury's only timber-framed

survival: timber-framed to the front, that is (cf. Cerne Abbas). It is much rebuilt, however, the last rebuilding completed in 1979. Behind this PARK LANE leads to the main promenade in Shaftesbury, PARK WALK, with the view one way, and the entrance to the Abbey Museum through the wall. The space was given to the town and an avenue planted in 1753, by a local citizen hoping to gain political favour. The trees were cut down and the space dreadfully municipalized in 1953–6. However, fresh trees are at last softening the scene. Beyond ABBEY WALK, on the r., the Gothic Revival WESTMINSTER MEMORIAL HOSPITAL, dated 1871, by *J.B. Corby* of Stamford. Additions of 1929–30 by *Marshall Sisson* and a polygonal-ended w extension of *c.* 1970 by *Brian Savage*. All partially obscured by a large 1980s octagonal s block by the *Salisbury Hospital Works Department*.

In the High Street proper (heading E) there is very little of note to look at after the Town Hall and church are past. On the N side LLOYDS BANK has the top two storeys of a suave late C18 façade, of Greensand ashlar. There is the favourite central bow, very shallow and elliptical, and the minimal Venetian windows in the side bays. Thereafter almost everything is Victorian, occasionally in a lively Neo-Tudor idiom. The former CROWN INN, also on the N side, dated 1862, is also Neo-Tudor, but its chief interest is the boldly handsome lintel of a Perp fireplace installed in the old public bar. This has encircled quatrefoils at the angles, and daggers head to toe in the centre. At the end of the street one should glimpse the view down Shooters Lane to the r., and the Post Office (*see* above) beyond.

BELL STREET (reached by turning l. up ANGEL LANE) runs back parallel to the High Street, and is a more attractive walk, with its grey stone cottages, occasional brick and scattering of thatch. At the junction with MUSTON'S LANE on the s side there is a pair of matching early C19 curved-cornered houses with contemporary shopfronts. Also the PUBLIC LIBRARY, by *J.R. Hurst*, County Architect, completed 1971, loosening the street's texture by its octagonal form. So back w past the Grosvenor Arms Hotel and l. into BIMPORT, before the turn, glimpsing ahead the gable of the C17 SHIP INN at the top of TOUT HILL. In Bimport, on the l., is Holy Trinity church (*see* p. 517). From the churchyard one sees the rubble-stone medieval wall of the abbey precinct, with an ogee-headed lancet. At the w end of the churchyard the former NATIONAL SCHOOL of 1847. Tudor Revival; buttressed and gabled. Around the corner to the s in ABBEY WALK, one sees ABBEY HOUSE, late C17 but with Georgianized fenestration. It has within the sw room downstairs an ambitious C17 plaster ceiling, decked with fruit, flowers and leaves; the staircase is contemporary with this. Back through the churchyard to continue w along Bimport. CASTLE HILL HOUSE on the r. is a parapeted box, three windows wide by two deep, of 1743. Doorcase with a broken segmental pediment. Wooden Venetian windows l. and r.

OX HOUSE, next door, must be early C17, a rough ashlar front, with a central projecting porch, an addition, because the string course over the window heads l. and r. does not carry round it. Drastically restored and enlarged behind in 1963. Still on the r. of Bimport, beyond the terrace of mid-C19 houses, lies the promontory called Castle Hill, the site of the medieval castle. Now EARTHWORKS only, dating back to the reign of King Stephen. The last house to note in Bimport (on the l.) is EDWARDSTOWE, a very long stone range, with origins in a three-roomed house of c. 1500. A mural stair led to an upper-floor hall, the roof of which partially survives. At each end an C18 cottage was added.

The road turns sharply l., downhill, and then becomes ST JOHN'S HILL* and seems to leave the town behind. But at the bottom one finds ST JAMES, a suburb on the spring line at a lower level. The first house on the l. at the foot of the hill (No. 101 St James's Street), originally partially thatched, has quite a show of mullioned windows. Hoodmoulds and hollow-chamfered mullions. There is even a two-storey bay with 1:3:1 lights on both floors. One would date it all c. 1600. In ST JAMES'S STREET continuous stone cottages, with hardly a jarring note. It is opened up once, at PUMP YARD, where a pump stands in a tiny open-ended quadrangle of late C18 to early C19 cottages. Those nearest the road were added in 1862.

MILLAND HOUSE, Breach Lane, ½ m. WSW. Built as a rectory to St James's church. By *J. E. Gill* of *Manners & Gill* of Bath, 1860. Brick. Tall steep gables – vaguely Puginian.

PENSBURY HOUSE, Motcombe Road, ⅓ m. N. A five-bay-wide mid-C18 ashlar-fronted house with a central pediment. Sash windows in keyed architraves. Extended at the NE end in 1863. Its qualities are missed as it backs on to the road.

BLYNFIELD FARM, 1¾ m. WSW. A good group with two dated buildings. FARMHOUSE, datestone MW 1812 on the chimney-stack, remodelled at that date with wide sash windows. The buttressed BARN is dated MW 1809. Lozenge-patterned ventilation openings formed in the brickwork.

SHAPWICK

A village of many thatched cottages, some cob, some timber-framed.

ST BARTHOLOMEW. Large, of flint and stone, partly banded. Long C12 nave (s wall rebuilt in the early C14) and plain C12 N doorway, buttressed early C14 W tower with C15 belfry, C14

---

*There was a medieval church of this dedication on the W side.

N chapel heightened and extended eastwards *c*. 1500. Chancel (and sympathetic restoration), 1879–80 by *Frederick Rogers*. The two-centred tower arch with chamfered imposts looks 1300 at the latest, and the N arcade has one bay of the mid C12 (round arch with one slight chamfer) and a second widened in the early C16 and given a panelled arch. A second C16 panelled arch leads from the chancel into the eastern extension of the N chapel. The N window of this is the usual straight-topped type, but the E window has some bleak uncusped tracery. – REREDOS. Triptych by *E. Swinfen Harris*, *c*. 1890. – FONT. Late C12. Big, octagonal, of Purbeck marble, with two blank arches each side. Wrought-iron COVER, exuberant, probably *c*. 1880. – STAINED GLASS. E window, 1882 by *Clayton & Bell*. – BRASS. Richard Chernok, vicar, †1538, 18 in. (45 cm.) (chancel floor). Clerical dress. Adapted from a civilian brass of *c*. 1490. – TOMB-RECESS, N aisle. Late C15, elliptical-headed, with traceried spandrels. It houses a chest tomb with worn shields: Thomas Hussey †1639. – MONUMENT. Rev. William Sherley †1657. Tablet with classical surround.

E of the church in the heart of the old village, the MARKET CROSS, nothing but a stump now, probably C15, set upon ironstone steps. Surmounted by a war memorial cross of 1920.

BISHOP'S COURT, 200 yds N. The former Shapwick Champayne of the Hussey family, now mostly of *c*. 1857, Gothic Revival, brick. Late C16 stone range at the back.

WHITE MILL (National Trust), 1½ m. SE, is of red brick, dated   92 1776 on the mill race. It must be later than the adjoining MILL HOUSE, according to the evidence of the S-facing elevation. WHITE MILL BRIDGE is of stone with eight arches. Triangular cutwaters and refuges. Round arches cut back in two layers. In origin a bridge of 1341, but also the product of successive remodelling from the C16 up to the early C19. Bridge and mill together make a lovely group, with ever-so-verdant vegetation all round.

BADBURY BARROW GROUP, 1 m. N. Five barrows on either side of the Blandford to Wimborne road. The beech avenue to Kingston Lacy House, planted 1835, included the 'Badbury Barrow', nearly levelled in 1845. This barrow yielded a central cairn enclosed by a ring of flints and a sandstone wall, three inhumations, fifteen cremations, food vessels and urns. At the centre was a huge sandstone slab bearing carvings of daggers and axes.

BADBURY RINGS BARROW GROUP, 1¾ m. NE. Nine BARROWS immediately W and NW of Badbury Rings, a linear group, once thought to be Roman. The earthwork of the ROMAN ROAD to Dorchester is aligned on the group.

CRAB FARM, 1 m. NE. An Iron Age SETTLEMENT of small rectilinear enclosures and tracks, occupied from the Middle Iron Age to the end of the Roman period, and spreading over at least 60 acres along the main Roman road to Dorchester. It has been identified as the Roman town *Vindocladia* of the Antonine Itinerary. A rectangular Roman fort of 7½ acres, bounded by a triple-ditch fortification, was constructed in the later C2 A.D. across the line of the Roman road.

BADBURY RINGS (National Trust), 1¾ m. NE. Iron Age HILL-FORT, multivallate, occupying the dome-shaped western knoll of Badbury Hill. On the eastern knoll, in High Wood, is an Iron Age D-shaped enclosure. The inner two ramparts of the hill-fort have inturned entrances on E and W, the latter with a protective barbican. The outermost rampart enclosed the whole with aligned E and W inturned entrances. This rampart, associated with late Roman finds, may have been refurbished in the Roman/post-Roman period. The interior of 17½ acres is covered in earthworks. An inner enclosure may be earlier; many rectilinear earthworks are Romano-British or later. Together with the adjacent earthworks to the SW and at Crab Farm (*see* above), the complex has been identified as *Vindocladia*, and also as the *Mons Badonicus* of the C6 monk and historian Gildas.

ROMANO-BRITISH TEMPLE, 1¾ m. NE, immediately alongside the Badbury Rings Barrow Group. The temple EARTHWORK, once thought to be a disc barrow, was attached to the NW side of a sub-rectangular enclosure of 15 acres, beside the outer ramparts of Badbury Rings. The TEMPLE has been shown to have been square in plan, with sides of 65 ft (20 metres) and with a possible porch on the SE side. It was surrounded by a *temenos* enclosure, some 200 ft (60 metres) square. The complex was in use from the later Iron Age through to the post-Roman period, and formed part of the *Vindocladia* complex.

6010

SHERBORNE

Sherborne stands at the headwaters of the River Yeo, just S of the main historic route from London to the south-western counties. Its development has been closely linked to the presence of the abbey, built first as the cathedral for St Aldhelm, its founding bishop, when in 705 the see was created here under the Saxon king Ine. The settlement, called Lanprobi, was dispersed within a curve to the N and E of the abbey, with Cheap Street at its centre, almost certainly the market street of the emerging Saxon town. In the later medieval period inns were concentrated at the N end of Cheap Street, around The Green, where they adjoined the E–W route. In 1540, Leland wrote that Sherborne was 'the best toun yn Dorsetshir', and that 'it stondith partely by making of Clothe, but most by al maner of craftes'. Cloth weaving was succeeded in the C17 by button- and lace-making, which survived until the late C18. Silk-weaving started in Sherborne in 1755 at Riverside Works, on the Dorchester road at the SW corner of the town. By 1769 the industry employed some 600 men, women and children in the area. It flourished until the 1830s, reviving periodically, and finally ceasing in 1956.

At the Dissolution, and certainly by the early C17, the town's fortunes were related to that of the Sherborne Castle estate of the Digbys. Several Digbys were generous patrons, promoting the preservation of the abbey and erecting civic buildings. In 1856 the wealthy George Wingfield Digby inherited the estate from his uncle, the bachelor 2nd Lord Digby, a change of ownership that was highly beneficial to a town that otherwise might have dwindled to a backwater. Initially concentrating his activities at the castle, Wingfield Digby later supported the continuing restoration programme at the abbey – one of the longest and most careful of the time – and contributed to the building of a hospital, a hotel, further growth at Sherborne School, and some commercial development. Much of the town is still owned by the estate. From their first engagement in 1849 throughout this period, the architectural firm of *R.C. Carpenter* with his partners and successors handled all of the major town projects. The grouping of the restored abbey with the almshouses, and with the medieval-inspired memorial to Wingfield Digby, creates a memorable ensemble, quite the Puginian dream of a medieval town.

ABBEY CHURCH OF ST MARY THE VIRGIN

In 705 Sherborne was made the see of the Bishop of Wessex, St Aldhelm, who was also Abbot of Malmesbury. He is credited with founding the church, on a possible Roman villa site (where a portion of Roman pavement is said to have been found 'a long time ago'). It remained a cathedral until 1075, when the see was moved to Old Sarum. Prior to this the importance of Sherborne was diminished by the subdivision of the Wessex diocese in 909, on the creation of the new sees of Wells, Ramsbury (partly formed also from the Winchester see) and Crediton. The cathedral fell under Benedictine rule in 998 under Bishop Wulfsin, and did not cease to be so until the Dissolution.

The present Anglo-Saxon remains appear to date from *c.* 1045 (under Bishop Ælfwold). Of this period, above-ground survivals include much of the core of the crossing tower substructure, and elements of the Saxon w wall and 'westwork'. Further rebuilding took place in the first half of the C12, much of which survives behind the later Perp framework. Early in the C13 a Lady Chapel was added axially at the E end, the first part of the building to incorporate the Gothic (E.E.) style. Immediately w of the abbey church, and using the abbey w wall as its E wall, the town church of All Hallows was built in the late C14.* Abbeys did not like parochial duties, for which the w part of their church had to be kept publicly open. A riot in 1437 sparked by a long-running dispute between abbey and town caused much of the abbey church to be burnt, and a major Perp reconstruction ensued; some Perp improvements had already been undertaken under Abbot John Brunyng (1415–36).

31

---

*Possibly on the site of St Aldhelm's original cathedral (Gibb).

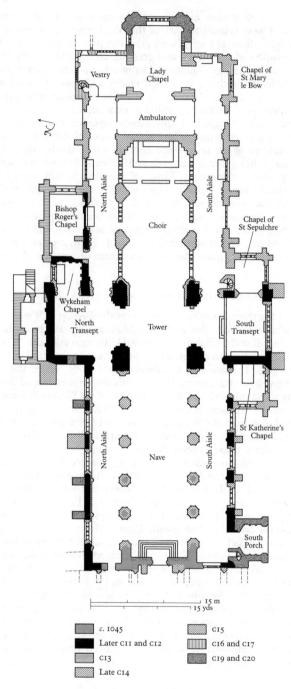

Vestry

Lady
Chapel

Chapel of
St Mary
le Bow

Ambulatory

Bishop
Roger's
Chapel

North Aisle

South Aisle

Choir

Chapel of
St Sepulchre

Wykeham
Chapel

North Transept

Tower

South
Transept

St Katherine's
Chapel

North Aisle

South Aisle

Nave

South
Porch

15 m
15 yds

	c. 1045		C15
	Later C11 and C12		C16 and C17
	C13		C19 and C20
	Late C14		

Sherborne Abbey.
Plan

At the Dissolution in 1540 the monastic property, including the abbey church, was purchased by Sir John Horsey of Clifton Maybank, who then sold the church to the town. They elected to retain the abbey as their church, and the surplus All Hallows was demolished. That the town kept up the whole of the abbey church instead of demolishing the E end or the W end is much to Sherborne's credit. Selby, Cartmel, Carlisle, Tewkesbury and Southwark did more or less the same; Bridlington, St John Chester, Dunstable, Leominster, Malmesbury, Holy Cross Shrewsbury, Waltham Abbey and Worksop preserved only the nave; Bristol and St Bartholomew London kept only the choir.

The present church has minor but important Anglo-Saxon features, C12 transepts and crossing, and an E.E. Lady Chapel, but is predominantly Perp. The Perp work was begun from the E c. 1425–30, and by the time of the fire in 1437 the crossing had been reached. The vaulting of the E end took place c. 1450. It was not until the last quarter of the C15 that the nave was rebuilt. The church is c. 255 ft (78 metres) long and of Ham Hill stone. Nave and transepts were restored in 1849–51 by *R.C. Carpenter* (who died in 1855); *William Slater*, his partner, restored the choir in 1856–8. Later the partnership was *Slater & R.H. Carpenter*, and the latter restored the tower in 1884. In 1921 the E chapels and vestry, which had been converted in 1561 for the Sherborne School headmaster's house, were returned to the church. The Tudor house structure was (controversially) removed by *W.D. Caröe* in order to recreate the Lady Chapel.

Exterior

The examination must start at the W front, although this faces us with what looks like extreme confusion. However, the confusion is fruitful; for it tells not only of the church in whose shadow we stand but also of its Anglo-Saxon predecessor and of the parish church of All Hallows.

THE ANGLO-SAXON CHURCH. The rough masonry of the W wall belongs to it, as is proved by a completely preserved doorway which leads into the N aisle. It is cut through the wall without any splays, is high in proportion to its width and is accompanied externally by the typical shafts l. and r. at a distance from the opening. The shafts once continued as an arch. In section they are semicircular. This doorway is protected externally by a flat-roofed porch (1947 by *W.H. Randoll Blacking* and *Robert Potter*). Excavations about 1875, and again in 1964–70, have shown that W of this Saxon wall was a westwork consisting of a tower and two side chambers or *porticūs* extending further N and S than the N and S aisles. There may also have been an atrium W of the W tower, but evidence for it is inconclusive. The NE corner of the extension was found in 1968 and is of good and telling long-and-short work (*see* Sherborne School, p. 536). A similar doorway to that to the N aisle has been found in the S aisle, although here only the N jamb survives, incorporated into a C12 doorway (now blocked). Late Saxo-Norman (i.e. C11) remains are also to be seen in the slype, accessible from Sherborne School.

ALL HALLOWS. It is not known when the parish church was built. The late C14 is the most likely date. What remains is the whole N wall to the height of the original window sills, with the wall-shafts dividing aisle bay from aisle bay, the E responds of the aisle arcades (they are of standard section), and, to the N and S of these, the responds of high arches leading into side chapels which extended N and S of the ambulatory. The springing of the S archway is still *in situ*. The blocked doorway into the S aisle of the church is C12, probably of *c.* 1120, incorporating the Saxon jamb as mentioned above. There is in addition a narrower C14 doorway inside the Norman one, inserted *c.* 1436. The main W doorway of the abbey appears contemporary with the building of All Hallows and may be the original W doorway of the latter, re-set when the parish church was demolished. It has tracery spandrels and a quatrefoil frieze over. Above, the late C15 W window of nine lights, the two principal mullions reaching right up into the principal arch. Its two lower rows of lights were added by *R.C. Carpenter, c.* 1850. In doing so he discovered remains of an Anglo-Saxon window which originally looked out from an upper floor of the Saxon tower into the nave. This would conform with other examples, as at Deerhurst, Gloucestershire, and Brixworth, Northamptonshire, where such windows survive.

EXTERIOR CONTINUED. The C12 church extended as far W as the Anglo-Saxon church, as the SOUTH PORCH proves. Norman rebuilding had probably begun early in the C12 at the E end and reached the S porch only *c.* 1170. The upper floor of the porch is of *c.* 1850 by *Carpenter*, in a somewhat fanciful, but attractive, Neo-Norman.* The monumental entrance arch has chevron at right angles to the wall surface and two orders of columns. The capitals are fanciful, with masks, beaded bands and foliage. There is also small nailhead l. and r., and round the corners to the W and E are blank arches with continuous roll mouldings. Such blank arches are also inside the porch. An upper tier of them again has chevron at right angles. The room is rib-vaulted. The S doorway is very large. It has an inner order of continuous chevron at right angles, one tall order of columns and a chevron arch, at right angles too. The columns of the doorway inside the building have trumpet-scallop capitals, another proof of a date *c.* 1170. In the niche over the porch, a cast of the STATUE inside the abbey of St Aldhelm by *Marzia Colonna,* 2005–6.

The S view of the church seems entirely Perp. The S aisle windows of the NAVE are of three lights and the aisle has a

---

*Replacing very plain C15 work, as shown in the 1655 Dugdale view. In the course of the work (as indicated in a 1851 print), the porch was entirely dismantled, so much of the stonework is of that date.

parapet with blank quatrefoils, many containing carved figures at their centre. The nave clerestory windows have steep two-centred arches, five lights with the two main mullions again reaching up into the main arch. Some of the sub-arches have straight shanks. The shallow buttresses between look C12 but are not. The SOUTH TRANSEPT is evidently C12, though the big S buttresses are Perp and so is the window. But in the E wall are exposed traces of the upper Norman windows. In the angle between nave S aisle and S transept is ST KATHER-INE'S CHAPEL, Perp too. Three-light windows and a quatre-foiled parapet. The S transept S window is of eight lights, again with the main mullions up into the main arch and again with some sub-arches with straight shanks. The CHAPEL OF ST SEPULCHRE (in the angle between the transept and the choir S aisle) is similar to that of St Katherine. The CROSS-ING TOWER of c. 1450 has pairs of two-light bell-openings with a transom and Somerset tracery. Set-back buttresses at the corners and at the centre of each face, each topped by a crocketed pinnacle, twelve in total. The double pinnacles at each corner create a lively effect (restored by *R.H. Carpenter* in 1884, *see* the Dugdale view). Before this there were eight. It is a close match to the contemporary tower at Milton Abbey (q.v.), where the parapet has pierced quatrefoils. Presumably the same was intended here but not completed.

The S aisle of the CHOIR has windows with depressed arches and four lights and another quatrefoiled parapet. A small doorway has leaf spandrels. In contrast with the nave, the choir clerestory has flying buttresses and wider windows of six lights. They have two-centred arches, and the main mullions once more reach into them. There are also the straight shanks and sub-arches. The E window is of nine lights, the main mullions as before. More quatrefoiled parapets. The choir S aisle ends in the CHAPEL OF ST MARY LE BOW. This looks curiously domestic, the reason being that this, its northern continua-tion (i.e. the larger part of the Lady Chapel) and the vestry block (*see* below) became the headmaster's house of Sherborne School in 1561, the date of the conversion recorded on the E side. Under the S gable are four-light mullioned windows. A multitude of shields of arms between them. Above the upper window is the coat of arms of Edward VI between twisted col-onnettes. This work is typical of that found on nearby country houses such as Sandford Orcas, Clifton Maybank or Melbury House (Melbury Sampford).

In its conversion to a school building, the three-bay C13 LADY CHAPEL was truncated to a single bay. It was restored as a war memorial in 1921–33 by *Caröe*, who gave it a new E end, full of unexpected Gothic invention, not out of place in this context, taking some motifs from the 1561 alterations to the Bow Chapel. SE of the chapel are handsome wrought-iron GATES of 1723.

The NORTH SIDE of the church is less easily seen, unless one visits the school (*see* below). The N side of the choir is like the s side. The vestry corresponding to the Bow Chapel is domestic-looking too. Three floors with mullioned windows, of six lights to the E. (The exterior of Bishop Roger's Chapel is only seen from the school side, *see* p. 535.) The W and E windows of the N transept are large and Perp, of six lights under depressed arches. Two transoms. The nave clerestory windows are as on the S side. But the aisle treatment is different. Three windows are replacements of *c*. 1850, that at the W end being entirely new as it would have been blocked when the upper storey of claustral buildings was standing. Before the nave restoration commenced, it was recorded that one of these aisle windows had reticulated tracery, the only Dec feature of the whole church.

Interior

The exterior having been treated as a perambulation, it may be useful to discuss the interior chronologically and always from E to W.

ANGLO-SAXON. We have already considered the evidence of the W end (also to be viewed internally); the slype arcading is described below (p. 535). Some further conjectures will appear presently.

NORMAN. Of the C12 choir nothing can now be seen except the plinths of the clasping buttresses of the E end visible below the stone bench in the ambulatory and some outer N walling inside BISHOP ROGER'S CHAPEL. This has three niches with continuous roll mouldings like the S porch and upper intersecting blank arcading, the colonnettes with three small scallops. Next, the CROSSING PIERS must be examined, and they are likely to be Anglo-Saxon, at least in their cores. What appears typically Saxon is the projection of the outer corners of the piers into the nave and choir aisles. That is exactly the type of crossing one finds in the early C11 crossing of Stow in Lincolnshire, and also at Milborne Port in Somerset and Norton in County Durham. In Dorset the same plan can be seen at Wimborne Minster. More puzzling are the nearly semicircular projections of the crossing piers into the transepts. They also do not tally in their bases with the C12 work, and while their tops disappear into the roof-space, there are string courses that link with the C12 work. They may well be Saxon (cf. Deerhurst chancel arch, Glos.). The piers were also partially rebuilt *c*. 1850–5 by *R.C. Carpenter*, and it is unclear whether any of their details were altered then.

Clearly C12 on the other hand are the crossing piers otherwise, with their twin demi-shafts. Capitals of big, i.e. early, scallops. The E arch is now Perp, the W arch has had its shafts removed (for stalls) in the lower parts. The arches are stepped and the transept arches are stilted. There is no evidence of Perp work being higher than C12 work; on the contrary, the s transept walls (less parapet) are the same height as originally built in the C12, as the marks of the C12 weathering of its roof on the s tower face prove. The nave arch is not stilted; the transept arches are stilted because they are narrower yet reach the same height as the nave arch. Beast-head keystones to each of the arches. The Perp crossing vault cuts into C12 lantern arcading in the tower. Seven arches, the middle one higher and wider.

The NORTH TRANSEPT has C12 walling, one odd shaft and capital exposed in the E wall and the complete arch to the nave N aisle. This also has tiny scallop capitals, except for one which has the kind of decoration like the porch capitals, i.e. may be a later alteration, as may be the roll attached to an edge of the arch. The WYKEHAM CHAPEL is C12 too. It has a straight E end, and on that side and the s large intersecting arches. A fragment of the C12 E window also remains.

The s transept walling can be seen exposed in ST KATHER-INE'S CHAPEL. The arch to the s aisle is like the N arch, but all capitals are scalloped. Of the C12 nave all that can be seen is a piece of string course on the NW crossing pier. Of the aisle walling nothing pre-C15 is to be noticed, and the W wall – to end the Norman description – is a mixture of C11, C12, C15 and C19 work. As has already been said, the C12 s aisle W doorway has a C14 doorway set in.

EARLY ENGLISH. This is mainly the LADY CHAPEL. It was originally three bays long, truncated by the 1561 conversion for the school. *Caröe*'s restoration quite rightly made no attempt to recreate the chapel in its early C13 form. The entry from the ambulatory is marked by responds with a group of detached Purbeck-like shafts carrying lively stiff-leaf capitals and a finely and intricately moulded arch.* Such capitals and shafting also for the former N and s windows. Short shafts on cornucopia-like corbels and again with stiff-leaf capitals mark the division between first and second bay. Rib-vault with a small boss and the springing of the ribs of the second bay.

The other E.E. contribution is BISHOP ROGER'S CHAPEL, but there is nothing to be remarked on inside except a good PISCINA and the Purbeck shafting of the E window, lancet lights as well as super-arch.

DECORATED. Signally absent, as has already been said.

PERPENDICULAR. This makes Sherborne what it is. *Caröe* was right to use it in 1921 for his E bay of the LADY CHAPEL, and his tripartite entry arches, narrow–wide–narrow with thin piers, are a charming conceit. Above the tripartite arch is an eight-light window, presumably installed *c.* 1561 as part of the headmaster's house conversion. The AMBULATORY is fan-vaulted with many bosses; so are the choir aisles. The wall-shafts are thin, but have the standard section. Panelled transverse arches W and E of the second bays from the W.

24

*Only the s shaft of the entrance arch is real Purbeck. The other shafts are replacements in local Forest marble.

The CHAPEL OF ST MARY LE BOW has in its E wall a fire-place, and domestic-looking S windows. These also belong to the alterations of 1561. The chapel itself dates probably from the C14 (see the S jamb of a former E window). The CHOIR has broad piers of complicated section. To the choir 'nave' the projection is the standard one, to the arches it is a triple shaft. The impressive thing is a broad panelled order which rises all the way up to embrace the clerestory window. There is one tier of panelling below these as well, and panelling against the E wall. The vault is a fan-vault, the earliest large-scale fan-vault known (completed c. 1450), and indeed still with ribs, thin and straight as matchsticks – as if it were a lierne vault. A vault of this type may have been intended from the start, as indicated by the nature of the piers and clerestory windows of before 1437. The work was no doubt interrupted by the fire of that year.

Christopher Wilson has shown that the apparently innova-tive format of the Perp choir at Sherborne was presaged by the remodelling of the choir of Glastonbury Abbey, Somerset (begun c. 1360).* Enough of this ruin survives to indicate that it had the low aisle arcades and high clerestory seen at Sher-borne. Also as at Sherborne, the wall surfaces at Glastonbury were panelled between the arcades and clerestory. What form the vault took at Glastonbury is, however, unknown. As for the author of the Sherborne choir vault, John Harvey (*Perpen-dicular Architecture*, 1978) suggested that the master mason *Robert Hulle* (†1442), the successor to William Wynford at Win-chester, may have been responsible, and that the design may have originated as early as c. 1425. Hulle was certainly working at the Sherborne almshouses between 1440 and 1442; before that, in 1426, he is recorded at Salisbury. The E window may be a post-fire replacement, following damage. Harvey linked its installation to repair works recorded in 1445–6, and considered it to be by a different designer from that of the vault.

The same fan-vaulting is used in the CROSSING. Broad pan-elling to the choir. The N transept is fan-vaulted too, whereas the S transept has a beamed ceiling with bosses, supported by late C14 carved corbels. The WYKEHAM CHAPEL has a veritable primer-book fan-vault. The CHAPEL OF ST SEP-ULCHRE is lierne-vaulted, the CHAPEL OF ST KATHERINE again fan-vaulted (with a square of liernes in the middle). The NAVE AISLES have lierne vaults, the nave a gorgeous fan-vault with many bosses. The nave piers are not placed at equal distances, and it has been suggested that the narrower distances towards the W end are those of the C12 (or even of the Anglo-Saxon) piers. The N side piers stand 14 in. (36 cm.) W of the corresponding ones on the S side and all the arches vary in width. What is implied by this may be the survival of the C12 (or Saxon) arcades until the C15 rebuilding, although

---

* *See* his chapter in *Gothic: Art for England*, Victoria and Albert Museum catalogue (2003).

why this should be the case is difficult to explain, especially as a perfectly regular clerestory was then built above them, the window spacings not coinciding with the arches blow. The piers (or pier casings) of the NAVE are broad and panelled all over. Shields at the apexes of the arches (including a bishop of Exeter in office 1509–19). Angel busts and fleurons along the string course below the clerestory. The angels hold shields (including that of Cardinal Morton, who died in 1500). The clerestory windows have one tier of blank panelling below.

William Smyth (†1490) may have been the architect of the nave and aisles (Harvey). He was master mason of Wells Cathedral; the fan-vaults in the N transept and Bow Chapel at Sherborne resemble Smyth's crossing vault at Wells, as do details of the blind tracery of his Camery Lady Chapel there (*see also* the crossing vault at Milton Abbey).

Furnishings

From E to W, and always N before S.

LADY CHAPEL. REREDOS. A sheet of glass engraved by *Laurence Whistler* in 1967–8 with a Sacred Heart and two cornucopias. Back-lit. – CHANDELIER. The earliest dated example in England of the familiar brass type, inscribed 1657. It is probably a Dutch import. Such chandeliers appear in innumerable C17 Dutch pictures. – STAINED GLASS. E window by *Christopher Webb*, 1937, and two side windows by him, 1934 and 1945.
AMBULATORY. A panel of floor TILES, C14 and C15.
CHAPEL OF ST MARY LE BOW. FONT. C15. Octagonal, of Purbeck marble. Panelled stem of Ham Hill stone. – Also some floor TILES. – SCREEN. Only the base is Perp. The upper part with the openwork inscription must be of *c.* 1930. It was designed by *Caröe*. – STAINED GLASS. Several fragments in E and S windows, C15.
CHOIR. REREDOS. By *Slater*, 1858, with elaborate Gothic canopies and large figures in relief by *James Forsyth*. It replaced a classical reredos given *c.* 1720 by William, Lord Digby. – STALLS. Also by *Slater*, and richly carved. They incorporate a series of C15 MISERICORDS. These include (N) a man pulling his mouth open, the Last Judgment, (S) a chained monkey, a man whipping a boy, an archer, a woman beating a man. – STONE SCREENS. 1856, probably by *Slater* or *R.H. Carpenter*. – PAINTING. The decoration on walls and vault is by *Clayton & Bell*, executed by *J.G. Crace*.* – STAINED GLASS. E window and six clerestory windows by *Clayton & Bell*, 1856–8. One of the finest large-scale schemes by the firm, adding to the rich effect of all of the furnishings and decorations in the choir.
CHOIR NORTH AISLE. MONUMENTS. Two of Purbeck marble to clergy. Of Abbot Clement only the head and the round arch

---

*An earlier (1849) unexecuted scheme for the vault was designed by *Pugin* at Crace's request, but not used.

above or behind his head is preserved. This is of *c.* 1180. The face is severely stylized, reminding one of Maya heads. – The other, of a priest in mass vestments, is easily C13. Shafts l. and r. of the effigy and a trefoiled arch.

CHOIR SOUTH AISLE. There is a third Purbeck marble MONU-MENT here, yet a little later. The priest's head is below a pointed-trefoiled arch with a gable. There are no shafts. The arch stands on corbels, one a head, the other stiff-leaf. – Tester of a C17 PULPIT, used as a table top.

BISHOP ROGER'S CHAPEL. Assembled here are a number of MONUMENTS, all tablets. Dominating the others is the enormous one to Carew Henry Mildmay †1784. Drapery hanging from the top of an obelisk against which stands an urn. Medallion of his wife above the urn, his medallion against the plinth. Hutchins says it is by *Thomas Carter* of Piccadilly. – John Eastmont †1723. Three urns, the top one in a scrolly open pediment, the other two on console scrolls at the base. Ionic side pilasters.

CHAPEL OF ST SEPULCHRE. PISCINA. Ogee-headed, late C14. – SCULPTURE. Wooden statue of St James, late C15. Spanish. – STAINED GLASS. E window by *Christopher Webb*, 1947.

CROSSING. PULPIT. A fine piece of 1899, designed by *Benjamin Ingelow* and carved by *James Forsyth*. Marble base with pink colonnettes; oak superstructure. Ingelow became R.H. Carpenter's partner in 1872. – LECTERN. 1869 by *R.H. Carpenter*, made by Messrs *Potter* of London. Puginian. – ORGAN CASE by *Gray & Davison*, 1856.

WYKEHAM CHAPEL. MONUMENT. Sir John Horsey †1546 and his son †1564. White stone. Tomb-chest with shields. Two recumbent effigies. Square pillars with arabesque decoration. Against the back wall the coat of arms in a lozenge (cf. Clifton Maybank, the frontispiece of *c.* 1535 now at Montacute in Somerset). Top with supporters and a small pediment on two sides.

SOUTH TRANSEPT. STAINED GLASS. Excellent S window with ninety-six figures. Designed by *Pugin* (assisted by *J.H. Powell*) and made by *Hardman*, 1851–2. – MONUMENTS. John Digby, 3rd Earl of Bristol †1698. Signed by *J. Nost I.* A vast *machine*, but not too large for its position. Reredos with upcurved top on two elegant Corinthian columns. Inside in front of blank arches the Earl, and a little lower down his two wives holding burning hearts. Two putti, almost quaintly small, outside the columns. – A son and a daughter of the 5th Lord Digby, †1726 and †1729, have a smaller tablet beneath the S window without any effigies. However, the epitaph is by Pope. – Opposite, in an E stone SCREEN by *J. Dudley Forsyth* (1909), a Gothic Revival tablet to J.K.D. Wingfield Digby †1904.

NAVE. STAINED GLASS. Magnificent W window by *John Hayward*, 1996–7. Expressionist in detail but with an overall colour scheme giving it coherence. It controversially replaced a window by *Pugin* (assisted by *J.H. Powell*) and made by *Hardman* in 1851. This had lost paint (like the other Hardman windows here),

78

but according to some experts could have been restored. Its panels are now in the possession of the Worshipful Company of Glaziers in London.

ST KATHERINE'S CHAPEL. STAINED GLASS. Many fragments are assembled here, including small whole bearded figures; C15. – MONUMENT. John Leweston †1584. White stone, the foot-end attached to the E wall. Tomb-chest with shields, recumbent effigies, six Corinthian columns, big top with putti. The underside of the canopy has the characteristically Elizabethan ornamental motifs of straight lines connecting circles and squares. Probably by *Allen Maynard* (cf. Longleat, Wilts.). – At the entrance to the chapel, STATUE of St Aldhelm by *Marzia Colonna*, 2007.

NORTH AISLE. STAINED GLASS. Four windows by *Pugin* (assisted by *J.H. Powell*), made by *Hardman*, 1851. Much paint loss.

SOUTH AISLE. FONT. Octagonal, with on the bowl a veritable pattern book of blank Perp three-light and four-light windows. It is of *c.* 1850 by *R.C. Carpenter*. – ROYAL ARMS of Henry, Prince of Wales, dated 1611, by *Charles Rawlings*. – STAINED GLASS. From E, 'School Window' by *Powell & Sons*, 1951; Butt memorial by *Clayton & Bell*, 1862; Millennium window by *J. Hayward*, 2001.

SOUTH PORCH. The wrought-iron GATE is of 1750 'to prevent indecencies'.

WEST PORCH (NORTH AISLE). STAINED GLASS. Depicting St Stephen Harding, by *Frederick Cole*, 1962 (made by *Wippell & Co.*).

SHERBORNE SCHOOL

The school, after having been monastic, was re-founded by Edward VI in 1550. From the early C17 it had purpose-built schoolrooms at the E end of the abbey, with the headmaster's house converted from the E abbey chapels. Significant expansion did not occur until after the appointment of a forceful headmaster, the Rev. H.D. Harper (1850–77). He transformed the school's character and scale, bringing in *R.C. Carpenter* and *W. Slater* as his architects. Converted monastic buildings were joined by new ones in a sympathetic Gothic style. The architecture changed into a slightly more bombastic Tudor with the appointment of *Sir Reginald Blomfield* in 1894, who, until 1926, was 'responsible above all others for the aspect of modern Sherborne'.* When Harper arrived there were forty boys, when he left 278. Today there are about 550, yet visually Harper and his architects still dominate the school.

The earliest post-Dissolution SCHOOL BUILDINGS are concentrated at the E end of the abbey, with the headmaster's house

*A.B. Gourlay, *A History of Sherborne School* (1971).

taken out of the three-storey vestry of the church (see its
domestic fenestration), the Lady Chapel and the Bow Chapel
(*see* above). Taking them chronologically, starting at the s
the first is the OLD SCHOOL ROOM, visually the most attractive of all the school buildings. Of 1606–8 by the master mason
Roger Brinsmeade and carpenter *John Reape*. The s front, faithfully reconstructed in 1884–6 (but with a new oriel, r.) is by

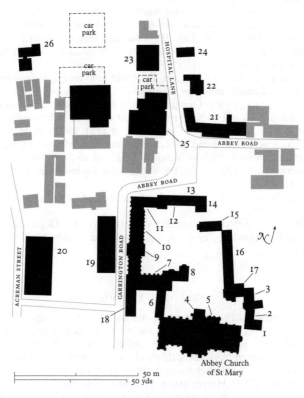

Abbey Church
of St Mary

50 m
50 yds

1	Old School Room	14	Porter's lodge
2	Oak Room	15	Medlycott
3	Bell Buildings	16	School House
4	Slype	17	Headmaster's House (former)
5	Bishop Roger's Chapel	18	Classrooms of 1870
6	Guesten Hall (now Library)	19	Carrington Buildings
7	Abbot's Hall (now Chapel)	20	Pilkington Laboratories
8	Abbot's Lodging	21	Abbey House
9	World War II Memorial Extension	22	Abbey Grange
10	Big School	23	Music School
11	North-west Classrooms	24	Music School (former)
12	Ranges by Blomfield	25	Gymnasium (former)
13	Entrance archway	26	Sanatorium

Sherborne School.
Plan

R.H. Carpenter. It has two large four-light mullioned windows with a transom under a string course. Ovolo mouldings. To the l., and in no relation to the windows, a four-centred-arched doorway in a classical surround with thin Doric pilasters. A second stage of Ionic pilasters, also thin, flanks the arms of Edward VI (by *Roger Moore*, 1608, but renewed in 1912), with a chronogram panel below, which reads:

Tecta Draco custos Leo vinDeX fLos Decus auctor
ReX pius haec servat protegit ornat aLit.

('The snake protects this building as guard, the lion protects it as avenger, the flower adorns it as decoration, the founder, the pious king, nurtures it.') Add the Roman numerals in pairs and get the foundation date 1550; add them singly and get 1670, which refers to a post-Civil War restoration. The top balustrade with vertically symmetrical balusters, and the pretty cresting – scrolls surmounting discs – are original (the balusters replaced in 1990). Inside, at the E end in a niche, a statue of Edward VI, carved in 1614 by *Godfrey Arnold*. Also much late C17 panelling.

To the N as a wing off the Old School Room, the OAK ROOM, a very humble range, dated 1670 on a panel and by *John Whetcombe the Elder*, wholly vernacular in character – mullioned windows with hoodmoulds. Next come the BELL BUILDINGS, dated 1835, and also modest, repeating the 1670 style. The three-storey entrance gable is leanly proportioned in the early C19 way. This part of the school was entered through a doorway in a wall along the N side of Church Lane, the alley connecting the abbey cemetery with the town. Over this doorway a panel recording the founding of the school by Edward VI.

Now moving W towards the surviving MONASTIC BUILD-INGS. First the C13 SLYPE immediately N of the N transept, in the SE corner of the former abbey cloister. There is a narrow passage with a pointed tunnel-vault, with to the N a yet smaller room with a tunnel-vault. E of these is a small square room with a rib-vault of single-chamfered ribs without a boss and springing from E.E. corbels in the N corners. Partly obscured by the vault wall arches on its S wall (i.e. on the N side of the N transept), now thought to be associated with the late Saxon building. The CHAPTER HOUSE must have followed to the N. The DORMITORY was on the upper floor, but only one much-altered window survives above the square rib-vaulted room. This has a lean-to roof against the transept gable, but a string course indicates the two-storey medieval height of this E cloister range. E of the transept is the C13 BISHOP ROGER'S CHAPEL, its E window with three stepped lancets under a single arch (now used as a choir vestry and not normally accessible).

As we swing around to the N side of the abbey aisle we see more substantial monastic remains. The CLOISTER itself was built probably *c.* 1350–70, and as indicated above stood W of the N transept, along almost the full length of the abbey nave. The wall-shafts and vault springers of the S and W ranges are recognizable. There are indications that the S range, at its W end, was two-storeyed from around the C14 onwards, as indicated by the upper doorway at the W end of the range. (The N aisle window here is a mid-C19 addition. Also, the two-storey portion – perhaps the abbot's chapel – could not have been of this height further E, as it would have blocked the three N aisle windows.) The upper doorway linked with the former W range. Also two-storeyed, with the cellarer's storage below and the great hall of the monastery, the GUESTEN HALL, above. Of the C13 but rebuilt and re-roofed in the C15, it has two heavy flying buttresses on the E side (part of the mid-C19 restoration) on the site of the W cloister range, the shafts and springers of which remain *in situ*. Tall two-light Perp windows with smaller single lights below, all much restored. Inside the hall a good nine-bay roof with arched collars and wind-bracing, the latter cusped. The detailing of the six S bays differs from the three N, suggesting a former partition wall. The hall was recovered in 1855 by *R.C. Carpenter* from an altered state, having served as a silk mill until then. This work was relatively sensitive to the surviving medieval fabric. On the ground floor in the SE corner is exposed Saxon long-and-short quoining, associated with the westwork of the Saxon abbey. It formed part of the NE corner to the N *porticus*. There are also on both floors small Dec doorways leading to a C14 spiral staircase and the missing upper floor of the S cloister range. – STAINED GLASS. S window by *Clayton & Bell*, 1888.

Of the N range which contained the REFECTORY there is no evidence, except for the LAVATORIUM, which was removed to the centre of the town (*see* p. 543).

The present school chapel forms the head of a T with the W range. It was the ABBOT'S HALL, and stands on an UNDERCROFT with one round C12 pier and four vaults with unchamfered ribs. The remaining Neo-Norman work is of 1855, except for one small doorway with a segmental arch and some nutmeg ornament in the hoodmould. The roof of the original Abbot's Hall (i.e. the E part) is C15, of five bays, and has wind-braces. NE of the hall is a former ABBOT'S LODGING, a picturesque C15 house with a pretty, quite elaborate doorway to the N, a bay, formerly staircase, to its l., and a N projection at the E end. This N projection has a large medieval chimney (of the monastic kitchen), with now hardly discernible signs of the four Evangelists carved on the N face. Beyond this are the purpose-built school buildings, forming a large courtyard known as THE COURTS.

Before moving away from the monastic buildings, however, closer inspection should be made of the former Abbot's Hall in the S range of The Courts. It was restored by *R.C. Carpenter* to become the school CHAPEL in 1855 and further lengthened to the W twice: an additional two bays in 1865 by *Slater & Carpenter*; and two further bays in 1922 by *Blomfield*. In 1877–81

Sherborne School, former Abbot's Lodging and Hall.
Lithograph, 1853

Carpenter & Ingelow added a N aisle above a cloister walk, both
elaborately Perp. Projecting to the N at the W end is the gable of
Blomfield's WAR MEMORIAL STAIRCASE (1922). This became
the new access into the lengthened chapel. – REREDOS. By
Powell & Sons, 1904, as a Boer War memorial. Perp stone
framework with *opus sectile* panels. – Marble SANCTUARY
PAVING by the same firm, 1907. – PANELLING and FUR-
NISHINGS by *Blomfield*, 1925. – STAINED GLASS. E window
by *Clayton & Bell*, 1896 (moved from the W end in 1925). On
the s side six further windows by the same, 1867–1902, and
another in the N aisle, 1922. (Other windows were destroyed
by a bomb in 1940.)

Continuing N, and linked to the Chapel by the cloister, is the
SECOND WORLD WAR MEMORIAL EXTENSION by *R. de
W. Aldridge* and *O.S. Brakspear*; 1955, Cotswold manor style,
with a staircase leading up to a doorway with a multi-light
window above, and a tiny two-light in the gable. It is really a
s extension to the BIG SCHOOL of 1877–9, by *Carpenter &
Ingelow*, with tall gabled windows converted from Gothic to
plain mullions and transoms in 1955 following bomb damage.
Within, panelling and fitting-out by *Sir Reginald Blomfield*,
1894 (his first work at the school), and inside a corridor at
the N end a classical niche (by *Blomfield*) containing a BUST
of Archbishop Frederick Temple of Canterbury by *Sir George
Frampton*, *c.* 1903. This is in a lobby attached to the next phase
of expansion, the NORTH-WEST CLASSROOMS by *Carpen-
ter & Ingelow*, 1883, which continue along the N side of The
Courts in an Early Tudor style.

An altogether bolder character was adopted by *Blomfield* for
two further ranges, of 1913 and 1923. The latter includes the
TOWER over the entrance archway. This cleverly incorporates
staircases to the range on its W. Now from the gatehouse E.
First the PORTER'S LODGE of the former gateway of 1853,

probably by *R.C. Carpenter*, then MEDLYCOTT, a detached
Cotswold-style house of 1954 by *Brakspear*. Then, running N–S,
the dormitories of SCHOOL HOUSE, 1860–1 by *Slater*, much
like his and Carpenter's work for the Woodard Schools* and
the first building at Sherborne to introduce Harper's new scale.
The range ends with the former HEADMASTER'S HOUSE,
breaking out from lancets into bay windows. The headmaster's
house adjoins the earlier school premises (described above).

Beyond this somewhat irregular quad, further new buildings
have been generally located to the N and W. In Carrington
Road to the W are the CLASSROOMS of 1870 by *Slater & Carpenter* with big gables S of the Chapel, and on the opposite side
are the CARRINGTON BUILDINGS of 1909–10 by *Blomfield*,
the first building for the school not in a Tudor style. It is a symmetrical composition in an Edwardian Free Style, not easily
defined. Angle pavilions with two shaped gables each, but
classical doorways and a centre cupola. Behind are former silk
mill buildings, and facing Acreman Street the PILKINGTON
LABORATORIES of 2000 by *Hopkins Architects*. In a minimalist
Neo-vernacular style, these fit sensitively into the town-fringe
street scene. To the NE the former GYMNASIUM by *Blomfield*,
1923 (now the dining hall). Rustic Neo-Georgian. Timber-framed and timber-clad. Further N the MUSIC SCHOOL
by *ORMS Architects*, 2008–10. Stone with vertical, colour-bleached timber boarding above under monopitch roofs. (For
an earlier music school, now a drama studio, *see* Hospital
Lane, p. 545.) The last building of interest is the SANATORIUM
of 1888 to the NW by *K.D. Young*, who specialized in hospital
buildings. Tudorish Gothic. Two blocks linked by a bridge at
upper-floor level.

CHURCHES

ST MARY MAGDALENE, Castleton. Reconsecrated in 1715,
probably incorporating structure of 1601. Pope recorded that
the designer was the *5th Lord Digby*. It is a very curious design.
The interior (which was without aisles until 1715) is simply a
continuation of the Gothic past: four bays of arcading N and
S with octagonal piers and single-chamfered arches. All is very
avant garde for the early C18, suggesting that the Digby was
very much setting the trend towards Gothic Revival. Typical
C18, and again advanced, the windows with Y-tracery. The
arcades were certainly in place before *W. Slater*'s 1863 restoration, so are presumably also of 1715. The façade has the three
gables of many a West Country Gothic church, and also four-centred arches to the doorways. The large circular windows
above the aisle entrances are the only recognizable Queen
Anne motif. – REREDOS. Classical (Wren style), with the Commandments in a pedimented centre, Lord's Prayer and Creed

---

*The eleven schools founded by the Victorian educationalist the Rev. Nathaniel
Woodard (1811–91), e.g. Lancing College, West Sussex.

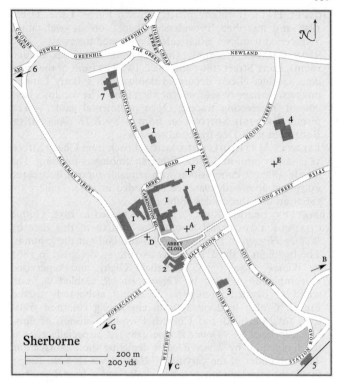

A   Abbey church of
    St Mary the Virgin
B   St Mary Magdalene
C   Sacred Heart and
    St Aldhelm (R.C.)
D   Gospel Hall
E   Union Chapel
F   Wesleyan Methodist
    church
G   Cemetery

1   Sherborne School
2   Almshouse of St John the
    Baptist and St John the
    Evangelist
3   Digby Memorial Church Hall
4   Public Library and
    Digby Hall
5   Railway station
6   Sherborne School for Girls
7   Yeatman Hospital

in side panels. – WEST GALLERY with a reused late Elizabethan
staircase. – ROYAL ARMS of Charles II, dated 1671, on the
gallery front. – CHANDELIER of brass, dated 1714. – FONT.
C18. A baluster with a small bowl. Plain compared with, e.g.,
Blandford Forum. – MONUMENT. Jonathan Beaton †1717, a
handsome cartouche.

SACRED HEART AND ST ALDHELM (R.C.), Westbury. 1893–4
by *A.J.C. Scoles*. Ham Hill rock-faced nave and chancel. C13
lancet triplets on the nave, heavily buttressed. Bellcote over E
end of nave. Triplet arcades E of sanctuary arch, N and S, the
N opening into a former nuns' nave at right angles. – STAINED
GLASS. Probably contemporary, designer unknown. – Large
CHURCH HALL, W end, 1998.

GOSPEL HALL (formerly Strict Baptist), Finger Lane. Dated
1838 and inscribed 'Providence Chapel' on an oval tablet.
Y-traceried windows either side of a pointed doorway.
UNION CHAPEL (formerly Congregational, now an auction
room), Long Street. 1803 and 1821. Two-bay front of the latter
date, Gothic. Nicely decorated doorways in a Batty Langley
manner, perhaps re-set from the 1803 front. The windows have
cusped intersecting tracery. Open pedimental gable. – The
former BRITISH SCHOOL in front is by *R.H. Shout*, 1852.
Buttressed with Dec-traceried windows.
WESLEYAN METHODIST CHURCH, set back from Cheap Street.
1841–2 but refronted 1862. Quite an ambitious building. The
façade a lancet composition with pinnacle-topped buttresses.
Polygonal apse with plate tracery added in 1884. Gallery (of
1862) around three sides within.
CEMETERY, Lenthay Road, ½ m. SW. Opened in 1856. Gothic
CHAPELS, LODGE and RECEIVING HOUSE of this date by
William Haggett of Sherborne, who also laid out the grounds.
The highlight is the DIGBY MAUSOLEUM, designed in 1862
by *William Slater* for G. Wingfield Digby, and supervised
to completion in 1877 by *Thomas Farrall*. Gabled W front,
apsed E. Banded stonework. Fine and elaborately carved
French Gothic W doorway with alternating coloured voussoirs (of Mansfield and Cornish Polyphant stone), as illustrated in Eastlake's *Gothic Revival* (1872).* Especially good is
the tympanum by *James Redfern* depicting the Resurrection.
The remainder of the carving by *Henry Poole & Sons*. Richly
fitted-out interior with polished shafts and a tunnel-vault in
Sienese-style banding. Also hydraulic hoists for the lowering
of coffins.

PUBLIC BUILDINGS

104 ALMSHOUSE OF ST JOHN THE BAPTIST AND ST JOHN THE
EVANGELIST, Abbey Close. Built in 1438–48 (on the site of
an earlier hospital), for twelve poor men and four poor women.
The chapel, completed in 1442, was by *Robert Hulle*, who was
paid in instalments between 1440 and that year. This remains
in an unusually complete state of preservation and is still used
as it was in the C15. The original part is the S range, laid out
in the manner of a monastic infirmary, the chapel to the E
internally open to the dormitory. Ground-floor refectory at
the W end. The peculiarity at Sherborne is that the dormitory
part is two-storeyed – because the almshouse was for women
as well as men. The men slept below, the women above. In
1858 the big expansion to the N gave separate rooms to the
inmates, and the dormitories became dining hall and board
room. *Slater* designed the new part, keeping exactly in style

*Also in *The Builder*, 7 March 1874. The portal was shown at the International
Exhibition in South Kensington of 1862.

Sherborne, cemetery, Digby Mausoleum, west front.
Engraving by Orlando Jewitt, 1872

as far as possible, but indulging in an E oriel overlooking the
entrance to the Abbey Close, and going E.E. in the open-ended
arcaded cloister. He thereby created a delightfully picturesque
grouping.

The S front, though much restored in 1861, makes a fine
show, two storeys of seven one-light windows, under big
square hoodmoulds, the lower linked continuously. Ground-
floor windows of two lights, and four lights at the W end for
the refectory. Four lofty octagonal chimneystacks. In the E
bay the chapel doorway, flanked by ogee-headed niches. The

chapel is truly a chancel only, narrower and lower than the rest. Large three-light windows E and S, set deeply in the wall, and given moulded surrounds and hoodmoulds. Normal Perp tracery. On the street, C19 cast-iron railings with mitre finials to the posts. The ensemble is completed by the robust LYCHGATE into the courtyard by *Slater*. – CHANCEL SCREEN. Of wood, two-storeyed and quite simple. Square-headed openings, 4:4:4, with cusped heads. – STAINED GLASS, in the S window. Three figures of the Virgin flanked by the two St Johns and some heraldry, dated to *c.* 1475 but re-set. Tenderly drawn and inevitably coarsened by restoration. – ALTARPIECE. An exceptionally fine triptych of *c.* 1480. North French, perhaps from the Picardy region, by an artist influenced by the circle of Rogier van der Weyden. In the centre the Raising of Lazarus, and other of Jesus's miraculous acts of healing in the wings. Standing saints in pairs on the backs of the wings.

DIGBY MEMORIAL CHURCH HALL, Digby Road. Surprisingly of 1909–10 (but looking 1810), by *C.B. Benson* of Yeovil. Tudorish except for the Perp oriel in the gable. Niche below with a statue of St Aldhelm. Spired roof vent.

PUBLIC LIBRARY AND DIGBY HALL, Hound Street. Of 1972 by *J.R. Hurst*, County Architect. Single-storeyed and flat-roofed. Panels of local rubble stone, divided by vertical slit windows. Horizontal window slits between the panels and roof eaves. The adjoining Digby Hall repeats the vertical windows, but with monopitched roofs at a low angle with clerestory lighting in the spandrels.

RAILWAY STATION, Station Road. Of 1860 to a standard design for a 'first class' station by *Sir William Tite* for the Salisbury & Yeovil Railway (cf. Gillingham). Two gables front and back, the taller for the stationmaster's house, the lower for a waiting room. Booking hall between the two.

SHERBORNE SCHOOL FOR GIRLS, Bradford Road. The school was founded in 1899 but work did not start on its present site until 1902. The initial scheme was by *John Harding & Son* of Salisbury. Completed after Harding's death (1910) by *W.D. Caröe*. A gabled Tudor range with higher cross-wings at the ends. Former science wing added at the SE corner by *Caröe*, whose high tower of 1925–6 at the junction is 'memorable and sophisticated' (Jennifer Freeman) in its free interpretation of Tudor. Slightly battered walls with a central buttress rising from a pair of low arches. Above these gilded inscriptions. Battlemented parapet incorporating clock faces. Inside, the ASSEMBLY HALL of 1902 has a hammerbeam roof and a classical plaster frieze (completed in 1920 after a fire).

Several of the BOARDING HOUSES are also by *Caröe*. That with the most inventive composition is ALDHELMSTED EAST (formerly Aldhelmsted East and Kenelm), over Horsecastles Lane to the W. Brick. Of two phases, 1926–8 and 1937–8. U-plan, the N wings terminated by tall paired chimneystacks. At the centre of the N and S fronts a steep pediment set within a gable of similar pitch.

YEATMAN HOSPITAL, Hospital Lane. By *Slater & Carpenter*, 1866. Gothic, indistinguishable from the firm's work for Sherborne School. Formerly a symmetrical composition centred on a gable, facing S. This now blocked out by a large S extension of 1965, approximately in a modern style. Caramel-coloured brick. Towards the road, the WARLEIGH WING, 1913 (rainwater head) by *Sir Edward Maufe*. In a neat classical style. Big hipped roof. Ground-floor loggias l. and r., arched at the centre in a Venetian-window way. Recent (1992) classical porch by *Studio Four Architects* set between the two builds.

PERAMBULATIONS

1. Northward from the Abbey

The starting point, just S of Sherborne Abbey (p. 523), is the ornate MEMORIAL to George Digby Wingfield Digby, of Sherborne Castle, whose money made so much of Sherborne's C19 works possible. Erected in 1884 to *Carpenter & Ingelow*'s design. It takes its inspiration from the Eleanor Crosses, and is elaborated at the corners above the base by four bronze figures by *J. W. Singer* of Frome, and by a mass of mini-buttresses and crockets above. The landscaping of the Abbey Close is by *Haggett & Pocklington*, 1858. The Town Hall, which blocked off the view of the Abbey and Close, was demolished in 1885.

Now E into HALF MOON STREET, where much of the N side is taken up by a continuous row of tenements. The W half of these is of *c.* 1532–4, built as a row of shops with a church room above. The matching E part has a datestone 1570–1, referring to an extension of that date. Another datestone WS. 1701 probably denotes a repair. Stone, the upper floor to both parts showing twelve identical windows of four arched lights not set in a surround. Two further windows at the W end, converted to sashes in the early C19. Shopfronts below, but one original doorway survives, with four-centred-arched head and a chamfer. Such humble Tudor town buildings have very rarely survived, and in this case, rarer still, with records of the date of erection and original purpose. Next a jump in scale, date and style to SAINTS JOHN BUILDING, of 1894 by *R. H. Carpenter*. Commissioned by the Master of the Almshouse as a home for church workers (and a hall for the Young Men's Society). Picturesque Gothic grouping, setting the character at this important crossroads. To its N the tiny square made before the E gateway to the abbey precinct. The CEMETERY GATE is a lofty C15 four-centred arch, moulded with a hollow and a wave, and with three worn, once-canopied niches above. Just beyond it, ABBEY GATEHOUSE, the former Almonry, with a frontage rebuilt in the mid C19. The CONDUIT in the centre of the space was built by Abbot Mere in the early C16 as the lavatorium in the abbey cloister. Hexagonal, with buttressed angles. Originally only the N side had a doorway. Panel tracery on the other five sides, uncusped, a sign of the late date. Of the surrounding houses, two are of timber-framed construction. That immediately adjoining the s side of the gateway (now a local history centre) is of *c.* 1600, jettied but with its framing otherwise hidden by plaster – no doubt its original finish. On the N side BOW HOUSE (part of Sherborne School since 1916) is of the same date, but with its exposed timber framing heavily restored.

Continuing from here up CHEAP STREET, the area around the conduit and the first row on the l., where the buildings are set back, is known as THE PARADE. A few quiet Italianate mid-C19 frontages; the best is ABBEY BOOKSHOP of the 1840s, w side, with delicately incised pilasters and a wrought-iron-balustraded balcony. Next a single bow-fronted bay with a Venetian window, raised on Ionic columns, opened as the Sherborne Savings Bank in 1818. The next shop is timber-framed, and beyond it, still on the w side, one C17 mullioned window with a hoodmould survives above the shopfront of MORTIMERS. On the E side, opposite The Parade, the early C18 ABBEY PHARMACY with good late C19 shopfronts, the first of several of various C19 dates to be found around the town. Adjoining on its l. a single stone bay, with a delicately bowed window at first-floor level with an oriel-like apron. Further on, LLOYDS BANK of the mid C19, probably by *George Evans* of Wimborne (built for the Wilts. & Dorset Bank), commercial Italianate. Beyond, where Hound Street joins on the r., the plainish *c.* 1930 Neo-Georgian of a BARCLAYS BANK. This has a fine fanlight over its main doorway, built on the angle.

On the w side, just after the (very restored) early C16 timber framing and heavy stone flank walls of NATWEST BANK, ABBEY ROAD breaks in. N of the corner, ABBEYLANDS, showing better than any other house the combination of timber framing and stone walls which must have been common in the town as it first developed. Towards Cheap Street a jetty, restored timbering, three oriels and three gables. The s return front has restored mullioned-and-transomed windows, with hoodmoulds.* Set back here a gabled full-height porch that must originally have belonged to the next-door house, dated 1649 over the round-headed entrance arch, which has the fat soffit roll and jewelled keystone and impost blocks that one would call Jacobean, and a hoodmould which looks Early Tudor. That must surely be reused. Continuous string courses above.

w down Abbey Road, on the s side the E.E. detailing of the former WESLEYAN SUNDAY SCHOOLS (now the Powell Theatre of Sherborne School), by *Lander* of Barnstaple, 1872. It adjoins the Methodist church (approached off Cheap Street, *see* p. 540). On the N side ABBEY HOUSE, the Georgian-looking ashlar front of which is detailed with astonishing gaucheness. The frieze of the Doric porch is carved with odd leaves, and the window above has a semicircular pediment and blowsy side

* On this part a date 157– was visible (A.B. Gourlay, *A History of Sherborne School*, 1971).

scrolls also embellished with scraps of foliage. Close inspection suggests that, even more astonishingly, the façade dates only from the early C19.

Now is the moment to turn r. for a brief sally up HOSPITAL LANE, to see ABBEY GRANGE, whose bizarre appearance is explained by its being just the transeptal porches of the abbey's tithe barn of c. 1400, whose four-bay-long buttressed ends* were removed and new E and W walls cobbled up in 1827. Pairs of gabled buttresses, and mullioned windows. The original arch into the S porch has a continuous chamfer and a hood-mould, and over it is a two-light Perp window. Beyond is the former MUSIC SCHOOL (now Drama School) of Sherborne School, 1926, Neo-Georgian by *R. Blomfield*.

CHEAP STREET continues N less eventfully. On the W side, after Abbeylands, timber framing of c. 1500, the jetty carried on curved brackets, and posts carved as clustered shafts, and inserted shopfronts. Another of about the same date further on with its framing exposed. On the E side, the boldly detailed Neo-Georgian-cum-Italianate frontage of the POST OFFICE by *Archibald Bulloch* of the *Office of Works*, c. 1930, added to an earlier house. Further up on the W side an early C19 house with a two-storey bow window. As the culmination on the E side the former DIGBY ESTATE OFFICE, a dignified stuccoed front of c. 1800, with a pair of shallow bowed shop windows.

Beyond the top of Cheap Street there is a leftward bend and THE GREEN opens out. Here there are several houses to note. Moving around clockwise, GREENHILL HOUSE, on the S side of The Green, is the only substantial C17 town house in Sherborne. Canted two-storey window bays, giving 1:4:1 lights, contribute the accent to a symmetrical façade under three gabled dormers – large, small, large – the large gables reached by moulded corbelling from the canted bays below. Spare bay to the l. The road named GREENHILL crosses the head of The Green, placing on its N side an Early Victorian terrace, GREENHILL COURT (built in 1843) to look across the widest space. The central pair of houses have pedimented doorcases. To the W, cottages continue attractively downhill behind raised walks. To the E the houses become grander, of the early C19. ANTELOPE PLACE, opened 1748 as a hotel, is of painted brick with small sashes. It has a porch with Tuscan columns projecting the full width of the pavement. Back to The Green, at right angles to Greenhill, on the E side, the former ANGEL INN of c. 1840, its raised entrance bay with porch on Tuscan columns still with the sign LICENSED TO LET POST HORSES on its frieze.

Back to the top part of Cheap Street, known as HIGHER CHEAP STREET, with a cluster of cottages on the corner of NEWLAND. One (No. 7) has two matching early C19 shopfronts. Further up, on the E side, a complete C16 timber-framed house with its

*As illustrated in an 1802 view by Buckler.

upper floor projecting; then THE JULIAN (now 'The Slipped Stitch'), a medieval inn, given to the Almshouse in 1437. Although restored, it is not much altered from its appearance in Buckler's sketch of 1803. The W end, curiously arranged with a full-height canted window bay between single-light windows, has stone flanking walls corbelled out at half-height, suggesting that a timber-framed upper storey has been replaced in stone. One or two original openings round the side, and in the adjoining GEORGE INN a contemporary stone archway, four-centred and moulded in the standard way, with wave and hollow. Inside, downstairs, intersecting ceiling beams with carved bosses, among them the arms of the abbey, and in the roof, kingposts and wind-braces.

Before returning to Newland, a detour to NETHERCOMBE FARM, by going W from Greenhill, then N up Coombe Road. The farmhouse is on the r. It was thought to have been the former church of St Emerenciana, the chief early feature of which is the C14 Perp two-light blocked window in the gable-end to the road. The evidence, however, suggests that the window is at the upper end of a small C14 house. The S-facing range runs W–E, with the former open hall at the centre and a service room at the E end. Four-bay upper cruck roof. Much late C16 or early C17 remodelling. Attached on the N side, a contemporary BARN with a small, two-centred-arched doorway to the road.

Now back and E into NEWLAND, for the town's best individual house, grandly set back from the road with its own twin-entrance forecourt. This, SHERBORNE HOUSE, was built c. 1720 (incorporating an early C16 rear wing) for Henry Seymour Portman as a halfway house between his properties in Somerset (Orchard Portman) and Dorset (Bryanston). In common with other such houses (e.g. Barrington Court, Glos., as originally built for Earl Talbot, 1737–8), it was exceptionally well appointed while relatively modest in size.* Seven-bay ashlar façade (alas, renewed in artificial stone) of great height and considerable *noblesse*. By the simplest means – breaking the centre three bays forward under a small pediment, close window spacing, moulding the window surrounds and employing angle quoins – its designer has imparted this air; for the central feature adds up to little, just a pilastered doorcase against a curtailed background of rustication, under a broken segmental pediment, and a triangular pediment to the window above. Top balustrade. Inside, the staircase hall has fine wall paintings by *Sir James Thornhill*, painted a year or two after completion of the house. The same system is used as in the signed paintings at Charborough Park (c. 1718, q.v.), grisaille low down, the upper walls and ceiling in polychromy. Diana on the ceiling, the myth of Meleager and the Calydonian boar

74

* Hutchins reports that his architect was Mr *Bastard*, although, given the date, it is more likely that the Bastard company of Blandford only provided internal joinery. *Thornhill* may have been its architect, seeing that he painted the fine stair-hall mural.

on the N and S walls. Fine-quality staircase, rising round three sides of the well. Three balusters per step, of an unusual shape, triangular in section and tapering downwards. The house passed into Digby ownership in the early C19, and from 1932 to 1992 was Lord Digby's School.

The MANOR HOUSE (now Town Council Offices) by the roadside immediately beyond is in origin of *c.* 1500. The oriel is of that date, although previously on the E gable; it was moved to above the doorway as part of a wild sub-gothicization of *c.* 1820. Canted, with one cinquefoiled light each way, corbelled on a worn demi-angel. Inside, in a first-floor corridor, a Perp piscina with a two-centred head, presumably imported. Elsewhere mullioned windows with hoodmoulds that come round at the sides like ears. Frenzied cusping.

To return to the centre, it is worth taking a last detour via HOUND STREET, further on the S side, beyond the Manor House. After 75 yds, on the E side, FOSTER'S SCHOOL. The Gothic Revival SCHOOL HALL is of 1875, the plainer BOARDING HOUSE behind of 1887 by *Farrall & Edmunds*. Further off to the SE, the Public Library (*see* p. 542). Halfway down, also on the E side, in the grounds of HARPER HOUSE (an early C19 stucco villa with its back to the street) is a remarkable SHELL GROTTO. Of *c.* 1740–60, circular externally, with a pyramidal thatched roof. Octagonal within, with an intensive decorative shell scheme in a classical style. Each of the seven closed wall faces has a niche, its back treated in varying patterns. Running around the wall above the niches is a series of floral swags made from lead (for the stalks and runners) and shells (for the leaves and flower petals).

89

2. South from the Conduit

From the Conduit S down SOUTH STREET, on the W side, at the junction with Half Moon Street, the ornate shopfront of the former WOODWARD'S DRAPERS shop of 1871 by *Thomas Farrall* (now Melbury Gallery and Barker Dry Cleaning). The detailing is somewhat ecclesiastical, with rich foliate carving on the capitals by *Grassby* of Dorchester. A plain upper floor was added in 1900. After some 200 yds, on the E side, two houses of note. The first, with an ashlar S front, is DUCK HOUSE of *c.* 1830, with its shallow pilaster strips and shallow round-headed depressions framing the major windows. Further on, LODBOURNE HALL (*c.* 1850) is more Italianate, especially in the block rustication of its Tuscan porch. Continuing S and turning r. into STATION ROAD, the former WOOLMINGTON HOTEL, of about the same date as the arrival of the railway (i.e. *c.* 1860) is a typical commercial hotel in a vague Italianate style. Opposite the railway station (*see* p. 542) the PAGEANT GARDENS were laid out in 1906. They give this corner of the town a setting of suitable gentility for the former DIGBY HOTEL, round the corner in Digby Road. Built in 1869 by

Slater & Carpenter for G. Wingfield Digby, partly to provide accommodation for his castle guests. Now a Sherborne School boarding house. Of three storeys with a row of gabled dormers and tall bay windows on the s front, giving it something of the air of a French château. A richly carved Digby coat of arms (by *Grassby*) on the porch parapet. To the w, an adjoining ballroom of 1878. Bland block added to the N side *c.* 1970, facing the road, for the school. Further along the road, the archway into the former COACH HOUSES AND STABLES, opposite which is a MASONIC LODGE dated 1896 and the Digby Memorial Church Hall of 1910 (*see* p. 542). The road then takes us back to the Digby Memorial and the abbey.

3. *From the Abbey to the east*

From the abbey E along Half Moon Street again, then N and almost immediately E into LONG STREET. The oldest evidence comes at the start; but it is nothing more than, on the s side, a timber front of *c.* 1500, the lower part only, with curved jetty brackets, re-erected in 1926, and on the N side an early C16 house with what remains of its two-storey oriel of mullioned windows built into the later shop facing Cheap Street. Of similar date further along the N side TUDOR ROSE, a cottage with a C17 five-light stone-mullioned window. Just to its l., GILYARD SCARTH ESTATE AGENT has a good shopfront dated to 1881, when this opened as the Sherborne Coffee Tavern. On the s side an excellent group, starting with the BANK HOUSE of *c.* 1740, with its Doric porch. More exotic is the OLD BANK HOUSE, a blend of genuine (i.e. C16) and Tudor Revival features, the former including a canted oriel with battlements and a lower frieze of sub-cusped quatrefoils. It became the Sherborne and Dorsetshire Bank *c.* 1750 and by 1773 was Pretor's Bank. The part to the r., entirely of the early C19 with a tall mullioned-and-transomed window, is a later banking hall. ABBOT'S LITTEN, next door, is a plain early C18 town house, just a five-bay ashlar front and a spare bay over a carriage entry to the l. Central pedimented doorcase on Doric half-columns.

Beyond, the street is interrupted on both sides: by the Gothic CONGREGATIONAL CHURCH and SCHOOL (*see* p. 540) on the N, and by the big early C19 former WHITTLE & CO. BREWERY on the s. The first buildings here were erected for the Dorsetshire Brewing Co. in 1796. Many new walls of local stone, from its conversion to flats in the 1960s, and just beyond a substantial stone house of 1971 by *Roydon Cooper Associates*, both projects intended to be sympathetic to the emerging preservationist spirit in Sherborne. Beyond the brewery on the N side another interruption, the red brick front of THE RED HOUSE, a remodelling *c.* 1730 of a late C17 house, much enlarged at the rear in the early C19. It stands back behind railings and brick gatepiers, but it is a truly urban façade. Ham

Hill stone dressings, channelled quoins set in slightly from the angles, channelling round the doorway, and Tuscan pilasters and entablature enclosing that. Then on the s side the mid-C18 red brick façade of the EASTBURY HOTEL with old-fashioned emphasis at the centre. Here the doorway is linked by a balustraded panel with the slightly more elaborate treatment of the window above.

Beyond this point buildings become more cottagey, with one or two pairs built by the Digby Estate. This is the way to Sherborne's castles (*see* below), and to walk the rest of the way gives a pleasant passage at last down CASTLETON ROAD, past what is left of the once-independent village of Castleton, which was cut off from the town by the arrival of the railway. Opposite St Mary's church (p. 538), the stone fronts and large mullioned-and-transomed windows of LATTICE HOUSE, MIDDLE HOUSE and RALEIGH LODGE. The first is taller and of *c.* 1700 in origin, but with an early C19 Gothick porch. Middle House is lower, with hoodmoulds only on its upper windows and an early C18 pedimented porch hood. It is probably of *c.* 1680. The last, probably of the same date, seems heavily restored in the C19. Beyond this group the present entrance to Sherborne Old Castle.

OLD CASTLE

Roger of Caen, Bishop of Sarum or Salisbury and *procurator regni* to Henry I, built the castle between 1122 and 1139. The property reverted to the Crown during the Anarchy following the succession of Stephen in 1138, but became an episcopal seat again in 1355 and remained with the Salisbury bishops until the Dissolution. In 1592 the lease was granted to Sir Walter Raleigh, who, following the precedent of Robert Dudley, Earl of Leicester, at Kenilworth some twenty years earlier, began converting it as his mansion. This scheme proceeded – often sporadically – until Raleigh was arrested for treason in 1603, and it seems likely that it was far from complete at his death. His eventual successor to the property, Sir John Digby, seems to have had little interest in Raleigh's Old Castle project, and from *c.* 1625 concentrated his resources on rebuilding the bishops' hunting lodge. The castle was initially held for Charles I during the Civil War. Several changes of hands, and its fall at a 1645 siege, brought about its present ruinous condition, for Fairfax's incapacitating of castles was nothing if not thorough. Even so, there is enough left to allow one to work out the unique plan of Bishop Roger's castle and to admire the new standard of ashlar masonry which he demanded: masonry that was, in William of Malmesbury's words, 'ita iuste composito ordine lapidum, ut iunctura perstringat intuitum, et totam maceriam unum mentiatur esse saxum' ('the courses of stone being laid so exactly that the joints defy inspection and give the whole wall the appearance of a single rock face'). Few indications remain, however, of the scope of Raleigh's work.

From 1617 the Old Castle became part of the Digby estate in Sherborne. It was transferred by Simon Wingfield Digby to the Ministry of Works in 1956, and is now an English Heritage property.

Sherborne was not a fortress, like Corfe, but a very strongly defended palace, set within a lake and adjacent to its own deer park. One approaches across a deeply excavated dry ditch to pass under the gate-tower. This is the SW of four towers which stood symmetrically straddling the castle's curtain wall. Little is left of the curtain wall, just a stretch at the SW, and another at the NE, with a few intermediate chunks. It was about 25 ft (7.6 metres) in height throughout. The area defined by the wall and further defended by the ditch was a rectangle c. 450 ft (135 metres) by c. 330 ft (100 metres), with its corner sections angled at forty-five degrees in plan. The total length is some 1,400 ft (425 metres).

10   The SOUTH-WEST GATEHOUSE is four-storeyed, ashlar-faced, relatively small and similar to those at Framlingham and Henry I's great castle of Arques-la-Bataille in Normandy. It rises from a battered plinth and a chamfered string course, but without further interruptions except a slight step halfway up, to its full height. Clasping buttresses to the outer angles;

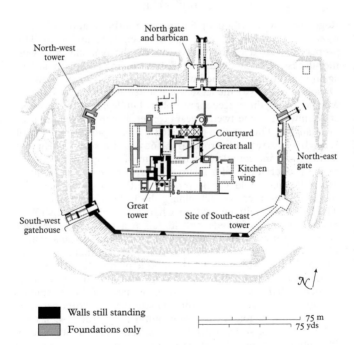

Sherborne, Old Castle.
Plan

SW stair-turret, the NW turret carried up into a chimney with a conical cap, probably of the late C16. Evidence of Norman windows on the side faces. They have unsplayed reveals. The best evidence that the style is still very much Early Norman is the semicircular inner archway and the window above it: their arch mouldings are little more than grooves. The windows of the top two storeys are of Raleigh's time, square-headed of three lights, the mouldings identical with those on the new Sherborne Castle (*see* below).

The foundations of the pedestrian NORTH GATE, near the centre of the N curtain wall, are almost overgrown. It was considerably larger in area than the other gateways, and had round turrets at the outer angles, these being a later, probably C13, strengthening of the defences. It extended forward with a barbican, crossing the ditch to give access to the lake. A further gateway is indicated in the NE corner; the two other mural towers were open gorge (i.e. open-backed) in plan.

Within this formidable enceinte, slightly to the W of its centre, stand the sadly reduced relics of BISHOP ROGER'S PALACE. It consisted of a great tower, attached to the SW corner of a great square block of buildings, four ranges round a central courtyard. For internal communications there were covered walks like a cloister on all sides of the courtyard. No parallel for this luxurious and indeed prophetic plan exists; Bishop Roger's palace at Old Sarum is similar, but there the great tower is free-standing.

Most of the facing and carved stone has been robbed, so that one can only point out odd features here and there. The GREAT TOWER is rectangular, N–S being the longer axis, with a latrine tower or annexe against the S end of its W wall. Clasping buttresses to great tower and annexe, and an intermediate W buttress. Only the S wall of the annexe stands to any height, and the steps and terrace against the W wall are Raleigh's doing. Also not original is the curious arrangement of the S wall of the great tower with a bulging central projection, and a groin-vaulted room inside carried on a reused Norman column with a scallop capital. This structure supported a large two-storey bay window (much like similar work at Kenilworth), the centre bowed and the whole raised above a high base. The cellar vaults of the great tower, inserted in the late C15 by Bishop Langton, are parallel, l. and r. of a N–S spine wall. The annexe and great tower communicated only at first-floor level and above. In the N wall traces of a newel staircase, clear evidence of the communication between great tower and W range.

Examination of the COURTYARD BLOCK may begin with the sole surviving evidence of the S range. This is an upper string course, with chevron decoration of its sloping under-side, running across the great tower's E wall. So there must have been an important room at ground level here, such as a great hall, evidence for which is scanty. It was demolished during Raleigh's alterations. For the E range one can only speak of undercroft level. External pilaster buttresses and three round-headed windows in the E wall. Springing of the tunnel-vault of the undercroft only as long as the courtyard walk, and in the W wall a small window splayed towards the W, showing that the courtyard walk was covered. Evidence of a staircase N of the undercroft.

The NORTH RANGE is preserved to a greater height, and shows an elaborately decorated room on the first floor, extending to the E wall. External pilaster buttresses mark it as four bays long; and it was supported on vaults: a tunnel in the W bay, and groin-vaults in the rest. Tufa vault-rubble. The E window of the main room has continuous chevron outside, and a scallop capital for an internal shaft. One N window has not only the continuous chevron but shafts l. and r. with bud-like volutes on the capitals, billet on the hoodmould, and big outward-pointing chevron, a memorably early example, i.e. hardly later than c. 1130, of the move from CII shallowness in decoration to something more sculptural. The internal face of the N wall has arcading of intersecting arches, with a roll moulding, set on shafts, the shafts gone, but not all the scallop capitals or all the bases, a long way below. The internal moulding of one window survives. This range is believed to have contained two chapels, the lower with its groin-vaulted three bays at the E end, the upper also vaulted and with the intersecting arcading around its walls.

Finally the WEST RANGE, where there is nothing to report except a further pilaster buttress, a string course linking the range with the great tower, and a tiny room in the thickness of the wall. This range most likely provided entertaining rooms for the bishop, his private rooms being close by in the great tower itself.

Attached to the SE corner were KITCHENS, nothing of which survives above ground. Outside the NE gate the buildings of a service court lie buried beneath a Civil War bastion.

SHERBORNE CASTLE

60   Queen Elizabeth leased the Old Castle to her favourite Sir Walter Raleigh in 1592, and in 1599 allowed him to purchase it together with a substantial estate. As we have seen, Raleigh carried out a scheme for the conversion of the CI2 castle, making it his main Dorset mansion. He then embarked on the construction of this new house (incorporating parts of a late CI5 bishop's hunting lodge) across the valley 400 yds to the S, and easily within its view. It was known as The Lodge, and must be one of the earliest lodges, those smallish, compact but flamboyant houses which one especially associates with the reign of James I. From its limited initial accommodation its purpose must have been to act as a centre for entertainment – hunting and banqueting – rather than as a main country seat. This was the function of the Old Castle.

Raleigh's lodge bore the date 1594 in stained glass, as noted by Hutchins, suggesting at least a start in that year. When first built its plan was a simple rectangle. A plan for 'Sherborne

Lodge' in the Hatfield collection signed by *Simon Basil* is for adding irregular polygonal corner turrets; it is thought to date from the visit by Robert Cecil and his family to Sherborne in 1600. This implies that the four corner turrets were additions, a point confirmed by what was seen when the E front was bared of its rendering in 1969, establishing that the turrets were not bonded into the body of the house. Each turret forms an irregular hexagon in plan. They are not quite as Basil drew them in that he must have had some idea of viewing angles, or some notional line-of-sight for weaponry, in his mind. The hall is set off-centre, occupying the W two-thirds of the S front, and the whole E third including the turrets forms the parlour. In the remaining NW corner what was a small withdrawing room (and later a dining room).

The ELEVATION of the house built upon this plan is correspondingly bizarre; but before it can be further described notice must be taken of the fact that, after Raleigh's downfall, Sherborne was eventually, in 1617, granted to Sir John Digby, the ambassador to Spain (made Earl of Bristol in 1622), and that the four wings are his, built between *c.* 1625 and 1630. These resulted in an H-plan, carrying on Raleigh's style faithfully, and complete a house doubly bizarre in outline. The entire house is rendered, with dressings of Ham Hill stone. Raleigh's Lodge is three-storeyed, three windows broad and two deep, with four-storey angle towers, and the main block rises to a fourth storey in the centre by way of shaped gables. Those on the N and S faces have a full mullioned-and-transomed window flanked by small rectangular lights; those on the E and W have two small arched windows only. This creates a flat balustraded platform running N–S on the rooftop.

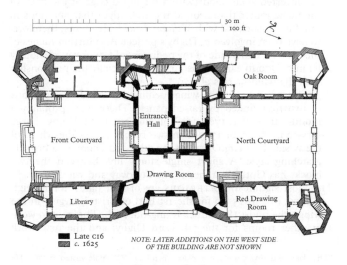

Sherborne Castle.
Plan

The tall square chimneystacks line up along its sides, and there
are more sprouting from the towers, alternating with heraldic
beasts. The windows are almost all restored, but not wholly
accurately (see the original survivors, with square-section mullions, in the NE wing). Originally the E windows were four-
lighters. Also, flanking the second-floor window were a pair of
œils de bœuf. Further *œils de bœuf* were incorporated at both
main levels where Digby's wings join Raleigh's towers. Simple
base-moulding and two thin string courses over the window
heads. The upper windows have architraves, not hoodmoulds.
Two-lighters in the towers, ranging with the main windows.
The upper rooms in the turrets could only be reached across
the roof leads, so must have been used as banqueting houses
à la Longleat.

Digby's balustraded wings continue the Raleigh idiom so
perfectly that one can hardly believe them to be of a later
date. Only the slightly richer base-moulding gives them away.
Artistically more important, they are only two-storeyed, thus
underlining the stress laid by Raleigh on the two lower storeys.
The towers sprout from the outer angles of the wings, and copy
the irregular hexagonal shape; but they too support the main
block without stealing its thunder, for they are three-storeyed
only. The only possible miscalculation is the straightforward,
not diagonal, projection of the wings, making a pinched composition (and narrow, deep forecourts) to N and S. Digby's
additions, so inconvenient yet so sympathetic, are a matter
for wonder. He did however introduce a few Renaissance
trappings, especially the gateways to the N and S forecourts.
Round-headed arch between square piers with niches, and
(for the S gateway only) strapwork panels and a demonstrative
armorial headgear. Balustrade to l. and r. The niches here have
the inverted shell-hood (with a scalloped edge at the back of
the niche rather than around the arch edge) that one finds in
buildings associated with *William Arnold.* He seems, therefore,
to have been involved in Digby's project. Also further niches of
this type on either side of the pedimented S doorway, obviously
let in *c.* 1770 to earlier masonry (see especially the relationship
with the window sills above).*

The E side has in the wings pedimented window surrounds
in two tiers linked by raised panels. These were probably a
modification of *c.* 1700 for William, 5th Lord Digby. Large
service addition of 1787–8 in two blocks across the whole of
the W side by *Evan Owen* for the 7th Lord Digby in a broadly
matching style. A short single-storey link between the two
blocks has Gothick arches to the doorway and windows.

The most significant INTERIORS are of four dates: for Raleigh
c. 1600; of *c.* 1625–30 for the 1st Earl of Bristol, largely in the
wings; the mid-C18 Gothick fitting-out of the library, and work
in other rooms for the 7th Lord Digby; and the new work

*The classical doorway was not in place when Horace Walpole visited in 1762. He
describes entering through a corner doorway into one of the turrets.

carried out for George Wingfield Digby in 1859–65 by *P.C. Hardwick*, with interior decoration by *Morant & Boyd*. The following rooms are described in the sequence along the route followed by the public.

After entering via the SE turret, the LIBRARY, in the SE wing, is Gothick, of 1757–8, the bookshelves set between slender shafts which carry arches with ogee heads. This work cost £250 and was by *William Ride*. The ceiling (1758) is in a Jacobean style, but with flower sprays that speak clearly of mid-C18 plasterwork, too naturalistic to convince. Its designer (remarkably) was *Francis Cartwright* of Blandford, who received a payment of £33. In Raleigh's Parlour (now the SOLARIUM), *Hardwick* made his biggest show. Especially fine is the Jacobean-style marble fireplace by *White & Co.* Mr *Cubit* (presumably the firm under Lewis Cubitt after Thomas's death in 1855) was also employed fitting up this room, being perhaps responsible for the Austrian oak panelling and 'Jacobethan' doorcases. The ceiling here must be early C17 with irregularities to accommodate the extensions into the two E turrets. The RED DRAWING ROOM in the NE wing is a creation for the 1st Earl of Bristol, complete by *c.* 1630. It has an early C17 ceiling, with roses and posies of flowers in the fields. Early C17 chimneypiece, the flanking columns Corinthian below, Composite above. Armorial overmantel in a gadrooned border. Above this room on the first floor is the PORCELAIN ROOM with a late C18 fireplace. It leads, via the original NE turret, into the GREEN DRAWING ROOM, Raleigh's original Great Chamber. This has three early chimneypieces, the main one with coupled columns of two orders, and a fine opening border decoration of overlapping circles. It is a wider version of very similar fireplaces at Montacute, Somerset, and Wolfeton (Charminster), both in great chambers built *c.* 1596–1601. All three may be early work by *Arnold*. The Bristol coat of arms appears to have been let in to the surrounding strapwork; perhaps it supplanted Raleigh's arms. Smaller chimneypieces in each of the turret recesses, these with single columns, also two orders. The ceiling, with its oak and acorn motifs and Tudor roses, is a grander version of that in the Solarium below.

Decoration in the BLUE DRAWING ROOM (above the Library) is late C18 in character (although mostly mid-C19) with a genuine late C18 fireplace. Its *c.* 1600-style ceiling is a C19 copy. LADY BRISTOL'S BEDROOM is the Great Bedchamber of Raleigh's house, but shortened in length. Its ceilings are of *c.* 1600 and consistent with others of this date in the house. They are also found in the corridor outside, taken off what was most likely an ante-room. This leads into the original NW turret. Here (and on the floor below) the outside corner of the original rectangular house has been retained, no doubt for structural reasons. The delicate stick-balustered 1770s STAIRCASE descends to the HALL of Raleigh's house. Simple Late Perp fireplace and doorways, the square surround ovolo-moulded. Much restoration here in the 1930s. Behind the hall,

61

facing N, the SMALL DINING ROOM is no doubt much as Raleigh would have known, with a typical C17 fireplace. Finally the OAK ROOM in the NW wing, a complete panelled interior of c. 1620, chiefly remarkable for the two internal porches, all of timber, with pilasters and pierced strapwork parapet. These, together with the panelling and fireplace, were introduced from elsewhere. The porch cresting was brought in in the mid C19. The arch at the N end is probably c. 1630 and has much in common with arches by *Arnold*.

On the top floor of the original NORTH-EAST TURRET (but not shown) is a small panelled room with a Serlian classical stone fireplace: diminishing Ionic pilasters with gadrooning and fluting. This is said to have been Raleigh's study. Adjoining this another room with a bed alcove. Both retain original plasterwork. Here also a late C16 staircase (from attic to roof) with tapering column balusters.

The PARK was laid out for the 6th and 7th lords Digby. It includes the serpentine LAKE to the N, between the two castles, designed by *Capability Brown* in 1753, and the GARDENS immediately around the house, also by Brown (1774–8). The broader LANDSCAPING may not have been by him, as there are no indications in the accounts of this. He must, however, have cast a continual influence over its development since he made regular visits even after the completion of his contract in 1778. The park to the S is now farmed, and wooded ground rises in the distance. But the Brownian landscaping is still detectable as the underlying structure here.

Immediately below the castle on the W side, a Gothick DAIRY of 1753–5, possibly by *Brown*. Its three-bay N loggia is of the same bamboo-like character as the library. Re-set on the floor, a Roman MOSAIC PAVEMENT from Lenthay Common (just over 1 m. SW of the abbey, S of the railway line), found in 1836. Apollo with a lyre and Marsyas with a double flute – a rustic version of a classical myth.

The Neoclassical ORANGERY of 1779 facing the dairy may have been designed by *Henry Holland*, Brown's son-in-law. The design (exhibited in the castle) is unfortunately unsigned. Ashlar-faced, five bays of full-height round-headed windows, the end ones surrounded by a Doric aedicule with stretched pilasters. Frieze of *Coade* stone.

STABLES, 300 yds WSW. Very large. Three ranges of stone, ashlar-faced towards the square courtyard. By *Benjamin Bastard* of Sherborne (for which he was paid one guinea for the drawing in 1758). The date 1759 on them refers to the centre range, and the start of the return ranges, which were extended to the S in the mid C19 by *Hardwick*. Arcading of that date. Without being given the date one would have supposed the main block to be rather late C17, with its naïve array of cross-windows and two-light mullioned windows above. A further STABLE BLOCK to the W, with tower-like ends, has detailing matching that on Hardwick's stable extensions, so must also be by him.

LODGE at the main entrance, 150 yds w of the stables. Of 1857 by *Hardwick*. Ornate 'Jacobethan' in rich, rock-faced, Ham Hill stone. Adjoining wrought-iron GATE SCREEN.* Piers topped by carved griffins holding coats of arms.

MIDDLE LODGE, ¾ m. E. Thatched *cottage orné* of 1857.

GOATHILL LODGE, 1¾ m. E. A near duplicate of the above, and of the same date.

RALEIGH'S SEAT, 400 yds NNW. Of *c.* 1600; overlooking the old road into the town. A simple stone alcove seat, heavily buttressed.

DENNY (or DINNEY) BRIDGE, just N of Raleigh's Seat. A medieval structure of two arches, probably contemporary with Bishop Roger's castle.

POPE'S SEAT, E of the bridge, on the N bank of the lake. A battlemented arched alcove of 1780, probably by *Holland*.

THE FOLLY, further E. A castle-style mock ruin of 1755–6. Behind (but not connected to it) stands a crenellated WALL of the same date, along the outer line of the Old Castle moat. In order to reach the Old Castle itself, a CARRIAGE ARCH was made through the outer bank in 1789–90 by *T.M. Cook* for Henry, 1st Earl Digby. To facilitate and frame the view back towards the New Castle, just w of the arch, a CLAIRVOIYÉE was made, *c.* 1790.

PINFORD BRIDGE, ⅞ m. E of Sherborne Castle. Suave classical bridge, meant for an ornament at the head of the lake – see the pilaster buttresses instead of cutwaters. A design by *Robert Adam* (1767) was not executed. Designs of 1768 at the castle showing the bridge largely as executed are by *Capt. the Hon. Robert Digby*, younger brother of Lord Digby. The builder was *William Privett*.

SHILLINGSTONE

A long, linear village on the A357 with buildings of various dates, which never quite adds up to a homogeneous whole.

HOLY ROOD. Early C12 nave and chancel of flint – see one s window and, visible inside above the N arcade, two more windows. There is also a chancel N window, now also internal. Late C15 two-stage w tower, ashlar-faced. The N arcade and N aisle are of 1888, by *F.W. Hunt. G.F. Bodley* was responsible for the charming roof decoration. He designed it in 1902–3 as part of a full restoration, and he was critical of Hunt's work. Bodley's chancel screen was regrettably removed in 1977. The present vestry was furnished as a Lady Chapel by *Comper* in 1914. Alas, nothing remains of this fitting-out. – PULPIT. Mid-C17, with some motifs still in the Jacobean tradition, others

---

* *J. Potter* was paid £827 for this in 1859.

already of the Wren type. – FONT. Square, Norman, of Purbeck marble, with the usual shallow blank arches. – STAINED GLASS. E window by *Burlison & Grylls*, 1903. Two colourful chancel S windows by *Warrington*, 1872. Former chancel E window, now vestry E window, *c.* 1888 by *Hardman*. Three *Comper* panels in the N aisle, 1914. At W end of N aisle three panels transferred from Shillingstone Grange, the central by *Powell & Sons*, 1907. W window of 1920 by *Mary Lowndes & Barbara Forbes*. – MONUMENTS. Incised outline of a figure, probably C13. – Eliza Acton †1817. By *Chantrey* (in the vestry). Large kneeling woman in relief.

LYCHGATE of 1903. Timber-framed.

VILLAGE CROSS. C15 steps, plinth and pedestal. Very well-executed shaft and carved cross-head of 1891.

SHILLINGSTONE GRANGE (now CROFT HOUSE SCHOOL), ¼ m. W. 1905–6. Arts and Crafts house by *C. E. Ponting* for Mrs Kyre Chapman. Gables and various bay projections. Largely unaltered on the SW (garden) front. Large additions and new buildings to the NE after it became a school, *c.* 1948.

LIME KILN HOUSE, 1 m. S. Large Arts and Crafts-inspired house, 2004 by *Gerald Steer* of *St Ann's Gate Architects* of Salisbury. Butterfly plan with tile-hanging and extensive tiled roofs. Large Gothic entrance arch.

SHIPTON GORGE

4090

ST MARTIN. In a splendid location, raised high above the Bredy valley to the S. The embattled W tower with polygonal higher stair-turret and a doorway with straight-shank arch and decorated spandrels is Perp of *c.* 1400. The church itself was built in 1861–2 by *John Hicks* of Dorchester. Perp-style windows. N aisle under a separate roof. Perp-style too the N arcade. Good roof corbels by *Grassby*. – PULPIT. By *Hicks*, carved by *Grassby*. Elaborate. – FONT. Heptagonal, with three blank trefoil-headed arches; early C14. It sits on a circular bowl and stem, probably C13. – Simple original FURNISHINGS by *Hicks*. – ROYAL ARMS. Of Queen Victoria. Gilded and enamelled.

SHROTON *see* IWERNE COURTNEY

SILTON

7020

The traditional grouping of church, former rectory and manor farm.

ST NICHOLAS. A gem of *Clayton & Bell* church decoration, in a medieval building dominated by the Wyndham monument (*see* below). Several phases making a harmonious whole. First, the s arcade of four bays is late C12. Round piers, round fluted capitals, double-chamfered pointed arches. The chamfers are still slight. The chancel is C15. Perp too, but of *c.* 1500, the two-stage, battlemented and pinnacled w tower. Also the s porch (entrance with leaf spandrels), the s fenestration and especially the charming chantry chapel, N (now vestry). This is opened by a large panelled four-centred arch into the chancel, within which is a screen of six lights (two blocked) and a doorway. The church was thoroughly restored by *Charles Buckeridge* of Oxford for the Rev. William Percy in 1869–70, when several sections of external wall were rebuilt, interrupting the bold Perp plinth moulding. At this time a new alcove for the Wyndham monument was created in the nave N wall. The chantry chapel has a single fan-vault bay of the same pattern as Gloucester Cathedral, also *c.* 1500. Excellent wagon roofs with bosses over chancel, nave and porch. The aisle roof is as good. C15 PISCINA and SEDILE, chancel s wall. – Fine painted REREDOS, contemporary with the 1869–70 restoration. – PAINTING. The interior was stencilled by *Clayton & Bell* at the time of the restoration. Recently restored by *Peter Larkworthy*, Clayton & Bell's biographer. – STAINED GLASS. A complete scheme by *Clayton & Bell*, 1869–70. Many of the windows were paid for and designed by *Alfred Bell* himself, on account of his birth in Silton. That in the w end of the s aisle is a memorial to his mother, Leah Bell. – MONUMENTS. Opposite the entrance, Sir Hugh Wyndham †1684. Made by *John Nost I* and set up by him in 1692. Large and grand standing monument, originally in the chancel, s side. Standing figure in judge's garments. At his foot his first two wives, mourning. Twisted columns l. and r. and a segmental pediment. – Dorothy Kingeswell †1638. Tablet with billet-moulded surround.

SILTON HOUSE (formerly the rectory), just N of the church. Late C18 with C19 additions. Entrance front with off-centre, gabled ashlar projecting bay. Sash windows, some with marginal panes.

SCHOOL (now VILLAGE HALL), ½ m. N. 1853. Large stained-glass window by *Clayton & Bell*, NE wall.

SIXPENNY HANDLEY   *9010*

Cob and thatch cottages lined the village street until a devastating fire in 1892. Much of the present village results from the post-fire rebuilding.

ST MARY. Flint and stone bands. Of the early C14 church (and N aisle of 1832), only the heavily restored chancel and repositioned s porch survive. Otherwise various C14 features were re-set when the church, including the C14 w tower, was almost

entirely rebuilt by *G.R. Crickmay* in 1877 (at a cost of £3,000).
The chancel has an E window with reticulated tracery and a
TOMB-RECESS inside. The two three-light windows in the S
aisle must be early C14, as must be those of the chancel S wall
(reticulated and cusped, intersecting tracery). Sturdy mid-C14
S porch, the stone roof carried on hoop-like pointed chamfered
transverse arches, expressed externally by buttresses. Roof of
stone slabs and raised copings in line with the buttresses.*
Lively articulation of the gabled organ loft (with traceried rose
window) and vestry at the NE corner. – PULPIT. By *Crickmay*.
Stone. Cylindrical and heavy, typical of Crickmay. – FONT.
Of the C12 Purbeck type. Square, with four flat blank arches
to each side. Five supports, the four to the corners added
later. – SCULPTURE. In the N aisle, a seated Christ within a
vesica, C12. It may once have been good, but it is very weathered. – STAINED GLASS. E window by *Powell & Sons*, 1901.
– MONUMENT. John Alie †1579. Standing stone monument,
without an effigy. Two Tuscan columns l. and r.; flat top. Quite
characteristic of Early Elizabethan monuments. The last line
of the long inscription tells us: Nemo felix ante obitum ('Call
no man happy until he is dead').

MANOR FARMHOUSE, Woodcutts, 1½ m. W. Early C18 with a
symmetrical five-bay front of chequerboard ashlar and flint.
Group of three diagonal brick shafted chimneystacks on each
gable-end.

WOR BARROW, 1 m. E. A Neolithic long barrow, aligned SE–NW.
The site has been left as excavated by General Pitt-Rivers
in 1893–4: the ditch, with four causeways, cleared to its original depth, and the soil from the mound and ditch left piled
up rough on the outside (to form a modern amphitheatre).
Towards the SE end of the mound was a rectangular wooden
structure, inside which were the primary burials: six inhumations, three crouched and three with bones in disorder, all
covered with turfs. A crouched male with a leaf-shaped arrow-
head in his ribs and a child close by were in the primary filling
of the SE end of the ditch.

On WOODCUTTS COMMON, ¾ m. NW of the hamlet of Woodcutts, is the site of an Iron Age and Romano-British FARM, also
excavated by Pitt-Rivers, who restored the earthworks.

SMEDMORE HOUSE

1 m. SE of Kimmeridge

The beautiful situation close to the sea was chosen by Sir William
Clavell early in the C17, not for its beauty but to exploit the

---

*Cf. a similar roof vault and slab arrangement on the Gyvernay Chapel, Limington,
Somerset (Sir Richard Gyvernay, †1329); and on the porch at Leverington,
Cambridgeshire.

bituminous shale of Kimmeridge Bay. His 'little newe House' is mentioned *c.* 1632. Of the C17, partially obscured by later work, at the back (facing NE) a symmetrical arrangement of three-light, two-light, two-light, three-light windows, in two storeys, the lower with transoms. This is vernacular in character. More impressive is the SW-facing façade added to the C17 house in a partial remodelling for Edward Clavell, probably just after *c.* 1696. This front must have been a little jewel before it lost its l. end. Originally a simple formula of five bays and two storeys with a parapet, transformed by the fine-wrought Purbeck stone dressings. Bolection-moulded window surrounds given a refined bulge, and raised panels to link them vertically. Central window with side-pieces on scrolls, carved with delicate foliage. One window retains its nine-over-nine arrangement of panes. Doorcase with a hood on carved brackets. This part was originally rendered, setting off the ashlar elements.

The entrance (NW-facing) range, dated 1761 on the rainwater heads, is entirely of ashlar (although recently rendered). It was added for George Clavell at right angles to the earlier house and was wider than what lay behind. Around 15 ft (4.5 metres) at the NW end of the older block were chopped off, which required the re-setting of two windows from the late C17 SW front on to its back wall.* For the SW front's style the NW range also showed no sympathy, for its own effect is made without embellishment, merely by projecting two semicircular window bows from the plain ashlar wall. 1761 is a notably early date for bows. Square window surrounds and string courses. At the same time the older part of the house was extended by a plain range to the SE, and the kitchen wing was remodelled with a SE elevation of about the same date: a big Venetian window between two peculiar Gothick sashes, under a trio of chopped-off gables.

The old entrance hall and staircase are in the late C17 part. The first has panelled wainscoting, while the oak staircase has two balusters per tread, one of the barley-sugar type. The rooms of the 1761 range have simple fittings: a white and mottled marble chimneypiece in the drawing room, brackets in the hall with a very little Rococo plasterwork, and in the dining room wall panels of a Kentian cast. These may have been by the *Bastard* family of Blandford, who in that year had just completed a phase of internal work at nearby Lulworth Castle. The best feature, however, is upstairs, an unrestrained Rococo chimneypiece.

CLAVELL TOWER. *See* Kimmeridge.

*'An Estimate to Build 3 Rooms &c agreeable to a Plan hereunto annexed' survives, although without the plan or any indication of the architect.

SOUTH PERROTT

A winding village street with the older buildings in two clusters: the first N of the church, the second to the E around Manor Farm. Many are of the C17 with stone-mullioned windows.

St Mary. A substantial church, with an apparent unity of conception. Nave, transepts, chancel and high central tower, all with plain parapets. Stair-turret to the tower in the angle of N transept and nave, rising higher than their parapets. So, externally all appears C15, except for the s organ chamber and vestry (on the site of a medieval chapel) added by *A. Southcombe Parker* of Plymouth, 1907–10. (The W porch is late C13, but also remodelled in the C15.) Internally the crossing is of *c.* 1200, the capitals left uncarved, the arches pointed and double-chamfered. The walls of the nave and transepts are also of this date, but later raised in height and refenestrated. Access to the vestry is from the s transept below a blocked long Perp window (C14 probably) with a depressed arch. The chancel was restored and given a new E window during the restoration of 1907–10. – FONT. Octagonal bowl, perhaps C14; stem with waterholding base, C13. – STAINED GLASS. The E and W windows have minor Art Nouveau glass; early C20. Two late C18 roundels in the chancel N window. Nave s window by *Lavers, Barraud & Westlake*, 1875. s transept s window by *Jones & Willis*, 1909.

Pickett Farm, ¾ m. s. Long rectangular C15 stone range, much altered in the C17. Externally one sees the diagonal buttresses at the W end, and a blocked E window, two lights with cusped heads and cusped tracery in the super-arch. A C17 range running s from the W end forms an L-plan. (Inside, the complete eight-bay roof remains, of the favourite collar-beam and arch-braced variety with wind-braces.)

SOUTHWELL *see* PORTLAND, p. 489

SPETISBURY

Spetisbury is a main-road village, sandwiched between the former line of the Somerset & Dorset Railway and the River Stour. Scattered cob and thatched cottages, but much recent bungaloid housing. Until its demolition in 1927, the centrepiece of the village was Spetisbury House (*c.* 1735, attributed to *Nathaniel Ireson*). The Chapel of St Monica (R.C.), *c.* 1830 by *J. Peniston* of Salisbury, formerly attached to the house, was pulled down in 1967.

St John the Baptist. Short late C15 three-stage W tower with battlements. Projecting stair on the N side, rising to belfry only.

The church, not at all small, is by *T.H. Wyatt*, 1859, except for the fine N arcade, which is partly early C13. Choir N aisle by *Wyatt*, 1868. Heathstone and flint on the tower; flint with ashlar blocks 'speckled' on Wyatt's work. – PULPIT. Early C17 with the usual blank arches, but with monsters in front of them and other enrichment. Base dated 1901. – Contemporary wooden HOURGLASS STAND behind. – STAINED GLASS. Three chancel windows and one in the tower, *c.* 1870, all possibly by *Wailes*. The chancel N window is by *Hardman*, 1862. Two three-light windows, N aisle (one depicting St Robert of Knaresborough, Charles I and Sir Thomas More), 1909 by *Powell & Sons*. One S window by *A.K. Nicholson*, described by Pevsner as 'anaemically sentimental', †1930. – MONUMENTS. John Bowyer †1599. Italian Renaissance style (i.e. looking more *c.* 1500 than *c.* 1600) standing monument. Tomb-chest with strapwork. Two coarse columns, a lively frieze and a pediment with strapwork in the tympanum. The inscription is still in black-letter.

In the churchyard, monument to the Rev. Thomas Rackett (†1840) and Dorothy Rackett (†1833). A trihedron, i.e. a three-sided pyramid. By *Marshall* of Blandford.

SPETISBURY HALL. Built as the rectory in 1716, for Dr Charles Sloper. Red brick. Two- and three-storeyed because the land falls. Pairs of sheer chimney-breasts at the side stress the height in a way typical of Baroque design at that moment. SW (road) front 1:3:1, altered in the late C18 by the addition of a broken pediment over the central bays and Adamish porch on columns with upright leaf capitals. An early C18 staircase indicates joinery work by the *Bastard* company. Otherwise much altered internally *c.* 1800 for the Rev. Thomas Rackett.

CRAWFORD BRIDGE, 1 m. SE. Stone. Nine low arches, of 1505 on the W side, which has cutwaters. E side of 1819, when the road was widened, with chequerboard masonry. (Re-set date-stone of 1719.) Very picturesque, among the water irises and fennel.

CRAWFORD CASTLE or SPETISBURY RINGS, ¾ m. SE. Iron Age HILL-FORT, univallate, enclosing 4 acres, with a NW entrance and hornwork. The railway cutting of 1857–8 exposed a mass grave within the NE ditch containing at least eighty skeletons, some with battle injuries. Associated weaponry indicates that they were victims of the advancing Roman army in A.D. 43. Saxon spearheads from the hill-fort belong to the period 450–5.

COMBS DITCH. *See* Winterborne Whitechurch.

STALBRIDGE   7010

A small linear town standing on a ridge, and on the once-important Blandford to Castle Cary highway. The Abbot of Sherborne was granted a market here in 1286, and by the early

C14 the town had grown to about the same size as Poole. It was largely the property of the owners of Stalbridge Park; in the C19 these were the Paget marquesses of Anglesey and, after sale in 1854, the Grosvenor marquesses, then dukes, of Westminster.

ST MARY. A large town church, mostly rebuilt in the C19. Of the medieval period, only the strong late C14 nave arcades of four shafts and convex curves in the diagonals as if of a circular core. Small capitals with fleurons. Also the rood-loft staircase in the N pier of the chancel arch. The N chapel itself is *c.* 1500 – see the typical straight-headed windows with the uncusped rounded arches to the lights. To the chancel a three-bay arcade with piers whose capitals display angel busts (cf. Holwell), each with a black-lettered scroll. A similar arch to the N transept with angel busts carrying monogrammed shields and with further lettering either side. Otherwise all is C19 of at least three phases. Bold S tower, dated 1868, built for the Rev. Henry Boucher of Thornhill and said to have been designed by him, although it looks more like the work of *G. Evans* (cf. Melbury Abbas). The remainder a vague Perp cloaking of an 1840-rebuilt nave and N aisle, 1877–8 by *T.H. Wyatt*. He also reconstructed the chancel and S transept and added a S chapel. Early C16 canopied Perp niche in the chancel N wall. – CHOIR STALLS and CLERGY SEATS by *Wyatt, c.* 1878. – CHANCEL SCREEN and PULPIT by *Ponting*, 1912. – FONT. Bowl, early C13 on C19 base. Wooden architectural Gothic COVER, by *William Brown, c.* 1900. – STAINED GLASS. E window by *Cox, Sons, Buckley & Co.*, 1892. Three N chapel windows by *N.H.J. Westlake*, 1910 and 1912. His also the N aisle W window, †1916. S aisle W window by *A.L. Moore*, 1904. Large W window by *Heaton, Butler & Bayne*, †1908. – ENGRAVED GLASS. Doors by *Tracey Sheppard*, 2007. – MONUMENTS. N chapel, head of a C13 coffin-lid with a foliated cross. – Two late C15 or early C16 tomb-chests with shields in quatrefoils, one under the chancel arcade, the other with a cadaver effigy. – Thomas Weston. C17, classical, angled across the NE corner. – William Boucher, †1836. Greek Revival by *Osmond* of Salisbury. – On the chancel S wall, John Douche †1674, and sons, by *R. Parr*. Large tablet with three inscription plates and a segmental pediment carried on two Corinthian columns. – Above the doorway, Bradford family (†1810 to †1837). Three-dimensional Gothic, by *H. Hopper* of London.

CONGREGATIONAL CHURCH (formerly Independent chapel), Station Road, ¼ m. SE. 1870 by *W.J. Stent* of Warminster. Banded brick and rubble with lancets.

WESLEYAN METHODIST CHAPEL (former), Ring Street, ⅓ m. SE. 1873–4. A bolder lancet-windowed composition of rock-faced masonry. Turrets with curiously precarious-looking tops flank the front gable.

N of the church, opposite Stalbridge Park gates, the former NATIONAL SCHOOL of 1832.

The main street runs S from the church, becoming the HIGH STREET. Its great moment is at a widening of the road, the MARKET CROSS, of the later C15 and surviving almost whole, if much eaten away by time. It must in its day have been a splendidly rich piece. The design has much in common with a series of churchyard crosses in Somerset at, e.g. Bishop's Lydeard and Drayton. The usual stepped base, supporting an octagonal pedestal carved with subject reliefs on the cardinal faces. Tapering octagonal shaft, with pinnacles half-buried against the diagonal faces, and to the W, carved out of the monolith, a large (but now terribly worn) figure on a decorated corbel and under a pinnacled canopy. The cross-head, with a relief of the Crucifixion under a canopy, is a modern copy of what toppled to the ground in 1950.

THE OLD RECTORY, just NE of the cross, is dated 1699 on a rainwater head. The characteristic seven-bay, hipped-roofed house of that moment stands behind a high wall. Opposite, GOLD STREET has the characteristic mix of rubble-built, occasionally stuccoed, unassuming cottages found throughout the town. Further S, as the HIGH STREET narrows after the cross, on the l., the SWAN HOTEL, early C18 with a front doorway of c. 1830. On the r., SILK HAY, while appearing C18, has early to mid-C16 intersecting chamfered ceiling beams within. This block steps forward from a long C15 range containing at least one arch-braced roof truss and a section of arched wind-bracing.* At THE RING, at the S end of the street, several ESTATE COTTAGES in pairs, of two distinct periods. The earlier set, built c. 1835 by the Anglesey Estate on the NE side, is Tudor, with low-pitched hipped roofs. Later gabled cottages, one dated 1866, built for the Grosvenor Estate on the SW side. At the centre of the green a fine Gothic WATER PUMP, c. 1850.

STALBRIDGE PARK, NW of the town. Nothing survives of the mansion, demolished without proper record in 1822. Between 1618 and 1620 the 2nd Earl of Castlehaven built a 'goodlie faire house', according to Coker. What is more tantalizing is that, in 1638, Richard Boyle, 1st Earl of Cork, was employing as his architect Inigo Jones's protégé, *Isaac de Caus*. Probably however nothing of significance was carried out for, where one looks for a Jonesian style, Hutchins's print of 1813 shows nothing but a house with Jacobean motifs of an idiosyncratic cast. What is left are the massive rusticated GATEPIERS N of the church. Late C17, and not of first-rate quality. Lion-crest terminals (the emblem of the Boyles) on a very large scale.** The fine PARK WALL, running from the corner of Stalbridge churchyard and extending some 5 m. around the 500-acre parkland, was added for Edward Walter in the 1750s. Although

---

* *See* the report on the house by Michael Laithwaite (1977), the summary by Pamela Cunnington (1982), and Hilary Townsend, *Silk Hay: One Woman's Fight for Architectural Heritage* (2012).
**The gatepiers must pre-date the death of the last Boyle owner in 1699.

broken down in a few places, it remains impressively complete, the stone beautifully silvery with lichen.

FRITH HOUSE, 1¾ m. W. Small country house by *Macpherson & Richardson*, 1910. Local vernacular NE front, but symmetrical on the SW garden side with a pair of hipped-roofed wings flanking a recessed centre.

STURT FARM, 1 m. SW. Rubble-stone farmhouse of the late C16. Symmetrical three-bay W front, plus a S addition. Windows of Ham Hill stone, 3:2:3 lights, mullioned with hoodmoulds.

STANBRIDGE *see* HINTON PARVA

4090

STANTON ST GABRIEL

OLD CHURCH, 1¼ m. WSW of Chideock. The only substantial walls remaining are those of the S porch and the nave N wall. Late C14 S doorway. For the church replacing it *see* Morcombelake.

ST GABRIEL'S HOUSE, 120 yds W. Mostly C18 with much rebuilding. A T-plan with the lower service range at the back. Picturesque and thatched, with walls of rubble stone giving way to brick in the upper parts.

0000

STAPEHILL
Ferndown

Former HOLY CROSS ABBEY (Cistercian nuns) and church of OUR LADY OF DOLOURS (R.C.), now deconsecrated. By *C.F. Hansom*, 1847–51. The church has two separately gabled naves, the r. behind the tower for the nuns, the l. for the congregation. Red brick, with lancet windows and windows with plate tracery. The congregational church has an outer aisle. This and the arcade between the naves have octagonal piers. The nuns' church carries a substantial bell-tower with a steep pyramid roof. Conventual buildings attached on the S side. One taller building, rendered, with battlemented parapets, probably predating the remainder. The others by Hansom more domestic in character. – Much FURNISHING, especially the opposing nuns' stalls, survives within.[*] – STAINED GLASS. In the E and W windows good glass, respectively by *Hardman* to *Pugin*'s designs, 1850, and *Powell & Sons*, 1853. – MONUMENT, in the churchyard. Cross to the Rev. Mother Augustine de Chabannes †1844. Also by *Pugin*.

---

[*]Seemingly threatened with removal (2014).

OLD THATCH PUB, 300 yds N. Incorporating at its w end part of the thatched *cottage orné* lodge of *c.* 1800 for Uddens (*see* Holt).

STEEPLE

Nothing more than the traditional grouping of church, rectory and manor house. All of the farms (and farm cottages) are some distance off.

ST MICHAEL. The S doorway is a simple Norman piece, the arch with two slight stop-chamfers, an odd detail. It dates the nave to the early C12, although nothing else of that date is evident. In the nave one C13 N lancet and several C15 S windows. Big and bold C16 Perp W tower with higher stair-turret on the N side. Plain parapets. There must have been a C16 rebuilding of the chancel, for this is the date of the plain chancel arch. The S chapel (now a vestry) is C16 too. A N chapel (called the 'North Pew') is of the early C17, entered separately. Above its doorway a panel with the arms of Edward Lawrence (of Creech Grange), dated EL 1616. In the mid C19 the chancel was replaced and a S porch added, both Perp. – Many of the FURNISHINGS are of the mid C19, the PULPIT and READING DESK being the best. – COMMUNION RAIL. These very thin balusters are typical early C19. – FONT. A tapering plain C13 bowl on an equally plain stem. – STAINED GLASS. E window by *Powell & Sons*, 1892. – MONUMENT. Francis Chaldicot †1636, and others (installed 1641). By *William Wright* (GF). Slate tablet in chancel, set in an alabaster surround with vaguely classical detailing.

Immediately NW of the church the RECTORY of *c.* 1840, perhaps by *Edward Mondey* of Dorchester.

MANOR HOUSE, NE of the church. SE-facing, with two gabled wings. The l. half is *c.* 1600 with a projecting wing of *c.* 1660 for Roger Clavell; the r. half is by *P. R. Morley Horder*, *c.* 1920 for Major Swann, and intended to match the earlier work. At the rear a projecting wing dated 1698 (and with the initials RCR for another Roger Clavell) with tall sashes in keyed architraves. This faces the road through a pair of contemporary GATE-PIERS. GARDENS by *Brenda Colvin*, laid out in 1923.

BLACKMANSTON FARM, ¼ m. SE, has a good unspoilt vernacular S front, two-storeyed with a two-storey porch not central. Mullioned windows with hoodmoulds. The l. part is late C16, while the porch and r. part were added in the early C17.

STINSFORD

A grouping of church, vicarage and country house. The few cottages on the approach lane are recent but sympathetic.

St Michael. Mostly early C13, but not readily detectable externally. Here the character is of plainness, except for the C15 s aisle with battlements and grotesque gargoyles on a string course. The w tower is C14, and buttressed only on its lowest stage. Its arch to the nave has three-quarter shafts with moulded capitals. On the tower w face a sculpture panel of St Michael, 2011 by *Rebecca Freiesleben*. Expressive and angular. (The original late C10 or early C11 sculpture has been moved inside, *see* below.) N aisle of 1630 (date on the N wall). A restoration of 1868 by *J. Hicks* replaced the chancel and N aisle windows, elaborated the window label moulds and made a new roof. (Prior to this the windows had C18 round arches, according to a print of *c.* 1790 in the church.) Within, the chancel arch and the s arcade are fine E.E. features. The chancel arch has rich, deep mouldings, all continuous – which is slightly unusual. The s arcade (two round-arched bays) has a beautiful w respond with three detached shafts carrying a stiff-leaf capital. The shafts fit into a sinking of the respond. The central pier has four shafts, while the E, matching the w, is a replacement of 1868. The N arcade (also two bays) has a central pier made quatrefoil and massive by crude cylinders. It, together with the matching responds, are probably of 1630. A niche in the s aisle (probably re-set) is C15 with crocketed canopy. Just below the niche, a C13 PISCINA with trefoil head.

FURNISHINGS. REREDOS and black-and-white SANCTUARY FLOORING by *F.C. Eden*, 1938. – CHOIR STALLS. Of 1925 by *Davis & Son* of Dorchester; above average. The panelling around them is also of this date. – PULPIT and READING DESKS. Oak, Gothic, from *Hicks*'s restoration. – FONT. Late C12. Square, of Purbeck marble, with six flat blank arches on each side. – ORGAN GALLERY, 1996. A replacement for the musicians' gallery, removed in 1843. – SCULPTURE. Re-set inside the s aisle at the w end, an extremely impressive Saxon (late C10 or early C11) relief of St Michael with spread wings and striding to the l., slaying the dragon. It is unfortunately not well preserved. – STAINED GLASS. E window and one other in the chancel by *Lavers, Barraud & Westlake*, 1868. They also did the E windows of both aisles. All have much loss of paint. In the s aisle a war memorial window by *Powell & Sons*, 1916. The finest in the church is the other s aisle window, a glowing work by *Douglas Strachan*, 1930. It depicts Elijah in a deep purple cloak (with a text from 1 Kings 9) and was installed as a memorial to Thomas Hardy.* – MONUMENTS. Audeley Grey, dated 1723. Tablet with Corinthian columns, side scrolls and armorial crest. – George Pitt †1734. Large tablet with long inscription and a bust on the top. – Set of memorials to the Hardy family in the churchyard, where Thomas Hardy's heart is buried.

Stinsford House, immediately w. Mostly stone, with a long, nine-bay single-storey range of tall sashes facing s. This is an

* *See* Hardy's poem 'Quid Hic Agis?' of 1916.

early C18 rebuilding for Thomas Strangways, over a basement of stone-mullioned windows retained from a C16 house. His is also the symmetrical w front, again single-storeyed except in the gabled wings. Melbury House came to Strangways in 1713, so the single-storey work may be an economy in anticipation of his inheritance of that large mansion. The three-bay Gothick stuccoed block at the E end of the S front was added in the 1770s for William O'Brien.

BIRKIN HOUSE, ½ m. N. Of 1875 for Reginald Thornton. Classical, with ashlar façades and a pedimented centrepiece to its w entrance.

FROME WHITFIELD HOUSE, 1¼ m. WNW. A stucco-faced villa of c. 1845, built for W.L. Henning. Wrought-iron trelliswork verandas either side of a central S projection.

MILESTONE, I m. NE. Possibly Roman; now with an OS bench mark, and located on the centre line of the Roman road (excavated 1987) to the E gate of *Durnovaria* (*see* Dorchester, p. 264).

STOCK GAYLARD
Lydlinch

7010

ST BARNABAS. Rebuilt by *W.J. Fletcher*, 1884–5, reusing much medieval fabric. Nave and chancel with a large N vestry and w bellcote. Tudor Perp style. Timber barrel-ceilinged interior. Mosaic flooring. – Original FURNISHINGS in the chancel, also by *Fletcher*. – English altar, c. 1900. – FONT. C15, Perp. Octagonal with quatrefoils. – PAINTING (vestry). Early C16. A large wooden panel thought to have come from a rood screen. It depicts an apostle. – STAINED GLASS. Small piece of the C15 with the Crucifixion. Two small saints, mid-C19, but re-setting medieval faces. – MONUMENTS. Cross-legged knight, late C13, in a heavily cinquefoiled recess. – Tomb-chest with cusped quatrefoils and panels (now the altar). – Large number of wall monuments to the various owners of Stock Gaylard House. The earliest is to the Lewys family, 1749. – Harry Farr Yeatman †1917. A striking bronze relief of a recumbent soldier. By *Henry Pegram*, 1919.

The church stands on the lawn of STOCK GAYLARD HOUSE, just to the N. Main block of 1712 for Charles Lewys. Seven bays with a pediment over the central three. Enlarged to the rear in the late C18 for John Berkeley Burland.

w of this an C16 DOVECOTE. Circular plan with conical roof. Rainwater head dated 1675, probably relocated. Converted to a summerhouse in the late C18 or early C19.

A fine DEER PARK with oak trees surrounds the group.

LODGE, ¼ m. S. Dated 1900, by *Arthur E. Bartlett*. Half-timbered.

STOCKWOOD

St Edwold (Churches Conservation Trust). The smallest church in Dorset, only 30 ft (9 metres) by 12 ft 8 in. (3.9 metres). Early to mid-C15 Perp. One early C16 three-light nave window. The others, including the three-light E window with panel tracery, are original. In 1638 a W porch was added. Round arch with bold imposts and a jewelled keystone in the Arnold manner. Also of this date a delightfully naïve bell-turret, round, with cap on four stumpy Tuscan columns and a big grotesque face.

Church Farmhouse, immediately SW. Of c. 1820. Brick front, rubble sides and back. Wide sashes in moulded stone surrounds. Also moulded eaves, platband and doorcase with keyed lintel.

STOKE ABBOTT

St Mary. C12 chancel – see one N window. Remodelled and probably lengthened in the early C13 – see three lancets (and watch for their rere-arches). C15 E window. Also early C13 the nave and tower arch of two slight chamfers, but the upper parts of the tower C15 (rebuilt shortly after a lightning strike in 1828, with only a plain parapet). One big Perp nave S window, to the E of the porch, and a late C14 Perp chancel arch. The N aisle is largely by *J.P. St Aubyn*, 1877–8 (with a major restoration of that date). It has a C15 E bay – either a chapel or a transept. Also here a re-set C13 two-light window. – Good choir stalls and clergy seats by *St Aubyn*. – Encaustic tiles by *Godwin* on the chancel floor. – pulpit. Early C17. Oak. Only three sides, with heavily enriched rails and posts but plain panels. – font. An exceptionally beautiful late C12 piece, not arbitrary and confused as they so often are, but rationally organized. Bowl and stem in one. Larger heads under arches, the latter taken off small grotesque heads. Hexagons with big leaves inside below. – stained glass. E window by *Cox & Son*, †1878. Chancel N window by *M.C. Farrar Bell*, 1956. N aisle E window by *Hardman*, †1880. Central N aisle window by *John Hayward*, 1999. – monument. Caroline Lucy Andrews †1920. Mosaic tablet by *Powell & Sons*, 1920.

Congregational chapel (former), 130 yds SW. 1838. Simple with round-arched windows.

Former rectory, just W of the church. 1864 by *St Aubyn*. Bold but somehow not Gothic. Mullioned-and-transomed windows in a two-storey bay window. Tall slabs of chimneystacks.

Among the loose group of stone houses that make up the village centre one can pick out one or two with instructive dates. Stoke Farm, SW of the church, displays the date 1613 on its modest, symmetrical front. Mullioned windows with a hollow chamfer, four-light to the ground floor, three-light above. Hoodmoulds. MANOR FARM, NW of the church, is dated 1748, very late for mullioned windows, even if the windows do have simple classical surrounds. Continuous drip-courses; thatched roof. And on the lane to the church with a hipped thatched roof, COURT ORCHARD, a five-bay ashlar front with the same reactionary windows, yet the dates are 1751 (under the eaves) and 1762 (on the porch).

BRIMLEY HOUSE, ⅝ m. WSW. Dated 1734. A symmetrical brick house; two parallel ranges. Porch hood on shaped brackets. Five bays of sash windows.

WADDON HILL, ¾ m. NW. A ROMAN FORT of the CI A.D. The defences are visible on the E side; on the N side they were lost in the quarry pits which progressively destroyed the S and W sides.

STOKE WAKE   7000

ALL SAINTS (now privately owned). 1872 by *G. R. Crickmay*, built for £900. Nave, chancel with apse, and N aisle. W bell-cote over five graded lancets. Three-bay arcade, the capitals of which are of the French Early Gothic foliage type, very similar to those of Crickmay's Turnworth (q.v.).*

MANOR HOUSE, immediately S. Early C18 N-facing range with mullioned windows, stone to the ground floor, timber above. Central doorway. Extended S in brick, c. 1920.

RAWLSBURY, ⅓ m. SE. Iron Age HILL-FORT, bivallate, enclosing 4½ acres; single entrance on the E with an outer barbican. For the cross-dykes 150 yds to the E, *see* Woolland.

STOURPAINE   8000

A cluster of cottages, some C17 and earlier in clunch and thatch, others of brick and flint of the C19.

HOLY TRINITY. C15 W tower of Greensand ashlar. Bold, cone-topped stair-turret in the NE corner. The rest 1858 by *T. H. Wyatt*. Flint with ashlar-block speckling, an unfortunate effect.** The N windows Perp and reused from the medieval church. Wyatt's own tracery is, as so often, incorrect without being fanciful. Graceful S aisle arcade. – FURNISHINGS. A complete *Wyatt* set. – TILES l. and r. of the altar. The style is reminiscent of Walter Crane. – STAINED GLASS. Three chancel windows (one

*The C15 FONT has been removed to St Peter (R.C.), Eastleaze, Swindon, Wilts.
** Seemingly 'pioneered' during Wyatt's work at Wimborne Minster (q.v.).

dated 1898); another in the S chapel dated 1872, all signed by *Lavers, Barraud & Westlake*. The W window of 1891 is also most likely theirs. – MONUMENT. In the tower, tablet of 1670 to John Straight, with a very naïve frontally kneeling effigy.

LYCHGATE, 1896, perhaps by *Ponting*. Quite a showpiece. Angled to the road with a fine wrought-iron lantern and crucifix finial.

S of the church are a medieval MOAT and ENCLOSURE, and beyond the EMBANKMENT of the former Somerset & Dorset Railway of 1863.

LAZERTON FARM, at Ash, ⅝ m. N. Though with westward enlargement, a typical compact C17 stone house. Two-storey symmetrical E entrance front, with four deep four-light windows below, and windows above of four, two, and four lights. End gables and central W staircase projection.

HOD HILL (National Trust), ¾ m. NNW. Iron Age HILL-FORT, bivallate, enclosing 54 acres: the largest in Dorset. Excavated in 1951–8 and surveyed by geophysics in 2005. There were four phases of Iron Age ramparts. Immediately inside are extensive quarry pits. Over 200 hut circles, unploughed in the SE sector,

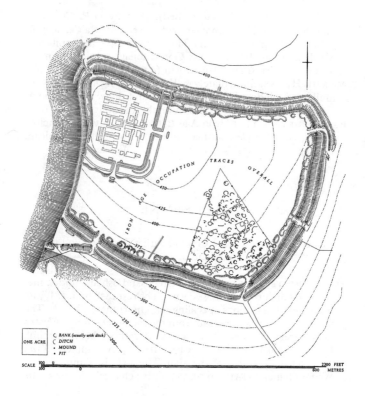

Stourpaine, Hod Hill, Iron Age hill-fort and Roman fort.
Plan by Ian Richmond, 1970

cover the interior. The Iron Age entrances are near the NE and SW corners. The NW gate is a Roman insertion, the one on the SE medieval or later. A street system fans out from the NE entrance, with aligned groups of huts and small enclosures, indicating focal points and urban planning throughout the Iron Age occupation.

Many ballista bolts, recovered from across a large hut circle, set within a hexagonal enclosure, are perhaps evidence for a Roman assault. After c. A.D. 44 a ROMAN FORT was built in the NW corner of the hill-fort, covering 7 acres. Excavations identified legionary barracks (with storage sheds) and cavalry barracks (with stables); also a hospital, granary and latrines, plus a headquarters building.

STOUR PROVOST   7020

The village centre is the best in this northern lobe of the county. Continuous cottage rows of local biscuit-coloured stone form a wedge-shaped space, tapering where the land falls to the N.

ST MICHAEL. A larger version of Fifehead Magdalen, with the C15 S tower here to the E of the porch. The upper stage of the tower was rebuilt, possibly to an increased height, in the C17. Extensive refenestration when the chancel was rebuilt in E.E. style, 1838. Is the one C13 lancet in the nave (to the l. of the porch) *in situ*? It is the only indication of so early a date. The main body of the church (with the exception of the N aisle) is dated by the RCHME to the early C14. The very heavy chancel arch is also C14. Excellent low-pitched, ceiled chancel roof, said to have come from the N aisle c. 1840. It has clearly been adapted to fit. The tower arch into the nave is blocked. The early C16 N arcade is of four bays, with standard elements and clumsy capitals. – COMMUNION RAIL. Late C18. – FONT. Octagonal, Perp, with simple panelling. – ROYAL ARMS of Queen Anne. A lozenge-shaped timber panel, dated 1701. – STAINED GLASS. E window by *Christopher Webb*, 1946, in a re-set C18 Gothick window. Chancel N window by *William Warrington*, 1847. Nave S window, Expressionist glass of 1959–60 by *Jasper & Molly Kettlewell*. N aisle E window of 1882 by *Alexander Gibbs*.

Two paths to the church, the shorter leading from the narrow end of the main village street. To the N, CHURCH HOUSE, set back, quite a big early C17 farmhouse. Long front with a gable l. and a gable r. but no symmetry. The lower windows are of four mullioned lights, without hoodmoulds; the upper have hoodmoulds, but only three lights. Two-lighter in the r. gable. At the back more three-lighters with hoodmoulds and a later staircase projection towards the r.

Opposite the church path, THE COTTAGE was two C17 cottages, now combined. Timber casements and thatch sweeping over the dormers and down to the porch.

Just W of the crossroads, DIAMOND FARM, Mill Lane, another variant on the C17 stone vernacular. Here the three-light windows (no hoodmoulds) have hollow-chamfered mullions, with a linking string course. No proper symmetry, but a pattern of two lower windows to one above.

Set back N from Church Lane, 20 yds E of the church, MANOR FARM. C15 in origin, rebuilt in the late C18 and extended W in the C19. Within are two bays of a former four-bay hall roof. Although much restored, this has arched collar-bracing and two tiers of arched wind-bracing.

THE OLD RECTORY, 150 yds NW. 1828 by *William Wilkins* for John Tomkyns, former Vice-Provost of King's College, Cambridge. Square block with subordinate wing. Low-pitched slate roofs. Robust Neoclassical pillared porch.*

At Woodville, 1 m. E, STOWER PROVOST COMMUNITY SCHOOL dated 1850. Gothic. Attached to it the SCHOOL HOUSE, dated 1904.

STOUR ROW

Stour Provost

ALL SAINTS (now redundant). By *John Hicks*, 1867–8. E.E.-style nave and chancel. W porch rising as a wide buttress to become a steeply gabled bellcote. Simple interior. Chancel arch with naturalistic foliage on corbel colonnettes. – STAINED GLASS. E and W windows, 1882 and 1883 respectively, by *Alexander Gibbs*. Three chancel windows by *Clayton & Bell*, 1907.

CONGREGATIONAL CHAPEL (now VILLAGE HALL), ¼ m. W. 1843. Lancet windows and a blind quatrefoil in the gable.

JOLIFFE'S FARM, 1 m. NE. An unspoilt late C17 stone farm. Telling arrangement of windows, the main ones below, four-lighters, a string course running along and up over their heads. Irregular fenestration in the middle because of the stairs. Little wood-mullioned windows under the eaves.

STOURTON CAUNDLE

A main street with farmhouses of the late C17, interspersed with modern dwellings.

---

*It closely resembles the house in Cambridge that Wilkins built for himself, now demolished.

St Peter. c13 chancel with lancets. Also two lancet heads re-set, one in the s porch, the other as a PISCINA in the s chapel. Three-stage, embattled c14 Dec w tower: see the reticulated tracery of the w window and also the bell-openings. The later c14 nave is Perp, as is the c15 s chapel. Two bays with a very large squint. There is a complete c15 rood-loft staircase in the N wall, together with the supporting corbels in the s and a small window above. Also c15 (or early c16) the nave wagon roof. The whole was sensitively restored by *Ponting*, 1900–2. – COMMUNION RAIL. Jacobean, with turned balusters. – PULPIT. Early c16. Hexagonal, the lower panels with linenfold, the upper with little canopied blank arches incorporating tracery. Crocketed pinnacles at the corners. – FONT. Of *c.* 1740, with gadrooning and rather wild enrichment. – ROYAL ARMS. Queen Anne, on a lozenge panel. – MONUMENTS. Recess with concave-sided gable and tomb-chest. Late c15. Some original painting surviving on the tomb-chest. The contemporary recumbent alabaster effigy of a lady is from elsewhere. – Tablet on the chancel N wall by *Eric Gill* (Aylen de Tavora Luis Fernandes †1921).

Manor Farm Chapel, in a field 300 yds sw. Small square E.E. nave of rubble stone, original in its w wall and the N wall with a simple doorway with two-centred head, and a lancet (trefoil-headed rere-arch). Chancel destroyed *c.* 1900.

Congregational chapel (former), 200 yds s. Dated 1859. Simple lancet style.

STRATTON

6090

Stratton was a small linear village until affected by much new development after the construction of a by-pass in 1967.

St Mary. Of the c12 only the plain N and s doorways, both with a later door surround inset. The s doorway now blocked. Stone w tower, nave and chancel of flint and stone bands. The early c15 tower is embattled, of three stages with bold buttresses. Not especially distinguished w doorway and window. Later c15 nave with four arched Perp windows and one with a square head, *c.* 1500. Chancel by *Crickmay & Son*, 1891. The nave was rebuilt at the same time, re-setting a number of old features. If the chancel arch is early c12, it has been so restored as to look late c19. Two image niches in the e splays of two of the nave s windows. The one feature of the church which will be remembered is the wooden cage of the TOWER STAIRS, with long linenfold panels and starting on a fan-corbel. It is no doubt early c16. – Panelled REREDOS by *Crickmay*, 1911. – FONT. Plain circular bowl, probably c13. Late c19 stem. – STAINED GLASS. Several c15 pieces in the tracery lights of the westernmost of the nave s windows. E window perhaps by *Percy Bacon Bros*, †1901. Two nave windows in contrasting early C20 styles. The more *recherché* is another by *Bacon Bros*, 1921. The other is thinly wrought and weakly coloured, a later work by *Clayton & Bell* (signed by *Reginald Bell*), 1939. – MONUMENT. Robert Pattison †1845 by *Marble Works* of Westminster. Tablet with draped urn. – In the churchyard the CROSS, C15. The base and steps are preserved; the shaft fragment is later.

LYCHGATE. By *Jem Feacey*, 1905. Timber-framed on stone side walls.

WAR MEMORIAL. By *Frederick Maltby*, 1919. Design based on the Cross of Sacrifice by Sir R. Blomfield.

MANOR HOUSE, SW of the church (now subdivided). C17, the earlier S part all stone, the later N part banded with stone and flint. The E front has a doorway with a four-centred-arched head and several two-light stone-mullioned windows. In the S part an early C17 overmantel with figures and much other enrichment.

ASHLEY MEMORIAL INSTITUTE, 150 yds NW. Dated 1898. By *Jem Feacey*. Purple Broadmayne brick with rather thin Gothic detailing in stone.

Former PARSONAGE, just W of the above. Of 1895 by *Crickmay & Son*, in an Arts and Crafts vein. (Alterations of 1902 by *Feacey*.) Red brick with stone elaboration. Bold corbelling out of the front gable. Also the W side brought forward on cast-iron columns. On the E, however, a picturesque jumble of gables and bays.

ALMSHOUSES, at the E end of the village. Dated 1900, probably by *Feacey*. Purple brick combined with strong red brick chimneys and stone dressings. First-floor balcony on cast-iron columns.

WRACKLEFORD HOUSE, 1 m. ESE. Of *c.* 1835, for Robert Pattison. Compact stucco villa, incorporating an earlier house to the rear. Paired sashes. Porch with Tuscan columns. High red brick screen wall alongside the A37.

LANGFORD FARM, 1½ m. NNW. 1987 by *Anthony Jaggard* of *John Stark & Partners* for Anthony du Boulay. Red brick Neo-Georgian villa. Five bays of sashes with walls sweeping up to a three-bay first floor in a mansard roof.

RAILWAY VIADUCT, Grimstone, 1 m. NW. 1857 by *I.K. Brunel* for the Great Western Railway. Rock-faced stone with a dressed entablature. Modelled on a triumphal arch, the main round-headed arch flanked by two smaller ones. Within the separating piers a row of four transverse arches. The design is an adaptation of that used by Brunel at Chippenham, Wilts., 1841.

GRIMSTONE DOWN, 1¼ m. NNW. 'CELTIC' FIELDS and a FARMSTEAD, covering more than 100 acres. Between the field banks several hollow tracks converge on a series of small enclosures of Iron Age and Romano-British date.

STUDLAND

Until *c.* 1900 Studland remained largely undiscovered by tourists. This changed gradually, with a brick terrace or two adding to the picturesque groupings of cob and thatch cottages. Building of a more suburban character developed away from the historic core, to the w, from the mid 1920s onwards. More recently, with the attraction of the bay as an anchorage, and with the proximity of Sandbanks on the opposite side of the entrance to Poole Harbour, the danger has arisen that the fragile character of the place could be damaged by excessive construction and tidying-up.

St Nicholas. Studland is one of the dozen or so most complete Norman village churches in England. There is hardly anything that isn't – only the E.E. window, the windows enlarged in the C18 and the jarring C17 s porch. Restore these in your mind to what the remaining Norman windows are, and you have perfection.*

What one sees is largely late C11, but with considerable remodelling carried out in the early, rather than mid, C12 (see the total absence of chevron). A corbel table of all kinds of faces and motifs runs along the nave N and s walls. N and s doorways both have solid tympana, and the tower E of the nave has buttresses, including a thin one in the middle of the s and N sides. These buttresses have a slight but steep set-off, an early case. But there are also curiosities, especially the N and s windows to the square chancel, where small windows like the others are set into large moulded surrounds. So the exterior is a craggy Norman such as one might find on the Cotentin peninsula, whereas the interior is a more intense expression of C12 forms, where both the tower space and the chancel space are rib-vaulted. The ribs are heavy, of a half-roll between two hollows, and they rest on two E shafts in the chancel, but on four fully developed arches on columns under the tower, even on the N and s, where such arches seem to postulate transepts. The w and E arches are lower than the N and s arches, but they are more fully shafted: three shafts with decorated scallops and simple chip-carving on the imposts and arches. The arches have strong rolls. Nave roof rebuilt by *H. Kendall* of Poole, 1930–1. – Font. Plain C12 bowl. – The west gallery seems to date from the careful restoration by *G.R. Crickmay*, 1883–4.** – stained glass. One elaborate nave s window by *Thomas Willement*, 1859. – monument. Short Purbeck marble tomb-chest with cusped quatrefoils. Early C16. – In the churchyard the railed chest tomb of the Bankes family, *c.* 1850. Neo-Norman arcading.

*Also, excavations indicate the likelihood that the nave stands on the foundations of a pre-Conquest church.
**With advice from *C.G. Vinell*, SPAB secretary at the time.

STUDLAND MANOR FARM, Church Road, immediately s, framing
the approach to the church. Early C18 house, partly of banded
brick. Big s cross-wing, c. 1870, in Purbeck crazy-paving
masonry. CARTSHED opposite with large C18 BARN behind.

CHURCH CROSS, 120 yds s. By *Treleven Haysom*, 1976 on a medieval base. Anglo-Saxon-looking in its form and rich carving.
Traditional imagery on the w side; the e has more modern
motifs, such as a violin, a Second World War bomb and Con-
corde. Also 'Saxon' interlace in the form of the double-helix
of DNA.

STUDLAND MANOR (now a hotel), 200 yds N. Built c. 1825 as a
'marine villa' for the Rt Hon. George Bankes. Some early C20
enlargements. Stucco with big Purbeck stone slates. Picturesque irregularity taken to the pitch of total disorganization,
with many gablets. In its details a pleasing stylistic jumble, but
principally Gothic. Enlarging the house was Bankes's retire-
ment pastime, 'supplying deficiencies as they gradually presented themselves, and inventing improvements when there
were no more deficiencies to supply', as Pouncy puts it.* Much
reused joinery within, part Jacobean, part C18. – Two small
thatched *cottages ornés*, by Ben Pentreath, 2014.

HILL CLOSE, ⅜ m. SW. Designed in 1896 by *Voysey* for Alfred
Sutro, the popular Edwardian playwright. It is, like every
Voysey house, an object lesson in creating picturesque irregularity within a unified frame. Roughcast walls, battered buttresses, long, low mullioned windows, all drawn snugly under
the deep sloping hips of the stone-tiled roof. That is what
Voysey would do anywhere. His only concession to local practice is the framing of the windows with rough-hewn blocks
of Purbeck stone. Hill Close was built as a studio house,
the studio window angled towards the view of Studland Bay.
Restored in 2003 by *Morgan Carey Architects*, who removed
some poor additions and added a sensitive one of their own
at the s end.

Former LODGE with garage ('motor house', rather) by the
road. Also *Voysey*'s, but of 1913; altered.

STUDLAND BAY HOUSE, ½ m. NNW. Of c. 1920, probably by
Sidney Tugwell of Bournemouth. Brick with stone dressings.
Handled in Norman Shaw's Bedford Park style, under a hipped
roof with strategically placed chimneys. Mixture of tile-hung
gables. Bold octagonal flat-roofed bay overlooking the sea.

THORNY BARROW GROUP, 1¼ m. WSW. A group of four round
barrows on the e side of the golf course, in a straight line.
Fishing Barrow is a bell barrow, the rest bowls.

AGGLESTONE, ¾ m. WNW, is a natural outcrop of weathered
gritstone; a prominent, but now fallen, landmark since prehistoric times.

NEWTON, 2⅓ m. NW, on the s end of the Goathorn Peninsula,
is the site of Edward I's proposed new town. There is nothing
to be seen.

* In *Dorsetshire Photographically Illustrated* (1857).

STURMINSTER MARSHALL

A large village with several thatched cob, brick and flint cottages, interspersed by mid- to late C19 brick houses (that came with the railway) and C20 development.

ST MARY. Brown heathstone with ashlar dressings. C12 nave, but almost entirely lost in later alterations. Late C15 N aisle. Broad W tower of 1805 with flat buttresses. Battlemented parapet and crocketed pinnacles added during a major restoration of 1859–60 by *Henry Woodyer*. He also largely rebuilt the chancel end of the nave, although this remained without a chancel arch. The N arcade of three bays with oblong piers with stop-chamfers and round arches is essentially C12, but the piers have been encased in stone. Even earlier must be the nave corbel table as one sees it from the N aisle. But is a single stone still original? The arch from chancel to N chapel appears early C13 but must be Woodyer. Tower arch also of 1859–60, enriched in a vaguely C12 style. – REREDOS. Mosaic Last Supper, *Powell & Sons*, 1901. – CHANCEL FURNISHINGS, ROOD SCREEN and PULPIT. All *c.* 1860. Some painted decoration to the easternmost S chancel window surround. The very tall painted timber screen has three very pointed arches. – FONT, *c.* 1860, but possibly incorporating a re-cut medieval bowl. – STAINED GLASS. Chancel windows by *Hardman & Co.*, 1860. N aisle, a window by *Powell & Sons*, 1893. N aisle W window by *Hardman*, 1863. Highly decorative W window, possibly by *Ward & Hughes*, 1860. – BRASS. Rev. Henry Helme †1581 (chancel floor). Clerical. – MONUMENTS. Two coffin-lids (S porch), one with a foliated cross. Purbeck marble, early C14. The inscription reads: 'Tu[m]ba Joh[ann]is Vicarii Quisquis ades qui morte cades, sta, perlege, plora. Sum quod eras [*scil.* 'eris'], fueram q[ue] quod es. Pro me precor, ora.' ('The tomb of John, vicar. Whoever you are whom death fells, stay, read, weep. I am as you will be, I was as you are. I beg you, pray for me.') – CROSS in the churchyard, C14. The shaft with eroded formerly crocketed rolls at the corners.

Beside the church, CHURCH COTTAGES, a long, low, thatched row with a curved cottage at the NE end. One C17, timber-framed. The remainder C18, cob, with a standard arrangement of two windows, one per floor, to l. or r. of the doorway, disturbed by C20 alterations following fire damage.

HENBURY HOUSE, 1½ m. SSE. Brick country house, the NW-facing block with stone quoins. Of *c.* 1715 for the 1st Earl of Strafford. Two-storeyed, of three bays, the centre one very wide, brought forward under a pediment. Low lunette window prominent above the front door. Doric porch, probably an addition. Enlarged SE *c.* 1770, and given a full-height canted bay on the SW elevation when altered and extended NE, probably by *W.M. Teulon* in 1854. Converted to flats in the 1990s.

FOREST HILL HOUSE, 3 m. SSE. By *Forsyth & Maule*, *c.* 1910. Brick and render with weatherboarded gables, Lutyens-style.

The original entrance front has been obliterated by nursing-home extensions, *c.* 1990.

STURMINSTER NEWTON

Viewed from the banks of the Stour, the town appears satisfyingly compact, centred on its triangular-plan market square with Bridge Street trailing down towards the strategically important bridge. There are indications that a small market town had developed here by the late C13; this gradually developed until, by the mid C17, it had become of middle size, comparable with Beaminster. As at Gillingham and Blandford, a major fire caused significant destruction, in this case in 1729, when sixty-seven houses were lost. Most of the brick building in the town post-dates the fire. In the outer areas, though, near to the church, several houses survive of earlier date, some of timber-framed construction.

The arrival of the Somerset & Dorset Joint Railway in 1863 made little impact on commercial activity. Significant growth of the town N of the railway, between Bath Road and Manston Road, started only in the late 1950s, creating the suburb of Rixon and the Butts Pond trading estate.

ST MARY. This is a strange building, big and serious, and to a large extent erected in 1825–8 to the design of *William Evans* for the Rev. T. Lane Fox. He started from an existing Perp church of the late C14 or early C15. The W tower was retained, together with the aisle walls with their three-light windows, the aisle arcades with their octagonal piers, and the late C15 or early C16 nave wagon roof. But the aisles were made to embrace the tower, a favourite early C19 motif, and transepts and chancel were added, with the three principal windows of five lights, and Perp of a correctness not exceeded even by Rickman. The tower top is more idiosyncratic, with its band of criss-cross ribbing below the battlemented parapet. Some internal walls were scraped in 1927. While this is aesthetically regrettable, it reveals, in the N aisle, blocked doorways at two levels, presumably to allow access to galleries from an external staircase. – FURNISHINGS of several phases: plain PEWS by *A.H. Green* of Blandford, 1884 (when the galleries and box pews were removed); carved oak CHOIR STALLS by *William Westcott* of Sturminster Newton, 1901; chancel screen, 1919 by *Ponting*, who added further screens in 1923 when the Warrior Chapel was created. – The finely carved FONT, of Marnhull stone, was designed by *W.D. Caröe*, 1927. – Mid-C19 ROYAL ARMS above the chancel arch. – STAINED GLASS. Fine E window by *O'Connor*, 1865 (costing £250). Two windows by *Mary Lowndes*, the vicar's daughter: in the tower of 1886–7, made by *Powell & Sons*; in the S choir aisle of 1901, with *Isobel Gloag*. N transept W, by *Alexander Gibbs*, *c.* 1865. N aisle, by

Geoffrey Webb, 1911. Finest of all in this exceptional collection is the s aisle window by *Harry Clarke* of Dublin, 1921. Sir Owen Morshead called it 'rich in textures, gorgeous in colours, *à la* Reynolds Stephens'.* Jewel-like and deeply expressionist, the central light depicts the Madonna with Child, while the side-lights contain St Elizabeth of Hungary and St Barbara. – MON-UMENT. s transept. James Michel of Whatcombe House, †1839, by the *Patent Works*, Westminster. Renaissance style, with a dove above the pediment. Flanked by marble benefaction boards.

CEMETERY CHAPEL, The Bridge, ¼ m. s. Gothic, rock-faced stone, *c.* 1882. Bellcote and buttresses. In the cemetery itself (opened in 1882), many of the original cast-iron PLOT-MARKERS are still in place. Matching LODGE, dated 1881.

PRIMITIVE METHODIST CHAPEL, Broad Oak, ⅝ m. s. Dated 1869. Simple, whitewashed, with marginal panes to the round-arched front windows.

WESLEYAN METHODIST CHURCH, Church Street, ⅛ m. w. Italian Gothic, red brick enlargement of 1869. The earlier chapel of 1832 was incorporated.

Apart from the detour to the church, a PERAMBULATION need only concentrate on the triangular MARKET PLACE and its immediate vicinity. As with so many market places, the broader end has been partly built upon, so the base of the C15 MARKET CROSS stands among houses. The two free-standing buildings at the s end (the thatched STURMINSTER NEWTON MUSEUM and the block immediately to its N) are of *c.* 1500 in their origins, although heavily rebuilt on several occasions. On the E side of the Market Place the plain stone front of the ASSEMBLY ROOMS, of *c.* 1800, with a central carriage arch and large sash windows above. Next door the bizarre mid-C18 brick façade of the SWAN HOTEL. Humble side parts, and a two-bay centre marked by blue as well as red brick, and by giant pilasters, the middle one – and this is the oddity – carrying a chunk of entablature with a triglyph. The pediment must be an alteration. On the w side, opposite, three imposing (at least for Sturminster) banks. LLOYDS BANK (formerly Wilts. & Dorset Bank) is Arts and Crafts-influenced Queen Anne of *c.* 1905, possibly by *Fletcher & Brett* of Wimborne. Another, heading s, the NATWEST (formerly National Provincial Bank) is *c.* 1860. The third, with rough ashlar ground floor, roughcast above and a mansard roof, now SUTCLIFFE & CO., was built in 1929 as Barclays Bank by *R.C. Fisher*. Between these, a number of C18 cottages, shops and an inn, several thatched, mostly whitewashed brick. The WHITE HART HOTEL, with its undulating thatched roof and various bay windows, is dated RWM 1708. CANDY'S, on the corner of Goughs Close, has a complete Regency shop frontage. Above a datestone inscribed RB 1730.

*A memorial panel to Sir Owen Morshead, †1977, by *Kenneth Wiltshire* is in the N transept.

PENNY STREET (formerly Tanyard Lane) curves circui-
tously from the SE corner of Market Place to the church.
Here, on the l. VINE HOUSE, a T-plan stone house of the C17,
the head of the T towards the road and lengthened to the r. in
the C18, the rear wing of *c*. 1700. Ashlar. Three- and four-light
windows, with hoodmoulds. (Contemporary staircase, through
the full height of the house. Flat, shaped balusters. Newels
with balls and pendants. RCHME) Just beyond, on the r.,
the eye-catchingly steep stone side of the SCHOOL of *c*. 1800.
Buttressed substructure. Further round, on the r., the whitewashed timber framing of TANYARD. The RCHME reports its
origins as a late C15 or early C16 open hall. After narrowing,
Penny Street ends at the SE entrance to the churchyard, with
its pair of early C19, mitre-topped GATEPIERS of wrought-iron
openwork.

Returning to the Market Place W from the church, on the l.
the mildly Italianate 1862 rear wing of the former VICARAGE
(now STOUR GRANGE), the main part of which is of *c*. 1800.
Turn r. into CHURCH STREET where many of the cottages
remain thatched, including Nos. 23–27, a long row of *c*. 1800
with burnt-header pattered brick walls on the r.

BONSLEA HOUSE, White Lane Close, ⅓ m. NW. An idiosyncratic
bungalow house for H. S. Senior, dated 1905. A blend of Italianate and Jacobethan. Colonnaded S front. A circular turret
at the SW corner.

STOUR VIEW HOUSE, Bath Road, ½ m. N. Built as the Union
Workhouse in 1836–8 to *Vulliamy*'s design. The Y-plan, with
single-storey workrooms lining the rectangular plot, is in
accordance with Sampson Kempthorne's recommendations
for workhouses. Adjacent, the former WORKHOUSE CHAPEL
of 1890.

TOWN BRIDGE, ¼ m. SW, over the River Stour. Six two-centred
arches, of stone. Late C15 or early C16, widened in the C17.
Corbelled-out refuge in the centre of each side.

CASTLE, S of the bridge. Not really a castle, for the grassy mound
overlooking the river is a natural outcrop of rock, and the small
ivy-enshrouded stone building upon it is identifiable as the
service end, perhaps with solar above, of an unfortified manor
house of the C14. In the S outer wall a blocked doorway low
down; stumps of buttresses and a two-light window towards
the E. Undergrowth hides the most significant features, which
are the four openings towards the N, giving entrance from this
block to the screens passage, and so to the hall. Nearby the
footings of what may have been a detached kitchen. The ruins
stand inside a crescent-shaped bank and ditch, possibly of an
Iron Age promontory fort, enclosing about 4 acres.

STURMINSTER NEWTON MILL, Newton, ½ m. SW. An impor-
tant example of a water mill of *c*. 1650, its position on the Stour
creating a satisfyingly picturesque effect. Stone, with mellow
brick on the large wing of *c*. 1800 projecting over the river. The
mid-C19 machinery is intact.

SUTTON WALDRON

ST BARTHOLOMEW. Rebuilt as a Puginian model church in 1847 by *George Alexander* for the Rev. Anthony Huxtable, built by *H. Green* of Pimperne and costing about £3,000. W tower with recessed spire, and flying buttresses up to it from the corner pinnacles (the tower rendered in 1897). The church is of flint with rusty-coloured Mapperton freestone dressings. Tracery mainly E.E. and Dec, with shafted rere-arches. S aisle, the W part forming a baptistery. Inside a major scheme of painted polychromy by *Owen Jones*, the most important surviving scheme by this pioneer of High Victorian design. Jones has painted every surface, framing the arches with the semi-oriental abstract patterns, stylized and repetitive, which he derived from the Alhambra and from his experiments in chromo-lithographic book production. The pale blue of the nave and aisle walls is a pastel shade which seems almost to foreshadow the 1920s. Dark blue and red are the other colours used, and the chancel roof is 'powdered with gilt stars', as described by *The Builder*, 27 November 1847. – The FITTINGS are also of high quality. REREDOS. Alabaster, with the sculpted emblems of the Evangelists. – SEDILIA, COMMUNION RAIL, PULPIT and READING DESK, all integral with the design and painted by *Jones*. – Encaustic TILES in chancel and baptistery by *Minton*. – BENCHES. A typical functional mid-C19 shape. – FONT. Chalice-shaped, with an ornate Gothic COVER of oak. – STAINED GLASS. Glowing E window depicting Christ and the Evangelists by *Charles Hudson*, 1847. Several windows by *Powell & Sons*, incorporating their patented stamped quarries. The others may also be by *Hudson*. – MONUMENT. Re-set in the E wall of the bell-chamber, a medieval monument no doubt marking a heart burial.

Contemporary GATE SCREEN by *Alexander*, including a pair of spiky stone gatepiers.

ALMSHOUSES, Nos. 17–24, The Street. Of *c*. 1860, brick, probably by *George Evans*. Central two-storey block of four; single-storey pair at either end.

SWANAGE

Swanage in 1821 was a large and populous village, its High Street about a mile long. One can still sense its character strongly near St Mary's church. At that time sixty quarries were open within the parish, the stone being shipped out by sea. Attention began to turn from hill to bay almost at once after this, although it was the coming of the railway in 1885 that killed Swanage as a place for the shipping of stone and brought, in its stead, large numbers of visitors. This reinforced a trend that had started earlier in the century, when William Morton Pitt determined to make Swanage a second Weymouth. He converted the symmetrically composed block at the E extremity of the High Street to a hotel in 1823, and erected baths and a library, with billiard and coffee rooms, close to the shore in 1825. Princess Victoria visited Swanage in 1835, and the new era was launched.

Architecturally there is nothing much to show for this; for an architectural show the town had to wait for the activities of George Burt (1816–94), general contractor and collector extraordinary. Burt imported large quantities of architectural salvage from London, thrown up by his business partner John Mowlem's building and development activities. This architectural enhancing of the town was reinforced by the arrival of Sir J. C. Robinson, director of the Victoria and Albert Museum, who also owned and developed large tracts of the town. Burt's was especially the controlling mind behind the boarding-house boom of the 1880s, which gave Swanage its present character of a popular resort. First, gentry villas were built on rising land to the S of the old town. Then, from c. 1900, the town began to expand northwards beyond the railway station to link up with New Swanage, a detached suburb on the curve of Ballard Down.

CHURCHES

ST MARY, Church Hill. A large church with a confusing plan. Pre-C19 is only the gaunt and vigorously erect C14 W tower, unbuttressed and with a plain parapet. Its upper part is of c. 1620. *T.H. Wyatt* in 1859–60 built a new nave, chancel and bulky transepts, all of an equally gaunt character. See particularly the under-scaled wheel window set in the otherwise blank S transept gable. A complete contrast came in 1906–8 with a new N aisle by *Clifton & Robinson*. This is almost as large as the nave, more architecturally elaborate, and provides a new W entry. At this point also Wyatt's N transept was rebuilt in a new position. Wyatt's intersection of diagonal arched braces over the crossing ought to be noticed. It is repeated at a slightly smaller scale in Clifton & Robinson's aisle. Wyatt's galleries remain *in situ* in the transepts. The E end of the N aisle is filled by a huge ORGAN CASE, presumably of 1906. – Most of *Wyatt*'s FURNISHINGS are still in place. – FONT. A granite bowl of c. 1860. – Some *Minton* encaustic TILES on the sanctuary steps. – STAINED GLASS. Much of the C19 scheme was lost in 1942 when the nearby Congregational church (*see* below) was bombed. The earliest windows are therefore in the N wall. Here a single light, probably by *Lavers & Barraud*, 1861, who did the original E window. This was replaced in 1948 by *Francis Skeat* (with *Goddard & Gibbs*). He also did one in the S transept, also 1948. In the N chapel, beneath the (N transept) gallery, windows by *Abbott & Co.*, 1936, and *Roy Coomber* for the *Wippell Mowbray Studio*, 1972. Another († Pitt) is perhaps by *Alexander Gibbs & Co.*, c. 1900. The chapel screen has three re-set panels from St Aldhelm's church (dem. 1973) by *A.L. Moore*, c. 1892. Nave S three-light by *Francis Skeat*,

1951. N transept wheel window by *Henry Haig*, 1994. – MONU-
MENTS. Many tablets, the biggest on the nave W wall, Joseph
Edmonds †1794. Sarcophagus with an oval panel depicting a
naval engagement in front of a grey obelisk. Two putti, in the
round, l. and r. In the N aisle, Nathan Chinchen †1840. Panel
with shrouded urn above. By *Gillingham & Son.*

ALL SAINTS, Ulwell Road. 1956–7 by *Robert Potter (Potter &
Hare)*. Purbeck rubble. Big gable-ends on a curved plan. The E
has a vesica-shaped window. Inside, tapering pre-cast concrete
fins define narrow aisles. Parabolic section to the nave ceiling.

ST MARK, Bell Street, Herston. 1869–72 by *John Hicks*, completed by *G.R. Crickmay*. Rock-faced, with lancets. No tower.
Bellcote over chancel arch. Short, two-bay N aisle. – FONT.
Dated 1663, from the years of many extremely simple fonts
all over England. This one is specially memorable because it
is a straight revival of the polygonal C12–C13 fonts of Purbeck
marble. – STAINED GLASS. E window, central light by *Martin
Travers*, 1948, the other lights by *Francis Skeat*, 1967.

HOLY SPIRIT AND ST EDWARD (R.C.), Victoria Avenue. 1902–4
by *A.J.C. Scoles*. Sanctuary added by *Francis Newbery*, 1924.
Purbeck rubble. Gothic style of *c.* 1300. Nave and chancel
in one, but with a chancel arch internally. Bellcote over the
chancel arch. (Liturgical) S transept. – PAINTINGS. Triptych
behind the high altar by *Newbery*, 1926. Another by him in the
Lady Chapel, 1930. – PRESBYTERY of *c.* 1904, E side. Brick.

METHODIST CHURCH, High Street. 1886 by *Bucknell & Jennings*. Tender £4,250; cost £5,800. The Gothic front with an
overstressed octagonal spired steeple, r., and flowing tracery,
especially mouchette wheels, is spectacular, the side (typically)
anti-climactically utilitarian. The SCHOOL continues the same
style as late as 1907.

EBENEZER WESLEYAN CHAPEL (former), Bell Street, Herston.
Dated 1861 on an oval panel. Gable-end to the road. Plain
openings.

EMMANUEL BAPTIST CHURCH, Victoria Avenue. 2012 by *CPL
Chartered Architects*. A variegated effect of gables and hips in
Purbeck rubble and brick. Bold monopitch-roofed tower.

UNITED REFORMED CHURCH (formerly Congregational), High
Street. The earlier chapel is a simple building of 1837 by *George
Gollop* of Poole. Off-centre plain tower to the road with twin
doorways. Its more imposing and elaborate replacement r., of
1901–2 (cost £2,500), by *Thomas Stevens* of Bournemouth.
Rock-faced, Perp, without a tower (although one was proposed
over the main entrance) but with corner turrets. The earlier
building retains a gallery around three sides supported on
cast-iron columns.

PUBLIC BUILDINGS AND PERAMBULATION

Most of the town may be seen in a walk from St Mary's church
E, ending at Peveril Point. First a short detour N, off CHURCH
HILL, below the W end of the church, for the picturesque
grouping of typically Purbeck cottages (with much sensitive

post-war rebuilding) around the MILL POND, fortunately kept clear of cars. The MILL HOUSE itself is as low as the cottages. There is a 1754 datestone. Up to the HIGH STREET to the s, turning l. and passing No. 6 Church Hill, a house dated 1793 with platband and sashes under segmental heads. A first indication of the arrival of more genteel architecture. After the two Congregational chapels on the High Street (*see* above), on the opposite side, the DAY CENTRE (built as a health centre) of 1959 by *E. J. Ricketts*. Like an overgrown bungalow, with a portico on cylindrical stone piers. Its shape, carefully considered, and its generous lawns break up the texture of the old High Street; and it certainly speaks volumes for the mid C20, set as it is beside the Methodist church (p. 585). Next on this side PURBECK HOUSE, now a hotel. Built in 1875 by *G. R. Crickmay* of Weymouth for George Burt as his private residence; an overweening name for an overweening house. The character is highly personal and a clear architectural expression of Burt's High Victorian taste. Its position right beside the pavement makes it impossible to avoid those crazy-paving walls, those crowstepped gables, that octagonal turret and all those bay windows. The style is perhaps nearer to Scots Baronial than anything.

In the GROUNDS a number of pieces salvaged by Burt from London at demolitions by his uncle's contracting firm, Mowlem & Co. The most important are the ARCHWAY erected in 1844 in Grosvenor Place, at the Hyde Park Corner end, and, around what is now a tennis court SE of the house, six cast-iron COLUMNS from *Bunning*'s short-lived Billingsgate Market of 1848–52. Also three C17 STATUES. One is of a figure in academic dress; the other two, little more than torsos in vaguely classical armour, are from the Royal Exchange. Excellent Baroque drapery. Finally the TEMPLE, another structure (after 1878) made up from reclaimed components including cast-iron columns from *John Rennie*'s Waterloo Bridge toll houses and a floor within of encaustic tiles salvaged from the House of Commons, *c.* 1880. It has an exaggerated concave pyramidal roof topped by a pair of oversized terracotta dragons. Some 650 yds SE, on the skyline, a WATER TOWER (in Purbeck Terrace Road), castellated to match Purbeck House. Built 1886, no doubt for Burt.

Back to the reality of the High Street. Opposite Purbeck House is the heavy brick SPRINGSIDE HOUSE, built as Craigside Boarding House for J. M. Burt (almost certainly by *Crickmay*), and dated 1900. Just beyond, opposite the last, smaller and ogee-domed corner turret of Purbeck House, the TOWN HALL. The gift of George Burt and built in 1881–4; *Crickmay* again (opened 1886). Quite plain apart from the spectacular frontispiece, the re-erected Portland stone façade of the Mercers' Hall, which Burt had salvaged from the City of London at its demolition. The façade, really a broad one-bay frontispiece, taller than the Town Hall, is an overwhelmingly undisciplined example of the City of London style of the mid C17. It was

designed by *John Oliver*, possibly taking over elements of an
earlier design by *Edward Jerman* (†1668), and built by the
master mason *John Young* in 1669–71. Panels carved with fruit,
curved volutes, a wide open segmental pediment, wreathed
ovals and roundel, all characteristic motifs, hustled together to
make three stages under a top balustrade (the last by *George
Smith*, 1813). Metal balcony bearing the date 1670. The best
part is the juicy carving under the balcony, drapery and flying
putti in relief, bearing a bust of the 'Mercers' Maiden', above
the tall round-headed entrance arch. The sculptor was *John
Young*. A bracket clock added in 1882 projects almost comically
through the pediment opening.

The character of Swanage owes much to the jauntily gabled
and half-timbered SHOP TERRACES by *Crickmay & Son*,
c. 1900, of which the first appears on the s side. Further on,
on the N side, at the junction with Kings Road East, THE
ARCADE (1896 by *Crickmay*), single-storeyed, with an open
loggia of only three bays. It was the first of an intended seven-
shop row. Beyond, in almost shocking contrast, the COUNTY
LIBRARY, 1965 by *J. R. Hurst*, County Architect. Dodecagonal,
all glazed, the upper storey projecting beyond the lower all
the way round. On the s side facing, a group of three buildings worthy of notice, surely designed as a set in contrasting
styles. First No. 45 with its jetty and timber-framed gable;
next the brick and stone No. 43, crowned by a Flemish gable;
and finally LLOYDS BANK (built as Williams & Co.), 1896
by *Clifton & Robinson*. Purbeck ashlar, classical with three
tiers of pilasters. At the crossroad junction with STAFFORD
ROAD on the r., the scale returns to pre-Victorian vernacular
with the WHITE SWAN, *c*. 1700, gabled but much altered.
Opposite, along INSTITUTE ROAD to the N, more regularly
gabled SHOP TERRACES, brick on the r. with Dutch gables,
half-timbered on the l. At the end of Institute Road on the r.
the square, flat-roofed block of THE MOWLEM, a theatre of
1967 (replacing the Mowlem Institute of 1862 by *Crickmay*).
A restaurant juts out on struts over the beach (cf. the 1962
former Festival Hall, Paignton, Devon, by C. F. J. Thurley).
Just beyond it the equally incongruous ALFRED THE GREAT
MONUMENT. 1862, erected by *John Mowlem*, 'In commemoration of a great naval battle fought with the Danes in Swanage
Bay by Alfred the Great, A.D. 877'.* Granite Tuscan column
with four cannonballs balanced at the top.

From in front of the theatre, STATION ROAD leads between
more shopping terraces (Peveril Terrace is 1893 by *Crickmay*)
to the RAILWAY STATION, 1885 by *W.R. Galbraith* for the
Swanage Railway (later London & South Western Railway).
Two-storey cottage style. Purbeck rubble stone. Extended E
and provided with glazed awnings running w, 1938 for the

*No such battle is known to have taken place.

Southern Railway, to provide for intensified holiday traffic.
Beyond it the GOODS SHED, also 1885.

Returning to the HIGH STREET and continuing W, i.e. behind
the seafront, the SHIP INN is early C19, stuccoed with wide
sashes (probably a remodelling of a late C18 structure), while
on the l. is NEW LOOK (originally the Wilts. & Dorset Bank),
1896 by *G.M. Silley*. Banded rustication on the ground floor,
keyed and blocked architraves above. Next, on the S side ahead,
the VICTORIA TERRACE, of 1835. Five houses, three storeys
high, with wide sashes. Originally all stuccoed. Wrought-iron
balcony at first-floor level. After a later C19 block attempt-
ing the same effect (but without the stucco), the ROYAL
VICTORIA HOTEL, the earliest response to the provision of
visitor accommodation in Swanage. A sprawling symmetrical
group as seen from the N with, at its centre, the five bays of
the former manor house of *c.* 1721, built for John Chapman.
Central three bays pedimented with Ionic pilasters. Windows
with keyed architraves. The small Venetian window in the
pediment suggests the involvement of either *Nathaniel Ireson*
or *John James*. Its enlargement was made in 1777 for William
Morton Pitt. It was converted to a hotel in 1823, and renamed
in 1835, following the Princess's visit of that year. The widely
spaced wings (of 1777) have large tripartite sashes under segmental arches in their ends, inserted *c.* 1823 to take advantage of the sea views. A conservatory link, probably later C19,
regrettably blocks off the central façade.

Opposite the long E wing of the hotel, on the corner of
Seymer Road, THE ROOKERY, 1825 by *Wallis* for Pitt as one of
the first tourist facilities. Stucco, as were all of the new developments of this time, built as a library and custom house. Behind
this is Prince Albert Gardens, a recent reworking of George
Burt's pleasure gardens of *c.* 1880. Continuing up SEYMER
ROAD, on the r. the PEVERIL HEIGHTS development. 1969 by
Raymond Spratley & Partners. An intelligent piece of infilling,
close to the seafront. A terrace of flats, a row of bungalows
and a trio of houses make three rows stepping up the hillside.
Red brick and white boarded monopitch tops. Rather coarsely
detailed, but weaving neatly into the fabric of the town, which
is the main thing. Beyond these TONTINE HOUSES, 1830,
by *Charles Wallis* of Dorchester for William Morton Pitt. An
informal stucco terrace, the last houses retaining more of the
original elaboration.

Returning to the seafront, the continuation of the High
Street E is Peveril Point Road. On the l., MARINE VILLAS of
1825, also by *Wallis* for Pitt. Stucco with a hipped roof. It contained baths, and billiard and coffee rooms. To the SW, in the
gardens, another of George Burt's waifs: two shortened stone
Ionic columns, presumably brought from London. SWANAGE
PIER is of 1897 by *R. St George Moore* of Westminster to cater
for paddle-steamers, replacing an earlier structure of 1861 (the
supports for which survive), built for the export of stone. A

tramway was also laid, the rails for which survive in a few places. The view s from the pier is of THE HAVEN, a housing development of *c.* 1992, replacing the Grosvenor Hotel (dem. 1988). Monopitched roofs and coloured stucco, in a lively (if over-dense) reinterpretation of Regency maritime. At its E end, the CLOCK TOWER, of two stages in an accurate Dec style. Burt also brought this to Swanage; originally erected in 1854 (designed by *Arthur Ashpitel*) on the s side of London Bridge as the Wellington Testimonial Clock Tower, in memory of the Duke, who had died two years before. Its odd domical top replaced a slender spire. There is no longer a clock, however.

OUTLYING BUILDINGS

At DURLSTON HEAD, 1 m. s, the climax of George Burt's gifts to Swanage, DURLSTON HEAD CASTLE, 1887 by *Crickmay*, built as a cliff-top restaurant. Burt clearly believed that the public should be instructed on holiday, for the castle walls bear inscriptions giving miscellaneous geographical facts. At its E corner a tourelle, again Scots Baronial. Repaired and sensitively extended by *Long & Kentish*, 2004–11. Glass and timber, contrasting well with the heavily battered Purbeck fortress walls. The most unusual, but typically educative of Burt's development, is the STONE GLOBE, 10 ft (3 metres) across, poised on its correct axis with carefully carved coastline and inscriptions. In the curved retaining wall around it more panels with instructive statistics.

LIGHTHOUSE to the SW at Anvil Point, by *James Douglass*, opened 1881. An unaltered group, the keeper's house within high enclosing walls. Low lighthouse tower to seaward, linked by outbuildings, making a T-plan.

GODLINGSTON MANOR, 1¼ m. NW. Something of a puzzle. Although much rebuilt (especially after a late C19 fire), the main range is, in its bones, a hall house of *c.* 1300. The date is given now only by the entrance doorway, a good bold piece with a two-centred head and big cusps to give a trefoiled inner outline. Curious fin-like decoration of the cusps. Hutchins mentions a similar doorway, uncusped, opposite, which suggests the usual cross-passage arrangement. C17 mullioned windows, not uniform, in the s wall, one reusing an early C16 hoodmould. Cross-wing of *c.* 1900 at the r. But what of the half-round tower at the l. end? Many accounts take this as medieval and an indication of a semi-fortified house. If so, there are no features here earlier than, say, the C16, and no record of such a structure. So what was it? One possibility is that its purpose was storage. There is evidence too of a raising of its height *c.* 1550, probably to make it a dovecote, since the inner faces of this part are lined with pigeon holes. Integrated dovecote structures are not unknown, and the later medievalizing augmentations, such as the one or two small square openings, given two-centred heads and long jambs inside, as if they were lancets, may well be mid- to late C19.

NEWTON MANOR, High Street, ½ m. w. At its core C18 but, together with the s wing, refronted *c.* 1876 for Sir Charles Robinson, Curator of Sculpture at the Victoria and Albert Museum. Ashlar-faced, with a battlemented parapet, also on the lower wing and porch. Of the C17 is a former barn at the rear, converted to a dining room and given assorted mullioned windows in its s wall, one multi-light set (improbably) under a pediment. Also C17 a cross-wing at the N end, incorporated and made the kitchen. Many salvaged features within.

WHITECLIFF MANOR FARM, 1¼ m. N. An E–W range, the w part with an end cross-wing early C17, the E part later (a datestone of 1683 on an adjacent barn may relate to this). Stone-mullioned windows and a Purbeck stone-slate roof. Long C18 secondary wing to the s, creating an L-plan.

SWYRE

HOLY TRINITY. Largely rebuilt in 1843–4 for the 7th Duke of Bedford, but with reused masonry and re-set features. The w tower is Perp of *c.* 1400 but with a plain parapet and a two-light bell-opening on the N side only (facing the village). Late C14 Dec N doorway. Chancel arch of *c.* 1400 (matching the tower arch). The interior is dominated by the plaster rib-vault (cf. Trent, 1840), the wall-shafts and the door surround, all still Gothick in the C18 sense.* The FURNISHINGS are a model of what was expected in the 1840s. – FONT. 1843, Perp style. COVER with Gothick superstructure. – ROYAL ARMS. Of Charles II. Wood panel with low-relief carving. – MONUMENTS. John Russell †1505. Brass inscription and armorial shield set in a later stone tablet. – James Russell †1509. A matching set, similarly mounted. – Napier family, 1692. Pilasters with bunchy garlands, open scrolly pediment with an urn.

In the village several COTTAGES for the Bedford estate, including a terrace of six of *c.* 1855.

BERWICK HOUSE, 1 m. NNW. E-facing block of *c.* 1820, with sash windows. Early C20 N wing incorporating some early C16 features within, surviving from a more substantial earlier house (the home of the ancestors of the 1st Earl of Bedford). In this wing the kitchen may represent the original hall; also an arched doorway (now with a window) leading to a screens passage. Further early C16 doorways within.

---

*The architect is unrecorded but more than likely to have been from Bridport, perhaps *J. Galpin* or *R. Cornick*.

SYDLING ST NICHOLAS 6090

Sydling St Nicholas, isolated on the bare downs, has its own little high street. Many cottages of banded flint, several with thatched roofs. Also early C19 sash-windowed terraces. The church, Court House and tithe barn are in a secluded group at the SW end.

St Nicholas. Banded flint and chalk blocks. Nothing earlier than the mid C15 (apart from the re-cut C13 voussoirs of the chancel arch). S aisle c. 1500 (but with a C19 rendered parapet). Mid-C18 brick chancel, rendered and given a new E window, battlements and buttresses in the mid C19. The w gallery was removed only in 1903, during a restoration by C.E. Ponting. Three-stage Perp w tower, the doorway with fleurons. Set-back buttresses. Battlemented parapet with undersized crocketed pinnacles, these apparently C18 replacements. Polygonal N stair-turret. Boldly carved gargoyles. The S belfry opening is blocked. The tower was built independently of the church – see the buttresses inside the nave. However the church must have come soon afterwards. The aisles, the S chapel and the N porch are also embattled, and the lights of the windows are uncusped. Instead of a S porch there is the curious arrangement of a small doorway between two heavy buttresses.* They were presumably added to support a leaning wall (the S arcade leans yet). More bold gargoyles here. Both doorways incidentally are placed in the middle of the aisle walls, not somewhere further w (cf. Frampton). Another curious feature is that the aisle walls are of five bays, but the arcades of four for the same distance. The piers are standard; the chancel responds tally. In the nave a wagon roof with bosses, c. 1500. The chancel roof was designed to match.

FURNISHINGS. PULPIT. C18 style, but more likely c. 1903. – FONT. C12. Round, with two moulded bands and between them short narrow and wide flutes. Polygonal tapering stem. – TOWER SCREEN. Late C17 or early C18. Turned baluster screen above fielded panelling. Dentil cornice. – PEWS. In the S aisle, box pews, C18. Elsewhere, benches made up from mid-C17 panelling, presumably the earlier box pews. – ROYAL ARMS. Painted canvas. George III or IV. – HATCHMENTS. Two in the S aisle, C19. Both Smith with different quarterings. – STAINED GLASS. Hanging panel with re-set fragments of various periods. – MONUMENTS. Many tablets, e.g. three cartouches †1704, †1724 and even †1768, still with putto heads. – Henry Devenish †1804 (behind the organ). Grecian, by *Raggett* of Weymouth. – Fine set of tablets to the Smith family of Court House in the chancel. – Elizabeth Lady Smith †1796. Large standing monument, but flat like a tablet. At the foot

---

*These are dated by the RCHME as C17, with reused quatrefoils, but they seem convincing late Perp and the plinth mouldings are continuous with the S wall.

her husband rises out of his tomb. At the top a kneeling mourning woman. The whole set in a pointed arch. – Elizabeth Smith †1811. By *King* of Bath, with a standing woman by an urn. – Sir John Wyldbore Smith †1852. By *Marshall* of Blandford. A large open book propped up on a larger closed bible. – Three on the chancel N wall by *Lancashire & Son* of Bath: Elizabeth Curtis †1793; four sons and five daughters of Sir John and Lady Smith, *c.* 1805; Mary Smith †1797. All are finely detailed with shaped slate backgrounds.

CONGREGATIONAL CHAPEL (former), at the N end of the village. Dated 1834. Stucco front with a swooping gable and big kneelers. Gothick windows.

WESLEYAN METHODIST CHAPEL (former), High Street. Built as a Congregational chapel *c.* 1790. Tall, round-arched, brick-lined windows, only one having survived domestic conversion.

COURT HOUSE, immediately N of the church. Dated 1771 (for Sir John Smith), incorporating an early C17 house, but subsequently altered. Picturesque Gothick E front, *c.* 1820. Battlemented at its centre. Low tower-porch with angle buttresses and pinnacles. Taller N front with a bay window.

TITHE BARN, just SE. Probably early C16 (although a date of 1590 was recorded by Hutchins). Externally of seven bays, but these do not entirely correspond with the nine-and-a-half bays within. Flint walls. Stone buttresses with one set-off. One porch on the N side, its corresponding S porch now lost. Shortened at the E end, but this rebuilt in flint with brick banding, perhaps at the date recorded. Fine aisle-post interior, the trusses with arched collar-bracing. In poor condition with corrugated-iron roofing.

At the S end of the HIGH STREET (on the W side) the most interesting houses, three in a row. EAST HOUSE is the odd man out, red brick, three bays, with the wide windows of say *c.* 1790, and a minimal Venetian window as the centrepiece. Huge central chimneystack. Hipped roof. The middle house (No. 3), barely fifty years older, is a very late survivor of the earlier tradition, as the datestone 1733 shows; for the walls are chalk- and flint-banded, the windows mullioned, with an ovolo moulding. But there is symmetry and, a telling detail, an inconspicuous stone modillion cornice. Joined to it, the OLD VICARAGE, dated 1640 at the back. Same banded walls. Mullioned windows. Restored in 1778, the date of the sash windows on the r. Also a mid-C19 elaboration in the form of picturesque curvy gable bargeboards. It was probably enlarged at this date and given the slate roof.

VILLAGE CROSS. In front of this group. C15; only the base and part of the shaft.

On SHEARPLACE HILL, ¾ m. SE, are a Bronze Age and Iron Age SETTLEMENT and associated fields (the Bronze Age settlement excavated in 1958). One of a series of settlements and field systems on either side of the valley N and S of the village, some of which are partly visible as earthworks.

SYMONDSBURY

Symondsbury is a village of great character and intimacy, between the rounded hill to the N and the rounded hill to the S.

ST JOHN THE BAPTIST. A cruciform church with a high central tower. The tower is early C14 Dec with a C15 top. The arches carrying it have two continuous mouldings to E and W, responds with C14 capitals to N and S. The outer mouldings above them are on corbels. The windows of the lowest stage of the tower are lancet-shaped but include ogee. Perp belfry openings and a battlemented parapet. Nave and transepts also Dec, but the nave extended to the W in the C15 and the chancel probably rebuilt in the C17. Further analysis of the dating is problematic owing to phases of later fenestration. Most of the Perp-style windows are of the major restoration by *C.E. Ponting*, with *H.W. Crickmay*, 1920–7. The large window of the N transept however is of 1818 (with wrought-iron glazing bars), and the equivalent S transept window of 1885 by *E.S. Prior* (who had married the rector's daughter that year). C15 S porch with bold gargoyles.

    FURNISHINGS. REREDOS. 1922 by *Ponting*. Gothic; unpainted. – COMMUNION RAIL. Of *c.* 1730–40, with turned balusters and swept handrails. It encloses the altar space rectangularly. – CHOIR STALLS and CLERGY SEATS. Of 1920–6, made by local volunteers. Distinctive carved roundel finials by *Ida Cox*. – PULPIT, *c.* 1725. Simple fielded panelling with a backplate. – FONT, *c.* 1920 by *Ponting*. Circular stone bowl with a floral band at mid-height. On a central stem with four marble colonnettes. – STAINED GLASS. E window by *Kempe & Co.*, 1927. Chancel S window by *Henry Holiday, c.* 1921. The S transept S window dates from 1885. Four large Evangelists, with expressive woodcut faces. *W.R. Lethaby* was the designer (and *Worrall* the maker). The style presupposes a study of French Romanesque sculpture, which was at this time a scarcely discovered field. Of Morris influence there is none. The E window in this transept is by *Christopher Webb*, 1936. Nave S window (with a rather Edwardian head on the r.) by *Powell & Sons*, 1940. Nave N window by *Lowndes & Drury*, 1924. – MONUMENTS. Mrs Thew †1782. Signed by *J.F. Moore*. A large tablet of bold design. No figures, but an unusual combination of shapes and coloured marbles. – Eadith Syndercombe †1748. The monument probably of *c.* 1786. Tablet with plain black surround, cornice and swept top in coloured marble. – John Pitfield †1838. Rather severe, with a shrouded sarcophagus above. By *Wilkins* of Bridport.

Opposite the church, RAYMOND'S CHARITY SCHOOL, of 1867–8 by *John Hicks*. Of yellowish stone and High Victorian fervour. Plate tracery and gables alternating little and big. THE MANOR HOUSE N of the church, largish and of the

C17, is too restored and altered to make a statement of any historical clarity. Buckler's drawing of 1814 shows a four-bay range, with end gables, and non-symmetrical mullioned windows, five-light below, mostly four-light above, and this is what we see today. There are also rear ranges making an overall H-plan. Big C17 BARN to the E and a long SHELTER SHED to an L-plan running S. Brick-walled with a thatched roof.

The third large building is the grandiose, if restrained, OLD RECTORY, behind thick bushes to the w. Ashlar-faced. It is hardly a surprise to learn that Symondsbury was the richest living in the county. Built by a rector of 1716–35 (c. 1730) as a five-bay, three-storey block, and given lower wings c. 1820. Recessed segmental panels over the large windows of the wings and the platbands between the row of sashes on the main block are the only embellishment.

Finally, worth a glance is the ILCHESTER ARMS, 150 yds S. Its central three bays are C15, the arch-braced collar roof in this part also having chamfered wind-braces. All is hidden by the standard C17 rebuilding. Thatched roof.

TARRANT CRAWFORD

9000

Tarrant Crawford had one of the richest NUNNERIES of England. It was founded before May 1228 by Bishop Poore of Salisbury, and was Cistercian. Nothing at all remains of it above ground, except for any possible structures buried within Abbey House, and the telling undulations in the paddock to the NW of the church. The long windowless wall of the parish church has been attributed to proximity to the nunnery.*

ST MARY (Churches Conservation Trust). One visits the church for its C14 wall paintings, but also finds a building seemingly untouched by the Victorians, and hardly noticed through the C18. Conservative repair by *Ponting*, 1910–11. A C12 chancel and slightly later nave, but no chancel arch between them. Probably there was a continuous building programme from E to W. Norman chancel doorway (altered in the C13) and Norman nave quoins. The small two-stage w tower may be of c. 1508 (a date reported by Hutchins), but has a cusped Y-traceried window of c. 1300 re-set. It is of banded stone and flint. Battlemented parapet. Chancel E window of about the same time (three stepped cusped lancet lights under one arch), and more two-light windows of c. 1300. Porch and one nave S window probably contemporary with the tower. – COMMUNION RAIL. Late C17. – PULPIT. Hexagonal, early C17. – BOX PEWS consisting of re-set C17 panelling. – FONT.

---

* Bishop Poore (†1237) and Queen Joan of Scotland (King John's daughter, †1238) are both buried among the footings of the abbey.

Plain and square bowl, probably C13. C16 pedestal. Pyramidal oak COVER, probably late C16. – Some C13 and C14 TILES, re-set in the chancel pavement. – PAINTINGS, mainly taking advantage of the largely blank nave S wall. The best is the Annunciation, nave SE, to the l. of the window. Of large figures; first half of the C14. To its r. two tiers of stories: top fourteen scenes depicting the legend of St Margaret of Antioch; bottom, the allegory of the Three Living and the Three Dead. They are also C14. To their r., beyond the blocked nave S doorway, a Crucifixion. More fragmentary paintings on the nave N wall. Conservation by *E. Clive Rouse*, 1948–9, and by *Ann Ballantyne* and *Andrea Kirkham*, late 1990s.

The church lies at the far end of a lane with nothing around but a farmhouse and a barn. The BARN is partly C15. Rubble and flint with ashlar buttresses. Upper parts of brick with a datestone of 1759 in the E gable. Inside the adjoining farm-building range, at the NE end, the roof has four fine hammerbeam trusses. TARRANT ABBEY HOUSE is probably what was built from the materials of the demolished nunnery. Main range of rubble stone, brick-faced in the C18. At the SW end a cross-wing projecting at the back. Its ground floor is medieval in origin, of rubble and flint. The only features here are a slit window and the chamfered jamb of a doorway. Above, late C15 timber framing with brick-nogging.

TARRANT GUNVILLE

Once in the shadow of Vanbrugh's Eastbury (q.v.), the church and the two houses beside it seem oddly large, as if to compete with the nearby demolished goliath. The remainder of the village is a string of cob and thatch, or brick and flint, cottages.

ST MARY. A large church, partly of C12 origin, but (except for the tower) rebuilt and enlarged to the E by *Wyatt & Brandon*, 1844–5. Evidence of the Early Norman church is some remarkably large wall arcading re-set improbably high up in the S wall of the N aisle. Plain pilasters with blocky imposts and intersected arches. As for the present church, the W tower of bands of flint and stone is C15 Perp. The rest of the church also flint with a speckling of ashlar blocks. A few C14 parts reused, notably the S porch. Two five-bay aisle arcades in unconvincing Dec; matching chancel arch. Nicely stencilled chancel decoration. – TILES by *Minton* in the chancel. – ROYAL ARMS. Of Victoria, 1843. Painted metal. – STAINED GLASS. E window by *C.E. Kempe & Co.*, 1908. Chancel side windows (also the tower window) by *William Miller*, 1845. Over the chancel arch (re-set by *Miller*) two C16 royal armorial panels. S aisle W window another armorial panel, C18, re-set. Aisles, E end windows (†1869 and 1872) probably by *Lavers, Barraud & Westlake*.

s aisle (†1895) by *A.O. Hemming & Co.* N aisle window by *James Powell & Sons*, 1921. – MONUMENT. Externally, on the chancel s wall, Thomas Daccomb †1567. Tablet with shield of arms above.

OLD RECTORY, E of the church. Extraordinarily bald and stolid block, of *c.* 1798 for the Rev. Francis Simpson. Perfectly square in plan. Three-bay elevations on three sides. Banded walls, of stone and flint.

GUNVILLE MANOR, immediately s. 'Newly erected' in 1798 for Anthony Chapman. Venetian windows under round-headed relieving arches low down l. and r. on the N front. The house belonged to Josiah Wedgwood II in 1799–1805, and many of the rooms have Adamish fireplaces, doors and dadoes in *carton pierre* installed for him. Small marble chimneypiece by *Flaxman*, 1800.

BUSSEY STOOL PARK, 1¾ m. NNE. An Iron Age ovate ENCLO-SURE, univallate, of 6 acres. Out-turned bank at the NW and SE entrances.

9010

TARRANT HINTON

The village, just N of the turnpike road, is mostly of the early C19. Brick and flint-banded cottages at the bottom, white thatched ones up the lane to the church.

ST MARY. The church looks splendid from the s, with its big C15 W tower and its oversized battlements on the later C15 s aisle and porch. Otherwise largely mid-C14, of banded flint and Greensand ashlar. From the N the unusual two-storey N transept has to its E a truncated N chapel. The chancel is of 1874, by *Benjamin Ferrey*. Restoration of the remainder in 1892 (date over the s door) by *A.W.N. Burder & J.S. Alder* was evidently careful. The interior is full of pleasant surprises. The continuous single-chamfered arches to the s arcade (three bays) are mid-C14, for an earlier aisle. The chamfers are terminated at the base by carved stops. A blocked lancet out of any possible context is at the SE corner of this aisle. Above the s door are a few yet older bits, including Norman chevron. The early C16 N transept was originally two-storeyed, with probably a priest's room above. Later this was a gallery. The windows show a Late Perp date. The chancel arch is also Perp, with the standard Perp responds. Yet the capitals are unmistakably C19 Dec replacements.

39   In the chancel is a gorgeous EASTER SEPULCHRE, carrying the initials of Thomas Wever, rector 1514–36. It is an early example of the conversion to the Italian Renaissance. Its recess still has a four-centred arch, but to the l. and r. are Early Renaissance columns, crudely tapering above a cylindrical fluted section. Freely carved capitals of considerable delicacy,

as are the roundels and fluttering ribbons in the spandrels. The elegant writing is no longer black-letter either. Above, and forming part of the composition, is a windowed recess flanked by two carved angels. This has niches set into the window reveals with further carving in their spandrels. Two brackets re-set in Ferrey's adjoining arch to the N transept are by the same hand. – COMMUNION RAIL. Surplus sections from Pembroke College Chapel, Cambridge. Of c. 1665, with heavy twisted balusters growing out of bulbous leaves. – *Minton* TILES in the chancel. – LECTERN. Given in 1909. Of iron and brass, and in an exceptionally convinced Art Nouveau. – FONT. Square, C12, of the standard Purbeck type with five flat arches each side. Five supports around a fat central stem. – ROYAL ARMS. Of George III, 1802. – STAINED GLASS. Two in the S aisle by *Percy Bacon Bros*, the first (1909) depicting Dorset saints. In the SW corner a Millennium window by *Tom Denny*, 2000. – MONUMENT. Michael Hankey †1942, by *Alfred F. Hardiman*, 1944. Bronze. A relief portrait in pilot's uniform.

OLD RECTORY, 150 yds S of the church. Of 1843 for the Rev. C.D. Saunders, by *Benjamin Ferrey*. Quite large, but tall and compact, not spreading. Mellow red brick. Stone dressings. (Puginian) Tudor style of course, and good of its kind.

BARTON FIELD, ¾ m. NW. A Romano-British settlement discovered in 1845 by Shipp, who recorded 'extensive remains of foundations and walls with stucco and coloured facings extending over an area of nearly twenty acres'. Further excavation started in 1968, and to date is involved with two buildings. Building I, 55 ft (16.8 metres) long and 42 ft (12.8 metres) at its widest, consists of an entrance hall and five rooms with a tessellated corridor in front of three of them. They were originally built as three rooms with a corridor; the two other rooms were tacked on later.

TARRANT KEYNESTON   9000

A straggle of farms and cottages along the Tarrant valley, crossing with the Blandford to Wimborne highway.

ALL SAINTS. The Perp two-stage W tower is somewhat overpowered by the replacement nave and chancel, of 1852–3 by *T.H. Wyatt* for Sir John Smith of Sydling St Nicholas (and costing £1,500). Banded stone and flint on the tower; flint with ashlar-block 'speckling' on the church. Full-blown N aisle with its own pitched roof (with a reused C18 Gothick window in the E bay). Wyatt's work is Perp, intended to match the tower. Competent interior with three-bay N arcade (and an additional opening beyond the chancel arch). – The only *Wyatt* fittings of note are the CHOIR STALLS. – LECTERN. Oak. Arts and Crafts-inspired,

1917, designed by *Adams & Holden*. – STAINED GLASS. Three chancel windows by *Powell & Sons*, 1853. Nave s window by *Hardman*, 1897. – MONUMENT. In the churchyard, table tomb to Thomas Bastard II †1731 and his son John †1778, 'mason and architect', and others.

TARRANT KEYNESTON HOUSE, ⅛ m. NE. Set back from the road. Early C19. Central L-plan block with single-storey symmetrical wings. Stucco with low-pitched slate roofs.

BUZBURY RINGS, 1¼ m. NNW. Iron Age hill-slope ENCLOSURE with Romano-British occupation to the end of the C5. An outer kidney-shaped enclosure and a sub-circular inner enclosure (3¾ acres) with hut hollows; much damaged by the present road. 'CELTIC' FIELDS integrated with linear DITCHES and TRACKS extend S, SW and E. A single-ditched ENCLOSURE (3¾ acres) lies *c.* 200 yds SE, buried by the golf course.

TARRANT LAUNCESTON
9010

A straggle of cob and thatch cottages. The chapel of ease to the w was demolished in 1762.

TARRANT MONKTON
9000

Tiny village, of nothing but diminutive cob and thatch cottages, gathered near the ford and in a street to the s of the church.

ALL SAINTS. Banded flint and stone. A chancel of *c.* 1400, reordered internally in the C18, when it was given a segmental vaulted plaster ceiling. C15 nave and two-stage W tower. N aisle (under a separate pitched roof) rebuilt during heavy restoration in 1873, when the chancel was refenestrated. s transept of *c.* 1840. Several C15–C16 square-headed windows. – PULPIT. Late C17, polygonal, with two panels per face with enriched edges. – FONT. C12. Purbeck stone, square with tapered side. Four flat blank arches to each side. Re-cut. Central stem support with a plain colonnette to each corner. – STAINED GLASS. E window, 1948, by *Abbott & Co.* of Lancaster.

BLANDFORD CAMP. *See* p. 124.

TARRANT RAWSTON
9000

ST MARY (now a private chapel). Immediately by the farm. A small early C14 church of flint and stone with hipped-roofed transeptal chapels added N and S. C16 s chapel, also the porch. C18 N chapel, also the chancel. Some straight-headed Dec windows, re-set in the chancel and N chapel. Semicircular arches to the chapels. Plaster barrel-roofs. – WEST GALLERY of 1805. – COMMUNION RAIL. Late C18, with handrail rising to meet the dado around the chancel. – PULPIT. Partly early C17. – PEWS. Early C19, some reusing C17 fielded panelling. – MONUMENT. Radford (†1788) and Thomas (†1805) Gundrey. Broken pediment and apron with skull-and-crossbones carving, entirely in the tradition of 1730–50.

RAWSTON FARM. An H in plan. The centre bar, of chequered flint and rubble, has on the S side windows with hoodmoulds, typical of the years before and after 1600, and on the N a huge projecting chimney-breast. The brick uprights of the H are a five-bay SE range of c. 1760 (the central bay flanked by pilaster strips) and a NW range of c. 1840.

TARRANT RUSHTON

ST MARY. Cruciform with long transepts. Banded flint and rubble, partly rendered. Early C12, twice rebuilt at the W end: in the later C12, and when a C14 tower of rectangular plan was hoisted over it, giving the impression of a church without a nave. Transepts added and chancel rebuilt in the C14, the N transept first, perhaps c. 1300. This has Early Dec windows. Slightly later the chancel, its E window with reticulated tracery. The S transept (narrower than the N) may be contemporary with the chancel. Straight-headed S window with ogee-arched lights, its tracery crudely adapted from a reticulated arched window. Norman chancel arch without mouldings or imposts (heavily restored). Sections of nave walling also early C12. Careful (for its date) restoration of 1875 by *Mr Legge* of Charlton Marshall. Above the S door is a re-set LINTEL, facing the inside of the church. Carved on it is the Agnus Dei, a man with a book, and a man with a bird. It was dated to the early C12 by George Zarnecki, who compared it with Daglingworth in Gloucestershire, though it is much coarser than Daglingworth. The delight of the church is three Dec SQUINTS, all with stone grilles, one an elongated six-cornered star, one a sexfoiled circle, one with reticulation units. In the chancel a fine cinquefoil-headed C14 PISCINA. – COMMUNION RAIL. C18, with widely spaced thin balusters. – PULPIT. Modern, of 1962 by *Potter & Hare*. – ARCHITECTURAL FRAGMENT. Early Norman volute capital converted to a piscina. – Two ACOUSTIC JARS of earthenware built into the chancel W wall. – ROYAL ARMS of George IV, dated 1825. – STAINED GLASS. E window by *Francis Skeat*, 1970. S transept E window by *Charles Evans & Co.*, 1887.

At the S end of the village a run of late C19 ESTATE COTTAGES at right angles to the lane.

THORNCOMBE

Set on a ridge, one street climbing steeply from the Stonelake Brook. They converge at the village hall. Much loss of earlier building in a fire of 1882.

ST MARY. Rebuilt in 1866–7 by *J. Mountford Allen*. A large town-sized church. The style chosen was Perp, some of the windows with tracery designs copied from the cloister range of Forde Abbey. High W tower. Embattled parapets. Aisles and transepts, arcade piers with four chamfered projections (cf. Bishop's Caundle and Maiden Newton). – REREDOS. Perp stone panelling, elaborated by some inlay and gilded painted panels. – CHOIR STALLS. Some linenfold panels, perhaps C16. – CLERGY DESK. Incorporating early C16 elaborated panels, separated and flanked by posts with standing figures. Also standing figures on the ends and an enriched top rail. – PULPIT. Early C16, with two tiers of linenfold panels re-set on a new base in 1867. – FONT. Medieval. Square bowl with sloping undersides. Stem and base, 1867. – STAINED GLASS. E window by *W.G. Taylor*, 1895. Two chancel side windows by *O'Connor & Taylor*, 1867, and one at the E end of the S aisle by the same, 1876. Another in the S aisle by *Taylor*, *c.* 1895. N aisle window perhaps by *Percy Bacon Bros*, 1924. – BRASS to Sir Thomas Brook †1419 and his wife †1437. The best brass in Dorset but, with the marginal inscription, heavily restored when it was re-set in the new church. The figures 5 ft 3 in. (160 cm.) high with shields. – OTHER MONUMENTS. William Bertram Evans †1850. Mildly Gothic tablet in veined marble surround. – Eleanor Isabella Evans †1898; Sarah Boyd Evans †1906. Two large brasses by *Gawthorp* of London.

THORNCOMBE CHAPEL, 130 yds S. Built for the Plymouth Brethren. Of 1883. Pointed, but not Gothic windows.

VILLAGE HALL, opposite the chapel. Of 1887–9 by *W.H. Evans* (paid for by his sister, Miss Evans of Forde Abbey). Arts and Crafts with decorative bargeboards and a big bay window.

SCHOOL HOUSE FARM, ¾ m. SW. C17 vernacular front, with hollow-chamfered mullioned windows (no hoodmoulds) and, in a different stone, central features of *c.* 1700, a classically moulded doorcase, and an oval window above.

FORDE ABBEY. *See* p. 292.

HOLDITCH COURT, 2 m. WSW. Sir Thomas Brooke obtained a licence to crenellate in 1397, and the surviving part of this semi-fortified manor must be of that date. It is without parallel in Dorset, and a sign of how close the wilder Far West is here. Just a round angle tower, faced with roughly squared flint, standing to almost its full height. There was a staircase inside. No windows. Boldly undercut string courses at two levels, the lower one sloping down at the NW, where the lost main part of the building stood. The adjoining HOLDITCH FARMHOUSE to the N is an adaptation of a C16 gatehouse. (Towards the S end of the farmhouse were two archways, removed *c.* 1900.)

Thorncombe, St Mary.
Brass to Sir Thomas Brook †1419 and wife †1437

SADBOROW, 1 m. s. Built, for £2,589 2s. 4½d., in 1773–5 by
John Johnson (who was County Surveyor for Essex), for John
Bragge. Neoclassical of the plain sort. Ashlar box, three-
storeyed, of five bays by seven. The entrance (E) front has the
ground-floor windows under slightly sunk arches, but is otherwise quite plain; the only enrichment is a plain sill band at first-
floor level and a cornice with Doric mutule-like decoration
below the blocking course of the thin parapet. The arcaded
skyline feature and the Soanic porch are additions, probably
of 1843 and for Col. William Bragge, mitigating the bareness. s
front with the centre three windows in a bold full-height bow.
The original Adamish front doorcase re-set. w wing of 1843,
part of a courtyard arrangement incorporating a greenhouse,
of which the free-standing pedimented arcade facing s was
another. The exterior then gives no hint that there is a domed
top-lit staircase in the centre of the house. Wrought-iron curly
balustrade panels separated by pairs of stick balusters. Simple
Adam-inspired decoration of the dome. It is approached down
a passage and beyond an arch treated on its inner side as part
of a columned Venetian motif. Spalatro capitals.

BROOM GRAVEL PITS, 3 m. WSW. A Lower Palaeolithic OCCU-
PATION SITE, the most important open-air archaeological site
of the earlier Palaeolithic age in south-west Britain.

THORNFORD

A collection of cottages and farmhouses, many thatched, on
the Sherborne to Yetminster road. Some recent infill mimicking
vernacular styles.

ST MARY MAGDALENE. Largely C14 Dec, especially the chancel
and three-stage embattled w tower. C15 E bay of the N aisle.
Restored 1865–6 by *R.H. Carpenter*. He added the porch and
extended the N aisle, the latter in Perp style with a fine arcade
inside. Dec tower w window with reticulated tracery. In the
two-light bell-openings pierced stone screens dated 1634. Also
Dec the arch to the nave resting partly on two big head corbels.
The tower ceiling has re-set C15 painted bosses. In the chancel
N wall a big ribbed rather than panelled arch, C16. E of this
a two-light Dec window. The chancel windows are otherwise
Perp, those on the s with a priest's doorway between. Nice C15
two-light window with cinquefoil heads re-set in the 1865–6
vestry. – REREDOS and PULPIT by *Carpenter*, both stone,
the former with mosaic by *Salviati*, the latter with polished
stone inlays. – PANELLING in the E corners of the chancel.
Early C17, reused from a pulpit. – SCREEN. C15. Five bays,
of stone (cf. Bradford Abbas). Two-light divisions, cinquefoil heads. Re-set under the 1865–6 chancel arch. – FONT.
C15. Octagonal with quatrefoils. Loose alongside a broken

C13 FONT BOWL. – Typical *Carpenter* (& *Slater*) FURNISH-
INGS. CHOIR STALLS with poppyhead ends, Y-ended open-
framed PEWS. – ROYAL ARMS. Painted on board, *c.* 1814–37.
– STAINED GLASS. C15 fragments in the chancel SE window.
Those in the tracery lights still *in situ*. E window and chancel
N both by *Clayton & Bell*, 1866. N aisle window by *Burlison &
Grylls*, †1892. W window also almost certainly by *Clayton &
Bell*, *c.* 1870–80. – BRASS. H.J.D. Wingfield Digby †1874. A
typical Victorian panel.

In the churchyard LYCHGATE, surely by *Slater & Carpenter*,
c. 1866. Also an exceptionally large Gothic Revival headstone
dated 1863.

WESLEYAN METHODIST CHAPEL (former), Longford Road.
1869. Lancets.

The church stands in a High Victorian enclave. To the N (beyond
the mid-C19 THORNFORD HOUSE) the former RECTORY of
1864–5 by *W. Slater*. The former SCHOOL dated 1862, S of the
entrance to Church Road, is also his.

At the centre of this large and urban-seeming village a Queen
Victoria Jubilee CLOCK TOWER, erected in 1897. Rubble
stone. Jacobean-looking top. Drinking-water spout in a niche.
The other buildings of note include PYT HOUSE, halfway
along Pound Road. Late C17. Symmetrical front, combining
hoodmoulded upper windows with lower windows under a
string course (hollow-chamfered mullions). Depressed-arched
doorway. WINGFIELD COTTAGE in Longford Road is similar
but with the doorway off-centre. Both are thatched.

On the road to Sherborne, two Gothic Revival farmhouses. LAKE
HOUSE (I m. NE) dated 1853. Steep gables. Bold chimneystacks. COURT HOUSE DAIRY (½ m. further NE) is smaller
but much the same. Dated 1850. Both by *R.H. Shout* for the
2nd Earl Digby.

THORNHILL HOUSE

2 m. s of Stalbridge

Status was something which artists of the Renaissance were seriously concerned about. And in England as late as the early
C18, Hogarth was complaining about the low social position of
the painter. But his father-in-law, *Sir James Thornhill*, not only
rose to a level where he could meet foreign artists on their own
ground, but gained a knighthood, and a fortune large enough
to buy back his ancestral estate in 1720 and build a country
house (largely demolishing the previous house on the site).
Thornhill was probably his own architect (cf. his design for
Blandford Town Hall) and created a modest but sizeable villa.
Its walls are rendered, rather than ashlar, with only stone for
the dressings, no doubt an economy.

Rectangular block with mildly Palladianizing pavilions at
the N and S ends, 1:3:1 bays, two-storeyed, with a hipped
roof and dormers, a somehow toy-like design. Small windows
in large areas of plain wall, but a large doorway in a broad,
channelled surround, a big round-headed window above. On
the N front only, swag panels to its l. and r., and a pediment
set up unexpectedly high. Quoins at all the angles. The S façade
is a simplified version and has been altered to accommodate
later additions. Seven-bay E front, the ends brought slightly
forward. Tudor fenestration on the ground floor by *John
Peniston* for William Boucher, 1829; W front rebuilt at the same
time.

Thornhill's gallery (recorded by William Barnes in 1832,
and in the 3rd edition of Hutchins) ran the length of the first
floor. It was subdivided by Peniston in about 1810. However,
a single carved chimneypiece of Thornhill's time survives in
the drawing room. Interiors again remodelled *c.* 2000 by *Tim
Reeve*. Of this date the bold plaster trophy on the main staircase
by *Geoffrey Preston*.

OBELISK, N of the house. Very tall and slender, erected by Thornhill in 1727 in honour of George II's accession. No doubt he
expected Court patronage. Blown down and reconstructed
in 1836.

TINCLETON

A strung-out village, with a few cottages with estate character
(some by *B. Ferrey*, *c.* 1850) interspersed between cob and thatch
cottages.

ST JOHN THE EVANGELIST. Rebuilt in 1849–50 by *Benjamin
Ferrey*. Nave with bellcote, and chancel. Mid-C13 (Early Dec)
style. – REREDOS. 1889. Of alabaster, elaborately cut. The
E wall l. and r. of the reredos has stone arcading. – OTHER
FURNISHINGS. *Ferrey*'s scheme is largely unaltered. – PULPIT
by *Ferrey*. Perp style, of Caen stone. – FONT. C12, round, re-
tooled, but interesting in form and decoration. From the stem
the outline tapers out and then tapers in again. The decoration
is upside scallops below, downward-pointing scallops above,
and their concave ends meet in a syncopated way. – STAINED
GLASS. Intensely coloured E window by *Mayer & Co.*, 1883.
In the N chancel windows, stamped quarries by *Powell & Sons*,
c. 1850. – MONUMENTS. Rachel Baynard †1667. Egg-and-dart-
bordered tablet with arms above and strapwork-framed apron
below. – Mary White †1717. At the foot of the tablet a skull
and two putto heads. – Henry Redhead Kindersley †1942 and
wife †1951. Beautifully carved inscription. By *David Kindersley*.
SCHOOL (former), just NW of the church. Of *c.* 1840 by *Ferrey*.
Brick with stone Tudor Revival windows. A carved panel with
a bishop's mitre in the gable-end.

CLYFFE HOUSE (now apartments), ½ m. NE. Built in 1842–4 for Charles Porcher by *Benjamin Ferrey*, in a Tudor or, in Eastlake's phrase, 'Manorial Gothic' style.★ It is manor-house size, and sits compactly before the wooded hillside; but close to it is nothing but Early Victorian, and the tall windows on the N (entrance) front impart a somewhat doleful look. Brown Broadmayne brick (English bond) and sharply cut Portland ashlar. Straight gables and scrawny chimneystacks, and exceedingly large mullioned-and-transomed windows. The N front has more incident than the others, where the E-plan is enlivened by gabled dormers as well as gables, and by the polygonal re-entrant projections. The internal planning is with rooms front and back of a spine corridor, crossed at intervals by lofty four-centred arches. The staircase is Pugin-inspired, but thinly designed in comparison.

TODBER

As is common in this area, a scattering of farmsteads and cottages, but here with only bungalows near the church. Shallow depressions in the fields tell of quarrying for the biscuit-coloured Todber limestone; the quarry-faces are visible here and there.

ST ANDREW. The S tower has medieval masonry. The saddleback roof, however, is Victorian, part of a rebuilding of the whole church in 1879, in E.E. and Perp styles, by *G. Hiscock* of Motcombe, paid for by Elizabeth, Marchioness of Westminster. – REREDOS. A reused part of the pulpit sounding-board, C17. – PISCINA. C15, with an ogee head. – FONT. C15, octagonal, extensively re-cut. – The churchyard CROSS was re-erected (somewhat incongruously) in the nave, at the W end, in 1983. It is made up partly of Anglo-Saxon pieces. The decoration is scrolly and indicates the late C10 or C11. – ROYAL ARMS. A lozenge dated 1663, with the motto 'Feare God, Honour the King'. – STAINED GLASS. Fragments of C15 glass in the small tracery lights of the E and nave N windows, the former the Carent arms. Chancel N window by *Lavers, Barraud & Westlake*, 1879.

ALLARDS QUARRY. *See* Marnhull.

TOLLER FRATRUM

The grey group of buildings on a knoll in the valley looks promising from afar, and lives up to its promise splendidly. Just the

---

★ Designs were exhibited at the Royal Academy in 1842 and 1844.

church and the farm, the one worth looking at inside, the other out.

St Basil. Rebuilt *c.* 1800, probably incorporating some medieval fabric. Restored 1854. Nave and chancel in one, mini bell-turret. Lancet windows, typical of 1800. But two Norman relics of importance. The SCULPTURAL FRAGMENT is of the scene of the Magdalene washing Christ's feet, in style close to the Chichester reliefs, and therefore *c.* 1125–50.* – FONT. Generally dated to the early C12, but the presence of interlace (*see* below) suggests an early C11 possibility. This is wholly different in style, the figures without any expression, the composition hardly to be called that. One half is doll-like figures, some larger acting as Atlantes, or doing this with one arm while the other reaches down to smaller half-figures. But on the other half of the bowl are just standing figures side by side and a whole scene with a quadruped simply shown turned by ninety degrees so that it all lies on its side. Also cable-moulding banding, and an upper band of interlace. COVER, *c.* 1800. Conical with a cross finial. – COMMUNION RAIL. C18 with turned balusters. – The other FURNISHINGS are largely of *c.* 1854.

Little Toller Farm. The house and the thatched outbuilding that lies forward to the r. are both the work of John Samways, who bought Toller Fratrum in 1539. The dressings are of Ham Hill stone, which no doubt explains why they are of unusual quality and include motifs found in other houses of the mid C16 near the Dorset–Somerset boundary. The house is a single long thin rectangular block, its w third a rebuilding (as the roof with collar-beam and arch-braced trusses runs the full length of the house, it seems that it is not an extension). The s front only is faced with ashlar, so was important; yet it does seem surprising that its single accent is a projecting gabled chimney-breast near the centre carrying two lofty twisted chimneystacks, and a gable finial carved as a monkey with a mirror. The chimneystacks themselves are replacements of the 1930s, not necessarily copying those of the C16. What seems likely is that there was built, or intended, a range at the w end (with the hall?) coming forward towards the s closer to the chimney-breast than the present w range, and possibly a third range with a gatehouse forming the s side of a quadrangle closed on the fourth side by the free-standing outbuilding which survives. Certainly the SE angle of the existing range was meant as a termination, for it has an octagonal buttress, fluted in its upper part, carrying a twisted shaft and wyvern as a finial. For such buttresses cf. Clifton Maybank, Athelhampton, and Bingham's Melcombe (Melcombe Horsey).

---

*It has been suggested that this piece may have come from Chichester, either when the screen there was dismantled in the C14, or in 1829 when stones from the screen were uncovered. *See* the Pastoral Measure Report, 2011.

Thinly detailed classical stone porch, probably added after 1867 by Lord Wynford of Wynford Eagle, who purchased the property in that year. Plinth moulding and first-floor string course, with a refined Perp moulding, are carried across the façade round buttress and chimney-breast, and the string course drops down tab-like labels for the ground-floor windows. The original windows here have been replaced by sashes, but those aligned above them remain, a two-lighter l. of the chimney-breast, and two of four lights to the r. Arched lights. Deep hollow enframing moulding. Tellingly, the string course vanishes in the w part of the range, reinforcing the argument for a s-projecting wing here. The E and N walls are of rubble, but the latter has the mid-c16 base-moulding and window hoodmoulds of the same refined profiles as their fellows round the front. The deep projection here must be for a staircase – see the irregular levels of the windows.

The mid-c16 OUTBUILDING looks humble enough, one-storeyed and thatched, but it is detailed in a way worthy of the house. From the string course above the two-light windows dangle, in lieu of labels, squat balusters of unmistakably Renaissance type, the only Renaissance detail at Toller Fratrum. Also, on a shield, Samways's initials and crest.

TOLLER PORCORUM 5090

A straggle of cottages along the confluence of the River Hooke and a side stream. It acquired a railway station on the Bridport branch in 1862.

St Peter and St Andrew. Dec chancel of flint and stone bands – see the ogee-headed squint and a small window, c. 1300. Late c14 nave, probably built from w to e, as the fine three-stage tower has Dec bell-openings, whereas the chancel arch is Perp. Complicating this progression is the Perp w window. The tower is embattled with good gargoyles, bold set-back buttresses and a polygonal s stair-turret. On the N side of the nave a blocked former N porch, late c14; a blocked w gallery doorway, probably of 1832–3 when a w gallery was installed; a high two-light window, seemingly c16 or c17; and a larger c15 window towards the e. But what makes a visit to the church worthwhile is the s aisle added in 1832–3. The windows are odd in a typical early c19 way. One mullion and one transom as if they were c17 work, and above tracery with the arch shanks straightened. The arcade on the other hand is of the restoration by *A.T. Taylor & G. Gordon*, of 1891–5: piers and segmental arches with continuous mouldings. At this time the plaster was stripped from the nave and aisle walls. – REREDOS. Perp-style Gothic stone framing to a painted triptych incorporating a Last Supper. Early c19. – Mosaic FLOORING in the sanctuary, late C19. – FONT. The Ham Hill stone bowl, small, octagonal and Perp with fleurons, is C15. It sits loosely upon a stem of white stone, probably the original C12 font. This has volutes resembling those on a capital. – ROYAL ARMS. Of William IV. A framed painted panel. – STAINED GLASS. E window by *Charles Evans & Co.*, 1890. Two chancel side windows by the same. Nave N window by *A.L. Moore*, 1924. S aisle window with sundial arrangement by *John Hayward*, 2000.

Former VICARAGE, just E. Of *c.* 1820, with Gothic glazing bars to its S front sashes. Good cast-iron GATES and GATEPIERS, also *c.* 1820.

TOLLER WHELME

5000

ST JOHN. Of *c.* 1868–71, designed by the donor, *William Pope* (the roof designed by his friend *R. Warr* of Beaminster). Nave, chancel and short S tower; E.E. S porch arch label stops carved by *B. Grassby*. All of the original FURNISHINGS are *in situ*, including the PEWS with fleur-de-lys ends. – FONT. Small and Gothic, perhaps by *Pope*. – STAINED GLASS. E window (1868) and nave N window by *Holland & Son* of Warwick. W window by *Cox & Son*, 1869.

MANOR HOUSE. At the rear a range with diagonal buttresses, probably *c.* 1470. It has a two-centred-arched doorway in the E wall, blocked and only partially visible. Also, at the E end, a large square-headed fireplace with mouldings. Front range of *c.* 1645 forming an L-plan. Thatched. Here typical stone-mullioned windows with hoodmouldings of that date. A second wing, parallel to the medieval one, added *c.* 1840 for William Pope. Much refitting internally of that date, including the twisting staircase with stick balusters.

TOLPUDDLE

7090

A long village, formerly on the main Dorchester to Poole road, thankfully bypassed in 1998. Mostly of cob and thatch, the many more recent infill houses successfully aping their appearance. There are several commemorative features relating to the Tolpuddle Martyrs, tried in Dorchester and transported in 1834.

ST JOHN THE EVANGELIST. Stone and flint. From tower arch to chancel arch a C12 nave. C12 S doorway with plain tympanum. Early C13 the flint lower parts of the W tower, with a corbel table. The W window and the rubble-stone bell-chamber are C15. Early C14 Dec chancel (see the doorway, re-set in the S wall) and N transept (pointed-trefoiled lancets). Also of this date the two-bay N arcade with continuous chamfers, and the arches into the N and the demolished S transept and the demolished chancel arch. Late C15 S nave window at high level. The chancel was remodelled in 1855 by *T.H. Wyatt*, hence the internal corbels with naturalistic vegetation. Much of the Dec-style fenestration elsewhere is of this date. In 2012 a nave N doorway was unblocked to give access to a new vestry by *Chris Romain Architecture*. On the aisle side its door covers the round arch. The nave has a C14 tie-beam roof. Crown-posts and four-way struts. – TILEWORK in the sanctuary by *Minton*. – STAINED GLASS. An extensive set by *Heaton, Butler & Bayne* of a variety of dates. An exception, and the earliest here, is the early and very fine chancel NE window by *Clayton & Bell*, *c.* 1860. This was probably designed by *R.T. Bayne*, who left to join *Heaton & Butler* in 1862. The E window is the earliest by that firm (†1866); two further chancel windows by them of *c.* 1873, perhaps contemporary with two N transept lancets. Then the large N transept window (†1893) and a nave S window (†1894). – MONUMENTS. Philip, a late C12 priest. Purbeck marble, the head closely surrounded by the cut-out shape of a stone block. Flat carving. Latin inscription in hollow-chamfered border. – A headstone in the churchyard commemorates James Hammett (†1891), one of the Tolpuddle Martyrs, 1934 by *Eric Gill*. Suitably underplayed.

METHODIST CHAPEL, ½ m. E. Dated 1861. Stucco and plain with a railed forecourt. In front the TOLPUDDLE MARTYRS ARCHWAY of 1912, the first commemoration of the Martyrs in the village.

MANOR HOUSE, just S. Dated 1656 on its handsome grey ashlar S front. It belongs to the group of mid-C17 manor houses which have abandoned the use of gables for effect in front, and rely solely on the stately rhythm of large windows. Tolpuddle is two-storeyed, of five bays, the windows of four mullioned lights with a transom. Wave moulding. One-storey porch with a round arch, and the date over the four-centred inner arch. Over the arch a bracket on vaguely classical consoles, carrying a monkey, crest of the Martyns of Athelhampton. End gables, of brick and brick banded with flint; an interesting sign that brick was not yet in mid-Dorset felt to be of equal beauty to stone. To the E of the church, on the small village green, the thatched SHELTER of 1934 (perhaps also by *Unwin, see* below) commemorates the Tolpuddle Martyrs.

T.U.C. MEMORIAL COTTAGES, at the W end of the village. Designed in 1934 by *Sir Raymond Unwin*. Six brick cottages with a gabled communal hall at the centre, now the TOLPUD-DLE MARTYRS MUSEUM, and return gables at the ends.

In front of the cottages, the MARTYRS' SCULPTURE by *Thompson Dagnall*, 2000. Six rough-stone pillars representing the six martyrs, with George Loveless, one of the men,

depicted realistically. On the back of his pillar, the poem by
Loveless:

> God is our guide! from field, from wave,
> From plough, from anvil, and from loom;
> We come, our country's rights to save,
> And speak a tyrant faction's doom:
> We raise the watch-word liberty;
> We will we will we will be free!

SOUTHOVER HOUSE, ⅜ m. s. Of 1861 for James Crane. Jacobethan in grey Portland ashlar. A rambling E–W range with
short cross-wings.

TOLPUDDLE BALL, 1 m. E. Iron Age and Romano-British SET-
TLEMENT, and CEMETERIES, with a post-Roman cemetery
to the w, excavated on the Tolpuddle by-pass, ¾ m. s of
Weatherby Castle hill-fort (*see* Milborne St Andrew).

5010   TRENT

A village on a hill, richly filled with late medieval and C17 houses
spread out, each in substantial plots. To this is added mid-C19
Gothic character, mostly at the behest of the Rev. W. H. Turner,
rector here from 1835 to 1875.

26   ST ANDREW. There are few churches in Dorset with so much
to enjoy, although its early C14 Dec architecture is unusual in
the county. This may be because Trent was, until 1896, part
of Somerset. The first joy is the exterior, with its slender Dec
s tower, best seen as the village is approached from the s. The
three stages of windows with Y-tracery, decreasing in elaboration as they rise, are a perfect preparation for the spire – one
of very few medieval spires in Dorset (rebuilt as part of a
sensitive restoration by *Temple Moore* in 1910–11). It is topped
by a copper WEATHERCOCK, dated 1698. The tower parapet
of pierced quatrefoils is above a trefoiled corbel table with
head corbels. Angle buttresses with carved gargoyles above the
topmost offset; crocketed corner pinnacles. The window to the
s is more complex; free tracery forms but no ogee yet. The N
chapel on the other hand has an E window with some ogee,
even if not conspicuous. Its N windows are of *c.* 1865 by *Slater
& Carpenter* as part of a restoration of the chapel; they are
more E.E. than Dec. The w window (blocked by the C19 organ
chamber) is a large lancet, probably C13. Attached to the tower
on its w side is the s porch, its sloping roof having an angled
version of the tower parapet on the front, this returning and
continuing along the nave (and repeated on the N side). The
chancel is C15 and lacks the elaborate C14 parapets. The nave
was lengthened by one bay to the w, perhaps in 1694 or 1729
(dates on the s wall), but refenestrated in Perp style in 1840–2

for the Rev. William Henry Turner by *R. J. Withers*. Of this date too the polygonal w vestry, quite a daring little addition (built as a baptistery), with re-set in its w wall a C15 doorway.

Turner's improvements of 1840–2 had even more effect within: the plaster rib-vault of the nave is of this date as are many of the FURNISHINGS. These alone are enough to keep one busy for hours. – REREDOS. Six bays of ogee-headed niches, presumably *c.* 1840, as is the faience work below dado level throughout the chancel. – Extensive floor TILEWORK here by *Minton*. – The Gothic COMMUNION RAIL seems also of the Turner period. – Good CHOIR STALLS of *c.* 1840, designed to match the screen. – Next the SCREEN itself, the best feature in a church full of good furnishings. Of the C15, no doubt installed as soon as the chancel was completed. It is the most gorgeous piece, up to the very best Devon standard. Five bays, the centre with matching doors, the l. bay forming a frame to the rood-loft doorway. Six-light divisions with elaborate Perp tracery; rib-vaulted coving, and top bands of foliage. Below the mid-rail the panels have crocketed flat canopies, but the painted images that would have filled each panel have gone. – A second low SCREEN to the N chapel. Early to mid-C17, with blank arches and a strapwork-like treatment above. – PULPIT. Brought in by Turner. This must be Netherlandish and may be of about 1600. Religious scenes and at the angles Mannerist nudes. An elaborate piece re-set on a plain stem with later steps and cornice. – LECTERN made up of panels of a Jacobean piece, probably the clerk's desk. – Perp-style FONT, C19. Octagonal. Its COVER is genuine C15. A pyramid of pierced tracery. – BENCH-ENDS. As complete a set as any, and only a few are not original work of *c.* 1500. The additional ones have the arms of W. H. Turner and the date 1840. The original ends have varied tracery, the Instruments of the Passion, and initials. Four ends bear the inscription 'Ave Maria gratia plena Dominus tecum Amen' ('Hail Mary full of grace, the Lord is with you. Amen'). They are straight-topped and again Devon–Cornwall in type. – Two BIERS, one *c.* 1900, the other dated 1757. – ROYAL ARMS. Painted wood in relief; Hanoverian.

STAINED GLASS. The E window is crowded with pieces from Germany, Switzerland and the Netherlands, collected by Turner. Arranged by *A. K. Nicholson*, 1932, restored 1947. The remaining chancel and nave windows are by *Wailes* of Newcastle, typically pre-Pugin Gothic and commissioned by Turner, 1842 and 1849. One nave S window contains an 1850 panel by *Joseph Bell* (Our Lord appearing to Mary Magdalene). The W window is also an assemblage, early glass at the top, then three figurative panels (maker unknown) dated 1842, and three further panels at the bottom. The other nave windows also incorporate European glass from Turner's collection. Fine S transept window by *O'Connor*, 1871. N chapel E window by *A. K. Nicholson*, 1931.

MONUMENTS. As there are so many here, it is best to take each location in turn. – S porch. Defaced priest in mass

vestments of the C14. Broken and loosely laid out on a medieval coffin. – Nave. Sir Francis Wyndham †1715, probably by
William Goodfellow of Salisbury (GF). Elegant white marble
tablet with classical surround. Corinthian columns. Four
putto heads in the corners of the inscription, a trophy in
the segmental pediment. – Chancel. Tristrum Storke †1530.
A painted stone panel with five shields of arms. – Thomas
Hussey †1630. Tablet with curved pediment and Corinthian
columns spaced away l. and r. – Mary Turner †1866 by *Forsyth
& Co.* Gothic niche, with a figure relief. – N chapel. In C19
tomb-recesses, a knight of the late C14 (see the helmet and
the low belt), and a C14 civilian in a gown, both with dogs at
their feet.* – William Gerard †1604. Tablet with pilasters and
a big coat of arms, tucked around the corner. – Ann Gerard
†1633. An achievement of arms with inscription panel below
and strapwork above, designed as the E respond of the N chapel
arch. Two supporting columns below. The painted decoration
on the back of the respond notes that it was restored by
J. Williams of Yeovil in 1792. – Rev. William Henry Turner
†1875. By *W. Theed*, dated 1853. Recumbent effigy; his hands
crossed over a bible. – Henry Danby Seymour †1877. Small
and pretty brass and enamel plaque, signed by *Barlow* of Old
Compton Street, Soho.

　　CROSS in the churchyard. C15 with the upper part of 1924.
A fine shaft with leaf motifs up the angles.

　　GATEPIERS. Mid-C19 Gothic, adding greatly to the picturesque effect.

The church is loosely surrounded by a remarkable group of stone
buildings of the C15 to the C17.

THE CHANTRY, the smallest, most complete and closest to the
church, was probably built *c.* 1500 for a chantry priest. Late
Perp. It is small perhaps, but tall and undeniably luxurious
with its handsomely moulded windows towards the road and
towards the churchyard. On both storeys they are of two lights,
with a transom, and two-centred, cinquefoiled above, under
the hoodmould. Some of them however look like modern
replacements. On the road front a big chimney-breast projects
immediately r. of the doorway. The doorway has a two-centred
head under a big square hoodmould. Its pair, on the churchyard end of a cross-passage, is similar but without the hood.
The fireplace opening inside is square, and on the deep rectangular panel above are three encircled quatrefoils displaying a
rose and two shields. Projecting chimney-breasts up the short
ends, and octagonal stacks for all three, the end ones very
short, the side one very tall.

DAIRY FARM, across the road, must be roughly contemporary.
The W end has original mullioned windows on two levels, with
typical Late Perp hoodmoulds with big square stops and deep

---

*Nigel Saul (*English Church Monuments in the Middle Ages*, 2009) suggests that the
second commemorates John Trevaignon † *c.* 1335, a lawyer.

hollow surrounds. Four square-headed lights below, the upper of two lights with cinquefoiled heads and a little tracery above. Mid-C17 S front, the continuous string course stepping up and down over the window heads.

CHURCH FARM, SW of the church. Here the worthwhile part is also of the C15, the only external clue to this date being the angle buttress at the SE corner. Inside there are three stone service doorways, two-centred-arched and broadly chamfered, the r. one with its original wooden door decorated like a blank Perp window. The hall, then, lay to the N, so what survives today was until the mid C16 the service end of the house. Its hall was meagrely rebuilt in the C17. In the S wall of a C17 extension, above an outbuilding, a re-set two-light traceried window, and hoodmould on crude headstops. Facing E, unexpectedly, a late C17 classical window, with a pediment on consoles and an eared surround. It looks as if it matches the windows on the E front of Sherborne Castle. Fine late C16 plaster ceiling in the drawing room. – PIGEON HOUSE, N of Church Farm. C17. Simple cob walls and a hipped thatched roof.

THE MANOR HOUSE, N of the church. Large and much altered. At its core a C15 hall house represented by a SE-facing range. Its windows are ovolo-moulded and probably of the same date as a seven-bay-long, NE-facing range, added at right angles in 1706 for Sir Francis Wyndham. Its two-light mullioned windows are an oddly out-of-date type to use, although these have a wave moulding and, instead of hoodmoulds, there are moulded architraves. A new twin-gabled NW front was added by *Carpenter & Ingelow* in 1876 for H.D. Seymour. Although this was taken down *c.* 1960, much of the remodelling carried out at that time remains, further complicating the accumulation.

THE RECTORY, across the road, NE of the church. C15 evidence too, though the front one first sees is modest mid-C18 classical, five bays wide. In the earlier rear wing a N doorway, low-set but of good quality, with a four-centred arch and large foliage spandrels under the hoodmould. Above a C16 or early C17 three-light window with more Continental glass from W.H. Turner's collection.

TURNER'S ALMSHOUSES. These too belong to the church group, at its N end, but date only from 1845–6 (perhaps by *R.J. Withers*). Tudor Gothic style. Stone, with tall octagonal chimneystacks and fish-scale tiled roofs. Charmingly arranged round a central courtyard with a Perp pump, one-storey blocks l. and r., and a four-centred archway in front and behind.

There is yet more to see in Trent if one follows the road to the E, though no built-up village street anywhere materializes. First comes MANOR FARM, on the l., bedrock C17 vernacular (dated 1660 on a re-set lintel), a symmetrical three-bay front towards the road. Then nothing more of note for a while until down Rigg Lane, FLAMBERTS, much more substantial vernacular of the C16 and C17. U-shaped towards the road. The r. arm must be earlier than the centre, which is cut back to avoid a pre-existing window. The centre in its turn must be earlier than the l. arm, for a hoodmould or two get lost behind the latter's walling. The date on the l. arm is 1658. But the central doorway, with a hoodmould parting company from the arched doorhead below, and two windows sharing a hoodmould, may well be very little earlier than that. Straight garden façade of seven bays, the windows uniformly ovolo-moulded, but not regular, and in the slight shifts in level suggesting work of different dates. Internally the layout is straightforward enough; hall in the centre running on behind the l. arm, where the kitchen is, and to the r. the private rooms. Two downstairs have moulded plaster ceilings, just beams covered up, and given thin ribs and sprigs of flowers in the main room.

OLD SCHOOL HOUSE, at the E extremity of the village. Of 1678 (according to a lost inscription), still in the mullioned-windowed vernacular. Four-, three- and two-light windows not quite making symmetry. Hoodmoulds to each lower window, one for all five upper windows together. Doorway slightly arched; stepped-up hoodmould. Successor SCHOOL by George Aitchison Jun., 1865.

HUMMER FARM, ¾ m. N. More C17 vernacular, but the facing is ashlar, not rubble. In the E wall a re-set C12 doorway on shafts with scalloped capitals.

TURNERS PUDDLE

Just the church and farm alongside a ford crossing the River Piddle.

HOLY TRINITY. Nave and chancel of c. 1500. Heavily rebuilt on the N side in 1759 following storm damage. Flint and stone. Short W tower, the top repaired. S wall of chancel rebuilt in 1859. – FONT. Late C12. Round, with tapering sides. Intersecting arches. Pellet enrichment of the spandrels and arch-heads. Contemporary round stem and base. (Brought from Affpuddle church.) – BENCH-ENDS. In the nave, of the type of Affpuddle, i.e. with small poppyheads, the arms rising into a scroll and Renaissance detail. The date no doubt also c. 1545–50. – STAINED GLASS. E window by *Joseph Bell* of Bristol, 1897.

TONERSPUDDLE FARMHOUSE, just E. Late C16 W range. Formalized and enlarged c. 1700 to create a symmetrical S front. Hipped roof.

THROOP, ⅓ m. SW, is a hamlet where characteristic thatched white-walled cottages line up with unusual formality in the bosky meadowland, headed at the N end by the red brick THROOP HOUSE, new-fronted in 1869.

CLOUDS HILL (National Trust), 1½ m. s. A forester's or labourer's cottage, built of cob in 1808. Gradually rebuilt in brick, 1922–33, by *T.E. Lawrence* for himself. Tiny. Greek inscription over the door: οὐ φροντίς ('Why worry').

TURNWORTH

8000

An estate village mainly of brick and flint cottage pairs of *c.* 1830. Turnworth House, a Gothick villa built *c.* 1800 for Mark Davis, lay up a valley to the w. It was demolished in the early 1960s.

ST MARY. Perp w tower of flint and greenstone. The church is of 1869–70 by *G.R. Crickmay*. The design is based on that by *John Hicks*, who received the commission just before his death in 1868. *Thomas Hardy* – working for Crickmay at that time – designed the capitals, which are of the French Early Gothic foliage kind (carved by *Boulton*). He probably also designed the corbels. – REREDOS. Also carved by *Boulton*. Three gabled niches with polished colonnettes. – Sanctuary TILES by *Minton*. – High-quality CHOIR STALLS, CLERGY DESK and PULPIT of the Crickmay–Hardy period. – FONT. Elaborately High Victorian with small figure scenes by *Boulton*. – STAINED GLASS. E window and one chancel s window by *Powell & Sons*, 1884 and 1903. Nave s window, †1876, by *Clayton & Bell*. w window, 1933 by *Burlison & Grylls*. – MONUMENT. Mark Davis †1832, by *Simmonds* of Blandford. Relief of a mourning woman by a sarcophagus.

RINGMOOR, 1 m. NW. A well-preserved prehistoric and Romano-British SETTLEMENT, unusual in that it includes two small circular enclosures with internal occupation features. There are 30 acres of associated fields, and field systems also exist over 60 acres of TURNWORTH DOWN to the e.

TYNEHAM

8080

Tyneham lies far inside the area owned by the Ministry of Defence and used for artillery practice. However, regular openings ensure that this tract of lovely hill and coast is at least occasionally accessible. Military activity has reduced the village buildings and Tyneham House to ruins, but the church is well preserved and the former village school is used as a small museum.

ST MARY. The plan of the church looks a Greek cross. Only parts of nave and N transept are C13 (E.E.). A PISCINA, *c.* 1300 with two trefoil heads. The chancel is late C19 in a plain E.E. style. Most of the furnishings have been removed and displays of village history installed around the walls. The best feature of the church is the Gothic s transept, built by *Ferrey* before 1852 for the Rev. William Bond. There are inscriptions round the windows and three MONUMENTS to members of the Bond family, identical canopied tablets. The dates recorded are 1846 (window), 1852, 1854, 1875, 1876, 1893 (monuments). – In the N transept a much-restored tablet to John Williams (†1580), the monument dated 1641, poorly and inaccurately repainted. Classical framing with armorial panel above. – STAINED GLASS. E window by *Martin Travers*, 1924. Two by *Powell & Sons*, 1911–12, the larger in the s transept.

In the village a K1 TELEPHONE BOX (replacement). Concrete panels, top cornice and iron finial cresting. The K1 was the first standard design of telephone box, first made in 1921.

TYNEHAM HOUSE, ⅜ m. E. The gabled E front was built for Henry Williams in 1583 (the date on the porch). It was taken down by the Ministry of Works in 1967, reportedly to be incorporated into Athelhampton Hall, and the porch doorcase rebuilt at Bingham's Melcombe, Melcombe Horsey (q.v.). The earliest part is a SW range, built for the Russell family in the C14. It still stands, mothballed against further damage (but not accessible to the public). An open hall with a roof structure of a collar-beam, arch-brace and wind-brace system, partially preserved. Here the cusping and the pierced quatrefoil above the collar show that it was designed for display as well as for stability. From 1683 Tyneham was owned by the Bond family of Creech Grange, from whom it was requisitioned in 1943.

FIVE BARROW HILL, 2¼ m. N. Two bowl barrows and three fine bells form a straight alignment along a low ridge.

WORBARROW BAY, HOBARROW BAY and BRANDY BAY. Evidence for Iron Age and Roman OCCUPATION and BURIALS, with shale working, Purbeck marble industries and salt extraction on the cliffs.

Medieval SETTLEMENT remains and fields cover much of the parish s of the chalk ridge, and 200 acres of strip fields survive.

UNDERHILL *see* PORTLAND, p. 490

6000

UPCERNE

Upcerne's position in a bowl of the downs is made lovely by the contrast between parkland trees in their prime and the bare backs of the hills.

CHURCH. Flint and stone bands. The church stands close to the manor house. It was rebuilt (except for the early C16 chancel) in 1870, including the W tower, in a C15 Perp style. Three-light re-set C15 E window. – PULPIT. Early C17. Octagonal with reeded panels. – FONT. Late C12, square, of the familiar Purbeck type. Tapering with scalloped decoration. Central column stem with four colonnettes. – SCULPTURE. Small figure over the porch entrance, C15. – STAINED GLASS. A memorial window by F.C. *Eden*, 1915.

UPCERNE MANOR. Built before 1624 by Sir Robert Mellor, but much altered *c*. 1840, and restored *c*. 1875–80 for John Batten. Further changes *c*. 1970. Rubble stone. As it stands the entrance (W) front is completely informal and largely of 1624. The E front is a symmetrical composition with battlemented centre and flanking four-sided window bays, added *c*. 1875–80. Its style seems more mid-C16 than early C17. That Batten was an antiquary is no doubt the explanation. The W front is aiming towards the normal E-plan, with gables slightly projecting, but with only a one-storey porch, and an extra, deeper projection r. of the N gable. Weird chimney-breast climbing across the S gable to get the smoke out of the gable-top. Windows of two and three lights, with hoodmoulds and arched lights, seemingly very *retardataire* nationally, but not so in Dorset (cf. Chantmarle, 1612, Lulworth Castle, *c*. 1608, and Stafford House, West Stafford, of as late as 1633). The transomed windows on the E front between the gables are of *c*. 1970. Oddly angled side doorway in the S gable-end. Compact plan, of rooms two deep. N projection, lower, with gabled dormers, basically contemporary with the house (see the E side), but the W wall rebuilt in brick, diapered, early in the C18 perhaps. A Great Chamber is recorded by Hutchins that ran the full length of the S wing on the upper floor. It had elaborate plasterwork and was no doubt comparable with that at Herringston (Winterborne Herringston). Together with its great stair, it was stripped out in the 1840s.

UPTON HOUSE

1¾ m. NW of Poole

A stuccoed villa in a small park, built *c*. 1815 for Christopher Spurrier, son of a Poole Newfoundland merchant. Rendered. The N front has a rusticated centre with a pediment and Ionic portico. The colonnaded screen walls (1825) have delicate curves and counter-curves, the finest feature of this front. On the routine S front, two-storey bows in the end bays. Pretty friezes of swags and bucrania everywhere. Central domed hall with circular landing. The plain single-storey E wing and chapel by *John Peniston* were added after 1830 for Sir Edward Doughty.

6080

UPWEY

A village following the valley of the Wey from just above its source to Broadwey, the next settlement.

St Laurence. A large church with a late C15 two-stage w tower, nave and N aisle with Late Perp arcade. Added to these, and changing the scale of the church, a s aisle and s arcade of 1838 (broadly matching the N),* a clerestory of 1841, and a chancel of 1906 by *Crickmay & Son*. There was also a restoration in 1891 by *J. T. Micklethwaite*, removing three galleries, including the w gallery of 1685; the nave FURNISHINGS are largely of that date. Of the late C15, the N windows and leaf-band capitals are good indicators. – PULPIT. Mid-C17, but still with Jacobean elaboration. Two tiers of blank arches and strapwork panels. – FONT. Re-cut C15, octagonal. Two rosettes to each face. – TILEWORK by *Minton* in the chancel. – SCULPTURE. Three panels with standing figures, about 4 ft (1.2 metres) high, re-set either side of the tower arch and on the chancel s wall. Brought from Italy in the late C18 and formerly incorporated in a pedestal raising the height of the pulpit. – WALL PAINTING. N wall, three fragments of C16 texts with borders. – ROYAL ARMS. Of Queen Victoria. Carved wood. – STAINED GLASS. E window, c. 1840, but re-set in 1909 tracery. A confection of strident, almost modern, colouring. It incorporates panels of C17 Flemish or German origin. N aisle window of 1894 by *C. E. Kempe*; another in the s aisle of 1909 by *Kempe & Co*. – MONUMENTS. The best is in the chancel: Rev. John Gould †1841. By *H. Hopper*. Large, with a female figure in high relief. She is standing by a pedestal with an urn. – N aisle, Sarah Floyer †1733. Curved pediment with cherub's head.

CHAPEL (formerly Congregational, later Methodist), Church Street, ½ m. SE. Dated 1809. Of Portland stone, originally all plain Gothic windows. A window of five ornate Gothic lights added to the front in the late C19.

CONGREGATIONAL CHAPEL (former), Dorchester Road, ¾ m. SE. 1880–1 by *R. C. Bennett*, built as a successor to the above. More boldly Gothic, its front gable flanked by spirelet-topped turrets. Big traceried w window. Transepts with rose windows above lancets.

Surrounding the roughly triangular green, at the junction of Church and Stottingway streets (⅝ m. SE), three large houses.

UPWEY MANOR, to the s. The earliest part is N-facing and roughly symmetrical. Centre dated 1639 (for John Gould), where the doorway was, now a large window. This between slightly projecting gabled wings. The gable apexes bear chimneystacks in the C17 way. Most windows renewed. Towards the E one original window, of three mullioned lights with a

---

*This may have been by either *John Barnes* of Dorchester or *John Spinks* of Charminster, according to ICBS records.

hoodmould, and a gable carrying two brick chimneystacks. s front planned like the N, but less regular and more heavily rebuilt. Hall window here. Later C17 block on the w side. Here a doorway with moulded jambs and paterae in the spandrels, probably relocated from the N front. Large sw wing of *c.* 1920, roughly doubling the size of the house.

Pair of fine GATEPIERS, *c.* 1700. Alternating rusticated blocks. Gadrooned urns.

WESTBROOK HOUSE, w, in its own small parkland. From the road a three-bay mid-C18 house is seen. But on the w side (much obscured by additions) are the remains of a sizeable early C17 house built for Sir Thomas Freke. This has a two-storey porch, not specially remarkable, with a low service wing to the N. Inside, occupying the centre of the N front, and lit by an C18 Venetian window, the hall, its flat plaster ceiling covered with the usual Jacobean interweaving ribs and small floral and heraldic devices. Here also a Gothick fireplace of *c.* 1760, the lower half copied from *Batty Langley*'s *Gothic Architecture Improved* (1747), plate 47. Three mid-C18 additions surround the C17 hall on the w, s and E sides, the latter forming the present entrance. These plain ashlar blocks were added for John Floyer. Doorway flanked by large Tuscan three-quarter columns. Tall sashes on the first floor of the s (garden) front, and the wrought-iron balcony there, are alterations of *c.* 1806 for Nicholas Daniel.

Fine mid-C18 rusticated GATEPIERS and a BRIDGE over the River Wey at the entrance.

EASTBROOK HOUSE, on the NE corner. Italianate of *c.* 1850.

Halfway between this group and the church, UPWEY MILL. A telling group, of three-storey mill and separate mill house with pedimented doorcase in front. The mill is dated 1802 and contains much of its original machinery.

UPWEY HOUSE, ⅓ m. SE. On the hillside, a picturesquely composed Tudor Revival house of *c.* 1840 for the Rev. George Gould. Gabled.

RIDGE HILL, 1 m. NW. Several linear groups of ROUND BARROWS are visible on the skyline along the South Dorset Ridgeway, on and near the parish boundary with Winterborne St Martin. They include 'RIDGEWAY 7', now an irregular mound next to a reservoir. Excavated in the 1880s, it contained burials accompanied by a bronze axe and three daggers, one with a gold pommel.

RIDGEWAY HILL, ¾ m. NE. Clusters of ROUND BARROWS, much reduced by ploughing (*see also* Bincombe).

VIKING MASS GRAVE, 1 m. NE. In 2009, in cutting the new road, a mass grave of some fifty-two executed males was excavated on RIDGEWAY HILL; dated to 970–1025. These victims of Scandinavian origin were beheaded at the prominent location at a time when Viking (Danish) raids are recorded. Possible historical contexts include the ravaging of Portland in 982, and of Dorset in 998, 1015 and 1016, or perhaps the St Brice's Day Massacre of 1002, when King Æthelred ordered that all Danes be killed.

WINDSBATCH, ¼ m. s. A CROSS-RIDGE DYKE, prehistoric.

VERWOOD

Until major post-war expansion, Verwood consisted of small groups of cob and thatch cottages built on former common land and a few larger late C19 and early C20 villas. The town is now almost as large as Ferndown.

St MICHAEL AND ALL ANGELS, Church Hill. A chapel with lancet windows of 1829 was refaced in red brick by *H.T. Shillito* of Hatfield, 1886. In 1893 *Adye & Adye* of Bradford-on-Avon added the ashlar-faced chancel (replacing a chancel of 1870) and refitted the nave. The chancel arch with naturalistic foliage is theirs. The fine painting of the chancel wall and roof appears original. A major extension of 1981 by *Pantlin & Bradbury* surrounds the nave. Concrete aisle arcades were introduced. – SCREENS by *Adye & Adye*. Alabaster dado, with wrought iron above. – The FONT is also by them. Octagonal alabaster bowl on a Purbeck marble stem. – STAINED GLASS. E window by *Burlison & Grylls*, 1906.

METHODIST CHURCH, Vicarage Road. 1909. Brick. Round-arched windows.

UNITED REFORMED CHURCH (formerly Independent), Manor Road. 1906. Brick. Lancet style with matching porch. It replaced a chapel of 1877 that stands alongside, now used as the LIBRARY.

THE HUB, Brock Way. A multi-function community centre by *NVB Architects*, 2007. Mixed materials, including brick, zinc cladding and timber boarding. Highly expressive of the volumes within.

WALDITCH

St MARY. 1849–51 by *Richard Cornick* of Bridport. Nave with bellcote and chancel. Also a N aisle. Lancets. A good E.E.-style chancel arch. – FONT. Late C12, a shallow square bowl. Purbeck marble. The leaf spandrels on the top are identical with Netherbury. On the sides variations of treatment: scalloped; fleurons; and, more curiously, radiating arrows. C19 stem and base. – FURNISHINGS. Not elaborate, but complete. All presumably by *Cornick*. – STAINED GLASS. The nave s window has intricate floral elaboration and roundels with inscriptions, †1877. – MONUMENTS. Edward Cameron Gundry †1869. A heavily Gothic piece with two colours of colonnette. – Daniel Joseph Stone †1862. Gothic of a simpler kind. By *W. Fry* of Bridport.

Walditch, The Hyde.
Lithograph, after J.H. le Keux, 1861

SCHOOL (former), immediately N. Dated 1860. By *John Hicks*.
Two gables to the front, the l. containing the schoolroom with
five graduated thin lancets (repeated at the back).

THE HYDE, 300 yds W. 1852–3 by *H. Bastow* for Joseph Gundry,
added to an earlier house at the rear (burnt down in 1929).
Multi-gabled Jacobethan. Many pinnacles to the gables and
tall octagonal multi-shafted chimneystacks. Vernacular-style
rear wing of the 1930s. Elaborate dining-room decoration with
gold-embossed Russian leather wall coverings. Drawing room
in a sub-Adam style.

   STABLES and REAL TENNIS COURT, just E. Of 1887 by
F. Cooper of Bridport. Here the Jacobethan looks thinly
stretched over the bulk of the tennis court. The latter was
built principally to entertain the Prince of Wales, a regular
visitor to The Hyde.

STRIP LYNCHETS to the N, E and S.

WAREHAM

9080

The great glories of the town's setting are its location between
two rivers, and its protection by a rectangle of low earth ramparts,
the *burh* defences, built up during the reign of Alfred the Great
(probably *c.* 880).* Of the stone wall added a century or so later
nothing is now to be seen. The flood plain of both rivers has forced
later C19 and C20 development away from the Anglo-Saxon core,

---

*The walls are on three sides of the town with the fourth to the S 'defended' by the
River Frome. There are also indications within or near the walls of occupation from
the Iron Age and Romano-British periods.

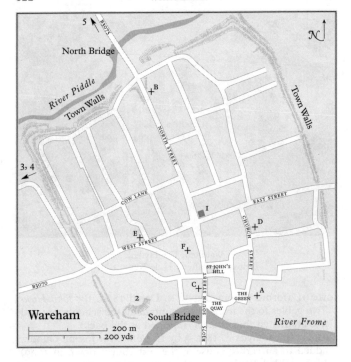

A	Lady St Mary	I	Town Hall
B	St Martin	2	Castle
C	Holy Trinity (former)	3	Lady St Mary Primary
D	Old Meeting House		School
E	Congregational church	4	Christmas Close Hospital
	(former)	5	Railway station
F	Free Unitarian church (former)		

so that the approaches to Wareham from the N, across the River Piddle, and from the S, across the broader Frome, are invitingly abrupt. The former is especially telling in the way that the road rises between two high retaining walls (with on the l. the late Saxon St Martin's church), and levels out several feet higher once the town interior is reached. Since the layout, almost certainly in place before the Conquest, is of two main streets crossing at the centre, there remain two further approaches to mention. A road from the W (from Dorchester) was the main access route prior to the building of bridges; here there is something of an excursion of more recent building beyond the town walls. To the E a lane left the town to reach the water meadows of Bestwall.

Settlement within the defences was initially concentrated around the River Frome and the town quay. Wareham was the main seaport in this part of the South Coast until superseded by Poole in the C14. By the C18 all four main streets had almost continuous frontages of buildings, many of which were destroyed by a great fire in 1762. (A total of 133 buildings were lost, some two-thirds of the town.) As a result, most houses today are post-fire rebuilds, although a few structures of the late C16, C17 and early C18 evidently survived the fire. The railway arrived (at Northport, the northern town suburb) in 1847. In the 1990s a by-pass to the W of the town was completed, which, together with hitherto largely successful planning policies, has continued to preserve the precious landscape setting of Wareham.

CHURCHES

LADY ST MARY. Apart from a few fragments, and some short lengths of wall at the W end of the aisles, nothing survives of the major early Anglo-Saxon minster, whose foundation c. 700 by St Aldhelm is recorded by William of Malmesbury. These fragments, and drawings of the church prior to rebuilding, suggest that what was destroyed may have been largely of the C10. The loss is mostly owed to *T.L. Donaldson*, who rebuilt the nave in 1841–2 (at a cost of £2,200). His style combines the Commissioners' type of long two-light lancets (four of them N, four S, widely spaced) with Perp arcades within. It must be admitted that what Donaldson destroyed was, according to an old drawing, not obviously attractive at that time. However, a more sensitive response could have revealed the pre-Conquest work, with some judicious pruning of the poorest and most recent of the additions. This was the opportunity that he missed. That much of the Saxon character still existed is evident from the survey carried out by Donaldson in 1840 and watercolours made based on sketches of the building before its restoration. The nave had round-arched arcades of six openings on the N and seven on the S sides. The piers were T-shaped, with cross-arches in the aisles (i.e. with the stem of the T supporting the aisle arches), there was a clerestory, and two *porticūs* stood at the location of the chancel arch (although not aligned with each other).

p. 19

So what then remains of St Mary to enjoy? The W tower is Perp, of c. 1500, four stages with a battlemented parapet, but the W window is 1869 (in a violently orange stone). The early C16 porch looks heavy-handed against the comparative delicacy of the Perp tower. Bold panels in the spirit of the Renaissance to the front parapet, which drops in height oddly on the sides. Two further attachments to the tower. The N vestry is contemporary with the porch. It has a blocked doorway with Tudor roses in the spandrels and an original two-light window on the N side. On the S side a lean-to porch of 1841–2 with a Norman-style doorway, *Donaldson*'s token nod at what he destroyed. Before entering it is worth looking at the chancel of c. 1325, especially the fine seven-light E window with a net of reticulated tracery in its head. Also here, on the S side, the tiny BECKET CHAPEL, contemporary with the chancel and built into an over-stout SE corner buttress, and, to its W, ST EDWARD'S CHAPEL of c. 1100 with an upper storey of the C13. Both fortunate to have been spared by Donaldson, these are the highlights to be visited within.

INTERIOR. *Donaldson*'s broad and lofty nave scarcely dis-
tracts attention from the chancel with its fine E window, previously mentioned. In the N wall a beautiful late C13 window
with bar tracery (three sexfoiled circles), presumably reused
from the previous chancel. A window of the same style, also
probably from the N aisle of the chancel, is re-set in the organ
chamber (1893 by *Crickmay & Son*). It has a circle in the
tracery too, but filled with six mouchettes. In the E wall of the
N aisle a circular window of *c.* 1100, and above it a C15 traceried window, both re-set. Also here a C13 DOUBLE PISCINA.
Inside the chancel the SEDILIA and DOUBLE PISCINA are
Dec too, with very thin shafts. S of the chancel are the two
vaulted chapels. The miniature early C14 BECKET CHAPEL is
the more unusual, 9 ft (2.7 metres) long inside, and covered by
an ingenious lierne vault starting from six wall supports with
the ribs running from each of them to two of the other points.
The result is a lozenge as the centre motif. The chapel has a
small C15 three-light E window. The ST EDWARD'S CHAPEL
of *c.* 1100 has its entrance from the E end of the S aisle. This is
Norman of the simplest. Above it is a scalloped arch with an
ogee gable peak, Dec in style, but is it C19? The chapel is sunk
by several steps. Above it was a room, perhaps for a chantry
priest. The present upper storey was built in the early C18. The
lower chapel has rib-vaulting of the early C13, in two bays. The
ribs are single-chamfered and rise from Purbeck shafts with
Purbeck capitals. In the chapel are two cinquefoiled TOMB-
RECESSES and a trefoiled PISCINA, both late C13.

20   FURNISHINGS. FONT. C12, hexagonal. One of the characteristic Norman lead fonts of England. Twelve statuettes of
Apostles under arches, two per face. Architecturally detailed
with grouped shafts and cushion capitals and bases. On a
C13 hexagonal Purbeck marble pedestal with attached corner
shafts. – Another FONT, octagonal and perfectly plain, except
for initials and the date 1620, in the N aisle. Brought from Holy
Trinity church (*see* below). – Most of the nave FURNISHINGS
are of 1882 by *John Colson & Son* of Winchester. Except for
the PULPIT, they are relatively unremarkable. – Five INSCRIP-
TIONS. In the S porch, and at the E end of the N aisle, a uniquely
instructive series of the C7 to the C9, similar to inscriptions in
Wales. They are cut on Roman architectural fragments. This
may imply post-Roman continuity of occupation, but no trace
of the settlement is yet known. Two (Nos. 2 and 4) are loose
fragments, one (No. 1) is re-set in the S porch, the others
(Nos. 3 and 5) are re-set at the E end of the N aisle. They
were uncovered in various locations in the church during the
1841–2 works. In chronological order: No. 1: VIDCV.../FILIVS
VIDA...; No. 2: IUDNNE.../FIL(I) QUI...; No. 3: CATGUG .C. ../
FILIUS . GIDEO; No. 4: DENIEL . FILIUS/AUPRIT . IACET;
No. 5: GONGORIE.*

---

*A more detailed analysis and interpretation of these stones is in RCHME, *Dorset*,
vol. 2 (1970).

STAINED GLASS. The great E window is by *Clayton & Bell*, 1886–90. The remaining windows are mostly a continuous campaign by *Percy Bacon Bros*, 1903–27. The earliest are almost as fine as Clayton & Bell, but the quality falls off. In the S aisle a window by *J. & L. Gilroy*, 2000. Brightly coloured and highly effective W window by *Andrew Johnson*, 2011, depicting the empty Cross and the town of Wareham. – MONUMENTS. Two Purbeck marble knights, both cross-legged, and both of before 1300. The earlier one – see the coif and the pillow – is chancel S, probably Sir Henry d'Estoke, mid-C13. The other is chancel N, probably Sir William d'Estoke †1294. – Also a number of fine tablets, including Arthur Addams †1724. A very pretty Rococo cartouche (N aisle W). – Anthony Trew †1771. Delicately designed, with a Baroque pediment. – John Barker †1819. Inscription on a shroud draped over a rectangular panel. By *Kendall* of Exeter. – Many other tablets, including a plain oval one (in the St Edward's Chapel) with inscription to John Hutchins, the county historian, †1773.

ST MARTIN, North Street. A small church standing on the town rampart, adjacent to the site of the north gate. Whereas for Lady St Mary the Anglo-Saxon state of the building has to be deduced from a drawing, here the majority of the nave and chancel fabric is Saxo-Norman of the C11. Tellingly the nave is relatively narrow for its height, another pre-Conquest indicator, as is the long-and-short quoining on the E corners of the nave and chancel. The S tower, for all its primitive appearance, is dated C16, with the top rebuilt in 1712 (as indicated on a panel over the doorway). It has a saddleback roof. Once inside, the atmosphere too is Saxo-Norman with later enhancements. Starting with the chancel arch, this is largely intact and has the characteristic opening surrounded on the wall at a distance from the arch itself by a hoodmoulding, semicircular in section, which originally ran down to the ground parallel to the arch reveals. Almost intact is the bold semicircular soffit moulding, taken up by attached half-colonnettes. An impost with chamfered lower edge extends l. and r. to the nave corners. The interruptions to this are two later squints and a trefoil-headed niche. A small chancel N window may also be original. The N aisle was added *c.* 1180. Two-bay arcade originally with paired Purbeck shafts at the responds and a cluster of four on the central pier. Only those of the E respond survive; the central pier is an C18 replacement. The C12 capitals are of the crocket variety. Most windows are C15, those in the W wall of the nave and aisle contemporary with rebuilding work here (hence no long-and-short at the W end). Sensitive restoration of 1936 by *W.H. Randoll Blacking*. 7

FURNISHINGS. FONT. Dated 1607. Square with angled corners. It stands on rough-hewn stone posts. Underneath (loose) is the base of the missing N arcade C12 pier. – MURAL PAINTINGS. These give the place much of its Romanesque character, although the work is of several periods. Traces of two scenes with horsemen on the chancel N wall (from the life of St Martin); c12. Also ornamental painting in the E window reveals, c15. On the nave E wall traces of a star pattern; c15. Also much later work, e.g. *c.* 1600 black lettering around the chancel arch and parts of a Decalogue, mostly overpainted in 1713 by a royal arms flanked by a contemporary Decalogue in two panels. – MONUMENT. T.E. Lawrence (of Arabia) †1935, who lived at the end of his life near Turners Puddle and is buried at Moreton church (qq.v.). Recumbent Purbeck stone effigy by *Eric Kennington* with Lawrence in full Arabian costume. Installed 1939.

HOLY TRINITY, South Street (now in community use). Early c16 two-stage W tower, c14 nave and chancel in one. E wall (to the street) rebuilt in the c17, when the window was simplified. Two-bay N arcade to a former chapel. Octagonal pier.

OLD MEETING HOUSE (Congregational, now United Reformed), Church Street. 1762. Arched upper windows, *c.* 1830. Sunday School wing, l., 1860. Long porch and r. wing, *c.* 1895. Internally the parallel roofs are supported on two rows of tall timber columns.

CONGREGATIONAL CHURCH (former), West Street. 1790, by *G. Gollop* of Poole and *J. Swetland*. Stuccoed. Three-bay front with panelled pilasters and pediment. Only the front retained in housing development, 1988.

FREE UNITARIAN CHURCH (former, now Wareham Conservative Club), South Street. 1830. Stuccoed. With a projecting giant portico of rather provincial unfluted Ionic columns and an attic. No pediment. Plaster barrel-vaulted interior.

PUBLIC BUILDINGS

TOWN HALL, North Street. 1869–70 by *G.R. Crickmay*. Vaguely Gothic, but almost French Renaissance in its upper storey – so a stylistic muddle. However, its spiky corner bell-turret is a suitable eyecatcher at the central crossroads of the town. Inside, the ROYAL ARMS of William III, in high relief.

CASTLE, Pound Lane. Nothing is left except a slight mound in the SW corner of the town, with a detached house (Castle Close) of 1911 sitting incongruously upon it. Excavation in 1952–3 found masonry foundations of a keep, datable to the early c12.

LADY ST MARY PRIMARY SCHOOL, Streche Road. 1969–70 by *J.R. Hurst*, County Architect. A grouping of flat-topped school and split-gabled caretaker's house.

CHRISTMAS CLOSE HOSPITAL (former), Christmas Close. Built as the workhouse in 1836–8 by *O.B. Carter & H. Hyde* on the approved Greek-cross plan. Octagonal centre part; nothing further by way of architectural elaboration. Converted to residential use in the 1990s.

RAILWAY STATION, Northport. Dated 1886 (opened the following year), for the London & South Western Railway. Rebuilt on a new site in connection with the Swanage branch line. Dutch-Flemish style. Red brick and ashlar. Two tall gables face the forecourt, one bearing the company arms, the other more elaborate.

The original station of 1847 (by *Sir William Tite*) stood further E, of which the GOODS SHED, standing at a curious angle to the track, survives. Converted to their offices by *Morgan Carey Architects*, 2010. Also a standard Southern Railway SIGNAL BOX of 1928.

PERAMBULATION

Wareham's streets are on a cruciform plan. We start at Lady St Mary church to the S and head up to the central crossroads, before turning E, N and W in turn.

First THE PRIORY HOTEL, immediately S of the church. Built on the site of a C12 priory, founded as a cell of Lire in Normandy and bestowed on the Carthusians in 1414. Nothing here is earlier than the C16, represented by a rectangular block on the S side of a central courtyard. Here there are traces of buttresses and of two transomed two-light windows for the one-storey hall, which lay W of the parlour. Some C17 fenestration dating from the insertion of an upper floor into the hall. To the r. a large chimney-breast. Assorted C17 ranges to the N, creating a rambling, cottagey group, part rubble stone and part C18 brick. Drawing room at the E end of the S range with intersecting ceiling beams, presumably representing the extent of the C16 parlour.

W from the church and priory is CHURCH GREEN, an informal space with two W exits. That to the l. leads between brick and tile cottages to THE QUAY, Wareham's happiest urban space if it were not for the continually parked cars. A large late C18 house on the E side with, beside it, a contemporary three-storey former WAREHOUSE, its gable (rebuilt *c.* 1930) facing the river. Simple mid- to late C18 whitewashed brick houses on the N side lead to SOUTH STREET and the brilliant white concrete of the SOUTH BRIDGE, 1927–9, replacing one of 1778.

So up SOUTH STREET towards the centre, passing the reticent COUNTY LIBRARY of 1976 on the E side, and Holy Trinity church on the W (*see* p. 626), taking a brief detour to the E to look at ST JOHN'S HILL, again used as a car park but with houses of greater gentility as one moves away from the quay. The best, MINT HOUSE on the S side, has a replacement brick frontage of *c.* 1800 and a strikingly casual sequence of bay window, pedimented doorcase and four-pane wide sash. On the E side of the space, other houses of the mid C18 have been refronted in the early C19 as well (see the use of stucco and sash windows with wide proportions).*

*The previous edition also mentioned TRINITY CLOSE, infill housing by *D.F. Martin-Smith*, 1968–9, in Pound Lane, W of South Street. It is described as 'thoughtful'.

Back in SOUTH STREET, the town's two best houses come next. The BLACK BEAR on the W side is that characteristic thing, a striking inn of *c.* 1800. Three storeys; full-height bows l. and r. of a columned porch carrying the eponymous bear. On the E side, set back behind railings and high hedge, the MANOR HOUSE, dated 1712 (for George Gould) on the lead roof. The house, of Purbeck stone, by its design asserts its superiority further. Three tall storeys and a top balustrade. Five bays, the centre brought forward a little. Small, even quoins here and at the angles. Plain window surrounds and string courses, throwing into even greater prominence the outstandingly elaborately carved and shaped doorway. Segmental pediment, and fluted obelisks in relief l. and r., set on shaped pedestals: a curious composition. Much of the architectural eccentricity continues within, especially a curiously elaborate cupboard recess in the drawing room to the l. of the entrance hall. Last on the E side, LLOYDS BANK, a mid-C18 house given a new stucco front with balustraded parapet in the mid C19.

At the central crossroads, the RED LION HOTEL on the NW corner is the best representative of the simple brick style of Wareham's rebuilding after the sweeping fire of 1762. White brick with red brick dressings. Facing it, on the SW corner, is its more normally coloured negative, red brick with white brick dressings. The roofs here, as throughout much of the town, are plain clay tiles with a characteristic two or three courses of large Purbeck stone slates at the eaves. On the NE corner, the Town Hall (*see* p. 626).

EAST STREET to the E has the same architectural coherence as the other town streets, but at a lower level of display. The only building to note is the former STRECHE ALMSHOUSES of 1741, immediately on the S side. What is remarkable is their bold brick rustication, even quoins at the angles and in the centre to support a pediment (with an *œil de bœuf* inscription panel in a rectangular frame), and in particular the door surround, where voussoirs get mixed up with a straight-sided outer frame. This all looks more like the 1660s than the 1740s; no doubt the builder was a local man. It is a pity that the façade has been colourwashed and that modern casements fill the windows. Beyond it are the familiar post-fire brick-built houses with, at the far E end, stucco cottages of *c.* 1840.

Back to the crossroads and N to NORTH STREET, which leads up to St Martin's church (p. 625). Glance to the l. for Nos. 11–13, header-bond brick in red and grey and Regency bowed shop windows. ANGLEBURY next door (Nos. 15–17) is a major C16 house of rubble stone, but showing externally only a big chimney-breast towards Cow Lane. Nos. 29–31, a pair of brick cottages of *c.* 1810 or so, have their doorheads neatly united by an ogee arch. That thatched roofing survives in the town (despite the fire) is illustrated by No. 33 and by the KING'S ARMS beyond. On the E side there is less coherence of scale, materials or building style, this having a mixture of small cottages, mid- to late C19 villas standing back from the road, and a three-storey town house (No. 16). Back near the Town Hall a neat Neo-Georgian POST OFFICE of 1936 by *David Dyke* of the *Office of Works*.

Finally, WEST STREET presents a coherent sequence of 1760s brickwork for a long way. After the widening of the street, in effect the town square, overlooked by the Red Lion Hotel, a number of fine Regency shopfronts and bay windows are to be found, e.g. Nos. 23–25 on the N side. Just beyond this the REX CINEMA, built as an Oddfellows' Hall, 1889; converted to a cinema, 1921. Gothic, presenting a big gable to the street. Original fitting-out of the cinema survives within the foyer and auditorium. None of the houses are large until ST MICHAEL'S, of *c.* 1760, well down on the N side. Exceptionally, this has a five-bay front. Unusually shapely shop-bow of *c.* 1800. Still on the N side, after St Michael's Road, the retained front of the former Congregational church (*see* p. 626). The street winds from its straight trajectory at this point, thrown off course by the site of the castle to the S. After passing through the town rampart, on the N side (in what has become WORGRET ROAD) are the replacement STRECHE ALMSHOUSES of 1908 by *Crickmay & Son*. Single-storeyed, forming three sides of a quadrangle. 'Jacobethan' brick and carved stone elaboration.

OUTLYING BUILDINGS

LIVABILITY HOLTON LEE, 3½ m. NE. Brick farm cottages, C19. Additions of 1999–2006 by *Tony Fretton Architects*. These include ARTISTS' STUDIOS to the NE with prominent north lights, a STUDY CENTRE attached to the cottages, and, immediately to the S, FAITH HOUSE. The last (of 2002) is modern of the most simplified and yet spiritual type, in accordance with its purpose. In plan, two overlapping rectangles. A flat-roofed timber-framed structure with horizontal and vertical timber cladding. At one point a colonnade of thin posts contrasts with the otherwise more robust corner detailing.

KEYSWORTH HOUSE, Keysworth Drive, 1½ m. NE. Neo-Georgian of 1978 by *Anthony Jaggard*, for Harry Clark. The usual proportions are reversed, with the higher storey on the upper floor.

TRIGON HOUSE, 2½ m. WNW. A brick house of 1911, extended 1926–9 by *Philip Sturdy*. Remarkably, the extension incorporates structure from the 1778 bridge at Wareham, then being replaced. One part forms a bastion-like feature (containing garages). Other masonry freely reused to create a fortified effect.

SEVEN BARROWS, 1 m. NW. Eight bowl barrows, straddling the road in an almost straight line, on the summit of a ridge. They were all probably dug into in 1844.

BESTWALL, ½ m. NE, over 77 acres as far as Swineham Point. Excavations in advance of quarrying recorded extensive 'CELTIC' FIELDS, Neolithic activity and SETTLEMENTS of the Middle Bronze Age, Late Bronze Age and Late Iron Age/ Romano-British periods, along with evidence for prehistoric and Roman pottery production.

WAREHAM SCHOOL, Worgret, ¾ m. WSW. Romano-British SETTLEMENT and POTTERY kilns, are known from excavations on the by-pass route.

WARMWELL

A small estate village centred on the church, rectory and country house group, so typical of Dorset.

HOLY TRINITY. C13 nave, refenestrated in the early C16, but with E.E. indications on the s side (see the blocked doorway and a small lancet to its r.). Short early C17 w tower; plain. Both somewhat overpowered by the E.E.-style, rock-faced chancel, higher than the nave. This is of 1881, by *R.C. Bennett* of Weymouth. – REREDOS. A miniature arcade in porphyry. Central Last Supper panel. – PULPIT and LECTERN. C18. A matching pair; plain. – FONT. C13. Octagonal, of Purbeck marble, with two blank pointed arches each side. – The FUR-NISHINGS are of 1881, not spectacular but a dignified set, especially in the chancel. – Sanctuary TILEWORK by *Minton*. – STAINED GLASS. E window probably by *Heaton, Butler & Bayne*, 1882.

64   WARMWELL HOUSE. Built for John Trenchard, who inherited in 1618. The plan surprises and confuses. It is best thought of as a hexagon with rectangular arms projecting from alternate faces, or rather that is what the symmetrical s front leads one to expect. At the back, however, a more complicated arrangement is found, perhaps owing to grafting the geometric plan on to an earlier building of uncertain plan. This N wing was in turn rebuilt in the early C19, increasing the jumbled effect. But most of this is hidden from the initial viewing. Here we see a Y-plan arrangement, quite possibly by *William Arnold*, since its central loggia has the same motifs as found, for example, at Cranborne Manor. The apparent intention behind the curious plan is the Jacobean enthusiasm for the incorporation of a device, often a letter of the alphabet, a Y being one of the more freakish examples. Two contemporary examples where the Y-plan is tidier are at Whiteparish, Wiltshire (before 1619) and Goodrich, Herefordshire (1636), both called 'New House'.

The house is built of silvery-grey limestone, the ashlar-faced s front a broad and tranquil composition, given life by the canting forward of the end bays. Two storeys and shaped gables

formed of a semicircle upon two quadrants and an intermediate step on which round-shafted chimneystacks are set l.
and r., to give an eventful skyline, such as Dorset designers
loved in Jacobean times. The S front is further singled out by
the extravagant size of the string courses and base-moulding
there, and in particular by the central recessed loggia, very
small, two round arches on Tuscan columns, set between dou-
ble-sized Tuscan half-columns. Chamfered doorway within,
flanked by shell-headed niches. Mullioned windows symmetrically arranged and rising to touch the string courses, two-,
three- and four-light, the ground-floor ones transomed and
taken down to the base-moulding. Original rainwater spouts
on curling brackets, throwing the water on to the ground. On
the E side a pair of re-set Perp windows, perhaps brought from
the church.

Inside, there are two memorable features. The main staircase, an integral part of the house, is of stone, carrying the
upper floor on thin Tuscan newel posts. The balusters are of
noble size, turned and tapering downwards. It is a real rarity;
but the Trenchards' main seat, Wolfeton House, Charminster,
has a stone staircase too, of the late C16. Was this brought from
Wolfeton at some point? The Long Gallery on the first floor
is not at all so special, just very pleasant to find, lined with
simple Jacobean panelling, in such a small, awkwardly shaped
house. Its chief curiosity is its position, off axis in the NE
wing. However, despite the geometry and jumble, the internal
planning of Warmwell is contrived so that all normal rooms
occur in their normal relationships: hence perhaps the external
confusion at the back. The Hall lies to the r. of the entrance.

The stone archway, with shafted jambs and banded chamfered arch, now re-set at the end of the central passage, led
originally from the Hall to the foot of the staircase, which
in turn led to the Long Gallery and to the Great Chamber
over the Hall. There is evidence that the Great Chamber
had a plaster barrel-vault. In the Hall (now dining room)
a Jacobean wood chimneypiece and overmantel, with caryatids below and above, installed c. 1850 for Augustus Foster,
and said to have come from the Old Rooms, Trinity Street,
Weymouth. In the Oak Room, to the N, Jacobean panelling
with pilasters, and a wood chimneypiece and overmantel with
coupled Ionic colonnettes below and above, also installed
c. 1850.

LODGE to the SW. Of c. 1850 for Augustus Foster. Gabled,
with a smaller gabled porch set parallel.

OLD RECTORY, between the church and Warmwell House,
behind a high wall. Late C18 wing to which a large classical
block was added in 1864 by E. Mondey of Dorchester.

Opposite the former rectory a late C18 brick GRANARY on small
supporting arches. N up the main road on the r. ESTATE COT-
TAGES and the former SCHOOL, the latter dated 1863, of pale
Broadmayne brick.

WATERSTON MANOR

1½ m. WNW of Puddletown

Among the C17 manor houses of Dorset none is more charming than the SOUTH RANGE of Waterston, and none employs
so much classical detail or treats it more cavalierly. Probably
added in 1641 for Sir John Strangways of Melbury House (who
purchased the estate in that year), it is tall and compact, three
bays by one, topped by one straight-sided gable per bay, with
finials like knob-ended handles. A semicircular bow, bearing
a balustrade, comes in front of the centre, and low down it
is brought forward squarely to take the Doric doorcase, its
attached columns carrying a seriously misunderstood entablature. Long stone cross-windows. So far so good. The first
cause for surprise is that the walling is all of red brick covered
in a black diaper. The upper part has long been rendered,
but the brickwork is clearly discernible beneath. Raised brick
quoins of even length at the angles, at the springing of the
bow and flanking the ground-floor windows, though in this
last place moulded capitals make them read as banded
pilasters à la Sanmicheli. Higher up the fun begins in stone.
The continuous string course is decorated with a sort of nailhead, and this recurs on the mullions of the window in the
bow. The string course round the bow and above the windows
goes one better, interspersing guilloche with the dogtooth.
The upper windows are pedimented, the pediments on entablatures on the oddest brackets, really tiny pilasters on scrolls.
Hoodmoulds turning into scrolls for the gable windows. A
shell-hood motif in the window pediments. The prettiest
motif of all is the arched links between the gables, with ser-
rated undersides. At the back a handsome brick chimneystack
set on the gable-top. It is rectangular and has sunk arched
panels.

56   That exhausts neither the beauties nor the splendours of
Waterston. Projecting from the EAST FRONT is a C17 gable,
ashlar-faced, with a finial like those of the S gables. Set into
its outer face is a classical frontispiece of considerable splendour, dated 1586 in the top pediment. Either Waterston has
undergone so many changes that the original context of the
frontispiece has been lost, or it may be resited from elsewhere on the house, or it was brought in by Lord Howard
of Bindon, the owner at that date, whose main residence was
at Bindon Abbey (q.v.). The fact that it is not *in situ* is reinforced by the cut-off entablature low down, and the change
in masonry further up. It has attached columns in three tiers,
Doric, Ionic, Corinthian, but there are the strangest shifts in
level and width. Shell-headed niches at the Doric level, niches
above with figures of armoured men. The top storey is only half
as broad, and here a niche houses a statue of Justice. Below
this a window at a half-level, the mullions in the form of Ionic

colonnettes. Top oculus window and triangular pediment. All this is of grey Purbeck stone; but in the oculus a rim of ochre dogtooth, a further shred of evidence that the frontispiece may have been re-erected here at the time when the s block was built. In 1863 the house was badly burnt, but old views show that the frontispiece had no doorway then, just a big window low down. The doorway was added in 1911 when the house was remodelled by *P. R. Morley Horder* for Major G.V. Carter.

Either side (to judge from early views) the elevations were quite informal, and seem to have had mullioned windows with hoodmoulds. Reconstruction in 1868 and the remodelling by *Morley Horder* after 1911 have left the rest of the house less humble than before but quite innocuous, so that the two show-pieces retain pride of place. The interiors were largely recon-structed after the fire, but retain a stone chimneypiece with wildly tapering Tuscan pilasters gadrooned below the capital (cf. a similar fireplace in Raleigh's study, Sherborne Castle, of *c.* 1600). Also a boldly balustered staircase, perhaps modelled on the pre-fire original, and a dining room with Jacobean-style panelling of the Morley Horder period.

The GARDENS, laid out by *Morley Horder*, make use of archways in the style of the s block. A stone-fringed rill-pond of this date is aligned on the frontispiece.

WEST BAY
Bridport

4090

In the early medieval period it seems likely that small ships were able to make their way to the southern end of Bridport. This route both silted up and was blocked by the encroachment of Chesil Beach shingle. A new harbour was finally constructed on the coast in 1740–4 by *John Reynolds* of Chester; later C18 and early C19 warehouses relating to this survive. Access from Bridport was improved by a new direct road in 1823, and by the former Great Western Railway branch of 1884 (closed to pas-sengers in 1930). No doubt with a view to promoting tourism, the harbour settlement was renamed West Bay.

ST JOHN. By *W. H. Randoll Blacking*, 1935–9. White rendering and stone with simple small three- and two-light windows and a plain bellcote – all rather reminiscent of Voysey and highly effective in this location. Inside also white, the s aisle arcade with plain, unmoulded, un-decorated square pillars. – FUR-NISHINGS. All by *Blacking*, in a simple late C17 style. – STAINED GLASS. E window, a memorial to Canon Farrer and Randoll Blacking. By *Christopher Webb*, 1958, and one of his finest.

METHODIST CHURCH. By *John Cox* (not an architect; he was leader of the Wesleyans and a shipbuilder), 1848. Stucco with incised ashlar. Round-arched windows. Curious Gothic detailing behind the swept roof of the porch.

PIER TERRACE. 1884–5 by *E.S. Prior*. Ten houses, built to a matching design originally, entered in pairs through large archways on the E side. Tall, tile-hung walls and tile-hung mansard roof at three different pitches. Tiny dormers and, facing W, oriels placed at the outer end of each pair. The pair at the S end are treated differently above first-floor level owing to rebuilding after a fire in 1929. On the W side these have four-storey canted bay windows. Prior's starting point must have been West Country vernacular (cf. especially The Nunnery, Dunster, Somerset), but the whimsical, and for the mid 1880s very fresh, design is all his own.

THE MOORINGS, N of the church, is less original. Of *c.* 1905 and probably by *F. Cooper* of Bridport, who knew Prior's local work. Late C17 style, with a central Venetian window, but gabled ends breaking through the hipped roof. Also tile-hung canted bays and a cupola.

QUAY WEST, on the W side of the harbour. A major development by *Western Design Architects*, completed 2007, for Wyatt Homes. Three white-walled, three-storey blocks with, detached at the S end, an oval-plan block (The Folly), slightly higher, with rubble-stone and vertical timber cladding. Tilted flat roof.

RAILWAY STATION (former), NE of the harbour. Opened in 1884 as the terminus of the extended Bridport branch (from Maiden Newton). Rubble stone. Tudor style. Bold moulded chimneystacks. Short canopy on the platform side.

5000

WEST CHELBOROUGH

ST ANDREW. C15 nave. Simple S tower dated 1638. Major restoration of 1894, probably by *J. Mountford Allen* of Crewkerne, who remodelled the chancel. – COMMUNION RAIL. Mid-C18. Turned balusters and fluted posts. – PULPIT. A two-decker by *Sir Charles Nicholson*, 1935. Quite simple; careful and appropriate detailing. – FONT. Late C12. Tub-shaped, with five bands of ornament. These are palmettes, decorated rope, St Andrew's crosses (or diaper), chevron and small dogtooth. – PEWS. A complete set from the 1894 restoration. – ROYAL ARMS. Hanoverian, before 1801. Relief of gilded metal or wood. – STAINED GLASS. E window by *Hardman*, 1894. – MONUMENTS. A lady of the Kymer family, early C17, badly carved, but interesting as a conceit. Recess with arch, flat big strapwork on the back wall, top with two small reclining allegorical figures. All that is current convention. But the lady is presented lying in bed with a small child also under the blanket. The lady's head is slightly turned on her pillow, and the blanket is not perfectly tidy, which produces, in spite of the bad quality of the workmanship, an exceptional sense of ease and relaxation. – Elizabeth Greenham †1715. Plain tablet. The inscription is worth reading.

WEST COMPTON
(*or* COMPTON ABBAS WEST)
2½ m. w of Compton Valence

5090

A hardly inhabited combe. *See also* West Compton, Compton Abbas, p. 216.

St Michael (private chapel). 1866–7 by *John Hicks*, retaining a chancel of 1858, probably also by Hicks. E.E. style. Small and built to a budget. Nevertheless, much is made of the bellcote by placing it over the gabled N porch. Also the vestry alongside the nave has movable partitions allowing it to function as a N aisle. Plain roof corbels; curiously sub-classical chancel arch capitals, their columns cut off on an angle. – FONT. Plain bowl, C13.

WESTHAM
⅓ m. w of Weymouth

6070

A late C19 suburb of Weymouth across the Backwater. Laid out on an informal grid, either side of Abbotsbury Road. It was reached by a bridge of 1859, built initially to serve the new cemetery (*see* below). This was replaced in 1921.

St Paul, Abbotsbury Road. Begun 1894–5 by *G.H. Fellowes Prynne*, who won a limited competition judged by William White in 1893. Three bays of the nave date from then, together with chancel and part of the aisles. The remainder, also by *Prynne*, including the low apsed w baptistery, finished in 1913. An apsed chancel chapel was added in 1903. Rock-faced, in the mixture of Dec and Perp details which Bodley had advocated. No tower, but a small double-arched bellcote over the chancel arch. The s side with two cross-gables. Large interior with octagonal piers to the four-bay aisles. – REREDOS. 1922, by *Prynne*. Oak. It incorporates mosaic panels. Carved cresting and riddel-posts with angel terminals. – FONT. C19 Perp. Brought from Christ Church, West Fordington, Dorchester (demolishd), 1932. – STAINED GLASS. *Percy Bacon Bros* did seven of the eight Lady Chapel lights, a chancel s window (high up), a N aisle window and lastly the large E window, all 1908–21. *A. O. Hemming & Co.* made the missing Lady Chapel window (St Margaret of Antioch), the w window, those in the baptistery and another in the N aisle, 1936–8. Finally three s aisle windows by *S. Walker* of *G. Maile & Son*, 1948–50.

St Edmund, Lanehouse Rocks Road, 1 m. w. Of 1952–4 by *Colin Crickmay* of *Crickmay & Son*. Modernized Arts and Crafts. Low-pitched pantile roof. A rectangular bell-tower breaks the horizontality.

MELCOMBE REGIS CEMETERY, Newstead Road, ⅛ m. N.
Opened in 1856. Gothic CHAPEL of rock-faced stone. Spired
turret on the SE corner. A similar (Nonconformist) chapel
to the S was demolished *c.* 1925. LODGE, and RECEPTION
HALL opposite, of matching style and date. The cemetery was
extended N in 1892.

RADIPOLE LAKE PUMPING STATION, Weymouth Way, ¼ m.
NE. 1979–82, by *Leonard Manasseh & Partners*. Rectangular
with diagonal boarding. Round-edged corrugated hipped
roofing.

7080

WEST KNIGHTON

A village in two parts. The northern end has the church, former
school and a farm, together with a number of cob and thatch
cottages. The southern is mainly a large development, suburban
in character.

ST PETER. The late C12 nave was extended to the W in the
early C13, when a S aisle was added. It was altered in the C16
to make a transept-like chapel. The S aisle was demolished
in the C18, leaving the chapel. The W tower is also early C13
in the lower two stages (see one lancet window), but C15 above.
The N doorway and one N lancet early C13. Either side of the
N porch large C15 windows, inserted when the roof was raised.
The chancel arch is late C12 (see the slight chamfer of the
arch). Chamfered abaci. Flanked by rectangular squints, probably C19. Early C13 S arcade, originally of four bays, but two are
now blocked, one bay infilled with a C17 window. The others
give access to the S chapel. Round piers with round abaci,
depressed two-centred double-chamfered arches. E.E. in part
the S chapel, or at least an E and a W lancet, the former *in situ*
at the E end of the former aisle, the latter re-set. There was a
careful restoration in 1893–4, and *Thomas Hardy* was in charge
(*The Builder*, 26 May 1894). The contractor was *Henry Hardy*,
Thomas's brother. – FONT. Late C12 square bowl; C19 colonnette pillars, stem and base. – BOX PEWS and a WEST GALLERY,
both part of a refurnishing by *Hardy*, 1894. Reordering by
Mark Richmond Architects, 2011, including a NAVE ALTAR and
LECTERN by *Ronald Emett* of Beaminster. – Two fragments of
WALL PAINTING: the lettering Jahveh, within a triangle above
the chancel arch; Lord's Prayer of *c.* 1800 above an aisle pier,
partly obscured by a later tablet. – The church retains OIL
LAMPS installed by Hardy. – STAINED GLASS. E window of
1920 by *Powell & Sons*. Chapel S window by *Hardman*, 1887.

WEST KNIGHTON FARM, opposite the church. The farmhouse,
of brick laid in English bond, is plausibly identified with one

wing of the house built late in the C17 by James Richards. Much altered in the early C19.

SCHOOL (former) and SCHOOL HOUSE, just NE. Dated 1865, by Mr *Stroud*, builder of West Stafford, for Dr Hawkins (*see* below). Gothic. Prominent porch-bellcote composition along the roadside. School house at the N end.

LEWELL LODGE, ½ m. N. Built *c.* 1796 for Adair Hawkins, an eminent surgeon, according to Hutchins. Three- by two-bay box, in the most elementary Gothic imaginable. Short but matching E wing added *c.* 1810.

TENANTREES, 1¼ m. NNE. Of *c.* 1896 by *C.E. Ponting* for Col. Egerton. Arts and Crafts, with bands of red tile-hanging and render. Three-storey front porch extending into the mansard roof.

LOWER LEWELL FARM, just E of the above. Farmstead group including a long barn, dated 1704 IR, end-on to the road. Another, shorter barn; both brick with thatched roofs. The FARMHOUSE is early C17, but largely rebuilt in the C18.

FRYER MAYNE. *See* Broadmayne.

WEST LULWORTH   8080

The village is in two parts, the upper on the windswept downland, and the lower along the lane approach to Lulworth Cove. Also on the coastline in this parish is the dramatic rock arch of Durdle Door.

HOLY TRINITY. Rebuilt on a new site, 1869–70. By *John Hicks* (but executed after his death by *G.R. Crickmay*). A sizeable church, with a SW tower and a N aisle. Window tracery of the Geometrical type, but with ogees. The tower has a complicated history. What stands now are the lower and top stages of what was a three-stage tower, only the lowest stage of which was of 1870. It was completed in 1888 by the addition of the upper two stages (to the original design) but reduced in 1952 by the extraction of the middle stage and lowering of the top.* Pier capitals inside of the French Early Gothic foliage variety (carved by *Grassby* of Dorchester). (Reused C16 arch in the vestry with black-letter inscription.) – REREDOS. Bavarian. Four carved panels by *Hans Meyr*. Bought 1895. – PULPIT and FONT. By *Crickmay*, 1870. The pulpit cylindrical with arcading on Purbeck marble colonnettes; the font on similar colonnettes. – STAINED GLASS. An extensive scheme (but with a weak E window). Several by *Kempe*, 1898–1901, the W window

---

*I am grateful to Richard Jones for this explanation.

exceptionally good. A close composition and sombre colours. By the pulpit, a window by *Herbert Bryans*, 1906. Next, one by *A.L. Moore*, 1903, with very bold colours. N aisle, one by *Kempe & Co.*, 1919; another by *William Morris & Co.* of Westminster, 1936. – MONUMENT. John Wordsworth, Bishop of Salisbury, †1911. Alabaster tablet by *Powell & Sons*.

THE OLD VICARAGE, just E. 1865 by *Hicks*. Gothic on the entrance side, diluting around the bay windows.

VILLAGE BUILDINGS of various dates, the earlier ones of local stone and thatch, of the C17 and C18. Interspersed with these some C19 red brick villas looking very out of place (brought here through the growth of the cove as a tourist attraction). At the entry to the lower settlement a series of facilities and car parks designed to handle the summer crowds. Further on, COVE COTTAGE is worth a look. Mid-C18 *cottage orné*. Stucco. Windows with criss-cross glazing bars. Thatched roof swept over the dormers. Opposite (to the W), a terrace of COAST-GUARD COTTAGES, early C19.

WESTON, Britwell Drive, ¾ m. SW. On the cliff top, a curious late house by *Lutyens*, 1927 for Sir Alfred Fripp (completed by the client). Brick, with extensive tile roofs, looking more at home in Surrey. A brilliant split-level plan on a steep slope, with direct access to the ground from each floor. Typical Tudor–Georgian vernacular detail. Otherwise surprisingly low-key for Lutyens.

LITTLE BINDON ABBEY, ¾ m. SE. This exposed cliff-top site close to Lulworth Cove was chosen by the Cistercians in 1149 for the first foundation of Bindon Abbey (q.v.). They soon moved to Wool (in 1172), but the cottage which occupies the place has at its E end a C13 chapel with an E lancet, and a two-centred N doorway slightly chamfered. Rough later buttresses, and brick lancets of the late C18. The roof is of *c.* 1500, a pointed tunnel-vault, plastered, but with thin timber ribs. The only C12 survivals are the reused corbels of the E gable, one carved as a bearded king, the other as a monster.

LULWORTH CAMP, 1 m. NE. Royal Artillery gunnery school. The same Neo-Georgian style as at Bovington Camp for the earliest parts, here of 1940. Mostly more recent and mundane in architectural character. The whole is something of a blot on this otherwise magnificent landscape.

HAMBURY TOUT, ½ m. SW. A BELL BARROW located on a prominent hill above the cliff. A central burial was excavated in 1790.

'CELTIC' FIELDS, 1 m. W. Spread over 850 acres from Newlands Warren westwards (*see also* Chaldon Herring).

BINDON HILL, 1 m. ESE. A bank and ditch along the northern side of the hill-crest, constructed in the Early Iron Age, probably as a defence. A single original inturned entrance ⅔ m. from the western end, which was enclosed by later cross-dykes above Lulworth Cove. The total length is 1¼ m. to Cockpit Head. Excavations showed that the entrance was not completed.

WEST MILTON
Powerstock

OLD CHURCH. Only the tower is left. Perp, of *c.* 1500, with a low arch to the former nave, the roof-line of the nave, and an embattled parapet. W aisle bays on either side embracing the tower. For more of the church *see* the primary school, Powerstock.*

CORFE FARM, ¾ m. SW. 2006–7 by *Stuart Martin Architects.* Neo-vernacular combined with Lutyens-style roofs and hipped dormers. Timber-framed room at the W end. Much weatherboarding on the N side.

WEST MOORS

A halt on the Southampton & Dorchester Railway was opened in 1847. Development of the present village, now largely suburban in character, gathered pace in the 1930s.

ST MARY, Station Road. 1897 by *W.H. Stanley* of Trowbridge. Ashlar; Geometrical tracery; polygonal, multi-gabled E apse. Extended westwards by *Herbert Kendall* in 1927. – REREDOS. 1920. Bath stone and marble. – FONT. Carved bowl on five marble supporting columns. Oak COVER incorporating a wrought-iron support for a brass ewer. – STAINED GLASS. Three fine apse windows of 1922 by *William Morris & Co.* of Westminster. W window by *A.K. Nicholson,* 1936.

Brick CHURCH HALL, 2010 by *David Illingworth Architects,* attached to N.

WEST ORCHARD

ST LUKE. A replacement chapel of ease of 1876–8 by *T.H. Wyatt,* paid for by the Marchioness of Westminster and the 2nd Lord Wolverton. Nave with aisles, bellcote and chancel, the last a heavy restoration of the late C15 predecessor. This set the style which Wyatt copied, in a lively idiom in fine Greensand ashlar. Two-bay arcades. Chancel arch on corbels. Contemporary FURNISHINGS, largely untouched.

*The church of ST MARY MAGDALENE of 1869–74 by *John Hicks,* completed by *A.B. Hansford,* was demolished in 1976.

WEST PARLEY

ALL SAINTS. Nave and chancel. The brown heathstone masonry
of the nave is C12 (but partially rendered), as is the segmental-
arched N doorway, sheltered by a C15 timber-framed porch.
C18 nave windows with ogee trefoiled heads. Repaired and
re-seated, 1840–2, by *Edmund Pearce*. His was the original
of the present handsome white W bellcote, re-clad in plastic
after storm damage. Chancel, with re-set C14 E window of two
cinquefoiled lights, rebuilt in 1896. Narrow two-centred C14
chancel arch (possibly incorporating reused C12 voussoirs)
flanked by lancet squints. The roof has a number of lozenge-
shaped wooden BOSSES. – FONT. Mid-C12 tapering bowl with
arcading decoration; on a cylindrical stem. Set on top of this
an octagonal bowl. Probably C14 or C15; plain. – PULPIT. C17,
hexagonal, with reading desk adjacent. C18 backplate and
tester. – Complete set of BOX PEWS of 1840–2, rebuilt from
an earlier set. Some are marked 'FREE' or 'CHOIR'; others
are numbered. – STAINED GLASS. E window †1869, probably by *Lavers, Barraud & Westlake*. Nave N window †1908 by
Joseph Bell & Son of Bristol. This firm may also have designed
the W window. – MONUMENT. Slab with a splayed-arm cross
in relief, leaning against the N porch. Probably C11, pre-
Conquest. – Externally, below the E window, a recess containing
an earthenware vase, said to be C14. According to the inscription, this is an 1893 re-interment of the Lady of Lydlinch.
DUDSBURY, ¾ m. NW. Iron Age HILL-FORT, bivallate, enclosing
about 8 acres. Original S and SW entrances.

WEST STAFFORD

Sited among the water meadows of the River Frome, the church
occupies the centre of the village picture, or rather the central
picture, for a walk down the winding street and back presents
church, barn, cottage and school very charmingly as a series of
vignettes. Occasional recent housing is generally away from these
groupings (to the S), but a few less sympathetic buildings have
intruded.

ST ANDREW. W tower early C16, with bellcote windows matching some of those on the nave. This is of 1640, wider than its
predecessor, with the S wall on the original alignment, hence
off-centre to the tower. The date is given on a stone in the nave
S wall. Re-set in the nave also C15 and early C16 windows. The
chancel, continuous with the nave, is an 1898 enlargement by
C. E. Ponting. His are the typically free Gothic N and S windows;
the E is Perp (restored and re-set). Inside the church 1640 is
much more prominent. First the plastered wagon roof is of

that date. In the chancel it is simply ornamented. Second, the late Jacobean SCREEN (i.e. also of *c*. 1640), with arches on colonnettes l. and r. of the doorway. (This was moved by Ponting some 15 ft (4.5 metres) E of its original position.) Third, the otherwise plain BENCHES, with an enriched top panel on the ends. – PULPIT. Of *c*. 1640. Panelled, the upper tier enriched with arabesque. Backboard with an inset painting of St Paul. Octagonal sounding-board with pendants at the angles. – COMMUNION RAIL. Of *c*. 1700. Strong balusters, the standards with ball finials. – FONT. Medieval. Plain, octagonal. – CHANDELIER of brass. Inscribed 1713. – ROYAL ARMS of James I on the mid-C18 WEST GALLERY. – WALL PAINTINGS. On the nave N and S walls remains of Decalogue and Creed, *c*. 1640.

STAINED GLASS. Splendid E window by *Christopher Whall*, 1913. Glowing colours, especially the pinks of the angels' wings. A N window by *Burlison & Grylls*, 1899, connected with Canon Southwell's effigy (*see* below). Nave S window by *Kempe & Co.*, 1926, described by Pevsner as 'disastrously retardataire'. Also an armorial window by *Hugh Powell*, 1980. – MONU-MENTS. Two big tablets, both unshowy but with some panache. The comparison is instructive. Richard Russell, 1674, attrib-uted to *Joshua Marshall* (GF), of slightly squarer proportions and more sedate and provincial; John Gould †1727, more vertical and more classically correct, with the Baroque flourishes of side scrolls, and a cresting of flaming urns and a central escutcheon. – Canon Reginald Southwell Smith †1895. (The chancel was also built as his memorial.) Recumbent effigy on a tomb-chest designed by *Ponting*; *Harry Hems* of Exeter was the sculptor. – Blanche Egerton †1913, probably also by *Hems*. A diminutive marble tablet with heavy classical, almost Byzantine, framework. The touching inscription also notes that the Whall E window is her memorial.

SCHOOL (now VILLAGE HALL), up the road to the E. Dated 1846. Lightly Gothic, the Ham Hill dressings contrasting with silver Purbeck rubble.

GLEBE COURT (formerly the rectory), Rectory Lane, at the W end, approached now through housing of a regrettably sub-urban character. Early C17, but largely rebuilt in red brick, creating a U-plan to the N. This part is dated 1767 (for the Rev. James Acton) and deploys the country classical vocabulary to make a show. Simplified Venetian window on the first floor of the centre, and on the wings. Central top bullseye, and pedi-mented doorcase on Ionic half-columns. (The hall, also 1767, has a pedimented chimneypiece.)

WEST STAFFORD MANOR, at the E end, presents an early C19 stuccoed appearance on the N (entrance) side, with panelled pilasters. Round to the E, however, a five-bay stone front with a cartouche of arms that dates a substantial remodel-ling to between 1702 and 1718 (for George White). The eaves kink up pedimentally to make room for it. The S front also goes with this date, the centre set far back and cramped between projecting wings, and round-headed windows on both storeys almost crowded out by the deeply projecting porch.

STAFFORD HOUSE, ¼ m. NNW. Stafford House has two façades, the E dated 1633, the W of 1848–50, both of pale grey limestone, rubble, and ashlar, and both unusually broadly and success-fully composed. The E front is on an E-plan, and symmetrical, except in the fenestration of the S wing. This wing provides a clue to the complicated evolution of the house. It is of *c.* 1560–70, built for Thomas Long and added to an existing, probably medieval, dwelling. In the late C16 the medieval main range was rebuilt. However, what we see of 1633 date, built for John Gould, is grafted on to this late C16 structure, much of which remains embedded in the present building. The S wing has a S-projecting stair-turret containing a stone newel staircase. Elsewhere, gables carry square chimneystacks on their heads, as so often in early C17 houses in these parts. The windows are of three arched lights with hoodmoulds, an archaism to be found also e.g. at Chantmarle of 1612, but rarely as late as this. Small two-storey gabled porch with a round-headed entrance arch but still Gothic mouldings, a typical combina-tion. What gives the façade its special flavour is the breadth of the recessed parts, with room for two bays l. and r. of the porch, and a gabled dormer over the inner of each pair of bays, which stresses the centre as it should be stressed. So a typically early C17 West Country front.

In contrast, the W front is by *Benjamin Ferrey* (for John Floyer), and is quite different from his slightly earlier Clyffe House, Tincleton. Here Ferrey has in window size and in massing taken his cue from the existing house, and produced a really convincing pastiche. Symmetrical front, except for the two-storey window bay under the l. gable, which reflects a pre-existing bay window at the W end of the N wing. Gables l. and r., gabled dormer in the centre, and a four-bay arcaded loggia across the centre part, the end bays blind and given niches: an expansion of a feature at Warmwell nearby. The quality of Ferrey's homage to early C17 Dorset architecture is high, as one might expect from an architect so familiar with the county.

Subdivided from the C17 hall, a MORNING ROOM of *c.* 1830 with a Regency Gothick fretwork cornice and matching fire-place. Of this date too, a pair of pointed arches, internally either side of the E main doorway. W STAIRCASE HALL by *Ferrey* (of 1848–50) in a Jacobean style; enriched plaster beams to the ceiling with pendants at the intersections.

A scheme of 1805 for Nicholas Gould by *Humphry Repton* to landscape the Stafford House riverside setting was largely unexecuted.*

---

* It was later published in Repton's *Fragments on the Theory and Practice of Landscape Gardening* (1816).

Talbothays Lodge, ½ m. e. Of c. 1890, by *Thomas Hardy* for his brother, Henry (who ran the family building firm). Neo-Georgian. Buff Broadmayne brick, grey-slated hipped roof. Three two-storey bays, asymmetrically placed, break up the formality, as do some very narrow windows on the bays. The round-arched front doorway is startlingly plain.

Talbothays Cottages, across the road, are by *Hardy* too.

Tenantrees and Lower Lewell Farm. *See* West Knighton.

Mount Pleasant, 1 m. wnw. A Neolithic henge monument stands on a low hill with a commanding view. It is much ploughed but covers 12 acres. Excavations in 1970–1 showed that the main bank and ditch had been constructed in the Late Neolithic and continued in use during the Chalcolithic. There were four causewayed entrances. At the same time a smaller ditched monument comprising five concentric circles of timber posts was added in the western sector of the interior. A little later the w entrance of the main enclosure was enlarged, and Conquer Barrow, on the Dorchester parish boundary (*see* p. 263), was completed over the bank. In the Early Bronze Age the small timber monument was replaced by a stone structure with a central setting and three outlying stones. At this time, just inside the outer earthwork an almost continuous palisade trench was dug, designed to hold tree trunks of telegraph-pole proportions. Entrances now lay on the n and w sides, and the enclosure continued in use during the Middle Bronze Age.

Frome Hill, ¾ m. wnw. The e end of the southern Dorchester Ridge (*see* Dorchester). A pair of prominent round barrows on the hill-crest.

WEST STOUR

7020

A mixture of brick and stone houses of modest size along a single village street, running n towards the church off the A30.

St Mary. A small church with s tower (cf. Fifehead Magdalen). c13, but almost entirely rebuilt in 1840 on the original plan (cost just over £330). The chancel has two c13 lancet n windows; the chancel se window could also be c13. Perp e window, but probably an c18 replacement. Panelled plaster ceiling, four-centred in section. Taken with the modest furnishings, a picture of the 1840s. – Pulpit. Simple, early c17. – Font. Supposedly c13 but heavily reworked. – Woodwork. The parapet of the w gallery, the front of a cupboard, and a door, all at the w end, are Perp and *ex situ*, probably from the screen.

Small former Primitive Methodist chapel of 1854, set back behind a railed screen, easily missed on the e side of the main village street.

WEYMOUTH

4 Weymouth is the Georgian seaside resort *par excellence*. Ralph Allen of Bath is said to have been the first to notice its possibilities in that line. He played host to the Duke of York, George III's brother, in 1758. Another brother of the king, the Duke of Gloucester, spent the winter here in 1780, and then built himself a house at the N end of the town. George III himself paid his first visit in 1789, and came regularly (on fourteen occasions) until 1805. The Court brought the place prosperity, and the king could not help but give it a cachet.

Little is now visible of the earlier Weymouth, or of the earlier Melcombe Regis,* for these were at first two separate towns, facing and antagonizing each other across the landlocked harbour, and earning a modest prosperity by trade. Melcombe, on the N side, became an incorporated borough in 1280. Weymouth, on the S, did not achieve that distinction until 1571, when it was forced to amalgamate with Melcombe as a united borough. A charter of 1616 gave the name 'Weymouth' to the whole. All surviving buildings post-date the union. These may be found close to the harbour, three on the S side where settlement is confined to a narrow strip, a few more in Melcombe. The latter was one of Edward I's planned towns, with a regular grid-pattern layout, narrowing towards the N where the isthmus linking it to the mainland was only a road's width. Bounded by the Backwater, harbour and seafront, it could only grow northwards. Soon after union came the construction of the first timber bridge across the harbour, in 1597. It was succeeded by two or three further timber bridges until a new stone structure was built in 1824. By *c.* 1700 the town had reached the line of Bond Street, with only the odd isolated building beyond. Late in the C18, after the erection of Gloucester Lodge and the visits of George III, sea-facing terraces spread up the bay, petering out only in the late C19 when villa-building took over.

The arrival of the Great Western Railway in 1857, with the line and terminus built on land reclaimed from the Backwater, allowed mass tourism to flourish. Many more terraces were constructed in the Park district of the town in the decade or so following, behind the Esplanade buildings. Many were destined to become guesthouses and small hotels. This development continued the trend of reclaiming the Backwater to thicken the previously narrow isthmus. A rail link with an enlarged cross-Channel ferry jetty (the former Pile Pier) was made in 1865, and from this point onwards Weymouth became a significant port. War damage and post-1950 reconstruction saw an unfortunate erosion of the town's scarce historic fabric, especially through the construction of the Council Offices in 1968–71, but also brought about the foundation of a Civic Society (1944) and the designation of a conservation area (1974). These, together with the more

*The earliest record of Melcombe being called 'Regis' dates from 1336.

Weymouth Bay.
Engraving by J. Crane, 1789

rigorous protection of listed buildings, have so far ensured that new development has been largely confined to the less sensitive W side of Melcombe.

CHURCHES

HOLY TRINITY, Trinity Road. To the harbour it presents an ashlar façade in the Perp typical of its construction dates: 1834–6 by *Philip Wyatt* for the Rev. George Chamberlain (completed by *Matthew Wyatt* after his uncle's death in 1835). It is dominated by one large seven-light window with vestigial buttresses either side that have become more vestigial, owing to the loss of their pinnacles. One enters the nave on axis at the N end, with surprisingly broad transepts of unequal length on either side. This all might seem as originally intended, but its history is more complex, for originally this entry was into the N transept of a church correctly orientated. The chancel was in the present E transept. *Crickmay & Son* reorganized the layout in 1886–7, remodelling the former chancel and completely rebuilding the nave (in rock-faced Portland rubble) to become the W transept. So we have a wide nave, and two large transepts, two bays deep in this airy building of unusual special quality. – CHANCEL REREDOS. By *C.E. Kempe & Co.*, 1918. A canopied triptych. – LADY CHAPEL REREDOS. By *Powell & Sons*, 1920. *Opus sectile* panel. – CHOIR STALLS and CLERGY CHAIRS. A good set of 1887 by *Crickmay*. – PULPIT of 1905. Alabaster, with carved figures in niches. – FONT. Of 1888 (originally in a baptistery under the N gallery). Alabaster. – STAINED GLASS. E and chancel side windows by *Heaton, Butler & Bayne*, 1895. N transept (Lady Chapel), E by *Martin Travers*, 1947, N almost certainly by *Heaton, Butler & Bayne*, 1904. Nave N by *Ward & Hughes*, 1909.

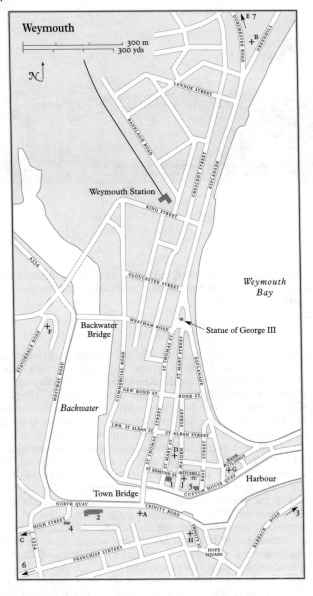

Weymouth

300 m
300 yds

N

DORCHESTER ROAD

E 7
+ B   GREENHILL

LENNOX STREET

RANELAGH ROAD

CRESCENT STREET
ESPLANADE

Weymouth Station

KING STREET

A354

GLOUCESTER STREET

Weymouth Bay

WESTHAM ROAD

Backwater Bridge

F +

Statue of George III

STAVORDALE ROAD

WESTWAY ROAD

Backwater

COMMERCIAL ROAD

ST THOMAS ST.
ST MARY ST.

ESPLANADE

NEW BOND ST.

BOND ST.

LWR. ST ALBAN ST.

ST THOMAS STREET
ST MARY STREET
MAIDEN STREET
EAST STREET

ST ALBAN STREET

D Z
+

BANK BUILDINGS

MITCHELL ST.

+ G

ST EDMUND ST.

J   5

Harbour

Town Bridge

CUSTOM HOUSE QUAY

NORTH QUAY

TRINITY ROAD

+ A

BARRACK ROAD

→ 3

HIGH STREET

2

4

TRINITY ST.

C ←
A354

6 ←

FRANCHISE STRTEET

+ H

HOPE SQUARE

A	Holy Trinity	I	Guildhall (former)
B	St John	2	Council Offices
C	St Martin (former)	3	Nothe Fort
D	St Mary	4	Old Town Hall
E	St Augustine (R.C.)	5	Custom House
F	St Joseph (R.C.)	6	Union Court
G	Baptist chapel	7	Weymouth College (former)
H	Hope United Reformed		and Weymouth College
	Church		
J	Methodist church		

St John, Dorchester Road and Greenhill. 1850–4 by *T. Talbot Bury*. Enlarged to the E to match, 1868 by *Bury*. Tractarian with the parts clearly expressed, but with lean-to aisle roofs. Portland ashlar. Local stone with Bath and Caen stone dressings. In the style of 1300 (Second Pointed). With a NW steeple, the spire well provided with lucarnes. Nave and aisles; double-width transepts. Very correct Dec arcades with octagonal piers. – REREDOS. Of 1883 by *E. F. Clarke*, carved by *T. Earp*. Caen stone, carved with Gothic gablets and a crocketed central gable. – *Minton* TILES in the sanctuary. – The furnishings have been stripped out leaving a standard Perp PULPIT and FONT, both by *Talbot Bury*. – STAINED GLASS. A very fine selection, mostly dating from the 1868 enlargement. The best are the brightly coloured E and W windows, by *O'Connor* and *Ward & Hughes* respectively. Tall chancel side windows by *Ward & Hughes*. Theirs also a window in the N transept, the other by *Lavers & Barraud*. The latter firm did the S transept windows, while two windows in the N aisle (1875 and 1876) are probably by *Ward & Hughes*. Another here by *Heaton, Butler & Bayne*, 1889. Two in the chancel S chapel (now partitioned off) by *Henry Hughes*, 1876.

Adjoining to the N, former VICARAGE, 1859, probably by *Talbot Bury*. Gothic with steep-pitched roofs.

St Martin, Chickerell Road (now St Martin's Court). 1908 by *C. E. Ponting*. Brick. A narrow front with two deep middle buttresses which embrace the porch, making the centre of the façade with a free Dec window seem to lie back. Arcaded sides (for intended aisles). Converted to flats, with an assortment of windows.

St Mary, St Mary Street. 1815–17, by the local architect *James Hamilton* (also designer of the George III statue, *see* p. 649). Built of Portland ashlar on a site where the façade is almost contiguous with houses on both sides, i.e. the churchyard is very cramped. Three-bay façade, the bays wide. Articulation by pilasters. For the middle bays they are coupled and carry a pediment (with two odd oculi in the tympanum). Flush with the pediment an undisguised truncated gable on which stands the cupola with an open rotunda of columns. Seven-bay side elevations, the central three in a slight break-forward. Rectangular windows to the aisles; arched to the galleries. Inside, the nave has a segmental tunnel-vault, quatrefoil piers and galleries on three sides. The aisles were partitioned off in 1971. – REREDOS with pilasters and the usual Commandment boards, Creed and Lord's Prayer between. Above it *Sir James Thornhill*'s large Last Supper of 1721 (painted just prior to his being elected M.P. for the town). Pevsner thought it a 'remarkably good picture, even by French standards'. – PULPIT. C17 style, but surely a late C19 piece. Oak. – STAINED GLASS. The best are a pair of circular windows lighting the organ loft in the W wall, and a rectangular window in the S aisle by *Henry Wilson* (made by *Powell & Sons*), 1922. Two further windows by *Powells* in the S aisle of 1923 and 1930, both by *J. H. Hogan* and both very good examples of his work. Here also one probably by *William Morris & Co.* of Westminster, 1922. N aisle, a window signed by *Abbott & Co.* of Lancaster, 1939 (but it looks fifty years earlier). – MONUMENTS. Several on the aisle walls. The best two are Bayles Wardell †1825, with a relief showing him on a couch, his disconsolate wife, and a hovering angel; and Roger Campden Cope †1818, by *Gray* of Weymouth, with draped urn and tablet on black marble ground.

ST AUGUSTINE (R.C.), Dorchester Road. 1832–5. No architect recorded. The classical ashlar façade is of *c.* 1900 (probably by *S. Jackson*). – STAINED GLASS. S window by *John Hardman Studios,* 1971.

ST JOSEPH (R.C.), Stavordale Road. 1933–4 by *George Drysdale*. Free Style with a memorably interconnected (liturgical) W bellcote, circular window and swept-up copper porch hood. Whitewashed brick with Cornish slate roofs. Aisled nave with primitive Gothic arches, but a large round arch for the sanctuary.

BAPTIST CHAPEL, Bank Buildings. 1813–14, the façade of 1859 by *Crickmay*. Five bays, the pedimented middle three with giant attached Roman Doric columns *in antis*. Arched windows between and a bold plaque at the centre. Gallery on three sides supported on cast-iron columns.

HOPE CONGREGATIONAL CHURCH (now UNITED REFORMED), Trinity Street. 1861–2 by *Haggett & Pocklington* of Sherborne. Ashlar. Five giant Doric pilasters carry stilted round arches. Heavy detailing with a heavy cornice to match. Pevsner asked, 'Can such a performance still be called classical? It isn't Italianate anyway.'*

METHODIST CHURCH, Maiden Street. 1866–7 by *Foster & Wood*. Brick with stone dressings. A startling essay in the Italian Romanesque. Badly damaged by a fire in 2002 and currently a roofless ruin.

PUBLIC BUILDINGS

101 GUILDHALL (former), St Edmund Street. 1836–8, by *George Corderoy*.** Quite impressive with its Ionic portico set above a rusticated arcade. The upper windows, between pilaster-like antae, give away the late date. (On the staircase in a niche a STATUE of Samuel Weston signed by *Joseph Theakston*, 1821, a white marble figure seated in a striking but easy pose.)

COUNCIL OFFICES, North Quay. 1968–71, typical of *Jackson & Edmonds*. A standoffish nonentity. And why had the whole street to be pulled down for it, including Weymouth's finest C16 house? Portland stone panels over a plum-coloured brick base. More plum brick on the back. Three under-scaled bay

---

*The 'crazily Norman' CONGREGATIONAL CHURCH in Gloucester Street, of 1864 by *R.C. Bennett*, was demolished in 1980.
**He is recorded as architect in a building agreement of 16 November 1836. The cost was £2,974 13s. (Weymouth Borough Archives).

windows: an attempt at emphasis over the off-centre entrance. Tower stump breaking the flat roof-line.*

NOTHE FORT, ½ m. E. Of *c.* 1860 to 1872 by the *Royal Engineers' Office* under *Col. J. Hirse.* Intended to guard the tip of land between the entrances to Portland and Weymouth harbours. Monumental Portland stone walls with embrasures for large guns facing over the water.

OLD TOWN HALL, High West Street. Of the humblest. Stone. C16 in origin, but largely rebuilt *c.* 1774 and heavily restored in 1896. Porch combined with bellcote at the N end.

CUSTOM HOUSE (former), Custom House Quay. Late C18. Brick with some diaper decoration. Stone only on the central pedimented door surround. Modern royal arms above. A pair of first-floor bow windows gives it a jaunty character.

UNION COURT (formerly Portwey Hospital), Wyke Road, ¼ m. WSW. 1836, built as the Weymouth Union Workhouse to designs by two of its Guardians, *Thomas Dodson* and *Thomas Hill Harvey.* Of Portland stone, laid out as low ranges enclosing four courtyards. Long two-storey road front (becoming three as the ground falls away) with central three-storey block.

WEYMOUTH COLLEGE (former), Dorchester Road, I m. N. Built in 1864 by *G.R. Crickmay* as a public school. Yellow brick with stone and red brick banding. Gabled and lightly Gothic. Roughly T-shaped block with an entrance and clock turret in the front angle.

The former CHAPEL to the SE, of 1894–6, is by *Crickmay & Son.* Gothic. Red brick.

The present WEYMOUTH COLLEGE is a separate campus on Cranford Avenue to the NE. Built from the 1970s onwards, main buildings completed in 2002. There is no unifying style apart from the weak classicism of the larger blocks.

PERAMBULATIONS

The first two perambulations must begin at the STATUE of George III which faces up The Esplanade near its S end, standing as patron saint, as it were, at the entrance to the old town. The statue is of *Coade* stone (supplied by that company in 1804), erected here in 1809, and has since 1949 been painted, most successfully, in naturalistic and heraldic colours. The king, a small figure, stands in full robes, before an outsize stool with a crown on it. On the gigantic slab of a pedestal in letters that seem intended for reading at the far end of The Esplanade an inscription proclaims, as well it might, the dedication by 'The *grateful* Inhabitants'. Also the designer's name, *J. Hamilton,* 'ARCH,ᵀ'. Two *Coade* stone figures of a lion and unicorn flank the pedestal. Thence the routes lie N and S.

97

---

*To be replaced by a housing development.

1. The Esplanade

First the simpler route, N up THE ESPLANADE, looking landward before returning S, looking seaward. Has any coast town
a more spectacular seafront than Weymouth, the terraces continuous for half a mile, fronting the expanse of Weymouth
Bay? The northward extension of The Esplanade can easily be
followed, for very little has been altered, in spite of the patchy
surface appearance.

Before heading N one should recap, as it were, to FREDER-
ICK PLACE of *c.* 1834, the first of the terraces facing on to the
last part of St Thomas Street. Here the pattern is established or
rather continued, from YORK BUILDINGS on the W side. Two-
storey bow windows in a three-storey block. At the S end the
MASONIC HALL. Façade of 1834 by *C.B. Fookes* of Weymouth.
Pedimented and Greek Doric with two columns *in antis*, the
order derived from the Hephaisteion, Athens. Central arched
and keyed doorway and blank niches.

Back N, to the first terrace facing the sea, ROYAL TERRACE.
Red brick but partly stuccoed, built in two parts, the N two-
thirds *c.* 1816, the rest soon after 1818. Three houses at each
end were higher, a symmetrical arrangement that was affected
by the demolition of the S end house in 1929 after the widening
of Westham Road. Here too many shopfronts of varying date.

Until the building of the terraces just described, the next
house (after Gloucester Street), built as GLOUCESTER LODGE
(later the Gloucester Hotel and now flats), was free-standing.
The N part of this was the original Gloucester Lodge, of *c.* 1780
for the Duke of Gloucester, occupied by King George III as
his summer residence from 1789, purchased by him in 1801,
and sold in 1820. Red brick, of 2:4:2 bays, the centre slightly
recessed, with big Venetian windows downstairs in the end
wings. Same at the back. Extended S on a bigger scale, *c.* 1850.
Heightened and rebuilt internally in 1927 (after fire damage).
It is, then, no Brighton Pavilion; but it did set a fashion in
facing the sea so uncompromisingly. Early resorts tended to
approach the sea only gingerly, and at Brighton the Prince of
Wales kept back a respectful distance. Attached at the N end,
GLOUCESTER ROW, a short terrace of *c.* 1790 by *J. Hamilton.*
Brick, but partly plastered over and the third house rebuilt in
the 1930s.

Next, the only break in the even flow of terraces, the ROYAL
HOTEL, 1897–9 by *C. Orlando Law*, in a florid Free Renais-
sance style. Brick with stone bands (*à la* New Scotland Yard,
London), and with octagonal domed corner pavilion turrets.★
Beyond, the ROYAL ARCADE of 1896, also by *C. Orlando Law.*
Then a further terrace length, also known as GLOUCESTER
ROW. Originally eight matching houses of *c.* 1790, the centre
two raised in height. Stucco with a rusticated ground floor

★It replaced the Royal Hotel of 1772, built as Stacie's Hotel by Andrew Sproule,
the Bath developer.

(part altered) and wrought-iron balconies above. Those in the centre have a hood covering. The house at the N end was replaced by another in 1911 by *Samuel Jackson* (Dutch-cum-Tudor brick over a shopfront). In KING STREET on the l. the commercial Italianate of the former FOUNTAIN HOTEL of *c.* 1860, and further on, the former CHRIST CHURCH HALL of *c.* 1874. The church of 1874 next door (probably by *Crickmay*) was demolished in 1956. Opposite, THE TIDES INN (originally Sun Inn). Free Style corner pub of *c.* 1895. Terracotta panel with the initials of the Weymouth brewers, J.A. Devenish & Co.

Back to the Esplanade, where the façade layout of Glouces-ter Row is continued on to ROYAL CRESCENT, a straight terrace of fifteen houses, where a crescent-plan terrace had been intended *c.* 1792; it was still incomplete in 1801. BEL-VIDERE, a terrace of sixteen beyond, was meant to have its brick exposed, as one or two of the houses still do. Most have been stuccoed, many with a rusticated ground floor. It was built sporadically between 1818 and *c.* 1855. Each three-window-wide house has slight elaboration of the central first-floor window, creating a fussy rhythm unlike the regularity of the earlier terraces. Wrought-iron-fronted balconies running continuously, but less refined than on the earlier terraces. VICTORIA TERRACE, which follows, is much grander, ashlar-faced, and in the bay windows of the raised centrepiece clearly of the debased classicism of the mid C19. Built in 1855–6, with the PRINCE REGENT HOTEL (formerly Burdon Hotel) as its higher centrepiece. Finally WATERLOO PLACE of 1835, and what one expects of that date. BRUNSWICK TERRACE, which begins afresh on the seaward side as the bay begins to curve, and which stands in front of Waterloo Place, is bowed at its s end, a happy echo of the s end of The Esplanade. Twenty houses built from 1823 to *c.* 1827 by *Morris Clarke & George Cox*. Further on, at another split in the roads (and in front of St John's church) is the STATUE of Queen Victoria, facing her grandfather from the N end of the Esplanade. 1902 by *George Simonds*. A version of his stone statue of 1887 at Reading, here cast in bronze on a stone plinth.

Following the road to the r. of the statue, later terraces on the r. and the odd 1930s semi-detached house intervene and break the spell. Only GREENHILL HOUSE is worth comment. A villa of *c.* 1840, stuccoed with a hipped roof and a Ven-etian window above a curious entrance: two fat Greek Doric columns, presumably intended to be covered by a porch. Ionic loggia facing the sea. Interiors remodelled by *Sir Aston Webb* for Sir Richard Howard, *c.* 1900. Continuing N along GREEN-HILL, almost at once there appear big detached houses of the 1860s and 70s, rather like North Oxford. Several of the late C19 and early C20 houses were designed by *Crickmay & Son*. Finally a detour further N along GREENHILL for the BEACH CHALETS of 1923. Two storeys, those at the top accessed from an iron-railed balcony. Cast-iron columns, the whole feeling like something of fifty years earlier. In GREENHILL GARDENS the STAINFORTH VANE by *Beresford Pite & Partners*, 1932, moved here from Weymouth College, 1952. The weathervane is a model of the 1931 Schneider Trophy-winning Supermarine S.6B aircraft. G.S. Stainforth, who flew the aircraft, was an alumnus of Weymouth College.

Having looked at the terraces, the other esplanade buildings associated with the beach need to be seen while heading back on the seaward side of the road to the George III statue. So, returning s, after passing the bowed end of Brunswick Terrace, the PIER BANDSTAND, 1939 by *V.J. Wenning*. What stands now is the entrance; a sad and mutilated section of a scheme with ambition. The open-air auditorium seating 2,400 projected over the sea (and, in poor condition, was demolished in 1986). After the CENOTAPH of 1921, by *F. Doyle Jones*, the first of a series of seven SHELTERS of 1889. Cast-iron structure and elaboration. Finally, opposite Gloucester Row, the frilly JUBILEE MEMORIAL CLOCK TOWER, for the Queen's Golden Jubilee of 1887–8, the clock given by Sir Henry Edwards, according to the plaque. Cast and wrought iron, jauntily painted. Just the thing to hang fairy lights on.

2. Melcombe Regis town, from the king's statue to the bridge

Starting again back at George III's statue and facing s, one sees that it is designed in combination with the bow-ended stuccoed blocks of STATUE HOUSE and its companion at the entrance to St Mary Street, both *c.* 1815. They with their shallow segmental bows and mansard roofs make a delightful group, built deliberately to create a townscape setting for the statue of some five years earlier. JOHNSTONE ROW, *c.* 1810, a terrace facing the sea, continues the bows seven times more. Then two poor contributions to the street frontage: the blocky 1970s addition to Barclays Bank and, set back, a rear elevation to MARKS & SPENCER. 1930s modernistic, called a 'disastrous lapse' in the earlier edition. Next, a more sympathetic recent insertion: the bow-ended block marking the start of YORK BUILDINGS of *c.* 1785, the first sea-facing terrace in Weymouth. After this the former HARVEY'S LIBRARY, CARD AND ASSEMBLY ROOMS of just before 1800. An upper storey of five bays carried on Ionic columns, the open ground floor later filled in. As first built it had an inner courtyard and a second block beyond. The original entrance was in the central bay. Beyond CHARLOTTE ROW (early C19), the thrillingly contrasting former STUCKEY'S BANK of 1883 by *Bonella & Paull*. French Renaissance. Lively front facing Bond Street with oriels and frilly Dutch gables, all stripy with brick and stone. The next block, AUGUSTA PLACE, is a jumble of late C18 houses of differing heights, typical of the early stages of esplanade development. On the corner of Alexandra Gardens across the road, the STATUE of Sir Henry Edwards, 1885 by

W. & T. Wills. Continuing along The Esplanade, a final set-piece is at the far end. DEVONSHIRE BUILDINGS and PULTENEY BUILDINGS, two linked red brick terraces begun in 1805. Bowed end to the former, an alteration ordered by an astute town council in 1819.

The town stops here, but beyond is the PILE PIER. Of early C17 origin, extended in 1729 (then resembling the Lyme Regis Cobb), and enlarged again on many occasions between 1840 and 1933, principally for the Great Western Railway ferry service to the Channel Islands. It was further transformed in 1971–2 for the larger ferries. On it, now stranded in a car park, the PAVILION THEATRE of 1958–60 by *Verity & Beverley* with *Oliver Hill* (Beverley's son-in-law), replacing an earlier building of 1908, burnt down in 1954. Attenuated fluted concrete Ionic pilasters with swags between the capitals. The infill panels had shell decoration, now covered. Finally the SEA LIFE TOWER, 2012 by *Huss Park Attractions*. A 174-ft (53-metre)-high shaft with a rising, doughnut-shaped, observation gondola.

Return to the l. of the prow of Devonshire Buildings, to head w along CUSTOM HOUSE QUAY, packed with fishing boats, yachts and pleasure boats, a contrast indeed with The Esplanade. After passing the back of the three-storey, pale brick block of the former EDWARD HOTEL (built as a house *c.* 1801, altered *c.* 1870 and in 1910), the diminutive former HARBOUR MASTER'S OFFICE of 1935. Brick with ashlar stone. Central oriel as a look-out. Further on, the round-arched, vaguely Venetian ROYAL DORSET YACHT CLUB, built as the Sailors' Bethel in 1866, by *Crickmay*. Several C19 brick warehouses here are testament to the working quayside. Turn r. at the CUSTOM HOUSE (*see* p. 649) into EAST STREET for more warehouses and, on the corner with Mitchell Street, l. the florid strapwork decoration of the Jacobethan-cum-Queen Anne GLOBE INN of 1905–6 by *Crickmay & Son*. Along MITCHELL STREET, on the r., the weak Neo-Norman of the WORKING MEN'S CLUB, dated 1873 on the elaborated porch. The ruin of the Methodist church (p. 648) is opposite. Continuing l. into MAIDEN STREET, the long early C17 ashlar-faced range of RAFA WINGS CLUB etc., is on the corner with St Edmund Street. Two gables at right angles, with kneelers at different heights. Mullioned windows arranged in diminishing sizes. The ground floor mutilated when it was converted to a public lavatory. Just down Maiden Street to the quay, on the l. corner the OLD FISH MARKET. One-storeyed, of stone. Big arched openings; roof on deep cantilevered eaves. Of 1854–5 by *Talbot Bury*. Back N, then w along ST EDMUND STREET, passing the former Guildhall (p. 648) on the l., there is the white-painted brick front of the late C18 GOLDEN LION HOTEL on the r. Opposite, a cast-iron balcony with honey-suckle ornament on an early C19 corner block.

We are now in ST MARY STREET, one of two parallel N–S shopping streets. Turning N up the street, passing St Mary's church (*see* p. 647) on the r., a crossroads is reached with St

Alban Street. On the l. corner a terracotta-enriched vestigial corner turret of No. 71, of *c*. 1900. Continuing N to the crossing with BOND STREET, on the r. is the Baroque former MIDLAND BANK (now HSBC) of 1923–4 by *Whinney, Son & Austen Hall*. Further N, on the l. LLOYDS BANK (built as the Wilts. & Dorset Bank), 1865, possibly by *George Evans* of Wimborne. Returning S down St Mary Street and turning r., the block on the SW corner along Bond Street, Nos. 84–86, is mid-C19. Composite pilasters, singly to the St Mary Street façade, coupled facing Bond Street. Following Bond Street W now, as it crosses St Thomas Street (the other main N–S street of old Melcombe), the elaborated corner of the late C19 NATWEST BANK is on the l. Continuing into the pedestrianized NEW BOND STREET, on the l., the WHITE HART TAVERN, the most substantial relic of the C17 town, recorded as the house of Sir John Browne of Frampton in 1617. C19 stuccoed front, but the sides N and S have Portland ashlar gables on elegantly scrolled corbels. (Stone newel staircase, and on the first floor an early C17 plaster ceiling.) It is isolated (but mercifully preserved) in a part of the town redeveloped as the NEW BOND STREET SHOPPING CENTRE, opened in 2000.*

Returning down ST THOMAS STREET S, towards the bridge, on the r., at the crossing with St Alban Street, the former POST OFFICE. Lively brick and stone Edwardian Baroque with a domed bow at the corner, of *c*. 1905 by *John Rutherford* (extended by *Roland Smith*, *c*. 1921). There is nothing of further note until the TOWN BRIDGE of 1930 (replacing that of 1824) by *H.W. Fitzsimons*, engineer. Bold ashlar abutments with a pair of metal lifting sections over the harbour.

3. Over the bridge to Weymouth old town

Across the bridge, old Weymouth consists largely of cottagey terraces. Before looking at these, turn r. in front of Holy Trinity church (p. 645), past the deplorable Council Offices (p. 648) to find behind HIGH STREET not only the Old Town Hall (*see* p. 649) but also the BOOT INN. C17, much restored, with five-light upper windows, four-light lower with hoodmoulds. Hollow-chamfered mullions. That is one early survivor. There are others in Trinity Street. This is reached by retracing our steps past the bridge and along TRINITY ROAD, lined on one side by terraces composed into unspoilt early C19 groups, shallow window bows and mansard roofs being the dominant motifs. At the widening of the harbour, where formerly there was an inlet (Hope Cove, infilled in the 1780s), the brick part of the OLD ROOMS INN, with a symmetrical sashed front. Built

---

*Nearby, in Nicholas Street, was the WHITE ENSIGN NAVAL CLUB, of 1905 by *Crickmay & Son*. Free classical, red brick banded in ashlar. It was demolished in 1970. John Newman described it as 'Weymouth's most distinguished building of the last hundred years'.

c. 1765 as an assembly room, the first in the town. Attached to the back, facing on to TRINITY STREET, a late C16 house and probably the earliest survival in the town. A gabled two-storey central porch boldly projecting. Square-headed doorway moulded with a hollow chamfer. The windows, one bay l. and r., are of six lights on both floors. Portland stone walling. Much restored. Opposite, Nos. 2–3 Trinity Street of *c.* 1600 is perhaps the best suggestion, with its Portland ashlar front and its pair of gables, of what the pre-C18 town looked like. Carefully repaired by *E. Wamsley Lewis* in 1958. The streets here, as in other areas near to the harbour, have C19 warehouses interspersed with houses.

A great leap in scale at the s end of the street in HOPE SQUARE, with the former GROVES BREWERY, 1903–4 by *Arthur Kinder & Son*. Mercantile Dutch brick. An earlier malt-house, of 1889 by *Crickmay & Son*, with 'Groves' picked out under the malting-roof eaves, is to the E, with, in front of it, a lower but more elaborate brick brewery building of 1878. Adjoining to the w, the buildings of the DEVENISH BREWERY (plain, red brick, mid-C19), with which Groves amalgamated in 1960. Regrettably, with closure in 1985 none of these survives as a working brewery.

OUTER WEYMOUTH

EDWARDS' HOMES, Rodwell Road, ¼ m. w. 1894 by *Crickmay & Son* for Sir Henry Edwards, in the character of almshouses. Pale Broadmayne brick with stone dressings. Five cottages facing the main road, five in James Street. At the corner between the blocks an armorial shield and inscription on a bold chamfer. Another, bulkier block (dated 1896), just SE in Rodwell Avenue. Tudor Revival. The same brick.

PORTLAND HOUSE (National Trust), Belle Vue Road, ½ m. s. 1935 by *Wellesley & Wills* for G.H. Bushby. Blended Spanish and Tuscan villa styles. White stucco walls and rich red Dutch pantiles. Casual L-plan, presenting a relaxed symmetry on the s front. Here a blend of Palladian and Mediterranean features. Sea-view terraces on two levels. Internal features generally Neo-Georgian, although the decorative tiled risers to the main stair continue the Mediterranean theme.

SANDSFOOT CASTLE, Old Castle Road, 1 m. SSW. Built as companion to Portland Castle (*see* p. 484) across Weymouth Bay, but through erosion of the shore and robbing of the stone facings sadly less well preserved. The castle was complete in 1541, having cost £3,887 4s. 1d. The octagonal gunroom has fallen into the sea, but the two-storey quarters for the garrison remain as a pockmarked shell, with a little of the Portland ashlar facing left round the window reveals. Entrance gate-tower at the landward end, with staircases in the depth of the wall l. and r. The gate-tower itself is square in plan and rises higher than the walls, as it always did. Its inner entrance arch has a flattened pointed head, as do the windows on both levels in the long sides. Fireplaces and garderobes in the depth of the wall at both levels. Large basement fireplace in the seaward wall. Internal walkways for public access added 2013.

WHITCHURCH CANONICORUM

A rather rambling village of many thatched cottages. There is no obvious centre apart from the splendid church, known locally as the Cathedral of the Vale.

ST CANDIDA (or ST WITE) AND THE HOLY CROSS. One of the most impressive parish churches of Dorset, and principally an E.E. one. But the s doorway is at once a reminder of yet older things.* It is late C12, with one order of columns, one of the capitals approaching the early C13 crocket form. Also, the arch has dogtooth; however, it is still round. This doorway led to the s aisle of a small Norman church, to judge from what survives, of only three bays in length.

Continuing with the exterior, on the chancel a s doorway with a trefoil head and trefoil hoodmould. The E group is of three single-stepped lancets, plain, without hoodmoulds. The s transept has two large w lancets and a Late Dec-style s window installed during the major restoration of 1848–9 by *Joseph Butler* of Chichester. His too the quatrefoil clerestory windows and the aisle windows. He was probably also responsible for the Perp-looking vestry to the E of the s transept. Its s window is Dec, but looking suspiciously C19, and one cannot count on the E lancet being genuine E.E. either. The N transept N window is however C15 Perp; one E window here is Dec, the other an E.E. lancet, both re-set after the E chapels were removed (see the relieving arch marking the former opening into one of the chapels). Perp too the s porch and above all else the early C15 three-stage w tower. It has a doorway with traceried spandrels, a quatrefoil frieze over, a transomed w window with niches l. and r., also a s niche, slender set-back buttresses and a battlemented top with eight pinnacles. The N aisle was rebuilt as part of *Butler*'s restoration.

The interior now. The late C12 s aisle of three bays (which relates to its s doorway) has two round arcade piers with square abaci, one very flat scallop capital, the other of a kind of broad waterleaf. Round arch of two slight chamfers. The church which went with that nave probably had a crossing tower. But the great campaign began immediately after that – probably *c.* 1200: a new chancel, new transepts, a new N aisle (replaced in 1848–9). The N aisle arcade of four bays (but of the same length as the earlier three-bay s aisle) seems to come first.

21

---

*Older still are the ROMAN TILES in the external walls of the N transept, the N wall of the chancel and under the NE and SE ends of the rebuilt E wall of the church.

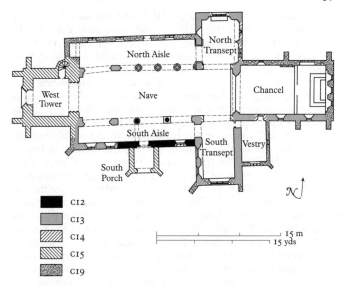

Whitchurch Canonicorum, St Candida and the Holy Cross.
Plan

Piers, two with four shafts and flat diagonals, one with four
main and four subsidiary shafts. The capitals are mostly of a
leaf kind neither Norman nor at all E.E. stiff-leaf. There is a
great variety of them, but there are also big trumpet scallops,
and that is a form rather contemporary with, than later than,
waterleaf. The arches are pointed, but also one of them still has
boldly undercut horizontal chevrons all up and all down. The
other arches have complicated rolls. The trumpets occur in the
arch to the N transept too. So that is likely to be contemporary.
The E arch of the S aisle has roll mouldings and was built to
link up with the S transept. The N transept has spectacular
wall-shafting with shaft-rings and still the same leaf capitals.
Originally there were chapels E of the transepts and also an
arch across the N end. The S transept is soberer. Only the W
wall has shafts with shaft-rings and still the same capitals.
Finally the chancel. The responds of its arch have major and
minor shafts and leaves perhaps nearer the stiff-leaf. Shafted E
window with rings. The N and S windows have continuous rolls
instead. What is remarkable is the condition of the carving,
especially in the nave – practically as fresh as the day it was
completed. The tower has a tall panelled arch to the nave. This
is late C15. It must be contemporary with the panelled arches
from the nave E bay to the transepts. What remains a puzzle is
the W arches of N and S arcades, for they seem to be intended
to link up with the new tower and yet are C13.

FURNISHINGS. PULPIT. Early C17. Oak, with two tiers of
elaborated arches. Further carving to the top and bottom rails.

– STALLS. The arabesque panels at the top and the mostly traceried panels at the ends are said to be early C16 French. – CLERGY DESK. This appears to be made up from C15 or C16 Perp panelling. – FONT. Late C12 bowl, cauldron-shaped, with intersecting arches. On a stem and base of 1849. – SHRINE OF ST WITE. A complete C13 *foramina* tomb shrine (i.e. with openings to allow access to the tomb within), which is an extreme rarity, but a totally plain one. Three mandorla-shaped openings in the front. – STAINED GLASS. Fragments in a chancel S window (including a hovering angel) and the N transept N window. Mostly C15. The E window is largely grisaille by *Powell & Sons*, 1849. – MONUMENTS. Part of the indent of the brass to Thomas de Luda, *c.* 1320, originally in Abbotsbury Abbey. The brass was a foliated cross. (For the rest *see* Askerswell.) – John Wadham †1584. An oddly crude tablet of two panels with tracery heads. Above is a steep pediment in which is a lozenge of circles. Against the top of the l. panel the inscription on brass. The base seems to be a medieval tomb-chest with two quatrefoils. – Sir John Jeffery †1611. A standing monument with recumbent effigy and much exceptionally intricate strapwork with masks, fleurons, cornucopias and other motifs. The strapwork is on the tomb-chest, as on the back wall. On the top two small, badly done allegorical figures and a shield.

p. 34

HIGHER ABBOTTS WOOTTON FARM, 1¼ m. NW. A complete small house of *c.* 1500, of the simple plan best expressed at the Abbots House Hotel, Charmouth. Here there is no addition to obscure the rectangular plan. Rubble, with big quoin stones. On the other hand the only original features are the S doorway and the window l. of it. The latter's deep mouldings, a hollow and ovolo here, and heavy hoodmould with big square labels are typical of the first decades of the C16. (C19 window inserted through it.)

HARDOWN HILL, ¾ m. SE. A cluster of five ROUND BARROWS, one pond and four bowls. In 1916 Saxon spearheads, axes and other metalwork of *c.* 450–550 A.D. were retrieved from one bowl barrow, perhaps a votive deposit.

CONEY'S CASTLE, 2 m. NW. Iron Age HILL-FORT, univallate, of half an acre, with a small enclosure abutting on the S, and a northern entrance disturbed by a road cutting through.

WHITCOMBE

The village had largely disappeared by the late C18, leaving only a farm hamlet to the S of the church.

CHURCH (Churches Conservation Trust). In a modest but perfect setting. The W two-thirds of the nave is C12, retaining a simple S doorway and a blocked N one opposite. In the late C15 the nave was refaced and extended E, with a new chancel, all in one with the nave. Perp windows, but in the E wall a group of three stepped C13 E.E. lancets. Late C16 W tower; mullioned bell-openings with Somerset tracery. On one panel (s) the date 1596 and initials MA. The nave S wall, E of the porch, was reconstructed in the C18, and the E wall rebuilt in 1912 as part of a restoration by *Jem Feacey* of Dorchester. This uncovered the wall paintings (*see* below) and a rood-loft stair in the N wall. – FONT. C13. Octagonal, of Purbeck marble, with two flat blank arches each side. – PAINTINGS on the N wall. Bold wall arcading, late C13. St Christopher, an impressive figure, late C15. – SCULPTURE. Two parts of an Anglo-Saxon cross-shaft with interlace of two different types.

LONG BARROW, 2 m. SSW. Aligned NE–SW, to the N of Culliford Tree Barrow group.

CULLIFORD TREE BARROW, 2¼ m. SSW. The largest barrow within a large linear group (*see* Broadmayne and Winterborne Came). Within a tree-clump enclosure planted in 1740, a bowl of 95 ft (29 metres) diameter and about 13 ft (4 metres) high. The barrow became the meeting place of the Hundred to which it gave its name. Excavation revealed a Wessex interment.

MEDIEVAL SETTLEMENT. Earthworks around the church, covering 14 acres.

WIMBORNE MINSTER

0090

Except for the Blandford road, approaching from the NW, every entrance to the town requires the crossing of a river, indicating its foundation on a relatively defensible site given the flatness of the surrounding land. From W and S arrival is over the broad River Stour, from N and E it is the slighter River Allen. Some settlement existed in the Roman period, demonstrated by a portion of tessellated pavement found beneath the Minster nave in 1857. Through the early medieval period the town grew up around the Minster, with the Cornmarket to its NW (part of the Dean's Market) and the High Street running N, where the main market was moved following its expulsion from the Minster churchyard in 1224. The Square, at the N end of the High Street, was until the early C16 a wooded area where St Peter's Chapel stood. It gradually developed to became an extension of the High Street. The chapel, having been converted to secular use by the early C16, had disappeared altogether when the first accurate town maps were made in the mid C18.

The Borough was a separate settlement outside the N edge of the medieval town, controlled by an independent manor court. Its development was more sporadic until the late C18, when it was incorporated into the main part of the town which expanded N towards Walford Bridge and its mill. Two parallel streets lined with fine houses, East Borough and West Borough, were more completely built up at this time. In the early C19 the beginnings of a suburb grew E from the Minster towards Leigh, reinforced by the arrival of the Southampton & Dorchester Railway in 1847, its station near to Canford Bridge in the SE corner of the town. A church for the area, St John, was built in 1876. To the N of Leigh Road, Rowlands, an area of fashionable villas, was completed by the 1880s. This eventually linked up with the similar villa areas of Colehill (q.v.). Continued expansion has been largely to the E and NE, the commendably preserved water meadows to the S and W giving the town a satisfyingly abrupt edge.

MINSTER CHURCH OF ST CUTHBURGA

Cuthburga, sister of King Ine, founded a nunnery at Wimborne before 705, of which she became abbess. The foundation also included a monastery where King Æthelred of Wessex was later buried in 871. Edward the Confessor revived religious life by creating a college of secular canons. The college was called a deanery under Henry III. Edward II in 1318 declared the church a free chapel, exempt from ordinary ecclesiastical jurisdiction. It was dissolved in 1547. Of the collegiate buildings nothing is preserved, but the church is there *in toto* – 186 ft (57 metres) long internally.

Wimborne Minster, as nowadays one drives around it, is imposing, but it is not obviously beautiful. The mixtures of stone patching and towers of two very different styles, with similar heights and both on the axis of the nave, may appear awkward, but they also speak of a structure that has evolved. The central tower once carried a tall stone spire, and much of the speckled character is the result of a Victorian desire to mimic the older, repaired masonry. The uncouth corbelling-out of the central tower parapet with its four heavy pinnacles can be related to

Wimborne Minster, from the south.
Engraving, 1800

more sophisticated contemporary tower design in Somerset. However, this formed part of the mid-C19 restoration, although engravings indicate that it is a reasonably accurate copy of a 1608 arrangement.

With the exception of a fragment of Roman tessellated pavement beneath the present nave floor (visible through an opening), the earliest fabric is of a cruciform Saxo-Norman church of the mid C11. The cores of the crossing piers and some inner parts of the transepts are of this date; the original length of the latter is indicated by a circular stair-turret projection on the W side of the N transept (originally its NW corner), and matching masonry on the W face of the S transept. In c. 1170–90 the nave and choir were rebuilt, the former acquiring a four-bay aisle and a clerestory. At this point the E end is thought to have been apsed, and flanked by four apsed chapels in echelon, as at Shaftesbury. The tower was also reconstructed and heightened. The E end was rebuilt further E around 1230, with a rectangular ambulatory and square-ended Lady Chapel to the E of the high altar (at that time located to the W of its present position). In the early C14 the floor of the Lady Chapel was raised, and a vaulted crypt created beneath. Around 1350 the crypt was extended by a further W bay, with new steps down into it from the ambulatory. The chancel was extended E to take in the Lady Chapel, with steps to the level of the raised floor above the crypt. N and S chapels were formed by widening the ambulatory. A vaulted S vestry and a N porch were also added in the C14, and the nave was extended westwards by two bays. A tall spire was added to the crossing tower in the early C15 (it collapsed in 1600), and in the mid C15 the W tower was erected. Almost immediately following, the nave roof was raised and a new clerestory added; the N porch and the S vestry were provided with upper floors, the latter now the library. C19 restoration took place chiefly in 1855–7 and 1866, both by *T.H. Wyatt*, and 1890–2 by *John Loughborough Pearson*, working with *W.J. Fletcher* of Wimborne.

Exterior

The CROSSING TOWER was no doubt first faced in creamy-white limestone. Years of repairs with a more local dark brown heathstone have led to a decidedly mottled colouring. Its first stage has two round-headed windows to each side with a blank pointed arch between. The windows are double-shafted. The capitals of the shafts have trumpet and crocket and stiff-leaf forms. So we are c. 1135–40 here. On the W side the nave roof cuts into that stage. The stage above has intersecting arches, and it is interesting to note that pointed lancet windows fit into the intersections. It was one of the theories of the late C18 and early C19 concerning the origin of the Gothic style that it had come about naturally by means of intersecting arches. Nowadays we know that styles do not come about in that way. All stages together have giant angle shafts with shaft-rings.

13

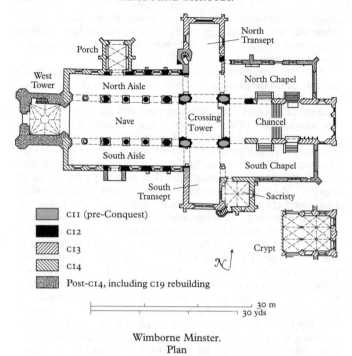

Wimborne Minster.
Plan

The distinctive corbelled-out top and pinnacles have already
been discussed.

The original extent of the TRANSEPTS is marked by the
round stair-turret on the W side of the N transept. Its string
courses, also found on the S transept, indicate that the latter
was of an equivalent length. The N extension can be dated
to *c.* 1260–70 from the correct, if over-restored, Geometrical
tracery. The N window has four lights, two quatrefoiled circles
and a larger sexfoiled one at the top. The E and W windows
are of two lights only, also with a foiled circle. The S transept
is different, first because the SACRISTY of *c.* 1350, with C15
upper floor (much rebuilt by *Pearson*), hides its E side, secondly
because the S window is of five stepped cusped lancet lights
under one arch. This is a product of the *Pearson* restoration
of 1890–2, replacing, according to Hutchins's engraving of
1803, Geometric tracery much like that of the N transept. All
the exposed Norman masonry in the transepts is of heathstone
rubble, uncoursed and very rough. It was surely first painted
or rendered, as seems to have been the case in many Norman
churches. The roof-lines of both transepts were re-profiled
by *Pearson* and much of the upper masonry is of this date,
although no doubt incorporating reused stone.

We continue first to the E. The EAST END has the choir
projecting by only one shallow bay. However, until the mid
C19 the E end of the choir and its N aisle approximately lined

up. The present arrangement is owed to *Wyatt*, who largely rebuilt the choir aisles in their present form, 1855–7. The main E window has three separate uncusped stepped lancets, with sexfoils and quatrefoils in plate tracery. This is of *c.* 1230 and was largely unaffected by the mid-C19 restoration. Beneath the E windows, and lighting the crypt, are five spherical-triangular windows, restored by *Wyatt*. The choir N aisle starts from the transept with one small Norman doorway, earlier obviously than the crossing tower, but re-set by *Wyatt*. Its tympanum has a segmental arch. The aisle windows, with cusped Y-tracery, are *Wyatt*'s. The stepped five-light windows of both choir aisle E windows, together with the gables in which they are set, are also his. The unfortunate flat-roofed sacristy and vestry of 1968 (by *R.K. Brett*) obscures the lower part of the S aisle.

The NAVE is the same both sides, except for the porches. C12 masonry from the crossing as far as the porch, with inserted two-light bar-tracery aisle windows of the later C13. Then, further W, the windows have C14 cusped Y-tracery – evidence for the extension of the nave westwards at this time. Three-light Perp clerestory windows, each with a straight top and elementary panel tracery between lights and top. *Wyatt*'s work of 1855–7 probably copied what had previously existed here, but reduced the number of windows from six to five. The sandstone ashlar of the clerestory is also mid C19, no doubt intended to match the early medieval masonry elsewhere.

The NORTH PORCH dates from *c.* 1350 but has a C15 upper storey. The lower storey is rib-vaulted in two bays, the ribs with fillets, the bosses with naturalistic foliage. The wall-shafts are of Purbeck marble. The entrance has continuous mouldings including a fillet, the doorway two continuous chamfers.

The Perp WEST TOWER is forbidding where the crossing tower is loquacious. It was built from 1448 to 1464 (according to Hutchins), is 87 ft (26.5 metres) high, and is almost sheer to the top. The Perp W doorway, together with the large six-light window above, are both *Wyatt*'s. The tower has polygonal clasping buttresses (cf. Bradford Abbas). The bell-openings are two each side, of two lights with a transom.

Interior

Here again we must begin at the CROSSING, and, as might be expected, because it can take some time to build a crossing tower, the four arches on which it stands are in fact more than a generation older than the rest. In fact the whole crossing as such may go back to the Saxo-Norman predecessor of the present building. The argument is the extruded outer angles of the crossing piers, the motif also found at Sherborne and e.g. at Stow in Lincolnshire. It means that the crossing was not strictly a crossing of identical chancel, transept and nave width, but was slightly wider in both directions. But even leaving this out of consideration the Norman crossing can hardly be

14

later than *c.* 1135–40. Two shafts rise to the round, single-step arches, depressed W and E, stilted N and S. In addition there are subsidiary single shafts. The capitals have comparatively large and few scallops. The next stage inside has a wall passage with Purbeck shafts arranged in groups of four lights with round arches under one pointed relieving arch. The top stage inside, corresponding to the lower outside, has shafted windows with blind pointed arches between. Banded corner shafts are found in the two tower stages also.

The crossing campaign extended into nave and choir, as we shall soon see. But first the TRANSEPTS. The arch from the N transept into the choir aisle is Dec above C12 imposts. Next to it, to the N, a C13 altar recess, very simple and totally undramatic, blocking off the original opening of the C12 outer chapel. (For the mural painting *see* below.) In the W wall is a small Norman doorway. It leads to the tower staircase, which continues high up as a corridor on corbelled courses. The C13 windows are shafted. The S transept has the arch to the choir aisle like the N one. In this case the C12 outer chapel arch, leading through to the choir aisle, was replaced with a pointed arch in the C13. The lancet to its S was blocked when the sacristy was built. In the S wall a PISCINA with trefoiled head, the moulding all studded with dogtooth.

14   There is good reason to continue with the NAVE rather than the choir: for it is in the nave that the Norman story continues. As a matter of fact Wimborne inside is largely a Norman building, which one would not guess externally. The Norman nave arcades begin from the crossing with a very narrow bay. That, as the scallops and fish-scales of the E corbels show, belongs to the crossing, although the single-step arch is pointed. This first bay had to be built to secure the job of carrying up the tower. It acted as W buttresses. The entrances from the transepts to the aisles on the other hand are not now Norman. They have C13 Purbeck shafts with Perp capitals but C13 arches. High up in the nave one can see the former roof-line and in the gable a small Norman window. The next three bays of the arcade start after a short bit of solid wall. They are Late Norman. Round piers, many-scalloped capitals, square abaci with nicked corners, higher pointed arches with chevron, also at right angles to the wall. On the apexes of the arches human and monster heads. Above, a course of small, shallow chevron serving to mark the sill of the Norman clerestory windows. Above all this is *Wyatt*'s Perp clerestory. The W respond of this Norman arcade is followed by some walling representing the Norman W wall. An extension took place early in the C14. It was of two bays, but the C15 tower cut into the second of them. The NE impost has ballflower. The piers are octagonal, the arches double-chamfered. The tower arch is very high and has large-scale Perp roll-and-wave mouldings. In the tower a tierceron-star vault. The hammerbeam nave roof was installed by *Wyatt*, reusing C17 carved wooden bosses.

The CHOIR starts with a Norman bay with responds like those of the crossing but capitals with small busy decoration. The arches are pointed and single-stepped like those of the nave E bay. Against the wall of the crossing, just as on the W wall, the former roof-line is marked, and in the gable is another small Norman window. The next bay is of *c.* 1350: it has three orders of shafts and a triple-chamfered arch. The upper windows are mid-C19. Steps lead up now to the high choir. The boundary is marked by giant triple shafts with thick leaf capitals. The E bay towards the choir aisles has Purbeck shafts, including a triple one and beautifully fine mouldings with fillets, *c.* 1230. Outstandingly good hoodmould stops, especially Moses, of *c.* 1200, re-set. Two clerestory windows of *c.* 1230 on each side. The three stepped lancets of the E wall are rather wilfully expressed inside by a string course which follows the arches but is blown up then to run round the foiled circles too. They have triple Purbeck shafts, a multiplicity of mouldings, and the central light emphasized by dogtooth enrichment. Against the S wall of the chancel is a delightful early C14 group of PISCINA and SEDILIA, with crocketed ogee gables; the exuberant finials are *Wyatt*'s.

That leaves the vaulted separate rooms – the sacristy and the crypt. The SACRISTY has an octopartite rib-vault, the ribs finely moulded, including the Dec sunk-quadrant moulding. The CHAINED LIBRARY above (founded in 1685 in the upper vestry, second largest in the country after Hereford) has no architecturally interesting features. The CRYPT is Dec too, but of two dates. The (more attractive) W bay with responds and continuous mouldings with fillets may be of *c.* 1350. This W bay as well as the two E bays are of three bays' width. The two parts are divided by three cusped arches.

Furnishings and monuments

CHOIR. The STALLS date from 1608. They are medieval in type but have the familiar blank arches on their fronts and foliage on the arms. The same is true of the READING DESKS. The rear stalls originally had ornate, high-canopied backs and the arrangement was completed by a screen. *Wyatt*'s 1855–7 restoration was unnecessarily destructive in that he removed both the stalls' canopies and an accompanying choir screen.* A fragment of Cosmatesque mosaic of *c.* 1270–80, thought to come from a shrine to St Cuthburga located in the sanctuary (after it was enlarged eastwards *c.* 1230), was rediscovered in 2008. The shrine was probably commissioned by Henry de Lacy, 5th Earl of Lincoln.** – STAINED GLASS. The middle E window

---

*The canopies and choir screen are illustrated in N. Whittock, *Views of the Exterior and Interior of the Collegiate Church of St Cuthburga, Wimborne Minster, Dorset* (1839).
**See L. Rees and M. J. T. Lewis, *Antiquaries Journal* 94, 2014.

has a Tree of Jesse, Flemish, early C16. Re-set by *Thomas Willement c.* 1840; the accompanying E and side windows are by him. – MONUMENTS. On the N wall St Ethelred, king of the West Saxons. Brass demi-figure, 14½ in. (39 cm.) long. Dated to *c.* 1440. The inscription plate is C17. – Within the arch through to the S aisle, John Beaufort, Duke of Somerset, †1444, and his duchess. Purbeck tomb-chest with cusped quatrefoils. On it two alabaster effigies, holding hands. Significant areas of the original paintwork survive. – Within the N arch, Gertrude, Marchioness of Exeter, †1558, yet a very similar tomb-chest still and not a touch of the Renaissance.

CHOIR NORTH AISLE (St George's Chapel). STAINED GLASS. E window of five lights, by *N.W. Lavers*, †1851. The heraldic window in the N wall is by *Willement*, 1838. To its l. a window by *Alexander Gibbs*, 1857. Next l. one by *Clayton & Bell*, †1890. – MONUMENTS. Damaged early C14 knight, SE corner. – Sir Edmund Uvedale †1606. Standing alabaster monument. He is lying on his side, his pose more relaxed than usual. Two columns, two obelisks, strapwork and ribbonwork. – Above a funeral HELM.

CHOIR SOUTH AISLE (Trinity Chapel). STAINED GLASS. A very fine five-light window in the E wall, by *Lavers*, 1857. The heraldic 'Beaufort' window in the S wall is by *Willement*, 1838. To its W the 'Lace Window' by *Heaton & Butler, c.* 1855. – MONUMENTS. Anthony Etricke, originally dated 1693 (altered to 1703). Black casket with painted shields. – William Et(t)ricke †1716. Large tablet without figures.

CROSSING. The majestic stone PULPIT is of 1868; the carving was done by *Thomas Earp.** – The equally majestic brass LECTERN of the eagle type is dated 1623.

NORTH TRANSEPT. The WALL PAINTING in the Norman recess is slightly clearer to read after conservation in 2008. It consists of five layers, dating from the late C12 to the late C14. The first is purely decorative; two of the later ones are Crucifixions. – STAINED GLASS. Four-light N window, †1891, by *Clayton & Bell*, who were also responsible for the two-light windows in the E and W walls.

SOUTH TRANSEPT. ORGAN. Rebuilt by *J.W. Walker & Sons*, 1965; the oldest pipes date from 1664. The sound is produced only partly through the conventional pipes. Above there is a display of musically functional gilded trumpets sticking out, a delightful idea. – STAINED GLASS. S window by *Powell & Sons*, 1892. – A number of TABLETS, the best John Moyle †1719.

NORTH AISLE. STAINED GLASS. The first from the E is a colourful window by *Baillie & Co.*, 1874. Next l. an early work by *Clayton & Bell*, †1859. To the l. (w) of the N door a later window, probably by the same (†1886), and further W a window depicting St Luke and St Cuthburga by *Bell & Beckham*, 1883. – MONUMENT. Thomas Hanham †1650, attributed to *William Wright*

---

* It replaced a wooden pulpit that was moved to Holt.

(GF). Two kneeling figures facing one another across a prayer-desk. This is a motif of Elizabethan and Jacobean funerary sculpture, but the pediment and the sparse foliage are post-Jacobean. – TABLETS. Harry Constantine, Sen. & Jun., †1712 and †1744. – Thomas Fox †1730.

SOUTH AISLE. STAINED GLASS. First from E by *Willement*, 1858. That to the r. of the doorway, by *Lavers & Barraud*, 1858. The last (W) probably by *Michael O'Connor*, †1857. – TABLETS. Bartholomew Lane †1679. – William Fitch who 'did in his life time cause this marble to be erected', 1705. – Warham family, 1746. – George Bethell †1782. Trophy at the top, but now also an Adamish oval patera at the foot.

TOWER. FONT. C13. With a Purbeck marble bowl, octagonal, with two blank pointed-trefoiled arches each side. Supported on eight Purbeck columns and a central spiral-moulded stem. – ROYAL ARMS, Stuart, C17, over the tower arch. – ASTRONOMICAL CLOCK. Said to be C14, but the case has early C17 reused panels. Supported on reused C12 corbels. – STAINED GLASS. The large W window is by *Heaton & Butler*, †1852. Beneath, in the tympanum of the W doorway, a memorial window by *Henry Haig*, 1992.

Outside the building against the bell-openings to the N is the QUARTER JACK, installed in 1612, with a Grenadier figure added in the early C19. – In front of the S side of the tower a monumental free-standing SUNDIAL on a high square base. It is dated 1676, but was placed here in 1894, having been removed from the S transept gable. – On the N, WAR MEMORIAL, 1921, by *Comper*. In the style of an Eleanor cross, with carved figures in the four faces of the crocket-enriched lantern.

OTHER CHURCHES AND PUBLIC BUILDINGS

ST JOHN THE EVANGELIST, on the corner of Leigh Road and St John's Hill, ⅜ m. E. Brick, with transepts and an apsed E end. Lancet windows. Bellcote on W gable. By *W. J. Fletcher*, 1876. Large brick additions of 1973, 1990 and 2005. The last, by *rlm Architects* of Bournemouth, included a complete reordering of the church interior. – STAINED GLASS. Chancel windows by *Heaton, Butler & Bayne*, 1904. They also did two windows in the N aisle, 1914 and †1922.

ST CATHERINE (R.C.), Lewens Lane, ¼ m E. By *P. A. Byrne*. Grey rubble stone very convincingly in the style of the 1830s. Slim W tower. Amazingly, it was completed in 1933, with the tower added 1936. The fin-like vaulting of the interior has a more contemporary flavour. – STAINED GLASS. Window in S transept by *Paul Woodroffe* of Chipping Campden, *c*. 1938.

Plain CHURCH HALL to the N, 1983, by *Pantlin & Bradbury*.

METHODIST CHURCH and COMMUNITY HOUSE, King Street. *See* p. 670.

UNITED REFORMED CHURCH (formerly Congregational), Chapel Lane. Gothic. 1846. Stuccoed, with a pair of turret-topped hexagonal buttresses on its gabled entrance front.

CEMETERY CHAPELS and LODGE. *See* Cemetery Road, Pamphill, p. 442.

COUNTY LIBRARY, Crown Mead. Of *c.* 1980 by the *County Architect's Department*, making good use of its mill-stream site. Brick. Picturesque massing of monopitches.

QUEEN ELIZABETH'S GRAMMAR SCHOOL, Grammar School Lane, s from the minster. 1849–51 by *Morris & Hebson*. Red diaper brick and Bath stone, very rich and imposing. The style of Henry VII, chosen because the school was founded in his reign. That justifies the ogee-domed turrets on either side of the central gable, which has a large Perp-style window. Converted to flats in 1982.

PERAMBULATION

A short circuit from the minster to the N and E, via The Square, will suffice to bring everything of interest into view.

First, then, from the E end of the minster, past the spiritless Perp-Gothic CHURCH HOUSE of 1905–6 by *W. J. Fletcher*, N into the HIGH STREET. Here, one of only two significant Tudor secular survivals in Wimborne, the PRIEST'S HOUSE, now a museum. (The other is St Joseph's, King Street, *see* below.) Towards the street all that shows is the stone gable-end at the l. The answering gable of the half-H-plan at the r. end, now a shop, was rebuilt in the C18. At the same time the originally recessed forecourt was filled in flush to the street, obscuring the w hall elevation. Rainwater heads of 1756 and 1783. Inside, the medieval building can be seen to be of Purbeck-Portland limestone. Lighting the hall one five-light window, with hoodmould, arched lights and a frame moulding of a deep hollow and roll. A date *c.* 1500 is suggested. A doorway with a four-centred head cuts into the r. light of the window, repositioned here when the original screens passage (to the r. of the window at the s end of the hall) was taken by the adjoining building. NE parlour with plaster ceiling of ribs in geometrical patterns, and an incised pattern on the frieze. This also has the wording 'AL PEOPLE REFRAYNE FROM SYN' and the initials IW AW, possibly John Woods, incumbent at the Minster 1604–20. At the back (E), facing one of the few remaining complete burgage plots in the town, evidence of two building periods. The lower part is all stone, with a four-light window to the l., like the window inside. Upper storey banded with stone and flint. The windows here the typical late C16/early C17 sort, with hollow-chamfered mullions and hoodmoulds. One stone (r.) and one timber-framed gable, off-centre over the hall. The arrangement roughly symmetrical about the doorway.

To the rear, the HILDA COLES OPEN LEARNING CENTRE, 2012 by *East Dorset District Council*. Timber-framed with vertical board cladding.

THE SQUARE opens towards the w. It wears quite a townish aspect, the main accents being the sandstone Baroque HSBC BANK (originally London Joint City & Midland Bank) of *c.* 1920 on the s side; the KINGS HEAD HOTEL (formerly Laing's Hotel), closing the w end, late C18, but significantly rebuilt with an additional storey and a new rendered classical façade of giant Tuscan pilasters in 1885; the ashlar Italianate façade of LLOYDS BANK (originally the Wilts. & Dorset Bank), of *c.* 1872 by *Evans & Fletcher*, in the middle of the N side; and BARCLAYS BANK in the NE corner, 1980 by *Pantlin & Bradbury*, dark brick with a courtyard behind. From the SW corner of The Square, CORNMARKET, the town's second square, can be reached down Church Street, where on the corner is the ODDFELLOWS' HALL, built by the town's Friendly Society in 1758 (on a tablet). Dutch gable above a Venetian window, the arcade below now glazed in. The WHITE HART is C17 with a front of *c.* 1800. Rusticated and arched C19 doorway. Also, on the s side, the former GEORGE INN, late C18 with a miniature early C18 Venetian window over its coach-way, and a fine C19 wrought-iron sign-bracket.

Back to The Square via WEST STREET, where No. 31 has a fine red brick later C18 façade of 1:5:1 bays, the outer bays C19. Segment-headed windows with white key blocks. Modern (but sympathetic) classical doorcase.

Wimborne's best street, WEST BOROUGH, runs N from the NW corner of The Square. It is a complete Georgian picture (marred now somewhat by bus shelters), red brick and white-rendered cottages, a pair of the latter still thatched, lining both sides, with just a few stronger accents, and in the distance a large tree to give a sense of scale. First, free-standing on the l., PURBECK HOUSE, *c.* 1830, rendered, three bays, two-storeyed, with a big Portland stone porch of starved Tuscan Doric columns. Next on the l. the NATWEST BANK: a mid-C19 three-bay house with banking hall of *c.* 1900 attached. The latter ashlar, with two Venetian windows and a Doric doorway on the corner entrance. Opposite, No. 10, a handsome red brick façade of *c.* 1780. Three-storeyed. Round-headed lower windows recessed in blank arcading. Broken pediment outlined over the centre three bays. Nos. 30–32, again late C18, tall and red brick, again with the lower windows (with Gothick glazing bars) in blank arcading of an odd alternating rhythm; but planned from the first as a pair of houses. The TIVOLI THEATRE opposite has a five-bay front of *c.* 1730, savagely mauled on the ground floor. A form very typical of this area, two-storeyed with a parapet. Keystones to the windows. The central upper window in an eared surround ending in scrolls. To the rear, CINEMA, 1936, by *E. de W. Holding*.

There is no need to walk further N, and one can turn r. down Priors Walk (widened in 1967) to reach ALLENDALE HOUSE, Hanham Road, now East Dorset Heritage Centre. Built 1823 by *Sir Jeffry Wyatville* for William Castleman, the Marquess of Anglesey's local agent and chief promoter of 'Castleman's Corkscrew', the Southampton & Dorchester Railway. Stucco, projecting bracketed eaves to low-pitched hipped roof. Porch on coupled Greek Doric columns. Over the bridge on the r., PIPPINS, children's home, 1968 by *J.R. Hurst*, the County

Architect. Compact, flat-roofed, two-storeyed. Formerly part of an earlier group of buildings, largely replaced by the STREETS MEADOW & HANHAM CENTRE elderly people's facility, 2004 by *R.J. Mitchell*. Banded brick with shallow-pitched roofs.

s from the bridge, alongside the River Allen, on the r. the CROWN MEAD shopping centre. 1978 by *Jackson, Greenen, Down & Partners*. Brick, bell-cast pitched slate roofs. Its alignment on the open space beyond the town centre raises it above the mundane. To the l., on former recreation grounds, the clean lines of WAITROSE, 2010 by *Farrell & Clark*. The return to the centre passes the County Library (p. 668). On the s side of King Street opposite the Minster, METHODIST CHURCH and COMMUNITY HOUSE, 1967, by *Pantlin & Bradbury*. Low-pitched gables typical of contextual architecture of the period, set back from the street with its own plaza, intended to group with the timber-framed ST JOSEPH'S (No.5, KING STREET) to its NW. This is C16 in origin. Single timber-framed range with a roof hipped with a narrower gabled bay towards the street. Further exposed framing and a broad brick chimney-breast on the E side. Originally an L-plan with heated rooms at the N (road) end.

OUTER WIMBORNE

75 DEAN'S COURT, ¼ m. S. A house in amazing seclusion so close to the town. It is one of the most swagger Early Georgian houses in the county, built, says Hutchins, in 1725 for Sir William Hanham. Two ranges conceal an earlier hall house in the SW corner of the block: possibly the remains of the medieval residence of the Dean of Wimborne. Two-storeyed, with a top parapet. N front of seven bays, E of five, each with a three-bay centre part broken forward a little. This, and the angles of the house, outlined in even stone quoins. Plenty more stonework set off against the red brick walls, in particular the doorcases, that on the N with columns and a pediment open to take a shield of arms, and the window over this with very flamboyantly designed side-pieces. Neo-Tudor refacing of the W front, 1868. Cantilevered stone staircase within, with elaborated wrought-iron balustrading and a mahogany handrail. Similar to that at Ranston (Iwerne Courtney; dated 1753), and therefore also probably by the *Bastards* of Blandford. Plaster cross-vaulted entrance vestibule of *c.* 1870. Kitchen wing remodelled in C18 style by the *Sarum Partnership*, 1990.

OLD MANOR FARM (formerly Leigh Farmhouse), Leigh Road, ¾ m. E. C16 lobby-entry house, with diaper brickwork. Timber ovolo-moulded mullioned windows. Partly rebuilt in the C17. Until at least 1845 it had a moat.

JULIAN'S BRIDGE, ⅜ m. W. 1636, widened on both sides, 1844. Eight very pointed stone arches, and corbelling for pointed refuges in the brick parapet. Datestones and cartouche on central s refuge. Causeway to the W, probably of 1844.

WALFORD BRIDGE, ½ m. N, across the River Allen. Quite inconspicuous. Basically a C17 packhorse bridge (built under an
order of 1666–7), of six arches, extensively repaired with an
additional N arch in 1802 by *W. Knott* and *W. Stainer* of Wimborne, possibly to the designs of *William Evans.*

CANFORD BRIDGE, ½ m. SE over the River Stour. The most
impressive of Wimborne's bridges, of Portland stone, in
three bold arches. Completed in 1813, by *John Dyson Jun.*
The viaduct S of the bridge makes a piquant contrast, having
six close-set arches, which are of red brick, with the lower
parts of local brown stone. For the design cf. Hurst Bridges,
Affpuddle.

WIMBORNE ST GILES   0010

Wimborne St Giles is an unusually sympathetic village. Its red
brick houses and cottages, many thatched, of the C17 and C18,
are complemented by Tudor Revival estate cottages added in the
mid C19, all spaced generously among lush fields and lusher trees.

ST GILES. A new church of 1732, the W tower possibly incorporating fabric from its medieval predecessor. The reason for
retaining the tower position was no doubt to avoid disturbance
to the almshouses next door (*see* below), but the church was
aligned centrally on the tower. There are stylistic similarities
with the new church at Blandford (1733–9) and other buildings
associated with *Nathaniel Ireson.* It is likely, therefore, that he
was the architect here, although no documentation survives to
support this. Walls of greensand and flint partly arranged cheq-
uer-wise. The fine W tower has rusticated corner pilasters in
the lower two stages, plain pilasters in the upper. These dimin-
ish in width as the tower rises, stage to stage. Keyed arches
and oculi, a pedimented round-arched doorcase with Tuscan
pilasters, and a moulded and keyed round-headed W window.
Along the nave and chancel there are three windows, widely
spaced. To the S is a porch (probably an addition) with pediment. To its r., a squire's doorway with alternatingly blocked
pilasters and above, integrated with it, a smaller version of the
standard arched windows. The thin buttresses are also additions, probably of the C19. The gable of the E end is given a
fully pedimented treatment, while at the W only a small part-
pediment on the S side is presented. No doubt its mirror was
to the N, but this was lost in subsequent work on the N side.
Here, towards the almshouses, an aisle with traceried windows
of C17 inspiration. This is by *Sir Ninian Comper,* who was called
in by the 9th Earl of Shaftesbury after a fire in 1908. He imitated the tracery of the hall of Oriel College, Oxford (where he
was designing new glass at the time), and also incorporated a
window from restoration in 1886–7 by *Bodley & Garner,* when
six-bay aisle arcades were first erected.

After the fire, the interior was once again remodelled: four-bay arcades of tall round piers supporting depressed four-centred arches were installed to replace the presumably fire-shattered C19 arcades. This results in a very narrow s aisle, although it simply repeated Bodley's perhaps wilful earlier work. The roof compartments have plasterwork modelled in a Late Gothic style, the main rafters on carved angel corbels with spreading wings. Comper's FURNISHINGS of 1910 are typically sumptuous. The SCREEN is a *tour de force*, very high, right across nave and aisles and largely Gothic. Figures of the Apostles under slender hoods and a rood above, flanked by St Mary and St John, each standing upon a dragon. Figures of seraphim flank the inner group. The attached box is the Shaftesbury Pew, only slightly less rich in decoration. Unlike screens elsewhere by Comper, there is some restraint in that the screen is not brightly painted and gilded, a treatment reserved for the altar and font cover. Beyond, a low alabaster REREDOS, painted blue and gold, with similar enrichment carried around the whole E window. High above is a TESTER, matching the magnificence of Comper's ensemble. The C17-looking FONT was given to the church in 1785. It is round and decorated with strapwork. The COVER is eminently *Comper* (added in 1940), with extremely elongated columns and with gold and sky-blue. Also by *Comper* the elaborate WEST GALLERY with ROYAL ARMS of George II (1730). The STAINED GLASS is mostly by *Comper*, and one of his best schemes. The E window depicts the Risen Christ. In the central s window some good panels of German early C16 glass, installed in 1785. Window by *Burlison & Grylls*, 1900, in the W wall.*

MONUMENTS. The Ashley monuments are a splendid series, though desperately displayed. The effigy of a cross-legged knight is a copy of what was there before the fire, which was an early C14 piece. (Some fragments from this were incorporated in the copy.) – Sir Anthony Ashley †1628 and wife. Two effigies, his behind hers and placed a little higher. Elaborate canopy of columns and arches. Big superstructure with two standing allegorical figures. On the floor kneels a daughter. By the parents' heads a helmet, by their feet a sphere of hexagons held by two mailed hands. This may be a stylized cabbage, since Sir Ashley is said to have introduced these to England. – 3rd Earl of Shaftesbury, the philosopher, †1712. Standing mourning female figure in a plain niche. Below, a granite sarcophagus. – 1st Earl †1683, but made only in 1732. Standing monument. Bust by *Rysbrack*, in front of an obelisk. It is a convincing likeness. Relief medallions with three female busts below. – 4th Earl †1771. Designed by *James Stuart*, made by *Thomas Scheemakers*. Bust before obelisk. Two weeping putti l. and r. of the sarcophagus. – 5th Earl †1811. Large tablet with the widow mourning over her dead husband. The three Fates

---

*A window by *Morris & Co.* was lost in the fire.

in the Roman Doric aedicule. Made in 1819 by *Rudolf Schadow*, son of the more famous Gottfried Schadow.

ALMSHOUSES. Attached to the NW corner of the church, and quite large enough to hold their own against it. The gift of Sir Anthony Ashley and built *c.* 1624, they are the only datable example of a style which makes a considerable contribution to the architecture of Wimborne St Giles. Single-storey red brick range with stone dressings, and three-bay stone arcade of a vaguely classical kind in the two-storey centre block. Above the arcade a fine armorial panel, a small oval in a brick panel and a gable on kneelers. This part is open to the roof now, but must surely originally have had a first-floor chapel, for the three-light window under the E gable at the back has trefoiled-arched lights. The other windows are of two square-headed lights with an ovolo moulding. That is a distinction in fenestration made e.g. in the chapels of Jacobean mansions such as Hatfield and Temple Newsam. Elaborated doorway into the former common room with arched pierced upper panel; this has a strapwork surround to a central roundel. Doorways with depressed heads and a chamfer. Originally the accommodation was ten one-room dwellings. They are indicated by the six pairs of tall diagonally set chimneystacks; the spare two heated the central common room and chapel above.

MILL HOUSE, ⅛ m. w. Of red brick set in English bond, and roughly of the date of the almshouses. Much restored, but the form of it seems to be authentic, a six-bay range, one room deep, with end gables. Symmetrical S front, the centre two bays brought forward slightly and rising to a gable. Large four-light mullioned windows, the lower all modern, the upper having ovolo mouldings and a straight architrave instead of a hoodmould. A mill race passes beneath the building and its original purpose, at least in part, was a paper mill.

ST GILES'S HOUSE, ¼ m. s. Since the early C15 St Giles has belonged to the Ashleys (later Ashley Coopers and since 1672 earls of Shaftesbury). The earliest evidence is a Late Perp doorway in the cellar of the main house; the earliest of architectural significance is the monumental early C17 outbuildings, for which *see* below. The architectural history of the present house began in March 1651, when Sir Anthony Ashley Cooper (later the 1st Earl) 'laid the first stone of my house at St Giles'. An estate map of 1659 indicates that the new house, forming an E-facing block added to earlier buildings, was complete. The earlier buildings, completely remodelled in the C18, formed an L-plan. This consisted of a N–S arm (later incorporating the White Hall), probably of 1639–43, closely followed by a N-facing E–W arm (later incorporating the Grand Dining Room). The E range started in 1651 connected to the latter to form a U, at first opened-sided to the S. In common with Kingston Lacy, the 1651 range was built of brick with ashlar dressings, although the angle quoins were brick rather than stone. As at Charborough, the house was of three storeys with a *piano nobile* above a ground floor, and the roof was hipped

71

with symmetrically arranged dormers and chimneys. This presented a formal, seven-bay-wide E façade, with five-bay side elevations. Internally, two large rooms of unequal size faced E, with three smaller rooms on the W side, beyond a spine wall. The central of these smaller rooms contained the stair hall, entered on the W side at ground-floor level. No architect is recorded for this work. Could it have been *Richard Ryder*, the assistant to John Webb who had in 1650 completed the W wing of the nearby Cranborne Manor, or *Webb* himself, who had in the same year finished work at Wilton House? Both are stylistically plausible.

The next phase, continuing the Commonwealth style, was the addition *c.* 1670 of a S range, linking the E block with earlier structures at the W end. *Thomas Glover* is mentioned in a memorandum book in connection with a contract for this, but the name of *William Taylor* is also noted; he may have been the architect. The range was substantially complete (according to another estate map) by 1672, as was a parallel range running W from the other end of the E block (and facing N). The 1672 map also indicates two long wings running W from the pre-1651 structures and framing a large service courtyard. The earlier N–S range projected at each end beyond the new E ranges, and a further step was made in the layout of the W wings, so that, as refronted, a symmetry was made when the whole composition was viewed from the E.

In 1740–4 *Henry Flitcroft* (probably assisted by *Francis Cartwright*) made extensive alterations for the 4th Earl. These must include the window surrounds and doorcase of the E front, and the new entrance on the N side, a composition typical of Flitcroft's brand of Palladianism. At about this time the hipped roofs of the C17 house were taken off and a series of flat roofs behind battlemented parapets installed. One further change, the addition of a raised terrace on the E side, extending to the W along the N and S façades, and causing the old ground floor to become a basement, brings the house to its appearance as illustrated by Hutchins in 1774. Cement stucco was added to the brickwork at some point after this, perhaps in connection with the engagement of *John Soane* in 1793 to prepare plans for improvements, although these seem generally not to have been acted upon. In 1816–20 a large library was created behind the S front for the 6th Earl, designed by *Thomas Cundy* (father and son). They also roofed over the inner courtyard (i.e. the space between the 1651 E block and the earlier N–S structures) and installed a new principal staircase in the E range on the site of the original.

Major changes of external appearance by the 7th Earl in 1853 were the addition of towers on the N and S fronts, each originally crowned by a tall French pavilion roof (removed in 1886), the rebuilding of the NW wing, and the reintroduction of pitched roofs. *P. C. Hardwick* was the architect, who no doubt intended to make the whole exterior more lively and Italianate but was constrained, perhaps wisely, by his client. The final addition was the installation of a private chapel in the ground floor of the SW wing, completed in 1907 by *Comper*.

A scheme of rationalization of this large house, begun in the mid 1970s, removed the NW and much of the SW wings, demolished Hardwick's towers and dismantled the N entrance. Bay windows added by the *Cundys* and *Hardwick* were also taken off, before work was abandoned. It has been revived only recently by the 12th Earl (*Philip Hughes Associates*, architects), with a phased programme intended to bring the house fully back into use. It includes the rebuilding of the N vestibule and entrance, thereby re-establishing its symmetry when viewed from the E.

The character of the 1651 house can most readily be appreciated from the seven-bay, two-storey EAST FRONT. Brick (the C18 render has been removed), with brick quoins and keyed moulded stone architraves to the windows, those to the ground floor extended downwards before 1774. Swan-neck pediment with an armorial cartouche above the central doorway; the central first-floor window has a triple keystone and spaced rustication blocks. Basement (the former ground floor) largely obscured by the C18 raised terrace. Parapet with ball finials. *Flitcroft*'s stone centrepiece to the NORTH FRONT is only roughly central. Rusticated Doric surround with a segmental pediment to a round-arched doorway, now a window. Above a window with a segmental pediment and scrolled architraves. Otherwise brick, as on the E front, but with the ground-floor windows less elongated. Battlemented parapet here and on the projecting entrance to the r. Here the fabric is pre-1651, as remodelled first by 1672, again when it formed *Hardwick*'s N tower entrance, and finally as part of the most recent reinstatement by the 12th Earl. The loggia with a rusticated arcade is a recreation of the *Hardwick* porch. The SOUTH FRONT is again the asymmetrical result of accumulative growth. Two areas of modern brickwork with sashed fenestration (intended to match the older work) mark the removal of bay windows. To the l. the façade steps out twice, first to accommodate the base of the S tower, now without its Hardwick top, and again to encompass a three-storey, three-bay C18 block (incorporating late C16 structure) with round-arched blank recesses between the first-floor windows. Facing the former WEST COURT are the older structures of the house, refaced and remodelled with sash fenestration in the C18. The *Comper*-decorated CHAPEL is now a free-standing box with a plain exterior.

The INTERIOR contains a continuous suite of rooms of 1740–4, largely *Flitcroft*'s creation. The N doorway from the rebuilt *Hardwick* loggia leads (via a vestibule) into the White Hall. E of this the Grand Dining Room, a major room, with a deep cove to give the room height, and a Palladian chimney-piece and overmantel, enriched frieze and cornice, and ceiling with enriched beams. It is a double cube in volume, similar to, although less elaborate than, Flitcroft's state saloon at Woburn Abbey, Bedfordshire of *c.* 1747. In the restoration for the 12th

Earl, some brickwork has been left exposed as testimony to the dire condition from which he rescued the house. The Tapestry Room was Flitcroft's entrance hall. The Large Drawing Room in the NE corner has the first of the mid-C17 survivals, a monster stone chimneypiece, very restrained and Jonesian.* Big cornice on big brackets. On the lintel flat swags, at the sides fat drops of fruit hung from lion masks. The Small Drawing Room (SE) is also dominated by the mid-C17 element, this time the ceiling. Bulging oval wreath of fruit, a broad outer wreath of oak leaves, and rectilinear side parts. Both C17 items make Flitcroft's work seem trifling by comparison, and tell of the changed, more elegant, less robust, ethos of the C18, in spite of the revival of Jonesian forms. They also look much more like work of the 1650s than of c. 1670, and are by an outstanding designer. An attribution to John Webb is tempting. Also in the Small Drawing Room however a fine mid-C18 marble chimneypiece with caryatid maidens l. and r. The Library by the *Cundys* is of 1816–20, the overdoors at each end made up of fragments of fine mid-C16 panelling, with foliage and projecting busts, of a Renaissance cast. The top-lit central hall was formed within the inner courtyard at the same time. A dramatic space, but awkwardly incorporating its staircase with iron balustrade at the E end.

The PARK, largely the creation of the 4th Earl, has trees of great size and splendour, a large serpentine lake S of the house, and several garden constructions. NW of the lake an ornamental GATEWAY of 1748, a fairly early example of the castle style. Round towers, banded alternately rough and smooth, flank a central rusticated archway. The GROTTO SE of the house, however, is a real extravaganza, recently carefully restored. This was constructed in 1745–52, by *Mr Castles* of Marylebone, as an outer chamber with side passages, behind the triple-arched opening, and an inner chamber with a fireplace. As described by Robert Andrews (in 1752) it is 'adorned with an immense profusion of the richest and most beautiful shells disposed in the wildest and most Grotesque Manner possible'. The anteroom (then still under construction) was 'to be enrich'd with several kinds of ores, minerals and fossils'.

'RIDING HOUSE', ⅛ m. NE of the house. Of 1616–18. Built as stables, the S range is a splendid example of Sir Anthony Ashley's Jacobean style. Red brick, irregularly bonded, with stone dressings. The S front has four gables with kneelers and small obelisks. Four-light windows with ovolo mouldings and, surprisingly, arched lights. Hybrid doorway with hoodmould and keystone. Similar doorway in the W end. Small oval windows in the gables and a set of three, arranged as a triangle, in the E end. (Undergoing conversion to accommodation, 2017.) The W range of the courtyard is lower and older, timber-framed with brick-nogging. Early C17 brick S end. Towards the courtyard

---

*It is identical to plate 16 in John Vardy's *Some Designs of Mr Inigo Jones and Mr William Kent* (1744).

both ranges have crudely carved timber carriage-arch-heads of the early C17.

LODGES, ¼ m. N of the house. A pair with octagonal ends with arched windows facing N. Stuccoed. Opposed porches. Contemporary with the *Hardwick* alterations to the house (i.e. *c.* 1853) and possibly also by him. A brick Tudor Revival LODGE a little further N, next to the church, is slightly later.

PHILOSOPHER'S TOWER, 1 m. ESE. Built *c.* 1700 by the 3rd Earl as a place of contemplation. Brick, domed, two-storeyed. Large sashes to the upper floor, one per face. An oval window on the W side lights the lower room. Cartouche with arms of the 2nd Earl on the S side. The 3rd Earl's major contribution to architectural history was his *Letter Concerning the Art, or Science of Design* written in 1712, critical of current British architecture and especially that by Wren.

MANOR FARM, Monkton Up Wimborne, 1½ m. NW. Rendered. The NW part originally a timber-framed structure of the C16, with an open hall and a solar end. Not obvious from its otherwise unprepossessing exterior.

DORSET CURSUS. *See* Gussage St Michael.

OAKLEY DOWN, 1 m. WSW of Pentridge church, in the N of the parish. A nuclear group of twenty-seven ROUND BARROWS, five of them discs, forming one of the finest Bronze Age barrow cemeteries in Wessex. An oval twin disc is cut across by Ackling Dyke (*see* Gussage All Saints). Finds from burials, which are in the Wiltshire Heritage Museum, Devizes, include urns, daggers, bone tweezers and amber necklaces.

WINFRITH NEWBURGH   8080

A linear village of many cob or brick cottages with thatched roofs, a stream flowing alongside the village street.

ST CHRISTOPHER. Quite large and, as one approaches from the E and N, Victorian-looking, the result of a heavy restoration with enlargements by *T.H. Wyatt*, 1852–3. At this date the sumptuous Norman N doorway was resited and largely remade. Only a few of the chevron voussoirs are original. The plain S doorway is genuine C12, and so are the jambs of the chancel arch. This has corbels and capitals of elongated, exaggerated trumpet scallops. Its pointed double-chamfered arch is C13. Also C13 the chancel, mainly seen in the S wall with its two lancets, one trefoiled, the other wider and cinquefoiled. There was major rebuilding at various stages in the C15. Early C15 W tower, with extremely thin angle shafts in the tower arch seeming more Dec than Perp. Slightly later nave S window of four lights.

Wyatt rebuilt the chancel E wall and added the N aisle. – PULPIT with mural doorway N of the chancel arch. By *Wyatt*.

– FONT. Octagonal, also by *Wyatt*. – STAINED GLASS. Three
early C15 fragments in a chancel s window. Also in the tracery
of the nave SE window. N aisle window by *A.R. Mowbray &
Co.*, 1922. – MONUMENTS. The best is Edward Berkeley (of
the Bryanston family) †1774, by *T. King* of Bath. Tablet with
shrouded urn on an oval grey marble ground.

LYCHGATE. Of 1924 by *C.E. Ponting*.

Former RECTORY behind the church. Early C19, three-
storeyed, brick.

The church stands beside (converted) barns at the s end of the
village, shielded from the village street by lime trees. LANG-
COTES MANOR (or the Manor House), across the lane to the
N, extends its brick front and the brick sides of its outbuildings along the street's beginning. The house itself is C16 but
refronted in brick in the early C19. Among the former farm
buildings the diapered brickwork of a C16 BARN. Then come
the usual thatched cottages, one by one. The good part ends
with more red brick at WINFRITH HOUSE. Late C18. Three
bays, extended to the l. (s), probably early C19. Porch with
Tuscan columns moved one bay l. at this time, when the flanking oval windows were installed. The house stands just behind
a red brick WALL, built in stages so that it now rises recklessly
high. Former GATEHOUSE, linked to the wall, just to its NW.
C18, castellated brick. Thought to be associated with a vanished
house to the w.

ATOMIC ENERGY ESTABLISHMENT (former), Winfrith Heath,
1¾ m. NE. Screened by belts of trees so that, except from a distance, the nuclear research buildings here are largely unseen.
Work started in 1957, with various experimental nuclear reac-
tors built subsequently, particularly the STEAM GENERATING
HEAVY WATER REACTOR (SGHWR). The others, except for
the drum-shaped DRAGON REACTOR of 1964 (shut down in
1976), have been decommissioned and removed, leaving the
SGHWR as the chief architectural feature of the site. Built in
1963–7 (and shut down in 1990). Its two cooling towers are
shaped for aerodynamic reasons like huge paper-racks, and
coloured pale green. Attached on one side a cylindrical office
tower. Also, in a weak attempt to break up its massing, a swirly
abstract mural on the top r. corner of its w front (described in
the previous edition as 'like a piece of cheap wallpaper much
enlarged'). These structures, at the w end of the site, will soon
also be removed, leaving the more run-of-the-mill four- and
five-storey slab-sided administrative buildings, with windows
in long bands, standing about haphazardly elsewhere. Most of
these have become DORSET GREEN TECHNOLOGY PARK.

WEST BURTON, 1¼ m. NE. A deserted MEDIEVAL VILLAGE,
covering 10 acres. There are two hollow ways, and slight
remains of ten rectangular closes. Surface pottery finds were
of the C12–C14.

WHITCOMBE HILL, 1¾ m. N. Mesolithic WORKING HOLLOWS
and STRUCTURES; pollen identified an open environment in
managed deciduous woodland.

A memorable grouping of silvery-grey classical country house,
perched up on a ridge, and small Perp church in a copse below.
The home farm and rectory are quite apart, on the opposite side
of the Wareham road.

St Peter (Churches Conservation Trust). All Perp, but of differing dates. C14 nave, early C15 chancel and late C15 W tower
(whose top seems to be Elizabethan or Jacobean), with an early
C19 bellringers' porch on the N side. Late C15 too a refenestration of the whole. Richly fitted-out interior, making it obvious
that the fortunes of the church were much affected by the
families of the house. – COMMUNION RAIL. Oak. Arcaded and
probably contemporary with the pulpit (see below). – SCREEN.
Early C16, but rebuilt and redecorated 1887. Of many one-light
divisions, each with a fretwork head. The dado with linenfold
panels. The top rail is Tudor classical with vine-trail carved
ornament. The black-letter frieze inscription is C19. – PULPIT.
Oak, dated 1624. With two tiers of enriched arches. – READING
DESK. Oak, mid- to late C19, with a carved figure of St Peter
below. – HATCHMENTS. Three lozenge panels of the Damer
and Dawson-Damer families. All C19. – STAINED GLASS.
In the chancel two windows by O'Connor, the earliest the E,
†1848. The other the S window, †1856. Also one signed by
J. & W. Warrington, 1867. In the nave, another probably by
Warrington, †1867. Three large figures (of Faith, Hope and
Charity) in the W window by Henry Holiday for Powell & Sons,
1882. – MONUMENTS. Dorothy Miller †1591. Plain tomb-
chest with an arch behind. This springs from short fluted
pilasters. – John Meller †1611 and wife. Tomb-chest with, in
niches, small, frontally kneeling figures of members of the
family, primitive Ionic pilasters between. Recumbent effigies
and two backplates. – Mary Frances Seymour Mills †1895
(made in 1908). White terracotta tablet above a realistically
modelled angel with outspread wings bearing an inscription
ribbon. In dance-like movement with foliage round her. One
would love to know the maker of this delightful piece. – Many
other tablets, Neoclassical and Gothic.
Came House. The mid-C18 masterpiece of a provincial master
mason, Francis Cartwright, whose monument in Blandford St
Mary church depicts the house, in the sense that this was his
worthiest memorial. His employer was John Damer, younger
brother of the creator of Milton Abbey. The N front is dated
1754, but there is evidence that interior work was not finished
until 1762, four years after Cartwright's death. The house is
a rectangle faced with Portland stone, two-storeyed, the top
balustraded. The S front was the original entrance, of five
bays, the central bay broken forward under a pediment and
really three in one. Pedimented doorcase with attached Ionic
columns in a composition of Ionic pilasters. This frontispiece

carries on above with a variant of a Venetian window, the columns here the Borrominesque Corinthian with inturned volutes so dear to West Country master masons. There is in fact much about the s front that suggests the influence of Nathaniel Ireson, whom Cartwright would have known from the post-fire rebuilding at Blandford.

The N front is more ordered, and more of a Palladian formula, with two bays l. and r. of an attached Corinthian temple front. Centre three *piano nobile* windows stressed by alternating pediments. Here the ground slopes, so that there is room for a channelled basement; at a still lower level to the E, a service block linked by a low passageway, with chains of rustication on its N wall. No doubt another to balance it to the w was envisaged.

The INTERIOR has a splendid set of Rococo plaster ceilings, not of course in the true Continental Rococo manner, but rather the English variety which uses rocaille among other motifs to create an effect lighter than the Kentian Palladianism of the 1720s and 30s; so that the immediate success of Adam's new delicate style in the 1760s is not surprising, for he offered new motifs not a new ethos. At Came the HALL has the heaviest forms, moulded beams creating rectangular fields, and a swirling rocaille centrepiece. Idiosyncratic cornice with brackets and small shells. This may have been the only interior designed by Cartwright before his death. The other central room, the DRAWING ROOM or SALOON, has the rectangular fields broken up by curves and the defining mouldings wreathed with flower trails. Eagle and thunderbolts in the centrepiece. Marble chimneypiece with female terms, and main doorcase with Corinthian half-columns, of the Early Palladian kind. This work was by *Vile & Cobb* of London, who took over the finishing of the house from Cartwright. The grisaille-painted overdoors are a little later. The Dining Room, in the NE corner of the house, has the most effervescent design, with putti cavorting in the centre. The staircase has a wrought-iron balustrade and more run-of-the-mill plasterwork on the ceiling and the underside of the landing, and, especially much of it, round the big w window.

The house has hardly been altered in more than two centuries. The one addition is the N porch, and back to back with it the CONSERVATORY, a deliriously frail cast-iron construction, both of *c.* 1845. The side walls carry most of the weight, helped by four slender columns with acanthus-bulb capitals. Central circular pergola, also of cast iron. The glazed roof rises in two convex curves.

OLD RECTORY, ½ m. NE. Of *c.* 1820, for the Rev. William England. Thatched *cottage orné*. French windows on the w front behind a thatched veranda. William Barnes, the dialect poet, lived here from 1862 to 1886, when he was rector of Winterborne Came.

CAME DOWN, 2 m. SW. Linear groups of BARROWS on the golf course, quite well preserved under grass.

CAME WOOD, 2 m. SSW. Well-preserved DISC and BELL BARROWS, surrounded by Second World War earthworks, in woodland W of Culliford Tree Barrow (*see* Whitcombe and Broadmayne).

CONYGAR HILL, ½ m. NW. Two BOWL BARROWS. One had a primary crouched inhumation with a food vessel and six especially fine barbed-and-tanged flint arrowheads, so named the Conygar Type; sealed by a massive Portland stone. The sites of two MINI-HENGES, ½ m. to the WNW, were excavated on the route of the Dorchester by-pass.

WINTERBORNE FARRINGDON, ¼ m. W, is a well-preserved deserted MEDIEVAL VILLAGE in two separate blocks. The E block, of 4 acres, may be incomplete. The W block, of 10 acres, divided by contemporary lanes running through it, has the site of St German's church. The wall standing on the site is a rebuilding, making use of a C14 window and stones from a C15 archway. There are several platforms for buildings. Strip lynchets cover 18 acres to the S.

WINTERBORNE CLENSTON

8000

Manor house set back from the road, largely hidden by a high wall. Next a large barn, and further S, in a memorably tree-backed setting, the spired estate church.

ST NICHOLAS. A rebuilding by *Lewis Vulliamy*, dated 1840, for Mrs Margaretta Michel of Whatcombe House. The typical estate church, though not a large one, i.e. standing on its own, almost as on a platter, and being entirely uniform. Also typical of the pre-archaeological C19 church, i.e. with transepts, no aisles and a short chancel (cf. Long Crichel). Flint and ashlar with large stone slates on the roof. Thin W tower with a spire rising from a stepping arrangement – so neither a broach spire nor splay-footed but a cross between the two. High, narrow doorways – not a proportion occurring in real Gothic churches. Lancet windows. High roofs, not reflected by the low-pitched ceilings within. – FONT. Early C19. Gothic, panelled and as attenuated as the lancets. (Made of composition and plaster.) – Transept and sanctuary FURNISHINGS of 1840; nave re-pewed, 1901. – STAINED GLASS. E window scheme of *c.* 1840. N transept quatrefoil with royal arms in glass. – MONUMENTS. Rev. James Michel †1839 (and Mrs Michel †1871) by the *Patent Works* of Westminster. Open book against a slate background. – Several tablets to members of the Mansel-Pleydell family of Whatcombe.

WINTERBORNE CLENSTON MANOR. A compact, two-storey, symmetrical Tudor house of considerable architectural power and ambition. The walls are of flint banded with greensand, the windows of warm Ham Hill stone, and other dressings of

Winterborne Clenston Manor.
Lithograph by Philip Brannon, 1861

a creamy colour: a delightful harmony. In date, although the
evidence is to a degree conflicting, it seems that the main
range is of *c.* 1480, built for Sir Thomas de la Lynde. The
striking stair-turret must be contemporary, although this poses
building-sequence difficulties (*see* below). T-plan, the upright
forming the service wing to the E. The main front faces W,
and was extended to the N, sympathetically but in a weaker
style, *c.* 1600. The E wing, three-storeyed but incorporating
earlier work, must also have been totally recast about the
same time.

From the W the frontage is dominated by the central porch,
octagonal and recklessly corbelled out towards the top by
means of two double waves and two waves, to make a gable
possible.* The front door is set modestly round the side,
and has modest mouldings, a hollow and a wave. The small
square-headed windows at random up the porch show that the
stairs are contained within it, this too a remarkable piece of
planning.

The windows of the W front are placed symmetrically, but
in a syncopated rhythm, a four-lighter each side at the upper
level, two closely spaced three-lighters below set nearer the
centre. They all have deep hollow mouldings and hoodmoulds
on lively headstops, the heads all looking inwards. The upper
windows have arched lights between the mullions, the lower do
not. These are of *c.* 1600 in form, and their insertion without
disturbing the surrounding banded masonry was carried out
with great skill. The S end of the main block has a big central

---

* Cf. the gabled projection at The Castle, South Street, Bridport.

projecting chimney-breast (with a later brick stack), a diagonal buttress at the sw corner and a lancet low down, perhaps not *in situ*. At the back there is an inserted two-storey window bay, which goes in date with the fenestration of the E wing. The windows in both these parts are mullioned and have shallower mouldings, chamfer, step and hollow, to the frames. One original E window is masked by a later outshot running along the N wall of the E wing.

The interior also has its remarkable features. The evidence of the roofs, supporting the evidence of fenestration, suggests that there were two rooms of equal importance on the first floor, divided by a central passage, and reached by the stone newel stairs in the porch-turret. These rooms are still separated by plank-and-muntin partitions, with one original doorway surviving in the partition to the l. At the opposite end of this corridor from the stair-turret, a recess containing a stone candleholder. In the main range the lower rooms have moulded ceiling beams forming square fields; the first-floor rooms however began life open to the roof. The N upper room (solar) has early C17 panelling and a timber inner porch. Above the present flat ceilings of both rooms the timber roof can be seen, running unbroken across the range, of major and minor arch-braced trusses, with three tiers of cusped wind-braces in three patterns. This is typical of the mid to late C15 and provides the principal dating evidence for the house. But could it have been brought in, like the roof of the adjoining barn? Above the solar, fragments remain of very fine mid-C16 plaster ceilings of close-set foliage designs, and part of a deep foliage frieze is still *in situ*. There are also pieces of a lozenge panel framed by candelabra, identical with one at Mapperton. So at this stage a ceiling had been introduced, but with a higher profile than the modern ceiling. However, if the stair-turret is contemporary with a *c.* 1480 erection date for the house, why does it have an upper flight of stairs leading to attics that could only have been formed when the upper rooms were ceiled in the mid C16? The service rooms must have always been in the back wing, which is entered via two plain stone doorways with two-centred-arched heads. `

The forecourt arrangement is of the C20. Late C17 TRO-PHIES of arms, brought from Milborne St Andrew, on the gatepiers. S of the forecourt a splendid BARN, the walls of this too banded in flint and stone, the roof with C19 red tiles of two types making a chequer pattern, a good effect (although now patched with corrugated iron). Cart entrance in the centre of each long side. But even all this does not prepare one for the grand roof inside, made of seven huge hammerbeam trusses, the arched members lavishly moulded. These must be reused timbers; they have been dendrochronologically dated to *c.* 1486. One can see how crudely missing pieces were here and there supplied. The suggestion that they came from the dissolved Milton Abbey, three miles away over the downs, seems very plausible.

6080   # WINTERBORNE HERRINGSTON

HERRINGSTON. The view along the drive from the N is of
Thomas Leverton's façade of *c.* 1803. It is of Portland ashlar,
and Gothic, by suggestion as much as in fact. Battlemented
centre, gabled wings, the gables oddly overlapping the centre.
In the centre the windows have hoodmoulds, at the sides they
are gathered in threes within a single big blind pointed arch.
Thus everywhere normal sashes (with Gothic glazing bars)
can be retained.

This Gothic is only a mask: the gables represent the fact
that Leverton demolished the N half of a courtyard house, and
thus had gable-ends to patch. A date of 1582 was reportedly
over an arched entrance into the S half of the house, lost in
the Leverton alterations, although this too must only indicate
a remodelling of a house of C14 origin, much of which remains
within the structure of the S and W parts of the present house.
The C14 house was most likely that built for John Heryng
(†1455). Nothing of this house can be seen externally. The W
wall is now simple Georgian of *c.* 1803, the E wall masked by
a Tudor-style wing of 1899 (for Edward Wilmot Williams), so
one must consider the earlier house from the S. Here the walls
are rendered, but the windows immediately reveal the later
development. Reading from the l. there is one bay of late C18
sashes. Then a window of 4:4 lights with a transom, the lights
arched at both levels. Hoodmould. This window is clearly for
the Hall and mid- to late C16. This part of the house is beneath
a lowered slate roof, a late C18 alteration. Then comes a gabled
projection, with two-light windows low down, but what must
be an important room, the Great Chamber in fact, above. Its
S wall is occupied by a window of 3:3 lights with a transom,
and there are further three-light windows round the sides.
Hoodmoulds; all lights arched. This all looks like work of a
single period, the period of Sir John Williams, who succeeded
in 1569 and died in 1617, i.e. what the date 1582 referred to.
The house, as remodelled in 1582 (and before *Leverton*'s alterations), is depicted in a pair of watercolours at the house by
John Upham, of *c.* 1790.*

Internally Leverton's front produces a compact block, with
a central top-lit staircase. The lofty HALL of *c.* 1600 must have
been splendid before its barrel ceiling was removed as part of
Leverton's alterations. Doorways in the Hall and at first-floor
level, and into the Great Chamber, are all crudely classical but
with wave-and-hollow impost mouldings and fat rolls round
the soffits of the arches, similar to the contemporary work of
William Arnold. Within the Hall, panelling (re-set in the later
C19) with carved biblical scenes, signed by *Wiliem Witting*. They
also have the number 26, thought to represent the year 1626.

62   The GREAT CHAMBER remains in all its spectacular splendour. Tunnel-vaulted plaster ceiling decorated with a grid of

---

*Reproduced in David Cecil, *Some Dorset Country Houses* (1985).

broad bands, broken to create square fields in which come large emblematic beasts, phoenix, swan, fishes, etc., and once, important for dating, the feathers of Charles Prince of Wales. That dates the ceiling to after 1616 (when Charles was made Prince of Wales) and before 1626 (when he was crowned king). Sprays of fritillaries and other flowers occupy the other L-shaped fields. From the crown of the vault grow down five large pendants, the three main ones exceedingly large, of openwork bars. Within the middle one little boys sit round a tree, up which another boy climbs. This plasterwork has much in common with the Great Chamber at Prideaux Place, Padstow, and the gallery at Lanhydrock, both in Cornwall and both thought to have been made by the same craftsmen. On the spandrel formed by the vault on the inner end wall, the plasterwork includes animals of all sorts – elephants and camels – dispersed without restraint. The outer end of the room, opened up with windows on three sides, has relentlessly decorated woodwork wherever there is free space. Basically the system is of figures under arcading alternately with panels of strapwork. The figures are a miscellaneous crowd, including Hope, Sisera, St John, Geometry, and Adam and Eve after the Fall. Larger pilasters between the windows, one left unfinished, perhaps at Sir John Williams's death in 1617. It is alarming to speculate what the room would have been like had the panelling been continued across all the walls. Now, the bare walls in the darker part of the room make a successful foil to the light and enriched part. The final item in the room is the CHIMNEYPIECE. Probably by *Godfrey Arnold* (cf. the statue niche to Edward VI at Sherborne School, 1614). However the sculptural details are a little odd, whereby Faith and Charity are large demi-figures l. and r. but Hope is a minuscule reclining figure at the top where the curve of the vault interferes.

WINTERBORNE HOUGHTON

8000

ST ANDREW. 1861–2 by *T.H. Wyatt*, retaining an earlier s aisle (remodelled by Wyatt). Flint, Perp, with a short unbuttressed but battlemented w tower. – FONT. C15, octagonal, with quatrefoils against the bowl, lancets on the stem.

On MERIDEN DOWN, 1 m. WNW, a ROMANO-BRITISH SETTLEMENT, with surrounding 'Celtic' fields and a system of tracks. It is one of the best of its type in Dorset.

WINTERBORNE KINGSTON

8090

ST NICHOLAS. Flint, grey ashlar, heathstone. Essentially C14 Dec, plus *G.E. Street*'s N aisle, vestry and chancel E window of 1873. Dec are the w tower (see the bell-openings and the tower arch dying into the imposts), the nave s doorway (with a cinquefoiled rere-arch), a s window and the chancel. Two other windows, of four lights, are early C16. The tower has battlements and buttresses but is otherwise plain. Four-bay N arcade and chancel arch with Street's bold clustered colonnettes. – REREDOS by *Street*, incorporating Cuenca-style tilework by *F. Garrard* of the *Millwall Pottery*. – Coloured TILES in the chancel (probably by *Godwin*), especially effective on the sanctuary step faces. – PULPIT. Early C17, octagonal. – FONT. 1736. A bulbous baluster. Contemporary domed oak COVER. – CRESSET STONE in the vestry, with two depressions. Probably medieval. – STAINED GLASS. e window by *Clayton & Bell*, 1873. Three other windows by the same firm of about this date.

WESLEYAN CHAPEL (former), just SW. Dated 1872, built by '*Mr Pike* of Blandford' (*Western Gazette*, 27 September 1872). Red and yellow brick. Lancets.

At Winterborne Muston (½ m. E) one can see from the road MUSTON MANOR, a thatched cottage of unusual pretension. Late C17, extended l. and r. in the mid C18 and given even a polygonal porch in imitation of Anderson Manor nearby. The interior also shows that the cottager built with unusual richness and desire for display. Panelling with egg-and-dart dado; ceiling cornice with acanthus enrichment.

On KINGSTON DOWN was a Romano-British settlement, well excavated in 1890. It is not located, but the contents of the well and associated finds imply a nearby shrine.

On MUSTON DOWN, 1¾ m. NNW of the church, was a prehistoric or Romano-British settlement covering an area of about 6 acres. It is now mostly ploughed out.

6080

WINTERBORNE MONKTON

ST SIMON AND ST JUDE. Early C13 nave and chancel, of which the E wall with pilaster buttresses and the plain, segmental-headed nave N doorway are the main indications. w tower of *c.* 1500, with a re-set Dec w window and an oddly raw arch to the nave. Early C16 s aisle and nave fenestration. The s arcade is standard, with four-centred arches. Capitals with foliage carving. Big organ chamber by *Ewan Christian*, 1874. (*Christian* had carried out an earlier restoration in 1870–1.) In the chancel a Dec PISCINA, C14. – The elaborate Gothic oak REREDOS of 1874 (by *Christian*) lies discarded in the tower. – SCREEN, PULPIT and READING DESK also by *Christian*. Oak, setting the *c.* 1870 character of the interior. The screen incorporates late C14 fretted tracery. – Encaustic and majolica TILEWORK by *Minton*, sanctuary walls and floor. – FONT. C14, octagonal, on a C19 base. – ROYAL ARMS of George III, after 1816. – STAINED

GLASS. S aisle, E window (behind the organ) by *Powell & Sons*, 1876. Nave N window, a memorial of 1937. – MONUMENT. Ellerie Williams, signed *Alex Elliott*, 1875.* Plaster. Recumbent maiden in bed, her hair down, the blanket not too tidy, her nightgown with lace borders showing. It is rather Parisian in style.

PENWITHEN, ½ m. NE, on the A354. A remarkable château-style house of *c.* 1910 for W. J. Watkins, a Dorchester builder, no doubt as a demonstration piece.

LONG BARROW, N of the W entrance of Maiden Castle (*see* Winterborne St Martin), on Hog Hill. A short long barrow, ploughed out.

LANCEBOROUGH, ⅓ m. N of the W entrance of Maiden Castle (*see* Winterborne St Martin). A LONG BARROW and a group of four ROUND BARROWS. Of these, one bell barrow is the largest of its type in Dorset and probably in Wessex. It is *c.* 250 ft (75 metres) in diameter and 20 ft (6 metres) high. Now infested by badgers. S of this great mound is a horseshoe-shaped enclosure (mini-henge), and to the W the long barrow, both ploughed out.

IRON AGE AND ROMANO-BRITISH SETTLEMENT, E of Lanceborough. *See* Dorchester, p. 265.

WINTERBORNE ST MARTIN

6080

Alias Martinstown. A linear village with a surprising number of larger gentry houses. Just W is the disappeared medieval village of Rew (*see* below).

ST MARTIN. Perp in two phases: the W tower and chancel, C15; the nave with N aisle, late C16. The tower is of three stages, battlemented, with the octagonal stair-turret (added later in the C15) rising above. Crocketed pinnacles at the corners and centres of each face; also smaller pinnacles at each angle of the stair-turret. Late Perp (i.e. Elizabethan) windows in the N aisle and S nave walls, the latter a C19 rebuild. Elizabethan also the arcade, with its short octagonal piers and the chunky shapes between the capitals and the arches – segmental arches. Shafts l. and r. of the altar, short, octagonal, with capitals, C15. Presumably re-set. What was their original function? A good PISCINA in the chancel: C14, ogee-headed, with a round-headed shelf-recess above. Careful restoration by *C. E. Ponting*, 1905. – COMMUNION RAIL (N aisle). Of *c.* 1700, with turned balusters. – PULPIT. Early C17, with one tier of blank arches and a band of guilloche ornament above. – FONT. Square, C12, of Purbeck marble, with five flat blank arches each side. Set upon a central pier with four colonnettes. Late C15 oak COVER with crocketed corner pinnacles matching those on

---

*Major-General Sir Alexander Elliott, an amateur painter and modeller.

the tower. – ROYAL ARMS of George II. – STAINED GLASS. E window with a mixture of coloured and grisaille glass. Of *c.*1870, perhaps by *A. Gibbs.* – MONUMENT. Arthur John Hawkins †1859, yet still entirely in the Georgian tradition. Standing woman by a pedestal with the inscription.

MANOR HOUSE, ¼ m. SE, set back behind a high wall. C17 (sundial dated 1654) but heavily rebuilt in the late C19. Gabled.

OLD VICARAGE, across the road to the SW. 1838 by *Edward Mondey* of Dorchester. Regency classical. E front with chimneys flanking the central three bays.

REW MANOR, ¾ m. NW. Of *c.*1840. Stucco with a veranda across the main front.

RYLSTONE, just E. Regency Tudor with a classical porch.

WEST END HOUSE, ½ m. W. Mid-C19. A hipped-roofed block and a secondary wing set back. Wide sashes throughout.

Up a lane running N, an unexpectedly well-built circular SHEEP DIP, probably early C19.

5 MAIDEN CASTLE (English Heritage), on the chalk ridge, 1½ m. SW of Dorchester.* An early Neolithic causewayed enclosure lies beneath the E end of a multivallate Iron Age hill-fort, one of the largest in Britain. Within the defences are visible the earthworks of a Neolithic long mound, two Bronze Age round barrows, and the stone footings of a Romano-Celtic temple uncovered in excavation. Three campaigns of excavation and survey have been undertaken: Cunnington 1882–4, Wheeler 1934–7 and Sharples 1985–6.

Ascend to the summit of the eastern knoll, on a footpath leading S from the car park, turning SE through the northern ramparts and past the stone foundations of the temple. Here the full circuit of the early Neolithic CAUSEWAYED ENCLOSURE, surrounding the eastern knoll, can be appreciated. The enclosure was built within woodland in the C36 B.C. (calibrated radiocarbon dates) and was in use only for about one generation (up to fifty years or so). Two concentric rings of interrupted ditch, now mostly obscured beneath the Iron Age ramparts, were investigated by excavation in the 1930s and 1980s. The ditches were 50 ft (15 metres) apart and 5 ft (1.5 metres) deep, enclosing 20 acres. The ditch fillings contained deliberate deposits of pottery, flint and animal bone. Possibly after a short interval, a LONG MOUND was built in a cleared landscape, from N of the western knoll to the NE side of the eastern knoll, perhaps in two or three stages between the late C36 and C34 B.C. The mound was 1,790 ft (545 metres) long and had parallel side ditches 60 ft (18 metres) apart and 5 to 6½ ft (1½ to 2 metres) deep. No contemporary burials are known.

The whole hilltop has been ploughed, but earthwork traces of the long mound are visible from a prominent eastern end, along the three-part alignment to the western tail end. During

---

*The name Maiden may be derived from the British-Celtic 'mai-dun', probably meaning great hill or great fortress.

the Bronze Age two ROUND BARROWS were built, on the western knoll and to the N of the long mound, both also visible as earthworks. The geophysical survey shows a dense palimpsest of features. Of these, a small rectangular ENCLOSURE, *c*. 130 ft (40 metres) square, on the S-facing slope between the two knolls and above and beside two undated dew-pond earthworks, may be of later Bronze Age date and associated with CROSS-RIDGE DYKES, of which one to the W on Hog Hill was incorporated as the outermost bank to the later hill-fort entrance.

The first HILL-FORT, constructed probably in the C5 B.C., enclosed 16 acres on the eastern knoll with a single rampart and ditch, and entrances on the W and E. The rampart was reinforced with timber front and back. The line of the western defences, surviving up to 5 ft (1½ metres) high, is visible running across the hill and cutting across the line of the long mound. A little later the single defences were extended to enclose the W knoll of the hill, and now covering 47 acres. From the western knoll the sheer size and scale of the occupation area now enclosed can be appreciated.

In the Middle Iron Age the ramparts and ditches were doubled in scale and extra lines of defence were added on the S and N sides. The entrances were elaborated, and round-houses, hearths, ovens and storage pits were built inside the rampart. Occupation debris included pottery, tools and personal ornaments, together with evidence for agriculture, which concentrated on the production of spelt wheat and the rearing of sheep. Later refashioning involved increasing the scale of the outer ramparts and further development of the complex entrances, with platforms for slingers. Finally, the now decaying inner rampart was repaired after *c*. 60 B.C.

Returning E along the southern ramparts and reaching the eastern entrance, the double-passageway entrance and outer earthworks are clearly visible. Outside the inner gate were zones used for iron smelting, and for many Late Iron Age burials of the C1 B.C. and C1 A.D. Many were accompanied by native Durotrigian bowls and food offerings. Originally interpreted as a war cemetery related to the burning of the gate by the Roman army in 43 A.D., the cemetery is now thought to have been a Durotrigian burial ground. Many bodies displayed weapon injuries, some of which had healed prior to death, and these may have resulted from inter-tribal skirmishes, ritual fighting or contact with the Roman army. One body was pierced by an arrowhead in the spine. After the Roman Conquest the E gateway was re-metalled and the hill-fort occupied, perhaps by a legionary garrison, until *c*. 70 A.D.

In the late Roman period the E entrance was remodelled to provide access to a *temenos* enclosure for a Romano-Celtic temple. The S portal was blocked, and a single entrance gate built in the N portal. This *temenos* reused the ramparts of the earliest Iron Age hill-fort, covering the E knoll. Walking NW uphill from the E entrance, one reaches the preserved foundations of the stone-built TEMPLE. Roughly 40 ft (12 metres) square, the temple comprised an inner *cella* (tower) surrounded by a covered passageway or open veranda. There were mosaic floors, and the flint walls, 2 ft (0.6 metres) thick, were covered inside and out with coloured plaster. Below the temple on the N is a smaller RECTANGULAR BUILDING which may have provided accommodation for the priests. Excavation just to the SW discovered an oval dry-stone building which probably functioned as a SHRINE well into the post-Roman period. This lay directly within the remains of a larger CIRCULAR BUILDING of the Late Iron Age, 40 ft (12 metres) across, which may have been an earlier shrine within the hill-fort. A nearby series of graves may have been post-Roman, and later some Anglo-Saxon burials were also interred. From the temple and oval shrine came votive objects including fragments from bronze and marble statues and the tinned bronze figure of a three-horned bull carrying three human busts.

From this point the site of *Durnovaria* (Roman Dorchester) is clearly visible, and the temple would have been a prominent landmark for the inhabitants of the town.

BRONKHAM HILL, 1¾ m. SW. Thirty ROUND BARROWS form a mile-long linear group along the South Dorset Ridgeway.

RIDGE HILL, 1¾ m. SSW to 1 m. S of Maiden Castle. ROUND BARROW GROUPS in linear array for 2 m. along the South Dorset Ridgeway, from Great Hill (W) to a bowl within a henge earthwork (E) on the parish boundary with Bincombe. The group includes the rich 'Ridgeway 7' burial. *See* Upwey.

FOUR BARROW HILL and EWELEAZE BARN, ¾ m. S. ROUND BARROWS in linear groups along the hill spur, many ploughed away.

CLANDON BARROW, ½ m. E on Clandon Hill, ¾ m. NW of Maiden Castle. This flat-topped bowl barrow, over 90 ft (28 metres) in diameter and 18 ft (5.5 metres) high, was excavated in 1882. The primary burial was not reached, but deposited in a stone cairn were a dagger, a gold breastplate, a jet macehead set with five gold-covered shale studs, an amber cup and a pottery incense cup. One of the richest votive groups in the county.

REW, ½ m. WNW. MEDIEVAL SETTLEMENT remains, with a long, narrow stretch of closes covering 5 acres.

8000

WINTERBORNE STICKLAND

Quite a big village, extending along the valley bottom, its focal points two aged lime trees. Near the N tree the church and several typical cob and thatch cottages; near the S tree more cottages, banded in flint and red brick.

St Mary. A C13 church of flint. Tall nave, probably raised *c.* 1500. The chancel has three plain E lancets and a nice Perp priest's doorway. W tower of *c.* 1500 with bands of flint and stone; battlemented parapet with crocketed pinnacles; S doorway, now blocked. The nave was remodelled again, probably in 1716; hence the tall round-arched windows, those at the W end raised to light the gallery. N tomb-chamber rebuilt in the second half of the C18, but incorporating a C16 E doorway. The elliptical-arched N window is of the later date, as is the pedimented internal surround to the E doorway. Gallery removed during a restoration by *W.J. Fletcher*, 1892. – PULPIT. Early C18; plain with balustraded steps. – FONT. Of *c.* 1740. Square baluster and octagonal bowl (cf. Blandford Forum). – CHANDELIER. Of brass; *c.* 1700. – SCULPTURE. A small tympanum with a C15 Crucifixion, re-set in the porch. Is it carved into a once-solid Norman tympanum? – STAINED GLASS. E windows almost certainly by *Clayton & Bell*, †1901. – MONUMENTS. Rachel Sutton, 1653. The monument is a black column with an Ionic capital and an entablature and it stands on a bracket. The long Latin inscription runs round the front of the column. It is a weird conceit, but the mid C17 was a time of weird conceits in funerary monuments. It is called at the beginning of the inscription 'Statua Sepulchri' ('image of the grave'). – Honor and Robert Clavering †1708. Pedimented tablet with urn, scrollwork and gadrooning. – In the tomb-chamber, Thomas Skinner (of Dewlish) †1756. Free-standing sarcophagus with a polished black marble lid.

METHODIST CHURCH (former), across the road to the E. Dated 1877. Brick with round-arched windows.

OLD RECTORY, 150 yds SE. Flint-banded throughout (except for a rebuilt gable). It consists of a main range, dated 1685 from the coat of arms over the front door, the arms of Robert Clavering, rector at the time of the first building. A NE wing is dated 1768. Mid-C19 range towards the street, sash-windowed with a pedimented Doric porch.

To the S a cottage with banded walls and prettily curvaceous thatch, and to the W the Gothic SCHOOL of 1861, still in the local materials.

As the road runs S down the valley modern bungalows break the spell.

QUARLESTON HALL, ½ m. S. L-shaped, a plain stone façade with C19 sashes towards the road, but round the back handsomely banded with stone and flint. The N range incorporates an early C15 hall, noted by Hutchins as existing in 1437 (straight joints mark its extent). No original window survives, so the banded walling, different on the two long sides, can hardly be original either. A partition on the E side of the cross-passage is C14, although much altered, so there must have been an even earlier house here. The hall roof, originally meant to be seen, has a standard arrangement of arched braces and wind-braces minimally enriched, but is now totally out of sight above an inserted floor. The C17 E range and the projection (for stairs) in the angle between the ranges are finely faced with knapped squared flints and ashlar bands. No hoodmoulds to the windows, which are mullioned of two and three lights. The house was enlarged to a full courtyard in the C17, but the S and W ranges were demolished in the mid C18 when it became a farmhouse. About 1700 the S doorway to the original screens was given a charmingly modish classical doorcase, with scrolly open pediment.

WINTERBORNE TOMSON

8090

Church, manor house and farm in the most idyllic of water-meadow locations. The approach – cropped grass beside the lane, and a single thatched cottage – is just right. A brick-walled compound surrounds the church, with farm buildings on one side, the churchyard raised above its surroundings to avoid flooding.

ST ANDREW (Churches Conservation Trust). Winterborne Tomson is a gem of a Norman village church, almost untouched, sufficiently different from others to arrest attention at once, and with an interior which fulfils all one's expectations. First half of the C12. Nave and chancel in one and with an apse of the same height. Over the W end a sweet little weather-boarded minimum bell-turret. Shallow buttresses to the apse. One Norman S window. Otherwise Tudor windows facing S, away from the farmyard. C18 W doorway and buttressing. The interior has most of its old furnishings under its charming plastered wagon roof whose arches include the apse, where they are set radially. Wooden bosses mask the rib-junctions, some with foliate decoration.

The FURNISHINGS are owed to Archbishop Wake of Canterbury (1716–37). They are unassuming and incidentally well preserved and sensitively, i.e. self-effacingly, restored: PULPIT, a two-decker with tester; BOX PEWS; WEST GALLERY with ladder-stair access; COMMUNION RAIL with slender twisted balusters. – FONT. Perp, octagonal, but with the top half of the bowl sliced off, leaving half-quatrefoils on the sides. – MONUMENT. Inscription tablet of 1962 to *A. R. Powys*, who restored the church for the SPAB in 1931, the year of his death. Beautifully cut inscription by *Reynolds Stone*. The money for the restoration was raised partially by a sale of Thomas Hardy manuscripts.* Hardy cared for the church in exactly the way we care now.

TOMSON MANOR, standing behind trees to the E, is a building of real architectural interest. From the S it appears a rectangular

---

*The architect Lionel Brett (Lord Esher) made up the deficit with a substantial contribution.

block, four bays by one with two storeys, mullioned windows of four lights with a hoodmould, the windows in the w wall one light bigger. Hollow mouldings on the windows indicate a date of *c.* 1600 (although much of the window stonework is recent replacement); built for Thomas Hussey. The hipped roof is unlikely to be the original configuration, but what did it replace? A simple gable-ended range seems the most likely precursor. Heathstone rubble walls; roofs of plain clay tiles with large stone slates at the eaves (as on Tomson church, and once common throughout the county).

On the N is an astonishingly picturesque display, of brown stone rubble walls, a vast chimney-breast l. and another r. with lozenge-shaped stacks, and attached to the l. side of the r. chimney-breast a square further-projecting porch, three-storeyed and gabled. In the recessed centre three-light windows like those in the other walls, and a similar ground-floor window masked by a later low outshot. Much late C18 and C19 rebuilding in brick to the upper parts of the porch and chimneystacks.

So this was the entrance front, the porch doorway with a minimal flattened four-centred head, set very low. It cannot be central because the porch contains a stone newel staircase rising through two storeys. This idiosyncratic arrangement is presumably copied from Winterborne Clenston Manor, which seems likely to be much earlier (*c.* 1480), and has a stress on symmetry and conscious display not in evidence here. The staircase, as at Clenston, leads straight to two upstairs rooms which occupy the entire length of the upper floor. This is entered through a two-centred-headed doorway with moulded jambs (the external doorways only have plain chamfers). Here the plaster ceilings, recently restored, have patterns of thin ribs, with motifs of fleur-de-lys etc. in the fields, typical of *c.* 1600. The larger w part – surely the Great Chamber originally – is divided off by a Jacobean partition with a reconstructed timber draught-lobby with pilasters. A fragment of plaster overmantel here does not appear *in situ*.

The house gives an impression of being a fragment of something larger. Indications of a mildly terraced FORMAL GARDEN, extensive in area, in the meadow to the s, support this.

WINTERBORNE WHITECHURCH

8000

Some cob and thatch, some brick and flint estate cottages, but much bungaloid infill and housing estate expansion.

St Mary. Flint. The chancel is *c.* 1300; it was probably accompanied by a contemporary nave and transepts, both of which have gone. Corbel table to the chancel. To its w a central tower, its crossing early C14 Dec and therefore a replacement, perhaps from the collapse of the previous tower. The tower superstructure is also Dec, in spite of the lancets. A disappeared N transept can be inferred from the arches inside. Ashlar banding on the tower and the remodelled C15 S transept. In 1844 *Benjamin Ferrey* rebuilt the nave and aisles. The E crossing arch has three continuous chamfers of that date, the S and W arches have responds of the Perp standard section and capital bands with very curious long fleshy leaves and heads. The arches are again triple-chamfered. Three C15 head corbels in the S transept S wall. A fourth in the crossing N wall. There is much original colour in the chancel, and when Ferrey rebuilt the nave and aisles he used much colour too.* Graceful three-bay arcades. – PULPIT. C15, with narrow niches crowned by crocketed ogee gables. Said to come from Milton Abbey. Restored 1867, when it was repainted, the niches were filled, and it was given a new base. – FONT. Mid-C15, and very odd indeed. An octagonal stem curving out to support the shallow bowl with its vine bands. In the corners four square pillars with shields and crocketed pinnacles unnecessarily supporting the bowl as well (cf. Bradford Abbas). Pyramidal C17 oak COVER. – STAINED GLASS. E window by *Lavers & Barraud*, c. 1865. Two chancel S windows, †1868, perhaps by *Clayton & Bell*. W window dated 1886, almost certainly by *Burlison & Grylls*. – MONUMENTS. In the S aisle, a specially attractive group of late C17 tablets to the Lawrence family. Also Ann and William Clapcott †1784, †1790. Pedimented tablet on a slate obelisk ground.

WHITECHURCH HOUSE (formerly the vicarage), opposite the church, was built in 1743. Red brick, sporting a white-painted window bay towards the garden. A similar mixture, making a similarly genteel picture, at WEST FARM, ½ m. SSE. Opposite the farm, a CIDER-PRESS HOUSE. C18. Circular, with a conical thatched roof.

WHATCOMBE HOUSE, ¾ m. N. Built for Edmund Morton Pleydell in 1750–3, when he left Milborne St Andrew (q.v.) for something neater and more convenient. Probably by *John* and *William Bastard* (cf. the earliest part of Crichel House, More Crichel). The two-storey, five-bay C18 house remains, and the SE room has a typical Rococo ceiling in the local manner with naturalistic wreaths of flowers looping round the rocaille-work centrepiece. The staircase, with wrought-iron balustrade, goes with this, as does the S façade, originally the entrance front. In 1802 another Edmund Morton Pleydell (while demolishing Milborne St Andrew Manor) enlarged this house and had it heightened by half a storey, stuccoed and given a main front of seven bays to the E. Yet in its new form it could easily be mistaken for a mid-C18 house, with its quoins, its broad stone window surrounds, its centre bay marked by Venetian windows one above the other, and the pairs of giant Ionic pilasters that flank them. Only details, such as the Spalatro capitals of the upper Venetian

36

---

* Michael Pitt-Rivers's *Shell Guide* (1966) says however that the arches were stencilled in 1882 by the wife of an incumbent.

window, and the armorial lunette over the door (of *Coade* stone), make it clear that the date is half a century later.

LODGE, ¼ m. NE of the house. Of *c.* 1802. Stuccoed to echo the enlarged house.

BRICKWHEAT BOTTOM, 1¾ m. ENE. By *Leonard Manasseh*, 1966. A gable-ended, white-painted rectangle with a central SW-facing cut-out, recessed and glazed.

COMBS DITCH, 1½ m. NE. A linear dyke, 2¾ m. long. This is an Iron Age and Romano-British boundary bank, with a ditch on the NE side. Remnants of 'Celtic' fields are associated in part. Excavation in 1965 revealed successive enlargement over a long period. Dating evidence shows that the dyke started as a prehistoric boundary in the Early Iron Age and was rebuilt as a defensive earthwork in the late Roman period, as was Bokerley Dyke (*see* Pentridge).

WINTERBORNE ZELSTON   *8090*

Several cob and thatch cottages. An especially good grouping alongside the river, near the church.

ST MARY. Unbuttressed C15 W tower of stone. Of three stages, with battlements and an octagonal N stair-turret. The rest flint and heathstone-banded by *T.H. Wyatt*, 1865–6, for J.J. Farquharson. Carefully crafted E.E. and Perp. Short, two-bay N aisle. Two C13 windows re-set in the N wall of the chancel. – FURNISHINGS by *Wyatt*, largely intact. – STAINED GLASS. E window, 1866 by *Lavers & Barraud*.

WINTERBORNE ZELSTON HOUSE, 100 yds N. Early C19 front with a recessed balcony at its centre. C18 behind.

HUISH MANOR, ⅓ m. ENE. Villa in its small park. Of 1792 for John Shittler. Stucco; hipped roof. Long matching service range to the E.

WINTERBOURNE ABBAS   *6090*

A linear village on the A35 on the upper reaches of the South Winterborne.

ST MARY. Early C13 nave and chancel, both much altered. What survives is the chancel N wall with two plain lancets and the nave S wall. In the latter an early C13 blocked archway, originally leading into a chapel or annexe. Otherwise the fenestration is C15, when much rebuilding was done, including the good three-stage battlemented W tower. This has a higher, octagonal stair-turret and big gargoyles. Set-back buttresses. Over the doorway an angel bust. Wide C17 porch. E chancel wall rebuilt in 1724 with a re-set C14 window. Careful restoration by *J. Arthur Reeve*, 1893–4, when the church was re-roofed. Inside, the chancel arch is early C13, pointed. Tower arch with small leaf capitals. In the chancel is an exceptionally fine mid-C14 PISCINA, Dec with a big finial. – Late C19 FURNISHINGS apart from the following. A group of C15 SLIP-TILES in front of the altar. – FONT, *c.* 1200. Cauldron-shaped, with beaded rope moulding on the underside. – NORTH GALLERY. Dated 1701, on spindly cast-iron columns of *c.* 1800. It extends E over the N doorway and has a curved end. – ROYAL ARMS. Dated 1661. On a lozenge-shaped panel. – STAINED GLASS. E window by *H. J. Stammers*, 1949.

LODGE to Bridehead (*see* Littlebredy), ½ m. w. Of *c.* 1822, by *P. F. Robinson*. Tudor Gothic (to match the house) with narrow corner turrets.

STRIP LYNCHETS, ½ m. S and 1 m. SSW. Medieval, and well preserved on NW-facing slopes and in Loscombe Wood.

NINE STONES, ½ m. W. A sarsen stone circle of which all the nine stones are standing, two large, seven small. They enclose an area 26 ft (8 metres) in diameter.

POOR LOT, 2 m. W, to the N and S of the A35. Forty-four ROUND BARROWS in a nuclear group. Despite damage to many of the barrows, this remains one of the most impressive groups in Wessex, though scarcely any finds are recorded. There are seven bells (two forming a double barrow), six discs, four (possibly five) ponds, two bell-discs, two triples and twenty-two bowls, twenty of them in Kingston Russell (*see* Littlebredy), six in Littlebredy and eighteen in Winterbourne Abbas. The parish boundary with Kingston Russell crosses the largest barrow. The core group is preserved in pasture, but two-thirds are now noticeably ploughed.

6080

WINTERBOURNE STEEPLETON

A nice grey grouping of church, rectory and manor house alongside the South Winterborne stream.

ST MICHAEL. 'Steepleton' because it has one of the three medieval spires of Dorset, a chunky C14 Dec spire, the pinnacles treated as little spires and the spire itself recessed behind a plain parapet. The tower has angled corner buttresses, and a buttress at the centre on the N and S sides. Not a large church, just nave and chancel, and seemingly C12 with C15 fenestration. But the church is yet older, and therein lies its surprise. The nave is Saxo-Norman of the first half of the C11, as an examination of three of the four quoin-sets will show. Much rebuilt in its N and S walls in the C12 and later. It has a blocked Norman N doorway, and a small Norman W window now looking into the C14 tower. The S doorway has a plain tympanum inside a roll moulding. Blocked C15 opening into a N chapel or transept. C15 chancel, the arch rebuilt in the C18. The most important item is a piece of SCULPTURE of national and maybe international reputation, formerly outside the S aisle, but brought into the chancel in 1990. A flying angel, dated by the *Corpus of Anglo-Saxon Sculpture* to the C10 or C11. The nearest parallel is Bradford-on-Avon, Wilts. Winterbourne Steepleton's is similar, with the angel's legs bent upwards from the knees. The l. arm appears to be holding a skull (or a flying fold of drapery). – ALTAR. A re-set stone slab with five consecration crosses, C12 or C13. Base of 1902. – PULPIT. C17 panels of blank arches and angle figures, re-set by *C.E. Ponting* in 1903. – FONT. C12, with round arches in pairs on triple shafts. Each pair has a pendant in the middle instead of a shaft. Cable moulding around the top. Stem C13 with attached corner shafts. – WEST GALLERY. Dated 1708 with the initials G C 8. Panelled front with balusters above. On it a ROYAL ARMS of 2002. – WALL PAINTINGS. A set on the N wall of the nave, including a C15 St Christopher with a C17 Lord's Prayer below, and traces of a Stuart royal arms. On the S wall, C13 painted masonry lines and C15 vine-scroll. – STAINED GLASS. C15 fragments in the tracery lights of the nave N and S windows. – MONUMENT. Daniel Sagittary †1756. Brass, of delectable quality, bright, almost as if gilded.

OLD RECTORY, just w. Of 1850–1, by *R.C. Hussey*. Gabled.

THE MANOR, standing apart opposite the church. By *T.H. Wyatt* for W.C. Lambert, 1870. Rock-faced Portland stone, which is no surprise. More unexpected is the relaxed Tudor style of the symmetrical half-H entrance front, a hipped-roofed centre block and gable-ended wings. On the garden front greater asymmetry, an oriel roughly balanced by a bay window.

Next w, MANOR COTTAGE, late C16 but with a raised roof, perhaps *c.* 1650. Thatched with hollow-chamfered mullioned windows. Staircase in a curved projection in the angle with a back wing.

At the w end MANOR FARM, with its banded back to the road. Late C16 or early C17 vernacular, but with a charming C18 central composition involving a three-light staircase window with a lunette, and a very long hoodmould between them, suggesting much rearrangement of fenestration. The front is quite straightforward, with a central gabled porch.

LOSCOMBE, 1 m. SW. BRONZE AGE 'CELTIC' FIELDS can still be traced across the chalk valleys and spurs below Black Down, now much reduced by ploughing. Within these, BARROWS are still preserved on Sheep Down and Cowleaze.

SHEEP DOWN, 1½ m. WSW. A LONG BARROW, aligned SE–NW, to the SW of a BARROW CLUSTER. This comprises five bowl barrows, one pond barrow and one twin bowl barrow with surrounding ditch. Excavation of the pond barrow showed that the depression was paved with flints, beneath which were thirty-five pits, some holding cremations, inhumations and urns of the Early Bronze Age.

COWLEAZE, 1½ m. SW, W of Loscombe Wood. Excavations in 1982 of the single BARROW within a Bronze Age field terrace uncovered the remnant mound and, to the NE, an adjacent sub-circular ENCLOSURE, across which cremation burials had been placed in pits. These were accompanied by amber and shale beads, a dagger, a jet toggle and an arrowhead of the Early Bronze Age Wessex Culture.

ROWDEN, ¾ m. WSW, high on the NE side of Loscombe Valley, NE of Loscombe plantation. A Middle Bronze Age HOUSE was excavated in 1981, within the remnant earthworks of the Bronze Age 'Celtic' fields.

BLACK DOWN, ½ m. SSW of Sheep Down barrows. A rectangular ENCLOSURE in the NW angle of a crossroads, 130 by 200 ft (40 by 60 metres), with an entrance in the middle of the SE side. Excavations in 1970 suggest construction in the Late Iron Age, CI A.D., and a Roman occupation.

WITCHAMPTON

A Crichel estate village, with picturesque timber-framed and thatched cottages interspersed with brick estate houses.

ST MARY, ST CUTHBERGA AND ALL SAINTS. Perp W tower with a rectangular staircase projection to the NE. Angle buttresses. Battlemented parapet. Heathstone and ashlar banding. Two grotesque heads in the arch towards the nave. S transept 1832–3, by *John Peniston* of Salisbury. Its S window has three stepped lancet lights. Nave, chancel and N transept 1844, probably by *J.M. Peniston*, for H.C. Sturt, costing £5,000. Perp. Banded flint. SE vestry and refurnishing 1898, by *C.E. Ponting*. – REREDOS. Painted wood, 1948, by *J. Wippell & Co.* – LECTERN. A wood-carved bunch of lilies, 1912. – PULPIT. Oak, *c.* 1730, probably by the *Bastards* of Blandford. – STAINED GLASS. Four-light E window by *Comper*, 1938. – MONUMENTS. Small brass figure of Isabel Uvedale †1572, together with all of the monuments in the N transept, removed from More Crichel church. – John Cole †1636. Tablet with paired black columns, two obelisks and an achievement.

LYCHGATE at the N entrance. 1899 by *Geldart*. Oak-framed on a stone base, with traceried sides and carved figure of St Cuthburga in a niche.

ABBEY HOUSE, just to the SE. The old brick garden walls diapered, with black headers (a remarkable survival) that run along the road opposite the church, go with the highly interesting house of *c.* 1530 which they enclose. Lofty two-storey rectangular brick range, gabled at the ends, but with a long S front, irregularly windowed. The original plan was a cross-passage

l. of centre with a parlour to its w and two rooms (the further a kitchen) to its E. An L-plan addition of 1874 by *Macvicar Anderson* is parallel to this on the N side. Diaper brickwork and fenestration originally matching the Tudor work. Altered in 1938 by the addition of a balancing NE wing and given Neo-Georgian fenestration. This resulted in a U-plan, with a five-bay centre and single-bay ends.

The only historical connection so far known is with the rector of Witchampton from 1505 to 1521, William Rolle. His initials are on the shield stops to a window on the s elevation above the blocked original doorway. Was this then the earliest of the noble parsonages which so many Dorset incumbents seem from time to time to have demanded? However, other heraldic frets indicate possible ownership by the FitzAlan earls of Arundel, lords of the manor in the early C16.

The first thing to remark is that the material is already brick. Diapering not only with the usual lozenge patterns but including letters and crosses. Ashlar dressings: big quoins, plinth moulding, an undercut string course at first-floor level, and all doors and windows, the last considerably but faithfully restored in 1874. The windows have hoodmoulds with square labels, and hollow-chamfered mullions (making two and, here and there, three lights). Pointed-arched lights. The w end of the s front has an original doorway (now a window) set in a deeply cut hollow-moulded surround. Its shield stops display a horse rampant before an oak tree, a device also found on a tablet high in the w gable. The three-light window above has the same moulding, a richer one than is used elsewhere. Roughly central lateral chimneystack, not projecting, and another at the E end, where a service addition of 1914 blocks some original windows. The w wall is the most restored, and the many chimneystacks with battlemented tops date from the 1874 alterations. Two four-centred-arched fireplaces survive at the w end, that in the parlour having a richly carved C17 oak overmantel.

MANOR HOUSE, ¼ m. SE. The ruins of a substantial unfortified manor house, perched on the bank of the River Allen, suffering from continued neglect. Flint walls with stone dressings. Probably a C13 solar on an undercroft at the NW end of a later hall (as indicated by investigations and excavations in 1961). The most substantial standing structure is a sw wall with tall slit windows below, and parts of two tall upper lancets, which had a transom and internal stone seats. Base of a possible stair-turret at the SE end of this wall. Pieces of walling further N.

Many of the red brick estate buildings were designed by *William Burn*, and later *Macvicar Anderson*, c. 1854–75. The CLUB HOUSE (also known as IVY HOUSE) was adapted by *Burn* from an older building in 1854. The OLD VICARAGE has an early C19 five-bay stucco front. Rear additions 1897, by *Ponting*.

HEMSWORTH ROMAN VILLA, 1½ m. WSW. Extensive buildings were uncovered in 1831 and 1908, including six pavements, three of them tessellated. One pavement from a large bath and the central roundel of another, depicting a horned and bearded head of a god, are now in the Dorset County Museum. Another fan-shaped pavement showing Venus, with an outer band of dolphins, small fish and scallop shells, is now in the British Museum.

WOLFETON HOUSE *see* CHARMINSTER

WOODLANDS

A scatter of mostly cob and thatch cottages. Some C20 development.

THE ASCENSION. Church of 1892 for the Countess of Shaftesbury by *Bodley & Garner*. Nave and chancel, and a bellcote turret set N–S, not W–E. Red brick and tiled roofs. Dec windows. There are two with a middle buttress W and two E, giving an indication of the surprising interior. It is two-naved (or twin-aisled with no nave), with only one high-pitched roof above. The broad four-bay arcade of octagonal piers rises up to the ridge – an odd spatial arrangement that works only because of the wide spacing of the piers.* The arcade terminates on corbels at the W and E end, the latter uncomfortably above the altar. DECORATIVE SCHEME of *c.* 1900 by the *Rev. C.F.C. Knapp* survives in part. – The SCREEN, ROOD and CHOIR STALLS are also to *Bodley*'s design of 1901, made by *Franklin & Co.* of Deddington. – FONT. C12 circular bowl, brought from Knowlton church and set on a late C19 base. – STAINED GLASS. Two E windows, 1901, designed by *Bodley*. Two S windows, 1929 and 1934, by *William Lawson*.
SCHOOL (former), opposite. Of *c.* 1860 for the Countess of Shaftesbury. Brick with broad pointed windows (cf. Hinton Martell). Chancel added to the E *c.* 1880, when it also served as the temporary church.
THE ROUND HOUSE, ⅛ m. W. A late C18 two-storey brick block with apsidal ends N and S, probably built as a workshop. Early C19 E wing at right angles.
WOODLANDS MANOR FARM, ½ m. SW. Part of a brick building of *c.* 1530, memorably early brickwork for Dorset (but cf. Witchampton). Red with a diaper of black brick. The S and E walls each have an upper and a lower two-light window, square-headed with cinquefoiled arched lights. Deeply sunk hollow-moulded surround, typical of the date. It is a fragment of Sir William Filiol's mansion which was visited in 1552 by

---

** *Bodley & Garner*'s other two-naved plans are St Luke at Warrington, South Lancashire, and the Trafford family chapel at Hom Green, Walford, Herefordshire. Michael Hall suggests that their use, although derived from historical sources, may also have been driven by the need for economy.*

Edward VI. Hutchins mentions a chapel, but this has disappeared. Two C16 fragments (a kitchen and chapel) were
incorporated in a mansion built *c.* 1710 for Mr Seymour 'of
the hanaper office', but this too was demolished (probably in
the early C19), leaving just the fragment described above, and
another – perhaps the kitchen – to the SW, also with diaper
brickwork. The present splendid long red brick range, ten
bays in all, now a house and stables in one, was also built
c. 1710 as the COACH HOUSE to Mr Seymour's demolished
mansion.

KNOWLTON. *See* p. 348.

WOODSFORD

7090

ST JOHN THE BAPTIST. Mostly 1861–2 by *T.H. Wyatt*, but the
lower part of the W tower and one nave lancet genuine E.E.
Wyatt followed the prompting, and his church has a long
chancel with lancets, and a S chapel with plate tracery. The
saddleback tower top is particularly effective. Quite a multi-
form interior. Robust two-bay N aisle arcade. – Carved stone
REREDOS by *Grassby* of Dorchester. – Sanctuary TILEWORK
by *Minton*. – STAINED GLASS. E triplet by *Burlison & Grylls*,
c. 1875–80. Two chancel S lancets by the same firm. Another
perhaps by *Charles Gibbs*, *c.* 1870.

OLD RECTORY, just W. 1850 by *Wyatt & Brandon*. Gabled, in
a vague Gothic.

Former SCHOOL, across the road to the S. Dated 1857, probably
by *Wyatt*. Gothic.

WOODSFORD CASTLE (Landmark Trust), ¼ m. SW. Even a   43
thatched roof and the loss of four of its five projecting towers
by no means obscure the defensive character of this C14 manor
house. Licence to crenellate was granted in 1335. The house
that ensued, of square Abbotsbury stone, was remarkable in
plan, a long, thin range, two storeys high, with towers projecting from all four corners and the fifth near the centre of the
long E wall. The NE tower survives, three of the others only by
the sockets of demolished walls. The surviving tower was for
a garderobe – see the blocked opening low down. Projecting
corbels suggest the original parapet height, and that the walls
have been heightened to form a gabled roof. On the main block
the W side has three tall square-headed first-floor windows,
two single-lighters, one of two lights, but all with transoms,
and trefoiled heads to the lights. These are either side of a
projecting staircase turret. Several C17 mullioned windows. On
the E side, at the junction with the NE tower, one large original
square-headed window, two lights with a transom, and trefoil-
ing at both levels, the upper ogeed. Another, matching it, in
the N wall. These were to light a room more important than
those at the S end. Just above the latter window a large corbel,
presumably associated with a parapet walk.

New Kitchen

'King's Hall'

Old Kitchen

'Queen's Room'

Bakehouse

Site of Tower

Guard Room

South Hall

Site of Tower

GROUND FLOOR

FIRST FLOOR

■ C14

▨ Major work, C17 and later

20 m
20 yds

Woodsford Castle.
Plan

The few internal features that survive help to clarify the layout. The ground floor is occupied by a series of intercommunicating tunnel-vaulted rooms. These can only have been service and store rooms. Wall recesses suggest that kitchen and bakehouse came in the middle. Only at the S end is there a larger room down here. At first-floor level the N room (called the King's Hall) was clearly the main living hall, with its garderobe tower. The adjoining room to the S was the chapel – see the piscina in the SE corner, finely moulded, ogee-headed, with shelf and drain perfectly preserved. Beyond this are four intercommunicating rooms, the middle two served by the stair-turret, the S room, which has the two-light W window, the largest. It seems then that there were two distinct suites of rooms served by the staircase, the N suite of four rooms, the S of two, and both having the main room at the furthest end. The first room entered in each suite may have served as a guardroom.

In the mid C17 the building was adapted for farmhouse (and farm building) use. It was then that the crenellations were removed and a thatched roof added. In place of the NW tower there is a small kitchen block of c. 1790. A sensitive restoration was carried out by *John Hicks*, 1850–1, for the 3rd Earl of Ilchester, its then owner.

WOODYATES

0010

Pentridge

Of the ruined church of West Woodyates nothing is now left.

WEST WOODYATES MANOR. A small gabled C17 flint house, refaced and extensively altered internally for the 5th Earl of Londonderry, c. 1720. His new E façade was originally five-bay and symmetrical, with sashes and pairs of bullseye windows. Extended N in c. 1820, and greatly enlarged by *Horace Farquharson* for F. B. Eastwood c. 1923. Of the latter phase is the two-storey sashed bow window on the main front.
BAILIFF'S COTTAGE to the SE. Brick and flint, also by *Farquharson*.

WOOL

8080

Until expansion after the Second World War, Wool was a village of two broadly parallel lanes of mostly cob and thatch cottages. A side lane leads SE to the church, while a station on the Southampton & Dorchester Railway (opened 1847) marks the northern limit. Beyond this are the water meadows of the River Frome, with the picturesque grouping of Wool Bridge and Woolbridge Manor. The presence within a couple of miles of Bovington Camp and the former Atomic Energy Establishment at Winfrith Heath, both expanded hugely in the 1950s and 1960s, has driven development, swamping the historic settlement. This has occurred to the W on either side of the Dorchester Road. Nevertheless, the old village still has much character and deserves to be cherished, and thankfully the all-important water-meadow approach from the N has been largely left intact.

HOLY ROOD. The church is C15 Perp in its squat grey ashlar W tower and its N aisle (with a curious triangular-headed doorway), but 1864–6 by *John Hicks* in the chancel and s aisle. Hicks's additions are in a brown ironstone speckled with lighter ashlar blocks that sits poorly against the medieval Purbeck freestone. The tower is three-stage with quatrefoil-pierced stone louvres in the bell-openings; battlemented, with a SE stair-turret rising to a pyramidal top. Internally the earlier origins of the church become more evident. We have now a two-bay early C13 N arcade of dark brown stone with round piers, base spurs, round caps and double-chamfered arches. The Perp W extension of this small original church reused another such respond, and for its own W respond provided a leaf corbel. The E extension, like the whole s arcade, belongs to Hicks's work. The late C14 chancel arch or CHANCEL SCREEN is tripartite with very thin octagonal piers. Although restored it is certainly something very rare. In the chancel N wall (where the organ is placed) a late C14 arch. – FONT. C15. Polygonal with quatrefoils. Built against the first N pier (originally on the E side of the same pier, moved in 1866). – CRESSET STONE. With four depressions (loose on a sill in the N aisle). – ROYAL ARMS of George III. Pre-1800 painted panel. – STAINED GLASS. E window by *Clayton & Bell*, 1887. Two chancel s windows (1878) and the s aisle E window (1905) by the same.

ST JOSEPH (R.C.), ⅓ m. NW. By *Anthony Jaggard* of *John Stark & Partners*, 1969–71. Fine example of a modern church responding to the precepts of the Liturgical Movement. A double square in plan, with walls of rendered brickwork. These are arranged as strips with windows between, rising in steps towards the E end. This rise is reflected in the Triodetic aluminium space-frame roof, whose depth forms a clerestory. The roof structure is punctuated at the E end by a lead-clad lantern, topped by a simple metal cross, and marking externally the position of the altar. There are four main additions to this volume in plum-coloured brick: a long low foyer or narthex at the W end; two cylindrical towers of unequal size on the s side; and a similar tower, to a larger oval plan, on the N. (The narthex is mirrored by a block at the E end containing the sacristy and related areas.) The function of these becomes clear within.

Areas of plain brickwork in different shades with light cast from the lantern, illuminating especially the free-standing altar at the spacious E end. On the s side, the larger of the two cylinders is the CHAPEL OF THE BLESSED SACRAMENT, housing a Tree of Life sculpture by *Geoffrey Teychenne* with a Dalmatian pelican in its upper branches. This is of welded steel and GRP resin, and rises from an altar towards the top lighting. Next to it the organ gallery, reached by a stair in the smaller of the brick cylinders. This ensemble is informally balanced on the N side by an oval-planned BAPTISTERY with the Weld family pew forming a gallery above. The space-frame roof, which is polished and lacquered, has dropping from it four boxes of strip lighting running E–W, breaking the openness of the interior only when viewed at an angle.

The FURNISHINGS are as installed in 1971. Surprisingly, the fixed PEWS are of concrete, with felt panels to the seat and back.

WESLEYAN METHODIST CHAPEL, Station Road, ¼ m. NNW. Of 1893. Red brick. Gothic, with a bellcote and a chancel-like porch at one end.

RAILWAY STATION, ⅜ m. NNW. 1969–70 by *British Rail Architect's Department, Southern Region*. A standard prefabricated box (*CLASP* system).

VILLAGE. For the survival of vernacular building character, SPRING STREET is the least altered. Here the typical thatched cottages stand back, so untypically for Dorset, behind broad grass verges. An exception is REGENCY COTTAGE, an early C19 *cottage orné* style at the junction with Church Lane. Its thatch curves over round-headed dormers. Decorative windows, some with octagonal panes, some with marginal lights. Further along Church Lane, a barn attached to Rowantree narrows and curves around the corner. Opposite, another cob and thatch cottage completes the tight grouping.

WOOLBRIDGE MANOR, ½ m. NNW, standing on the River Frome and reached by Wool Bridge (*see* below). The survival of Woolbridge Manor in a mellow unspoilt condition is a triumph. Long may it remain exactly as it is now. The contrast too of grey stone end walls and brick N front, and the contrast of the single end-gabled main range with a projecting N porch and a pair of big projecting chimney-breasts on the S side, bearing up slab-like panelled brick stacks, are equally piquant. The house clearly belongs to the C17, and a date of 1635 is found on the porch, although re-set. According to Hutchins the stone also had the initials IS, now illegible, but this may be a misreading of IT. This would accord with ownership by Sir John Turberville, who reached his majority in that year.

The gable walls are each three-storeyed, a two-light mullioned window with a hoodmould in the gable, and the main windows transomed, of four and three lights, also with hoodmoulds. Ovolo mouldings. One expects such details in the second quarter of the C17. Does the brick entrance front with its quite different motifs belong with the gables? It may seem improbable, but cf. the gatehouse at Poxwell where the brick details are very similar and the date is 1634. Also the quoin stones are common to front and sides, indicating one build. The real interest and puzzle however concerns the brick detailing. It is not a matter of moulded and cut brick, just of creating patterns in the laying. The entrance archway – which is odd enough itself, segmental and with a pendulous keystone carved with brackets back to back – has long thin niches l. and r., overlapped by brick rustication. The gateways in the garden wall l. and r. repeat the motif. At first-floor level there are similar niches in the plain walling on either side of all three windows. The moulded first-floor string course is brick, rendered, and above it are segmental relieving arches, which show that originally there was a rhythm of narrow, wide, narrow windows

l. and r. of the porch. The present mullioned-and-transomed
windows are from refenestration *c.* 1670. In the chimneystacks
similar niches, making arcading.

Taken in itself it is all rather fidgety, and more curious than
beautiful – should one call it primitive or debased? The classically moulded stone roundels on and flanking the porch are
clearly insertions, also of *c.* 1670, which give the façade just
the cachet it needs. A single-storey rear wing (to the sw) was
added at the time of the roundels (another was later removed),
increased to two storeys in the c18. (This wing has a simple
plaster ceiling of the later c17 type within. Upstairs on the
landing the wall paintings, made famous in Hardy's *Tess of
the d'Urbervilles*. They depict the heads and shoulders of two
female figures.)

N of the house an attractive group of OUTBUILDINGS, some
stone, some brick. c16 barn beside the road, with characteristic
low buttresses, and a re-set cinquefoil opening at the SE end,
a relic of Bindon Abbey, no doubt. Herringbone masonry in
the N wall.

WOOL BRIDGE over the River Frome. c16, and repaired in 1607
and 1688. Five arches of stone. Pointed cutwaters carried up
as refuges.

At BRAYTOWN, ¾ m. W, a major development of 2007–12 by
Simon Cooper Associates for Barrett Southampton and the Weld
Estate. Cottages in an assortment of blocks and terraces,
well scaled and broken up by the use of varied colours and
materials.

BOVINGTON CAMP, 2 m. NW. Established in 1917, at first as
a tented and hutted camp for the Royal Tank Corps, now
the ARMOUR CENTRE. Its main building periods were the
late 1930s and the 1960s, the effect being one of architectural
muddle, typical of military camps.

The major buildings here are of course those of the TANK
MUSEUM. Standard industrial buildings to which *Kennedy
O'Callahan Architects* have made an extensive and expressive
addition in 2007–8, intended as the first phase of exhibition
and storage facilities. A fan of pitched roofs orientated on a
central conning tower, this intended as a viewing and control
point for tank manoeuvres on the nearby events field.

STANLEY BARRACKS, to the W, opposite the museum.
Of 1958–65 by *Sutcliffe, Brandt & Partners*. Long and low
flat-roofed blocks. Yellow brick. Multi-storey mess buildings
further W, of 1964 and 1968, by the same practice.

BOVINGTON PRIMARY SCHOOL, ¼ m. NNW in Holt Road.
1966–7 by *J.R. Hurst* and the *County Architect's Department*.
The original buildings are the typical brown brick with grey
tile-hanging of the period. A central area with raised flat roof
and clerestory.

WOOLLAND

In the C19 the village was dominated by the church and Woolland House, a picturesque Gothic composition of 1833 by *W. J. Donthorn* (of Highcliffe Castle, Hants, fame) for G. Colby Loftus. Apart from the outbuildings, the house was demolished in 1962.

CHURCH. 1855–6 by *Sir George Gilbert Scott*, for Montague Williams of Woolland House. It cost around £1,800. Nave and chancel and a polygonal apse. On the w end of the nave, supported inside by an arch, is a polygonal bell-turret with a spire. The bell-openings are shafted lancets, but the other windows are all in Scott's beloved Second Pointed, i.e. late C13 in style. The chancel and apse are moreover rib-vaulted. This, the full polished Devon and Derbyshire stone shafting, and the lush foliage capitals, carved by *Farmer & Brindley*, make a climax which the scale of the building would not lead one to expect. There is also a chapel N of the chancel, with a fat pier, again with a rich capital. The arch for the bell-turret has two more. – Minton TILEWORK in the chancel. – PULPIT. Of Caen stone with mural stair entry, also finely carved, probably *c.* 1860. – FONT. Octagonal, C15, with quatrefoils; C19 stem and base. – A full set of contemporary FURNISHINGS. – STAINED GLASS. An extensive scheme by *Wailes* in sepia-toned grisaille, especially fine in the chancel. Coloured armorial window in the chapel. – MONUMENTS. Mary Argenton †1616, with a large kneeling brass figure and a long rhymed inscription. – John Feaver †1788. Tablet carved as if suspended on rope from a buckle. – Mrs Colby Loftus †1842. By *E. H. Baily*. With an excellent relief of a young woman with two young children seated by a sarcophagus on a high base.

WOOLLAND HOUSE, immediately E. The name adopted for the stables of the demolished house (*see* above), now a substantial dwelling itself. Banded brick and flint. In the grounds to the E a STUDIO by the sculptor *Elizabeth Frink* for herself, 1979. Brick cube with one wall completely glazed.

OLD RECTORY, immediately W. Former C17 manor house, enlarged to W and S in the mid C19.

Former SCHOOL, opposite, 1855. Rock-faced rubble Gothic.

CHITCOMBE HOUSE, ½ m. E. By *Stuart Martin Architects*, 2011. Inspired by Lutyens's classical mode. Entrance in the courtyard formed by the H-plan. Open pediment and vestigial pilasters. On the S front, a three-bay Tuscan loggia.

BUL BARROW, ¾ m. S, on Bulbarrow Hill. BOWL BARROW, the centre dug into.

CROSS-DYKES, ¾ m. S. One across the narrow centre of Bulbarrow Hill, one 300 yds NW across the spur and another 650 yds E on Woolland Hill to Delcombe Head. All lie E of Rawlsbury Camp (*see* Stoke Wake).

3090

WOOTTON FITZPAINE

Church and country house grouped together in landscaped grounds. The village, including some estate cottage pairs of *c.* 1880, is ½ m. w.

CHURCH.* A major restoration of 1872 by *George H. Birch* has removed much dating evidence. However, the central tower is C13 E.E., but without any form of elaboration to the parapets. What is left of the crossing arches inside confirms this date, especially the w arch. The chancel is in better shape: C14 Dec – see the reticulated E window and the two-light side windows. C15 s chapel with an over-restored straight-headed window; good gargoyles above the buttresses. N transept of 1872. The nave w window is, if not genuine, at least in its C13 shape trustworthy: two trefoiled lights and a vesica over. Well-carved C19 roof corbels. – Complete FURNISHINGS by *Birch*, including the REREDOS with tile and mosaic inlay. – PULPIT. Incorporating a series of early C17 panels, each with blank arches in two tiers. Elaboration to the surrounds and an arabesque frieze. – FONT. Octagonal bowl, re-cut, possibly from a medieval original. Stem with scalloped capital, probably late C12. – STAINED GLASS. E window by *Heaton, Butler & Bayne*, †1881. s aisle E window by *George Cook*, 1872. – MONUMENT. Thomas Rose Drew †1815. Grecian surround but a Gothick tablet.

WOOTTON HOUSE. A thin range of *c.* 1765 for Thomas Rose Drewe. Seven bays by three, built to the s and incorporating an earlier house. The s front is tall and plain, two-and-a-half storeys below a parapet, the centre three bays canted; red brick with big stone quoins and broad stone strings. What saves it from being a bore is the facing of the projecting bay, the parapet and a strip over the upper string with slates that glint like fish-scales. The modest interior fittings – chimneypieces in the sw and central rooms, a plaster ceiling in the se room – are in a busy sub-Rococo manner totally at odds with the outside, but quite what one would expect for the date. A new E front was created in 1896–7 as part of an enlargement by *Sir George Oatley* for Alfred Capper Pass. Here a smooth salmon-pink brick. The spacing of the five bays of sashes seems strange, accounted for by the need to maintain the l. three from the earlier house in their existing positions. Ballroom added at the w end for Mrs Capper Pass, 1905–6, also by *Oatley* (later converted to a swimming pool).

VILLAGE HALL, ¼ m. wsw. Dated 1906, by *F. W. Troup*. The gift of Mrs Capper Pass. Typically Arts and Crafts, in the mode of a barn. Weatherboarding and tile-hanging in the gable; brickwork, especially the heavy pair of buttresses (with decorative

---

*No dedication recorded, but *The Builder*, 28 December 1872, refers to it as the church of St Paul.

leadwork panels) clasping the narthex-like lobby at the N end, and a big clay-tiled roof. Roughcast to the lower parts of the walls. Side room with, above it, a complicated chimney with tile patterns. Inside, the roof structure is derived from medieval cruck construction.

WORTH MATRAVERS

The village has a unified centre, the cottages of local Purbeck stone. Its looks have been adjusted for tourists, however; the duck pond seems incongruous on the waterless slope of the hill.

ST NICHOLAS. Here is one of the two almost complete Norman churches of Purbeck (*see* Studland for the other). Both nave and chancel are of *c*. 1100, and both have corbel tables to indicate that date. These have grotesques of human and animal heads. The plainest imposts to the tower arch (with a rebuilt arch above), together with the several windows, and pilaster buttresses at the nave corners, are all of this period. But the large and heavy scallop capitals and the chevron decoration at the chancel arch suggest a later date of *c*. 1170. Of this date too the S doorway, and between them these suggest two phases of work. However this is a false trail, as the latter features were brought into the church from elsewhere, probably in the C16; their source is unknown.* Opposing nave doorways, that on the N within a later raised surround with a parabolic arch. The W tower is of *c*. 1100, of three stages, and with clasping buttresses on the W corners only rising to half the tower height. It also has a corbel table (not as sculpted as that to the nave and chancel) and a pyramid roof, restored in a surprisingly conservative repair of 1869–72 by *Anthony Salvin* for the Rev. J. G. Richardson and the 3rd Earl of Eldon. The church also has some C13 lancets, especially in the rebuilt S wall of the chancel. Its E wall is C14, hence the Dec E window with reticulated tracery.

But to return to the S doorway, one would love to have seen the tympanum in its prime. As it is, one hardly recognizes that it represents the Coronation of the Virgin with two angels l. and r. However, one can say for certain that this was a well-informed composition, inspired probably by French work. The subject poses an interesting dating problem. The Coronation of the Virgin became accepted in French sculpture only at the end of the C12 (Senlis) and the early C13 (Notre-Dame, Paris; Chartres transept). How late can the Worth Matravers tympanum be? It is placed in a surround with chevron, and the chevron very oddly develops out of two thin vertical rolls

---

* Richard Jones suggests that the chancel arch may have come from Bindon Abbey.

running up the jambs l. and r. of a broad convex moulding.
Chevron re-set also inside the porch entrance, the porch itself
being C18.

FURNISHINGS. The FONT is C19 Perp, looking weak
against the robust Norman work. – At the W end a C19
GALLERY. – One does not come to Worth Matravers especially to see the STAINED GLASS. E window by *Christopher
Webb*, 1955, who also did a nave S window (1960). Of an earlier
style, a nave N window by *Powell & Sons*, 1921. Two small nave
windows by *Jane Grey*, 1979 and 1985. In the tower doorway
a panel by *J. H. Bonnor*, brought in.

ST ALDHELM'S CHAPEL. *See* p. 509.

DUNSHAY MANOR (Landmark Trust), 1½ m. NNE. Small,
squarish manor house of late C16 origin. Extended in 1642
(rainwater heads on the E front dated with initials JDA for John
and Ann Dolling). Broad gable l. and r. of a parapeted projecting porch, a symmetrical composition. The details are typical
of the mid C17: chimneystacks on the gable-tips, three-light
windows without hoodmoulds except for the porch window,
round-headed porch entrance. Much rebuilt in 1906 by *Philip
Sturdy* for G. M. Marsden.

Several SCULPTURES in the gardens by *Mary Spencer Watson*,
who left the property to the Landmark Trust in 2006.

EAST AND WEST MAN, southwards from a point ½ m. SSE.
Medieval STRIP LYNCHETS are clearly visible over 100 acres,
and identifiable over another 190 acres, on each side of the
valley leading S to Winspit and on the spurs East Man and
West Man.

WRAXALL

ST MARY. Small. Late C12 nave and C13 chancel. Octagonal
bell-turret with a chamfered pyramid roof. The S doorway is
of the very late C12, which accounts for the pointed arch on
chamfered imposts. But are the narrow lancets on the nave and
chancel contemporary or slightly later? Two square-headed
C15 nave S windows. The bell-turret and nave N projection on
the site of a chapel date from restoration *c.* 1840, as does the
E triplet window. Pointed late C12 chancel arch with one step
and one hollow chamfer. Responds with scalloped capitals
and square abaci. A squint with a two-centred head to the
l., serving a disappeared chapel. – FURNISHINGS. Modest
in character, of two phases (e.g. the different pews on the N
and S sides). – MONUMENTS. William Lawrence †1681. Nicely
framed inscription in script. It reads:

Welcome deare Death let sweetest Sleep here take me
In thy cool Shades and never more awake mee
Like a rich Cortege draw thy Darkness round

Like a closed Chamber make my Grave profound
In it I'le couch secure no Dreames affright
A silent Lodger here no Cares dare bite
Making thy Bed seeme hard or long thy night
Let not thy armes oh Grave yet still enfold mee
Alas think not thou canst for ever hold mee
Wee'le breake at length thy marble wombe asunder
Reissue thence and fill the world with wonder
Envy thou'll then to see the Power divine
Nevre digge his Diamond Saints from thy deepest myne
Cleanse cleare and polish them then shall by farre
Each dust of theirs outshine the Morning Starre

Nearby is a BRASS to Mrs Lawrence †1672 (formerly on the side of a chest tomb). Her inscription is this:

Goodness in Heauen gaue a Birth
in here to Goodness here on Earth
And having Tyme long n^{th} here Bless'd
Tooke her to Heauen there to Rest
Goodness in Earth doth now in Mourning goe
Because she hath noe Patterne left Below

WRAXALL MANOR HOUSE, Higher Wraxall, 5/8 m. NW. An orderly and harmonious stone house of 1610 for William Lawrence, large, but quite without idiosyncrasies. Just a block, four gables wide, two deep, given a steady rhythm by large four-light windows, transomed and with hoodmoulds, and by the straight gables, each crowned with a chimneystack. Central porch set uncomfortably overlapping two bays; the entrance arch four-centred. On the w side there are blocked windows with arched lights, perhaps indicative of an earlier building incorporated. Addition of c. 1905 along the roadside, linking the rear with a coach house.

WYKE REGIS

1¼ m. S of Weymouth

6070

A separate village until overtaken by the suburban growth of Weymouth in the 1930s. Something of its former character can still faintly be felt, however, thanks to the dominance of the church, and to the stone walls which run hither and thither along the roads.

ALL SAINTS. An impressive church, all of Portland ashlar, and an important one; for the dedication date 1455 represents evidently the building as we see it now. The three-stage battlemented w tower is tall and has a w doorway to which the base course rises oddly, a three-light w window with cusped lights and a transom, cusped two-light bell-openings and set-back buttresses. The chancel does not project far and has a five-light E window, with cusped lights too. But the aisle windows are all already uncusped. They are of three lights, with panel tracery. The arcades inside are of five bays, and the piers are not quite standard. They have four shafts, and instead of the four diagonal hollows four of the familiar sunk convex quadrants. Tower arch and chancel arch are the same. So we have an uncommonly unified and capacious interior. The only detectable alteration (apart from furnishings, *see* below) is the installation of a roof of lower pitch. A steeper roof most likely had its principals supported at the heads of the wall-shafts set between the arcade arches. – FURNISH-INGS. Generally of a high standard, especially PEWS with their poppyhead ends. All of 1859 by *Henry Hall*. – FONT. C15, octagonal. The stem curves out towards the top and carries a shallow bowl. The stem has vertical roll mouldings rising from colonnette bases and big leaves between, the bowl fleurons in narrow panels. – ROYAL ARMS. Tudor. Relief carving. Said to have come from Sandsfoot Castle (*see* p.655). Also a painted panel, George III. – STAINED GLASS. E window by *Thomas Willement*, 1841, but 'barbarously treated' in a simplification of 1951.* One window in each aisle probably by *Clayton & Bell* (1881 and 1898). S aisle window by *Powell & Sons*, 1891. In the N aisle another, perhaps by *Shrigley & Hunt*, 1904. – MONU-MENTS. Many tablets, e.g. Lydia Harden †1800 with a small standing female by a vase, and Samuel Weston †1817, which is specially large. The latter, with a shrouded urn, is by *Thomas Cooke*. – Also Charles Meyrick Hickes †1862, a ceramic plaque by *Powells*, 1906.

WESLEYAN METHODIST CHURCH, Portland Road, ⅓ m. SSE. 1903. Gothic. Y-traceried W windows above a lean-to porch with central gablet.

COUNTY INFANT SCHOOL AND NURSERY, Shrubbery Lane. 1949–53 by *E. Wamsley Lewis*. The post-war school style handled with refreshing suggestions of vulgarity, e.g. the arched doorway with balcony high on the tower. Large L-plan. A series of class-rooms in echelon converge on the entrance and administration block at the centre. Low, except for the porch-tower feature. Portland stone laid crazy-paving fashion, and strawberry-ice colourwash. Chequerboard and porthole windows.

WYKE REGIS MEMORIAL HALL, All Saints' Road, just down from the church. 1897, by *Crickmay & Son*. A nice example of the style of that date. Red brick. Low-sweeping roof, and gables.

MANOR FARM, All Saints' Road, opposite the church. Now surrounded by converted farm buildings and suburban devel-opment. It has a powerful C17 N gable-end of Portland ashlar, with a gable on kneelers, and a vast chimney-breast, part of its weight taken on corbels. String courses continue to the E front, but here the bay window is C19.

* Michael Kerney, 'The Victorian Memorial Window', *Journal of Stained Glass* 31, 2007. The simplifiers were *Reece & Margaret Kaye Pemberton*.

WYKE CASTLE, Westhill Road, ⅜ m. SW. A firmly planned but tentatively detailed mock castle. Built *c.* 1855, apparently for a French exile. A V, open towards the sea; not a plan that takes most advantage of the view. Low round tower at the apex, low square towers at the ends of the arms.

COASTGUARD LOOK-OUT, Westhill Road, just N of the above. Of *c.* 1880. Small brick look-out kiosk. Two-storeyed to gain views over Weymouth and Lyme bays.

BELFIELD HOUSE, Belfield Park, ⅓ m. E. Of *c.* 1780, and mentioned in *The Weymouth Guide* of five years later as 'a neat house ... designed and executed by Mr Crunden, which does credit to the architect'. This was *John Crunden*, best known as the architect of Boodle's Club. For Isaac Buxton, a London merchant. A villa in an Adam style, very well proportioned and bold in the details. Buff brick and stone dressings. Rusticated stone basement. One-and-a-half storeys above. Five-bay E façade, the centre three under a free-standing Ionic portico, bays one and five wide and on the *piano nobile* given Venetian windows under semicircular super-arches, that Adam favourite. Three-bay side elevation under a pedimental gable (in stone on the more visible S end only). Inside there are just four main rooms: a semicircular hall, the staircase rising against the curve to an upper landing with pairs of columns with Spalatro capitals; an octagonal room behind (expressed externally in a canted bay); and identical rectangular drawing room and dining room, l. and r. The drawing room was refitted *c.* 1820 (reeded architraves with paterae), when an enlarged window with trelliswork veranda was added to take advantage of the views towards Portland and the sea. Later C19 conservatory to the rear. 95

Buxton built his house on a wooded hill behind the town (as depicted in Pouncy's *Dorsetshire Illustrated* of 1857). Its present situation, among suburban houses, would have dismayed him.

GREYSTONES, Belfield Park Drive, to the W of the above, is by *E. Wamsley Lewis*, 1933–4 (for H. Bartle Pye). Hipped, green-glazed pantile roof. Short curved 'sun-trap' wings, one no more than a screen wall.

Two more by *Lewis*, the comparatively undemonstrative No. 54 Buxton Road, 1937, and No. 59 Wyke Road (for L. Samphier), 1953. Both of Portland rubble with pantile roofs, the latter with two porthole windows.*

WYNFORD EAGLE

5090

ST LAWRENCE. Of 1840, either by *Edmund Pearce* (who submitted the plans) or *S. & H. Osborn* (who signed off on completion). Small, of the Commissioners' type. Three-bay nave, short

---

*No. 59 Wyke Road was awarded a medal by the Ministry of Housing in 1955.

canted chancel (with an E gable), W porch. But the chancel arch is from the predecessor building and early C15. Re-set in the W wall is an early C12 tympanum with two affronted monsters: birds (eagles?) with long thin tails. An inscription reads 'Mahad Delegele' (eagle?) and '*Alvi* me feci(t)'. There is also the scalloped head of a C12 PILLAR PISCINA. – The FURNISHINGS are of 1840. – Two two-tier C18 brass CHANDELIERS. – STAINED GLASS. E window by *Powell & Sons*, 1904.

MANOR FARM, 200 yds E. This is the manor house rebuilt in 1630 (see the date on the porch) by William Sydenham. It remains externally quite unaltered. Rectangular block two rooms deep, without projections, except the central three-storey porch. The roof at the back is hipped. Towards the W however, to make the show front, the greater height of gables was still preferred, so the house is transitional between the standard early C17 gabled form and the hipped-roofed blocks of the mid century. There is only one gable each side of the porch, to the two bays of windows below, and this involves an ugly splaying of the outer leg of the gable to fit it to the roof behind while keeping the front symmetrical, an instructive compromise. Along the spine wall two chimneys, each originally with four diagonal-set stacks (one stack is missing). Eagle perched on the porch gable. Windows regularly of three lights, the longer ground-floor ones with transoms. Ovolo mouldings. Hoodmoulds only for the gable windows, for continuous string courses run round above the heads of the main windows. Round-headed porch arch, with a keystone, but still Gothic mouldings. Ham Hill ashlar throughout, except on the N side, where local materials, stone and flint in bands, had to suffice. (A first-floor room fireplace has a contemporary arcaded overmantel of wood, painted later in the C17 with fantasy landscapes under the arches.)

YETMINSTER

Owing to a notably secure system of tenancy, farmhouses in Yetminster were well built and numerous, hence the architectural richness of the village. With its major church, and with a close supply of fine building stone, Yetminster is as good a place as any in Dorset for learning the vernacular range in stone buildings from, say, the C15 to the early C18, many of which retain their thatched roofs.* The main streets are an E–W High Street with, leading off to the S, Church Street.

ST ANDREW. Long C13 chancel with wide, paired uncusped lancets and a triplet of similar lancets to the E, stepped and under one arched hoodmould. A consecration is recorded for 1312, but one would expect at least the first hints of Dec by

---

* See R. Machin, *The Houses of Yetminster* (1978).

that date. Mid-C15 Perp the rest, of one build; embattled. Fine three-stage W tower with rectangular NE stair projection. Set-back buttresses. Five-light W window. Boldly carved gargoyles. Of this date too the aisles and large N porch. Large four-light windows. Arcades of three bays, tall piers of the standard section. Small round leaf capitals to the shafts only. Small grotesque beasts on the S aisle, including geese hanging a fox. The tower arch and chancel arch are similar. Two foliate brackets on the W face of the chancel arch, either part of a support for the rood loft or for images. Nave roof of the wagon kind, with bosses. Low-pitched lean-to aisle roofs, also with bosses. (The restored bosses are unpainted.) Restoration by *Ewan Christian* (chancel, including a new roof) and *G.R. Crickmay* (nave), 1889–90, completed by *C. & C.B. Benson* of Yeovil. There are a remarkable number of CONSECRATION CROSSES, eleven from the full set of twelve, all mid-C15.

FURNISHINGS. COMMUNION RAIL. Early C18 with turned balusters. – War Memorial PULPIT. 1921, carved by *Edward Woollen* of Yeovil to a design by *C.B. Benson*. Almost Art Nouveau carving. Now mounted on casters. – BENCHES. C15, with simple poppyheads. These are at the W end of the nave. Those towards the front are part of the *Crickmay* restoration, intended to match. – FONTS. Only the base of a typical Purbeck C12 or C13 font remains, made for five supports. A C15 font is built into a pier of the S aisle. Octagonal with moulded stem. – TOWER SCREEN. 1906 by *Benson* (carved by *Woollen*). Perp style and more competent than his later pulpit. Now part of support for the organ loft. – PORCH SCREEN. Also Perp in style and by *Benson*. – PAINTING. Much of the original C15 colour scheme survives on the arcades and the N aisle roof, with its repetitive design. – Some encaustic TILES in the sanctuary, 1890 by *Godwin* of Hereford. – SCULPTURE. Small part of an Anglo-Saxon cross-shaft, perhaps C10. Part cut down, but two sides each with a bust, interlace and rope banding. – Bracket with carved angel, late C14 (in the N aisle). – WEATHERCOCK. Dated 1752. Gilded. – STAINED GLASS. E window by *Burlison & Grylls*, 1890. Two later chancel windows by the same firm. – MONUMENTS. Bridgett Minterne †1649. Kneeling effigy at her prayer-desk between pairs of columns. Achievement and shields of arms above the entablature. Coloured. – John Horsey †1531, and Elizabeth, *née* Turges, his wife. Brass of gentleman and lady. Many separate additional brasses, including shields of arms, scrolls and a long inscription plate. Re-set in a concrete panel, 1890. – William Taunton †1691. Slate tablet in an enriched stone surround.

WESLEYAN METHODIST CHAPEL, Chapel Lane. 1850, by *James Wilson* of Bath. Lancet Gothic.

VILLAGE. First one of the earliest houses in Yetminster, UPBURY FARM, immediately SW of the church, set back from Church Street. C15. Long and low, showing evidence of the open hall in the centre by a big blocked two-light window with a transom and traceried head, and by the head of a smaller but similar window l. of it, and by the doorway to the r., moulded with wave and hollow. Quatrefoil panel above the doorway. Above the former open hall a collar-beam and arch-brace roof structure. Upper floor inserted in the late C16, with the hall fireplace of that date backing on to the cross-passage. Hall ceiling with moulded beams. Late C20 stone-mullioned windows, replacing wooden casements.

Now N down CHURCH STREET. On the E side a number of mid- and late C19 buildings, starting with the OLD VICARAGE, opposite the church. Tudor Revival with mullioned windows at the front, sashes on the sides, under a hipped roof. Next a terrace (one house dated 1901, no doubt the date for the whole) with the OLD SCHOOL at the end, again Tudor Revival (and a very late example of the style). Finally on this side HILL HOUSE, departing from the traditional forms. Of c. 1800, three-storeyed, with paired sashes and a roof hidden behind the parapet. The chief concessions to the C17 here are the terminal PIERS to the front railings with oversized stone finials.

At the junction between Church Street and High Street, the range of vernacular buildings is immediately discernible. On the W side, CROSS FARMHOUSE is probably early C17. Hollow-chamfered mullioned windows of three and four lights. Early C18 doorway and one sash window above, minimal alterations to the new styles. On the N side of the triangular central green, in the HIGH STREET, MANOR FARM is of two dates. With its gable on the road a mid-C17 range facing W, its stone-mullioned fenestration arranged symmetrically. On its E side, alongside the road, a later range, probably mid to late C18, still with stone-mullioned windows. Going E along High Street from the junction, after about 50 yds, set back to the r., GABLE COURT. Dates of 1600 and 1601 on the gabled dormers of the N front, the original cottage. Standard mullioned windows of three lights, the mullions hollow-chamfered. Hoodmoulds. It was extended towards the road, l., in the C18.

In CHAPEL LANE, opposite Gable Court, on the r., GABLE COTTAGE. Early C16, with a former open hall to the r. of its cross-passage. Inside on the l. a plank-and-muntin partition. Externally, C17 timber-mullioned windows giving no clue to its early date. An indication of the vernacular style continuing into the C18 is at LOWER FARM, at the N end of the lane, beyond the chapel (see above). It is dated 1707 on the porch, although this refers to an addition and change of ownership. The oval window in the W gable suggests a late C17 date, and its windows with hoodmoulds and four-centred-arched doorway would confirm this.

Back to HIGH STREET, where the main group lies to the W. After Manor Farm (see above) on the same (N) side, a pair of cottages (MINSTER COTTAGE and the former OAK HOUSE STORES, perhaps originally built as an inn), with, above the central doorway, an elaborate datestone of 1607. The initials are probably those of John Reade. The doorway has an arched head with the hoodmould rising higher than over the adjoining mullioned windows. Curious plan with lateral chimneystacks at the rear. Late C19 shopfront to the r. with contemporary casements above. Similar mullioned windows at CLARE COTTAGE next door, but here the roof has clearly been raised, probably *c.* 1800. After a few more cottages on the N side (some thatched), DEVON HOUSE, an interesting early C18 version of the theme. Mullioned windows of three lights above, four below, but in simple surrounds with classical mouldings, with plain chamfered mullions. Classical doorcase. Symmetrical front, which had rarely been a boast of village houses in the earlier C17.

Standing apart further W, the MANOR HOUSE was originally a range end-on to the street. It was rebuilt from a C16 house, probably in the 1670s, to present a two-storey façade to the street. Several C16 features are reused, such as the first-floor hollow-chamfered mullioned windows and the doorway, with a wave-and-hollow moulding, though the head is straight, not arched. Of the later date the ground-floor ovolo-moulded mullioned windows and the central oval window, the latter perhaps moved from an end gable. After another group of thatched cottages, the WHITE HART INN, also thatched. Here there are mid- to late C17 stone-mullioned windows on the ground floor and timber casements above, indicating that its roof has been raised, probably in the early C19. The ovolo mouldings and hoodmoulds appear to get a date at HIGHER FARM, a little further on, where the l. part of the front is dated 1624, the r. part 1630. However these datestones are not *in situ* (although at least one is from this house) as the front range was substantially rebuilt in the early C20 from a gabled form, the date of its present hipped roof.* On the S side, ROCK HOUSE, *c.* 1720, has a two-storey bow window of *c.* 1800, unique in Yetminster. Finally, back on the N side, BOYLE'S SCHOOL, founded in 1691 and built in 1697. Mullioned windows with hoodmoulds, the lower ones, for the schoolroom, longer and given transoms. The jumped-up hood to the doorway is such as Yetminster could show nearly a century before.

HAMLET HOUSE, 1¼ m. SSE. A former farmhouse of two parallel ranges, the S front dated 1688, the rear C18, stuccoed with sash windows. Four irregular bays to the front, with windows of three and four lights, the lower with hoodmoulds, and a one-storey porch.

MALTHOUSE, continuing this range to the E. Dated 1816. Thatched roof. Three storeys (but with a similar eaves height to the farmhouse). Openings to each floor with timber lintels. The ground floor was the steep (where the grain was soaked), the upper two floors were fitted with barley bins.**

---

* Information and an early photograph from the owner, Dr Peter Newton.
** *See* report by Amber Patrick, 1974.

GLOSSARY

Numbers and letters refer to the illustrations (by John Sambrook)
on pp. 728–735.

ABACUS: flat slab forming the top of a capital (3a).

ACANTHUS: classical formalized leaf ornament (4b).

ACCUMULATOR TOWER: *see* Hydraulic power.

ACHIEVEMENT: a complete display of armorial bearings.

ACROTERION: plinth for a statue or ornament on the apex or ends of a pediment; more usually, both the plinth and what stands on it (4a).

AEDICULE (*lit.* little building): architectural surround, consisting usually of two columns or pilasters supporting a pediment.

AGGREGATE: *see* Concrete.

AISLE: subsidiary space alongside the body of a building, separated from it by columns, piers, or posts.

ALMONRY: a building from which alms are dispensed to the poor.

AMBULATORY (*lit.* walkway): aisle around the sanctuary (q.v.).

ANGLE ROLL: roll moulding in the angle between two planes (1a).

ANSE DE PANIER: *see* Arch.

ANTAE: simplified pilasters (4a), usually applied to the ends of the enclosing walls of a portico *in antis* (q.v.).

ANTEFIXAE: ornaments projecting at regular intervals above a Greek cornice, originally to conceal the ends of roof tiles (4a).

ANTHEMION: classical ornament like a honeysuckle flower (4b).

APRON: raised panel below a window or wall monument or tablet.

APSE: semicircular or polygonal end of an apartment, especially of a chancel or chapel. In classical architecture sometimes called an *exedra*.

ARABESQUE: non-figurative surface decoration consisting of flowing lines, foliage scrolls etc., based on geometrical patterns. Cf. Grotesque.

ARCADE: series of arches supported by piers or columns. *Blind arcade* or *arcading*: the same applied to the wall surface. *Wall arcade*: in medieval churches, a blind arcade forming a dado below windows. Also a covered shopping street.

ARCH: Shapes *see* 5c. *Basket arch* or *anse de panier* (basket handle): three-centred and depressed, or with a flat centre. *Nodding*: ogee arch curving forward from the wall face. *Parabolic*: shaped like a chain suspended from two level points, but inverted. Special purposes. *Chancel*: dividing chancel from nave or crossing. *Crossing*: spanning piers at a crossing (q.v.). *Relieving or discharging*: incorporated in a wall to relieve superimposed weight (5c). *Skew*: spanning responds not diametrically opposed. *Strainer*: inserted in an opening to resist inward pressure. *Transverse*: spanning a main axis (e.g. of a vaulted space). *See also* Jack arch, Triumphal arch.

ARCHITRAVE: formalized lintel, the lowest member of the classical entablature (3a). Also the moulded frame of a door or window (often borrowing the profile of a classical architrave). For *lugged* and *shouldered* architraves *see* 4b.

ARCUATED: dependent structurally on the arch principle. Cf. Trabeated.

ARK: chest or cupboard housing the

tables of Jewish law in a syn-
agogue.

ARRIS: sharp edge where two
surfaces meet at an angle (3a).

ASHLAR: masonry of large blocks
wrought to even faces and square
edges (6d).

ASTRAGAL: classical moulding of
semicircular section (3f).

ASTYLAR: with no columns or
similar vertical features.

ATLANTES: see Caryatids.

ATRIUM (plural: atria): inner court
of a Roman or C20 house; in a
multi-storey building, a toplit
covered court rising through all
storeys. Also an open court in
front of a church.

ATTACHED COLUMN: see Engaged
column.

ATTIC: small top storey within
a roof. Also the storey above the
main entablature of a classical
façade.

AUMBRY: recess or cupboard to
hold sacred vessels for the Mass.

BAILEY: see Motte-and-bailey.

BALANCE BEAM: see Canals.

BALDACCHINO: free-standing canopy, originally fabric, over an
altar. Cf. Ciborium.

BALLFLOWER: globular flower of
three petals enclosing a ball (1a).
Typical of the Decorated style.

BALUSTER: pillar or pedestal of
bellied form. Balusters: vertical
supports of this or any other form,
for a handrail or coping, the whole
being called a balustrade (6c).
Blind balustrade: the same applied
to the wall surface.

BARBICAN: outwork defending the
entrance to a castle.

BARGEBOARDS (corruption of
'vergeboards'): boards, often
carved or fretted, fixed beneath
the eaves of a gable to cover and
protect the rafters.

BAROQUE: style originating in Rome
c.1600 and current in England
c.1680–1720, characterized by
dramatic massing and silhouette
and the use of the giant order.

BARROW: burial mound.

BARTIZAN: corbelled turret, square
or round, frequently at an angle.

BASCULE: hinged part of a lifting (or
bascule) bridge.

BASE: moulded foot of a column or
pilaster. For Attic base see 3b.

BASEMENT: lowest, subordinate
storey; hence the lowest part of a
classical elevation, below the piano
nobile (q.v.).

BASILICA: a Roman public hall;
hence an aisled building with a
clerestory.

BASTION: one of a series of defensive semicircular or polygonal projections from the main wall of a
fortress or city.

BATTER: intentional inward inclina-
tion of a wall face.

BATTLEMENT: defensive parapet,
composed of merlons (solid) and
crenels (embrasures) through
which archers could shoot; sometimes called crenellation. Also used
decoratively.

BAY: division of an elevation or
interior space as defined by regular
vertical features such as arches,
columns, windows etc.

BAY LEAF: classical ornament of
overlapping bay leaves (3f).

BAY WINDOW: window of one or
more storeys projecting from the
face of a building. Canted: with
a straight front and angled sides.
Bow window: curved. Oriel: rests
on corbels or brackets and starts
above ground level; also the bay
window at the dais end of a medieval great hall.

BEAD-AND-REEL: see Enrichments.

BEAKHEAD: Norman ornament
with a row of beaked bird or beast
heads usually biting into a roll
moulding (1a).

BELFRY: chamber or stage in a
tower where bells are hung.

BELL CAPITAL: see 1b.

BELLCOTE: small gabled or roofed
housing for the bell(s).

BERM: level area separating a ditch
from a bank on a hill-fort or
barrow.

BILLET: Norman ornament of small
half-cylindrical or rectangular
blocks (1a).

BLIND: see Arcade, Baluster, Portico.

BLOCK CAPITAL: see 1a.

BLOCKED: columns, etc. interrupted by regular projecting

blocks (*blocking*), as on a Gibbs surround (4b).

BLOCKING COURSE: course of stones, or equivalent, on top of a cornice and crowning the wall.

BOLECTION MOULDING: covering the joint between two different planes (6b).

BOND: the pattern of long sides (*stretchers*) and short ends (*headers*) produced on the face of a wall by laying bricks in a particular way (6e).

BOSS: knob or projection, e.g. at the intersection of ribs in a vault (2c).

BOWTELL: a term in use by the C15 for a form of roll moulding, usually three-quarters of a circle in section (also called *edge roll*).

BOW WINDOW: *see* Bay window.

BOX FRAME: timber-framed construction in which vertical and horizontal wall members support the roof (7). Also concrete construction where the loads are taken on cross walls; also called *cross-wall construction*.

BRACE: subsidiary member of a structural frame, curved or straight. *Bracing* is often arranged decoratively e.g. quatrefoil, herringbone (7). *See also* Roofs.

BRATTISHING: ornamental crest, usually formed of leaves, Tudor flowers or miniature battlements.

BRESSUMER (*lit.* breast-beam): big horizontal beam supporting the wall above, especially in a jettied building (7).

BRICK: *see* Bond, Cogging, Engineering, Gauged, Tumbling.

BRIDGE: *Bowstring*: with arches rising above the roadway which is suspended from them. *Clapper*: one long stone forms the roadway. *Roving*: *see* Canal. *Suspension*: roadway suspended from cables or chains slung between towers or pylons. *Stay-suspension* or *stay-cantilever*: supported by diagonal stays from towers or pylons. *See also* Bascule.

BRISES-SOLEIL: projecting fins or canopies which deflect direct sunlight from windows.

BROACH: *see* Spire and IC.

BUCRANIUM: ox skull used decoratively in classical friezes.

BULL-NOSED SILL: sill displaying a pronounced convex upper moulding.

BULLSEYE WINDOW: small oval window, set horizontally (cf. Oculus). Also called *œil de bœuf*.

BUTTRESS: vertical member projecting from a wall to stabilize it or to resist the lateral thrust of an arch, roof, or vault (IC, 2c). A *flying buttress* transmits the thrust to a heavy abutment by means of an arch or half-arch (IC).

CABLE OR ROPE MOULDING: originally Norman, like twisted strands of a rope.

CAMES: *see* Quarries.

CAMPANILE: free-standing bell-tower.

CANALS: *Flash lock*: removable weir or similar device through which boats pass on a flush of water. Predecessor of the *pound lock*: chamber with gates at each end allowing boats to float from one level to another. *Tidal gates*: single pair of lock gates allowing vessels to pass when the tide makes a level. *Balance beam*: beam projecting horizontally for opening and closing lock gates. *Roving bridge*: carrying a towing path from one bank to the other.

CANTILEVER: horizontal projection (e.g. step, canopy) supported by a downward force behind the fulcrum.

CAPITAL: head or crowning feature of a column or pilaster; for classical types *see* 3; for medieval types *see* Ib.

CARREL: compartment designed for individual work or study.

CARTOUCHE: classical tablet with ornate frame.

CARYATIDS: female figures supporting an entablature; their male counterparts are *Atlantes* (*lit.* Atlas figures).

CASEMATE: vaulted chamber, with embrasures for defence, within a castle wall or projecting from it.

CASEMENT: side-hinged window.

CASTELLATED: with battlements (q.v.).

CAST IRON: hard and brittle, cast in a mould to the required shape.

Wrought iron is ductile, strong in tension, forged into decorative patterns or forged and rolled into e.g. bars, joists, boiler plates; *mild steel* is its modern equivalent, similar but stronger.

CATSLIDE: *See* 8a.

CAVETTO: concave classical moulding of quarter-round section (3f).

CELURE OR CEILURE: enriched area of roof above rood or altar.

CEMENT: *see* Concrete.

CENOTAPH (*lit.* empty tomb): funerary monument which is not a burying place.

CENTRING: wooden support for the building of an arch or vault, removed after completion.

CHAMFER (*lit.* corner-break): surface formed by cutting off a square edge or corner. For types of chamfers and *chamfer stops see* 6a. *See also* Double chamfer.

CHANCEL: part of the E end of a church set apart for the use of the officiating clergy.

CHANTRY CHAPEL: often attached to or within a church, endowed for the celebration of Masses principally for the soul of the founder.

CHEVET (*lit.* head): French term for chancel with ambulatory and radiating chapels.

CHEVRON: V-shape used in series or double series (later) on a Norman moulding (1a). Also (especially when on a single plane) called *zigzag*.

CHOIR: the part of a cathedral, monastic or collegiate church where services are sung.

CIBORIUM: a fixed canopy over an altar, usually vaulted and supported on four columns; cf. Baldacchino. Also a canopied shrine for the reserved sacrament.

CINQUEFOIL: *see* Foil.

CIST: stone-lined or slab-built grave.

CLADDING: external covering or skin applied to a structure, especially a framed one.

CLERESTORY: uppermost storey of the nave of a church, pierced by windows. Also high-level windows in secular buildings.

CLOSER: a brick cut to complete a bond (6e).

CLUSTER BLOCK: *see* Multi-storey.

COADE STONE: ceramic artificial stone made in Lambeth 1769–*c.*1840 by Eleanor Coade (†1821) and her associates.

COB: walling material of clay mixed with straw. Also called *pisé*.

COFFERING: arrangement of sunken panels (coffers), square or polygonal, decorating a ceiling, vault, or arch.

COGGING: a decorative course of bricks laid diagonally (6e). Cf. Dentilation.

COLLAR: *see* Roofs and 7.

COLLEGIATE CHURCH: endowed for the support of a college of priests.

COLONNADE: range of columns supporting an entablature. Cf. Arcade.

COLONNETTE: small medieval column or shaft.

COLOSSAL ORDER: *see* Giant order.

COLUMBARIUM: shelved, niched structure to house multiple burials.

COLUMN: a classical, upright structural member of round section with a shaft, a capital, and usually a base (3a, 4a).

COLUMN FIGURE: carved figure attached to a medieval column or shaft, usually flanking a doorway.

COMMUNION TABLE: unconsecrated table used in Protestant churches for the celebration of Holy Communion.

COMPOSITE: *see* Orders.

COMPOUND PIER: grouped shafts (q.v.), or a solid core surrounded by shafts.

CONCRETE: composition of *cement* (calcined lime and clay), *aggregate* (small stones or rock chippings), sand and water. It can be poured into *formwork* or *shuttering* (temporary frame of timber or metal) on site (*in-situ* concrete), or *pre-cast* as components before construction. *Reinforced*: incorporating steel rods to take the tensile force. *Pre-stressed*: with tensioned steel rods. Finishes include the impression of boards left by formwork (*board-marked* or *shuttered*), and texturing with steel brushes (*brushed*) or hammers (*hammer-dressed*). *See also* Shell.

CONSOLE: bracket of curved outline (4b).

COPING: protective course of masonry or brickwork capping a wall (6d).

CORBEL: projecting block supporting something above. *Corbel course*: continuous course of projecting stones or bricks fulfilling the same function. *Corbel table*: series of corbels to carry a parapet or a wall-plate or wall-post (7). *Corbelling*: brick or masonry courses built out beyond one another to support a chimney-stack, window, etc.

CORINTHIAN: see Orders and 3d.

CORNICE: flat-topped ledge with moulded underside, projecting along the top of a building or feature, especially as the highest member of the classical entablature (3a). Also the decorative moulding in the angle between wall and ceiling.

CORPS-DE-LOGIS: the main building(s) as distinct from the wings or pavilions.

COTTAGE ORNÉ: an artfully rustic small house associated with the Picturesque movement.

COUNTERCHANGING: of joists on a ceiling divided by beams into compartments, when placed in opposite directions in alternate squares.

COUR D'HONNEUR: formal entrance court before a house in the French manner, usually with flanking wings and a screen wall or gates.

COURSE: continuous layer of stones, etc. in a wall (6e).

COVE: a broad concave moulding, e.g. to mask the eaves of a roof. *Coved ceiling*: with a pronounced cove joining the walls to a flat central panel smaller than the whole area of the ceiling.

CRADLE ROOF: see Wagon roof.

CREDENCE: a shelf within or beside a piscina (q.v.), or a table for the sacramental elements and vessels.

CRENELLATION: parapet with crenels (*see* Battlement).

CRINKLE-CRANKLE WALL: garden wall undulating in a series of serpentine curves.

CROCKETS: leafy hooks. *Crocketing* decorates the edges of Gothic features, such as pinnacles, canopies, etc. *Crocket capital*: see 1b.

CROSSING: central space at the junction of the nave, chancel, and transepts. *Crossing tower*: above a crossing.

CROSS-WINDOW: with one mullion and one transom (qq.v.).

CROWN-POST: see Roofs and 7.

CROWSTEPS: squared stones set like steps, e.g. on a gable (8a).

CRUCKS (*lit.* crooked): pairs of inclined timbers (*blades*), usually curved, set at bay-lengths; they support the roof timbers and, in timber buildings, also support the walls (8b). *Base*: blades rise from ground level to a tie- or collar-beam which supports the roof timbers. *Full*: blades rise from ground level to the apex of the roof, serving as the main members of a roof truss. *Jointed*: blades formed from more than one timber; the lower member may act as a wall-post; it is usually elbowed at wall-plate level and jointed just above. *Middle*: blades rise from half-way up the walls to a tie- or collar-beam. *Raised*: blades rise from half-way up the walls to the apex. *Upper*: blades supported on a tie-beam and rising to the apex.

CRYPT: underground or half-underground area, usually below the E end of a church. *Ring crypt*: corridor crypt surrounding the apse of an early medieval church, often associated with chambers for relics. Cf. Undercroft.

CUPOLA (*lit.* dome): especially a small dome on a circular or polygonal base crowning a larger dome, roof, or turret.

CURSUS: a long avenue defined by two parallel earthen banks with ditches outside.

CURTAIN WALL: a connecting wall between the towers of a castle. Also a non-load-bearing external wall applied to a C20 framed structure.

CUSP: see Tracery and 2b.

CYCLOPEAN MASONRY: large irregular polygonal stones, smooth and finely jointed.

CYMA RECTA and CYMA REVERSA: classical mouldings with double curves (3f). Cf. Ogee.

DADO: the finishing (often with panelling) of the lower part of a wall in a classical interior; in origin a formalized continuous pedestal. *Dado rail*: the moulding along the top of the dado.

DAGGER: *see* Tracery and 2b.

DALLE-DE-VERRE (*lit.* glass-slab): a late C20 stained-glass technique, setting large, thick pieces of cast glass into a frame of reinforced concrete or epoxy resin.

DEC (DECORATED): English Gothic architecture *c.* 1290 to *c.* 1350. The name is derived from the type of window tracery (q.v.) used during the period.

DEMI- or HALF-COLUMNS: engaged columns (q.v.) half of whose circumference projects from the wall.

DENTIL: small square block used in series in classical cornices (3c). *Dentilation* is produced by the projection of alternating headers along cornices or stringcourses.

DIAPER: repetitive surface decoration of lozenges or squares flat or in relief. Achieved in brickwork with bricks of two colours.

DIOCLETIAN OR THERMAL WINDOW: semicircular with two mullions, as used in the Baths of Diocletian, Rome (4b).

DISTYLE: having two columns (4a).

DOGTOOTH: E.E. ornament, consisting of a series of small pyramids formed by four stylized canine teeth meeting at a point (1a).

DORIC: *see* Orders and 3a, 3b.

DORMER: window projecting from the slope of a roof (8a).

DOUBLE CHAMFER: a chamfer applied to each of two recessed arches (1a).

DOUBLE PILE: *see* Pile.

DRAGON BEAM: *see* Jetty.

DRESSINGS: the stone or brickwork worked to a finished face about an angle, opening, or other feature.

DRIPSTONE: moulded stone projecting from a wall to protect the lower parts from water. Cf. Hoodmould, Weathering.

DRUM: circular or polygonal stage supporting a dome or cupola. Also one of the stones forming the shaft of a column (3a).

DUTCH or FLEMISH GABLE: *see* 8a.

EASTER SEPULCHRE: tomb-chest used for Easter ceremonial, within or against the N wall of a chancel.

EAVES: overhanging edge of a roof; hence *eaves cornice* in this position.

ECHINUS: ovolo moulding (q.v.) below the abacus of a Greek Doric capital (3a).

EDGE RAIL: *see* Railways.

E.E. (EARLY ENGLISH): English Gothic architecture *c.* 1190–1250.

EGG-AND-DART: *see* Enrichments and 3f.

ELEVATION: any face of a building or side of a room. In a drawing, the same or any part of it, represented in two dimensions.

EMBATTLED: with battlements.

EMBRASURE: small splayed opening in a wall or battlement (q.v.).

ENCAUSTIC TILES: earthenware tiles fired with a pattern and glaze.

EN DELIT: stone cut against the bed.

ENFILADE: reception rooms in a formal series, usually with all doorways on axis.

ENGAGED or ATTACHED COLUMN: one that partly merges into a wall or pier.

ENGINEERING BRICKS: dense bricks, originally used mostly for railway viaducts etc.

ENRICHMENTS: the carved decoration of certain classical mouldings, e.g. the ovolo (qq.v.) with *egg-and-dart*, the cyma reversa with *waterleaf*, the astragal with *bead-and-reel* (3f).

ENTABLATURE: in classical architecture, collective name for the three horizontal members (architrave, frieze, and cornice) carried by a wall or a column (3a).

ENTASIS: very slight convex deviation from a straight line, used to prevent an optical illusion of concavity.

EPITAPH: inscription on a tomb.

EXEDRA: *see* Apse.

EXTRADOS: outer curved face of an arch or vault.

EYECATCHER: decorative building terminating a vista.

FASCIA: plain horizontal band, e.g. in an architrave (3c, 3d) or on a shopfront.

FENESTRATION: the arrangement of windows in a façade.

FERETORY: site of the chief shrine of a church, behind the high altar.

FESTOON: ornamental garland, suspended from both ends. Cf. Swag.

FIBREGLASS, or glass-reinforced polyester (GRP): synthetic resin reinforced with glass fibre. GRC: glass-reinforced concrete.

FIELD: see Panelling and 6b.

FILLET: a narrow flat band running down a medieval shaft or along a roll moulding (1a). It separates larger curved mouldings in classical cornices, fluting or bases (3c).

FLAMBOYANT: the latest phase of French Gothic architecture, with flowing tracery.

FLASH LOCK: see Canals.

FLÈCHE or SPIRELET (lit. arrow): slender spire on the centre of a roof.

FLEURON: medieval carved flower or leaf, often rectilinear (1a).

FLUSHWORK: knapped flint used with dressed stone to form patterns.

FLUTING: series of concave grooves (flutes), their common edges sharp (arris) or blunt (fillet) (3).

FOIL (lit. leaf): lobe formed by the cusping of a circular or other shape in tracery (2b). Trefoil (three), quatrefoil (four), cinquefoil (five), and multifoil express the number of lobes in a shape.

FOLIATE: decorated with leaves.

FORMWORK: see Concrete.

FRAMED BUILDING: where the structure is carried by a framework – e.g. of steel, reinforced concrete, timber – instead of by load-bearing walls.

FREESTONE: stone that is cut, or can be cut, in all directions.

FRESCO: al fresco: painting on wet plaster. Fresco secco: painting on dry plaster.

FRIEZE: the middle member of the classical entablature, sometimes ornamented (3a). Pulvinated frieze (lit. cushioned): of bold convex profile (3c). Also a horizontal band of ornament.

FRONTISPIECE: in C16 and C17 buildings the central feature of doorway and windows above linked in one composition.

GABLE: For types see 8a. Gablet: small gable. Pedimental gable: treated like a pediment.

GADROONING: classical ribbed ornament like inverted fluting that flows into a lobed edge.

GALILEE: chapel or vestibule usually at the w end of a church enclosing the main portal(s).

GALLERY: a long room or passage; an upper storey above the aisle of a church, looking through arches to the nave; a balcony or mezzanine overlooking the main interior space of a building; or an external walkway.

GALLETING: small stones set in a mortar course.

GAMBREL ROOF: see 8a.

GARDEROBE: medieval privy.

GARGOYLE: projecting water spout often carved into human or animal shape.

GAUGED or RUBBED BRICKWORK: soft brick sawn roughly, then rubbed to a precise (gauged) surface. Mostly used for door or window openings (5c).

GAZEBO (jocular Latin, 'I shall gaze'): ornamental lookout tower or raised summer house.

GEOMETRIC: English Gothic architecture c. 1250–1310. See also Tracery. For another meaning, see Stairs.

GIANT or COLOSSAL ORDER: classical order (q.v.) whose height is that of two or more storeys of the building to which it is applied.

GIBBS SURROUND: C18 treatment of an opening (4b), seen particularly in the work of James Gibbs (1682–1754).

GIRDER: a large beam. Box: of hollow-box section. Bowed: with its top rising in a curve. Plate: of I-section, made from iron or steel plates. *Lattice*: with braced framework.

GLAZING BARS: wooden or sometimes metal bars separating and supporting window panes.

GRAFFITI: *see* Sgraffito.

GRANGE: farm owned and run by a religious order.

GRC: *see* Fibreglass.

GRISAILLE: monochrome painting on walls or glass.

GROIN: sharp edge at the meeting of two cells of a cross-vault; *see* Vault and 2c.

GROTESQUE (*lit.* grotto-esque): wall decoration adopted from Roman examples in the Renaissance. Its foliage scrolls incorporate figurative elements. Cf. Arabesque.

GROTTO: artificial cavern.

GRP: *see* Fibreglass.

GUILLOCHE: classical ornament of interlaced bands (4b).

GUNLOOP: opening for a firearm.

GUTTAE: stylized drops (3b).

HALF-TIMBERING: archaic term for timber-framing (q.v.). Sometimes used for non-structural decorative timberwork.

HALL CHURCH: medieval church with nave and aisles of approximately equal height.

HAMMERBEAM: *see* Roofs and 7.

HAMPER: in C20 architecture, a visually distinct topmost storey or storeys.

HEADER: *see* Bond and 6e.

HEADSTOP: stop (q.v.) carved with a head (5b).

HELM ROOF: *see* 1C.

HENGE: ritual earthwork.

HERM (*lit.* the god Hermes): male head or bust on a pedestal.

HERRINGBONE WORK: *see* 7ii. Cf. Pitched masonry.

HEXASTYLE: *see* Portico.

HILL-FORT: Iron Age earthwork enclosed by a ditch and bank system.

HIPPED ROOF: *see* 8a.

HOODMOULD: projecting moulding above an arch or lintel to throw off water (2b, 5b). When horizontal often called a *label*. For label stop *see* Stop.

HUSK GARLAND: festoon of stylized nutshells (4b).

HYDRAULIC POWER: use of water under high pressure to work machinery. *Accumulator tower*: houses a hydraulic accumulator which accommodates fluctuations in the flow through hydraulic mains.

HYPOCAUST (*lit.* underburning): Roman underfloor heating system.

IMPOST: horizontal moulding at the springing of an arch (5c).

IMPOST BLOCK: block between abacus and capital (1b).

IN ANTIS: *see* Antae, Portico and 4a.

INDENT: shape chiselled out of a stone to receive a brass.

INDUSTRIALIZED or SYSTEM BUILDING: system of manufactured units assembled on site.

INGLENOOK (*lit.* fire-corner): recess for a hearth with provision for seating.

INTERCOLUMNATION: interval between columns.

INTERLACE: decoration in relief simulating woven or entwined stems or bands.

INTRADOS: *see* Soffit.

IONIC: *see* Orders and 3c.

JACK ARCH: shallow segmental vault springing from beams, used for fireproof floors, bridge decks, etc.

JAMB (*lit.* leg): one of the vertical sides of an opening.

JETTY: in a timber-framed building, the projection of an upper storey beyond the storey below, made by the beams and joists of the lower storey oversailing the wall; on their outer ends is placed the sill of the walling for the storey above (7). Buildings can be jettied on several sides, in which case a *dragon beam* is set diagonally at the corner to carry the joists to either side.

JOGGLE: the joining of two stones to prevent them slipping by a notch in one and a projection in the other.

KEEL MOULDING: moulding used from the late C12, in section like the keel of a ship (1a).

KEEP: principal tower of a castle.

KENTISH CUSP: *see* Tracery and 2b.

KEY PATTERN: *see* 4b.

KEYSTONE: central stone in an arch or vault (4b, 5c).

KINGPOST: *see* Roofs and 7.

KNEELER: horizontal projecting stone at the base of each side of a gable to support the inclined coping stones (8a).

LABEL: *see* Hoodmould and 5b.

LABEL STOP: *see* Stop and 5b.

LACED BRICKWORK: vertical strips of brickwork, often in a contrasting colour, linking openings on different floors.

LACING COURSE: horizontal reinforcement in timber or brick to walls of flint, cobble, etc.

LADY CHAPEL: dedicated to the Virgin Mary (Our Lady).

LANCET: slender single-light, pointed-arched window (2a).

LANTERN: circular or polygonal windowed turret crowning a roof or a dome. Also the windowed stage of a crossing tower lighting the church interior.

LANTERN CROSS: churchyard cross with lantern-shaped top.

LAVATORIUM: in a religious house, a washing place adjacent to the refectory.

LEAN-TO: *see* Roofs.

LESENE (*lit.* a mean thing): pilaster without base or capital. Also called *pilaster strip*.

LIERNE: *see* Vault and 2c.

LIGHT: compartment of a window defined by the mullions.

LINENFOLD: Tudor panelling carved with simulations of folded linen. *See also* Parchemin.

LINTEL: horizontal beam or stone bridging an opening.

LOGGIA: gallery, usually arcaded or colonnaded; sometimes free-standing.

LONG-AND-SHORT WORK: quoins consisting of stones placed with the long side alternately upright and horizontal, especially in Saxon building.

LONGHOUSE: house and byre in the same range with internal access between them.

LOUVRE: roof opening, often protected by a raised timber structure, to allow the smoke from a central hearth to escape.

LOWSIDE WINDOW: set lower than the others in a chancel side wall, usually towards its W end.

LUCAM: projecting housing for hoist pulley on upper storey of warehouses, mills, etc., for raising goods to loading doors.

LUCARNE (*lit.* dormer): small gabled opening in a roof or spire.

LUGGED ARCHITRAVE: *see* 4b.

LUNETTE: semicircular window or blind panel.

LYCHGATE (*lit.* corpse-gate): roofed gateway entrance to a churchyard for the reception of a coffin.

LYNCHET: long terraced strip of soil on the downward side of prehistoric and medieval fields, accumulated because of continual ploughing along the contours.

MACHICOLATIONS (*lit.* mashing devices): series of openings between the corbels that support a projecting parapet through which missiles can be dropped. Used decoratively in post-medieval buildings.

MANOMETER or STANDPIPE TOWER: containing a column of water to regulate pressure in water mains.

MANSARD: *see* 8a.

MATHEMATICAL TILES: facing tiles with the appearance of brick, most often applied to timber-framed walls.

MAUSOLEUM: monumental building or chamber usually intended for the burial of members of one family.

MEGALITHIC TOMB: massive stone-built Neolithic burial chamber covered by an earth or stone mound.

MERLON: *see* Battlement.

METOPES: spaces between the triglyphs in a Doric frieze (3b).

MEZZANINE: low storey between two higher ones.

MILD STEEL: *see* Cast iron.

MISERICORD (*lit.* mercy): shelf on a carved bracket placed on the underside of a hinged choir stall seat to support an occupant when standing.

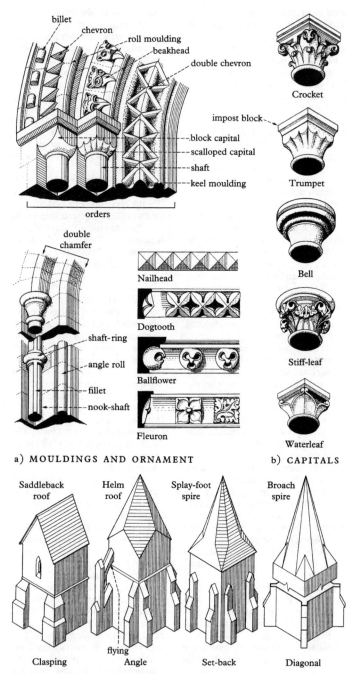

a) MOULDINGS AND ORNAMENT

b) CAPITALS

c) BUTTRESSES, ROOFS AND SPIRES

FIGURE 1: MEDIEVAL

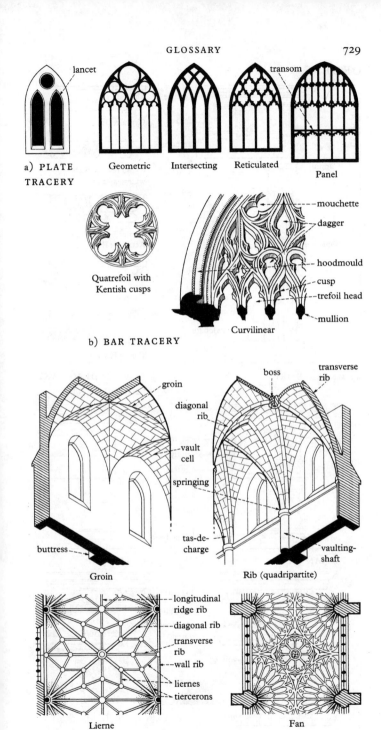

a) PLATE TRACERY

lancet

Geometric Intersecting Reticulated

transom

Panel

Quatrefoil with Kentish cusps

mouchette
dagger
hoodmould
cusp
trefoil head
mullion

Curvilinear

b) BAR TRACERY

groin
diagonal rib
vault cell

buttress

Groin

boss
transverse rib
diagonal rib

springing
tas-de-charge

vaulting-shaft

Rib (quadripartite)

longitudinal ridge rib
diagonal rib
transverse rib
wall rib
liernes
tiercerons

Lierne

Fan

c) VAULTS

FIGURE 2: MEDIEVAL

ORDERS

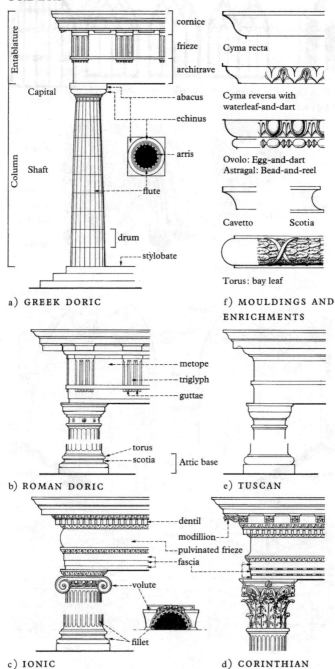

a) GREEK DORIC

- cornice
- frieze
- architrave
- abacus
- echinus
- arris
- flute
- drum
- stylobate

Entablature · Capital · Column · Shaft

f) MOULDINGS AND ENRICHMENTS

Cyma recta

Cyma reversa with waterleaf-and-dart

Ovolo: Egg-and-dart
Astragal: Bead-and-reel

Cavetto   Scotia

Torus: bay leaf

b) ROMAN DORIC

- metope
- triglyph
- guttae
- torus
- scotia   } Attic base

e) TUSCAN

c) IONIC

- dentil
- modillion
- pulvinated frieze
- fascia
- volute
- fillet

d) CORINTHIAN

FIGURE 3: CLASSICAL

a) PORTICO

Distyle in antis   Prostyle

Anthemion & Palmette   Guilloche   Key pattern

Rinceau   Husk garland   Vitruvian scroll

Console   Diocletian window   Acanthus

Broken pediment   Lugged architrave

Segmental pediment   Shouldered architrave

Venetian window

Open pediment   Swan-neck pediment   Gibbs surround

b) ORNAMENTS AND FEATURES

FIGURE 4: CLASSICAL

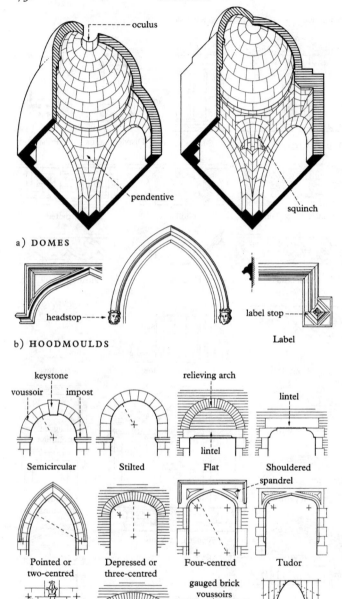

a) DOMES

b) HOODMOULDS

Label

c) ARCHES

FIGURE 5: CONSTRUCTION

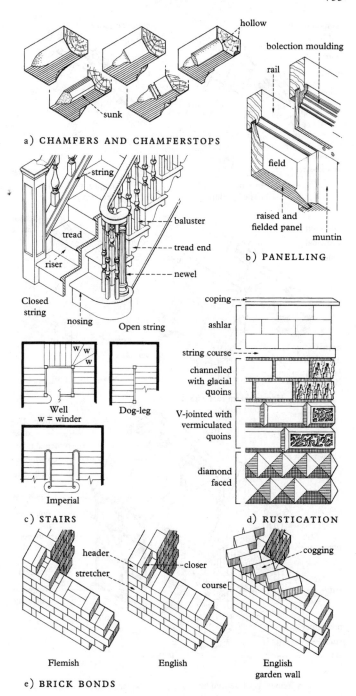

a) CHAMFERS AND CHAMFERSTOPS

b) PANELLING

c) STAIRS

d) RUSTICATION

e) BRICK BONDS

FIGURE 6: CONSTRUCTION

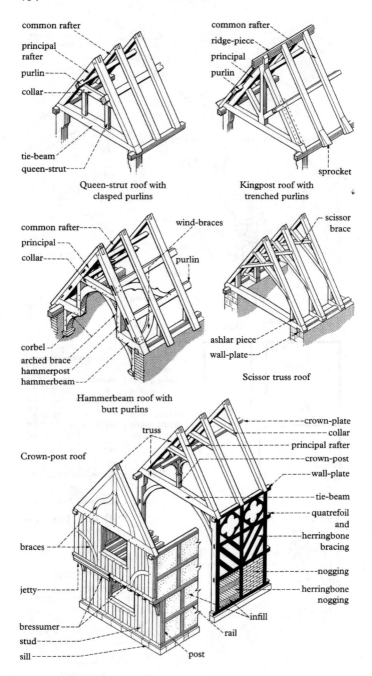

Queen-strut roof with clasped purlins

common rafter
principal rafter
purlin
collar
tie-beam
queen-strut

Kingpost roof with trenched purlins

common rafter
ridge-piece
principal
purlin
sprocket

Hammerbeam roof with butt purlins

common rafter
principal
collar
wind-braces
purlin
corbel
arched brace
hammerpost
hammerbeam

Scissor truss roof

scissor brace
ashlar piece
wall-plate

Crown-post roof

truss
crown-plate
collar
principal rafter
crown-post
wall-plate
tie-beam
quatrefoil and herringbone bracing
nogging
herringbone nogging
braces
jetty
bressumer
stud
sill
post
rail
infill

Box frame: i) Close studding   ii) Square panel

FIGURE 7: ROOFS AND TIMBER-FRAMING

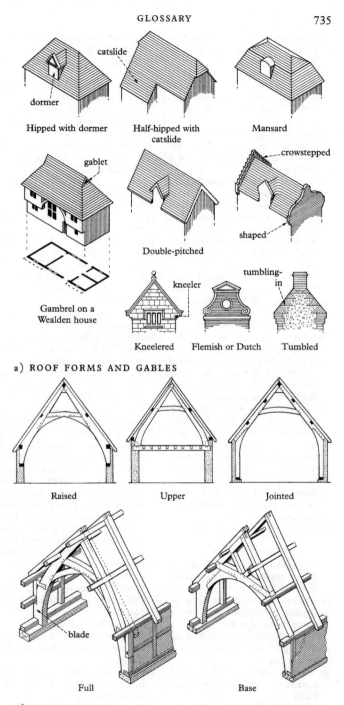

a) ROOF FORMS AND GABLES

b) CRUCK FRAMES

FIGURE 8: ROOFS AND TIMBER-FRAMING

MIXER-COURTS: forecourts to groups of houses shared by vehicles and pedestrians.

MODILLIONS: small consoles (q.v.) along the underside of a Corinthian or Composite cornice (3d). Often used along an eaves cornice.

MODULE: a predetermined standard size for co-ordinating the dimensions of components of a building.

MOTTE-AND-BAILEY: post-Roman and Norman defence consisting of an earthen mound (motte) topped by a wooden tower within a bailey, an enclosure defended by a ditch and palisade, and also, sometimes, by an internal bank.

MOUCHETTE: see Tracery and 2b.

MOULDING: shaped ornamental strip of continuous section; see e.g. Cavetto, Cyma, Ovolo, Roll.

MULLION: vertical member between window lights (2b).

MULTI-STOREY: five or more storeys. Multi-storey flats may form a *cluster block*, with individual blocks of flats grouped round a service core; a *point block*, with flats fanning out from a service core; or a *slab block*, with flats approached by corridors or galleries from service cores at intervals or towers at the ends (plan also used for offices, hotels etc.). *Tower block* is a generic term for any very high multi-storey building.

MUNTIN: see Panelling and 6b.

NAILHEAD: E.E. ornament consisting of small pyramids regularly repeated (1a).

NARTHEX: enclosed vestibule or covered porch at the main entrance to a church.

NAVE: the body of a church w of the crossing or chancel often flanked by aisles (q.v.).

NEWEL: central or corner post of a staircase (6c). Newel stair: see Stairs.

NIGHT STAIR: stair by which religious entered the transept of their church from their dormitory to celebrate night services.

NOGGING: see Timber-framing (7).

NOOK-SHAFT: shaft set in the angle of a wall or opening (1a).

NORMAN: see Romanesque.

NOSING: projection of the tread of a step (6c).

NUTMEG: medieval ornament with a chain of tiny triangles placed obliquely.

OCULUS: circular opening.

ŒIL DE BŒUF: see Bullseye window.

OGEE: double curve, bending first one way and then the other, as in an *ogee* or *ogival arch* (5c). Cf. Cyma recta and Cyma reversa.

OPUS SECTILE: decorative mosaic-like facing.

OPUS SIGNINUM: composition flooring of Roman origin.

ORATORY: a private chapel in a church or a house. Also a church of the Oratorian Order.

ORDER: one of a series of recessed arches and jambs forming a splayed medieval opening, e.g. a doorway or arcade arch (1a).

ORDERS: the formalized versions of the post-and-lintel system in classical architecture. The main orders are *Doric, Ionic,* and *Corinthian.* They are Greek in origin but occur in Roman versions. Tuscan is a simple version of Roman Doric. Though each order has its own conventions (3), there are many minor variations. The *Composite* capital combines Ionic volutes with Corinthian foliage. *Superimposed orders:* orders on successive levels, usually in the upward sequence of Tuscan, Doric, Ionic, Corinthian, Composite.

ORIEL: see Bay window.

OVERDOOR: painting or relief above an internal door. Also called a *sopraporta.*

OVERTHROW: decorative fixed arch between two gatepiers or above a wrought-iron gate.

OVOLO: wide convex moulding (3f).

PALIMPSEST: of a brass: where a metal plate has been reused by turning over the engraving on the back; of a wall painting: where one overlaps and partly obscures an earlier one.

PALLADIAN: following the examples and principles of Andrea Palladio (1508–80).

PALMETTE: classical ornament like a palm shoot (4b).

PANELLING: wooden lining to interior walls, made up of vertical members (*muntins*) and horizontals (*rails*) framing panels: also called *wainscot*. *Raised and fielded*: with the central area of the panel (*field*) raised up (6b).

PANTILE: roof tile of S section.

PARAPET: wall for protection at any sudden drop, e.g. at the wall-head of a castle where it protects the *parapet walk* or wall-walk. Also used to conceal a roof.

PARCLOSE: *see* Screen.

PARGETTING (*lit.* plastering): exterior plaster decoration, either in relief or incised.

PARLOUR: in a religious house, a room where the religious could talk to visitors; in a medieval house, the semi-private living room below the solar (q.v.).

PARTERRE: level space in a garden laid out with low, formal beds.

PATERA (*lit.* plate): round or oval ornament in shallow relief.

PAVILION: ornamental building for occasional use; or projecting subdivision of a larger building, often at an angle or terminating a wing.

PEBBLEDASHING: *see* Rendering.

PEDESTAL: a tall block carrying a classical order, statue, vase, etc.

PEDIMENT: a formalized gable derived from that of a classical temple; also used over doors, windows, etc. For variations *see* 4b.

PENDENTIVE: spandrel between adjacent arches, supporting a drum, dome or vault and consequently formed as part of a hemisphere (5a).

PENTHOUSE: subsidiary structure with a lean-to roof. Also a separately roofed structure on top of a C20 multi-storey block.

PERIPTERAL: *see* Peristyle.

PERISTYLE: a colonnade all round the exterior of a classical building, as in a temple which is then said to be *peripteral*.

PERP (PERPENDICULAR): English Gothic architecture *c.* 1335–50 to *c.* 1530. The name is derived from the upright tracery panels then used (*see* Tracery and 2a).

PERRON: external stair to a doorway, usually of double-curved plan.

PEW: loosely, seating for the laity outside the chancel; strictly, an enclosed seat. *Box pew*: with equal high sides and a door.

PIANO NOBILE: principal floor of a classical building above a ground floor or basement and with a lesser storey overhead.

PIAZZA: formal urban open space surrounded by buildings.

PIER: large masonry or brick support, often for an arch. *See also* Compound pier.

PILASTER: flat representation of a classical column in shallow relief. *Pilaster strip*: *see* Lesene.

PILE: row of rooms. *Double pile*: two rows thick.

PILLAR: free-standing upright member of any section, not conforming to one of the orders (q.v.).

PILLAR PISCINA: *see* Piscina.

PILOTIS: C20 French term for pillars or stilts that support a building above an open ground floor.

PISCINA: basin for washing Mass vessels, provided with a drain; set in or against the wall to the S of an altar or free-standing (*pillar piscina*).

PISÉ: *see* Cob.

PITCHED MASONRY: laid on the diagonal, often alternately with opposing courses (*pitched and counterpitched* or *herringbone*).

PLATBAND: flat horizontal moulding between storeys. Cf. stringcourse.

PLATE RAIL: *see* Railways.

PLATEWAY: *see* Railways.

PLINTH: projecting courses at the

foot of a wall or column, generally chamfered or moulded at the top.

PODIUM: a continuous raised platform supporting a building; or a large block of two or three storeys beneath a multi-storey block of smaller area.

POINT BLOCK: *see* Multi-storey.

POINTING: exposed mortar jointing of masonry or brickwork. Types include *flush, recessed* and *tuck* (with a narrow channel filled with finer, whiter mortar).

POPPYHEAD: carved ornament of leaves and flowers as a finial for a bench end or stall.

PORTAL FRAME: C20 frame comprising two uprights rigidly connected to a beam or pair of rafters.

PORTCULLIS: gate constructed to rise and fall in vertical grooves at the entry to a castle.

PORTICO: a porch with the roof and frequently a pediment supported by a row of columns (4a). A portico *in antis* has columns on the same plane as the front of the building. A *prostyle* porch has columns standing free. Porticoes are described by the number of front columns, e.g. tetrastyle (four), hexastyle (six). The space within the temple is the *naos*, that within the portico the *pronaos*. *Blind portico*: the front features of a portico applied to a wall.

PORTICUS (plural: porticūs): subsidiary cell opening from the main body of a pre-Conquest church.

POST: upright support in a structure (7).

POSTERN: small gateway at the back of a building or to the side of a larger entrance door or gate.

POUND LOCK: *see* Canals.

PRESBYTERY: the part of a church lying E of the choir where the main altar is placed; or a priest's residence.

PRINCIPAL: *see* Roofs and 7.

PRONAOS: *see* Portico and 4a.

PROSTYLE: *see* Portico and 4a.

PULPIT: raised and enclosed platform for the preaching of sermons. *Three-decker*: with reading desk below and clerk's desk below that. *Two-decker*: as above, minus the clerk's desk.

PULPITUM: stone screen in a major church dividing choir from nave.

PULVINATED: *see* Frieze and 3c.

PURLIN: *see* Roofs and 7.

PUTHOLES or PUTLOG HOLES: in the wall to receive putlogs, the horizontal timbers which support scaffolding boards; sometimes not filled after construction is complete.

PUTTO (plural: putti): small naked boy.

QUARRIES: square (or diamond) panes of glass supported by lead strips (*cames*); square floor slabs or tiles.

QUATREFOIL: *see* Foil and 2b.

QUEEN-STRUT: *see* Roofs and 7.

QUIRK: sharp groove to one side of a convex medieval moulding.

QUOINS: dressed stones at the angles of a building (6d).

RADBURN SYSTEM: vehicle and pedestrian segregation in residential developments, based on that used at Radburn, New Jersey, USA, by Wright and Stein, 1928–30.

RADIATING CHAPELS: projecting radially from an ambulatory or an apse (*see* Chevet).

RAFTER: *see* Roofs and 7.

RAGGLE: groove cut in masonry, especially to receive the edge of a roof-covering.

RAGULY: ragged (in heraldry). Also applied to funerary sculpture, e.g. *cross raguly*: with a notched outline.

RAIL: *see* Panelling and 6b; also 7.

RAILWAYS: *Edge rail*: on which flanged wheels can run. *Plate rail*: L-section rail for plain unflanged wheels. *Plateway*: early railway using plate rails.

RAISED AND FIELDED: *see* Panelling and 6b.

RAKE: slope or pitch.

RAMPART: defensive outer wall of stone or earth. *Rampart walk*: path along the inner face.

REBATE: rectangular section cut out of a masonry edge to receive a shutter, door, window, etc.

REBUS: a heraldic pun, e.g. a fiery cock for Cockburn.

REEDING: series of convex mouldings, the reverse of fluting (q.v.). Cf. Gadrooning.

RENDERING: the covering of outside walls with a uniform surface or skin for protection from the weather. *Limewashing*: thin layer of lime plaster. *Pebbledashing*: where aggregate is thrown at the wet plastered wall for a textured effect. *Roughcast*: plaster mixed with a coarse aggregate such as gravel. *Stucco*: fine lime plaster worked to a smooth surface. *Cement rendering*: a cheaper substitute for stucco, usually with a grainy texture.

REPOUSSÉ: relief designs in metalwork, formed by beating it from the back.

REREDORTER (*lit.* behind the dormitory): latrines in a medieval religious house.

REREDOS: painted and/or sculptured screen behind and above an altar. Cf. Retable.

RESPOND: half-pier or half-column bonded into a wall and carrying one end of an arch. It usually terminates an arcade.

RETABLE: painted or carved panel standing on or at the back of an altar, usually attached to it.

RETROCHOIR: in a major church, the area between the high altar and E chapel.

REVEAL: the plane of a jamb, between the wall and the frame of a door or window.

RIB-VAULT: *see* Vault and 2c.

RINCEAU: classical ornament of leafy scrolls (4b).

RISER: vertical face of a step (6c).

ROACH: a rough-textured form of Portland stone, with small cavities and fossil shells.

ROCK-FACED: masonry cleft to produce a rugged appearance.

ROCOCO: style current *c.* 1720 and *c.* 1760, characterized by a serpentine line and playful, scrolled decoration.

ROLL MOULDING: medieval moulding of part-circular section (1a).

ROMANESQUE: style current in the C11 and C12. In England often called Norman. *See also* Saxo-Norman.

ROOD: crucifix flanked by the Virgin and St John, usually over the entry into the chancel, on a beam (*rood beam*) or painted on the wall. The *rood screen* below often had a walkway (*rood loft*) along the top, reached by a *rood stair* in the side wall.

ROOFS: Shape. For the main external shapes (hipped, mansard, etc.) *see* 8a. *Helm* and *Saddleback*: *see* 1c. *Lean-to*: single sloping roof built against a vertical wall; lean-to is also applied to the part of the building beneath.

Construction. *See* 7.

Single-framed roof: with no main trusses. The rafters may be fixed to the wall-plate or ridge, or longitudinal timber may be absent altogether.

Double-framed roof: with longitudinal members, such as purlins, and usually divided into bays by principals and principal rafters. Other types are named after their main structural components, e.g. *hammerbeam*, *crown-post* (*see* Elements below and 7).

Elements. *See* 7.

Ashlar piece: a short vertical timber connecting inner wall-plate or timber pad to a rafter.

Braces: subsidiary timbers set diagonally to strengthen the frame. *Arched braces*: curved pair forming an arch, connecting wall or post below with tie- or collarbeam above. *Passing braces*: long straight braces passing across other members of the truss. *Scissor braces*: pair crossing diagonally between pairs of rafters or principals. *Wind-braces*: short, usually curved braces connecting side purlins with principals; sometimes decorated with cusping.

Collar or *collar-beam*: horizontal transverse timber connecting a pair of rafter or cruck blades (q.v.), set between apex and the wall-plate.

Crown-post: a vertical timber set centrally on a tie-beam and supporting a collar purlin braced to it longitudinally. In an open truss lateral braces may rise to the collar-beam; in a closed truss they may descend to the tie-beam.

Hammerbeams: horizontal brackets projecting at wall-plate level like an interrupted tie-beam; the inner ends carry *hammerposts*, vertical timbers which support a purlin and are braced to a collar-beam above.

Kingpost: vertical timber set centrally on a tie- or collar-beam, rising to the apex of the roof to support a ridge-piece (cf. Strut).

Plate: longitudinal timber set square to the ground. *Wall-plate*: plate along the top of a wall which receives the ends of the rafters; cf. Purlin.

Principals: pair of inclined lateral timbers of a truss. Usually they support side purlins and mark the main bay divisions.

Purlin: horizontal longitudinal timber. *Collar purlin* or *crown plate*: central timber which carries collar-beams and is supported by crown-posts. *Side purlins*: pairs of timbers placed some way up the slope of the roof, which carry common rafters. *Butt* or *tenoned purlins* are tenoned into either side of the principals. *Through purlins* pass through or past the principal; they include *clasped purlins*, which rest on queenposts or are carried in the angle between principals and collar, and *trenched purlins* trenched into the backs of principals.

Queen-strut: paired vertical, or near-vertical, timbers placed symmetrically on a tie-beam to support side purlins.

Rafters: inclined lateral timbers supporting the roof covering. *Common rafters*: regularly spaced uniform rafters placed along the length of a roof or between principals. *Principal rafters*: rafters which also act as principals.

Ridge, ridge-piece: horizontal longitudinal timber at the apex supporting the ends of the rafters.

Sprocket: short timber placed on the back and at the foot of a rafter to form projecting eaves.

Strut: vertical or oblique timber between two members of a truss, not directly supporting longitudinal timbers.

Tie-beam: main horizontal transverse timber which carries the feet of the principals at wall level.

Truss: rigid framework of timbers at bay intervals, carrying the longitudinal roof timbers which support the common rafters.

Closed truss: with the spaces between the timbers filled, to form an internal partition.

See also Cruck, Wagon roof.

ROPE MOULDING: *see* Cable moulding.

ROSE WINDOW: circular window with tracery radiating from the centre. Cf. Wheel window.

ROTUNDA: building or room circular in plan.

ROUGHCAST: *see* Rendering.

ROVING BRIDGE: *see* Canals.

RUBBED BRICKWORK: *see* Gauged brickwork.

RUBBLE: masonry whose stones are wholly or partly in a rough state. *Coursed*: coursed stones with rough faces. *Random*: uncoursed stones in a random pattern. *Snecked*: with courses broken by smaller stones (snecks).

RUSTICATION: *see* 6d. Exaggerated treatment of masonry to give an effect of strength. The joints are usually recessed by V-section chamfering or square-section channelling (*channelled rustication*). *Banded rustication* has only the horizontal joints emphasized. The faces may be flat, but can be *diamond-faced*, like shallow pyramids, *vermiculated*, with a stylized texture like worm-casts, and *glacial* (frost-work), like icicles or stalactites.

SACRISTY: room in a church for sacred vessels and vestments.

SADDLEBACK ROOF: *see* IC.

SALTIRE CROSS: with diagonal limbs.

SANCTUARY: area around the main altar of a church. Cf. Presbytery.

SANGHA: residence of Buddhist monks or nuns.

SARCOPHAGUS: coffin of stone or other durable material.

SAXO-NORMAN: transitional Romanesque style combining Anglo-Saxon and Norman features, current *c.* 1060–1100.

SCAGLIOLA: composition imitating marble.

SCALLOPED CAPITAL: *see* 1a.

SCOTIA: a hollow classical moulding, especially between tori (q.v.) on a column base (3b, 3f).

SCREEN: in a medieval church, usually at the entry to the chancel; *see* Rood (screen) and Pulpitum. A *parclose screen* separates a chapel from the rest of the church.

SCREENS or SCREENS PASSAGE: screened-off entrance passage between great hall and service rooms.

SECTION: two-dimensional representation of a building, moulding, etc., revealed by cutting across it.

SEDILIA (singular: sedile): seats for the priests (usually three) on the S side of the chancel.

SET-OFF: *see* Weathering.

SETTS: squared stones, usually of granite, used for paving or flooring.

SGRAFFITO: decoration scratched, often in plaster, to reveal a pattern in another colour beneath. *Graffiti*: scratched drawing or writing.

SHAFT: vertical member of round or polygonal section (1a, 3a). *Shaft-ring*: at the junction of shafts set *en delit* (q.v.) or attached to a pier or wall (1a).

SHEILA-NA-GIG: female fertility figure, usually with legs apart.

SHELL: thin, self-supporting roofing membrane of timber or concrete.

SHOULDERED ARCHITRAVE: *see* 4b.

SHUTTERING: *see* Concrete.

SILL: horizontal member at the bottom of a window or door frame; or at the base of a timber-framed wall into which posts and studs are tenoned (7).

SLAB BLOCK: *see* Multi-storey.

SLATE-HANGING: covering of overlapping slates on a wall. *Tile-hanging* is similar.

SLYPE: covered way or passage leading E from the cloisters between transept and chapter house.

SNECKED: *see* Rubble.

SOFFIT (*lit.* ceiling): underside of an arch (also called *intrados*), lintel, etc. *Soffit roll*: medieval roll moulding on a soffit.

SOLAR: private upper chamber in a medieval house, accessible from the high end of the great hall.

SOPRAPORTA: *see* Overdoor.

SOUNDING-BOARD: *see* Tester.

SPANDRELS: roughly triangular spaces between an arch and its containing rectangle, or between adjacent arches (5c). Also non-structural panels under the windows in a curtain-walled building.

SPERE: a fixed structure screening the lower end of the great hall from the screens passage. *Spere-truss*: roof truss incorporated in the spere.

SPIRE: tall pyramidal or conical feature crowning a tower or turret. *Broach*: starting from a square base, then carried into an octagonal section by means of triangular faces; and *splayed-foot*: variation of the broach form, found principally in the southeast, in which the four cardinal faces are splayed out near their base, to cover the corners, while oblique (or intermediate) faces taper away to a point (1c). *Needle spire*: thin spire rising from the centre of a tower roof, well inside the parapet: when of timber and lead often called a *spike*.

SPIRELET: *see* Flèche.

SPLAY: of an opening when it is wider on one face of a wall than the other.

SPRING or SPRINGING: level at which an arch or vault rises from its supports. *Springers*: the first stones of an arch or vaulting rib above the spring (2c).

SQUINCH: arch or series of arches thrown across an interior angle of a square or rectangular structure to support a circular or polygonal superstructure, especially a dome or spire (5a).

SQUINT: an aperture in a wall or through a pier usually to allow a view of an altar.

STAIRS: *see* 6c. *Dog-leg stair*: parallel flights rising alternately in opposite directions, without an open well. *Flying stair*: can-tilevered from the walls of a stairwell, without newels; some-times called a *Geometric* stair when the inner edge describes a curve. *Newel stair*: ascending round a central supporting newel (q.v.); called a *spiral stair* or *vice* when in a circular shaft, a *winder* when in a rectangular compartment. (Win-der also applies to the steps on the turn.) *Well stair*: with flights round a square open well framed by newel posts. *See also* Perron.

STALL: fixed seat in the choir or chancel for the clergy or choir (cf. Pew). Usually with arm rests, and often framed together.

STANCHION: upright structural member, of iron, steel or re-inforced concrete.

STANDPIPE TOWER: *see* Man-ometer.

STEAM ENGINES: *Atmospheric*: worked by the vacuum created when low-pressure steam is con-densed in the cylinder, as de-veloped by Thomas Newcomen. *Beam engine*: with a large pivoted beam moved in an oscillating fashion by the piston. It may drive a flywheel or be *non-rotative*. *Watt* and *Cornish*: single-cylinder; *com-pound*: two cylinders; *triple ex-pansion*: three cylinders.

STEEPLE: tower together with a spire, lantern, or belfry.

STIFF-LEAF: type of E.E. foliage decoration. *Stiff-leaf capital see* 1b.

STOP: plain or decorated terminal to mouldings or chamfers, or at the end of hoodmoulds and labels (*label stop*), or stringcourses (5b, 6a); *see also* Headstop.

STOUP: vessel for holy water, usually near a door.

STRAINER: *see* Arch.

STRAPWORK: late C16 and C17 dec-oration, like interlaced leather straps.

STRETCHER: *see* Bond and 6e.

STRING: *see* 6c. Sloping member holding the ends of the treads and risers of a staircase. *Closed string*: a broad string covering the ends of the treads and risers. *Open string*: cut into the shape of the treads and risers.

STRINGCOURSE: horizontal course or moulding projecting from the surface of a wall (6d).

STUCCO: *see* Rendering.

STUDS: subsidiary vertical timbers of a timber-framed wall or par-tition (7).

STUPA: Buddhist shrine, circular in plan.

STYLOBATE: top of the solid plat-form on which a colonnade stands (3a).

SUSPENSION BRIDGE: *see* Bridge.

SWAG: like a festoon (q.v.), but rep-resenting cloth.

SYSTEM BUILDING: *see* Industrial-ized building.

TABERNACLE: canopied structure to contain the reserved sacrament or a relic; or architectural frame for an image or statue.

TABLE TOMB: memorial slab raised on free-standing legs.

TAS-DE-CHARGE: the lower courses of a vault or arch which are laid horizontally (2c).

TERM: pedestal or pilaster tapering downward, usually with the upper part of a human figure growing out of it.

TERRACOTTA: moulded and fired clay ornament or cladding.

TESSELLATED PAVEMENT: mosaic flooring, particularly Roman, made of *tesserae*, i.e. cubes of glass, stone, or brick.

TESTER: flat canopy over a tomb or pulpit, where it is also called a *sounding-board*.

TESTER TOMB: tomb-chest with effigies beneath a tester, either free-standing (tester with four or more columns), or attached to a wall (*half-tester*) with columns on one side only.

TETRASTYLE: *see* Portico.

THERMAL WINDOW: *see* Diocletian window.

THREE-DECKER PULPIT: *see* Pulpit.

TIDAL GATES: *see* Canals.

TIE-BEAM: *see* Roofs and 7.

TIERCERON: *see* Vault and 2c.

TILE-HANGING: *see* Slate-hanging.

TIMBER-FRAMING: *see* 7. Method of construction where the structural frame is built of interlocking timbers. The spaces are filled with non-structural material, e.g. *infill* of wattle and daub, lath and plaster, brickwork (known as *nogging*), etc. and may be covered by plaster, weatherboarding (q.v.), or tiles.

TOMB-CHEST: chest-shaped tomb, usually of stone. Cf. Table tomb, Tester tomb.

TORUS (plural: tori): large convex moulding usually used on a column base (3b, 3f).

TOUCH: soft black marble quarried near Tournai.

TOURELLE: turret corbelled out from the wall.

TOWER BLOCK: *see* Multi-storey.

TRABEATED: depends structurally on the use of the post and lintel. Cf. Arcuated.

TRACERY: openwork pattern of masonry or timber in the upper part of an opening. *Blind tracery* is tracery applied to a solid wall.
Plate tracery, introduced *c*. 1200, is the earliest form, in which shapes are cut through solid masonry (2a).
Bar tracery was introduced into England *c*. 1250. The pattern is formed by intersecting moulded ribwork continued from the mullions. It was especially elaborate during the Decorated period (q.v.). Tracery shapes can include circles, *daggers* (elongated ogee-ended lozenges), *mouchettes* (like daggers but with curved sides) and upright rectangular *panels*. They often have *cusps*, projecting points defining lobes or *foils* (q.v.) within the main shape: *Kentish* or *split-cusps* are forked (2b).
Types of bar tracery (*see* 2b) include *geometric(al)*: *c*. 1250–1310, chiefly circles, often foiled; *Y-tracery*: *c*. 1300, with mullions branching into a Y-shape; *intersecting*: *c*. 1300, formed by interlocking mullions; *reticulated*: early C14, net-like pattern of ogee-ended lozenges; *curvilinear*: C14, with uninterrupted flowing curves; *panel*: Perp, with straight-sided panels, often cusped at the top and bottom.

TRANSEPT: transverse portion of a church.

TRANSITIONAL: generally used for the phase between Romanesque and Early English (*c*. 1175–*c*. 1200).

TRANSOM: horizontal member separating window lights (2b).

TREAD: horizontal part of a step. The *tread end* may be carved on a staircase (6c).

TREFOIL: *see* Foil.

TRIFORIUM: middle storey of a church treated as an arcaded wall passage or blind arcade, its height corresponding to that of the aisle roof.

TRIGLYPHS (*lit.* three-grooved tablets): stylized beam-ends in the Doric frieze, with metopes between (3b).

TRIUMPHAL ARCH: influential type of Imperial Roman monument.

TROPHY: sculptured or painted group of arms or armour.

TRUMEAU: central stone mullion supporting the tympanum of a wide doorway. *Trumeau figure*: carved figure attached to it (cf. Column figure).

TRUMPET CAPITAL: *see* 1b.

TRUSS: braced framework, spanning between supports. *See also* Roofs and 7.

TUMBLING or TUMBLING-IN: courses of brickwork laid at right-angles to a slope, e.g. of a gable, forming triangles by tapering into horizontal courses (8a).

TUSCAN: *see* Orders and 3e.

TWO-DECKER PULPIT: *see* Pulpit.

TYMPANUM: the surface between a lintel and the arch above it or within a pediment (4a).

UNDERCROFT: usually describes the vaulted room(s), beneath the main room(s) of a medieval house. Cf. Crypt.

VAULT: arched stone roof (sometimes imitated in timber or plaster). For types see 2c.
Tunnel or *barrel vault*: continuous semicircular or pointed arch, often of rubble masonry.

Groin-vault: tunnel vaults intersecting at right angles. *Groins* are the curved lines of the intersections.

Rib-vault: masonry framework of intersecting arches (ribs) supporting *vault cells*, used in Gothic architecture. *Wall rib* or *wall arch*: between wall and vault cell. *Transverse rib*: spans between two walls to divide a vault into bays. *Quadripartite* rib-vault: each bay has two pairs of diagonal ribs dividing the vault into four triangular cells. *Sexpartite* rib-vault: most often used over paired bays, has an extra pair of ribs springing from between the bays. More elaborate vaults may include *ridge ribs* along the crown of a vault or bisecting the bays; *tiercerons*: extra decorative ribs springing from the corners of a bay; and *liernes*: short decorative ribs in the crown of a vault, not linked to any springing point. A *stellar* or *star* vault has liernes in star formation.

Fan-vault: form of barrel vault used in the Perp period, made up of halved concave masonry cones decorated with blind tracery.

VAULTING SHAFT: shaft leading up to the spring or springing (q.v.) of a vault (2c).

VENETIAN or SERLIAN WINDOW: derived from Serlio (4b). The motif is used for other openings.

VERMICULATION: *see* Rustication and 6d.

VESICA: oval with pointed ends.

VICE: *see* Stair.

VILLA: originally a Roman country house or farm. The term was revived in England in the C18 under the influence of Palladio and used especially for smaller, compact country houses. In the later C19 it was debased to describe any suburban house.

VITRIFIED: bricks or tiles fired to a darkened glassy surface.

VITRUVIAN SCROLL: classical running ornament of curly waves (4b).

VOLUTES: spiral scrolls. They occur on Ionic capitals (3c). *Angle volute*: pair of volutes, turned outwards to meet at the corner of a capital.

VOUSSOIRS: wedge-shaped stones forming an arch (5c).

WAGON ROOF: with the appearance of the inside of a wagon tilt; often ceiled. Also called *cradle roof*.

WAINSCOT: *see* Panelling.

WALL MONUMENT: attached to the wall and often standing on the floor. *Wall tablets* are smaller with the inscription as the major element.

WALL-PLATE: *see* Roofs and 7.

WALL-WALK: *see* Parapet.

WARMING ROOM: room in a religious house where a fire burned for comfort.

WATERHOLDING BASE: early Gothic base with upper and lower mouldings separated by a deep hollow.

WATERLEAF: *see* Enrichments and 3f.

WATERLEAF CAPITAL: Late Romanesque and Transitional type of capital (1b).

WATER WHEELS: described by the way water is fed on to the wheel. *Breastshot*: mid-height, falling and passing beneath. *Overshot*: over the top. *Pitchback*: on the top but falling backwards. *Undershot*: turned by the momentum of the water passing beneath. In a *water turbine*, water is fed under pressure through a vaned wheel within a casing.

WEALDEN HOUSE: type of medieval timber-framed house with a central open hall flanked by bays of two storeys, roofed in line; the end bays are jettied to the front, but the eaves are continuous (8a).

WEATHERBOARDING: wall cladding of overlapping horizontal boards.

WEATHERING or SET-OFF: inclined, projecting surface to keep water away from the wall below.

WEEPERS: figures in niches along the sides of some medieval tombs. Also called mourners.

WHEEL WINDOW: circular, with radiating shafts like spokes. Cf. Rose window.

WROUGHT IRON: *see* Cast iron.

INDEX OF ARCHITECTS, ARTISTS, PATRONS AND RESIDENTS

Names of architects and artists working in the area covered by this volume are given in *italic*. Entries for partnerships and group practices are listed after entries for a single name.

Also indexed here are names/titles of families and individuals (not of bodies or commercial firms) recorded in this volume as having commissioned architectural work or owned, lived in, or visited properties in the area. The index includes monuments to members of such families and other individuals where they are of particular interest.

Maldon, Thomas 35, 218
Malet, Col. 210
Malet, Sir Thomas 495, 496
Malpas, Henry 68, 302
Maltby, Frederick 576
Manasseh, Leonard 695
Manasseh (Leonard) & Partners 636
Mandeville (de) family 387
Maners, Abbot Richard de 35, 122
Manger family 303
Manners & Gill 80, 167, 520
Manning, Samuel 350
Mansel, M.G. 503
Marble Works (Westminster) 93, 576
Marochetti, Baron Carlo 343
Marsden, G.M. 710
Marshall (sculptor) 563, 592
Marshall, Joshua 641
Marshall, W. 96
Martin, Stuart 361
Martin (Stuart) Architects 639, 707
Martin-Smith, D.F. 627n.
Martyn family 104, 499, 511–12, 609
Martyn, Nicholas 104n., 499
Martyn, Robert and Elizabeth 104n.
Martyn, Sir William 36, 102, 499
Mason, Augustus 138
Mason Richards Partnership 462–3
Matravers, John, Lord 35, 374–5
Matthews family 417
Matthews, Major 305
Matthews, H.E. 83, 250
Matthews, Thomas 417
Maufe, Sir Edward 84, 157, 543, Pl. 121
Mauley, Hon. William Ponsonby, 1st Lord de 62, 171, 174
Maw & Co. 136, 387, 513, 517
Mawson, Thomas 106, 139, 354
Mayer & Co. 233, 313, 385, 437, 488, 604
Maynard, Allen 45, 49, 198–9, 533, Pl. 58
Meadway, Richard 49, 209
Medd, H.A.N. 318
Melcombe, George Bubb (Dodington), 1st Baron 59, 268, 278
Mellor, Sir Robert (late c16) 356
Mellor, Sir Robert (early c17) 617
Mere, Abbot 543
Merrifield, L.S. 430
Metters, Colin 451
Meyr, Hans 637
Michel family 240–1
Michel, David 241
Michel, Rev. James 681
Michel, John 347
Michel, Mrs Margaretta 681
Micklethwaite, J.T. 618
Middleton family 143

Middleton, H.N. 141, 143
Middleton, Abbot William 25, 30, 405, 406, 409, 410, 411, 412
Milburn, G.W. 340
Mildmay, Carew Henry 532
Miller, Alec 476
Miller, William 205, 595
Millwall Pottery 686
Milne-Watson family 100
Milne-Watson, Sir David 100
Milton, Lady 69, 410–11, Pl. 81
Milton, Lord *see* Dorchester, 1st Earl of
Ministry of Works 349n.
Minton (tilemakers) 92, 134, 159, 168, 179, 180, 205, 243, 269, 281, 291, 298, 311, 319, 331, 338, 350, 375, 388, 403, 421, 426, 431, 435, 437, 487, 492, 495, 507, 510, 583, 584, 595, 597, 609, 611, 615, 618, 630, 647, 686, 701, 707
Minton, Hollings & Co. 395
Mitchell, Arnold 371, 372
Mitchell, Eddie 84, 470
Mitchell, Nicholas 379
Mitchell, R.J. 670
Mitchell, W.R. 513
Moffatt, W.B. 70, 517
Mohun, Robert 287
Monde, John 517
Mondey, Edward 251, 285, 338, 490, 567, 631, 688
Montagu family *see* Salisbury, earls of
Montague, Rev. Phillip 445
Moore, A.L. 138, 148, 243, 321, 490, 564, 584, 608, 638
Moore, Gabriel 43, 189
Moore, J.F. 66, 112, 428n., 593
Moore, R. St George 588
Moore, Roger 535
Moore, Temple 72, 179, 180, 486, 610
Moore, A.L. & C.E. 249
Morant & Boyd 555
More family 401, 432
More, Sir Thomas 401
Morgan, Robert 380
Morgan (Ken) Architects 94, 227, 259
Morgan Carey Architects 578, 627
Morley, James George 283
Morley (David) Architects 165
Morris, Colwyn 490
Morris, Roger 59, 268
Morris, William 247, 448n., 593
Morris (William) & Co. 77, 181, 216, 247, 385, 672n., Pl. 115
Morris (William) & Co. (Westminster) 283, 318, 351, 472, 638, 639, 648
Morris & Hebson 668
Morris (John) & C.G. Hebson 205

INDEX OF PLACES